J.R.R. Tolkien Encyclopedia

J.R.R. Tolkien Encyclopedia

Scholarship and Critical Assessment

Michael D.C. Drout
EDITOR

Routledge
Taylor & Francis Group
New York   London

Routledge is an imprint of the
Taylor & Francis Group, an informa business

Routledge
Taylor & Francis Group
270 Madison Avenue
New York, NY 10016

Routledge
Taylor & Francis Group
2 Park Square
Milton Park, Abingdon
Oxon OX14 4RN

© 2007 by Taylor & Francis Group, LLC
Routledge is an imprint of Taylor & Francis Group, an Informa business

Printed in the United States of America on acid-free paper
10 9 8 7 6 5 4 3 2 1

International Standard Book Number-10: 0-415-96942-5 (Hardcover)
International Standard Book Number-13: 978-0-415-96942-0 (Hardcover)

Library of Congress Cataloging-in-Publication Data

J.R.R. Tolkien encyclopedia : scholarship and critical assessment / [edited by] Michael D.C. Drout.
    p. cm.
  Includes bibliographical references and index.
  ISBN-13: 978-0-415-96942-0 (acid-free paper)
  ISBN-10: 0-415-96942-5 (acid-free paper)
  1. Tolkien, J. R. R. (John Ronald Reuel), 1892-1973--Encyclopedias. 2. Tolkien, J. R. R. (John Ronald Reuel), 1892-1973--Criticism and interpretation. 3. Middle Earth (Imaginary place)--Encyclopedias. 4. Fantasy fiction, English--Encyclopedias. I. Drout, Michael D. C., 1968- .

PR6039.O32Z664 2006
828'.91209--dc22
                                                  2006026700

Visit the Taylor & Francis Web site at
http://www.taylorandfrancis.com

and the Routledge Web site at
http://www.routledge-ny.com

CONTENTS

EDITOR

Michael D.C. Drout
Wheaton College, Norton, MA

ASSOCIATE EDITORS

Douglas A. Anderson
Marcellus, MI

Marjorie Burns
Portland State University, Portland, OR

Verlyn Flieger
University of Maryland, College Park, MD

Thomas Shippey
Saint Louis University, St. Louis, MO

CONTRIBUTORS

Nils Ivar Agøy
Telemark University College, Norway

Julaire Andelin
Salt Lake City, Utah

Douglas A. Anderson
Marcellus, Michigan

Don N. Anger
Brock University

Robert G. Anger
The Presbyterian Church in Canada

Roberto Arduini
Rome, Italy

Helen Armstrong
Bedfordshire, United Kingdom

Cecilia Barella
Editor, J.R.R. Tolkien, a Webliography

Jane Beal
Wheaton College

Raffaella Benvenuto
Rome, Italy

Beregond, Anders Stenström
Uppsala, Sweden

Bradley J. Birzer
Hillsdale College

Alexandra Bolintineanu
University of Toronto

David Bratman
San Jose, California

Clair Buck
Wheaton College

Marcel R. Bülles
University of Cologne

Anthony S. Burdge
Chairman, Heren Istarion, The Northeast Tolkien Society

Jessica Burke
Co-Chair, Heren Istarion, The Northeast Tolkien Society

Marjorie Burns
Portland State University

Alice Marie Campbell
Altadena, California

Christine Chism
Rutgers University

Joe R. Christopher
Tarleton State University

Hal Colebatch
Nedlands, Western Australia

Michael Coren
Toronto, Canada

Janet Brennan Croft
University of Oklahoma

Patrick Curry
Bath Spa University

Penelope Davie
Queensland University of Technology

Alex Davis
Independent Scholar

Ivan Derzhanski
Bulgarian Academy of Sciences

Merlin DeTardo
Cleveland, Ohio

CONTRIBUTORS

Michael Devaux
Livarot, France

Matthew Dickerson
Middlebury College

Leslie A. Donovan
University of New Mexico

Sarah Downey
University of Toronto

Michael D.C. Drout
Wheaton College

Kathleen E. Dubs
Pázmány Péter Catholic University

Jo-Anna Dueck
Burlington, Ontario, Canada

Colin Duriez
Cumbria, United Kingdom

Robert Eaglestone
University of London

Dustin Eaton
Grand Rapids, Michigan

Bradford Lee Eden
Las Vegas, Nevada

Jonathan Evans
University of Georgia

Matthew Fensome
Columbus, Ohio

Cath Filmer-Davis
Flosswyr Press

Dimitra Fimi
Cardiff University

Jason Fisher
Dallas, Texas

Verlyn Flieger
University of Maryland

Thomas Fornet-Ponse
University of Bonn

Mike Foster
Metamora, Illinois

Martin K. Foys
Hood College

Michele T. Fry
Oxford, United Kingdom

Christopher Garbowski
Maria Curie-Sklodowska University

John Garth
London, United Kingdom

David Gay
Indiana University

Gene Hargrove
University of North Texas

Jeniffer G. Hargroves
Conifer, Colorado

Amelia Harper
Nashville, North Carolina

Christina M. Heckman
Augusta State University

Kanerva Heikkinen
University of Helsinki

Katherine Hesser
Harvard College Fund

John R. Holmes
Franciscan University

Thomas Honegger
Friedrich-Schiller-Universität, Jena

Simon Horobin
Glasgow, Scotland

Carl F. Hostetter
Crofton, Maryland

John William Houghton
Canterbury School

Rod Jellema
Washington, DC

Rachel B. Kapelle
Brandeis University

Yvette L. Kisor
Ramapo College

Scott Kleinman
California State University, Northridge

Gisela Kreglinger
University of St. Andrews

Barry Langford
University of London

Reno E. Lauro
University of St. Andrews

Andrew Charles Lazo
Rice University

Kristi Lee
Harrisonburg, Virginia

Carol A. Leibiger
University of South Dakota

Miryam Librán Moreno
Caceres, Spain

Jared Lobdell
Eastern University

John F.G. Magoun
Chappaqua, New York

Olga Markova
Russian Academy of Sciences

James I. McNelis III
Wilmington College

Marcin Morawski
Warsaw, Poland

Gergely Nagy
University of Szeged, Hungary

Dale J. Nelson
Mayville State University

R. Scott Nokes
Troy University

David D. Oberhelman
Oklahoma State University

Victor L. Parker
University of Canterbury, New Zealand

Joseph Pearce
Ave Maria College

Michael W. Perry
Seattle, Washington

Anne C. Petty
Crawfordsille, Florida

Carl Phelpstead
Cardiff University

Joseph Piela
Blakely, Pennsylvania

Kathryn Powell
University of Manchester

Aline Ripley
Mount Saint Vincent University

Brian Rosebury
University of Central Lancashire

Geoffrey Russom
Brown University

Friedhelm Schneidewind
Hemsbach, Germany

Chester N. Scoville
University of Toronto

Gerald Seaman
Lawrence University

Eduardo Segura
Universidad Católica San Antonio

William Senior
Broward Community College

Tom Shippey
Saint Louis University

Alfred K. Siewers
Bucknell University

CONTRIBUTORS

Anna Skyggebjerg
The Danish University of Education

William Smith
Weatherford College

Arden R. Smith
Albany, California

Anna Smol
Mount Saint Vincent University

L. Lara Sookoo
Toronto, Canada

Lisa L. Spangenberg
University of California, Los Angeles

Michael N. Stanton
University of Vermont

Sandra Ballif Straubhaar
University of Texas at Austin

Amy H. Sturgis
Belmont University

L.J. Swain
University of Illinois at Chicago

Jeff Sypeck
University of Maryland

Paul Edmund Thomas
Manatt, Phelps & Phillips, LLP

Daniel Timmons
University of Toronto

Patricia Tubbs
Massena, New York

Allan Turner
University of Greifswald

Christopher Vaccaro
University of Vermont

René van Rossenburg
University of Leiden

John Walsh
Hult Library, Boston College

Christina Ganong Walton
Rocklin, California

Richard C. West
University of Wisconsin

Elizabeth A. Whittingham
SUNY College at Brockport

Shana Worthen
University of Toronto

Hilary Wynne
University of Toronto

Stephen Yandell
Xavier University

Arne Zettersten
University of Copenhagen

ALPHABETICAL LIST OF ENTRIES

THEMATIC LIST OF ENTRIES

Coghill, Nevill Henry Kendal Aylmer
Dundas-Grant, Jim
Dyson, Hugo
Havard, Humphrey
Inklings
Lewis, C.S.
Lewis, Warren Hamilton
Mathew, Fr. Anthony Gervase
McCallum, Ronald Buchanan
Sayers, Dorothy
Wain, John
Williams, Charles Walter Stansby

TCBS

Gilson, Robert Quilter
Smith, Geoffrey Bache
TCBS (Tea Club and Barrovian Society)
Wiseman, Christopher

Literary Sources

Anglo-Saxon

Alcuin
Battle of Maldon
Caedmon
Charms
Christ: "Advent Lyrics"
Cynewulf
Deor
Elf–Shot
Genesis
Guthlac: Poem
Juliana
Leechbook and *Herbarium*
Riddles: Sources
Runes
Saint Oswald
Seafarer, The
Solomon and Saturn
Wanderer, The
Ylfe, Alfr, Elves

Classical

Greek Gods
Latin Literature
Plato
Tertullian
Virgil

Continental Europe

Carolingians
Dante
German Folktale: *Deutsch Mythologie*
Mythology, Celtic
Mythology, Germanic
Old French Literature
Old High German Literature
Romances: Middle English and French

England

Brut by Layamon
Shakespeare
Spenser, Edmund
Milton

Middle English

Arthurian Literature
Orfeo, Sir

Scandinavia

Danes: Contributions to English Culture
Finland: Literary Sources
Old Norse Literature
Saxo Grammaticus

Literature

Unpublished by Tolkien

Arthurian Romance
Beowulf Translations
Old Norse Translations

Theoretical Concerns

Christian Readings of Tolkien
Class in Tolkien's Works
Environmentalist Readings of Tolkien
Feminist Readings of Tolkien
Fictionality
Gaze
Gender in Tolkien's Works
Jungian Theory

Scholars, Medieval

Scholarship by Tolkien: Medieval Literature

Sources

Medieval History

Medieval Literature

Stylistic Elements

Themes and Thematic Elements

Theological/ Philosophical Concepts and Philosophers

Sin
Suicide
Time

Tolkien's Contemporary History and Culture

Capitalism
Communism
England, Twentieth Century
Environmentalism and Eco-Criticism
France and French Culture
German Race Laws
Germany
Industrialization
Judaism
Literary Context, Twentieth Century
Nazi Party
Philo-Semitism
Politics
World War I
World War II

Works of Literature

Elvish Compositions and Grammars
Farmer Giles of Ham
Father Christmas Letters
Hobbit, The
I·Lam na·Ngoldathon: The Grammar and Lexicon of the Gnomish Tongue
Leeds University Verse, 1914–24
Letters of J.R.R. Tolkien, The
Lord of the Rings, The
Manuscripts by Tolkien
Mr. Bliss
"Mythopoeia"

"Nomenclature of *The Lord of the Rings*"
Qenyaqetsa: The Quenya Phonology and Lexicon
Road Goes Ever On, The
Roverandom
Silmarillion, The
Smith of Wootton Major
Spring Harvest, A: G. Bache Smith, ed. J.R.R. Tolkien
Tolkien Reader, The
Tree and Leaf
Unfinished Tales

History of Middle-earth

Book of Lost Tales I
Book of Lost Tales II
History of Middle-earth: Overview
Lays of Beleriand
Lost Road, The
Morgoth's Ring
Peoples of Middle-earth
Return of the Shadow
Sauron Defeated
Shaping of Middle-earth, The
Treason of Isengard, The
War of the Jewels, The
War of the Ring, The

Poems

Adventures of Tom Bombadil
Poems by Tolkien in Other Languages
Poems by Tolkien: *The Adventures of Tom Bombadil*
Poems by Tolkien: *The History of Middle-earth*
Poems by Tolkien: *The Hobbit*
Poems by Tolkien: *The Lord of the Rings*
Poems by Tolkien: Uncollected

INTRODUCTION

Because of their beauty, richness, and complexity, the works of J.R.R. Tolkien greatly reward close attention. Readers receive intense gratification from puzzling over difficult passages, linking together seemingly disparate observations, and connecting Tolkien's creations to the wider realms of literature and history. Very few authors inspire readers to learn invented languages (or invent languages of their own), teach themselves new alphabets, or struggle to master the complexities of history and politics written in the form of thousands of years' worth of annals. Very few authors drive students to learn Old English, Old Norse, and Gothic and to study the fragments of literature left to us in these languages. And very few authors have so encouraged the formation of communities of so many kinds: communities of fans, gamers, scholars, collectors, writers, artists, musicians, scholars, and teachers. Tolkien and his works—and the adaptations and development of those works, from stage to page to screen to game to song—have created communities and inspired individuals who want more understanding.

This encyclopedia is intended to be valuable to as many as possible of the varied and interconnected communities and individuals who are interested in Tolkien. Its contents are meant to bridge gaps and bring together separate branches of knowledge. Even within the specializations of Tolkien scholarship, there is a significant divide between (to use John Ellison and Patricia Reynolds' terminology) "Tolkien Studies"—scholarship about Tolkien the author and his works of literature—and "Middle-earth Studies"—analysis of Tolkien's invented worlds, histories, languages, creatures, etc. But each field is impossible without the other. "Tolkien Studies" without "Middle-earth Studies" would make no sense: how could someone comment intelligently on Tolkien's views of immortality without understanding how exactly the Elves are immortal and the interconnection between their bodies and spirits? What kind of critical insights could a critic have about the madness and despair of Denethor without understanding what exactly it was that Denethor saw in the palantír? (Hint: this information must be ferreted out of the timelines in Appendix B). Likewise, "Middle-earth Studies" without "Tolkien Studies" is impoverished. How can the language of the Rohirrim be understood without knowing that it is Old English? Is not the texture and detail of Middle-earth made that much richer by seeing its possible interconnections with medieval history and culture? Why would an enthusiast of Middle-earth wish to know *less* about that world's sources and about Tolkien's inspirations? Why would someone inspired by Peter Jackson's *Lord of the Rings* films not want to catch further glimpses of the world that Tolkien created and Jackson interpreted?

Thus, this encyclopedia seeks to be in both camps at once, drawing connections between the inside and the outside, showing how each type of study enriches the other. It is certainly not as comprehensive, in terms of "Middle-earth Studies," as Robert Foster's *A Guide to Middle-earth*, which gives almost complete coverage to everything that is fully within Tolkien's secondary world. But it is far more complete in gathering together discussions of Tolkien's life, scholarship, inspirations, cultural contexts, and social effects. There are plenty of monsters, elves, dwarves, hobbits, and heroes, and there are many entries on manuscripts, philology, and language, but there are also explanations of gaming, fandom, collecting and even an entry on the features of the undersea landscape named after Tolkien's characters.

Disentangling the web linking one man to another, one idea to another, or one text to another, is a task that has no real end. The book could easily have been five times as long and it still would not be completely comprehensive. Some limits had to be set, and I hope they are not capricious. But despite my best intentions, there will be omissions, both deliberate and accidental. In choosing which elements to discuss, therefore, I have focused on characters, places, artifacts, and ideas that have connections *outside* of Middle-earth, things that could not be comprehensively covered entirely within the rubric of "Middle-earth Studies." Thus, it was obvious that an entry on Rohan and the Rohirrim would have to discuss Anglo-Saxon history as much as it would have to clarify the migrations of the Rohirrim from the North to the Mark. Likewise, the entry on the Haradrim not only discusses the Middle-earth history of this people, but also examines the possible connections with medieval history and literature. Most of the entries also go beyond internal explanation and external sources to talk about reception and significance. Thus the discussion of Éowyn mentions not only her deeds within *The Lord of the Rings* but also interpretations of her character (though feminist studies and other forms of contemporary criticism) and her possible parallels in twentieth-century culture.

Tolkien's own scholarship, and thus many of his sources, was highly advanced and is not always accessible or understandable to the lay reader. This Encyclopedia is the first resource, to my knowledge, that contains a complete evaluation of Tolkien's scholarly works written by experts in the individual specialities. For example, Professor Arne Zettersten, one of J.R.R. Tolkien's students, explains the significance of Tolkien's work on the Middle English *Ancrene Wisse* and the "AB Language" that Tolkien discovered, while Tom Shippey investigates the influence of scholars of medieval literature on Tolkien. Readers who do not have extensive training in medieval studies and philology (i.e., most of the readers of this Encyclopedia) will now be able to see how Tolkien's scholarship is in fact an integral part of both Tolkien the man and Tolkien the author. Medieval literature was not, for Tolkien, merely a quarry for interesting names or images; it was in fact the vineyard in which he labored every day and to which he devoted years of study and contemplation. Reading the entries on his scholarship will demonstrate his penetrating intellect and the range of his thought.

The interpretation of Tolkien's works and the analysis of his themes is also an important part of this Encyclopedia. I know that there is an impulse in a field as young as Tolkien Studies to get all the ducks in a row, to assemble all of the possibly relevant information and only then make judgments, but I think this is a mistake. It is of course possible, even probable, that time will supersede some of the views now put forth, but I have used two methods to hedge against setting down incorrect or merely trendy viewpoints as facts. First, more than 120 contributors, from various countries have written 542 entries for this volume, thus presenting the widest possible range of interpretations and angles of vision. Second, I asked contributors to approach disputed questions without tendentiousness and to attempt to explain the various sides of difficult issues. Contributors responded by explaining the conflicts, noting the objections, and presenting what I think is a reasonable and even-handed approach to the most contentious debates (sadly, we will still not determine whether or not the balrog has functional wings—that is a question beyond any resolution). For instance, entries on Christian approaches to Tolkien, environmental readings, or political readings include caveats and point to contrasting views. Readers should therefore not only be able to see current consensus opinions but should also be able to recognize debatable propositions and unsettled cruces.

Tolkien was a part of a group of intellectual friends, The Inklings, who produced some of the most widely read books of the twentieth century. It was very difficult to know where to stop: this volume could very easily have become *The Tolkien and C.S. Lewis Encyclopedia* or *The Inklings Encyclopedia*. Readers will find that the entries on the Inklings (as individuals and as a group) and the Tolkien's Oxford milieu hang together quite well as a narrative of their own—most likely because they were written by some of the leading scholars of C.S. Lewis and the Inklings. Although he may have written most of his works late at night, the only one awake in his house, Tolkien was not the stereotypical lonely genius: he gathered with the other Inklings for fellowship and the exchange of ideas. Readers who work to fit him into this social and cultural context will be rewarded with a deeper understanding of how Tolkien's mind worked.

Tolkien needs to be seen in the matrix of his historical period as well as within the specific contours of his own life. The Encyclopedia therefore contains a great deal of information about Tolkien's life and work in Oxford and other historical and cultural events of his country and century. From the great wars to artistic movements (such as Art Nouveau or Arts and Crafts), to trends in politics and literature, a picture of a century (and going back even further) can be developed from the entries. Likewise, an examination of subsequent interpretations and adaptations of Tolkien's works—most visibly the Peter Jackson films, but also many other works of literature, art and film—cast light not only on Tolkien's work itself but also on the time periods and cultural contexts in which the adaptations were made. This is another place where the Encyclopedia could have grown exponentially and where I had to make difficult decisions about limiting the range of inquiry for the volume (should there be entries on the hundreds of individual writers and artists influenced or inspired by Tolkien? How much Oxford history was necessary?) I have tried to err on the side of explanation, so that perhaps even the college system at Oxford might be made at least as clear as the kindreds and migrations of the elves.

A more open and expansive definition of literature and a slowly developing historical perspective is now allowing us to look back on the twentieth century and see that Tolkien was one of the most distinctive and influential writers of that time period. My own opinion is that he was a genius in the very old-fashioned sense of the word: the smartest individual in whichever room he was seated, but also an inspired person, someone who had been to the top of the tower and seen the faraway sea. As readers of the Encyclopedia will see for themselves, the more one learns about Tolkien—both inside and outside his sub-created worlds—the more his genius stands out.

How to Use This Book

The entries in the *J.R.R. Tolkien Encyclopedia* range from very short descriptions of people, places and things (both inside and outside of Middle-earth) to much longer analytical approaches to Tolkien's life, works and context. The entries are arranged in alphabetical order and are cross-referenced within the volume. Thus a reader who wants to know more about the Inklings can read not only that particular entry (indexed under I, of course), but also the entries on each individual member of the group given in the "See Also" section at the end of the entry. Necessary bibliography is included in each entry in the "References and Further Reading" section. Entries are designed to be copious, so readers should look for both balrogs and orcs under "Monsters." A thematic list of entries is also included to assist readers in gathering together multiple entries on similar subjects. Readers are also encouraged to use the Analytical Index.

Citations to Tolkien's works follow the conventions developed by the journal *Tolkien Studies*. Readers are advised to refer to the next section, Conventions and Abbreviations.

Acknowledgments

I would first like to express my sincere gratitude to the many contributors who wrote entries. I may officially have been your editor, but in actuality I was your student. When I began this project I thought I knew quite a bit about Tolkien, his works and his influences. I have now been humbled in the face of the *immense* amount of learning, insight, and expertise that have been displayed in the hundreds of entries I have read, and I am a much better scholar (and a much better-informed person) than I was, thanks to all of you.

I want to note one contributor in particular. Daniel Timmons, who wrote some of the most important and difficult entries in the Encyclopedia, passed away after a long illness in December 2005. Best known in Tolkien studies as the editor (with George Clark) of *J.R.R. Tolkien and His Literary Resonances*, Dan was an excellent scholar, a talented critic, and, most of all, a warm and generous person. His entries are testament to his first rate scholarship and, even more importantly, his essential fair-mindedness. The field will miss the many additional contributions he would have made over the years, but even more, we will miss him.

Marie-Claire Antoine at Routledge believed in this project from the beginning and guided me through all of the difficult initial steps. I would like to thank her for all of her help, and for Marjorie Burns for suggesting me as the editor of the project. Jamie Ehrlich, my editor, has never failed to return an e-mail or answer a question and has been exceedingly patient with me. She has also handled all of the incredibly complex logistics of the Encyclopedia so well that there have never been any problems on that front, and for this and her ability to project calmness in all circumstances, I am particularly grateful. James Palmer has made the production of the volume a pleasure.

The Advisory Board, Douglas A. Anderson, Marjorie Burns, Verlyn Flieger and Tom Shippey, worked with me to shape the Encyclopedia and have saved me from many mistakes. Even more importantly, they have continued to encourage me throughout the project and have provided excellent advice. Their own entries—some of the most difficult—have also contributed enormously to the book.

At Wheaton College, my student research partners, Stephanie Olsen and Melissa Smith-MacDonald, were instrumental in helping me to develop the original table of contents for the Encyclopedia. Marcel R. Bülles and Rebecca Epstein were invaluable in completing the work. My colleagues in the English department and beyond have continued to support my work, and Marilyn Todesco has saved me from my own mistakes and generously provided the friendship and encouragement (as she always does) that allow me to work.

Finally, and most importantly, I want to thank my wife, Raquel M. D'Oyen, my daughter, Rhys Miranda Drout, and my son, Mitchell D.C. Drout, for their love and infinite patience. You three make all the work worthwhile.

Michael D.C. Drout, Dedham and Norton, Massachusetts

CONVENTIONS AND ABBREVIATIONS

Because there are so many editions of *The Hobbit* and *The Lord of the Rings*, citations will be by book and chapter as well as by page-number (referenced to the editions listed below). Thus a citation from *The Fellowship of the Ring*, book two, chapter four, page 318 is written (*FR*, II, iv, 318). The "Silmarillion" indicates the body of stories and poems developed over many years by Tolkien; *The Silmarillion* indicates the volume first published in 1977.

Abbreviations

B&C	*Beowulf and the Critics.* Michael D. C. Drout, ed. Medieval and Renaissance Texts and Studies 248. Tempe, AZ: Arizona Medieval and Renaissance Texts and Studies, 2002.
Bombadil	*The Adventures of Tom Bombadil.* London: George Allen & Unwin, 1962; Boston: Houghton Mifflin, 1963.
FR	*The Fellowship of the Ring.* London: George Allen & Unwin, 1954; Boston: Houghton Mifflin, 1954. Second edition, revised impression, Boston: Houghton Mifflin,1987.
H	*The Hobbit.* London: George Allen & Unwin, 1937. Boston: Houghton Mifflin, 1938. *The Annotated Hobbit*, ed. Douglas A. Anderson. Second edition, revised. Boston: Houghton Mifflin, 2002.
Jewels	*The War of the Jewels.* Christopher Tolkien, ed. London: HarperCollins; Boston: Houghton Mifflin, 1994.
Lays	*The Lays of Beleriand.* Christopher Tolkien, ed. London: George Allen & Unwin; Boston: Houghton Mifflin, 1985.
Letters	*The Letters of J.R.R. Tolkien.* Humphrey Carpenter, ed. with the assistance of Christopher Tolkien. London: George Allen & Unwin; Boston: Houghton Mifflin, 1981.
Lost Road	*The Lost Road and Other Writings* Christopher Tolkien, ed. London: Unwin Hyman; Boston: Houghton Mifflin, 1987.
Lost Tales I	*The Book of Lost Tales, Part One.* Christopher Tolkien, ed. London: George Allen & Unwin, 1983; Boston: Houghton Mifflin, 1984.
Lost Tales II	*The Book of Lost Tales, Part Two.* Christopher Tolkien, ed. London: George Allen & Unwin; Boston: Houghton Mifflin, 1984.
LotR	*The Lord of the Rings* by J.R.R. Tolkien; the work itself irrespective of edition.
MC	*The Monsters and the Critics and Other Essays.* London: George Allen & Unwin, 1983; Boston: Houghton Mifflin, 1984.
Morgoth	*Morgoth's Ring.* Edited by Christopher Tolkien. London: HarperCollins; Boston: Houghton Mifflin, 1993.
PS	*Poems and Stories.* London: George Allen & Unwin, 1980; Boston: Houghton Mifflin, 1994.
Peoples	*The Peoples of Middle-earth.* Christopher Tolkien, ed. London: HarperCollins; Boston: Houghton Mifflin, 1996.
RK	*The Return of the King.* London: George Allen & Unwin 1955; Boston: Houghton Mifflin, 1956. Second edition, revised impression, Boston: Houghton Mifflin, 1987.
S	*The Silmarillion.* Christopher Tolkien, ed. London: George Allen & Unwin, 1977. Boston: Houghton Mifflin, 1977. Second edition. London: HarperCollins, 1999; Boston: Houghton Mifflin, 2001.

Sauron	*Sauron Defeated*. Christopher Tolkien, ed. London: HarperCollins; Boston: Houghton Mifflin, 1992.
Shadow	*The Return of the Shadow*. Christopher Tolkien, ed. London: Unwin Hyman; Boston: Houghton Mifflin, 1988.
Shaping	*The Shaping of Middle-earth*. Christopher Tolkien, ed. London: George Allen & Unwin; Boston Houghton Mifflin, 1986.
TL	*Tree and Leaf*. London: Unwin Books, 1964; Boston: Houghton Mifflin, 1965. Expanded as *Tree and Leaf, Including the Poem "Mythpoeia" [and] The Homecoming of Beorhtnoth Beorhthelm's Son*. London: HarperCollins, 2001.
TT	*The Two Towers*. London: George Allen & Unwin, 1954; Boston: Houghton Mifflin, 1955. Second edition, revised impression, Boston: Houghton Mifflin, 1987.
Treason	*The Treason of Isengard*. Christopher Tolkien, ed. London: Unwin Hyman; Boston: Houghton Mifflin, 1989.
UT	*Unfinished Tales of Númenor and Middle-Earth*. Christopher Tolkien, ed. London: George Allen & Unwin; Boston: Houghton Mifflin, 1980.
War	*The War of the Ring*. Christopher Tolkien, ed. London: Unwin Hyman; Boston: Houghton Mifflin, 1990.

AB LANGUAGE

In 1929 Tolkien published an essay in *Essays and Studies of the English Association*, 14, in which he showed that the Corpus MS of the *Ancrene Wisse* (= A) and MS Bodley 34 of the Katherine Group manuscripts (= B) were written in the same standard literary language from the West Midland area. Tolkien called this consistent system of spelling habits "the AB language." See also *Ancrene Wisse* and *Katherine Group*.

The Katherine Group is a closely related group of five prose texts, most fully preserved in MS Oxford, Bodleian Library, Bodley 34, namely, *St. Katherine, St. Margarete, St. Juliana, Hali Meidenhad,* and *Sawles Warde.* Nowadays, the so-called Wooing Group of texts, represented by *The Wohunge of ure Lauerd,* is also counted among the AB texts.

The following comment on Tolkien's essay by Tom Shippey has been much quoted: "the most perfect though not the best-known of his academic pieces" (*The Road to Middle-earth*). Tolkien aimed to show in his essay that the scribes of MS Corpus Christi College, Cambridge, the *Ancrene Wisse* (= A), and of MS Bodley 34, the Katherine Group (= B), used a language and spelling nearly "as indistinguishable as that of two modern printed books."

There are clear signs indicating that literary standards had existed in Old English besides Late West Saxon. This is true of the Mercian type of dialect found in the Vespasian Psalter Gloss from the ninth century. There is an obvious continuity of writing traditions from this westerly part of England in Old English times to the West Midlands of England in the thirteenth century, where the AB language was located. Due to the fact that the Franciscans and the Dominicans are mentioned in the *Ancrene Wisse,* we may assume that the manuscript was written after the time when these two categories of friars arrived in England (1224 and 1221, respectively), most probably in the second quarter of the thirteenth century.

The connections between the manuscripts of the *Ancrene Wisse* and those of the Katherine Group had been touched on by some previous scholars. It was, however, J.R.R. Tolkien who pointed out the close relationship in language and spelling, almost amounting to identity, between the *Ancrene Wisse* and the Bodleian manuscript of the Katherine Group. Nowhere else in Middle English literature do we find two different manuscripts of two different literary works copied by different scribes that show such obvious similarities. It is clear that the two manuscripts must be connected in time and place.

These unique circumstances led Tolkien to suppose (i) that A or B are both originals, (ii) that A or B are in whole or part accurate translations, or (iii) that the vanished originals of A and B were in this same language (AB) and so belonged to practically the same period and place as the copies we have. The first possibility can at once be dismissed. Neither A nor B can be originals. Tolkien does not think that an accurate translation is credible. He firmly believes that the originals of A and B were written in the same language and spelling (AB) as the copies. He admits that the spelling suggests obedience to some school or authority. This school was the center of learning where the AB language was taught, read, and written. Tolkien placed the AB language in the West Midlands, more specifically in Herefordshire.

Since there are so many obvious links between the *Ancrene Wisse* and the Katherine Group, many scholars have suggested that they may have been written by the same author. However, there is no substantial reason for such an assumption. There are naturally numerous similarities in vocabulary, phraseology, and syntax, but this could be expected in texts that have been composed in close proximity or in the same religious or cultural center or in the same scriptorium.

Tolkien continued to exert his influence on one particular study of the AB language in an indirect way. In Simone d'Ardenne's edition of *Seinte Iuliene* from 1936, the author analyzed the orthography, phonology, morphology, and vocabulary of the AB language in great detail. It was, however, obvious that the supervisor of her thesis, J.R.R. Tolkien, had influenced d'Ardenne's description of the AB language quite clearly. This edition received considerable praise from reviewers at the time; it was considered the best edition of a Middle English text to date and was particularly admired for its originality of outlook.

In spite of the fact that J.R.R. Tolkien became especially famous for his studies not only of *Beowulf* but also of Chaucer and *Sir Gawain and the Green Knight,* his research on various aspects of the AB language was more extensive. In 1962, Tolkien continued his studies of the AB language by completing his edition of the *Ancrene Wisse* for the Early English Text Society, Oxford University Press. His interest in the AB texts and the West Midland literary tradition had started as early as the middle of the 1920s and continued until well into the 1960s. This period represents the best part of Tolkien's adult research life, nearly half a century.

ARNE ZETTERSTEN

Further Reading

Black, Merja Riitta. "AB or Simply A? Reconsidering the Case for a Standard." *Neuphilologische Mitteilungen* 100 (1999): 155–74.

Dance, Richard. "The AB Language: The Recluse, the Gossip and the Language Historian." In *A Companion to Ancrene Wisse,* edited by Yoko Wada, 57–82. Cambridge: D.S. Brewer, 2003.

D'Ardenne, S.R.T.O. *Þe Liflade ant te Passiun of Seinte Iuliene.* EETS 248. London: Oxford University Press, 1961.

Dobson, E.J. *The Origins of the Ancrene Wisse.* Oxford: Clarendon Press, 1976.

Laing, Margaret. *Catalogue of Sources for a Linguistic Atlas of Early Medieval English.* Cambridge: D.S. Brewer, 1993.

Millett, Bella, with the assistance of George B. Jack and Yoko Wada. *Ancrene Wisse, the Katherine Group, and the Wooing Group: Annotated Bibliographies of Old and Middle English Literature.* Vol. 2. Cambridge: D.S. Brewer, 1996.

Shippey, T.A. *The Road to Middle-earth.* Boston: Houghton Mifflin, 2005.

Smith, J.J. "A Linguistic Atlas of Early Middle English: Tradition and Typology." In *History of Englishes: New Methods and Interpretations in Historical Linguistics,* edited by Matti Rissanen et al., 582–91. Topics in English Linguistics 10. Berlin: Mouton de Gruyter, 1992.

Thompson, W. *The Wohunge of Ure Lauerd.* EETS 241. London: Oxford University Press, 1958.

Tolkien, J.R.R. "Ancrene Wisse and Hali Meiðhad." *Essays and Studies by Members of the English Association* 14 (1929): 104–26.

———. *The English Text of the Ancrene Riwle, Ancrene Wisse, Edited from MS Corpus Christi College Cambridge 402.* EETS o.s. 249. London: Oxford University Press, 1962.

Wada, Yoko, ed. *A Companion to Ancrene Wisse.* Cambridge: D.S. Brewer, 2003.

———, ed. and trans. *Temptations from Ancrene Wisse.* Vol. 1. Kansai University Institute of Oriental and Occidental Studies, Sources and Materials Series 18. Osaka: Kansai University Press; Cambridge: D.S. Brewer, 1994.

Zettersten, Arne. "The AB Language Lives." In *The Invented Worlds of J.R.R. Tolkien: Drawings and Original Manuscripts from the Marquette University Collection.* Milwaukee, WI.: Marquette University, 2004.

———. *Studies in the Dialect and Vocabulary of the Ancrene Riwle.* Copenhagen and Lund: Ejnar Munksgaard & G.W.K. Gleerup, 1965.

See also **Ancrene Wisse**, **Ancrene Riwle; D'Ardenne, S.R.T.O.; Katherine Group; MS Bodley 34, "Ancrene Wisse and Hali Meiðhad"**

ADVENTURES OF TOM BOMBADIL

The Adventures of Tom Bombadil and Other Verses from the Red Book is a collection of sixteen poems or songs published as a group in 1962, many of which were first published in the 1920s and 1930s, long before Tolkien began writing *The Lord of the Rings.* Within the world of Middle-earth, the collection represents a selection of material from the *Red Book of Westmarch,* the main body of which is *The Hobbit* and *The Lord of the Rings.* The authorship of the poems varies, but most are attributed to Bilbo, Frodo, and Sam, though many may have originated elsewhere in Middle-earth before becoming part of Shire folklore. Three of the poems appeared in *The Lord of the Rings:* "The Man in the Moon Stayed Up Too Late," which Frodo sang in Bree; "The Stone Troll," which Sam sang on the road to Rivendell; and "Oliphaunt," which Sam sang on the road south from the Black Gate. Three of the songs deal with alleged adventures of Tom Bombadil, the first two in the collection plus "The Stone Troll." "The Adventures of Tom Bombadil," which first appeared in *Oxford Magazine* in 1934, recounts how Tom escapes from traps set by Goldberry (supposedly a wraith), Willowman (probably a treelike Huorn), a family of badgers, and a barrow-wight (an undead human spirit). After a good night's sleep, Tom captures, pacifies, and marries Goldberry, accounting for the family situation that the Hobbits find on visiting Tom in his home. Tom sings a variant of the first two lines of the song in *The Lord of the Rings*, and much of his other singing is reminiscent of this song. The second song, "Bombadil Goes Boating," written especially for this volume, tells of a visit by Tom to Farmer Maggot of the Marish, a Hobbit who assisted Frodo and his fellow Hobbits in getting across the Brandywine River early in their adventures. On the way, Tom interacts with a wren, a kingfisher, an otter, a swan, and some Hobbits and then parties with Farmer Maggot and his family. Interestingly, the poem refers to Hreidmar's son Otter in the *Prose Edda* and mentions "tall Watchers by the Ford," Aragorn's rangers guarding the Shire. The first two songs are said to be folklore of Buckland. "Errantry," originally published in *Oxford Magazine* in 1933, is the nonsensical adventures of a tiny messenger knight who falls in love with a butterfly and battles various insects. It was written by Bilbo and is related to Bilbo's serious account of Eärendil's quest in *The Lord of the Rings*. "Princess Mee," originally published as "Princess Ni" in *Leeds University Verse, 1914–1924*, tells of an Elven princess who falls in love with her reflection in the ice. "The Man in the Moon Stayed Up Too Late," published as "The Cat and the Fiddle" in *Yorkshire Poetry* in 1923, is supposed to be the original version of the famous nursery rhyme. The sun and the moon in Middle-earth mythology are two vessels containing the flower and fruit of the Two Trees piloted by two Maiar, Arien and Tilion (the Man in the Moon). "The Man in the Moon Came Down Too Soon," published as "Why the Man in the Moon Came Down Too Soon" in *A Northern Venture* in 1923, is at most a Hobbit nursery rhyme, since the depiction of the Man in the Moon is not consistent with Middle-earth mythology. "The Stone Troll," originally "The Root of the Boot" in *Songs for the Philologists* in 1936, recounts an encounter between Tom and a troll, who is supposedly eating the shin of his (dead) Uncle Tim. This song is said to have been written by Sam, along with the next, "Perry-the-Winkle," another humorous story about a troll trying to make friends with Hobbits (a revision of an early unpublished poem). "The Mewlips," originally "Knocking at the Door" in *Oxford Magazine* in 1937, is a nursery

rhyme about monsters probably modeled on Orcs. The next three songs are examples of bestiary lore. "Oliphaunt," published in *Stapeldon Magazine* in 1927, is referred to by Sam in *The Lord of the Rings* as "speaking poetry" and as a nonsense rhyme based on "news out of the South" of the Swertings or Haradrim in the Sunlands. The Oliphaunts or Mumakil were used as weapons of war in the Battle of the Pelennor Fields. "Fastitocalon," published as "Adventures in Unnatural History and Medieval Metres" in *Stapeldon Magazine* in 1927, provides a rare glimpse of the fears of sailors traveling on the High Seas. The song warns of a giant turtle, who pretends to be an island and drowns those who land on him. "Cat," previously unpublished, examines the similarities of house cats with lions. "Shadow-bride," also previously unpublished, tells of a man under a spell and without a shadow who captures and marries a lady (probably an elf) and dances with her once a year thereafter making a single shadow. "The Hoard," published in *The Gryphon* in 1923, recounts the story of Elven wealth that successively is hoarded by a Dwarf, a dragon, and a human warrior and is finally lost behind doors that none can unlock. Although the preface suggests that it contains echoes of the Númenorean story of Túrin and Mîm, there is little relationship to the actual story. "The Sea-bell," published as "Looney" in *Oxford Magazine* in 1934, is said to be a dream of Frodo, related to his illness from the Morgul knife, in which, after riding in a mysterious boat, he is no longer able to interact with humans and other living creatures. "The Last Ship," first published as "Fíriel" in *The Chronicle of the Convent of the Sacred Heart* in 1934, tells of a human woman, Fíriel ("mortal woman"), who is offered the chance to sail to the Uttermost West with the Elves on the last ship from Middle-earth. She refuses, since she was born "Earth's daughter," and the song (and the memory) of the Elves fades from Middle-earth with her natural death years later.

GENE HARGROVE

Further Reading

Bertenstam, Åke. "A Chronological Bibliography of the Writings of J.R.R. Tolkien." http://www.forodrim.org/arda/tbchron.html (September 2002).

Kocher, Paul H. *Master of Middle-earth: The Fiction of J.R.R. Tolkien*. Boston: Houghton Mifflin, 1972.

Noel, Ruth S. *The Mythology of Middle-earth*. Boston: Houghton Mifflin, 1978.

Shippey, T.A. *The Road to Middle-earth*. Boston: Houghton Mifflin, 2000.

See also **Goldberry; Monster (Barrow-wight); Poems by JRRT:** *Adventures of Tom Bombadil*; **Rhyme Schemes and Alliteration; Tom Bombadil**

ÆLFWINE (OLD ENGLISH "ELF-FRIEND")

Ælfwine is a common Anglo-Saxon name (cf. Ælfwine [died 937 in the Battle of Brunanburh], grandson of King Alfred; or Ælfwine, abbot of the New Minster, Winchester, 1031–57) and comprises the equally common Anglo-Saxon name-elements *ælf* ("elf," cf. Ælfric, Ælfthryth, Ælfhelm, etc.) and *wine* ("friend," cf. Leofwine, Tatwine). Although an Anglo-Saxon could have easily deciphered the meaning of Ælfwine, it is assumed that it was regarded as a conventional name already in Old English times and that it no longer carried any associations with "elves."

Ælfwine/Elf-friend occurs in Tolkien's writings not only as a proper name in various forms, such as Elendil, Ælfwine, Alboin, and Alwin, but also as an honorific title and a concept (Flieger, "The Footsteps of Ælfwine"). However, the focus of this entry will be on the first of these, namely, Ælfwine as a protagonist in Tolkien's writings.

The earliest Ælfwine figure, at this stage called Eriol, appears in *The Book of Lost Tales I*. Eriol, also called Ottor, Waefre, and Angol, is a native of Angel, that is, the region of the Danish peninsula between the Flensburg fjord and the river Schlei— the very same region that was the home of the Angles before they set out for Britain. Eriol settles on the island of Heligoland in the North Sea. Together with a woman named Cwen (Old English for "woman"), he has two sons called Hengest and Horsa. After the death of Cwen, Eriol journeys westward over the ocean to Tol Eressëa, where he marries an Elvish woman with whom he has another son, Heorrenda. During his sojourn, Eriol also learns the "Lost Tales of Elfinesse" from the Elves themselves and even witnesses the ruin of Elvish Tol Eressëa. He, together with his son, afterward returns to his homeland.

The tales of the Elves were written down either by Eriol himself or by Heorrenda. The latter joins his half-brothers Hengest and Horsa, who are to be identified with the semimythical Jutish leaders of the Germanic tribes that came over to Britain in the fifth century AD. They conquer Britain and thus provide an explanation as to why the legendarium found its home in England. Christopher Tolkien comments "Thus it is that through Eriol and his sons the Engle (i.e., the English) have the true tradition of the fairies [... and] a specifically English fairy-lore is born, and one more true than anything to be found in Celtic lands." (*Lost Tales II*, 290).

Tolkien, at one stage of the development of the legend in the 1930s, equated Eriol with Ælfwine the Englishman (cf. *Lost Tales II*, 300).

This change of name signals a change in conception. Eriol's function is taken over by Ælfwine the Englishman (see *Lost Tales II*, 312–22), here an eleventh-century Anglo-Saxon from Wessex. In the early versions, he is of the kin of Ing, a king who ruled over Luthany (Britain) when it was not yet an island. Ing was friendly with the Elves, and, on his journey to Tol Eressëa, he was shipwrecked and became the ruler of the Ingwaiar, a people in the Northeast of Europe. He taught the Ingwaiar the lore of the Elves, and they later invaded Britain and thus came "back into their own." Ælfwine has, therefore, from his family background, an affinity to Elves, and he has the gift of seeing them. Ælfwine sails from England to Tol Eressëa, where he learns the lore from the Elves themselves. Yet while Eriol's Tol Eressëa was envisioned as the island that would become England, and thus makes the legendarium indeed "a mythology for England," this is no longer the case with Ælfwine the Englishman, who sets out from England westward and arrives at a Tol Eressëa that no longer occupies the same geographical space as Britain.

Ælfwine also occurs as one of the ancestors of Alboin Errol in *The Lost Road* (c. 1937) and of Alwin Loudham in *The Notion Club Papers* (c. 1945/46). Alboin, like Alwin (both names mean "Elf-friend"), "travels back in time" in dreams and visions by means of his ancestral memory and thus gets to know the story of Ælfwine (*869 AD), an Englishman of the time of King Alfred (died 899) and King Edward the Elder (reigned 900–24). Ælfwine and a companion (his son Eadwine in *The Lost Road*; his friend Treowine in *The Notion Club Papers*) sail to Ireland and then into the West, where they catch a fleeting glimpse of Tol Eressëa. Tolkien's ideas of what would happen afterward are not clear. On the one hand, we find sketches that have Ælfwine set foot on Tol Eressëa, where he is welcomed by the Elves. Ælfwine stays with the Elves, learns their lore, and writes it down in the Golden Book of Tavrobel, which he deposits, after his return to Britain, at Old Tavrobel (Great Haywood in England). On the other hand, Tolkien thought about having Ælfwine blown back by an adverse wind so that he never actually reached Tol Eressëa. There are also indications that Tolkien had planned to rewrite the Eriol-saga as the continuation of Ælfwine's tale, but rejected it in favor of the drowning of Númenor ("Atlantis") (cf. *Sauron*, 281–82).

Tolkien, by making Ælfwine both temporally and spatially distant from the events he records, turns him into a more detached chronicler of Elvish history and legend than his predecessor Eriol, who is portrayed as actively taking part in the events and as being an eyewitness to the defeat and the fading of the Elves. Eriol thus plays an active role and is both inside the tale as a protagonist as well as outside as a chronicler. Ælfwine, being placed several centuries after the time of Eriol and the events he describes, is a figure no longer directly involved in the stories and legends of the Elves and thus provides a more appropriate figure of identification for the modern Elf-friend Tolkien.

THOMAS HONEGGER

Further Reading

Flieger, Verlyn. "The Footsteps of Ælfwine." In *Tolkien's Legendarium*, edited by Verlyn Flieger and Carl F. Hostetter, 183–98. Westport, Conn.: Greenwood Press, 2000.

Tolkien, Christopher. "Commentary on The Cottage of Lost Play." In *Lost Tales I.*

———. "The History of Eriol or Ælfwine and the End of the Tales." In *Lost Tales II.*

See also **Anglo-Saxon;** *Beowulf*; *Book of Lost Tales I and II*; **Frame Narratives; Geatas;** *Lost Road*; *Notion Club Papers*

ALCUIN (CA. 735–804)

Born in England, Alcuin was a leading scholar and teacher of the Carolingian period and a close advisor to Charlemagne. His important works include several educational treatises, poems, and, especially, a series of more than three hundred letters. In a letter of 795 addressed to "Speratus" (usually identified as Bishop Higbald of Lindisfarne), Alcuin complains of monks listening to stories of pagan heroes, asking the rhetorical question, "*Quid Hinieldus cum Christo?*" ("What does Ingeld have to do with Christ?"). Alcuin here echoes the early Christian Father Tertullian, who argued that the study of pagan philosophy had no place in the Christian world, asking "*Quid ergo Athenis et Hierosolymis?*" ("What does Athens have to do with Jerusalem?"). Although Ingeld is mentioned only briefly in *Beowulf*, scholars, including Tolkien, have often applied Alcuin's question to the study of the poem, in an attempt to reconcile the pagan and Christian elements evident in it. In "*Beowulf*: The Monsters and the Critics," Tolkien suggests that the poem is inspired, at least in part, by questions like the one asked by Alcuin and argues that *Beowulf* resolves this debate by presenting the tragedy of pagan life not in a condemnatory way but in an attempt to stir Christian sympathy. The *Beowulf*-poet is able to blend successfully pagan and Christian elements, according to Tolkien, because he is writing at a time when Christianity had replaced paganism in England but had not erased the pagan past from popular memory.

WILLIAM SMITH

Further Reading

Allott, Stephen. *Alcuin of York, c. A.D. 732 to 804: His Life and Letters.* York: William Sessions Ltd., 1974.

See also ***Beowulf and the Critics;* "*Beowulf*: The Monsters and the Critics"; Carolingians; Tertullian**

ALDHELM (d. 709 OR 710)

Aldhelm was the abbot of Malmesbury and bishop of Sherborne. He was evidently descended from Wessex nobility and had connections with the royal court there. Aldhelm is the earliest native-born English scholar to leave behind a body of writing in Latin, including prose and metrical versions of his treatise *De virginitate* ("On Virginity") and a collection of one hundred poetic *enigmata*, or riddles. According to William of Malmesbury, Aldhelm was also an accomplished vernacular poet and a favorite of King Alfred's, although no example of his Old English verse survives. His name has frequently been associated with the *Liber monstrorum*, or "Book of Monsters," an anonymous Latin prose work thought to have been composed in England during the late seventh or early eighth century that shares source material with *Beowulf*. Although it seems unlikely that Aldhelm himself wrote the *Liber*, its sources suggest that its author, like Aldhelm, was working in Wessex and had access to the same monastic library.

Tolkien mentions Aldhelm in the early drafts of his 1936 Gollancz Lecture, "*Beowulf*: The Monsters and the Critics," as an example of an English, Christian scholar who both esteemed and contributed to a vernacular poetic tradition, but he edits this reference out of his final version.

KATHRYN POWELL

Further Reading

Lapidge, Michael. "'Beowulf,' Aldhelm, the 'Liber Monstrorum' and Wessex," *Studi Medievali*, ser. 3, v. 23 (1982).

Malmesbury, William of. *Gesta Pontificum*, edited by S.A. Hamilton, 332–33. London: Rolls Series, 1870.

Orchard, Andy. *The Poetic Art of Aldhelm.* CSASE 8. Cambridge: Cambridge University Press, 1994.

See also ***Beowulf and the Critics;* "*Beowulf*: The Monsters and the Critics"; Latin Language; Latin Literature; Old English**

ALLEGORY

Tolkien is regularly quoted as having written, "I cordially dislike allegory in all its manifestations, and always have done so since I grew old and wary enough to detect its presence" (*FR*, Foreword 7). However, his relationship to allegorical writing was much more complex than such a flat denial would indicate. Tolkien was not above using allegorical elements when it suited his purpose, but he emphatically refuted attempts to ascribe it to his fiction where it had not been intended.

In general, allegory is the one-to-one correspondence between characters or plot with historical persons, places, events, or even philosophical ideas. The basic operation of allegory, as Tom Shippey explains it, "is to start making equations" (*Road*, 40). Two well-known literary examples are John Bunyan's *Pilgrim's Progress* (in which Christian's journey to the Celestial City equals the soul's struggle toward Heaven) and George Orwell's *Animal Farm* (wherein farm animals stage a revolution that mirrors the Russian Revolution). The challenge in writing allegorical fiction is to create three-dimensional characters who live in their own right and are not simply flat cartoons of the thing they represent. That is not to say that vibrant, well-written fiction cannot have allegorical elements, as Tolkien himself admitted: "I dislike Allegory—the conscious and intentional allegory—yet any attempt to explain the purport of myth or fairytale must use allegorical language," he wrote to Milton Waldman of the Collins publishing house (*Letters*, 145).

Tolkien's Dislike of Allegory

Tolkien's objections to allegorical interpretations of his works are to be found mostly in his letters, in addition to his statement in the foreword to the second edition of *The Fellowship of the Ring*, quoted at the beginning of this essay. The letters reveal that his major animosity toward allegory was the result of its misapplication to *The Hobbit* and *The Lord of the Rings* by critics or readers who assumed allegory was Tolkien's major intention. He spent a good deal of energy writing denials to questions about the allegorical meaning of the books and got quite put out with literary commentators and overly analytical fans who wanted to read interpretations into the books that Tolkien insisted were not there. "I have already had one letter from America asking for an authoritative exposition of the allegory of *The Hobbit*," he complained to his publisher in 1938 (*Letters*, 41).

To another such letter, he responded, "There is no 'symbolism' or conscious allegory in my story.

Allegory of the sort 'five wizards = five senses' is wholly foreign to my way of thinking... . To ask if Orcs 'are' Communists is to me as sensible as asking if Communists are Orcs" (*Letters*, 262). He was especially rankled by Åke Ohlmarks's introduction to the 1961 Swedish translation of *The Lord of the Rings*, which suggested correspondences between Sauron and Stalin, or between Mordor and Russia. "I utterly repudiate any such 'reading', which angers me," Tolkien wrote to his publishers Allen & Unwin. "The situation was conceived long before the Russian revolution. Such allegory is entirely foreign to my thought" (*Letters*, 307). It was a statement that he would repeat numerous times when asked what *The Hobbit* and *The Lord of the Rings* were really about.

Applicability

Tolkien suggested more than once that readers who wanted to ascribe allegorical meaning to his fiction did not understand his approach to fiction writing. Just because something in a work of fiction resonates with a reader's knowledge of certain elements in history, religion, or politics does not mean there is an intended correspondence. As he observed in a response to questions from Walter Allen of the *New Statesman* in 1959, "most readers appear to confuse [allegory] with significance or applicability" (*Letters*, 297). The resonance a reader experiences is more universal, allowing for a much wider interpretation than the narrow assignments of allegory. "That there is no allegory does not, of course, say there is no applicability. There always is," (*Letters*, 262) he wrote in 1957.

Tolkien's essay "On Fairy-Stories" explores this notion in the context of fantasy. Further, Shippey points out that the fine-line balance between allegory and applicability that Tolkien was aiming for is evident in his famous defense of *Beowulf* (44). In this speech (published as "*Beowulf:* The Monsters and the Critics"), Tolkien argued for the poem as a work of literary art rather than mere didactic Christian allegory: the dragon does not equal the Devil or Leviathan, as one finds in typical medieval literature, nor is it a literal beast. It has both symbolic value and plot significance wider than that of mere allegory. In Tolkien's posthumously published introduction to the fifteenth-century poem "Pearl," he takes this idea further, arguing that the poem cannot be read as a simple allegory because "there are a number of precise details in *Pearl* that cannot be subordinated to any general allegorical interpretation" (9) even though they relate directly to the central figure of the poem. Thus, the necessary one-to-one correspondence of the work "*as a whole*" with some other event or philosophical idea is missing.

Interpreting *The Lord of the Rings*

The most prevalent allegorical interpretations of *The Lord of the Rings* are (1) biblical readings based on Tolkien's expressed Catholicism and (2) historical interpretations in which the War of the Rings is understood to be a cognate for World War I or World War II. For example, these arguments conclude that Saruman = Judas or industrialism/technology, Sauron = Satan or Hitler or Stalin, Gandalf = God or Churchill, Aragorn = Christ or MacArthur, the Ring = the atomic bomb, Mordor = Hell or Russia or Germany. Historically speaking, it is very tempting to equate the wastes of Mordor with the World War I battlefield Tolkien personally witnessed in France during the Battle of the Somme or to see the fell beasts of the Nazgûl as strafing bombers from World War II. In a letter to Sir Stanley Unwin discussing *The Lord of the Rings*, Tolkien admitted that the looming darkness of the state of the world in 1938 "has had some effect on it. Though it is not an 'allegory'" (*Letters*, 41). The general horror of war was applicable, but not as a specific war.

Regarding biblical cognates, as Michael W. Maher, S.J., suggests, "elements from the Christian tradition of salvation history frequently tempt readers into believing the work is a retelling of that history. When reading the trilogy, who could not think of Gandalf's descent into the pits of Moria and his return clothed in white as a death-resurrection motif?" (*Medievalist*, 225). One fairly unique biblical argument is Charles Nelson's interpretation of Tolkien's opus as a morality tale in which his races can be equated with the Seven Deadly Sins: Dwarves = Greed, Men = Pride, Elves = Envy, Ents = Sloth, Hobbits = Gluttony, Wormtongue = Lechery, Orcs = Anger (*Medievalist*, 84).

The problem with such a narrow interpretation is that it stifles the reader's imagination by insisting that only one consistent meaning can be ascribed throughout the saga to characters such as Gandalf or to events such as the overthrow of Sauron and his deadly weapon the Ring. If one allows applicability, however, readers can comprehend the books through a wide range of individual emotional and intellectual reactions.

Occasionally, according to Shippey, Tolkien comes perilously close to the realm of allegory, as witnessed in the Field of Cormallen scene in *The Return of the King* in which the eagle's song sounds suspiciously like Psalms 24 and 33: "Sing and be glad, all ye children of the West, / for your King shall come again, / and he shall dwell among you / all the days of your life" (*RK*, VI, V 241). Such parallels suggest Aragorn as a Gondorian Christ figure.

Tolkien's method of "combination of the familiar with the unfamiliar" (Kocher, *Master*, 17) is what adds authenticity to his subcreated world, but it does not constitute allegory with our real world events in any sense. Robert Plank's psychological reading of "The Scouring of the Shire" chapter, for example, labels it "a realistic parable of reality" (*Compass*, 118) rather than an outright allegory.

Allegorical Elements in Tolkien's Shorter Fiction

The allegorical content of Tolkien's short fiction is well documented by Shippey, Flieger, Kocher, Brian Rosebury, Richard Purtill, Jane Chance, Randel Helms, Bradley Birzer, and many others. In the short story "Leaf by Niggle," the character Niggle who spends much of his life trying unsuccessfully to complete the painting of a great tree before death takes him, is seen as representing Tolkien himself, who feared that *The Lord of the Rings* had grown far beyond his ability to write it all down in his lifetime. Niggle's "long journey" takes him through death, Purgatory, and eventually Paradise, where his Great Tree attains actuality. *Smith of Wootton Major*, a slightly longer piece, can be read as an allegorical depiction of Tolkien's struggle between his mundane academic life and his pursuit of fantasy writing, or as the representation of a man forced to give up his role in life (retirement) and pass the torch to younger aspirants. Tolkien's novella, *Farmer Giles of Ham*, is often seen as a parody (and parable) of "linguistic scholarship" in which both Tolkien and his fellow philologists are held up for mild ridicule.

Marjorie Burns best presents the caveat against assigning too much allegorical meaning to Tolkien's fiction: "There are a great number of literary themes or figures from a great number of literary traditions that could equally well demonstrate how Tolkien borrowed from other works and other ages in everything that he wrote. We need to remember, as well, that the ways in which Tolkien uses any individual theme or character are themselves highly complex" (*Legendarium*, 220).

ANNE C. PETTY

Further Reading

Birzer, Bradley J. *J.R.R. Tolkien's Sanctifying Myth: Understanding Middle-earth.* Wilmington, DE: ISI Books, 2002.

Carpenter, Humphrey. *Tolkien: A Biography.* Boston, MA: Houghton Mifflin, 1977.

Chance, Jane, ed. *Tolkien and the Invention of Myth: A Reader.* Lexington, KY: University Press of Kentucky, 2004.

———. *Tolkien's Art: A Mythology for England.* New York: St. Martin's Press, 1980.

———, ed. *Tolkien the Medievalist.* London and New York: Routledge, 2003.

Flieger, Verlyn. *A Question of Time: J.R.R. Tolkien's Road to Faërie.* Kent, OH: Kent State University Press, 1997.

Flieger, Verlyn, and Carl F. Hostetter, eds. *Tolkien's Legendarium: Essays on the History of Middle-earth.* Westport, CT.: Greenwood Press, 2000.

Kocher, Paul H. *Master of Middle-earth: The Fiction of J.R.R. Tolkien.* New York: Ballantine Books, 1972.

Lobdell, Jared, ed. *A Tolkien Compass.* La Salle, IL: Open Court, 1975.

Purtill, Richard L. "Heaven and Other Perilous Realm." *Mythlore* 22 (Fall 1979): 3–6.

Rosebury, Brian. *Tolkien: A Cultural Phenomenon.* New York: Palgrave Macmillan, 2003.

Shippey, Tom. *The Road to Middle-earth: Revised and Expanded Edition.* Boston, MA: Houghton Mifflin, 2001.

Tolkien, J.R.R., trans. *Sir Gawain and the Green Knight, Pearl, and Sir Orfeo,* edited by Christopher Tolkien. New York: Ballantine Books, 1975.

See also **"*Beowulf*: The Monsters and the Critics"; Criticism of Tolkien, 20th Century; *Farmer Giles of Ham*; Good and Evil; Industrialization; "Leaf by Niggle"; Marxist Readings of Tolkien; "On Fairy-Stories"; *Smith of Wootton Major*; Theological and Moral Approaches in Tolkien's Works; *Tree and Leaf*; War**

ALLITERATION

Anglo-Saxon alliterative poetry was a pervasive influence on Tolkien's writing. He periodically composed alliterative poetry in Anglo-Saxon itself, notably in *The Lost Road* and *The Notion Club Papers.* He also took pride in demonstrating how well alliterative meter could be adapted to Modern English, both in original works such as "The Lay of the Children of Húrin" and "The Homecoming of Beorhtnoth Beorhthelm's Son" and in his scholarly translations from such Anglo-Saxon and Middle English poems as *Beowulf, The Battle of Maldon, Pearl,* and *Sir Gawain and the Green Knight.*

Tolkien believed that Anglo-Saxon alliterative verse is often misjudged by critics attuned only to modern metrical regularities or to classical poetic forms. Anglo-Saxon verse requires study because its structures have become remote and unfamiliar. Each line of Anglo-Saxon alliterative poetry is divided into two half-lines, and each half-line usually carries one or two stresses. The most strongly stressed syllables begin with the same sound or with more complex patterns of alliteration. In *Beowulf and the Critics,* Tolkien analyzes Anglo-Saxon alliterative verse as a structure of balanced contrasts, whose six varying rhythmic patterns may differ between the half-lines. The half-lines are bound together by alliteration on stressed syllables. Thus "in [Anglo-Saxon meter] there is no single rhythmic pattern progressing from the beginning of the line to the end; the lines do not go according to a tune. They depend on a balance and weight and emotional content, which are more often rhythmically contrasted rather than similar. They are more like masonry than music" (59). Two pivotal lines from *The Battle of Maldon* may serve as an illustration of this idea:

> H̲ige scealþe h̲eardra, h̲eorte þe cenre
> M̲od sceale m̲aree ure m̲aegen litlad

The first line is alliteratively bound together by the letter "H," while the second line alliterates on "M." There is no rigid pattern of stressed and unstressed syllables, either between consecutive lines or across the half-line. Tolkien translates these lines as "Heart shall be bolder, harder be purpose / More proud the spirit as our power lessens," and his Modern English translation enriches the stressed alliteration of "H" and "P" with concatenating secondary alliterations of "B" and "S" on unstressed syllables. Yet while the alliteration binds each half-line together, the half-lines construct images in opposition. The first line balances the fiery courage of the heart with the stiffening of resolve in the mind, while the second line weighs the strengthening spirit against the weakening body.

This combination of rhythmic variation, alliterative flow, and compressed, juxtaposed images achieves a poetic power that Tolkien felt and tried passionately to convey to readers. In "*Beowulf*: The Monsters and the Critics," he writes of how in Anglo-Saxon poetry "profound feeling, and poignant vision, filled with the beauty and mortality of the world, are aroused by brief phrases, light touches, short words resounding like harpstrings, sharply plucked" (59). Alliteration helped tie the composition together, not into the repeating rhythms of modern poetic "music," but something more ancient, the Anglo-Saxon *scop* (minstrel/bard) in the mead hall: an image of artistic creation deeply rooted in the ancient English past.

Thus the archaism of Anglo-Saxon alliterative poetry was not a failing to Tolkien, but rather a link to history, for those who could—by study, reading, and creative composition—tune their ears to hear it; and in his view the prize was well worth the venture. Its power resounds throughout his characterization of the Rohirrim in *The Lord of the Rings*, where even the language barrier cannot prevent the hobbit Merry's heart from leaping when "some Rider would lift up his clear voice in stirring song."

CHRISTINE CHISM

Further Reading

Tolkien, J.R.R. "*Beowulf*: The Monsters and the Critics." In *MC*.
———. "On Translating *Beowulf*." In *MC*.

See also **Alliterative Revival;** *Lays of Beleriand***;** *Sir Gawain and the Green Knight***;** *Pearl***;** *Orfeo, Sir***; Rhyme Schemes and Alliteration; Auden, W.H.**

ALLITERATIVE REVIVAL

From the untrustworthy evidence of the surviving manuscript record, English alliterative poetry had a checkered medieval career. A rich tradition of Anglo-Saxon alliterative poetry extended from the seventh through the eleventh centuries, mostly extant in tenth- and eleventh-century manuscripts, but after the Norman Conquest in 1066, English literary culture seems to have faded from the scene, replaced for the next two hundred years by literary writing in French and Latin. Alliterating, rhythmic prose occurs in sermons and exhortations, yet the few English alliterative poems—such as *Layamon's Brut*—that do survive from this post-Conquest period only draw attention to the echoing gap. When English poetry begins to reappear in the thirteenth century, it has generally adopted the syllabic and rhymed meters in use on the continent. Yet, apparently suddenly in the mid-fourteenth century, alliterative poetry emerges again, in surprisingly sophisticated forms; indeed, some of the greatest poems of the medieval period are written in a fluid, erudite, alliterative long-line that seemingly has no immediate precedent. *William of Palerne* led the brigade followed by *Winner and Waster*, *St. Erkenwald*, William Langland's *Piers Plowman* in at least three different versions, its successors *Mum and the Soothsegger*, *Richard the Redeless*, and *The Crowned King*; the great historical romances of *The Wars of Alexander*, *The Destruction of Troy*, *The Siege of Jerusalem*, the *Alliterative Morte Arthure*, and *Gologrus and Gawain*; the cautionary *Awntyrs off Arthure*, *The Three Dead Kings*, and *Somer Sunday*; and closest to Tolkien's heart, the stunningly beautiful works of the *Gawain*- (or *Pearl*-) poet: *Pearl*, *Sir Gawain and the Green Knight*, *Patience*, and *Cleanness*. What can explain this apparent eruption of late-medieval alliterative verse? If knowledge of Anglo-Saxon alliterative poetry dwindled after the

conquest, and indeed, the very ability to read Anglo-Saxon was lost amidst the rapidly evolving new structures of Middle English, where did poets as brilliant as William Langland and the *Gawain*-poet learn their craft?

Tolkien's friend R.W. Chambers hypothesized that after the Norman Conquest, when French became the language of culture in England, Old English poetic forms went underground, surviving in oral culture and performance through the exigencies of the next two hundred years, and finally reemerging into writing in the late fourteenth century in a deliberate revival. Tolkien agreed with this theory. He treated the writer of *Sir Gawain and the Green Knight* as an inheritor of "the old alliterative meter" ("*Ofermod*," 23). To Tolkien, however, this worthy attempt to revive the Anglo-Saxon poetic inheritance was doomed, and the *Gawain*-poet "paid the price for its failure, for alliterative verse was not in the event revived. The tides of time, of taste, of language, not to mention political power, trade and wealth were against it" ("Introduction" to *Sir Gawain*, 14). In effect, Tolkien tried to redress this failure, undertaking a one-man twentieth-century alliterative revival of his own. On July 18, 1962, he wrote to Jane Neave: "I never agreed to the view of scholars that the metrical form was almost impossibly difficult to write in, and quite impossible to render in modern English. No scholars (or, nowadays, poets) have any experience in composing themselves in exacting metres. I made up a few stanzas in the metre to show that composition in it was not at any rate 'impossible' (though the result might today be thought bad)." His metrically exact translations of the works of the *Gawain*-poet attempt to convey to modern readers the complex beauty and learnedness of these half-lost works, and he used alliterative meters in original works such as "The Lay of the Children of Húrin."

The "Alliterative Revival" has since become a site of critical dispute, and questions remain as to whether there is a single "old alliterative meter" at all. Does the alliterative long-line used so gorgeously by the *Gawain*-poet really have anything to do with Anglo-Saxon poetic traditions, or is it fundamentally different in structure? Is the apparent late–medieval efflorescence of alliterative verse a fluke of manuscript survival? Can we find evidence that earlier alliterative works once existed? Was late medieval alliterative verse an antiquarian revival of past poetic forms, or were those half-lost forms freely reinvented for contemporary purposes? Or, to cut closer to Tolkien's quick, is the Alliterative Revival a nativizing invention of twentieth-century scholars with an investment in rescuing the ancient English past from the encroachments of other cultural traditions? The debate continues.

CHRISTINE CHISM

Further Reading

Cable, Thomas. *The English Alliterative Tradition.* Philadelphia, PA: University of Pennsylvania Press, 1991.

Chambers, R.W. "On the Continuity of English Prose from Alfred to More and His School." In *Nicholas Harpsfield's Life of Sir Thomas More*, ed. E.V. Hitchcock and R.W. Chambers, xi, xiv–clxxiv. EETS 186. Oxford: Oxford University Press, 1932.

Lawton, David, ed. *Middle English Alliterative Poetry and Its Literary Background: Seven Essays.* Cambridge: D.S. Brewer, 1982.

Tolkien, J.R.R., trans. *Sir Gawain and the Green Knight, Pearl, and Sir Orfeo.* Boston: Houghton Mifflin, 1975.

Tolkien, J.R.R., and E.V. Gordon, eds. *Sir Gawain and the Green Knight.* Oxford: Clarendon Press, 1925.

See also **Alliteration; Arthurian Literature; *Brut* by Layamon; *Lays of Beleriand*; *Pearl*; *Sir Gawain and the Green Knight*; *Orfeo, Sir*; Auden, W.H.**

ALLITERATIVE VERSE BY TOLKIEN

Tolkien wrote substantial bodies of alliterative verse in Modern English several times, in several different circumstances. Between 1920 and 1925, he composed rather more than three thousand lines of an earlier and a revised version of "The Lay of the Children of Húrin" (see *Lays,* 3–130). At about the same time, he began two further poems in the same meter on subjects from the "Silmarillion," "The Flight of the Noldoli from Valinor," and "The Lay of Eärendil" (*Lays,* 131–44); and nine alliterating lines precede the 1925 poem on Beren, "Light as Leaf on Lindentree" (see *Shadow,* 180). More than a decade later, his unfinished story "The Lost Road" includes 153 lines of a poem on "King Sheave," based on a story hinted at the start of *Beowulf. The Lord of the Rings* contains eight passages of alliterative verse, most of them short, all but one connected with the Riders—the exception is Treebeard's twelve-line excerpt from "The Long List of the Ents," to which he later adds three more lines, having rejected one suggested by Merry and Pippin. Of the seven Rider-poems, three are calls to arms; four are dirges: two of the dirges, the "Lament for Théoden" and the "Song of the Mounds of Mundburg," are relatively long, twenty-one and twenty-seven lines, respectively, and are perhaps Tolkien's finest expositions of the art of alliteration. Sixteen lines of an untitled poem on wizards are given in the essay "The Istari," in *Unfinished Tales* (395–96).

Tolkien further translated the whole of the Middle English alliterative romance *Sir Gawain and the Green Knight* into Modern English alliterative verse and wrote most of the play fragment of "The Homecoming of Beorhtnoth Beorhthelm's Son" in similar meter. The Middle English *Pearl,* probably also by the author of *Sir Gawain,* is in a complex meter that uses both alliteration and rhyme, faithfully reproduced in Tolkien's translation of it. Tolkien seems to have worked on all three of these pieces between the late 1930s and 1953 or 1954. His poem "The Nameless Land," published in 1927 but existent in several versions, is in the same highly unusual meter and stanza-form as *Pearl.* In 1967, Tolkien wrote a praise-poem in Old English alliterative verse, "For W.H.A. [Auden]," to which he added a translation in the same meter. Tolkien is known to have made a partial translation of *Beowulf* into alliterative verse, which has not been published; he uses some of it to illustrate points in his essay "On Translating *Beowulf.*" Mention should also be made of a poem Tolkien wrote in 1933 for R.W. Chambers. It is modeled on *Piers Plowman,* was called "Doworst" with allusion to *Piers Plowman*'s "Vision of Dobest," describes Oxford students taking an oral exam conducted by (among others) Lewis and Tolkien, and may be seen as a companion piece to "The Clerkes Compleint," modeled on Chaucer, which describes a similar ceremony at Leeds University. Nineteen lines of this poem, from a manuscript since lost, were published in an Australian fanzine in 1978.

From what has been, said it will be clear that Tolkien's alliterative compositions were quite various in date, intention, and even literary model. Alliterative poetry is an old form, extending from at least the seventh century to the sixteenth, and it changed markedly from the Old English period (i.e., before 1066) to the later Middle English period of *Pearl, Sir Gawain,* and *Piers Plowman.* Changes in the language have meant that Middle English, and even more Modern English, contain more unstressed syllables, more little filler-words (especially articles and prepositions) than Old English: translations from Old to Modern English always come out longer. Since alliterative poetry is based overwhelmingly on stress, this makes its older formats hard to imitate. One might say that where Old English tramps, Modern English patters. In between, Middle English poets, and even the poet of the late Old English *Battle of Maldon,* Tolkien's model for "Beorhtnoth," allowed themselves metrical liberties at which the *Beowulf*-poet would have shaken his head disapprovingly.

Tolkien reacted to these issues in different ways. The poems in *Lays of Beleriand* are based on Old English models (with hints also of Old Norse), but are inevitably somewhat slack or unorthodox metrically. One brief way of testing is to see how many half-lines contain unstressed syllables both before the first stress and after the second. In strict Beowulfian meter, this is allowed only under certain conditions, but in these early poems Tolkien permits it quite often. The demands of meter also lead to frequent archaic word-order patterns: Old English was much more flexible in this respect than Modern English. The effect is increased by deliberate use of archaic words such as "dreed" ("endured," from Old English *dreogan*) or "leasows" ("pastures"). One can see why this experiment found little favor.

Translating Middle English was rather easier, since most of the important linguistic changes had already taken place in the original poems, and Tolkien's translations of *Pearl* and *Sir Gawain* read more freely and naturally. It is important to remember, though, that alliterative poetry is very much an oral form; what matters is how the stressed syllable is pronounced, not how it is written, while the stressed syllable need not be at the start of a word. Tolkien scrupulously followed his originals here, though his scrupulosity is concealed by standard English as printed. It is clear, for instance, that the *Gawain*-poet, like so many Englishmen, did not pronounce all his "aitches." When he wrote "Ay watz Arthur the hendest, as I haf herde telle," he meant the first three stresses to fall on "Arth-," "hend-," and "herd-." But for strict meter to be preserved, all three stressed syllables should begin with a vowel. Tolkien's translation accordingly should be pronounced, "ever was ARTHur most 'ONoured, as i 'ave 'EARD men tell." The fact that this in later ages would be regarded as "vulgar" would not have bothered Tolkien at all. His own native Birmingham dialect was not dissimilar to the *Gawain*-poet's.

"The Homecoming" also benefits from the relatively loose meter of *Maldon*, which Tolkien's characters repeatedly quote or allude to. The poem of "King Sheave" approaches much more closely to the effect of classical Old English, both in meter and in rhetorical devices; and Treebeard's gnomic "List" imitates well the similar list in the Old English poem *Maxims II*. However, the best of Tolkien's alliterative poetry is to be found in *The Lord of the Rings*. "Théoden's Battle-Cry" echoes in form and content both the Old English "Finnsburg Fragment" and the Old Norse *Völuspá* (or "Prophetess's Spell)," the former describing a historical battle, the latter the Old Norse Armageddon. The "Lament for Théoden" and the "Song of the Mounds of Mundburg" could be used as textbook examples of Old English metrics in Modern English, and are yet completely comprehensible. In context, they give a powerful sense of the

sadness at the heart of the Riders' heroic culture—and, Tolkien would have added, at the heart of all pre-Christian heroic cultures, real or fictional.

TOM SHIPPEY

Further Reading

Cable, Tom. *The English Alliterative Tradition*. Philadelphia, PA: University of Pennsylvania Press, 1991.

Lewis, C.S. "The Alliterative Metre." In his *Rehabilitations and Other Essays*, 119–32. London: Oxford University Press, 1939.

Shippey, Tom. "Tolkien and the *Gawain*-Poet." In *Proceedings of the J.R.R. Tolkien Centenary Conference*, edited by Patricia Reynolds and Glen H. Goodknight, 213–19. Milton Keynes: Tolkien Society; Altadena, CA.: Mythopoeic Press, 1995.

Zimmermann, Manfred. "Rendering of Tolkien's Alliterative Verse." *Mythlore* 8, no. 2 (Summer 1981): 21.

See also **Alliteration; *Homecoming of Beorhtnoth*; *Lays of Beleriand*; *Sir Gawain and the Green Knight*; Tolkien's Translations of *Beowulf*; Auden, W.H.: Influence of Tolkien**

ALPHABETS, INVENTED

The writing systems invented by Tolkien, most of them associated with the Elves of his mythology, exhibit a variety of forms appropriate to the putative users of the various scripts. These alphabets also display varying degrees of linguistic sophistication, with a more systematic application of symbol to sound than is found in most scripts in general use.

Tengwar

One of the two main Elvish writing systems presented in *The Lord of the Rings* is the *Tengwar* (Quenya "letters," singular *tengwa*), invented by Fëanor, the most skilful of the Noldorin Elves. The letters have a rounded, flowing quality that allows elegant calligraphic representation, as seen in the inscriptions on the One Ring and the West-gate of Moria.

The system is not a linear series of letters with arbitrary sound values, like the Greek and Latin alphabets, but is instead based on a matrix of letters that can be applied to different sounds, depending on the phonological system of the language being represented. The different applications of the letters are known as modes.

As described in Appendix E to *The Lord of the Rings* (*RK*, 395–401), the twenty-four primary letters are each formed of a *telco* (stem) and at least one *lúva* (bow) and are arranged in a grid of four columns (*témar,* series) and six rows (*tyeller,* grades). The four *témar* are constructed thus: (1) open bow to the right of the stem, (2) closed bow to the right of the stem, (3) open bow to the left of the stem, and (4) closed bow to the right of the stem. These four series correspond to points of articulation in the mouth and usually represent the following classes of sounds: (1) dentals, (2) labials, (3) velars (palatals and palato-alveolars in some modes), and (4) labiovelars (velars in some modes). The six *tyeller* are constructed thus: (1) single bow with normal (i.e., descending) stem, (2) double bow with normal stem, (3) single bow with raised stem, (4) double bow with raised stem, (5) double bow with reduced stem, and (6) single bow with reduced stem. The six grades correspond to different manners of articulation and voicing and most frequently represent the following classes of sounds, though applications differ in some modes: (1) voiceless stops, (2) voiced stops, (3) voiceless fricatives, (4) voiced fricatives, (5) nasals, and (6) semivowels and other sonorant consonants.

In addition to the primary letters are additional letters, varying in number according to the mode in question, which are used to represent sounds not covered by the grid of primary letters. The shapes of these are usually derived from primary letters representing similar sounds. A number of diacritical marks or *tehtar* (signs) are also used, either to indicate modifications of consonantal sounds (e.g., indicating a doubled consonant or marking a preceding nasal) or to indicate vowels. In modes employing *tehtar* to indicate vowels (*ómatehtar*), the diacritic may be placed above the preceding consonant or the following consonant, depending on whether words in a given language more frequently end in a vowel (as in Quenya) or a consonant (as in Sindarin). In some modes, however, vowels are represented by full letters, which may themselves be modified by *tehtar* (e.g., to indicate diphthongs).

The most usual application of the system to Quenya is exemplified by a *tengwar* text of "Namárie" (*Road,* 65). In this mode, the *ómatehta* is placed above the preceding consonant, and grades 2 and 4 have unusual values, representing clusters of nasal + voiced stop and nasal + voiceless stop, respectively. The "full-names" of the *tengwar* are Quenya words containing the relevant letter, according to this particular mode.

In contrast to the Quenya mode, modes in which the *ómatehta* is placed above the following consonant include the Sindarin mode in the third copy of the King's Letter (*Sauron,* 131), the Black Speech mode in the Ring-inscription (*FR,* I, ii, 59), the Old English mode in text I of Lowdham's manuscript (*Sauron,* 319–20), and the English mode on the title page of *The Lord of the Rings.* Several modes in which vowels are represented by full letters are also attested. These include the Sindarin Mode of Beleriand on the West-gate of Moria (*FR,* II, iv, 319) and in the text of "A Elbereth Gilthoniel" (*Road,* 70), a different Sindarin mode in the first copy of the King's Letter (*Sauron,* 130), and a variety of English modes seen in the King's Letter (*Sauron,* 130–131), the Book of Mazarbul, and assorted samples of Elvish calligraphy (Tolkien, *Pictures,* nos. 24 and 48).

Cirth (Angerthas)

The other general type of Elvish writing seen in *The Lord of the Rings* consists of angular alphabetic characters called *cirth* (Sindarin "runes," singular *certh*). The name *Angerthas* (Sindarin "long rune-rows") is applied to the alphabets comprised of these *cirth*. The *cirth* were invented by the Sindar of Beleriand, who designed them to be carved into wood or stone. The Elvish *Angerthas Daeron* is named after the minstrel of Doriath who was credited with its elaboration and arrangement; the Noldor of Eregion later expanded this alphabet. The *Angerthas Moria* is a modification of this, used by the Dwarves of Khazad-dûm. The Dwarves of the Lonely Mountain made further changes, resulting in the *Mode of Erebor.*

The *cirth* generally have a less elegant look to them than the Noldorin *tengwar,* which is appropriate to their use by the more rustic Sindar and the Dwarves. Nevertheless, the inscription on Balin's tomb (*FR,* II, iv, 333) exhibits the Dwarves' skill in stonework, with straight lines of serifed *cirth* that recall inscriptions on Roman monuments rather than Scandinavian rune stones.

Although the *cirth* resemble the historical Germanic runes in shape, the organization of the *Angerthas* is much more systematic. The relationship of letter to phonetic value in the *Angerthas Daeron* is not as flexible as in the Fëanorian *Tengwar,* but some of the same principles are employed in its arrangement. The *Angerthas* is divided into ten groups of *cirth,* separated in Tolkien's table (*RK,* Appendix E, 402–3) by double circles, which represent different classes of sounds (labial consonants, dental consonants, vowels, etc.). *Cirth* within each of these groups generally share some similarity in construction; the *cirth* for the labial consonants, for example, consist of a stem and at least one angular bow. Other similarities in form apply to *cirth* in more than one group. For example, the addition of a stroke to a consonantal rune normally indicates voicing, and a *certh* representing a stop consonant is generally reversed to produce that representing the corresponding fricative.

In addition to the inscription on Balin's tomb, noted above, *cirth* appear on the title page of *The Lord of the Rings* and in the facsimile of the Book of Mazarbul (*Pictures*, 24). Earlier versions of the *Angerthas*, including a cursive variety called the Alphabet of Dairon, appear in the "Appendix on Runes" (*Treason*, 452–65). Other early runic-style alphabets invented by Tolkien include the Gondolinic Runes ("Early Runic Documents," 111–13) and the Taliskan *skirditaila* or "runic series" (mentioned without examples in *Treason*, 455). The runes used in *The Hobbit* are not of Tolkien's own invention, but are instead an adaptation of the Old English runic alphabet.

Alphabet of Rúmil

The alphabet credited to Rúmil, the Noldorin sage of Valinor, is the oldest Elvish alphabet in the chronologies of both the primary and secondary worlds. The Rúmilian letters, or *sarati* (singular *sarat*), were the first written characters invented by the Elves. First created in 1919, the Alphabet of Rúmil was also the first invented script that Tolkien associated with his invented Elvish languages and mythology.

The *sarati* were usually written vertically, from top to bottom, but they could also be written horizontally, either left to right, right to left, or in boustrophedon (lines alternating left to right, right to left). They were sometimes attached to stems, which could be short and attached to individual letters or could run for the entire length of a line. The various extant Rúmilian texts therefore give different visual impressions: stemless lines of vertical text are somewhat reminiscent of Japanese *hiragana* in style, whereas horizontal lines attached to long stems more closely resemble Indian *devanāgarī*.

In basic structure, however, the *sarati* were somewhat similar to the *tengwar*. Though their arrangement was not as systematic as that of the Fëanorian letters, the Rúmilian letters employed such features as the doubling of bows to indicate the voicing of consonants and the use of diacritical marks to indicate vowels. Tolkien modified the alphabet several times, and there are also different applications for different languages: samples of Rúmilian script are extant in Qenya, Goldogrin (Gnomish), and Middle and Modern English.

Nearly all of the published corpus of Rúmilian appears in Tolkien, "The Alphabet of Rúmil."

Valmaric

Tolkien applied the term "Valmaric" to a group of related alphabets that he invented in the early to mid 1920s and did not appear to use after that. The Valmaric script was written horizontally from left to right, with vowels denoted by diacritical marks, but the level of systematic organization in these alphabets is more similar to that found in Rúmilian than to that of the Fëanorian *tengwar*. In addition to general phonetic varieties of the script, there are also applications to specific languages. Examples in Qenya, Noldorin, and Old and Modern English are extant.

An example of Valmaric script is the caption to the 1925 "Lunar Landscape" drawing from *Roverandom*, first published in Hammond and Scull (78). A nearly complete corpus of Valmaric documents appears in Tolkien, "The Valmaric Script."

Goblin Alphabet

Two invented alphabets appear in the letters that Tolkien wrote to his children in the guise of Father Christmas and his friends at the North Pole. The Elvish script used by Ilbereth is simply a spidery variety of the *tengwar* (*Father Christmas*, 120). The Goblin Alphabet used by Karhu, the North Polar Bear, is very different. Based on goblin cave-drawings illustrated in the 1932 letter, it consists of crude, mainly humanoid figures. It is, however, more sophisticated than a simple substitution code for English, since it contains a number of characters representing diphthongs and common consonant combinations. Karhu sent a letter written in the alphabet, followed by a key to the script (Tolkien, *Father Christmas*, 75, 77, 80, 113).

Other Alphabets

Another early example of Tolkien's alphabetic invention can be seen in the Gnomic Letters, an alphabet for Noldorin containing angular, rounded, and lowercase forms ("Early Runic Documents," 108–10). The New English Alphabet, dating from the later years of Tolkien's life, applies structural principles of systems like the *Angerthas* and *Tengwar* to characters that look more like Greek and Latin letters (examples in Hammond and Scull, 189–90).

ARDEN R. SMITH

Further Reading

Björkman, Måns. *Amanye Tenceli: The Writing Systems of Aman.* http://at.mansbjorkman.net/ (August 2005).

Hammond, Wayne G., and Christina Scull. *J.R.R. Tolkien: Artist & Illustrator.* Boston: Houghton Mifflin, 1995.

Mellonath Daeron. http://www.forodrim.org/daeron/md_home.html (August 2005).

Tolkien, J.R.R. "The Alphabet of Rúmil," edited by Arden R. Smith. *Parma Eldalamberon* 13 (2001): 3–89.

———. "Early Runic Documents," edited by Arden R. Smith. *Parma Eldalamberon* 15 (2004): 89–121.

———. *Letters from Father Christmas.* Edited by Baillie Tolkien. Boston: Houghton Mifflin, 1999.

———. *Pictures by J.R.R. Tolkien.* 2nd ed. with foreword and notes by Christopher Tolkien. Boston: Houghton Mifflin, 1992.

———. *The Road Goes Ever On: A Song Cycle.* Music by Donald Swann. 2nd ed., rev. Boston: Houghton Mifflin, 1978.

———. "The Valmaric Script," edited by Arden R. Smith. *Parma Eldalamberon* 14 (2003): 87–134.

See also **Languages Invented by Tolkien; Runes**

AMERICA IN THE 1960S: RECEPTION OF TOLKIEN

For ten years after its first publication in 1955, *The Lord of the Rings* had enjoyed steady, satisfactory sales.

But an unexpected party began in 1965, a long, loud boom in J.R.R. Tolkien's popularity in the United States that spread internationally and continues yet.

Three factors contributed to this. One was the tenor of the times, the era of hippies, Vietnam, dissent, demonstrations, conscience, community: a homely ideal of benevolent, natural, ungoverned, mellow freedom like that of the Shire.

Another factor was America's cultural Anglophilia. From the car radio to the movie theater to the fashion magazines, Britannia ruled pop culture from 1964 on.

But the primary cause was an unauthorized paperback edition published by Ace Books, a New York science fiction firm, in June 1965.

This piratical move, spawned by an alleged copyright loophole, prompted Tolkien's publishers to produce an authorized version. Although delayed by Tolkien's procrastination on revisions needed to file for a new copyright, the authorized Ballantine Books paperback was released in October 1965. Within a year, it was in its ninth printing.

Thus *The Lord of the Rings* was inexpensive and omnipresent, sold at the corner drugstore. Paperback sales boosted Tolkien's readership from the tens of thousands to the millions.

The bootlegged Ace paperbacks sold for seventy-five cents each; the Ballantines were ninety-five cents.

Publicity from the legal brouhaha over Ace's pilfered publication probably benefited sales of the Ballantine version. By 1966, the authorized three-volume edition was the top-selling paperback in the United States, with over three quarters of a million copies in print. Now a passport to Middle-earth cost less than three dollars. Until then, a hardcover set, when available, was at least fifteen dollars.

Ever alert for the newest youth trend, the popular press swiftly anointed Tolkien as the next B.M.O.C., Big Man on Campus.

"The Tolkien people may be less noisy than the LSD-heads but there are more of them," wrote Henry Resnik in the *Saturday Evening Post* on July 2, 1966, concluding that "the time cannot be far away when not having read it will be, in most literary and academic circles, tantamount to complete boorishness."

In "The Hobbit Habit" on July 15, 1966, *Time* magazine declared: "Holden Caulfield is a moldy fig; the Lord of the Flies is swatted. This year, the unquestioned literary god on college campuses is a three-foot-high creature with long curly hair on his feet, the passion for six vast meals a day, and the improbable name of Frodo Baggins."

Tolkien was called "the literary darling of an entire generation of high school and college students, who have made him a flagrant best-seller—smack at the top of the 1966 paperback list" by *Life* magazine associate editor Charles Elliott in a belated book review published February 24, 1967.

Extolling Tolkien's "high seriousness" and "construction of literary and philological sand castles of astounding complexity," Elliott nonetheless dismissed *The Lord of the Rings* as an "undemanding, comfortable child-sized story" with "no symbolism, no sex, no double meanings ... just a good yarn on the level of *Tom Swift and his Electric Runabout*."

Elliott's snide derision of the Tolkien "fad" was typical of the establishment and academic response. Tolkien fans, with their earnest energy, "pipeweed," costumes, and "Frodo Lives" and "Go Go Gandalf" buttons, were easy targets for mockery.

But while some reviewers, including W.H. Auden, C.S. Lewis, and Michael Straight, extolled the work as literature, many others linked it to the emerging counterculture. The ecological and social concerns of many American readers were incarnated in Tolkien. The triumph of the Ents over Saruman could be read as a victory of nature over the military-industrial complex. The racial diversity of the Fellowship could not be overlooked: Legolas and Gimli conquer prejudice and become lifelong best friends. Frodo, a brave but reluctant hero, emerges as a pacifist in "The Scouring of the Shire." Small and humble folks press on, and by persistence, despite overwhelming odds, good defeats evil. Mordor is cast down; the Shire is saved.

The emphasis on personal conscience was also attuned to the philosophical and religious thinking of the times. After the nihilism of *The Catcher in the Rye* and *Lord of the Flies*, this best-seller was more encouraging.

Coincidentally or not, a cultural Anglophilia began to dominate popular film, fashion, and music as well as literature mid-decade. The top-grossing films in the United States during those years were the thrillers *Goldfinger* (1964) and *Thunderball* (1965), starring Sean Connery as British secret agent James Bond. *Blow-Up, Alfie,* and *Georgie Girl* also drew crowds. Meanwhile, Mary Quant and other London designers exported the miniskirt and the Twiggy look.

And on Sunday, February 9, 1964, an estimated 73 million viewers watched the Beatles, a charming, cheery English foursome not unlike *The Lord of the Ring*'s four Hobbits, debut on Ed Sullivan's variety show. The band would become another 1960s phenomenon that endured, perhaps because, like Tolkien's, their work was original, well crafted, and at once English and universal. Hot on the Beatles's boot heels, other British bands would soon occupy the top spots on US charts.

Had the Beatles succeeded with their 1968 plan to make a film out of *The Lord of the Rings* with a two-record soundtrack, a triumvirate fusing all three media would have been created. Apple film executive Denis O'Dell chronicles how the group's enthusiastic plans, featuring Paul as Frodo, Ringo as Samwise, and John as Gandalf, were shattered when designated director Stanley Kubrick declared that a cinematic adaptation of Tolkien was "unmakable."

The Tolkien boom was expedited by paperback publication, American Anglophilia, and the U.S. social situation. No bust has followed this boom. At least 10.5 million copies of *The Hobbit* and *The Lord of the Rings* were sold even before the Peter Jackson film trilogy brought many millions more to Tolkien from 2001 on.

Although Tolkien's worldwide popularity began in America in the 1960s, his themes—power, choice, nature, technology, loyalty, loss, and redemption—are not the concerns of one time and place. They resonate in all times and all places.

Mike Foster

Further Reading

O'Dell, Denis, with Bill Neaverson. *At the Apple's Core: The Beatles from the Inside.* London: Peter Owen Ltd., 2002.

See also **Technological Subcultures**

ANCRENE WISSE

The *Ancrene Wisse* (meaning "a guide for female recluses") is considered one of the finest prose works in the Middle English period. It was originally written for three daughters of good family, who had withdrawn from the world to lead a solitary life in a West Midland convent.

The word *wisse* ("guide") is based on the Old English verb *wissian* ("to guide, instruct"). The first word *ancrene* is the genitive plural form of the word *ancer*, meaning "anchorite" "recluse," or "person who lives in solitude."

The title *Ancrene Riwle* is not recorded as a phrase in any of the existing manuscripts, while *Ancrene Wisse* is recorded on folio. 1r of Corpus Christi College, Cambridge, MS 402. One may therefore point out that, though *Ancrene Riwle* has the same meaning, it has none of the medieval authority *Ancrene Wisse* has. The Early English Text Society decided to use *Ancrene Riwle* when it published the seventeen extant manuscripts between 1944 and 2000 (nine of which are in English, four in Latin, and four in French). More scholars now tend to prefer the latter title, *Ancrene Wisse*.

J.R.R. Tolkien started as early as 1926 to work on the Corpus MS, which is the earliest and most important of the seventeen manuscripts. In 1929, Tolkien published an essay in *Essays and Studies of the English Association*, 14, in which he showed that the Corpus MS of the *Ancrene Wisse* (= A) and MS Bodley 34 of the Katherine Group manuscripts (= B) were written in the same standard literary language. Tolkien called this consistent system of spelling habits "the AB language." See also *AB Language* and *Katherine Group.*

Tolkien completed his edition of the Corpus MS of the *Ancrene Wisse* for the Early English Text Society, Oxford University Press, in 1962. The aim of the society was to publish all the manuscripts, starting with the Latin and French editions in 1944. The whole project was completed by Zettersten-Diensberg's edition of MS Vernon in 2000.

Tolkien placed the origin of the AB language in the West Midlands, in Herefordshire, on purely linguistic grounds. E.J. Dobson developed Tolkien's research even further and concluded that Wigmore Abbey in northwest Herefordshire was the place of origin of the *Ancrene Wisse.* He further suggested that the author was "Brian(us) of Lingen," a secular canon of Wigmore. Dobson proposed that the sentence "Inoh meful Ich am, þe bidde se lutel" = "I am moderate enough, who ask for so little" (fol. 117v) conceals a pun on Brian's name (Lat. *Bria* = "moderate") and an anagram of Linthehum ("of Lingen"). See Dobson's *Origins of Ancrene Wisse* (349–53).

Such a conclusion, based on a pun and an anagram, would certainly have been to Tolkien's liking had he still been alive when it was put forward (in 1976). Dobson's proposition was later doubted, and the localization now regarded as the most credible is the one based on the data of the *Linguistic Atlas of Late Middle English* (forthcoming). According to Jeremy Smith, the localization based on the *Atlas* is North Herefordshire or the southern tip of Shropshire. (See B. Millet et al., *Ancrene Wisse,* 11, n.7.)

The first scholar to analyze the stemma of the *Ancrene Wisse* in great detail was E.J. Dobson in "Affiliations of the Manuscripts of *Ancrene Wisse,*" published in the Festschrift for Professor Tolkien on the occasion of his seventieth birthday in 1962. Yoko Wada in her "Temptations from *Ancrene Wisse*" provides an "extended stemma," in which she illustrates Dobson's views of the influence of the revised text based on a lost copy. As Wada observes (82), "No proper assessment of Dobson's textual history or of his extraordinary comprehension and precise account of the early history of *Ancrene Wisse* can be undertaken, however, until these have been studied in the cold light of variorum texts of those parts of the work which can be so treated."

In the course of the latter half of the twentieth century, *Ancrene Wisse* studies were characterized by a large scholarly output, due to a great number of interesting, unsolved problems connected with authorship, provenance, sources, relations between the manuscripts, vocabulary, style, and so on. Toward the end of the twentieth century, many new research areas came into focus, such as feminist readings of several AB texts. This is made clear by Bella Millett's comprehensive annotated bibliography published in 1996 with the assistance of George B. Jack and Yoko Wada. Additional bibliographic material is also provided by Roger Dahood in his article "The Current State of *Ancrene Wisse* Group Studies" and by Robert Hasenfratz in *Ancrene Wisse* (38–54). An excellent example of how much *Ancrene Wisse* research has moved forward at the beginning of the new millennium can be found in Yoko Wada's *A Compendium to Ancrene Wisse* (2003).

Furthermore, there are many new possibilities regarding textual analysis that have been brought to light with regard to the use of modern electronic techniques. One such innovation has been introduced by a Japanese research group headed by Tadao Kubouchi, The Tokyo Medieval Manuscript Reading Group. In 1996, it launched a project for an "Electronic Corpus of Diplomatic Parallel Manuscript Texts as a Tool for Historical Studies of English." *Electronic Parallel Diplomatic Manuscript Texts of the Ancrene Wisse* (2001) was their first undertaking.

The final version of their *Ancrene Wisse* texts will contain all the relevant English manuscript texts in computer-readable format.

With regard to future directions in *Ancrene Riwle* studies, it would seem that rewarding paths are likely to be found in the large and promising area of electronic publishing. Bella Millett, who is currently working on a critical edition of the *Ancrene Wisse* together with Richard Dance, has also inserted a trial electronic edition of the preface to the Ancrene Wisse on the World Wide Web with a view to presenting a complete edition and a new translation as well.

Almost without any doubt, *Ancrene Wisse* was originally composed in English and later translated into Latin and French versions.

The manuscripts of the *Ancrene Wisse*, which have all been edited by the Early English Text Society, are listed below, with indications of the approximate datings:

A: Cambridge, Corpus Christi College, MS 402
   Tolkien, J.R.R., ed. *The English Text of the Ancrene Riwle, Ancrene Wisse, Edited from MS Corpus Christi College Cambridge 402.* EETS o.s. 249 (London, 1962). Date: second quarter of the thirteenth century.

C: London, British Library, MS Cotton Cleopatra C. vi
   Dobson, E.J., ed. *The English Text of the Ancrene Riwle Edited from B.M. Cotton MS Cleopatra C. vi.* EETS o.s. 267 (London, 1972). Date: second quarter of the thirteenth century.

F: London, British Library, MS Cotton Vitellius F. vii
   Herbert, J.A., ed. *The French Text of the Ancrene Riwle Edited from British Museum MS Cotton Vitellius F vii.* EETS o.s. 219 (London, 1944). Date: early fourteenth century.

G: Cambridge, Gonville and Caius College, MS 234/120
   Wilson, R.M., ed. *The English Text of the Ancrene Riwle Edited from Gonville and Caius College MS 234/120.* EETS o.s. 229 (London, 1954). Date: second half of the thirteenth century.

N: London, British Library, MS Cotton Nero A. xiv
   Day, Mabel, ed. *The English Text of the Ancrene Riwle Edited from Cotton Nero A. XIV.* EETS o.s. 225 (London, 1952). Date: second quarter of the thirteen century.

O: Bodleian Library, MS Eng. th. c. 70 (The Lanhydrock Fragment)
   Mack, Frances M. and A. Zettersten, eds. *The English Text of the Ancrene Riwle Edited from Cotton MS Titus D. XVIII, Together with the*

Lanhydrock Fragment, Bodleian MS Eng. th. c. 70. EETS o.s. 252 (London, 1963). Date: first half of the fourteenth century.

P: Cambridge, Magdalene College, MS Pepys 2498

Zettersten, Arne, ed. *The English Text of the Ancrene Riwle Edited from Magdalene College, Cambridge MS Pepys 2498.* EETS o.s. 274 (London, 1976). Date: second half of the fourteenth century.

R: London, British Library, MS Royal 8. CI

Baugh, A.C., ed. *The English Text of the Ancrene Riwle Edited from British Museum MS Royal 8 CI.* EETS o.s. 232 (London, 1956). Date: fifteenth century.

T:London, British Library, MS Cotton Titus D. CVIII

Mack, Frances M., and A. Zettersten, eds. *The English Text of the Ancrene Riwle Edited from Cotton MS Titus D. XVIII, Together with the Lanhydrock Fragment, Bodleian MS Eng. th. c. 70.* EETS o.s. 252 (London, 1963). Date: second quarter of the thirteenth century.

L: Merton College, Oxford, MS C. I. 5

d'Evelyn, Charlotte, ed. *The Latin Text of the Ancrene Riwle.* EETS o.s. 216 (London, 1944). Date: first half of the fourteenth century. The edition contains variant readings from the following MSS:

Magdalen College, Oxford, Latin MS 67

Date: late fourteenth or early fifteenth century.

British Museum Cotton MS Vitellius E. VII

Date: first half of the fourteenth century.

British Museum MS Royal 7 C.X.

Date: first half of the sixteenth century.

S: Trethewey, W.H., ed. *The French Text of the Ancrene Riwle Edited from the Trinity College Cambridge MS R. 14. 7.* EETS o.s. 240 (London, 1958).

V: Bodleian, MS Eng. poet. a 1 (MS Vernon)

Zettersten, Arne and B. Diensberg, eds. *The English Text of the Ancrene Riwle Edited from Oxford, Bodleian Library MS Eng. Poet. a.1.* EETS o.s. 310 (London, 2000). Date: second half of the fourteenth century.

ARNE ZETTERSTEN

Further Reading

Dahood, Roger. "The Current State of *Ancrene Wisse* Group Studies." *Medieval English Studies Newsletter* 36 (June 1997): 6–14.

Dobson, E.J. "The Affiliations of the Manuscripts of *Ancrene Wisse.*" In *English and Medieval Studies Presented to J.R.R. Tolkien on the Occasion of his Seventieth Birthday,* edited by Norman Davis and C.L. Wrenn, 128–63. London, Early English Texts Society 1962.

———. "The Date and Composition of *Ancrene Wisse.*" *Proceedings of the British Academy* 52 (1966): 181–208.

———. *The Origins of Ancrene Wisse.* Oxford: Clarendon Press, 1976.

Hasenfratz, Robert, ed. *Ancrene Wisse.* Kalamazoo, MI., Medieval Institute Publications 2000.

Kubouchi, Tadao, et al., eds. *The Ancrene Wisse: A Four-Manuscript Parallel Text, Preface and Parts 1–4.* Studies in English Medieval Language and Literature, 7. Frankfurt a.M.: Peter Lang.

McIntosh, Angus, M.L. Samuels, and Michael Benskin. *A Linguistic Atlas of Late Mediaeval English.* 4 vols. Aberdeen: Aberdeen University Press, 1986.

Millet, Bella. "The Ancrene Wisse Group." In *A Compendium to Middle English Prose,* edited by A.S.G. Edwards. Cambridge: D.S. Brewer, 2004.

———. "The Origins of *Ancrene Wisse*: New Answers, New Questions." *Medium Aevum* 61 (1992): 206–28.

Millet, Bella, with the assistance of George B. Jack and Yoko Wada. *Ancrene Wisse, the Katherine Group, and the Wooing Group: Annotated Bibliographies of Old and Middle English Literature.* Vol. 2. Cambridge: D.S. Brewer, 1996.

Tolkien, J.R.R. "*Ancrene Wisse* and *Hali Meiðad.*" *Essays and Studies of the English Association* 14 (1929): 104–26.

Wada, Yoko, ed. *A Companion to Ancrene Wisse.* Cambridge: D.S. Brewer, 2003.

———, ed. and trans. *Temptations from Ancrene Wisse.* Vol. 1. Kansai University Institute of Oriental and Occidental Studies Sources and Materials Series 18. Osaka: Kansai University Press, 1994; Cambridge: D.S. Brewer, 1994.

Zettersten, Arne. "Editing the *Ancrene Riwle* for the Early English Text Society: Past Experience and Future Prospects." *Studies in Medieval English Language and Literature* 12 (1997): 1–28.

———. *Studies in the Dialect and Vocabulary of the Ancrene Riwle.* Copenhagen & Lund: Ejnar Munksgaard & G.W. K. Gleerup, 1965.

See also **D'Ardenne, S.R.T.O.; Katherine Group; Manuscripts: Medieval; MS Bodley 34: A Re-collation of a Collation**

ANGBAND

Angband was Morgoth's immense subterranean fortress in the northwest region of Beleriand. Situated behind the fence of the curved Ered Engrin (Iron Mountains), it lay a mere one hundred and fifty leagues north of Menegroth, and from it great colds swept down, affecting the climate of neighboring areas such as Hithlum. The name is Sindarin for "Iron Prison" or "Iron-Gaol," but is often rendered "Hell of Iron"; the Quenya form, *Angamandos,* is related to *Mandos,* or "castle of custody" (*Morgoth,* 350), and Tolkien associated it with the Old English *Engbend,* from *enge,* "narrow, strait, oppressive, cruel," and *bend,* "bond, fetter" (*Shaping,* 209). In the published *Silmarillion,* Angband originally served as the fallen Vala's western outpost, guarding against attack from the West while Utumno to the east along the Iron Mountain range was his primary stronghold. During their imprisonment in Valinor, Sauron and the Balrogs remained in the deepest recesses of Angband that escaped destruction, and Morgoth reestablished his dominion there upon his return. Morgoth bored a massive entry passage in front of Angband, and above it reared the three peaks of the Thangorodrim, artificial mountain-towers "made of the ash and slag of his subterranean furnaces and the vast refuse of his tunnellings" (*S*, 118) from which noxious vapors and even rivers of flame could erupt. The 1977 map of Beleriand does not mark the precise location of Angband, but Tolkien's "Second Silmarillion" map depicts Thangorodrim encircled by a small mountain range and nowhere shows the "great curving wall" of the Ered Engrin. Christopher Tolkien notes that his father never corrected this obvious discrepancy (*Lost Road*, 271).

Angband was the focus of the many conflicts with the Elves and Edain during the First Age. Its many smithies and caves functioned as the breeding grounds for Morgoth's armies of Orcs as well as monsters and other fell creatures such as dragons. The fortress also contained vast dungeons and mines where Morgoth could torment slaves and captives such as Gwindor and Maeglin. Morgoth imprisoned his mightiest opponents on the cliffs of Thangorodrim: Maedhros was chained like the classical Prometheus to the rocks, and Húrin was forced to sit on a high seat to survey the devastation of his homeland, a perversion of Odin's seat in Asgard. For much of the First Age Morgoth never left the nethermost hall of Angband, his power becoming increasingly bound to the depths of the fortress he made (Kocher, *Reader's*, 81). "The Lay of Leithian" offers the most vivid description of the interior of Angband as Beren and Lúthien descend through the echoing corridors of this "many-tunnelled tomb" to Morgoth's cavernous throne room with its forest of "devil-carven" pillars (*Lays*, 294–96).

From Angband, Morgoth launched the first battles in the Wars of Beleriand, but after the Dagor Aglareb his fortress was besieged for four hundred years. The Siege of Angband was broken by the fires that spewed forth from Thangorodrim in the Dagor Bragollach, turning the grassy plains of the Ard-galen into the arid wasteland of the Anfauglith, and Morgoth's forces prevailed until the armies of the Valar came in the War of Wrath. During that legendary battle, the body of winged dragon Ancalagon the Black shattered the peaks of Thangorodrim, and the pits of Angband were violently unearthed as Morgoth was bound and cast into the Timeless Void.

Angband becomes the terrestrial embodiment of the Christian hell in Tolkien's legendarium as well as a dark counterpart to the underworlds of various Northern European mythologies. In *The Book of Lost Tales*, the Vala Fui (later Nienna) reads the hearts of mortal Men and sends some to Mandos, but the wicked "she drives forth beyond the hills and Melko seizes them and bears them to Angamandi, the Hells of Iron, where they have evil days" (*Lost Tales I*, 77). Tolkien later abandoned this early conception of Angband as a place of punishment for the souls of Men, but it still represents a "hell" in opposition to the "heaven" of Valinor in later writings. The Norse tradition of Niflheim or Niflhel—the cold, fog-enshrouded underworld ruled by the goddess Hel (Lindow, *Handbook*, 240–41)—greatly influenced Tolkien's image of frozen hell to the north. John Garth notes that Tolkien was also creating a negative version the Celtic myth of an underworld ruled by faërie races such as the Tuath Dé Dannan in making Angband a prison for the Gnomes/Noldor (Garth, 222). Angband is moreover the prototype for all the industrial "hells" in Tolkien's work, such as Saruman's blighted, machine-ridden Isengard (Petty, 63). Sauron's tower of Barad-dûr and the desolation of Mordor clearly echo the dark grandeur and terror of Morgoth's fortress and the ravaged nature around it. Indeed, even though Angband was destroyed forever at the end of the First Age, its legacy, like the taint of Morgorth in Arda Marred, endures even in later ages.

DAVID D. OBERHELMAN

Further Reading

Fonstad, Karen Wynn. "Thangorodrim and Angband." In *The Atlas of Middle-earth*. Rev. ed. Boston, MA: Houghton Mifflin, 1991.

Garth, John. *Tolkien and the Great War: The Threshold of Middle-earth*. Boston, MA: Houghton Mifflin, 2003.

Kocher, Paul. *A Reader's Guide to the Silmarillion*. London: Thames & Hudson, 1980.

Lindow, John. *Handbook of Norse Mythology*. Santa Barbara, CA: ABC-Clio, 2001.

Petty, Anne C. *Tolkien in the Land of Heroes: Discovering the Human Spirit*. Cold Spring Harbor, NY: Cold Spring Press, 2003.

See also **Beren; Christianity; Darkness; Heaven; Hell; Lúthien; Maps; Middle-earth: Monsters; Mordor; Morgoth and Melkor; Mythology: Celtic; Mythology: Germanic; Sauron; Valar; Valinor**

ANGELS

Gandalf is an angel—there it was in black and white, in the interview with Henry Resnik in *Niekas*, in the master's own living words in 1967. Gandalf's name in that capacity was Olórin (*TT*, IV, V, 279), and he was one of the Maiar. In *The Silmarillion*, in Tolkien's description of the creation of the Ainur—the Valar and Maiar before the beginning of time—we find that the "Wisest of the Maiar was Olórin," a name Gandalf said (*S*, 30, 279) was his "in his youth, in the West that is forgotten." In the chapter "The Istari" in *Unfinished Tales* is a rough version of a narrative describing the council of the Valar in which they discuss sending emissaries (messengers = [Gk] αγγλοι = angels) to Middle-earth to help in the struggle against Sauron: "Who would go? For they must be mighty, peers of Sauron, but must forego might, and clothe themselves in flesh so as to treat on equality and win the trust of Elves and Men" (UT, 393). A peer being someone of equal stature with another, and Sauron being himself a Maia ("in his beginning he was of the Maiar of Aulë" in *The Silmarillion*), the Valar clearly intended to send other Maiar as their emissaries (*Istari*). Tolkien wrote elsewhere that "we must assume that they [the *Istari*] were all Maiar."

In Pseudo-Dionysius (or Dionysius the Pseudo-Areopagite), the angels were the lowest of the nine orders of the celestial hierarchy—the orders are given in the Anglican Hymn, "Ye Watchers and Ye Holy Ones / Bright Seraphs, Cherubim, and Thrones / Raise the glad strain! Alleluia! / Cry out Dominions, Princedoms, Powers! / Virtues! Archangels! Angels choirs!"—that is to say, the Nine Orders of the Celestial Hierarchies are Seraphim, Cherubim, Thrones, Dominions (or Dominations), Princedoms (or Principalities), Powers, Virtues, Archangels, and Angels. (In some accounts, there is a different order.) Dionysius, in *De Caelestis Hierarchia*, develops in fifteen chapters the doctrine of the celestial hierarchy, comprising nine angelic choirs that are divided into closer groupings of three choirs each (triads). First triad: seraphim, cherubim, thrones; second triad: virtues, dominations, powers; third triad: principalities, archangels, angels (*C.H.*, vi, 2 in *P.G.*, III, 200 D). The grouping, as noted, shows some variation. The first three face inward to God always, the second three face both inward (to God and the first three) and outward to the last three. The last three, including the lowest order, the Angels, face always outward, toward men. They are thus ideally situated to be messengers between God and men. Dionysius believes that the different choirs of *angels* are less intense in their love and knowledge of *God* the farther they are removed from him, just as a ray of light or of heat grows weaker the farther it travels from its source—also (as noted) that the highest choirs transmit the light received from the Divine Source only to the intermediate choirs, and these in turn transmit it to the lowest. Note that the discussion of the three triads is

itself arranged in the triad of *prologos*, *mysterion*, *theoria*.

While this Christian (or perhaps neo-Platonic) ordering is not necessarily Tolkien's ordering, and while the Valar/Maiar/Archangels/Angels parallel is too easily drawn, there is no doubt that Gandalf (Olórin) is an angel (messenger) from the Valar. The Tolkienian pun on angels/eagles (with the eagles being also messengers in *The Lord of the Rings*) emphasizes the role of the *Istari* ("wizards") as angels (αγγλοι). Also, it is notable in "Myths Transformed" in *Morgoth's Ring* how much of the rebellion of Melkor (= Morgoth) had to do with light and the extinguishing of light (see also *Sin*).

JARED LOBDELL

Further Reading

[Pseudo-]Dionysius (floruit ca. 500 CE in Syria), *De Caelestis hierarchia*, in Migne, Jacques-Paul, ed. S. Dionysii Areopagitae Opera Omnia Quae Exstant. Patrologia Graeca, vol. III (Paris: Garnier Fratres, 1889).

See also **Gandalf**; *Silmarillion, The*; **Sin**; **Theology**; *Unfinished Tales*; **Wizards**

ANIMALS IN TOLKIEN'S WORKS

Animals are an integral part of Tolkien's storytelling, and he initially included speaking animals as a lighter element in the story. As the story of Middle-earth became broader and deeper, the animals also became entrenched characters and plot movers. Animals have varying levels of sentience, or self-awareness, and express different moral standards. There is a marked difference between sentient animals and "Speaking Peoples" in Tolkien's writing that aids in understanding questions of responsibility. Animals also give Middle-earth's spiritual aspect more depth in subtle ways, as Tolkien uses particular animals to perform eschatological functions such as prophecy.

Sentient and Nonsentient Creatures

In the mythology of Middle-earth, the Vala Yavanna was responsible for creating the *kelvar* (animals and living things that can move freely). Among the *kelvar* are those with both greater and lesser sentience and intelligence. (Sentient creatures such as dragons that were created by Morgoth are not *kelvar* and are not discussed here.)

Eagles are depicted with the greatest level of self-awareness, especially the lineage of Thorondor, King of the Eagles. Although Yavanna created the *kelvar*, it was in the Song of the Ainur that the thoughts of Manwë, the highest of the Valar, and Yavanna mingled to create their race.

In *The Silmarillion*, eagles are depicted as the vassals of Manwë whom he sends to Middle-earth to watch over the Elves and report on the doings of Morgoth. Thorondor and his eagles intervene in many tales at key moments, such as the rescues of Beren and Lúthien and Maedhros or the transportation of Húrin and Huor to Gondolin. Thorondor's descendents, the Eagles of the Misty Mountains (the Lord of the Eagles in *The Hobbit* and Gwaihir, Landroval, and Meneldor in *The Lord of the Rings*), retain this sentience along with Thorondor's advanced ability to make decisions, stand against evil (thereby inferring an ability to make certain moral determinations), and give advice to their allies.

Shelob is also a highly sentient creature, but her foremother Ungoliant was not of the *kelvar*; she was a Maia who chose the form of a spider to fit her nature and her desire to feed on light and spin webs of darkness. Her children inhabited Middle-earth, creating nightmarish regions with their presence and their webs. As Ungoliant's offspring, Shelob was more intelligent and self-aware than the spiders of Mirkwood, who were further descendents. Her actions as well as her thoughts, emotions, and memories are portrayed to the reader. Without Shelob using verbal language, Tolkien establishes an intimate understanding of her power, the motives behind her interactions with other beings, and her internal state of awareness.

Huan was a hound of Valinor who, in *The Silmarillion,* was given to Fëanor's son Celegorm by the Vala Oromë. He became involved in the story of Beren and Lúthien and is shown as capable of higher emotions such as love for Lúthien (vs. loyalty), as able to plan and give advice, and as able to make certain kinds of moral determinations (he voluntarily left Celegorm's service when he and his brother attacked Beren and Lúthien).

There are animals that range between the levels of sentience discussed above and regular animals. Shadowfax, one such example, is depicted as more noble and intelligent than regular horses, and his interactions with Gandalf demonstrate a higher understanding. Shadowfax's sentience is communicated through Gandalf's words and through their relationship where, though Gandalf rides him, he is more of a friend than a servant.

Wargs are also sentient creatures, and in *The Hobbit* they speak in their own tongue, taunting Bilbo, Gandalf, and the Dwarves. Orcs often rode the Wargs to battle, and they often shared plunder with them. This indicates that Wargs have some capacity to negotiate with Orcs and appreciate plunder. The race of ravens and Röac, who converse with the Dwarves and Bilbo in *The Hobbit*, and the *crebain* of Dunland, who act as spies in *The Lord of the Rings*, are also intelligent birds whose sentience is greater than most other birds.

> What of talking beasts and birds with reasoning and speech? These have been rather lightly adopted from less "serious" mythologies, but play a part which cannot now be excised. (*Morgoth*, 409–10).

The line between animals and Speaking Peoples is clear in Tolkien's writing. The Speaking Peoples are the Children of Ilúvatar and are all equal beings (but not necessarily with equal power), having derived their original minds and spirits, or *fëa*, from him. Tolkien distinguished between the *fëa* (individual spirit) and the *hröa* (body or form). Only Ilúvatar could instill *fëar* (spirit, mindful being) in living beings. Although the Valar had subcreative powers and could create many different *hröa* for creatures and bring them to life, the creatures they created were not equal to them. (The exception is Aulë's creation of the Dwarves. Ilúvatar took pity on them and imbued them with *fëar* and free will.) The fact that certain animals can speak does not indicate that they are rational beings; this is rather an indicator of intelligence.

> The same sort of thing can be said of Huan and the Eagles; they were taught language by the Valar, and raised to a higher level—but they still had no *fëar*. (*Morgoth*, 411).

The mind of each rational being, by virtue of the *fëa*, is equal and distinct. Even the Valar cannot control the mind or actions of a *fëa*; this is the sole province of Ilúvatar, who does not intervene in this manner. The actions of rational beings like the Speaking Peoples are also independent of any other source, and they have true free will, making them more than sentient or self-aware. They are sapient creatures with functions of higher consciousness and choices in the matters of their inner nature and destiny. Thus Yavanna's *kelvar*, no matter how sentient, do not have *fëar* and are not truly rational.

Eschatological Functions

Unlike other well-known fantasies such as *The Chronicles of Narnia* by C.S. Lewis, animals do not play an active part in the eschatology of Middle-earth. In *Chronicles*, the lion Aslan takes the characters through the final battle and destruction of

Narnia into a realm beyond, which equates to Paradise. Tolkien only wrote of the destruction of Middle-earth through prophecy since it is presented as a prehistory of our own world. There are two notable and subtle uses of animals, specifically birds, to denote ideas about the eschatology, or end times, for Middle-earth.

Eagles perform two functions related to eschatology. The first establishes a particular perception for their intervention in the affairs of Middle-earth. It is the dramatic device of "deus ex machina" where they save the protagonists from certain doom by appearing in a way that is not foreshadowed in the story and is literally the "mechanism of God," or in this case, the device of the Valar. In both the Battle of the Five Armies (*The Hobbit*) and the battle before the Black Gates of Mordor (*The Lord of the Rings*), Eagles arrive unexpectedly at the last moment and turn the tide, saving the heroes of the stories. Their rescues of Maedhros and Beren and Lúthien in *The Silmarillion,* of Bilbo, Gandalf, and the Dwarves in *The Hobbit*, and of Gandalf and Frodo and Sam in *The Lord of the Rings* can be viewed in the same light.

Tolkien also relates Eagles to eschatological prophecy as portents of doom or change in the world. This is powerfully illustrated in Tolkien's tale *Akallabêth* when the Valar send warnings to the Númenórean king Ar-Pharazôn in the form of immense eagle-shaped clouds as a sign of impending catastrophe. The appearance of Eagles at the battle before the Black Gates could be viewed as having the same prophetic weight regarding impending doom and the ending of an age.

The seagull or sea-bird is also used as a subtle eschatological prophecy. This is most clearly evidenced in the rhyme Galadriel sends to Legolas in *The Lord of the Rings*: If thou hearest the cry of the gull on the shore, / Thy heart shall then rest in the forest no more. (*TT*, III, v, 106)

The sea-bird is indicative of the journey across the sea to the West, where all the Elves eventually find their rest. The land of Aman is deathless and the equivalent of Paradise for those beings that were created to remain within the Circles of the World. Although the Elves are born in Middle-earth, by the end of the Third Age, Aman has become their place of rest and belonging, and Middle-earth a place where they fade. The sea-bird serves as a sign of that ultimate home for the Elves.

Although Tolkien included animals in his story, he did not create what he termed a "beast-fable" by including sentient creatures. His animals are not anthropomorphized conduits for human traits. Instead, they present the reader with unique ways to interpret the moral, spiritual, and psychological dimensions of Middle-earth, and they enrich his writing in its breadth and depth.

LARA SOOKOO

See also **Beren; Christianity; Death; Dragons; Free Will; Frodo; Gandalf; Good and Evil; Heaven; Lúthien; Misty Mountains; Paradise; Prophesy; Redemption; Sam; Shelob; Valar**

AQUINAS, THOMAS

Though the name of Thomas Aquinas never appears in any of Tolkien's published writings or letters, it would be impossible for a Roman Catholic of his generation not to have been influenced by Thomism. In 1879, Pope Leo XIII set the stage for the revival of Thomism with his highly influential encyclical *Æterni Patrus,* naming Aquinas patron saint of Catholic universities, colleges, and schools. Aquinas also holds the very rare title of Doctor of the Church (given in 1568; he is only one of thirty-three as of the year 2005). Born in 1225 and dying in 1274, Aquinas synthesized the ideas of Aristotle with traditional Catholic thought, making the Greek philosopher compatible with medieval Catholic philosophy and theology. Aquinas almost always refers to Aristotle as "the Philosopher" and St. Paul as "the Apostle." Mostly written as logical tracts against Islamic thought and doctrine, Aquinas's many works argued three things: (1) the sovereignty of God and the necessity of faith, (2) the uniqueness of each created thing, each having its own purpose in the larger Economy of Grace, and (3) the acceptance of Reason, properly understood, as a gift of God. While Aquinas had a very strong mystical side, as well as a profound love of the role of the imagination, many prominent Thomists and Neo-Thomists have neglected this side of him, focusing almost exclusively on his use of reason and his belief in free will. In reality, though, Aquinas argued that revelation always trumps reason, if the two appear to be in conflict, and that free will could only be understood within God's sovereignty and predestination. In his most important work, *The Summa*, Aquinas wrote:

> Thus, it is impossible that the whole of the effect of predestination in general should have any cause as coming from us; because whatsoever is in man disposing him towards salvation, is all included under the effect of predestination; even the preparation for grace. For neither does this happen otherwise than by divine help, according to the prophet Jeremias (Lam. 5:21): "convert us, O Lord, to Thee, and we shall be converted." Yet predestination has in this way, in regard to its effect, the goodness of God for its reason; towards which the whole effect of predestination is directed as to

an end; and from which it proceeds, as from its first moving principle.

And, perhaps most importantly, toward the end of his life, Aquinas experienced a profound vision. "I can write no more," he told a close friend. "I have seen things which make all my writings seem like straw." Aquinas spent much of the remainder of his life in contemplation and prayer.

One finds an implicit rather than explicit Thomism in Tolkien's work. The first and most significant Thomistic element is in the character of Aragorn, especially once he has returned as the king. Aragorn, indeed, represents the ideal of the Thomist king. From Socrates through Aquinas, much ancient and medieval political philosophy dealt with the necessity of the virtuous leader for a well-ordered and virtuous society. In his famous book, *On Kingship,* Aquinas argued that the only truly good king is one who acts as Christ. Just as Christ sacrificed himself for the good of the church, so, too, should a king sacrifice himself for the good of the people (the *res publica*). In the most succinct formulation of this concept, Aquinas wrote: "If, therefore, a multitude of free men is ordered by the ruler towards the common good of the multitude, that rulership will be right and just, as is suitable to free men. If, on the other hand, a rulership aims, not at the common good of the multitude, but at the private good of the ruler, it will be an unjust and perverted rulership." Aragorn certainly represents the highest ideal of Thomistic kingship. He reveals his virtue (from *virtu* or "manly power") slowly through *The Lord of the Rings.* In the beginning, the reader finds him a shadowy figure, dedicated to protecting a population that neither respects nor trusts him. During the journey from Bree to Rivendell and in his assumption as the head of the Fellowship with the death of Gandalf, Aragorn reveals his true nature. This proves especially true in his challenge to Sauron in the palantîr, and his ability to heal (to give of one's self) in the Houses of the Healing. Indeed, it is only after his actions in the House of the Healing that word spreads: "King! Did you hear that? What did I say? The hands of a healer, I said" (RK, V, viii, 142). As Tolkien noted in letter 250, "Now I pray for you all, unceasingly, that the Healer (the *Hælend* as the Saviour was usually called in Old English) shall heal my defects, and that none of you shall ever cease to cry *Benedictus qui venit in nomine Domini*" (*Letters*, 340).

Aragorn's coronation remarkably resembles the crowning of Charlemagne, itself an imitation of the Old Testament crowning of David. As Gandalf crowns him, he states, "Now come the days of the King, and may they be blessed while the thrones of the Valar endure!" (RK, VI, v, 246) Through the use of the great medieval institution, the Council, as well as through his own virtues of "mercy and justice," Aragorn rules wisely.

Nicolo Machiavelli ended nearly two thousand years of such thought with his letter *The Prince,* which argued that while a king might need to appear virtuous, he need not necessarily behave in such a manner. Machiavelli replaced the notion of love or sacrifice as the highest good with the notion of power as the necessity to control populations. But, in his own mythology, Tolkien challenged the Machiavellian notion of power, noting that the return of the king would reunite Middle-earth under a virtuous leadership, akin to an effective Holy Roman Empire.

BRADLEY J. BIRZER

See also **Aragon; Christianity; Fate/Fortune; Incarnation; Kingship; Theology**

ARAGORN

Aragorn provides *The Lord of the Rings* with its chief epic hero. As Aragorn II, son of Arathorn II and Gilraen the Fair, he is the chieftain of the northern Dúnedain, the people of the fallen kingdom of Arnor. Born in Third Age 2931 and crowned king of Gondor in Third Age 3019, he lived for two hundred and ten years and ruled for one hundred and twenty years (one hundred and ninety years and one hundred years in earlier editions), dying in 1541 (Shire Reckoning). He is descended through an unbroken male line from the Númenórean Elendil the Tall, founder of Arnor and its co-kingdom Gondor, through Elendil's elder son Isildur.

Aragorn appears first as Strider, a rough-hewn traveler with graying dark hair. He carries the broken halves of Narsil, the sword of Elendil, the symbol of his royal Númenórean heritage; due to that heritage, he is older (at eighty-seven) than he looks. Strider becomes the companion and guide of the Hobbits.

In Rivendell, an exalted side to Aragorn's nature begins to emerge. His life is dedicated to the war against Sauron, and the poem made and recited by Bilbo reveals that he also carries the hope that one day he will reclaim the kingship of Gondor, restore Arnor, and reunite the two kingdoms.

Aragorn's natural authority is tempered by his reverence for Gandalf, but after Gandalf's fall in Moria, Aragorn becomes the leader of the Fellowship. In Lothlórien there are further hints that he is a man of destiny, but at Parth Galen he experiences a crisis when he must choose to abandon either Frodo or Merry and Pippin. He chooses to follow those whose need is most immediate, and from then on he acts decisively in supporting Rohan against Saruman, confronting Sauron in the palantír, and most essentially in taking the Paths of the Dead. At Minas Tirith, his royalty is revealed in his healing power, but he does not offer himself to the people as king until Sauron has been defeated. With Gandalf, he initiates and leads a desperate expeditionary force to the gate of Mordor to distract Sauron from the Ringbearer's quest.

Aragorn's final hour of doubt comes when he seeks a sign that his hope of marriage will be granted. The union of Aragorn and Arwen renews the two kingdoms and unites the ruling houses of Elves and Men.

Tall and dark, Aragorn in his charisma appears still taller in moments of crisis. Otherwise, his manner is quiet but decisive and occasionally sharp-tongued. Described as "the most hardy of living men," his experiences have made him serious, even grim, but he remains capable of humor and self-deprecation. His authority and dedication to his cause make his times of anxiety and self-doubt the more striking.

Aragorn, both as Strider and as Elessar, is courteous and considerate of those smaller, more foolish, or of lower rank than himself. He remains Strider informally to the hobbits, who knew him first by that name. He is a hero in the romantic and epic mold popular in the late nineteenth and early twentieth century.

Aragorn's family belongs to the royal line of Númenor, which traces back to Elros, brother of Elrond, and through Elros to Lúthien Tinúviel. This Elvish heritage emerges in his occasional flashes of foresight.

Though he is Isildur's heir, Aragorn cannot simply claim the kingship of Gondor. Gondor's direct royal line (the heirs of Isildur's younger brother Anárion) died out generations earlier. Aragorn's ancestor Arvedui claimed the kingship, but Gondor quietly ignored Arvedui and chose its own king. After two generations, that line also failed (Third Age 2050), and Stewards were appointed to await the return of a royal heir. In the meantime, the heirs of Isildur had declined into chieftains, lacking the authority to claim the throne. The events of *The Lord of the Rings* unfold some 968 years later.

Aragorn has powerful counselors in his foster-father Elrond and the wizard Gandalf, but in a more archetypal sense his journey to kingship is a series of decisions that he must take largely alone. When Aragorn falls in love with Arwen, Elrond enjoins that his daughter will marry no man but the king of Gondor and Arnor. Aragorn responds by going alone into the wild to pursue the feud with Sauron.

For Tolkien's "true king," there is no simple dragon to slay. Aragorn spends nearly seventy years in the wilderness or as a paladin in the service of other rulers. Through his devotion to his cause, he becomes a leader of men, and he follows his long apprenticeship by turning aside from the direct path to Minas Tirith, risking all to fight the dangers on Gondor's flanks. Ultimately, Aragorn's claim rests upon his heredity, but it is his long dedication and decisive action that bring him to the kingship. Crucially, he also displays humility and mercy, winning the love of those who know him and of the people he is to rule.

Aragorn has many of the marks of a mythical "hidden king" and true hero. His mother (and in an earlier draft his grandmother) prophesies on his behalf. At moments of drama a white flame appears on his brow. He loves a princess of the Elves. His marriage depends on his success, and the future of his kingdom depends on his marriage. He is supported and advised by a powerful otherworldly woman, Galadriel, and carries tokens of his heritage and destiny (Andúril, the Elfstone). The last sapling of the White Tree of Gondor flowers to herald his marriage, and he is crowned in Gondor by Gandalf, the hierophant in the story, and later, in Arnor, by his Elvish queen. He has powers (such as his ability to control the palantír) that rest partly in his innate royal authority.

The Sword Narsil, reforged and renamed Andúril, is an important part of Aragorn's identity. Like Arthur of Britain, Aragorn is raised in secret and learns his true identity when he gains his sword. Andúril also parallels Gram, the sword of Sigmund, broken by Odin and reforged by the Dwarf Regin for Sigmund's son Sigurd in the Old Norse *Volsunga Saga*.

Aragorn is well endowed with names even by heroic standards. As a child, he was called Estel, meaning "hope" in Sindarin. This theme recurs throughout the story. In the countryside, his nickname is Strider, which occasionally irritates him. In Rivendell he is called the Dúnadan ("Man of the West") as chieftain of the Dúnedain (Númenóreans) of the North. As king he is called Elessar ("Elfstone") for the green stone that he wears, as foretold by Galadriel, and he takes as his family name Telcontar, a Quenya rendering of Strider. He names himself Envinyatur, "renewer," in the Houses of Healing. Most often he is referred to, by himself and others, as "the heir of Isildur" and occasionally of Elendil, Valandil, or (after his accession) Anárion. He is called Captain of the West and later Lord of the Western Lands and King of the West. Other epithets given by friend or foe include Longshanks (Bill Ferny), Stick-at-naught Strider (Bill again), Wingfoot (Éomer), Lord of the White Tree (Legolas), and Elfstone in the Common Speech. When in the past he served both King Thengel of Rohan and the steward Ecthelion II of Gondor, he bore the pseudonym Thorongil ("Eagle of the Star").

In the early stages of the writing of *The Lord of the Rings*, the part of the guiding Ranger was played by a hobbit (later a Man) named Trotter. Gradually, this character evolved into Aragorn, but the name Trotter stuck till a late stage, when it was replaced by Strider.

A late note interprets "Aragorn" as "kingly valor" but does not analyze it. In an early draft, the name Aragorn was assigned to Gandalf's horse (later Shadowfax). Late in the tale, Frodo gives the name Strider to his pony.

HELEN ARMSTRONG

Further Reading

Auden, W.H. "The Quest Hero." In *Tolkien and the Critics*, edited by Neil D. Isaacs and Rose A. Zimbardo, 40–61. Notre Dame, IN: University of Notre Dame Press, 1968.

Byock, Jesse L., trans. *The Saga of the Volsungs*. Berkeley: University of California Press, 1990.

Flieger, Verlyn. "Frodo and Aragorn: The Concept of the Hero." In *Tolkien: New Critical Perspectives*, edited by Neil D. Isaacs and Rose A. Zimbardo, 40–62. Lexington, KY: University Press of Kentucky, 1981.

Kocher, Paul H. "Aragorn." In *Master of Middle-earth: The Achievement of J.R.R. Tolkien*, 130–60. London: Thames & Hudson, 1972.

Zimbardo, Rose A. "Men, Halflings, and Hero-Worship." In *Tolkien and the Critics*, edited by Neil D. Isaacs and Rose A. Zimbardo, 109–27. Notre Dame, IN: University of Notre Dame Press, 1968.

See also **Arwen; Beren; Elendilmir; Elessar; Elrond; Elves; Galadriel; Gondor; Middle-earth: Men; Palantíri; Rivendell; Weapons: Named**

ARDA

In *The Silmarillion* Arda is the earth, a "habitation set within the vast spaces of the World" (19); elsewhere Tolkien defines Arda as the solar system (*Morgoth*, 337). Tolkien's cosmogony, the *Ainulindalë*, recounts how Ilúvatar, Father of All, proposes a great theme of music to the Ainur, his angelic servants, who develop it. But Melkor, the greatest of the Ainur, obtrudes his own desire for power into their symphony, creating new discord every time Ilúvatar restores harmony with a new theme. Silencing the symphony, Ilúvatar makes the music played so far visible to the Ainur, showing them the world and its unfolding history, whose glory even Melkor's discord only serves to increase. Making the vision disappear, Ilúvatar commands Arda into being. Into this new, as yet unformed world, the greatest of the Ainur (including Melkor) descend, to participate in its making (*S*, 15–22).

In the cosmogony's earliest version, Arda is a flat-earth world "globed amid the Void" (*Lost Tales I*, 56). An illustrated description from the 1930s shows its constitution. The Walls of the World form its spherical surface, transparent but impassable. The sphere's upper half consists of air, its lower half of Middle-earth, a flat surface floating on the ocean. This ocean reaches almost to the Walls of the World, except that it is bounded in the east by the Walls of the Sun and in the west by Valinor (*Shaping*, 238–51).

Arda's geography suffers massive changes during the battles of the Valar against Melkor, and even greater ones when Ilúvatar himself intervenes to stop the Númenórean attack on Valinor, removing Valinor from Men's reach, creating new seas and continents, and making the earth round (*S*, 278–79, 281–82).

Between the 1940s and the 1950s, Tolkien tried to make his invented world's astronomy more realistic. First, he placed the enclosed flat-earth cosmos into a vast universe, among countless stars (*Morgoth*, 12, 27–29), as in *The Silmarillion*. In later versions, the round earth and the sun exist from the beginning of creation (*Morgoth*, 369–90), and Arda comes to designate the entire solar system (*Morgoth*, 337). However, Tolkien never completed these revisions, having come to see his mythology as "too interlocked in all its parts, indeed its roots too deep, to withstand such a devastating surgery" (Christopher Tolkien, *Morgoth*, 383).

Comparing Old and New Testament cosmogonies to Tolkien's, Verlyn Flieger points out theological and narrative correspondences, but also important differences. In Tolkien, God shares the work of creation with his angelic servants, the Valar (Flieger, 49–55). In Tolkien, as in Milton, the fall of the rebel angels immediately precedes the earth's creation (Flieger, 55–58), a pattern that also appears in the Old English poem *Genesis A* (familiar to Tolkien from his work on *The Old English Exodus*).

As to the process of creation, Bradford Lee Eden links the medieval concept of the angelic "music of the spheres" to the importance of music in Tolkien's legendarium, from the symphony of Arda's creation onward. John William Houghton compares Tolkien's cosmogony to St. Augustine of Hippo's interpretation of Genesis. In this interpretation, God first created the angels, then created their knowledge of what was to be made, and then created a physical world that developed gradually, under the Holy Spirit's guidance, to its present state. The *Ainulindalë*, Houghton argues, "fits neatly amongst the real cosmogonies known to early medieval Europe" (171).

ALEXANDRA BOLINTINEANU

Further Reading

Chance, Jane, ed. *Tolkien and the Invention of Myth.* Lexington, KY: University Press of Kentucky, 2004.

———, ed. *Tolkien the Medievalist.* London and New York: Routledge, 2003.

Dobbie, Elliott Van Kirk, and George Philip Krapp, eds. "Genesis A." In *The Anglo-Saxon Poetic Records: A Collective Edition,* 1:3–87. New York: Columbia University Press, 1931–53.

Eden, Bradford Lee. "The 'Music of the Spheres': Relationships between Tolkien's *The Silmarillion* and Medieval Cosmological and Religious Theory." In *Tolkien the Medievalist,* edited by Jane Chance, 183–93. London and New York: Routledge, 2003.

Flieger, Verlyn. *Splintered Light: Logos and Language in Tolkien's World.* Grand Rapids, MI.: Eerdmans, 1983.

Gordon, R.K., trans. "Genesis A." In *Anglo-Saxon Poetry,* 95–111. London: J.M. Dent & Sons Ltd.; New York: E.P. Dutton & Co., 1962.

Houghton, John William. "Augustine in the Cottage of Lost Play: The *Ainulindalë as Asterisk Cosmogony.*" In *Tolkien the Medievalist,* edited by Jane Chance, 171–82. London and New York: Routledge, 2003.

Noad, Charles E. "On the Construction of 'The Silmarillion.'" In *Tolkien's Legendarium: Essays on "The History of Middle-earth,"* edited by Verlyn Flieger and Carl F. Hostetter, 31–68. Westport, CT: Greenwood Press, 2000.

Tolkien, J.R.R. *The Old English Exodus: Text, Translation and Commentary,* edited by Joan Turville-Petre, 33–36. Oxford: Clarendon Press, 1981.

See also **Ainulindalë; Astronomy and Cosmology, Middle-earth; Eru; Middle-earth; Morgoth and Melkor; Valar; Valinor**

ARKENSTONE

The Arkenstone is the greatest treasure and heirloom of the Dwarves of Erebor. This precious white stone, a globe of crystalline light, is otherwise known as the Heart of the Mountain. The origins of Arkenstone can be derived from numerous forms of the Anglo-Saxon word *eorclanstān,* or "precious stone." An example of an *eorclanstān* appears in *Beowulf* in relation to the King of the Geats, Hygelac, upon the occasion of his death (Anderson, 293). In describing the Silmarils, as Tolkien translated portions of the "Annals of Valinor," into Anglo-Saxon, he utilized the word *eorclanstān*as (Anderson, 294).

In *The Hobbit,* while standing atop a mound of treasure, when Smaug is away from his hoard, Bilbo finds the Arkenstone. The large gem, cut and fashioned by the Dwarves, radiates and reflects light that falls upon it from a thousand facets. The Arkenstone is hidden within Bilbo's pocket and later given to Bard to barter for peace between the warring armies of Elves, Dwarves, and Men. The Arkenstone, a central plot theme for Tolkien, relates in symbolism to alchemy's Philosopher's Stone or the *lapis philosphorum.* The Philosopher's Stone transforms base metals into gold, uniting opposites into a new whole (Bloom, 91). While in Bag End, Thorin promises Bilbo one fourteenth of the treasure, which Bilbo interprets to be applicable to the Arkenstone. The Hobbit decides to sacrifice his share of the treasure to unite the opposites of the story—the forces of Men, Elves, and Dwarves. Open war ensues between the armies, but is quickly averted as they are attacked by goblins, and bitter truce prevails.

It is the act of burglary, or theft, that leads to the significance of Bilbo's sacrifice, of his assumed share of the treasure, which is the turning point of the story's moral character. The fundamental evils within *The Hobbit* and the events of the War of the Ring, are pride, possessiveness, and greed (Kocher, 24). Tolkien translated a medieval English poem, *Pearl,* which details a jeweler who loses his pearl in a garden. But the poem can stand as an allegory or symbolic look into faith, Christ, salvation, and redemption. The pearl also symbolizes wealth, pleasure, pride, and possessiveness of rank or station. Thorin's lament of the missing Arkenstone parallels the opening lines of the poem as we learn of the missing pearl. The jeweler falls asleep in a garden and dreams of an alternate landscape filled with "precious stones," similar to those of King Hygelac in *Beowulf.* Within the jeweler's dream, he finds the pearl, which is transformed into a maiden of Paradise. The maiden teaches the jeweler about pride and possessiveness through faith, imagery, and symbolism (Zatta, *Pearl*).

Tolkien and the doctrines of his Catholic faith condemn the three cardinal sins: pride, possessiveness, and greed. Through Bilbo's actions, and Thorin's repentance upon his death, Elves, Dwarves, and Men all receive a generous share from the dragon's treasure hoard. The Arkenstone remains with Thorin after Bard lays it upon his breast when he is laid to rest.

ANTHONY BURDGE

Further Reading

Anderson, Douglas, ed. *The Annotated Hobbit: Revised and Expanded Edition.* Boston, MA: Houghton Mifflin, 2002.

Helms, Randel. *Tolkien's World.* Boston, MA: Houghton Mifflin, 1974.

Kocher, Paul. *Master of Middle-earth: The Fiction of J.R.R. Tolkien.* Boston, MA: Houghton Mifflin, 1972.

O'Neill, Timothy R. "The Individuated Hobbit." In *Modern Critical Views: J.R.R. Tolkien.* Harold Bloom, ed. Philadelphia: Chelseq House Publishers, 2000.

Zatta, Jane. *Pearl: An Introduction.* The ORB: On-line Reference Book for Medieval Studies. http://www.the-orb.net/textbooks/anthology/middleenganon/zatta.html.

ARMS AND ARMOR

The basic model for the arms and armor of Middle-earth was established very early in Tolkien's writing career. During the course of writing "The Fall of Gondolin," beginning in 1916, Tolkien established that the High Elves of Gondolin made various coats of mail, helms, vambraces and greaves, shields, swords, bows, axes, spears, and bills. Tolkien consistently adhered to this model during all of his Middle-earth writings and artwork for the next fifty-five years. This model carries much the same flavor of armor and weapons of the Dark Ages or Ancient period, most notably derived from such writings as *Beowulf* and the Norse Epics. Any variations to the model were fairly subtle, mainly in the way war gear was adorned or stylized.

The coats of mail were most often of small linked rings (commonly know as chain mail), which was first contrived by the Dwarven Smiths of Belegost in the ancient days before the Noldor returned to Middle-earth. Mail coats could be made longer (hauberks) or shorter (byrnies or corselets). Mail made by the Free Peoples of Middle-earth tended to be of better quality, more strongly made, with a closer weave for keeping the tips of weapons and arrows out. Mail made by the Orcs seemed to usually be of much lower quality, with a looser, less protective weave. Sometimes a variation was encountered: "Fishes' Mail," usually known as scale armor. It is a good possibility that scale armor was the predominant form of armor (both in Middle-earth and in Valinor) before the Dwarves contrived mail of linked rings. This is due to the simple fact that fish and reptiles are clad in scales naturally, so it easily observed and imitated.

Helms seemed to be most often of high, conical profile, though this does not preclude the use of lower, rounder styles. Such helms were often made entirely of iron or other metals, but sometimes a type of helmet construction was used that was of Tolkien's own design. This helm construction consisted of a frame of metal hoops covered with leather; an exterior metal brim could be added at the bottom, and at least in some cases a tall spike of metal could be added at the top. The most famous helm of this design was the one Bilbo received from Thorin, which can be seen in a rough sketch that Tolkien did of the Battle of Five Armies. Even when made entirely of metal, there is some evidence that helms were forged in a similar fashion to the metal-and-leather variety. For example, the sketches that Tolkien did of the Crown-Helm of Gondor show the use of hoops in reinforcing the plates of the helm, much like the hoop frame of the leather-and-metal helms.

Weapons throughout the history of Middle-earth were usually designed for use in one hand in conjunction with a shield in the other hand. Long, straight swords were the primary melee weapon of Elves and Men, while the Dwarves leaned toward the use of axes (though these are generalizations; there are cases when Elves used axes and Dwarves used swords). Spears were also frequently used by all the Free Peoples. There is also evidence for shorter swords or long knives carried as backup weapons. Some tales tell of the use of two-handed weapons (usually axes, mattocks, spears, and pikes), but the use of the shield is so commonly noted that it seems that two-handed weapons were not nearly as common as weapon and shield. Tolkien apparently knew well from his research that warriors eagerly sought out the practical protection of a shield (both in real history and the created history of Middle-earth). One of the best illustrations of this occurs when Thorin's shield was destroyed at the Battle of Azanulbizar. He took his axe to an oak tree and cut off a sturdy limb, to use both as a kind of shield to block blows and to wield in turn as a club. Tolkien noted that curved swords were almost never used by the High Elves, so much so that it was quite remarkable that Egalmoth of Gondolin carried one.

Elves and Dwarves had great renown in forging weapons of unparalleled quality, having great sharpness and durability. The Noldor of the First Age forged blades that glowed when Orcs (and perhaps other evil creatures) were nearby. The Númenoreans also had great ability in weapon-smithing (though not perhaps as great as Dwarves and Elves) as shown by the four barrow blades carried by Frodo and his companions.

Archery plays a great part in the history of Middle-earth warfare. Elves and Men in various times and places are very famous for their various type of long-bows made of yew or other suitable wood. In the First Age, Beleg Cuthalion was a renowned Sindarin archer armed with his mighty yew bow Belthronding. The High Elves of Gondolin had many skilled archers among them, in particular those from the Companies of the Swallow and the Heavenly Arch. The Wood Elves of Thranduil's realm used shorter bows, though they were greatly skilled archers. The Numenoreans had a unique type of bow made of hollow steel. Even the Dwarves had some skill in archery, as shown by Thorin and Company.

From the time of the earliest drafts of the "Silmarillion," the trademark weapon of the Orcs was the scimitar, a sword with a curved blade. Orcs had a variety of other weapons that they used also, most notably broad-bladed spears, as well as axes, bows, and daggers, but they were most famous for their scimitars. This being so, it was a notable difference that the Orcs of Isengard used short, broad-bladed stabbing swords. These short swords were also handy for cutting, as illustrated by the Orc captain Ugluk hewing the heads off several rebellious Orcs not of his Isengard band of Uruk-Hai. The various Orcs through time were handy with bows of a shorter nature, whereas the Orcs of Isengard used longbows much like those used by men.

JOSEPH PIELA

See also **Dwarves; Fëanor; Mithril; Technology in Middle-earth; Violence; War; Weapons: Named**

ART AND ILLUSTRATIONS BY TOLKIEN

While his literary critics have struggled to determine where Tolkien stands among twentieth-century writers—particularly in the face of a literary establishment that sniffs that he doesn't belong there at all—the problem of evaluating Tolkien's status as a visual artist is even more daunting. Even if the literary work of his heart, the "Silmarillion," languished in editorial limbo, *The Hobbit* and *Lord of the Rings* had a vast public. His drawings and paintings, on the other hand, mostly remained a private hobby—except as illustrations of his fiction. The publication of Tolkien calendars near the end of his life, however, had raised awareness among his fans of the quality and quantity of his visual art. After his death in 1973, an exhibition of Tolkien's drawings at the Ashmolean Museum in Oxford in December of 1976, moving to the National Book League in London the following spring, increased interest in the visual element in Tolkien's imagination. Yet even then, in the foreword to the catalog for that exhibition, K.J. Garlick, speaking for the custodians of Tolkien's art in the Bodleian Library at Oxford, could assert: "Few can be aware that he was a practicing draughtsman, and watercolourist, over a long period."

Later exhibitions in 1987, commemorating the fiftieth anniversary of *The Hobbit*, and in 1992, on the centenary of Tolkien's birth, served notice that Tolkienists could scarcely ignore the author's role as a visual artist. At the 1987 exhibition at Marquette, in fact, Christopher Tolkien went as far as to say that the study of Tolkien is incomplete without a consideration of his drawing and painting. The publication of Christopher Tolkien's *Pictures by J.R.R. Tolkien* in 1979 (a reproduction of the Tolkien calendar artwork, revised in 1992) and Wayne G. Hammond and Christina Scull's more comprehensive *J.R.R. Tolkien: Artist & Illustrator* in 1995 made reproductions of some of Tolkien's most obscure drawings available to a mass audience.

But the dilemma still remained: how to evaluate Tolkien the artist? In Rudyard Kipling's poem "The Conundrum of the Workshops" (1890), after Adam created the world's first drawing, the Devil whispered to him, "It's pretty, but is it Art?" Tolkien, who liked Kipling more than twentieth-century men of letters were supposed to, might have heard that same whisper. Critics are certainly susceptible to the seduction of that whisper, though very little has been written about Tolkien's art in comparison with his fiction. Yet in point of fact, J.R.R. Tolkien became a professional illustrator the moment he became a professional novelist: with the publication of *The Hobbit* in 1937. Ten black-and-white line drawings by Tolkien graced the first British edition of *The Hobbit*, and the American edition added four watercolor paintings. Tolkien's illustrations can in no way be considered a "composite art" with his fantasy, as both literary and art critics have come to speak of the illuminated poetry of William Blake, but certainly the drawings (and particularly the maps) serve to realize Tolkien's Middle-earth in a way complementary to his writing.

Tolkien's earliest literary critics understood the extent to which his linguistic and mythological backgrounds to his fantasy helped create verisimilitude by implying what lay beyond the borders of the books; maps and pictures of Middle-earth could only do the same. A few pages into chapter 3 of *The Hobbit*, for instance, the reader could, by consulting the map labeled "Wilderland" in the front of the book, see that Thorin and Company have reached Rivendell, which suggests (both etymologically and cartographically) a pass through increasing elevations of rock. Yet long before Tolkien prepared the map for publication, he had sketched two traveler's-eye views of Rivendell, one looking east, as the Dwarves would have seen it on approach, and one looking west, as Bilbo and Gandalf would have seen it coming back in chapter 19. Tolkien had visualized the landscape beyond verbal description, not only in three dimensions, but in 360 degrees.

The status of Tolkien's drawings as illustrations of his fiction is precarious, according to a footnote in his landmark lecture "On Fairy-Stories." "However good in themselves," he wrote, "illustrations do little good to fairy-stories. The radical distinction between all art (including drama) that offers a visible presentation and true literature is that it imposes one visible form" (67). But in one of the earliest discussions of Tolkien and "the Visual Image," Nancy-Lou Patterson pointed out, first, that Tolkien did not take his own advice, illustrating some of his works and seeking illustrators for others, and second, that the dilemma of illustrating fantasy was anticipated by Tolkien's nineteenth-century influences, particularly William Morris, who, as both a Northern-inspired teller of tales and a Pre-Raphaelite painter, worked out some of the problems Tolkien would face in realizing imaginary realms both poetically and visually. "You may be sure," Morris wrote, "that any decoration is futile, and has fallen at least into the first stage of degradation, when it does not remind you of something beyond itself, of something of which it is but a visible symbol" (Morris, 152, cited by Patterson, 13). Morris's principle helps us take one step toward answering the question of Tolkien's status as an artist: Tolkien's pictures succeed as art even when they begin life as an illustration of a separate work in another genre, because they point to a reality beyond the work. So Tolkien was right to say that "illustrations do little good to fairy-stories" *unless* they are considered as entirely separate enterprises in rendering a discrete reality apprehended by the imagination.

Tolkien's visual art was not limited to illustration of his legendarium, however. His early paintings and sketches from life reveal an ability to, with Wordsworth, "look steadily at [his] subject" and to render that subject accurately—with the remarkable exception of the human figure. So lifelike are his renderings of trees, flowers, landscapes, and architecture, that Tolkien's cartoonish attempts to draw people seem works of a different hand. If by his oft-repeated avowal to publishers that he "cannot draw," Tolkien meant that he could not draw people, it was simply the truth; if he was denying any artistic ability or draftsmanship, it was mere modesty, and a false modesty at that. Tolkien's pictures and designs are nearly as important a window into his imagination as is his fiction.

The visual dimension entered his scholarly life as well. The philological nature of Tolkien's professional training as a medievalist, with its emphasis on the word, particularly its sound, can hide how very visual medieval studies were in Tolkien's lifetime. Tolkien certainly availed himself of the best editions, but he also knew the Old English classics from their manuscripts (though he considered himself a dilettante at paleography), admiring them as artifacts and imitating those artifacts in his own calligraphy. Two of Tolkien's watercolors from September of 1927, *Glorund Sets Forth to Seek Túrin* and *Hringboga Heorte Gefysed*, are lettered in a hand worthy of an eighth-century Mercian scribe, with the *yogh* form of the "g," and a descending initial "s" and "r." Clearly this is a hand in love with the shape of the letter, as a thing of beauty apart from its role as a vehicle of meaning. Hammond and Scull, in their appendix on calligraphy in *J.R.R. Tolkien: Artist & Illustrator*, report that Tolkien learned calligraphy from his mother and that even his functional "fair hand" was based on tenth- and eleventh-century models in Edward Johnston's *Writing & Illuminating, & Lettering* (1906). Poet W.H. Auden, in his 1967 liner notes to the Caedmon recording of *Poems and Songs of Middle Earth* expressed envy of Tolkien's "gift for calligraphy."

Of course, Tolkien's calligraphy was not limited to his scholarly interests; it colored his fantasy as well. Integral with Tolkien's invention of his Middle-earth languages was the invention of the corresponding alphabets. Just as Tolkien's philological interest led to Elvish dialects that developed and changed like historical languages, and just as Old English and Old Norse were recorded in more than one alphabet (the runic and the Greco-Roman), Tolkien's Elvish is found in different scripts: the delicate *tengwar,* consisting of stems and "bows," and the more angular *cirth*, adapted from Germanic runes. Even within alphabets Tolkien sought variation, developing a "pointed" style of *tengwar*. The shape is as important to the character of the script as the sound, or what Tolkien called "'phonaesthetic' pleasure" (*Letters,* 176) to the spoken word.

Tolkien's sense of writing as artifact extended to paleography in the great pains he took to produce a facsimile of the *Book of Mazarbul*, on which, according to Hammond and Scull (163), Tolkien spent more time than on any other illustration to *The Lord of the Rings*. Having seen and touched ancient parchments himself, Tolkien knew the textures he sought in a facsimile: mottled in coloring, stained with blood, dirt, and the mysteries of long years of oxidation; torn, burned, and pierced for binding. Tolkien's treatment of the drafting materials as artifacts can be seen in the fact that the burns, tears, and binding lacunae are not drawn in, but actually burned, torn, and punched in the paper. Other instances of Tolkien's engagement of the viewer in manipulating the artifact—what Hammond and Scull call "mechanical effects"—include a watercolor from his undergraduate period, *The Land of Pohja* (1914), the original version of "Thror's Map" for *The Hobbit* (1937), and the meticulous reproduction of North Pole stamps and postal cancellations in the envelopes to the "Father Christmas letters" (1920–43). *The Land of Pohja* is painted on two leaves of a sketchbook, the first of which is cut diagonally so that the top flap can be opened to reveal a second view behind it. One view is a cheery sun touching the tops of a fir tree; the other is a cold, sunless landscape. As a sequence, the painting illustrates an incident in the Finnish *Kalevala* in which the evil Louhi steals the sun.

In inviting the viewer to participate in the shaping of the image in *The Land of Pohja*, Tolkien is being essentially modern. Yet in bringing in an element of temporal change to the drawing, Tolkien was imitating medieval artists that he must have been discovering at the time. The technique of temporal movement in visual art can be seen in any medieval triptych or in paintings as late as Sassetta's *The Meeting of Saint Anthony and Saint Paul* (c. 1440), representing events widely separated in time simultaneously on the canvas. Sassetta's painting is a useful analogue to Tolkien's *Pohja*, because it, too, divides the composition diagonally with a grove of trees that separates three different moments in St. Anthony's journey, each with a different linear perspective. Each event is separated historically by several days, as events in a biblical triptych by centuries, but typologically they are the same "moment." In inviting the viewer to change the temporal vantage point, then, Tolkien exhibits the same paradoxical amalgam of modernism and medievalism that often perplexes his literary critics.

Another example of Tolkien's modern adaptation of the medieval triptych can be seen in the first page of his "Father Christmas letter" for 1932. Formally, it is indeed a triptych, divided horizontally into three unequal panels, the middle one itself dividing into two, as it depicts a cutaway view of Father Christmas exploring caves beneath the North Pole. All three panels contain Father Christmas, so the events they depict cannot be simultaneous. The top panel is extraordinary, one of Tolkien's best compositions, a rare study of light and shade bordering on impressionism. It is the Oxford skyline at night, as seen from the west, with the dome of Sir Christopher Wren's Camera in the center and the spires of the Bodleian Library to the left; from the upper right, Father Christmas flies down to the rooftops, headed north (the direction, in this picture, of the Tolkien home at 20 Northmoor Road). The night sky in this panel is typical of Tolkien's pen-and-ink imitations of copperplate engravings, shading the sky with parallel lines, though carefully backgrounding the reindeer and the sleigh with a large white cloud, leaving the reindeer (except for the lead pair) in silhouette.

The cityscape, however, is done in a gray wash that perfectly captures the nature of architectural detail at night. Tolkien paints the buildings in various shades of gray, but instead of choosing the shade to maximize contrast of neighboring elements, as he does with the sleigh and the cloud, he actually minimizes

contrast, achieving the essence of what we see—or don't see—at night. In general, the shade of gray indicates distance: the farther away, the lighter. The gray value of pillars differs only slightly from that of the shadows between them, so that the eye first sees a single dark outline and then gradually makes out details, just as it would if observing the real building from downtown Oxford. It is a masterful piece of draftsmanship.

Tolkien's development as a visual artist might be described in terms of three categories (four, if his juvenilia is included), which may in turn be thought of in either generic or chronological terms (since the genres tend to fall into chronological periods, yet the periods overlap): Holiday Landscapes, Abstract Visions, and Middle-earth Landscapes. Each period or group influences the others. Tolkien's juvenilia, is, as one might expect, of interest only in terms of hints at later themes: these early drawings (1902–10) survive in a sketchbook belonging to Tolkien's mother, Mabel Tolkien; another sketchbook of his own begins with some sketches from Tolkien's early youth (aged four to five) on the first few pages, but then, starting from the other side, resuming about 1904.

The first category after Tolkien's juvenilia might be called "Holiday Landscapes," since the bulk of Tolkien's drawings and watercolors after his mother's death in 1904 date from his summer holidays— though this category includes works as late as 1952. His sketches at Hove, where he lived in 1904 for a brief time with his aunt Jane Neave, just after his mother's death, might be placed in this category, though they are certainly not "holiday" pictures. The Holiday Landscapes are sketches from nature, and while such mimetic artwork began after 1914 to recede in favor of the imagined landscapes of Middle-earth that began with Tolkien's first poetic evocations of his legendarium, Tolkien returned to sketches from life during his convalescence from "Trench Fever" in 1917–18, and from time to time they would crop up again. *Spring 1940*, for example, a colored pencil sketch, captures the moment the blossoms appeared on the Victoria Plum tree in Tolkien's garden at 20 Northmoor Road, Oxford. A summer holiday to Ireland resulted in a last spurt of Holiday Landscapes in August of 1952.

In the middle of Tolkien's undergraduate years at Oxford (1911–14), before his Holiday Landscapes yielded to his visionary landscapes of Middle-earth, Tolkien produced a different, more abstract type of visionary art, in a separate sketchbook he labeled *Book of Ishness*. Even the titles were abstractions: *Before, Afterwards, Beyond, Thought, Eeriness, Wickness, Undertenishness, Grownupishness*—the latter two explaining the title *The Book of Ishness*. The collective title resonates with Tolkien's literary art in two ways: first, by dealing with abstraction without resorting to the post-Enlightenment trick of Latinate diction—preferring the Anglo-Saxonism *-ishness* to a Latinism like *abstraction*. Second, in 1912–13 Tolkien is already thinking of his visual art, as he would soon think of his legendarium, as pieces of a larger artistic vision. Each story in *The Book of Lost Tales*, or later in *The Silmarillion*, is part of a larger mythological framework, just as *Beyond* and *Before* are parts of *The Book of Ishness*.

Some of the "Ishnesses" develop stylistic abstractions that later characterize the Middle-earth landscapes Tolkien painted first to visualize, and then to illustrate, the matter of *The Hobbit*, *The Lord of the Rings*, and *The Silmarillion*. In *Beyond*, for example, painted in *The Book of Ishness* January 12, 1914, mountains are reduced to simple triangles on a horizon line only partially delineated by their shadows, and fir trees are reduced to inverted black cones, a stylized evergreen that will reappear later that year in *The Land of Pohjah*, already mentioned (and also placed in *The Book of Ishness*), and again in later Middle-earth landscapes like *Mithrim* (1927, also in *Ishness*) and certain trees in the middle ground of his watercolor versions of *The Hill: Hobbiton-across-the-Water* and *Rivendell* (both 1937), two of Tolkien's most-recognized paintings. The stylization he perfected in the *Ishness* paintings of his undergraduate days would serve him later in his more mimetic *Hobbit* paintings, where he could create depth by detailing trees leaf by leaf in the foreground and by allowing the middle and background trees to become mere masses of color—which is how distance makes them appear to the eye in life. Baillie Tolkien considers this "deceptive combination of naturalism and formality" characteristic of her father-in-law's work as a whole.

Another result of the compositional use of colored shapes in the *Ishness* paintings is a freeing of Tolkien's brush. By the time Tolkien returned to the *Ishness* sketchbook in 1927, he no longer depended on the pencil line to compose the figures. This is true even when pencil guidelines can be detected on the paper: they are there to compose or to guide the brush, but not to serve as a visible outline. In watercolors before 1927, the brush seems to be decorating compositions already finished by pencil and sometimes ink. After 1927, the brush is part of the composition process. One masterful watercolor from September of that year, *Hringboga Heorte Gefysed,* outlines the sinuous curves of a coiled dragon in pencil but details the dragon's scales in painted shapes of various shades of green. Baillie Tolkien commented on Tolkien's preference for greens and his ability to produce a

subtle variety of that color. Certainly his colored pencil sketches tend toward greens, and not just when the subjects are trees (or great green dragons). The mountains of *Lunar Landscape* (1925), an illustration intended for *Roverandom*, are shaded and tinged with green, and not just at the base where they are presumably covered with grass (or maybe green cheese?). In his ink and colored pencil illustration of *The Lord of the Rings* entitled *Barad-dûr* (undated), there is not a blade of grass or leaf in sight—yet the brickwork in the mountain fortress is done in varying shades of green, and some green highlights can be seen in the shadings of the rocks at its base. And, of course, readers who remember the dust jackets to the original editions of *The Hobbit* and *The Lord of the Rings* will recall the deep green of *The Hobbit* and the dark green body color of the covers to *The Two Towers* and *The Return of the King*, all of which Tolkien designed.

Yet the primary association with green for Tolkien is certainly the leaves of trees, and it is perhaps the most common observation on his art that trees are his favorite subject. Nor is this to be wondered at by anyone who has read his fiction or his personal letters, where trees are revered. Most discussions of Tolkien's art turn sooner or later to the major artist figure in his fiction, the painter Niggle in his short story "Leaf by Niggle." Niggle "was the sort of painter who can paint leaves better than trees." As self-criticism (and there is no doubt among Tolkien's readers that Niggle is an autobiographical, or at least self-mythologized character), this is about as fair as Tolkien's protest that he "cannot draw": a partial truth. Tolkien certainly has a mind for detail: as a philologist he operated on the level of the word, a focus that had an effect on his writing. But that focus in no way implies a lack of architectonic sensibilities, either as a fiction writer, mastering incredible complexities of interlaced plots in *The Lord of the Rings*, or as a composer of pictures.

The dragon picture already mentioned, *Hringboga Heorte Gefysed* (1927), is a case in point. Each scale of the dragon's body is carefully and separately painted; some even are shaded in contrasting values of green to make them stand out. And yet part of the beauty of the painting is compositional: the gradual modulation of the shape of the scales, from near squares in the central, thickest part of the body to more and more elongated diamonds, and later leaf shapes as the tail narrows; the variety of shades of green (and some gray) providing contrast to the overlapping portions of the sinuously coiled worm (the very meaning of the Old English word *hringboga*, literally "bent into a ring"; the phrase is from *Beowulf* 2561); the very interlace structure of the composition itself, imitating the interwoven rings of Anglo-Saxon metal-work and graphic design. It is a triumph of design—and yet it also shows a niggling attention to detail.

But green, as we saw, primarily suggests trees. Trees appear in Tolkien's art in variety nearly as infinite as nature's. They are an early interest: an untitled watercolor landscape circa 1904 foregrounds an alder, its black trunk starting at the lower right and bending into the composition, overhanging a stream: the leaves are not quite individualized (some of them merge together, though clearly they began as separate dabs of the brush). The use of trees as foreground to create depth continued in later paintings and allowed for the characteristic combination of naturalism and formalism cited by Baillie Tolkien, which in practice became a combination of niggling detail and abstract form. In *King's Norton from Bilberry Hill*, for example (July 8, 1913), Tolkien uses fine strokes of a pointed brush to suggest individual needles on a few branches of a pine that forms the left-hand margin of the watercolor, while all of the background trees are blobs of various shades of green. The contrast between the sharp focus of the foreground tree and the panorama of King's Norton far below is heightened by the muting of the background both in terms of color and detail. Even his undergraduate sketch of *Turl Street, Oxford* (c. 1913), which is unusual for Tolkien in its architectural subject, sets the rows of buildings behind the overhanging branches of a tree from the vantage point of an upper-story window. Some three decades later, Tolkien's colored pencil sketch *The Forest of Lothlórien in Spring* (early 1940s) frames the composition with a tree whose trunk, highlighted in gold, forms the left-hand margin and whose overhanging lower limbs form the top margin, spangled with individually outlined leaves dotted with yellow blossoms. Yet every other visible tree is stylized, a few leaf lines appearing above the trunks and limbs, but mostly just blocks of color, greens and yellows.

Niggle notwithstanding, some of Tolkien's most detailed tree drawings are entirely or virtually leafless. In July of 1928, Tolkien produced two pencil and ink studies of Grendel's Mere in *Beowulf*, both entitled *Wudu wyrtum fæst* ("Wood Clinging by the Roots," *Beowulf,* 1364a). They are all twisted trunks and branches, except for one tree in one version whose few remaining leaves droop toward the surface of the mere as the trees hang over the surrounding cliffs. There is no attempt to texture the trunks, which look more like serpents than trees: there is not a single line or dot within the outline of the trunk or branches. Yet so organically do the branches twist and overlap one another that the overall impression is of detail rather than outline. The same curves that in Tolkien's

dragon pictures connote vitality here convey only decay and foreboding. A third study of a gnarled tree from the same period added texture and the suggestions of a face and was copied by Tolkien into his 1937 illustration *The Front Gate* in *The Hobbit*.

A drawing from the same month (July 1928), sketched again in pencil and ink, but this time finished in watercolor, is one of Tolkien's most visually engaging works: *Taur-na-Fúin*, later entitled *Fangorn Forest*. Once again, the trees are totally without leaves, except for a few gray ones belonging not to the trees but to the parasitic vines that envelop them. Again the forest scene suggests decay, but this time the decay seems but a natural part of the life cycle of an ancient forest, and Tolkien conveys an infectious fascination with the gnarled and intricately individualized roots and trunks. From the horizon line up, the composition is a mass of verticals, a seeming endless succession of fairly straight trunks (in various hues and textures) gradually merging into the black background. Below the horizon, the foreground is all a coil of twisted roots. Unlike the *Beowulf* illustrations, each of the trunks here has its own pattern of bark or shading: some scaly, some striated, some maculate, but all conveying character. In 1937, Tolkien redrew the scene for black-and-white reproduction in *The Hobbit* as *Mirkwood*.

The use of trees more directly as decorative border in something close to art nouveau fashion occurs a few times, notably in the watercolor *The Shores of Faery* (May 10, 1915) in *The Book of Ishness*, and in the only noncartographic illustration in *The Lord of the Rings*, the *Doors of Durin* (1954). The curled tendrils of the two trees in Tolkien's line drawing wrap themselves around the pillars and imitate the curls of the Feänorian script. In fact, the translated calligraphy below the illustration imitates both the insular characters of Old English manuscript and the very Feänorian characters it translates. The simplicity of the design (like the *Beowulf* trees, in outline only) belies the effort it cost Tolkien to produce the printed version: a series of preliminary sketches, each a refinement of the last, shows how Tolkien labored to produce that simplicity.

One tree design in particular, and this perhaps his most highly stylized, haunted Tolkien's visual imagination across four decades. Called *The Tree of Amalion*, it exists in three colored pencil versions, dated August 1928, in *The Book of Ishness*, reproduced in the 1979 Tolkien calendar; near the end of his artistic and literary career, Tolkien produced another version as the cover illustration for the 1964 paperback edition of *Tree and Leaf*. The prospect of coming up with a design for the book led publisher Rayner Unwin to connect Tolkien's sense of design with his professional interests in medieval manuscripts. Perhaps, Unwin suggested near the end of 1963, Tolkien could find an illustration ready-made in some parchment illumination. Tolkien's reply was surprising. "Medieval MSS," he said, "are not (in my not very extensive experience) good on trees" (*Letters*, 342). It is one thing for a writer dabbling in illustration to say "I cannot draw," but quite another for a celebrated Oxford medievalist to call his experience with medieval MSS "not very extensive." We can think of the assertion as Tolkien's characteristic modesty, but it may be simply a frank explanation to a nonspecialist that his expertise was philological and not art historical.

But just as puzzling is Tolkien's assertion that medieval MSS are "not good on trees." After all, trees, particularly the stylized curlicues of arboreal tendrils such as we see in Tolkien's *Amalion* designs, abound in medieval MSS. In fact, the preferred border design for medieval illuminators appeared to be, in most cases, the very sort of branches and leaves and nesting birds we find in Tolkien's *Tree(s) of Amalion*. How, then, are medieval MSS not good on trees? Perhaps one answer is William Morris's assertion, mentioned above, that designs not drawing the imagination to "something beyond itself" are futile, a sign of degraded art. In illuminated texts such as the fourteenth-century *Roman de la Rose* (several MSS of which resided in Tolkien's Oxford), we can see the sort of degradation Morris warned about: leaves that are mere geometric patterns, spacing dictated by the textual frame, with no attempt to create even the illusion of organic growth. There is no sense of a real tree behind these patterns.

Certainly there are fourteenth-century illuminations of trees that meet Morris's criterion of manifesting a reality beyond itself, as well as Tolkien's of being "good on trees." The English "Queen Mary's Psalter" and several French Books of the Hours come to mind. Yet the undeniable existence of medieval MS art that did not share Tolkien's love of trees must have led to Tolkien's resolve to produce his own art for the *Tree and Leaf* cover—the image for which, he told Unwin, "crops up regularly at those times when I feel driven to pattern-designing." The tree in its various manifestations is an emblem of arboreal lushness and variety. The branching curls of the tree are random and asymmetrical enough to remind us of real trees, yet artificial enough to place these drawings in the category of decorative rather than mimetic art. As Tolkien put it, they are "more suitable for embroidery than printing."

The details of any version of *The Tree of Amalion* illustrate the tension in fantasy art between the familiarity of mimetic landscape art—images of this world—and the estrangement of faerie. Leaves and flowers sprout from the ever-narrowing growth, their weight pulling the supple branches into natural curves. Yet Nature gives us trees whose leaves and flowers reproduce the type: individual leaves are not perhaps identical, yet each expresses a single form. Not so the leaves and flowers of *Amalion*: a bewildering variety of shapes, colors, and forms, each expressing not just a different individual, but even a different species. No real tree, not even the most man-tormented hybrid, could realize such variety. It is a pure expression of human imagination, a triumph of fantasy.

The Tree of Amalion does, in Morris's language, point to something beyond itself, but not in the natural world. Perhaps the image abided with Tolkien so tenaciously because, like Niggle's tree in his short story, it expressed his entire artistic life. As in "Leaf by Niggle," Tolkien the notorious allegorophobe had no qualms about attributing large allegories to *The Tree of Amalion*. The tree as a whole is an expression of an abstraction, the very idea of variety. Tolkien's readers have had no difficulty associating Niggle's tree with Tolkien's entire literary output; the variety in the blossoms on *The Tree of Amalion* similarly points to the literary works of Middle-earth. "The tree," Tolkien told Unwin, "bears besides various shapes of leaves many flowers small and large signifying poems and major legends." *Amalion*, then, might be a fit emblem for all of Tolkien's work, literary and visual, and of the interrelation between the two.

JOHN R. HOLMES

Further Reading

Ashmolean Museum, Oxford. *Drawings by Tolkien*. Oxford: Ashmolean Museum, 1976.

Hammond, Wayne G., and Christina Scull. *J.R.R. Tolkien: Artist & Illustrator*. Boston: Houghton Mifflin, 1995.

Morris, William. *Selections from the Prose Works of William Morris*. Edited by H.R. Pall. Cambridge: Cambridge University Press, 1931.

Patterson, Nancy-Lou. "Tree and Leaf: J.R.R. Tolkien and the Visual Image." *English Quarterly* 7 (1974): 11–26.

Tolkien, Christopher, ed. *Pictures by J.R.R. Tolkien*. London: HarperCollins 1992.

Tolkien, J.R.R., "On Fairy Stories." In *TL*.

See also **Artistic Movements; Artists and Illustrators' Influence on Tolkien;** *Father Christmas Letters*

ARTHURIAN LITERATURE

In the section of his lecture "On Fairy-Stories" that is concerned with children, J.R.R. Tolkien, looking back on his own childhood, remarked that "fairy-stories were plainly not primarily concerned with possibility, but with desirability. If they awakened *desire*, satisfying it while often whetting it unbearably, they succeeded" (134). From this, he described his earliest literary tastes; Tolkien loved stories that elicited the "desire of Faërie" (135), a wish to enter into another world, with all its strangeness and adventures. Among these stories were the tales of the "land of Merlin and Arthur" (134–35), which, unlike *Alice in Wonderland* or *Treasure Island*, captivated Tolkien from a young age. Into adulthood, in his professional life as a philologist and creative writer, the "desire of Faërie" sustained and inspired Tolkien. His decision to edit and translate *Sir Gawain and the Green Knight* was almost certainly guided by his fascination with fairy stories and, more particularly, by his early familiarity with Arthurian literature. This is not because Tolkien liked stories about fairies necessarily, nor does it mean that Arthurian literature is exclusively about fairies; it is about knights, kings, wizards, and queens. As Tolkien notes elsewhere in his lecture, "Arthur, Guinevere, and Lancelot are not [fairies]; but the good and evil story of Arthur's court is a 'fairy-story'" (112). In this sense, "Faërie" is properly described as "the realm or state in which fairies have their being," a realm whose borders sometimes cross with ours, inexplicably and unpredictably, "when we are enchanted" (113). As a consequence, Tolkien wrote, "most good 'fairy-stories' are about the *aventures* of men in the Perilous Realm or upon its shadowy marches" (113).

Tolkien did not use the word *aventure* lightly or by accident; he chose it deliberately, because *aventure* is a quintessentially Arthurian term. It comes from a precise language—Old French—and a specific literary genre—romance. This genre had its earliest origins in the twelfth and thirteenth centuries. It started with Wace's *Roman de Brut* and was perfected by Chrétien de Troyes, whose *Erec et Enide,* was fashioned significantly from a *conte d'avanture* (tale of adventure). Tales of Arthurian adventure continued in Chrétien's other romances of Cligés, Lancelot, Yvain, and Perceval (whose story's other main character is Gawain) and grew into many thirteenth-century continuations, culminating in Malory's fifteenth-century *Le Morte D'Arthur.* Each of Chrétien's romances, like Arthurian romance generally, told the stories of Arthurian knights errant who journeyed through the countryside and the wilderness and came upon adventure at nearly every turn. Some notable adventures involved the enchanted garden (Erec), the mysterious fountain (Yvain), the sword-bridge (Lancelot), and, of course, the Grail procession (Perceval). The romances also told tales of unrequited love or conflicted companionship, as in the famous story of Lancelot and Guinevere, and in the lesser known unions of Cligés and Fénice, Yvain and

Laudine, and Perceval and Blanchefleur. Finally, they also told of the quest for the Grail, and ultimately described the end of Arthur's life and reign.

In the late fourteenth-century story of *Sir Gawain and the Green Knight, aventure* occurs four times, in lines 29, 250, 489, and 2482, and in a variety of different spellings, which is not uncharacteristic of the period or of the manuscript means of textual transmission. Tolkien and Gordon correctly glossed *aventure* as "adventure or marvellous event," though, in his later translation, Tolkien also cast the term as "wonder" and "marvel," which adds an important texture to its meaning and draws it closer to the French "merveil," which is a near synonym. Tolkien and Gordon assumed, as do most scholars still, that *Sir Gawain and the Green Knight* had both Old French and Celtic origins. They also believed, somewhat chauvinistically, that *Sir Gawain* surpassed its French Arthurian predecessors in quality: "This is a story shaped with a sense of narrative unity not often found in Arthurian romance," they wrote. "Most of the Arthurian romances, even the greatest of them, such as the French *Perlesvaus*, or Malory's *Morte Darthure* (which is much better knit than its French originals), are rambling and incoherent" (*Sir Gawain*, introduction, x).

Some French originals, such as Chrétien's *Le Chevalier de la Charrette*, which is the first vernacular story of Lancelot and Guinevere, provided a lens through which scholars, Tolkien included, came to understand important features of Arthurian romance in general. Specifically, the detection of a system of so-called courtly love within this romance assisted the subtle and ingenious interpretation of Sir Gawain's temptation that Tolkien made in his lecture on "Sir Gawain and the Green Knight." Based on the terms of the relationship of Lancelot and Guinevere, and first described by the nineteenth-century French philologist Gaston Paris, courtly love consists of the following: courtly love is secret, risky, illegitimate, and adulterous; the status of the courtly lover is inferior to his beloved; the beloved lady has a capricious and disdainful nature; the lover idealizes the lady; and the lover serves the lady as a vassal serves a lord. Tolkien's friend and colleague C.S. Lewis also and later wrote on courtly love in ways that are consistent with Paris's thesis. In addition, Lewis enumerated courtly love's characteristics as humility, courtesy, adultery, and what he called the religion of love. Aware of this scholarly framework, Tolkien carefully analyzed Sir Gawain as a courtly lover who, obedient to a higher law, actually overcame the constraints of the lady and thus redeemed himself in a way that Lancelot in the Old French tradition never did. As Tolkien wrote of Gawain: "We have seen a gentle courtly knight learn by bitter experience the perils of Courtesy, and the unreality in the last resort of protestations of complete 'service' to a lady as a 'sovereign' whose will is law; and in that last resort we have seen him prefer a higher law" ("Sir Gawain," 99).

Knowledge of Arthurian literature clearly defined Tolkien's career as a scholar. The influence of this literature on Tolkien's creative works, however, is not immediately visible, although *aventure* in the Perilous Realm clearly pervades his fiction. There are much more explicit Arthurian connections in the scholarship and fiction of his friend C.S. Lewis. Tolkien did, of course, write a major poem entitled "The Fall of Arthur" around 1930. Never finished or published, the poem was known essentially only among a circle of scholarly colleagues, including E.V. Gordon, and it is mostly notable as one of the few instances in which the author "deals explicitly with sexual passion" (Carpenter, 168). Echoes of Avalon, the mythical Arthurian place across the sea whence the wounded king will someday return, abound in Tolkien's mythology and can be found in *The Silmarillion*, *The Hobbit*, and *The Lord of the Rings*. In this last work, the departures of the Elves, Gandalf, Bilbo, and especially Frodo clearly recall the departure of the wounded Arthur for a place where all will be healed and made whole again. Tolkien's mythology, however, was meant for England; in this sense, it is not Arthurian either in essence or in substance. In fact, it sought to replace the myth of Arthur with a myth of greater depth, history, and authentic connection to the ancient English land and language. For, as Tolkien the philologist knew very well, the myth of Arthur was a late import to the island, one that followed on and coincided roughly with the Norman Conquest. In all Tolkien's inventions, therefore, it may be the absence of Arthurian material that most clearly indicates the author's preoccupation with the conquest. Without Arthur, Tolkien's mythology follows a clear central impulse, which he indirectly intimates in his lecture on "English and Welsh": to return to a time before the Normans and to rediscover, as it were, Mercia's roots.

GERALD SEAMAN

Further Reading

Anderson, Douglas A. "'An industrious little devil': E.V. Gordon as Friend and Collaborator with Tolkien." In *Tolkien the Medievalist*, edited by Jane Chance, 15–25. London and New York: Routledge, 2003.

Carpenter, Humphrey, ed. *Tolkien: A Biography*. Boston, MA: Houghton Mifflin, 1977.

Chance, Jane. *The Lord of the Rings: The Mythology of Power*. Rev. ed. Lexington, KY: University Press of Kentucky, 2001.

————. *Tolkien's Art: A Mythology for England*. Rev. ed. Lexington, KY: University Press of Kentucky, 2001.

Chrétien de Troyes. *Oeuvres Complètes*. Paris: Gallimard, 1994.

Lazo, Andrew. "A Kind of Mid-wife: J.R.R. Tolkien and C.S. Lewis—Sharing Influence." In *Tolkien the Medievalist*, edited by Jane Chance, 36–49. London and New York: Routledge, 2003.

Lewis, C.S. *The Allegory of Love*. Oxford: Oxford University Press, 1936.

Paris, Gaston. "Etudes sur les romans de la Table Ronde: Lancelot du Lac. II. *Le Conte de la Charrette*." *Romania* 12 (1883): 459–534.

Shippey, Tom. *J.R.R. Tolkien: Author of the Century*. Boston and New York: Houghton Mifflin, 2000.

————. *The Road to Middle-earth*. Boston, MA: Houghton Mifflin, 1983.

Tolkien, J.R.R. "On Fairy-Stories." In *MC*.

————. "Sir Gawain and the Green Knight." In *MC*.

Tolkien, J.R.R., and E.V. Gordon, eds. *Sir Gawain and the Green Knight*. Oxford: Clarendon Press, 1925.

See also **Alliteration; Alliterative Revival;** *Brut* **by Layamon; France and French Culture; Gordon, E.V.; Lewis, C.S.; Old French Literature; "On Fairy-Stories";** *Pearl; Sir Gawain and the Green Knight; Orfeo, Sir;* **Unpublished Poems**

ARTHURIAN ROMANCE

Other than that it exists, little information is available at present about Tolkien's only creative venture into the world of Arthur, his long, unfinished, and as-yet unpublished poem, "The Fall of Arthur." Aside from his comment in a 1955 letter to his publisher that he still hoped to finish it, all available information about the poem comes from Humphrey Carpenter's account in his biography of Tolkien. Carpenter dates the poem to sometime in the 1930s and cites approving comments by R.W. Chambers and E.V. Gordon. According to Carpenter, Tolkien's poem, in Modern English, is written in the alliterative meter and two-part poetic line of Anglo-Saxon poetry such as *Beowulf*. Tolkien's choice of the word "Fall" rather than the more traditional "Death" or "Morte" to describe the poem's trajectory suggests a conscious effort to distinguish it from its probable Middle English precursors, the heroic, alliterative *Morte Arthure* and the stanzaic romance *Morte Arthur*. The alliterative *Morte* presents a heroic warrior king whose foreign wars leave England open to the usurper Mordred, while the stanzaic romance, beginning after the Grail quest, makes the adulterous relationship between Lancelot and Guinevere the root cause of Arthur's downfall. According to Carpenter, there is no Grail in Tolkien's poem, and although references to Guinever as a temptress and fatal woman suggest elements of the romance tradition, the emphasis seems to be more on Arthur's continental wars and his final battle with Mordred. The character of Gawain figures prominently.

Although Tolkien made use of Arthurian motifs in *The Lord of the Rings* (the withdrawal of a sword, a tutelary wizard, the emergence of a hidden king, a ship departure to a myth-enshrined destination), these are reinvented to fit the context of his own story. Given his explicit dismissal of the Arthurian world as England's mythology, his one explicit poem on the subject may, when published, shed new light on his relationship to Britain's most enduring story.

VERLYN FLIEGER

Further Reading

Benson, Larry D., ed. *King Arthur's Death: The Middle English Stanzaic Morte Arthur and Alliterative Morte*. Exeter Medieval Texts and Studies. Exeter: University of Exeter Press, 1995.
Carpenter, Humphrey. *Tolkien: A Biography*. Boston, MA: Houghton Mifflin, 1977.

See also **Alliterative Poetry; Arthurian Literature; Malory; *Sir Gawain and the Green Knight*; Unpublished Manuscripts**

ARTISTIC MOVEMENTS

The artistic movements of the Pre-Rapahaelites, Arts and Crafts, and art nouveau overlapped and were interconnected; accordingly, they will be discussed together here.

The Pre-Raphaelites were a group of writers and artists founded in 1848 by William Holman Hunt, D.G. Rossetti, and John Everett Millais. Its best-known members and associates are Edward Burne-Jones, the author and artist William Morris (of whom more below), Dante Gabriel Rossetti, Christina Rossetti, and John William Waterhouse. Their foundational goals, applauded and supported by John Ruskin, were to produce good art in the context of the appreciation of nature and rejection of convention (in the visual arts, rejecting the Mannerism of Raphael and the artists who followed him), and they were greatly interested in medieval themes. Waterhouse's lushly erotic paintings, typically depicting knights entranced by slender and diaphanously clad maidens in sylvan settings, are the most familiar Pre-Raphaelite works to a modern audience; reproductions may be found in almost any poster shop. The Birmingham Museum and Art Gallery contains a major collection of Pre-Raphaelite paintings that Tolkien presumably saw during his years at King Edward's School, including works by Burne-Jones, D.G. Rossetti, Ford

Madox Ford, Millais, and Morris. Tolkien would certainly have known the murals painted by the Pre-Raphaelites in the old Oxford Union Debating Chamber, which had become the Old Library by his time. Rossetti commissioned the young Morris and Burne-Jones, along with others, to paint the frescoes, which depict scenes from Malory's *Morte D'Arthur*. Although the frescoes began to decay almost immediately, their remnants can still be seen in the building.

The Pre-Raphaelites were also instrumental in launching the British Arts and Crafts movement, of which Morris was the most prominent member and which inspired the American movement subsequently. These artists laid emphasis on manual arts and artisanship and appreciation of well-made art, furniture, and buildings; and they valued the virtues of natural materials, elegant and practical design, suitability to purpose, and the premise that good art should be affordable to ordinary people—in opposition to the mechanically mass-produced, overly ornamented, and socially pretentious tendencies of mainstream Victorian furnishing and decoration.

Art nouveau, begun in the 1880s, continued the graceful aesthetics and focus on natural motifs of the Pre-Raphaelites (though in a more stylized presentation), but as its label suggests, it was oriented toward the modern rather than the archaic and made full use of mechanical reproduction, contemporary materials, and had an eye toward commercial success. Like the Pre-Raphaelites, nouveau encompassed a wide range of painting, printing, crafts, furnishing, architecture, and other arts. Art nouveau and Arts and Crafts encompassed the work many of the major artists of the late nineteenth and early twentieth centuries, including Frank Lloyd Wright, Gustav Klimt, Gustav Stickley, René Lalique, and Louis Comfort Tiffany.

The relevance of these movements as possible influences on Tolkien is obvious, in spite of Tolkien's admission that he "was not well acquainted with pictorial Art" (*Letters,* 413); they pervaded the British culture of Tolkien's youth and have endured ever since. It has been argued that the Elven jewelry described in *The Lord of the Rings* is essentially identical to art nouveau jewelry (although it might be argued that the Elves would hardly be likely to use anything but natural motifs in their designs) and that a number of well-known illustrations from Pre-Raphaelite and nouveau works show more than a passing resemblance to Tolkien's own art (see Podles, which reproduces several relevant illustrations). His drawings resemble their work in their emphasis on natural elements and in a two-dimensional flatness that, while understandable in a self-trained "primitive" artist, is also consistent with medieval artistic conventions—both those of Europe and those of Japanese prints, which Tolkien collected (and which were also sources for art nouveau).

The most significant figure across all three movements, as well as in the renaissance of modern printing and the book arts of hand-lettering, papermaking, and binding, was William Morris. As a translator of sagas and author of medievalist romances, Morris was by far the most influential of the Pre-Raphaelites for Tolkien. He "fell under the spell of Morris" while at Birmingham (Carpenter, *Inklings*, 29), and used his 1914 Skeat Prize money (five pounds) to buy Morris's *Life and Death of Jason*, translation of *Völsunga-saga*, and *House of the Wolfings* (*Biography,* 69). Morris, too, had attended Exeter College (*Biography,* 69). Writings of Tolkien that show Morris's influence include his "Story of Kullervo," the first draft of *The Book of Lost Tales*, and "The Fall of Gondolin" (*Biography,* 73, 92). C.S. Lewis's own fondness for Tolkien's writing came about in part because it reminded him of Morris's (*Inklings*, 32). Tolkien explicitly acknowledged the influence of *Wolfings* and of *The Roots of the Mountains* as sources for the Dead Marshes and the Morannon (*Letters*, 303).

Morris's influence in terms of book arts, while less documented, may have been equally great. The books he designed, printed, and bound at the Kelmscott Press were characterized by lush illustration, some of it with woodblocks, his own font designs for the text, and ornate natural motifs used in borders and illustration. The effect was less of an attempt to imitate medieval book arts than to pay tribute to the artists and artisans of the premodern world in the contemporary rerendering of medieval and other texts. Kelmscott was central to the modern revival of interest in the book arts of handpress printing, font design, hand-binding, and papermaking, all of which continue to enjoy a strong revival to the present day. The culmination of the Kelmscott works was the epochal *Works of Geoffrey Chaucer Newly Imprinted*, finished shortly before Morris's death. While Tolkien's calligraphy derives largely from medieval influences, from runic inscriptions to uncial Irish early medieval lettering and the clear fluid lines of ninth-century Carolingian minuscule, Morris is a likely inspiration there as well; one of his creations was a complete hand-lettered manuscript of Virgil's *Aeneid*.

As an illustrator as well as calligrapher in his manuscripts, Tolkien's synthesis of both the visual and textual arts—like those of Morris, and the Romantic poet William Blake before him (see Blake's self-illustrated, lettered, and printed *Songs of Innocence and Experience*)—represents a more or less complete refusal to compromise with the technical or fiscal limitations of mid-twentieth–century commercial book production. It was not until the fiftieth anniversary single-volume edition of *The Lord of the Rings*, published in 2004, that features Tolkien had always desired (including the Ring Inscription printed in red and color plates of the Book of Mazarbul inserted at the beginning of the chapter "The Bridge at Khazad-dûm") were finally realized in print.

JAMES I. MCNELIS III

Further Reading

Banham, Joanna, and Jennifer Harris. *William Morris and the Middle Ages*. Manchester: Manchester University Press, 1984.

Chaucer, Geoffrey. *The Works of Geoffrey Chaucer Now Newly Imprinted*. London: Basilisk Press, 1975. A facsimile of the Kelmscott Chaucer published as a two-volume set with Duncan Robinson, *A Companion Volume to the Kelmscott Chaucer*. Reprinted as *William Morris, Edward Burne-Jones and the Kelmscott Chaucer*. Kingston, RI: Moyer Bell Ltd., 1986; UK edition, London: Gordon Frazier, 1982.

Cumming, Elizabeth, and Wendy Kaplan. *The Arts and Crafts Movement*. London: Thames & Hudson, 1991. Reprint, 1995.

Greenhalgh, Paul. *Art Nouveau, 1890–1914*. New York: Harry N. Abrams, 2000.

Hammond, Wayne, and Christina Scull, *J.R.R. Tolkien: Artist and Illustrator*. New York: Houghton Mifflin, 2000.

Hilton, Timothy. *The Pre-Raphaelites*. Oxford: Oxford Publication, 1995.

Latham, David, and Sheila Latham. *Annotated Critical Bibliography of William Morris*. London and New York: Harvester Wheatsheaf and St. Martin's Press, 1991.

Peterson, William S. *The Kelmscott Press*. Oxford: Clarendon Press, 1991.

Podles, Mary. "Tolkien and the New Art: Visual Sources for *The Lord of the Rings*." In "Tolkien and the Christian Imagination," special issue, *Touchstone* 15, no. 1 (January/February 2002): 41–47.

See also **Artists and Illustrators' Influence on Tolkien; Tolkien's Art and Illustrations; Morris, William**

ARTISTS AND ILLUSTRATORS' INFLUENCE ON TOLKIEN

Tolkien's visual debt to illustrators and artists parallels his literary debt to writers and storytellers, though it was less wide-ranging, more ad hoc, and more unconscious. According to his purpose, he either absorbed elements of style so that they became part of his repertoire, or he incorporated subjects and details directly, using the original as a template. Visual art also had a direct impact on Tolkien's writing.

Perhaps the most abiding and productive artistic influence on Tolkien was William Morris (1834–96), instigator of the Arts and Crafts ethos that valued the handicrafts or "lesser arts" as much as painting and sculpture. Tolkien's absorption of similar ideals is apparent in his frieze patterns and decorative picture-borders, his Númenórean tiles and Elven heraldic devices, and particularly his book-jacket designs.

Art nouveau, descended from Arts and Crafts, appears in the stylings of landscape pictures such as *The Vale of Sirion*, which Hammond and Scull compare to the work of Danish fairy-story illustrator Kay Nielsen (1886–1957). The writhing forms of illustrator Arthur Rackham (1867–1939) have often been perceived in Tolkien's depictions of trees (e.g., *Old Man Willow*). Although Tolkien told Pauline Baynes to avoid Rackham's style in her illustrations for *Farmer Giles of Ham*, his own *Beleg Finds Gwindor in Taur-nu-Fuin* closely evokes the Golden Age illustrator's work.

Tolkien's stylistic debts extended to his maps and calligraphy. *Thror's Map* in *The Hobbit* is reminiscent of the work of anonymous medieval cartographers, but other maps recall hand-drawn First World War trench charts, such as the one of Regina Trench attributed (probably wrongly) to Tolkien. For calligraphic guidance, he consulted *Writing & Illumination, & Lettering* (1906) by Edward Johnston (1872–1944); he also derived decorative features from the same book.

Some pictures held sufficient appeal for Tolkien to adapt them directly, particularly for illustrations not intended for publication. *Eeriness* (1914) suggests Rudyard Kipling's illustration for "The Cat who Walked by Himself" (*Just So Stories*, 1902). The animals in cave paintings from the "Father Christmas letter" of 1932 were copied from Baldwin Brown's *The Art of the Cave Dweller*; the men hunting them recall South African cave images reproduced by Baldwin Brown and in the collection of the Pitt-Rivers Museum, Oxford. The drawing of the trolls in *The Hobbit* borrows from a print by Jennie Harbour in Edric Vredenburg's *The Fairy Tale Book* (c. 1934). An early conception of Orthanc recalls the concentric circles of Brueghel's *Tower of Babel*.

Other adaptations, especially in *The Hobbit*, reflect a concern for scientific accuracy. Tolkien's golden eagle (*Bilbo Woke Up with the Early Sun in His Eyes*) is a close copy of an 1891 chromolithograph by Alexander Thorburn reprinted in T.A. Coward's *The Birds of the British Isles and Their Eggs* (1919). J.S. Ryan points out that *Beorn's Hall* is modeled on an image of a Norse hall interior by Tolkien's colleague E.V. Gordon for *An Introduction to Old Norse* (1927). Drawings of Esgaroth (*Lake Town*) recall early twentieth-century visualizations of prehistoric lake villages.

Among the visual influences on Tolkien's writing, William Morris is once again prominent. The "lesser arts" he popularized appear in carvings and tapestries, Dwarven ironwork, and the Silmarils; a claim has been made for the influence of French art nouveau jeweler René Lalique (1860–1945) on Tolkien's descriptions of jewelry (Podles). The case for other, more specific influences on Tolkien's writings is more debatable. The Mirror of Galadriel and other elements have been compared to illustrations by Walter Crane (1845–1915) for Grimm's *Fairy Tales*; Podles also suggests the mark of Swedish illustrator John Bauer (1882–1918) on Hobbits themselves. Attributes of Gandalf have been related by Anderson to illustrations of the central European Rübezahl mountain spirits; he also likens the Ents to a picture of an ogre in oak-tree garb for E.H. Knatchbull-Hugessen's fairy-tale "Puss-cat Mew."

When asked about the striking congruences between *The Lord of the Rings* and a number of pictures, Tolkien denied that his "imagination had fed on pictures, as it clearly had been by certain kinds of literature and languages," declaring himself "not well acquainted with pictorial Art." However, on other occasions he admitted a literary debt to visual art. Rackham's drawings probably suggested Old Man Willow's propensity to catch unwary passers-by in a crack of his trunk, he said. He also noted that a German postcard by Josef Madlener (1881–1967) of an old man, *Der Berggeist* ("The Mountain Spirit," related to the Rübezahl figures) was the "origin of Gandalf."

JOHN GARTH

Further Reading

Baldwin Brown, Gerald. *The Art of the Cave Dweller*. London: John Murray, 1928.

Carpenter, Humphrey. *J.R.R. Tolkien: A Biography*. London: Allen & Unwin, 1977.

Garth, John. *Tolkien and the Great War: The Threshold of Middle-earth*. London: HarperCollins, 2003.

Hammond, Wayne G., and Christina Scull. *J.R.R. Tolkien: Artist and Illustrator*. London: HarperCollins, 1995.

Podles, Mary. "Tolkien and the New Art: Visual Sources for *The Lord of the Rings*." In "Tolkien and the Christian Imagination," special issue, *Touchstone* 15, no. 1 (January/February 2002): 41–47.

Ryan, J.S. "Two Oxford Scholars' Perceptions of the Traditional Germanic Hall." *Minas Tirith Evening-Star*, no. 1 (Spring 1990): 8–11.

Scull, Christina. "The Influence of Archaeology and History on Tolkien's World." In *Scholarship and Fantasy: Proceedings of the Tolkien Phenomenon, Turku, May 1992*, ed. K.J. Battarbee, 33–51. Turku: Turku University, 1993.

Zimmermann, Manfred. "The Origin of Gandalf and Josef Madlener," *Mythlore*, 9, no. 4 (Winter 1983).

See also **Art and Illustrations by Tolkien; Artistic Movements; Artists and Illustrators of Tolkien's Works;** *Father Christmas Letters*; **Manuscripts, Medieval; Prehistory: Cavemen**

ARWEN

Arwen in *The Lord of the Rings* is the daughter of Elrond Halfelven and the beloved of Aragorn. Her mother, Celebrían, is the daughter of Galadriel and Celeborn. Arwen's two brothers, the twins Elladan and Elrohir, play a small part in the story.

Arwen was born in Third Age 231, nearly three thousand years before the action of *The Lord of the Rings*. She marries Aragorn in Third Age 3019, reigns with him for one hundred and twenty years, and bears a son, Eldarion, and several unnamed daughters. Her death follows Aragorn's. It is implied that, like Aragorn and their Númenórean kin, she can choose the time of her own death, provided she does not delay too long.

Yet Arwen makes few appearances in the story. She is first seen by Frodo in Rivendell and not again until she rides into Minas Tirith on Midsummer's Eve to become Aragorn's bride. Soon after her marriage, Arwen comforts Frodo and tells him that he may cross the sea to the Undying Lands in her place. (But this is not a "ticket transfer"; see *Letters,* 327.) She is the first to see that Frodo is burdened by his memories.

Arwen, unlike Éowyn and Galadriel, has little action function within the story other than to marry Aragorn. Her symbolic role is to elevate their marriage, and Aragorn's kingship, to an act of destiny. In a later essay (UT, 271–285), it is Arwen, as Queen of Elves and Men, who crowns Aragorn again as Lord of Arnor.

As Elrond's daughter, Arwen can choose whether she will complete her life as Elf or Man—to be immortal within the life of the world or to die and depart to an unknown fate. By marrying Aragorn and remaining in Middle-earth when her father leaves, Arwen becomes a mortal woman.

Elrond and his children are of joint Elvish and Mannish descent. The "daughter of Elrond" appeared at a late stage in the composition, first named Finduilas. Tolkien tried several names in quick succession but settled soon on Arwen ("Royal Maiden") with the *epessë* (additional name) Undómiel ("Evenstar"). She was said to be "the evenstar of her people." In the published drafts of *The Lord of the Rings*, she arises first as the maker of the royal banner brought to Aragorn by her brothers. Subsequently, she comes to Minas Tirith, makes the "choice of Lúthien," and marries Aragorn.

In introducing her, Tolkien replaced his earlier intention that Aragorn should marry Éowyn and opened the door to the reuniting of the royal houses of Elves and Men and the evocation of the First Age story of her ancestress Lúthien Tinúviel, whom Arwen is said to resemble. Her great beauty is emphasized. Like the fairy-tale heroine "Rose Red" and the hero Noisiu in the Irish legend of the Sons of Uisliu, she has pale skin and very dark hair. This coloring is a mark of many of the descendants of Lúthien and her mother Melian, as well as of the Noldorin High Elves. It may be a reflection of Tolkien's regard for his wife Edith, but this is not certain.

Like many of Tolkien's vast dramatis personae, Arwen is sketched in a few lines, her actions more important than her inner personality. The reader must respond to her words and deeds. She appears by turns inspirational, remote, generous, and, like Elbereth, watchful of the well-being of others.

The marriage of Aragorn and Arwen represents the renewal of the part-Elvish royal line of Númenor. It is one of only three marriages of High Elves and mortal Men. (There is a fourth marriage, often overlooked, between the sylvan Elven-lady Mithrellas and the Man Imrazôr, ancestor of Imrahil of Dol Amroth. See UT, 248.) In the other two, the hero's potential is raised by marriage to a courageous and proactive Elvish princess. Tuor aids Idril in saving the refugees from Gondolin. Lúthien and Beren win the Silmaril from Morgoth by going into danger together.

But Tolkien's Arwen is not a warrior and lives out her marriage in regal domestic peace. Her union with Aragorn restores the High Elven heritage to Men, though the future remains uncertain, as always, in Arda. But it is the choice of the children of Elrond, not her marriage to a Man, that makes Arwen a mortal woman at last.

Tolkien wrote "A Part of the Tale of Aragorn and Arwen" as an extra episode. At the conclusion, Arwen and Aragorn talk intensely to each other about the nature of death. It could be said that Arwen finally speaks on behalf of mortals everywhere. Published as part of Appendix A, the tale was to Tolkien sufficiently important to be included in editions where the other appendices were omitted. He discussed this in a letter (181) to Michael Straight in 1956.

HELEN ARMSTRONG

Further Reading

Armstrong, Helen. "There Are Two People in This Marriage." *Mallorn: The Journal of the Tolkien Society* 36 (1998): 5–12.

Chance, Jane. "Tolkien's Women (and Men): The Films and the Book." *Mallorn: The Journal of the Tolkien*

Society 43 (2005): 30–37. Originally published in *Tolkien on Film: Essays on Peter Jackson's "The Lord of the Rings*," edited by Jay Brennan Croft, 175–93. Altadena: Mythopoeic Press, 2004.

Rawls, Melanie. "Arwen, Shadow Bride." *Mythlore* 43 (1985): 24–25, 37.

Shippey, T.A. "When All Our Fathers Worshipped Stocks and Stones." In *The Road to Middle-earth*, 148–54. London: Allen & Unwin, 1982.

Tolkien, J.R.R. "The Disaster of the Gladden Fields." In *UT*.

———. "History of Galadriel and Celeborn." In *UT*.

See also **Aragorn; Ëarendil; Elendilmir; Elrond; Elves; Elves: Kindreds and Migrations; Elves: Reincarnation; Galadriel; Gondor; Lúthien; Rivendell**

ASCETICISM

Throughout his works, Tolkien emphasizes the value of self-discipline and self-denial as fundamental for preserving purity of heart and dedication to one's purpose. Such self-discipline requires the endurance of physical discomfort, fasting, fatigue, and isolation. These sufferings, in Tolkien's view, are both obligatory and freeing. They reduce life down to its essentials. Through them, the sufferers can demonstrate the primacy of love and unity, and the necessity of preserving good and fighting evil.

Tolkien's view of asceticism was influenced by the value of self-discipline in medieval culture. Monastics, hermits, and *peregrini* provided precedents for Tolkien, as these ascetics chose lives of isolation to more thoroughly immerse themselves in prayer and contemplation. Anglo-Saxon elegiac poems, notably *The Wanderer* and *The Seafarer*, lament the ephemeral nature of earthly pleasures and observe that permanence resides only in heaven. In these sources, denying the needs of the body and despising the things of this world free the spirit, bringing the soul closer to God.

Many characters in Tolkien's works pursue an ascetic lifestyle, maintaining through self-discipline their purity of heart and dedication. Men, because of their weakness and mortality in comparison to Elves, are most often distinguished by their ascetic lives. In *The Silmarillion*, Beren lives alone in desolate places, spends years wandering in solitude, and endures a horrific journey through the Ered Gorgoroth before emerging from his torment into Doriath (S 182, 192–93). In *The Lord of the Rings*, Aragorn, Beren's descendant, likewise endures painful hardships in the wilderness, offering his suffering service without recognition, as he emphasizes to Boromir during the Council of Elrond (*FR,* II, ii, 261). The Rangers fulfill their purpose by enduring hardship and danger to preserve the safety of other peoples. Gimli and Legolas join Aragorn in this task during the chase of the Three Kindreds, pursuing Merry and Pippin across the plains of Rohan (*TT*, III, 410). Gandalf, like Aragorn, spends years wandering throughout Middle-earth, suffering discomfort and danger in his fight against Sauron (*FR*, I, x, 182). Following Gandalf's fall from the bridge in Moria, both the Elves of Lothlórien and Frodo, who refer to Gandalf as a "pilgrim," honor his ascetic life in their laments (*FR*, II, viii, 374).

The hobbits likewise assume an ascetic lifestyle on their journeys through Middle-earth, an especially difficult task for them because of their love for comfort, safety, and regular and plentiful meals (*H,* 4). Initially, the hobbits mourn the loss of their feasts, firesides, and warm beds. As they persevere in their quest, their endurance grows, and ultimately their hardships release the "seed of courage" residing within them (*FR*, I, viii, 151). Deprivation allows them to discover and demonstrate their inner strength. Frodo's increasing weakness on the journey allows Sam to recognize his own courage and strength, crucial for the future of Middle-earth and the Shire. On the final stages of their pilgrimage to Mordor, their endurance of hunger, thirst, exhaustion, and despair makes them even more determined in their purpose to destroy the Ring and end the reign of Sauron.

CHRISTINA M. HECKMAN

Further Reading

Krapp, George P., and Eliott Dobbie, eds. *The Exeter Book*. New York: Columbia University Press, 1935.

See also **Aragorn; Beren; Frodo; Gandalf; Gimli; Hobbits; Legolas;** *Lord of the Rings***; Merry; Pilgrimage; Pippin; Sam; Sauron;** *Seafarer***;** *Silmarillion***;** *Wanderer*

ASTRONOMY AND COSMOLOGY, MIDDLE-EARTH

The sun, the moon, and the stars are an insistent presence in *The Hobbit* and *The Lord of the Rings*. Good characters look to the lights of heaven as they observe their surroundings or the passage of time; the sun, moon, and stars feature in their greetings, riddles, songs, and verse (*H,* III, 91; V, 122; *FR*, I, iii, 90 etc.). Evil characters, on the contrary, hate and fear the lights of heaven: the trolls turn to stone at sunrise; Gollum cannot endure sunlight and moonlight; ordinary Orcs will not venture into sunlight; and before his first attack on Middle-earth, Sauron darkens the sun (*H,* V, 136; *TT*, IV, 783).

In its more systematic picture of the universe surrounding Middle-earth, *The Silmarillion* maintains and elaborates the moral significance of Middle-earth's astronomy. Arda, the earth, flat during its early history, coexists with distant stars in an infinite space. The Valar create the lights of heaven, which eventually take the form of the nearer stars, the sun, and the moon, to sustain life on earth and to combat evil. This light, however, is subject to the "long defeat" of the world's history, diminishing, fragmenting, and drawing ever farther away from Middle-earth (Flieger, 89).

The Valar's initial attempts to illumine the earth do not involve heavenly bodies at all. First, they make two vast lamps to light all of Middle-earth, but Melkor casts these down. Then they make the Two Trees, Telperion and Laurelin, each of whose radiance waxes as the other's wanes. The two trees illuminate Valinor, but Middle-earth lies under Melkor's dominion, in darkness under the faraway stars. To check Melkor's power, Varda, Queen of the Valar, creates stars nearer to the earth (their real life counterparts are suggested in *Morgoth*, 434–36 and *S,* 313–65): Carnil (Mars), Luinil (Neptune), Nénar (Uranus), Lumbar (Saturn), Alcarinquë (Jupiter), Ellemírë (Mercury), and Helluin (Sirius). Varda also assembles constellations (identified in *S,* 354, 340, 353 and *Morgoth,* 388): Wilwarin (perhaps Cassiopeia), Telumendil, Soronúmë, Anarríma, Menelmacar (Orion), and Valacirca (the Great Bear or the Plough). Of these, Menelmacar, the Swordsman of the Sky, and Valacirca, the Sickle of the Valar, stand in the heavens as a threat to the powers of evil. The Elves, who awake under these new stars, will always love their light. In *The Lord of the Rings*, Elves begin to sing when the Swordsman (called here Menelvagor) appears in the sky (*FR*, I, iii, 91). Other stars named in *The Lord of the Rings* are red Borgil, variously identified as Aldebaran, Betelgeuse, or the planet Mars, and Remmirath, the Netted Stars, identified as the Pleiades (Larsen, 161–70).

Like the stars, the sun and the moon are a riposte to Morgoth's evil. After Morgoth mortally wounds the Two Trees and the Valar try in vain to heal them, Telperion produces a last silver flower, and Laurelin a last golden fruit. The Valar bless them, place them in vessels that may traverse the firmament, and give them guides: a silver-loving spirit named Tilion for the silver flower that becomes the moon (Isil) and a mighty spirit of fire, the maiden Arien, for the golden fruit that becomes the sun (Anar). In Middle-earth, Men awake at the first sunrise.

At first the sun and moon travel the sky concurrently: each rises from Valinor and moves toward the east as the other returns from the east to Valinor. But because Tilion draws so near the sun that the moon is scorched, and because the constant daylight banishes rest and hides the stars, Varda changes her mind. She ordains that the sun descend in the West, rest in Valinor, and then pass under the earth to rise again in the east. She also ordains the moon to travel the sky at night, but he remains wayward, sometimes appearing in the day sky, sometimes eclipsing the sun altogether.

The youngest heavenly body is Eärendil, the evening or morning star, whom the Valar set sailing the heavens with a Silmaril on his brow. When the people of Middle-earth first see the new star in the sky, they call it "the Star of High Hope" and are comforted (*S,* 250).

In *The Silmarillion*, the count of time begins when the older of the Two Trees of Valinor, Telperion, first grows bright. The Valar count a day as twelve hours, six illuminated by Telperion and six by Laurelin. After the death of the Trees, the Valar count the days according to the sun; accordingly, Elves, Men, and eventually Hobbits use various solar calendars (RK, Appendix D, 384–390).

Tolkien's mythical cosmology changes considerably over time, as Charles E. Noad demonstrates. Between the early 1920s and the early 1930s, his invented world consists of a flat earth, as in *The Silmarillion* (*Lost Tales I*, 56, 68; *Shaping,* 232–61), but placed in a finite cosmos: Middle-earth and its attendant heavenly bodies are enclosed in the Walls of the World, outside of which lies a starless void (*Shaping,* 235). The astronomy is more mythical: Some of Varda's stars, as well as the sun and moon, are light-filled vessels, traversing the heavens under the guidance of spirits; and in addition to a guide, the moon also has a stowaway, an old Elf who becomes known as the Man in the Moon. The phases of the moon occur as Telperion's flower periodically wanes and descends to Valinor (*Lost Tales I,* 177–206)

In the late 1930s, Tolkien devised and integrated into his mythology the story of Númenor's fall, in which the flat earth becomes round (*Lost Road,* 7–104).

In the 1940s, Tolkien began to revise his cosmogonic myths to fit more closely with the "real world." A late 1940s *Ainulindalë* places the enclosed flat-earth cosmos of the *Ambarkanta* into a vast astronomical universe, among countless stars (*Morgoth*, 12, 27–29). This is essentially the cosmology of *The Silmarillion*. Another *Ainulindalë* from this period, soon abandoned, makes the earth round and redefines Arda as the solar system. In this version, in a radical departure from the myth of the Two Trees, the sun predates the earth, and the moon is a piece of the earth torn away by Melkor (*Morgoth,* 3–6, 39–44).

In the late 1950s, Tolkien again envisioned a round earth in the midst of starry space, its sun coeval with the earth, and its moon made by the Valar, possibly from the substance of the earth (*Morgoth,* 369–90). This version reduces Varda's role as subcreator; her stars merely imitate real constellations on the protective dome that covers Valinor. No fully developed narrative integrates this more astronomically realistic cosmology with the rest of Tolkien's legendarium.

ALEXANDRA BOLINTINEANU

Further Reading

Bolintineanu, Alexandra. "'On the Borders of Old Stories': Enacting the Past in *Beowulf* and *The Lord of the Rings.*" In *Tolkien and the Invention of Myth,* edited by Jane Chance, 263–73. Lexington, KY: University Press of Kentucky, 2004.

Flieger, Verlyn. *Splintered Light: Logos and Language in Tolkien's World.* Grand Rapids, Mich.: Eerdmans, 1983.

Larsen, Kristine. "A Definitive Identification of Tolkien's 'Borgil': An Astronomical and Literary Approach." *Tolkien Studies: An Annual Scholarly Review* 2 (2004): 161–70.

Noad, Charles E. "On the Construction of 'The Silmarillion.'" In *Tolkien's Legendarium: Essays on "The History of Middle-earth,"* edited by Verlyn Flieger and Carl F. Hostetter, 31–68. Westport, CT: Greenwood Press, 2000.

See also **Arda; Calendars; Eärendil; Elements; Light; Middle-earth; Morgoth and Melkor; Valar; Two Trees; Silmarils**

AUDEN, W.H.: INFLUENCE OF TOLKIEN

Perhaps the most dominant English poet of his time, and a distinguished critic, W.H. Auden (1907–73) was in both these professions a student of things medieval, and especially of Anglo-Saxon language and literature. Throughout his career, he paid special tribute to the influence of Professor J.R.R. Tolkien, whom he had encountered in his student days at Oxford. Years later, he was the first important critic to regard Tolkien's fiction as a major literary achievement. But the influence upon himself that Auden cites is always the philologist, never the author of *The Lord of the Rings.* Curiously, Auden received a mere third-class degree and was found in tears after the Old English examination paper. He remarked often that the deep influence came not from scholarly lectures but from hearing Tolkien reading *Beowulf* aloud.

Spellbound by the sounds of Tolkien's voice, Auden said years later of the lectures, "I do not remember a word he said."

These two giants of literary imagination share not only Old English. In a skeptical age that makes them look nearly subversive, they also share deep commitments to historic Christianity. Yet their relations are filled with contradictions and complexities. Auden is a mythic but very modernist poet, Tolkien a weaver of magic but an exacting medievalist word-digger. A grateful Tolkien bristles with some annoyance at Auden's assessments of *The Lord of the Rings.* There is a fairly petty altercation in the late sixties about the appearance of Tolkien's house. But they survive into a final quiet if nervous friendship before the deaths of both of them in 1973.

As Tolkien's second career as a novelist rose, Auden was there to hail it in three reviews, in a BBC talk, and in a critical essay. He saw in Tolkien the resurgence of deep and universal mythic consciousness, the recovery and revitalizing of an alternative way of seeing what human beings and history are. Auden saw *The Lord of the Rings* as a glorious triumph of human imagination, while linking it to old traditions of the Quest Hero. But even so, Auden's personal thanks go to the scholar. In "A Short Ode to a Philologist," he notes that

> Dame Philology is our Queen still
> Quick to comfort
> Truth-loving hearts in their mother tongue
> ... [so that] A poor commoner [can] arrive at
> The Proper Name for his cat.

A language is not immortal, Auden goes on, until it dies,

> But a lay of Beowulf's language too can be sung
> Ignoble, maybe, to the young,
> Having no monster and no gore
> To speak of, yet not without its beauties
> ... A lot of us are grateful for
> What J.R.R. Tolkien has done
> As bard to Anglo-Saxon.

But here too, it is neither the Ring trilogy nor the scholar's scholarship, but his making the old language sing, that means most to Auden.

Tolkien took very little notice of Auden's praises—little public notice, that is. There exists among his *Letters* a belabored eight-page response to Auden's reviews. Strangely, it was revised once but never sent or shown to anyone. What it reveals is a distrustful scholar-turned-myth-maker feeling rankled by a modernist poet's sense of the word "imagination." "I am historically minded. Middle-earth is not an imaginary world ... but the historical period is imaginary."

And so Tolkien lays out to himself a sense of tale-telling, journey, and quest that is far less "politically purposive" and allegorical, far less psychological, and far less concerned with "our experience of social-historical realities," than Auden's. Obviously, Tolkien sees Auden the poet, for all his fealty, as coming from some other orientation.

In 1966, Auden proposed writing a forty-eight-page monograph on Tolkien for a series called *Contemporary Writers in Christian Perspective.* Sensitive to Tolkien's silence, he may have seen this as a chance to reconstruct and clarify his praise, this time enriched by a shared religious context. But Tolkien, in letters to the publisher and to Auden, asked that the project be scrapped, arguing to Auden that it would be a "premature impertinence" and to the publisher that, among other things, "he does not know me." Tolkien then cited to the publisher something Auden had reportedly said, quoted in the *New Yorker*, about Tolkien's house, calling it "a hideous house—I can't tell you how awful it is—with hideous pictures on the wall." Auden, who had reportedly been drinking heavily before making his strange impromptu pronouncement, never explained it, but immediately withdrew ("If Professor Tolkien does not wish me to publish it, I shall not publish it"). He apparently destroyed the working draft of the manuscript. One careless sentence and some sensitivity to it deprived the world of a book that would certainly have deepened our insights into both these masters.

In less than a year, the relationship, always an uneasy one for Tolkien, had become almost a friendship. Tolkien contributed a poem, "For W.H.A.," to a Festschrift gathered for Auden's sixtieth birthday, in 1967. Upon Auden's death in 1973 at age 66, Tolkien, then 74, expressed in print his gratitude for Auden's support of his work and placed him "as one of my great friends."

Auden's profound respect and gratitude were always constant. But though he wrote brilliantly about Tolkien's literary achievement, indicating paths into it for serious readers and other critics, it was the sound of the professor reading *Beowulf* that remained the biggest influence. From then on, the sounds of Old English resonate in Auden's poetry (e.g., "Doom is dark and deeper than any sea dingle"). Professor Tolkien, slightly suspicious of imagination and very suspicious of dream, may not have understood how meaningful the sounds of a voice would be to a poet. But Auden may well have had his old Oxford professor in mind when he wrote, in his *Obiter Dicta,* still grateful, that "a professor is someone who talks in someone else's sleep."

ROD JELLEMA

Further Reading

Auden, W.H. *Collected Poems.* New York: Vintage, 1991.
———. *The Dyer's Hand and Other Essays.* New York: Random House, 1962.
———. "The Quest Hero." In *Understanding the Lord of the Rings*, edited by Rose Zimbardo and Neil D. Isaacs, 31–51. Boston, MA: Houghton Mifflin, 2004.
Carpenter, Humphrey. *Tolkien: A Biography.* Boston: Houghton Mifflin, 1977.
Jellema, Rod. "Auden on Tolkien: The Book That Isn't and the House That Brought It Down." In *W.H. Auden: A Legacy*, ed. David Garrett Izzo, 39–46. West Cornwall, CT: Locust Hill Press, 2002.
———. *Later Auden.* New York: Farrar Straus & Giroux, 1999.

AUGUSTINE OF CANTERBURY, SAINT, FIRST ARCHBISHOP OF CANTERBURY (d. c. 604)

Generally called the Apostle of England, Augustine was prior of St. Andrew's on the Coelian Hill in Rome, when Pope Gregory I (the Great) sent him with a band of forty monks to preach the gospel to the pagan English in 596. Gregory's famous incident of seeing English slaves being sold in the Roman marketplace and relating their name (Angli) with the word "angel" is considered the genesis for the English mission, although more emphasis should be placed on the needs of the English king, Ethelbert of Kent. Ethelbert had married a Frankish princess, Bertha, who was a Christian, and part of the marriage arrangement was the construction of a Christian place of worship as well as providing a Christian priest to conduct ceremonies. Ethelbert soon joined the Christian faith once Augustine arrived in 597, and many of the English followed his example. In 601, Pope Gregory I sent reinforcements to England, including personnel, books, sacred vessels, and relics to consecrate altars. Augustine tried twice to work with the local British/Celtic priests who still practiced Christianity to some degree in the north and western portions of Britain, but their supposed stubbornness regarding certain practices and customs led Augustine to bring updated Roman practices to British Christianity.

Augustine's extensive correspondence with Pope Gregory I survives and was quoted by the Venerable Bede in his history of the English race in the eighth century. Topics related to the destruction of pagan shrines, the adaptation of Gallican and British customs in the Roman liturgy, and the establishment and daily life of monks were some of the discussions for which Augustine asked for help from the Roman pontiff. Augustine was able to establish two other episcopal sees during his lifetime, one in London for the East Saxons and one in Rochester. During his seven–year apostolate, Augustine was able to plant the seeds that would eventually bring Christianity to the whole of Britain. His feast day is celebrated on May 26 in England and on May 28 elsewhere.

BRADFORD LEE EDEN

Further Reading

Attwater, D. *The Penguin Dictionary of Saints*. Baltimore, MD: Penguin Books, 1965.

Deansley, M. *Augustine of Canterbury*. London: Nelson, 1964.

Farmer, H. "Augustine of Canterbury, St." In *New Catholic Encyclopedia*, 1:1058. New York: McGraw-Hill, 1967–79.

Matz, T. "St. Augustine of Canterbury." In *Catholic Online Saints*. http://saints.catholic.org/saints/augustinecanterbury.html.

See also **Christianity; Conversion; Gregory the Great; Missions from Anglo-Saxon England; Saints**

AUGUSTINE OF HIPPO

Augustine writes in his *Confessions* that he was born in Tagaste, in Roman Africa, to a Christian mother, Monnica, and a pagan father, Patricius. Educated at Madaura and Carthage, he taught in Africa and at Rome before becoming professor of rhetoric in Milan (384). There, under the influence of Neoplatonist philosophers and of St. Ambrose, and after a divine directive to read Romans 13 (*Conf.* 8.8), he was converted to Catholic Christianity and baptized by Ambrose at Easter in 387. He returned to Tagaste in 389; in 391, the church of Hippo Regius (some sixty miles away) persuaded him to be ordained a priest. In 395, he succeeded to the bishopric, holding it until his death, as the Vandals besieged the city, on August 28 (now his feast day) in 430.

Two prominent issues in Augustine's extensive writings have particular resonances in Tolkien's work: creation (including the nature of evil), and free will and predestination. Responding to the dualistic Manicheanism he had himself practiced, Augustine argues that the one, good God created the universe good and that (as Neoplatonists taught) evil is fundamentally nothing. While developing this doctrine in several commentaries, he also interprets other aspects of Genesis, explaining, for example, in *On the Literal Meaning of Genesis [De Genesi ad litteram]* that the repetitive language of Genesis 1 reflects, in part, God announcing the divine plan to the angels before creating the world. The *Ainulindalë* presents a similar process, with Eru first proclaiming themes

to the Ainur, then giving their music being with a word. More significantly, Augustine's Neoplatonist idea of evil as nothing occurs throughout the legendarium, for example, in the idea that Morgoth and Sauron can only corrupt, rather than create. How far Tolkien means to follow Augustine on this point has been much discussed (see Houghton and Keesee, "Tolkien," with references to Shippey, *Road*, and others).

Free will and predestination are topics within Augustine's doctrine of grace, a body of teaching largely shaped by the Pelagian controversy. Offended (as Augustine reports in *On the Gift of Perseverance* [*De dono perseverantiae*] 20.53; Mourant and Collinge, 323) by the prayer in *Conf.* 10.29.40, "give what you command and command what you will" (*da quod iubes et iube quod vis*), Pelagius argues that God commands no more than people are able to will and perform. Augustine replies that only by God's prevenient grace, given without regard to the person's antecedent virtue, can the will choose the good: in *On Grace and Free Will [De gratia et libero arbitrio]*, he notes "Lead us not into temptation" in the Lord's Prayer would be pointless if the will could resist temptation unaided (13.26; Russell, 280). Similarly, Tolkien suggests that Frodo is predestined to receive the Ring ("you also were *meant* to have it," *FR*, I, ii, 65) and describes the Sammath Naur scene as a meditation on "lead us not into temptation but deliver us from evil" (Shippey, *Road*, 164; *Letters*, 252).

JOHN WM. HOUGHTON

Further Reading

Augustine. *Confessiones*. Corpus Christianorum Series Latina 27. Edited by L. Verheijen. Turnhout: Brepols, 1981. Translation by Henry Chadwick published as *The Confessions* (Oxford World's Classics. Oxford: Oxford University Press, 1991).

———. *De dono persverantiae*. Patrologia Latina 45:993–1034. Translation by John A. Mourant and William J. Collinge published as "On the Gift of Perseverance," in *Four Anti-Pelagian Writings: On Nature and Grace, On the Proceedings of Pelagius, On the Predestination of the Saints, On the Gift of Perseverance*, 271–340 (The Fathers of the Church: A New Translation 86. Washington, D.C.: Catholic University Press, 1992).

———. *De Genesi ad litteram libri duodecim*. Edited by Josephus Zycha. Corpus Scriptorum Ecclesiasticorum Latinorum 28, 1. Vienna: Tempsky, 1894. Translation by Edmund Hill published as *On the Literal Meaning of Genesis*, in *On Genesis*, 155–507 (Hyde Park, N.Y.: New City Press, 2004).

———. *De gratia et libero arbitrio*. Patrologia Latina 44:881–912. Translation by Robert P. Russell published as "On Grace and Free Will," in *The Teacher; The Free Choice of the Will; Grace and Free Will*, 245–308 (The Fathers of the Church: A New Translation 59.

Washington, D.C.: Catholic University of America Press, 1968).

Brown, Peter. *Augustine of Hippo: A Biography*. London: Faber & Faber, 1967. New ed., 2000.

Houghton, John William. "Augustine in the Cottage of Lost Play: The *Ainulindalë* as Asterisk Cosmogony." In *Tolkien the Medievalist*, edited by Jane Chance, 171–82. London: Routledge, 2003.

Houghton, John William, and Neal K. Keesee. "Tolkien, King Alfred and Boethius: Platonist Views of Evil in *The Lord of the Rings*." *Tolkien Studies* 2 (2005): 131–59.

Shippey, Tom. *The Road to Middle-earth: Revised and Expanded Edition*. Boston and New York: Houghton Mifflin, 2003; London: HarperCollins Publishers, 2005.

See also: **Free Will; Good and Evil; Mercy; Satan and Lucifer;** *Silmarillion, The***; Time**

AUTHORSHIP

Tolkien's attitude to authorship was a peculiar one, owing to his conceptions about fiction (including his own), his method of work, and his Roman Catholic religion. In "On Fairy-Stories," he explains that the making of "secondary worlds" (largely = literary fictions) is an inborn human faculty, which humans possess because they are made in the likeness of a creating God (74–75); consequently, he sometimes voiced an opinion that his work might be "inspired" or "revealed" (*Letters,* nos. 87, 89, 153, 328). This may also be connected to his method of work, which he always reported as "discovering" rather than "inventing" (*Letters,* nos. 98, 131, 163, 180, 214), parallel to how the philologist "discovers" (reconstructs) unattested linguistic forms (Shippey, *Road,* 48–50). Tolkien's own author position in most of his works is covered over by his fiction of the editor/translator, in the literary tradition of "the old manuscript found and published." He thus consistently disavows control over his text in various senses, both in terms of their creation and in their interpretation. In his preface to the second edition to *The Lord of the Rings* and in his letters, he frequently made the point that he had no explicit "intention" (especially allegorical or didactic) in writing.

As far as authorship of the texts is concerned, *The Silmarillion* (1977) is sometimes singled out as a problematic case, since the text of this publication in the form it appears was not finalized by Tolkien. The text as it stands was compiled and edited by Tolkien's youngest son, Christopher Tolkien, from those of his father's manuscripts that he at that time was aware of and thought to contain the latest version of any story, with the aim of producing (as Tolkien certainly intended) a "coherent and consistent" narrative.

Resulting from Tolkien's preoccupation with the presentation of his works as translated accounts, authorship is also a theme that gains an important place in them. The fictional authorship of the stories he wrote had always been a crucial point for him, and most of the proposed frame narratives of *The Silmarillion* are bound up with the question of who the supposed author (or mediator between author[s] and audiences) is. In the works published in his lifetime, Tolkien maintained a clearer situation: *The Hobbit* is according to the fiction authored by Bilbo Baggins, while various characters (including Frodo and Sam as well as a Gondorian scribe) are involved as authors in the fictional writing of *The Lord of the Rings.* In the published *Silmarillion,* owing to the final framing device (*The Silmarillion* seen as Bilbo's "translations from the Elvish"), authorship is a concept much differentiated, since the (fictionally) translated and compiled text always suggests as its sources further works with further authors, and since the textual activities these authors (and Bilbo) perform are not uniform. With these distinctions among author, complier, translator, and other author functions, Tolkien brings into play medieval conceptions about authority and authorship (e.g., St. Bonaventure's) and contributes an aspect to the general concern with authority discernible in his work (this is also connected to his opinion about inspiredness, since medieval conceptions of authority often referred to God's inspiration of the author). The author writing a text is one of Tolkien's central figures and exemplifies one aspect of his own attitude to texts, their use, and meaning: author-heroes such as Frodo or Bilbo are nearly always scholar-heroes as well. Different types of authors also problematize the several modes of writing Tolkien uses in the intentionally compendious *Silmarillion*: poetic, historical, or mythological texts suppose as many authorial attitudes to material, sources, audiences, and linguistic/stylistic variety, and consequently as many possible modes of reception. A concern with reception is the other side of Tolkien's preoccupation with authorial activities, since authors' attitudes in writing necessarily show their interests and interpretive choices in reading as well.

Authorship is thus closely connected to Tolkien's use of textuality and the stress he places on showing the dynamics of how cultures preserve, interpret, and use stories (ultimately, their past); he shows these processes to happen in textual activities, the different handlings of texts or textually conceived compositions, and to be traceable by philological methods. His own models in creating his "body of connected legend" were authors very similar to his own central author figure, Bilbo: for example, Elias Lönnrot (1802–84), who is responsible for collecting and editing Finnish oral songs to produce the *Kalevala*, the Finnish national epic.

GERGELY NAGY

Further Reading

Flieger, Verlyn. *Interrupted Music: The Making of Tolkien's Mythology*. Kent, Ohio, and London: Kent State University Press, 2005.

Shippey, Tom. *The Road to Middle-earth*. 3rd ed. Boston: Houghton Mifflin, 2004.
Tolkien, J.R.R. "On Fairy-Stories." In *The Tolkien Reader*, 31–99. New York: Ballantine, 1966.

See also **Fictionality; Frame Narratives; "On Fairy-Stories";** *Silmarillion, The***; Textuality**

B

BAKSHI, RALPH (1938–)

Although neither contemporary critical reception nor posterity (nor, come to that, the box office) has been kind to Ralph Bakshi's animated film *J.R.R. Tolkien's The Lord of the Rings*—which misleadingly claims the title of the entire work but offers an adaptation of only *The Fellowship of the Ring* and about two thirds of *The Two Towers*—the film is at least historically important as the first theatrical feature to eventuate from the rights deal Tolkien signed in 1967 with United Artists.

Production History

J.R.R. Tolkien's The Lord of the Rings originated in Bakshi's longstanding fascination and affection for Tolkien's novel (he has described his efforts to secure the film rights as a "yearly trek" to the halls of the interconnected studios MGM/United Artists following his first unsuccessful attempts to persuade his then employer, Terrytoons, to undertake the project in the mid-1960s). A pioneer of "adult animation" in the early 1970s with the hugely commercially successful adaptation of Robert Crumb's underground strip *Fritz the Cat* (1972) and the more complex and personal *Heavy Traffic* (1973), Bakshi came to the project committed to delivering a more traditionally styled animated fantasy feature that would nonetheless appeal to adults, as well as children, on the basis of both its dramatic seriousness and its technical and stylistic ambition. The film, developed initially

at MGM following John Boorman's failure to deliver a satisfactory script for his mooted live-action adaptation, eventually returned to MGM's partner studio United Artists following acquisition of the film rights by independent producer Saul Zaentz, fresh from the success of *One Flew Over the Cuckoo's Nest* (1975). With an animation team totalling some six hundred artists and a budget of more than $7 million, *The Lord of the Rings* could fairly claim to be the most ambitious animated film attempted to that point.

Narrative

The shooting script prepared by Bakshi's scenarists, Chris Conkling and Peter Beagle, provides a generally faithful rendering of Tolkien's narrative while compressing, eliding, and editing in ways both predictable and defensible. (Earlier versions took considerably greater liberties with Tolkien's narrative organization, one draft beginning *in medias res* with Merry and Pippin meeting Treebeard in Fangorn and narrating the Company's adventures to that point as flashback.) The film sets trends that both the BBC radio adaptation and Peter Jackson would subsequently follow: opening the narrative with a mostly comprehensible (for the non-Tolkien *aficionado*) if somewhat tendentious digest of the prehistory of the Ring synthesizing various widely scattered statements in the novel by Gandalf, Elrond, and others, and pruning much of the action in Book I of *The Fellowship of the Ring*, notably omitting in their entirety the chapters centring on Tom Bombadil, the Old Forest, and the Barrow-Wights and expediting Frodo's dilatory departure from Bag End to heighten both dramatic economy and narrative tension.

Whereas Peter Jackson would later expand and alter in significant ways the character arcs and motivations of some key figures—including Aragorn, Théoden, and Arwen—Bakshi generally attempts an accurate if abbreviated rendering of the novelistic characters. The generally unimpressive vocal performances unfortunately mean that the literally two-dimensional figures depicted here tend to enhance the received view of Tolkien's characters as flat and undifferentiated. The film also apes Tolkien's strictly epic (as opposed to novelistic) structure, content to retain Sauron as an invisible and unvisualizable off-screen antagonist rather than enhancing Saruman's role as Sauron's ally and surrogate, as Jackson would.

Finally, however, as a narrative experience, Bakshi's *The Lord of the Rings* is critically impaired by the missing limb of Bakshi's proposed and intended second film. The claim on the part of cowriter Beagle—who has characterized the film as a "partial-birth abortion"—that producer Zaentz reversed the sequence of the first film's scenes, in the knowledge that a sequel would not be forthcoming and with the intention of providing a more rousing conclusion to the amputated narrative torso that remained, cannot be verified. Zaentz "flatly denies it" (Plesset); however, as Smith and Matthews note, it would help account for the stuttering and disjointed quality of the ending of the film as it stands. However, the absurd attempt to sketch in Tolkien's missing denouement with an obtuse and inexact voiceover résumé—"the forces of darkness were driven from Middle-earth forever by the valiant friends of Frodo"—would scarcely be acceptable as an appetizer for a forthcoming sequel; as the conclusion of an ostensibly autonomous text, it is disastrous.

Technique

Bakshi's film is distinguished technically by his decision to employ rotoscope animation techniques throughout the film. Pioneered by Max Fleischer at RKO in the 1930s and widely practiced (though little advertized) in Hollywood animation thereafter, rotoscoping essentially involves drawing over previously filmed live action in the interests of a more naturalistic effect, particularly in the dimension of organic movement. For *The Lord of the Rings,* Bakshi filmed the entire screenplay on largely undressed soundstages using movement doubles (whose lack of screen credit

went to guild arbitration), handing the ensuing footage over to his team of animators to transform the mapped-out live action into animated characterizations on some ten thousand painted backgrounds (compared to the thousand-odd typically prepared for an animated feature at this time).

The advantages of this technique for a project reliant on a relatively small, young, and unseasoned team of animators like Bakshi's are evident: the manifold difficulties of achieving a plausible imitation of biomorphic movement, especially on a large scale, are mitigated by the use of real human actors as the basis for the blocking. Bakshi himself waxed predictably rhapsodic, finding the results "staggering . . . the most realistic animation I've ever seen" (Bruce, 34). Its disadvantages, however—at least as far as this particular film is concerned—are unfortunately glaringly evident. Most importantly, even with visual characterization and dialogue added subsequently, rotoscopy's effectiveness depends on the quality of the live-action performances used to originate the animated action. Few of the performances elicited by Bakshi—admittedly at great speed and with little opportunity for either rehearsal or retakes—are particularly impressive. In the fireside scene between Frodo and Gandalf at Bag End, for example, not only does the wizard's explanation of the Ring's fatal nature involve a great deal of pacing, circling, and hand-waving to no obvious purpose (at one point he performs a pirouette) but also, having thrown the Ring into the fire with the stated purpose (as per Tolkien) of finally proving its identity, the resultant fire-writing simply goes unmentioned, nor is it indicated visually. The underlying problems that must have beset the rotoscope animators are suggested by the nonrotoscoped prologue, in which the story of the Ring's creation, loss, and theft by Gollum unfolds in a series of sketchy tableaux filmed as silhouetted dumb show through red filters presumably suggestive of fire, blood, or both. The quality of the mime in this sequence—the actors' movement and interaction—is extremely poor, notably in the Battle of Dagorlad, which far from the apocalyptic confrontation envisioned by Tolkien here seems barely a skirmish among actors lumpishly wielding prop swords (as Smith and Matthews note, the voiceover narration also inexplicably declares the battle a defeat for Last Alliance of Elves and Men, which makes nonsense of much of the subsequent action). In short, either through distraction (from the many challenges of a complex and straitened production) or inexperience, Bakshi's direction of his live actors seriously constrains the quality of the resultant rotoscope animation. At other times the poverty of Bakshi's material resources is distressingly evident, as in the Mines of

Moria where the Company appears to confront at most two dozen Orcs. There are also odd sequences in which the overdrawing on the rotoscoped footage varies from one shot to the next—at Khazâd-Dûm again, for instance, in the long shots the live-action actors are scarcely overdrawn, and both their movement and their appearance differ markedly from the rest of the film. Such inconsistencies bear out Vincent Canby's observation (in the *New York Times*) that although the results of Bakshi's rotoscopy are occasionally impressive, at other times the viewer has the impression of simply being confronted with badly developed film stock.

Bakshi's technique comes into its own, perhaps ironically, when live-action footage is made to serve the interests not of realism but of stylization. The minimal and suggestive rather than the mimetic overdrawing on the rotoscoped Orcs, for example, effectively suggests their bestial and monstrous nature. The flight to the ford, by contrast, sets the animated characters against abstract live-action backdrops—broiling clouds, and so on—that equally effectively suggest Frodo's hallucinatory experience as he falls further under the Shadow. The devices Bakshi adopts here seem to owe a debt to the pop-psychedelic underground style he pioneered so successfully for *Fritz the Cat* and to succeed largely by abandoning the film's overall commitment to a realist *mise-en-scène*.

The film perplexingly abjures some opportunities where animation could (before the advent of contemporary effects technologies) realize some of Tolkien's larger-scale descriptive effects: the Hobbits' visions in the Mirror of Galadriel are narrated rather than seen, and Frodo's vision of warring Middle-earth from the seat of Amon Hen is cut altogether.

The success of any animated film, from traditional cel animation to contemporary computer-generated imagery productions, relies heavily on the quality of the characterisations visualized. Here, too, Bakshi's *The Lord of the Rings* compares unfavorably with the animated classics to which it begs comparison. Although the ingenuous Frodo is a persuasive presence (who may have had some influence on Peter Jackson's subsequent casting of the not-wholly-dissimilar Elijah Wood), the clodhopping, serf-like portrayal of Sam, with bulbous nose and tombstone teeth, not only does the character a disservice but seems to operate in a different, more crudely caricatural graphic domain than most other principal characterizations. Many of the human characters—such as a wildly hirsute and rather callow Saruman; Aragorn, distinctly unkingly in a thigh-high skirt; a redbearded Viking Boromir; the notably Romanesque Elrond; the simpering cheerleader Galadriel; and the bald Dwarf Gimli—seem drawn from generic (perhaps Arthurian) preconceptions of medieval epic figures more appropriate to the bargain-basement "Animated Classics" series than to a serious adaptation of Tolkien's mythology. The Balrog—a Wookie adorned with moth wings—is no more felicitously conceived. If these judgments seem uncharitable, they are made in light of Bakshi's own stated ambition for *The Lord of the Rings* to "get away" from the "cartoon look" of his previous work and "reach a level of painting in animation" (Bruce, 34).

Critical Reception and Influence

Reviews of *J.R.R. Tolkien's The Lord of the Rings* upon its release in November 1978 were at best mixed: the *New York Times'* Vincent Canby's assessment of the film as "both numbing and impressive" summed up the view of many others. Reviewers generally faulted the film for both the inadequacy of its explication of Tolkien's mythology to the uninitiated (*Variety* found the picture not only "confusing" but ultimately "boring," and Canby faulted its "incomprehensible exposition") and the unadvertized truncation of the narrative (which made the staid Canby want to "rip up a seat" in frustration). The film's perceived artistic failure—and its modest box office performance—confirmed Zaentz's decision to forego the intended second feature.

Notwithstanding, Peter Jackson at least has gone on record to attest to the impact of first viewing the cartoon at age thirteen—indeed, it apparently impelled him to read the novel for the first time. Certain scenes in Jackson's trilogy, such as the Black Riders' nocturnal assault on the Hobbits' room at The Prancing Pony, strongly echo Bakshi (the escape from the first Nazgûl on the Road in the Shire is lifted almost shot for shot from the earlier film). Inevitably, Bakshi's film has received renewed visibility on repackaged home video in the wake of the blockbuster success of Jackson's trilogy. Given Bakshi's stated rationale (wholly defensible in the mid-1970s) that the physical universe of Middle-earth and all its inhabitants could only be plausibly rendered through animation, there is a certain irony in his film's recovery from obscurity through the massive success of a live-action film (with enormous amounts of digital manipulation and inserted animated effects).

BARRY LANGFORD

Further Reading

Bruce, S. "Ralph Bakshi on *Lord of the Rings*." *Cinefantastique* 8.1 (1978): 33.

Plesset, R. "*The Lord of the Rings:* The Animated Films." *Cinefantastique* 34.1 (2002): 52–53.

Smith, J., and J.C. Matthews. *The Lord of the Rings: The Films, the Books, the Radio Series*. London: Virgin, 2004.

Zito, S. "Bakshi among the Hobbits." *American Film* 3.10 (1978): 58–63.

See also **Art Inspired by Tolkien; Illustrations; Peter Jackson Films; Reception of *Lord of the Rings***

BARFIELD, OWEN (1898–1997)

Owen Barfield was born in London on November 9, 1898, the older of two sons of Arthur Owen Barfield, a London solicitor, and Elizabeth Shoults Barfield, an ardent feminist and suffragette. After army service in World War I, Barfield became an undergraduate at Wadham College, Oxford, and while there formed a close friendship with C.S. Lewis, himself an undergraduate at University College. Barfield took a First Class at Wadham and went on to write a D.Litt. thesis on the changing meanings of the word *ruin*. In 1923 he married Matilda Douie and about the same time became interested in the thought and works of Rudolf Steiner, founder of the metaphysical philosophy Anthroposophy. Though by inclination and chosen vocation Barfield was a writer and a philosopher of language, he reluctantly went to work in his father's firm of Barfield and Barfield in 1929 to support his growing family. His interest in anthroposophy continued for the rest of his life; he took for his special concentration Steiner's theory of the evolution of consciousness, humanity's ever-growing awareness of itself as separate from the world around it.

The focus of Barfield's work was the mutual development of language and consciousness. His thesis on *ruin* became the basis for and a chapter in his best-known book, *Poetic Diction,* first published in 1928. This explored the breaking down of once-comprehensive perceptions and words into ever smaller and more precise units of meaning. He subsequently published a number of books and essays on the history of consciousness, ranging from the philological *History in English Words* to the philosophical *Romanticism Comes of Age* and *What Coleridge Thought,* the Socratic dialogue *Worlds Apart,* and the metaphysical *Saving the Appearances* and *Unancestral Voice*. All express the same fundamental, simple, yet radical perspective on humanity's constantly changing way of knowing the world around it. He retired from law practice in 1959 and embarked on a second career, lecturing on Anthroposophy in Britain and the United States. He died in Sussex on December 14, 1997, a month into his hundredth year.

In *Poetic Diction,* Barfield argued that language and perception are interconnected and interdependent. Perception gives rise to language, which then houses and further develops perception. Furthermore, he hypothesized that in its beginnings language did not separate the abstract from the concrete or distinguish between the literal and the figurative or metaphoric. Each word embodied an "ancient semantic unity" of meaning that has over time divided and subdivided into ever narrower, more precise, and often more abstract units of meaning. He gave as an example the Greek word *pneuma,* now of necessity translated variously as "wind," "breath," or "spirit" depending on the context but originally encompassing all of these aspects, whose interlocking meanings were perceived as essentially the same. Following this hypothesis, he suggested that increasingly precise vocabulary indicates increasing awareness and ability to make distinctions. More particular percepts require more exact, and therefore more limited, words to express them. In turn, these narrowing definitions fine-tune perception, giving rise to even more exact meanings. Words thus both express and foster ongoing development in human consciousness.

It is in this notion of the interconnection of consciousness and language that Barfield's mind and thought met those of Tolkien. Both men were friends of C.S. Lewis, and it was through occasional attendance at Inklings meetings (at which Tolkien was a regular) in Lewis's rooms in Magdalen College in the 1930s and 1940s that Barfield came to know Tolkien. Barfield's theory had a direct impact on Tolkien's view of the function and the power of language. After reading *Poetic Diction* some time in 1928, Tolkien remarked to Lewis that Barfield's concept of an ancient semantic unity fragmented over time had modified his whole outlook on language and that he was always just going to say something in a lecture when Barfield's conception stopped him. "It is one of those things," Lewis reported him saying, "that when you've once seen it there are all sorts of things you can never say again" (Carpenter, 42). At that time, Tolkien, whose hobby since childhood had been inventing languages, had also been for some ten years at work on the vast and comprehensive mythology he hoped to dedicate "to England" and to which he gave the overall title the "Silmarillion." He had begun the first tales of his mythology when he was sent home from the Western Front with trench fever in 1917. He said later, "It was just as the 1914 War burst on me that I made the discovery that 'legends' depend on the language to which they belong; but a living language depends equally on the 'legends' which it conveys by tradition" (*Letters,* 231).

What Barfield's theory added to this discovery was the centrality of human consciousness as both generator and reflector of language and legend. Language, as Barfield hypothesized and Tolkien actualized in his invented world, does not occur in a vacuum but develops from and manifests its speakers' awareness of the world around them. As words name and organize phenomena, they bring them into being. This is obvious once you have seen it but not until it is pointed out, like Gandalf's insight concerning the password to the doors of Moria. We may compare Barfield's idea of the links among myth, language, and consciousness with Tolkien's statement in "On Fairy-Stories" that, "to ask what is the origin of stories . . . is to ask what is the origin of language and of the mind." Or there is his declaration later in the essay that, "the incarnate mind, the tongue, and the tale are in our world coeval." Both state, at once more simply and more sweepingly, what Barfield's theory postulates: that human consciousness, language, and myth are interdependent and mutually supportive, arising and existing in relation to one another. There is no myth without a language to express it, no language without a people who speak it, no people without a myth that describes their world to them.

Tolkien's invented world is the illustration *par excellence* of Barfield's theory. His migrating and fragmenting Elven communities, their proliferating languages, and their perceptions of the world around them enact exactly the process that Barfield described.

Just eleven months short of his hundredth year, Barfield died on December 14, 1997, at his residence in The Walhatch, a retirement home in Forest Row, East Sussex.

VERLYN FLIEGER

Further Reading

Carpenter, Humphrey. *The Inklings: C.S. Lewis, J.R.R. Tolkien, Charles Williams and Their Friends.* Boston, MA: Houghton Mifflin, 1977.

See also **Inklings; Lewis, C.S.; Oxford; Theories of Language**

BARRIE, J.M. (1860–1937)

J.M. Barrie, dramatist and novelist best known for his play and fiction about Peter Pan, the boy who would not grow up, occupies an important place in the development of twentieth-century British fairy literature and fantasy. References in his personal writings and literary scholarship point to Tolkien's familiarity with the invented world of Neverland and with Barrie's work in general. Tolkien wrote in his diary after viewing a production of *Peter Pan* in Birmingham in April 1910: "Indescribable but shall never forget as

long as I live" (Carpenter *Biography*, 47). Barrie then appears in the 1939 lecture "On Fairy-Stories," in which Tolkien offered some critical comments on his use of the fantastic. Although the fantasy aesthetics of the two writers differ considerably, there are nonetheless parallels that suggest Barrie was present in the "pot of soup" out of which Tolkien's imaginative depictions of Faërie emerge in the legendarium and other stories.

Barrie occupies an important place in the history of fantasy because he helped create the fairy craze in early Edwardian children's books and illustrations (Carpenter *Gardens*, 170). He is heir to the tradition of George MacDonald and other writers of the late 1800s; MacDonald's allegorical *At the Back of the North Wind* (1870) with a boy flying the wind to heaven is one of the sources of the Peter Pan tales (Birkin, 105). The play *Peter Pan* (1904), the short stories republished as *Peter Pan in Kensington Gardens* (1906), and the novel *Peter and Wendy* (1911) all center around attempts to forestall death, adulthood, and sexuality by creating a protagonist locked in an eternal youth, doomed to repeat his tale of seeking a new young girl as a mother figure. Humphrey Carpenter reads the Peter Pan story as a study of the limits and dangers of the imagination in which Neverland is a "deliberately unreal Arcadia" requiring a belief that children cannot sustain as they mature (Carpenter, 180). Others read Peter as a self-consciously sentimental means of avoiding adult fears of sexuality and death and Neverland as but a coded emblem for death under the guise of a domain of boyish adventure (Gilead, 286).

Barrie further explores fantastic worlds and their effect on human aging in dramas such as *Dear Brutus* (1917) in which an enchanted wood allows characters to see what they would have become if they had made different choices in the past. His 1920 play *Mary Rose,* a work like "Rip Van Winkle" centering on a character removed from the passage of time (Geduld, 163), portrays a mother who disappears into an unknown, unsettling counterpart of "Neverland" and there ceases to age. But in the end she becomes a ghost mourning her loss of the child she had wanted to keep forever young. These thematic preoccupations with mysterious otherworldly realms and immortality versus human mortality figure prominently in Tolkien's fiction as well.

Tolkien specifically discusses Barrie's fantasy twice in "On Fairy-Stories," first to refer to the role of the childhood in *Peter Pan* and then to comment upon drama as a vehicle for fairy-stories and Barrie's refusal to picture the frightening implications of the unseen fairy world he alludes to in *Mary Rose*. In criticizing the traditional view that fairy-stories are intended for children, and the related notion that childhood is an idealized state as opposed to the corruption of adulthood, Tolkien remarks, "Children are meant to grow up, and not to become Peter Pans" (*MC,* 136). He then adds, "it is one of the lessons of fairy-stories . . . that on callow, lumpish, and selfish youth peril, sorrow, and the shadow of death can bestow dignity, and even sometimes wisdom" (*MC,* 136). Tolkien later turns his attention to the use of fantasy in drama and concludes that true fantasy cannot be conveyed on stage. He cites *Mary Rose* as an example of Barrie's attempt to present "the impact upon human characters of some event of Fantasy, or Faërie" but explains that "that is not fantasy in dramatic result" (*MC,* 159). Verlyn Flieger has published some of Tolkien's unused manuscript notes on *Mary Rose* in which he takes Barrie to task for not presenting the inhuman dimension of the fairy world to which his damaged heroine was drawn: "It was as if Barrie, extending his art in making a notion of Celtic fantasy 'credible' in the centre of the stage, and enchanted with his Elvish heroine, had simply ignored the torment in the wings" (Flieger, 53). In effect, Tolkien sees Barrie as one who hinted at the "ghostly deathlessness" in store for those "entangled in 'Faërie'" (Flieger, 53) but who ultimately shrank from bringing that terrifying world to the stage.

Despite his reservations about Barrie's dramatic fantasies, Tolkien seems to have been inspired at some level by Barrie's worlds in fashioning his own magical realities. John Garth observes that Tolkien's earliest conception of Faërie or Valinor in the 1915 poem *You and Me and the Cottage of Lost Play* clearly evokes Barrie's Neverland (Garth, 73). Moreover, his early notion "of the coming of mortal children in sleep to the gardens of Valinor" (*Lost Tales I,* 31), the conceit from "The Cottage of Lost Play" frame narrative in *The Book of Lost Tales,* recalls the nocturnal journey of children to Neverland. Mike Foster has proposed that *The Hobbit* has several structural similarities to *Peter Pan:* Gandalf's voice trick with the Trolls recalls Peter's ruse at the Marooners' Rock; both narratives had their genesis as stories told to an audience of boys; both contain a Faërie realm in which warring peoples compete but then unite against a common enemy; and both are tales of *There and Back Again* with travels to a Neverland/Wilderland of adventure. The effect of the One Ring upon its bearers is a nightmarish version of the arrested development, the "ghostly deathlessness" that Barrie's unaging characters suffer. Even the repetitive cycle of choosing a new child to receive the star with which to visit Faery in *Smith of Wootton Major* echoes the cycle the gay yet melancholy Peter Pan is doomed to repeat with each new generation of children.

Tolkien resisted Barrie's sentimental, quasi-Victorian depiction of fairies such as Tinker Bell in his own image of fairy beings, perhaps the biggest difference between the fantasy of the two writers, and he rejected Barrie's use of drama for staging his magic tales. Nevertheless, the two have much in common in their conceptions of alternate realities apart from human reality and in their attention to issues of death and deathlessness in a time-bound world. Indeed, Tolkien's immortal Elves, the ones forever barred from understanding the Gift of Men, might well find themselves repeating Peter's famous line: "To die will be an awfully big adventure" (Barrie 1930, 94).

DAVID D. OBERHELMAN

Further Reading

Barrie, J.M. "Peter Pan, or the Boy Who Would Not Grow Up." In *The Works of J.M. Barrie.* Peter Pan edition. Vol. 10, *Peter Pan and Other Plays.* New York: Charles Scribner's Sons, 1930.
Birkin, Andrew. *J.M. Barrie and the Lost Boys.* New Haven, CT: Yale University Press, 2003.
Carpenter, Humphrey. *Tolkien: A Biography.* Boston: Houghton Mifflin, 1977.
———. *Secret Gardens: A Study of the Golden Age of Children's Literature.* Boston, MA: Houghton Mifflin, 1985.
Flieger, Verlyn. *A Question of Time: J.R.R. Tolkien's Road to Faërie.* Kent, OH: Kent State University Press, 1997.
Foster, Mike. Telephone interview. January 28, 2006.
Garth, John. *Tolkien and the Great War: The Threshold of Middle-earth.* Boston, MA: Houghton Mifflin, 2003.
Geduld, Harry M. *Sir James Barrie.* New York: Twayne, 1971.
Gilead, Sarah. "Magic Abjured: Closure in Children's Fantasy Fiction." *PMLA* 106.2 (1991): 277–93.

See also **Fairies; Children's Literature; Literary Influences, Nineteenth and Twentieth Century; "On Fairy-Stories"**

BATTLE OF MALDON, THE

After *Beowulf,* the Old English poem that most influenced Tolkien's fiction may be *The Battle of Maldon.* Tolkien's dramatic "sequel" to the poem, "The Homecoming of Beorhtnoth, Beorhthelm's Son," is only the most concrete sign of the poem's influence on Tolkien: more general is the poem's iconic status as the classic expression of what Tolkien in "*Beowulf:* The Monsters and the Critics" called "Northern courage." The speech of Beorhtnoth in lines 312–13 of *Maldon* crystallizes this "theory of courage":

> *Hige sceal þe heardra, heorte þe cenre,*
> *mod sceal þe mare þe ure mægen lytlað.*

("Will shall be the sterner, heart the bolder, spirit the greater as our strength lessens"—Tolkien's translation).

This *gnome* or traditional proverb stayed in Tolkien's mind: he cited it in the *Beowulf* essay in 1936 (footnote 11) and repeated it in his introduction to "The Homecoming" nearly two decades later. In the same work, he defined Northern courage succinctly as "uttermost endurance in the service of indomitable will."

Tolkien summarized the critical consensus on the poem as "an extended commentary on, or illustration of" Beorhtnoth's saying. The poem as it survives is a fragment, lacking a beginning and end, running 325 lines. It is the true, if romanticized, story of a valiant final stand of a British army hopelessly outnumbered by Scandinavian invaders in 991. The Vikings taunt the English by offering to leave if the English pay them enough. The commander of the English forces, Beorhtnoth (or Byrhtnoth as the now-lost manuscript spells it: Tolkien reconstructs the eastern form presumably altered by the West Saxon scribe) replies that the Vikings will be paid with spears. The numerical advantage of the Norsemen was mitigated by a river that lay between them and the English, and the attackers could only advance one at a time over a "bridge" of hardened earth. The Vikings sneeringly imply that the English aren't being good sports, provoking Beorhtnoth to allow them to pass over, an act that ensures the death of every English soldier.

Tolkien would have been deeply immersed in *Maldon* during the composition of his famous *Beowulf* lecture. The edition of the poem by his Leeds University colleague E.V. Gordon appeared only a year later and must have taken a good bit of Tolkien's attention in the 1930s. Like so many projects originally envisioned as a "Tolkien and Gordon" collaboration, it slipped, as deadlines passed Tolkien by, into a single-editor volume, though Gordon's preface acknowledged that Tolkien shared with F.E. Harmer the editor's "greatest debt of gratitude" and attributed to Tolkien "the solution to many of the textual and philological problems" in the poem.

One of these "textual and philological problems" was certainly the single word of the poem on which the most commentary has been generated, including Tolkien's nearly 1,500-word appendix to "The Homecoming": *ofermod.* Tolkien's commentary demonstrates the moral complexity of his concept of heroism in a way surprising to readers of his fiction. These readers recognize that he stands out in the twentieth century for reasserting an older model of heroic courage as an absolute good, which had been rejected by literary critics. Now, with his interpretation of Beorhtnoth's *ofermod,* Tolkien was doing the opposite: denying the absolute good of heroic courage even though other critics were attempting to prop it up.

The word *ofermod* was the key. The root *mod* is the most common word for "courage" in Old English heroic poetry, so *ofermod* should mean something like "too much courage," "foolhardiness," or the meaning Tolkien assumed in translating it as "overmastering pride." Tolkien's appendix on the word became the "orthodox" view from which critics like Frederick Whitehead, Warren A. Samouce, N.F. Blake, and George Clark dissented in the 1960s, suggesting that the *ofer* in *ofermod* might simply mean "great." Richard C. West, in a discussion of Tolkien's interpretation of *ofermod* in the story of Túrin, points to the irony that a similar ambiguity surrounds Tolkien's German surname, which could be read positively as an oxymoron (*toll,* "mad," + *kühn,* "bold," = "fiercely bold") or negatively as simply "foolhardy," as Tolkien himself translated it to an American publisher in 1955 (*Letters,* 218). Yet Tolkien's contention that even a virtue can be overdone is standard classical and Christian moral theory (and not limited to the west), the "doctrine of the mean." Aristotle's *Nichomachean Ethics* lists courage as the mean between rashness and cowardice.

Tom Shippey hears in *The Lord of the Rings* an echo of another speaker in *Maldon,* Ælfwine (a name Tolkien borrowed for his unfinished novel *The Lost Road*), who says in line 215, *nu mæg cunnian hwa cene sy,* "now we may know who is bold" (*cene* being cognate with the *kien* in *Tolkien*). Shippey finds the same sentiment in Aragorn's response to Boromir's thinly veiled taunt in "The Council of Elrond" (*FR,* II, ii, 260, II, ii), wondering if Aragorn's prowess can match his ancestry: Aragorn simply replies, "We shall put it to the test one day."

Oddly enough, a final parallel between battle scenes in *The Lord of the Rings* and *Maldon* involves an apparent slacking off of "uttermost endurance." In Book V, chapter x, Aragorn meets a bedraggled host of recruits "unmanned" by terror. Instead of rousing them with a never-say-die Northern courage speech, as the reader might expect, he tells them they may go home (though he hopes they would relieve the garrison at Cair Andros; *RK,* V, x, 162). While this may seem to set the bar of courage rather low, it is parallel to a contrast in Beorhtnoth's addresses to the troops in *Maldon.* There we find a sharp distinction between his instructions to the men of the *fyrd,* reserves called up from the farms who don't even know how to stand or hold a shield (lines 19–20), and his speech to his *heorðwerod,* his personal guard, his "hearth companions" (lines 29–41). Nowhere in *Maldon* does Beorhtnoth tell anyone to go home, but Aragorn's pity seems closer to the spirit of

Maldon once we realize that the men he excuses are the equivalent of Beorhtnoth's *fyrd*.

JOHN R. HOLMES

Further Reading

Gordon, E.V., ed. *The Battle of Maldon*. London: Methuen, 1937.

West, Richard C. "Túrin's *Ofermod:* An Old English Theme in the Development of the Story of Túrin." In *Tolkien's Legendarium: Essays on "The History of Middle-earth,"* edited by Verlyn Flieger and Carl F. Hostetter, 233–45. Westport, CT: Greenwood, 2000.

See also **The Homecoming of Beorhtnoth, Beorhthelm's Son**; **Northern Courage**; **Pride**

BEDE (ST. BEDE THE VENERABLE, OLD ENGLISH *BÆDA*) (672?–735)

Bede's family presented him at age seven to be an oblate in St. Benedict Biscop's twin monasteries of Wearmouth and Jarrow in the Anglo-Saxon kingdom of Northumbria; St. John of Beverly ordained him deacon at the uncanonically early age of nineteen and priest at thirty. He spent the rest of his life at the monastery, rarely traveling even a small distance away, and yet became the "venerable and admirable teacher of modern times" [*venerabilis et modernis temporibus doctor admirabilis Beda,* so named by the Council of Aachen, 835]. He said of himself, in a postscript to the *Ecclesiastical History of the English People [Historia Ecclesiastica Gentis Anglorum],* "it has always been my pleasure to learn, or to teach, or to write" [*semper aut discere, aut docere, aut scribere dulce habui* (5.24)].

An eyewitness reports that Bede died at Jarrow after sundown May 25, on the eve of the Ascension. In the eleventh century, a monk of Durham Cathedral stole Bede's supposed remains: they were placed in the coffin of St. Cuthbert in the cathedral and later moved to a separate shrine at the opposite end of the building. Reburied at the Reformation, they were exhumed and placed in a new monument in 1831. Bede was honored as a saint within fifty years of his death; his feast (now May 25, earlier May 27) dates from the eleventh century and was added to the *Book of Common Prayer* in 1661. In 1899, Pope Leo XIII declared him a Doctor of the Church, authorizing universal observance of the feast. His invariable title of "the Venerable" apparently stems from his being so named in the eighth-century *Homiliary* of Paul the Deacon and has no connection with the modern use of *venerable* to designate one at the first stage of canonization.

Bede wrote more than forty books, some so popular that his monastic brothers eventually developed a new handwriting to satisfy the demand for manuscripts by copying more quickly. Contemporaries valued particularly his many commentaries on the scriptures, his sermons, and his treatise on the calendar and the calculation of Easter. The twelfth-century Ordinary Gloss *[Glossa Ordinaria]* on the Bible draws heavily on Bede's commentaries, particularly in books for which there was no patristic commentary tradition, such as the Acts of the Apostles. Since the Reformation, attention has shifted to his historical works and particularly to the *Ecclesiastical History.* The *History,* which popularized Dionysius Exiguus' system of dating *Anno Domini* (and extended it to events that occurred before Christ), remains a central source for study of early medieval England.

Tolkien's most widespread debt to Bede comes in *The Lord of the Rings.* Tolkien remarks in "Guide to the Names in the *Lord of the Rings*" that "All the month names in the Shire Calendar are (worn-down) forms of the Old English names" (199, s.v. "Lithe"). Tolkien's source for the Old English (OE) names is the fifteenth chapter of *On the Reckoning of Time [De temporum ratione],* where Bede gives them with his translations and comments (Jones, 329–32; Wallis 1999, 53–54). In the somewhat Latinized forms Bede uses, the names are January, *Giuli* ("from the day the sun turns back," i.e., Yule); February, *Solmonath* (month of cakes); March, *Hredmonath* (from the goddess Hretha); April, *Eosturmonath* (from the goddess Eostre); May, *Thrimilchi* ("three milks," because in the legendary past the cows produced so much at this season that they had to be milked three times a day); June, *Lida* (from a word meaning "gentle," because the sea at this season was calm and navigable); July, also *Lida;* August, *Weodmonath* (weed month); September, *Halegmonath* (month of holy things); October, *Winterfilleth* (month of the first full moon of winter); November, *Blodmonath* ("blood month," month of sacrifices); and December, *Giuli* again. When an extra lunar month was required, about every three solar years, a third *Lida* was inserted. Compare the Shire's Afteryule, Solmath, Rethe, Astron, Thrimidge ("archaically Thrimilch"), Forelithe, Afterlithe, Wedmath, Halimath, Winterfilth (retained from a year that "began after the harvest"), Blotmath, and Foreyule, with an extra day at Lithe in leap years. The concept of "ages" of the world, used throughout *The Lord of the Rings,* also plays a role in *Reckoning* and other Bedan works, though it is not unique to Bede.

In Book I of the *Ecclesiastical History,* Bede gives an account of the *Adventus Saxonum,* the fifth-century invasion of post-Roman Britain by the

Germanic Angles, Saxons, and Jutes. This narrative (along with the later accounts of Nennius and *The Anglo-Saxon Chronicle,* which mirror Bede's but use some independent sources) lies behind the early history of the Shire and had a place in the early form of the legendarium's "framing story." The tripartite division of the Hobbits before their coming to Eriador mirrors the threefold ancestry of the invaders, and the Fallohide brothers Marcho and Blanco (from OE *marh, "horse," and *blanco,* "white horse," a word found only in *Beowulf*) reflect the real-world Hengest and Horsa ("stallion" and "horse"), who led the Anglo-Saxon invasion of Kent (Marmor, 181; Shippey, 116). In that stage of the development of *The Book of Lost Tales* at which the wandering listener was to be Eriol, an Anglo-Saxon named in his own tongue Ottor and called "Wæfre," Hengest and Horsa would have been his sons, their names reminiscent of Ottor's father Eoh (yet another OE word for horse) (*Lost Tales I,* 23–24).

The story of Hengest and Horsa had considerable importance for Tolkien's scholarly work, because a character named Hengest appears both in *Beowulf* (first at line 1091) and in the Finnsburg Fragment (line 17). In *Finn and Hengest,* Tolkien argued that the Hengest of these two poems was a historical character and the same person as Bede's Hengest (still a debated position). In "English and Welsh," Tolkien refers to Hengest and cites Bede's *History* (5.23) in reference to Uualchstod, Bishop of Hereford, whose name comes from an OE noun *wealhstod,* meaning roughly "one who translates between Welsh and English."

JOHN WM. HOUGHTON

Further Reading

Brown, George Hardin. *Bede the Venerable.* Boston: Twayne, 1987.

Colgrave, Bertram, trans., *The Ecclesiastical History of the English People.* With the *Greater Chronicle* and "Letter to Egbert" translated and edited, with introduction and notes, by Judith McClure and Roger Collins. Oxford World Classics. Oxford: Oxford University Press, 1999. [Same translation as the 1969 edition.]

Colgrave, Bertram, and R.A.B. Mynors, ed. and trans. *Bede's "Ecclesiastical History of the English Peoplex,"* Oxford: Clarendon, 1969. [Latin and English.]

Jones, Charles W., ed. *Bede: De Temporum Ratione.* Bedae Venerablis Opera VI: 2. Corpus Christianorum Series Latina 123B. Turnhout, Belgium: Brepols, 1977.

Marmor, Paula. "An Etymological Excursion among the Shire Folk." In *An Introduction to Elvish,* edited by Jim Allan, 181–84. Hayes, Middlesex: Bran's Head, 1978.

Nennius. *British History and the Welsh Annals.* Edited and translated by John Morris. History from the Sources Series. London: Phillimore; Totowa, NJ: Rowman & Littlefield, 1980. [Latin and English.]

Shippey, Tom. *The Road to Middle-earth.* Revised and Expanded edition. Boston: Houghton Mifflin, 2003. London: HarperCollins, 2005.

Sims-Williams, P. "The Settlement of England in Bede and the *Chronicle.*" *Anglo-Saxon England* 12 (1983): 1–42.

Swanton, Michael, ed. and trans. *The Anglo-Saxon Chronicle.* London: Dent, 1996. Revised ed. London: Phoenix, 2000.

Tolkien, J.R.R. "Guide to the Names in the *Lord of the Rings.*" In *A Tolkien Compass,* edited by Jared Lobdell, 153–201. La Salle, IL: Open Court, 1975.

Wallace-Hadrill, J.M. *Bede's "Ecclesiastical History of the English People": A Historical Commentary.* Oxford: Clarendon, 1988.

Wallis, Faith, trans. *Bede: The Reckoning of Time.* Translated, with introduction, notes, and commentary. Translated Texts for Historians series, 29. Liverpool: Liverpool University Press, 1999.

See also **Book of Lost Tales I; "English and Welsh"; Finn and Hengest;** History, Anglo-Saxon; *Lord of the Rings*

BENNETT, JACK ARTHUR WALTER (1911–81)

Jack Arthur Walter Bennett, a New Zealander, was a colleague of C.S. Lewis's at Magdalen College, Oxford, from 1947, teaching Anglo-Saxon. It was at this time that he was invited to meetings of the Inklings. While studying at Merton College in the thirties, he attended the lectures of C.L. Wrenn, Tolkien, and C.T. Onions. In 1935, he gained a First Class degree in English and a D.Phil. in English in 1938. Between 1956 and 1980, he was editor of *Medium Aevum,* succeeding C.T. Onions. This was a demanding task, requiring a huge range of competence, because the journal has for its subject the major literature of medieval Western Europe. In 1964, he took on Lewis's post as professor of medieval and renaissance literature at Cambridge University, but as a lecturer he lacked his predecessor's popular touch. His inaugural lecture was devoted to the subject of Lewis, titled "The Humane Medievalist" (1965). He brought out many editions of medieval texts, including *Devotional Pieces in Verse and Prose* (1955). He also wrote three studies of Geoffrey Chaucer, including *Chaucer at Oxford and at Cambridge* (1974). He contributed an entry on Lewis for the *Dictionary of National Biography.* One of the most daunting tasks Bennett took on was a volume in the *Oxford History of English Literature* (known, with feeling, as the "Oh-Hell" by its contributors, one of whom only produced a contents list in the course of nearly sixty years). The original brief for the series was broad-ranging: to encompass "the whole range of letters" within each of its demarked periods of English literature. Bennett worked on *Middle English Literature* in the series for most of his working life but had not completed it at his sudden death in 1981. Douglas Gray "edited and completed" it for publication in 1986. Norman Davis described Bennett as "one of the most active and influential of the medieval scholars of his generation."

COLIN DURIEZ

Further Reading

Davis, Norman. "Jack Arthur Walter Bennett, 1911–1981," *Proceedings of the British Academy* 68. 1982, 481–94.
Hooper, Walter. *C.S. Lewis: A Companion and Guide.* London: HarperCollins, 1996.

See also **Inklings; Lewis, C.S.; Oxford**

BEORN

Beorn is a shape-changer who takes the form of a bear. Bilbo and Thorin's Dwarven company meet Beorn at his home on the plains between the Misty Mountains and the Mirkwood Forest after fleeing the Orcs (*H*, XVIII). Although initially hesitant at the intrusion, Beorn, not known for his hospitality, eventually accepts the Dwarves after they are introduced two at a time by Gandalf and invites them into his hall. The hall and its contrast to prior displays of hospitality provide a social example of the relationship between Beorn and the natural world, beyond the obvious example of his shape-changing ability. The other inhabitants of the hall are intelligent animals, and the hall itself is devoid of metal with the exception of a few dinner knives. Beorn's reluctant hospitality contrasts with Elrond's gracious reception of the company at the Last Homely House, where the party is well received. Elrond possesses knowledge of metals and weapons, but when the Dwarves talk about metals and smithcraft, Beorn begins to fall asleep. Beorn's lack of refined goods, his use of natural materials in crafting his entire hall, and his animal servants all tie him to the natural world.

In addition to his association with animals and the natural world, Beorn has a relationship with Old English and Norse sources. The etymology of his name is Old English and Old Norse. In Old English *Beorn* means "man, warrior." The Old Norse word *bjorn* means "bear." In literature, "The Saga of Hrolf Kraki" featured a character named Beorn who could also transform into a bear. Beorn also has ties to Beowulf. *Beo*, in Old English, means "bee" and *wulf*, obviously enough, means "wolf." Taken together, *Beowulf* translates into "bee's wolf" or euphemistically, "honey-eater," meaning a bear. Gandalf, upon

entering Beorn's territory, comments that Beorn keeps bees. Another etymology used by Rider Haggard in "Eric Brighteyes" of "Bear-sark" is that *berserkr* means "bear-shirt" or "bare-shirt." This possible connection comes from Old English as well, with *bera*, the feminine form of "bjorn," and *serkr*, "shirt." Hence bear-shirt. This is based on the belief that berserkers gained their name from wearing a bear's skin into battle in a totemistic fashion.

Naming conventions aside, Beorn and Beowulf display similarity in size and strength. They also have a similar habit of displaying war trophies. The evening after his meeting with the Dwarves, Beorn transforms into a bear and meets with the bears of the area. Across the Anduin river, he captures a goblin who verifies Gandalf's tale. The next day Beorn displays the head of the goblin he interrogated on his gate and nails a warg's skin to a tree, just as Beowulf displayed Grendel's arm in Heorot hall. Yet another parallel is the relationship of both Beowulf and Beorn to their respective halls. Bilbo and company are cautioned not to leave the hall after dark for fear of Beorn in bear shape. In Heorot, Beowulf and party are cautioned about the danger that comes into the hall. Although the dangers differ, one inside the hall, the other without, the perfect reversal of these situations shows a clear connection to Beorn's Old English sources.

Beorn figures into the story of Middle-earth again at the Battle of Five Armies. In his bear shape, he carries the injured Thorin out of combat then slays Bolg, the goblin leader, causing the goblin forces to rout. After the Battle of Five Armies, Beorn becomes a chieftain, and his people were known as the Beornings. The Beornings' land lay between the Misty Mountains and the Mirkwood and they kept the High Pass open and the ford across the Anduin safe for travelers.

JOHN WALSH

Further Reading

Shippey, Tom. *The Road to Middle-earth.* Boston, MA: Houghton Mifflin, 2000.

BEOWULF AND THE CRITICS

Some time between 1933 and October 23, 1935 (most likely in 1934), Tolkien began the composition of a series of Oxford lectures on *Beowulf* and its critical reception and interpretation. Originally titled *Beowulf with Critics* and later changed to *Beowulf and the Critics* (a nod to one of the chapters of R.W. Chambers' *Widsith*), the lectures were the antecedent of the famous 1936 British Academy lecture, "*Beowulf: The Monsters and the Critics.*"

The manuscript, Oxford, Bodleian Library, A26/1–4, was donated to the Bodleian Library in 1985. It was edited and published in 2002. *Beowulf and the Critics* contains two versions, labeled "A" and "B" by Christopher Tolkien, with the B-text including all revised A-text and then continuing. The contours of the final, British Academy lecture are present in the A-text, but Tolkien develops the argument more slowly and less allusively: veiled references in the published lecture are spelled out in the A- and B-texts. Tolkien also gives a more thorough treatment of the history of *Beowulf* criticism than his "Babel of Voices" in the published lecture (although this history is cribbed from John Earle's *The Deeds of Beowulf*). *Beowulf and the Critics* also includes two poems on dragons, one by C.S. Lewis (*The Northern Dragon* from Lewis's *The Pilgrim's Regress*) and one by Tolkien himself (a variant of *Iúmonna Gold Galdre Bewunden,* a revised version of which was published as *The Hoard*).

The main critical foils for Tolkien in *Beowulf and the Critics* are not, as they are in "*Beowulf: The Monsters and the Critics,*" the critics W.P. Ker and R.W. Chambers (Tolkien is far less politic in his criticism of these major figures) but the lesser-known Archibald Strong and J.J. Jusserand. Tolkien spends a great deal of time dissecting their many errors. However, the original impetus for Tolkien's lecture almost certainly was dissatisfaction with the way W.P. Ker treats *Beowulf* in his *The Dark Ages:* notes found by Christopher Tolkien in J.R.R. Tolkien's copy of *The Dark Ages* are directly connected with the A-text of *Beowulf and the Critics.*

Beowulf and the Critics is particularly valuable in shedding light upon Tolkien's methods of working and the rhetorical development of his arguments, showing that Tolkien produced important rhetorical set pieces even before he was clear about the eventual direction of his argument. At other times, his revisions were particularly effective, such as when he created the famous "allegory of the tower" from an original allegory of a rock garden. *Beowulf and the Critics* (in Appendix I) also contains a passage of Tolkien's hitherto unpublished *Beowulf* translation.

MICHAEL D.C. DROUT

Further Reading

Drout, Michael D.C. "How the Monsters Became Important: The Logical and Rhetorical Development of 'The Monsters and the Critics.'" In *Fabelwesen, mostri e portenti nell'immaginario occidentale*, edited by Carmela Rizzo, 1–23. Torino: Edizione dell'Orso, 2004.

———. "The Rhetorical Evolution of '*Beowulf:* The Monsters and the Critics.'" In *The Lord of the Rings, 1954–2004: Scholarship in Honor of Richard E. Blackwelder*, edited by Wayne Hammond and Christina Scull, 183–215. Milwaukee: Marquette University Press, 2005.

Earle, John. *The Deeds of Beowulf: An English Epic of the Eighth Century Done into Modern Prose.* Oxford: Clarendon, 1892.

Ker, W.P. *The Dark Ages.* London: Blackwood and Sons, 1904.

See also **Beowulf: Tolkien's Scholarship;** **Beowulf: Translations by Tolkien;** **Exodus, Edition of;** **Homecoming of Beorhtnoth, Beorhthelm's Son**

"*BEOWULF*: THE MONSTERS AND THE CRITICS"

On November 25, 1936, Tolkien delivered the Sir Israel Gollancz Memorial Lecture to the British Academy. Printed in *Proceedings of the British Academy,* volume 22, "*Beowulf: The Monsters and the Critics*" is the most important essay ever written about *Beowulf.* Even if Tolkien had never published *The Lord of the Rings,* his academic reputation would have been made with this one essay.

"*Beowulf: The Monsters and the Critics*" has perhaps become (in the tongue-in-cheek words of R.D. Fulk) "the object of mindless veneration," and it certainly is not often enough read in its proper scholarly context. Nevertheless, the essay is more than a touchstone, and it is fair to say that "*Beowulf: The Monsters and the Critics*" marks the beginning of modern scholarship on *Beowulf.* After "*Beowulf: The Monsters and the Critics,*" scholars refocused their attention on *Beowulf* itself rather than examining what was missing from the poem or was only tangentially discussed. Tolkien set the monsters at the center of *Beowulf* criticism, and there they have remained (though it is important to note that he was by no means the first scholar to discuss their importance).

"*Beowulf: The Monsters and the Critics*" began as a series of Oxford lectures (eventually published many years after Tolkien's death as *Beowulf and the Critics*), and the essay's originally oral form contributes to both the rhetorical effects and the logical complexity of the published argument. Tolkien begins with the assertion that the accretions of modern scholarship have obscured the poem and that what is needed is criticism of *Beowulf* itself. He argues that seeing the poem as primarily a historical document is not an effective approach to *Beowulf* studies because it ignores the poetry. Tolkien then develops the famous "allegory of the tower":

A man inherited a field in which was an accumulation of old stone, part of an older hall. Of the old stone some had already been used in building the house in which he actually lived, not far from the old house of his fathers. Of the rest he took some and built a tower. But his friends coming perceived at once (without troubling to climb the steps) that these stones had formerly belonged to a more ancient building. So they pushed the tower over, with no little labour, to look for hidden carvings and inscriptions, or to discover whence the man's distant forefathers had obtained their building material. Some suspecting a deposit of coal under the soil began to dig for it, and forgot even the stones. They all said: "This tower is most interesting." But they also said (after pushing it over): "What a muddle it is in!" And even the man's own descendants, who might have been expected to consider what he had been about, were heard to murmur: "He is such an odd fellow! Imagine his using these old stones just to build a non-sensical tower! Why did not he restore the old house? He had no sense of proportion." But from the top of that tower the man had been able to look out upon the sea.

The man who builds the tower is the *Beowulf*-poet, the stones are the ancient songs and lays, and the friends who push the tower over are the later critics. As Tom Shippey notes, the allegory implies that no one but Tolkien had, heretofore, understood the *Beowulf*-poet's purpose. This allegory has been immensely rhetorically effective.

After the allegory of the tower, Tolkien depicts a Babel of voices (in which all major opinions on *Beowulf* are expressed in pithy phrases). Having thus set up almost all other critics as misguided or misinformed (and having shown how contradictory opinions were), Tolkien then turns to the criticism of W.P. Ker and his pupil R.W. Chambers, excellent *Beowulf* scholars who, Tolkien felt, had not adequately understood the poem as a poem.

Much of "*Beowulf:* The Monsters and the Critics" is devoted to rebutting Ker's analysis of *Beowulf* in *The Dark Ages*. Ker thought the monsters to be a childish flaw, but Tolkien shows that they are essential to the design of *Beowulf* and that dragons in particular are quite rare in the poetry of the north of Europe. Tolkien argues that the "dignity" of *Beowulf* that Ker and Chambers both praise is due to the theme of the poem, which he attached to the monsters: "that man, each man and all men and all their works shall die." This theme, and its dignity, arises from a Christian poet looking back on a pagan past. Tolkien thought *Beowulf* to have been written in "the Age of Bede" (ca. 700–750), but (to the sorrow of many subsequent readers) he does not explain this deduction. The poet had an antiquarian temper, Tolkien asserts, thus explaining archaisms in the language of *Beowulf* and linking the poem to the pre-Christian historical events supposed to underpin the narrative.

Tolkien then argues that the poem is not meant to "advance" but is rather a balance of two moments in a great life; this balance is then linked to the Anglo-Saxon poetic line, an opposition of two halves. This structural description of *Beowulf* has often been critiqued (some critics see the poem as having three parts, some as having four parts), but it is fair to say that it remains the mainstream critical consensus that the poem is balanced between Beowulf's adventures in Denmark (the fights against Grendel and his mother) and his later exploits in his own country (the fatal fight against the dragon).

Tolkien concludes the essay by (allusively) setting *Beowulf* in a larger context: "Yet it is in fact written in a language that after many centuries has still essential kinship with our own, it was made in this land, and moves in our northern world beneath our northern sky, and for those who are native to that tongue and land, it must ever call with a profound appeal—until the dragon comes." In 1936, the identity of the dragon looming over England (and all of Europe) was perhaps all too clear.

This conclusion is followed by appendices on "Grendel's Titles," the words "'Lof,' and 'Dom,' 'hell,' and 'heofon,'" and lines 175–88 (Tolkien says that lines 181–88 "have a ring and measure unlike their context, and indeed unlike that of the poem as a whole," and speculates that the second half of 180 has been altered, with the current lines 180b–88 replacing an originally shorter passage). In these appendices, we see Tolkien's more technical (as opposed to integrative and interpretive) approach to Old English: the appendices are detailed and philological rather than literary-critical.

But Tolkien's greatest successes in the essay are rhetorical rather than philological or even scholarly. He never defends one of his most important claims (about the date of the poem—and note that this was far less controversial in 1936 than it is today) his discussion of a possible interpolator is removed to the appendix, and it is not clear that there is a single technical breakthrough in the essay. Yet "*Beowulf:* The Monsters and the Critics" has been overwhelmingly influential for so long not only because it told critics what they wanted to hear (that *Beowulf* was an effective work of art) but also because the essay addresses very big questions of literary and artistic worth. There is not much criticism in the world like this.

MICHAEL D.C. DROUT

Further Reading

Drout, Michael D.C. "Introduction: Seeds, Soil and Northern Sky." In *Beowulf and the Critics*, by J.R.R. Tolkien, edited by Michael D.C. Drout, 1–29. Medieval and Renaissance Texts and Studies, Vol. 248. Tempe: Arizona Center for Medieval and Renaissance Studies, 2002.

———. "How the Monsters Became Important: The Logical and Rhetorical Development of 'The Monsters and the Critics.'" In *Fabelwesen, mostri e portenti nell'immaginario occidentale*, edited by Carmela Rizzo, 1–23. Torino: Edizione dell'Orso, 2004.

———. "The Rhetorical Evolution of 'Beowulf: The Monsters and the Critics.'" In *The Lord of the Rings, 1954–2004: Scholarship in Honor of Richard E. Blackwelder*, edited by Wayne Hammond and Christina Scull, 183–215. Milwaukee: Marquette University Press, 2005.

Ker, W.P. *The Dark Ages*. London: Blackwood and Sons, 1904.

Shippey, Tom. "Introduction." In *Beowulf: the Critical Heritage*, edited by Tom Shippey and Andreas Haarder, 1–74. London: Routledge, 1998.

———. *The Road to Middle-earth*. Revised and Expanded edition. Boston: Houghton Mifflin, 2003.

———. "Tolkien's Academic Reputation Today," *Amon Hen* 100 (1989), 18–22.

See also *"Beowulf*: The Monsters and The Critics"; *Beowulf*: Tolkien's Scholarship; *Beowulf*: Translations by Tolkien

BEOWULF: TOLKIEN'S SCHOLARSHIP

Although Tolkien is famous as a scholar of *Beowulf*, he published relatively little research on the poem during his lifetime. "*Beowulf*: The Monsters and the Critics" is the most important article ever written about *Beowulf*, but aside from this landmark essay, Tolkien only published a short piece on translating the poem and a discussion of *ofermod* in *The Battle of Maldon* that also touches on *Beowulf*. The larger, book-length studies *Finn and Hengest* and *Beowulf and the Critics* were both published after Tolkien's death and have not been widely influential on *Beowulf* scholarship.

Nevertheless, Tolkien's shadow looms long over *Beowulf* scholarship. Much of this influence is because of the enormous success of "*Beowulf*: The Monsters and the Critics," which is viewed as the beginning of modern *Beowulf* criticism. But Tolkien also shaped *Beowulf* studies through his Oxford lectures to several generations of students, some of whom went on to distinguished careers of their own. As Bruce Mitchell notes, "Tolkien was very generous with his ideas to those who sat at his feet." Inspection of the many, many pages of unpublished *Beowulf* commentaries by Tolkien held in the Bodleian library shows that he wrote on almost every aspect of the poem at one time or another, and although he never assembled this material into publishable form, he obviously communicated much of it to colleagues and students.

It is thus difficult to determine whether Tolkien should be credited with specific technical contributions to *Beowulf* study. "*Beowulf*: The Monsters and the Critics" only briefly touches on the most controversial contemporary topic in *Beowulf* scholarship— the date of the poem—and Tolkien asserts without explanation his conclusion that the poem dates from the "age of Bede" (ca. 670–735). His assertion in the appendix of "*Beowulf*: The Monsters and the Critics" that lines 181–88 of *Beowulf* are likely an expansion or reworking of an earlier, shorter version of the passage by an interpolator is credited to his "ear and judgment" and given only a brief explanation (Tolkien was not the first scholar to note the problems posed by lines 175–88). Likewise, in the brief passage of his verse *Beowulf* translation that appears in "On Translating *Beowulf*," Tolkien equates the Geats of *Beowulf* with the Goths, but he does not explain this intriguing (and controversial) identification. There are more technical contributions in *Finn and Hengest*, the most important of which is the idea that in the Finnsburg episode in *Beowulf* and the Finnsburg Fragment there were Jutes on both sides of the conflict, and this analysis is backed up with so much philological and historical evidence that it becomes clear that Tolkien had thought deeply on the dark historical relationships among the various peoples of the north and west of Europe. Unfortunately, the main arguments in *Finn and Hengest* take place in the textual commentaries and are hard to put into narrative form. They have thus, sadly, been almost entirely neglected by mainstream *Beowulf* criticism.

Tolkien was so influential in *Beowulf* studies—at least during his lifetime—not because he made specific, technical contributions but because he developed a big-picture reading of the poem that has found favor with several generations of critics. Although it is untrue to assert that no one before Tolkien had viewed *Beowulf* as a coherent work of art, Tolkien made the first widely accepted case for viewing *Beowulf* as aesthetically successful, and he showed how the monsters in *Beowulf* were symbolic (not allegorical) representations of chaos and night, set in opposition to stability and civilization. The poet's use of such symbols allowed him to create a poem that focuses not on enmeshed loyalties of heroes but on the larger cosmic drama of which they are a part. Thus, Tolkien interpreted the theme of *Beowulf* to be that "man, each man and all men and all their works shall die," a theme consistent with the heathen past but one that "no Christian need despise." It was this theme, Tolkien argued, that brought the great dignity to the poem that even scholars who had regretted the monsters had noted.

Tolkien also argued that the macrostructure of the poem was akin to the microstructure of the Anglo-Saxon poetic line: both were based on the balance of one part against another. The poetic line is divided into two roughly equal halves by the caesura (Tolkien used the more descriptive term "breath pause" in "On Translating *Beowulf*"); likewise, the poem is divided into two roughly equal halves, the first in Denmark, the second in Geatland. This view of the structure of the poem remains to this day the consensus among Anglo-Saxonists (although there are dissenters who argue for a three-part or four-part structure, their arguments have not been widely accepted).

Tolkien's historical claims are somewhat more controversial. As noted previously, he accepted a date for the composition of the poem of between 670 (immediately after the conversion of the last pagan kingdom, Sussex) and 735 (the date of Bede's death). The *Beowulf*-poet, he argued, was a Christian looking back (but not too far back) on a pagan past. The poet's antiquarian interests and attempts at writing a kind of historical fiction could then explain why there are no references to Christ, the Trinity, or other major Christian terms anywhere in the poem (of all the names in scripture, only Cain and Abel appear in *Beowulf*): the poet knew that the days he was depicting had been heathen even though he was not. This figure of a deliberately archaizing poet has had enormous influence on the subsequent criticism of the poem, because it allows critics to integrate the conflicting data (linguistic, historical, and syntactic) of *Beowulf* into any number of coherent wholes. From his posthumously published edition of *Exodus,* it is possible to infer that Tolkien thought that this poem and *Beowulf* to be closely related, and both poems were "old" (i.e., written before the end of the eighth century), but Tolkien never was able to publish or even put in order his thoughts on the connections between *Beowulf* and *Exodus.*

The strange, two-part article "The Homecoming of Beorhtnoth, Beorhtwald's Son" (composed of a poem and a subsequent essay) is about *The Battle of Maldon,* not *Beowulf.* But in his analysis of Beorhtnoth's *ofermod,* Tolkien discusses *Beowulf,* arguing that the hero's expedition against the dragon, without his retainers, was brought about by an irresponsible excess of chivalry that ends in Beowulf's people losing their king "disastrously." Tom Shippey has noted how widely influential Tolkien's views on *Maldon* have become (although there has been some more recent critical reaction against the view expressed in "Homecoming"), and likewise this interpretation of *Beowulf* has been adopted by many critics. The

connected idea, also propounded by Tolkien in his essay, that the final word of *Beowulf, lofgeornost* (most eager for praise) is "ominous" is also influential. These ideas appear to contradict Tolkien's earlier views on Beowulf's fight against the dragon that "a man can but die upon his death day." Perhaps here is evidence of the evolution in Tolkien's thought also possibly indicated by his not translating "Geats" as "Goths" in his later prose translation of *Beowulf:* in both cases, the more traditional, heroic vision of the Anglo-Saxons (apparently at one time shared by Tolkien and E.V. Gordon) had evolved toward a more Christian, ironic view of heroism and Northern courage.

The massive influence of "The Homecoming" and "*Beowulf:* The Monsters and the Critics" is in some ways ironic. The great majority of Tolkien's work on *Beowulf* was of the sort represented by the textual commentary in *Finn and Hengest*—detailed, philological, historical, and infinitely painstaking. Yet the most influential of Tolkien's discussions of the poem are those in which he makes the greatest unsupported (or lightly supported) generalizations and in which he discusses the poem in the broadest possible terms. Tolkien would perhaps have seen a fundamental continuity between the detailed and philological and the broader and more interpretive work, but because of the accidents of publication—and because of Tolkien's great gift for rhetoric—only the latter has shaped the field of *Beowulf* criticism.

MICHAEL D.C. DROUT

Further Reading

Drout, Michael D.C. "How the Monsters Became Important: The Logical and Rhetorical Development of 'The Monsters and the Critics.'" In *Fabelwesen, mostri e portenti nell'immaginario occidentale*, edited by Carmela Rizzo, 1–23. Torino: Edizione dell'Orso, 2004.

———. "The Rhetorical Evolution of '*Beowulf:* The Monsters and the Critics.'" In *The Lord of the Rings, 1954–2004: Scholarship in Honor of Richard E. Blackwelder*, edited by Wayne Hammond and Christina Scull, 183–215. Milwaukee, MN: Marquette University Press, 2005.

Earle, John. *The Deeds of Beowulf: An English Epic of the Eighth Century Done into Modern Prose.* Oxford: Clarendon, 1892.

Ker, W.P. *The Dark Ages.* London: Blackwood and Sons, 1904.

Shippey, Tom. "Introduction." In *Beowulf: the Critical Heritage*, edited by Tom Shippey and Andreas Haarder, 1–74. London and New York: Routledge, 1998.

———. *The Road to Middle-earth.* Revised and Expanded edition. Boston: Houghton Mifflin, 2003.

———. "Tolkien's Academic Reputation Today," *Amon Hen* 100 (1989), 18–22.

See also **Beowulf and the Critics**; "**Beowulf**: The Monsters and the Critics"; **Beowulf**: Translations by Tolkien; **Exodus, Edition of; Homecoming of Beorhtnoth, Beorhthelm's Son**

BEOWULF: TRANSLATIONS BY TOLKIEN

Tolkien made a complete prose and a partial verse translation of *Beowulf*. Small fragments of these translations have been published in "On Translating *Beowulf*," *J.R.R. Tolkien: Artist and Illustrator,* and *Beowulf and the Critics.* The manuscripts are held by the Bodleian Library at Oxford.

While a professor at Leeds (between October 1920 and December 1925), Tolkien began his alliterative translation (MS Oxford, Bodleian Library, Tolkien A 29 A) at the same time that he was seriously engaged in writing alliterative poetry of his own. This translation was most likely never completed, but it seems likely that Tolkien returned to this translation in 1940 when called upon to write "Preface: On Translating *Beowulf*" for C.L. Wrenn's revision of J.R. Clark Hall's *Beowulf and the Finnsburg Fragment: A Translation into Modern English.* The published excerpt of the verse translation is most notable for Tolkien's efforts to mimic the rhythm of each of the major Sievers' "types" of verse in Modern English and for his use of "Gothland" to translate Old English "Geatland," thus indicating that Tolkien at least entertained the idea of equivalence between the Geats and the Goths.

Some time after Tolkien had moved from Leeds to Oxford (thus after 1925) he produced a prose translation of *Beowulf* (Tolkien A 29 B), which was corrected by C.S. Lewis. At some later time, an amanuensis typescript of this translation was made, perhaps by Christopher Tolkien.

Examples of Tolkien's *Beowulf* translation were exhibited by the Bodleian Library at the 1992 Tolkien Centenary Conference, but the Estate has not yet allowed the translations to be published.

MICHAEL D.C. DROUT

Further Reading

Hammond, Wayne G., and Christina Scull. *J.R.R. Tolkien: Artist and Illustrator.* Boston: Houghton Mifflin, 1995.
Tolkien, J.R.R. "On Translating *Beowulf*." In *Beowulf and the Finnsburg Fragment: A Translation into Modern English.* Translated by J.R. Clark Hall, revised by C.L. Wrenn. London: George Allen & Unwin, 1940. Reprinted in *The Monsters and the Critics and Other Essays,* edited by Christopher Tolkien, 49–71. London: George Allen & Unwin, 1983.

See also **Beowulf and the Critics**; "**Beowulf**: The Monsters and the Critics"; **Beowulf**: Tolkien's Scholarship; "On Translating *Beowulf*"

BEREN

Also named Erchamion the One-handed and Camlost the Empty-handed, Beren is the son of Barahir of the house of Bëor and Emeldir the Manhearted. He is the father of Dior, the grandfather of Elwing, and the great-grandfather of Elrond.

Tolkien referred to the story of Beren and his beloved Lúthien as "the kernel of the mythology" and said it "arose from a small woodland glade filled with 'hemlocks' (or other white umbellifers) near Roos on the Holderness Peninsula—to which I occasionally went when free from regimental duties while in the Humber Garrison in 1918" (*Letters,* 221). Tolkien must have begun visiting the glade earlier than 1918 because "The Tale of Tinúviel," published in *The Book of Lost Tales: Part II,* was written in 1917. In this earliest version, Beren is not a Man but rather a Gnome of the Noldoli from Hisilómë, a northern land, and his father is Egnor, a hunter. Beren wanders into Artanor, the Elven realm of King Tinwelint, where he observes the King's daughter, Tinúviel, dancing in the woods and falls in love with her. When Beren tells Tinwelint he desires Tinúviel, Tinwelint scornfully says that if Beren brings him a Silmaril from the crown of Melko, he will allow Beren to marry Tinúviel. Beren scornfully accepts the challenge and journeys to Melko's stronghold, but he is captured by Orcs and brought before Melko, who makes him a thrall of Tevildo, Prince of Cats. Tinúviel rescues Beren with the help of Huan, Captain of Dogs. They journey to Angamandi, and Tinúviel, who wears a magic robe, woven from her hair, that induces sleep, makes Karkaras, the wolf guarding the entrance, fall asleep. Once inside, Tinúviel beguiles Melko with dancing, and he falls asleep as her robe brushes him. Beren cuts the Silmaril from the crown. Departing swiftly, they find Karkaras awake. Beren fights him, and Karkaras bites off Beren's hand that holds the Silmaril. Driven mad by the Silmaril within him, Karkaras runs away. With Huan's and Tinwelint's help, they hunt and slay Karkaras and recover the Silmaril, but Beren is killed. Tinúviel appeals to Mandos, who from pity reanimates Beren and sends the lovers back into Middle-earth but makes both mortal. Tolkien later commented that "It was in Ossiriand, a forest country, secret and mysterious before the west feet of the Ered Luin, that Beren and Lúthien dwelt for a while after Beren's return from the Dead (*Letters,* 334). In the "Quenta Silmarillion," as revised after the publication of *The Lord of the Rings,* Tolkien stated more specifically that they lived on the island of Tolgalen in the river Adurant in Ossiriand (*Jewels,* 195). Tolkien also commented that Beren's return from death makes the story "a kind of Orpheus-legend in reverse, but one of Pity not of Inexorability" (*Letters,* 193).

The resurrected Beren appears at the end of "The Nauglafring," the last of the *Lost Tales* to be written. When Beren learns that the Dwarves have conquered Artanor, he attacks them and kills Naugladur in single combat. (Tolkien later commented, perhaps tongue-in-cheek, that "it seems clear that Beren, who had no army, received the aid of the Ents" in this battle [*Letters,* 334]). Beren takes the Nauglafring and gives it to Tinúviel, who wears it only briefly, but Mîm's curse falls on her, her decreed mortality comes, and she fades from life. Beren dies shortly thereafter.

In 1925, Tolkien decided to tell the story in verse and so began six years of composing *The Lay of Leithian,* his ambitious narrative poem of more than four thousand iambic tetrameter lines set in rhymed couplets. In 1931, he left it unfinished at the point at which the wolf Carcharoth bites off Beren's hand. The poem is published in *The Lays of Beleriand.*

Although following the story of the tale, the *Lay* enriches it in many ways, and several passages involve Beren. At the outset, Beren's father Barahir lives as an outlaw in northern lands conquered by Morgoth. Gorlim, one of Barahir's men, is tricked by Morgoth into betraying Barahir, and Barahir is slain. Gorlim's repentant spirit speaks to Beren in a dream, and Beren kills his father's killers and recovers his father's ring, a gift of friendship from the Elven King Felagund, to whom Barahir gave aid after the Siege of Angband. Then, fleeing Morgoth, he goes south into Doriath (formerly Artanor), the kingdom of Thingol (formerly Tinwelint), where he sees Lúthien (Canto II). After accepting Thingol's challenge to obtain the Silmaril, Beren journeys to Felagund's kingdom of Nargothrond, where Felagund vows to assist Beren. However, Celegorm and Curufin, two of the sons of Fëanor who have vowed to destroy any who keep the Silmarils, persuade all but ten not to accompany Felagund and Beren (Canto VI). Morgoth's lieutenant Thû captures the twelve, and all except Beren are devoured by wolves. Beren is rescued by the hound Huan and Lúthien (Canto IX). Beren seeks Lúthien's safe return to Doriath, but they are attacked by Celegorm and Curufin, and Beren is shot by Celegorm. Lúthien heals his wound, and Beren returns her to Doriath (Canto X). Beren then resumes his quest, but Lúthien, unwilling to stay in Doriath, rejoins him as he nears Thangorodrim (Canto XI).

After the publication of *The Lord of the Rings,* Tolkien returned twice to the story of Beren and Lúthien, first in recommencing the *Lay* and rewriting it from the outset (*Lays,* 330–63), and then in the "Grey Annals" and the "Later Quenta Silmarillion," both published in *The War of the Jewels.*

In 1972, Tolkien wrote to his son Michael that in 1909 he "met the Lúthien Tinúviel of my own personal 'romance,' with her long dark hair, fair face and starry eyes. . . . But now she has gone before Beren, leaving him indeed one-handed, but he has no power to move the inexorable Mandos" (*Letters,* 417). The name Lúthien appears beneath Edith Tolkien's name on her gravestone; beneath Tolkien's, the name Beren appears.

PAUL EDMUND THOMAS

See also **Alliterative Poetry; Angband;** *Book of Lost Tales II***; Death; Dwarves; Eärendil; Elves; Elves: Kindreds and Migrations; Elves: Reincarnation; Fairies; Fëanor; Heroes and Heroism;** *History of Middle-earth: Overview***; Jewels;** *Lays of Beleriand, The***;** *Letters of J.R.R. Tolkien, The***; Maiar; Melian; Middle-earth: Men; Monsters, Middle-earth; Middle-earth: Peoples; Morgoth and Melkor; Mountains; Mythology for England; Northern Courage; Resurrection; Sacrifice;** *Silmarillion, The***; Silmarils; Thingol**

BIBLE

Although not a theologian, Tolkien was familiar with the Bible in all its aspects because of his religious devotion and his work as a philologist. He saw it as a powerful vessel of truth. This familiarity informs all his fiction but primarily *The Silmarillion.*

Tolkien used the Bible professionally. His studies of medieval literature were often related to the Bible, such as his translations of the *Ancrene Wisse,* whose author frequently refers to the medieval Bible, and *The Old English Exodus.* He valued the Welsh Bible for its preservation of that language (*MC,* 165). He read the Latin Vulgate and original Greek texts. He referred to the French Bible de Jérusalem and the original Hebrew to translate the Book of Jonah for the Jerusalem Bible (published 1966), the first Catholic Bible translated into English from the original languages. Although listed as a principal collaborator, other demands forced him to resign, and he referred to the title as an "undeserved courtesy" (*Letters,* 378).

As a devout Catholic, Tolkien believed the story of Christ is the ultimate fairy-story because "it is true" (*TL,* 72). While recognizing that the Gospels had greater historicity than Genesis, he believed in the reality of Eden and its repercussions (*Letters,* 109–10, 147). In a time when the Bible, particularly Genesis, was under attack from modernism and science, Tolkien strove to restore the power of myths in general and the Bible in particular (Houghton, 180).

The exact Bibles in Tolkien's library are not publicly known, but he probably used the Catholic Douay Version, as well as the Authorized (King James) Version. Pieter Collier of Tolkienlibrary.com wrote (in a June 15, 2005, e-mail) that in 1923 Tolkien obtained an 1865 copy of *The Lindisfarne and Rushworth Gospels.* This is an Anglo-Saxon translation of the Gospel of John, whose divine *Logos* (Word) had great significance for Tolkien. He saw words as fragments of the *Logos* of John and writing or subcreating as something intrinsic to those made in the Creator's image (Flieger, 41).

Tolkien's philosophy of myth and truth hinged on precepts from Genesis and John. He regarded myths and fairy-stories as imperfect attempts to express truths that only God can tell perfectly, such as in the Gospel, where "Legend and History have met and fused" (Wood, 8; *TL,* 72).

Tolkien avoided overt biblical references in his fantasy because he believed it "fatal" for art to be explicitly religious (*Letters,* 144). Rather, his presuppositions, patterns, symbols, and themes parallel those of the Bible, such as Providence (*FR,* I, vii, 162; *TT,* III, xi, 254) and the self-destructive nature of evil (*TT,* III, xi, 255; Prov. 1:10–19). Darker biblical themes are expressed as well, such as the futility of all human endeavors and the conviction that life is an ongoing struggle (Ecclesiastes; *FR,* II, ii, 319–20).

More than *The Lord of the Rings, The Silmarillion* draws openly on the Bible but avoids retelling the Genesis account by focusing on the Ainur and the Elves (*Letters,* 146; Shippey, 236). Tolkien makes biblical metaphors literal and recombines biblical elements to be particular to Middle-earth (Flieger, 58). Both Genesis and *The Silmarillion* assume an all-powerful creator-God, although Tolkien's Eru Ilúvatar is more remote than God in the Bible. Beginning earlier than the Genesis account, Tolkien describes Ilúvatar's creation of the Ainur. Synthesizing Genesis, John, and Job 38:4 and 7, Tolkien tells how the Ainur "took part in the making of the world as 'sub-creators'" (*Letters,* 284) by harmonizing with Ilúvatar's musical theme, forming everything except Elves and Men (Flieger, 59). Their genders and roles as sub-creators make them unorthodox angels, though perhaps they embody aspects of the majestic plural name of God used in Genesis 1:1 (Flieger, 54–55).

As in Genesis 1:31, "Nothing is evil in the beginning" of Middle-earth (*FR,* II, ii, 351). Evil is not Eru's creation but a perversion, the Ainu Melkor's misuse of free will when he pridefully rejects Eru's theme and makes his own melody (*S,* 16; Isa., 14). Repeatedly, Eru reincorporates Melkor's melody into his own theme, illustrating God's sovereignty in bringing good out of evil (*S,* 17; Gen. 50:20; Acts 2:23). In an allusion to Satan, Melkor "descended through fire and wrath into a great burning, down into Darkness" with his own demons, fallen Maiar (*S,* 31; Rev. 12:9, 20:1–3, 10).

Ilúvatar brings the music to life in Arda with one word: *Eä!*—"Let these things Be!" Echoing Genesis's "Let there be . . . ," *Eä!* sends forth into the void "the Flame Imperishable" to be the heart of the world. Tolkien said this flame characterizes the Holy Spirit, God's agent of creation (Kilby, Isa. 4:4, Acts 2:3).

One Ainu "wrought two mighty lamps" (*S,* 35), like the "two great lights" of Genesis 1:16, and soon flora and fauna appear in the Genesis pattern. In a departure from Genesis, night results from sin, coming after Melkor destroys the Lamps (*S,* 48). Here, the symbolism of John resonates strongly, as darkness manifests that which opposes God (John 8:12). The first killing of Elf by Elf at Alqualondë is like the murder of Abel by Cain on a larger scale.

Long after the Elves, Men appear in the story from the east, already fallen. Tolkien avoided retelling the Fall of Man to prevent contradicting the Bible (Shippey, 236) and to emphasize the prehuman origins of sin (Evans 2002, 206–7). As Adam and Eve are uniquely made in God's image, Men and Elves are created exclusively from Ilúvatar's theme (*S,* 18).

Both Elves and Men have a satanic adversary on earth and are alienated from the divine. As in the Bible, they are unable to save themselves but await a mediator to plead "for pardon on their misdeeds and pity on their woes" (*S,* 244). Eärendil is a Christ figure: recalling John 18:37, the Valar say of Eärendil, "For this he was born into the world" (Helms, 39). Eärendil and the Silmaril become the Evening and Morning Star, alluding to Christ as the "bright and morning star" of Revelation 22:16 (Duriez, 194).

Tolkien describes *Akallabêth* as "the Second Fall of Man," blending the Atlantis myth with the biblical stories of Noah and Lot. The Númenóreans desire not forbidden fruit but eternal life. They deny the existence of God, make altars and human sacrifices to Melkor, and persecute and kill the "Faithful" (*S,* 273; Gen. 6:5). Tolkien refers to Elendil, the righteous man who escaped the destruction of Númenor with his sons, as a "Noachian figure" (*Letters,* 156, 206).

Tolkien relied on the Bible academically and spiritually, both as a window into old languages and as a moral structure for his fictional work. Biblical images and references powerfully reinforce his extensive use of world mythic archetypes in his writing of an imaginative new cosmology.

CHRISTINA GANONG WALTON

Further Reading

Duriez, Colin. *Tolkien and "The Lord of the Rings": A Guide to Middle-earth.* Mahwah, NJ: Hidden Spring, 2001.

Evans, Jonathan. "The Anthropology of Arda." In *Tolkien the Medievalist*, edited by Jane Chance. London: Routledge, 2002.

Flieger, Verlyn. *Splintered Light: Logos and Language in Tolkien's World.* Revised edition. Kent, OH: Kent State University Press, 2002.

Helms, Randel. *Tolkien and the Silmarils: Imagination and Myth in "The Silmarillion."* New York: Houghton Mifflin, 1981.

Houghton, John William. "Augustine in the Cottage of Lost Play." In *Tolkien the Medievalist*, edited by Jane Chance. London: Routledge, 2002.

Kilby, Clyde S. "Meeting Professor Tolkien." *Christian History & Biography*, 2003. http://www.ctlibrary.com (accessed August 14, 2005).

Shippey, Tom. *The Road to Middle-earth.* Revised and Expanded edition. Boston: Houghton Mifflin, 2003.

Wood, Ralph C. *The Gospel According to Tolkien: Visions of the Kingdom in Middle-earth.* Louisville, KY: Westminster John Knox, 2003.

See also **Angels; Catholicism, Roman; Childhood of Tolkien; Christ; Christian Readings of Tolkien; Christianity; Darkness; Death; Fall of Man; Genesis; Good and Evil; Heathenism and Paganism; Heaven; Hell; Immortality; Incarnation; Law; Mercy; Paradise; Pride; Prophecy; Redemption; Renewal; Resurrection; Sacrifice; Saints; Satan and Lucifer;** *Silmarillion, The***; Sin; Time**

BILBO BAGGINS

Bilbo Baggins, traveler, writer, and the first hobbit to become famous in the world at large, was born September 22, 2890, Third Age, at The Hill, Hobbiton, the Shire. His father, Bungo Baggins, was a well-to-do and most respectable Hobbit, conventional in appearance and conduct. He built a fine hobbit-hole called Bag End for his family, a dwelling in which Bilbo, aged fifty, was still living when the adventures recounted in his diary and reproduced in *The Hobbit* began.

The susceptibility to adventures came from his mother's side of the family, for she was Belladonna Took, one of the daughters of the Old Took, head of the clan that lived in Tookland across The Water. The Tooks were known for a certain flamboyance and dashing spirit. As Tolkien sums up Bilbo's somewhat unusual heritage, "the Tooks were not as respectable as the Bagginses, though they were undoubtedly richer" (*H*, I, 31). This tinge of raffishness added to independent wealth creates a certain propensity for adventures; it was perhaps this potential that Gandalf the wizard spotted; he therefore treated Bilbo to the string of remarkable incidents that began with The Unexpected Party in the spring of 2941.

The partygoers were thirteen Dwarves who arrived on Bilbo's doorstep that fine morning, and their and Bilbo's exploits are recounted in *The Hobbit*. A few aspects of their journey there and back again should be mentioned here: First, Bilbo revealed an unexpected streak of ingenuity and practical wisdom at various points, even though the Dwarves, who tended to be somewhat patronizing, continually expressed doubts about his abilities. Bilbo repeatedly showed resourcefulness, but the Dwarves operated on the principle of "what have you done for us lately?" Second, in an exploit quite unrelated to the purpose of his journey with the Dwarves, Bilbo acquired a magic ring that usefully made him invisible when he wore it. Other properties of the ring became manifest later. Third, Bilbo acquired two valuable objects: a short sword, which he named Sting after it helped him vanquish the spiders of Mirkwood, and a coat of mail made of *mithril*, or true silver, that Thorin gave him from the wealth of Smaug's horde. Fourth, the journey enabled Bilbo, already well-to-do, to amass dragon treasure and troll gold and return to his beloved homeland a very rich hobbit. (Frodo later said that Bilbo gave away the gold because it had been obtained in the first instance by theft.)

It might be noted here that although Bilbo was a typical hobbit in many ways, loving his snug home, his creature comforts, and his daily routines, he was also unusual in being able to reach beyond ordinary existence. Writing to Rayner Unwin about a new edition of *The Hobbit* in 1965, Tolkien remarked that most Hobbits are devoid of any "spark": "Bilbo was specially selected by the authority and insight of Gandalf as *abnormal:* he had a good share of hobbit virtues: shrewd sense, generosity, patience, and fortitude, and also a strong 'spark' yet unkindled. The story and its sequel are not about 'types' or the cure of bourgeois smugness by wider experience, but about the achievements of specially graced and gifted individuals" (*Letters,* 365).

In any case, after his return to Bag End in June 2942, Bilbo resumed his peaceful ways: the Took part receded, and the Baggins part came forward. He spent later years in quiet deeds of good: he adopted his orphaned cousin Frodo and raised and educated him at Bag End. He taught his gardener's son, Sam Gamgee, to read and write. One of the odd qualities of the ring he had found seemed to be to slow the aging process. By the time Bilbo reached the age of 111, his eleventh-first birthday, he was looking remarkably well preserved.

But the ring's evil (for it was a very evil Ring) began to gain on Bilbo. He finally determined to give an immense party for his eleventh-first birthday, which also happened to be Frodo's thirty-third, and thereafter to leave the Shire. The Long-Expected Party was an amazing success: Gandalf the wizard provided fireworks; there was food and drink enough even for hobbits; at last Bilbo made a short speech at the conclusion of which he put on the Ring and instantly vanished. He did leave the Shire, and he was constrained to leave the Ring behind.

He made his way toward Rivendell, the Last Homely House East of the Sea and the home of Elrond Half-elven, which he had visited during his journey with the Dwarves, and he stopped there. After visiting Dale, he returned to Rivendell and made it his permanent home, writing memoirs and poems and napping. Frodo found him there on his own journey to the east many years later and found him again on the return from his quest.

We hear nothing of Frodo in *The Hobbit* and rather little of Bilbo in *The Lord of the Rings,* yet the relationship of the two hobbits colors the latter book. They are cousins, as Gaffer Gamgee explains, yet given their age and circumstances the terms uncle and nephew seem more truly descriptive. As Frodo sets out from Rivendell on his quest to lose the Ring, Bilbo bestows on him his own little sword, Sting, and the mail coat of *mithril* that the Dwarves had given him decades ago. These are not sentimental gifts; they turn out to be of lifesaving importance later. Thus, Bilbo's role in *The Lord of the Rings,* though indirect, is vital.

In the end, Bilbo finally achieves one of his cherished goals, to outlive the Old Took and become the longest-living Hobbit in recorded history by reaching his 131st birthday.

That day came September 22, 3021, as Bilbo was journeying to the Grey Havens with Elrond, Galadriel, and Gandalf. On September 29, he met Frodo there and with him and the others took a ship to the West and left Middle-earth forever.

His Actions and Their Meaning

Bilbo Baggins may be unusual among Hobbits, as Tolkien suggested, but as Tom Shippey says, always in these works of Tolkien's "hobbits are the bridge" (48).

The world of Middle-earth bears the coloration of medieval epic and romance, but Bilbo is unquenchably English and middle-class; he lives in the Shire, a world of high tea, umbrellas, and postal service. His anachronistic way of living is a means of entry, a mediating device, for readers. Beginning in the familiar and the unthreatening, we can more easily move into the strange, the glamorous, and the dangerous. Of course, Bilbo's Edwardian England is itself to some extent an anachronism to the twenty-first-century reader, but if it is archaic, it is not wholly arcane. Shippey's calling Bilbo a bourgeois burglar (Shippey, 10) suggests both the actuality and the potential of this remarkable individual. One small mark of Bilbo's unusual capabilities may be his rhetorical skill: few creatures of any sort can speak to dragons with any façade of self-possession, but Bilbo the hobbit can address Smaug with courtesy and aplomb.

A more important achievement of Bilbo's as the "gifted individual" Tolkien mentioned is his literary art. Bilbo's writings begin all that we know of Middle-earth. Tolkien's pose as historian, transcriber, and translator of Middle-earth records starts with *The Red Book of Westmarch* that, with additions, was the later name for Bilbo's account of his adventures, called *There and Back Again,* to which Frodo added the story of his own quest. Bilbo began writing his story before he left the Shire in 3001, continued it sporadically during his stay in Rivendell, but at last gave it to Frodo to supplement and finish when the younger Hobbit passed back through Rivendell after the Quest was over. At the same time, he gave Frodo three books bound in red leather titled *Translations from the Elvish, by B.B.* Tolkien quite rightly describes these volumes as "a work of great skill and learning" (*FR*, Prologue, 24). Frodo gave the entire compendium, now known as the *Red Book,* to Sam when the former left Middle-earth in September 3021, so as "to keep alive the memory of the age that is gone" (*RK*, VI, ix, 309).

Skillful as Bilbo may be as historian and translator, he is equally accomplished and better known as a poet, or at least a lyricist. (Many of his verses seem to have been set to music.) In *The Fellowship of the Ring* alone, there are ten poems composed by hobbits: of these, Bilbo wrote eight (Sam has one on trolls, and Frodo has one on the passing of Gandalf). His poems include several that are favorite songs among his hobbit acquaintances, such as "The Road Goes Ever On and On" and "I Sit Beside the Fire and Think." Certainly, in a hobbit society in which "many never reach" their letters, Bilbo's work as a prolific versifier is not the least of his accomplishments.

MICHAEL N. STANTON

Further Reading

Crabbe, Katharyn. "The Quest as Fairy Tale." Chap. 2 in *J.R.R. Tolkien*. Revised and Expanded edition. New York: Continuum, 1988.

Green, William H. *"The Hobbit": A Journey into Maturity*. New York: Twayne, 1995.

Helms, Randel. "The Hobbit as Swain." Chap. 3 in *Tolkien's World*. Boston: Houghton Mifflin, 1974.

Matthews, Dorothy. "The Psychological Journey of Bilbo Baggins." In *A Tolkien Compass*, edited by Jared Lobdell, 29–42. La Salle, IL: Open Court, 1975.

Scull, Christina. "*The Hobbit* Considered in Relation to Children's Literature Contemporary with Its Writing and Publication." *Mythlore* 14, no. 2, whole no. 50 (1987): 49–56.

Shippey, Tom. *J.R.R. Tolkien: Author of the Century*. Boston, MA: Houghton Mifflin, 2000.

Wytenbrook, J.P. "Rites of Passage in *The Hobbit*." *Mythlore* 13, no. 4, whole no. 52 (1987): 5–8.

See also **Beorn; Dwarves; Frodo; Gandalf; Hobbits; Hobbiton; Shire**

BIOLOGY OF MIDDLE-EARTH

In principle, the biological rules of our primary world also apply to Middle-earth; after all, Middle-earth is our world (*Letters,* 186; 220). The same is true for the basic principles of evolution—variation and natural selection—which result in adaptation to differing environmental circumstances. Tolkien was aware of these principles, and he knew the correct definitions of "species" and "race" in zoology: two animals belong to one species if they can produce fertile offspring. If clearly definable differences occur within one species, the developing systematic units are called subspecies, breeds (domesticated), and races.

Tolkien noted that "Elves and Men are evidently in biological terms one race, or they could not breed and produce fertile offspring" (*Letters,* 189), thereby describing an inbreeding group that is not a race but a species. However, he often uses biological terms correctly—for example, when describing Hobbits as "really meant to be a branch of the specifically human race" (*Letters,* no. 131, p. 158), in pointing out that the Drúedain show "racial difference[s]" (*UT,* 385), and in counting Men as "Second Race" (*Letters,* no. 153, p. 189).

However, Elves, Men, and Dwarves are created differently, which poses a problem in using scientific terms. Tolkien usually circumvents this by introducing "kindred" for races. Thus Eärendil is "representative of both Kindreds, Elves and Men" (*Letters,* 150). This shows that, for Tolkien, the concept of *origo gentis* (history of bloodline) was more important than the point of view of the biological sciences.

Examples of "regular" evolution in Middle-earth are hobbits and Drúedain. Their dwindling is explained by typical processes of selection; the dwindling of the hobbits "must be due to a change in their state and way of life" (*UT,* 287). Similar circumstances are reported for the Drúedain (*UT,* 383).

Although Trolls and dragons are products of deliberate breeding, this is not explicitly clear for Orcs. *The Silmarillion* gives two Elvish theories on the origin of Orcs. The first one states that Melkor bred Orcs from Elves "by slow arts of cruelty . . . corrupted and enslaved" (*S,* 47), designed to be "mockeries of the Children of Ilúvatar" (*S,* 310). The second hypothesis assumes Orcs were "perhaps . . . Avari who had become evil and savage in the wild" (*S,* 102), which would be a case of typical evolution. Other texts show further theories ranging from "Morgoth . . . bred Orcs from various kinds of Men" (*UT,* 385) to crossbreeding with lesser "spirits" like Maiar (*Morgoth,* 409–24). The fact is that Orcs are ordinary living beings; they "had life and multiplied after the manner of the Children of Ilúvatar" (*S,* 47) and did not spring from mud holes.

The exact origin of Trolls, perhaps from giant apes but possibly from Men, Orcs, or "Spirits," is not known, but all of these were breeds for the purposes of Melkor and Sauron (*Morgoth,* 414). Tolkien calls Trolls "the older race of the Twilight" (*RK,* Appendix F, 410), but whether the different kinds of Trolls really belonged to one species remains unknown: "But there are other sorts of Trolls beside these . . . Stone-trolls, for which other origins are suggested" (*Letters,* 190).

Dragons belong to the "many evil things that Morgoth has devised in the days of his dominion" (*S,* 310) and were probably bred from snakes (they have "serpent-eyes" [*S,* 255]). The first dragons were the wingless Urulóki (Quenya: "fire serpent"), which were intelligent and able to breathe fire. Later, Melkor bred two variants: cold-drakes, which were capable of flight but could not breathe fire, and firedrakes, which were bad fliers but could produce a fire strong enough to destroy Rings of Power, except the One Ring (*FR,* I, ii, 70). Some of these creatures were still living in the Third Age (like Smaug). To achieve this, Melkor might have inbred giant eagles with snakes or Urulóki, and it is unclear whether they are races or separate species.

The giant spiders of Middle-earth all descended from "Ungoliante the primeval devourer of light" (*Letters,* 188). This is an example of evolution through successive degeneration: in comparison, Shelob is only as big as a horse, and the giant spiders mentioned in *The Hobbit* are even smaller and less intelligent.

Ents occupy a place between fauna and flora, showing characteristics from both realms. They could be intelligent and mobile plants that, because of a lack of roots, receive nutrition from various fluids. Or they could be animals with certain plant-like characteristics. However, both explanations fit the description of the creation of the Ents as given in *The Silmarillion* (41).

The *longevity* of Elves, whose spirits endure as long as the world lasts, and some Men is altogether different from the *immortality* that, for example, the Ainur possess (*Letters*, 285; 189). Longevity can actually be explained in biological terms. Single-celled organisms are potentially immortal. Differentiation in multi-celled organisms is paid for with mortality. If this were different with Elves, their aging could come to near-total standstill. In Half-elves, Quarter-elves, and so on, different aging processes could then take place.

Longevity in the Ring-bearers, on the other hand, is a modification caused by the external influence of the Ring. Regarding longevity and immortality, Tolkien wrote "that each 'kind' has a natural span, integral to its biological and spiritual nature" (*Letters*, 155). If this natural span is extended beyond its limit, it becomes "like stretching a wire," as in Bilbo's case. Even in the "immortal lands" nobody becomes actually immortal, since this "is strictly only a temporary reward: a healing and redress of suffering" (*Letters*, 198). The only exceptions to this, Lúthien and Tuor, are the result of "a direct act of God" (*Letters*, 194)—which is no longer part of the explanatory powers of biology.

FRIEDHELM SCHNEIDEWIND

Further Reading

Schneidewind, Friedhelm. "Biologie, Abstammung und Moral." In *Eine Grammatik der Ethik: Die Aktualität der moralischen Dimension in J.R.R. Tolkien's literarischem Werk*, edited by Thomas Honegger et al. Edition Stein und Baum. Saarbrücken: Verlag der Villa Fledermaus, 2005.

———. "Biologie, Genetik und Evolution in Mittelerde." In *Tolkien's Weltbild(er)*, edited by Thomas Fornet-Ponse et al. Hither Shore 2. Interdisciplinary Journal on Modern Fantasy Literature. Jahrbuch der Deutschen Tolkien Gesellschaft e. V. (DTG). Düsseldorf: Scriptorium Oxoniae, 2006.

———. "Einfach in sie eintreten: Biologie, Genetik und Evolution in Mittelerde." In *Das dritte Zeitalter*, edited by Thomas Le Blanc. Tagungsband zu den 25. Phantastischen Tagen 2005. Wetzlar: Phantastische Bibliothek Wetzlar, 2006.

———. "Drachenfeuer: Biologie und Mythos. Die biologischen Grundlagen real möglicher Drachen." In *Wie es wirklich war: Mittelerde ist unsere Welt*, edited by Friedhelm Schneidewind and Frank Weinreich. Edition Stein und Baum. Saarbrücken: Verlag der Villa Fledermaus, 2006.

See also **Dragons; Elves; Ents; Men; Spiders; Trolls; Ungoliant**

BLISS, ALAN (1921–1985)

In the years between 1928 and 1937, Tolkien lectured specifically on the story of Finn and Hengest, each lecture varying in focus. After presenting his work "Hengest and the Jutes" to the Dublin Medieval Society, Alan Bliss discovered that he would not be able to publish this paper because Tolkien had anticipated his conclusions. When meeting with Tolkien in 1966, Bliss explained how his own work would be impossible to publish because Tolkien's work precluded his own. Tolkien offered all of his material to Bliss, but he wished to organize it before giving it up. Upon Tolkien's death in 1973, Bliss had not received the work. It was not until 1979, when providing "indispensable information about his father's methods of work," Christopher Tolkien encouraged Bliss to undertake the project (Bliss 1998, ix).

From this material Bliss sought to produce a text completely in Tolkien's own words. The lectures and material, which had never been prepared for publication, dated from 1928 through 1960. Bliss faced with the problem of dating the various manuscripts and then organizing them into a definitive version. The help of Professor Jack Arthur Walter Bennett, who lent Bliss his 1934–35 notes on Tolkien's lectures, partly solved this issue. As editor, Bliss provided four parts compiled from "a patchwork of material" (Bliss 1998, vii): a study of names, a chronology of the story Fragment and Episode, notes on the Episode text, and a reconstruction of the overall tale (Bliss 1998, vi). The completed text by Bliss provides Tolkien's most comprehensive version of his lectures. Bliss supplies a few words of his own within brackets where ideas or the argument is not clearly explained from the material. The fruits of his labor would later become *Finn and Hengest: The Fragment and the Episode*. It was first published in the United Kingdom in 1982.

ANTHONY S. BURDGE and JESSICA BURKE

Further Reading

Bliss, Alan, ed. *Finn and Hengest: The Fragment and the Episode*. London: HarperCollins, 1998.

See also **Bennett, Jack Arthur Walter;** *Finn and Hengest*; **Tolkien, Christopher; Tolkien, J.R.R.**

BODLEIAN LIBRARY, OXFORD

The Bodleian Library is the main research library of the University of Oxford. It is the largest of many libraries, including college and department faculty libraries, that are part of the university. Its principal building, the Old Bodleian, dates from the fifteenth to seventeenth centuries and includes Duke Humfrey's Library and the Divinity School. Besides book stacks, the Bodleian contains many reading rooms where research may be conducted, because no borrowing from the library is permitted. Dons and students of the university frequently visit the Bodleian to consult books and manuscripts as their research and study interests dictate.

Tolkien worked with medieval manuscripts from many libraries. His principal published works studying material held in manuscript at the Bodleian are his edition of and commentary on *The Old English Exodus,* found in the Bodleian's MS Junius 11, and several scholarly papers on the Middle English collection known as the Katherine Group, MS Bodley 34. Much of this work, particularly two studies of MS Bodley 34 written in collaboration with Simonne d'Ardenne, is based on close physical examination of the manuscripts.

Many of Tolkien's papers have been donated by his family to the Bodleian Library. These holdings include manuscripts, typescripts, proofs, and correspondence relating to most of his books (except for the material acquired by Marquette University); unpublished fictional material; artwork including illustrations to his books (some formerly held by the Ashmolean Museum); lecture drafts and other academic working papers, including translations of *Beowulf;* editions and translations of his works (many donated by HarperCollins); books from his personal collection; and family papers. The Department of Western Manuscripts holds the Tolkien papers and has organized exhibitions of this material. Except for the family papers, which are still restricted, the Tolkien papers are open to scholarly use.

DAVID BRATMAN

See also **Education;** *Exodus,* **Edition of; Katherine Group; Manuscripts; Oxford; Manuscripts: Unpublished**

BOOK OF LOST TALES I

The Project

Published in 1983, three years after *Unfinished Tales, The Book of Lost Tales: Part I*—the first of twelve volumes of *The History of Middle-earth (HoM–e)*—is composed of ten principal sections plus a foreword, "Appendix on Names," (English) glossary, and index. These chapters correspond, roughly, to the first part of the published *Silmarillion.* That correspondence points to the difference between *HoM–e* and Tolkien's other posthumous publications—whereas *The Silmarillion* presented a finished text and *Unfinished Tales of Númenor and Middle-earth* offered edited drafts of previously unpublished material, accompanied by Christopher Tolkien's notes and commentary, *HoM–e* was to consist largely of drafts and alternate versions of *already published* tales.

In the foreword, Christopher Tolkien sets out his intention for *HoM–e*—to provide a "longitudinal" view of the legendarium, as opposed to the "transverse" view created by publication of *The Silmarillion* (*Lost Tales I,* 7–8). He begins from his response to Tom Shippey's *The Road to Middle-earth.* Shippey postulates that part of the force of *The Lord of the Rings* comes from the "depth" created by references to such stories of the Elder Days as the "Tale of Beren and Lúthien" (Shippey, 260–61). Citing Tolkien's letter of September 20, 1963 (*Letters,* 353), Shippey argues that in the "Silmarillion" the author faced the problem of telling stories from such early times that there could be no "impression of depth." Christopher Tolkien responds, first, that depth cannot be the sole criterion of literary success and, second, that depth depends not on the time of the story but rather on the reader's imagined viewpoint. Although the stories in *The Silmarillion* narrate events of various periods, the compilation as a whole is to be thought of as an artifact of the end of the Third Age; moreover, the "compendious" style of the collection preserves a sense of distance (*Lost Tales I,* 4).

Christopher Tolkien feels, nonetheless, that once *The Lord of the Rings* had appeared it was a mistake to publish *The Silmarillion* without a fictional provenance, as if it were "self-explanatory." His father had abandoned the original framing device of *Lost Tales* without explicitly developing another. *The Lord of the Rings* suggests, however, that the "Silmarillion" formed part of Bilbo's translations from the Elvish included in *The Thain's Book* (*FR,* Prologue, 24). Christopher Tolkien had been reluctant to rely on this idea in preparing *The Silmarillion*—a decision that, in retrospect, he regrets. That the book would appear without a "history" led to the presentation of its contents as a single coherent text, and the single text has, in turn, produced critical misapprehensions about the place of the "Silmarillion" in his father's work and about the nature of his own contribution to *The Silmarillion* (*Lost Tales I,* 5–7).

HoM–e will, then, correct the misunderstandings created by *The Silmarillion;* its editor hopes, however, that the development of his father's conception over the course of some five decades will be of interest in itself. The series will also present elements of the legendarium that did not survive into *The Silmarillion* but had not necessarily been explicitly rejected by Tolkien. To accomplish these purposes, Christopher Tolkien adopts a format like that of *Unfinished Tales of Númenor and Middle-earth,* presenting a master version of each narrative and giving separately at the end of the chapter notes, name changes (frequent in his father's palimpsestic pencil-and-pen notebooks), and commentary. This conscious compromise between an ordinary reader's text and a variorum edition with a formal scholarly apparatus (*Lost Tales I,* 10) has predictably left some members of the general public, as well as some scholars, dissatisfied.

Summary and Discussion

Although Christopher Tolkien presents the ten chapters of *Lost Tales I* in their fictional historical order— "The Cottage of Lost Play" (13–44); "The Music of the Ainur" (45–63); "The Coming of the Valar and the Building of Valinor" (64–93); "The Chaining of Melko" (94–112); "The Coming of the Elves and the Making of Kôr" (113–39); "The Theft of Melko and the Darkening of Valinor" (140–61); "The Flight of the Noldoli" (162–73); "The Tale of the Sun and Moon" (174–206); "The Hiding of Valinor" (207–28); and "Gilfanon's Tale: The Travail of the Noldoli and the Coming of Mankind" (229–45)—he is at pains to establish their actual dates. He traces "Cottage"—the earliest stratum of *Lost Tales I* itself, though not the oldest part of the legendarium—to 1916 and 1917, when his father was twenty-five (*Lost Tales I,* 8). Tolkien comments in a 1964 letter that he wrote a "cosmogonical myth" (presumably "Music") when he was working at the Oxford English Dictionary—that is, between late 1918 and early 1920 (*Letters,* 345). As the other eight chapters seem to have been composed continuously with "Music," and in several cases follow on directly in the manuscripts, they appear to date from the same period. In addition to the narrative chapters, Christopher Tolkien includes in his commentary an early sketch map (*Lost Tales I,* 81), a drawing of the world conceived as a ship (84), and a number of his father's poems, sometimes in multiple versions but all originally dating from 1914 to 1916: *You and Me and the Cottage of Lost Play* (27–31); *Kortirion among the Trees* (32–43); *Habbanan beneath the Stars* (91–92); *Tinfang Warble* (108); *Over Old Hills and Far Away* (108–10); *Kôr*

(136); *A Song of Aryador* (138); and *Why the Man in the Moon came down too soon* (204–6). Finally, the appendix (246–73) draws on two dictionaries: the *Qenya Lexicon* (so-named by the editor), datable to 1915 (and thus reflecting an earlier stage of development than most of the stories), and *i·Lam na·Ngoldathon* (The Tongue of the Gnomes): *Goldogrin,* which actually bears the date 1917.

Nearly every page of *Lost Tales I* contains some new information, not all of it equally significant: early versions of particular names (Melko versus Melkor, Inwë versus Ingwë) attract less attention than the first account of the creation of the Sun and Moon. Most noteworthy among the major items is the "framing story" already alluded to (Christopher Tolkien points out that it is not precisely a frame, because its resolution would also resolve the included narrative). In Tolkien's 1915 conception, Tol Eressëa, the Lonely Island, was the dwelling of those fairies who, having left Valinor to battle Melko and retreated in defeat after the Fall of Gondolin, were now awaiting a "Faring Forth" to rescue their Noldorin kindred still in the "Great Lands" (Tolkien did not adopt "Middle-earth" until the 1930s). Ulmo would uproot the island and draw it near the Great Lands in preparation for this new battle. The fairies would be defeated again, through human treachery, and retreat to the island, followed closely by humans. As the fairies diminished, the island would become human England. Eriol "Wæfre" (Old English "wanderer," parallel to Old Norse "Gangleri," "Wanderer," in Sturulson's *Prose Edda,* cf. Flieger 2000, 186), a human mariner—a figurative "son of Eärendil"— would come to the Lonely Island between the Fall of Gondolin and the Faring Forth and hear, first in the tiny Cottage of Lost Play then later in Kortirion at the house of Meril-i-Turinqui, the stories that made up the projected *Book of Lost Tales* (*Lost Tales I,* 23–27). The first of these would be the story of the Cottage of Lost Play itself, built to replace the Cottage of the Play of Sleep, near Kôr in Valinor, to which human children once came in their dreams.

For readers of the later works, the most noteworthy overall feature of these early drafts is how much Tolkien would later reject. Some of this abandoned material is on the grand scale of mythology—the archaizing style (mandating the glossary) and Valar who, like Olympians, have children. Other concepts hint of late-Victorian preciousness, for example, the diminutive Elves and Valinor as a children's dreamland. At the same time, some rejected elements clarify Tolkien's oft-cited desire to remedy the "poverty" of English story and legend (cf. *Letters,* 144): Tol Eressëa is Great Britain, with Kortirion ancestral to Warwick and Tavrobel to Great Haywood, and Eriol the mariner is an Angle, father of the Hengest and Horsa who were the leaders of the fifth-century Anglo-Saxon invasion. Moreover, some rejected materials reinforce that mapping of the legendarium onto the romance of Edith Bratt and Ronald Tolkien to which the couple's tombstone, with its inscription of "Lúthien" and "Beren," testifies. Warwick/Kortirion is where Edith lived for the three years before her marriage, and Great Haywood/Tavrobel where she lived after it; *You and Me and the Cottage of Lost Play* depicts the fair-haired speaker and his dark-haired love as children who met in that dream-cottage.

JOHN WM. HOUGHTON

Further Reading

Carpenter, Humphrey. *J.R.R. Tolkien: A Biography*. London: George Allen & Unwin, 1977.

Flieger, Verlyn. *A Question of Time: J.R.R. Tolkien's Road to Faërie*. Kent, OH: Kent State University Press, 1997.

———. "The Footsteps of Aelfwine." In *Tolkien's Legendarium: Essays on "The History of Middle-earth,"* edited by Verlyn Flieger and Carl F. Hostetter, 183–98. Westport, CT: Greenwood, 2000.

Garth, John. *Tolkien and the Great War: The Threshold of Middle-earth*. Boston, MA: Houghton Mifflin, 2003.

Shippey, Tom. *The Road to Middle-earth*. Revised and Expanded edition. Boston, MA: Houghton Mifflin, 2003. London: HarperCollins, 2005.

See also **Arda**; *Book of Lost Tales II*; **Elves; Fairies; Fall of Man;** *Finn and Hengest*; **Frame Narrative; Great Haywood; History, Anglo-Saxon;** *History of Middle-earth:* **Overview; Kôr; Mythology for England;** *Silmarillion, The*; **Tavrobel; Tol Eressëa; Valar; Valinor; Warwick**

BOOK OF LOST TALES II

The Book of Lost Tales was Tolkien's first attempt to tell the history of Valinor and Middle-earth. He began the tales in 1916 when he was in his twenties and still a soldier in the Great War. He left the work unfinished when, approximately ten years later, he began writing narrative poems based on his developing mythology of the Elder Days. Published in two volumes in 1983 and 1984, the tales are arranged according to Tolkien's ordering and not according to their chronological composition. *Part II* contains four complete tales written in archaic but vigorous prose: "The Tale of Tinúviel," "Turambar and the Foalókë," "The Fall of Gondolin," and "The Nauglafring." In addition, the volume contains detailed examination of materials for the unwritten "Tale of

Eärendel," and discussion of the materials constituting "The History of Eriol or Ælfwine and the End of the Tales."

"The Tale of Tinúviel"

"The Tale of Tinúviel," written in 1917, is the first of three tales in *Part II* set partly in the Elven realm of Artanor, ruled by King Tinwelint and Queen Gwendeling, and hidden from Melko by Gwendeling's magic. It tells the love story of Beren and Tinúviel and their capture of a Silmaril from Melko's crown.

Beren, a Gnome from Hisilómë, a northern land of Gnomes and Men, crosses the Iron Mountains and wanders into Artanor, where he observes the Elven maiden Tinúviel, daughter of Tinwelint and Gwendeling, dancing in the woods, and immediately loves her. Tinúviel is fearful at first, but perceiving his love, she loses her fear and leads Beren before her parents. Tinwelint views Beren with suspicion and asks what he desires. Beren says he desires Tinúviel. Tinwelint scornfully says that if Beren brings him a Silmaril from the crown of Melko, he will allow Beren to marry Tinúviel. Beren returns his scorn by saying he will fulfill the King's small desire and so departs, leaving all in astonishment and Tinúviel in tears, because she knows Beren will likely die in the perilous attempt.

Beren makes an arduous journey to Melko's stronghold, but he is captured by Orcs and brought before Melko, who spares his life but makes him a thrall of Tevildo, Prince of Cats.

Meanwhile, through magic Gwendeling perceives Beren's peril and informs Tinúviel, who vows to rescue him, but Tinwelint imprisons her in a high tree house to prevent her attempt. Tinúviel casts a spell that makes her hair grow to an extraordinary length. From her hair she weaves a robe imbued with magic to induce sleep and a long rope with which she descends from the tree house and escapes.

Journeying towards Tevildo's castle, Tinúviel is befriended by Huan, Captain of Dogs, the chief foes of Tevildo. They lure Tevildo into a surprise attack, and Huan forces him to reveal the secret spell of cats. Armed with this, Tinúviel shrinks the cats in the castle to puny size, and they flee in fear. Thus unimpeded, she rescues Beren from his oppressive thralldom.

Once Beren recovers his strength, he and Tinúviel devise a plan to capture a Silmaril. Tinúviel disguises Beren as one of Tevildo's thanes, she dons her magic robe, and they proceed towards the fortress of Angamandi. Tinúviel's robe makes Karkaras, the fierce wolf who guards the entrance, fall asleep. Once inside, Tinúviel beguiles Melko and all his folk with dancing, and as her robe touches them, they fall asleep. When Melko's head droops, the iron crown falls off, and Beren cuts out the Silmaril. Departing swiftly, they find Karkaras awake. Beren fights him, and Karkaras bites off Beren's hand that holds the Silmaril. Driven mad by Fëanor's jewel burning within his belly, Karkaras runs into the wilderness.

Beren and Tinúviel return to King Tinwelint, who is moved to love Beren for his courage. With Huan's help, they hunt and slay Karkaras and so recover the Silmaril, but Beren is hurt to death in the fight. Tinúviel appeals to Mandos, who has pity and reanimates Beren but makes both lovers mortal. Nevertheless, they spend many years together in happiness.

"Turambar and the Foalókë"

This tale, which was in existence by the middle of 1919, takes place when Men first inhabited Hisilómë after the Battle of Unnumbered Tears, in which Melko destroyed nearly all his adversaries and enslaved the Noldoli. Mavwin, wife of Úrin, a lord of Men who was captured by Melko in the battle, sends her young son Túrin to be fostered by King Tinwelint in Artanor, over Túrin's tearful objections. An outsider among the Hidden Elves, Túrin grows into a strong but gloomy young man of rough appearance and manners. After killing a taunting Elf in a moment of anger, Túrin spends his days in self-imposed exile, hunting in the far reaches of Artanor with his friend Beleg. There Túrin is captured by Orcs, and Beleg wanders long in search of him with the help of Flindling of the Noldoli. At last they find Túrin asleep and bound in an Orc camp, and Beleg frees him, but Túrin, startled awake and mistaking Beleg for an Orc in the dark, swiftly kills him. Anguished when he sees what he has done, Túrin thinks himself accursed.

Flindling takes Túrin to dwell with the Rodothlim Elves in their secret caves. There Túrin becomes so great a warrior and kills so many marauding Orcs that Melko becomes aware of the secret caves and sends against the Rodothlim a great host of Orcs and a fearsome dragon, a Foalókë, named Glorund. Nearly all Rodothlim warriors are slain in the fight, and Glorund captures the famed gold hoard of the Rodothlim. Glorund casts a tormenting spell on Túrin, tells him he is doomed to an evil fate, and puts in his heart a desire to return to his mother and sister, Nienóri, who was but an infant when he went to Artanor. Defying Glorund, Túrin renames himself

Turambar, Conqueror of Fate, but he is nevertheless spurred with the desire to seek his mother and sets out for Hisilómë.

When Turambar reaches his mother's house, he finds it empty and gone to seed because several years earlier Mavwin and Nienóri, now a grown woman, had gone to Artanor in search of him. Having no news of him, and thinking that perhaps Glorund has enthralled Túrin, Mavwin persuades Tinwelint to attack the Foalókë, who guards his hoard in the desolation of Rodothlim. The attack fails; Tinwelint's men are scattered, and Mavwin and Nienóri are captured by Glorund. The Foalókë casts a spell on them so that they swoon, and Nienóri awakens alone and without memory of her name or her past. She wanders, is captured by Orcs, and is rescued by Turambar, who takes her to dwell with Men known as the wood-rangers. He names her Níniel, one of little tears. They grow to love each other and eventually marry. Happy days follow; Turambar prospers, and his people grow strong.

The prosperity of Turambar's folk stirs envy in Glorund, and he attacks Turambar's realm. Turambar fights and mortally wounds the Foalókë but nearly dies. Níniel cannot revive him and thinks him dead. Glorund stirs and, with his dying breath, reveals to Níniel her true identity and that Turambar is her brother. In despair, Níniel casts herself over a waterfall to her death. Turambar awakens, learns what has befallen Níniel, and slays himself. Turambar and Níniel are entombed together. Many years later, Mavwin, bent with age, visits the tomb, and later folk believe that her anguished spirit haunts the spot.

Melko, holding Úrin imprisoned all this while, shows him a vision of the destruction of his family, persuades him that Tinwelint's cowardice led to their deaths, and releases him to work malice against Tinwelint. Úrin leads a band of men to recover the hoard of Glorund from the caves of the Rodothlim, which none have despoiled for fear of the spirit of the Foalókë. Úrin kills the hoard's only guardian, the Dwarf Mîm, who, dying, utters a curse that death shall follow the gold while it remains on earth. Úrin takes the gold to Artanor and casts it at Tinwelint's feet with scornful words. Tinwelint replies in kind. Úrin departs in anger, and their exchange later breeds estrangement between Elves and Men.

"The Fall of Gondolin"

"The Fall of Gondolin" was begun in 1916 in Birmingham or Great Heywood during Tolkien's convalescence from "trench fever" caused by a lice-borne bacterial infection he acquired at the Somme. The tale underwent extensive revisions before Tolkien read it aloud to the Essay Club of Exeter College in 1920. The published version is largely the 1920 text with some minor retentions from the 1916–17 version.

The focal character is a Man of Dor Lómin named Tuor, a huntsman and musician. Longing to wander unknown lands, Tuor leaves home and journeys to the shore of the Great Sea, where he dwells for several years alone. But, one day, seeing three swans flying south, he follows them until he comes to the Land of the Willows. Ulmo appears and tells Tuor that he must seek Gondolin, the hidden city of the Gondothlim Elves, and that there Ulmo shall give him a message for the Gondothlim. Tuor sets out and, with the aid of Voronwë of the Noldoli, finds after long searching the secret gate to Gondolin.

Tuor is brought before Turgon, King of the Gondothlim. Ulmo inspires him to say that Melko will muster forces to conquer Gondolin, and therefore Turgon must lead his people to safety in Valinor and must persuade the Valar to overthrow Melko. Turgon, whose people have spent many years fortifying the city, declines and says he will put his trust in the city's defenses. Voronwë weeps for what he fears will come from Turgon's decision.

Tuor remains in Gondolin, where he becomes highly esteemed. Tuor marries Turgon's daughter Idril, the first marriage of mortal Man and Elven maid, which pleases all save Meglin, a lord whose betrothal suit was refused by Idril. Gifted with foresight, Idril fears that Meglin's jealousy will grow malicious, and she asks Tuor to begin delving a secret escape tunnel from the city through the mountains. Tuor begins the work, which takes many years, but its secret is preserved.

Meanwhile, Meglin, quarrying outside the city, is captured by Orcs and brought before Melko, where, in exchange for his life, he divulges much information about Gondolin and its defenses and assists Melko in planning the conquest of the city. Melko musters forces for seven years and then attacks Gondolin with fire-drakes, Balrogs, and a great host of Orcs. While Tuor and the hosts of Gondothlim meet Melko's onslaught, Meglin threatens to kill Eärendel, the child of Idril and Tuor, unless Idril shows him the secret tunnel of which he has heard rumors. Returning at that moment to secure his family, Tuor kills Meglin. The forces of Melko finally overwhelm the Gondothlim, kill King Turgon, and burn the city. Tuor leads the survivors to safety through the escape tunnel. Nevertheless, they are pursued over the mountains by Orcs, whom they defeat with the help of eagles. Tuor leads the people to dwell by the Great Sea at the mouth of the river Sirion.

"The Nauglafring"

The last of the *Lost Tales* to be written, "The Nauglafring" tells the tragic history of the accursed gold of Glorund. After the angry departure of Úrin from Artanor, the Men with whom he recovered the hoard fight Tinwelint's Elves for the gold. Tinwelint's warriors prevail, but the fight is bitter, and the gold, in accord with Mîm's curse, is drenched with blood. Gwenniel (alternately, Gwendelin) counsels Tinwelint to cast the gold away, but Ufedhin, a Gnome who had dwelt among the Dwarves (the Nauglath) of Nogrod, guilefully counsels Tinwelint to allow half the gold to be worked by the Dwarves, whose skill in metalcraft is unsurpassed, and, if Tinwelint approves the treasures they make, to allow them to craft the other half. Tinwelint, whose heart has been pierced by the gold's glamour, agrees but holds Ufedhin hostage as a surety for the Dwarves' return.

The Dwarves craft wondrous vessels, rings, bracelets, collars, and coronets. Delighted, Tinwelint gives the Dwarves the remainder but holds them imprisoned in Artanor to craft it. The Dwarves fashion more treasures, and last of all they make the Nauglafring, a necklace of matchless beauty, and they persuade Tinwelint to allow them to set in it the Silmaril recovered by Beren and Tinúviel. Dazzled, Tinwelint puts on the Nauglafring. The Dwarves then request a rich reward for their labor, including an Elven maid for each Dwarf. Tinwelint, whose mind now works under the curse of Mîm, has them whipped for their insolence and sends them away with only a few trifling jewels.

The Dwarves return home to Nogrod, where their lord, Naugladur, hearing of their treatment, resolves to attack Artanor with a host of Dwarves of Nogrod, their kindred allies the Indrafangs, and Orcs. Narthseg, a traitorous Elf, leads Naugladur's forces through Gwendelin's magic defenses into Artanor. They slay Tinwelint and many Elves and ransack the kingdom, and Naugladur takes the Nauglafring. Ufedhin attempts unsuccessfully to steal the Nauglafring, and fighting breaks out among the Dwarves, which results in an age–long feud among the Dwarf kindred. Ufedhim gains nothing for his effort but grief and flees alone into wild lands.

Huan, Captain of Dogs and friend of Tinwelint, goes to Hithlum and tells Beren of the conquest of

Artanor. Beren leads a host of Elves against the Dwarves as they attempt to cross the river Aros. The Dwarves are slain, and Beren kills Naugladur in single combat and takes the Nauglafring, but the rest of the golden treasures are lost in the river Aros. Beren gives the Nauglafring to Tinúviel, who wears it only briefly before declining to keep it. The curse of Mîm nevertheless falls upon her, the mortality decreed by Mandos quickly comes to her, and she fades from life. Beren, wretched without her, fades into death shortly thereafter and leaves the Nauglafring to his son Dior, who wears it openly in Hisilómë.

Word of the Nauglafring reaches the sons of Fëanor, who, having vowed to regain the Silmarils, resolve to conquer Dior's folk in the first premeditated war of Elves with Elves. The battle is bitter for both sides: Dior, his son Auredhir, and several sons of Fëanor are slain. Though Fëanor's sons prevail, they do not win the Silmaril, for Dior's unhappy people scatter and bear the Nauglafring away with them. The fortunes of the Elves reach their nadir, because on the same day of this battle, Melko launches his attack on Gondolin. Elwing, the sole surviving descendant of Beren, journeys to the lands by the mouth of the Sirion and joins Tuor's people, the survivors of the destruction of Gondolin.

"The Tale of Eärendel"

Had "The Tale of Eärendel" been written, it would, according to Christopher Tolkien, have been nearly half the length of all completed *Lost Tales* combined. The extant outlines and notes are contradictory and thus tell an unclear story of Eärendel's voyages, but the main events and features can be summarized.

The tale begins where "The Nauglafring" ends, with the coming of Elwing, granddaughter of Beren, to Tuor's folk, the survivors of Gondolin, dwelling at the mouth of the Sirion. Elwing and Eärendel fall in love as children. Tuor, now growing old, hears Ulmo's conches and sets sail in secret to find Ulmo. Believing her husband Tuor may have gone to the halls of Mandos, Idril, grieving, asks Eärendel to pursue his father even to Mandos. Eärendel obeys, but his ship is wrecked, perhaps because of Mîm's curse. He is saved by Ulmo, who tells him, for a reason never explained, that he must sail to Kôr, the Elves' city in Eldamar. Eärendel returns to the mouth of the Sirion. He sets sail a second time, perhaps to search for Tuor or to reach Kôr, and is again wrecked, this time by Ossë, who is attempting to fulfill the curse of Mîm. Mermaids save Eärendel, and he

returns to Sirion. There he hears Ulmo's conches, builds a great ship named Wingilot, and sails to Kôr, but he finds it empty because the Elves have gone into the world. In Kôr he is covered with gleaming diamond dust. Returning to Sirion, he finds it has been sacked and is deserted. He journeys by land to the ruins of Gondolin. He learns from Men that Melko has been bound after great wars, that the Elves have departed to Tol Eressëa, and that Elwing has faded under the curse of Mîm and has become a seabird. He sails for seven years in search of Elwing but perhaps also in search of Mandos. He reaches the edge of the world and sets sail in the oceans of the firmament to gaze over the world and continue his search for Elwing. His great grief makes him shine like a star.

"The History of Eriol or Ælfwine and the End of the Tales"

Christopher Tolkien devotes the last section of *Part II* to piecing together the diverse early materials concerning the end of the earliest version of the mythology. The story elements can be summarized chronologically as follows.

The Eldar depart from the Great Lands for Valinor against the will of the Valar. The Valar refuse to allow the Eldar to reenter Valinor. The Eldar settle on Tol Eressëa. Tulkas defeats Melko. The Man Eriol sails to Tol Eressëa, dwells in Kortirion, learns the ancient lore of the Valar and the Elves, and writes it down. Eriol marries and has a Half-elven son named Heorrenda. The Lost Elves overcome the servants of Melko and journey to Tol Eressëa. Ulmo and Uin the whale drag Tol Eressëa eastward to the geographic position of England, but Ossë tries to drag the island back westward and breaks off the portion that becomes Ireland. Evil Men and Orcs conquer Tol Eressëa. The Elves fade to near invisibility to the sight of Men. The sons of Eriol conquer Tol Eressëa but are not hostile to the faded Elves. Tol Eressëa becomes England, and Kortirion becomes Warwick. Then, Heorrenda compiles and completes Eriol's writings as the *Golden Book of Tavrobel*, which contains the *Lost Tales*.

In 1920 or later, subsequent to the writing of the *Lost Tales*, Tolkien made notes and outlines for a reframing of the entire work. In the second scheme, whose materials Christopher Tolkien discusses in detail, Eriol is replaced by Ælfwine, a Man of eleventh-century Wessex. Ælfwine sails from England, called Luthany, where Elves once dwelt, to Tol Eressëa, where they came to dwell, and there he learns and records the lore of the Elves.

Christopher Tolkien's Commentary

In his foreword to *Part I,* Christopher Tolkien discusses the ambivalent reception that greeted *The Silmarillion* in 1977. The foreword is partly Christopher's defense of his decision to publish the legends of the Elder Days as a coherent narrative in a single volume, but he acknowledges that this decision led to the misperception that the scheme of *The Silmarillion* is his invention and not his father's. To some extent, this misperception motivated Christopher to publish the *Lost Tales* and their diverging attendant materials in all their complexity.

To aid understanding and correct misapprehension, Christopher's commentary for each of the completed tales compares their features to their counterpart versions in *The Silmarillion.* Where applicable, Christopher comments on related texts. In "The Tale of Tinúviel," he discusses *The Lay of Leithian,* Tolkien's ambitious narrative poem published in *The Lays of Beleriand,* which, although based on the tale, contains extensive development of several elements: the most notable change is that Beren is a Man and not a Gnome. "Turambar and the Foalókë" includes discussion of "Narn i Hîn Húrin," published in *Unfinished Tales.* And, "The Fall of Gondolin" includes commentary on "Of Tuor and His Coming to Gondolin," also published in *Unfinished Tales.*

Additional Reading

In addition to the related texts listed above, several critical works offer help in understanding the tales of *Part II* and the context in which Tolkien created them. Humphrey Carpenter's *Tolkien: A Biography* is the baseline text for understanding Tolkien's life and work: the first three sections of the book are relevant to *Part II.* John Garth's *Tolkien and the Great War* provides an invaluable background to *Part II* by elucidating the life, thought, ambitions, writings in verse and prose, and influential friendships of young Tolkien from his childhood to 1919. Garth's book comments on several of the tales and gives extensive treatment to "The Fall of Gondolin" in the specific context of Tolkien's wartime experiences.

Two essays in the anthology *Tolkien's Legendarium* provide helpful discussions of specific tales: Verlyn

Flieger's "In the Footsteps of Ælfwine" comments on "The History of Eriol or Ælfwine" in the context of Tolkien's "elf-friends," and Richard West's "Túrin's *Ofermod*" provides insight on "Turambar and the Foalókë" in discussing the development of the Túrin legend.

Several works discuss *Part II* in the context of the larger "Silmarillion." Christina Scull's "The Development of Tolkien's Legendarium" in *Tolkien's Legendarium* treats the progress of several important themes from work to work and provides helpful discussion of "The Tale of Tinúviel" in particular. Charles Noad's "On the Construction of 'the Silmarillion,'" also in *Tolkien's Legendarium,* comments on the place of *Part II* in the entire structure of the published materials of the Elder Days. Tom Shippey comments on elements of *Part II* in discussing the "Silmarillion" as a whole in his fifth chapter of *J.R.R. Tolkien: Author of the Century.*

PAUL EDMUND THOMAS

Further Reading

Carpenter, Humphrey. *Tolkien: A Biography.* Boston, MA: Houghton Mifflin, 1977.

Flieger, Verlyn, and Carl F. Hostetter, eds. *Tolkien's Legendarium: Essays on "The History of Middle-earth."* Westport, CT: Greenwood, 2000.

Garth, John. *Tolkien and the Great War.* London: HarperCollins, 2003.

Shippey, Tom. *J.R.R. Tolkien: Author of the Century.* Boston, MA: Houghton Mifflin, 2000.

See also **Ælfwine; Angband;** *Book of Lost Tales I;* **Caves; Doors and Gates; Dwarves; Eärendil; Eldamar; Elves; Elves: Kindreds and Migrations; Elves: Reincarnation; Fairies; Fëanor; Frame Narrative; Gilson, Robert Quilter; Heroes and Heroism;** *History of Middle-earth:* **Overview; Jewels; Kôr;** *Lays of Beleriand, The;* **Maiar; Middle-earth: Men; Middle-earth: Monsters; Middle-earth: Peoples; Morgoth and Melkor; Mountains; Mythology for England; Northern Courage; Oral Tradition; Prose Style;** *Silmarillion;* **Silmarils; Smith, Geoffrey Bache; Tavrobel; TCBS (Tea Club and Barrovian Society); Thingol, Elwë, Elu Singolo; Tol Eressëa; Tolkien Scholarship: Since 1980; Túrin;** *Unfinished Tales;* **Valar; Valinor; Violence; War; Warwick; Wiseman, Christopher Luke; Women in Tolkien's Works; World War I**

BOROMIR

By the time of his inclusion in the Fellowship commissioned to destroy Sauron's Ring, Boromir has few rivals in Middle-earth for lineage, courage, or strength of arms. He is the defender of Osgiliath,

High Warden of the White Tower, and heir to the Steward of Gondor; he is, as Aragorn assures Frodo, "a valiant man" (*FR,* I, iii, 289). But from his arrival at Imladris in search of counsel regarding a recurrent dream he claims to share with his brother, Faramir, Boromir's arrogance not only mars his heroism, it foreshadows his role as breaker of the Fellowship.

Born in 2978 (Third Age) to Lady Finduilas of Dol Amroth and Denethor II, Boromir's Númenórean heritage is equaled by few and surpassed only by Aragorn. From his father, Boromir inherits impressive physical stature and pride; otherwise, he resembles the last of Gondor's vanished Kings, the brash Eärnur, who did not marry but found pleasure "chiefly in arms" and who cared "little for lore, save the tales of old battles" (*RK,* Appendix A, 337). Consequently, Boromir is reckless, arrogant, and reliant on power. After deprecating Bilbo's offer to destroy the Ring, scolding Gandalf before the Door of the Watcher, and speaking ill of Lothlórien and the Lady Galadriel, he attempts to seize the Ring from Frodo on Amon Hen. "The fearless, the ruthless," he tells the Ring-bearer, "these alone will achieve victory" (*FR,* II, x, 414). After his treachery, however, a repentant Boromir gives his life to defend Merry and Pippin from Saruman's Uruk-hai. It is a sacrificial and redeeming act, one that Aragorn calls "a victory" (II, III, i, 16) and Gandalf, in turn, an escape (II, III, v, 99).

Critics generally center their comments around how Boromir's inner conflicts work within the story. Tom Shippey concentrates on the meaning of his fall within Middle-earth's cosmology of power. Shippey observes how Boromir's patriotism, his "never-quite-stated opinion that 'the end justifies the means,'" provides an access point through which the Ring of Power gains influence over him (125). Other critics approach Boromir's fall through dramatic terms. Marjorie Burns points to the story's many layers of tension, noting, "If we are going to have a story, we need disruption in one or another form. We need a snake in every garden, a Melkor or Loki in every pantheon, and a Boromir in every Fellowship" (176). Expanding the discussion into Tolkien's legendarium, Katharyn Crabbe considers Boromir in context of the history of Middle-earth. Crabbe contends that Boromir represents the sad decline of human glory from its Númenórean grandeur to a merely physical greatness (74).

In rebuttal to those critics who found *The Lord of the Rings* "simple-minded, just a plain fight between Good against Evil," Tolkien pointed specifically to Boromir (*Letters,* 179). As a figure torn between King and father, Fellowship and country, honor and pride, power and wisdom, Boromir reflects many of the moral and dramatic complexities found in *The Lord of the Rings.*

ALEX DAVIS

Further Reading

Burns, Marjorie. *Perilous Realms: Celtic and Norse in Tolkien's Middle-earth.* Toronto: University of Toronto Press, 2005.

Crabbe, Katharyn. *J.R.R. Tolkien.* Revised and Expanded edition. New York: Continuum, 1988.

Shippey, Tom. *The Road to Middle-earth.* 2nd ed. London: Grafton, 1992.

See also **Men; Pride; Temptation**

BOURNEMOUTH

Bournemouth is a town on the south coast of England, thirty miles west of Southampton. During Tolkien's lifetime, it was part of the county of Hampshire (local government boundaries have since changed). Noted for its beach and mild weather, it has been a popular vacation and retirement resort since the early nineteenth century.

Tolkien and his family vacationed at seaside resorts in various parts of England throughout his life. He visited Bournemouth as early as 1902 with his brother and godfather (*Artist & Illustrator* 13). After his retirement in 1959, he and Edith frequently took holidays at the Miramar Hotel in Bournemouth. When they decided to move from Oxford, they looked to Bournemouth and bought a small modern home at 19 Lakeside Road, two miles from the Miramar just over the Dorset county line in the suburb of Branksome Park. The move in August 1968 had been delayed by Tolkien's leg injury and hospitalization, and the packing inevitably disrupted his papers, but over the three-and-a-half years he lived there he was slowly able to organize his work and do some writing, some of it published in *Unfinished Tales* and *The Peoples of Middle-earth.*

Tolkien regretted the lack of intellectual companionship in Bournemouth, but he appreciated the comfort and the absence of disruption. His address was kept secret; all his fan mail went to George Allen & Unwin, where it was dealt with by Joy Hill, who regularly visited with material needing Tolkien's personal consideration.

Tolkien moved back to Oxford after Edith's death in November 1971, but he retained friends in Bournemouth and was visiting there when he fell ill on

August 30, 1973. He died in a local private hospital three days later.

DAVID BRATMAN

BOYENS, PHILIPPA

Philippa Boyens was one of the three screenwriters for *The Lord of the Rings* film trilogy (New Line Cinema, 2001–3). A playwright, drama teacher, and former head of the New Zealand Writers Guild, Boyens joined the husband and wife writing team of Peter Jackson and Fran Walsh in August 1997 after they had drafted a ninety-page treatment of the film. She worked with the other two writers through the end of principal photography in 2000 and wrote additional dialogue for reshoots from 2001 to 2003. In February 2004, Boyens, along with Jackson and Walsh, received an Academy Award for Best Adapted Screenplay for *The Lord of the Rings: The Return of the King*.

Her familiarity with the novel aided her in the writing process as she and her cowriters composed the script. As she commented in an interview, "When I began the first draft of the first screenplay, I went about as far away from the source material as you would want to go. Then it was a gradual process of finessing, of bringing in more and more of the books as I fine-tuned the screenplay" (Smith, 6). Boyens said that "both prose narrative and film narrative have their own rules" (Ryfle, 40), and accordingly she and the others sought to balance fidelity to Tolkien's text with the demands of a feature film script. For example, she notes that they did not reduce the number of hobbits from four to two, a more logical number from a cinematic perspective, and they retained the two villains, Sauron and Saruman, making Saruman a major opponent in the first two films.

There has been much debate in the scholarly community over the changes the writers introduced as they adapted the book for the screen (see the essays in *Tolkien on Film*, edited by Janet Brennan Croft, for an overview of the critical response to Peter Jackson's trilogy). Boyens defends the choices she and her collaborators made in their departures from the text as means of bringing out conflicts and themes in the story. In the audio commentary track for *The Two Towers* Special Extended edition DVD, she explains that they always sought to leave "room for journey and for reversals" in their characterizations and alterations of the plot. Boyens maintains that she and the other filmmakers were offering their vision of *The Lord of the Rings* but that they always remained true to the spirit of the novel and "tried to leave the foundations of Tolkien's myth intact" (Mattingly).

DAVID D. OBERHELMAN

Further Reading

Croft, Janet Brennan, ed. *Tolkien on Film: Essays on Peter Jackson's "The Lord of the Rings."* Altadena, CA: Mythopoeic, 2004.

"Director and Writers Commentary." *The Lord of the Rings: The Two Towers.* Special Extended edition DVD. New Line Home Entertainment, 2003.

Mattingly, Terry. "Good, Evil, and 'The Lord of the Rings,'" *Scripps-Howard News Service.* http://www.shns.com/shns/g_index2.cfm?action=detail&pk=RELIGION-FAITH-12-11-02 (accessed December 11, 2002).

Ryfle, Steve. "*The Lord of the Rings:* The Two Towers." *Creative Screenwriting* 9.6 (2001): 40–42.

Smith, Patricia. "Patricia Burkhart Smith Talks with Philippa Boyens." *Creative Screenwriting* 8.2 (2001): 4–8.

See also **Fandom; Film Scripts, Unused; Jackson, Peter**

BRUT BY LAYAMON

Layamon (or Laȝamon, with the Middle English letter "yogh," or Lawman) was a priest at Arley Kings in Worcestershire around 1200. His *Brut* is a poem of more than sixteen thousand lines of alliterative verse, written sometime between 1199 and 1225. It chronicles the legendary history of Britain from the settlement of the island by Brutus, an exile from the destruction of Troy in the Trojan War, to the reign of Cadwallader in the seventh century. The poem is based mainly on a French poem by Wace, which is itself a version of Geoffrey of Monmouth's mid-twelfth-century Latin prose work, *Historia regum Britanniae* (History of the Kings of Britain). Layamon's *Brut* is one of the most important surviving texts from the period 1100–1300, and it features the first appearances in English of King Lear, Cymbeline, and King Arthur.

Layamon's alliterative line is similar to that used in Old English poetry: two half-lines each with two stressed syllables and a variable number of unstressed syllables are linked by alliteration, which fulfils a structural rather than decorative or rhetorical purpose. Layamon also employs poetic diction used in earlier English poetry, but his verse is freer than that of the Old English period, and he makes occasional use of rhyme.

In a note to his essay "On Translating *Beowulf*," Tolkien refers to the "decadent alliterative verse of Middle English" (*MC*, 67), and *Brut* may have been among the texts he had in mind. However, Layamon was, according to Tom Shippey, the poet "whom Tolkien regarded as the last preserver of Old English tradition" (*Road*, 56). In a note to his lecture "English and Welsh," Tolkien argues that the major division in the history of the English language occurs not around 1066, where the conventional division between Old and Middle English is located, but in the thirteenth century (*MC*, 195 n. 9), and this would put Layamon in the same period as his Anglo-Saxon predecessors. Like other early Middle English writers whose work Tolkien believed showed continuity with the Anglo-Saxon period, Layamon was from the West Midlands—from the same county as Tolkien's maternal ancestors. His English is a West Midlands dialect of the kind that Tolkien claimed to have taken to as soon as he encountered it.

Tolkien makes a small number of passing references to Layamon's *Brut* in his published work. A brief comparison between Layamon's account of Lear and Shakespeare's play appears in *Beowulf and the Critics* (97) and in Tolkien's essay "On Fairy-Stories" (*MC* 1997, 120). Michael Drout (*B&C*, 15) quotes a passage from unpublished lecture notes in which Tolkien uses Layamon's *Brut* to illustrate a hiatus in the continuity of English cultural life.

Shippey has identified some echoes of Layamon's *Brut* in Tolkien's creative work: the association of Elves with the sea and their taking of Frodo to the Undying Lands at the end of *The Lord of the Rings* is like Layamon's version of the passing of King Arthur (Shippey, 56). In *The Lord of the Rings*, Éowyn's word *dwimmerlaik* is derived from Layamon (Shippey, 300), and one of Gollum's riddles in *The Hobbit* has an analogue in *Brut* (Shippey, 25).

The only complete published edition of *Brut* available to Tolkien was that edited by Sir Frederick Madden in 1847; selections edited by J. Hall were published in 1924. The standard edition is now that of the Early English Text Society; Rosamund Allen (1992) provides a translation into modern English.

CARL PHELPSTEAD

Further Reading

Hall, J., ed. *Layamon's "Brut": Selections.* Oxford: Clarendon, 1924.

Lawman. *Brut.* Translated by Rosamund Allen. London: Dent, 1992.

Layamon. *Brut.* edited by G.L. Brook and R.F. Leslie, 1963–78. 2 vols. Early English Text Society Original Series 250, 277. London: Oxford University Press.

Madden, Sir Frederick, ed. *Layamon's "Brut," or Chronicle of Britain: A Poetical Semi-Saxon Paraphrase of the Brut of Wace.* 3 vols. London: Society of Antiquaries, 1847.

Shippey, Tom. *The Road to Middle-earth.* 2nd ed. London: HarperCollins, 1992.

———. *J.R.R. Tolkien: Author of the Century.* London: HarperCollins, 2000. Paperback edition, 2001.

See also **Arthurian Literature**

BUCHAN, JOHN (1875–1940)

Tolkien is known to have admired the novels of John Buchan, a liking often taken as proof of his Philistinism. Buchan was, however, a more complex and certainly a more productive and varied writer than his popular image would suggest. There are good grounds for seeing why Tolkien sympathised with and perhaps learned from him.

Buchan had a long career as a writer, publishing his first novel in 1895, his last appearing posthumously in 1941. He was also a prominent politician, ending his career as governor-general of Canada. He is currently best known for a sequence of thrillers centred on the character of Richard Hannay, which began with *The Thirty-Nine Steps* (1915). The first three of these became part of the British propaganda effort in World War I, in which Buchan took a leading role; there are some similarities of incident and phrasing with Tolkien's works. More significant, however, are a string of novels written after the war celebrating British stability and conservatism, the best and funniest centring on the Glasgow grocer Dickson MacCunn. Like Bilbo Baggins, Dickson is a figure of the greatest bourgeois respectability—Gloin says disparagingly that Bilbo "looks more like a grocer than a burglar!" But like Bilbo, Dickson has a buried romantic streak, and in the first of the MacCunn novels, *Huntingtower* (1922), he finds himself an illicit guardian of rescued jewels and committed to storming "the Dark Tower" to rescue a princess.

It is, however, Buchan's relatively little-known historical novels that seem most likely to have roused Tolkien's admiration. The most strikingly Tolkienian is *Midwinter: Certain Travellers in Old England* (1923). Among many connections, it uses the word "halfling" in chapter 1, where we also meet characters strongly reminiscent of Bill Ferny and Tom Bombadil; a volunteer corps of "Rangers" appears near the end. In the climactic chapter 13, the hero is about to be thrown down a deep limestone cleft into an underground river from which a roaring of rocks can be heard—"Journeyman John" grinding his teeth. Gypsy Ben offers to kill the hero quickly and mercifully if he will give him the ring he is wearing, but it must be freely given, "that I may wear it and kiss it and call to mind my darling dear." The hero is saved on the brink, and Gypsy Ben falls into the cleft instead. There are obvious parallels with the Ring, the Sammath Naur, Gollum, and even Gollum's way of speaking.

Even more significant, and a recurrent theme with Buchan, is the idea of "Old England." It should be noted that Buchan was firmly Scottish but strongly Anglophile. *Midwinter* could be seen as a riposte to Walter Scott's *Waverley* (1819). Both are set in the 1745 rebellion, but where *Waverley* shows an Englishman joining the Highland army, *Midwinter* presents a Scot who comes to appreciate the virtues not of the Hanoverian cause but of something more English and deeper rooted. In another historical novel, *The Blanket of the Dark* (1931), Buchan again presents a secret society that exists below the level of government and politics but preserves the traditions and the core of Old England, which remain regardless of changing alien dynasties. This theme of hidden continuity, which we see in Strider, also appears in Buchan's sequence of novellas, *The Path of the King* (1923), which traces a ring and its wearers generation by generation from Viking times to Abraham Lincoln, who eventually fulfils the destiny of his family. It is possible that Tolkien had the idea of doing something similar with the story sequence begun in "The Notion Club Papers."

Douglas Anderson's *Tales Before Tolkien* (2003) has furthermore picked out a Tolkien theme in Buchan's "The Far Islands," a story of a man with a recurrent dream, first published in 1899. Another motif that both writers share is the repeated image of a girl dancing alone in a wood, found in Buchan's *Witch Wood* (1927) and in *The Dancing Floor* (1926). Tolkien no doubt further appreciated Buchan's essay on "The Novel and the Fairy-tale" (1931), along with his readiness to see the mythical coexisting with the everyday and to sense fairyland, or in Scottish dialect *Elfhame,* as forever present on the margins of Old England. It is here, rather than in the political works and thrillers, that we should see a link between the two writers.

TOM SHIPPEY

Further Reading

Giddings, Robert, and Elizabeth Holland. *J.R.R. Tolkien: The Shores of Middle-earth.* London: Junction Books, 1981.

Lownie, Andrew. *John Buchan: The Presbyterian Cavalier.* London: Constable, 1995.

See also **England, Twentieth Century; Frame Narrative; Literary Context, Twentieth Century; Mythology for England**

BUTLER, SAMUEL (1835–1902)

Samuel Butler, English novelist and man of letters, published the satirical dystopian novel *Erewhon* in 1871. Using the rugged backcountry of New Zealand (where Butler had lived for several years in the 1860s) as the setting for his imaginary land, Butler told how his Erewhonians had first relied upon and then been enslaved by various machines and mechanical devices. Butler borrowed the then-novel idea of Darwinian evolution to suggest how machines advanced in sophistication. Eventually, the Erewhonians rose up and banished all such devices from their land. So antimechanistic are they that as soon as he enters Erewhon, the protagonist/narrator of Butler's novel is arrested for wearing a watch.

In a 1944 letter to his son Christopher, Tolkien, speaking of military bombers and other engineering marvels being used to prosecute World War II, notes that "old Sam Butler" had glimpsed the truth about the new and horrid evils brought upon us by our machines and devices in this fallen world (*Letters,* 88).

It is doubtful that Tolkien was influenced by Butler in any significant way, but certainly he agreed with the Victorian writer. Butler as a satirist could exaggerate for effect, but there is little exaggeration in Tolkien's fear of and contempt for mechanical "Progress." Even in *The Hobbit* Tolkien says of the Goblins (later known as Orcs), "It is not unlikely that they invented some of the machines that have since troubled the world, especially the ingenious devices for killing large numbers of people at once, for wheels and engines and explosions always delighted them" (*H,* IV, 109).

Similarly, in *The Lord of the Rings* Saruman's fall from excellence and wisdom takes the form of mechanization: "Once [Isengard] had been green and filled with avenues, and groves of fruitful trees. . . . But no green thing grew there in the latter days of Saruman. The roads were paved with stone-flags, dark and hard; and beside their borders instead of trees there marched long lines of pillars, some of marble, some of copper and iron, joined by heavy chains" (*TT,* III, viii, 160).

And again, when the Hobbits return to the Shire, they find its degradation displayed in mechanical terms (with Saruman's hand in the work here also): trees cut down and houses torn down or dug up, replaced by misshapen sheds and huts; the old gristmill now polluting The Water with industrial waste; and more to the same effect.

The destructive nature of industrial civilization is a symptom and a sign for Tolkien of evil. The unrelenting mechanization of the world, of which

Samuel Butler made satirical play, was for Tolkien grim reality.

MICHAEL N. STANTON

Further Reading

Birzer, Bradley J. "Middle-earth and Modernity." Chap. 6 in *J.R.R. Tolkien's Sanctifying Myth: Understanding Middle-earth*. Wilmington, DE: ISI Books, 2003.

Butler, Samuel. *Erewhon*. London: Penguin, 1970.

Holt, Lee E. "*Erewhon*." Chap. 2 in *Samuel Butler*. Revised edition. Boston, MA: Twayne, 1989.

Stanton, Michael N. "Tolkien in New Zealand: Man, Myth, and Movie," in *Tolkien's Modern Middle Ages*, edited by Jane Chance and Alfred Siewers, 281–91. New York: St. Martin's, 2005.

See also **Industrialization; Saruman**

C

CAEDMON

Caedmon was an Old English poet whose poetry was one of the primary sources for the word "Middle-earth." Caedmon died about 680 CE and is often referred to as the "father of English poetry," though many scholars, including Tolkien, have argued that the term, "father of Christian English Poetry" is more accurate. In *The Old English Exodus*, Tolkien referred to Caedmon as an "inspired peasant" whose poetry "deeply stirred his generation."

The most well–known poem commonly attributed to Caedmon is "Caedmon's Hymn." This nine-line poem was ascribed to Caedmon by the Venerable Bede, an ancient historian who first recorded a Latin version of the poem in his work *An Ecclesiastical History of the English People* sometime before his death in 735. However, at a slightly later date, two Old English versions of the poem were added to the Latin text, one in West Saxon and one in Old Northumbrian, the native dialect of both Caedmon and Bede. Though some scholars now feel that the authorship of the Old English version of the poem is somewhat doubtful, the historical importance of the poem itself cannot be debated.

Line seven of the poem states that the Holy Creator created "Middle-earth." The term "Middle-earth" was originally written in Old English as *Middangeard*, a description of the habitation of man. In his *Letters* (no. 165), Tolkien explained to publishers at Houghton Mifflin that it was this word that inspired his own use of the term "Middle-earth."

The story of the poet Caedmon is, in itself, both curious and inspiring. According to accounts by Bede, Caedmon was an ignorant cowherd who lived near Whitby in the North of England, working on grounds of a monastery. As the other laborers would gather at feasts, passing the harp and sharing poems and songs, Caedmon would often retire to his byre, ashamed of his own lack of ability. One evening, as he left such a feast, he was visited by a vision of a man (or angel) who commanded him to sing. The result was *Caedmon's Hymn,* a well-composed alliterative poem praising the Creator. The abbess, learning of the miraculous gift bestowed upon the humble herdsman, began to educate him and to encourage his poetic efforts.

According to Bede, Caedmon later went on to compose more complete and elaborate poems (dealing with a variety of spiritual subjects) that retell sacred history in the form of alliterative verse. Though poems resembling these survive in Old English documents, the true authorship of these "Caedmonian poems" remains in dispute. Many critics, including Tolkien, felt that these works, though likely inspired and influenced by Caedmon, could not be directly attributed to him.

In his book, *The Road to Middle-earth*, Tolkien critic Tom Shippey translates a portion of the Old English version of *The Ecclesiastical History of the English People*, which was written in that form by a Worcester monk of the ninth century. This description of Caedmon and his influence on English literature, Shippey asserts, could as easily be applied to

Tolkien himself: "Whatever he learned of scholars, he brought forth adorned with great sweetness and inspiration.... And many others following him began also to make songs of virtue among the English people.... But just the same, none of them could do it like him."

AMELIA HARPER

Further Reading

Gibson, E.C.S. "St. Caedmon" (edited version). http://www.britannia.com/bios/saints/caedmon.html (September, 2005).

Harper, Amelia. *Literary Lessons from the Lord of the Rings*. Nashville: Homescholar Books, 2004.

Shippey, Tom. *The Road to Middle-earth: Revised and Expanded Edition*. Boston: Houghton Mifflin, 2001.

See also **Old English; Places in Tolkien's Work: Middle-earth; Scholarship by Tolkien:** *Exodus*, **Edition of; Bede**

CALENDARS

Tolkien generally gives dates in the history of Middle-earth in terms of four ages, each of which has a separate count of years. Dates in the First Age appear in Valian Years, reckoned from the beginning of time, Years of the Trees, counted from their first flowering, or Years of the Sun, counted from its first rising. Where Hobbits are concerned, dates often appear in their Shire Reckoning. Appendix D of *The Lord of the Rings* (*RK*, 384–90) presents the calendrical systems used by the Elves, Dúnedain, and Hobbits in detail, with additional information appearing in the drafts of this appendix (*Peoples*, 119–39).

The Four Ages

In *The Silmarillion*, time begins with the entry of the Valar into Eä, but the Count of Time does not begin until Valinor is completed and the Two Trees are created (*S*, 20, 38–39). In "The Earliest Annals of Valinor" (*Shaping*, 262–93) and "The Later Annals of Valinor" (*Lost Road*, 109–23), time is reckoned in years of the Valar, which are equivalent to ten solar years, and three thousand Valian Years elapse from the beginning of time to the first rising of the sun. The later version in "The Annals of Aman" (*Morgoth*, 47–138, esp. 50–51, 59–60) reckons time in Valian Years (or Years of the Trees) that are equivalent to about 9.58 solar years, with the first flowering of the trees occurring in Valian Year 3500 and the rising of the moon and sun in Valian Year 5000.

The latter part of the First Age is reckoned in Years of the Sun from its first rising to the defeat of Morgoth in the Great Battle. "The Earliest Annals of Beleriand" (*Shaping*, 294–341) places the end of the First Age in the year 250, but "The Later Annals of Beleriand" (*Lost Road*, 124–54) in the year 397, emended to 597. Tolkien abandoned "The Grey Annals" (*Jewels*, 3–170) at the death of Túrin and Nienor in the year 499, which corresponds to the emended chronology of "The Later Annals of Beleriand."

The Second Age ends with the first defeat of Sauron and the taking of the One Ring by Isildur in the year SA 3441 (*RK*, App. B, 363–65). Although the island of Númenor was destroyed, the Undying Lands were removed from the physical world, and the shape of the earth was changed from flat to round in SA 3319 (*S*, 278–82), this was not of enough significance to warrant the beginning of a new age.

The Third Age ends, not with the destruction of the One Ring and the downfall of Sauron on March 25, TA 3019, but with the departure of the Three Keepers (Elrond, Galadriel, and Gandalf) on September 29, TA 3021 (*RK*, App. B, 377, App. D, 390). In Gondor, the first year of the Fourth Age was held to have begun on what would have been March 25, TA 3021. The final entry in "The Tale of Years" is dated Fourth Age 120 (*RK*, App. B, 378).

In a letter to Rhona Beare, dated October 14, 1958, Tolkien stated that he imagined the gap between the end of the Third Age and the present day to be about six thousand years and that we were now "at the end of the Sixth Age, or in the Seventh" (*Letters*, 283).

The Elvish Calendar

As explained above, the Elves of Valinor reckoned time in Valian Years, which were on the order of ten solar years in length. Longer periods were measured in terms of the *randa* (cycle, age), equivalent to a hundred Valian Years (*Lost Road*, 382). In each Valian Year, there were one thousand Days of the Valar, each consisting of twelve hours, Valian hours being equivalent to seven of our hours (*Morgoth*, 50; *S*, 38–39).

In Middle-earth, after the rising of the sun, the Eldar measured time in terms of the *yén*, which consisted of 144 solar years or 52,596 days. The *yén* was also divided into 8,766 six-day weeks, called *enquier* (singular *enquië*). In the Calendar of Imladris (Rivendell), the solar year, called *coranar* (sun-round) or *loa* (growth), was divided into six seasons, called in Quenya and Sindarin, respectively, *tuilë/ethuil* (spring), *lairë/laer* (summer), *yávië/iavas* (autumn), *quellë/firith* (fading), *hrívë/rhîw* (winter), and *coirë/echuir* (stirring).

Lairë and *hrívë* each contained seventy-two days, and the others fifty-four each. Three *enderi* (middle-days) were inserted between *yávië* and *quellë*, and these were doubled every twelve years. Elvish New Year (*yestarë*) corresponded approximately with Astron (April) 6 in the Shire Calendar.

The six days of the *enquië* were named *Elenya/Orgilion* (for the Stars), *Anarya/Oranor* (Sun), *Isilya/Orithil* (Moon), *Aldúya/Orgaladhad* (Two Trees), *Menelya/Ormenel* (Heavens), and *Valanya/Orbelain* (or *Tárion/Rodyn*, the Valar or Powers) (*RK*, App. D, 385–90).

Calendars of the Dúnedain

In the King's Reckoning, used in Númenor and in Arnor and Gondor until the end of the kings, the year began in mid-winter and was divided into twelve *astar* (months). These were called *Narvinyë/Narwain, Nénimë/Nínui, Súlimë/Gwaeron, Víressë/Gwirith, Lótessë/Lothron, Nárië/Nórui, Cermië/Cerveth, Urimë/Urui, Yavannië/Ivanneth, Narquelië/Narbeleth, Hísimë/Hithui,* and *Ringarë/Girithron*. Each month contained thirty days, except *Nárië* and *Cermië*, both of which contained thirty-one. Outside of the months were *yestarë, loendë,* and *mettarë*. Every fourth year, except the last of a century, *loendë* was replaced by two *enderi*.

Mardil, the first Ruling Steward of Gondor, introduced a new system, taking effect in TA 2060, which was called Stewards' Reckoning. This system was eventually used throughout the Westron-speaking areas of Middle-earth, except among the Hobbits. In this calendar, all the months had thirty days, and there were five holidays outside of the months: *yestarë, tuilérë, loendë, yáviérë,* and *mettarë*.

In the New Reckoning, beginning in TA 3019, the year began on former *Súlimë* 25, the anniversary of the downfall of Sauron. *Yavannië* 30 (former *Yavannië* 22, Frodo's birthday) was doubled in leap years and celebrated as *Cormarë* (Ringday).

The Númenórean week, unlike that of the Eldar, consisted of seven days, adding *Eärenya/Oraearon* (Sea-day) after *Menelya/Ormenel*. The Dúnedain also changed *Aldúya/Orgaladhad* to *Aldëa/Orgaladh*, referring to the White Tree only (*RK*, App. D, 386–88).

Shire Reckoning

The hobbits of the Shire reckoned their years from the founding of the Shire in TA 1601, those of Bree from TA 1300.

The hobbits used a calendar in which each month had thirty days, with two Yuledays at the beginning and end of the year and three Summerdays or Lithedays between the sixth and seventh months. An additional Litheday (Overlithe) was added every four years. In the Shire, the names of the months were *Afteryule, Solmath, Rethe, Astron, Thrimidge, Forelithe, Afterlithe, Wedmath, Halimath, Winterfilth, Blotmath,* and *Foreyule*. These are translations of the genuine Hobbitish names and are in fact modernized forms of Old English month names; Modern English names are given instead in the main text of *The Lord of the Rings* and in Appendix B.

The hobbits adopted the seven-day Númenórean week, translating the Elvish names into their own language. The weekday names given in Appendix D are anglicized renditions of these, which are also to some extent puns of the English weekday names: *Sterday, Sunday, Monday, Trewsday, Hevensday, Mersday,* and *Highday*. The hobbits also introduced an innovation called Shire-reform, which established that Mid-year's Day (and Overlithe in leap years) should have no weekday name, which allowed the same date to fall on the same weekday in every year (*RK,* App. D, 384, 387–89).

Dúrin's Day

Little is said of the Dwarvish calendar, though it is said in *The Hobbit* that the Dwarves' New Year, called Dúrin's Day, is "the first day of the last moon of Autumn on the threshold of Winter" (*H,* III, 96).

ARDEN R. SMITH

See also **Astronomy and Cosmology, Middle-earth; Two Trees**

CAPITALISM

About capitalism as a means of production, Tolkien said virtually nothing directly. He attacked industrial ugliness and pollution, which can be present with capitalist societies but which in practice are more essentially features of Communist ones, as the examples of Eastern and Western Europe or the Soviet Union and the United States show.

While Tolkien did not explicitly endorse capitalism, the logic of his hatred of any type of coercion, particularly state coercion, points to an economic order with as much freedom as possible. He wrote in 1956: "I am not a 'socialist' in any sense—being adverse to 'planning' (as must be plain) most of all because the 'planners', when they acquire power, become so bad."

There are no capitalist heroes in Tolkien's tales. Nor, though they are common in other fiction, are there capitalist villains. The principal enemies, Morgoth, Sauron, and Saruman, build industrial bases by coercive force, not through investing the profits of production. They are not interested in securing *economic* domination. Morgoth steals the Silmarils but does nothing with them except place them in an iron crown. The enemies have none of the financial accoutrements, or weapons, attributed to capitalism such as banks, credit, collateral, mortgages, joint stock companies, predatory pricing, monopolies, or lawyers. Their aim is *power*, and they are far less interested in *money* than the average hobbit appears to be.

Although several of Tolkien's villains—Smaug and other dragons, the crooked and greedy Master of Lake-Town, and the trolls in *The Hobbit*, for example—hoard treasure, none can sensibly be described as capitalists; they have no idea of investing it productively. They are thieves and misers, and they destroy rather than produce.

Smaug and the Master of Lake-Town are also the only characters who show an interest in "tolls"—that is, not in trade but in money extracted from putting barriers in the way of trade. However, at the Council of Elrond, Gloin also mentions the tolls of the Beornings, which are "high," at least for Dwarves, whom the Beornings do not love. Possibly as colonists of a wild area they need all the income they can get and also need to finance the effort of keeping the passages and trade-routes open. The Numenoreans also exact tribute from Middle-earth. Like tolls, this is a form of institutionalized robbery and suggestive of their potential and growing corruption. It is not, however, capitalism in action.

The good and happy societies in Middle-earth—Gondor, Rohan, Esgaroth and Dale, and (normally) the Shire—apparently have an open and liberalistic rather than a coercive economic order. In peacetime, Men, Elves, and Dwarves trade, and they prosper by doing so, whereas the economy and production of Mordor needs slaves; "Where there's a whip there's a will!" as one Orc slave-driver puts it.

Perhaps the closest things to capitalists in Middle-earth are the Dwarves, who love making things and live by trade. One can at least imagine Dwarves investing the profits of trade to expand their productive ability. Thorin Oakenshield's recounting of their fortunes to Bilbo in *The Hobbit* touches on this: having sunk low economically after the disaster of Smaug's attack, they have since managed to improve their fortunes somewhat, even by resorting to the lowly occupation of coal mining. The contract of employment the Dwarves give Bilbo at the beginning of *The Hobbit* also shows they are a "businesslike" people. The faults into which they are most likely to fall are greed and, closely related, the cherishing-up of grudges, but they are not intrinsically evil.

Tolkien was not greatly concerned with economics in his writing, but he was aware that some economic background had to exist in any world, primary or "subcreated." He stated in a letter that "it would no doubt be possible to defend poor Lotho's introduction of more efficient mills, but not Sharkey's and Sandyman's use of them (*Letters,* 200)."

In the Shire, we see something near the Catholic Social Movement's vision of a community of small farms and small trades. Individuals are property owners. Some are employees of others, but even the Gamgees, though poor and ill-educated, seem to be independent, with their own little house and garden. The inhabitants of the Shire are quite keenly interested in money and property. However, anything like building up an industrial conglomerate is out of the question. The ideal appears to be independent and "comfortable" rather than rich. The rich Brandybucks are, like the English aristocracy, not treated with reverential awe by the rest, and the acquisitive Sackville-Bagginses are ridiculous. There is at first a definite social gap between Sam and Frodo, Pippin and Merry, but it is not huge, and by the end of the tale it has disappeared.

The Shire's economy is unregulated or minimally regulated and is a free market, though a small-scale one (where the money used in the Shire and Bree comes from and how its supply is controlled we don't know, but it may be a relic of the old north kingdoms). This economic freedom is destroyed by Sharkey's men under socialistic slogans of "gathering" and "sharing." However, while Tolkien saw the Shire as a good and lovable society, he was also aware of the shortcoming of such a limited way of life. Little is said about the economy of Gondor, but there is a reference to "the lampwrights's street," suggesting again craftsmen working in small trades.

Tolkien's values regarding political economy seem in harmony with the classic economic tradition stemming from Adam Smith, for example, seeing trade as a win-win rather than a zero-sum situation and seeing barriers to market-entry as destructive, but this is a matter of inference and implication rather than direct statement.

When Pope John Paul II said in *Centesimus Annus*: "Not only is it wrong from an ethical point of view to disregard human nature, which is made for freedom, but in the long run it is impossible to do so," he might have been speaking for Tolkien as well as for Adam Smith.

Tolkien never made the error, to be found in some Catholic writing, of seeing capitalism and Communism as equivalents or mirror-images of one another. He saw that capitalism—a means of production—had no spiritual pretensions, unlike Communism or German National Socialism. Tolkien never demanded of capitalism or of the market answers to the human condition that they were not equipped to give and that lay, if anywhere, in other realms.

Tolkien disliked the ugly by-products of "commerce" as they touched his own life but was obviously aware that commerce was necessary. The things against it (this is again more a matter of inference than direct statement) were that it distracted attention from the High and Numinous, and ultimately from the Holy, and pandered to the lowest common denominator in tastes. This meant, he saw, in a fallen world, the promotion of the raucous, ugly, trivial, and generally Orkish—litter, noise, "Morlockian" factories were all aspects of this. The curing of these evils and uglinesses lay not in coercive regulation but in morality.

Although Tolkien could hardly be described as having much interest in "consumerism" in his own life, he lived as a modern man. He was keenly interested in the financial rewards of *The Lord of The Rings* and had the normal enjoyment of modern amenities.

He detested Henry Ford's great icon of consumerism, the motorcar, as the countryside round Oxford was being despoiled for car factories, and motorborne tourists and trippers spread noise and litter in previously unspoiled places. The only relatively modern machine to be shown in a positive light in his fiction is "the pleasant little local train" in "Leaf by Niggle," which consists of "one coach, and a small engine, both very bright, clean and newly painted." (He did in old age write with affection of one motorcar that his family owned: "poor old o, that valiant sorely-tried Morris.")

To say that Tolkien disliked modern consumer society but used its products is not to suggest he was hypocritical, simply that he was a man living in the industrial twentieth century while his visions, longing, and artistic impulses were directed elsewhere.

HAL G.P. COLEBATCH

See also **Acquisitiveness; Communism; Kingship; Politics; Possession**

CAROLINGIANS

The Carolingians were the dynasty holding the throne of France from the eighth century to 987 and centering on Charlemagne (742–814; ruled 768–814; created emperor 800). They seem to have played little

role in Tolkien's imagination—though he used some of their names for contrast with the homely family names of the Hobbits, as with Pippin Took. The first Carolingian was Charles Martel, mayor of the Palace, whose son Pippin (Pepin) III dethroned the last Merovingian king Chilperic. Charles the Great (Charlemagne) was Pippin's son, and Charlemagne's son was Louis (Ludovic), who was succeeded by three sons, including Lothair. About the only connection of any interest between Tolkien and the Carolingians seems to have been the occasional use of Carolingian or related first names (e.g., Lotho) in combination with Hobbit last names, for comic purposes. But Meriadoc is a Merovingian name; Frodo (correctly Froda) is Danish or Old English; Samwise is Old English, and the use of Carolingian names is relatively uncommon in *The Lord of the Rings* and certainly not essential to the comic effect.

There is of course a parallel between the mayors of the Palace who became kings and the ruling steward of Gondor who would not step down to be "dotard chamberlain of an upstart... last of a ragged house long bereft of lordship and dignity" (*RK,* V, vii, 130)—in other words, who sought the powers of the kingship, though not to be king. The recorded complaint against the Merovingians was indeed that they were bereft of lordship and dignity (perhaps they were, though the Carolingians wrote the history). But Denethor came of a lineage far greater than Charlemagne's.

JARED LOBDELL

Further Reading

Wallace-Hadrill, J.M.W. *Early Germanic Kingship.* New ed. Oxford: Clarendon Press, 2000.
———. *The Frankish Church.* Oxford: Clarendon Press, 1983.
———. *The Long-Haired King.* Toronto: University of Toronto Press, 1982.

See also **Hobbits; Pippin**

CATHOLICISM, ROMAN

In 1900, much to the dismay of her family, Mabel Tolkien was confirmed in the Roman Catholic Church. Her family strongly disapproved of her decision—though they tended to be only nominally Protestant—cutting her and her boys off from all family monies and support. Four years earlier, her husband had died, leaving her a widow with two boys, Ronald and Hilary, to raise. Four years after her conversion to Roman Catholicism and the resulting ostracization from her family, Mabel died of diabetes, a disease that might have easily been treated with sufficient finances. She "was a gifted lady of great beauty and wit, greatly stricken by God with grief and suffering, who died in youth (at 34) of a disease hastened by the persecution of her faith," Tolkien remembered in 1941. It would be impossible to stress too much the influence her death had on Tolkien. He was almost thirteen when she died, and she had served, effectively, as his only parental figure to this point in his life. She had influenced him in everything, and Ronald attempted to live up to her memory for the rest of his life. This was especially true in his religious devotions. "I witnessed (half-comprehending) the heroic sufferings and early death in extreme poverty of my mother who brought me into the Church," he reflected in 1963. The impress of his mother's death lay on him his entire adult life, and it permeated his academic work as well as his mythology.

With her untimely death, Mabel left Ronald and Hilary to the care of a Roman Catholic priest at John Henry Cardinal Newman's Birmingham Oratory. Though he struggled with him at times, especially over dating his future wife Edith, Ronald considered his legal guardian, Father Francis Morgan, his true father. Indeed, Tolkien credited Father Morgan with solidifying the faith into which his mother brought him. "I first learned charity and forgiveness from him," Tolkien wrote in 1965, and Morgan's example and teaching "pierced even the 'liberal' darkness out of which I came, knowing more about 'Bloody Mary' than the Mother of Jesus—who was never mentioned except as a object of wicked worship by the Romanists." At the Oratory, importantly, Tolkien absorbed Newman's profound presence and shaping of the institution. Newman had been the most famous Catholic of the English-speaking world in the nineteenth century, with his *Apologia* and his *Idea of the University* serving as core texts in the Catholic world. Additionally, Newman was a devout follower of St. Augustine, who served as a significant influence on Tolkien as well. Tolkien was also intimately familiar with the teachings of Saints John and Thomas Aquinas.

From his mother and Father Morgan, Tolkien learned a traditional, Tridentine Roman Catholicism. The church grew like a tree, Tolkien argued, changing over time and branching out. Like all Catholics of his generation, Tolkien believed in scripture, tradition, and the power of the magisterium (the Catholic Church's teaching over and through time). The Protestant fascination with the early, primitive Christian church, Tolkien wrote, simply resulted in a morbid fascination with ignorance, as the church needed time to grow. By entering time, Christ sanctified history, and his sacraments continue the Incarnation across the ages. To trap the church in one era as the

Protestants attempt to do, means the retardation of the church and the denigration of the Incarnation and sacraments. In essence, by denying tradition, Protestants paradoxically forced the church into stasis or regress.

Tolkien was greatly disappointed with the Catholic Church at the end of his life. The changes brought about by the Vatican II Council (1962–65) disturbed him. Clyde Kilby described one of reactions to the changes:

> Worst of all briar patches was what [Tolkien] persistently regarded as the spiritual decay of our times and particularly of his own Roman Catholic church, of which he was a longtime and devout member. The Church, he said, "which once felt like a refuge now feels like a trap." He was appalled that even the sacred Eucharist might be attended by "dirty youths, women in trousers and often with their hair unkempt and uncovered" and, what was worse, the grievous suffering given by "stupid, tired, dimmed, and even bad priests." An anecdote I have heard involved his attendance at mass not long after Vatican II. An expert in Latin, he had reluctantly composed himself to its abolishment in favor of English. But when he arrived next time at services and seated himself in the middle of a bench, he began to notice other changes than the language, one a diminution of genuflection. His disappointment was such that he rose up and made his way awkwardly to the aisle and there made three very low bows, then stomped out of the church (13).

Though disturbed by the changes, Tolkien remained publicly quiet regarding his disappointment and continued to attend mass until he died. "I know quite well that, to you as to me, the Church which once felt like a refuge, now often feels like a trap. There is nowhere else to go!" he wrote to his son John. "I think there is nothing to do but to pray, for the Church, the Vicar of Christ, and for ourselves; and meanwhile to exercise the virtue of loyalty, which indeed only becomes a virtue when one is under pressure to desert it."

Though never as public about his Christianity as was his closest friend, C.S. Lewis, Tolkien never hid his faith, and his Catholicism manifested itself in a number of profound and often surprisingly public ways. First, Tolkien was always quite open about his faith with his friends. With his closest friends, such as C.S. Lewis and the various members of the Inklings, he discussed issues of faith and theology often. But, even in front of typically agnostic or atheistic academic audiences, Tolkien openly confessed that he rarely held "strong views" about his major subject of scholarship, philology, as he deemed it "[un]necessary to salvation." To his literary friends, those beyond the Inklings, Tolkien frequently admitted his fondness for scripture. Tolkien willingly expressed his religious fervor to his students as well. Once, after distributing the beginning to St. John's Gospel written in Anglo-Saxon, he informed his students that "English was a language that could move easily in abstract concepts when French was a still a vulgar Norman patois." With the exception of Lewis, most English academics kept their religious proclivities a private matter. Tolkien, like Lewis though, embraced it, making it inform and determine the questions and directions of his scholarship, if not the answers to his questions. Indeed, he argued that one must always seek truth first, alone and unhindered by fundamentalist zealotry. When an overly eager Roman Catholic sought to uncover the Catholic heritage of a particular place in England, Tolkien objected strongly to the man's method. "With reference to the letter of 'H.D.' on the subject of COVENTRY I am at a loss to know how the etymology of any place-name can be pursued 'in keeping with Catholic tradition,' except by seeking the truth without bias, whether one ends up in a convent or not" (*Letters,* 112). This proves a telling example.

Due to the example set by his mother and Father Morgan, Tolkien also strove to live out the forms and good works necessary for sanctification within the Roman Catholic tradition. He told his son Christopher, for example, to memorize a variety of prayers as well as the entirety of the Mass in Latin. "If you have these by heart you never need for words of joy," Tolkien advised. Considering his strong devotion to the Blessed Virgin Mary discussed below, he most likely said the rosary frequently. He kept one by his bed, even during his nights spent on watch for Nazi bombings of Oxford during World War II. In addition to his strong devotion to Mary, Tolkien often asked for the prayers of various saints. Tolkien also believed that God answered his prayers directly, even miraculously healing ills and sickness.

Most importantly for his prayer life, he believed in frequent reception of the Eucharist and even more frequent confession. The Eucharist, fully the Body and Blood of Christ in Catholic theology, especially had meaning for Tolkien. "I put before you the one great thing to love on earth: the Blessed Sacrament," Tolkien wrote to his son Michael. "There you will find romance, glory, honour, fidelity, and the true way of all your loves upon earth"(*Letters,* 112). Tolkien even once experienced a profound vision. During Adoration of the Blessed Sacrament (praying before the transubstantiated Bread and Wine, which Catholics believe to be the actual Body and Blood of Christ), he revealed, "I perceived or thought of the Light of God

and in it suspended one small mote (or millions of motes to only one of which was my small mind directed), glittering white because of the individual ray from the Light which both held." Tolkien claimed to have witnessed his guardian angel in the vision, not as a go-between but as the personalization of "God's very attention." Further, Tolkien only had one "dry" period in his religious life, sometime during the early 1920s. It was his love of the Eucharist, he claimed, that brought him back to the church. "But I fell in love with the Blessed Sacrament from the beginning— and by the mercy of God never have fallen out again: but alas! I did not live up to it," he admitted to his son Michael. "I brought you all up ill and talked to you too little. Out of wickedness and sloth I almost ceased to practice my religion—especially at Leeds, and 22 Northmoor Road. Not for me the Hound of Heaven, but the never-ceasing silent appeal to the Tabernacle, and the sense of starving hunger" (*Letters,* 340). Perhaps most tellingly, Tolkien believed that Pope Pius X's call for frequent communion and attendance at daily mass would reform the church far more than any of the official reforms of the second Vatican Council.

The mythological equivalent of the Eucharist finds its place in Tolkien's legendarium as the Elvish *lembas.* Properly translated from the Elvish, *lembas* means "journey bread" in Sindarin and "life-bread" in Qenya. With the normal reception of the Eucharist in the Catholic mass, the Body of Christ is referred to as the "bread of life." During the reception of last rites or extreme unction, most likely the last sacrament a Catholic will ever receive before dying, the Eucharist is known as the *Viaticum,* "food for the journey."

Tolkien also held a profound devotion for the Theotokos, the mother of God or the Blessed Virgin Mary. Having lost his own mother, Tolkien especially felt a closeness to Mary. He spoke of her often in conversation with friends, and Mary appears frequently in Tolkien's letters and even in some of his writings of the legendarium, most notably in Tolkien's own commentary and notes regarding his piece "Athrabeth Finrod ah Andreth." Mary provided him with his sense of "beauty in majesty and simplicity." From Tolkien's perspective, God offered the image and life of Mary to the world as worthy of devotion to "refin[e] so much our gross manly natures and emotions, and also of warming and colouring our hard, bitter, religion." The very idea that she served as the human tabernacle for the Second Covenant, the Christ, meant that she must be impeccably and awesomely beautiful, Tolkien argued. Anything, therefore, of beauty that Tolkien created, he claimed, came from his own limited notions and understanding of Mary. "There is something missing from any form of 'Christian thought' that could make such an omission. A failure (I think) to accept fully *all* the consequences of the Incarnation-story as it is told to us in scripture," Tolkien wrote in an unpublished letter to Clyde Kilby. In his attitude, Tolkien reflected the decisions of some of the earliest ecumenical church councils. They proclaimed the dogmas about Mary not to elevate Mary, but to elevate Christ. Without an understanding of the Incarnation, Tolkien argued, one could never fully understand that the Incarnate Word was both fully God and fully man.

Mary, as the only "unfallen human," also demonstrates for Tolkien what death was to have been like prior to the fall of Adam and Eve. The "'assumption' [of Mary] was the natural end of each human life, though as far as we know it has been the end of the only 'unfallen' member of Mankind." Strangely, this finds its fullest expression in the "death" of Aragorn, when Aragorn chooses his time to leave the world. Here, he follows, almost exactly, the Catholic understanding of Mary's assumption into Heaven.

One can also find several Marian figures in the legendarium, in addition to Aragorn. Certainly, none actually holds a one-to-one correspondence to Mary, but they often share a number of things in common with her. Galadriel, the Elven queen of Lorien, a timeless realm she created and sustained with the ring Nenya, is probably the most obvious representation of Mary. Galadriel spent much of the Second and Third Ages resisting the power of Sauron. She also created the White Council, the council dedicated to overthrowing the darkness. Even though she must repent for her blasphemy against the Valar in the First Age, Tolkien wrote, "it is true that I owe much of this character to Christian and Catholic teaching and imagination about Mary." Elbereth serves as another significant Marian figure in the legendarium. The angelic wife of Manwë and maker of light and stars, she serves, like Mary in Roman Catholic theology, as the "Queen of Heaven" and "Star of the Sea." The Elves invoke her in prayer and revere her more than any other of the Valar. In turn, she listens to their prayers. Her graces flow to more than just the Elves, though, as she answers the prayers of Hobbits, including Sam's pleas for aid during battle with Shelob. Wielding the Phial of Galadriel, for example, Sam receives strength from Elbereth when attacking the spawn of Ungoliant, Shelob. Together with Manwë, Elbereth sends Gandalf to aid Middle-earth against Sauron. Prior to the "Last Battle," Tolkien's mythological equivalent of Ragnorak and St. John's Apocalypse, the final triumph of Ilúvatar and his allies over Morgoth and all forms of disorder and evil, Elbereth forms the constellation of Menelmakar

as a sign of coming of the Last Battle. Chapter 12 of the "Apocalypse of St. John" reads: "A great and wondrous sign appeared in heaven: a woman clothed with the sun, with the moon under her feet and crown of twelve stars on her head." In Roman Catholic thought, the woman "clothed with the sun," ready to give a second birth to the messiah, is Mary. Other female Vala have attributes of Mary, as does the Fairy Queen in Tolkien's non-Middle-earth work *Smith of Wooton Major*.

Though Tolkien said that the Roman Catholicism only entered *The Lord of the Rings* consciously in its revision, one finds prayer, notions of hierarchy, and Catholic sacramental elements in the earliest conceptions of legendarium. In Tolkien's *Qenya Lexicon*, written and compiled in the 1910s, for example, he already included words for crucifixion, monks, demon, Father (as in the "1st Person of the Blessed Trinity"), saint, Christian missionary, gospel, nun, and crucifix. Tolkien even describes "Eldamar" as "the rocky beach in Western Inwinóre (Faëry), whence the Solosimpeli have danced along the beaches of the world. Upon this rock was the white town built called Kor, whence the fairies came to teach men song and holiness." Tolkien also gives the names for Christ (*Ion*) and the Holy Spirit (*Sā*) (35).

None of this, however, should suggest that Tolkien meant any of his legendarium as mere Christian propaganda. Tolkien rejected all propaganda as an insult to the dignity, complexity, and freedom of the human person. Instead, he argued for a Christian art, a subcreation, as he described in his "On Fairy-Stories." Art or subcreation should glorify God, creation, and the human person. In this, Tolkien followed one of the oldest traditions on the Roman Catholic Church, the sanctification of the pagan. St. Paul first used this in his speech and actions on Mars Hill in Athens. While challenging the philosophies of the Stoics and Epicureans, Paul congratulated the Athenians for being religious. Specifically, he noted, he was impressed with their statue to the "unknown God." Christ, he told them in no uncertain terms, was their unknown God. All of their religion, philosophy, and culture had pointed them to him. Paul even quoted approvingly, though sanctifying the meaning, of two Stoic philosophers and poets, Aratus and Cleanthes, in Acts 17:28: "In him we live and move and have our being" and "For we are indeed his offspring." Such became the model for the Christian church. One finds its clearest expression in the commands of St. Gregory the Great to St. Augustine of Canterbury: "But if you have found customs, whether in the Church of Rome or of Gaul or any other that may be more acceptable to God, I wish you to make a careful selection on them, and teach the Church of the English, which is still young in the Faith, whatever you have been able to learn with profit from the various Churches. For things should not be loved for the sake of places, but places for the sake of good things. Therefore select from each of the Churches whatever things are devout, religious, and right; and when you have bound them, as it were, into a sheaf, let the minds of the English grow accustomed to it." Hence, one finds elements of Christ, Odin, and St. Michael in Gandalf. One finds elements of the Arthurian Lady of the Lake and the Blessed Virgin Mary in Galadriel.

BRADLEY J. BIRZER

Further Reading

Kilby, Clyde. Unpublished parts of chapter, "Woodland Prisoner," p. 13 in Kilby Files, 3–8, Wade Collection Wheaton College, Wheaton, IL.
Tolkien, J.R.R. "Quenye Lexicon," *Parma Eldalamberon* 12 (2003).

See also **Christian Readings of Tolkien; Christianity; Incarnation; Life**

CAVE, THE

In Humphrey Carpenter's *The Inklings* (London 1978; reprint, New York, 1981), he mentions in passing—as one of the "gatherings" of the English School "junto" at Oxford in the 1930s (and thereafter)—"quite a large group, known as 'Cave'"; the Cave is named after the Cave of Adullam in which David organized the conspiracy against Saul (I Samuel 22:1–2)—Saul being, in this case, David Nicol Smith. Carpenter gives as members of the Cave (61n) Lewis, Tolkien, Coghill, Dyson, Leonard Rice-Oxley, and H.F.B. Brett-Smith (1884–1951). To these may be added, from conversations with the late Cleanth Brooks in 1991–92, Brooks himself (1906–94) (whose tutor was Coghill), R.B. McKerrow (1872–1940), and perhaps F.P. Wilson (1879–1954).

McKerrow and Brett-Smith were distinguished textual scholars. Besides his editions of *The Gull's Hornbook* (1904, 1907), *The Tragedy of Locrine* (1908), *The Virtuous Octavia* and *The Play of Patient Grissell* (both 1909), *The Works of Thomas Nashe* (1910), and *Apius and Virginia* (1911), McKerrow was noted for his great collections, such as the *Dictionary of Printers and Booksellers in England, Scotland, and Ireland* (1910–22), *Printers and Publishers Devices in England and Scotland, 1485–1640* (1913), and *Title Page Borders Used in England and Scotland, 1485–1640* (1932).

Herbert Francis Brett Brett-Smith (1884–1951) was principally known for his *Works of Thomas Love Peacock* (1924) and *Dramatic Works of Sir George Etherege* (1927); but he also edited *The Unfortunate Traveller* (1919?), *Gammer Gurtons Needle* (1920), *Nimphidia: The Court of Fayrie* (1921), *Seven Deadly Sins of London* (1922), *Incognita, or Love and Duty Reconcild* (1922), *Loves of Clitophon and Leucippe* (1923), and *Ovyde hys Booke of Metamorphose Books X–XV* (1924).

Leonard Rice-Oxley was noted chiefly for his book *Oxford Renowned* (1925, 2nd ed. 1934, 3rd ed. 1947, 4th ed. 1950, etc.); he was also editor of *Fielding: Selections, with Essays by Hazlitt, Scott, Thackeray ...* (1923, a companion volume to Dyson's on Pope), editor of *The Poetry of the Anti-Jacobin* (1924), editor of Smollett's *The Expedition of Humphrey Clinker* (1925) for the World's Classics, and author of the 1914 Stanhope Prize Essay, *Memoirs as a Source of English History*. He seems to have fallen into the "literary document as social history" basket, but that at least is not a form of purely "literary" (or Nicol Smith?) appreciation of literature.

When his brother retired to Oxford in 1933 (but could not come to the Cave), C.S. Lewis seems to have raided the Cave for those like-minded scholars who became part of the Inklings—Tolkien, Coghill, Dyson, perhaps Lord David Cecil (another "literary document as social history" scholar)—though the Cave still met at least up to Gordon's death in 1942, perhaps up to Brett-Smith's in 1951. Yet the Cave was not merely an Inklings predecessor (or even Kolbitár successor). Cleanth Brooks, in conversation, summarized what he learned from the Cave: (1) concentration on what the text *says* is necessary to find out what the text *means* and (2) the biographer, the literary historian, and the lexicographer hold the keys necessary for unlocking a poem's full meaning. Tolkien did not need to learn those lessons, but his participation in the Cave was part of his continuing effort to make sure those lessons were learned, in this case in good humor around the dinner table at the Mitre.

JARED LOBDELL

See also **Coalbiters/Kolbitár; Coghill, Neville; Dyson, Hugo; Inklings; Lewis, C.S.; Oxford**

CAVES AND MINES

Caves and mines are a recurring image throughout Tolkien's work. Caves serve as symbols with mythological, psychoanalytical, and philosophical implications, as well as an important narrative element in Tolkien's tales, especially in *The Hobbit* and in

The Lord of the Rings. Mines, however, reflect the complexity of Middle-earth, revealing the intricacies of the cultures and societies as created by Tolkien.

Caves

There are structures that could be deemed caves, ranging from the Dwarven halls beneath the Lonely Mountain to Shelob's Lair at the pass of Cirith Ungol to the Caves of Menegroth.

In the world of myth, caves are catalysts through which the hero achieves his stature as Hero. Joseph Campbell outlines the importance of the cave, often symbolizing the unknown, the threshold that the hero must cross, the first test the hero must face (Campbell, 77, 91–92). Psychoanalytically, caves symbolize what comes before and what comes after life. Caves therefore symbolize the womb from which we are all born, and the grave we all come into. Philosophy, however, has a unique approach to the symbolic function of the cave, which stems from Plato and his great work *The Republic*. Plato's "Theory of Forms" derives from an allegory of the cave, which can be found in Book VI, lines 506–21. The cave in this allegory serves as a means to hide truth from mankind. If one leads a life with the inability to recognize Truth, Plato likens one to a slave chained within a cave. Once light—which symbolizes Truth and the world in its true form—is perceived, the slave is released from the cave.

In his writing, Tolkien is keenly aware of all the symbolism behind the use of the cave image. Caves are at the beginning of both *The Hobbit* and *The Lord of the Rings*—Hobbit holes are a kind of cave. Randel Helms succinctly outlines the Freudian approach by stating that Bag End can be seen as the womb from which the hero is born (Helms, 41–46). The crossing of thresholds and the delving of caves mark each stage of the Hobbits' journey—for both Bilbo and Frodo. Bilbo earns Sting, the mark of his stature as hero, from the trolls' lair (*H*, II, 80–83), and Frodo takes a bold step forth as a hero as he saves his companions from the wights in "Fog on the Barrow Downs" (*FR*, I, viii, 150–54). Bilbo's journey beneath the Misty Mountains and his fortuitous meeting with Gollum serves as another narrative break, a crossing to a new level, another threshold. In *The Lord of the Rings*, Moria serves to transform Gandalf through his battle with the Balrog and reveals Frodo as a warrior with his mail shirt, and Frodo's final test on Mount Doom is again in a cave. Most of Tolkien's stages of transition occur within cavelike structures.

Mines and Mining

Mines, as opposed to caves, were not specifically named in many of Tolkien's writings. The primary named mine was Khazad-dûm, or the Mines of Moria, where the Dwarves mined for many precious metals but most predominantly for mithril. Mining was essential to life in Middle-earth, but Tolkien focuses on the craftsmanship as an ultimate product from what is mined rather than on the mining itself. Evidence of mining, however, can be gleaned from discussions of craftsmen and the making of weaponry, the shaping of stone, and the carving of gems, dating back to the creation of Eä and the beginning of days. Aulë was the master of all crafts from metalwork to stone craft (*S*, 27). He created and taught the Dwarves all his skill (*S*, 43), and we can assume mining was one of theses fundamental skills. Melkor, however, is associated with the first named mine: Utumno, where he created his fell beasts and delved the earth for his foul crafts (*S*, 36, 47, 51). Angband, the fortress of Sauron, is another parallel to Utumno, housing dungeons, caves, and quite possibly mines (*S*, 47, 118). The Noldor were the foremost craftsmen of all the Eldar; named Gwaith-I-Mírdan or jewel-smiths, they wrought all the precious things of the earth (*S*, 286). The Noldor were reputed for their work delving and crafting gems. Mahtan was the first named Eldar smith and stonewright who learned his craft from Aulë (*S*, 64). Fëanor, however, was the greatest of all the Noldorin craftsmen (*S*, 64–65). After their flight from Valinor, the House of Fëanor settled in Eregion, the lands west of the Misty Mountains, and were renown among the Noldorin smiths. Known simply by Men as Hollin, the Noldorin smiths settled this place to be close to the mithril of Moria (*S*, 286).

Yet the only race specifically noted as masters in the craft of mining were the Naugrim, the Dwarves (*S*, 91–92). In his essay "Of Dwarves and Men," Tolkien discusses the cultural relationship of the Dwarves to the different peoples of Middle-earth, particularly Men. Dwarves traded throughout Middle-earth, especially with the Elven kingdoms of Eregion. Men were known for providing food, for which the Dwarves exchanged their skill as stonemasons and miners (*Peoples*, 302). The most ancient Dwarven settlements, where undoubtedly mines existed, were Belegost, Nogrod, and Khazad-dûm, and later the Blue Mountains, the Iron Hills, and the Lonely Mountain. The Naugrim delved for stone, gold, silver, copper, iron, and mithril.

A brief list of specific caves and mines in Tolkien follows:

- Glittering Caves, Aglarond, or the Caverns of Helm's Deep
- Henneth Annûn, the Window of the West, or the Window of Sunset
- Khazad-dûm, Moria
- Paths of the Dead (*LotR*, 775, 780, 781–83, 867, 874, 877)
- Caves of Menegroth, Hidden Kingdom of Doriath (*S*, 56, 93–94, 96–97, 108, 121–22, 183–86, 199–202, 231–36)
- Caverns of Narog, Nargothrond (*S*, 114–15, 120–22, 151–52, 156–57, 168–71, 190–92, 230–31)
- Caves of the Forgotten in the Pélori Mountains (*S*, 279)
- Utumno (*S*, 36, 47, 51, 365)

JESSICA BURKE

Further Reading

Anderson, Douglas. *The Annotated Hobbit: Revised and Expanded Edition*. Boston, MA: Houghton Mifflin, 2002.

Campbell, Joseph. *The Hero with a Thousand Faces*. Princeton, NJ: Princeton University Press, 1972.

Helms, Randel. *Tolkien's World*. Boston, MA: Houghton Mifflin, 1974.

Jung, Carl Gustav. *The Portable Jung*. Edited by Joseph Campbell. New York: Penguin Books, 1971.

Plato. *The Republic*. Translated by A.D. Lindsay. New York: Everyman's Library, 1976.

See also **Allegory; Darkness; Dwarves; Fëanor; Gondor; Good and Evil; Hell; Jungian Theory; Light; Lonely Mountain (Erebor); Misty Mountains; Mithril; Moria; Quest Narrative; Plato; Symbolism in Tolkien's Works; Theological and Moral Approaches to Tolkien's Works**

CECIL, LORD DAVID (1902–86)

Aristocrat David Cecil taught English literature and modern history as a fellow at Wadham College, Oxford, where he gave up his post in 1930 to devote himself to writing, before returning to teaching (which he missed) in 1938 to become a fellow of English at New College. He married happily, to Rachel McCarthy, daughter of one of the original members of the Bloomsbury group, and Virginia Woolf recorded their marriage in her diary: "David and Rachel, arm-in-arm, sleep-walking down the aisle, preceded by a cross which ushered them into a car and so into a happy, long life, I make no doubt" (*The Diary of Virginia Woolf*, ed. A.O. Bell, [1982], 4:128). Both were practising Christians. Like C.S. Lewis, Cecil was a popular lecturer at Oxford. His health

prevented him from serving in the war—he had been a sickly child. From 1948 to 1970, he was Goldsmith's Professor of English Literature, remaining a fellow of New College. A brilliant conversationalist, he was a valued member of the Inklings and, unlike some members, was enthusiastic about the "new hobbit" as Tolkien read installments. He was author of many books, some of them reaching a wide readership, including *Poets and Storytellers* (1949), *Visionary and Dreamer: Two Poetic Painters—Samuel Palmer and Edward Burne-Jones* (1969), and his most popular study, *A Portrait of Jane Austen* (1978). His first biography was *Striken Deer* (1929), a portrait of William Cowper, which later won the Hawthornden Prize. His anthology *The Oxford Book of Christian Verse* (1940) included Charles Williams's "At the 'Ye who do truly.'" He knew Williams through Oxford University Press, and they became warm friends through the Inklings meetings. Sir Isaiah Berlin described him as "one of the most intelligent, irresistable, attractive, gifted, life-enhancing, shrewd and brilliant man of letters of his time." His portrait was painted in oils by Augustus John (1935, Tate collection).

COLIN DURIEZ

Further Reading

Cecil, David. *The Cecils of Hatfield House*. London: Constable, 1973.

———. *A Portrait of Jane Austen*. London: Constable, 1978; New York: Hill & Wang, 1979.

———. *The Stricken Deer, or The Life of Cowper*. London: Constable, 1929; New York: Oxford University Press, 1935.

Cecil, David, and Rachel Trickett. "Is There an Oxford 'School' of Writing? A Discussion between Rachel Trickett and David Cecil." *Twentieth Century* (Melbourne, Australia), June 1955, 559–70.

Cranborne, Hannah, ed. *David Cecil: A Portrait by His Friends*. Stanbridge, England: Dovecote Press, 1991.

Lewis, W.H. *Brothers and Friends: The Diaries of Major Warren*. San Francisco: Harper & Row, 1982.

Trickett, Rachel. "Lord David Cecil." In *Dictionary of National Biography*. Oxford: Oxford University Press, 2004–6.

See also **Inklings; Lewis, C.S.; Lewis, W.H.; Oxford; Williams, Charles**

CHARMS

As a philologist and professor of Anglo-Saxon, Tolkien was familiar with "minor" works of Old English (OE) literature like the Anglo-Saxon charms. These texts were communicative acts, applications of verbal magic in which language was used to affect material reality (Nöth, 63). As in most Indo-European languages, OE charms consisted of an optional epic introduction, which identified the evil or related an analogous situation (e.g., illness or infection) and how it was overcome, demonstrating the power of the cure (Grendon, 111) and the incantation itself, in which the desired result was "modeled in language" (Zimmer, 68–69). Underlying the charms was the assumption of the "power of the word" to change reality (Grendon, 119). We find echoes of OE charms in the verbal magic performed in *The Lord of the Rings*, and the charms also shaped aspects of the story.

Two charms from the eleventh-century Anglo-Saxon magico-medical text *Lacnunga* (MS Harley 585, British Library), the "Nine Herbs Charm" (*Nigon Wyrta Galdor*) and "Against a Sudden Stitch" (*Wið Færstice*) appear to have influenced Tolkien's writing of *The Lord of the Rings*. The "Nine Herbs Charm" was an incantation uttered over nine powerful plants (mugwort, plantain, chamomile, apple, fennel, chervil, betony, nettle, and lamb's cress [Dobbie, cxxxiii]) to intensify their ability to counteract nine poisons and nine infections or illnesses from *onflygnum*, flying infections thought to enter their victim through the mouth and ears (Storms, 196–97; Abernethy, 21–22). Pettit has suggested that Tolkien used this nine versus nine opposition in Elrond's assembling of the nine-member Fellowship of the Ring to oppose the nine Black Riders of Mordor (41n; *FR*, II, iii, 275). The numbers three and nine occur with greater frequency than any other numbers in the Anglo-Saxon charms (Grendon, 122; Grattan and Singer, *Anglo-Saxon*, 44); as Chevalier and Gheerbrant point out, three is a number used in Indo-Europeans cultures and, in fact, almost universally, to represent wholeness or completeness (997). Nine, as the square of three, shares and perhaps intensifies this quality.

The second charm used by Tolkien, "Against a Sudden Stitch," is meant to counteract rheumatism or lumbago (Storms, 140; Hauer, 250) or a sudden stabbing pain of unknown origin (Pettit, "Tolkien's," 39), understood as the result of a dart or knife shot into the victim by mysterious riders, witches, demons (i.e., Germanic gods from a Christian perspective [Grendon, 215]), or elves on a burial mound or hill. The exorcist uses the herbs feverfew, nettle, and plantain and a knife to extract or neutralize this dart, which then melts. Pettit argues convincingly that this charm influenced Tolkien in his depiction of the Black *Riders'* attack on the Fellowship on the *hill* Weathertop, Frodo's stabbing by the *Witch* King of Angmar using a Morgul *Knife*, and Frodo's experience of "pain like a *dart*" (*Anglo-Saxon Remedies*, 195–96; *FR*, I, xi,) and his subsequent healing by Elrond, who finds the sliver of the knife and extracts and

melts it (Pettit, *Anglo-Saxon Remedies*, 41; *FR*, II, I, 221–22; my emphasis).

There are several instances of actual charms in *The Lord of the Rings*, most of them associated with Tom Bombadil (his charming of Old Man Willow [*FR*, I, vi, 120] and the barrow-wight's spell [*FR*, I, viii, 141] and Tom's counterspell [*FR*, I, viii, 142]). Zimmer adduces these instances of magic and adds Gandalf's breaking of Saruman's staff in *The Two Towers* (67; *TT*, III, x, 583). Interestingly, Tolkien's charms lack an epic introduction, but they do contain the conclusion of the typical Anglo-Saxon metrical charm, in which an evil being is deprived of power, sent to sleep, or cast out of its habitation through the use of language.

CAROL A. LEIBIGER

Further Reading

Abernethy, George William. "The Germanic Metrical Charms." Diss., University of Wisconsin–Madison, 1983.

Chevalier, Jean, and Alain, Gheerbrant. *A Dictionary of Symbols.* Trans. John Buchanan-Brown. New York: Penguin, 1997.

Chickering, Howell D., Jr. "The Literary Magic of 'Wid Faerstice.'" *Viator* 2 (1971): 83–104.

Dobbie, Elliott Van Kirk, ed. *The Anglo-Saxon Minor Poems.* New York: Columbia University Press, 1942.

Grattan, J.H.G., and Charles Singer. *Anglo-Saxon Magic and Medicine.* Publications of the Wellcome Historical Medical Museum, New Series, 3. New York: Oxford University Press, 1952.

Grendon, Felix. "The Anglo-Saxon Charms." *Journal of American Folklore* 22, no. 84 (1909): 105–237.

Hauer, Stanley R. "Structure and Unity in the Old English Charm 'Wid Faerstice.'" *English Language Notes* 15, no. 4 (1978): 250–57.

Horn, Wilhelm. "Der Altenglische Zauberspruch Gegen Den Hexenschuß" [The Old English Charm against a Sudden Stitch]. In *Probleme Der Englischen Sprache und Kultur*, edited by Wolfgang Keller, 88–104. Heidelberg: Carl Winter, 1925.

Jolly, Karen Louise. "Anglo-Saxon Charms in the Context of a Christian World View." *Journal of Medieval History* 11 (1985): 279–93.

Nöth, Winfried. "Semiotics of the Old English Charm." *Semiotica* 19 (1977): 59–83.

Pettit, Edward, ed. *Anglo-Saxon Remedies, Charms, and Prayers from British Library Ms. Harley 585: The Lacnunga.* Vol. 1, *Introduction, Text, Translation, and Appendices.* Lewiston, NY: Edwin Mellen, 2001.

———. "J.R.R. Tolkien's Use of an Old English Charm." *Mallorn* 40, no. 11 (2002): 39–44.

Skemp, A.R. "Notes on Anglo-Saxon Charms." *Modern Language Review* 6 (1911): 289–301.

Storms, Gotfrid. *Anglo-Saxon Magic.* The Hague: Martinus Nijhoff, 1948.

Thun, Nils. "The Malignant Elves: Notes on Anglo-Saxon Magic and Germanic Myth." *Studia Neophilologica* 41 (1969): 378–96.

Weston, L.M.C. "The Language of Magic in Two Old English Charms." *Neuphilologische Mitteilungen* 86, no. 2 (1985): 176–86.

Wrenn, C.L. *A Study of Old English Literature.* New York: W.W. Norton, 1967.

Zimmer, Mary. "Creating and Re-creating Worlds with Words: The Religion and Magic of Language in *the Lord of the Rings.*" *Seven* 12 (1995): 65–78.

See also **Elf–Shot; Health and Medicine;** *Leechbook* **and** *Herbarium;* **Plants**

"CHAUCER AS PHILOLOGIST: THE REEVE'S TALE"

Chaucer's *Reeve's Tale* concerns two Cambridge undergraduate students, both of northern origin, and as part of their characterization Chaucer gives them northern accents. This is the earliest example of the representation of dialect speech in English literature and is thus of some considerable significance. Tolkien's article is based on a paper read at a meeting of the Philological Society in Oxford on May 16, 1931, in which he provided a detailed analysis of the linguistic features that characterize the northern dialect, which continues to provide the foundation for every modern discussion of this feature of Chaucer's language. Tolkien was interested less in the stylistic and functional reasons behind Chaucer's decision to represent dialect speech and more in the philological detail of its representation. Tolkien's concern is to demonstrate that Chaucer, like his audience, was a philologist and that the depiction of northern speech was primarily a "linguistic joke" that can now only be understood by a philologist. This emphasis is understandable given his audience, though it does lead Tolkien to assume that Chaucer aimed at greater consistency and authenticity in his portrayal of dialect than is probably true.

Tolkien's philological discussion is accompanied by a critical text of the relevant passages from *The Reeve's Tale*, based upon seven of the earliest surviving manuscript witnesses. In reconstructing these passages Tolkien adopted the premise that Chaucer's scribes did not recognize his attempt to represent northern speech and so unconsciously replaced northern forms with their own southern forms, with less concern than they would show brushing a fly off their nose. In order to reconstruct Chaucer's original, Tolkien adopted every northern form found in these seven manuscripts, producing a text "very nearly purely and correctly northern." The result is a text in which the northern dialect is represented with philological consistency and rigor, but which probably goes further than Chaucer in accurately reproducing northern dialect features. This is because several of the manuscripts used by Tolkien were copied by scribes using northern dialects who added northern forms of their own to those introduced by Chaucer. It is now generally accepted that the earliest surviving manuscript, known as the Hengwrt manuscript, which shows a much less consistent depiction of the northern dialect, was copied by an accurate scribe close to Chaucer so that this text is probably a fair reflection of Chaucer's original. Tolkien's assumption that scribes paid no attention to details of spelling has also been challenged by more recent work on Middle English dialectology, which has shown that many scribes consciously and methodically "translated" the dialect of their original copies into their own native dialects, demonstrating a much greater awareness of dialect and spelling than Tolkien assumed.

The reconstructed northern dialogue is accompanied by a linguistic analysis that displays Tolkien's masterly philological skills. It is divided into two separate sections dealing with sounds and forms and vocabulary and draws on considerable linguistic knowledge of Middle English and Old Norse. This detailed consideration of the northernisms introduced by Chaucer is followed by a discussion of features where Chaucer used a southern form where he could have used a northern equivalent. Of these Tolkien found just six instances, although he added to this total several examples where southern forms have been erroneously introduced by Chaucer's scribes. This led Tolkien to the conclusion that Chaucer was extremely thorough and accurate in his depiction of northern dialect, though the small number of inconsistencies is of course partly a result of Tolkien's reliance upon his own reconstructed northern text.

Tolkien concluded that Chaucer's detailed knowledge of northern dialect must have derived from face-to-face interaction with northern speakers, as well as from reading northern texts. He speculated that time spent in Hatfield, Yorkshire, may have provided Chaucer with such an opportunity, although there were northern speakers in London during Chaucer's lifetime. While Chaucer does not attempt a precise localization of the dialect, the students are said to come from a town called Strother, "fer in the north." Tolkien identified a number of places in both Northumbria and Scotland as possible contenders for Chaucer's Strother, including two places of the same name: Strother (Boldon) and Strother (Haughton), also pointing out that ME *strother* was a dialect word meaning "marsh." Tolkien was, however, not concerned with attempting to tie Strother with a particular place, which, like speculating as to the reason behind the use of dialect in this tale, he sees as more suitable questions for a literary scholar than a serious philologist: "To guess is not, in any case, the province of the philologist."

SIMON HOROBIN

See also **Scholarship by J.R.R. Tolkien**

CHILDHOOD OF TOLKIEN

John Ronald Reuel Tolkien was born in Bloemfontein (Orange Free State), January 3, 1892, the older child and older son of Arthur Reuel Tolkien (1857–96) and Mabel Suffield Tolkien (1870–1904). His younger brother, Hilary Arthur Tolkien, was born in February 1894, also in Bloemfontein. His father had come out to be manager of the Bloemfontein branch of the Bank of Africa; his mother had followed in 1890, and they were married at Cape Town Cathedral (Anglican) in 1891. He recorded many years later (in "English and Welsh," 1955) that "My cradle-tongue was English (with a dash of Afrikaans)"—Afrikaans was the tongue of his nurse, also the maid and the "house-boy" Isaak, who all appear in a family picture in *The Tolkien Family Album* (16). Tolkien was, at the age of two, in 1894, borrowed by Isaak to be taken to the kraal where the residents had never seen a white baby.

The year 1894–95 was a particularly hot year in South Africa, and in April 1895 Mabel Tolkien took John Ronald and Hilary, aged three and one, to England, where they stayed with her family. "Years later, Ronald described to us [his wife and children] the powerful sense he had during the preparations for that voyage of the weight of emotion between his parents at their coming separation. He retained an image of extraordinary clarity of his father painting A.R. Tolkien on their cabin trunk, an item that Ronald kept and treasured in memory of his father" (*Tolkien Family Album*, 18). Then, of the long voyage home on the *Guelph*, "he remembered two brilliantly sharp images: the first of looking down from the deck of the ship into the clear waters of the Indian Ocean far below, which was full of lithe brown and black bodies diving for coins thrown by the passengers; the second was of pulling into a harbour at sunrise, seeing a great city set on the hillside above, which he realised much later in life must have been Lisbon" (18). Though Tolkien spent only three years in South Africa, it made a great impression on him, not least through the impression the round green land of England made on him on his arrival there.

In February 1896, Mabel Tolkien received a telegram that Arthur had rheumatic fever and, almost immediately thereafter, news of his death. That summer she found a cottage near Moseley, just south of Birmingham. They were in an area almost entirely rural, wild daffodils in the fields, near Sarehole Mill—the mill fascinating the boys, but "they were terrified of the miller's son, whom Ronald named 'the White Ogre'" (*Tolkien Family Album*, 20). Their mother left the boys in long hair and baby clothes longer than was customary, so the boys were called wenches by the local children.

In 1900, Mabel converted to Roman Catholicism, losing the support of both her family and the Tolkiens: the boys were of course thenceforward raised as Roman Catholics. That year Ronald started school at King Edward's Grammar School on New Street in Birmingham, which necessitated the family's moving near the (Oratorian Fathers') Oratory on Hagley Road in Birmingham. Mabel was teaching her sons the elements of Latin, French, English, and drawing, as well as of the Roman Catholic faith, at the time Ronald first attended King Edward's. In 1902–3 the boys attended St. Phillip's School, conducted by the Oratory, but in 1903 Ronald earned a scholarship to go back to King Edward's. Among the fathers at the Oratory was Father Francis Morgan, of an Hiberno-Spanish family notable in the wine trade, whose "Spanish connection contributed to the young Ronald's developing interest in languages" (*Tolkien Family Album*, 24). When Ronald Tolkien won his scholarship and his mother developed diabetes, Father Francis arranged for the family to rent rooms in the Oratory's lodge cottage at Rednal, where Mabel died in November 1904, leaving Father Francis as guardian to her sons.

After a brief and unsatisfactory period with their aunt (by marriage) Beatrice Bartlett Suffield, widow of Mabel's younger brother William (1874–1904), the boys were lodged in Duchess Road, and with this the period of their childhood may be said to have come to an end. It was while Mabel Tolkien was still alive, perhaps, that young Ronald first fell in love with the Welsh language, through the Welsh names on the coal trucks. We know for sure at least one story familiar to him in those days, "Puss Cat Mew" (by E.H. Knatchbull-Hugessen, 1829–93). This story has ogres, both hero (Joe Brown) and ogre becoming trees, and the story is an explanation of a nursery rhyme. He also read Andrew Lang's varicolored collections of fairy tales, especially the *Red Fairy Book* with Sigurd and Fafnir. He also read Fenimore Cooper's Leatherstocking saga.

It may be that his reading *The Black Douglas* also dates from this time (see *Sauron*), though this is not sure. It has been asked whether Tolkien in his childhood read E. Nesbit's *The Story of the Amulet*, with its great overarching wave coming over Atlantis, but *The Story of the Amulet* was published in 1906, which makes it unlikely (it could of course come from another Atlantean story). On the other hand, it has been suggested that the Psamathist in *Roverandom* derives from Nesbit (see *Roverandom*). What is clear is that Tolkien's childhood reading and his childhood experiences, like C.S. Lewis's, can be seen in his literary subcreation throughout his life. Buchan he read later in life, but Rider Haggard was early, possibly in part because of the South African scene. Of one influence we are certain: his mother's ornamental script influenced his handwriting and indeed his creation of alphabets (see her 1892 letter from "The Bank House Maitland Street Bloemfontein," in *Tolkien Family Album*, 17).

In speaking of himself as a child (in "On Fairy–Stories," in *MC*, 135), Tolkien wrote, "speaking for myself as a child, I can only say that a liking for fairy-stories was not a dominant characteristic of early taste," and going on to speak of "the years between learning to read and going to school. In that... time I liked many other things as well, or better: such as history, astronomy, botany, grammar, and etymology." The unusual in this list (from our common point of view) are the most Tolkienian entries—grammar and etymology. These were part of what his mother taught him in those not "happy and golden" but "troublous times" from age four to age eight, when they lived near the mill at Sarehole, after his father's death.

Two passages in his letter to W.H. Auden (June 7, 1955) are of particular interest here: "I was actually born in Bloemfontein, and so those deeply implanted impressions, underlying memories that are still available for inspection, of first childhood are for me those of a hot parched country. My first Christmas memory is of blazing sun, drawn curtains and a drooping eucalyptus" (*Letters*, 213) And at the end of the letter, discussing Shelob, "if that has anything to do with my being stung by a tarantula as a small child, people are welcome to the notion (supposing the improbable, that anyone is interested). I can only say that I remember nothing about it, should not know it if I had not been told; and I do not dislike spiders particularly, and have no urge to kill them. I usually rescue those whom I find in the bath" (*Letters*, 217).

JARED LOBDELL

Further Reading

Carpenter, Humphrey. *Tolkien: A Biography*. Boston, MA: Houghton Mifflin, 1977.
Shippey, Tom. *J.R.R. Tolkien: Author of the Century*. Boston, MA: Houghton Mifflin, 2000.
Tolkien, John, and Priscilla Tolkien. *Tolkien Family Album*. Boston, 1992.

See also **Morgan, Father Francis; King Edward's School; Oxford; Suffield Family; Tolkien, Arthur; Tolkien, Mabel; Tolkien, Hilary**

CHILDREN'S LITERATURE AND TOLKIEN

While Tolkien's major works, *The Hobbit* and *The Lord of the Rings*, are among the best–known and most popular works of the twentieth century, he also wrote and illustrated other children's stories. Three main strands of criticism exist: an analysis of *The Hobbit* as one of the classics of English-language children's literature, an approach by which it is argued that *The Hobbit* is suitable reading for adult Tolkien fans as a prequel to *The Lord of the Rings*, and a less frequent tendency to dismiss it as "juvenile." Much less critical writing on Tolkien's other children's works exists.

Tolkien's Children's Books

These other works, written for his own children and published posthumously, are *Mr. Bliss, Roverandom,* and *Letters from Father Christmas.* Wayne Hammond and Christina Scull (83) suggest, based on surviving fragments of text and illustration, that Tolkien wrote and illustrated several other stories for his children as well.

Walter McVitty writes that it is "no coincidence that many classic children's books were first written for (or told to) particular children, usually with no thought of publication at all," and he includes Tolkien in a list of classic authors along with A.A. Milne, Lewis Carroll, Kenneth Grahame, E. Nesbit, and C.S. Lewis. *The Hobbit*, however, was extensively rewritten from the original stories told to the Tolkien children. Other stories that have been described as children's works include *Farmer Giles of Ham* (although this was rewritten as an adult tale), *Smith of Wootton Major, Leaf by Niggle,* and several of the poems in the *Tom Bombadil* collection. These, however, are more commonly treated as works for adults. Although *The Lord of the Rings* was begun as a simple sequel to *The Hobbit*, it quickly became clear that it would be a large-scale work intended for adult readers. This has not stopped generations of children from enjoying the work. Tolkien comments in "On Fairy Stories" that he never regarded fairy tales and fantasy as being only, or even particularly, suited for a child audience. Tolkien later repented writing *The Hobbit* for children at all, commenting that "the desire to address children had nothing to do with the story as such in itself or the urge to write it" (*Letters*, 215). Notably, *Roverandom* and *Mr. Bliss* have only been published posthumously to feed a desire for Tolkieniana, rather than as books for children, despite their consideration for publication contemporaneously with *The Hobbit*. Apart from *The Father Christmas Letters*, especially the letters-in-envelopes edition published in 1995, these children's books are framed with introductions, facsimile text in Tolkien's handwriting, or other apparatus aimed at an adult, or even a scholarly, audience.

Children's Literature

Children's literature critics, including Peter Hunt, Walter McVitty, Anita Silvey, David Whitby, Maurice Saxby, and Glenys Smith, all claim *The Hobbit* as a children's classic. This position has become an assumption in the later part of the twentieth century, and as C.W. Sullivan argues, many critics go no further in their critical engagement with the text (253). Sullivan also argues that despite *The Hobbit*'s constant popularity, many "critics and readers alike" engage with it as a prequel to Tolkien's adult work.

Children's literature criticism has largely ignored Tolkien's other children's works. What little critical matter exists on these is largely from critics who work within a tradition of Tolkien scholarship and engage with all of Tolkien's works from an adult reader's perspective, such as Janet Croft or Hammond and Scull.

The Hobbit was initially well received by reviewers, particularly C.S. Lewis writing anonymously in *The Times*, and the book sold well (Green, 11). It was not, however, until the publication of *The Lord of the Rings* in 1954 that *The Hobbit* became a consistent best-seller as we know it today. Although never selling in quite the same astonishing numbers as *The Lord of the Rings*, it remains in print, is still popular with children, and is still regarded as a classic. McVitty defines "classic" as a book that remains constantly popular, despite changing "standards, tastes and fashions," which *The Hobbit* most certainly has; but Tolkien's other children's works have not. Other children's authors listed as classic by McVitty, and also by Hunt, Elizabeth Hoke, and Perry Nodelman, include A.A. Milne, Kenneth Grahame, E. Nesbit, Lewis Carroll, and C.S. Lewis. Hoke also writes of *The Hobbit* as *the* most popular of all twentieth-century fantasies for children and argues that

Tolkien's influence on other children's writers is notable.

Tolkien (*Letters,* 31) claims some influence from George Macdonald, author of several children's and adult fantasies, but suggests that he was more directly influenced as a child by the mythologies and languages of Europe that so fascinated him in his professional life. Andrew Lang is also mentioned approvingly in "On Fairy-Stories," in contrast to Tolkien's own stated dislike of diminutive fairies found in most children's "fairy-stories." Tolkien's own early verse indicates, however, that he may have felt rather differently about diminutive fairies earlier in his life. Several times in his letters he also displays a familiarity with the books his own children were reading and his own position among contemporary works (*Letters*).

Other Children's Authors

Several children's authors have acknowledged Tolkien's direct or indirect influence on their work. Diana Wynne Jones comments that a number of well-known British writers of children's fantasy attended Oxford while Tolkien taught there. Her list includes herself, Penelope Lively, and Jill Paton Walsh. Susan Cooper (143) makes the same point; fantasy was not encouraged at Oxford, even by Tolkien, but the course of study in English was influenced by Tolkien to include the kinds of mythological elements that cemented a preference for fantasy and myth already present in these authors. Assumptions about the ongoing influence of Tolkien on later children's writers go largely unquestioned by newspaper writers, fans, and critics, who frequently attribute the existence of the children's fantasy genre to Tolkien, regardless of evidence of earlier writers in the genre. Comments such as "Garner exhibited Tolkien's influence style as well as teleological concerns'" (Johansen, 28) or that Harry Potter is "not nearly as brilliant or literary as, say, *The Hobbit* or *Alice in Wonderland*" (Bernstein, E1) are common.

Tolkien Scholarship and Tolkien's Children's Works

For Tolkien scholars, the major interest has been in *The Lord of the Rings* and *The Silmarillion*. Several, however, have addressed Tolkien's children's work in some detail. William H. Green in *The Hobbit: A*

Journey into Maturity argues that *The Hobbit* is a growth-to-maturity text, a theme common to many children's literature texts. Green also discusses the linguistic and literary elements of *The Hobbit* and its critical reception by children's literature and Tolkien scholars. Hammond and Scull discuss both *The Hobbit* and Tolkien's other works, particularly in light of Tolkien's illustrations and visual artwork in *J.R.R. Tolkien: Artist and Illustrator*, but contextualize much of the visual material in terms of story, character, and genre. Croft advocates for a greater awareness of *Roverandom, The Father Christmas Letters,* and *Mr. Bliss* in her article "Beyond *The Hobbit*: J.R.R. Tolkien's Other Works for Children," while Paul Hyde argues that Tolkien's "care and concern for detail" (23) are as evident in his linguistic constructions within *The Father Christmas Letters* as anywhere else in his adult work.

As Green concludes, *The Hobbit* is a book of "unquestionable importance," both as a children's book and as part of Tolkien's larger body of work. Questions still exist regarding the value of Tolkien's other children's books, and there is scope for further critical work in this field.

PENELOPE DAVIE

Further Reading

Bearne, Eva. "Myth, Legend, Culture and Morality." In *Where Texts and Children Meet*, edited by Eva Bearne and Victor Walson, 183–97. London: Routledge, 2002.

Bernstein, Richard. "The Reality of the Fantasy in the Harry Potter Stories." *New York Times* (New York, NY). 1999: E, 1:2.

Collins, David R. *J.R.R. Tolkien: Master of Fantasy.* Minneapolis: Lerner Publications, 1991.

Cooper, Susan, "There and Back Again: Tolkien Reconsidered." *The Horn Book Magazine*, March/April 2002, 143–50.

Croft, Jane Brennan. "Beyond *The Hobbit*: J.R.R. Tolkien's Other Works for Children." *World Literature Today*, January–April 2004, 67–70.

Green, William H. *The Hobbit: A Journey into Maturity.* New York: Twayne Publishers, 1995.

Hammond, Wayne, and Christina Scull. *J.R.R. Tolkien: Artist and Illustrator.* London: HarperCollins, 1995.

Hunt, Peter, ed. *An Introduction to Children's Literature.* Oxford: Oxford University Press, 1994.

Hyde, Paul Nolan. "A Philologist at the North Pole: J.R.R. Tolkien and the *Father Christmas Letters Mythlore.* 15 (1 [55]) (1988 Autumn): 23–27.

Johansen, K.V. "The Sixties: Alan Garner, Madeline L'Engle, William Mayne, and Joan Aiken." *Resource Links* 8:3. Feb. 2003.

Jones, Diana Wynne. "The Official Diana Wynne Jones Website." http://www.leemac.freeserve.co.uk/autobiog. htm (August 2005).

Mathews, Richard. *Fantasy: The Liberation of Imagination.* New York: Routledge, 2002.

McVitty, Walter. *Classic Children's Authors and Illustrators.* Pymble: Collins Angus & Robertson, 1988.

Saxby, Maurice, and Gordon Winch, eds. *Give Them Wings: The Experience of Children's Literature.* South Melbourne: Macmillan, 1991.

Shippey, T.A. *The Road to Middle-earth.* Hemel Hempstead: Allen & Unwin, 1982.

Silvey, Anita, ed. *Children's Books and Their Creators.* Boston: Houghton Mifflin, 1995.

Sullivan, C.W., III. "J.R.R. Tolkien's *The Hobbit*: The Magic of Words." In *Touchstones: Reflections on the Best in Children's,* edited by Perry Nodelman, 1:253–61. West Lafayette, Ind.: Children's Literature Association, 1985.

Whitley, David. "Fantasy Narratives and Growing Up." In *Where Texts and Children Meet*, edited by Eva Bearne and Victor Walson, 172–92. London: Routledge, 2000.

Zimbardo, Rose A., and Neil D. Isaacs, eds. *Understanding the Lord of the Rings: The Best of Tolkien Criticism.* New York: Houghton Mifflin, 2004.

See also **Adventures of Tom Bombadil**; **Art and Illustrations by Tolkien**; **Bilbo Baggins**; **Farmer Giles**; **Farmer Giles of Ham**; **Father Christmas**; **Father Christmas Letters**; **Gandalf**; **Garm**; **Lewis, C.S.**; **Hobbit, The**; **Literature, Twentieth Century: Influence of Tolkien**; **Mr. Bliss**; **North Polar Bear**; **"On Fairy-Stories"**; **Publications, Posthumous**; **Ransome, Arthur**; **Roverandom**; **Smith of Wootton Major**; **Tolkien Scholarship: An Overview**; **Tolkien, Baillie**; **Tom Bombadil**

CHRIST

Tolkien stated on December 2, 1953, that "*The Lord of the Rings* is of course a fundamentally religious and Catholic work; unconsciously so at first, but consciously in the revision." Five years later, on October 25, 1958, he discussed the existence of a "scale of significance" appertaining to the relationship between himself and his work. At the very top of this scale of significance, as the single-most important of the "really significant" elements, was the fact that "I am a Christian (which can be deduced from my stories), and in fact a Roman Catholic." According to Tolkien's friend George Sayer, "*The Lord of the Rings* would have been very different if Tolkien hadn't been a Christian. He thought it a profoundly Christian book." Since, however, and as Tolkien explained, "the religious element is absorbed into the story and the symbolism," the accurate discernment of the presence of this "absorbed" religious element is necessary for anyone seeking an understanding of the deeper meaning of *The Lord of the Rings*.

The centrality of the hidden presence of Christ is discernible most insistently in the date that Tolkien ascribes to the destruction of the Ring. In one of the appendices to *The Lord of the Rings*, he states that

March 25 is "the date of the downfall of the Barad-dûr," adding that the New Year began on March 25, "in commemoration of the fall of Sauron and the deeds of the Ring-bearers." This date is of singular significance in the Christian calendar. It is the Feast of the Annunciation, the date on which Christians celebrate the Incarnation of Christ, the Word becoming Flesh in the womb of the Blessed Virgin. It is traditionally believed to be the date on which Christ's Crucifixion occurred. Annunciation Day, as it was called, was also the start of the New Year in most countries in Christian Europe during the Middle Ages.

The theological connection between the Incarnation and the Crucifixion, and hence the logical assumption that the two events happened on the same significant date, is that both events were necessary for the redemption of man from original sin. Put simply, Christians believe that original sin was "unmade" by the life, death, and resurrection of Christ. Original sin is "the One Sin to rule them all and in the darkness bind them," and this "One Sin" is "unmade" by the Crucifixion of Christ on the hill of Golgotha, the place of the skull (Mount Doom).

March 25 is, therefore, the key that unlocks the deepest meaning of *The Lord of the Rings*. If the Ring is synonymous with sin in general and original sin in particular, the Christocentric aspects of the work become apparent. Frodo, as the Ring-bearer, emerges as a Christ figure, the one who bears the Cross, and with it the sins and the hopes of humanity. He emerges also as an Everyman figure, in the tradition of the medieval Mystery Plays, who takes up his own cross in emulation of Christ. His journey through Mordor (Death) to the summit of Mount Doom (Golgotha/Death) is thus a reminder both of Christ's archetypal *via dolorosa* and also of the path of sorrows that Everyman is called to follow in the quest for sanctity and salvation. In similar vein, Sam emerges as a faithful Christian who follows in his master's footsteps.

Although Frodo emerges as the most obvious Christ figure, it should be remembered that Tolkien disliked formal or crude allegory. As such, Frodo is only a Christ figure insofar as he is the Ring-bearer and insofar as the Ring can be seen to signify sin. In every other respect, he is simply a hobbit of the Shire. He is not a figure of Christ at all times in the way that a character in a formal allegory is merely a personified abstraction of the thing or person he represents, such as, for example, the character of "Reason" in C.S. Lewis's *The Pilgrim's Regress*. In this context, it is important to recall Tolkien's distinction between the formal allegory he despised and the allegorical *applicability* he espoused. According to Tolkien's understanding of applicability, aspects of a story can be applicable to the world beyond the story, most notably to the world inhabited by the reader.

With regard to Christological applicability, it can be seen that other characters in the story, besides Frodo, emerge as Christ figures at certain *applicable* moments. Gandalf clearly reminds us of Christ in his "death," "resurrection," and "transfiguration," especially in the way that Tolkien's description of Gandalf's "resurrection" resonates unmistakably with the Gospel accounts of Christ's Transfiguration. Aragorn's descent to the Paths of the Dead reminds us of Christ's descent into hell following the Crucifixion. Aragorn, like Christ, is "King of the Dead" who has the power to set the suffering souls free of the death curse. Similarly, Aragorn is a Christ figure in his role as healer. As Ioreth, wise woman of Gondor, proclaimed: "The hands of the king are the hands of a healer, and so shall the rightful king be known" (RK, V, viii, 142).

For Tolkien, as he insisted so memorably in his famous conversation with C.S. Lewis on the nature of mythology in September 1931, Christianity was the "True Myth," the myth that really happened, the myth that gives ultimate meaning to all the lesser myths. Similarly, the Person of Christ is the True Hero who gives ultimate meaning to the heroism of all the lesser heroes. It is no surprise, therefore, that Tolkien's heroes emerge as Christ figures, reminding his readers of the archetypal Hero who gives his own lesser heroes their meaning and their very raison d'être.

JOSEPH PEARCE

Further Reading

Birzer, Bradley J. *J.R.R. Tolkien's Sanctifying Myth*. Wilmington, DE: ISI Books, 2002.

Caldecott, Stratford. *Secret Fire: The Spiritual Vision of J. R. R. Tolkien*. London: Darton, Longman & Todd, 2003.

Pearce, Joseph, ed. *Tolkien: A Celebration*. London: HarperCollins, 1999.

——. *Tolkien: Man and Myth*. London: HarperCollins, 1998.

Purtill, Richard. *J.R.R. Tolkien: Myth, Morality and Religion*. San Francisco, CA: Harper & Row, 1984.

See also **Allegory; Christianity; Fall of Man; Incarnation; Redemption; Resurrection**

CHRIST: "ADVENT LYRICS"

The opening texts of the Exeter Book, one of the four main surviving manuscripts of Old English poetry, are known to modern scholars as *Christ I, Christ II,* and *Christ III* (some, including Tolkien, use the Old English spelling *Crist*). Tolkien's discovery of the name Earendel in *Christ I* (also known as the *Advent*

Lyrics) was the seminal moment in the development of his mythology.

The "Advent Lyrics" are a series of short poems, most of which paraphrase and elaborate on Latin antiphons looking forward to the birth of Christ that are sung before and after the Magnificat at Vespers on the days leading up to Christmas (December 17–23). *Christ II* is loosely based on an Ascension Day sermon by Gregory the Great, and *Christ III* is a poetic meditation on Judgment Day.

Runic letters toward the end of *Christ II* spell the name of Cynewulf, a poet who similarly "signs" three other surviving Old English poems. The three *Christ* poems were long read as a single sequence ascribed to Cynewulf, and Tolkien refers to him as the author of lines from *Christ I*. However, only *Christ II* is certainly Cynewulfian, and *Christ I* is now generally thought to be anonymous.

The reference to Earendel that caught Tolkien's attention is in lines 104–5 of *Christ*:

Eala earendel, engla beorhtast,
ofer middangeard monnum sended.
(O Earendel, brightest of angels, sent
to men over Middle - earth)

In a letter to Clyde Kilby at Christmas 1965, Tolkien quotes these lines and describes them as "Cynewulf's words from which ultimately sprang the whole of my mythology" (Kilby, *Tolkien,* 57). The lines are the beginning of the fifth lyric in the sequence, a poem based on the Magnificat Antiphon for December 21.

Tolkien read *Christ* while a student at Oxford in 1913. He later wrote a fictionalized account of his encounter with the poem (published posthumously in *The Notion Club Papers; Shaping,* 236–37). The earliest evidence of its effect on his imagination is the poem "The Voyage of Éarendel the Evening Star," written in September 1914 (*Lost Tales II,* 267–69). Characteristics acquired by the character Éarendel/ Eärendil as Tolkien's mythology developed were directly related, as Hostetter has shown, to Tolkien's interpretation of the Earendel mentioned in *Christ*.

Tolkien refers in a letter to being struck by the "great beauty" of the name Earendel in *Christ* and its unusually euphonious form (*Letters*, no. 297), but he was also attracted by what could be deduced about the word's earlier history. In a letter to Milton Waldman, Tolkien notes that his Earendil "is in actual origin Anglo-Saxon: *earendel* 'ray of light' applied sometimes to the morning-star, a name of ramified mythological connexions (now largely obscure)" (*Letters*, no. 131). He says that it appears originally to have been a proper name and argues that cognate forms in other Germanic languages indicate it must

once have been the name of a star or star group in astronomical myth (Tolkien was aware that in Snorri Sturluson's *Edda* the Norse equivalent of *earendel*, *Aurvandilstá*, is certainly a star); noting that *earendel* is used to refer to a star presaging the dawn, he equates it with Venus, the Morning Star. In a note to the letter, he explains that the lines from *Christ* are often taken to refer to Christ (or Mary), but in fact refer to a herald and messenger, the dawn that precedes the arrival of Christ, the true sun. In an anonymous Anglo-Saxon sermon collection, *The Blickling Homilies, earendel* clearly refers to John the Baptist, and Tolkien concludes that the word is used of Venus, the Morning Star, and figuratively refers to John the Baptist.

The invocation of Earendel in *Christ I* is echoed in the line *Aiya Eärendil Elenion Ancalima* ("Hail Earendil brightest of Stars") in *The Lord of the Rings* (TT, VI, ix, 329) and in Fionwë's greeting to Eärendel in *The Shaping of Middle-earth* (154).

Tolkien probably knew Cook's edition of *Christ* (1900). A Modern English translation of the poem is in Bradley (*Anglo-Saxon,* 203–16). The philological background and Tolkien's use of *Christ I* are discussed in Helms (*Tolkien,* 37–40), Shippey (*Road,* 218–19), and Hostetter ("Over").

CARL PHELPSTEAD

Further Reading

Bradley, S.A.J., ed. and trans. *Anglo-Saxon Poetry*. London: Dent, 1982.

Cook, Albert S., ed. *The Christ of Cynewulf.* Boston: Ginn & Co., 1900.

Helms, Randel. *Tolkien and the Silmarils.* London: Thames & Hudson, 1981.

Hostetter, Carl F. "Over Middle-earth Sent unto Men: On the Philological Origins of Tolkien's Eärendel Myth." *Mythlore* 65 (1991): 5–10.

Kilby, Clyde. *Tolkien and the Silmarillion.* Berkhamsted: Lion Publishing, 1977.

Muir, B.J., ed. *The Exeter Anthology of Old English Poetry.* 2 vols. Exeter: Exeter University Press, 1994.

Shippey, T.A. *The Road to Middle-earth.* 2nd ed.. London: HarperCollins, 1992.

See also **Cynewulf; Eärendil; Old English**

CHRISTIAN READINGS OF TOLKIEN

Since the publication of *The Lord of the Rings* in the mid-1950s, numerous reviewers, scholars, and fans have sought meaning, significance, allegory, and parable within Tolkien's works. Some have desired to find parallels to contemporary world problems, while others have attempted to discover Western pagan (classical and northern European) and Christian symbolism and sources within the works. Tolkien, though, on several occasions denied the possibility of a strict allegorical interpretation of *The Lord of the Rings*, and he often expressed his profound dislike of allegory. More often than his denial of allegory, though, Tolkien credited real and invented languages, northern myth, and Roman Catholicism as the primary inspirations for his mythology. As Tolkien told an American evangelical: "I am a Christian and of course what I write will be from that essential viewpoint."

Several writers, such as the *Wall Street Journal*'s Edmund Fuller, Marquette University's William Ready, and one of Tolkien's last undergraduate students, John Ryan, commented on Tolkien's faith in the 1960s in their own works. In 1973, however, Sandra Miesel offered the first full exploration of the Christian element within Tolkien's mythology in her fine *Myth, Symbol, and Religion in "The Lord of the Rings."* For a theoretical underpinning to her book, Miesel relied heavily on Tolkien's "On Fairy-Stories" and on the various works of the French Christian Humanist Mircea Eliade. Miesel nicely ties in the Christian understanding of myth with the northern understanding of myth as found in such works as the *Völuspá* and *Beowulf*.

The following year, a professional logician and fantasy novelist, Richard Purtill, published his first of two scholarly books on Tolkien's faith, *Lord of Elves and Eldils*, also dealing with the faith of C.S. Lewis. Ten years later, he published *J.R.R. Tolkien: Myth, Morality, and Religion.* Tolkien, according to Purtill, created a literary myth that got as close to original myth as possible. In other words, Tolkien's myth is morally, ethically, theologically, and philosophically true, and, in terms of reality and plot, not entirely untrue. Certainly, for Tolkien, it would have been impossible to write an original myth, as the original myth, completely true, has been recorded in the Old and New Testaments. To change it would be blasphemy and heresy. Instead, Tolkien created a literary myth that glorified the original myth.

An American evangelical and professor of English at Wheaton College in Illinois by the name of Clyde S. Kilby wrote, perhaps, the best Christian exploration of Tolkien's mythology. Kilby had the advantage of knowing Tolkien personally, having carried on an extensive correspondence with him in the 1960s as well as having worked with him to prepare *The Silmarillion* during the summer of 1966. The memoir, *Tolkien and the Silmarillion* (1976), discusses in detail the many conversations the two had that summer. In chapter 4, "Tolkien as Christian Writer," Kilby describes Tolkien's belief in miracles, his devotion to the Virgin Mary, his view that creativity came from

God, and his identification of the "Secret Fire" of his mythology with the Holy Ghost of the Trinity.

In his 1981 *England and Always: Tolkien's World of the Rings*, Jared Lobdell argued that while "Middle-earth has no Christian 'feel' to it," one must distinguish between the Catholic religion and Catholic theology. Once separated, Lobdell claimed, it becomes possible to recognize that the theology of the trilogy "is uncompromisingly Christian and Catholic." Within the trilogy, Lobdell argued, one can find sin, love, and redemption. In other words, Tolkien's worldview is utterly Catholic, whether he presents the figure of God (or any person of the Trinity) blatantly or not.

Between 1984 and 1998, very little appeared specifically discussing Tolkien's Catholicism or the religious symbolism within his legendarium. In 1998, though, this changed dramatically with Joseph Pearce's outstanding *Tolkien: Man and Myth*, a book that inspired a whole new wave of Christian evaluations of Tolkien. Pearce argues that *The Lord of the Rings* is a theological thriller, and he explores specifically Catholics ideas and theology found within the legendarium. By 1998, of course, all of Tolkien's corpus had been published, giving the newer books a definite advantage over those published between 1973 and 1984. Not all of the Christian authors following Pearce, however, employed these advantages, and many of them focused only on *The Lord of the Rings*.

This new wave of post-Pearce books ranges from the brilliantly insightful to the absurdly incoherent. Using the philosophy of Josef Pieper and the theology of Karl Barth, Protestant theologian Ralph C. Wood argues in his *Gospel According to Tolkien: Visions of the Kingdom in Middle-earth* (2003) that the Christian Gospel is embedded into the very foundations of Tolkien's mythology. Matthew Dickerson, a Protestant Evangelical and novelist, explores the themes of heroism and free will in *Following Gandalf: Epic Battles and Moral Victory in "The Lord of the Rings"* (2003). Another Protestant Evangelical, Mark Eddy Smith, examines *The Lord of the Rings* as a personal journey, informed by a scriptural worldview, in his *Tolkien's Ordinary Virtues* (2001). Indeed, his chapters and thoughts follow, exactly, Tolkien's plot. An Episcopal minister, Fleming Rutledge, argues that Tolkien wrote a superficial narrative and a deep narrative. Her book, *The Battle for Middle-earth: Tolkien's Divine Design in "The Lord of the Rings,"* follows the superficial narrative while constantly commenting on the deeper narrative, which she argues has an invisible but active God at the very center of the plot. Bradley J. Birzer, a professional historian, considers Tolkien's Catholicism in light of one of the oldest questions of the Christian Church, "What has Athens to do with Jerusalem?" In his *J.R.R. Tolkien's Sanctifying Myth* (2003), Birzer claims that Tolkien followed a long tradition beginning with St. Paul in Athens, attempting to sanctify the pagan. The best of the post-Pearce Christian works is Stratford Caldecott's *Secret Fire: The Spiritual Vision of J.R.R. Tolkien* (2003; published in a revised edition as *Power of the Ring* [2005]), a work brimming with theological insight about Tolkien's particular brand of Catholicism. Caldecott, a Catholic theologian, argues that Tolkien offers the reader an anti-ideological book, thus celebrating creativity and freedom, in the best sense of these words.

Among the worst of the post-Pearce books is *Finding God in "The Lord of the Rings"* (2001) by Kurt Bruner, vice president of Focus on the Family, and Jim Ware, a professional Christian author. Seemingly written for Bible study groups, Bruner and Ware's book come across as trite, and the reader wonders how the proof-texting of scripture really fits into Tolkien's mythology. Even worse is Greg Wright's *Tolkien in Perspective: Sifting the Gold from the Glitter* (2003). Filled with a welter of pop-cultural references, poorly developed arguments, and unsupported assertions, *Tolkien in Perspective* hopes, first, to show Christians that they should read Tolkien, and, second, to "persuade the Tolkien fan that there may be good reasons to maintain a cool relationship with Middle-earth" as the "Book of the 20th century was not *The Lord of the Rings*. It was the Bible." With books such as these, it should surprise no one that many scholars and fans fear that Christians have attempted to co-opt Tolkien's works and create a hagiographic image of Tolkien as many of C.S. Lewis's fans have done to Lewis. In a not atypical response to the outpouring of works on Tolkien's religion by those who openly profess Christianity, one reviewer stated, "the essential motive behind many of these books is for the fundamentalists to claim Tolkien as one of their own." The reviewer entitled his article "Wake Up and Smell the Dogma."

Other scholars—such as Verlyn Flieger, Jane Chance, Tom Shippey, Colin Duriez, and Anne Petty—while not setting out explicitly to consider the Christian elements of Tolkien's work, have made significant contributions to an understanding of his Catholicism. In his *Author of the Century*, for example, Shippey points out that *The Fellowship of the Ring* departs from Rivendell on December 25, with its success and the fall of Sauron on March 25. While the symbolism of the departure date is obvious, March 25 is more obscure. It is, however, Shippey notes, a very important day in the old English calendar. On that day, the English once acknowledged

the fall of Adam and Eve, and celebrated both St. Gabriel's Annunciation to Mary, and, of course, the Resurrection of Christ. Shippey labels the time between December 25 and March 25, significantly, "mythic space."

BRADLEY J. BIRZER

See also **Catholicism, Roman; Christ**

CHRISTIANITY

It would be difficult to overemphasize the importance of the Christian religion to J.R.R. Tolkien. From his mother's controversial conversion to Roman Catholicism in 1904 until he died in 1973, Tolkien remained a pious and devout Roman Catholic. "I have consciously planned very little; and should chiefly be grateful for having been brought up (since I was eight) in a Faith that has nourished me and taught me all the little that I know," Tolkien wrote to his friend Father Murray, a Jesuit. That "I owe to my mother, who clung to her conversion and died young, largely through the hardships of poverty resulting from it." Only in the early 1920s when at Leeds University did Tolkien falter in his faith. It was a time he remembered with bitterness and self-loathing. It was, however, in the big scheme of things, a very brief part of his life. His Roman Catholic faith not only defined his spiritual life, it also pervaded his family life, his academic life, and his social life. According to his son Michael, Roman Catholicism "pervaded all his thinking, beliefs and everything else." In an interview in 1997, Tolkien's close friend George Sayer stated that *The Lord of the Rings* "would have been very different, and the writing of it very difficult, if Tolkien hadn't been a Christian. He thought it a profoundly Christian book." And, famously, Tolkien admitted that *The Lord of the Rings* was unconsciously Catholic in its original and consciously so in its revision. Tolkien's larger legendarium—as found in *The Book of Lost Tales* and "The Silmarillion"—offers an even more blatant Christian vision. From the first *Qenya Lexicon,* which contains words for each member of the Blessed Trinity, monks, nuns, missionaries, saints, and the crucifix, to his last writings of his legendarium, especially those printed in the last three volumes of the *History of Middle-earth*, Tolkien's mythology is filled with Christian imagery, symbolism, and significance.

For Tolkien, Christianity meant specifically Roman Catholicism. While each culture may express its faith in its own individual manner, each should adhere to certain universals. In other words, Tolkien believed that the essence of true faith was that held by the Roman Catholic Church, but like Pope Gregory the Great in his instructions to St. Augustine of Canterbury, he also believed that each culture had the right to express itself through the accidents of certain liturgical practices, prayers, and so on. Tolkien, along the same lines, also believed that Catholicism must sanctify the pagan. One can find Tolkien's clearest vision of this in his essay on *Beowulf*. The Christian should not reject paganism; he should instead learn from it and incorporate the best of it into the larger Catholic tradition. Here, again, Tolkien believed in the diversity of accidents, as long as the essence (Christian theology) remained universal. In this belief, Tolkien followed a long line of Catholic tradition, from St. Paul in Athens and his discussion of the Unknown God to St. Augustine's *City of God*, which incorporates into Christianity the philosophies and some of the metaphysics of Plato, Aristotle, and Cicero and St. Thomas Aquinas's synthesis of Catholicism and Aristotelianism.

When pushed on it, Tolkien offered a broad-tent vision of Christianity. But in the main, he held Protestants in low regard. First, he resented the Reformation with an intense bitterness. "It was against this [the Blessed Sacrament] that the W. European revolt (or Reformation) was really launched—'the blasphemous fable of the Mass'—and faith/works a mere red herring," Tolkien wrote in 1963 to his son Michael. Tolkien reserved his greatest anger for the Church of England. The true foundation of the Anglican church, Tolkien once wrote to his son Christopher, was merely a deep hatred of Roman Catholicism and sheer "cockiness." He thought Anglicanism "a pathetic and shadowy medley of half-remembered traditions and mutilated beliefs." When the allied forces entered Rome during World War II, Tolkien expressed his shock at the utterances of elderly, bigoted Englishmen.

Second, the Protestant love of "primitivism" grated on him. He believed that it destroyed the organic nature and existence of the church, which St. Paul described as "the Body of Christ" numerous times in his New Testament letters. The church, like a tree, must be allowed to grow and branch. Tolkien, then, believed the Reformation to be a regressive step rather than a progressive one. It ignored in particular the power of the Logos to transform the world through the sacraments, a fundamental Catholic belief about the nature and history of the world after the Incarnation, death, and resurrection of Christ.

The resentment Tolkien held for Protestants often revealed itself in his occasionally volatile relationship with C.S. Lewis. Tolkien played a vital role in C.S. Lewis's acceptance of Christianity in the fall of 1931.

The two had talked theology frequently after meeting in 1926. It was shortly after a late-night conversation between Lewis, Tolkien, and another Inkling, Hugo Dyson, that Lewis converted to Christianity. Lewis, of course, became the most important Christian apologist of the twentieth century. Much to Tolkien's chagrin, Lewis never became Roman Catholic but instead reawoke to "the prejudices so sedulously planted in childhood and boyhood." Additionally, Lewis's Everyman "Mere Christianity" theology frequently annoyed Tolkien. Even worse for Tolkien, Lewis's seeming indifference to persecutions of Catholics greatly bothered him. When the infamous Roman Catholic convert and poet Roy Campbell visited the Inklings in the autumn of 1944 and discussed the Communist atrocities against the church in Spain, for example, Tolkien noted that the martyrdom of Roman Catholic priests rarely affected Lewis. "I daresay [he] really thinks they asked for it," Tolkien commented. Tolkien noted with further irony that Lewis was ready to go to war over a jailed Protestant, even though he dismissed the murder of Catholics.

Perhaps Tolkien's most profound statement regarding Christianity comes from his academic address given at the University of St. Andrews in the 1930s, "On Fairy-Stories." After a long and profound discussion of the role of mythology and fairy in awakening the best within each person and confronting the evils of modernity, Tolkien discussed the nature of the most complete joy possible in this earth, the eucatastrophe, a foreshadowing of the joy to come.

> I would venture to say that approaching the Christian Story from this direction, it has long been my feeling (a joyous feeling) that God redeemed the corrupt making-creatures, men, in a way fitting to this aspect, as to others, of their strange nature. The Gospel contains a fairy-story, or a story of a larger kind which embraces all the essence of fairy-stories. They contain many marvels—peculiarly artistic, beautiful, and moving: "mythical" in their perfect, self-contained significance; and among the marvels is the greatest and most complete conceivable eucatastrophe. But this story has entered History and the primary world; the desire and aspiration of subcreation has been raised to the fulfillment of Creation. The Birth of Christ is the eucatastrophe of Man's history. The Resurrection is the eucatastrophe of the story of the Incarnation. The story begins and ends in joy. It has pre-eminently the "inner consistency of reality." There is no tale ever told that men would rather find was true, and none which so many skeptical men have accepted as true on its merits. For the Art of it has the supremely convincing tone of Primary Art, that is, of Creation. To reject it either leads to sadness or wrath (*MC*, 155-56).

That Tolkien would speak so bluntly of his faith to a group of academics, most of whom would have been secularized, in the 1930s speaks volumes about the importance of his faith to him.

BRADLEY J. BIRZER

See also **Catholicism, Roman; Eucatastrophe; Lewis, C.S.; Life; Roman Catholic Church; Theology; Tolkien, Edith**

CHURCH OF ENGLAND

Tolkien's troubled relationship with the Church of England was linked to the painful memories of his mother's untimely death. He believed that her death, at the age of thirty-five, when he was only twelve years old, was the result, indirectly at least, of the persecution she had suffered from her Anglican relatives following her conversion to Catholicism in 1900. "When I think of my mother's death ... worn out with persecution, poverty, and largely consequent, disease, in the effort to hand on to us small boys the Faith ... I find it very hard and bitter, when my children stray away." Tolkien considered his mother a martyr for the Catholic faith, writing nine years after her death that "my own dear mother was a martyr indeed, and it was not to everybody that God grants so easy a way to his great gifts as he did to Hilary and myself, giving us a mother who killed herself with labour and trouble to ensure us keeping the faith." His insistence that his future wife, Edith, a very active member of the Church of England, must become a Catholic before he would marry her should be seen in the light, or gloom, of this lingering resentment of, and antagonism toward, the anti-Catholicism of the Church of England. There is little doubt that he held the Church of England in considerable contempt, declaring it "a pathetic and shadowy medley of half-remembered traditions and mutilated beliefs."

JOSEPH PEARCE

Further Reading

Pearce, Joseph. *Tolkien: Man and Myth.* San Francisco: Ignatius Press, 1998.

See also **Catholicism, Roman; Christianity; Tolkien, Edith**

CLASS IN TOLKIEN'S WORK

Critics have long noted Tolkien's conservative views on social class and the prominence of traditional class structures in his universe. He is often seen as a spokesman for royalist, aristocratic values, although his social origins in Sarehole and the Birmingham region were "impoverished" middle class and poorer than those of many other twentieth-century British writers (Rosebury, 135). Indeed, Tolkien had a strong affinity for working-class men during his wartime experiences because of his early experiences with rural and urban laborers (Garth, 149). Humphrey Carpenter sums up Tolkien's attitudes on social station that permeate his writings thus: the professor believed that each person "belonged or ought to belong to a specific 'estate', whether high or low," and saw that those who were unsure of their status or who put down others could be "ruthless" (Carpenter, 127–28). Respecting one's social betters is a natural corollary to this idea, for as Tolkien said, "Touching your cap to the Squire may be damn bad for the Squire but it's damn good for you." (Carpenter, 128). Tolkien's literary works support his belief that all must respect their positions in the class hierarchy and should bolster the system for the greater good.

In *The Hobbit*, Tolkien portrays Bilbo Baggins as a model of "respectable" English class values while also poking fun at him and his society for its stodginess. Tom Shippey comments that Bilbo is a "middle-middle" to "upper-middle class" member best described as "bourgeois"; nevertheless, the name "Baggins" comes from the food a laborer would take with him to work, thus introducing a mildly "vulgar" aspect to his character (Shippey, 8–9). Bilbo is labeled "queer" upon his return after his adventures, and Tolkien uses the outrage of his neighbors to laugh at the provincial narrow-mindedness of the "respectable" classes (Kocher, 25–26). Yet *The Hobbit* also praises traditional social values by promoting rule by a benevolent steward over the mob rule of the people—Bard the heir to the Lord of Dale versus the Master of Lake-town who rules as a "politician" trying to appeal to the masses. This pattern fits in with Tolkien's overall dislike of democracy as a form of government and his preference for an "unconstitutional" monarchy. The anachronism of a middle-class hobbit existing in a world of kings and hereditary rule underscores the extent to which Tolkien regarded the bourgeois culture represented by Bilbo as a complement to the older social hierarchy.

The other parts of the legendarium further combine a faith in a highly structured society culminating in the king as the ultimate authority with depictions of familiar, quasi-English array of socio-economic levels in a continuum from the working classes to the more prosperous orders. The *Silmarillion* accounts focus upon the upper tiers of the divine and worldly hierarchies of Arda: the pantheon of the Valar and the kings and princes of Beleriand in their struggles against Morgoth. Even outlaws such as Túrin Turambar or Beren belong to highest orders of their races. In *The Lord of the Rings*, the members of the Fellowship and even the other major players (such as Sméagol) are all from the top of their respective social hierarchies (Burns, 2004). Aragorn becomes the rightful ruler in the end, asserting the role of the king as the natural ruler over the other layers of society from the highest to the lowest. Some readers have mapped the different races onto a grid of economic classes, with hobbits representing the "peasants," Elves the aristocrats, Men the promoters of "democratic rulership," and Dwarves standing for "factory workers and hard laborers" (Houston), showing how complex the hierarchical functioning of class can be in Tolkien. Yet it is principally within the hobbit culture that we can see the peaceful dealings of different classes with each other and can thereby understand how overarching concepts such as the divine right of kings relate to the bonds of master and servant on a smaller scale.

The cultural and economic organization of the Shire expands upon the ambiguously middle-class image of Bilbo's home described in *The Hobbit*. In letter 181, Tolkien explains that "as an Englishman brought up in an 'almost rural' village of Warwickshire on the edge of the prosperous bourgeoisie of Birmingham (about the time of the Diamond Jubilee!)," he used the world he knew in his depiction of hobbit communities (*Letters*, 235). As such, the Shire is "half republic half aristocracy" in nature (*Letters*, 241), administered by the high Fallohidish families such as the Tooks led by the Thain (an originally military title to represent authority on behalf of the absent king), the Brandybucks with their manor-like Brandy Hall, and the bourgeois Baggins, as well as the elected mayor of Michel Delving. The remaining farming and other laboring families, chiefly the Stoors and Harfoots, resemble traditional Victorian images of the rural poor.

The harmonious interaction of the classes in the Shire demonstrates how societies should function for Tolkien. Bilbo's teaching Sam how to read reflects the Victorian ideal of educating the poor, and he displays "genteel deference to his servant" the Gaffer on matters of vegetable gardening (Chance, 29). The close tie between Frodo and his gardener Sam during their trek into Mordor is the most vivid instance of class cooperation. Many have viewed their relationship in terms of that between a gentleman military office in the World War I era and his

batman, or officer's valet, but their dependence upon each other and the emergence of greatness even in those not born to it reflects the change that occurred in class relations resulting from wartime experiences (Hooker, 131). Master and servant come to rely upon each other, adding some fluidity to the class divide, but ultimately showing how the classes can work in concert with each other for the betterment of both. Sam climbs in social station in the end when he becomes the mayor, but he keeps true to his roots (Hooker, 132), and like the rise of the healing king Aragorn, the rise of a gardener to the office of mayor signifies the restoration of fertility to the community after the upheavals of Saruman's brutal social reorganization (Chance, 126).

Though some critics assert that "Tolkien was introduced into a world of privilege (if only middle-class privilege) in which racial distinctions and levels in class were assumed" (Rearick, 866), they should note that Tolkien does not regard class differences as a form of oppression, but rather as a necessary condition of his universe. Respecting boundaries and recognizing distinctions form the basis for both social and cosmic order.

DAVID D. OBERHELMAN

Further Reading

Burns, Marjorie. "King and Hobbit: The Exalted and Lowly in Middle-earth and Beyond." Paper presented at "The Lord of the Rings, 1954–2004: Scholarship in Honor of Richard E. Blackwelder," Marquette University, Milwaukee, WI., October 22, 2004.

Carpenter, Humphrey. *Tolkien: A Biography*. Boston: Houghton Mifflin, 1977.

Chance, Jane. *The Lord of the Rings: The Mythology of Power*. Rev. ed. Lexington, KY: University Press of Kentucky, 2001.

Garth, John. *Tolkien and the Great War: The Threshold of Middle-earth*. Boston, MA: Houghton Mifflin, 2003.

Hooker, Mark T. "Frodo's Batman." *Tolkien Studies* 1, no. 1 (2004): 125–36.

Houston, Julia. "Tolkien, Racism, and Paranoia." *About.com: Sci-Fi/Fantasy*. http://scifi.about.com/cs/lordoftherings/a/aa012303.htm (November 9, 2003).

Kocher, Paul. *Master of Middle-earth: The Fiction of J.R.R. Tolkien*. Boston, MA: Houghton Mifflin, 1972.

Rearick, Anderson, III. "Why Is the Only Good Orc a Dead Orc? The Dark Face of Racism Examined in Tolkien's World." *Modern Fiction Studies*, 50, no. 4 (2004): 861–74.

Rosebury, Brian. *Tolkien: A Cultural Phenomenon*. Houndmills: Palgrave Macmillan, 2003.

Shippey, Tom. *J.R.R. Tolkien: Author of the Century*. Boston, MA: Houghton Mifflin, 2000.

See also **Capitalism; Communism; England, Twentieth Century; Frodo; Hierarchy; Kingship; Marxist Readings of Tolkien; Politics; Sam**

COGHILL, NEVILL HENRY KENDAL AYLMER (1899–1980)

Nevill Coghill was professor of English literature at Oxford from 1957 to 1966 and a member of the Inklings, where, especially in the early days, he could be seen with a cigarette at his lips, his large head nodding at some comment. He hailed from Ireland, the younger son of an Anglo-Irish baronet. After serving at the tail end of World War I, he went as a scholar to Exeter College, Oxford, gaining a First Class degree in English in 1923. In 1924, he was elected a research fellow there, the following year also becoming librarian. As an undergraduate attending the Essay Club at Exeter College with his friend H.V.D. "Hugo" Dyson, he heard Tolkien read aloud "The Fall of Gondolin." The tale was enthusiastically received. He was also a member of the Coalbiter (Kolbítar) Club set up by Tolkien, which included a number of dons such as C.S. Lewis; George Gordon, the president of Magdalen College; C.T. Onions from the Oxford English Dictionary project; R.M. Dawkins, the professor of Byzantine and Modern Greek; and others. The formation of the Inklings in the fall of 1933 coincided with the natural ending of the Coalbiters, which by now had fulfilled its purpose. Three of the Coalbiters, Tolkien, Lewis, and Nevill Coghill, became Inklings. After the early years of the Inklings club, Coghill's attendance became intermittent, probably because of his many activities.

Among the many students he oversaw were the poet W.H. Auden and the actor Richard Burton, who first acted in Coghill's theatrical productions as an undergraduate fresh from the South Wales valleys. In 1945, Coghill gave the Sir Israel Gollancz Memorial Lecture at the British Academy on the subject "The Pardon of Piers Plowman," which was subsequently published. He also brought out a study, *The Poet Chaucer,* in 1949.

Coghill was renowned for his theatrical productions, appreciated by Tolkien with his own dramatic bent. Coghill's notable productions included *Samson Agonistes* (1930), *Troilus and Cressida* (1937), *Hamlet* (1940), *The Winter's Tale* (1946), and *The Tempest* (1949). Coghill made a movie of Christopher Marlowe's *Doctor Faustus* (1968), starring Richard Burton, Elizabeth Taylor, and members of the Oxford University Dramatic Society, adapted from his theatrical production in Oxford in 1966. He began to translate from Middle English as opportunities arose for broadcasting with the BBC. Radio listeners were able to enjoy his renderings of such works as *The Canterbury Tales* (1946–47), Langland's *Piers Plowman* (1947), and Chaucer's *Troilus and Criseyde*. The publication of his famous translation of Chaucer's *Canterbury Tales* into Modern English couplets resulted from the broadcasts.

Tolkien and Coghill were long-standing friends. A mutual friend was C.S. Lewis, and it was inevitable that Coghill was therefore drawn into the circle of the Inklings. Tolkien confided to Coghill that he had modeled Treebeard's manner of speaking (*Hrum, Hroom*) on the megaphonic voice of C.S. Lewis. Coghill, with the poet John Masefield, arranged "Summer Diversions" in Oxford. At the 1938 and 1939 events, Tolkien presented himself as Chaucer and from memory recited *The Nun's Priest's Tale* and *The Reeve's Tale*, demonstrating his acting talents.

Coghill indirectly was responsible for Charles Williams's introduction to the Inklings. While visiting Nevill Coghill at Exeter College one evening in February 1936, Lewis discovered Charles Williams's novel *The Place of the Lion*. Lewis heard from Coghill the basic plot of the "spiritual shocker" in vivid terms. Recalled Lewis, "No man whom I ever met describes another man's work better that Mr. Coghill (his descriptions of Kafka always seemed to me better even than Kafka himself) and I went home with his copy." Soon the book passed around the other Inklings, Tolkien sharing the excitement of the discovery, according to Lewis in a fan letter to Charles Williams.

In 1965, W.H. Auden invited Tolkien to contribute to a Festschrift to mark Coghill's retirement. Tolkien expressed himself grieved that he had nothing he could offer. He was amused in later life by the recollection of Coghill's adjective "hobbit-forming," applied to his books.

COLIN DURIEZ

Further Reading

Carpenter, Humphrey. *The Inklings: C.S. Lewis, J.R.R. Tolkien, Charles Williams and Their Friends.* London: Allen & Unwin, 1978.

———. *J.R.R. Tolkien: A Biography.* London: Allen & Unwin, 1977.

Coghill, Nevill, trans. *Canterbury Tales Translated in Modern English.* Harmonsworth: Penguin Books, 1951.

Gray, Douglas, ed. *The Collected Papers of Nevill Coghill: Shakespearian and Medievalist.* Brighton: Harvester, 1987.

Lawlor, John, and W.H. Auden, eds. *To Nevill Coghill from Friends.* London: Faber, 1966.

See also **Inklings; Lewis, C.S.; "Chaucer as Philologist: The Reeve's Tale"; Oxford**

COLLECTING

Since the publication of *The Lord of the Rings*, collecting related to Tolkien—from his published work to criticism to related journals, toys, and other paraphernalia—has grown in popularity as quickly as Tolkien's name has entered fandom. The collectibles trend in general is a major industry. Since 2001, the collecting phenomenon has drastically increased due to the release of Peter Jackson's film interpretation of *The Lord of the Rings*, which has added a plethora to the collectibles market.

Prior to the recent film interpretations of Tolkien's work, the primary form of collecting with regard to Tolkien has been to seek out Tolkien's published works, rare manuscripts of his unpublished work, drawings, and even letters by his own hand. Many beginning collectors start with a modern edition of *The Hobbit* or *The Lord of the Rings*. The enthusiast will then move onto earlier editions of either work or other titles by Tolkien, which begin to become expensive, depending upon publication details. How obscure the item is determines the price. Examples of rare Tolkien collectibles are original articles or journals Tolkien edited or was published in, such as "Iþþlen in *Sawles Warde*" (reprints Tolkien's essay from *English Studies* 28, no. 6 [December 1947]), *The Devil's Coach Horses* (1925), *Songs for the Philologists* (1936), or *Medium Aevum* (1940–59). The price of any item depends upon its scarcity and the demand for it.

Various editions of Tolkien's work are highly desired by collectors. To obtain an edition inscribed by Tolkien himself elevates the collector to heights of rapture. First editions range from priceless to the thousands, while early or rare editions have sold for the hundreds or thousands. An inscription by the author will double the value of such a collectible.

For the novice literary collector, many Tolkien scholars provide resources about where to obtain books and related material. Two resources of great repute provide excellent scholarship in Tolkien studies as well as invaluable material to the collector: originally entitled the *J.R.R. Tolkien Collecting and Bibliography Special Interest Group Magazine*, *The Tolkien Collector* has been produced and edited by Christina Scull and Wayne Hammond since 1992; and Hammond's *J.R.R. Tolkien: A Descriptive Bibliography*, published in 1993 with the assistance of Douglas A. Anderson, details a historical account of Tolkien's publishing history, a bibliography, and every known detail of Tolkien's work. It is a standard reference for scholars, librarian, students, and collectors with a growing interest in Tolkien. One of the most comprehensive collections of Tolkien material available for public viewing and research would be the Tolkien collection at Marquette University. Marquette is also the home of the S. Gary Hunnewell Collection, which is the largest compilation of journal publications and fanzines dedicated to Tolkien.

For those collecting items other than literature by Tolkien, the 1960s began what is today considered the "Tolkien cult." Buttons and bumpers stickers declaring "Gandalf for President" or "Frodo Lives!" along with the first production of Tolkien calendars, which featured the work of renowned artists Ted Nasmith, the Hildebrandt Brothers, and a multitude of other artists, are greatly sought. The 1970–80s began the trend of role-playing games dedicated to Tolkien's world, eventually leading to action figures based on the Ralph Bakshi films. The games produced by Iron Crown Enterprises (ICE) are no longer produced, having been replaced by games based on the 2001–3 *Lord of the Rings* films, thereby creating a demand for the ICE games. This is the same for the earlier action figures, which have been uncommon with the release of action figures bearing the likenesses of Jackson's film interpretations.

The Internet has made collecting an easier trade for old and new enthusiasts. A simple search for a book or item can produce hundreds of Web sites advertising the item or distributors selling it across the planet. For the collector, whether it is for personal, sentimental value or monetary gain, the Tolkien collecting phenomenon has a wide spectrum of items to offer. It has never been a singular collecting area, but one that offers something for everyone.

ANTHONY S. BURDGE and JESSICA BURKE

Further Reading

Drout, Michael D.C., ed. "Bibliography (in English) for 2001–2002." *Tolkien Studies* (West Virginia University Press) 1 (2004).

———. "Bibliography (in English) for 2003." *Tolkien Studies* (West Virginia University Press) (2005).

Hammond, Wayne, and Anderson, Douglas. *J.R.R. Tolkien: A Descriptive Bibliography*. Newcastle, DE: Oak Knoll Press, 1993.

Hammond, Wayne, and Scull, Christina, eds. *The Tolkien Collector*. http://bcn.net/~whammond/collect.html.

Marquette University Special Collections. J.R.R. Tolkien. http://www.marquette.edu/library/collections/archives/tolkien.html.

Tolkien Library. "Collecting Tolkien." http://www.tolkienlibrary.com/collectingtolkien.htm.

See also **Artists; Gaming;** *Lord of the Rings,* **Adaptations; Jackson, Peter**

COLORS

Ambiguity inheres in the symbolism of colors in general (Hermann and Cagiano di Azevedo, 434), and Tolkien's works provide no exception. Nonetheless, the color white in Western culture has traditionally indicated purity and perfection (Hermann and Cagiano di Azevedo, 431, 434)—one thinks, for example, of the eponymous "pearl" without spot in the Middle English poem—and Tolkien often avails himself of this association unproblematically: for example, the White Tree of Gondor represents (explicitly) all that is good in Middle-earth. Opposed to white is black: the Nazgûl, for example, wear black robes and ride black horses. Yet one must not suppose that Tolkien employs such symbolism methodically: the banner that Arwen sews for Aragorn has a black field, and however white the snow on Caradhras, it still hinders the Fellowship.

Moreover, Tolkien's use of white grows complicated. For white is also unbroken light, that is, light before, in diminution, it is split into the colors of the spectrum. When Saruman falls from grace, his erstwhile white garments become multihued. "White" and "light" thus often coincide in Tolkien's conception: the priceless gem in *The Hobbit*, the Arkenstone, is white and emits light. The most precious objects in Tolkien's works emit light, for example, the Silmarils (the eponymous jewels of *The Silmarillion*). "Black," by contrast, is but the absence of light. Tolkien's symbolic use of "black" and "dark" to describe evil thus harmonizes with the Boethian view of evil as merely the absence of good (on this in Tolkien, see Shippey, 128–35).

Green also has significance in Tolkien's works. The most prominent gem in *The Lord of the Rings* is the Elessar, the emerald that gives the returned king, Aragorn, his regnal name. As a ranger, Aragorn had also worn green. The Hobbits commonly wear green garb; and the Elessar's name ("Elf-Stone") associates green with the Elves. Green, besides its obvious natural associations with vigor and vitality, also had in medieval thought a connection with light: it suggested "seeds [which] burst into light" (Hugh of St. Victor, *De tribus Diebus*, 821B) and has "roots in the Sun" and "lights in whitest serenity" (Hildegard of Bingen, "O nobilissima uiriditas"). In Hildegard's conception, green was "the earthly expression of the celestial sunlight" (Dronke, 84). This may help explain the positive associations of green in *The Lord of the Rings*: Middle-earth's Elessar corresponds to the divinely lit Silmarils as the green grass of Rohan does to the sunlight. Still, one may easily become overlearned: just because gray in medieval art represented temptation (Haupt, 115), we need not analyze under this association Gandalf the Grey's fear of temptation through the Ring. All the same, much remains for investigation in this regard.

Finally, Tolkien often uses color as a simple distinguishing device—much as the liturgical colors of purple, white, green, black, and red distinguish the ecclesiastical seasons. His wizards wear white, grey,

brown, and blue. The three Elven rings are blue, white, and red. The color chosen need not lack a symbolic value (e.g., the red ring is that of fire and serves to kindle men's hearts), yet we should not always expect to find one.

VICTOR L. PARKER

Further Reading

Biggam, C. P. "Aspects of Chaucer's Adjectives of Hue." *Chaucer Review* 28, no. 1 (1993): 41–53.

Dronke, P. "Tradition and Innovation in Medieval Western Colour-Imagery." *Eranos* (Leiden) 41 (1972): 51–107.

Haupt, A. "Die Farbsymbolik in der sakralen Kunst des abendländischen Mittelalters." Diss., Leipzig, 1941.

Hermann, A., and M. Cagiano di Azevedo. "Farbe." *Reallexikon für Antike und Christentum* 7 (1969): 358–447.

Hildegard of Bingen. *Lieder*. Edited by P. Barth et al. Salzburg: Otto Muller, 1969.

Hugh of St. Victor. *De tribus Diebus*. Edited by D. Poirel Turnhout: Brepols, 2002.

Mengis, C. "Farbe." In *Handwörterbuch des deutschen Aberglaubens*, edited by H. Bächtold-Stäubli, 2:1189–1215. 1930.

Shippey, Tom. *J.R.R. Tolkien: Author of the Century*. Boston: Houghton Mifflin, 2000.

See also **Elessar; Silmarils; Two Trees**

COMEDY

Comic elements are unevenly spread in Tolkien's works. They are most abundant and straightforward in his children's stories, like *The Hobbit* or *Roverandom*. In *The Silmarillion* there is very little comedy. In his major work, *The Lord of the Rings*, comedy plays a more significant role but works within certain bounds. The author himself claimed the work was intended to "delight" the reader. Moreover, at the structural level it is possible to detect "the essentially comedic (in contradistinction to tragic) nature of *The Lord of the Rings*" (Rosebury, 70). Related to this is the importance of eucatastrophe in the aesthetic fulfillment of the work. The comic characters and incidents contribute to the ultimately benign character of Middle-earth.

However, Tolkien felt that on account of the evident artificiality of the subcreated "Secondary World," the moment "disbelief arises, the spell is broken" ("On Fairy-Stories," 132). Consequently, a fantasy world cannot withstand much irony, and very little is found in his fiction. One has to look beyond the Middle-earth universe to a story like *Farmer Giles of Ham* for a more sustained, albeit gentle, example of irony.

Thus, comedy and comic situations in *The Lord of the Rings* tend toward simplicity. Most are centered round the hobbit world and characters. Frodo is one of the rare major hobbit characters that is not comic in any way. Significantly, describing Sam as the quintessential hobbit, Tolkien claimed he possessed a vulgarity that displayed itself in his "mental myopia which is proud of itself, and a readiness to measure and sum up all things from a limited experience, largely enshrined in sententious traditional 'wisdom'" (*Letters*, 329). Understandably, then, he is often the source of comic relief, much like his fellow hobbits, who share the above characteristics to a greater or lesser degree.

The novel's narrator introduces hobbits in a good-naturedly tongue-in-cheek manner, especially when talking about their customs. This is continued in the first chapter with Bilbo's birthday party, instilling the impression of a Breughel canvas of peasant-like characters and activities. Such an introduction to the hobbits purposefully misleads the reader, who, along with the more obviously heroic characters, has initial misgivings of the depth of this "race."

At an individual level, a hobbit character, like Merry, for instance, might go from an initial stage, where he is more comic, to a weightier presence as events allow him to develop. Even then, however, he may surprise us, as when Aragorn lays his hands on the unconscious Hobbit in the Houses of Healing and Merry awakens to say "I am hungry. What is the time?" (*RK*, viii, 145). The function of the comic utterance at this juncture is to gently prick the high tone of the preceding narrative.

The culture of the hobbits likewise tends toward the comic. For instance, hobbit poetry is generally characterized by "plain language [and] proverbial sentiment" (Shippey, 172), which lends itself well to comic verse, like Frodo's "The Man in the Moon" song at the Prancing Pony and Sam's "Rhyme of the Troll" near Weathertop. The first exemplifies the Shire's "high style," skillfully extending folkloric themes, and the second is an example of hobbit black humor, featuring the exchange between a hobbit and a troll gnawing the latter's uncle's bones. Combined, they reinforce the impression of the fundamentally benign nature of hobbit culture.

Even though the world of Middle-earth is treated with the utmost seriousness, the same is not true of every theme. Paradoxically, the theme that is the most imposing, of power and domination, is undercut by the character of Tom Bombadil. On the one hand, the character is among the most mysterious, since it is never clear why the One Ring has no hold on him; on the other hand, with his garish clothing and nonsensical calls of "hey dol" and "merry dol," he is perhaps the most comical non-hobbit in *The Lord of the Rings*.

Most often, when minor characters are comic, such as Barley Butterbur of the Prancing Pony, the fun is never too demeaning and adds to the humanity of the individual depicted. Moreover, a character like Lobelia Sackville-Baggins may start out as a nasty comic character, but she ends up heroic, demonstrating that in the overall scheme of the work characters are not necessarily set in one particular role, no matter how minor they may be.

CHRISTOPHER GARBOWSKI

Further Reading

Rosebury, Brian. *Tolkien: A Cultural Phenomenon*. Palgrave MacMillan, 2003.
Shippey, T.A. *The Road to Middle-earth*. HarperCollins, 1992. First published 1982.
Tolkien, J.R.R. "On Fairy-Stories." In *MC*, 109–61.

See also **Eucatastrophe; Hobbits; Humor; "On Fairy-Stories"; Tom Bombadil**

COMMUNISM

Opposition to totalitarianism of both the German National Socialist and Communist varieties (Communism here being used in the twentieth-century sense of Marxism-Leninism) is implicit throughout Tolkien's mythology and is explicit in several passages in his letters.

The reasons included its actual record of murderous cruelty and aggression, its coercion and claim to control every aspect of life, and most of all its denial of the existence of God and even of absolute values beyond the needs of the Party. Lenin's statement to a Komsomol Congress on Communist ethical thought is an example of the antithesis of Tolkien's values: "Morality is what serves to destroy the old exploiting society and to unite all the working people around the proletariat, which is building up a new society ... we do not believe in an eternal morality, and we expose all the falseness of fables about morality."

Further, the practice of Communism was associated with ugliness, drabness, enforced conformity, and a hatred and contempt for the past. Tolkien's admiration of ancientry, proper hierarchy, including proper kingship, and ritual splendor were absolutely at odds with Communism and the drabber aspects of socialism (some socialist visions, like that of William Morris, were more colorful).

Communist thought would have dismissed Tolkien's work, interests, and values as bourgeois sentimentality or reactionary propaganda. It is significant that *The Lord of the Rings* received many hostile reviews from the Left in general, even when these reviews did not undertake an ideological analysis of the work.

Probably Tolkien's most explicit statement of his view of Communism is to be found in the notes written on W.H. Auden's review of *The Return of the King* in 1956, in which he states that since Sauron aspired to divine honors:

> [E]ven if in desperation ''The West'' had bred or hired hordes of Orcs and had cruelly ravaged the lands of other men as allies of Sauron, or merely to prevent them from aiding him, their cause would still have been indefeasibly right. As does the cause of those who now oppose the State-God and Marshal This or That as its High Priest, even if it were true (as it unfortunately is) that many of their deeds were wrong, even if it were true (as it is not) that the inhabitants of ''The West,'' except for a minority of wealthy bosses, live in fear and squalor, while the worshippers of the State-God live in peace and abundance and mutual esteem and trust (*Letters,* 244).

During the second part of World War II, when the myth of Stalin as kindly ''Uncle Joe'' was being officially promoted, Tolkien, unlike many other writers and intellectuals, was not taken in even temporarily, describing Stalin as ''that bloodthirsty old murderer'' in December 1943, probably near the high point of Stalin's popularity in Britain. (*Letters,* 65).

Writing to Christopher Tolkien on October 6, 1944, Tolkien was full of admiration for the anti-Communist poet Roy Campbell, who had fought for Franco on the Nationalist side in Spain and later joined the British Army, and who, after meeting him at the ''Eagle and Child,'' Tolkien likened to Trotter (an early name for Aragorn). In the same letter, he ridiculed the Leftist poets (the ''corduroy Panzers'') who fled to America when the war started (*Letters,* 95–96). Ironically, one of these, W.H. Auden, later, and by then thoroughly disillusioned with Communism, became a friend and great supporter of Tolkien's work.

Although Tolkien obviously welcomed the end of World War II and the defeat of German National Socialism, he took no joy in the advance of the Russian armies into Europe.

Tolkien strongly denied his stories were allegory, but the regime in Mordor looks very like Stalinist Communism (even Hitler hardly claimed the demidivinity that Stalin seems to have aspired to).

It is easy to believe that the drab, joyless, coercive, and destructive order set up by Sharkey in the Shire under gangs of bullying ''gatherers'' and ''sharers''— which if successful would have turned it into a desert—owed much to the drabness, bleakness, and bureaucratic regulation of postwar Britain under the Attlee Labour Government. Tolkien said that though

there was no allegory in *The Lord of The Rings,* this did not mean that there was no applicability. Though the Attlee Government was strongly anti-Soviet (banning pro-Soviet propaganda stunts such as ''peace'' conferences, maintaining large armed forces, pushing ahead with developing a British atom bomb at a time when the Soviet Union was the only possible enemy, and otherwise fighting the cold war quite energetically), many of its policies, including nationalization of key industries and the great expansion of regulation and bureaucracy into many new areas of life, looked to many like an embryonic form of Communism. In Sharkey's Shire, the language of equality and justice had been perverted to disguise massive theft and the seizure of power by a new ruling class. Similarly, in Attlee's Britain, some (e.g., Evelyn Waugh) saw the emergence of a new two-class state of proletariat and officials, with the latter by no means indifferent to their own comforts and benefits at the expense of the masses.

While some on the Left have attacked Tolkien's work, others have at times tried to enlist it for the adversary culture (it is said the Beatles were once interested in making a film of *The Lord of the Rings*), but it is so plainly incongruous with and at odds with Leftism generally that none of these attempts has been successful.

Tolkien would probably have been delighted as well as astonished by the fact that in 1991, during the ''eucatastrophic'' collapse of Soviet Communism, anti-Communist groups in Moscow set up barricades against the attempted Communist countercoup under the banner ''Frodo is with us!''

HAL G.P. COLEBATCH

Further Reading

Berezhnoj, Serge V. ''The Long Hot Summer of Russian Fandom.'' In Edward James, *Science Fiction in the Twentieth Century.* Oxford: Oxford University Press, 1994.

Colebatch, Hal G.P. *Return of the Heroes: The Lord of the Rings, Star Wars, Harry Potter and Social Conflict.* Christchurch, New Zealand: Cybereditions, 2003.

Kolakowski, Leszek. *Main Currents of Marxism.* Vol. 2, *The Golden Age.* Oxford: Oxford University Press, 1978.

See also **Capitalism; Good and Evil; Marxist Readings of Tolkien; Saruman**

CRITICISM OF TOLKIEN, TWENTIETH CENTURY

This entry is to be devoted to so-called mainstream criticism—not to Tolkien scholarship and certainly not to criticism of Tolkien by ''Tolkien scholars'' or ''Tolkien critics.'' It is aimed rather at mainstream critics—like Edmund Wilson or Philip Toynbee or Auberon Waugh or Edwin Muir or Harold Bloom—or, possibly the poet-critic W.H. Auden (though he was favorable). The fundamental problem with discussing "criticism of Tolkien" as something separate from Tolkien scholarship and as therefore limited to writers known as critics is that it tends to limit "criticism of Tolkien" to criticism in the popular sense—that is, negative criticism. There were reviews early on by C.S. Lewis (but he was a friend) and Edmund Fuller (but he was a Christian—and actually, of course, Lewis was both a friend and a Christian). But these were more or less considered (by other "critics") as the work of interested parties.

Edmund Wilson, of course ("Oo! Those Awful Orcs!"), was well known as an enemy of religion, popular culture (especially popular books *not* by his friends), and the old guard or indeed conservatism in any form. For all that, he was in many ways a perceptive critic (he recognized, e.g., that Marx wrote mythopoetically), so his first negative reaction to Tolkien was widely quoted—much more widely (at least in the United States) than Auberon Waugh's or Philip Toynbee's. Lewis's and Fuller's reviews were also quoted, and many of the early reviews appear in part or whole in Isaacs and Zimbardo, *Tolkien and the Critics*. Harold Bloom and Isaac Asimov both tried their hands at Tolkien criticism—Bloom as a critic and anthologist of criticism and scholarship (and self-proclaimed polymath and expert) and Asimov, of course, as a self-proclaimed polymath and expert.

Bloom decided Edwin Muir was the best (partly) favorable critic of Tolkien (he himself not caring for the author or the book he was compiling commentaries on). Asimov, of course, did not need (or need to quote) anyone's opinion but his own. Bloom's views count as criticism of Tolkien (though he came late to the gate); Asimov's most-quoted comments on Tolkien were (he said) a commentary on the symbolism of the One Ring and (I believe) a claim that modernity (or perhaps the modern world) wasn't all bad. But Tolkien never said it was, and there's a world of difference between "not all bad" (which Tolkien could have agreed with) and (in the vernacular) "not all *that* bad" (which he would not have, if ever he would have accepted the phrase long enough to consider it).

It could be said, fundamentally, that no "mainstream critic" appreciated *The Lord of the Rings* or indeed was in a position to write criticism on it—most being unsure what it was and why readers liked it (not to say loved it, doted on it, used it as a lens through which to view the world). The best possible exception would be Colin Wilson in his 1974 Capra Press pamphlet *Tree by Tolkien,* in which he compares Tolkien somewhat oddly (but in the end perhaps perceptively) with Jeffrey Farnol. Brian Aldiss was a critic of fantasy and science fiction—thus not a mainstream critic because not a critic of mainstream literature—but he was a critic recognized by some mainstream critics and his comparison of Tolkien with P.G. Wodehouse echoes Colin Wilson. The critics—including to some extent Edmund Wilson—were recognizing the "Edwardian adventure story" at the root of *The Lord of the Rings* and either liking it or disliking it as they would.

At least one observer has suggested that the best single essay in Tolkien criticism is Richard C. West's "The Interlace Structure of The Lord of the Rings." West was the compiler of the *Annotated Checklist of Tolkien Criticism* (2nd ed., Kent, OH: Kent State University Press, 1981): the essay first appeared in the journal *Orcrist* and then in revised form in *A Tolkien Compass* (1st ed., LaSalle, IL: Open Court, 1975; paperback ed., New York: Ballantine Books, 1980; 2nd ed., LaSalle and Chicago, IL: Open Court, 2003). When he wrote the paper West was a graduate student under the great Eugène Vinaver, the expert on *entrelacement*. It is indeed criticism, but it is scholarly—one might say, academic—form-criticism. By the standards of this entry, it falls into another place. And that illustrates a paradox of Tolkien criticism, as of any criticism of a new thing—Eliot's *Waste Land*, Pound's *Cantos*, Joyce's *Finnegan's Wake* or *Ulysses*, and *The Lord of the Rings*, to take four (or five) great twentieth-century examples. As with Lewis's corkscrew or cathedral, first we have to know what the thing is before we can criticize it. But the inquiry into what it is—what *The Lord of the Rings* is—does not itself fall into the category of criticism as often understood. Professor Bloom's reactions are evidence here, suggesting a perceptive "critic" in a quandary.

JARED LOBDELL

Further Reading

Lobdell, Jared. "Afterword." In *A Tolkien Compass.* 2nd ed. Open Court: Chicago, 2003.

———. "Far from the Madding Critics." In *The Rise of Tolkienian Fantasy*, 1–20. Open Court: Chicago, 2005.

———. *The World of the Rings.* Open Court: Chicago, 2004.

Shippey, Tom. *J.R.R. Tolkien: Author of the Century.* Boston, MA: Houghton Mifflin, 2000.

See also **Lord of the Rings: Success of; Tolkien Scholarship**

CRUCES IN MEDIEVAL LITERATURE

A crux, according to the *Oxford English Dictionary*, is, on the one hand, "a difficulty which it torments or troubles one greatly to explain, a thing that puzzles the ingenuity; as 'a textual crux,'" and, on the other hand, "the chief problem; the central or decisive point of interest." Both meanings are relevant to Tolkien's professional life, as to the inspirations of his fiction.

Textual cruxes, or cruces, take on particular significance when one is dealing, as Tolkien almost always was, with ancient manuscripts in long-forgotten languages. Quite often, a manuscript was written down at a remove of decades or even centuries from the original composition and was copied by a scribe or scribes who may not have understood very well what they were writing. The modern editor, then, is faced with something that appears to make no sense as it stands. To understand the poem, one has to use all one's ingenuity to work out what seems to have been intended, as Tolkien did repeatedly, for instance, in his edition of the Old English poem *Exodus*, posthumously published in 1981. Furthermore, in many cases the textual crux is of particular importance because the word or idea that the copyist failed to understand may represent something that has faded from memory, but which in its garbled form offers us the hope of an insight into vanished heroic or mythological tradition.

A good example is the plural noun *wodwos* in line 721 of *Sir Gawain*, edited by Tolkien and E.V. Gordon in 1925. This cannot be correct as it stands, for it implies a singular *wodwo. Tolkien and Gordon concluded that it must derive from a lost and never-recorded word, Old English *wudu-wasa, which ought to have given, in the Middle English dialect of the *Gawain*-poet, *wodwosen—and perhaps did, only the scribe misunderstood the irregular plural. The question of what is a "woodwose" is then answered in *The Return of the King*, where the Riders encounter the Woses of Ghân-buri-Ghân. In similar style, Tolkien may have derived his idea of Gandalf from stanza 12 of the Old Norse poem *Völuspá*, where the name *Gandálfr*—seemingly the name of an Elf—is found in what is clearly a list of Dwarves. What is an Elf doing mixed up with Dwarves, and what does the first part of his name mean? Tolkien's solution, expressed from the very start of *The Hobbit*, is that *gand*- means "wand" or "staff," that this is the traditional property of a wizard, and that the name implies that once upon a time a wizard, a person with Elvish powers, had something to do with a Dwarvish expedition.

Even single words, then, may tell a story to the imaginative editor. Many cruces, however, demand explication of longer passages, such as lines 3071–5 of *Beowulf*, which seem to imply that the hero has fallen under a curse, or a spell, connected with the dragon's gold. Did he, and if so what kind of a spell was it? One answer is given in Tolkien's poem "The Hoard," printed in *The Adventures of Tom Bombadil* (1962), but based on a poem of 1923 with a title drawn, this time, from line 3052 of *Beowulf*. Cruces may also require cross-comparisons. Tolkien did this in his early scholarly analysis of variant forms of the rare Old English word *sigelhearwan*; his consideration of the variant uses of Old English *searu*, *searwian*, perhaps played a part in the creation of Saruman. The textual crux was a vital part of Tolkien's thinking at every level.

TOM SHIPPEY

Further Reading

Minnis, Alistair J., and Charlotte Brewer, eds. *Crux and Controversy in Middle English Textual Criticism.* Cambridge: D.S. Brewer, 1992.
Shippey, Tom. *The Road to Middle-earth: Revised and Expanded Edition.* Boston, MA: Houghton Mifflin, 2001.

See also **Beowulf**; **Exodus, Edition of; *Finn and Hengest*; Gandalf; Poems by J.R.R. Tolkien; Scholarship; *Sir Gawain and the Green Knight*, Edition with E.V. Gordon**

CYNEWULF

Cynewulf was an Anglo-Saxon poet of the ninth or tenth century, author of several Christian poems featuring distinctive runic signatures, including *Elene*, *Juliana*, *The Fates of the Apostles*, and *Christ*.

In "*Beowulf*: The Monsters and the Critics," Tolkien demonstrates his knowledge of Cynewulf's poetry by emphasizing the "dignity" shared by *Beowulf* and other Anglo-Saxon poems, including those of Cynewulf (14). In response to critics' comments on *Beowulf* as a flawed epic, Tolkien argued that the dignified tone of the poem demonstrated its worth. According to Tolkien, the works of Cynewulf and the other Anglo-Saxon poets could not compare to *Beowulf*, which he considered "more beautiful" (14). In his appendix to the essay, Tolkien further critiques Cynewulf's use of "the old heroic language," which was "strained or misused in application to Christian legend" (41).

Tolkien's best-known comment on Cynewulf relates to the name of *Eärendil*, husband of Elwing and father of Elrond and Elros. In a letter intended for a certain Mr. Rang, Tolkien located the origins of Eärendil's name in the Anglo-Saxon *éarendel*. Tolkien translated this term as "the name of a star or star-group ... a star presaging the dawn ... what we now call *Venus*: the morning-star as it may be seen shining brilliantly in the dawn, before the actual rising of the Sun" (*Letters*, 385). The term *éarendel* appears in several Old English texts, most notably in the *Christ* of Cynewulf: "*Eala Earendel engla beorhtast / ofer middangeard monnum sended*" (104–5) ("Hail, Earendel, brightest of angels, sent to men throughout Middle-earth"). Tolkien described Cynewulf's lines as "rapturous words" in a letter to Clyde Kilby (Birzer, 31, 152 n45). Later, Tolkien wrote that in reading these words, "I felt a curious thrill ... as if something had stirred in me, half wakened from sleep. There was something very remote and strange and beautiful behind those words ... far beyond ancient English" (Carpenter, 64). Tolkien later incorporated *éarendel* into his works, as he explained to Rang: "I adopted him [Earendel] into my mythology—in which he became a prime figure as a mariner, and eventually as a herald star, and a sign of hope to men" (*Letters*, 385). His early poems on Earendel were later developed into the *Lay of Eärendil*, mentioned in *The Silmarillion* (Carpenter, 295, 309). In *The Fellowship of the Ring*, Eärendil is also the subject of verses composed and sung by Bilbo in the Hall of Fire at Rivendell (*FR*, II, i, 246–49). Due to the name's origins in Cynewulf's poem, Eärendil might easily be associated with angelic messengers or other figures in Christianity. Tolkien, however, denied this connection in the letter to Rang (*Letters*, 387).

Tolkien also traced linguistic connections between Cynewulf's poems, including *Juliana* and the Middle English texts of the Katherine Group, detailed in his essay "Some Contributions to Middle-English Lexicography" (1925). Tolkien postulated an "AB language" used in the Katherine Group texts, a standardized dialect of the Southwest Midlands, which linked them with Middle English versions of the *Ancrene Wisse*. He believed that MS Bodley 34 was likely lineally connected to Cynewulf's poetry.

CHRISTINA M. HECKMAN

Further Reading

Birzer, Bradley J. *J.R.R. Tolkien's Sanctifying Myth: Understanding Middle-earth*. Wilmington, DE: ISI Books, 2002.

Carpenter, Humphrey. *Tolkien: A Biography*. Boston, MA: Houghton Mifflin, 1977.

Krapp, George P., and Eliott Dobbie, eds. *The Exeter Book*. New York: Columbia University Press, 1935.

Tolkien, J.R.R. "'*Ancrene Wisse*' and '*Hali Meiðhad*.'" *Essays and Studies* 14 (1929): 104–26.

———. "*Beowulf:* The Monsters and the Critics." In *MC*, 5–48.

———, ed. *The English Text of the Ancrene Riwle: Ancrene Wisse: Edited from MS. Corpus Christi College, Cambridge 402*. EETS o.s. 249. London: Oxford University Press, 1962.

———. "Some Contributions to Middle-English Lexicography." *Review of English Studies* 1, no. 2 (1925): 210–15.

See also **AB Language; Anglo-Saxon;** *Beowulf*; **"*Beowulf*: The Monsters and the Critics"; "MS Bodley 34: A Re-collation of a Collation";** *Christ*: **"Advent Lyrics"; d'Ardenne, S.R.T.O.; Eärendil; Elrond;** *Juliana*; **Katherine Group;** *Lord of the Rings*; **Middle English; Old English;** *Silmarillion, The*

D

DAGNALL, SUSAN (1910–52)

Margery Kathleen Mary Dagnall, known familiarly as Susan, was born in 1910. She read English at Oxford (BA, 1932), where her classmate in the Society of Home-Students (later renamed St. Anne's College) was Elaine Griffiths (1909–96). Dagnall went to work for the London publisher George Allen & Unwin in 1933, and sometime in the late spring or early summer of 1936 she visited Oxford to discuss with Griffiths the status of a projected revision of a translation of *Beowulf* by John R. Clark Hall that was a popular undergraduate crib. Griffiths had been engaged to do this on Tolkien's recommendation, but she hadn't completed the work (and never did). Instead, she directed Dagnall to visit Tolkien and borrow from him the manuscript of *The Hobbit*, which Griffiths thought good and deserving of publication. Dagnall did so, and after reading the manuscript encouraged Tolkien to complete the book for consideration by George Allen & Unwin. She also worked closely with Tolkien during the production of the book and through its publication in September 1937. In April 1939, Dagnall married Richard Edmund Grindle, and afterwards she left the employ of George Allen & Unwin. She was killed in an automobile accident on July 1, 1952. In a letter to Charlotte and Denis Plimmer of February 8, 1967, Tolkien wrote: "It is sad that Miss Dagnall, to whom in the event I owe so much, was, I believe, killed in a car-accident not long after her marriage."

DOUGLAS A. ANDERSON

DANES: CONTRIBUTIONS TO ENGLISH CULTURE

The culture of England in its present form might not have developed were it not for contributions from Danish culture, and Tolkien's academic and literary career might not have been possible apart from the influence of Denmark in the Middle Ages and the early modern period. The intermittent raids and systematic campaigns of hostile invasion and peaceful settlement from the late eighth through the early eleventh centuries galvanized the defensive policies of English monarchs early in this period, strengthening the emerging concept of "England" as a distinct, unified nation. The narrow military victory against the Danish *micel here* (great army) won by King Alfred of Wessex in 878—literally a "last-ditch" effort in the swamps of Somerset—followed by the diplomatic accommodations of the Treaty of Wedmore in 886 established most of northeast England as the Danelaw, a territory under the customary laws of the Danish settlers. What remained was, in a legal sense, English, and while King Alfred cannot be said to have ruled a unified Kingdom of England *per se*, a rising sense of national identity in the face of the ongoing Danish threat continued to grow throughout the reign of Alfred and his sons and grandsons.

On the other hand, later in this period the reconquest of the Danelaw in the tenth century drew heavily Danish-influenced portions of the island under English rule, and in these areas—mostly in Yorkshire, Lincolnshire, Leicestershire, and Northamptonshire —relatively peaceful coexistence between originally

English and more recently acculturated, Anglicized Scandinavian settlers created conditions favorable to cultural interchange and the adaptation of Danelaw customs to English usage. Judicious tolerance of the Scandinavian minority by Alfred's great-grandson Edgar (959–75) contributed to further accommodations between the English and the Danish portions of his kingdom, and (following a period of political turbulence) England was finally united for the first time under the rule of a single king, Cnut (1016–35)—a Dane.

Although foreign influence from other Scandinavian sources, including Norway and Viking strongholds in Ireland, played a role, particularly in the northwest, in the Danelaw and post-Danelaw period of the late ninth to the mid eleventh century, English culture was influenced significantly by Danish customs. This is evidenced partly by the large number of loanwords adopted during this period by English-speakers from a Scandinavian dialect best described as Anglo-Danish. Inhabitants of the Danelaw of both English and Danish ancestry enjoyed particular legal and political freedoms and—perhaps as a result—economic success unknown elsewhere in England during this period. As Sir Frank Stenton, Cyril Hart, and others have shown, ideas of representative local government, trial by jury, and other legal and political customs adopted from practices in the Danelaw have been established permanently among the English.

Certain intersections of Danish and English culture have particular bearing upon the life and work of Tolkien. For example, it was a Dane—Rasmus Rask (1787–1832), a librarian and philologist in the University of Copenhagen—who initially formulated the theory of consonant alternation known as the First Consonant Shift, popularized later by Jacob Grimm and known subsequently in Germanic philology as Grimm's Law. Rask also published grammars of Old English, Old Norse, and Modern Icelandic, and his work played an important part in the nineteenth-century development of the philological paradigm essential to Tolkien's academic and creative career. In addition, manuscript collections housed in the University of Copenhagen and the Danish Royal Library preserved the most important works of medieval Scandinavian literature—the *Poetic Edda,* Snorri Sturluson's *Prose Edda,* the *History of the Danes* by Saxo Grammaticus, and most of the Icelandic sagas, including the *Saga of the Volsungs*—which were crucial to the development of Tolkien's philological and literary pursuits.

Beowulf, the earliest English epic, was central to Tolkien's academic and literary interests; it begins with an encomium on the ancient Danish warrior-kings, and two-thirds of the poem is set in Denmark.

As a result of the prominence of Denmark and legendary Danish history in the poem, the first edition of *Beowulf,* published in Copenhagen in 1815, was titled *De Danorum Rebus Gestis Seculis III et IV: Poema Danicum Dialecto Anglosaxonica,* or *A Danish Poem in the Anglo-Saxon Dialect on Danish History in the Third and Fourth Centuries,* betraying its editor Grímur Thorkelín's convictions concerning the poem's origins and authorship. Scholars have associated the origins of *Beowulf* with various English dynasties having real or putative Danish ancestry and/or Danish sympathies. The precise time and place of composition and the intended audience of the poem have not been determined, but some favor has been accorded to the middle to late-tenth-century Danelaw period, with some even considering a time of composition as late as the early-eleventh-century reign of the Danish King Cnut.

While the Old English poem *The Battle of Maldon* describes the attackers of 991 as *Dene,* "Danes," the Viking force victorious at Maldon was in all likelihood composed primarily of Norwegian seamen possibly led by Olaf Tryggvason, later King of Norway. Nevertheless, the poem is consistent with the general history of recurrent hostilities with Scandinavians—mostly from Denmark—throughout the period, and the poem's development of the theme of doomed heroic valor is crucial to an understanding of the tragic heroism Tolkien found in Northern Germanic literature and mythology.

JONATHAN EVANS

Further Reading

Bjork, Robert E., and John D. Niles, eds. *A Beowulf Handbook.* Lincoln: University of Nebraska Press, 1997.

Graham-Campbell, James, Richard Hall, Judith Jesch, and David N. Parsons, eds. *Vikings and the Danelaw.* Oxford: Oxbow, 2001.

Hadley, Dawn M., and Julian D. Richards, eds. *Cultures in Contact: Scandinavian Settlement in England in the Ninth and Tenth Centuries.* Turnhout, Belgium: Brepols, 2000.

Hart, Cyril. *The Danelaw.* London: Hambledon, 1994.

Niles, John D. "The Danes and the Date." In *Beowulf: The Poem and its Tradition,* 96–117. Cambridge, MA: Harvard University Press, 1983.

Roesdahl, Else. *The Vikings.* Translated by Susan M. Margeson and Kireten Williams. New York: Viking Penguin, 1991.

Stenton, Sir Frank Merry. *Anglo-Saxon England.* 3rd ed. Oxford: Clarendon, 1971.

———. "The Historical Bearing of Place-Name Studies: The Danish Settlement of Eastern England." *Transactions of the Royal Historical Society,* 4th ser., 24 (1942): 1–24. Reprinted in *Preparatory to Anglo-Saxon England,* edited by Doris Mary Stenton, 298–313. Oxford: Clarendon, 1970.

See also **Battle of Maldon, The; "Beowulf: The Monsters and the Critics"; Danish Language; Heroes and**

Heroism; History: Anglo-Saxon; *The Homecoming of Beorhtnoth, Beorhthelm's Son*; **Northern Courage; Old Norse Literature; Old Norse Translations; Saxo Grammaticus**

DANISH LANGUAGE

A member of the North Germanic or Scandinavian language family, Danish is grouped geographically in the eastern branch of that family, which includes Swedish and Gutnish. Norwegian, Icelandic, and Norn (extinct) belong to the western branch. Linguistically, Danish is the most progressive among the Scandinavian languages: its noun morphology has given up all earlier case distinctions except for the possessive, and the verb conjugations have been simplified to include—besides the infinitive—only a present and a preterit form without inflections for person or number. In addition, gender differences between masculine and feminine nouns disappeared in the early modern period, resulting in two remaining grammatical genders: *common gender* and *neuter.* Danish vocabulary includes many lexical items adopted earlier from Latin, Plattdeutsch, Hochdeutsch, and French and, since the nineteenth century, from English. In the period of Viking conquest, settlement, and—briefly—monarchal rule in England by Danish-speakers (c. 790–1042), the English language was influenced markedly by Anglo-Danish, a Scandinavian dialect spoken in England and closely related to medieval Danish. The impact upon English was second only to the French influence following the Norman Conquest of 1066; however, because surviving manuscripts in medieval Scandinavian literature have been preserved primarily in Old Norse (ON) or Old Icelandic, for comparative purposes in scholarly literature, evidence for Danish influence upon English is illustrated mostly by classical ON forms.

Place-name evidence provides some indication of the linguistic impact of Danish settlement in northeast England, where many geographical names are based on Scandinavian personal names or on words ending in the suffix *-by* (village, homestead) and *-thorpe* (farm, hamlet). Perhaps more important are the hundreds of everyday words that entered the English vocabulary following Danish settlement in the portion of England known as the Danelaw under King Alfred. In "A Middle English Vocabulary" appended to Kenneth Sisam's edition of *Fourteenth Century Verse & Prose* (1921), Tolkien cites Scandinavian words in the normalized spelling of Geir T. Zoëga's *Old Icelandic Dictionary* and lists about 186 headwords, with additional morphological derivatives and spelling variants, deriving from forms related to ON. These include such terms such as *ay,* "always, ever"; *felawe,* "fellow, companion"; and *harwen,* "harrow"—words destined to remain in standard English permanently—alongside *grayþed,* "got ready, prepared"; *layne,* "conceal"; and *tyte,* "quickly"— terms that enjoyed some currency in Middle English but later dropped out of English usage. In his foreword to *A New Glossary of the Dialect of the Huddersfield District* by Walter E. Haigh (1928), Tolkien commented insightfully on Huddersfield's location in an area of dialect competition between Northern and Western Midlands speech in the Old and Middle English periods. Surviving evidence of both Danish and Norwegian influence overlaps in the linguistic geography in and around Huddersfield; Haigh estimates the ratio of words in his glossary derived from Scandinavian sources to be about 25 percent; examples Tolkien draws particular attention to include *ælsh* ("loop, knot," from ON *hālsa,* "to clasp, embrace"), *gredli* ("proper, good-looking," from ON *greithiliga,* "readily"), and *kār* ("marsh, pond," from ON *kjarr,* "marshy grove, pond").

The glossary to the Tolkien/Gordon edition of *Sir Gawain and the Green Knight* (1925) includes several hundred Scandinavian loanwords, many destined for success in the subsequent history of English. These include *glyter* (from ON *glitra,* "glitter"), *lawe* (from ON *laga,* "law"), and *wrang* ("wrong," from ON *vrangr*). Alongside these may be found terms like *aghlich,* "terrible"; *bigge,* "settle, found, build"; and *lyndes,* "loins"—popular words destined for extinction in standard English. Tolkien commented in great detail on pronunciation and spelling differences between Southeast Midlands (London) English and the Northern dialect of Middle English as represented in Geoffrey Chaucer's "The Reeve's Tale," noting also a number of loanwords including, for example, *hail* (from ON *heill*), *il* (evil), *imell* (from Old Danish *i mellae*), and *laþe* (from ON *hlaða,* "barn"). Despite their general nature, Tolkien's article "Philology: General Works" in the *Year's Work in English Studies* (1923–25) comments in passing on topics related to Danish/English language contacts then arising in linguistic scholarship.

Hundreds of Anglo-Danish vocabulary items adopted during the Middle Ages remain in everyday usage in Modern English. These include such common nouns as "bag," "bread," "cake," "dirt," "egg," "leg," "skin," "skirt," "wing," and "window"; verbs including "blend," "call," "cut," "get," "give," "seem," "take," and "want"; and modifiers like "awkward," "happy," "ill," "odd," "sly," "ugly," and "wrong." Many of these loanwords seem to bespeak the violence associated with Viking invasion— for example, "die," "hit," "kick," "ransack," "rive," "scar," "scare," "scathe," "scorch," and "thrust," as well as "anger," "club," "knife," "scar," "slaughter," and "snare." Friendly, even intimate, relations are implied, however, by such words as "fellow," "husband," "kid," "sister," and "tyke." The total displacement of standard Old English (OE) verbs such as *niman, giefan,* and *gietan* by ON *taka, gefa,* and *geta*—Modern English "take," "give," and "get"—suggest the linguistic depths to which the Danish impact reached. The remarkable borrowing of abstract terms such as "fro" (cf. "to and fro"), "hence," "thence," "though," and "till," and especially the plural pronoun forms "they," "them," and "their" (ON counterparts of OE *hie, heom,* and *heora,* which were abandoned), indicate linguistic and social relations between speakers of English and speakers of Anglo-Danish were close indeed during the Middle Ages. Contributions in the postmedieval period reveal the ongoing productivity of language contacts between Danish and other Scandinavian languages and English well into the twentieth century—for example, "fjord," "gauntlet," "maelstrom," "muggy," "troll," "smorgasbord," and "ombudsman."

JONATHAN EVANS

Further Reading

Björkman, Erik. *Scandinavian Loan-Words in Middle English.* Halle: Niemeyer, 1902.
Evans, Jonathan. "Scribal Error as Linguistic Evidence in the *Peterborough Chronicle:* Anglo-Scand/eME *þeora.*" *NOWELE* (North-West European Language Evolution) 37 (2000): 53–122.
Fellows-Jensen, Gillian. *Scandinavian Settlement Names in the East Midlands.* Copenhagen: Akademisk Forlag, 1978.
Jespersen, Otto. *Growth and Structure of the English Language.* Chicago, IL: University of Chicago Press, 1982.
Townsend, Matthew. *Language and History in Viking Age England: Linguistic Relations Between Speakers of Old Norse and Old English.* Turnhout, Belgium: Brepols, 2002.

See also **"Chaucer as Philologist: The Reeve's Tale"; Danes: Contributions to English Culture; Denmark: Reception of Tolkien; Middle English Vocabulary; *New Glossary of the Dialect of the Huddersfield District, A*; Old Norse Literature; *Pearl*: Edition by E.V. Gordon; *Sir Gawain and the Green Knight*; Viking Raids**

DANTE

"He's full of spite and malice. I don't care for his petty relations with petty people in petty cities." Tolkien, reminded of his comments on Dante Alighieri, called these words "outrageous" and identified Dante

as "a supreme poet," but he maintained that Dante's writing was sometimes marred by "pettiness" (*Letters,* 377). Nevertheless, Tolkien knew Dante's work well and referred to it in his scholarship, and Tolkien's fiction shares many of Dante's concerns in its examination, on a vast narrative scale, of subjects such as free will and the nature of evil.

"Pettiness" might refer to Dante's criticism of his political enemies in *The Divine Comedy,* or perhaps Tolkien, who could forgive "stupid, tired, dimmed and even bad priests" (*Letters,* 338), disliked the poem's placement of four popes in Hell. Also, *The Divine Comedy* is an allegory, a form that Tolkien famously disliked (*FR,* Foreword, 7). Naturally, one Tolkien work that several scholars have linked to Dante is allegorical: "Leaf by Niggle," which Rogers and Rogers (57) call "Tolkien's little *Purgatorio.*" Niggle's labors in the Workhouse, his release to a kind of paradise before he ascends the Mountains, and the refreshing Spring all echo the middle part of Dante's masterwork (Christopher, 105).

However, these similarities might simply show Tolkien and Dante working from the same theological ideas, and connections to Dante in Tolkien's other stories are more difficult to identify: Grant (164) sees *The Lord of the Rings* as deriving its morality from "the Dantesque form of Christian epic" in a post-Romantic shape; Rosebury (47) thinks Dante and Tolkien share a view of evil as dull and squalid; and Houghton (29–32) finds *The Divine Comedy* to be an early demonstration of Tolkien's concept of eucatastrophe. More specifically, Flieger (179) notes that *ele* (behold), the first word of Tolkien's Elves, resembles *El* (God), Adam's first word in Dante's linguistic treatise, *De Vulgari Eloquentia.* In addition, *The Lord of the Rings* and *The Divine Comedy* have in common main characters, Frodo and Dante, who are precisely halfway through their natural life spans (In his introdution to *Pearl,* Tolkien notes Dante's age elsewhere in comments about the role of biography in medieval narratives [Tolkien, *Sir Gawain,* 20–21]). And the insatiable *lupa* (she-wolf) that menaces Dante as he races to the summit in *Inferno* (I, 13–99) may presage Tolkien's gluttonous monsters, Carcharoth and Shelob.

Duriez (121) suggests "Leaf by Niggle" was partly inspired by Charles Williams, an influence that Tolkien denied (*Letters,* 209), though he knew Williams's "plunging, soaring" Dante scholarship (Carpenter, 123). Tolkien, like Williams, followed C.S. Lewis in joining the Oxford Dante Society and was a member from 1945 to 1955 (Oxford Dante Society, 147). The Bodleian Library has notes for a talk, "A Neck-verse," that Tolkien gave to the Society about the word *lusinghe* (flatteries)—from

Cato's admonition to Virgil in *Purgatorio* (I, 92) and Middle English *losenger* (flatterer), whose etymology was the subject of a 1953 study by Tolkien. Here, one aspect of Tolkien's interest in Dante is clear: when a work "throws light on words and names," as he observes in a 1958 letter (*Letters,* 264), then he responds as "a *pure* philologist."

MERLIN DETARDO

Further Reading

Carpenter, Humphrey. *The Inklings: C.S. Lewis, J.R.R. Tolkien, Charles Williams, and Their Friends*, by Humphrey Carpenter, 123–6. Boston, MA: Houghton Mifflin, 1979.

———. Uncatalogued papers. A13/1, fols. 167–77. New Bodleian Library, University of Oxford.

Christopher, Joe R. *C.S. Lewis*. Boston, MA: G.K. Hall & Co., 1987.

Dante Alighieri. *De Vulgari Eloquentia*. Edited and Translated by Steven Botterill. Cambridge: Cambridge University Press, 1996.

———. *Divina Commedia*. In *Tutte le opere*. Rome: Grandi Tascabili Economici Newton, 1993.

———. *The Divine Comedy: The Inferno, The Purgatorio, The Paradiso*. Translated by John Ciardi. New York: New American Library, 2003.

Duriez, Colin. *Tolkien and C.S. Lewis: The Gift of Friendship*. Mahwah, NJ: Hidden Spring, 2003.

Flieger, Verlyn. *Splintered Light: Logos and Language in Tolkien's World*. Revised edition. Kent, OH: Kent State University Press, 2002.

Grant, Patrick. "Tolkien: Archetype and Word." In *Understanding "The Lord of the Rings": The Best of Tolkien Criticism*, edited by Rose A. Zimbardo and Neil D. Isaacs, (163–82). Boston, MA: Houghton Mifflin, 2004.

Houghton, John William. "Commedia as Fairy-story: Eucatastrophe in the Loss of Virgil." *Mythlore* 17, no. 2, whole no. 64 (1990 Winter): 29–32.

Oxford Dante Society. *Centenary Essays on Dante*. Oxford: Clarendon, 1965.

Rogers, Deborah Webster, and Ivor A. Rogers. *J.R.R. Tolkien*. Boston: G. K. Hall & Co., 1980.

Rosebury, Brian. *Tolkien: A Cultural Phenomenon*. New York: Palgrave Macmillan, 2003.

Tolkien, J.R.R. "Introduction to *Pearl*." In *Sir Gawain and the Green Knight, Pearl, and Sir Orfeo*. Translated by J.R.R. Tolkien, 18–23. Boston, MA: Houghton Mifflin, 1975.

See also **Allegory; Angband; Angels; Aquinas, Thomas; Astronomy and Cosmology, Middle-earth; Bible; Catholicism, Roman; Christian Readings of Tolkien; Christianity; Cruces in Medieval Literature; Death; Descent; Devils; Dreams; Epic Poetry; Eucatastrophe; Free Will; Frodo; Heaven; Hell; Italian Language; Latin Language; Latin Literature; Lewis, C.S.;** *Lord of the Rings, The;* **Lothlórien; Middle English; "Middle English "Losenger": Sketch of an Etymological and Semantic Inquiry"; Mordor; Morgoth and Melkor; Mountains; Oxford; Paradise;** *Pearl:* **Edition by E.V. Gordon; Penance; Poems by Tolkien: Uncollected; Satan and Lucifer; Sauron; Sayers, Dorothy; Shelob; Sin; Taniquetil;** *Tree and Leaf;* **Valar; Valinor; Virgil; Williams, Charles Walter Stansby**

D'ARDENNE, S.R.T.O. (1899–1986)

The Belgian medievalist Simonne Rosalie Thérèse Odile d'Ardenne published work under her initials, both as "S.T.R.O" and "S.R.T.O." d'Ardenne. She came to Oxford in 1932 for graduate study in Middle English and lodged with the Tolkien family, with whom she made close and lifelong friendships. On the recommendation of C.T. Onions, Tolkien supervised her work. She earned her B. Litt. in 1933, and her thesis, revised and considerably enlarged, was published in 1936 as *An Edition of þe Liflade ant te Passiun of Seinte Iuliene*. As d'Ardenne herself admitted, it should have been appeared under both her and Tolkien's names, in collaboration, but published under her name alone, as a thesis for a Belgian degree, it allowed her to be elected as a university professor. Dedicated to Tolkien, it ironically contains more of Tolkien's own views on early Middle English and on the West Midlands dialect than Tolkien published under his own name during his lifetime. It was reprinted by the Early English Text Society in 1961, with the title shortened to *Þe Liflade ant te Passiun of Seinte Iuliene*. In 1938, d'Ardenne was appointed the professor of comparative grammar at the University of Liège.

Tolkien and d'Ardenne planned other work together, including an edition of *Seinte Katerine*. Begun in 1938, it was soon afterward delayed by World War II and the collaboration was never resumed. D'Ardenne's edition, coedited with E.J. Dobson, was published by the Early English Text Society in 1981.

While in Oxford from 1945–47 as a British Council Scholar, d'Ardenne and Tolkien published two short collaborative works of scholarship. "'Iþþlen' in Sawles Warde" appeared in *English Studies* for December 1947, and "MS. Bodley 34: A Re-Collation of a Collation" was published in *Neophilologica* for 1947–48. At this time d'Ardenne also translated into French Tolkien's then-unpublished story *Farmer Giles of Ham*, as a way of urging Tolkien to publish the English version, thereby making it possible for her translation to appear. Tolkien did publish *Farmer Giles of Ham* in 1949, but d'Ardenne's translation, as *Maître Gilles de Ham*, did not appear until 1975.

In 1950, Tolkien visited d'Ardenne to take part in the sixtieth anniversary of the Departments of Germanic and Romance Philology at the University of Liège. He returned in September 1951 to speak at the Congrès International de Philologie Moderne, but arrived without a prepared lecture. D'Ardenne recalled a short study of the Middle English word *losenger* she had planned to do and had discussed with him on a short trip to Oxford. Knowing his interest in the word, she thought it would be a suitable topic for his lecture, and Tolkien agreed. The resulting essay appeared in the proceedings volume, *Essays de Philologie Moderne* (1953).

Tolkien's last visit to d'Ardenne was in October 1954, when on her initiative Tolkien was awarded an honorary doctorate by the University of Liège.

D'Ardenne contributed an essay to Tolkien's Festschrift, *English and Medieval Studies Presented to J.R.R. Tolkien on the Occasion of His Seventieth Birthday* (1962), and also a short essay on "The Man and the Scholar" to the memorial volume *J.R.R. Tolkien: Scholar and Storyteller* (1979), edited by Mary Salu and Robert T. Farrell.

DOUGLAS A. ANDERSON

Further Reading

Schweicher, Eric. *Department of Germanic Languages and Literatures, University of Liège, J.R.R. Tolkien, The Lyf so short, the Craft so lone to lerne . . . Exhibition Catalogue, From May 16 to May 22 1992.* Belgium: University of Liège, 1992.

Tolkien, John, and Priscilla Tolkien. *The Tolkien Family Album.* Boston: Houghton Mifflin, 1992.

See also **Farmer Giles of Ham; Katherine Group; "'Iþþlen' in *Sawles Warde*"; "MS. Bodley 34: A Re-Collation of a Collation"; Middle English**

DARKNESS

> In the beginning . . . the earth was a formless void and darkness covered the face of the deep. . . . Then God said, "Let there be light"; and there was light. And God saw that the light was good; and God separated the light from the darkness.

The opening lines of the first book of Genesis are paralleled by Tolkien in *Ainulindalë*, the Music of the Ainur, his own version of the Creation myth. Thus speaks Ilúvatar, the All-father (God), at the beginning of time: "'Therefore I say: *Eä!* Let these things Be! And I will send forth into the Void the Flame Imperishable, and it shall be at the heart of the World, and the World shall Be.' And suddenly the Ainur saw afar off a light, as it were a cloud with a living heart of flame" (*S*, 20). Light is, therefore, at the heart of Creation, and its absence, Darkness, is associated from the beginning with evil. Thus, Tolkien says of Melkor: "He began with the desire of Light, but when he could not possess it for himself alone, he descended

through fire and wrath into a great burning, down into Darkness" (*S*, 31).

At its deepest, this primal and primeval dichotomy of light and darkness is a reflection of orthodox Christian theology. St. Augustine and other great Christian philosophers and theologians have taught that evil has no existence of its own but is merely the absence of that which is good. It is, therefore, easy to see why good is synonymous with, and symbolized by, light, whereas evil is synonymous with, and symbolized by, the absence of light, that is, darkness. It is for this reason that Tolkien describes Sauron as "a huge shape of shadow" or as "a shadow of Morgoth." Like evil, a shadow has no existence of its own but is only visible insofar as it obstructs or hides the light. "Above all shadows rides the Sun," states Samwise Gamgee in the Tower of Cirith Ungol, reflecting Tolkien's own Christian understanding of the deepest theological truths (RK, VI, i, 185). In Sam's hope-filled words, uttered amid the terrible darkness on the edge of Mordor, the Sun can be seen as a metaphor for Ilúvatar, the All-father, God Himself, and the shadows a metaphor for the evil that cannot prevail.

In the meantime, however, the children of Ilúvatar (Elves and Men) are doomed, through the rebellion of Melkor (Satan), to dwell in his shadow. "So great was the power of his uprising that . . . through long years in Arda [he] held dominion over most of the lands of the Earth" (*S*, 31). Yet from the beginning the Elves are given the light of the stars as a promise of their final deliverance from the darkness of evil. Varda, greatest of the angelic Valier, forged the brightest of the stars in the heavens to serve as an everlasting light over the darkness of Middle-earth. "It is told that even as Varda ended her labours . . . in that hour the Children of the Earth awoke, the Firstborn of Ilúvatar. By the starlit mere of Cuiviénen, Water of Awakening, they rose from the sleep of Ilúvatar; and while they dwelt yet silent by Cuiviénen their eyes beheld first of all things the stars of heaven. Therefore they have ever loved the starlight, and have revered Varda Elentári above all the Valar (*S*, 38)." Thus, in Tolkien's Creation myth, God chooses the moment that Varda finishes the forging of the stars, including the constellation of Menelmacar (Orion) "that forebodes the Last Battle that shall be at the end of days" (the final victory of light over darkness), as the time to bring the Elves into Being (*S*, 48). Thereafter, the Elves look to the stars, and to Varda, the maker of the stars, whom they call Elbereth, as a promise of the triumph of light over darkness, good over evil. If Samwise Gamgee, the hobbit, looks to the light of the sun as a promise of deliverance from darkness, the Elves look to the light of the stars.

JOSEPH PEARCE

Further Reading

Pearce, Joseph. *Tolkien: Man and Myth*. London: Harper-Collins, 1998.

———, ed. *Tolkien: A Celebration*. London: HarperCollins, 1999.

See also **Augustine; Astronomy and Cosmology, Middle-earth; Christianity; Eru; Fall of Man; Good and Evil; Incarnation; Morgoth and Melkor; Redemption; Satan and Lucifer; Sauron; Valar**

DEATH

Tolkien claimed in his correspondence that, with immortality, death is a dominant theme in *The Lord of the Rings*. The theme of death pervades the novel structurally through "the mystery of the love of the world in the hearts of a race 'doomed' to leave and seemingly lose it [and] the anguish in the hearts of a race 'doomed' not to leave it, until the whole evil-aroused story is complete" (*Letters,* 186). Tolkien is referring to the contrast between Men, with their short life spans, and Elves, who possess the potential of deathlessness. Thus, the contrasting state of the latter acts as a thematic foil. After the posthumous publication of *The Silmarillion* and the volumes of *The History of Middle-earth,* it is evident that the theme is central to Tolkien's entire mythopoeic writing.

The theme encapsulated in Tolkien's letter is found clearly represented in *The Silmarillion,* wherein death is claimed to be a "Gift of Ilúvatar," Ilúvatar being the godhead of the mythology. In a passage after Ilúvatar blesses the created earth, which "shall be a mansion for [Elves and Men]," he goes on to claim that people have the power of self-determination but that this freedom bears the weight of finding no rest upon this earth. The narrator continues: "Death is their fate, the gift of Ilúvatar, which as Time wears even the Powers shall envy" (*S,* 42). Part of the "gift" includes the promise "that Men shall join the Second Music of the Ainur," meaning that they shall join Ilúvatar at the end of time.

Tolkien effectively implies that people are pilgrims on Middle-earth, yet the pilgrimage is liberating and people rise above the determinism that subordinates even sentient beings such as Elves. Death in this context has strong echoes of the Christian "may s/he rest in peace" benediction, as well as Augustine's claim that because we were made for our Creator our only true rest is in God.

Consequently, if the gift is a fulfillment of rest in the Creator/Ilúvatar, trust must be placed in Ilúvatar that he has the best intent of his creatures in mind despite appearances to the contrary. What makes this

trust difficult is the satanic Melkor's intervention, because "Melkor cast his shadow on [the gift], and confounded it with darkness, and brought forth evil out of good, and fear out of hope" (*S,* 42). At this juncture, Tolkien's mythology approaches the doctrine of original sin. However, since he did not wish to parody Christian scripture in his work, he only tentatively explored the origins of the darkness mentioned, discussing it most fully in his unfinished works written after *The Lord of the Rings.*

In contrast to people, the Elves are "by nature" deathless, or if they are slain, as we are informed in *The Silmarillion,* they can return to Middle-earth through reincarnation—albeit no instances of this happening (with the possible exceptions of Finrod and Glorfindel) are given. Although the theme of death with the elf-human contrast is largely structural in *The Lord of the Rings,* there is a point at which it is particularly dramatized: in the romance of Arwen and Aragorn. The conceit that Tolkien introduces into his mythology is that a union between an elf and a human is possible if the former sacrifices his or her immortality. The most dramatic juncture of this arrangement is presented in the "Tale of Aragorn and Arwen," hidden in the appendices of the novel, when Aragorn accepts his time of death, which is considerably sooner than his wife's. Although Arwen knew this moment had to arrive, she tells her husband at his deathbed: "If this is indeed, as the Eldar say, the gift of the One to men, it is bitter to receive" (*RK,* Appendix A, 344).

Arwen's questioning of the "gift" is taken a step further and is virtually undermined in Tolkien's post-*Lord of the Rings* writings, especially in the tale "Athrabeth Finrod ah Andreth." The story is chronologically set in the First Age, and the theme of death figures largely in the dialogue between Finrod and Andreth. When the High-elf Finrod hints at the special status of people, the wise woman Andreth reiterates the different experience of death among Men and Elves, concluding the fate of people means that "dying we die, and we go out to no return. Death is an uttermost end, a loss irremediable" (*Morgoth,* 311).

When the possibility of a fate beyond mortal life is discussed, Finrod displays a dualist understanding of the separation of the body and the soul, which is inherent in the reincarnation of the Elves; for her part, Andreth comes close to the Christian comprehension of the unity of the body and the soul. Andreth rejects the idea that the body can be left behind: "For that would be contempt for the body, and is a thought of the Darkness unnatural in any of the Incarnate whose life uncorrupted is a union of mutual love. The body is not an inn to keep the traveller warm for a night, ere he goes on his way, and then to receive another" (*Morgoth,* 317). The dialogue even comes close to suggesting a premonition of Ilúvatar becoming incarnate to bring true salvation to Middle-earth.

Generally, the tenor of the reflection on death between the High-elf and the wise woman is quite dark and more open-ended than is suggested in the earlier mythology, where the rather optimistic concept of death as the Gift of Ilúvatar comes to the fore, or at least remains unquestioned. Arwen's despair after Aragorn's death is symbolically contrasted with the latter's unnaturally beautiful corpse, proof of the righteousness of his acceptance of the gift. Significantly, Arwen likewise seems posthumously rewarded for her suffering in the flowers that grow on her burial mound, although her despair could be understood as a result of Melkor's shadow. This demonstrates that *The Lord of the Rings* is at the juncture where the author's earlier optimism crosses with the later somber thoughts, adding to the novel's nuanced expression of the theme of death.

CHRISTOPHER GARBOWSKI

See also **Elves: Reincarnation; Fall of Man;** *Morgoth's Ring*; **Reincarnation; Theological and Moral Approaches in Tolkien's Works**

DENETHOR

Denethor II, son of Ecthelion, is sworn "to hold rod and rule in the name of the king," until that King should return (*RK,* Appendix A, 333). Described as "a proud man, tall, valiant, and more kingly than any man that had appeared in Gondor for many lives of men," Gondor's twenty-sixth Ruling Steward appears suited for the task (*RK,* Appendix A, 336). Even when compared with Gandalf, a being of a higher spiritual order, Denethor appears "much more like a great wizard. . . more kingly, beautiful, and powerful; and older" (*RK,* V, i, 129). Yet despite his considerable gifts, hubris and mistrust of others ultimately lead Denethor to madness and suicide.

Overconfident in his strength of will and eager to find power by which to withstand the attacks of Mordor, Denethor has long sought knowledge through the *palantír* of Anarion. Because of its close connection with a sister stone in the possession of Sauron, use of the *palantír* is a risk no other Steward or King has dared take. And while Denethor succeeds in gaining great knowledge through its use, the stone not only ages him prematurely but also allows Sauron to distort Denethor's view of the world.

Accordingly, when finally introduced in the opening chapter of *The Return of the King,* it is a cynical and despairing Steward who accepts Pippin into his service. Denethor berates Gandalf's plan to destroy the Ring as "a fool's hope," contending that it should have been locked away under Gondor, close to him (*RK,* V, iv, 87). He tells his second son, Faramir, that he wished his older and more pliable son, Boromir, were the one still alive (*RK,* V, iv, 86). And when he uses the *palantír* during the siege of Gondor, as Tom Shippey points out, Denethor not only mistakes the fleet with black sails for reinforcements of Mordor but also (as a reading of the timeline in Appendix B shows) appears to have been shown and wrongly assumes that Sauron has taken possession of the Ring (Shippey, 172). Embracing "pride and despair" (*RK,* V, vii, 129), Denethor renounces both his Stewardship and the powers of the West, attempting to kill himself and Faramir (*RK,* V, vii, 128). Although Pippin, Gandalf, and Beregond rescue Faramir, they cannot stop Denethor from burning himself alive (*RK,* V, vii, 130–31).

Critical responses to Denethor are wide ranging, but many focus on the nature of his fall and his corrupted Stewardship. After comparing him to other models of leadership in the story, Jane Chance concludes that "Denethor fails as a father and as Steward-ruler because he gives in too readily to hopelessness and despair" (2001, 111); it is a specific lack, then, that founds his tragedy. Richard Purtill, on the other hand, characterizes Denethor by his possession of pride and egoism. As Purtill puts it, Denethor "'serves' Gondor but thinks of it as his. He is very close to saying, and thinking, 'There is no purpose higher in the world than my rule'" (85). In a more hermeneutical approach, Shippey translates Denethor into twentieth-century political terms, likening him to "an arch-conservative," that particularly modern type of despot who guards "a mean concern for his own sovereignty and his own boundaries" (155). Translated into whatever terms, however, Denethor represents many of the intertwined issues of power and knowledge that underlie *The Lord of the Rings.*

ALEX DAVIS

Further Reading

Chance, Jane. *The Lord of the Rings: The Mythology of Power.* Revised edition. Lexington, KY: University Press of Kentucky, 2001.

Purtill, Richard. *J.R.R. Tolkien: Myth, Morality, and Religion.* San Francisco, CA: Ignatius, 2003.

Shippey, Tom. *The Road to Middle-earth.* 2nd ed. London: Grafton, 1992.

———. *J.R.R. Tolkien: Author of the Century.* Boston, MA: Houghton Mifflin, 2000.

DENHAM TRACTS, THE

The Denham Tracts, edited by James Hardy and published in two volumes by the London Folklore Society, is a collection of North English folk sayings compiled by folklorist Michael Aislabie Denham between 1846 and 1859. Included in the second volume of *The Denham Tracts* is a brief article in which the first reference to the word *hobbit* is recorded. *The Denham Tracts* were reprinted in 1974 by Frank Graham, Newcastle Upon Tyne.

Denham was born in Gainford, County Durham, England, on April 8, 1800, and died in Piercebridge on September 10, 1859. A fervent collector of Northumberland, Newcastle, and Berwick folklore, his six-section anthology, titled *Folklore,* consists of Northern English proverbs, weather sayings, and prophesies. Denham also published two political tracts: *The Slogans and War* and *The Gathering Cries of the North of England.*

According to the brief article found in *The Denham Tracts* titled "Ghosts Never Appear on Christmas Eve": "every lone tenement, castle, or mansion-house, which could boast of any antiquity, had its bogle, its specter, or its knocker." The article lists two hundred such specters, including a creature called a hobbit. Also included in Denham's list are several more names with the prefix *hob-,* including *hobgoblins, hobhoulards, hobby-lanthorns, hob-thrushes,* and *hob-headlesses.*

Other creatures found in both Denham's catalogue and Tolkien's legendarium are wizards, elves, dwarves, wraiths, trolls, goblins, and corpse lights. No further descriptions of the hobbit or any other of Denham's creatures are given, and it is unclear whether the majority of the beings cited were truly active in the English folk imagination or were simply literary inventions of Denham.

Denham's primary source for his inventory of spirits seems to derive from *The Discoverie of Witchcraft* by Reginald Scot, first published in 1584. Scot wrote *The Discoverie* as a declaration of his vehement opposition to the witch-hunting craze of the sixteenth century, which he believed to be a galling manifestation of irrational and unchristian superstitions.

Since 1989, *The Second Edition of the Oxford English Dictionary* has attributed the invention of the word *hobbit* solely to Tolkien. In the *Oxford English Dictionary's* newsletter dated December 2003, however, the dictionary's chief editor, John Simpson, writes that the word *hobbit* "has since turned up in one of those 19th-century folklore journals, in a list of long-forgotten words for fairy-folk or little people" and that future editions of the dictionary will take "evidence for earlier use into account." As of this writing,

the online and print editions of the *Oxford English Dictionary* still credit Tolkien with the sole invention of the word *hobbit* and make no mention of either Michael Denham or *The Denham Tracts.*

DUSTIN EATON

Further Reading

Bilton, Harry. "Great Aycliffe Archive." Street names in Newton Aycliffe, 1980. http://www.round-our-way.co.uk/acley/BodyPages/denham_place.htm.

Hardy, James, ed. *The Denham Tracts,* vol. 2, 76–80. London: Folklore Society, 1895.

Myers, Alan. "Michael Denham." In *Myers Literary Guide to North-East England,* 2004. http://pages.britishlibrary.net/alan.myers/lit/m-denham.html.

Scot, Reginald. *The Discoverie of Witchcraft.* New York: Dover Publications, 1972.

Simpson, John. "Words of Choice." *Oxford English Dictionary* newsletter, December 2003. http://www.oed.com/newsletters/2003-12/wordsofchoice.html.

See also **Folklore; Hobbits**

DENMARK: RECEPTION OF TOLKIEN

Tolkien broke through in Denmark in the 1970s when *The Lord of the Rings* became cult reading. His books were first associated with the youth revolts at the end of the 1960s and the collective movement of the 1970s. One famous Danish author, Ebbe Kløvedal Reich (1940–2005), took the name Kløvedal from the Danish translation of Rivendell in Tolkien's universe as a gesture to promote "power to fantasy." In 1977, Queen Margrethe II of Denmark (1940–) illustrated *The Lord of the Rings* with original Jugend-style-inspired drawings.

Tolkien's books still sell extremely well in Denmark, and *The Lord of the Rings* is one of the most popular books with Danish children and young adults (according to a survey of reading habits carried out in 2004). Tolkien's books are also widely read by adults and continue to be published by the adult literature section of the Danish publishing house Gyldendal. Of course, *The Hobbit* and *The Lord of the Rings* have appeared in Danish translation, but so have *The Father Christmas Letters, Farmer Giles of Ham* (with the humorous Danish title *Niels Bonde fra Bol), Mr. Bliss, Roverrandom, Silmarillion, Tree and Leaf,* and several shorter stories.

The Hobbit and *The Lord of the Rings* have had a special influence on Danish fantasy writing. Since the beginning of the 1980s, several books have appeared that were inspired by Tolkien's secondary universes. They generally have been published as children's literature, but they work in the same way that Tolkien's books did—as crossover literature with a broad spectrum of adult and child readers. In 1985, one of the best-known living Danish writers, Bjarne Reuter (1950–), published the novel *Shamran—den som kommer [Shamran: He Who Will Come]* about a boy chosen to save a whole world from perdition because it had been taken over by Evil. The story has mythological features, and the novel is reminiscent of Tolkien's universe in minor detail and broad storyline.

More recently, there have been several Danish female fantasy writers influenced by the Tolkien tradition. These writers have constructed universes that evoke an allegorical interpretation as a criticism of modern civilisation. This is true of Josefine Ottesen (1956–) and not least Lene Kaaberbøl (1960–). The latter translated her *Shamer*-tetralogy (2000–2003) into English. The Shamer stories take place in a medieval-like feudal society with magic and dragons as features of everyday life. The eponymous Shamer is a kind of witch who acts on behalf of Good by awakening a sense of shame in criminals, thus touching upon themes such as guilt, shame, and justice.

In an article about her writing, Kaaberbøl subscribes to Tolkien's idea about the eucatastrophe, which he presented in "On Fairy-Stories" (published in *Tree and Leaf*). The eucatastrophe (meaning an ending that brings harmony) is seen as necessary to observe the pact previously agreed between writer and reader. In modern Danish fantasy writing, however, we can discern a tendency to use more open endings and to break with Tolkien's theoretical demands.

ANNA KARLSKOV SKYGGEBJERG

See also **Eucatastrophe; "On Fairy-Stories"**

DEOR

Deor or *Deor's Lament* (the original has no title) is a forty-two line Anglo-Saxon poem found in the *Exeter Book* (a manuscript of the tenth century, although the date of the poem is uncertain). The poem is usually divided into seven sections, the first six being marked in the manuscript by large, beginning capital letters. The first five and the seventh end with a refrain, "Þæs ofereode; þisses swa mæg" ("That passed; this may also"—or, in Tolkien's paraphrase, "Time has passed since then, this too can pass" [*Lost Tales II,* 323]). Those five and the seventh each have an example of a personal problem from the Germanic heroic age—the last one personal to the poet. The first two stanzas deal with an episode in the life of the smithy god, Weland—in the first, Weland has been captured by

Niðhad, a human king, and made to work as a blacksmith; in the second, Beadohilde, Niðhad's daughter, has been raped and impregnated by Weland. Weland's grief passed because he later escaped; Beadohilde's grief passed because she later married Weland and their son became a hero. The next three sections involve people whose problems—or their subjects' problems—have been identified by scholars from cognate versions of the stories. (See the discussions of Mæðhilde, Ðeodric, and Eormanric in Malone [8–14] and Pope [93–95].) Eormanric receives a brief discussion by Tom Shippey in *The Road to Middle-earth* (13–14). The sixth section is a Christian meditation on adversity: on earth, God gives both prosperity and sorrow. In the final section, the author calls himself Deor (meaning brave or bold), a scop (or bard) who was honored for many years by the Heodenings but then lost his position and his land grant to Heorrenda, another scop. The latter appears in at least four Scandinavian or Germanic works as a good poet. Thus, the author puts his fictionalized self into the heroic age of Heorrenda.

Tolkien was interested in this final section in several literary ways. First, he occasionally referred to the author of *Beowulf* as Heorrenda (*Lost Tales II,* 323; Drout, 244, n. 20)—presumably in his scholarly work as a *jeu de sprit,* for the *Beowulf*-poet was also a better poet. Second, he identified with Deor. That is, at one point in the early work on the "Silmarillion" mythos, he said Déor the singer was married to an Elven woman called Éadgifu (whose name Drout [231] identifies as the Anglo-Saxon source of the name Edith); Déor and Éadgifu lived at the town Kortirian (Warwick) (*Lost Tales II,* 291–92, 313). Edith Bratt was living in Warwick from 1913 until her marriage in 1916, and Tolkien visited her there (*Lost Tales I,* 25). As the Beren and Lúthien story incorporated some elements of the Tolkien-Bratt love (e.g., her dancing for him), so this marriage of a poet and an Edith (the Anglo-Saxon name means "gift") incorporates others (her name, the town). Third, in an odd contrast to the second point, in a different account Éadgifu is the wife of Ælfwine and mother of Heorrenda. In this tradition, Heorrenda is the editor of *The Golden Book,* based on his father's writings (*Lost Tales II,* 290–91). *The Golden Book* is thus *The Book of Lost Tales* (*Lost Tales II,* 310). Because Ælfwine means "elf-friend" in Anglo-Saxon (*Lost Tales I,* 24), and because in these early writings he is "an Englishman of the Anglo-Saxon period" (*Lost Tales II,* 309), perhaps he is another projection of Tolkien (an Englishman who loves Anglo-Saxon and the concept of elves), explaining this second marriage of Éadgifu; their child as the greater poet and a book compiler may be a projection of the great literary work(s) that will be produced by Tolkien with his wife as his inspiration. Fourth, the preceding three points are involved in varying degrees with Tolkien's early attempt directly to tie his mythos to England's history—for example, in "Ælfwine of England" (*Lost Tales II*, 312–22). That account contains the information of the second point. It takes place in the time of the English in England, but before the departure of the Elves (*Lost Tales II*, 313). In connection with the third point, Heorrenda is the half-brother of Hengest and Horsa, and with them conquered England (*Lost Tales II*, 290–91). Hengest's capital was at Warwick, Horsa's at Oxford, and Heorrenda's at Great Haywood, Staffordshire—the latter where the newly married Tolkiens lived in 1916–17 (*Lost Tales II*, 292). In Bede's history, Hengest and Horsa led the Jutes in the conquest of Kent—a more limited area than in Tolkien's reworking. Perhaps, at Great Haywood, Heorrenda spent his time writing *Beowulf* (point 1). Finally, for completion of this survey of the influence of *Deor* on Tolkien, a passing mention of Heorrenda as a poet who turned an Elvish song into English occurs in the interlude before "The Fall of Gondolin" (*Lost Tales II*, 145). Tolkien evidently felt that the appearances of Deor and Heorrenda in an Anglo-Saxon poem were cause enough to depict them in his fictionalized Anglo-Saxon (and Elvish) England.

JOE R. CHRISTOPHER

Further Reading

Drout, Michael D.C. "A Mythology for Anglo-Saxon England." In *Tolkien and the Invention of Myth: A Reader*, edited by Jane Chance, 229–47. Lexington, KY: University Press of Kentucky, 2004.

Malone, Kemp, ed. *Deor*. 4th ed. Methuen's Old English Library. New York: Appleton-Century-Crofts, 1966.

Pope, John C., ed. *Seven Old English Poems*. Library of Literature. Indianapolis, IN: Bobbs-Merrill, 1966. *Deor* is on pp. 39–40; its commentary and notes are on pp. 91–96.

Shippey, Tom. *The Road to Middle-earth*. Boston, MA: Houghton Mifflin, 1983.

See also **Ælfwine; Book of Lost Tales II; Frame Narratives; Great Haywood; Kortirion; Mythology for England; Warwick**

DESCENT

The theme of the descent into the underworld appears in Tolkien's work in several places, such as the journey through Moria, the Goblin caves, Shelob's Lair, the Paths of the Dead, and Angband.

The Fellowship's experience mirrors that of Aeneas from Virgil's *Aeneid* in several key ways that establish the literary motif. The parallels of the two journeys begin before the Fellowship even reaches Moria and before Aeneas arrives at Hades. Both Aeneas and the Fellowship cross a bleak and foreboding land that features a dark lake. In each case, there is a guide to escort them during the descent and assist them in navigating the perils of the underworld. Frodo Baggins is guided in the descent into Moria by Gandalf, and Aeneas is shown the way by the Sibyl. Both journeys are plagued by a lack of potable drinking water. The Fellowship is warned against drinking the water in Moria, and Aeneas faces the swampy Stygian stream of Hades.

A guardian figure is another prominent feature of the descent into the underworld. Frodo and Aeneas must pass by the guardian figure of the realm. During the course of Aeneas' journey, he hears Tisiphone, the Guardian of Tartarus. In the case of the Fellowship, it encounters the monstrous Balrog. These guardians of the underworld have much in common aside from their role; both hold whips in their left hand and bladed weapons in their right.

To clearly demarcate the passage across the underworld, a physical barrier and obstacle are used. Aeneas passes over the River Styx, and the Fellowship passes over a bridge. The passage over these physical locations is obstructed in both cases by a guardian figure, Charon the Ferryman and the Balrog, respectively.

A great loss also occurs during the descent to show that one cannot descend into the underworld and leave unscathed. Aeneas is reunited with his father Anchises but must leave him behind to continue his journey. The Fellowship must leave Gandalf behind to move on with their quest to save Middle-earth from Sauron.

The descent and passage through the underworld ultimately end in a pleasant destination as the journey draws to a close. Aeneas' journey ends in the Fields of Elysium, a paradise for him where he can recover from the ordeal of his journey. For the Fellowship a similar respite occurs in Lórien.

Thus, Tolkien's descent into the underworld, as shown in the example of the journey through Moria, follows the classical motif that appears in Virgil's *Aeneid*. The Fellowship encounters the same geography; the same undrinkable water; and similar guardians, barriers, and loss, and both descents end in a type of paradise.

Another appearance of the underworld in Tolkien's work is in *The Hobbit* when the Dwarves and Bilbo enter the Goblin caves. Seeking shelter in the

Misty Mountains, the company enters a cave and is taken prisoner and brought to the Goblin city. Bilbo eventually slips away and encounters Gollum in the lake. This journey through the Goblin caves mirrors three distinct motifs of the underworld. First, caves can serve as entrances to the underworld, which hearkens back to the legends of the Sibyl of Delphi and Aeneas' journey to Hades. Second, within the caves/underworld there exist monsters, in this case the Goblins. Lastly, within the underworld there are guardian figures, such as Cerebrus or Beowulf's dragon, which protect treasures, such as Gollum did with the ring.

Shelob's Lair is another example of a journey through the underworld. Sam and Frodo travel through the cave network of Cirith Ungol to reach Mount Doom. Again this mirrors the classic underworld quest. Sam and Frodo have a guide on their journey, Gollum, much as Aeneas had the Sibyl. In addition, Sam uses the light of the Phial of Galadriel to overcome the guardian of the cave, Shelob, much as Aeneas used the golden bough to gain passage from Charon the Ferryman. The last similarity between the underworld and Shelob's Lair is Frodo's "death." Shelob poisons Frodo, placing him in a state resembling death. This "death" shows how thin the liminal border between life and death can be in the underworld. Often in classical literature, a hero would descend into the underworld to attempt to return one of the dead to life. Although these tasks mainly ended in failure, they showed how transitional death could be in the underworld.

Aragorn traveling the Paths of the Dead is yet another example. Aragorn descends through the Dark Door into the Paths of the Dead, an unhallow place full of the shades of the people who betrayed Isildur. The Paths of the Dead mirrors the Norse underworld of Hel, which was home to the spirits of oath breakers. Upon reaching the Stone of Erech, Aragorn reveals that he is the heir of Isildur and commands the specters to attack the corsairs of Umbar, which will lift the curse Isildur placed on them for their treachery. To marshal the ghosts to aid in the war against Sauron, Aragorn has to travel beyond the realm of the living into the underworld.

Angband is another example of an underworld in Middle-earth. Lúthien descended into Angband to rescue Beren, who took the Silmaril from the Iron Crown. This rescue is reminiscent of the Orpheus legend in which Orpheus traveled to Hades to free Eurydice. Angband was guarded by the great wolf Carcharoth, who bit off Beren's hand, which held the Silmaril. While a wolf biting off the hand of a hero is more in line with Fenrir and Tyr, the use of a wolf as an underworld guardian comes directly from the classical mythological creature Cerberus.

Thus, from numerous sources, both classical and Norse, Tolkien crafted the various descents into the underworld as they appeared in Middle-earth: Moria, the Goblin caves, Shelob's Lair, the Paths of the Dead, and Angband.

JOHN WALSH

Further Reading

Obertino, James. "Moria and Hades: Underworld Journeys in Tolkien and Virgil." *Comparative Literature Studies* 30, no. 2 (1993): 153–69.

DESPAIR (WANHOPE)

The Old English noun "wan 'hope'" (Want of hope; despair; melancholy; delusion; weariness) was replaced by "despair (d-spâr)" (ca. 1325). Both *despair* and *wanhope* are generally defined as a complete loss or lack of hope and being overcome by sense of futility or defeat. In Christianity, despair is not an emotional but a moral state. It is also a sin. Despair is the polar opposite of hope, a Christian virtue. The sinner in moral degradation doubts the Christian God's ability to save him or herself and becomes uncertain whether he or she can earn salvation within the most desperate circumstances. From as early as the eleventh century, "the problem of pride and despair among the powerful" has been among the greatest themes in English Literature (Drout 2004, 137). A myriad of Tolkien's works deal with wanhope or despair.

In the fourteenth century, William Langland's *The Vision of the Piers* dealt with the sin of despair. The B-text of William Langland's *Piers Plowman* (ca. 1370) introduces the reader to *wanhope*: "Ware thee—for Wanhope wolde thee bitraye" is translated as "And said, 'Beware of Despair who would thee betray.'" This treatment in relation to sin and loss of hope is similar to Chaucer's vivid and powerful picture of despairing in the mercy of God within *The Parson's Tale*: "Now cometh wanhope, that is despeir of the mercy of God" (Benson 1987). To die in despair, or wanhope, is not to allow room for salvation, the ultimate sin in Christianity. Chaucer's tale is a handbook on how to treat the effects of despair and encourage the way of the pilgrim. The Parson describes each of the seven deadly sins, providing a remedy accompanied by a reestablishment to Grace through penance.

Tolkien's characters all deal with despair in its various manifestations; some, such as Samwise, never truly give into it, and others, such as Denethor, completely lose hope. Denethor is an exploration into a leader who is a product of despair. Like King Lear, Denethor is essentially the aged monarch who falls from the highest elevation and is driven to madness, stripped of all humanity, and set to suffer from the woes of misery and despair. Denethor's suffering, misery, and despair result from fear: the possible loss of his throne to Aragorn, the war with Sauron, the death of his son Boromir, the potential mortal wounding of Faramir, and the fear of his own mortality. These fears create a despair that permeates, preventing Denethor from accomplishing the duties of his Stewardship. Without hope of reprieve or salvation, Denethor immolates himself and attempts to force Faramir's death upon the pyre (*RK*, V, vii, 130–131, 825, 850–57). "Of Túrin Turambar" (*S*, 242–79) is primarily inspired by Tolkien's interest in the Finnish "Story of Kullervo" from the *Kalevala*. The despair and fate of Túrin and Kullervo do not allow room for salvation; both end their lives tragically after it is revealed each had slept with his sister, whom he had blindly taken for a wife.

Despair is also the ultimate tragedy of Tolkien's Elves. From his Elves in "The Cottage of Lost Play" to the majesty of Galadriel, despair is the "long defeat" they must battle against (*LotR*, , , 357). This is a theme relevant to the time and tide of Tolkien. For Tolkien, the will to carry on and to persevere in the face of despair, qualities he instills in most of his characters, are encapsulated in a few lines of the Old English poem *The Battle of Maldon,* which Tolkien translated. As a summation of ancient heroic code, the lines read: "Will shall be the sterner, heart the bolder, spirit the greater as our strength lessens" (Garth, 71).

ANTHONY S. BURDGE and JESSICA BURKE

Further Reading

Benson, Larry D. *The Riverside Chaucer*. Boston, MA: Houghton Mifflin, 1987.

Drout, Michael D.C. "Tolkien's Prose Style and Its Literary and Rhetorical Effects" *Tolkien Studies: An Annual Scholarly Review*, 1 (2004): 137–62.

Garth, John. *Tolkien and the Great War: The Threshold of Middle-earth*. Boston, MA: Houghton Mifflin, 2003.

Hammond, Wayne G., and Christina Scull. *The Lord of the Rings: A Reader's Companion*. Boston, MA: Houghton Mifflin, 2005.

Wood, Michael. *Shakespeare*. New York: Basic Books, 2003.

See also **Anglo-Saxon History; *Battle of Maldon, The*; Chaucer, Geoffrey; Denethor; Finland: Literary Sources, Kalevala; Langland, William; Old English; Túrin**

DEVIL'S COACH-HORSES

In one of his earliest philological studies (but after his work on the *Oxford English Dictionary* and the *Year's Work in English Studies*), Tolkien looked at the curious passage in *Hali Meiðhad*), "Bi hwam it is iwriten þus þurh þe prophete, þet ha in hare wurðinge as eaueres forroteden . . . Þe ilke sari wrecches þe i þe fule wurðinge unwedde waleweð beoð þe deofles eaueres, þet rit ham & spureð ham to don all ðet he wule"(Furnivall, 18)—translated as "Of whom it is written thus by the prophet, that they in their filth rotted like boars . . . the same sorry wretches that unwedded wallow in the foul mire are the devil's boars, who rides them and spurs them to do all he will." The Old English (OE) for "boar" is *eofor*, and the OE for "draught-horse" (West Midlands dialect) would be *eafor*, (as we will see = *jumentum*), which would give Middle English *eaueres* as here—and OE *eofor* would give *eoueres*.

As Tolkien remarks, "It can hardly be doubted that Joel i.17 *computruerunt jumenta in stercore suo* is the prophet referred to." *Jumentum* has the original meaning of "a yoked team, " then of "one of a team of draught animals," then of "draught-horse" (but not "ox"). Tolkien suggests that the early use of *eaueres* in this form in *Hali Meiðhad* virtually proves a pre-Conquest origin for the term and thus independence from *aver* (property). But others have suggested a later date, as we will see. The word *aver* as "draught-horse" in Northern and Scottish speech, he notes, is well attested from Dunbar (ca. 1500) to Scott (ca. 1800).

After going through his philological argument, Tolkien emphasizes that the Devil is apparently riding a different kind of horse from what might be expected (336): "The fact remains that there was something irregular in the devil's behavior. We can abandon the picture of him riding upon rotting boars, but neither was an *aver* a beast for a gentleman to ride. . . . The devil appears to have ridden his coach-horses like a postillion, but he was in worse case than Geoffrey Chaucer's shipman who 'rood upon a rouncy as he couthe'; his steeds seem indeed to have been heavy old dobbins that needed all his spurring." But if the word is indeed pre-Conquest, is this all unexpected?

It is notable that the word in the form *eafor* occurs only once in OE, with *cumfeorm* as part of the obligation of the king's tenants to harbor the king's messengers and further them with transport facilities (*cumfeorm* and *eafor* for "entertainment" and "transport"), and indeed, the king's messengers were among the few mounted men in the England of (say) the *Vita Sancti Cuthberti* (seventh century). If the underlying implication is that the Devil rides the horses when we invite him in as the king's messenger (but which king?), there need be no particular reference to draught-horses, as there is no particular reference to coach-horses. And given the kind of horses that would be necessary for later knights, we should not be surprised to find beasts of burden bearing the burden of the Devil—or any devil. It might be worth knowing whether the king's messengers of early days rode with stirrups: if not, perhaps heavy draught-horses would be advisable, rather than more spirited steeds.

There is more of interest here than this. In a footnote on *aferian, eafor,* referring to Liebermann's long note in *Herrigs Archiv* (109, 75), Tolkien adduces a "striking but purely accidental parallel . . . in OHG *gûl* originally 'boar' > mod. Germ. 'Gaul' = nag." Of course, *gûl* in Tolkien, even in a 1925 philological note, brings to mind the *nazgûl*—the ringwraiths on their steeds (but not horses), the Devil's beasts of burden indeed. And is it purely coincidental that a little later we have a discussion of the rare OE words in *Hali Meiðhad,* for example, *sabaz,* "sabbaths" (334)? *Praemonitus praemunitus*—Professor Tolkien warned me long ago about finding in him the kind of echoic borrowing we find in C.S. Lewis, Tor and Tinidril from Tuor and Idril, but it is still curious.

Tolkien dates *Hali Meiðhad* to ca. 1150, but later scholars suggest a time from 1210 to 1220. The text is in MS Bodley 34 and has been most fully edited by Tolkien's friend Simonne d'Ardenne in her *The Katherine Group edited from MS Bodley 34* (1977), which was originally to be a joint publication with Tolkien. The Katherine Group includes lives of St. Katherine, St. Margaret, St. Juliana, Sawles Warde, Ancrene Wisse, and *Hali Meiðhad.* That MS Bodley 34 comes from the first quarter of the thirteenth century seems to be a popular view, but what that says about the date of original composition of *Hali Meiðhad* is not clear. It might be as early as Tolkien suggests, or it might not. However, although the word might not be pre-Conquest, the form *eaueres* suggests it is.

To be sure, the phrase "the Devil's coach-horses" has indeed more of the seventeenth (or eighteenth or nineteenth) than the twelfth or thirteenth (or seventh) century about it. The famous description of the Devil's coach-horses comes from "Touching the Trial of one Major Weir, a Warlock," in Roughead's *12 Scots Trials* (1913) and in much the same words from Stevenson's *Edinburgh: Picturesque Notes* (1879) of the Devil who transported Major Weir and his sister Jean from Edinburgh to Musselburgh and back in 1648, in his coach with six black horses that seemed all of fire (or whose eyes seemed all of fire). Scott adopted the

story for "Wandering Willie's Tale" in *Redgauntlet,* but he made little of the Devil's coach or horses. The Devil's coach-horses, as of 1925, were the six black, fire-eyed steeds of Roughead or Stevenson. Tolkien's use of the phrase may be anachronistic humor (as with the definition of blunderbuss by the clerks of Oxenford in *Farmer Giles*).

JARED LOBDELL

Further Reading

d'Ardenne, Simonne R.T.O., *The Katherine Group.* Paris: Société d'Edition Les Belles Lettres, 1977.
Furnivall, F.J., ed. "Hali Meidenhad." EETS OS 189 (London: Oxford University Press, 1922).
Tolkien, J.R.R. "The Devil's Coach-Horses." *Review of English Studies* 1, no. 3 (July 1925): 331–36.
———. "Ancrene Wisse and *Hali Meiðhad.*" *Essays and Studies, by members of the English Association* 14 (1929): 104–26.

*See also **Ancrene Wisse**; Katherine Group; "MS Bodley 34: A Re-collation of a Collation"*

DEVILS

Tolkien very much believed in the devil, or "the Enemy," sin, and the human capacity for evil and temptation, as can be seen in his *Letters* (48). Humphrey Carpenter in *The Inklings* suggests that Tolkien, who felt it was dangerous to study too closely the methods of evil, found the discussion of how best to tempt humanity in C.S. Lewis's *The Screwtape Letters* personally horrifying and even dangerous. In a letter, Tolkien mentions reading that Lewis was not very fond of *The Screwtape Letters* and says that he now knows why Lewis dedicated it to him (*Letters,* 342), which Tolkien found less than flattering.

In Anglo-Saxon literature, devils are rebel angels, cast out of heaven and condemned to hell with Satan, and tempters of mankind, as in the Old English "Genesis B" and the Blicking and Vercelli Homilies. Devils debate saints in hagiographic texts such as Cynewulf's *Juliana.* In Felix of Crowland's Latin "Life of Saint Guthlac," the devils that torment St. Guthlac speak cacophonous Welsh, as Tolkien notes in "English and Welsh" (*MC,* 182). The invisible arrows of the devil, like the arrows that the devil in Hrothgar's "sermon" in *Beowulf* sends under the unwary warrior's helmet, provide transport for sin and temptation. Grendel and his mother are called *deofla,* devils (line 1,680) in *Beowulf,* as Tolkien notes in Appendix A of "*Beowulf:* The Monsters and the Critics." Tolkien observes that as a creature of flesh and blood, an ogre, although Grendel is kin to devils, he is not a true devil. Grendel is a mere monster and chooses to sin. Tolkien's reference to Morgoth as a "Diabolus" who "fell," and to Morgoth's rebellion as "Satanic" suggest that he saw Morgoth's role as roughly equivalent to that of the fallen angel Lucifer (*Letters,* 195, 202).

LISA L. SPANGENBERG

Further Reading

Carpenter, Humphrey. *The Inklings*. London: George Allen & Unwin, 1978.
———. *J.R.R. Tolkien: A Biography*. London: George Allen & Unwin, 1977.
Dendle, Peter. *Satan Unbound: The Devil in Old English Narrative Literature*. Toronto: University of Toronto Press, 2001.

See also **"Beowulf: The Monsters and the Critics"; Beowulf: Tolkien's Scholarship; Elf-Shot; Genesis; Juliana**

DOORS AND GATES

In Middle-earth, doors and gates have both practical and symbolic functions. They mark exclusion or admission. They test character and wisdom. They suggest mystery, secrecy, and privilege. They serve as barriers, confrontation points, riddles, or thresholds to adventure and status. Doors and gates come in many shapes and forms, from the charming round doors of hobbit dwellings, through the tower-gate of Cirith Ungol with its baleful watchers, to the frowning Black Gate, the Morannon, which seals off northwestern Mordor.

A number of gates or doors are mentioned only in passing, such as the gate of the village of Bree or the new gates the hobbits find barring the Shire when they return. Still, there are at least a dozen named gates or doors in *The Hobbit* and *The Lord of the Rings*. There are also natural features called gates, such as the Redhorn Gate, the pass over Carardhas, and natural features associated with gates, such as the Sirannon, the Gate-stream, at the west door of Moria. That entrance, like several others, bears many names: the Doors of Durin, the West-Door, the Elven Door, the Door, the Gate, or Westgate. The journey through that door is echoed when Aragorn and his companions are forced to seek the Dark Door in Dwimorberg and walk the Paths of the Dead. Here, as in Moria, they must endure a dread underground journey, but to a much happier end.

Certain doors or gates are associated with particular characters: In *The Hobbit*, the secret door into the Lonely Mountain lets Bilbo Baggins enter Smaug's treasure hoard. Its existence is noted in the ordinary runes on Thror's Map. How to gain access can be demonstrated only by someone (like Elrond) who can read the moon-runes on that Map. The location of its keyhole can be found only by someone (like Bilbo) who is observant and quick-witted.

Three further examples involve Gandalf:

- In *The Lord of the Rings*, the western entrance to the Mines of Moria can be opened by anyone who knows the correct spell or command. Finding the word is a challenge to Gandalf's resources of language, but the real challenge is to realize, as he eventually does, that the needed word is in plain sight.
- The major public entrance to the city of Minas Tirith (usually called the Gate, it also has half a dozen other names) provides the site for a great confrontation between good and evil. Gandalf sitting on Shadowfax, forbids the Captain of the Nazgûl entry once the gate itself is down. The timing is superb: a moment after Gandalf says "You cannot enter here," a rooster crows for dawn, and far away the horns of Rohan are heard (*RK,* V, iv, 103).
- The Black Gate of Mordor appears twice in the tale of the Ring. Finding it closed, Frodo and Sam reach one of the low points of their journey. It seems "they were come to the bitter end" (*TT,* IV, iii, 246). They turn aside and head southwest. Later, Gandalf tries to protect Frodo's mission by a desperate feint at that same Black Gate, and the final battle of the War takes place there just as Frodo reaches the Cracks of Doom.

MICHAEL N. STANTON

Further Reading

Huttar, Charles. "Hell and the City: Tolkien and the Traditions of Western Literature." In *A Tolkien Compass*, edited by Jared Lobdell, 117–42. La Salle, IL: Open Court, 1975.

See also **Caves; Moria; Towers**

DOUBLES

Tolkien has a pattern of creating matched, parallel, or double individuals, a pattern that allows him not only to emphasize certain personality traits but also to suggest internal splits or negative potentiality within his characters. In *The Lord of the Rings*, Gollum and Frodo are closely and purposefully linked. The implication is clear: Gollum is the Ring-destroyed soul that Frodo could become. Moreover, Gollum has his own duality. Like Bilbo, whose nature is split between Baggins and Took, Gollum's internal division is suggested by double names: Sméagol and Gollum (or, in Sam's terms, Slinker and Stinker).

Most of Tolkien's key characters have their shadow side. As a "servant of the Secret Fire, wielder of the flame of Anor," Gandalf briefly faces a form of antithesis in the Balrog, the "flame of Udûn," a worker of "dark fire" (*FR*, II, V, 344). However, Gandalf's most significant double (in appearance, wisdom, and age) is Saruman—"like, and yet unlike" (*TT*, III, x, 183). Where Saruman yields to temptation and ultimately falls, Gandalf resists temptation, avoids the offer of the Ring, and becomes greater than before. He becomes, in fact, what Saruman "should have been" (*TT*, III, v, 98). Though Galadriel remains physically distant from her shadow self (Shelob the Great), the two—Lady and spider—are nonetheless closely connected. Both are equally ancient; both live in isolated realms; both work with webs; both are called Lady or Ladyship. They are also vividly matched in opposition. Shelob creates darkness and lives in darkness; she desires a glutting, swelling increase for herself and "death for all others" (*TT*, IV, ix, 333). Galadriel preserves life, is willing to diminish, and gives Frodo the phial that brings light into Shelob's tunnels.

Among Men, Boromir (the proud and rash seeker of glory) is balanced by Faramir, his brother (the wiser, more restrained, and more peaceable of the two). In a similar way, Denethor is balanced by Théoden. (Note the almost mirror image spelling of their names.) Where Denethor yields to despondency, takes his own life, and would take Faramir's life as well, Théoden overthrows despair, rides at the head of his army, and dies an honorable death.

Tolkien's various races and sometimes even his settings have their contrasting doubles too. Orcs are the antithesis of Elves; Trolls are balanced by Ents, and Minas Tirith has its negative match in Minas Morgul (the enemy's Tower of Sorcery). However, not all of Tolkien's doubles are contrasts between good and evil. Some are repetitions that reinforce specific character types (generally on differing hierarchical levels). Like her mother, Ungoliant (the light-hating and light-devouring monster of *The Silmarillion*), Shelob has her own darkness and her own insatiable lusts. But Shelob is a less powerful version of Ungoliant, just as Sauron is an imitative and lesser version of Morgoth and just as Saruman (whose Isengard is "only a little copy" of Barad-dûr) is an imitative and lesser version of Sauron (*TT*, III, viii,161).

On the positive side, Galadriel serves as a Middle-earth representative for Varda (Elbereth), Queen of the Stars. Both Varda and Galadriel are called upon the way Catholic saints might be; like Varda,

Galadriel is a bestower of light. In a more homey way, Goldberry is a version of Galadriel. Both live in and tend to isolated, tree-filled realms; both are associated with water; and to Frodo, Goldberry appears like "a fair young elf-queen" (*FR*, I, vii, 134). A more significant parallel for Galadriel, however, is Melian, the enchantress from *The Silmarillion*. Melian is a queen; Galadriel is sometimes called a queen. Lúthien (Melian's daughter) marries into the race of Men; Arwen (Galadriel's granddaughter) does the same. Melian is placed in opposition to Ungoliant; Galadriel is placed in opposition to Shelob. Like Galadriel, Melian maintains a protected realm.

Parallels and repetitions are also prevalent in Tolkien's incidents, objects, and scenes. See Randel Helms's *Tolkien and the Silmarils* and Michael N. Stanton's *Hobbits, Elves, and Wizards* for examples that include stolen treasures, eagle rescues, underground descents, and much more.

MARJORIE BURNS

Further Reading

Burns, Marjorie. *Perilous Realms: Celtic and Norse in Tolkien's Middle-earth.* Toronto: University of Toronto Press, 2005.

Helms, Randel. *Tolkien and the Silmarils: Imagination and Myth in "The Silmarillion."* New York: Houghton Mifflin, 1981.

Keenan, Hugh T. "The Appeal of *The Lord of the Rings*: A Struggle for Life." In *Tolkien and the Critics: Essays on J.R.R. Tolkien's "The Lord of the Rings,"* edited by Neil D. Isaacs and Rose A. Zimbardo, 62–80. Notre Dame, IN and London: University of Notre Dame Press, 1969.

O'Neill, Timothy R. *The Individuated Hobbit: Jung, Tolkien and the Archetypes of Middle-earth.* London: Thames and Hudson, 1980.

Stanton, Michael N. *Hobbits, Elves, and Wizards.* New York: Palgrave Macmillan, 2001.

Zimbardo, Rose A. "Moral Vision in *The Lord of the Rings*." In *Tolkien and the Critics: Essays on J.R.R. Tolkien's "The Lord of the Rings,"* edited by Neil D. Isaacs and Rose A. Zimbardo, 100–8. Notre Dame and London: University of Notre Dame Press, 1969.

See also **Boromir; Denethor; Faramir; Frodo; Galadriel; Gollum; Shelob; Théoden**

DRAGONS

These extraordinarily large, reptilian creatures appear in Middle-earth as preternaturally evil monsters, created in the First Age by Morgoth. Dragons are inimical to all the Children of Ilúvatar but in particular to Dwarves and Men. They appear as characters in *The Hobbit* and *The Silmarillion*, with references in *The Lord of the Rings* confined to brief allusions.

Tolkien modeled his dragons on classical and medieval Germanic exemplars; his dragon-slayer narratives equal or exceed his sources in dramatic effect.

Tolkien said his first story, composed about age seven, was about a dragon (*Letters*, 214, 221). He was influenced probably by the Old Norse *Völsunga saga* translated by William Morris and published in condensed form in Andrew Lang's *Red Fairy Book*, a source he acknowledges in "On Fairy-Stories." Later—at age twenty-two—the first serious story he attempted to write was the germ of the tragic account of Túrin Turambar and Glaurung the dragon (*Letters*, 7, 434), published later in *The Silmarillion*.

Besides Lang and Morris, Tolkien's sources include material from Old English (OE) and Old Norse (ON) literature and culture. *Beowulf* alludes to a legendary fight with a dragon, ascribing the victory to Sig(e)mund—father of Sigurd, the preeminent dragon-slayer in Germanic tradition; the poem concludes with Beowulf's death in a dragon-fight. Both dragons are associated with fabulous treasure hoards, a Germanic commonplace. Tolkien thought the *Beowulf* dragon and the dragon slain by Sigurd the only effective ones in early medieval literature; he considered the monsters, including the dragon, central to the theme of *Beowulf* and the mechanics of its plot ("*Beowulf:* The Monsters and the Critics"). Together with the *Poetic Edda*, the *Prose Edda* of Snorri Sturluson, and the *Völsunga saga*, which develop similar mythic material, ON *skáldic* verse from many sources—some as early as *Beowulf*—suggests the legend of Sigurd, slayer of the dragon Fáfnir, was the *Königsmythe*, the "master myth" of early Germanic culture. Carved scenes depicting the slaying of Fáfnir have been found in archaeology in wood and stone throughout northern Europe. Proverbs concerning dragons and their paradigmatic greed survive in OE and ON manuscripts; Jacob Grimm recognized this as a mythic motif and mentions the related concept of the dragon as a transformed human in the *Deutsche Mythologie*. OE *draca* and modern English "dragon" are cognate with Latin *draco*, from a Greek term meaning "sharp-sighted." The OE word *wyrm*, "worm, serpent," was a synonym; Tolkien uses "worm" sometimes for archaizing literary effect.

Tolkien treated Germanic dragon motifs as fragments of a once-unified corpus of prehistoric Germanic dragon lore, imaginatively reassembling them into a mythic "natural history" of dragons spanning all three ages of the history of Middle-earth. In *The Silmarillion*, Glaurung appears about 260 (First Age) during the Wars of Beleriand half-grown, his armor not yet fully developed, the first of the Urulóki (fire-serpents) and "the father of dragons." He is repulsed by archers under the command of Fingon, prince of Hithlum. Two hundred years later, in the Battle of Unnumbered Tears, Glaurung reappears in full strength accompanied by a brood of other dragons. There he slays Azaghâl, Dwarf-lord of Belegost; before dying, Azaghâl drives a knife into Glaurung's belly, forcing his retreat. Decades later, Glaurung reappears in Beleriand, wreaking widespread ruin; he is fought and slain by Túrin Turambar. Glaurung's depredations, the paralyzing spell of his gaze, and the devastating evil of his insidious, ironic prophesies make him Tolkien's most effective dragon. The story of Túrin's fight with Glaurung is one of the most moving dragon-slayer narratives ever written, outmatching Tolkien's sources in the strength and subtlety of its tragic themes.

The account of the Fall of Gondolin mentions a host of dragons, "the brood of Glaurung," among the terrible forces unleashed by Morgoth. An earlier, lengthier version of the story published in *The Book of Lost Tales: Part II* shows Gondolin besieged by monstrous mechanical dragons of iron cunningly linked and filled with armed Orcs, bronze and copper dragons with hearts of fire, and Balrogs mounted on dragons of pure flame.

The Urulóki, of which Glaurung is foremost—fire-breathing reptiles, but not winged—are but one class of dragons invented by Tolkien. In the sixth and final War of Wrath in Beleriand, winged dragons first appear, the mightiest of which is Ancalagon the Black. At the climax of this war, Ancalagon is slain by Eärendil in a titanic battle ending with the dragon's cataclysmic fall upon the towers of Morgoth's realm. In the victory over their Enemy, the Valar destroy "well-nigh all the dragons"; an earlier version of the "Quenta Silmarillion" published in *The Shaping of Middle-earth* says two escaped into the East. These were apparently male and female, for they are said to have bred in the dark places of the earth to afflict the world, "as they do still." *The Lord of the Rings'* Appendix A mentions their multiplying and growing strong in the wastes of Ered Mithrin north of Mirkwood—yet another class of dragons called colddrakes, apparently lacking fire—which slay King Dain I and Frór his son and drive the Dwarves out. About two hundred years later, Smaug—the fiery dragon of *The Hobbit*—descends on the Lonely Mountain.

The Hobbit has been seen as a dragon-slayer narrative of the *Beowulf* type rewritten as a comic children's story (Stein). Bilbo's adventures climax with the slaying of Smaug by Bard, a Man from Laketown, by an arrow-shot to a small unarmored spot on the dragon's underbelly—a motif borrowed from Germanic sources. A speaking dragon like Glaurung, Smaug is modeled on Fáfnir, whose dying speech prophesies Sigurd's doom. Despite its comic tone, Smaug's voice has the unsettling effect of malevolent threat masked in jocularity. Smaug and other dragons are presented as extremely old, a characteristic mentioned in *Beowulf* and probably based ultimately on the biblical dragon of the Apocalypse, the *draconem serpentem antiquum qui est diabolus,* "the dragon, that old serpent, which is the Devil" (Rev. 20:2). The narrator of *The Silmarillion* says "long and slow is the life of the dragons." Also mentioned in *The Hobbit* are the "Wild Were-worms of the Last Desert" (*H,* I, 49) otherwise unexplained but seemingly a reference to the human-to-dragon transformation motif of Germanic tradition (cf. *werewulf,* "man-wolf").

Dragons as such do not appear in *The Lord of the Rings.* In the Shire, Ted Sandyman scoffs at them as relics of children's stories; Gandalf comments that dragon-fire could melt the Rings of Power, but no dragons left on earth are hot enough and not even Ancalagon the Black could have melted the One Ring. At the end of the book, Merry Brandybuck is awarded a Dwarf-made horn taken from the hoard of Scatha the Worm by Fram—a Man of Rohan, slayer of the dragon. The poems "The Dragon's Visit" and "The Hoard" exemplify dragon motifs in the Middle-earth corpus; Chrysophylax, the dragon in *Farmer Giles of Ham,* belongs to the genre of mock-heroic, pseudo-legendary comic romance and has little to do with the main body of dragon lore in Middle-earth.

JONATHAN EVANS

Further Reading

Evans, Jonathan. "As Rare As They Are Dire: Old Norse Dragons, *Beowulf,* and the *Deutsche Mythologie.*" In *The Shadow-Walkers: Jacob Grimm's Mythology of the Monstrous,* edited by Tom Shippey, 207–69. Tempe: Arizona Center for Medieval and Renaissance Studies, 2005.

———. "The Dragon-lore of Middle-earth: Tolkien and Old English and Old Norse Tradition." In *J.R.R. Tolkien and His Literary Resonances: Views of Middle-earth,* edited by George Clark and Daniel Timmons, 21–38. Westport, CT: Greenwood, 2000.

———. "The Dragon." In *Mythical and Fabulous Creatures,* edited by Malcolm South, 27–58. Westport, CT: Greenwood, 1987.

Lionarons, Joyce. *The Germanic Dragon: The Nature of the Beast in Germanic Literature.* Middlesex: Hisarlik, 1998.

Rauer, Christine. *Beowulf and the Dragon: Sources and Analogues.* Cambridge: D.S. Brewer, 2000.

Stein, Ruth M. "The Changing Styles in Dragons—From Fáfnir to Smaug." *Elementary English* 45 (1968): 179–83.

See also **"***Beowulf***: The Monsters and the Critics"; Bible;** *Book of Lost Tales II;* **Childhood of Tolkien; Gaze;** *Hobbit, The;* **Lonely Mountain (Erebor);** *Lord of the Rings, The***; Middle-earth: Monsters; Poems by Tolkien: Uncollected; Poems by Tolkien: "Adventures of Tom Bombadil"; Old Norse Literature; Possessiveness;** *Shaping of Middle-earth, The***;** *Silmarillion, The***;** Túrin

DRAMATIZATIONS: STAGE AND SPOKEN

Stage productions of Tolkien's works have been few in number except for *The Hobbit,* which has been a perennial favorite of many children's theatres. Script adaptations by Patricia Gray (1967), Markland Taylor (1992), Edward Mast (1996), Glyn Robbins (1999), Kim Selody (1999), Gilly McInnes (2005), and others continue to be performed around the world, in many countries and many languages. Although most productions are strictly dramatic, others are musicals—most notably Ruth Perry's 1972 adaptation with music by Allan Jay Friedman and lyrics by David Rogers, as well as Brainerd Duffield's 1977 adaptation with music by John Morris. Reducing *The Hobbit* to a performance length that will hold the attention of young audiences is a challenge, and Mast and Selody have produced popular texts.

The Lord of the Rings presents greater challenges than *The Hobbit,* including the varying heights of the characters, a flaming Balrog and other fantastic beings, major battles, and an incredibly long, complicated text. As a result, no major stage production has been attempted until recently. An adaptation of the three books separately was undertaken by Blake Bowden and produced in Cincinnati, Ohio, one each year from 2001 through 2003. *The Fellowship of the Ring* had a disappointing run, but *The Two Towers* and *The Return of the King* attracted much larger audiences.

The Shaun McKenna and Matthew Warchus adaptation of *The Lord of the Rings* presents the entire epic in a three-and-a-half-hour musical, which opened to preview audiences in Toronto in February 2006. Directed by Warchus, the musical score is by A.R. Rahman, the Finnish band Värttinä, and Christopher Nightingale. As opposed to traditional musicals, the singing grows from natural circumstances. Promoted as a stage extravaganza, the Toronto run is exclusive for nine months with plans to open in London next.

Audio productions of Tolkien's works, which do not have the special effects problems of theatrical performances, have abounded. Tolkien himself made the earliest recordings. The author's readings from *The Two Towers* and *The Return of the King* date to a 1952 tape recording. It is now available in a four-CD set (2001), that also includes a recording of Tolkien's Christopher reading from *The Silmarillion*, though Tolkien's reading from *The Hobbit* is not included. Christopher's stately voice is a pleasure to listen to and seems fitting for *The Silmarillion*. To hear the dynamic voice of the creator of Middle-earth, however, and his colorful depictions of the various characters is a particular delight.

A BBC production of *The Hobbit* originally aired on BBC radio in 1988 and, like many audio productions, has been formatted in both audio cassette (1989) and compact disc (1997). The recording features Anthony Jackson as narrator and involves a full cast of characters. Their voices are nicely complemented by music and sound effects such as thunder, lightening, and splashing water.

The National Public Radio recording (1979/1994) is also an ensemble performance, with Ray Reinhardt as Bilbo and Bernard Mayers as Gandalf. Gail Chugg performs superbly as narrator using the script adaptation by Bob Lewis. With songs, background music, and extensive sound effects throughout, this production is one of the most elaborate versions of *The Hobbit*.

Some audio recordings involve a single reader, and Martin Shaw's performance of *The Hobbit* is a solid one, which he carries off without music or sound effects. His recordings are popular and just the right production for those listeners who find that the music and sound effects detract from Tolkien's words. The only unabridged reading (1991) of this text is by Rob Inglis, a remarkable performance in which he provides distinctive voices for the various characters and sings the songs in the story.

Like *The Hobbit*, many audio recordings have been made of *The Lord of the Rings*. The 1987 BBC production, with script adaptation by Brian Sibley and Michael Bakewell (1999/2002), features Ian Holm as the narrator and as Frodo. Holm is best known in recent years for his portrayal of Bilbo in the Peter Jackson movies. The recording is produced and directed by Jane Morgan and Penny Leicester, with music composed and conducted by Stephen Oliver. One noteworthy feature is the story's beginning with an account of the One Ring that includes a scene in Mordor of Gollum being tortured for information.

The American audio production (1979/2001) of *The Lord of the Rings* is based on the script adaptation by Bernard Mayers. It includes several first-rate character portrayals including Mayers as Gandalf, James Arrington as Frodo, and Tom Luce as Aragorn. One distinctive characteristic is that the pronunciation of names unwaveringly stresses the penultimate syllable, misinterpreting Tolkien's guidelines in the appendices,

which produces such surprising results as Sa-RU-man and Le-GO-las. This production has two notable faults: Merry, Pippin, and Sam possess the voices of little boys, and Gandalf's use of his staff produces a sound reminiscent of a ray gun in a poorly made 1950s space opera.

One of the best of the audio productions showcasing a single reader is the 1974 performance of *The Hobbit* by accomplished actor Nicol Williamson, whose vocal mastery is evident throughout. The only unabridged reading (1990) of *The Lord of the Rings* is by Rob Inglis, and though he sings the songs in the story, as he does in *The Hobbit*, his voices for the characters are less dramatic, and there are no sound effects. It is, nonetheless, a superb performance.

Audio recordings have also been made of some of Tolkien's other works. Recorded Books produced a 1990 reading from the appendices, an unabridged recording of "The Annals of the Kings and Rulers." Martin Shaw narrates the only unabridged audio recording (1998) of *The Silmarillion*. His rich, solemn voice is appropriate for such topics as the creation of the world, the evil works of Morgoth, and the struggles of Elves and Men in the First Age. As in his recording of *The Hobbit*, there are no sound effects and virtually no background music. In addition, HarperCollins AudioBooks has produced recordings of *Sir Gawain and the Green Knight, Pearl, Sir Orfeo, Farmer Giles of Ham*, and *Roverandom*.

ELIZABETH A. WHITTINGHAM

DREAMS

What is particularly interesting in Tolkien's attitude toward dreams and his use of dreams is his rejection (or apparent rejection) of George MacDonald and the German Romantic tradition going back to Novalis (Friedrich von Hardenberg, 1772–1801). It was Novalis who gave us the Bergmann, the Miner in the Depths of the Mountain, who is certainly one of the progenitors of Tolkien's Dwarves. But it was also Novalis who said "Life is not a dream but it should—and perhaps must—become one" ("Unser leben ist kein Traum– aber es soll und wird vielleicht einer werden," Aphorism no. 237 in *Novalis Schriften*, III, 281), which ties in well enough with MacDonald but not well at all with Tolkien. Tolkien is writing feigned history, not dream vision, but in his history there are of course dreams, and those dreams do obey two other Novalis *dicta*. First, dreams are often meaningful and prophetic because in them the orderly operations of time are suspended (Aphorism no. 959 in *Novalis Schriften*, III, 452). Second, the genuine poet of *Märchen* (the "fairy tale"?) is a seer of the future ("Der achte Marchen muss zugleich Prophetische Darstellung . . .Der achte Märchendichter ist ein Seher der Zukunft," Aphorism no. 234, *Novalis Schriften,* III, 280–81).

That Tolkien was aware of Novalis can scarcely be doubted, given his Germanic heritage and interest and the age in which he grew up. Certainly, Frodo and Sam, the folktale tellers *(Märchendichter),* are the dreamers of *The Lord of the Rings*—and Frodo, as Verlyn Flieger has suggested, is the dreamer-in-chief. It has been argued that Frodo's important dreams are three in number and that the first, his dream of Goldberry, is pretty much a "mood piece" without significance in the development of the story. The other two—the visions of Gandalf rescued from Orthanc and of the coast of Aman "under a swift sunrise"—are more than merely evocative. But they are neither the gates to the action of the story nor dreams are part of the story (as dreams are, for example, in *The Notion Club Papers,* where the name Errol seems to repeat Eriol, who dreams alone). But they certainly add to the quality of romance and perhaps (all of these three) of Faërie.

There are meaningful dreams, as far back as Homer, and we need not look to Novalis to understand "Tolkien on Dreams." But we should understand that in Tolkien the dreams (and they may be veridical) are part of the story *in* his world—not the gate *to* his world or even the gate to the story in his world. (cf., for example, Jane Studdock's dreams in C.S. Lewis's *That Hideous Strength,* which are a key ingredient in the story.) Also, in Tolkien's world, the *Märchendichter* (the poet of *Märchen*) is preeminently Frodo, secondarily Sam, and as Richard West observed in *A Tolkien Compass* (1975), Frodo is the visionary and dreamer of *The Lord of the Rings,* "and no one else in the romance has so many dreams or such varied ones."

JARED LOBDELL

Further Reading

Flieger, Verlyn. *A Question of Time: J.R.R. Tolkien's Road to Faërie.* Kent, OH: Kent State University Press, 1997. Using a (J.W.) Dunnean interpretation of time and dream.
Kocher, Paul. *Master of Middle-earth*, Boston, MA: Hughton Mifflin, 1972.
Lobdell, Jared. *The Rise of Tolkienian Fantasy.* Chap. 6. Chicago, IL: Open Court, 2005.
Samuel, R., ed. *Novalis Schriften*, vol. 3. Stuttgart: Kohlhammer, 1977.
West, Richard C. "The Interlace Structure of *The Lord of the Rings*." In *A Tolkien Compass*, edited by Jared Lobdell, 90. La Salle, IL: Open Court, 2003.

See also **Prophecy**

DRUIDS

Tolkien studied Latin and Greek as a schoolboy and as an undergraduate, and he would certainly have been familiar with the writings of Caesar, Tacitus, Pliny, and Plutarch, all of whom discuss continental druids. He would know that the duties of the druid included officiating as priest during ritual sacrifices, possibly overseeing other rituals in a sacred grove, counseling the king, and making judgments. He would be aware that in medieval Irish texts the druid is a cross between a prophet and a wizard or sorcerer. He was familiar with the Irish saints' lives in Latin, as well as some from medieval Irish, where Patrick and Bridget in particular prove that the magic of the druid is less significant than the divine miracles of the Christian priest.

Tolkien would have known that English borrowed "druid" from Latin *druides* but that *druides* has a Celtic origin. He might even have recognized that "druid" contains the Indo-European root **deru,* or **dreu,* and that "druid" is likely a Celtic compound **dru-wid-,* "strong seer," with the second syllable, **wid-,* "seeing," from the Indo-European **weid-.* Shippey points out that the Drúadan Forest mentioned in "The Ride of the Rohirrim" in *The Return of the King* is probably formed from Gondorin *-adan,* with the first syllable *druí* (*UT,* 385) likely being "magic," borrowed, much as Anglo-Saxon itself borrowed *dry-craeft,* "magic," from the Celtic *druid.*

John Arnott MacCulloch's *The Religion of the Ancient Celts* would certainly have been available, should Tolkien have chosen to read an early scholarly study of Celtic religion. But even references in Tolkien's earliest drafts to what become the Istari, wizards of Middle-earth, including Radagast the Brown and Gandalf, show a marked resemblance to Norse mythology, not Celtic.

Gandalf and the other Istari, or wizards of Middle-earth, bear little resemblance to the druids of medieval Irish tales and saints' legends. Gandalf does not preside over sacrifices or make judgments. Gandalf is closer to wizards, like Merlin or Gwydion in the fourth branch of the Welsh *Mabinogion,* than to druids, yet Gandalf behaves far more ethically than either. In his letter to Robert Murray, SJ (*Letters,* 202), Tolkien compares Gandalf and the other Istari to angels given human form. Gandalf's use of magic is limited, his behavior restricted, as Tolkien's letter implies, by rules. This is less true of the druids of Irish myth, who behave in ways that Tolkien would find reprehensible. They are more willing to interfere in the lives of others, or use magic and charms, than Gandalf is.

It is somewhat paradoxical to see the enormous influence that Tolkien's wizards have had on neo-pagan druids, many of whom see Tolkien's mythology, and Gandalf in particular, as direct inspirations for their faith, perhaps because of the historical druid's association with a sacred grove and Tolkien's fondness for trees.

LISA L. SPANGENBERG

Further Reading

Burns, Marjorie. "Gandalf and Odin." In *Tolkien's Legendarium: Essays on "The History of Middle-earth,"* edited by Verlyn Flieger and Carl F. Hostetter, 219–31. Westport, CT: Greenwood, 2000.

MacCullough, J.A. *The Religion of the Ancient Celts*. Edinburgh: T. and T. Clark, 1911.

Piggott, Stuart. *The Druids*. New York: Thames and Hudson, 1985.

Shippey, Tom. *The Road to Middle-earth*. Revised and Expanded edition. Boston, MA: Houghton Mifflin, 2003.

See also **Arthurian Literature; Celtic; Gandalf; Latin Literature; Mythology; Old Norse Literature; Two Trees; Wizards**

DUNDAS-GRANT, JIM (1896–1985)

James Dundas-Grant was a member of the Inklings, known to them as D.G. He was a Catholic, born in London of Scottish parentage, who served in the Royal Navy during World War I. As a member of the Royal Naval Volunteer Reserve, he was recalled to service in World War II. In October 1944, he was appointed commander of the Oxford University Naval Division, with residence at Magdalen College.

In a memoir, "From an 'Outsider'" (published in *C.S. Lewis at the Breakfast Table,* ed. James T. Como), Dundas-Grant recalled arranging for C.S. Lewis to tutor him and his cadets in philosophy. Through this acquaintance, he was introduced to the Inklings. In his memoir, Dundas-Grant names Tolkien among the people he met in Lewis's rooms and, after the war, at morning pub sessions at the Eagle and Child.

Dundas-Grant and his wife Katherine settled in Oxford after the war, running a house in Iffley for Catholic undergraduates. He stayed in touch with the Inklings through pub sessions and lunches. A few days after Lewis's death in 1963, Tolkien had a mass said in his memory, which Dundas-Grant and Dr. Robert Havard attended.

DAVID BRATMAN

Further Reading

Como, James T. *C.S. Lewis at the Breakfast Table and Other Reminiscences*. New York: Harvest, 1992.

See also **Lewis, C.S.; Havard, Humphrey; Oxford**

DUTCH LANGUAGE

As a philologist, Tolkien had a working knowledge of the Germanic languages, including Dutch. He showed this by his involvement with the Dutch translation of *The Lord of the Rings.* In 1956 Tolkien received from his publisher a list of proposed Dutch translation of the nomenclature. For instance, Max Schuchart, the Dutch translator, wanted to translate "hobbit" into "hobbel," living in "Hobbelland" because that sounded like "Holland," and Schuchart felt that this would make the book more appealing to Dutch readers. Tolkien wanted none of it. On July 3, 1956, Tolkien wrote to Rayner Unwin that he was "actually very angry indeed." He stated that in principle the whole nomenclature should not be translated, and he objected to the Dutch names in the Shire because—as Tolkien felt—"Dutch toponymy, in spite of the affinity of the Dutch language and in many respects of its idiom, was specially unsuitable." To prove his point, Tolkien translated a number of Dutch place-names into English (making a mistake by using in one instance a German word instead of Dutch). Tolkien limited his criticism to the translation of individual words and especially names. With his knowledge of the history of words and—as he said—a good Dutch dictionary, he could judge the translation of words. But he did not have enough understanding of modern Dutch to be able to judge the style of the translation.

Later, Tolkien mellowed on his refusal to have names translated, and to assist future translators he wrote a "Guide to the Names in *The Lord of the Rings.*" By that time, the Dutch translation and the second one, the Swedish, were published, and in the Guide, Tolkien gave examples of both to show what he meant. For instance, he now felt that the Shire could be translated "by sense" because it is a word from the Common Speech. He approved the Dutch word *Gouw* because, as he wrote, "the Old English *scír* seems very early to have replaced the ancient Germanic word for 'district', found in its oldest form in Gothic *gawi,* surviving now in Dutch *gouw.*"

Tolkien also displayed his knowledge of Dutch during his visit to Holland in March 1958. He was guest of honour at a "Hobbit Maaltijd," a Hobbit dinner, held in Rotterdam. Tolkien gave a speech in which he—to the delight of the audience—spoke some Dutch. During the day, he was shown the city of Rotterdam. Tolkien was particularly interested in the many parks. He asked his Dutch guide for the Dutch names of the trees and flowers he saw, and when his companion did not know, Tolkien would translate the English or Latin name of the flower into Dutch to see if that would ring a bell.

Later that day, when they visited the bookshop that organized the meeting, Tolkien noticed a book he found appropriate for his somewhat fat guide. He took *Word slank en blijf gezond* from the shelves, wrote the translation "Get slim and stay in trim" on the title page, and presented the book to his guide, showing both his knowledge of Dutch and his sense of humor.

RENÉ van ROSSENBERG

Further Reading

Tolkien, J.R.R. "Guide to the Names in *The Lord of the Rings.*" In *A Tolkien Compass*, edited by Jared Lobdell. La Salle, IL: Open Court, 1975.

Van Rossenberg, René. "Tolkien's Exceptional Visit to Holland: A Reconstruction." In *Proceedings of the J.R.R. Tolkien Centenary Conference 1992*, edited by Patricia Reynolds and Glen H. Goodknight. Milton Keynes and Altadena: The Tolkien Society/ Mythopoeic, 1995.

See also **"Nomenclature of *The Lord of the Rings*"; *Lord of the Rings*: Success of; Netherlands: Reception of Tolkien**

DWARVES

This race of people was created by Aulë in imitation of Elves and Men. Named in Sindarin the Naugrim and Gonhirrim, "the Stunted People" and "Masters of Stone," Dwarves call themselves the Khazâd. The appendix of *The Lord of the Rings* describes them as "a tough, thrawn race . . . secretive, laborious . . . lovers of stones, of gems," and things made by "the hands of the craftsman." In the *Silmarillion*, they are "stone-hard, stubborn, fast in friendship and enmity," and long-lived (*S*, 44). In *The Hobbit* we learn they "can make a fire almost anywhere out of almost anything" (*H*, II, 68). Tolkien's Dwarves exhibit attributes found in earlier Germanic myth and folklore: diminutive, bearded, stout of stature, miners of ores and gems, they dwell secretively in subterranean places, especially mines and caves; they are smiths and forgers of great skill.

Like their creator Aulë, they are skilled builders and makers of jewels and weapons. *The Silmarillion* tells of Nauglamir, "the Necklace of the Dwarves," made for Finrod Felagund; it also speaks of their fabulous stone strongholds—Gabilgathol and Tumunzahar, excavated in Beleriand, and in Eriador, Khazâd-Dûm (Moria). Telchar of Nogrod is called the greatest weapon-smith of the First Age. As artificers, they care little for "things that live by their own life"; their need for wood to fuel forge-fires sparks

Aulë's spousal quarrel with Yavanna, who creates and nourishes life in Arda (*S*, 45).

The myth of the Dwarves' creation illustrates Tolkien's theory of subcreation as expressed in "Mythopoeia" and may indicate anxieties about the independent value of art. Ilúvatar regards Aulë's unauthorized, independent creation of the Dwarves as an offense; he ultimately grants them life but orders them to await, in sleep, for the awakening of Durin and the Seven Fathers of the Dwarves waken later in eastern Middle-earth; some eventually enter Beleriand, where they encounter Sindarin Elves under King Thingol, whom they serve as builders, artisans, and weapon-makers.

Charles Nelson says the Dwarves' chief temptation is greed; "It needs gold to breed gold," a Dwarvish proverb, exemplifies this (*RK*, Appendix A, 354). The Dwarves Bilbo meets at Bag End are jealous to reclaim the treasure hoard accumulated by their ancestors and later usurped by the dragon Smaug. The song describing their mission tells of ancient Dwarves' hammers ringing in "hollow halls beneath the fells"; their forging of bejeweled swords, goblets, and crowns; and their love of "pale enchanted gold" (*H*, I, 44–45). The song wakens in Bilbo a similarly "fierce and jealous love" of "beautiful things made by hands and by cunning and by magic" (*H*, I, 44-45); Thorin's greed, focused on a lost jewel, the Arkenstone, is his eventual downfall.

The word "dwarf," from Old English *dweorh/dweorg*, has cognates including Old Norse *dvergr*, Danish *dværg*, and German *zwerg*, from Common Germanic **dwergo-z* and Indo-European **dhwérg-whos*, but this family of words had nothing to do originally with short stature. Norwegian *dvergskot*, "animal-disease, murrain" and Old Indic *drva-*, "malady, ailment," point to a possible Indo-European root **dhuer-*, "harm, hurt, injure," and Old Indic *dhvaras*, "demonic spirit," suggests underlying **dhreugh-*, "fantasy, delusion," with "phantom, hallucination" as possible alternative meanings. Early English usage, however, assumes diminutive size as a principal attribute: Anglo-Saxon glossaries equate Old English *dweorg* with Latin *nanus, pygmaeus, pumilio, humiliamanus* (midget, pygmy, little person, dwarf). In a 1937 letter and in *The Lord of the Rings'* Appendix F, Tolkien defended his use of plural "dwarves" philologically as "a piece of private bad grammar," citing by analogy "elf/elves" and pointing to "dwarrows" as a more correct form (*RK*, Appendix F, 415).

Traditional English literature and folklore are silent concerning dwarves. Until the modern period, "dwarf" meant simply "stunted, diminutive human." In medieval romance, Spenser's *Faerie Queene,* and

Malory's *Morte D'Arthur,* they have none of the supernatural powers seen in Scandinavian tradition. Mythic associations in later English fairy tales reflect influence from German folklore and Scandinavian mythology in translations appearing earliest in Percy's *Northern Antiquities* (1770) and later in Victorian translations of Grimm, Lang's *Fairy-books,* William Morris, and others. An exception, Walter Scott's *The Black Dwarf* (1831), is based on a Highlands legend of "the Brown Man of the Muirs," a supernatural protector of wildlife, reported to Scott as authentic by Robert Surtees of Mainsforth.

Tolkien's ultimate sources are German or Scandinavian. In Old Norse literature, dwarves are subterranean smiths associated with treasure, supernatural knowledge, the subterranean world, and the dead. Nearly two hundred dwarf names are extant in Old Norse manuscripts, and dwarves play a significant role in several mythic narratives. The *Völsunga saga* and the Eddic poem *Völuspá* furnished important ideas. In the *Völsunga saga,* the dwarf Andvari has a fabulous treasure hoard and a magic, gold-generating ring. Eight of the thirteen Dwarves named in *The Hobbit*—Dwalin, Bifur, Bofur, Bombur, Nori, Fíli, Kíli, and Thorin—Thorin's byname Oakenshield, and the name Gandalf—are taken virtually unchanged from a section of the *Völuspá* traditionally called the *Dvergatál,* the "Dwarf-tally." Tolkien borrowed other Dwarf names found elsewhere in Old Norse or modeled them on authentic exemplars. In Middle High German literature, Alberîch the dwarf controls the Nibelungs' treasure.

Possibly as a linguistic joke, Tolkien's description of Dwarves as "thrawn"—twisted, misshapen; crossgrained, ill-tempered—suggests the Old Norse adjective *þrá,* "obstinate, stubborn"; the noun-form *þráinn,* "obstinate one," is closely homophonous with "thrawn" and identical to Thráinn, a name from the *Dvergatál* appearing twice in the genealogy of Thorin Oakenshield.

Dwarves' love of wealth, their migratory lives as artisans, traders, and "traffickers", and their alien status among other races suggest tinges of anti-Semitism. In a 1955 letter, Tolkien said "like Jews" they are "at once native and alien in their habitations . . . speaking the languages of the country, but with an accent due to their own private tongue." They guard their language, Khuzdul, "as a treasure of the past"; *The Lord of the Rings'* Appendix F calls it a "strange tongue" few of other races learn, and the Elves regard it as "cumbrous and unlovely" (*S,* 92). Yet, Dwarves later "gave their friendship . . . readily" to the Noldor, an attribute exemplified in *The Lord of the Rings* in Gimli's deep friendship with Legolas. In *The Silmarillion,* Mîm the Petty-dwarf's friendship with

Túrin Turambar is clouded by tragic betrayal and revenge.

JONATHAN EVANS

Further Reading

Battles, Paul. "Dwarves in Germanic Literature: *Deutsche Mythologie* or Grimm's Myths?" In *The Shadow-Walkers: Jacob Grimm's Mythology of the Monstrous,* edited by Tom Shippey, 29–82. Tempe: Arizona Center for Medieval and Renaissance Studies, 2005.

Funk, David A. "Explorations into the Psyche of Dwarves." In *Proceedings of the J.R.R. Tolkien Centenary Conference 1992,* edited by Patricia Reynolds and Glen H. GoodKnight, 330–33. Milton Keynes and Altadena: The Tolkien Society / Mythopoeic, 1995.

Gould, Chester N. "Dwarf-Names: A Study in Old Icelandic Religion." *PMLA* 44 (1929): 939–67.

Motz, Lotte. "Of Elves and Dwarves." *Arv* 29–30 (1973–74): 93–127.

———. "The Craftsman in the Mound." *Folklore* 88 (1977): 46–60.

Nelson, Charles. "The Sins of Middle-earth: Tolkien's Use of Medieval Allegory." In *J.R.R. Tolkien and His Literary Resonances: Views of Middle-earth,* edited by George Clark and Daniel Timmons, 83–94. Westport, CT: Greenwood, 2000.

Shippey, Tom. *The Road to Middle-earth.* Revised and Expanded edition. Boston, MA: Houghton Mifflin, 2003.

———. "Creation from Philology in *The Lord of the Rings.*" In *J.R.R. Tolkien, Scholar and Storyteller: Essays in Memoriam,* edited by Mary Salu and Robert T. Farell, 286–316. Ithaca, NY: Cornell University Press, 1979.

See also **Arkenstone; Arthurian Literature; Children's Literature; Dragons; Finrod; Folklore; Gandalf; German Folktale:** *Deutsche Mythologie***; Gimli; Jewels; Judaism; Literary Influences, Nineteenth and Twentieth Century; Lonely Mountain (Erebor); Moria; Mythology; Old English; Old High German Literature; Old Norse Language; Old Norse Literature; Philo-Semitism; Possessiveness; Spenser; Thingol; Thorin**

DYSON, HUGO (1896–1975)

Born in 1896 in Hove, Henry Victor Hugo Dyson was educated at Brighton College and at the Royal Military College at Sandhurst. He was always known as Hugo. He served in the First World War and was seriously wounded at Passchendaele. He attended Exeter College, Oxford, in 1919, where he read English. He became a tutor and lecturer at the University of Reading from 1921 until 1945, when he became a Fellow of Merton College, Oxford, in which position he remained until 1963.

His works include *Pope* (1933), *The Emergence of Shakespeare's Tragedy* (1950), and various essays on Jacobean and eighteenth-century literature. A powerful, loud, and sometimes difficult man, he was loved by many of his students but feared and disliked by others. He once introduced himself to a group of new acquaintances with "I'm Hugo Dyson. I'm a bore," and there were several who would have agreed with him.

Yet he was also greatly respected as a lecturer, perhaps more than as an author, and his classes at university were the stuff of college legend. Tutorials were even more entertaining, often beginning with beer being served to the assembled class. "Bring out the buckets, men," he would bellow. His style led to a certain public reputation, and he was asked to and did deliver a series of unscripted talks on television on the subject of William Shakespeare, about whom he was a genuine authority.

He also had a minor role in director John Schlesinger's film *Darling,* playing an elderly writer. "I think I've never been happier," he said about his brief television and film career. "The mere fact of being on television or in the cinema is so enormously flattering to a vain man."

That vanity continued and even survived through declining health. Dyson became arthritic and was obliged to use a cane when he walked. It was, however, a cane with a silver top. The style never left him. He died in 1975.

His connection to Tolkien began shortly after the end of the First World War when the two men met at Exeter College. Dyson was one of the first people to hear Tolkien read *The Fall of Gondolin* at the college's Essay Club. It is surprising, given that he did not enjoy public readings and was later to resist much of Tolkien's work, that he offered absolute approval and praise on this occasion. A committed Christian and an active member of the Church of England, he was an intensely witty and clever man with whom Tolkien formed an immediate bond.

Dyson became a member, albeit an occasional one, of The Inklings, along with Tolkien, C.S. Lewis, Charles Williams, and others. He appreciated the company and the conversation of the group rather than the readings that took place, and he was to become one of the harshest critics within the Inklings circle of *The Lord of the Rings* when it was read aloud by Tolkien.

Although his criticisms were expected, they were sufficiently intense to sting the usually forgiving and thick-skinned Tolkien. So strong was Dyson's dislike of these readings at gatherings of The Inklings that it was thought wise to give him a power of veto over any work being read aloud by any other member. C.S. Lewis's brother Warnie noted that on one occasion Dyson entered the room just as "we were starting on *The Hobbit,* and as he now exercises a veto on it—most unfairly I think—we had to stop."

Dyson and Tolkien had a profound influence on the beliefs of C.S. Lewis, who claimed that his life was changed by a conversation the three men had September 19, 1931. They dined at Magdalen College, Oxford, together and then strolled in nearby Addison's Walk. Lewis explained to his two friends that while he accepted God, the Gospels, and even Jesus Christ as the Messiah, he could not embrace other Christian ideas and found it impossible to accept the organized and sacramental church.

Lewis insisted that there were many myths and only some of them were true and meaningful. Tolkien argued that most myths originated in God and that some of them contained godly truth. As he spoke, a strange gush of wind blew through the trees and Lewis felt as if he had felt the real presence of God. The men walked and spoke on, with Tolkien eventually going home to his bed at three o'clock in the morning.

Dyson remained with Lewis, walking along the country lanes and in the corridors of the Oxford college. By the end of the conversation, Lewis had become a new person, writing that he now believed in Christ and that "my long night talk with Dyson and Tolkien had a good deal to do with it."

Tolkien and Dyson enjoyed a close but strained friendship. They joked to and about each other, and at times the humor was somewhat barbed. On one occasion, Lewis read from his book on hell titled *Who Goes Home,* a reference to the ceremonial cry of the policeman who locked the doors of the British parliament at night. Tolkien suggested that a more suitable title for a book about hell might be *Hugo's Home.*

Part of the problem was that Dyson never quite accepted the appeal and worth of Tolkien's fiction writing and was sometimes mocking to the point of rudeness. It is possible that he, along with other so many other academics, resented Tolkien's public success. Yet Tolkien was always stimulated by the man's boisterous charm, their shared experienced of the trenches of the First World War, and Dyson's compelling self-confidence, sheer sense of fun, tomfoolery, and acute intelligence.

MICHAEL COREN

Further Reading

Bratman, David. "Hugo Dyson: Inkling, Teacher, Bon Vivant." *Mythlore*, v. 21, no. 4 (Winter, 1997; whole number 82): 19-34.

Carpenter, Humphrey. *The Inklings.* New York: Ballantine, 1981.

Duriez, Colin. *The C.S. Lewis Chronicles.* New York: Bluebridge, 2005.

See also **Inklings; Lewis, C.S.**

E

EÄRENDIL

According to *The Silmarillion,* Eärendil is the world's greatest mariner, whom the Valar set to sail the heavens in his ship Vingilot, transforming him into the Evening and Morning Star. Eärendil, whose name means "Lover of the Sea," is one of the Half-elven, the son of Tuor (a Man fostered by Elves, the messenger of Ulmo to Gondolin) and Idril (an Elf, the king of Gondolin's daughter). He possesses the virtues of both races and his father's longing for the sea. As a child, he escapes with his parents from the sack of Gondolin and joins the Elves of Sirion. After his parents sail west and fail to return, Eärendil marries Elwing, a descendant of Beren and Lúthien, and they have two sons, Elrond and Elros. Longing for the sea, Eärendil sets sail, seeking both his parents and the uttermost West and desiring to implore the Valar for mercy on Elves and Men.

While Eärendil is away at sea, the sons of Fëanor hear that Elwing still possesses Beren and Lúthien's Silmaril. When they attack Sirion, Elwing leaps into the sea with the Silmaril. Transformed into a white bird by Ulmo, she flies to Eärendil, and together they sail to Valinor, arriving there by the power of the Silmaril. They come ashore, and Eärendil delivers the message, asking the Valar for "mercy upon Men and Elves and succour in their need" (*S,* 249). The Valar grant his prayer but ordain that neither he nor Elwing may return to Middle-earth. Also, both of them must elect to which kindred they will belong; they choose the Elves.

The Valar hallow Vingilot, Eärendil's ship, endow it with light, and place it in the heavens. Eärendil, Silmaril bound on his brow, journeys in it alone in the starless void; when he returns to haven, Elwing rejoins him in bird shape. As a new star, Eärendil is most visible at sunrise and sunset; and the people of Middle-earth take the new star's appearance as an omen, calling it "Gil-estel, the Star of High Hope" (*S,* 250).

Though Eärendil never again sets foot on Middle-earth, he fights in the host of the Valar from the air and kills the greatest of Morgoth's winged dragons, Ancalagon the Black. After the Valar casts Morgoth out of the world and into the void, Eärendil keeps watch against him in the sky (*S,* 255).

Tolkien first encountered the word *earendel* in an Old English lyric, now known as *Christ I* (Shippey, 245–46). There the word, which literally means "dawn" or "a ray of light" (Cameron), designates a divine messenger—either Christ, as the Latin original of the lyric suggests, or John the Baptist, as other Old English texts imply and Tolkien believed (*Letters,* 385). Drawn by the word's beauty and intrigued by the tangle of myth surrounding it, Tolkien adopted it into his invented languages and mythology, incorporating the "philological possibilities" of the word *earendel* in Old English into his invented character (Hostetter, 5–10).

Earendel [*sic*] first appears in a handful of poems written between 1914 and 1915, which depict him with varying amounts of detail as a mariner sailing into the uttermost West and then into the sky in a luminous

137

ship named Vingilot (*Lost Tales II,* 267–77). Numerous "highly condensed and often contradictory" drafts and notes from this period, and even a fragment of alliterative verse, describe his parentage and recount his many sea adventures, including his slaying of Ungweliantë (Ungoliant) the monstrous spider and his encounters with mermaids, fire mountains, tree-men, pygmies, and cannibal-ogres (*Lost Tales II,* 254). Throughout, Eärendil's purpose is to search for his vanished seafaring father. His journey to Valinor, accomplished on Ulmo's command, is fruitless: his errand is not what convinces the Valar to send help to Middle-earth. Also, his love story with Elwing, where it exists, ends unhappily. Not until 1930 does Eärendil's voyage acquire its final motivation—to search for his parents and to entreat the "Gods and Elves of the West" for help for Middle-earth; and not until the second draft of that narrative, written the same year, does Eärendil accomplish his task (*Shaping,* 148–50, 151–55).

The version of his story that appears in *The Silmarillion* dates between 1930 and 1937 (*Lost Road,* 323–38), just before Tolkien began to write *The Lord of the Rings.* It includes an apocalyptic prophecy according to which Morgoth will return from the void, Eärendil will drive him from the sky, and the Valar with heroes of Men and Elves will kill him; then the Two Trees will be healed with the recovered Silmarils and give light to the renewed world.

Tolkien points out the importance of Eärendil in the legendarium as a bridge between the story of the "Silmarillion" and that of the later Ages: Eärendil brings the former to a close, and his descendants (Elrond, lord of Rivendell, and Elros, ancestor of the kings of Númenor) figure prominently in the latter. Eärendil's story embodies some of the basic thematic patterns of *The Silmarillion,* most notably that of eucatastrophe intertwined with loss: Eärendil accomplishes his errand to Valinor, and the host of the Valar defeats Morgoth, but Eärendil is forever banished from his home country, and the light of the Silmarils —only a fragment of the original light of Valinor—is almost lost to Middle-earth (Flieger 1983, 89).

Every reference to Eärendil in *The Lord of the Rings* emphasizes the continuity between the legendary past and the present: Eärendil appears as a descendant of Beren and Lúthien and as the father of Elrond, for whom the Elder Days are a living memory; Galadriel catches Eärendil's light in a phial for Frodo; Sam and Frodo, climbing the stairs of Cirith Ungol, consider Eärendil in the continuum of "great tales" they remember to encourage one another; and Frodo uses the light of the phial to fend off Shelob, calling on Eärendil with an ancient Elvish invocation patterned on the original Anglo-Saxon

verse in whose context the name struck Tolkien (*TT,* IV, ix, 329). The parallel between Eärendil's fate and Frodo's (the former discernible from Bilbo's poem, *FR,* II, i, 246–49) strengthens the continuity between past and present (Bolintineanu 2004, 271). Like Frodo, Eärendil carries a great jewel and undertakes a dangerous quest; his exile from Middle-earth foreshadows Frodo's final realization that, in saving the Shire, he has lost it. A reference to Eärendil in *The Lost Road* clearly echoes this: "He [Eärendil] forsook all whom he loved, ere he stepped on that shore. He saved his kindred by losing them" (60).

ALEXANDRA BOLINTINEANU

Further Reading

Bolintineanu, Alexandra. "'On the Borders of Old Stories': Enacting the Past in *Beowulf* and *The Lord of the Rings.*" In *Tolkien and the Invention of Myth,* edited by Jane Chance, 263–73. Lexington, KY: University of Kentucky Press, 2004.

Cameron, Angus, Ashley Crandell Amos, and Antonette diPaolo Healey, eds. *Dictionary of Old English A–F* [CD-ROM]. Toronto: Pontifical Institute of Mediaeval Studies, 2003.

Carpenter, Humphrey. *Tolkien: A Biography.* Boston, MA: Houghton Mifflin, 1977.

Dobbie, Elliott Van Kirk, and George Philip Krapp, eds. "Christ." In *The Anglo-Saxon Poetic Records: A Collective Edition,* vol. 3, pp. 3–15. New York: Columbia University Press, 1931.

Flieger, Verlyn. *Splintered Light: Logos and Language in Tolkien's World.* Grand Rapids, MI: Eerdmans, 1983.

Hostetter, Carl F. "Over Middle-earth Sent unto Men: On the Philological Origins of Tolkien's Eärendel Myth." *Mythlore* 65 (1991): 5–10.

Shippey, Tom. *The Road to Middle-earth: How J.R.R. Tolkien Created a New Mythology.* Revised and Expanded edition, 244–47. Boston, MA: Houghton Mifflin, 2003.

See also **Astronomy and Cosmology, Middle-earth;** *Christ:* **"Advent Lyrics"; Eucatastrophe; Light; Morgoth and Melkor; Old English; Silmarils; Valar; Valinor**

EARTH

Tolkien's original legendarium featured an Earth that was flat, with three "airs" and a dome of stars created by Varda. At the end of the First Age, in the cataclysm that destroyed Númenor, Ilúvatar remade the Earth into a globe. The Undying Lands of the old West—Valinor (home of the Valar) and Eressëa (Elven-home)—were then removed from the physical world. As Tolkien put it, "Men may sail now West, if they will, but return only into the east and so back again; for the world is round, and finite, and a circle inescapable—save by death. Only the "immortals," the lingering Elves, may still if they will, wearying of the circle of the world, take ship and find the "straight way," and come to the ancient or True West, and be at peace" (he adds elsewhere that this was also granted to a "few 'mortals'. . . by special grace") (*Letters,* 156, 411).

After the flat Earth of his original mythology was in place, Tolkien struggled for years to devise a way to reconcile it with modern scientific cosmology. Every attempted solution failed, however. For example, his attempt to attribute the old picture to Númenórean misunderstanding of Elvish truth left unresolved the "actual" places of Valinor and Eressëa. It also introduced new inconsistencies: how, and where, could the Valar be imagined in the vast emptiness of geophysical space? And did Varda create all the stars, some, or none? In any case, this ongoing and ultimately unsuccessful effort undoubtedly contributed to the "Silmarillion" remaining unfinished at the time of his death.

PATRICK CURRY

Further Reading

Noad, Charles. "On the Construction of *The Silmarillion.*" In *Tolkien's Legendarium: Essays on "The History of Middle-earth,"* edited by Verlyn Flieger and Carl F. Hostetter, 31–68. Westport, CT: Greenwood, 2000.

See also **Astronomy and Cosmology, Middle-earth; Middle-earth;** *Shaping of Middle-earth*

EAST, THE

Tolkien's legendarium focuses on the relationship of Northern peoples with a paradise to the West. Drawing on mythic traditions close to his own heart and homeland, he overlaid his stories onto an imaginary northwestern European landscape (*Letters,* 163, 212). In the resulting moral geography of this subcreated world, the East is defined negatively as "not West," or an antiparadise.

The East as a geographic place serves several story functions in the mythological cycle. In *The Silmarillion* it is the "Land of the Sunrise," which is the literal meaning of Quenya *romen,* Sindarin *rhûn* (east), where the Elves, and later Men and Dwarves, awaken. After the Elves have gone to the West, the East is farthest from the heavenly light of Valinor, and the latecoming races of Men and some Dwarves tend to fall into evil under Morgoth's influence. Finally, in *The Lord of the Rings,* the East, or Rhûn, is dominated by Sauron of Mordor, and its wild Men, the

"Easterlings," are a constant threat to Gondor and the West. In *The Lord of the Rings,* the East is also symbolically the direction associated with evil and the Enemy. The East in *The Hobbit* is somewhat outside this tradition and is a place of mythic wilderness and adventure rather than evil.

Tolkien's East evokes the eastern regions of Eurasia in real history, which were the source of the migrating tribes that first settled northwestern Europe and of the nomadic nations that later invaded or made war on those western lands (Kocher, 16). Some critics draw on these parallels to accuse Tolkien of a kind of racial or moral bias against nations as diverse as Nazi Germany and Stalinist Russia and peoples as diverse as the Slavic peoples, the Seljuk Turks, the Lombards, and the Vandals. Others, following Tolkien himself (*FR,* Foreword, 7), reject these too-literal or allegorical readings (Rosebury, 14).

Scholars have long noted Tolkien's symbolic use of the east-west axis. Of the outstanding interpretations, perhaps Verlyn Flieger's is strongest because she works within Tolkien's own schema, contrasting the Light of the West with the Darkness of the East. She notes how movement in both directions is necessary to produce the creativity and growth that Elves and Men experience in *The Silmarillion* (Flieger, 119–26).

Other scholars take Jungian approaches that see West and East as the healthy and unhealthy unconscious, together representing the conflicted souls of the Men and Elves of Middle-earth (O'Neil, 94), or draw on the somewhat overused image of the hero traversing underground from West to East to experience a solar rebirth (Green, 65). Another likens the moral extremes of East and West in Middle-earth's geography to the traditional medieval three-tiered cosmology (Lobdell, 60).

All these interpretations recognize that one of Tolkien's major digressions from European Christian cosmology is his removal from Middle-earth of the idea of an eastern Edenic paradise, replacing it with a metaphoric Hell on Earth. Middle-earth does not orient its maps to holy Jerusalem in the East but to heavenly Valinor in the West. Tolkien's moral geography gives the ongoing struggle with satanic Evil an actual geographic locus, in the East.

JOHN F.G. MAGOUN

Further Reading

Chism, Christine. "Middle-earth, the Middle Ages, and the Aryan Nation: Myth and History in World War II." In *Tolkien the Medievalist,* edited by Jane Chance. London: Routledge, 2003.

Day, David. *The World of Tolkien.* New York: Gramercy Books, 2003.

Flieger, Verlyn. *Splintered Light: Logos and Language in Tolkien's World.* Revised edition. Kent, OH: Kent State University Press, 2002.

Garbowski, Christopher. *Recovery and Transcendence for the Contemporary Mythmaker.* Lublin: UMCS Press, 2000 (as quoted in Rosebury).

Green, William H. *"The Hobbit": A Journey into Maturity.* New York: Twayne, 1995.

Kocher, Paul. *Master of Middle-earth: The Fiction of J.R.R. Tolkien.* Boston, MA: Houghton Mifflin, 1972.

LeGuin, Ursula. "Rhythmic Pattern in *The Lord of the Rings.*" In *Meditations on Middle-earth,* edited by Karen Haber. New York: St. Martin's, 2001.

Lobdell, Jared. *The World of the Rings: Language, Religion and Adventure in Tolkien.* La Salle, IL: Open Court, 2004.

Markova, Olga. "When Philology Becomes Ideology: The Russian Perspective of J.R.R. Tolkien." Trans. Mark T. Hooker, *Tolkien Studies* I (2004): 163–70.

O'Neill, Timothy R. *The Individuated Hobbit: Jung, Tolkien, and the Archetypes of Middle-earth.* Boston, MA: Houghton Mifflin, 1979.

Rosebury, Brian. *Tolkien: A Cultural Phenomenon.* Hampshire: Palgrave Macmillan, 2003.

Schwarz, Guido. "Jungfrauen im Nachthemd-Blonde Krieger aus dem Western" (Maidens in Nightgowns–Blond Warriors out of the West). Reviewed by Shaun F.D. Hughes in "Tolkien Worldwide." *Modern Fiction Studies* 50, no. 4 (Winter 2004): 980.

Tolkien, J.R.R. "Guide to the Names in *The Lord of the Rings.*" In *A Tolkien Compass,* edited by Jared Lobdell. La Salle, IL: Open Court, 1975.

———. "The Etymologies." In *The Lost Road and Other Writings: Language and Legend before "The Lord of the Rings,"* edited by Christopher Tolkien. New York: Ballantine, 1996.

See also **Astronomy and Cosmology, Middle-earth; Bible; Christian Readings of Tolkien; Dwarves; Elves; Elves: Kindreds and Migrations; Fall of Man; Goths; Hell; Huns; Jungian Theory; Koivië-néni and Cuiviénen; Maps; Middle-earth; Men, Middle-earth; Missions from Anglo-Saxon England; Mordor; Morgoth and Melkor;** *Morgoth's Ring;* **Peoples of Middle-earth; Race and Ethnicity in Tolkien's Works; Racism, Charges of; Sauron; Symbolism in Tolkien's Works; Valar;** *War of the Jewels;* **Wilderland; Wizards**

EASTERLINGS

Easterlings is a term used to denote various alien tribal groups originating in the eastern parts of Middle-earth, presumably in the land of Rhûn (which is simply the Sindarin word for "east"). The Edain and subsequent western Mannish cultures had inimical encounters with these Easterlings in both the First and the Third Ages. Like the Haradrim and the Variags, Easterlings were classified as "Wild Men" by the "Free Peoples" not necessarily because of their primitivity but because of their status as infidels (not drawn to the West in the same ways as the Eldar and the Edain) and their dubious allegiances.

The most prominent Easterlings of the First Age, Ulfang (the Black) and Bór, as well as their sons and followers, migrated into western Middle-earth (Beleriand) a few decades before the Battle of Nirnaeth Arnoediad ("Unnumbered Tears"), at the end of the First Age. Newcomers in the area, these Easterling warriors attached themselves variously to Morgoth or to factions supporting different sons of Fëanor—or, more accurately, to both in turns. Although Bór originally offered his service to Morgoth, he and his sons later repented, swearing fealty to Maedhros and Maglor. Bór's three sons died in the great battle, but not before they slew two of Ulfang's three sons, who had been followers of Caranthir and (later) Morgoth. (Ulfang's third son, Uldor the Accursed, was slain by Maglor.) Morgoth gave to the Easterling chieftains Lorgan and Brodda (one of Ulfang's surviving liegemen) the land of Hithlum after the battle. Brodda then took a woman of the Edain (Aerin of the house of Hador) by force to wife; he was later slain by Túrin, son of Húrin, of that same house.

That these First-Age Easterlings were akin to those equestrian (and sometimes Wainriding) "Easterling" confederations of tribal invaders who harried Gondor at various times in the Third Age, challenging at least six of Gondor's kings, is not specifically stated but likely. Two of these kings took the name Rómendacil (East-victor) to commemorate their victories, although the first of them (d. 541 Third Age) was subsequently slain by his eastern foes. Rómendacil II (d. 1366 Third Age) made strategic alliances with the Northmen of Rhovanion against the eastern invaders. King Narmacil II and his heir Calimehtar (in a battle in 1899 Third Age on the old battleplain of Dagorlad) both fought the Wainriders; a subsequent Easterling attack, in the reign of Calimehtar's heir Ondoher, resulted in the death of the king and both his sons (1944 Third Age). Six hundred years after that, the Balchoth, an otherwise unknown fierce Eastern people owing fealty to Sauron and perhaps designatable as Easterlings, were defeated by Eorl the Young and his newly arrived Northern horsemen (the Éothéod, "Horse-people," descendants of Rómendacil II's allies) in alliance with Cirion, Ruling Steward of Gondor, at the Field of Celebrant. In the War of the Ring (3018–19 Third Age), tribes of Easterlings renewed their enmity to Gondor and the West, participating alongside the Haradrim and the Variags of Khand as vassals of Sauron.

As (sometimes) mounted tribal invaders out of the east, and the harriers of western, more urbanized peoples, the Easterlings are probably based at least partly on historical and legendary images of the Huns in our primary-world histories, such as the xenophobic account of the Huns and their origins in Jordanes' sixth-century *History of the Goths*.

SANDRA BALLIF STRAUBHAAR

Further Reading

Mierow, Charles Christopher, ed. and trans. *The Gothic History of Jordanes*. Cambridge: Speculum Historiale, 1966.

Said, Edward. *Orientalism*. New York: Pantheon Books, 1978.

See also **Goths; Jordanes:** *History of the Goths*

EDUCATION

Tolkien's early education greatly affected the direction of his later writings. He received a strong classical education with heavy emphasis on linguistic training and was considered a brilliant, if dilatory, scholar who, despite his successes, never quite lived up to his academic potential. His love of obscure languages and creative invention often distracted him from acquiring the type of knowledge more commonly required for the highest levels of academic distinction in England at the beginning of the twentieth century. Yet these same distractions later formed much of the basis for his creation of Middle-earth.

Early Education

His mother was his first teacher. Tolkien often gave her the credit for his academic success and for exciting his interests in the fields of knowledge that would later shape his life. Though Mabel Tolkien, like most women of that age, did not have an extensive formal education, she had a good academic background and had served as a governess for a time before her marriage. She taught young Ronald Tolkien alone until he reached the age of eight.

From the beginning, Tolkien showed an interest in words. He learned to read before the age of four and learned to write easily, developing what biographer Humphrey Carpenter called an "elegant and idiosyncratic" form of penmanship inspired by his mother's unusual and flowing style. Tolkien once commented in a letter that his mother's interest in etymology, alphabets, and handwriting inspired his own fascination with these areas (*Letters,* 294). He later used these interests in his development of the Dwarvish runes and the flowing Elvish script found in *The Lord of the Rings*.

Lessons in language were his favorites. Mabel Tolkien began to instruct him in the rudiments of Latin before he reached the age of six. He was attracted to the sound of the language and progressed quickly. His mother soon noted his extraordinary aptitude for languages and introduced French, a language Tolkien did not find appealing. He was as much enthralled with the sounds and shapes of words as their actual meaning and soon developed a strong personal taste for the "phonetic aesthetic" of certain languages, basing his preferences on the linguistic sounds that most attracted him. He also began to experiment with creating languages almost as soon as he could write. However, none of these early attempts survived. Young Tolkien destroyed them because his mother did not approve, feeling that this hobby distracted him from his more serious studies. This early scholastic conflict foreshadowed a linguistic distraction that would continue to plague Tolkien throughout his academic life.

Mabel also tried to instruct her son in piano, an effort that failed miserably. Artistic training was more successful, and young Tolkien soon proved adept at drawing. He was especially good at drawing landscapes and trees, the feel and shape of which fascinated him more than the scientific botanical details that his mother taught him. However, his love of nature and botany would remain with him throughout his life and would be reflected in his later works of fantasy.

Mabel Tolkien was also responsible for introducing Tolkien to works of literature in the form of fairy tales, myths, Arthurian romances, and the works of such writers as George MacDonald. Tolkien was particularly fond of the stories like that of "Sigurd the Dragon Slayer" found in Andrew Lang's *Red Fairy Book*. Carpenter quotes Tolkien as once stating, "I desired dragons with a profound desire." He wrote his first story during this period, a lost story of a "great, green dragon." In a letter to his American publishers at Houghton Mifflin, Tolkien later commented on this phase of his education, "It is to my mother who taught me . . . that I owe my tastes for philology, especially of Germanic languages, and for romance" (*Letters,* 165).

King Edward's School

Despite Mabel Tolkien's tutelage, Tolkien failed at his first attempt to pass the entrance exam to the prestigious King Edward's School in Birmingham, his father's *alma mater*. Tolkien was seven at the time of this first attempt and remained under the instruction of his mother for another year. She increased her efforts hoping that he would, in time, not only win a place in the school, where entrance was quite competitive, but also secure a scholarship that would cover the cost of his tuition.

The next year, in 1900, Tolkien again took the entrance exam and this time was accepted, though he did not secure a scholarship. A Tolkien uncle came forward and offered to pay the fees, which amounted, at that time, to twelve pounds per year. Money was extremely tight for Mabel Tolkien and her sons. At the time that Tolkien was accepted at King Edward's, the family was still living in a country cottage at Sarehole, which was four miles from the school. Because there was no money for train fare and no tram service, Tolkien had to walk the distance to school for the first few weeks.

Finally, Mabel Tolkien was able to secure lodgings in the Birmingham area on the tram route. Though the transportation dilemma was now solved, this situation created new problems for the family. Young Tolkien missed his country life and found that the confusion, din, and clamor of the crowded school and town bothered him. He suffered from bouts of ill health in his first year that often caused him to miss school altogether. He soon adjusted to the school and began to improve, though he still, at that time, did not seem to tower above his classmates academically.

King Edward's was what Tolkien termed a "first-rate" school, rich in tradition, renowned for its academic excellence, and, as Tolkien described it, based on an "ultimately medieval foundation" (*Letters*, 199). The school was founded in honor of King Edward VI, the son of Henry VIII. The educational standard was unrivalled in that part of England, and the school had a reputation for producing many scholars who won awards at major English universities. When Tolkien attended, King Edward's was located on New Street in an impressive Victorian Gothic structure. Though the school had branch schools throughout the area, the main school on New Street accepted only the best and brightest students. It consisted of two "high" schools, one a classical school, which Tolkien attended, and one modern. The combined student body of these two schools was about five hundred day students, all male. Though a girls' school (a recent addition) adjoined the campus, the classes were not co-educational.

Tolkien was at King Edward's for a little over a year when another dramatic change took place. Mabel Tolkien discovered the Birmingham Oratory, a large Catholic church founded by Cardinal Newman in 1849. Attached to the church was the Grammar School of St. Philip, a school where Mabel felt that her sons could receive a strong Catholic education at a cost far lower than that of King Edward's. In addition, she was able to find a house for rent next door. It seemed to her a good solution. The family moved to Edgbaston, a Birmingham suburb where the school was located, and Tolkien entered St. Philip's in early 1902 at the age of ten.

Though Mabel found there a kind and helpful adviser in the form of a parish priest named Father Francis Xavier Morgan, she quickly discovered that the educational standards at the St. Philip's were far lower than those of King Edward's. Tolkien soon surpassed his classmates, and Mabel began to be concerned that he would lose academic ground if he remained there much longer. She removed both Ronald and his younger brother Hilary and began to teach them again at home. This time, she set up a rigorous program for Ronald and taught him all the subjects herself, except for geometry, which was taught by her sister. Carpenter's biography of Tolkien records a letter from Mabel Tolkien to a relative stating that, by the time Tolkien was eleven, a clergyman commented that he "read too much, everything fit for a boy under fifteen, and he didn't know a single classical thing to recommend him."

His mother's efforts paid off. Tolkien again took the exam at King Edward's and not only regained his place but also won a scholarship. In the autumn of 1903, Tolkien went back to King Edward's and resumed his training there. He was then introduced to Greek, which attracted him from the first. Carpenter notes Tolkien's first reaction to the language: "The fluidity of Greek, punctuated by hardness, and with its surface glitter captivated me. But part of the attraction was antiquity and alien remoteness (from me): it did not touch home." This introduction also brought him into contact with new literary experiences. In *Tolkien and the Great War*, biographer John Garth quotes Tolkien as saying that he "first discovered the sensation of literary pleasure in Homer."

A year after his return to King Edward's, his mother died of complications from diabetes at the age of thirty-four. At Mabel's request, Father Francis, a generous and compassionate man, assumed the guardianship of Ronald and Hilary. Father Francis arranged for the boys to remain at King Edward's, even though it was not a Catholic school. He even allowed Ronald to attend classes in the New Testament in Greek with the King Edward's headmaster. In a letter to his son Michael, Tolkien later commented that this concession made it easier for him to navigate his way in non-Catholic professional society (*Letters*, 306).

His linguistic interests were again piqued in the literature classes of George Brewton, who was at heart a medievalist and would recite portions of Chaucer's *Canterbury Tales* to the class in the original Middle English. The sound of the language and its historical context intrigued Tolkien, and he began to explore and study the language on his own. Brewton later discovered Tolkien's private interest and, delighted with the boy's progress, began to tutor him in Anglo-Saxon.

About this time, Tolkien also began to find solace in scholastic male companionship. He developed a close friendship with a fellow classmate, Christopher Wiseman, the son of a Wesleyan minister whom Tolkien greatly respected. By this time, Tolkien was displaying considerable academic promise, and Wiseman, who was a year younger, was his intellectual match. Both boys led their class academically, usually with Tolkien in first place and Wiseman a close second. Their good-natured academic rivalry and shared love for Latin and Greek resulted in a firm friendship. According to Tolkien biographer John Garth, the two young scholars referred to themselves as "The Great Twin Brethren." Spurred on by this intellectual partnership, Tolkien excelled at the study of Latin and Greek, which made up the core of the classical curriculum at King Edward's. He became adept at both languages and reached the First (or senior) Class level just before his sixteenth birthday. He then began to set his sights on an Oxford scholarship.

Preparing for Oxford

Tolkien's final years at King Edward's were eventful. He gained enormous ground in the area of philology, his special interest and the academic field that would become his focus in his Oxford years. He also developed a widening group of friends who were to play important roles in his development and in the shape of the future course of his life. However, he also found many distractions, both linguistic and personal, which interfered with his goal of an Oxford scholarship, a necessary step if he were to have the funds to pursue his studies.

Tolkien joined the Debating Society in his final years. He had a reputation for poor oratorical delivery, yet he was renowned for his impassioned speeches. His language training stood him in good stead, because the debates were typically held entirely in Latin. However, Tolkien found this approach too easy and often took on the roles of "foreign" ambassadors to the "Senate" so that he could deliver his lectures in Greek, Gothic, or Anglo-Saxon.

He also took up rugby, a game he played enthusiastically. At first, Tolkien was rejected from the house teams because of his light frame. However, as he later explained in a letter to his son Michael, Tolkien decided to make up for his weight by "legitimate ferocity" (*Letters,* 16). By the end of his first season of play, he was made house captain, and he was awarded his colors the next season. His involvement in rugby also resulted in an accident in which he broke his nose and nearly severed his tongue. In later years, he blamed the improper healing of his nose for repeated bouts of nasal problems and suggested that the tongue injury was the source of his reputation as an indistinct lecturer. In truth, this reputation preceded the accident. Tolkien generally played down his own abilities as a rugby player but was surprised to discover in later years that many of his younger schoolmates primarily remembered him for his skills at rugby and for his "taste in coloured socks" (*Letters,* 58).

It was at this time that Tolkien also came in close contact with the concept of philology. The headmaster, Robert Cary Gilson, taught the First Class and encouraged the study of classical linguistics, which suited Tolkien's interests in the scientific aspects of language. Tolkien began to develop an interest in the general language principles that would shape the course of his career. His fascination led him to begin to collect German works of philology and to explore the common roots and interconnectedness of various languages. His language explorations led him deeper into the roots of modern English. He read *Beowulf,* both in translation and in the original Anglo-Saxon, and was fascinated with the poem. He read *Sir Gawain and the Green Knight* and *Pearl* and explored the dialect of the Middle English language that produced these masterpieces. He delved into Old Norse and finally read the story of Sigurd in its original language.

He also renewed his interest in language creation and experimented with the sounds of language that attracted him. He began to invent a "private" language called Naffarin, which was heavily influenced by Spanish but had its own system of grammar and phonology. However, his enthusiasm for this project waned when he encountered Joseph Wright's *Primer of the Gothic Language.* This historic language that survived only in fragmented form delighted him, and he began to construct "extra" Gothic vocabulary words to supplement the limited surviving vocabulary. This activity blended his love for linguistic creation with his desire to expose the "bones" of language.

Though these intellectual explorations were fascinating and made important contributions to

Tolkien's later work, in the realms of scholarship and of fantasy literature, they acted as distractions to Tolkien in his quest for an Oxford scholarship; Oxford entrance exams rarely presented questions dealing with obscure languages, philology, or linguistic invention. Tolkien was also distracted by his burgeoning romance with Edith Bratt, an orphan girl who roomed at the same boarding house that Tolkien and his brother then inhabited. The romance was discovered by Father Francis, and he forbade Tolkien to see Edith, fearful that she would divert the young scholar from his academic goals. This emotional upheaval took place just before Tolkien sat for his Oxford entrance exams, and he failed to win a scholarship, despite his academic brilliance and the high expectations of his instructors.

After this failure, Father Francis may have felt justified in his decision to part the young lovers. However, Tolkien did not feel that his relationship with Edith had affected the results of the exam. Instead, he placed the blame squarely on his own shoulders. He later wrote in a letter to his son Michael, "I was clever, but not industrious or single-minded; a large part of my failure was due to simply not working (at least not on classics) not because I was in love, but because I was studying something else: Gothic and what-not"(*Letters,* 43).

In his final year, Tolkien redoubled his efforts at the study of the classics, determined to win the scholarship that represented his only hope for future studies. Yet he was still involved in many extracurricular activities and served as a prefect, secretary of the Debating Society, and football secretary. He also participated in the Officer Training Corps that sprang up at schools in the prewar England of 1910. As one of his final acts as a representative of the school, he was chosen with eleven other cadets to line the route to Buckingham Palace as George V ascended the throne in the summer of 1911.

The severing of his relationship with Edith forced Tolkien to find other social distractions at this time. He and a group of other senior boys were given the title of school librarians and began to form their own academic and social club based on their common interests and a thirst for the special knowledge that each of them possessed. This developed in Tolkien a taste for academic male camaraderie that would remain with him the rest of his life. The TCBS (Tea Club and Barrovian Society) consisted primarily of Tolkien, Wiseman, and Robert Gilson (the son of the headmaster). Tolkien contributed his knowledge of ancient languages, and he often recited passages from *Beowulf, Pearl, Sir Gawain and the Green Knight,* and the Norse *Völsunga saga.*

Another primary member of the group was Geoffrey Bache Smith, a promising young poet who inspired Tolkien's new-found interest in poetry, an area that had been neglected in the course of his schooling. Later, in letter to poet W.H. Auden, Tolkien explained that he spent much of his time at school learning Latin and Greek but little in the study of English literature. He had limited contact with poetry in the classroom except for Shakespeare, whom he "disliked cordially." His main contacts with poetry were in translation of the Latin poets (*Letters,* 163). Smith changed all that, and Tolkien began not only to read English poetry but to write it as well. His early poems often contained some mention of dancing elves, fairies, or sprites, elements likely traced to his fascination with the works of Catholic mystic poet Francis Thompson.

Tolkien's fascination with language also continued. He encountered the Finnish language, which appealed to him greatly, not only because of its "phonetic aesthetic" but also because it opened up a whole new world of mythology before his eyes. He also continued to delve into philology. During the winter (Lent) term of 1910, he presented a paper to the First Class on "The Modern Languages of Europe—Derivations and Capabilities." He read the lecture for three one-hour class periods, and the master had to stop him before he even reached the "Capabilities" part of the paper.

Yet he also pursued the classics with greater zeal in an effort to win the highly prized Oxford scholarship. In December 1910, he was awarded an Open Classical Exhibition (a partial scholarship based on knowledge and merit) to Exeter College, Oxford. He did not receive as much praise as one would expect for this accomplishment. Most of his instructors felt that, given his extraordinary abilities, he should have scored even higher and won a full scholarship. However, it was enough. With this scholarship, a school-leaving bursary from King Edward's, and Father Francis's aid, he would be able to attend Oxford in the fall of 1911.

Tolkien left King Edward's in the summer of 1911 with mixed feelings of anticipation for the future and sadness at leaving the academic world that had stimulated his intellect and exposed him to new ideas and friendships. Carpenter the author quotes Tolkien as saying: "I felt like a young sparrow kicked out of a high nest." Young Tolkien would leave a world filled with the peaceful quest for knowledge and face a world that would ultimately be clouded by war and the loss of many of his boyhood friends. According to Garth's biography, in July 1911 an editorial ascribed to Tolkien appeared in his school newspaper: "'Twas a good road," Tolkien wrote, "a little rough, it may be in places, but they say it is rougher further on."

AMELIA HARPER

Further Reading

Carpenter, Humphrey. *J.R.R. Tolkien: A Biography*. Boston, MA: Houghton Mifflin, 2000.

Duriez, Colin. *The J.R.R. Tolkien Handbook*. Grand Rapids, MI: Baker Books, 1992.

Garth, John. *Tolkien and the Great War: The Threshold of Middle-earth*. Boston, MA: Houghton Mifflin, 2003.

Grotta, Daniel. *J.R.R. Tolkien: Architect of Middle-earth*. Philadelphia, PA: Running Press, 1992.

See also **Alphabets, Invented; Childhood of Tolkien; Morgan, Father Francis; Languages: Early Introduction and Interest; Languages Invented by Tolkien; Marriage; T.C.B.S. (Tea Club and Barrovian Society); Tolkien, Mabel**

EGYPT: RELATIONSHIP TO NÚMENÓREANS

In his *Letters*, Tolkien states that "The Númenóreans of Gondor were proud, peculiar, and archaic, and I think are best pictured in (say) Egyptian terms. In many ways they resembled 'Egyptians'—the love of, and power to construct, the gigantic and massive. And in their great interest in ancestry and in tombs" (*Letters*, 281). The ancient Númenóreans were accomplished builders who constructed many architectural wonders from stone, such as the Pillars of the Kings (the Argonath), and inexplicable artifacts like the Black Stone of Erech, the Pinnacle of Orthanc, and the Seats of Amon Hen.

Also in *Letters* (no. 211), the crown of Gondor as depicted in a drawing by Tolkien, shows a striking similarity to the pharaonic crown of the Upper and Lower Kingdoms of dynastic Egypt. Both have the same conical bullet shape, the only visible difference being that the crown of the Númenóreans has wings instead of the cobra head an Egyptian crown would have.

The last Númenórean King was named Ar-Pharazôn the Golden. The name sounds suggestively Egyptian, and the honorific term "the Golden" is especially intriguing, given the ancient Egyptian relationship to sun worship and their god-kings the pharaohs.

Thus, the Númenóreans show their connection to the ancient Egyptians by way of monuments, the depiction of the crown, and the name of the last king.

JOHN WALSH

ELDAMAR

Eldamar, Elven-home, is the dwelling of the Elves on the eastern shore of Aman, the Blessed Land, between the encircling Pelóri mountains and the sea. It is also the name of the great bay in this land, in the center of which is the lonely isle, Tol Eressëa. The shores of Eldamar are described thusly in *The Silmarillion*:

> There they dwelt, and if they wished they could see the light of the Trees, and could tread the golden streets of Valmar and the crystal stairs of Tirion upon Túna, the green hill; but most of all they sailed in their swift ships upon the waters of the Bay of Elven-home, or walked in the waves upon the shore with their hair gleaming in the light beyond the hill. Many jewels the Noldor gave them, opals and diamonds and pale crystals, which they strewed upon the shores and scattered in the pools; marvelous were the beaches of Elendë in those days. And many pearls they won for themselves from the sea, and their halls were of pearl, and of pearl were the mansions of Olwë at Alqualondë, the Haven of the Swans, lit with many lamps. For that was their city, and the haven of their ships; and those were made in the likeness of swans, with beaks of gold and eyes of gold and jet. The gate of that harbour was an arch of living rock sea-carved; and it lay upon the confines of Eldamar, north of the Calacirya, where the light of the stars was bright and clear. (*S*, 61)

Tolkien's descriptions of Eldamar give us a good idea of his conceptions of absolute beauty. The combination of the natural (the waves, the arch of rock, the light of the stars) and the wrought (the halls, the city, the haven, the ships) show that for Tolkien Elvish beauty was found in the harmony of the natural and the cultural, not in the domination of one over the other. In this way, the descriptions of Eldamar show a similarity with the description of the paradisiacal land in the Middle English poem *Pearl* (which Tolkien translated), from the gems scattered in the water to the stairs made of crystal: both the works of nature and the works of man are combined to generate further beauty. This ability to work with nature without dominating it, to generate a landscape that is natural but has also been shaped and improved, is a key characteristic of the Elves and illustrates how Tolkien saw them as taking the noblest and most mystical attributes of human beauty and extending them still further.

MICHAEL D.C. DROUT

ELEMENTS

In the introduction to *The Psychoanalysis of Fire,* the literary critic Northrop Frye underlines that "earth, air, water and fire are still the four elements of imaginative experience, and always will be." The four elements as ancient backbone of the Earth is a concept deeply rooted in the Western culture. It derives from the Greek philosopher Empedocles, who conceived the theory that the entire material world is composed of four basic elements: water, air, earth, and fire. One century later, Aristotle developed it into a scientific system. Through combination with the inorganic opposite principles of cold and hot, moist and dry, the elements had their equivalent in the organic world in the four humors: choler (yellow bile), blood, phlegm, and melancholy (black bile).

Nowadays, the elements of the periodic table are the successors of air, fire, earth, and water. Nonetheless, they remain "the elements of imaginative perception," Frye remarks—that is, the archetypes, the representation of the very essence of the created universe—and for that reason are powerfully evocative. The clearest examples of these old symbols in Tolkien's works are the three rings of the Elves: Narya, the Ring of Fire (red); Vilya, the Ring of Air or the Ring of Sapphire (blue); and Nenya, the Ring of Water or Ring of Adamant (white), the one Galadriel wore. In *The Silmarillion,* Tolkien deals with the basic elements of nature in the tale of the creation of Arda, the Earth. They are connected to the Ainur: Ulmo turned his thought to water, Manwë to air and wind, Aulë to earth, and Melkor to fire.

It would be wrong to make a distinction between good elements and evil elements. To the Greek philosophers and to Tolkien, the four elements as a whole stand for nature and for life. On the contrary, Mordor is characterized by the lack of living nature, where destruction reigns. When Frodo and Sam are in the land of Mordor heading toward Mount Doom, among obstacles and dangers, the lack of natural elements is a dramatic distress they have to cope with physically and psychologically. Sam is obsessed by the lack of water. He is also haunted by memories of the Shire, Rivendell, and Lórien. On the contrary, as the burden of the Ring becomes increasingly heavier, Frodo cannot recall the Shire, its rivers, and its breeze; his sense are numb.

There is evidence that the Nazgûl fear at least two of the elements: fire and water. The Black Riders hesitated on the shore of the Bruinen, then they were drowned in the river. Aragorn armed himself and the Hobbits with fire on Weathertop. As the Nazgûl were inhabitants of the shadow world, some elements of the natural world were inimical to them—Tolkien must have devised them as a form of opposition to Mordor. Fire is perhaps the most dual-natured of the elements, used both in creation and in destruction; for example, Balrogs wielded whips of flame.

CECILIA BARELLA

Further Reading

Curry, Patrick. *Defending Middle-earth. Tolkien: Myth and Modernity*. London: HarperCollins, 1997.

Frye, Northrop. "Introduction." In *The Psychoanalysis of Fire*, edited by G. Bachelard. Boston, MA: Beacon Press, 1987.

See also **Colors; Nature; Rings of Power;** *Silmarillion, The*; **Symbolism in Tolkien's Works**

ELENDILMIR

The Elendilmir was the single white gem that the Kings of Arnor and, afterward, the Chieftains of the Dúnedain bore on their brow, in lieu of the Southern crown, as the token of royalty (*RK,* Appendix A, 323). The gem was also called "Star of the North," "Star of Elendil," and "Star of the Northern Kingdom." The Elendilmir ("star/jewel of Elendil" in Quenya) was a white star of Elvish crystal bound by a mithril fillet that represented the Star of Eärendil, which had guided the founders of Númenor (*RK,* Appendix A, 315). Silmariën (b. 548 Second Age), eldest child of Tar-Elendil (the fourth king of Númenor), had passed the jewel to her descendants (*UT,* 277). Silmariën's great-grandson Elendil the Tall, father of Isildur and Anárion (ca. 3319 Second Age), established the Elendilmir as the symbol of royalty for Arnor, the Northern Kingdom (*UT,* 271). In this, he followed the example of Tar-Aldarion, the sixth ruler of Númenor, and his wife Erendis: Erendis set her betrothal gift as a star in a silver fillet, and her betrothed bound the jewel on her forehead. Thus, it became the custom of later Kings and Queens to wear as a star a white jewel upon their brow, instead of a crown (*UT,* 184, 215 n. 18, 284 n. 33). Thirty-six Kings of Arnor and Chieftains of the Dúnedain wore the Elendilmir, down to Elessar himself (*UT,* 284 n. 33), who put the jewel on for the Battle of the Pelennor Fields (3019 Third Age) as a sign of his royal claim (*RK,* V, vi, 123; V, viii, 137).

The potency and brilliance of the Elendilmir were astounding (*UT,* 277). The light of the Star of Elendil could not be extinguished, even by the invisibility conferred by the One Ring (*UT,* 274, 283 n. 25). However, the authentic Elendilmir had been lost, after the violent and unexpected death of Isildur (2 Third Age), whose corpse was never found. Thus, the Elven-smiths made for Valandil, heir of Isildur, a replica of the missing Elendilmir in their forges at Imladris (*UT,* 277). This second Star of Elendil, although much weaker in power, became one of the heirlooms of King Arvedui's house after the fall of Arnor (1974 Third Age) with such other insignia of Northern royalty as the ring of Barahir, the shards of Narsil, and the sceptre of Annúminas (*RK,* V, viii, 137; Appendix A, 323).

The real Elendilmir was given up for lost until Aragorn unexpectedly found the jewel hidden in a casket during the restoration of Orthanc, more than three millennia after its disappearance (*UT,* 276–77). It soon became evident that Saruman had stolen the original Star of Elendil from the corpse of Isildur and had kept it concealed in Isengard. When Aragorn returned to the North and took up again the full kingship of Arnor, Arwen, after the manner of the Kings and Queens of Númenor, bound upon his brow the true Elendilmir (*UT,* 277). During his long reign, Elessar assumed the true Elendilmir only for special days and only while staying in the North. At all other times, he wore the second Elendilmir that had been passed to him. The "Star of the Dúnedain" that he gave Mayor Samwise Gamgee on occasion of the King's visit to Brandywine Bridge (14 Fourth Age) was a different jewel (*UT,* 284 n. 33).

As a reading of *Smith of Wootton Major* will attest, Tolkien invested having a star upon the brow with great symbolic and almost sacral significance. He may have been inspired by a similar Roman artistic convention that indicated the wearer's closeness to the divine (*Aeneid* 8.681–82, "Servius" on Virgil's *Aeneid,* 8.681). Although wearing jewels on the brow was also a medieval secular fashion (e.g., *Sir Gawain and the Green Knight* 26.615–20; Dante, *Purgatorio* IX 4), when creating the concept of the Elendilmir Tolkien may have had the Roman imperial diadem *(diadema)* in mind as well. The diadem (cf. *Letters,* 281) was a headband or fillet of white cloth fitted with jewels (see especially *Historia Augusta* 24.30.14 for a description), which late Roman emperors since Constantine (d. 337 CE) wore as a token of their sovereignty (Hurschmann, 335–36). Two historical anecdotes concerning the *diadema* may throw some light on the history and usage of the Elendilmir. After deposing Romulus Augustulus, the last western Roman emperor (476 CE), the Herulian chieftain

Odoacer had the Roman senate convey to the eastern Roman emperor Zeno the imperial diadem, along with the rest of royal insignia Romulus Augustulus had worn, for its safeguard in Constantinople (477 CE), on the premise that the western Roman empire had effectively ceased to exist (Cresci, Malchus fr. 10). Compare this with the keeping of the heirlooms of Arnor at Imladris after the fall of the Northern Kingdom (*RK,* Appendix A, 323). Charlemagne's habit of wearing the diadem only on high feast days (Einhard, *Life of Charlemagne,* 23) may offer a parallel for Elessar's refusal to bear the true Elendilmir except for special festive occasions.

MIRYAM LIBRÁN MORENO

Further Reading

Cresci, L.R. *Malco di Filadelfia. Frammenti.* Byzantina et neohellenica neapolitana. Naples: Bibliopolis, 1982.

Einhardi Vita Karoli Magni. Post G.H. Pertz recensuit G. Waitz, editio sexta curavit O. Holder-Egger. Monumenta Germaniae Historica. Scriptores rerum Germanicarum. Hannover, Leipzig: Hahnsche Verlagsbuchhandlung, 1911.

Hoh, Ernestus, ed. *Scriptores Historiae Augustae.* Addenda et corrigenda adiecerunt Ch. Samberger et W. Seyfarth. Leipzig: Teubner, 1971.

Hurschmann, R. "Diadema." In *Brill's New Pauly,* 335–36. Leiden: Brill, 2004.

"Servius Maurus Honoratus Grammaticus." *In Vergilii carmina comentarii.* Servii Grammatici qui feruntur in Vergilii carmina commentarii. recensuerunt Georgius Thilo et Hermannus Hagen. Leipzig: Teubner, 1,881–902.

Tolkien, J.R.R., and E.V. Gordon, eds. *Sir Gawain and the Green Knight.* Revised by Norman Davies. Oxford: Clarendon, 1967.

See also **Aragorn; Jewels; Kingship**

ELESSAR

Elessar is an Eldarin word whose English equivalent is "elfstone." It has two meanings, both associated with Aragorn. It first appears in Tolkien's writings in *The Lord of the Rings* when Galadriel uses the word in both its senses. First, Elessar is the name of a gemstone possessed by Galadriel and given by her to Aragorn: "Then she lifted from her lap a great stone of a clear green, set in a silver brooch that was wrought in the likeness of an eagle with outspread wings; and as she held it up the gem flashed like the sun shining through the leaves of spring." As she gives him the stone, Galadriel uses the term in its second sense, as a name for Aragorn: "In this hour take the name that was foretold for you, Elessar, the Elfstone of the house of Elendil!" When Aragorn pins "the brooch upon his breast," the Elessar manifests both ennobling and restorative qualities: "Those who saw him wondered; for they had not marked before how tall and kingly he stood, and it seemed to them that many years of toil had fallen from his shoulders" (*FR*, II, viii, 391).

The effect of the Elessar upon Aragorn suggests further detail in regard to both meanings of the word. In stating that the stone made him appear "kingly," Tolkien implies the precise meaning of Elessar as a name for Aragorn: it is the name that he takes when he becomes King of Gondor and Arnor. However, Aragorn initiates use of it long before that event, albeit infrequently: he first uses the name when the Company's boats pass the Argonath (*FR*, II, ix, 409) and, shortly thereafter, when he reveals himself to Éomer (*TT*, III, ii, 36).

In stating that that the elfstone made "many years of toil" fall from Aragorn's shoulders, Tolkien implies the healing power associated with the stone. In the Houses of Healing in Minas Tirith, after the Battle of the Pelennor Fields, Aragorn uses the name in both its senses but emphasizes his abilities as a healer: "'In the high tongue of old I am *Elessar*, the Elfstone, and *Envinyatar*, the Renewer': and he lifted from his breast the green stone that lay there" (*RK*, V, viii, 139). It is in ministering to the wounded in the Houses of Healing that Aragorn reveals himself to the people of Gondor as their King, and so they proclaim him: "And word went through the City: 'The King is come again indeed.' And they named him Elfstone, because of the green stone that he wore, and so the name that was foretold at his birth that he should bear was chosen for him by his own people" (*RK*, V, viii, 147).

The unforeseen appearance of the elfstone in Galadriel's hand raises questions about its origin that Tolkien did not answer until after *The Lord of the Rings* was published. In a short piece published in *Unfinished Tales,* Tolkien provides two stories of the elfstone's appearance in Middle-earth.

First, the stone is made by Enerdhil, a jewel-smith of Gondolin, who loved the appearance of sunlight shining through leaves and captured that light in the stone. Enerdhil gave the stone to Idril, daughter of King Turgon, and it did not perish when Gondolin was destroyed. Idril gave the stone to Eärendil, her son by Tuor. The Elessar bestowed healing powers on one who touched it, and Eärendil, so empowered, healed Elves and Men in Sirion and made the land fair. When Eärendil sailed from Middle-earth, the Elessar departed with him. The Elessar of Eärendil came to Valinor, where Yavanna gave it to Olórin (Mithrandir) to give to Galadriel when he went to Middle-earth. Olórin instructed Galadriel to use the elfstone to make Lórien the most beautiful place in Middle-earth and to keep it until the coming of the man named Elessar, Aragorn.

The second story is a variation that begins after the departure of the Elessar with Eärendil. Another less-powerful Elessar was made in later years for Galadriel by Celebrimbor, who was also of Gondolin and was Enerdhil's friend. Galadriel used the stone to make Lórien verdant. Later, when Celebrimbor gave Galadriel the Elven ring Nenya, she no longer needed the Elessar to preserve Lórien. She gave it to her daughter Celebrían, who gave it in turn to her daughter Arwen, who gave it to Aragorn (*UT*, 248–51).

In *Unfinished Tales,* Tolkien does not say which version of the story is definitive, and both can be reconciled with the facts of *The Lord of the Rings.*

PAUL EDMUND THOMAS

See also **Aragorn; Arwen; Eärendil; Galadriel; Gandalf; Jewels;** *Lord of the Rings;* **Lothlórien; Magic in Middle-earth;** *Unfinished Tales*; **Valar; Wizards; Women in Tolkien's Works**

ELF-SHOT

Elf-shot is a term occurring in Old English medical texts and charms in reference to a sudden pain or a disease located in a specific part of the body in animals or humans. Although beginning in the sixteenth century sources use the term elf-shot to denote prehistoric arrowheads found in Britain and Scotland, Anglo-Saxon references suggest elf-shot was generally attributed to internal injuries from invisible, magical, projectile weapons wielded by unseen, malevolent elves or witches. Among the possible ailments scholars have identified as elf-shot are muscle spasms, digestive cramps, rheumatism, and heart attacks. Anglo-Saxon treatments for it typically involved a combination of physical or herbal actions and verbal incantations or inscriptions. One Old English charm, "For a Sudden Stitch" (Wið Færstice), likens elf-shot to injuries from spears cast by a band of fierce warrior women and recommends a treatment that involves the efforts of a smith to counter its debilitating suffering. As a magical object with Elvish origins, the fairy star in Tolkien's *Smith of Wootton Major* evokes elf-shot similarities, but the stabbing pain occurs when it is given up rather than when it is taken in. The protagonist's name and occupation further recall the smiths referred to in "For a Sudden Stitch." In *The Fellowship of the Ring,* the Nazgûl blade used to stab Frodo on Weathertop also echoes elf-shot traditions in that it is a piercing weapon wielded by an unseen, malevolent, supernatural assailant that causes intense, specifically located pain ameliorated only by a combination of herbal and magical remedies.

LESLIE A. DONOVAN

Primary Sources

Cameron, Malcolm Laurence. *Anglo-Saxon Medicine.* Cambridge Studies in Anglo-Saxon England, 7. Cambridge: Cambridge University Press, 1993.
Dobbie, Elliott Van Kirk, ed. "For a Sudden Stitch." In *The Anglo-Saxon Minor Poems.* Anglo-Saxon Poetic Records, vol. 6, pp. 122–23. New York: Columbia University Press, 1942.
Hall, Alaric. "Getting Shot of Elves: Healing, Witchcraft and Fairies in the Scottish Witchcraft Trials." *Folklore* 116 (2005): 19–36.
Jolly, Karen Louise. *Popular Religion in Late Saxon England: Elf-Charms in Context,* 139. Chapel Hill: University of North Carolina Press, 1996.

See also **Charms; Frodo;** *Smith of Wootton Major*

ELROND

One of the most important Elves in Middle-earth, Elrond is Half-elven on both sides of his family: his father is Eärendil, son of Tuor (a Man) and Idril (Elven daughter of King Turgon of Gondolin), and his mother is Elwing, granddaughter of Beren (a Man) and Lúthien (Elven daughter of Thingol and Melian).

Elrond first appears in the "Sketch of the Mythology" of 1926. When the sons of Fëanor attack Sirion to obtain the Nauglafring, Eärendil has already set sail in search of his father, and Elwing has already been transformed into a seabird and flown in search of Eärendil. Elrond, left alone as a child, is saved by Maidros, the only surviving son of Fëanor. When the Elves return to the West, Elrond, "bound by his mortal half," elects to stay in Middle-earth (*Shaping,* 38). Elrond, in fact, makes two choices: being "bound by his mortal half" means he chooses to refrain from going into the West but not that he chooses to be a mortal Man, because unlike his brother, Elros, who elects Manhood, Elrond chooses to remain an Elf (*Shaping,* 70).

The saving of infant Elrond by Maidros is maintained in the "Quenta," begun in 1930, and late additions to the "Quenta" introduce Elros, who is also saved (*Shaping,* 150, 153, 155).

In the first outline of "The Fall of Númenor," Elrond assists King Amroth in the Last Alliance against Thû. In the second, Elrond becomes the first king of Númenor and builds the tower of Númenos (*Lost Road,* 18, 23, 25).

Tolkien describes Elrond's appearance in *The Hobbit* as "a fortunate accident, due to the difficulty of constantly inventing good names for new characters." He used the name "casually" and not with deliberate intent to connect the Elrond of *The Hobbit* with the namesake in the mythological writings, but he nevertheless made Elrond Half-elven (*Letters,* 346–47). In *The Hobbit,* Elrond is the master of the Last Homely House in the valley of Rivendell, where "Evil things did not come." In addition to providing Thorin and company with food, rest, mended clothing, and advice, Elrond functions as a loremaster: he reads the runes on the Gondolin swords that Gandalf and Thorin took from the Trolls' lair, and he reads the moon-runes on Thrór's Map, which reveal the process for discovering the keyhole to the Side-door into the Lonely Mountain (*H,* III, 95, 96).

It is not until Elrond appears in *The Lord of the Rings* that Tolkien connects him to the son of Eärendil of the "Silmarillion" writings: he is "the great-grandson of Lúthien and Beren" and, as the master of Imladris and bearer of Vilya, mightiest of the three Elven rings, he is "a great power and a Ringholder" (*Letters,* 347). In *The Lord of the Rings,* Elrond commands the Bruinen to flood when the mounted Ringwraiths attempt to cross it in pursuit of Frodo; he heals, as much as possible, Frodo's wound from the Morgul-knife; he hosts the Council in Rivendell and tells the history of the One Ring and of his part in the Last Alliance as herald of Gilgalad; he helps choose the members of the Fellowship; he attends the wedding of his daughter Arwen to Aragorn (King Elessar); and he leaves Middle-earth from the Grey Havens with Galadriel, Gandalf, and Frodo.

Appendix A, I [iii], to *The Lord of the Rings* tells of Elrond's healing of his wife Celebrían, daughter of Galadriel, from Orc wounds and her departure for the West more than four hundred years before the events narrated in *The Hobbit.*

In "Concerning Galadriel and Celeborn" written after the publication of *The Lord of the Rings,* Tolkien describes the expulsion of Sauron from Eriador during the Second Age and Elrond's part in the war against him. The piece concludes with Gil-galad giving Elrond Vilya and making Elrond his vice-regent in Eriador (*UT,* 233–40).

In a 1958 letter, Tolkien says that *rondō* means "cavern" and that Elrond was so named because he was found in a cave (*Letters,* 282). In the essay "Quendi and Eldar" of 1959–60, Tolkien interprets *rondō* as derived from the verb *rono,* "to arch over."

He says the term is used to represent the heavens, so Elrond's name can means "star-dome" (*Jewels*, 414–15).

PAUL EDMUND THOMAS

See also **Aragorn; Arwen; Beren; Bilbo;** *Book of Lost Tales II;* **Eärendil; Elves; Elves: Kindreds and Migrations; Elves: Reincarnation; Frodo; Galadriel; Gandalf; Glorfindel;** *Hobbit, The;* **Legolas;** *Lord of the Rings;* *Lost Road;* **Lúthien;** *Return of the Shadow;* **Ring-Giving; Rings; Rings of Power; Rivendell;** *Shaping of Middle-earth;* **Silmarils;** *Silmarillion, The;* **Towers;** *Treason of Isengard;* *Unfinished Tales;* **War;** *War of the Jewels*

ELVES

Of all the peoples with which Tolkien inhabited Middle-earth, none involved more of his creative energy and love than the Elves. His ideas regarding Elves go back to both medieval and Victorian depictions of these peoples, which were developed early in his life through his learning and reading of ancient and medieval languages and literatures, and eventually to the development of his own languages.

Early on, Tolkien read many of the Victorian fantasy writers, not really caring for their depictions of elves as a diminutive, fairy-like, pointy-eared people. Of all the Victorian writers, only George MacDonald's fantasies influenced Tolkien. In his examination of and fascination with medieval literatures and languages, however, Tolkien quickly found a different depiction of elves: powerful, strange, and as tall as humans but living in a different space and time. *Sir Gawain and the Green Knight* and *Sir Orfeo* are just a few of the tales that have survived from the medieval period that document the results of confrontations or encounters with elves or otherworldly beings, usually with disastrous effects for the humans involved. Not only is there a strong connection between music and elves from the medieval period, but the time-space continuum often has humans following elves into their realm for a day only to return and find that years have passed in Earth time. Other medieval literature has survived indicating cures for or protection against elfish trickery or contact.

At the same time that Tolkien was reading medieval literature, he was learning medieval languages. As is well documented, he was already writing and inventing languages based on medieval languages in his early teens, Tolkien invented two languages: one based on Finnish and Greek, and one based on Welsh. It was the phonetic sounds and almost musical qualities of these languages that influenced Tolkien's creation of new languages based on them. The former one Tolkien called Quenya, or High-elven; the name "Elves" is a translation of the word *Quendi*. Quenya is similar to Latin in our society; it was rarely used as a living language, especially during the time of *The Hobbit* and *The Lord of the Rings*, but can be found in abundance in Tolkien's earlier writings and in *The Silmarillion*. The latter language, based on Tolkien's well-documented encounter with railroad cars bearing Welsh words as a child, became the living language of the Elves in Middle-earth and was called Sindarin or Grey-elven. Tolkien mentions that Sindarin, for him, was attractive linguistically because of its British-Welsh origins and that it fit well with the "Celtic" quality that so fascinated him.

The emanation of these two languages naturally led Tolkien toward his concern that no mythology had survived from the medieval period for the British people. He thus began to write stories using his invented languages, similar to medieval tales, that appeared to document events in human history that had not survived into modern times. Central to these stories were the Elves, a race of beings whose might and power were once central in our historical past but whose record of existence had not survived into modern times. To distinguish Elves from the race of Men, Tolkien made them almost demigods in their appearance and abilities: they were immortal; they were at least as tall, if not taller, than the human race; they were prolific in craftsmanship and music, able to make weapons and songs both powerful and magical; and they were able to fight and sometimes defeat deities and gods. But they were also flawed (or cursed), in that their "tale" or "history" was filled with woe and doom, concepts of significance and meaning in medieval language and literature, as is so well illustrated in Tolkien's major scholarly contribution to the academy, his defense of the earliest surviving poem in the English language, *Beowulf*. The slow decline in power of Tolkien's Elves in our own undocumented past is similar to medieval cosmological and musical theory; therefore, it is important to understand the Elves and their history, as documented in *The Silmarillion*, in order to understand their eventual role and appearances in Tolkien's later and more popular works, *The Hobbit* and *The Lord of the Rings*. (Earlier developments and versions of Tolkien's Elves can be found in *The History of Middle-earth* series but will not be related here.)

According to the Ainulindalë, or the Music of the Ainur, the Elvish race has its origins in one of the themes of music expounded by the One and the Ainur before the beginnings of time. When Ilúvatar actually turned the Music into being and created Eä, the Ainur witnessed the history of Middle-earth and the coming of Elves and Men in a sort of "predetermined" cinematic preview. Some of them wished to "descend into" this created world and participate in its history and in the eventual rise of the Firstborn, or Elven, people. When they did this, they became known as the Valar. Their purpose as the "gods" of Middle-earth were to prepare the way for the coming of the Elves and encourage their growth and destiny. The Elves as a people first awoke in the far eastern land of Cuiviénen on Middle-earth, on the shores of the Inland Sea of Helcar and beneath the mountains of the Orocarni. At first, the Valar had no knowledge of their awakening; Melkor discovered them first and captured some of them. It is thought that the race of Orcs was the result of experimentation by Melkor on these hapless Elves. Hearing the sound of water flowing soon after their awakening, the Elves were always thereafter drawn to the sea and to water, which, according to The Silmarillion, carried the sounds of the Music of the Ainur continuously and forever in its waves. When Oromë, the great hunter god of Middle-earth, discovered the Elves, he named them Eldar, the People of the Stars, because they had awakened under the starlight of Yavanna during the Years of the Trees. Soon after their discovery by the Valar, and to protect them, the Valar went to war against Melkor and captured and imprisoned him in Valinor. After Melkor's defeat, the Valar offered to transport the Elves to Valinor to live under their protection. The Elves, still suspicious, were leery of this journey and chose three ambassadors to travel to Valinor with Oromë to help the Elves decide whether to stay in Middle-earth or make the long journey to Valinor. These three Elves were Ingwë, Finwë, and Elwë. After visiting Valinor and returning to Middle-earth, these three counseled the Elves to travel to and live in Valinor.

The Great Journey, as it was known, saw the first Sundering of the Elvish people, as those who choose to stay in Middle-earth were known as the Avari, the Unwilling. Those who did follow the three ambassadors from Middle-earth became known as the Three Kindreds: the Vanyar, the Noldor, and the Teleri. The Vanyar, under Ingwë, were the least numerous yet the most loyal to the Valar. The Noldor, under Finwë, became the most proficient in craftsmanship and power in Valinor, especially Finwë's son Fëanor, who crafted the three Silmarils, gems of power and magic that captured the light of the Two Trees in their making. The Teleri were the last to reach Valinor and lived for a time on the shores of eastern Beleriand, during which time they lost their leader, Elwë, who

encountered a Maia named Melian and fell in love with her. He eventually stayed in Middle-earth, became known as Thingol, and established a kingdom there. It was Thingol and Melian's daughter, Lúthien, who would become one of the main characters in the First Age of Middle-earth. The Teleri, disheartened by the loss of their leader, split into two groups, those who went with the Valar to live in Valinor and those who remained in Middle-earth to wait for the return of Elwë. Those who remained were known as the Sindar, or Grey-elves.

Tolkien focused on the history of the Noldor in The Silmarillion, because it is their history that is filled with the doom and fate so typical of medieval literature that determines the entire history of Middle-earth from the First Age to the time of The Lord of the Rings. Tolkien incorporated many parallel stories and tales from medieval literature and epics into the doom of the Noldor, from the rise of the race of men, to the love of Lúthien the Elf and Beren the man, to the rise of the kingdom of Gondolin and Nargothrond and their eventual fall and defeat due to their own ties to the doom and fate of the Noldor, to the love of Arwen the Elf and Aragorn the man at the end of the Third Age. There are many other threads that Tolkien weaves throughout his mythology, which cannot be described here. It is enough to know that when Tolkien finished the Tale with The Lord of the Rings Elves had diminished as the dominant power on Middle-earth and either faded into obscurity or took the Long Road to Valinor and that Men had become the new power on Middle-earth, and thus the recorded history of our own Earth begins.

Tolkien, a devout Catholic, made specific references in The Silmarillion and in his Letters that Elves, if they died due to disease or violence, were reincarnated and returned to Middle-earth, whereas Men were granted the gift of "mortality" and waited for the End of Time in a place the Elves could not go. In a letter from 1954, Tolkien goes to great lengths to explain more of his theology and reasoning behind this decision. Tolkien, wrestling with his religious viewpoints and his medieval philosophical background, states that denial of the possibility of reincarnation as a mode of existence is impossible and then goes into the biologic and scientific, if not metaphysical and theological, reasonings behind this possibility. Reading through his earlier drafts and versions of stories contained in The Silmarillion, we can see that this topic is fairly consistent throughout his writings regarding the Elves. His letter from 1956 continues to expound on this interesting possibility. Because Elves cannot escape from time, due to their immortality, the destruction of their incarnate form means that they must remain *in* this world, either as discarnate beings or as reborn beings. Tolkien chooses to reincarnate Elves who die because they are a part of the Story and cannot escape it, whereas men, who are mortal, have the gift of death (which they often consider a curse) that allows them to leave the Story and become part of something greater and more mysterious.

BRADFORD LEE EDEN

Further Reading

Burns, Marjorie. *Perilous Realms: Celtic and Norse in Tolkien's Middle-earth.* Toronto: University of Toronto Press, 2005.

See also **Elves: Kindreds and Migrations; Elves: Reincarnation of; Music in Middle-earth;** *Silmarillion, The*

ELVES: KINDREDS AND MIGRATIONS

A hint of the diversity in the Elven race can be found in *The Hobbit* when the narrator distinguishes between Wood-elves and High-elves, further dividing the later category into Light-elves, Deep-elves, and Sea-elves. Douglas Anderson notes that "over time, Tolkien's names of the divisions of the Elves went through very complicated changes, with shifting meanings assigned to the same names" (*H*, VIII, 218–19). Nonetheless, in the published *Silmarillion,* there was a consistent scheme. Though *The Hobbit* and *The Lord of the Rings* are "anthropocentric" ("seen mainly through the eyes of Hobbits"), *The Silmarillion* and the earlier legends are "seen through Elvish eyes" (*Letters,* 160). They focus on histories of the Elves, in which only the greatest heroes of Men play a significant role, Dwarves only a minor roll, and Hobbits no roll. Much of this Elven history deals with the rises and falls of various Elven kingdoms and the complex interactions among the kindreds.

Overview: Calaquendi and Moriquendi

When the Vala Oromë first finds the Elves wandering in Cuiviénen in the east of the world, they have already developed speech, named themselves the *Quendi* ("those that speak with voices"), and begun to act in kindred groups. Because of the violence of Morgoth against Middle-earth, the Valar summon the Quendi to Valinor, the Guarded Realm, part of the Blessed Realm of Aman, in the Undying Lands of the West (Faërie in *The Hobbit*). There the Elves can enjoy the protection of the Valar and the light of the Two Trees. When Elves are at first unwilling to go, the Valar invite three of their number, Ingwë, Finwë, and Elwë, to come as ambassadors. "Filled with awe by the glory and majesty of the Valar," and desiring "greatly the light and splendour of the Trees," these three return to Cuiviénen and councel their people to accept the summons. The most significant division of the Elves occurs then: Ingwë's people, and the majority of Finwë's and Elwë's, agree to depart for the West. Those who begin the journey keep the name given to the Elves by the Valar: *Eldar* (equivalently the *Eldalië*), meaning "People of the Stars." Those who refuse are known as the *Avari,* the "Unwilling." The Avari are thus sundered from the Eldar and play little role in the events of the legendarium (*S,* 49–52).

Because the Elves appear in the east of Middle-earth, the answer to the summons results in a long migration west. This takes many years, and not all travel together at the same pace. Those who complete the journey are known as the *Calaquendi,* or "Elves of the Light," because they see the light of the Two Trees of Valinor and the glory of Aman before the Two Trees are destroyed. They are also called High-elves. However, some (mostly among the kindred of Elwë and Olwë) become lost on the road, or linger in Middle-earth, and never come to Valinor to see the light of the Two Trees. Those who begin but do not complete the journey are called the *Úmanyar,* "those not of Aman." The Úmanyar and Avari together are known as the *Moriquendi,* or "Elves of Darkness," because they never behold the light of the Two Trees (*S,* 52–53).

The Three Kindreds of the Eldar

Of the Three Kindreds who begin the migration, that of Ingwë is the smallest. They set forth from Cuiviénen first, arrive first in Valinor, and become known as the *Vanyar,* the "Fair-elves." Ingwë becomes the high king of all the Elves of Aman. (Though "Elves of Light," as previously noted, comes to mean all Elves who complete the migration, the name "Light-elves" in *The Hobbit* certainly refers to the Vanyar, who in earlier versions are known as the Lindar.) The Vanyar are closest to Manwë and Varda but play little role in the history of Middle-earth. However, Indis of the Vanyar weds Finwë of the Noldor and bears him two sons, Fingolfin and Finarfin. Fingolfin becomes high king of the Noldor, who return to Middle-earth.

The people of Elwë and Olwë travel the slowest. When those who continue westward under Olwë finally arrive in Aman, they remain in the east of the Guarded Realm by the seashore and settle the city of Tol Eressëa. They build great ships and are close in friendship with the Vala Ulmo and his vassal the Maia Ossë. They become known as the *Teleri,* which means "Last-comers," but are also known as "Sea-elves" and call themselves the *Lindar,* meaning "singers" (a name used for the Vanyar in earlier versions.) Eärwen, daughter of Olwë, weds Finarfin and becomes the mother of Galadriel, and thus Galadriel has the blood of all three kindreds of the Calaquendi: Noldor, Vanyar, and Teleri. Many of the Teleri of Tol Eressëa become victims of the Kinslaying at Alqualondë, when the Noldor are exiled, but play little role otherwise in the history of Middle-earth.

Finwë's people are known as the *Noldor,* the "Deep-elves." The Noldor are most beloved by the Vala Aulë and learn much from him. They become famous craftsmen and workers with Earth-gems and love words and names. The Noldo loremaster Rúmil is the first to devise letters and fitting signs for recording of speech. Curufinwë, son of Finwë and Míriel, later called Fëanor, is the most skilled of hand in the history of Elves and the proudest and most famous. He devises improved letters for writing and creates the famed Silmarils, in which he captures the light of the Two Trees. When Morgoth steals the Silmarils, Fëanor and his sons swear a terrible oath and lead many of the Noldor back to Middle-earth, returning of their free will but also under exile. The Noldor are thus the only Eldar to return to Middle-earth and to become important in its subsequent history.

The Sindar and the Kindreds of the Úmanyar

Many Elven kindreds and kingdoms also emerge from the Úmanyar. The greatest is that of Elwë, later named Elu Thingol. During the migration, Elwë is enchanted and falls in love with Melian of the Maiar. He abandons the migration and with her aid establishes the hidden kingdom of Doriath. When the exiled Noldor return, they give the name *Sindar* to all the Elves in the west of Middle-earth under Thingol's overlordship. However, the Sindar, though sundered from the Teleri of Aman, still hold bounds of kinship with the victims of the Kinslaying and are unwelcoming of the returning Noldor. Much strife arises between the Sindar and the returning Noldor.

Included among the Sindar are the *Falathrim,* Elves of the Falas ruled by Círdan the Shipwright, who acknowledge the overlordship of Thingol. Thranduil, father of Legolas and king of the Silvan Elves of northern Mirkwood, is also of the Sindar. The name Sindar means "Grey-elves," or "Elves of the Twilight," perhaps because they are not Calaquendi (Light-elves), never having been to Valinor, yet neither are they Moriquendi (Dark-elves), because they are ruled by Thingol and Melian, both of whom had dwelt in the light of the Two Trees. The name Sindar may also come from their lord Thingol, who is also called "Grey-mantle."

Lúthien, the most famed of all Elves, is Sindar, the only child of Thingol and Melian. She weds a mortal, Beren. Later, Celeborn, a kinsman of Thingol, weds Galadriel of the Noldor, and they also establish a Sindar kingdom in Lothlórien. Their daughter Celebrían, who marries Elrond Half-elven, thus has the mingled blood of all three kindreds of the Eldar, as well as the Sindar ancestry of her father. Elrond is descended from Beren and Lúthien and has the blood of all three kindreds and of the two noblest kindred of men and of the Maia Melian.

The *Nandor* are another group, of Teleri, not counted among the Sindar, who, under the leadership of Lenwë, abandon the westward march. Lenwë's son, Denethor, eventually leads some of the Nandor westward into Ossiriand, where they become known as the "Green-elves" or *Laiquendi.*

Conclusions

While Humphrey Carpenter suggests that Elves represent "Man before the Fall which deprived him of his powers of achievement" (Carpenter 1977, 93) and Tolkien describes them as "Men with greatly enhanced aesthetic and creative faculties" (*Letters,* 176), there is nothing in the biography and little in Tolkien's *Letters* about the philosophical, theological, or moral significance of the kindreds. One letter suggests only that the Noldor represent the trend toward technology as manifest among Elves (*Letters,* 190). Verlyn Flieger makes a good case that "taken together, the (Vanyar, Noldor, and Teleri) are a paradigm of the spectrum of human spirituality and response to God." The Vanyar, the smallest group, are "most spiritual, least material," and the Teleri (tellingly the largest group) are "least eager for the light" and "vacillate, hesitate, and are changeful in mind and spirit" (Flieger 1983, 90–91). The Noldor fall in the middle.

What the sundering of Elves certainly provides—especially the most significant distinction between the

Eldar (Calaquendi) and the Sindar (Moriquendi)—is the opportunity for Tolkien the philologist to develop two related and yet wholly separated languages: Quenya, the language spoken by the Eldar, and Sindarin, the language spoken by the Sindar. Tolkien notes that the "'stories' were made rather to provide a world for the languages than the reverse" (*Letters,* 219). (Indeed, the few references in his *Letters* to the kindreds refer mostly to linguistic matters.) Thus, Tom Shippey suggests, "Accordingly, one might well say that the major root of *The Silmarillion* and all that followed from it was the invention of the Elvish languages, Quenya . . . and Sindarin." And "the real root was the relationship between them, with all the changes of sound and semantics which created two mutually-incomprehensible languages from one original root" (Shippey, 230–31).

MATTHEW DICKERSON

Further Reading

Carpenter, Humphrey. *Tolkien: A Biography*. Boston, MA: Houghton Mifflin, 1977.
Flieger, Verlyn. *Splintered Light: Logos and Languages in Tolkien's World*. Grand Rapids, MI: Eerdmans, 1983.
Shippey, Tom. *J.R.R. Tolkien: Author of the Century*. Boston, MA: Houghton Mifflin, 2003.

See also **Elves; Fëanor; Finwë and Míriel; Languages Invented by Tolkien; Maiar; Melian; Thingol; Valar**

ELVES: REINCARNATION

The main theme of *The Lord of the Rings* is death and immortality (*Letters,* 246). This issue, on a wider scale, orders the conception of the whole legendarium. The very existence of Elves, who are immortal, raises the issue of the death of the other races. If it already seems to be a scandal when all creatures naturally die, it appears to be a crucial problem when one race does not die. Yet are Elves completely immortal? Tolkien speaks of a "serial longevity" (*Morgoth,* 331; *Letters,* 224): Elves live *while the world lasts,* and they are immortal in Arda (*Morgoth,* 212, 214, 218, 259, 331; *S,* 48). Their immortality is a relative one, depending on particular conditions (Devaux 2002, 14–23). Besides, they can even die in Arda: "For though Eru appointed to you to die not in Eä, and no sickness may assail you, yet slain ye may be, and slain ye shall be; by weapon and by torment and grief," so says the prophecy of Mandos (*S,* 88). The immortality of Elves, which

entails a passage through death, is tantamount to reincarnation. This theological possibility (*Letters,* 189) separates them from men. We know, in the legends, of at least one man if not reincarnate, who came back from the dead: Beren. It also seems that some Dwarves (the Fathers) return, Dúrin in the first place (*Peoples,* 383). Does his mind go to another body, or is his body brought back to life? Tolkien wavered depending on the versions (384). However that may be, the issue of *Elvish* reincarnation is the most critical one, in particular with Glorfindel and Míriel.

Elvish reincarnation is related to the issue of death; it crops up, here or there, in the major texts that Tolkien dedicated to death: the "Laws and Customs among the Eldar" and "Athrabeth Finrod ah Andreth" (in *Morgoth's Ring*). Yet shorter texts specifically deal with it: "The Converse of Manwë and Eru" (1959), "Reincarnation of Elves" (1959–66), and "Some notes on 'rebirth,' reincarnation by restoration, among Elves" (1972). Those texts were first partially published or summarised, respectively, the first two in *Morgoth's Ring* (361–65) and the last one in *The Peoples of Middle-earth* (382–83), before being published (again), *in extenso,* in *Tolkien, l'effigie des elfes.* It appears that the parts that were not included in *The History of Middle-earth* were of a more technical nature (there can be found the principle of the identity of the indiscernibles).

The philosophical presuppositions of the doctrine of reincarnation are, first, the distinction between *feä* and *hroä* (spirit and body); second, the identification of the principle of personal identity in the *feä* (see again *Morgoth,* 227, 330); and finally, the argument according to which the *feä* remembers, exactly though mainly unconsciously, the *hroä.*

Tolkien envisages (*Morgoth,* 362) that reincarnation is carried out through rebirth (of the mind) or through remaking (of the body). This duality in the *modus operandi* of reincarnation reveals the duality of those who carry it out: remaking is up to the Valar, rebirth up to Eru. As far as the latter is concerned, if "The Converse" leaves the prerogative to Eru, this possibility is rejected in "Reincarnation of Elves" and in "Some notes." And Tolkien is prone to repent concerning who is to carry out the remaking. Thus, in "The Converse" the body is remade by the Valar, but in "Reincarnation of Elves" the *feä* itself is at work and "Some notes" is a return to the previous stance (the Valar). Would Tolkien have forgotten by 1972 his positions and arguments of 1966? However that may be, the first version of "The Converse" (published in *Morgoth's Ring*) should not be considered his last word.

According to the revised and enlarged edition of "The Converse" the *post mortem* events unfold as follows: The houseless *feär* are summoned to Aman. Once there, they are instructed by the Valar before being judged by Mandos. For the remaking of the body, two situations arise, depending on whether the Elf died innocent or guilty of misdemeanours. The innocent ones will be able to choose whether to return among the living or not. If they choose to do so, they will join them quickly. The guilty ones have to be instructed by the Valar. If they wish, once their feelings have been improved they may be reincarnated. In both cases, the Valar decide when they are to return. Elves may choose reincarnation through rebirth, but Eru will choose when they are to return. Their past will be veiled; innocent youth shall be the reward for their wounds, but their past shall return to them. It is better for those who are born again to be wise, to have died recently, and not to be married. Tolkien analyses clearly the difficulties of rebirth in "Reincarnation of Elves." It represents a lack of consideration towards the new parents who have a child who already has his own character. The best solution then dawned upon Tolkien (on a day of June 1966): reincarnation is carried out through reconstruction of the body (and not through rebirth by Eru), and it is the *feä* (not the Valar) that makes it again. And to avoid psychological problems (in particular in relation to marriage), the rehoused *feär* shall stay in Aman, with a few odd exceptions (*Tolkien, l'effigie des elfes,* n. REF, p. REF).

If there is no unique answer to the issue of Elvish reincarnation within the legendarium; likewise far from obvious is the issue of the conceptual models that Tolkien may have drawn inspiration from to think out what he calls reincarnation. If the term reincarnation may call to mind Buddhism, we should keep in mind that it is there conceived as a complete change: the one who goes through reincarnation is no longer the same; he is not human anymore (Nârada, chapter 8). Yet the issue of identity is essential in Tolkien. Celtic reincarnation, insofar as we know it, was not limited by the species barrier either. In Scandinavian lore, some think that rebirth was conceived as the passage of a part of the person who had died into a child, who was also given the name of the deceased (Ellis, 139). Finally, Elvish reincarnation is that of the same into the same, which is much closer to the resurrection of the Catholic tradition as is highlighted by Stratford Caldecott (88–89). For further details on this whole issue, see the presentation that goes with the edition of the texts, "L'effigie des elfes."

MICHAËL DEVAUX
Translation by DAVID LEDANOIS

Further Reading

Caldecott, Stratford. *Secret Fire: The Spiritual Vision of J.R.R. Tolkien.* London: Darton, Longman & Todd, 2003.

Devaux, Michaël. "'The Shadow of Death' in Tolkien." In *2001: A Tolkien Odyssey. Proceedings of Unquendor's Fourth Lustrum Conference, Brielle, The Netherlands, 9 June 2001*, edited by Ron Pirson and translated by David Ledanois, 1–46. Leiden: De Tolkienwinkel, 2002.

———. "L'effigie des elfes." In *Tolkien, l'effigie des elfes* (*La Feuille de la Compagnie,* no. 3), edited by Michaël Devaux, REF. Genéve: Ad Solem, 2005.

Ellis, Hilda Roderick. *The Road to Hel: A Study of the Conception of the Dead in Old North Literature.* New York: Greenwood, 1968.

Nârada, Thera. *The Buddhist Doctrine of Re-birth.* Colombo: W.E. Bastian and Co., 1939.

Tolkien, J.R.R. "Fragments on Elvish Reincarnation." In *Tolkien, l'effigie des elfes* (*La Feuille de la Compagnie,* no. 3), edited by Michaël Devaux, REF. Genéve: Ad Solem, 2005.

See also **Elves; Finrod;** *Morgoth's Ring*; **Peoples of Middle-earth; Theology in** *The Lord of the Rings*

ELVISH COMPOSITIONS AND GRAMMARS

The following is an annotated chronological list of Tolkien's chief writings in and concerning his invented languages that have been published to date. Because the publication of Tolkien's linguistic writings is at this writing an ongoing project, this list will continue to grow for some years to come, chiefly through the continuing publication of such writings in the journals *Parma Eldalamberon (PE)* and *Vinyar Tengwar (VT)*.

- 1915–ca. 1919—*Qenyaqetsa: The Qenya Phonology and Lexicon* (see separate article). Excerpted in the appendices to *The Book of Lost Tales.* Published in full in *PE* 12 (1998), incorporating in the editorial notes a second, later (ca. 1917), selective word-list called "The Poetic and Mythologic Words of Eldarissa."
- 1915–16—*Narqelion* ("Autumn"). An untranslated Qenya poem of twenty lines on the theme of autumn. Published in facsimile with analysis in *VT* 40 (April 1999).
- ca. 1916–20—Various fragmentary charts of "Early Qenya Pronouns." Published in *PE* 15 (2004).
- ca. 1917–20—Various of the "Early Qenya Fragments" associated with the *Qenya Lexicon* and *The Book of Lost Tales,* including "The Creatures of the Earth," a hierarchical list of the Qenya names for various races and creatures,

with glosses; a Qenya and Goldogrin bilingual list titled "The Names of the Valar"; "*Otsan* and *Kainendan*," Qenya names for the days of the week; "*Matar* and *Tulir*," two brief verb paradigms; and "The Qenya Verb Forms," a set of early Qenya verb conjugations tucked into the front of the *Qenya Lexicon.*

- ca. 1917–19—"Sí Qente Feanor" ("Now said Fëanor"), an untranslated Qenya prose passage of thirteen lines, apparently giving Fëanor's rather contemptuous view of the nature of Men. Published in *PE* 15 (2004).

- 1917–ca. 1919—*I·Lam na·Ngoldathon: "The Grammar and Lexicon of the Gnomish Tongue* (see separate article). Excerpted in the appendices to *The Book of Lost Tales.* Published in full *PE* 11 (1995).

- ca. 1917–20—Various of the "Early Noldorin Fragments" associated with *The Book of Lost Tales,* including "Heraldic Devices of Tol Erethrin," three drawings with Goldogrin names of associated English towns; "Goldogrin Pronominal Prefixes," in three persons and two numbers; "Early Chart of Names," occurring in the *Lost Tales* in parallel Qenya and Goldogrin lists with glosses and contemporary with "The Poetic and Mythologic Words of Eldarissa"; and "The Official Name List," a similar list of names occurring in "The Fall of Gondolin." Published in *PE* 13 (2001).

- ca. 1917–20—"Name-list to 'The Fall of Gondolin'," a list of names derived from the earlier "Official Name List." Excerpted in the appendix to *The Book of Lost Tales: Part II.* Published in full in *PE* 15 (2004).

- ca. 1917–20—"Names and Required Alterations," a parallel list of Qenya names from "The Cottage of Lost Play" with suggested Goldogrin equivalents. Published with an appendix giving other early, fragmentary texts relating to Qenya and Goldogrin in *PE* 15 (2004).

- ca. 1918–20—"The Gnomish Lexicon Slips," loose slips inserted into the back of the Gnomish Lexicon, the start of an unfinished recapitulation of that lexicon, with additional entries. Published in *PE* 13 (2001).

- ca. 1918–25—Charts of and inscriptions in various runic alphabets, collected and analyzed as "Early Runic Documents." Published in *PE* 15 (2004).

- ca. 1919–25—Various charts of and inscriptions in the early Rúmilian alphabet, collected and analyzed as "The Alphabet of Rúmil." Published in *PE* 13 (2001) with an addendum in *PE* 15 (2004). A few of the latest examples in

this corpus date from 1930 and later. One of the earliest Rúmilian texts, and the lengthiest, a transliteration of a passage from the ca. 1919 "Tale of Turambar," was published with analysis in *VT* 37 (December 1995).

- ca. 1920–25—Various others of the "Early Noldorin Fragments," including a concise "Early Noldorin Grammar," covering the article and its mutations, plural formation in nouns and adjectives, comparison, and various verb paradigms, and a set of short "Noldorin Wordlists." Published in *PE* 13 (2001).

- ca. 1920–25—The "Early Qenya Grammar," a concise but complete descriptive and historical grammar, treating phonology, including root modifications and the evolution of the accent; the article, definite and indefinite; noun classes, declensions in nine cases and two numbers, and compounds; adjective and adverb formation and comparison; cardinal, ordinal, and quotiential numbers; pronouns, personal, reflexive, and deictic; and verbs, in three persons, two numbers, and twelve tenses. Published in *PE* 14 (2003).

- ca. 1920–25—"Index of Names for *The Lay of the Children of Húrin*," comprising a list of Noldorin names in that lay with notes and a chart of the phonological development of diphthongs. Published in *PE* 15 (2004).

- ca. 1922–25—A partial English–Qenya dictionary with Qenya forms written in Valmaric. Published in *PE* 15 (2004).

- ca. 1922–25—Various charts of and inscriptions in the early Valmaric alphabet, collected and analyzed as "The Valmaric Script." Published in *PE* 14 (2003) with an addendum in *PE* 15 (2004).

- ca. 1923—A partial Noldorin dictionary, incorporating entries from the "Noldorin Wordlists." Published in *PE* 13 (2001).

- ca. 1924–36—"The *Entu, Ensi, Enta* Declension," of (probably) two deictic pronouns, in thirteen cases and two numbers (singular and dual). Published in facsimile with analysis in *VT* 36 (July 1994).

- 1929—A farewell in "Arctic," actually Qenya *(Mára mesta. . .).* Published in *The Father Christmas Letters* (1976).

- ca. 1930—Various Qenya and Noldorin poems with translations given in "A Secret Vice," including *Oilima Markirya* (Q. "The Last Ark') in two closely contemporary early versions, the earlier in twenty-seven lines and the later in thirty-six lines, on the theme of the end of days; *Nieninque* (Q. "Snowdrop') in eight lines about a dancing maiden; *Earendel,* a Qenya poem in nine lines about the intrepid mariner at the helm of his ship; and an untitled Noldorin poem *(Dir avosaith a gwaew hinar. . .)* in eight lines on the hunter Damrod. Published in *The Monsters and the Critics and Other Essays* (1983).

- ca. 1936—"The Bodleian Declensions" of five Qenya noun classes, in eleven cases and four numbers (singular, general/total, particular/partitive plural, and dual). Published with analysis in *VT* 28 (March 1993).

- 1936—Noldorin inscription ("*Lheben teil. . .*") on an early draft of Thrór's Map for *The Hobbit*. Published in *J.R.R. Tolkien: Artist and Illustrator* (1995).

- ca. 1937—Untitled Qenya prose fragments, in seven lines with interlinear English glosses, describing the Downfall of Númenor; "Fíriel's Song," an untitled Qenya poem in fourteen lines, with translation, on the theme of creation and mortality; and other Qenya dialogue, all occurring in the story "The Lost Road." Published in *The Lost Road and Other Writings* (1987).

- ca. 1937—"The *Lhammas*" (Noldorin, "Account of Tongues"), a story and internal history of the descent of all languages of Arda from (at this conceptual stage) the language of the Valar, with a later and shorter version of the same account, "*Lammasethen*" (Noldorin, "Shorter Account of Tongues"). Also "The Etymologies," an extensive etymological dictionary of the Eldarin languages, organized by Eldarin base. Both texts published in *The Lost Road* (1987). An extensive "Addenda and Corrigenda to 'The Etymologies'," compiled from the original manuscript, was published in two parts, in *VT* 45 and 46 (November 2003 and July 2004, respectively).

- ca. 1937—"The Elvish Alphabets" and "The Alphabet of Dairon," brief discussions of the origins of Elvish scripts and runes. Published in *The Treason of Isengard* (1989).

- ca. 1937–41—The "Koivieneni Manuscript," Tolkien's workings on two Qenya prose sentences, one concerning the awakening of the Elves at Koivieneni and the other concerning the planting of the Two Trees in Valinor. Also his workings on several Noldorin names, with various phonological notes. The first Qenya sentence was published with analysis in *VT* 14 (November 1990), and a facsimile and analysis of the entire manuscript page was published in *VT* 27 (January 1993).

- 1946—"Lowdham's Fragments" of Qenya and Adûnaic prose, depicting the Downfall of Númenor, with interlinear English glosses, one

version in facsimile, and Edwin Lowdham's Old English texts in *tengwar* transliteration, in facsimile; both occurring in Part II of the story "The Notion Club Papers." Also "Lowdham's Report on the Adûnaic Language," an extensive story and internal historical sketch of Adûnaic, including phonology, noun declensions, and verb conjugations. Published in *Sauron Defeated* (1992).

- ca. 1951–54—Various poems, spells, exclamations, and inscriptions as published in:

1. *The Fellowship of the Ring* (1954), including the English inscription in *tengwar* and *cirth* decorating the title pages; the Black Speech Ring-inscription in *tengwar (Ash nazg. . .)*; Frodo's Qenya greeting of Gildor *(Elen síla. . .)*; Glorfindel's Sindarin greeting of Strider *(Ai na vedui. . .)* and urging-on of Asfaloth *(noro lim. . .)*; the Sindarin poem *A Elbereth. . .*; Gandalf's Sindarin spell of fire against the wolves *(Naur an edraith. . .)*; the Sindarin inscription, in *tengwar,* on the West-gate of Moria *(Ennyn Durin. . .)*; Gandalf's Sindarin spells of opening *(Annon edhellen. . .* and *Edro!)*; the Khuzdul inscription, in *cirth,* on Balin's tomb *(Balin Fundinul. . .)*; the Lórien sentry's Sindarin command to stop *(Daro!);* Aragorn's Qenya farewell to Arwen *(Arwen vanimelda. . .);* and Galadriel's Qenya lament, also often called *Namárië, (Ai! laurië. . .)*. Published draft versions of these compositions include Frodo's greeting and both Glorfindel's greeting and his urging-on of Asfaloth, all arising in 1938 and published in *The Return of the Shadow* (1988), with a subsequent intermediate version of Glorfindel's greeting from ca. 1940 published in *The Treason of Isengard* (1989); "Elbereth," the Moria-gate inscription Gandalf's opening spells, and the Mazarbul-pages, all arising ca. 1939 in *Return;* later intermediate versions of the gate-inscription and the Mazarbul-pages given in *The Treason of Isengard* (1989); Gandalf's fire spell, Galadriel's lament, and Balin's tomb inscription, all arising ca. 1940 and published in *Treason.* Various other draft versions of the Moria-gate inscription, and variant versions of the Ring-inscription, were published in *J.R.R. Tolkien: Artist and Illustrator* (1995).

2. *The Two Towers* (1954), including the debased Black Speech curse of the Orc of Mordor *(Uglúk u bagronk. . .)*; Treebeard's long, descriptive Qenya names of Lórien *(Laurelindórenan lindelorendor. . .)* and

Fangorn Forest *(Taurelilómëa-tumbalemorna. . .)*; Gimli's Khuzdul battle cry *(Baruk Khazâd!. . .)*; Frodo's Quenya cry at raising aloft the phial of Galadriel *(Aiya Eärendil. . .)*; and Sam's Sindarin invocation of Elbereth *(A Elbereth. . .)*. Published draft versions of these compositions include Treebeard's description of Fangorn Forest, arising ca. 1942 and published in *The Treason of Isengard* (1989); Gimli's battle cry, arising ca. 1942 and published with some grammatical notes in *The War of the Ring* (1989); and Frodo's cry and Sam's invocation, both arising ca. 1944 and published in *War*.

3. *The Return of the King* (1955), including the Quenya *(A laita te. . ., Cormacolindor. . .)* and Sindarin *(Cuio i Pheriain. . ., Daur a Berhael. . ., Eglerio!)* exclamations of praise for Frodo and Sam at Cormallen; Aragorn's coronation oath *(Et Eärello. . .)* and his exclamation at finding the sapling of the line of Nimloth *(Ye! utúvienyes!)*, both Quenya; and Treebeard's Quenya address to Galadriel and Celeborn *(A vanimar. . .)* and his unflattering Quenya descriptive name of orcs *(Morimaite Sincahonda.)* Also, in Appendix A, Gilraen's Sindarin *linnod (Ónen i Estel. . .)*. Published draft versions of these compositions include the Cormallen praises, Aragorn's oath and exclamation, and Treebeard's address and description, all rising co. 1948 and published in *Sauron Defeated* (1992). Various other draft versions of Aragorn's oath were published in *J.R.R.Tolkien: Artist and Illustrator* (1995).

Further among the appendices are the following: D, on the calendars, contains various Quenya and Sindarin calendaric names; E, on writing and spelling, contains much information on the *tengwar* and the *cirth;* and F, on the languages and peoples of the Third Age, presents a general history of those languages of Middle-earth that figure in the novel, including most of the attested vocabulary of the Common Speech. Extensive draft versions for both D and F are given in *The Peoples of Middle-earth* (1996), including, in the former, additional Quenya and Sindarin calendaric names and, in the latter, considerably more information on the Common Speech *(Sōval Phare)*.

- ca. 1951–59—Quenya translations of five Catholic prayers, including *Átaremma (Pater Noster), Aia María (Ave Maria), Alcar i Ataren (Gloria Patri), Ortírielyanna (Sub Tuum Praesidium),* an incomplete translation of the Litany of Loreto, *Alcar mi Tarmenel na Erun* (an incomplete translation of *Gloria in Exclesis Deo*), and *Ae Adar Nín,* an incomplete Sindarin translation of the Lord's Prayer. Collected and published in facsimile with analysis, in two parts, in *VT* 44 and 45 (January and June 2003, respectively).

- ca. 1951–59—"*Dangweth Pengoloð*" (Sindarin, "The Answer of Pengoloð') to the question of how the languages of an immortal race such as the Elves could become so changed and divided. Also "Of Lembas," a brief and partly philological discussion of the waybread of the Elves. Published in *The Peoples of Middle-earth* (1996).

- ca. 1952—Three versions of "The King's Letter" from Aragorn to Sam, in Sindarin, written in both *tengwar* and roman letters. Versions one and three were published in facsimile in *Sauron Defeated* (1992); version two was published in facsimile in *VT* 29 (May 1993).

- ca. 1953—Tolkien's facsimile pages from the "Book of Mazarbul," in *cirth*. Published in *Pictures by J.R.R. Tolkien* (1979); republished in *J.R.R. Tolkien: Artist and Illustrator* (1995).

- ca. 1955—An untitled and untranslated Sindarin poem of five lines *(Ir Ithil ammen Eruchín. . .)* occurring in "The Lay of Leithian Recommenced." Published in *The Lays of Beleriand* (1985).

- ca. 1959–60—"Quendi and Eldar," a lengthy and important philological essay on the names used for and by the various Elvish peoples, chiefly the Ñoldor, the Teleri, and the Sindar, as well as Elvish names for Men, Dwarves, and Orcs. The essay includes historical and etymological consideration of the names and their earliest origins and elements. This essay also contains essentially all that Tolkien ever wrote concerning the language of the Valar. Published in *The War of the Jewels* (1994). A substantial, largely phonological, and unused portion of Appendix D to this essay was subsequently published in *VT* 39 (July 1998).

- ca. 1959–60—"*Ósanwe-kenta*: Enquiry into the Communication of Thought," a philological essay incorporating many Quenya metaphysical terms. Published in *VT* 39 (July 1998), with associated etymological notes published in *VT* 41 (July 2000).

- ca. 1963–72—The third and latest version of the Quenya poem *Oilima Markirya* (see section on ca. 1930) in thirty-eight lines. Published in "A Secret Vice" in *The Monsters and the Critics* (1983).

- 1967—Tolkien's *tengwar* transcriptions of the poems *Namárië* (Quenya) and *A Elbereth Gilthoniel* (Sindarin), with his interlinear English glosses and grammatical notes on these poems and on Sam's invocation of Elbereth. Published in *The Road Goes Ever On* (1967).

- ca. 1966–67—"The Plotz Declension," sent by Tolkien to Dick Plotz, of two Quenya nouns, in eight cases and four numbers (singular, general/total plural, particular/partitive plural, and dual). First published in *Beyond Bree* (March 1989); republished with Tolkien's accompanying notes in *VT* 6 (July 1989); and republished in facsimile in Nancy Martsch's *Basic Quenya*.
- ca. 1968—"The Shibboleth of Fëanor," a philological essay concerning the change of original þ to *s* in Quenya among the Ñoldor in Valinor and the role this change played in the political strife between the Ñoldor and the Vanyar. The essay also touches on the giving of names among the Eldar and discusses the forms and etymologies of the Quenya names of the descendants of Finwë and their conversion to Sindarin. Published in *The Peoples of Middle-earth* (1996). A few unused phonological and etymological notes from this essay were subsequently published in *VT* 41 (July 2000).
- ca. 1968—"Notes on *Óre*," presenting various fragmentary texts comprising a philological discussion of the Elvish *óre,* an inner warning and advising faculty of the mind, and associated concepts, with etymological notes. Published in *VT* 41 (July 2000).
- ca. 1968–70—"The Problem of Ros," an (unsuccessful) attempt by Tolkien to re-etymologize the Sindarin element *-ros* to accord with his later concepts of that language. Published in *The Peoples of Middle-earth* (1996).
- 1969—"The Rivers and Beacon-hills of Gondor," a lengthy philological essay concerning the etymology of the names of those and other geographic features and regions in and about Gondor, with a lengthy etymological digression on the Eldarin numerals. Short excerpts from this essay were published in *Unfinished Tales* (1980); the remainder of the essay was published in *VT* 42 (July 2001).
- ca. 1969—"Cirion's Oath" in Quenya *(Vanda sina. . .),* with English translation and grammatical notes, occurring in the story "Cirion and Eorl." Published in *Unfinished Tales* (1980).
- ca. 1969–70—"Of Dwarves and Men," including a general discussion of the history and character of the languages of both races. Published in *The Peoples of Middle-earth* (1996).

There are also a few Quenya sentences that were first published in *The Silmarillion* (1977) but date (for the most part) from the 1950s, arising in texts published in *Morgoth's Ring* and *The War of the Jewels,* including Eru's word of creation *(Eä!),* Fingon's cry at the Nirnaeth Arnoediad *(Utúlie'n aurë!)* and the response *(Auta i lómë!),* and Húrin's cry at the same battle *(Aurë entuluva!).* There is also one Sindarin phrase, Túrin's epitaph *(Túrin Turambar Dagnir Glaurunga).* Similarly, there are two Quenya sentences occurring in certain texts given in *Unfinished Tales* (1980), of uncertain but probably similar or later date: Gelmir's farewell to Tuor *(Anar kaluva tielyanna!)* and Nienor's despairing lament for Túrin *(A Túrin Turambar turún' ambartanen!).* There are also three Sindarin sentences: Tuor's curse of the Orcs *(Gurth an Glamhoth!),* Voronwë's exclamation upon sighting the mountains encircling Gondolin *(Alae! Ered en Echoriath. . .),* and the battle cry of the Edain of the North *(Lacho calad! . . .).* Finally, a Sindarin exclamation of vengeance by Húrin *(Tôl acharn!)* occurs among a displaced section of the "Grey Annals" published in *The War of the Jewels.*

CARL F. HOSTETTER

See also **Alphabets, Invented; Languages Invented by Tolkien; Publications, Posthumous**

ENCHANTMENT

In Tolkien's essay "On Fairy-stories" (delivered as a lecture in 1939 and first published in 1947) he articulated two related concepts, magic and enchantment, which are of considerable interest in their own right and significant for understanding his fiction. Magic is treated elsewhere in this encyclopedia, but because the two form a linked pair it is necessary briefly to spell out the contrast.

Tolkien pointed out the semantic confusion attending the word "magic" and suggested that magic should be understood as essentially the will to power: that is, an exercise of the will, and thence power and domination, to create changes in the "Primary World" (granted, this, whether the means employed are material or spiritual, is a secondary consideration). Enchantment, in contrast, "produces a Secondary World into which both designer and spectator can enter." It is, he wrote, "artistic in desire and purpose," and that purpose is "the realisation, independent of the conceiving mind, of imagined wonder" (*TL,* 49–50, 18). So if the hallmark of magic is will, that of enchantment is wonder.

Several important points follow. One is that enchantment (and reenchantment) cannot be pursued programmatically, although willpower is certainly needed to create the conditions for it to happen.

Enchantment is literally useless, and any instrumentalist appropriation of it turns into magic instead. It does not follow, however, that it has no effects in the Primary World. Any Secondary World necessarily draws its substance from attributes of the Primary, and the experience of enchantment feeds back into the latter in various ways and contexts—emotional, spiritual, sexual, political—to a powerful if usually unpredictable effect. As Tolkien rightly remarked, enchantment can be "perilous" (*TL*, 50).

In distinguishing magic from enchantment, he once wrote that "the Elves are there (in my tales) to demonstrate the difference" (*Letters*, 146). He suggested that enchantment is the defining characteristic of Faërie and the art, or simply the mode, that is natural to elves (*TL*, 15, 18). In a remark that would give the most insouciant postmodernist pause, he added that the effect of being present at a Faërian drama (upon a human being, that is) is so potent that "you give in to Primary belief, however marvellous the events" (*TL*, 49).

The Elvish connection is significant because the immortal elves in Tolkien's literary mythology are arguably of the Earth in a way that human beings, whose death takes them beyond "the circles of the world," are not. He also described the motive of Elvish art as "the adornment of Earth, and the healing of its hurts" (*Letters*, 151–52). The implication is that enchantment is integrally linked to the more-than-human world—that is, the natural world as including, but much more than, humanity.

Interestingly, these same issues are central to the tradition of critical theory of the Frankfurt School and its ancestors and heirs, such as Max Weber, Theodor Adorno, Max Horkheimer, and Michel Foucault. What they have in common with Tolkien is a deep concern about the corrosive effects of pathological modernity. Thus, the affinity between Tolkien's championing of enchantment against modernist magic and Weber's analysis of "the disenchantment of the world" is not coincidental; nor is it with Horkheimer and Adorno's diagnosis of the Enlightenment as the enemy of gods, qualities, and nature alike.

The value Tolkien placed on enchantment is also reflected in the fiction that was his principal preoccupation. There can be little doubt that he saw himself as a storyteller whose art, ideally at least, entailed enchantment. And enchantment is a theme within the stories, particularly in association with the Elves. It constitutes Frodo's experience (and is named such) of the songs in the Hall of Fire in Rivendell (*FR*, II, i, 306). But it is strongest in "the heart of Elvendom on Earth," Lothlórien (*FR*, II, vi, 439). Here, it transcends even the need for art as anything special: "Nothing seems to be going on," as Sam observes, "and nobody seems to want it to" (*FR*, II, vi, 468).

"It's sunlight and bright day, right enough . . . but this is more elvish than anything I ever heard tell of. I feel as if I was *inside* a song, if you take my meaning" (*FR*, II, vi, 455). This, of course, is the etymological meaning of enchantment.

Another marker, well known to students of enchantment (especially mystical experience) is that time slows and even stops—or else, as Tolkien said of fairy stories, "they open a door on Other Time, and if we pass through, though only for a moment, we stand outside our own time, outside Time itself, maybe" (*TL*, 32). Thus, the departing Company sees Galadriel as "present and yet remote, a living vision of that which has already been left far behind by the flowing streams of Time" (*FR*, II, vi, 485). And they feel that it is Lórien that is slipping away, leaving them "helpless upon the margin of the grey and leafless world"—as good a description of disenchantment as any (*FR*, II, vi, 490).

PATRICK CURRY

Further Reading

Curry, Patrick. "Magic vs. Enchantment." *Journal of Contemporary Religion* 14, no. 3 (1999): 401–12.

Horkheimer, Max, and Theodor W. Adorno. *The Dialectic of Enlightenment*. New York: Continuum, 1994 [1944].

See also **Capitalism; Elves; Environmentalism and Eco-Criticism; Faërie; Magic in Middle-earth; Nature; "On Fairy-Stories"**

ENGLAND, TWENTIETH CENTURY

This section does not include coverage of World War I and World War II, which are separately covered. The twentieth century, in this context, means preeminently the period after the "long nineteenth century" (in world-systems terms) that ran from 1789 to 1914. In those terms, the "long twentieth century" in England has not yet ended and may not end for twenty years. On the other hand, the twentieth century could be defined in traditional terms as beginning with Queen Victoria on the throne (January 1, 1901) and ending midnight December 31, 2000–January 1, 2001. In either case, Tolkien died before the century was over, and most of sources of information on what he thought about anything other than his own work cease before the first half of the century was over. What are principally considered here are Tolkien in the twentieth century and especially his views of it.

Unlike his friend C.S. Lewis, Tolkien was a reader of newspapers. Like Lewis, he listened to the BBC during World War II (possibly at other times), though with no great enthusiasm. Tolkien was not quite the *laudator temporis acti* that Lewis was, and some twentieth-century developments (like the automobile, at least in *Mr. Bliss*) attracted his not-entirely unfavorable attention. Some of his concerns were those of the twentieth century, not only the environment but also apartheid, which he detested in all its forms. Nevertheless, his political views were certainly out of tune with the twentieth century in England. His letter to Christopher dated November 29, 1943, is a primary (though exaggerated) text here:

> My political opinions lean more and more to Anarchy (philosophically understood, meaning abolition of control, not whiskered men with bombs)—or to "unconstitutional" Monarchy. I would arrest anybody who uses the word State (in any sense other than the inanimate realm of England and its inhabitants, a thing that has neither power, rights nor mind); and after a chance of recantation, execute them if they remained obstinate. If we could get back to personal names, it would do a lot of good. Government is an abstract noun meaning the art and process of governing and it should be an offence to write it with a capital G or so as to refer to people. If people were in the habit of referring to "King George's Council, Winston and his gang," it would go a long way to clearing thought, and reducing the frightful landslide into "Theyocracy." Anyway, the proper study of Man is anything but Man, and the most improper job of any man . . . is bossing other men. (*Letters*, 63–64)

Note the (portmanteau?) neologism, *Theyocracy*—government by "Them!"—the faceless and unknown.

Tolkien not only was out of tune with the twentieth century but also was scarcely in tune with even the Augustan Age. The next year (in a letter dated December 28, 1944), he took off after Anthony Eden, then principal secretary of state for foreign affairs (*Letters*, 107): "Mr. Eden in the House [of Commons] the other day expressed pain at the occurrences in Greece, 'the home of democracy.' Is he ignorant, or insincere? δημχρατία was not in Greek a word of approval but was nearly equivalent to 'mob-rule'; and he neglected to note that Greek philosophers—and still more is Greece the home of philosophy—did *not* approve of it." Eden did so no more than Tolkien in this twentieth-century context. Because this was written during World War II, it could be considered under that heading, but what it really speaks to is the politicization of life in the modern world and the forgetting (willful or careless) of the past. In that sense, Tolkien, like the socialist George Orwell, stands firmly on the side of the horses and the professors of Greek and against the twentieth century. I informed him once of a notepad a friend of mine had created with the label "The Ad-Hoc Committee to Send the Twentieth Century Back to the Factory"—

but he thought that the factory (any factory) was the wrong place to send it and, humor aside, that *we* are not given the leave to send God's works back once we have spoiled them.

Perhaps the best summary of Tolkien's view of the twentieth century (at least as of 1945) comes in a letter to Christopher dated January 30, 1945 (*Letters*, 111): "The first War of the Machines seems to be drawing to its final inconclusive chapter—leaving, alas, everyone the poorer, many bereaved or maimed and millions dead, and only one thing triumphant: the Machines. As the servants of the Machines are becoming a privileged class, the Machines are going to be enormously more powerful. What's their next move?"

He did not believe current literature should be part of the canon (if indeed there should be a canon). He was sympathetic to the kind of literary scholarship that developed into the New Criticism of Brooks and Warren (which had some of its origins with "The Cave" in the early 1930s). In some ways, he was very much of the twentieth century—even in some of the things he opposed, he was taking a stand with a twentieth-century opposition. His view on the machines (which, after all, included the computer) and the question he asked ("What's their next move?"), leaves some doubt as to whether he thought the servants or the machines were making that next move. Whichever it was, he did not expect to like it—any more than his younger contemporary Orwell, whose political views were so far from his and whose love and lament for England were so close.

His views on the destruction of Sarehole and the English countryside in general are well known, and Sandyman's new mill brings that view into *The Lord of the Rings*. But it is important to remember that his views were learned from experience, though on the base of a recollection of childhood idylls. He was a child of the Edwardian Age—when he went back many years later to an alumni reunion at his school, he found to his surprise that he was remembered as a rugger player and for his colored socks. (Had Tolkien the makings of a knut?) He was a survivor of the generation that did not survive, and that, I believe, stayed with him till he died. When he and Edith went to the Miramar at Bournemouth, they were perhaps returning to the Edwardian Age but were not turning their backs on the twentieth century—except in terms of the "long nineteenth," to which they were indeed returning. The phrase "Winston and his gang" suggests the reaction of the Spanish-Welsh "Tory" Father Francis in 1906 (to Winston's apostasy), rather than a reaction to the defender of England in 1940, but that may be an oversimplification (and compare the "cherub" reference quoted under the entry titled "World War II"). Nevertheless, how the twentieth century is defined has a good bit to do with any discussion of Tolkien in it or his reaction to it. He was a man of the twentieth century but also, and especially, of the "long nineteenth."

JARED LOBDELL

Further Reading

Shippey, Tom. *J.R.R. Tolkien: Author of the Century.* Boston, MA: Houghton Mifflin, 2001.

See also **Cave, The; Lewis, C.S.; World War I; World War II**

"ENGLISH AND WELSH"

A 1955 paper delivered by Tolkien to inaugurate the O'Donnell Lectures, which were established to promote interest in the Celtic element in the English language, "English and Welsh" has been called Tolkien's "last major learned work" (Shippey 2001, 113.) Despite Tolkien's private view that much of his lecture was unoriginal and "rather dull except to dons," it includes a valuable contribution to the study of the place of Britons in Anglo-Saxon England, a warning against theories of "race," a daring hypothesis about inborn linguistic tastes, and the clearest expression of Tolkien's views on linguistic aesthetics, the driving force in his creation of Middle-earth.

Tolkien's passing observations on the Old English noun *w(e)alh,* "foreigner, slave, or Celt," (plural *w(e)alas,* whence "Wales") have led to the clarification of a major historical enigma: what happened to the Britons and their Celtic language when the Anglo-Saxons invaded. In the absence of written records by or about the Britons under English rule, a nineteenth-century view lingered that they had fled west or been wiped out; at best it was accepted that the Britons' ongoing presence was virtually invisible to history. The evidence of *wealh* in laws and place-names was largely ignored, partly because of the perceived difficulty of distinguishing when it meant "Celt" and when it meant "slave." However, Tolkien argues that *wealh* was "basically a word of linguistic import" applied to foreigners who spoke a Celtic language (or Latin) or to slaves of British origin and that a different word, *théow,* was reserved for any non-British serf. He concludes that Britons continued to form a distinctive element in England after the invasion, only adopting English gradually. It has been left to others to prove his thesis. A comprehensive analysis of *w(e)alh* in law codes, literature, and personal names by Margaret L. Faull in 1975 is noted for providing "the sober documentation for Professor

Tolkien's inspired rhetoric" (Gelling). Taking "English and Welsh" as its starting point, a 1979 O'Donnell lecture by Kenneth Cameron examines place-names containing *w(e)alh,* reinforcing Tolkien's conclusions.

On other linguistic matters of detail, Tolkien redefines *wealhstod,* "interpreter," as "a man who could understand the language of a *walh*" and notes that the Celts knew the word, using it in the *Mabinogion* in the name Gwrhyr, *Gwalstawt Ieithoed* (Interpreter of Tongues). He argues for a Celtic influence on the English language in terms of morphology (giving Old English forms of the verb "be" as an example) and phonology: linking the Old English system of vowel changes including *i*-mutation with the similar Welsh process of *i*-affection and noting the preservation in English, uniquely for a Germanic language, of both *th* and *w,* common sounds in Welsh.

With the assertion that "Language is the prime differentiator of peoples—not of 'races,'" Tolkien stresses a people's right to cultural self-realization but challenges views of "racial" identity. On the one hand, he defends the distinct cultural identities of the Welsh and the English, abjuring the imposition of the term "Britain" to the nation-state since Tudor times, "when in a quite unnecessary desire for a common name the English were officially deprived of their Englishry and the Welsh of their claim to be the chief inheritors of the title British." On the other hand (as Christine Chism has pointed out), Tolkien counters the key ideas of race, soil, blood, and immutable essence used by Nazi ideologues and their antecedents in philology to define the "Nordic" ideal, noting that these are attitudes "still alive . . . in this land at large." He observes (1) that a people is a mutable and heterogeneous grouping, and being "English" implies descent not only from the Anglo-Saxons but also from the Britons and their Bronze Age and Neolithic predecessors; (2) that none of these peoples was indigenous to the "British Isles"; (3) that extensive intermarriage makes a Celtic surname no warrant of much Celtic "blood"; and (4) that the essentialist "modern myth" differentiating his countrymen as "the wild incalculable poetic Celt, full of vague and misty imaginations, and the Saxon, solid and practical when not under the influence of beer" was historically groundless and perceptibly false.

Tolkien's most contentious assertion is that ancestry shapes linguistic taste, giving rise to a "personal linguistic potential" or notional "native language," which is quite distinct from one's "cradle tongue" or first language. The idea is well discussed by Paul Bibire; Tolkien had previously fictionalized it as a psychic key to access prehistory in "The Lost Road" and "The Notion Club Papers." Therefore, Tolkien says, the absorption of Celtic stock into the English population means that Welsh "rings a bell, or rather it stirs deep harp-strings in our linguistic nature." He states that as a result "most English-speaking people . . . will admit that *cellar door* is 'beautiful,' especially if dissociated from its sense (and from its spelling)" because (by chance) the phrase combines sounds common in Welsh phonology. Largely through an unattributed reference in Richard Kelly's 2001 movie *Donnie Darko,* the observation has been widely cited (misattributed to Edgar Allen Poe, H.L. Mencken, and others) and misquoted as a claim for "the most beautiful" phrase in English without regard to the notion of inherited tastes or the Welsh substrate in the language.

Tolkien's more general assertions here about the intrinsic value of linguistic aesthetics are crucial to a critical understanding of his legendarium, which had its origins in his desire to provide a setting for the invented languages he modelled on Welsh and Finnish. Tolkien alludes to this in a valuable account of his own aesthetic responses to Welsh and Finnish, as well as Latin, French, Greek, and Gothic. In his statement that *The Lord of the Rings* "contains, in the way of presentation that I find most natural, much of what I personally have received from the study of things Celtic," Tolkien was alluding not only to the literary influences he had taken from Celtic myth but also to his construction of Sindarin in the phonological style of Welsh. Tolkien's comments on the kinship of Welsh and Latin bear comparison with the relationship between Sindarin and Quenya; and his interest in the Celtic element in English place-names is reflected in the toponymy of Bree in *The Lord of the Rings:* mostly Celtic adapted to English (Archet, Bree) or hybrid Celtic–English compounds (Bree-hill and Chetwood). The fascination with the interplay among peoples, languages, and history evidenced in the lecture is also a central creative theme.

Tolkien had been appointed as the first O'Donnell lecturer in 1954. He delivered "English and Welsh" in Oxford on October 21, 1955, the day after the publication of *The Return of the King.* The paper was first published in 1963.

JOHN GARTH

Further Reading

Bibire, Paul. "Sægde seþe cuþe: J.R.R. Tolkien as an Anglo-Saxonist." In *Scholarship and Fantasy: Proceedings of the Tolkien Phenomenon, Turku, May 1992,* edited by K.J. Battarbee, 111–29, see especially 115–20. Turku: Turku University, 1993.
Burns, Marjorie. *Perilous Realms: Celtic and Norse in Tolkien's Middle-earth.* Toronto: University of Toronto Press, 2005.
Cameron, Kenneth. "The meaning and significance of Old English *walh* in English place-names." *Journal of the English Place-Name Society* 12 (1979–80): 1–53.
Chism, Christine. "Middle-earth, the Middle Ages, and the Aryan Nation: Myth and History in World War II." In *Tolkien the Medievalist,* edited by Jane Chance, 74. London: Routledge, 2003.
Faull, Margaret L. "The semantic development of Old English *wealh.*" *Leeds Studies in English* 8 (1975): 20–44.
Gelling, Margaret. *Signposts to the Past.* 3rd ed., 93–94. Chichester: Phillimore, 1997.
Hammond, Wayne G., with the assistance of Douglas A. Anderson. *J.R.R. Tolkien: A Descriptive Bibliography,* 243–44, 310. New Castle, DE: Oak Knoll Books, 1993.
Shippey, Tom. *The Road to Middle-earth: How J.R.R. Tolkien Created a New Mythology.* Revised and expanded edition. Boston, MA: Houghton Mifflin, 2003.
Tolkien, J.R.R., "English and Welsh." In *Angles and Britons: O'Donnell Lectures,* ed. Henry Lewis. Cardiff: University of Wales Press, 1963. 1–41. Reprinted in J.R.R. Tolkien. *The Monsters and the Critics and other essays,* ed. Christopher Tolkien. London: George Allen & Unwin, 1983. 162–97.
Tolkien, J.R.R. "Nomenclature." In *The Lord of the Rings: A Reader's Companion,* edited by Wayne G. Hammond and Christina Scull, 765. London: HarperCollins, 2005.
Wikipedia. "Cellar door." http://en.wikipedia.org/wiki/Cellar_door. [date]

See also **Languages Invented by Tolkien;** *Lost Road, The***; Racism, Charges Of; "A Secret Vice"**

ENTS

The Ents, also called the Onodrim, are described in Appendix F as "the most ancient people surviving in the Third Age" (*RK,* Appendix F, 408). They are a notoriously unhasty folk who take a form best described as tall walking trees. Growing fourteen feet and more in height, they have size and tremendous strength surpassing that of Trolls, man-like arms and legs, hide like the bark of a tree, and deep, penetrating eyes (*TT,* III, iv, 66). Though they hold these features in common, two Ents may differ in appearance from one another as much as two trees of disparate species might differ.

The origin of the Ents can be traced to the First Age of Middle-earth and the tale "Aulë and Yavanna." When Yavanna complains of Melkor's marring of life in Middle-earth, Manwë foresees the coming of "spirits from afar" who will both protect the trees and avenge their loss with "just anger." The reference to spirits suggests beings of the order of Maiar, though this is not explicitly stated. The title Manwë gives to these protecting spirits is the Shepherds of the Trees (*S,* 46). When Gandalf, speaking to Théoden, uses that same title to describe the Ents, the connection to the spirits of Manwë's prophecy is made explicit (*TT,* III, viii, 155).

By the end of the Third Age, Ents survive only in Fangorn Forest, also called Entwood, a remnant at the edge Rohan of the One Wood that once extended across all of Middle-earth. There the Ents are led by Treebeard, or Fangorn, the chief of the Ents—*the* Ent, as he calls himself—and the oldest living creature on Middle-earth. As Treebeard·tells the Hobbits Merry and Pippin, the Ents had long ago become separated from the Entwives, and no new Entings had been born in many years. As a result of their dwindling population and dwindling role, the Ents are largely forgotten in Middle-earth. Even in neighboring Rohan they are remembered only in children's tales.

Nonetheless, Treebeard and the Ents play a significant role in the events at the end of the Third Age and the victory over Sauron and Saruman. After being roused by Treebeard, who himself is roused by Merry and Pippin, the Ents attack and destroy Isengard and bring an end to the power of Saruman. Treebeard also sends Huorns to the Battle of Helm's Deep, where they aid in the destruction of the Orcs. In doing so, however, Treebeard makes it clear that the Ents are not particularly on the side of Rohan or Gondor but are acting primarily as defenders of the trees.

One of the most striking characteristics of the Ents is their language and ability with languages. The Entish tongue—which like the Ents themselves is unhasty and which none except Ents could ever learn—is described as "slow, sonorous, agglomerated, repetitive, indeed long-winded; formed of a multiplicity of vowel-shades and distinctions of tone and quality which even the masters of the Eldar had not attempted to represent in writing." Linguistically, this represents a well-recognized primitive stage in the development of the Indo-European languages. Their interest in speech, though not their language itself, is said to have been awakened by the Elves. The Ents are "skilled in tongues, learning them swiftly and never forgetting them" (*RK*, Appendix F, 409). In other words, the Ents are gifted philologists, which may make them of all characters in the legendarium (with the possible exception of Gandalf) the most like Tolkien (who often associated himself with trees). Given Tolkien's views on the close association between language and myth, it is not surprising that story is also important to Ents, for whom it is closely connected with names and language. As Treebeard tells the young Hobbits Merry and Pippin, his name would take a long time to tell. "My name is growing all the time, and I've lived a very long, long time, so my name is like a story. Real names tell you the story of the things they belong to in my language, in the Old Entish as you might say. It is a lovely language, but it takes a very long time to say anything in it" (*TT*, III, iv, 68).

The actual word *ent*, though obsolete in Modern English, comes from Old English *ent* and the related *eoten*. The genitive plural form *enta* appears in *Beowulf* (2,717, 2,774) in the phrase *enta geweorc* (the work of Ents), and the adjectival form is in *entische helm* (Entish helmet, 2979). The *eoten* variant shows up in the phrase *eotenas ond ylfe ond orcneas* (112) connecting the Old English Ents with both Elves and Orcs. The word is usually translated as giant, but Tolkien's gloss was probably closer to "troll"; thus, his Ettenmoors are called the "troll-fells" (*FR*, I, xii, 212), and the Ettendales are "troll-country" (*FR*, I, xii, 215). Tom Shippey suggests that the connection between *ent/eoten* and trees was entirely Tolkien's own invention, though the inevitable extinction of Ents from Middle-earth (foreseen by the end of *The Lord of the Rings*) comes from the idea that the Anglo-Saxon ents, whatever they were, existed only in artifacts and were no longer a threat (2001, 88–89). Tolkien's glossing of *ent* as "troll" would explain why in his early concepts for *The Lord of the Rings* the Giant Treebeard was the hostile being responsible for Gandalf's imprisonment (*Shadow*, 363) and his later connection that Trolls were counterfeits made in mockery of Ents (*TT*, III, iv, 89).

Jonathan Evans points out that although Tolkien dismisses any association of the word with the philosophical language of ontology, the *Oxford English Dictionary* gives several citations related to the word, which it relates both to the botanical world (as in a "scion" or "graft") and to the abstract terms associated with essential being. The first sense of the word may well have suggested to Tolkien something from the world of forestry. As to the second sense, the *OED* editors also suggest that *ens* and *entia* mean "essence" and are related to the form of present-participial suffixes in Latin, Greek, and Old English. If we see *ent* as a back-formation of *ens*, carrying the meaning of "essence/being," then despite Tolkien's denial we might see *ent* not merely as a tree but as a tree "rooted in" the essence of being. This understanding is given considerable plausibility, not only by the connection with Yggdrásil, the "World Ash" that is the pillar of the world in ancient Scandinavian mythology, but also by the nature of the Ents and their close association with language and story (and thereby with meaning).

MATTHEW DICKERSON

Further Reading

Dickerson, Matthew, and Jonathan Evans. *Ents, Elves and Eriador: The Environmental Vision of J.R.R. Tolkien.* Lexington, KY: University Press of Kentucky, 2006.

Shippey, Tom. *J.R.R. Tolkien: Author of the Century.* London: HarperCollins, 2001.

See also **Treebeard; Trees**

ENVIRONMENTALISM AND ECO-CRITICISM

The natural environment plays a major role in Tolkien's fiction. It is no mere setting for human (and quasi-human) drama but is treated in a way that clearly conveys a concern for its integrity independent of human interests. Its destruction is not justified by our purposes alone. Furthermore, the instrumental exploitation and destruction of nature is identified as integral to moral evil in this world. That is made plain by "the desolation that lay before Mordor," its "lasting monument . . . a land defiled, diseased beyond all healing" (*TT*, IV, ii, 296). It is equally evident in the havoc wrought on Fangorn Forest by the Dark Lord's chief imitator, Saruman, in his own pursuit of power. Indeed, the One Ring of Power is positioned as the ultimate enemy of the Earth. As Galdor says at the Council of Elrond, Sauron "can torture and destroy the very hills" (*FR*, II, ii, 348).

Conversely, the most enchanted places in Middle-earth are so, at least partly, because they are loved and cared for. As Sam says of Lothlórien, "Whether they've made the land, or the land's made them, it's hard to say" (*FR*, II, vii, 468). Perhaps even more fundamental, however, is Goldberry's response to the question of whether Tom Bombadil owns the Old Forest: "No indeed! . . . The trees and grasses and all things growing or living in the land belong each to themselves" (*FR*, I, vii, 172). It follows that any attempt to defend nature by directly contesting the Ring of Power would end by betraying it; the only hopeful path is cooperating with nature, which implies not mastery but relationship.

One of the major dimensions of Tolkien's work is thus eco-centric (nature-centred), as opposed to anthropocentric (human-centred). These are terms originating in environmental philosophy, especially environmental or ecological ethics, beginning in the 1970s; in the 1990s, they became central to the still newer field of eco-criticism. In terms of eco-centric literature, there are obviously precedents for Tolkien's values in Blake, Wordsworth, Thoreau, Morris, Lawrence, and Edward Thomas, among others, as well as in Ruskin's essays. (The extent to which Tolkien was directly influenced in this respect by any of these writers is another question and seems doubtful.) However, in the context of modern and especially modernist literature, Tolkien's eco-centrism certainly stands out. Indeed, given the ongoing environmental crisis, it was relatively prescient when the books first appeared. Recognition of this even among "green" critics has been hampered, however, by their residual modernist commitment to a literary canon that excludes *The Lord of the Rings* as not a novel, not self-conscious or ironic, and insufficiently difficult to read.

There can be little doubt that the eco-centrism of Tolkien's work is one of the things to which so many readers, in contrast, have responded so positively. Some it has even spurred into action. Tolkien was enthusiastically taken up by the same counterculture, beginning in the 1960s, that gave birth to the ecology movement. One of the founders of Greenpeace, David Taggart, was reading *The Lord of the Rings* on a seminal action on behalf of the environment, sailing into an exclusion zone to protest against nuclear testing in 1972. A few years later, an advocate of a road bypass through Dartmoor attacked opponents of the scheme as "Middle-earth hobbits." A later generation of environmentalists took nonviolent direct action to resist new motorways running through green places in England in the 1990s: Newbury, Twyford Down, Batheaston, and elsewhere. These young people set a moral example all the more striking in the context of the materialism of the time, with its destructive ecological consequences. And for them, Tolkien's work was a—perhaps even the—principal inspiration.

All this surely gives the lie to the accusation (seemingly commonest among the critics who know his work least) that Tolkien encourages a reactionary escapism or political quietism. His fictional Middle-earth is a site of struggle against ecological, as well as social and political, disaster, just as is our own. His readers are finally directed back into this world, not another, and that is how they have responded. The best way to understand his most-read and best-loved work, *The Lord of the Rings,* is thus as an instance of what Fraser Harrison memorably called "radical nostalgia" (162–72).

PATRICK CURRY

Further Reading

Coupe, Laurence, ed. *The Green Studies Reader: From Romanticism to Ecocriticism.* London: Routledge, 2000.

Curry, Patrick. *Defending Middle-earth: Tolkien, Myth and Modernity.* 2nd ed. Boston, MA: Houghton Mifflin, 2004.

Harrison, Fraser. "England, Home and Beauty." In *Second Nature,* edited by Richard Mabey, 162–72. London: Jonathan Cape, 1984.

Veldman, Meredith. *Fantasy, the Bomb, and the Greening of Britain: Romantic Protests, 1945–1980.* Cambridge: Cambridge University Press, 1994.

See also **Capitalism; Industrialization; Nature**

ENVIRONMENTALIST READINGS OF TOLKIEN

The rising popularity of Tolkien's fantasy in the counterculture of the 1960s and 1970s paralleled rising popular interest in the United States and Europe in ecology and the environment as political and scientific movements. This parallel engendered from the start critical interest in Tolkien's focus on nature in *The Lord of the Rings,* as exemplified in particular by his distinctive creation of the Ents, a culture of tree shepherds, and his use of natural landscape as, in effect, a central character in storytelling. The latter was also one of the nonaction elements of his writing most clearly translated into film by director Peter Jackson in his stunning use of New Zealand landscapes as Middle-earth. Although Tolkien's work to date has not been examined in a sustained and systematic way in mainstream discussions within the discipline of eco-criticism or environmental literary studies (which began to emerge discretely in the 1970s and has tended to focus on nineteenth- and twentieth-century canonical works), analysis of the environmental meaning of his fantasy has been an important subtext in Tolkien criticism and promises to gain more prominence in the future, both within and beyond the discipline. (Eco-criticism involves a foregrounding of the background of a work, to focus and read it through its construction of nature, and involves what this can reveal about the cultural context of the narrative, especially in terms of how human subjectivity and social norms are formed in relation to the natural world. Often it parallels postcolonial approaches to literature in examining the formation of the Other by which a culture or individual defines itself.)

Environmental criticism of Tolkien's work to date generally has found in it an example of "eco-centric" literature, narrative that provides a central place for the natural world, treated as a larger force than a mere tool for human allegorizing and semiotics, as contrasted to much Western literature from the late Middle Ages until recent decades. An eco-centric text tends to engage with nature in an integrative way rather than to marginalize it as Other, as apparent in Tolkien's treatment of Middle-earth as a predecessor to our world. However, Tolkien's approach to nature, which appears to fit well in many ways with postmodern views of life as an ecological network, stems largely from his love for and knowledge of ancient texts and traditions that stand in opposition to more impersonal views of nature fostered by modern science and technological advancement. In this, his work still fits well with one goal of the eco-critical movement, as advanced by influential writers such as Lawrence Buell and in the beginnings of medieval eco-critical studies in *ISLE* (the field's main journal) and more mainstream journals (see, for example, my "Landscapes of Conversion," which references Tolkien's Anglo-Saxon scholarship): to reach into the Western literary past and highlight environmentally conscious traditions as alternatives to modern culture.

Besides his distinctive creation of the Ents (echoing earlier myth and folklore including the medieval Welsh *Cad Goddeu* poem) and the centrality of landscape, an eco-centric reading of Tolkien's fantasy romance epic is also supported by his depiction of Tom Bombadil, Goldberry, and the Old Forest; the associations of the Elves and Dwarves with the natural world; the role of the rising river in repulsing the Black Riders from Rivendell (echoing a theme in the early Irish *Cattle-Raid of Cooley*); a place in the narrative for animals suggesting lives independent from human concerns—from the great eagles to a contemplative fox in the Shire; and the unnatural magic of Sauron and Saruman that creates industrial-style wastelands and various artificial depravities (including the Orcs). And in many ways, Tolkien was the first eco-critic of his own writing in a self-referential glossing reminiscent (in its modernist context) of T.S. Eliot's *The Waste Land* (and dealing with similar issues of modern life as a type of wasteland echoing medieval literature, though with a more explicitly environmental component than Eliot's work). Tolkien noted, in the foreword to the second edition of his fantasy romance epic, the effect on him of the scouring of the English countryside by modernization. Tolkien's childhood is often cited as the reason for purported eco-centricity in his writing, including dim memories of South African gardens and idyllized views of his family's ancestral Midlands rural countryside, mixed with a love for northern mythology filtered through derivative Edwardian romanticism.

Just how far the reading of Tolkien's interest in nature has gone from these roots is indicated by often relatively informal pieces of recent scholarship, such as Andy Letcher's 2001 article in the journal *Folklore* on the role of Tolkien in "Eco-Protest Culture" and Andrew Light's reflection on Tolkien's "Green Time." But perhaps the greatest "debate" in Tolkien scholarship on the author's eco-centricity to date was, typical of the still maturing field of Tolkien studies, somewhat off base from the start, in centering on criticism of Patrick Curry's *Defending Middle-earth,* the most extensive book-length treatment of Tolkien's allegedly "Green" (in a capital-G political sense) approach to nature. Curry argued that Tolkien's fantasy involved subtle but strong advocacy for a communitarian and ecological vision of society. Verlyn Flieger's thoughtful response to Curry's book, from a more mainstream position in Tolkien scholarship, revealed the gaps in Curry's rather free-form, advocacy approach. She argued persuasively for viewing Tolkien's approach to nature not as simplistically Green in politics or approach but as an interlaced pattern of nature and culture that does not clearly favor nature in the end. Flieger's critique, like Curry's polemic, took place largely outside of the discourse of eco-criticism as a field, in which the integration of the human with the natural, as in the praxis of ecological restoration, can be a part of an eco-centric framework, not necessitating the clear privileging of nonhuman nature in a binarized way. In that sense, Tolkien's viewpoint can be usefully paralleled with that of fellow Catholic E.F. Schumacher's sustainable Green-style economics, as in the latter's *Small is Beautiful* manifesto, a topic of study also for Tolkien scholar Joseph Pearce.

Brian Bates took a twenty-first-century "pop culture" approach to Tolkien's views of nature in assigning the latter to the author's imbibing of pagan mythology. However, I have argued, drawing on Tolkien's scholarship, that it is possible to place his view of nature within the context of early medieval Celtic otherworldly literature, which in turn was reflective of patristic Christian thought, as shown by John Carey's studies on early Irish literature. In this analysis, Tolkien's sense of a personalized and spiritually energized nature (as in the overlay landscapes of the Elven realms) reflects a non-Augustinian view of nature, developed from desert monasticism as promoted by John Cassian and articulated most explicitly by Maximus the Confessor and his intellectual protégé in the West, the Irish philosopher John Scottus Eriugena. In this sense, Tolkien's Augustinian Catholicism melded with an earlier Christian worldview reflected in early Irish and Welsh stories of the Otherworld that formed a basis for his initial and ongoing focus on the Elves. What the theological scholar Dumitru Staniloae has called the "sparkle in creation," or paradisiacal divine energies in patristic writing, that influenced such early stories became the natural magic infusing many of the landscapes of Middle-earth—not Green in a partisan way, but eco-centric in a Christian sense all the same.

ALFRED K. SIEWERS

Further Reading

Bates, Brian. *The Real Middle-earth: Exploring the Magic and Mystery of the Middle Ages, J.R.R. Tolkien and "The Lord of the Rings."* New York: Palgrave Macmillan, 2003.

Buell, Lawrence. *The Environmental Imagination: Thoreau, Nature Writing, and the Formation of American Culture.* Cambridge, MA: Belknap, 1995.

Carey, John. *A Single Ray of the Sun: Religious Speculations in Early Ireland.* Andover, MA: Celtic Studies Publications, 1999.

Curry, Patrick. *Defending Middle-earth: Tolkien, Myth and Modernity.* New York: St. Martin's, 1997.

Flieger, Verlyn. "J.R.R. Tolkien and the Matter of Britain." *Mythlore* 23, no. 1, whole no. 87 (2000): 47–59.

Letcher, Andy. "The Scouring of the Shire: Fairies, Trolls and Pixies in Eco-Protest Culture." *Folklore* 112 (2001): 146–61.

Light, Andrew. "Tolkien's Green Time: Environmental Themes in *The Lord of the Rings*." In *The Lord of the Rings and Philosophy: One Book To Rule Them All*, edited by Gregory Bassham and Eric Bronson, 150–63. Chicago, IL: Open Court, 2003.

Schumacher, Barbara Wood, and Joseph Pearce. *Small is Still Beautiful: The Sequel to Small is Beautiful.* London: HarperCollins, 2001.

Siewers, Alfred K. "Landscapes of Conversion: Guthlac's Mound and Grendel's Mere as Expressions of Anglo-Saxon Nation-Building." *Viator* 34 (2003): 1–39. Reprinted in *The Postmodern Beowulf*, edited by Eileen Joy, Mary Ramsey, and Bruce Gilchrist. Morgantown, WV: West Virginia University Press, 2006.

———. "Tolkien's Cosmic-Christian Ecology: The Medieval Underpinnings." In *Tolkien's Modern Middle Ages*, edited by Jane Chance and Alfred K. Siewers, 139–53. New York: Palgrave Macmillan, 2005.

Staniloae, Dumitru. *Orthodox Spirituality.* Translated by Archimandrite Jerome Newville and Otilia Kloos. South Canaan, PA: St. Tikhon's Seminary Press, 2003.

See also **Animals in Tolkien's Works; Dwarves; Elves; Ents; Environmentalism and Eco-Criticism; Nature; Trees**

ÉOMER

Rider of Rohan and Third Marshal of the Riddermark, Éomer later succeeded Théoden as the eighteenth king of Rohan. According to Appendix A in *The Lord of the Rings,* Éomer was born in 2991 to Theodwyn (sister of King Théoden) and Eomund (the Chief Marshal of the Mark). His sister, Éowyn, was born in 2995. After the death of Éomer and Éowyn's parents, King Théoden took the children into the courts of Edoras and raised them as his own.

Éomer became Third Marshal of the Mark in 3017 and served as a loyal and brave warrior throughout Théoden's incapacitation. Spurred on by suspicion of Grima Wormtongue's treachery and the need to protect Rohan against an invading army of Orcs, Éomer rode with his army against the Orcs and defeated them. It was after this battle that Éomer met Legolas, Gimli, and Aragorn for the first time. After hearing Aragorn's explanation of their situation, Éomer allowed the travelers to continue on to Fangorn Forest. He gave them two horses on the condition that they return to Edoras.

Upon his return to Edoras, Éomer was arrested by order of Grima Wormtongue, a servant of Saruman then acting as the king's adviser. Éomer was pardoned after Gandalf's healing of Théoden and with

Aragorn led the defense of the Hornburg at the Battle of Helm's Deep. After this battle, he accompanied Gandalf, Aragorn, and Théoden to Isengard. During the exchange between Saruman and Théoden, Éomer interjected to remind Théoden of Hama's grave at Helm's Deep and the outrage the Rohirrim had suffered: "Have we ridden forth to victory, only to stand at last amazed by an old liar with honey on his forked tongue?" (*TT*, III, x, 185).

Éomer accompanied his king to the battlefield at the Pelennor Fields in front of the city of Minas Tirith in Gondor. When King Théoden fell in battle, he named Éomer successor by directing that his banner be given to the young warrior. Éomer, greatly saddened by the king's death, wept at his side. Not long after, he found that his sister, Éowyn, had also fallen in battle and, from her sickly pallor, thought that he had lost her as well. In his grief and anger, he took up a horn and rode over the field, shouting "Death! Ride, ride to ruin and the world's ending!" (*RK*, V, vi, 118).

After the War of the Ring had ended, Éomer returned to Minas Tirith and was reunited with his sister, healed of her wounds. It is told in Appendix A that Éomer ruled Rohan for sixty-five years and was later known as Éomer Éadig. He kept good relations with Gondor and visited there often. He was succeeded by his son, Elfwine the Fair (*RK*, Appendix A, 357).

Éomer's name originates in the Old English word for horse *(eoh)*. His name as king, Éadig, is Old English for "blessed." As Tom Shippey notes, Éomer represents dashing valor in battle. This is emphasized by the white horse's tail on his helmet, the technical term for which is *panache*, a word that also describes Éomer's and his Riders' behavior in battle. Their sudden, overwhelming rush is perhaps to be credited to the vigor and strength that, Faramir says, the Men of Gondor find so appealing in the "younger" or "lower" Rohirrim (*TT*, IV, v, 287).

HILARY WYNNE

Further Reading

Shippey, Tom. *The Road to Middle-earth: How J.R.R. Tolkien Created a New Mythology*. Revised and Expanded edition. Boston, MA: Houghton Mifflin, 2003.

See also **Rohan; Théoden; War**

ÉOWYN

The character of Éowyn sets herself apart from Tolkien's other female characters by refusing to remain among them. The rebellious Lady of Rohan desires nothing more than to go off to battle and fight with the men of her country and win glory. She enters the male realm of war to fight in battle dressed as a man—the soldier Dernhelm. Éowyn is seen as masculine even before she puts on men's clothes just because she longs to be part of the male society of war, which is forbidden to her as a woman. Éowyn knows that though she is an accomplished fighter, her gender prohibits her from being a soldier. Tolkien takes care to conceal her sexual features while allowing her to be recognized as a woman through nonsexualized features, such as her hair and demeanor. When she appears before Merry for the first time, Tolkien describes her as if she is clearly female, though dressed as a man for battle:

> As they drew near Merry saw that the rider was a woman with long braided hair gleaming in the twilight, yet she wore a helm and was clad to the waist like a warrior and girded with a sword. (*RK*, V, iii, 68)

According to this description, Éowyn seems to be dressed in plated armor that covers her breasts and a skirt that hinders her agility while fighting.

In contrast to Éowyn's strong desire for glory, she is a nurturing figure in the work as she nurses the bewitched and ailing King Théoden, who serves as a father figure to her, and worries about her banished brother Éomer. Her battle lust must be muted due to the restrictions placed on her gender, resulting in deep personal frustration:

> "Shall I always be chosen?" she said bitterly. "Shall I always be left behind when the Riders depart, to mind the house while they win renown, and find food and beds when they return?" (*RK*, V, ii, 57)

Interestingly, Éowyn does not take ownership over the domestic tasks she describes. She says that the Riders will find food and beds when they return; she does not say that she will provide them. Following this plea, Éowyn offers and at times begs to go to battle to give her life for victory. Every time the men of Rohan march off to battle, Éowyn is faced with the possibility that they may not return in need of her care and housekeeping. She will find herself useless, so to die with glory would be far better than to live without purpose.

Even though Éowyn attempts to participate in battle, as would an authentically male soldier, her displayed heroism is quite different from that of the male soldiers. In Éowyn's encounter with the Nazgûl and their prebattle conversation, we see her engaging in feminine fighting. Éowyn acts defensively rather than aggressively as she warns the Nazgûl to stay away from the body of Théoden:

> "Be gone, foul dwimmerlaik, lord of carrion! Leave the dead in peace!"
> A cold voice answered: "Come not between the Nazgûl and his prey! Or he will not slay thee in thy

turn. He will bear thee away to the houses of lamentation, beyond all darkness, where thy flesh shall be devoured, and thy shriveled mind be left naked to the Lidless Eye.''

A sword rang as it was drawn. "Do what you will; but I will hinder it, if I may." (*RK*, V, vi, 116)

Éowyn does not attack the Nazgûl on sight but warns him before she even draws her sword. Then, with her sword in hand, she gives him another warning, saying that she will "hinder" his action rather than kill him. It is clear that she acts out of the need to provide familial protection rather than the need to kill.

Éowyn attempts to rectify her "relegation to the female sidelines" by dressing as the Rider Dernhelm and going off to battle. Éowyn's cross-dressing does allow her to actively participate in the war as a combatant; it only allows her to do so as a man. Éowyn's identity is concealed under that of Rider Dernhelm and is not revealed until she tells the Nazgûl that though "no *man* can stand between the Nazgûl and his prey," she will be able to because she is a woman (*RK*, V, vi, 116). She attempts to reconcile the contradiction between her desire and her gender through the term "shieldmaiden," which she calls herself. The concept of a shieldmaiden comes from an exclusionary rhetoric that keeps women who provide the same services as men in a distinctly separate category. As a woman, Éowyn cannot simply be a Rider of Rohan; she is defined as the opposing and lesser other.

The painful side of Éowyn's experience living the life of a male soldier is that she begins to feel that she *is* a soldier, which is, by definition, male. This is especially true when she relates to Aragorn, the Ranger who leads the Hobbits on their journey and who later becomes King of Gondor and Arnor. Being both man and woman at once causes her to struggle with two diverse emotional experiences—being in love with Aragorn, as a woman, and being as mesmerized by Aragorn as a thane would be by his lord. Faramir, who eventually becomes Éowyn's husband, explains to her why her love for Aragorn was not the love she thought it was:

> You desired to have the love of the Lord Aragorn. Because he was high and puissant, and you wished to have renown and glory and to be lifted far above the mean things that crawl on the earth. And as a great captain may to a young soldier he seemed to you admirable. For so he is, a lord among men, the greatest that now is. But when he gave you only understanding and pity, then you desired to have nothing unless a brave death in battle. (*RK*, VI, v, 242)

Here, Faramir points out to Éowyn that part of her attraction to Aragorn was his position and class. He tells her that seeking battle is, for her, an attempt

to rise above the "mean things that crawl on the earth." If we interpret "mean" as ordinary or average, then we can see that Éowyn wants to surpass her common life of a woman tending an old king and keeping house for an army. But there is another layer of intensity on Éowyn's want of battle—she attempts a suicide mission, choosing death over living without the love of Aragorn. This sentiment was shared by many medieval fighters who would rather die than be in exile, separated from their lords.

Before Éowyn accepts Faramir and her new life as a healer, her relational identity in the text is questionable. She is neither daughter nor sister because her parents died when she was young, her father figure King Théoden is ailing and eventually dies, and her brother Éomer is imprisoned. She is neither wife nor anyone's betrothed, and she is truly neither man nor woman.

When, amid much celebration, Éowyn finally becomes betrothed to Faramir, her identity is then clearly defined—as a possession. As Aragorn praises her brother for delivering to Gondor the "fairest thing in his realm," all of Éowyn's successes in battle, her fierce loyalty to her country, and her enduring devotion to her family are forgotten as she is placed among Arwen and Galadriel, the other idealized females whose beauty is defended and debated throughout the work. The forced transformation of Éowyn alongside Arwen's controversial choice to forgo her immortality to spend an abbreviated eternity with Aragorn asserts that the gender and familial harmony of Middle-earth reject the existence of working mothers in favor of trophy wives.

KATHERINE HESSER

EPIC POETRY

During the Renaissance, epic, or heroic, poetry was considered the highest form of poetry one could compose: Sir Phillip Sidney praised the heroic form for teaching "the most high and excellent truth" (1992, 615). In the early twentieth century, scholars began to codify the role of the epic hero. An epic poem, characterized primarily by a greater length over other poetic forms, deals with heroic, often superhuman, individuals, events, and deeds, which follow a traceable pattern. As a student of the classics, Tolkien studied many epics, learning the elements of style and function that compose the epic form. As he worked on constructing his own languages, he turned first to the poetic form in creating a vehicle for his languages before abandoning it in favor of his prose epics, *The Lord of the Rings,* and, unpublished in his lifetime, *The Silmarillion.*

Epic poetry in the English language can be divided into two stylistic categories based on the source of influence: Old English and Classical. The more familiar form is the Classical; English poets from Chaucer to Milton incorporated the stylistic elements of the Classical epic used by Homer, Virgil, and Dante in their own works. This form is dominated by a steady meter and rhyme scheme, most often in the form of iambic pentameter but not exclusively so. Stanzas are grouped so that the meter carries evenly, emphasized by a stylized end-rhyme of various forms with the end point of a canto emphasized with the heroic couplet. By contrast, the Old English form of poetry, used in the epic *Beowulf,* is dominated by an alliterative style instead of rhyme.

As a philologist, Tolkien gained aesthetic pleasure "from the form of words (and especially from the fresh association of word-form with word-sense)" (*Letters,* 172). He was drawn to works of foreign languages, including those of Anglo-Saxon origins. Word-form affects the meaning of words by playing upon the ear—a series of sibilants create different connotations than a grouping of hard consonants. In the process of creating linguistic patterns for his languages, this technique would play a part. His studies of word-form and word-sense, and their corresponding interweaving of rhyme, meter, meaning, and alliteration, lend themselves to the crafting of his two epic poems, *The Lay of the Children of Húrin* (*Lays,* 5) and *The Lay of Leithian* (*Lays,* 189). Abandoned and unpublished in his lifetime, these two works have the stylistic elements of the Old English and Classical epic styles, respectively.

Tolkien's background in Old English and Anglo-Saxon philology would give him a clear understanding of the nature of the stylistic elements of the Old English alliterative verse, clearly indicated in his translation of *Sir Gawain and the Green Knight.* Tolkien's clear semantic translation of the Middle English text preserves the alliterative patterns of the original, showing his understanding of the Old English poetic form, an understanding which is demonstrated again in *The Lay of the Children of Húrin.*

Tolkien felt that *The Lay of Leithian,* in particular, had "grave defects" (*Lays,* viii), despite many strong passages. The weakness lay in the form he chose for the work: octosyllabic heroic couplets; iambic tetrameter with an AABBCCDD rhyme scheme. Such a structure falls easily into a singsong rhythm, which he tried to avoid—with greater or lesser success in various passages.

In his Middle-earth cosmology, Elvish and Dwarvish poems generally contain the stylistic elements of the Classical style, and the poems of the races of Men contain a mix of the Old English and Classical styles. Those races of Men who mingled most with the Elves, like the Númenóreans and Men of Gondor, adopted the Classical poetic styles into their works, and those with little exposure to the Elves, such as the early Edain and the Rohirrim, maintained the Old English style.

In his epic poems, as well as in his prose epics, Tolkien followed the heroic model common to myth and epic works like *Beowulf* and *The Kalevala,* from which he drew inspiration. Scholars like Carl Jung and Joseph Campbell, who based their studies and theories of the heroic model on many of the same works that he emulated in crafting his Middle-earth cosmology, outlined and codified this model. In his two lays, both of his heroes, Túrin and Beren, follow Campbell's outline of the hero's journey, including elements like the tragic hero's flaw, evidenced by Túrin, and the descent into the Underworld that Beren and Lúthien undertake in their quest to retrieve a Silmaril.

Tolkien started and abandoned various other original poems of an epic nature in their early stages or used them solely to hint of a longer piece extant in the cosmology of Middle-earth; examples include *The Lay of Gil-Galad,* which Samwise quotes in part (*FR,* I, xi, 197–98); the *Song of the Mounds of Mundburg* by an unnamed Rohirric poet (*RK,* V, viii, 124–125); and *The Flight of the Noldoli from Valinor* (*Lays,* 159).

JULAIRE ANDELIN

Further Reading

Campbell, Joseph. *The Hero with a Thousand Faces.* 2nd ed. Princeton, NJ: Princeton University Press, 1980.

Shippey, Tom. *The Road to Middle-earth: How J.R.R. Tolkien Created a New Mythology.* Revised and Expanded edition. New York: Houghton Mifflin, 2003.

Sidney, Sir Phillip. "The Defense of Poesy." In *The Renaissance in England: Non-dramatic Prose and Verse of the Sixteenth Century,* edited by Hyder E. Rollins and Herschel Baker, 605–24. Prospect Heights, IL: Waveland, 1992.

Tolkien, J.R.R., trans. *Sir Gawain and the Green Knight, Pearl, and Sir Orfeo.* New York: Ballantine, 1980.

See also **Alliteration; Alliterative Verse by Tolkien; Arthurian Literature;** *Beowulf and the Critics;* **"Beowulf: The Monsters and the Critics";** *Beowulf:* **Tolkien's Scholarship;** *Beowulf:* **Translations by Tolkien; "Chaucer as Philologist: The Reeve's Tale"; Dante; Heroes and Heroism; Jungian Theory;** *Lays of Beleriand;* **Middle English Vocabulary; Milton; Old English; Old Norse Literature; "On Translating** *Beowulf"*; **Poems by Tolkien in Other Languages; Quest Narrative; Rhyme Schemes and Meter; Shakespeare;** *Sir Gawain and the Green Knight, Pearl, and Sir Orfeo:* **Edited by Christopher Tolkien; Spenser, Edmund; Virgil**

ERU

In the beginning, there "was Eru, the One, who in Arda is called Ilúvatar; and he made first the Ainur, the Holy Ones, that were the offspring of his thought, and they were with him before aught else was made." Eru spoke to them through song, offering themes of music; the Ainur sang as well. He gave to each of them an individual purpose, and only slowly did they understand their singular role within the larger community of creation. Eru "kindled" each "with the Flame Imperishable" and commanded the Ainur to make a "Great Music," each to add a unique contribution to the theme of Eru's own devising. With song, creation of the material universe began. When Melkor, the greatest of the Ainur, created with things of his own, contrary to the Order of Eru, discord ensued, and Eru stopped the music. Calmly, Eru began a second theme. Melkor again challenged the order of Eru, and there arose "a war of sound more violent than before." Again, Eru began a third theme; this time the music was "wide and beautiful, but slow and blended with immeasurable sorrow, from which its beauty chiefly came." Melkor once again challenged the music of Eru. Eru stopped the music and chastised Melkor. In the third theme, Eru alone created His Children, Elves and Men, and the beauty and sorrow were the Incarnation, Death, and Resurrection. He also, it seems, gave shape to the Later Ages, the Apocalypse or Ragnarök, though He refused to show the Ainur its shape. After the chastisement of Melkor, Eru revealed the world that the Ainur had helped create through song. He then gave the vision Being. "*Eä!* Let these things Be!" Filled with joy, many of the Ainur departed the realms of Eru and entered time to continue the work begun by their song.

From this point forward, Manwë, one of the Valar, becomes the vice-regent of Eru, and Eru remains, mostly, offstage during the remainder of Tolkien's legendarium. He does, however, appear and intervene in two vital moments. The first deals with Dwarves, and the second deals with the reshaping of the world. In the first, Aulë, one of the Valar and similar to Melkor "in thought and in powers," though loyal to Ilúvatar, attempts to make his own creatures. In secret, "he made first the Seven Fathers of the Dwarves" in Middle-earth. When Ilúvatar demanded to know by what authority Aulë made the Dwarves, Aulë offered a fatherly answer: "I desired things other than I am, to love and to teach them," to have them love creation. Ilúvatar, out of compassion, then gave the Dwarves life and will, commanding that they must sleep until after the Elves and the Men had been born into the world.

The Dwarves even earned a vital purpose, to remake the world after the Last Battle.

Equally important, Ilúvatar reshapes the corruptions and marrings of evil not only to make His plan work out but also to create something entirely better than the original. At each of the vital moments of Tolkien's legendarium—the Creation, the end of the First Age, the end of the Second Age, and the Last Battle—Ilúvatar intrudes directly. When Melkor sang his own tune during the Creation, Ilúvatar incorporated it into the larger design and began anew. When Morgoth became too powerful in Middle-earth, Ilúvatar ended his reign: God ended it at the end of the First Age, and he will do so again at the Last Battle. When the Sauron-allied Númenóreans attempted to invade the Blessed Realm at the end of the Second Age and become gods themselves, Ilúvatar destroyed their island and made Arda round, preventing further contact with the Blessed Realm. Ilúvatar ultimately ends Morgoth's reign of terror at the Last Battle, an event foreshadowed by Ilúvatar's destruction of Númenor.

In his mythological conception of God, Tolkien combined Judeo-Christian theology, Stoic and Platonic philosophy, and, to a lesser extent, Northern Germanic and Scandinavian mythology. Eru (translated from Qenya as "The One" or "He that is Alone") or Ilúvatar (translated from Qenya as "All-Father," "Heavenly Father," or "Father of All") is Tolkien's mythological representation of the First Person of the Christian Trinity, God the Father. In the later version of the "Silmarillion," Tolkien labeled Eru "The Lord of All." At times, though, Tolkien employs Eru, translated as "The One," to mean the entire Trinity. For example, in his later writings, Tolkien wrote Arda "was made by Eru, but He is not in it. The One only has no limits." In an interview in 1968, the interviewer asked who the "One God of Middle-earth" was. "*The* one, of course!" Tolkien answered. "The book is about the world that God created—the actual world of this planet." The mythological representation of the Third Person of the Trinity, the Flame Imperishable or the Secret Fire, also appears relatively frequently in Tolkien's legendarium. Tolkien admitted to Clyde Kilby in the summer of 1966 that this was the Holy Spirit. The nature of the Second Person of the Trinity, the Logos, appears only in the abstract in the story "Athrabeth Finrod Ah Andreth." Finrod and Andreth's conversation, though, does anticipate the Incarnation. "They say that the One will himself enter into Arda, and heal Men and all the Marring from the beginning to the end," Andreth skeptically states. "Even if He in Himself were to enter in," Finrod answers, "He must still remain also as He is: the Author without."

BRADLEY J. BIRZER

See also **Arda; Astronomy and Cosmology, Middle-earth;** *Morgoth's Ring*; **Shaping of Middle-earth;** *Silmarillion, The*

ESPERANTO

Esperanto is an artificial language designed as a neutral means of international communication, first published as *Lingvo internacia* by its inventor, L.L. Zamenhof, in 1887. Its vocabulary is constructed primarily on a Romance and Germanic basis and is easily expanded by a variety of prefixes and suffixes. The grammar is simplified and regular, summarized in the form of sixteen rules, for ease of learning.

Tolkien learned Esperanto in his adolescence, and short texts in the language appear in a notebook called the *Book of the Foxrook*, composed in 1909, which also contains a system of code-writing invented by the seventeen-year-old Tolkien, consisting of a phonetic alphabet and a number of ideographic symbols. Tolkien never became a "practical Esperantist," as he put it, and he wrote in 1932, "I can neither write nor speak the language. . . . 25 years ago I learned and have not forgotten its grammar and structure, and at one time read a fair amount written in it" (Smith and Wynne, 35).

In his essay "A Hobby for the Home," written in 1931 and published posthumously as "A Secret Vice," Tolkien wrote that he believed in the desirability of an artificial language "at any rate for Europe . . . as the one thing antecedently necessary for uniting Europe, before it is swallowed by non-Europe," and he added that he particularly liked Esperanto "not least because it is the creation ultimately of one man" (*MC*, 198). The following year, Tolkien became a member of the Board of Honorary Advisers to the Education Committee of the British Esperanto Association, and a letter he wrote to the committee's secretary was published under the title "A Philologist on Esperanto" in the May 1932 issue of *The British Esperantist*. In this letter, he goes into greater detail regarding his interest in the international language movement and his reasons for supporting Esperanto, the chief of these being that it had "the widest measure of practical acceptance" and "the most advanced organization" of all international auxiliary languages (Smith and Wynne, 35–36).

Later in his life, however, Tolkien appears to have abandoned any hope of Esperanto achieving its goals. In a draft of a letter to a Mr. Thompson, dated January 14, 1956, he writes that Esperanto and other languages of the same sort "are dead, far deader than ancient unused languages, because their authors never invented any Esperanto legends" (*Letters*, 231).

Esperanto does not appear to have been a significant influence on Tolkien's own invented languages. Words in the languages of Tolkien's Middle-earth resemble Esperanto vocabulary only to the extent that they resemble words in the languages on which Esperanto was based. Furthermore, the grammars of Tolkien's languages were devised to mimic the complexities found in natural languages (including the ways in which they change over time) and thus bear little similarity to the simplified grammar of Esperanto.

ARDEN R. SMITH

Further Reading

Janton, Pierre. *Esperanto: Language, Literature, and Community*. Edited by Humphrey Tonkinand translated by Humphrey Tonkin, Jane Edwards, and Karen Johnson-Weiner. Albany, NY: State University of New York Press, 1993.

Smith, Arden R., and Patrick Wynne. "Tolkien and Esperanto." *SEVEN: An Anglo-American Literary Review* 17 (2000): 27–46.

See also **Languages Invented by Tolkien "A Secret Vice"**

ESSAYS PRESENTED TO CHARLES WILLIAMS

This memorial volume of essays by Dorothy Sayers, J.R.R. Tolkien, C.S. Lewis, Owen Barfield, Gervase Mathew, and W.H. Lewis was edited by C.S. Lewis and published by the Oxford University Press in 1947.

Charles Williams (1886–1945), novelist, poet, playwright, historian, scholar of Dante, lecturer on literature, and professional editor, befriended C.S. Lewis in 1936 when they exchanged letters expressing admiration for each other's books. When the Oxford University Press moved from London to Oxford in 1939, Williams joined the Inklings group that met in Lewis's rooms at Magdalen College, and was a frequent participant for five years. When Williams failed to regain consciousness after an intestinal operation and died unexpectedly on May 15, 1945, C.S. Lewis's brother, Warnie Lewis, wrote in his diary "The blackout has fallen, and the Inklings can never be the same again" (*Brothers & Friends* 182). In his Preface to the book, C.S. Lewis emphasizes

Williams's learning, courteousness, playfulness, flamboyant yet unaffected manners, and love of ritual, and says "he gave to every circle the whole man: all his attention, knowledge, courtesy, charity, were placed at your disposal." (x)

Dorothy Sayers: "'. . . And Telling you a Story'"

Sayers's essay is a panegyric on Dante. She wrote it amid the joy of early enthusiasm, for she was still in the first stages of her extraordinary translation of *La Divina Commedia*, which remained unfinished at her death in 1957. She speaks of her early reluctance to read Dante and of her astonishment when she did: "the plain fact is that I bolted my meals, neglected my sleep, work, and correspondence, drove my friends crazy . . . until I had panted my way through the Three Realms of the Dead" (2). She then examines and praises Dante's story-telling ability ("the most incomparable story-teller who ever set pen to paper" (2)), the poem's structure ("What Dante in fact does is to take the whole thing and cram it, as though into a steel corset, into three sets of concentric and similar rings" (7)), its style ("The miracle of the style is its fluidity – it moves like water, taking on every contour of the great rock-sculptured mass over which it flows" (15)), the realism of the allegorical figures ("Cerberus is not simply a projection of gluttonous desire; he is a dog" (17)), the realism of Beatrice ("she is *that* real woman: the same Florentine girl who once made fun of Dante at a party, who once cut him in the street, whose mere presence in the city filled him with inexplicable anguish and ecstasy" (18)), the appropriateness of the first-person narrative ("It enables him to dissect himself with almost alarming acuteness and candour" (20)), the poem's humor ("There are, at every turn, lines and similes through which irrepressible little chuckles bubble up" (21)), the similes ("from first to last they are earthy, homely, and concrete" (35)), and she closes by commenting on the "massive unity" and "architectural beauty which is the poem's chief glory." (36)

Tolkien: "On Fairy-Stories"

Tolkien's essay was an expansion of a lecture he gave at the University of St. Andrews on March 8, 1939. For a detailed discussion, see the entry "On Fairy-Stories."

C.S. Lewis: "On Stories"

Lewis attempts to define the nature of the literary experience of story, in particular, the kind of pleasure we experience in reading "those forms in which everything else is there for the sake of the story" (90). Lewis argues that in the best stories "the *plot* . . . is only really a net whereby to catch something else," a theme "that has no sequence in it" and that is "something other than a process and much more like a state or quality" (103). Lewis is not interested in the traditional satisfactions derived from a well-told tale, such as the sheer excitement and suspense associated with thrillers and cliff-hangers; he is after a subtler quality that can only be called Platonic. To illustrate his point, he discusses diverse stories that, in his view, are nets that succeed, wholly or partly, to catch and "hold the bird" (105). For example, the folktale "Jack the Giant-Killer," is not "simply the story of a clever hero surmounting danger" because "the whole quality of the imaginative response is determined by the fact that the enemies are giants" and "that heaviness, that monstrosity, that uncouthness, hangs over the whole thing" (94). Other successes Lewis analyzes are H. Rider Haggard's *King Solomon's Mines*, H.G. Wells's *First Men in the Moon*, Homer's *Odyssey*, David Lindsay's *Voyage to Arcturus*, Kenneth Grahame's *Wind in the Willows*, Sophocles' *Oedipus Rex*, Tolkien's *The Hobbit*, E.R. Eddison's *The Worm Ouroboros* and Zimiamvian novels, the short stories of Walter de La Mare, and William Morris's *The Well at the World's End*.

It is a bold thing for a writer who matured in the age of Eliot and Pound to elevate "story" above other literary qualities, such as style or intellectual content. While Lewis is not alone (he finds sympathetic, critical precursors in Aristotle, Boccaccio, and Jung), there is an undercurrent of polemic in his efforts, couched as they are in an avuncular style. Some of Lewis' examples are from genres that have been routinely despised and ignored by the literary power-brokers: children's literature, fantasy, science fiction. Lewis' essay is a provocative protest to this omission. It is also a marvelous defense of literature in an age in which literature has been all but denuded of respectability by the various hermeneutists of suspicion, for Lewis provides an articulate definition of the pleasures of reading. These pleasures, and the desire for them, exist already in the reader's mind: when, for example, a reader encounters a title such as *The Well at the World's End*, his imagination already knows and longs for a story that will fulfill the expectations raised by that title. Lewis believes that reading a good story is not unlike religious experience because "In life and art both . . . we are always trying to catch in our net of successive moments something that is not successive" (105). Reading provides us with the delight of enjoying a quality or state of being that, conscious or not, we already crave—we yearn for poetry's unheard music, the suggested delights of a novel's untold story. That a handful of works actually make good on their promise is a reason to keep on reading.

Owen Barfield: "Poetic Diction and Legal Fiction"

In an essay that could be an appendix to his seminal *Poetic Diction*, Barfield discusses the creation of meaning through the process of making metaphors. Based on the German word "tarnung," Barfield coins the term "tarning" to refer to this process. He demonstrates tarning in verse, and then asserts that it is seen most clearly in the small metaphoric expressions we use everyday: "We all speak of *clear* heads, of *brilliant* wit, of *seeing* somebody's meaning, of so and so being *the pick of the bunch*." Barfield then observes that "We seem to owe all these tropes and metaphors embedded in language to the fact that somebody at some time had the wit to say one thing and mean another, and that somebody else had the wit to tumble to the new meaning, to detect the bouquet of a new wine emanating from the old bottle" (113).

In all the examples the tarning has already occurred. To slow the process and see it at work, Barfield discusses the creation and use of legal fictions, personified abstractions, such as the creation of a corporation as a "person" that can sue and be sued. Barfield analogizes that legal fictions operate in law to create new conditions of social life, usually in response to new circumstances, in the same way that metaphors operate in language to create new meaning, usually in response to new ideas.

Barfield strengthens his analogy by observing the paradox that exists in both law and language: both must have constant meanings to operate effectively and be comprehended, and yet both must be flexible to meet the needs of changing social conditions. Addressing the paradox in language, Barfield comes to the heart of his essay. "Logic presupposes first and foremost that the same word means the same thing in one sentence as it does another . . . repetition is inherent in the very meaning of the word 'meaning.'" But, if a person, in response to changing life, has "something new to say, something new to mean," that person "must use language – a vehicle that presupposes that he must either mean what was meant before or talk nonsense!" To break out of constancy and create new meaning, we must "resort to tarning" and make "that which was hitherto unconscious" conscious by saying "what is nonsense on the face of it, but in such a way that the recipient may have the new meaning suggested to him" (123). In Barfield's view, the making of metaphors is the source of the inherent adaptability of language to meet new conditions, and it is why Aristotle called metaphor "the 'most important'" of the figures available to the poet.

Gervase Mathew: "Marriage and *Amour Courtois* in Late Fourteenth-Century England"

In a brief but learned essay that reflects careful reading of French and English texts from the 12th to 15th centuries, Mathew argues that the romantic ideals of courtly love, which included service, courtesy, and constancy, but which, in the 12th century, were aspects of adulterous and forbidden love, became united with the ideals of marriage by the age of Chaucer. Mathew is careful to say that the union exists in literature but that "there can never be sufficient evidence to determine the exact extent to which the ideal of love and marriage in the romances either influenced or reflected contemporary social custom" (134).

W.H. Lewis: "The Galleys of France"

An expert in French history, Warnie Lewis illuminates details of primary accounts to give a horrifyingly vivid picture of the 17th century galériens and the cruel galleys they inhabited, which, "until the coming of the concentration camp . . . held an undisputed pre-eminence as the darkest blot on Western civilization" (136). Lewis sees the galley, with "all its gilded splendour and hidden misery" as a symbol of the age of Louis XIV. The starved and flogged convicts who worked the crowded galleys lived "literally in close contact with each other until the end of their days" and "ceased to be men" as they became mere extensions of the oars. (140) In closing, Lewis reminds us, "there is a tendency . . . to assume that because a man is ill-treated, he must be a good fellow," but the "in our indignation against the whole system," we should not waste sympathy on the galérien because the 17th century criminal, perpetrator of horrors and atrocities, "is not a sympathetic object."

CHARLES H. FISCHER and PAUL EDMUND THOMAS

Primary Sources

Lewis, C.S., editor. *Essays Presented to Charles Williams*. Grand Rapids, MI: William B. Eerdmans, 1966.

Further Reading

Barfield, Owen. *History in English Words*. London: Faber & Faber, 1953.
———. *Poetic Diction: A Study in Meaning*. London: Faber & Gwyer, 1928.
Carpenter, Humphrey. *The Inklings: C.S. Lewis, J.R.R. Tolkien, Charles Williams, and Their Friends*. London: George Allen & Unwin, 1978.
———. *Tolkien: A Biography*. Boston, MA: Houghton Mifflin Company, 1977.
Dante Alighieri. *The Comedy of Dante Alighieri, The Florentine: Cantica I, Hell*. Sayers, Dorothy L., Translator. Harmondsworth, Middlesex: Penguin Books, 1949.

————. *The Comedy of Dante Alighieri, The Florentine: Cantica II, Purgatory.* Sayers, Dorothy L., trans. Harmondsworth, Middlesex: Penguin Books, 1955.

————. *The Comedy of Dante Alighieri, The Florentine: Cantica III, Paradise.* Reynolds, Barbara and Sayers, Dorothy L., Translators. Harmondsworth, Middlesex: Penguin Books, 1962.

Lewis, C.S. *The Allegory of Love: A Study in Medieval Tradition.* Oxford: Clarendon Press, 1936.

————. *Dymer.* London: J.M. Dent, 1926.

————. *English Literature in the Sixteenth Century, Excluding Drama.* Oxford: Clarendon Press, 1954.

————. *The Great Divorce: A Dream.* London: Geoffrey Bles, 1946.

————. *A Preface to 'Paradise Lost.'* Oxford: Oxford University Press, 1942 J.M. Dent, 1926.

————. *The Screwtape Letters.* London: Geoffrey Bles, 1942.

————. *Till We Have Faces: A Myth Retold.* London: Geoffrey Bles, 1956.

Lewis, W.H. *Brothers & Friends: The Diaries of Major Warren Hamilton Lewis.* Kilby, Clyde S. and Mead, Marjorie Lamp, Editors. San Francisco, CA: Harper & Row, 1982.

————. *The Splendid Century: Some Aspects of French Life in the Reign of Louis XIV.* London: Eyre & Spottiswoode, 1953.

————. *The Sunset of the Splendid Century: The Life and Times of Louis Auguste de Bourbon, Duc de Maine, 1670–1736.* London: Eyre & Spottiswoode, 1953.

Mathew, Gervase. *The Court of Richard II.* London: John Murray, 1968.

Williams, Charles. *All Hallows' Eve.* London: Faber & Faber, 1945.

————. *The Figure of Beatrice: A Study in Dante.* London: Faber & Faber, 1943.

————. *The Place of the Lion.* London: Victor Gollancz, 1931.

————. *Taliessin Through Logres, The Region of the Summer Stars, and Arthurian Torso.* Grand Rapids, MI: William B. Eerdmans, 1974.

————. *War in Heaven.* London: Victor Gollancz, 1930.

See also **Allegory; Barfield, Owen; Catholicism, Roman; Chaucer, Geoffrey; Children's Literature and Tolkien; Christianity; Coghill, Nevill; Eucatastrophe; Fall of Man; Folklore; Homer; Inklings; Lewis, C.S.; Lewis, W.H.; Literary Context, 20th Century; Literature, Twentieth Century: Influence of Tolkien; Manuscripts, Medieval; Mathew, Gervase; Mythology for England; "On Fairy-Stories"; Oxford; Sayers, Dorothy; Tolkien, Christopher; Williams, Charles**

ESTATE

The Tolkien Estate represents the children of J.R.R. Tolkien regarding their financial and legal rights to his writings. The Estate controls the copyrights for all of Tolkien's fiction, poetry, letters, published drafts such as the volumes of *The History of Middle-earth,* and unpublished works. It has a well-deserved reputation for enforcing its copyrights with vigor. The Estate has been involved over the years in often controversial legal disputes with people attempting to use names and other trademarks from Tolkien's writings. Although the Estate is officially executed by Christopher Tolkien (the youngest of Tolkien's surviving children), it does not do business directly with anyone seeking licensing permissions but typically grants or denies them either through its representatives at HarperCollins UK or through its legal counsel, Cathleen Blackburn at the London firm Manches LLP. Blackburn is a specialist in intellectual property law who represents a variety of high-profile clients, including a number of libraries and museums and other authors and publishers. Recently, Christopher Tolkien and the Estate founded the Tolkien Copyright Trust, whose function is to protect the copyright and the interests of the Estate in perpetuity.

There has sometimes been confusion over the ownership of Tolkien's copyrights because of the two unrelated entities that hold them: the Tolkien Estate and Tolkien Enterprises. Tolkien Enterprises is owned not by the Tolkien family but by the American film and music mogul Saul Zaentz. Zaentz has produced many award-winning films, including *One Flew Over the Cuckoo's Nest, Amadeus, The Unbearable Lightness of Being,* and *The English Patient,* and he produced Ralph Bakshi's 1978 animated film of *The Lord of the Rings.* Zaentz's Tolkien Enterprises holds marketing and licensing rights for the titles *The Hobbit* and *The Lord of the Rings,* as well as proper names and short phrases from those books. Tolkien Enterprises also owns all stage and cinema rights to the books. It licensed New Line Cinema to produce Peter Jackson's recent film trilogy, as well as licensing a musical version of the trilogy now in production in Toronto. The enormous quantity of film merchandise that has been marketed in the past few years has all been licensed by Tolkien Enterprises. The Estate was not involved in any way in the films or in the musical. The Estate was, apparently, invited to be involved in the films but declined.

The Tolkien Estate, by contrast, owns the licensing rights to all of Tolkien's other writings, both published and unpublished, and the copyrights to the text of all of Tolkien's writings, including *The Hobbit* and *The Lord of the Rings.* It authorizes editions of Tolkien's writings and monitors books and other writings about Tolkien for possible copyright infringement. Due to Tolkien's great popularity, the Estate has frequently acted to protect its copyright from people that it has perceived to be attempting to breach it. This process has become more complicated since the explosion of the Internet and its many Tolkien fan sites. For example, in early 2004, the estate successfully sued a Canadian company that had registered the Internet domain name jrrtolkien.

com. In 2002, by contrast, the Estate brought but later dropped a lawsuit against author and self-publisher Michael W. Perry, who had written a book-length chronology of *The Lord of the Rings*. The Tolkien Estate has, as a result of these and similar legal actions, developed a reputation among some for being unreasonable; however, given Tolkien's immense popularity and the enormous potential for copyright abuse, its vigor in protecting its rights is understandable.

CHESTER N. SCOVILLE

See also **Bakshi, Ralph; Jackson, Peter; Merchandising; Tolkien, Christopher; Tolkien, Priscilla**

EUCATASTROPHE

Eucatastrophe is a concept that Tolkien introduced in his Andrew Lang lecture at the University of St. Andrews, titled "On Fairy-stories," describing the effect that he felt the "fairy story," or fantasy, ideally has on the reader. According to Tolkien, fairy stories have the capacity to lead to the "imaginative satisfaction" of profound human desires, among others the "escape from death," but he concludes that of much greater importance "is the Consolation of the Happy Ending." He defines eucatastrophe as "the good catastrophe, the sudden joyous 'turn'" and coined the term to mean the opposite of tragedy, "the true form of Drama." The dénouement of a tragedy is known as the catastrophe; consequently Tolkien adds a prefix to create a noun that literally means "a happy or fortunate ending" (cf. Northup, 831).

The concept has a good deal in common with comedy as it was understood in the Middle Ages, where, as Francesca Murphy puts it: "The hero ascends toward a community of love. He uses prudence and discernment to reach it. He suffers as much as the tragic hero; he struggles against evil forces. But the swing of the comic plot hauls him up" (7). Suffering on the part of the hero, the possible experience of both "sorrow and failure," is accepted by Tolkien and termed "dyscatastrophe," but eucatastrophe gives the fullest resolution for fantasy. Part of the imaginative satisfaction of eucatastrophe likewise involves achieving what the author calls "recovery" and "restoration": a sense of defamiliarization of the known world to better appreciate its qualities.

Since the concept is affective, there is no formula for achieving eucatastrophe: of primary significance is attaining the desired emotional effect in the reader. Tolkien claims that in the best fantasy the improbable nature of the story events or plot turns is of secondary

importance as long as "the 'turn' comes." The concept is thus fairly open-ended as far as narrative form is concerned. Moreover, since it relies on a relationship with the reader, this likewise hearkens back to the medieval esthetics, where beauty was understood as that which gives a purer form of delight.

In the lecture of 1939, Tolkien hints at a religious dimension of eucatastrophe through the employment of the telling expression *evangelium* in association with joy. He clarified the idea in the "epilogue" of the printed version of his essay in 1947, wherein he claims that in it there may occur "a far off gleam or echo of *evangelium* in the real world." He explains that the Gospel story of the Incarnation, the life of Christ on Earth, "begins and ends in joy" and is the true eucatastrophe of which those occurring in stories are a manner of premonition. At any rate, with this point the concept becomes closely associated with his concept of "subcreation," which is introduced in the same essay. In subcreation, by telling stories or inventing worlds the artist effectively imitates the "Primary Creator."

This idea is further clarified in a letter of 1944 to his son Christopher in which Tolkien suggests a theology of narrative in relation to eucatastrophe, wherein he claims, "Man the story-teller would have to be redeemed in a manner consonant with his nature: by a moving story" (*Letters*, 100–1). Consequently, since the Primary Creator ultimately intends humans to be happy, the artist that evokes eucatastrophe is creating in consonance with God. Moreover, if the deepest sense of story is consonant with revelation, the concept approaches natural theology with a Christian humanist perspective.

On account of its relationship to fantasy, the idea of eucatastrophe has been treated as something of an artistic manifesto on the part of Tolkien; consequently, it is a useful key to understanding his major fiction. However, because Tolkien's original reflections centered on the fairy story, a short form primarily associated with children's reading, the question arises of how eucatastrophe can be evoked in a modern prose work like the author's *The Lord of the Rings*.

Unsurprisingly, the numerous Christian interpretations of the work draw heavily on the concept of eucatastrophe. For instance, the concluding chapter of Richard Purtill's *J.R.R. Tolkien: Myth, Morality, and Religion*, one of the earlier book-length studies from this perspective, bears the indicative title: "The Sudden Joyous Turn." These discussions generally remain within the framework established by Tolkien. Since in contemporary theology, as in a number of other disciplines, narrative has developed into a prominent matter of reflection, attempts have also been undertaken to enlist the concept for a better understanding of narrative for theology. Regardless of the success of such efforts, a more enriched application of the concept of eucatastrophe likewise seems possible from this perspective for narrative art.

While recognizing the religious implications underlying eucatastrophe, in his analysis of *The Lord of the Rings*, Brian Rosebury concentrates on its humanistic implications. Rosebury reflects on the comic nature of the novel and notes that "the reader must be delighted in Middle-earth in order to care that Sauron does not lay it desolate" (41). Thus the "eucatastrophe is compelling . . . because its optimism is emotionally consonant with the work's pervasive sense of a universe hospitable to the humane" (71). Among others, Tolkien achieves this by the variety of the good—for instance, in the multiculturalism of the benign societies of Middle-earth. From this perspective, evoking a powerful sense of the good life based on its diversity undergirds the attainment of the correct emotional tenor and its resolution in the work; the concept of eucatastrophe thus becomes enriched in Tolkien's opus. Because the question of human flourishing has returned to a number of fields of public discourse, it becomes evident why this aspect gives Tolkien's work a contemporary ring.

Eucatastrophe is closely connected with hope in both the religious and the humanistic senses. Hope has been defined as the unique human capacity for generating positive expectations concerning the future regardless of present circumstances. Eucatastrophe is most simply understood as a forceful expression of the esthetic fulfillment of hope.

CHRISTOPHER GARBOWSKI

Further Reading

Murphy, Francesca. "The Human and Divine Comedy." Chap. 1 in *The Comedy of Revelation: Paradise Lost and Regained in Biblical Narrative*, 1–28. Edinburgh: T & T Clark, 2000.

Northup, Clyde B. "The Qualities of a Tolkienian Fairy-Story." *Modern Fiction Studies* 50, no. 4 (2004): 814–37.

Purtill, Richard. *J.R.R. Tolkien: Myth, Morality, and Religion*. San Francisco, CA: Harper & Row, 1981.

Rosebury, Brian. *Tolkien: A Cultural Phenomenon*. Hampshire: Palgrave Macmillan, 2003.

See also **Comedy; "On Fairy-Stories"; Theological and Moral Approaches in Tolkien's Works**

EUCHARIST

Tolkien's understanding of the Eucharist is expressed most clearly in a letter of November 1963 to his son Michael. Tolkien there emphasized the importance of will to faith and stated: "The only cure for sagging of faith is Communion. Though always Itself, perfect and complete and inviolate, the Blessed Sacrament does not operate completely and once for all in any of us. Like the act of Faith, it must be continuous and grow by exercise. Frequency is of the highest effect." He thereby expressed the Catholic doctrines that a sacrament operates *ex opere operato* and *ex opere operantis* and that it sustains and augments the supranatural life of the soul. While he did not explicitly mention the recipient's union with Christ as the main effect of the Eucharist, this is implied in this letter too.

For the most part of his life, Tolkien tried to attend Mass daily. He explained that by the mercy of God that he never has fallen out of his love with the Blessed Sacrament. Furthermore, Tolkien was convinced that Christ plainly intended to put the Blessed Sacrament in the prime place. In a letter of March 1941 to Michael, he calls it "the one great thing to love on earth" and continues that there one will find "the true way of all your loves upon earth, and more than that: Death: by the divine paradox, that which ends life, and demands the surrender of all, and yet by the taste (or foretaste) of which alone can what you seek in your earthly relationships (love, faithfulness, joy) be maintained, or take on that complexion of reality, of eternal endurance, which every man's heart desires." The nexus between Eucharist and Death might be surprising but perhaps hints at the sacrificial character of the Eucharist, because on the one hand the sacrifice of Christ is remembered, and on the other hand the congregation prays to become an offering in Christ. Furthermore, the belief of the Communion as pledge of the coming resurrection is present.

Since Tolkien's expressed convictions are harmonious with the Catholic doctrine of his time, it seems rather unlikely that *lembas* is a conscious reference to the Eucharist, although many critics point out the similarities between both in feeding the will, and so on. In a letter to Deborah Webster, Tolkien mentioned a critic who saw in *lembas* a derivation of the Eucharist and added, "(That is: far greater things may colour the mind in dealing with the lesser things of a fairy-story.)" But there are great differences between *lembas* and the Eucharist: the Eucharist was instituted by Christ; it is not only used for journeys or "the hurt whose life was in peril" ("Of Lembas," "Peoples," 404); it has to be received in a service; it is intended for all Men and not restricted to the Elves and few exceptions; and in some cases a confession is necessary before receiving communion. While a certain similarity to the effects of the Eucharist and the effects of *lembas* is possible, it seems not a central one, although in "Quenya it was most often named *coimas* which is 'life-bread'" ("On Lembas").

THOMAS FORNET-PONSE

Further Reading

Birzer, Bradley J. *J.R.R. Tolkien's Sanctifying Myth: Understanding Middle-earth.* Wilmington, DE: ISI Books, 2002.

Caldecott, Stratford. *Secret Fire: The Spiritual Vision of J.R.R. Tolkien.* London: Darton, Longman & Todd, 2003.

Pearce, Joseph, ed. *Tolkien: A Celebration.* London: HarperCollins, 1999.

See also **Catholicism, Roman; Christ; Christianity; Food; Resurrection**

EXILE

The concept of exile in Tolkien's works derives partly from the legacy of Anglo-Saxon culture and literature. Historical records attest to exile not only as a legal punishment for crime but also as a state in which a retainer might find himself bereft of kin, lord, and community as a result of war or treachery. Such a separation of the individual from hearth and companions severed more than access to simple material comforts of food and shelter; exile also ruptured the social and emotional foundations upon which family honor, personal reputation, and future fulfillment were built. In Old English literature, typically the theme of exile is accompanied by *ubi sunt* imagery, in which lost hall-joys and absent companions are enumerated and lamented, and ruined halls serve as testimonies to the transitory nature of earthly life. While many Old English literary and religious works employ the exile motif, perhaps the most central witnesses to the theme are *The Seafarer* and *The Wanderer.* These short, elegiac poems offer the dramatic monologues of speakers identified as exiles who contemplate their present state and seek consolation for their hardships by looking beyond the mutabilities of mortal life toward an everlasting life with God.

While the Old English theme of exile is most often associated with a lone survivor or solitary pilgrim, the Anglo-Saxons also understood that groups of people might endure a shared state of exile as a result of political feud or geographic displacement. One model for this type of exile may be found in the biblical story of Exodus, a story retold in an Old English poem that was edited by Tolkien and published posthumously in 1981. In addition, from a spiritual standpoint, as both *The Wanderer* and *The Seafarer* suggest, the transient nature of the temporal world exiles all humans from the constancy of their true homeland in heaven. Like the Old English texts with which he was so familiar, Tolkien's fiction frequently explores exile through peoples sundered from communities central to their heritage. Foremost among the races presented as exiles in Middle-earth are Noldor Elves, who were expelled from their beloved homeland in the Undying Lands for disobeying the Valar and killing some of their Elven kindred. As a result of these events narrated in *The Silmarillion,* the sudden and painful change in the Noldor's fortune and their loss of former glory echo themes of exile common in the Old English elegies. One of these Noldor, Gildor, the leader of the Elves the Hobbits first meet in the woods in *The Fellowship of the Ring,* specifically refers to his people as exiles in Middle-earth. Other groups or races that Tolkien describes as serving in exile because of the poor choices made by their leaders are Thorin Oakenshield's band of Dwarves in *The Hobbit,* the Númenóreans in *The Silmarillion* and *The Unfinished Tales,* and the Dúnedain in *The Lord of the Rings.* Even though they were not displaced from their ancestral homeland as are some of Tolkien's other races, the Ents also may be considered exiles because their separation from the Entwives is portrayed as an emotional state, much like that described of the Old English exiles, in which they mourn the loss of their female counterparts and despair of regaining the completeness of community they once provided.

Tolkien also incorporates exile themes with individual characters. Aragorn, for instance, is initially portrayed as an exile wandering in the wilds without home, physical comfort, or companionship. As *The Lord of the Rings* unfolds, Aragorn is further described, like the speaker in *The Seafarer* especially, as a Man bereft of the former glories of his people who chooses a self-imposed exile from his homeland and friends. In *The Fellowship of the Ring,* the four Hobbits also voluntarily go into exile from their beloved Shire when they undertake the journey to destroy the Ring. In characteristic exile fashion, at some point in the text, Tolkien has each of the Hobbits articulate a longing for the simple pleasures and pastoral life of his home. Even after Frodo returns to the Shire, his experiences in exile have so changed his state of mind that he continues to perceive himself as distanced from his home and community. Recalling the conclusions reached by the exiles in *The Wanderer* and *The Seafarer,* however, Tolkien allows Frodo to realize an eternal permanence beyond the confines of Middle-earth when he sails with the Elves into the Undying Lands at the end of *The Return of the King.*

LESLIE A. DONOVAN

Further Reading

Alexander, Michael. *A History of Old English Literature*. Peterborough, ON: Broadview, 2002.

Crossley-Holland, Kevin, trans. *The Seafarer*. In *The Anglo-Saxon World: An Anthology*, 53–55. Oxford: Oxford University Press, 1999.

———, trans. *The Wanderer*. In *The Anglo-Saxon World: An Anthology*, 50–52. Oxford: Oxford University Press, 1999.

Fell, Christine. "Perceptions of Transience." In *The Cambridge Companion to Old English Literature*, edited by Malcolm Godden and Michael Lapidge. Cambridge: Cambridge University Press, 1991.

Gordon, Ida L., ed. *The Seafarer*. London: Methuen, 1960.

Greenfield, Stanley B. *Hero and Exile: The Art of Old English Poetry*. Edited by George H. Brown. London: Hambledon, 1989.

Krapp, George Phillip, and Elliot Van Kirk Dobbie, eds. *The Seafarer*. In *The Exeter Book*. Anglo-Saxon Poetic Records, vol. 3, pp. 143–47. New York: Cambridge University Press, 1936.

———, eds. *The Wanderer*. In *The Exeter Book*. Anglo-Saxon Poetic Records, vol. 3, pp. 134–37. New York: Cambridge University Press, 1936.

O'Brien O'Keeffe, Katherine, ed. *Old English Shorter Poems: Basic Readings*. New York: Garland Publishing, 1994.

Senior, W.A. "Loss Eternal in J.R.R. Tolkien's Middle-earth." In *J.R.R. Tolkien and His Literary Resonances: Views of Middle-earth*, edited by George Clark and Daniel Timmons, 173–82. Contributions to the Study of Science Fiction and Fantasy, 89. Westport, CT: Greenwood, 2000.

Tolkien, J.R.R. *The Old English Exodus*. Text, translation, and commentary by J.R.R. Tolkien. Edited by Joan Turville-Petre. Oxford: Oxford University Press, 1981.

See also **Aragorn; Christian Readings of Tolkien; Elves; Ents;** *Exodus,* **Edition of; Frodo; Hobbits; Legolas; Men, Middle-earth;** *Seafarer;* **Thorin;** *Wanderer*

EXISTENTIALISM

It is extremely unlikely that Tolkien had anything more than an anecdotal familiarity with the major twentieth-century existentialist thinkers Martin Heidegger (1889–1976) and Jean-Paul Sartre (1905–80), and he certainly did not share the former's prewar fascism and the latter's communism. However, some of the major themes in his work clearly echo some of the concerns of these thinkers. Overall, this may be because all three writers are concerned with how meaning is to be made in the modern world. Here I will discuss only three issues: authenticity, technology, and language.

Both Heidegger and Sartre were much concerned by the question of "authenticity": like much in existentialist thought, this central concept is at once extremely complex and—because it's something that each of us experiences in our daily life—quite simple. For both thinkers, authenticity is what marks each of us as ourselves, living a life of our own on which we have reflected. Heidegger, indeed, describes a state of being in thrall to the "they-self" of received opinion and attitudes from which one must try to escape. Similarly, it is possible to see Tolkien's work as a meditation on making authentic decisions. However, where, for example, Sartre might see such decisions as running against social convention, for Tolkien these decisions are often in support of the society: when, for example, Théoden, decides to fulfil his oath and ride to the aid of Minas Tirith, this is an authentic choice, regardless of whether society approves of it or not.

Heidegger and Tolkien also share a concern with the problem of technology in the modern world. For Heidegger, the development of technology was more than the encroachment of machines into nature. Rather, "technological thinking" is a way of engaging with the world, including plants, creatures, and people, that sees living beings solely as tools or resources to be used. Clearly, in *The Lord of the Rings* Sauron and more explicitly Saruman are examples of this. Indeed, the Ring and its evil might be seen simply as the "spirit of technology." For example, its power of invisibility means that the possessor need not engage with people as people but can simply avoid them, as one might avoid a heedless object, and so reduce them to objects. In contrast, Heidegger and Tolkien both tried (in different ways) to rediscover ways of being in the world that did not do this. For example, in Lothlórien, Frodo touches a tree climbing to a flet: "Never before had he been so suddenly and keenly aware of the feel and texture of the tree's skin and of the life within it. He felt a delight in the wood and the touch of it, neither as forester nor as carpenter, it was the delight of the living tree itself" (*FR,* ii, VI, 460–61). Here, Frodo engages with the tree not as a resource to be cut down, or preserved, but simply as its being as a tree.

Finally, there is a complex relationship between language and the world for both Heidegger and Tolkien. Language, as many twentieth-century philosophers have argued, is more than a means to convey information: Stanley Cavell puts it like this: "In 'learning language' you learn not merely what the names of things are, but what a name is . . . not merely what the word for 'father' is but what a father is; not merely what the word for 'love' is, but what love is." Language, that is, conveys a world. In Tolkien, too, there is something of this: language, and languages, does not simply exist to convey information. It shapes the views that peoples share and makes the world. As Tom Shippey argues, Tolkien believed "there might often be a close connection between thing-signified, person-signifying and language signified-in." But language has an even more significant role. In his influential "Letter on Humanism" from 1945, Heidegger posits a profound but hard-to-explain—indeed, it is often seen as a mystical—relationship between what to be and language. Man, he writes, is the "shepherd of Being"—meaning that we have responsibility towards our own (perhaps communal) being, and this is constituted in language: "Language is the language of Being as clouds are the clouds of the sky." There is a sense of responsibility that exists between the peoples in Tolkien's fiction and their languages and in the passing down of those languages, stories, songs, and worlds: indeed, if Sauron obtained the Ring, as Sam says, "there'll be no more songs" (*TT*, IV, x, 430). In part, this sense of "stewarding" accounts for the complex relationship between melancholy (at the passing of things) and hope (at their preservation and passing on through time) that characterises Tolkien's work.

ROBERT EAGLESTONE

Further Reading

Shippey, Tom. *The Road to Middle-earth: How J.R.R. Tolkien Created a New Mythology.* Revised and Expanded edition. Boston, MA: Houghton Mifflin, 2003.

See also **Language, Theories of; Environmentalism and Eco-Criticism**

EXODUS, EDITION OF

Tolkien, as is well known, taught Old English language and literature. One of the texts that he taught often during the 1930s and 1940s is the *Old English Exodus.* According to Humphrey Carpenter (139), he intended to produce an edition of the poem, "and indeed he nearly completed this task, but it was never finished to his satisfaction."

The *Old English Exodus* is a poem of 590 lines included in a single manuscript, Oxford, Bodleian's MS Junius 11. The poem is a fascinating combination of the heroic tradition stemming from the Germanic culture of the Anglo-Saxons and the biblical and patristic traditions imported with Christianity from Rome. The poet relates the story of Israel's departure over the Red Sea out of Egypt, but only the outlines of the story are followed; much of the poem is creative invention based on patristic commentary.

In 1981, a former student of Tolkien's, and a scholar of renown in her own right, Joan Turville-Petre, published Tolkien's notes, edition, and partial translation of the poem. Tolkien began the edition in 1925 and never completed it. Turville-Petre used Tolkien's notes for his lectures during the 1930s and 1940s, with some revisions by Tolkien to the notes in the 1950s, no doubt in preparation for Tolkien's own planned edition. The editor is careful to note that what is now published was never intended as an edition, so the problems of the text derive from its unfinished nature. The edition consists of Tolkien's text with critical apparatus, Tolkien's translation of the poem up to line 505, and Tolkien's commentary on the text comprising largely discussion of words and emendations.

The poem is notoriously difficult, partly because the copy in the Junius manuscript is incomplete. Tolkien emends several of the readings; some of these changes have been found worthy by subsequent scholars, some not so. Of the latter type, Tolkien without much justification transposed lines and sections of the poem, such as lines 43–44 and 49, and with justification transposed lines 93–107 and 108–24, a long-standing problem in the poem in Tolkien's day. Often Tolkien takes the scribe to task. His commentary on lines 46–47 of the edition remarks that *on helle* in the line is "nonsensical" ("nonsense" and the like seem to be favorite words and the most significant censure) and that the opposition of heaven and hell in these lines is scribal invention and so not part of the original poem. Similarly, at line 253 Tolkien says that the word *beohata* is a "scribal falsehood." Other changes that Tolkien makes in the text are designed to make the poem readable for students. Thus, Tolkien "fixes" a number of forms and "misspellings," such as at line 79 *dægscealdes* has been emended to *-sceld.*

As a creative writer himself, Tolkien has a feel for the beauty and language of the poetry. Regarding lines 81–85 he says, "The artistry of the language here should affect our judgment of the apparent confusions in the passage beginning 93ff." At line 71 he remarks on the "queer, strained language," and he calls the speech of Abraham "well-constructed" at line 418ff. Other passages could be mentioned in this regard, but these comments alone illustrate Tolkien's appreciation of the artistry of the poet in contrast to what he calls the failures of the scribe.

The translation is mostly, though not entirely, based on the edition. Tolkien's emendations to the text are not always reflected in the translation. Overall, however, the translation not only is good English prose but also renders the original in creative and fascinating ways, giving the reader a genuine feel of the original. At line 115b, *Heofoncandel barn* becomes "the torch of Heaven blazed," and at line 482 *Lagu land gefeol, Lyft wæs onhrered* is translated as "sea fell back on the land, the sky was shaken." A personal favorite is the use of the form "blent" as the past tense of "blend" to render *geblanden* in line 476.

Tolkien's teaching and notes on *Exodus* have had some impact on subsequent scholarship. The most notable to date is Peter Lucas's edition of the same poem, published in 1977, four years before

Turville-Petre's. Lucas accepts a number of Tolkien's emendations and thus has influenced subsequent scholarship on the poem. Even some of Tolkien's unnecessary emendations are accepted; for example, at line 280 *nu* (now) becomes *hu* (how), and later at line 518b in the Tolkien text the poem's *dægweorc nemnað* (day's deeds invoked) becomes *dægweorc ne mað* (day's deeds were not hidden). The latter is unnecessary, though in Tolkien's translation it comes across well: "the deeds of that day he did not in silence keep." Lucas acknowledges his debt to Tolkien's lectures in the introduction to his edition.

Another former student of Tolkien's, Bruce Mitchell, praises highly Tolkien's translation of the poem. He also reflects on Tolkien as a teacher, relating that at the end of the first term he recalls Tolkien apologizing to the class for not having arrived yet at the Red Sea (line 134). He recommends Tolkien's translation at least twice in his magisterial *An Invitation to Old English and Anglo-Saxon England.*

Exodus seems to have influenced Tolkien's creative work as well. One place that has been clearly demonstrated is the development of the Balrogs. The poem mentions *Sigelwara land,* the land of the Sigelware. Usually, this is taken as a reference to the Ethiopians. Tolkien thought that this was an error and that the name should be **sigel-hearwa.* He argued in a two-part essay that this name should be understood as a fire giant: *sigle* is a word for the "sun" (and the name of the rune "s") and could mean "jewel." The second element of the compound name *hearwa* Tolkien argued was cognate with Latin *carbo,* "soot." Thus, the name means something like "sun-soot" and in pre-Christian Old English would have referred to Múspell, the Old Norse fire giant who brings about Ragnarök. The Sigelware, then, are the children of the fire giant: gigantic, fiery, deadly, and destructive. The similarity between this interpretation of the word on Tolkien's part and the Balrogs is apparent.

Coupled with this is the conflation of the meanings and forms of *sigel, sigle, sigil* as "sun, jewel." Surely this must lie behind Tolkien's concept of the Silmarils, jewels that capture the light of the main light source in Arda. One of these jewels is now a star, like the sun, in the heavens on the brow of Eärendil, an influence from another Old English poem. Less fearsome, but only in difference of degree, is the Orc chieftain who stabs Frodo in Moria with "swart-face, red tongue, and 'eyes like coals,'" a description that would fit both the Sigelware as Ethiopians (or at least medieval conceptions of them in literature) and the Sigelware as offspring of the fire giant.

This is not the only place where such influence may be felt. One of the themes of the poem is hopelessness. The children of Israel are caught between the Red Sea on one side and the enemy host on the other, "their lands canopied with a cloudy veil." "Now were the hearts of men without hope, when they saw from the southward ways the army of Pharaoh marching on, their crests like a forest moving, their cavalry shining, their banners towering. . . . The people of Israel were in despair" (from Tolkien's translation). Careful readers will notice that several of the battle scenes in *The Lord of the Rings* bear a striking resemblance to this description. Like the Israelites in *Exodus,* one army, the good guys, is caught between a natural barrier (in *Exodus,* the Red Sea; in *The Lord of the Rings,* against the mountains of the Hornburg and the White Mountains behind the city of Minas Tirith), and a host of enemies, rank upon rank, are arrayed against them under cover of a cloudy darkness. And in both *Exodus* and *The Lord of the Rings* there is a figure both powerful and martial, sent by the divine, who speaks hope and in the end opens the way for victory.

The parallel is especially to be seen in the Battle of the Hornburg whereas in the poem, there is a night's respite from harrowing by the enemy force, but at dawn the Israelites are delivered by an opening in the sea. And in each case when the form of deliverance is noticed by the army of the heroes, they are afraid. Until, that is, Moses and Gandalf tell them to not fear and go through the waves or the trees. It would seem that Tolkien adapted the narrative of the *Exodus* to *The Lord of the Rings* in ways similar to his adaptation of *Beowulf.*

Other moments in *The Lord of the Rings* also recall the *Old English Exodus.* When Frodo faces the Nine Riders at the Fords of Bruinen in Book I, the eucatastrophe of the river's destruction of the Black Riders is reminiscent of the water's destruction of pharaoh's army in *Exodus,* as one example.

L.J. SWAIN

Further Reading

Carpenter, Humphrey. *Tolkien: A Biography.* Boston, MA: Houghton Mifflin, 1977.

Lucas, Peter J. *Exodus.* London: Methuen, 1977.

Mitchell, Bruce. *An Invitation to Old English and Anglo-Saxon England.* Oxford: Blackwell, 1995.

Shippey, Tom. *The Road to Middle-earth: How J.R.R. Tolkien Created a New Mythology.* Revised and Expanded edition. Boston, MA: Houghton Mifflin, 2003.

Tolkien, J.R.R. *The Old English Exodus.* Text, translation, and commentary by J.R.R. Tolkien. Edited by Joan Turville-Petre. Oxford: Clarendon, 1981.

———. "Sigelwara Land" [1]. *Medium Aevum* 1, no. 3 (December 1932): 183–96.

———. "Sigelwara Land" [2]. *Medium Aevum* 3, no. 2 (June 1934): 95–111.

See also **Bible; Old English; Publications, Posthumous**

F

FAËRIE

Faërie (or Faery or Fayery—his spelling varied over time) was an idea of central importance to Tolkien's imagination and his art. His essential concept never altered, that the word did not denote a supernatural creature but rather a supernatural region of enchantment and strange adventure. However, the rationale behind the concept and the exact nature of the supernatural region underwent shifts and changes over the course of time. Furthermore, his creative depictions of Faërie tended to outpace his rational explications of it. Despite his declaration that "Faërie cannot be caught in a net of words," he never stopped trying to do just that—more effectively in his imaginative depictions than in his critical analyses. In his fiction, Tolkien's words netted marvelous and believable Faërie worlds for his readers and for his characters to appreciate—the playful yet increasingly dark and mysterious Wild into which Bilbo travels in *The Hobbit,* the perilous regions of Middle-earth with their unforeseen enchantments and dangers that the Hobbits encounter in *The Lord of the Rings,* and the Elf-inhabited mythic world of *The Silmarillion.*

His less creative, more analytic efforts to examine or explain Faërie met with varying degrees of success. Over the course of twenty-five years, he wrote two major essays and part of a third on the subject. These are, in order of their composition, his long critical essay, "On Fairy-stories," written in 1939; his brief unfinished introduction to George MacDonald's story, *The Golden Key,* written in 1964; and its direct outcome, the longer *Smith of Wootton Major,* written

concurrent with the story of the same name from 1964–1966. All are attempts to elucidate what he meant by the term *Faërie,* both for a general readership and for his own clarification. Trying to capture the various shades of meaning in so indefinable a term, he swung, in the two major essays, between apparently contradictory views. In "On Fairy-stories," he made the psychologically defensible argument that Faërie is an effect, an altered state of consciousness brought about by the manipulation of language. In *Smith of Wootton Major,* he took what was for a man of the rational twentieth century the far riskier position that Faërie is or could be an actuality.

Essential as they are for understanding his use of the term, the two essays appear also to be part of an interior debate or process of reflection and self-questioning, an ongoing conversation Tolkien had with himself over the course of some twenty-five years. Their distinct positions notwithstanding, part of this ongoing conversation brought each essay, at one point or another, into argument with itself. "On Fairy-stories" includes the remarkable qualifier: "if elves are true, and really exist independently of our tales about them"; *Smith of Wootton Major* concludes by suggesting that "Faery might be said indeed to represent Imagination." The opposing notions that elves "really exist" and that their world "represents Imagination" could not in either essay be fully reconciled, yet they are held in tension in a mind that could accept the paradox.

"On Fairy-Stories," the earliest, most formal, most academic essay, made what Tolkien felt to be the essential but often-overlooked point that fairy stories are stories not about fairies but about "the *aventures* of men in the Perilous Realm." The word *realm*, as opposed to a more neutral term such as *place*, *country*, or *region*, is worth noting, for it carries clear connotations of rule or dominion by some power. Tolkien cautioned his audience about the perils of this realm, warning that in addition to beauty and enchantment it contained "pitfalls for the unwary and dungeons for the overbold," and by these he meant the readers of the stories as well as the characters in them. He described the world of Faërie as containing all the standard trappings of fairyland— elves, fays, trolls, dwarves, and dragons, as well as the phenomena of the primary world—earth and sea and sky, and most important, "ourselves, mortal men, when we are enchanted" (and here again he meant readers as well as characters). The word *enchanted* is the key to his concept of Faërie in this essay.

Some etymology will help clarify that concept. During the development of his mythology, Tolkien came to reject the modern English word *fairy,* with its connotations of delicacy and prettiness, in favor of the more archaic spelling *faërie* and its deeper, darker implications. This older orthography is formed by the addition of the suffix *erie/ery* to the Old French noun *fay/fae* (fairy). Spelled thus, *faërie* does not refer to a supernatural creature but to a supernatural activity (the act of enchanting) and/or condition (the state of being enchanted). A comparable modern form would be *slavery,* which can mean both the act of enslavement and the condition thus brought about of being enslaved. To push the etymology even farther back, *fay/fae* is derived from Latin *fata* (fate), the past participle of *fari*, "to speak," hence *spoken.* The connection of *faërie* to the spoken word is essential for the understanding of Tolkien's use of the term in "On Fairy-stories," because his concept is predicated on the power of language to enchant not just those within the story but also its hearers or readers.

Tolkien's purpose in the abortive *Golden Key* discussion, where he spelled the word as *fairy,* was essentially the same: to convince the reader of the power and serious meaning of the word. Focused more narrowly on specific usage, his effort here was to correct what he saw as the common misunderstanding and misuse of the word. Addressing its use as an adjective rather than a noun, he gave a series of examples— fairy tale, Fairy Queen, fairyland—where he felt the word should connote power and majesty, even danger.

The last essay to be written, *Smith of Wootton Major,* contained the most extreme view, discussing Faery at length as (within the world of the story) an actual if alternate reality with its own consistency and its own laws. In this later, more private consideration of Faery (note the modified but still etymologically significant spelling), enchantment becomes its own reality. Here, the real and Faery worlds are presented not as different states of mind but as explicit and definable parallel planes of existence. The model here was the Otherworld of Celtic myth and folktale, called by the Welsh Annvwyn, by the Irish Tír-na-nOg, the Land of the Ever-young, traditionally conceived as actual alternate space into which unwary mortals may stray. This essay gave careful attention to the exact nature of Faery and to the precise circumstances of its temporal, geographic, and spiritual/psychological relationship to the real world, in particular the villages of the story—Wootton Major on the wood's edge, Wootton Minor within the wood, and Walton deep inside the wood. In this exploration, as in the story that is its companion, the real and Faery worlds coexist side by side, but although those from the world of Faery can enter the "real" world at will, entry by humans into the Faery world is limited and only allowable upon conditions.

The variation in perspectives among the essays can be accounted for, if not completely reconciled to a single view, in part by the disparate circumstances of their composition. "On Fairy-stories" was originally given as the annual Andrew Lang Lecture at St. Andrews University, Scotland. It was therefore designed for public hearing by an audience presumably interested in and knowledgeable on the subject. Subsequently published as an essay, it has become a classic in the field and is now recognized as Tolkien's major statement on his own art, as well as a landmark critical examination of the uses and importance of fairy story and myth. It was also the only one of the three essays to be published during Tolkien's lifetime. The introductory fragment was written for and to the presumed readers of *The Golden Key,* but it was left unfinished. The last essay, "Smith of Wootton Major," was not intended for publication nor aimed at any audience but Tolkien himself. It was a wholly personal exploration undertaken to clarify for his own understanding the background, both natural and supernatural, of the short story. It was clearly his effort to explore one last time, and capture if he could, the nature of Faery. Written by himself and for himself, it had the express purpose of explicating and illuminating his own understanding. In such a private venue, he felt free to let his imagination off its critical leash and gave it free play.

Examples from Tolkien's fiction may serve to illustrate the difference between the perspectives demonstrated in the two major essays. The first example is the Faërie world of Lórien in *The Lord of the Rings,* the second its equivalent Faery in *Smith of Wootton Major.* Entering Lórien only on sufferance and by the grudging permission of its guardians, Frodo in *The Lord of the Rings* is still physically in the real world of Middle-earth. Yet he can experience a dramatic change of perception so that it *seems* to him that he has stepped into "a corner of the Elder Days." Alternatively, in *Smith of Wootton Major,* Smith not only seems to but can in actuality (as long as he possesses the star that is his passport) leave Wootton Major in the morning, physically enter the contiguous Faery world, spend any length of time there from hours to days, and return home on the same evening.

Setting aside their supernatural inhabitation and their obvious ability to enchant the visitor, the chief commonality in both these Otherworlds is alteration of the passage of time. This, too, derives obliquely from traditional Celtic Otherworlds stories, wherein time can be either slowed down or speeded up in comparison to the outside world. What might seem to be years spent in the Otherworld can take place in a moment of mortal time so that the traveler returns in the same instant at which he left, older in experience but not in days. Conversely, a single day in the Otherworld may span years of mortal time, so that the returning traveler finds himself overtaken by age, his family and friends all dead, his world gone on without him and his very existence passed out of living memory. While no such dramatic alterations happen to either Frodo or Smith—indeed, in the "Smith of Wootton Major" essay Tolkien explicitly rejected such extremes as stretching credibility—Tolkien nevertheless took care to ensure that both his characters would experience a shift in time, albeit each in a different way.

The time the Fellowship passes in Lórien *seems* to be slowed from the pace of ordinary time. They cannot count the days. Their embarkation on the River (which Frodo associates with "the time that flows through mortal lands") constitutes a return to the "real" world. Here, Sam has difficulty reconciling his time spent in Lórien with observable phenomena such as the phases of the moon. Tolkien was careful, however, to keep the whole presentation in the context of experience, couching his description in terms of subjective rather than objective reality. To this end, the Tale of Years in Appendix B of *The Lord of the Rings* gives a careful count of the days, adding up to a month, that the Fellowship spent in Lórien. He was bolder in *Smith of Wootton Major,* explicitly providing that Smith can and does go and return after spending extended periods of time in Faery without dislocation of his normal human life.

It is not unreasonable to conjecture that in both instances Tolkien was writing out of immediate and highly personal experience; that his own visitations to the Faërie world that so enchanted him could seem to encompass days or years or even Ages of Middle-earth time while he sat at his desk in the small hours of the night writing about Fëanor and Fingolfin, and Frodo and Sam, and the rise and fall of kingdoms. Here, if we had a way to confirm it, is where his two visions of Faërie would merge and the paradox be resolved, for the ring of truth in his narratives shows that while he was engaged in creating them he was indeed (and whether in truth or in seeming does not really matter) in an alternate but to him actual reality, the Perilous Realm of his own Faërie.

VERLYN FLIEGER

Further Reading

Tolkien, J.R.R. "Introduction to *The Golden Key*" and "Smith of Wootton Major." In *Smith of Wootton Major*, edited by Verlyn Flieger. Expanded edition. London: HarperCollins, 2005.

See also **Enchantment; Magic in Middle-earth; "On Fairy-Stories";** *Smith of Wootton Major*

FAIRIES

In his earliest poems and stories, Tolkien was already thinking and writing about fairies. At first, his fairies were similar to the tiny people and creatures popularized by Drayton and Shakespeare and later wholeheartedly endorsed by the Victorians. In *Goblin Feet,* his first professionally published poem, Tolkien refers to goblins, gnomes, and "tiny leprechauns," and most of the imagery derives from flowers or insects. According to Humphrey Carpenter, Tolkien wrote *Goblin Feet* to please his fiancée Edith Bratt, who favored flowers and small elfin folk.

In some respects, as Tom Shippey and Carpenter have both noted, the creatures of *Goblin Feet* are typical of exactly the sort of fairy Tolkien later came to loathe as he became increasingly interested in another, older sort of fairy, the elves and fairies of medieval texts. Tolkien read widely even as an undergraduate, and as his stories and poems gradually reflected his increasing linguistic interest and expertise, his fairies did as well, changing first in size and then in name as he began to refer to them as Elves and his invented "fairy language" as Elvish. Gradually, Tolkien's references to his fairy language (*Letters,* 8) become references to "Elf-Latin" (*Lost Road,* 41), then to Elvish, and later Quenya and Sindarin.

In rejecting the Victorian associations of *fairy* with diminutive winged folk, Tolkien turned to older medieval sources, not only the Norse and Old English poems he loved but also Middle English texts and even those in medieval Welsh and Irish. Some of his earliest poems describe fairies dancing in a forest glade, an allusion, surely to Orfeo's witness of fairy women dancing in *Sir Orfeo,* a text that Tolkien translated and taught. The image of a fairy woman dancing in a glade also had personal meaning for Tolkien, inspired by a memory of Edith Bratt dancing in a glade in Roos, Yorkshire (*Letters,* 420). Tolkien used the image in the poem *Light as Leaf on Linden-tree,* early versions of which are discussed in *The Lays of Beleriand* (120–26). A version of the poem was printed in 1925, and another was inserted as a portion of the tale of Tinúviel sung by Aragorn on Weather-top (*FR,* I, xi, 204–205).

Tolkien made a deliberate, philologically informed decision to reject *fairy* in favor of the Germanic *elf* as he created the mythologies and peoples of Middle-earth. As Shippey observes, Tolkien would have recognized that *fairy* has a French derivation from *fée.* Moreover, the associations of fairies and fairy stories with the works of people like Drayton were not associations Tolkien wished to advance. Tolkien turned then to Elf, Elves, and Elvish, reserving *Faërie* for special use.

In his essay "On Fairy-stories" Tolkien makes it abundantly clear that by Faërie (sometimes spelled by him Faerie or Faery) he means both a place—the Otherworld, the world of subcreation, a complete secondary world, inhabited by elves, fairies, dragons, nature, and even mortal humans—and the creative aspect of faërie, the quality that makes the place possible. He describes the creative aspect of Faërie not as magic but as enchantment, the ability to create rather than control. Tolkien makes a similar distinction between *magia* and *goetia* (*Letters,* 199–200). Faërie as the secondary world is thus the world of enchantment. Tolkien explicitly states that one of the essential qualities of Faërie expressed in fairy stories is that its inhabitants partake of "Other Time." The quality of Other Time, of time that is not in synch with the time of this world, is one that Faërie shares with other secondary worlds, including the Otherworld of Celtic mythology, the fairy Otherworld of medieval romance and ballad, and Tolkien's Middle-earth. Verlyn Flieger thoroughly explores Tolkien's Other Time and the relationship and function of time in Tolkien's works.

LISA L. SPANGENBERG

Further Reading

Flieger, Verlyn. *A Question of Time: J.R.R. Tolkien's Road to Faërie.* Kent, OH: Kent State University Press, 1997.

Shippey, Tom. *The Road to Middle-earth: How J.R.R. Tolkien Created a New Mythology.* Revised and Expanded edition. Boston, MA: Houghton Mifflin, 2003.

———. Tolkien Studies I article.

Tolkien, J.R.R. "On Fairy-stories." In *The Monsters and the Critics and Other Essays,* edited by Christopher Tolkien. Boston, MA: Houghton Mifflin, 1984.

See also **Arthurian Literature; Elf-Shot; Elves; Enchantment; Faëry; Folklore; Middle English Vocabulary; Mythology, Celtic; Mythology, Germanic; "On Fairy-Stories"; *Orfeo, Sir*; Romances: Middle English and French; Shakespeare; *Sir Gawain and the Green Knight*; Spenser; Ylfe, Alfr, Elf**

FAIRYOLOGY, VICTORIAN

Tolkien's writing commenced in the Edwardian era (1901–1910), when Victorian culture was lingering on, and before the dramatic changes brought about by the Great War. During the Victorian period fairies were a prominent feature of contemporary art and culture, represented in literature and painting and on the stage. Victorian fairy painting, which had its heyday in the 1840s, popularized the image of tiny, beautiful, winged fairies that inhabited flowers and frequented toadstools and woodlands (Maas). The emerging scholarly interest in folklore and the publication of numerous collections of fairy lore and fairy-tales provided more source material for painters and writers alike. The performing arts contributed to this trend: Shakespeare's two plays involving fairies, namely *A Midsummer Night's Dream* and *The Tempest,* which were very popular at that time, and romantic ballet performances which revolved around themes of fairy lore, enhanced the visual familiarity of such creatures (Lambourne). In the Edwardian period "fairy-plays" superseded Victorian panto-mimes. Tolkien had seen one of these in 1910: J.M. Barrie's *Peter Pan* (Carpenter, 47), a work that produced one of the best known fairies of modern times, Tinkerbell.

Tolkien's early poems are often populated by creatures very close to the fairies of Victorian art. Part of his poem "Wood-sunshine", written in 1910, is an invocation of "fairy things" and 'sprites of the woods', while his 1914 poem "Goblin Feet" describes tiny fairy creatures that seem to infest the air (Carpenter 1977, 47, 74–5). The same imagery is also retained in parts of "You and Me / and the Cottage of Lost Play", another poem Tolkien wrote in 1914, where "happy white-clad shapes" dance in "fairy rings" and weave daisy-strings. This last poem came to be associated with Tolkien's mythology as first conceived in *The Book of Lost Tales,* where the term 'fairy' is still used to refer to the creatures that later evolved into his Elves, but the issue of their diminutiveness is left ambiguous, while the image of the happy tiny fairy beings of the earlier poems gradually disappears. The *Qenyaqetsa: The Quenya Phonology and Lexicon*, which preserves some very early layers of the 'Lost Tales' that never came to be written down, includes a few entries describing fairies inhabiting flowers, which seem to originate in the Edwardian fad for flower-fairies, but the fairies/elves of the *Book of Lost Tales* are closer to Tolkien's later Elves than to such popular fancies.

Tolkien eventually rejected the popular image of the Victorian fairies, declaring openly his dislike for "flower-fairies and fluttering sprites with antennae" and explaining the diminutive fairy as a product of literary fancy. The sentimentality and enchantment associated with Victorian fairyology did not survive the Great War, and the incident of the Cottingley fairies marked the end of the cult of fairies in literature and other arts (Bown, 187–97). In the same way, Tolkien's Elves evolved into much more sombre and tragic characters, associated with profound beauty rather than ephemeral prettiness, and rooted more in Northern mythology than in popular Victorian fairyology.

DIMITRA FIMI

Further Reading

Bown, Nicola. *Fairies in Nineteenth-Century Art and Literature*. Cambridge: Cambridge University Press, 2001.

Carpenter, Humphrey. *Tolkien: A Biography*. London: Allen and Unwin, 1977.

Fimi, Dimitra. "'Come Sing ye Light Fairy Things Tripping so Gay': Victorian Fairies and the Early Work of J.R.R. Tolkien," In *Working with English: Medieval and Modern Language, Literature and Drama*. 2(2006).

Garth, John. *Tolkien and the Great War: The Threshold of Middle-earth*. London: HarperCollins, 2003.

Lambourne, Lionel. "Fairies and the Stage." In *Victorian Fairy Painting*. Ed. Jane Martineau. London: Royal Academy of Arts, 1997. pp. 47–53.

Maas, Jeremy. "Victorian Fairy Painting." In *Victorian Fairy Painting*. Ed. Jane Martineau. London: Royal Academy of Arts, 1997. pp. 11–21.

See also **Book of Lost Tales I; Book of Lost Tales II; Elves; Faerie; Poems by Tolkien; Qenyaqetsa: The Quenya Phonology and Lexicon; Shakespeare; Ylfe, Alfr, Elf**

FALL OF MAN

Tolkien never explained in great detail anywhere in his legendarium the Fall of Man. He found it a terribly difficult thing to do. "Tolkien described to me his problem in depicting the fall of mankind near the beginning of *The Silmarillion*," Clyde Kilby explained after a conversation with Tolkien in 1966. "'How far we have fallen!' he exclaimed—so far, he felt, that it is impossible even to think in the right pattern about it or how to imagine the contrast between Eden and the world which followed." Kilby, however, discovered a "Job-like conversation" in the papers of Tolkien.

In the "Job-like conversation," titled the "Conversation between Finrod and Andreth," the two characters muse over the power of Morgoth. Although Melkor had the power and will to tempt or corrupt an individual here or there, he could never corrupt an entire creation of Ilúvatar—that is, the entire race of Men. When Finrod pushes Andreth to explain the reasons for the Fall, Andreth merely answers that neither she nor any of the wise will speak of the matter to those who are not Men. Further, she admits, no Man really knows what happened to cause his Fall. There exist many speculations, but there are few answers. "Thereafter we were grievously afflicted, by weariness, and hunger, and sickness; and the Earth and all things in it were turned against us. Fire and Water rebelled against us," Andreth explained. "The birds and the beasts shunned us, or if they were strong they assailed us. Plants gave us poison; and we feared the shadows under the trees" (*Morgoth*, 348). In this interpretation, Tolkien offers a Fall that implicitly resembles the Judeo-Christian understanding of the Fall in the first three chapters of the book of Genesis. It is, however, not identical in its intent or implications and therefore should not be regarded merely as a mythological version of the Christian understanding. Tolkien explained in 1958:

> I suppose a difference between this Myth and what may be perhaps called Christian mythology is this. In the latter the Fall of Man is subsequent and a consequence (though not a necessary consequence) of the "Fall of the Angels": a rebellion of created free-will at a higher level than Man; but it is not clearly held (and in many versions is not held at all) that it affected the "World" in its nature: evil was brought in from outside, by Satan. In this Myth the rebellion of created free-will precedes creation of the World (Eä); and Eä has in it, subcreatively introduced, evil, rebellions, discordant elements of its own nature already when the *Let it Be* was spoken. (Letter no. 212)

Because of this, all things in the nature of Arda (trees, Elves, Men) may "go bad" as Tolkien wrote it. In addition, by not making it explicitly Christian, Tolkien implicitly incorporated classical Greek and Roman understandings of humans as terribly flawed though gifted.

Though keeping the Fall offstage for the legendarium, Tolkien believed in the necessity of the Fall—in the primary world and in his subcreated world. "There cannot be any 'story' without a fall—all stories are ultimately about the fall—at least not for human minds as we know them and have them," Tolkien wrote in 1951 (Letter no. 131). Tolkien therefore brought in many "falls": the fall of Morgoth, the fall of Fëanor and his kin, and the fall of the Númenóreans. Each represents—in its own way—the Fall of Man in the primary world. The fall of the Númenóreans in the Second Age especially resembles the essence of the Judeo-Christian Fall, even if the form seems quite distinct from the Genesis account. Sauron, like Lucifer in the guise of the snake, appears to them as tempter and offers them power. In their pride, the Númenóreans accept his knowledge and leadership and thus become at first slowly corrupted and then almost utterly corrupted as they attempt to stave off mortality.

BRADLEY J. BIRZER

See also **Christianity; Devils; Morgoth and Melkor; Satan and Lucifer; Sin**

FAMILY BACKGROUND

Tolkien was the son of Arthur Reuel Tolkien and Mabel Suffield. Tolkien ever saw a contrast between the Tolkiens and the Suffields, and he identified himself largely with the latter. The Tolkiens several generations before his birth had been German immigrants, and the name gave rise to family myths of its origin, as is common in such situations. One story that appealed to Tolkien was that the name derived from *Tollkühn,* "foolhardy," a nickname given to an ancestor who, it was supposed, took part in a daring and unauthorized raid against the Turks. (Tolkien later gave himself a fictional name of Professor Rashbold in his unfinished "The Notion Club Papers.") The recent generations were piano makers who had fallen on hard times. The Suffields, in contrast, he felt were thoroughly English, rooted in the Evesham area of Worcestershire. As West Midlanders, they belonged to a region that Tolkien loved for its dialect and its geography and that inspired the Shire in his fiction and was a central source of his "mythology for England." His mother, Mabel, represented for him all that was best in the Suffields. He wrote, "Though a Tolkien by name, I am a Suffield by tastes, talents and upbringing." Worcestershire was, for him, home: "Any corner of that county (however fair or squalid) is in an indefinable way 'home' to me, as no other part of the world is." The sense of difference between his Tolkien and his Suffield heritage was heightened by his mother's conversion to Roman Catholicism. The Tolkiens were Protestant (as were the Suffields), but his mother's new faith, it seems likely, was to her son quintessentially English and West Midland and rooted in the long medieval period. His own Roman Catholic convictions were emotionally tied strongly to his mother.

COLIN DURIEZ

Further Reading

Carpenter, Humphrey. *J.R.R. Tolkien: A Biography.* London: George Allen & Unwin, 1977.
Tolkien, John, and Priscilla Tolkien. *The Tolkien Family Album.* London: HarperCollins, 1992.

See also **Catholicism, Roman; Tolkien, Arthur; Tolkien, Mabel**

FAMILY TREES

Tolkien's subcreation is a world dominated by trees, both literal and figurative, of which family trees are one important manifestation. Tolkien provides family trees for the principal houses of the Quendi and the Edain in *The Silmarillion* and for the more important Hobbit families and the Dwarves of Erebor in *The Lord of the Rings.* Family trees serve a plenitude of functions for Tolkien, both inside and outside the world of Middle-earth. Some of these are more superficial, and others fulfill more fundamental thematic purposes.

On the surface, epics and legends, such as the medieval Icelandic sagas (unquestionably of great influence on Tolkien), often provided extensive genealogical background. This established the lineage of heroes and villains, and the relationship among them, their families, and their gods. In this sense, Tolkien's use of family trees follows long-established tradition. Family trees also supply a backdrop for tales of such ambitious scope. They bring essential details, texture, and verisimilitude to the created world. Without them, such a world lacks depth.

Tolkien was foremost a lover of languages and their interrelationships. Indeed, he reputedly said, "I am a philologist, and all my work is philological." As such, family trees serve another purpose: they allowed Tolkien to play with the meanings and etymologies of his characters' names, as well as with how these derivations related characters to one another, to families and forebears, and even to a particular time or place. The analogy between the names in a family tree and the central linguistic concerns of Tolkien's academic work is clear. Tolkien alludes to this connection, perhaps a little obliquely, in "On Fairy-stories" as "the desire to unravel the intricately knotted and ramified history of the branches of the Tree of Tales," which is "closely connected with the philologists' study of the skein of Language."

A highly practical benefit to developing detailed family trees was the mitigation of error. As Tolkien wrote to Hugh Brogan in October 1948, "It is astonishingly difficult to avoid mistakes and changes of name and all kinds of inconsistencies of detail in a long work." In this sense, the family trees served a mechanical (in addition to a thematic) purpose: to help Tolkien keep his characters and their relationships straight.

Another rationale behind the family trees in *The Lord of the Rings* revolves around point of view. The fundamental narrative angle is that the work is, at its heart, a Hobbit's tale. *The Lord of the Rings* is, in fact, *The Red Book of Westmarch*. Therefore, the inclusion of the genealogies of key hobbit families comes as no surprise, given hobbits' predilections for genealogy and given the book's decidedly hobbitish perspective. As Tolkien conveys in the prologue, "all hobbits were, in any case, clannish and reckoned up their relationships with great care. They drew long and elaborate family-trees with innumerable branches. In dealing with hobbits it is important to remember who is related to whom, and in what degree." The family trees in Appendix C are a consistent commitment to this point of view.

In *The Silmarillion*, we find a similar relationship between the family trees and the perspective of the tales. In this case, the legends unfold through the eyes of the Elves and, to a lesser degree, the Edain rather than hobbits. For instance, through their family trees we can more easily see the relationship between Fëanor and Fingolfin, both sons of Finwë, though their mothers were Míriel and Indis, respectively. The gulf between them, so evident in the unfolding of the "Quenta Silmarillion," can be visualized at a glance in their family tree.

In addition to highlighting rifts such as those between Fëanor and Fingolfin, family trees emphasize the significance of the *unbroken* line and illuminate the *mingling* of lines. Through family trees, we can visualize the mingling of Elf, Maia, and Man in the person of Aragorn. Moreover, through Aragorn's marriage to Arwen, the sundered kindreds of Elros and Elrond are joined together again. The declaration in the "Quenta Silmarillion" that "from these brethren alone has come among Men the blood of the First-born and a strain of the spirits divine that were before Arda" is made plainly visible through their family trees.

Bilbo, likewise, is a similar distillation of the best of two families. As Gandalf puts it in "The Quest of Erebor," "'So naturally thinking over the hobbits

that I knew, I said to myself, "I want a dash of the Took . . . and I want a good foundation of the stolider sort, a Baggins perhaps." That pointed at once to Bilbo.'" And Frodo is no different, bringing together a comparable mixture of Baggins and Brandybuck.

And in the end, family trees also help us see how the various families of the key characters join together at later points—or where they end. As already mentioned, Bilbo's parents were a Baggins and a Took, and Frodo's were a Baggins and a Brandybuck. Further down their trees, Sam's daughter Rose marries Peregrin's son Faramir. An even more famous example concerns Meriadoc's marriage to Estella Bolger (Fredegar Bolger's sister), absent from the published family trees until after 1966 (but restored subsequently) even though Tolkien drew genealogical charts for the Bolgers (and the Boffins). These latter two trees made it as far as the type script but, inexplicably, were dropped before *The Return of the King* went to print. Fortunately, these family trees have been restored to readers in the fiftieth-anniversary omnibus edition of *The Lord of the Rings,* illuminating further connections among the hobbits of the Shire. The family trees even hint at future events beyond the end of the narrative, for example, that, like Frodo, Merry never had any children, yet Pippin and Sam did. For interested readers, the genesis, evolution, and considerable amendment of the family trees in *The Lord of the Rings* are chronicled in *The Peoples of Middle-earth.*

JASON FISHER

See also **Aragorn; Bilbo; Frodo; Melian; Nature; Old Norse Literature; Renewal; Trees; Two Trees**

FAN ART

Given the vivid imagery and often detailed descriptions found in Tolkien's works, it is no surprise that there exists a decades-old cache of readers who extended their appreciation of the texts from pure readership to become fan artists. These individuals have used their skills to create their own artistic interpretations inspired by the characters, geographies, and structures found in Middle-earth and in Tolkien's short stories and poems. Working outside the realm of official Tolkien illustrators, many fan artists create their works without the expectation of earning any money. Tolkien was a reluctant recipient of art from his fans, who wished to thank him with gifts from paintings to engraved goblets. With the explosion of interest in *The Lord of the Rings* in the United States in the mid-1960s, the first organized Tolkien fan groups formed, and with them fanzines (fan-published magazines). One of the first

Tolkien-oriented fanzines, *Niekas,* included fan art in its pages; four issues in 1966 featured alternative dust jackets for the unauthorized Ace and subsequent Ballantine edition of *The Lord of the Rings.* Fan art has been an historic and integral element of science fiction conventions; following this tradition, entities such as the Mythopoeic Society in the United States and the Tolkien Society in the United Kingdom commonly include showings of fan art in their conference activities.

Unlike fan art based on movies or television shows, Tolkien fan art for the first twenty years necessarily drew its inspiration from the canonical texts and professional illustrations, including Tolkien's own drawings. Film interpretations of Tolkien's works provided additional sources of visual imagery with animated movies released between 1977 and 1980. *The Hobbit* and *The Return of the King,* produced by Rankin/Bass Studio, and much of *The Lord of the Rings* by Ralph Bakshi, however, were not embraced enthusiastically by many fans. Peter Jackson's commercially successful live-action films, released over three years from 2001 to 2003, changed the fan art landscape. Beginning with the initial published cast photos, much subsequent Tolkien fan art has been influenced by, and incorporates, the physical qualities of the actors in Jackson's films. This is especially true of the newest generation of Tolkien fans, many of whom have admitted that they read the original texts only after seeing the Jackson-directed films.

Fan art remains an expected element at Tolkien conventions and fan-oriented gatherings, at which artists can sell their representations of Tolkien's stories and characters to fellow fans. Fan art has proliferated through the digital realm as well, because artists are now able to scan their artwork, showcasing and selling it online. Fan artists also illustrate fan fiction, providing visual images for stories that go beyond Tolkien's texts. Most Tolkien fan fiction is posted in online form, and fan fiction authors consider it quite a privilege to have their stories illustrated by a fan artist. Today's Tolkien fan art may derive its genesis exclusively from Tolkien's texts and his illustrations, from Jackson's live-action films or the animated interpretations, or from a blending of these several sources, making it a rich realm indeed.

KRISTI LEE

Further Reading

Bacon-Smith, Camille. *Enterprising Women: Television Fandom and the Creation of Popular Myth.* Philadelphia, PA: University of Pennsylvania Press, 1992.
Jenkins, Henry. *Textual Poachers: Television Fans and Participatory Culture.* New York: Routledge, 1992.
Meskys, Ed. "Tolkien Fandom." *The View from Entropy Hall,* no. 12 (1997). http://www.worldpath.net/~bullsfan/entropy/issues/12.html.
Resnik, Henry. "The Hobbit-Forming World of J.R.R. Tolkien." *Saturday Evening Post* 239, no. 14 (1966): 90–94.
The Mythopoeic Society. "Annual Society Conference: Mythcon" http://www.mythsoc.org/conferences.html.
The Tolkien Society. "Oxomoot." http://www.tolkien society.org/oxon/index.html.

See also **America in the 1960s: Reception of Tolkien; Art and Illustrations by Tolkien; Bakshi, Ralph; Fandom; Fan Fiction; Jackson, Peter; Publishing History; Rankin/Bass**

FAN FICTION

The contemporary fan fiction phenomenon began with the publication of the first *Star Trek* fanzine, *Spockanalia,* in 1967—which, significantly, ended with the words "Frodo lives!" Tolkien fan fiction itself has a notable history. Past publications from the Tolkien Society, the American Tolkien Society, and the American Hobbit Association, to name but a few groups, prove that some Tolkien fans feel an ongoing literary impulse to contribute to the landscape of Middle-earth through original poetry and prose.

Due to the widespread popularity of Peter Jackson's *The Lord of the Rings* film trilogy and the instant accessibility of electronic texts, multiple generations of fans are now involved together in the production and critique of Tolkien fan fiction. Traditional fan fiction outlets and by-products such as conventions, printed fanzines, and awards continue to thrive, but the World Wide Web also allows online fan fiction archives, discussion boards, lists, blogs, live journals, role-playing games (RPGs), and multiuser shared hallucinations (MUSHs) to flourish. These channels have expanded greatly the opportunities for experiencing fan fiction at every stage of its production: collaborators "act out" narratives in virtual environments before committing them to the page; writers post works in progress for friends' eyes only to gain useful feedback for the revision process; and readers list and link to stories they recommend to others.

Many of the fan fiction categories identified by pioneering scholars in media studies, such as Henry Jenkins and Camille Bacon-Smith, apply well to works by the Tolkien fan fiction community. Among these are "slash" (homoerotic), "h/c" (hurt-comfort), "Mary Sue" (self-insertion), "crossover" (blending Tolkien's universe with the world created in another work of fiction), and "AU" (alternate universe) stories and poems. For example, some slash stories explore the romantic relationship between Frodo

Baggins and Samwise Gamgee; some h/c stories explore the recovery of Merry Brandybuck and Pippin Took from their wounds during the War of the Ring; some Mary Sue stories allow authors to create idealized versions of themselves to travel with the Fellowship and woo its members; some crossover stories explore what might happen if Tolkien's characters met those from J. K. Rowling's Harry Potter series; and some AU stories explore what might have occurred if Boromir had survived or Galadriel had taken the Ring for herself. Other, more specific categories used by the Tolkien fan fiction community include "bookverse" (fiction based exclusively on Tolkien's writings), "movieverse" (fiction based exclusively on Jackson's films), "RPS" (real person slash, using actors from the films as main characters in homoerotic stories), "Legomances" (romances featuring Legolas), and "Silmfic" (fiction based on *The Silmarillion*).

Some Tolkien fan authors also use the unique opportunities provided by "gap filler" and "bridge" fiction. Gap fillers represent attempts to address scenes implied but not elaborated upon, such as Rosie Cotton's time in the Shire while waiting for Samwise Gamgee's return or Arwen's time in Lothlórien with her grandparents. Bridges reflect the desire to negotiate a space between Tolkien's texts and Jackson's films, blending the most compelling aspects of each while attempting to reconcile the points at which they diverge. For example, a bridge story might introduce the film character Figwit and explain how he relates to the characters and events described by Tolkien in *The Lord of the Rings.*

The Tolkien fan fiction community has exploded in the twenty-first century, and it shows every sign of a long life. At the time of this writing, the fan fiction clearinghouse Web site Fanfiction.net alone houses 37,870 individual *The Lord of the Rings* stories and 1,789 *Silmarillion* tales, many with multiple chapters. Specialized archives for Tolkien fan fiction number in the dozens and range in size from exclusive sites that include an editorial board vote on each story such as *Henneth Annûn,* which boasts 1,537 stories based on Tolkien's various works, to narrower ones like *Emyn Arnen,* which includes 117 stories focusing specifically on the characters of Éowyn and Faramir. The popular Yahoo! Groups forum includes 245 different lists devoted solely to Tolkien fan fiction. Among the largest of these groups is "Aragorn and Legolas: The Mellon Chronicles" with 1,987 members, "Henneth Annûn" with 1,543 members, and "LOTR-FANFIC" with 1,128 members. Fan fiction is now the subject of university courses not only in media studies but in Tolkien studies as well.

AMY H. STURGIS

Primary Sources

Emyn Arnen. Tribute site to Éowyn of Rohan and Faramir of Gondor. http://www.emyn-arnen.net/ (accessed February 10, 2006).

Henneth Annûn. Story archive. http://www.henneth-annun.net/ (accessed February 10, 2006).

"Entertainment & Arts > Humanities > Books and Writing > Genres > Science Fiction and Fantasy > Authors > Tolkien, J.R.R. > Fan Fiction." Directory. Yahoo! Groups. http://dir.groups.yahoo.com/dir/1601410403 (accessed February 10, 2006).

Further Reading

Bacon-Smith, Camille. *Enterprising Women: Television Fandom and the Creation of Popular Myth*. Philadelphia, PA: University of Pennsylvania Press, 1992.

Booker, Susan. "Tales Around the Internet Campfire: Fan Fiction in Tolkien's Universe." In *Tolkien on Film: Essays on Peter Jackson's "The Lord of the Rings,"* edited by Janet Brennan Croft, 259–82. Altadena, CA: Mythopoeic, 2004.

Brobeck, Kristi Lee. "Under the Waterfall: A Fanfiction Community's Analysis of Their Self-Representation and Peer Review." *Refractory* 5 (2004). http://www.refractory.unimelb.edu.au/journalissues/vol5/vol5.html (accessed February 10, 2006).

Jenkins, Henry. *Textual Poachers: Television Fans and Participatory Culture*. New York: Routledge, 1992.

Sturgis, Amy H. "Make Mine 'Movieverse': How the Tolkien Fan Fiction Community Learned to Stop Worrying and Love Peter Jackson." In *Tolkien on Film: Essays on Peter Jackson's "The Lord of the Rings,"* edited by Janet Brennan Croft, 283–305. Altadena, CA: Mythopoeic, 2004.

———. "Reimagining Rose: Portrayals of Tolkien's Rosie Cotton in Twenty-First Century Fan Fiction." *Mythlore* 24, no. 93–94 (Winter 2006). Forthcoming.

See also **Artistic Movements; Fan Art; Fandom; Jackson, Peter**

FANDOM

Tolkien fandom is as diverse a subject as Middle-earth. Its complexity has only been deepened in the years subsequent to Peter Jackson's cinematic interpretations of *The Lord of the Rings (LotR)*. In the years pre-Jackson, Tolkien fandom could have been divided into perhaps two fundamental groups. There were those who study the life and works of Tolkien, sometimes called "Tolkienists" or Tolkien scholars. Here would be the professional scholar and casual fan completely enmeshed in Tolkien's Middle-earth. Fans in this category have read most of Tolkien's works on Middle-earth, from *The Hobbit* to *The Silmarillion,* and some have gone beyond its borders to read his many scholarly works. On the other hand were the fans who only seem lured by Tolkien's work on *The*

Hobbit and *LotR*. Post-Jackson, however, the divisions have become even more multifarious, and not all are of an accord. Some might even say that there has been more bickering and more strife in Middle-earth now than ever before.

Tolkien "Speak"

The terminology of Tolkien fandom has likewise metamorphosed into something beyond the simple "Tolkien fan." In the years since the Internet and post-Jackson, we have Ringers and writers of fanfic, fangurls (fangirls), purists, canon freaks, newbies, film nuts, swooners, Elf Fanciers, Tolkienites, Legomaniacs, and Hobbitophiles, and the list could go on. One point to note, as opposed to other areas of fandom, is that not all Tolkien fans agree on the "designation" of their particular group. There are multiple terms defining the myriad branches of Tolkien fandom, and many of the terms used to denote a particular branch reveal the hostility in the world post-Jackson.

On one side of the great divide are the original Tolkien fans. The Tolkienists who study the life and works of Tolkien—those who hold *LotR* as a book that ultimately should not have been tampered with—are the so-called book purists, otherwise called, with an air of disdain in the film fan community, "canon freaks." This branch includes those relatively new to reading Tolkien and those who read his works habitually. There are casual fans and hard-core Tolkien obsessives who devote entire bookshelves to works of Tolkien and works on Tolkien. While there are fans in this category who admire aspects of the Jackson films, there is a large basis of fandom here that finds innumerable faults in the Jackson interpretations and prefers to get back to the roots of Tolkien. Scores of book purists hold a certain amount of contempt for film fans, especially those who seem to have forgotten (or fail to realize) that Tolkien was the creator of Middle-earth, not Jackson. Rather than resort to any dissemination of terminology, folks in this category are simply called Tolkien fans or Tolkien scholars.

On the other side are the diametrically opposed film fans—those who freely confess that they prefer Jackson's *LotR* to Tolkien's Middle-earth. A good percentage of these fans have never read or never completed reading any of Tolkien's works, and others have read his major works, *The Hobbit* and *LotR*, but found the original lacking. A certain ambivalence bordering on dislike for the books has unfortunately arisen in this community, as can be seen in the appellation "canon freak" used to describe those who do not concur with adulation for the Jackson films. Into this category we would find the fangirls, or a type of fan comparable only to the groupies prevalent in the rock music genre. These fangirls have extensive Internet-based communities solely devoted to the actors from the Jackson films. Quite a number of these fans travel from convention to convention, tracking the actors' appearances. More of these fans still are admirers of the lesser-known actors, in addition to the previously established actors, present in the films. Whole Internet communities, primarily comprising women ranging from fourteen to forty years of age, have grown up around actors and characters in the film with little screen time and lines that may not have survived to the theatrical edition of the films. Part of this group are the "swooners" (a community of women who attend conventions to literally swoon over film stars) and writers of Legomances (a brand of fan fiction devoted to Legolas, or, more accurately, to Orlando Bloom who portrayed Legolas in the Jackson films). For an interesting account of the engineering behind the fan of the Jackson films and the explosion of Tolkien fandom post-Jackson, refer to Simone Murray's "Celebrating the Story the Way It Is: Cultural Studies, Corporate Media, and the Contested Utility of Fandom."

A third branch may be the most important in that it spans the divide, consisting of fans of both the book and the film. Into this category could go the fan known as the Ringer. This term was primarily adopted by the film-based Web site TheOneRing.net and is loosely applied to the *LotR* fan. Ringer is more precisely used to denote a fan who frequents this particular site and could be extended to denote a Tolkien fan who admires the films as well. Ringers often accept alterations in the text, the overall story and purpose of Tolkien's original with a mind toward compromise and the necessity of changing such a complex tale into the realm of cinema. There is undoubtedly cross-pollination between this group and the other two camps. Fans in this group may consist of hard-core Tolkien scholars who appreciate the monumental effort accomplished in the production of the Jackson films and fangirls who have moved beyond the film into Tolkien's original.

Fandom: A History

Tolkien's works have been in print for the better part of the last century. Tolkien fandom, however, did not reach its epitome until nearly thirty years later in the mid-1960s, a full decade after the publication of *LotR*.

Initially, admirers of Tolkien participated in an activity dear to the professor's heart but now almost lost to society: letter writing. To the mind of his publishers, who often had to wait many months for revisions and other requested materials, the hours Tolkien spent writing to fans were an apparent waste of time (Carpenter, 231). This "waste" would prove crucial in launching sales of Tolkien's work and would help secure Tolkien's fan base for generations to come. Unfortunately, there is no public record of any early letters to Tolkien from fans and admirers of his work. As noted in the *Letters,* many of Tolkien's letters before World War I until a few years before World War II do not survive. However, fans did write to Tolkien, and—perhaps more importantly—he wrote back. Over the years, it was common for Tolkien to establish correspondences with a good number of his "fans." Tolkien would routinely be asked for signed copies of his books, explanations on character development, advice on the naming of cattle, and he was happy to oblige in cordial, and sometimes lengthy, letters. In the years after the publication of *LotR,* as Tolkien fandom exploded in the mid to late 1960s and early 1970s, Tolkien's secretary prudently kept the more erratic or unusual letters from Tolkien so that the unstable ramblings of many an erstwhile fan would not "upset" the professor. Tolkien fans made impromptu visits to Tolkien's home and telephoned him regardless of time zone prudence. As evidenced in a letter by Tolkien dated May 1966, Tolkien opted to follow his publisher's advice and change his telephone number, rather than take an approach followed by his close friend W.H. Lewis. Lewis, accustomed to answering his brother's phone, repeated the phrase "Oxford Sewage Disposal Unit" until the caller simply hung up (*Letters,* 368–69).

The dawn of the paperback wars between the U.S. publishing houses of Ace and Ballantine in 1964–65 denotes a watershed in Tolkien fandom. First published in 1954, *LotR* existed for more than a decade without a paperback edition. During this time, sales of Tolkien's works were not voluminous, and fandom per se had not reached the fevered height that it would in the 1960s. The Tolkien fan community—if indeed it could be called a community at this time—more closely resembled a private club rather than a public forum, mirroring Tolkien's own literary group, the Inklings. Tolkien's own fan base precedes the publication of *LotR* by many years. The Inklings—C.S. Lewis and Charles Williams, along with others— were the original Tolkien fans, being privy to Tolkien's works before publication. After *LotR* was published, Tolkien was not completely accepted in so-called literary circles, as displayed in the literary battle between W.H. Auden and Edmund Wilson. Many, such as

Wilson, held Tolkien in contempt for being a professor who succumbed to the wiles of juvenile escapist literature. Many more transferred distaste for C.S. Lewis, himself a writer of some controversy, to Tolkien because Lewis wrote one of the first laudatory reviews of *FR* in 1954 titled "The Gods Return to Earth." During this time, Tolkien enjoyed a healthy boost from fans through their letters and kind words—many of which can be read in *Letters.* It is interesting to note that as fandom grew, Tolkien's letters became shorter and less cordial, particularly after a few readers wrote Tolkien obsequiously proposing sequels to *LotR* that they themselves would write.

In the decade after the publication of *LotR,* sales were rather low in the United States. *LotR* sold fewer than 20,000 copies nationwide. Ace Books, an American publisher specializing in science fiction and the growing fantasy market, decided that it would publish its own paperback *LotR*—without seeking permission from Tolkien or his publishers and without paying royalties. The Ace paperbacks sold for seventy-five cents each, and they were obtainable throughout the United States. This "pirated" edition was poorly printed, included many textual errors, and showed ridiculous cover art that included a deranged wizard and a man with a duck on his head. Tolkien and his publishers decided to make editorial changes, revising the text into an authorized edition that would be released in paperback. In a letter to his son Michael in October 1965, Tolkien freely admitted that the Ace editions offered publicity hitherto unavailable to his works. He further hoped that such public focus would herald an increase in sales (*Letters,* 363–64). When the long-awaited "authorized" edition was released by Ballantine Books in late 1965, about six months after the Ace editions had flooded the market, sales did not favor the authorized edition, which cost nearly twenty cents more; the frugal teenage and college markets, cajoled by the Ace editions, weren't buying. Tolkien's relationship with his fans is what ultimately saved *LotR.* In advertisements, letters to the public, and personal letters to fans, Tolkien loudly professed the inaccuracies of the Ace editions and steered readers toward the authorized edition. Because of Tolkien's so-called wasted hours writing to what became a devoted fan base, many Tolkien fans in America banded together (*Letters,* 258). Tolkien's American readers not only defended him but also forced booksellers to remove all copies of the Ace editions from the market. With the efforts of the established Science Fiction Writers of America, combined with those of the newly formed Tolkien Society of America, Ace contacted Tolkien, promising not only that it would pay royalties to him for every Ace edition sold but also that it would cease printing once stock was depleted (Carpenter, 231–32). The Ace editions sold around one hundred thousand copies in 1965 alone and were far surpassed by the authorized Ballantine edition. Despite the indignities of the Ace editions, the controversy surrounding them had the lasting effect of launching Tolkien from the quiet realm of the literary aficionado to the world of the rabid Tolkien maniacs.

Fan Societies and Publications

As noted earlier, perhaps the first fan society that included discussions of Tolkien's works could be Tolkien's own group, the Inklings. Tolkien, however, would have disapproved of this categorization, because he largely looked on the pervasive fervor surrounding *LotR* as deplorable, lamenting that American audiences—indeed, many young readers— were absorbed in the tales in ways that Tolkien himself never would have been (Carpenter, 233). The first traceable links to any fan society could be seen in the adoption of Tolkien's works by many science fiction associations across America throughout the late 1950s and early 1960s, most notably the Los Angeles Science Fiction Society (LASFS). An offshoot of LASFS was Fellowship of the Ring, founded by Bruce Pelz around 1960. With Pelz's society came the publication of what may be the first Tolkien fanzine—fan-published magazine—in the United States: *I Palantír*. Avid Tolkien scholar and collector S. Gary Hunnewell has amassed one of the world's most extensive collections of Tolkien fandom, the S. Gary Hunnewell Collection, available in Marquette University's Department of Special Collections and University Archives. Included are issues of *I Palantír*, along with more than two hundred fan titles since 1960. Among them one can find such titles as *Ilmarin, Henneth Annûn, Eldritch DreamQuest, Belladonna's Broadsheet, Simbelmyne, Yrch!*, and *A Few Words About Bilbo*.

Tolkien societies sprang up and disappeared almost overnight. In the United States, 1965 saw the birth of the New York Tolkien Society (NYTS), later known as the Tolkien Society of America (TSofA), originally founded by Dick Plotz. In a letter to Tolkien in the summer of 1965, W.H. Auden expressed concerns that NYTS would be run by "lunatics." In his response, Tolkien asserted that genuine lunatics didn't associate with such organizations but that such societies did fill him with "alarm" (*Letters*, 359). Tolkien corresponded with Plotz, but he expressed his discomfort at a society solely devoted to discussion of his work. Ed Meskys became

the second Thain of TSofA in 1967, and by 1968 America saw its first Tolkien Conference, held in New Hampshire and sponsored by TSofA. Meskys published, with the editorial help of Plotz, *The Tolkien Journal (TTJ)* around 1968. Another instrumental fanzine, published independent of TSofA by the University of Wisconsin Tolkien Society, was *Orcrist,* edited by Richard West. But by 1969, *Orcrist* and *TTJ* had merged. By 1972, TSofA was absorbed into the Mythopoeic Society, which was originally established in California in 1967 to study the life and works of Tolkien, C.S. Lewis, and Charles Williams. Starting in 1970, the Mythopoeic Society held its first Mythcon event, which has met annually ever since. The American Tolkien Society (ATS) was founded in 1975, although its publication, *The Minas Tirith Evening Star,* began in 1967 and has continued without interruption in the decades that followed. Europe and the United Kingdom saw similar activity in both Tolkien societies and Tolkien fanzines. One of the first European societies is Forodrim, the Tolkien Society of Sweden, founded in the mid-1960s a few years before the Tolkien Society UK (TSUK) in 1967. The societies hitherto discussed have been continued, almost without disruption, for over thirty years. The Mythopoeic Society, along with Forodrim, TSUK, and ATS, all actively seek new members. In 2000, the tradition was continued with the reestablishment of a Tolkien Society in New York, also called NYTS. By 2005, NYTS had become the North East Tolkien Society.

Elaborationists

In his article "The Evolution of Tolkien Fandom," Philip Helms discusses the first important change in the realm of Tolkien fandom. During the 1960s, Tolkien was adopted as part of the countercultural movement. After the brouhaha surrounding the Ace editions, along with the societal instabilities in American culture, hippies, college students, and many cultural rebels embraced Tolkien's works. But in the 1970s, the Tolkien fan ceased to be some "bizarre" entity (Helms, 108). Tolkien was remembered for his medieval roots, his philological passion, and his work in Anglo-Saxon literature. Tolkien fans were no longer content to merely read Tolkien's works innumerable times: they thirsted for information. Helms notes how Tolkien fans of this period, and for many years to come, fell into three distinct categories:

1. Fans who seek an analysis of Tolkien's works

2. Those who explore Tolkien's languages, geography, and mythologies, treating Middle-earth as a historically real world and not a subcreation
3. Fans who wish to elaborate on Tolkien's creation

Fan fiction (fanfic) and the world of gaming emerge from this "elaborationist" approach. Fanfic in its "purest" form can be defined as "any kind of written creativity that is based on an identifiable segment of popular culture . . . and is not 'professional' writing. Fan authors borrow characters and settings . . . for use in their own writings" (Tushnet 1997).

In her comprehensive article on Tolkien fanfic, "Make Mine Movieverse," Amy Sturgis traces fanfic to the Middle Ages when authors expanded on Arthurian tales to create their own tales of Camelot. Meredith McCardle tracks a more "definitive" evolution in fanfic to the fan-driven fiction written in the 1860s parodying and elaborating on Lewis Carroll's writings (McCardle, 8). Modern fanfic, however, was born in the same cultural hothouse as Tolkien fandom: in the turbulent 1960s. The first fanfic to officially be recognized as such came in 1967 with the second season of *Star Trek.* Tolkien-related fanzines were publishing what could be considered fanfic as early as 1960s. Alongside fanfic came other outlets for Tolkien fans to express their appreciation of Tolkien's Middle-earth—most notably fan art. Both subgenres of Tolkien fandom would be significantly altered with the coming of the Peter Jackson films.

Fanfic, fantasy role-playing games employing scenarios based in fanfic, and fan art may have been spawned by a comment Tolkien made in a letter to Milton Waldeman in late 1951. In discussing his desire to create an interconnected mythology, Tolkien designed to leave a great many of the tales incomplete, thereby creating a yearning for others to complete them. He also remarks how "absurd" this idea is, perhaps taking the humble and somewhat defeatist view that none of his other tales would ever see completion by his own hand, let alone suffer contributions from the hands of others (*Letters,* 145). Tolkien did expressly note that such contributions, however, should be "purged of the gross" and should be categorized as high literature (*Letters,* 144). Many fan authors and artists have taken these comments as an invitation to play in the universe Tolkien has created.

Fanfic has seen a significant expansion post-Jackson. In the fanfic world before the Internet, the genre was distributed primarily through fanzines or circulated privately or at conventions. The World Wide Web has made the dissemination of fanfic easier than ever. According to Susan Booker, in "Tales Around the Internet Campfire," in 2004 Tolkien fanfic counted for no less than 10 percent of the 3.5 million fanfic international Web sites. These sites, however, can be divided into some easily digestible categories. There are tales of fanfic solely concentrated on Tolkien's writings, setting the tales in what is known as "bookverse." There are tales on the opposite end of the spectrum, dealing with Jackson's "movieverse." And there are tales that take characters or settings from either universe into a unique alternate universe (AU). Another brand of fanfic is "slash" fiction. Such a categorization arose from the Kirk/Spock tales that put the *Star Trek* characters into sexually explicit roles. Slash fiction deals with sexuality on all levels, from romances of either a heterosexual or homosexual nature to hard-core pornography. Sturgis discusses a new genre of fanfic, arising from the apparent obsession with the films: real person slash (RPS), which deals with actors from the Jackson films. As outlined in Charlotte Evans's article "Is it Fair to be a Fan?" many authors of fanfic falsely believe their works do not infringe upon the rights of the original. For more information regarding the legalities of fanfic, please refer to Evans as cited in Further Reading.

Fan art, likewise, has been altered post-Jackson. Along with the germination of Tolkien societies, fanzines, and fanfic, many fan artists chose to express their love for Tolkien's works in art—from sketches appearing in the earliest fanzines to full-color paintings. Tolkien's descriptive prose begged to be rendered into visual media, and in the previously mentioned letter to Waldeman, Tolkien expressed a craving to see such renditions. Some of the most notable Tolkien fan artists are Patrick Wynne, Ted Nasmith, and Pauline Baynes. Wynne's works can be seen in the many Tolkien publications from the Mythopoeic Society. Nasmith's art gained popularity, propelling his work from the realm of fan to professional, with his works on Tolkien calendars and the art he provided for many editions of Tolkien's tales. Baynes was perhaps the first Tolkien fan artist, illustrating many of Tolkien's works and collaborating directly with the author. For decades, Tolkien's words inspired breathtaking pictures by artists, as can be seen in the many Tolkien calendars. Tolkien fan art, however, has not escaped the influence of the Jackson films. In the years before the films, when seeking to render a particular landscape or character, the artist inevitably went to the source or used pure imagination to make the image possible. Now, countless fan artists are depicting the actors from the films as the characters and the computer-generated landscapes from Jackson's studios as the backdrop for their work.

ANTHONY BURDGE and JESSICA BURKE

Further Reading

Carpenter, Humphrey. *Tolkien: A Biography*. Boston, MA: Houghton Mifflin, 2000.

Evans, Charlotte. "Is it Fair to be a Fan? Fan Site Infringement and Fair Use." *Law and the Internet: Fall 2003 Georgia State University College of Law Papers*, December 22, 2003. http://gsulaw.gsu.edu/lawand/papers/fa03/evans/#fiction.

Helms, Philip. "The Evolution of Tolkien Fandom." In *A Tolkien Treasury*, edited by Alida Becker, 104–9. Philadelphia: Running Press, 1989.

McCardle, Meredith. "Fan Fiction, Fandom, and Fanfare: What's All the Fuss?" *Boston University School of Law Journal of Science & Technology Law* 9, no. 2 (Summer 2003). http://www.bu.edu/law/scitech/OLJ9-2.htm.

Murray, Simone. "Celebrating the Story the Way It Is: Cultural Studies, Corporate Media, and the Contested Utility of Fandom." *Continuum: Journal of Media & Cultural Studies* 18, no. 1 (March 2004): 7–25.

Sturgis, Amy. "Make Mine 'Movieverse': How the Tolkien Fan Fiction Community Learned to Stop Worrying and Love Peter Jackson." In *Tolkien on Film: Essays on Peter Jackson's "The Lord of the Rings,"* edited by Janet Brennan Croft, 283–305. Altadena, CA: Mythopoeic, 2004.

Tushnet, Rebecca. "Legal Fictions: Copyright, Fan Fiction, and a New Common Law." *Loyola of Los Angeles Entertainment Law Journal* 17 (1997). http://www.schrag.info/tushnet/law/fanficarticle.html.

See also **America in the 1960s: Reception of Tolkien; Gaming; Inklings; Tolkien Scholarship: First Decades; Tolkien Scholarship: Institutions; Tolkien Scholarship: Since 1980**

FARAMIR

A character in *The Lord of the Rings,* Faramir, Captain of Gondor, is the younger son of Finduilas, daughter of Adrahil of Dol Amroth, and Denethor II, son of Ecthelion II and twenty-sixth Steward of the house of Anárion, Kings of Gondor in Minas Tirith. Faramir is five years younger than Finduilas and Denethor's elder son, Boromir, Captain of the White Tower.

Faramir enters the novel in *The Two Towers*. A capable commander, he defends the eastern border of Gondor by leading war parties against Southrons and Orcs in Ithilien. There he captures Frodo, Sam, and Gollum, closely questions them, discovers that Frodo bears the Ring, withstands the temptation to take the Ring for himself, and defies Denethor's standing order to bring captives to Minas Tirith by letting Frodo proceed eastward. After sending his men to Osgiliath, Faramir is pursued to Minas Tirith by Nazgûl on winged steeds and only gains the safety of the city with Gandalf's help. There he is questioned by Denethor, who strongly disapproves of him allowing Frodo to continue eastward with the Ring. He volunteers to lead the defense of Osgiliath and, as the remnants of his defeated men retreat over the Pelennor, he is sorely wounded by a flying dart while standing fast with the rearguard against forces led by the Nazgûl. Carried unconscious into Minas Tirith, he nearly dies when Denethor, giving in to madness and despair, ignites a funeral pyre to burn himself and his son. But Faramir is rescued by Pippin and Gandalf. He is healed by Aragorn, formally recognizes Aragorn as King of Gondor, and calls for the crown of Eärnur to be given to him. When peace has been restored in Gondor, Faramir becomes engaged to Éowyn, sister of King Éomer of Rohan, in Edoras.

Section I [iv] of Appendix A to *The Lord of the Rings* describes Faramir's characteristics: "He read the hearts of men as shrewdly as his father, but what he read moved him sooner to pity than to scorn. He was gentle in bearing, and a lover of lore and of music, and therefore by many in those days his courage was judged less than his brother's. But it was not so, except that he did not seek glory in danger without a purpose. . . . Yet between the brothers there was great love, and had been since childhood, when Boromir was the helper and protector of Faramir" (*RK,* Appendix A, 337). Faramir shows all these characteristics in the novel: love for Boromir, and pity when he perceives that the Ring was too strong a temptation for Boromir (*TT,* IV, v, 274–5, 289); courage without seeking glory when he volunteers to defend Osgiliath (*RK,* V, iv, 90); knowledge of history when he tells Frodo of the Men of Númenor (*TT,* IV, v, 286); a gentle bearing when he professes his love to Éowyn (*RK,* V, iv, 238); and shrewd perception when he rightly discerns that Frodo has not told him the truth of his errand and that Gollum has committed murder (*TT,* IV, vi, 302).

Faramir's qualities are illumined by comparisons with other characters. When Faramir first appears, Tolkien does not describe him directly in detail but describes his men: "goodly men, pale-skinned, dark of hair, with grey eyes and faces sad and proud," who bear long bows and spears and speak both the Common Speech and an Elven tongue, "Dúnedain of the South, men of the line of the Lords of Westernesse" (*TT,* IV, iv, 265, 267). In contrast to Denethor, Faramir immediately acknowledges Aragorn as King (*RK,* V, viii, 142). Unlike both Boromir and Denethor, Faramir says he would not take the Ring if he "found it on the highway" (*TT,* IV, v, 289). And Sam says that Faramir has an air that reminds him of "Gandalf, of wizards" (*TT,* IV, v, 291).

Faramir appeared in the writing of *The Lord of the Rings* unexpectedly in early May 1944. "A new character has come on the scene . . . walking into the woods of Ithilien . . . Faramir, the brother of Boromir," Tolkien wrote to his son Christopher on May 6, 1944, and commented, "I am sure I did not invent him, I did not even want him, though I like him" (*Letters*, 79). In another letter written in 1956, Tolkien said, "As far as any character is 'like me' it is Faramir—except that I lack what all my characters possess (let the psychoanalysts note!) *Courage*" (*Letters*, 232).

PAUL EDMUND THOMAS

See also **Aragorn; Boromir; Denethor; Éowyn; Frodo; Gandalf; Gollum; Gondor;** *Letters of J.R.R. Tolkien;* *Lord of the Rings***; Men, Middle-earth; One Ring, The; Sam**

FARMER GILES OF HAM

A short novel that originated as a story told to Tolkien's children in the late 1920s, *Farmer Giles of Ham* was revised several times before being published in 1949, after *The Hobbit* and before *The Lord of the Rings*. In 1938, a version was read to the Lovelace Society in lieu of an expected paper on fairy tales and was well received. Its finished form successfully combines an amusing and exciting children's story with a number of sophisticated philological jokes, and it adds a mock-serious foreword that pokes fun at the scholars Tolkien criticized in his *Beowulf* essay for ignoring the importance of the story itself. The illustrations by Pauline Baynes are perfectly matched to the tone of the story.

The tale is set in the semilegendary medieval time between the reign of King Coel and that of King Arthur. England is divided into a number of small kingdoms, and in the village of Ham in the Middle Kingdom lives Ægidius Ahenobarbus Julius Agricola de Hammo, vulgarly known as Farmer Giles of Ham. One night Giles's dog Garm awakens him to announce that a giant has squashed his favorite cow; in an anachronism similar to those in *The Hobbit,* Giles frightens off the giant by firing a blunderbuss, a weapon not invented till the 1700s. The king sends him an old sword as a reward for his bravery. Then a genuine dragon invades the kingdom, and Giles bests it with luck, cunning, some ring mail hastily cobbled together by the pessimistic smith, market-honed bargaining skills, and the unexpected magic help of his sword Caudimordax, or Tailbiter. When the king hears of the dragon's vast wealth, he mounts an expedition to claim it, forcing Giles to accompany his quite useless knights (who turn tail and run at the sight of the dragon). Through good luck, a bit of stout rope, and the common sense of his gray mare, Giles wins the dragon's hoard (and the dragon's

help) for his village. Disillusioned with his glimpses of the king and his court, Giles sets up his own Little Kingdom in Ham and rules long and happily.

The fiftieth-anniversary edition edited by Christina Scull and Wayne Hammond includes an earlier version of the text and Tolkien's notes toward a sequel featuring Giles's son George and his page, Suet, and the Battle of Otmoor, which was never completed. This edition also includes a newly drawn map by Baynes. Typescripts and manuscripts are located in the Tolkien Collection at Marquette University.

While the feel of the story is quite different from that of *The Lord of the Rings* and the rest of the Middle-earth legendarium, there is a certain kinship. Giles, like Bilbo and Frodo, is a reluctant hero with more about him than one might guess. His personality is reminiscent of both the blustering braggadocio of the Tom Bombadil of the early poems and the bulldog tenacity of Sam Gamgee. The dragon, Chrysophylax Dives, is similar to Smaug in his trickiness, lack of conscience, and financial acuity. The theme of an enchanted sword giving warning when enemies are nearby parallels Bilbo's and Frodo's sword Sting, and the bit of rope that comes in handy reminds the reader of Sam's Elven rope. In the unfinished sequel, Suet's search for his captured master by making barnyard noises outside of caves both echoes Blondel's search for King Richard I (as Hammond and Scull point out) and presages Sam's hunt for Frodo in Cirith Ungol. Like the hobbits, Giles is unimpressed by knightly honor and far more concerned with military practicality. And in both the Middle Kingdom and Middle-earth, the successful adventurer is the one who knows how to make the most of his luck.

The story initially grew from speculations about the place-name Worminghall and its draconian implications during family drives in the countryside. As a linguist, Tolkien had an interest in place-names and folk etymology, and part of the fun of *Farmer Giles* are the explanations given for the origins of place-names in the Oxfordshire area and the gentle ribbing, in the foreword, of scholars who pore over old stories solely for this sort of information. Real places mentioned or referred to in the text include the town of Thame and the river Thames, Worminghall, Oakley, Oxenford (Oxford), Tamworth, Farthingho, the Rollright Stones, and the Pennine Mountains, all but the last of which were within about twenty miles of where Tolkien lived when he wrote the story.

Tolkien's love for the English Midlands countryside, and his concern with environmental themes and the depredations of war, are also evident in the descriptions of the desolation of the well-ordered landscape wrought by the giant and the dragon, not to mention the king and his knights during their self-invited visit to Ham (*Letters*, 113). Various critics point out references to the works with which Tolkien was concerned as a scholar: *Beowulf,* Chaucer's "The Reeve's Tale," *Sir Gawain and the Green Knight* and other Arthurian materials, *King Lear,* old nursery rhymes and aphorisms, the *Oxford English Dictionary,* Fafnir's hoard, the medieval calendar of saints, Geoffrey of Monmouth's *Historia Regum Britanniae,* and so on. The story also exhibits elements from medieval genres such as epic, romance, fabliau, fable, chronicle, and saga (Johnson). And Tom Shippey half-jokingly suggests that Tolkien intended the story in part as an allegory on creativity and dry academic scholarship (99); this view could be supported by the fact that the story is structured around the Oxford academic calendar (Rateliff, 47).

If not an allegory, *Farmer Giles* is at least a highly amusing parody and *jeu d'esprit.* In none of Tolkien's other stories is there such a sustained use of rollicking humor and philological jokes, nor such delightfully depicted animal characters as Giles's dog Garm and his old gray mare (though *Roverandom* may come close). Giles and Chrysophylax are also memorable personalities, and even minor characters like the parson, the miller, the smith, and the king have their charms. Too frequently overshadowed by Tolkien's Middle-earth legendarium, this story is worthy of far more attention.

JANET BRENNAN CROFT

Primary Sources

Tolkien, J.R.R. *Farmer Giles of Ham: The Rise and Wonderful Adventures of Farmer Giles, Lord of Tame, Count of Worminghall, and King of the Little Kingdom,* edited by Christina Scull and Wayne G. Hammond and illustrated by Pauline Baynes. Boston, MA: Houghton Mifflin, 1999.

Further Reading

Croft, Janet Brennan. "Beyond *The Hobbit:* J.R.R. Tolkien's Other Works for Children." *World Literature Today* (2003): 67–70.
Hammond, Wayne G., with the assistance of Douglas A. Anderson. *J.R.R. Tolkien: A Descriptive Bibliography.* Winchester, UK: St. Paul's Bibliographies, 1993.
Johnson, J.A. "*Farmer Giles of Ham:* What Is It?" *Orcrist* 7 (1973): 21–24.
Kocher, Paul Harold. *Master of Middle-earth: The Fiction of J.R.R. Tolkien.* Boston, MA: Houghton Mifflin, 1972.
Lewis, Alex. "The Lost Heart of the Little Kingdom." In *Leaves from the Tree: J.R.R. Tolkien's Shorter Fiction,* edited by Tom Shippey, 33–44. London: The Tolkien Society, 1991.
Linley, Steve. "*Farmer Giles: Beowulf* for the Critics?" *Amon Hen* 98 (1989): 11–12.
Petty, Anne C. *Dragons of Fantasy.* Cold Spring Harbor, NY: Cold Spring Press, 2004.
Rateliff, John D. "Early Versions of *Farmer Giles of Ham.*" In *Leaves from the Tree: J.R.R. Tolkien's Shorter Fiction,* edited by Tom Shippey, 45–48. London: The Tolkien Society, 1991.
Shippey, Tom. *The Road to Middle-earth: How J.R.R. Tolkien Created a New Mythology.* Revised and Expanded edition. Boston, MA: Houghton Mifflin, 2003.

See also **Beowulf: Tolkien's Scholarship; Dragons; Environmentalist Readings of Tolkien; Farmer Giles; Garm; Heroes and Heroism; History, Anglo-Saxon; Humor; Oxford; Possessiveness; Weapons, Named**

FARMER GILES

Farmer Giles of Ham is a delightful story of novelette length completely unrelated to the history and mythology of Middle-earth, although it was written during and shortly after the time of the writing of *The Hobbit.* The story is focused around three events in the life of Farmer Giles: first, his defense of his farm against the intrusion of a nearsighted giant; second, his defeat of a dragon named Chrysophylax, lured into the area by misinformation from the giant; and third, his revolt against his king and the establishment of his own kingdom with the help of the dragon. In addition to Giles, the giant, the dragon, and the king, the main characters include a talking dog named Garm and an unnamed gray mare. Although Giles has a wife, her role in the story is fairly marginal, her primary role being to encourage him to go out into the fields to see if a giant really was there. The main theme of the story is courage, an important focus of Tolkien's academic writing. None of the characters are particularly brave, but Giles grows more confident and heroic as various events work to his favor. In his "Ofermod" (Excessive Pride) at the end of "The Homecoming of Beorhtnoth, Beorhthelm's Son," Tolkien presents a medieval theory of courage characterized by responsibility from above and loyalty from below. Because the king fails to act responsibly in light of the threat from the dragon with regard to his subjects, especially Giles, Giles's revolt becomes justifiable. Interestingly, the dragon in turn becomes loyal to Giles, serving him faithfully until Giles eventually releases him from service. Aside from play with pompous-sounding Latin names, the primary insider joke in the book involves an anachronistic blunderbuss, which Giles uses to shoot the giant and scare him away. The definition of the blunderbuss cited in the story is the one included in the *Oxford English Dictionary* ("Now superseded in civilized countries by other firearms"), and the Four Wise Clerks of

Oxenford who supply the definition are the four editors of the dictionary, with whom Tolkien worked on the dictionary. Tolkien also has fun with the geography of England, using actual place-names in England as the locations where events in the story took place— for example, Worminghall, Oakley, perhaps Tamworth, and Thame. The giant and the dragon supposedly came from Wales. According to the story, the name of the village of Ham (village) became corrupted into the name Thame because of confusion about Giles's titles: Lord of the Tame Worm became Lord of the Tame, which was then confused Lord of Ham, producing Lord of Thame, affecting the name of the village and the nearby rivers. As with the pre-*Hobbit* Bombadil poems, Tolkien associated Giles's Little Kingdom with the countryside of England. Sadly, by March 1945 he abandoned interest in a sequel to *Farmer Giles* because "the heart has gone out of the Little Kingdom, and the woods and plains are aerodromes and bomb-practice targets."

GENE HARGROVE

Further Reading

Kocher, Paul Harold. *Master of Middle-earth: The Fiction of J.R.R. Tolkien*, 178–86. Boston, MA: Houghton Mifflin, 1972.

Shippey, Tom. *The Road to Middle-earth*, 74–76. Boston, MA: Houghton Mifflin, 1983.

Tolkien, J.R.R. *Farmer Giles of Ham: The Rise and Wonderful Adventures of Farmer Giles, Lord of Tame, Count of Worminghall, and King of the Little Kingdom*, edited by Christina Scull and Wayne G. Hammond and illustrated by Pauline Baynes. Boston, MA: Houghton Mifflin, 1999.

———. "The Homecoming of Beorhtnoth, Beorhthelm's Son." In *Poems and Stories*. Boston, MA: Houghton Mifflin, 1994.

See also **Garm; Oxford**

FATHER CHRISTMAS LETTERS

Letters from Father Christmas belongs to the category of Tolkien's writings inspired by his family life. Between 1920 and 1943, he adopted the persona of Father Christmas and composed letters to his children at Christmastime. These letters were edited after Tolkien's death and published in 1976. They begin simply and create a more complex picture over time. Father Christmas develops a personality early. He is old and so dislikes disruptions but is affectionate to his friends and has a sense of humor. Supporting characters become numerous as the correspondence continues. The North Polar Bear Karhu, Father Christmas's assistant, is the first to appear. His comic mishaps are often the subject of the letters, though he

interjects his own notes and drawings. Later, Tolkien included many other characters, such as Polar Bear's nephews, elves, the Snow Man, the Man in the Moon, and goblins. In the letters, Father Christmas relates events from the previous year. He also discusses how he and his helpers make and distribute presents.

The author brought some of his characteristic preoccupations to the letters. His interest in language, first of all, is evident. Besides a general linguistic playfulness, he invented a goblin alphabet and included bits of Elvish, "Arctic," and Icelandic. Second, he exercised his drawing skills. Most of the letters are accompanied by illustrations in pen and ink, watercolors, or colored pencils; many contain marginal decorations in imitation of illuminated manuscripts (Hammond and Scull 1995, 68–77). Some elements of Tolkien's other fiction appear in the letters, but the connections are few. Friendly elves and war-like goblins are both included. Father Christmas's elven secretary bears the familiar name of Ilbereth. The piece of Elvish Ilbereth writes in 1937 has been identified by Paul Nolan Hyde as Simplified Sindarin Tengwar (24). But neither race closely resembles those in his prominent works. The elves are small, and the goblins are compared to rats (1932). Father Christmas's voice, however, is not unlike the conversational tone used in *The Hobbit* and *Roverandom*.

As usual, Tolkien's treatment of legend and folklore results in a figure that resembles his traditional depiction but exceeds it. Before the Victorian period, when he grew more like Santa Claus, Old Father Christmas was England's representation of the season. He lacked any connection to gift giving but served as a presenter in Christmas mummers' plays (Pimlott, 111–12). A link between this figure and Tolkien's version is discernable because Tolkien's is also linked to the year's cycle, as Deborah and Ivor Rogers explain. His father's name is Yule (as mentioned in 1932), and in 1931 he refers to his "Green Brother" who, Rogers and Rogers argue, probably represents the summer solstice (64). But this character, whose first name is Nicholas, is clearly also related to Santa Claus/Saint Nicholas. He lives at the North Pole, employs elves, and drives reindeer. He wears a long white beard and a fur-lined red coat and hood.

Tolkien also, perhaps unknowingly, contributed to the tradition of presenting Father Christmas in wartime. Beginning in 1939, Father Christmas often mentions the Second World War. The displacements it has caused are making his duties difficult. In 1941, goblins take advantage of the conflict to conduct a particularly fierce attack on the North Pole. Two years later, Tolkien's daughter Priscilla is hanging up her stocking for the last time, and Father Christmas implies that he must retire while the war continues. Tolkien was not the first to imagine Father Christmas's response to war. The character had appeared in British war-related advertisements since the 1870s (Golby and Purdue, 117). In some he deplored the violence, but in others he was militaristic and armed (Brown 2004, 51, 58, 121). It does not seem, however, that this portrayal was common in fiction. One exception is American author L. Frank Baum's *The Life and Adventures of Santa Claus* (originally published in 1902), in which Santa Claus's friends raise an army to save him from monsters called Awgwas. Tolkien's goblins somewhat resemble the Awgwas, who also steal presents. But Baum's Santa does not fight like Tolkien's Father Christmas does.

As a collection, *Letters from Father Christmas* differs from other Christmas stories in terms of both content and mood. The events it describes are considerably more varied than those in most other works about the figure. Before 1943, it was not uncommon for writers to explore Father Christmas's home life, but it was unusual to find so many details unrelated to his standard role. Its mood, meanwhile, is not as moralistic or religious as some Father Christmas or Santa stories were, as Nancy Willard notes (90). He only, for example, mentions the nice versus naughty children distinction once, in 1930. In addition, although he reminds the children occasionally that he was born in the year 1 AD on Christmas, there is no other attempt to connect him to Christ's birth, as writers like British-born novelist Coningsby Dawson had in his Father Christmas stories.

Paul Nolan Hyde, Wayne Hammond, and Christina Scull have convincingly argued that Tolkien did not fail to focus his considerable attention to detail upon the letters. This attention extends to practical and material aspects of the characters' lives and contributes to the vividness of the letters. We learn, for example, about which winds the reindeer hate (1929) and the numbering system Polar Bear invents to keep track of children (1936). But perhaps because the book as a whole lacks a plot structure, its significance as a children's story has not been thoroughly evaluated. It is generally deemed entertaining but minor. What has been written tends to praise its illustrations and comic elements, especially the character Polar Bear. Critics have, in addition, appreciated the lack of a conventional moral or religious emphasis, as well as the voice Father Christmas employs; he shares jokes with children instead of condescending to them. And for Tolkien's fans, the letters are an opportunity to observe one of his subcreations evolving. They are also a valuable example of how he imagined a magical world and our own could connect.

RACHEL KAPELLE

Primary Sources

Baum, L. Frank. *The Life and Adventures of Santa Claus*. New York: Henry Holt and Company, 2003. Originally published 1902.
Tolkien, J.R.R. *Letters from Father Christmas*, edited by Baillie Tolkien. Revised edition. Boston, MA: Houghton Mifflin, 1999.

Further Reading

Brown, Mike. *Christmas on the Home Front 1939–1945*. Phoenix Mill, UK: Sutton Publishing, 2004.
Golby, J.M., and A.W. Purdue. *The Making of the Modern Christmas*. Athens, GA: University of Georgia Press, 1986.
Hammond, Wayne G., and Christina Scull. *J.R.R. Tolkien: Artist and Illustrator*. Boston, MA: Houghton Mifflin, 1995.
Hyde, Paul Nolan. "A Philologist at the North Pole: J.R.R. Tolkien and *The Father Christmas Letters*," *Mythlore* 15, no. 1 (1988): 23–27.
Pimlott, John Alfred Ralph. *The Englishman's Christmas: A Social History*. Atlantic Highlands, NJ: Humanities Press, 1978.
Rogers, Deborah Webster, and Ivor A. Rogers. *J.R.R. Tolkien*. Boston, MA: G.K. Hall & Co., 1980.
Willard, Nancy. "The Father Christmas Letters." *The New York Times Book Review*, December 5, 1976, 90.

See also **Animals in Tolkien's Works; Art and Illustrations by Tolkien; Comedy; England, Twentieth Century; Father Christmas; Humor; North Polar Bear; War**

FATHER CHRISTMAS

For more than twenty years, Tolkien's children received annual letters from the North Pole (first from Christmas House, then and for most of the time from Cliff House)—from Father Christmas himself; from his sometimes silly and trouble-seeking assistant, North Polar Bear, and on occasion from Father Christmas's secretary, the Elf Ilbereth. Father Christmas is the figure better known in the United States as Santa Claus (Sinterklaas, Saint Nicholas). The letters were published as *The Father Christmas Letters,* the first edition under that title; *The Father Christmas Letters,* edited by daughter-in-law Baillie Tolkien; and then a new selection as *Letters from Father Christmas,* also edited by Baillie Tolkien, with reproductions of letters in reproductions of their envelopes and incorporating partial text from the original edition and further material (from the Tolkien MS in the Bodleian Library).

The letters begin when eldest son John is two or three and continue until daughter Priscilla (the youngest) is almost to her teens—the last, to "Dear children," reads in part, "Now I shall have to say goodbye, more or less. I shall not forget you. We always keep the names of our old friends, and their letters, and later on we hope to come back when they are grown up and have houses of their own, and children." Along the way, the children heard Father Christmas wondering, "When is Michael going to learn to read and write his own letters to me?" (Christmas 1925), and next year they heard about the time when North Polar Bear turned off the tap for the Aurora Borealis ("Rory Bory Aylis"), and there was "the biggest bang in the world" that "shook all the stars out of place, broke the moon into four—and the Man in it fell into my back garden. He ate quite a lot of my Xmas chocolates he said he felt better and climbed back to mend it and get the stars tidy" (Christmas 1926). By 1933, the letter is to Christopher and Priscilla, and Father Christmas tells them about the worst attack of goblins for centuries. In that letter, Father Christmas refers to himself as "your old great-great-great-etc. grandfather at the North Pole"—which hints, curiously, at North American tribal mythologies (which also include the Aurora Borealis and polar bears—at least in the versions my father told me). The letter from Ilbereth the Elf, though his name is Elvish (cf. Elbereth), shows a sketch of Ilbereth not devoid of Pigwiggenry. The 1926 letter shows the North Pole in its arctic expanse looking rather like a Chesley Bonestell rocket ship on Mars. Even the picture of Father Christmas in bed in his bedroom shows the chill outside, but the polar landscapes are more than merely chilly. In one of the letters, the Red Gnomes who live in the caves under the North Pole promise Father Christmas and North Polar Bear that they will get rid of the goblins that seem to have taken up residence there. The caves are good, with appropriate cave drawings on the walls.

Like *Mr. Bliss* (though that was not written in installments over twenty years), *The Father Christmas Letters* is virtually a picture-book, more than a book with pictures. Like *Mr. Bliss* and *Roverandom* (and to some extent *The Hobbit*), it shows Tolkien as *paterfamilias,* and (like these and *Farmer Giles*), it shows Tolkien's sense of humor (and his sense of the comic). Other children should be so lucky as to have such a correspondent.

JARED LOBDELL

Further Reading

Hammond, Wayne G., and Christina Scull. *J.R.R. Tolkien: Artist and Illustrator.* Boston, MA: Houghton Mifflin 1995.
Tolkien, J.R.R. *The Father Christmas Letters,* edited by Baillie Tolkien. London: George Allen & Unwin, 1976.
——— *Letters from Father Christmas,* edited by Baillie Tolkien. Boston, MA: Houghton Mifflin 1995.
Tolkien, John, and Priscilla Tolkien. *The Tolkien Family Album.* Boston, MA: Houghton Mifflin 1992.

See also **Father Christmas Letters**

FËANOR

In Fëanor we confront one of Tolkien's most complex and fascinating creations. The greatest of the Noldor, and perhaps even of all the Eldar, he exhibits a powerful ambition to create and to devise objects of wonder and beauty for their own sake. At the same time, however, veins of pride and arrogance run through him, as deeply as those of the precious metals and gemstones so revered by his people. In fact, the complex harmony between these two passions, jointly hastening Fëanor's downfall, is voiced even in his names. He was first known as Finwë, after his father, but this was "afterwards enlarged as his talents developed" to Curufinwë—adding the element *curu* (skill). But his mother, recognizing his impetuous and passionate character, called him Fëanáro (spirit of fire), which eroded over time to Fëanor. The two names, then, embody two parallel aspects of Fëanor's personality, mutually reinforcing each other and leading him to his untimely ruin.

Tracing the path of Fëanor *qua* Creator begins with his mother, Míriel. She was called Serindë (the Broideress), "for her hands were more skilled to fineness than any hands even among the Noldor." Fëanor established his reputation early, improving on Rúmil's alphabet with his own Fëanorian letters. Around the same time, he learned to create by his own hands gems that surpassed those his father's people had mined from the earth. These early stones— "white and colorless, but being set under starlight they would blaze with blue and silver fires brighter than Helluin"—were probably the beginnings of the Fëanorian lamps described in *Unfinished Tales*. Also among his chief creations were the *palantíri*, "crystals . . . wherein things far away could be seen small but clear, as with the eyes of the eagles of Manwë."

Fëanor wedded Nerdanel, probably with the explicit purpose of learning from her father Mahtan, a great craftsman and favorite of Aulë. In the days that followed, Fëanor created the mysterious substance, *silima,* and from it the legendary Silmarils, in which he preserved the blended light of the Two Trees of Valinor. In this act, Fëanor reached the zenith of his skill, believing he could never make their like again. At this point, creatively content, other aspects of his overwhelming personality began to dominate.

Finwë remarried following his loss of Míriel, and he had two sons by his new spouse, Indis, a Vanyarin Elf. From the outset, Fëanor mistrusted and disliked his half-brothers, Fingolfin and Finarfin, perhaps in part because of their Vanyarin blood, perhaps out of loyalty to his mother. Later, fed by Melkor's lies, Fëanor's innate distrust of his half-brothers blossomed wickedly. Fëanor threatened Fingolfin's life, irrationally believing he intended to usurp Fëanor's place within his father's heart and among the Noldor. Later, after the devastation of the Two Trees, Fëanor would not suffer the Silmarils, in which the light of the Trees still lived, to be broken, even though Yavanna could have resurrected them thereby. Instead, he claimed them greedily to himself alone, unaware they had already been wrested from Formenos. Then, near madness on learning of the theft of the Silmarils, Fëanor swore with his seven sons a dreadful oath, thus weaving the Doom of the Noldor. From these events unraveled still further deeds of misery—the Kinslaying at Alqualondë, the abandonment of Fingolfin in the wastes of Araman, and Fëanor's own sudden death at the hands of Gothmog. Even in death, "so fiery was his spirit that as it sped his body fell to ash, and was borne away like smoke."

Yet despite his failings in life and his long penance in the Halls of Mandos, Mandos foretells that "the Silmarils shall be recovered out of Air and Earth and Sea. . . . Then Fëanor shall take the Three Jewels and bear them to Yavanna Palúrien; and she will break them and with their fire rekindle the Two Trees."

JASON FISHER

Further Reading

Helms, Randel. *Tolkien and the Silmarils: Imagination and Myth in "The Silmarillion."* London: Thames and Hudson, 1981.

Kocher, Paul Harold. *A Reader's Guide to "The Silmarillion."* Boston, MA: Houghton Mifflin, 1980.

Lewis, Alex. "Fëanor: Archetype and Prototype." *Amon Hen* 1, no. 108 (1991): 17–20.

See also **Alphabets, Invented; Elves; Exile; Finland: Literary Sources; Finwë and Míriel; Free Will; Galadriel; Jewels; Palantíri; Possessiveness; Pride; Prophecy; *Silmarillion, The*; Silmarils; Sin; Treason**

FEMINIST READINGS OF TOLKIEN

Despite (or perhaps because of) the dearth of female characters in *The Lord of the Rings* and other works, Tolkien's life and fiction have been the subject of debate by feminist critics. Often they begin with the man himself, pointing to his membership in all-male groups like the Inklings and the TCBS, which generated a "male culture" (Fredrick and McBride, 1) mirrored in the camaraderie shared by his male characters and in the perceived exclusion of any major role for his female characters (Partridge, 183). Tolkien's negative personal opinions on feminism (*Letters*, 48–54, 65–66) suggest that he held conventional views on the role of women rather than the more radical opinions available during his lifetime (Lewis and Currie, 181–93).

A few critics have derided Tolkien's representation of female characters in *The Lord of the Rings*, expressing their disappointment that given the opportunity to create a totally new world, Tolkien chose not to redefine the role of women but instead preserved the gender hierarchy of his own familiar patriarchal society (Fredrick and McBride, 109; Myers, 18–19). Catherine Stimpson (18) and Doris Myers (14) claim that in Tolkien's predominantly male secondary world, the female characters are nothing more than traditional stereotypes, who, according to Candice Fredrick and Sam McBride (110–11), perform such typically feminine roles as housekeeper (Goldberry), nurse (Ioreth), or love interest of the active male heroes (Arwen, Rosie). In some views, even the characters of Galadriel and Éowyn do not fulfill their potential of being active, nontraditional heroines: Galadriel is most helpful to the Fellowship through her feminine skill in weaving the fabric of the cloaks she gives them (Fredrick and McBride, 112), and Éowyn is motivated not by duty or honor but by her unrequited love for Aragorn (Partridge, 192). But it is the grotesque spider Shelob who elicits harsh accusations of Tolkien's misogyny (Stimpson, 19; Partridge, 191). As the only evil female in *The Lord of the Rings*, yet not subordinate to any male, her monstrous spider shape can be viewed as the manifestation of Tolkien's fear of the powerful female in a patriarchal world (Pretorius, 38).

Other feminist critics who commend Tolkien's representation of women examine the powerful agency of female figures in his stories, emphasizing their strength and importance. Galadriel, Melian, and Lúthien each possess powers that their husbands do not, and unlike conventional wives, Galadriel acts independently of Celeborn, leaving him behind when she returns to the West (Hopkins, 365). Belladonna Took, though not even a character in *The Hobbit*, is credited for the adventurous personality traits with which Bilbo is endowed (Green, 188). In *The Silmarillion*, the Valier are powerful female figures equal in number and wielding complementary powers to their male counterparts, making Tolkien's creation story an improvement over many myths where female spiritual power is lacking (Crowe, 273).

Specific literary sources also support the narrative importance of Tolkien's female characters. Galadriel may be compared to the Homeric figures of Circe and Calypso in *The Odyssey* in offering the hero advice and gifts of food, cloaks, and light (Fenwick, 17–18). In a Christian context, she may be compared to the Virgin Mary by association with the symbols of light and seeds (Pretorius, 37; Richmond, 14). On the other hand, the radiance of Galadriel, the malevolence of Shelob, the martial skill of Éowyn, and the woven gift from Arwen to Aragorn may be seen as some of the Valkyrie-like traits found in the Old Norse mythology that Tolkien evokes (Donovan, 106–32).

Examining gender traits offers another approach to assessing the importance of the feminine in Tolkien's works. Melanie Rawls (5–13) focuses on masculine and feminine "principles" inherent in both male and female characters and determines that Tolkien viewed the feminine as complementary rather than subordinate to the masculine. William Green (188–95) provides a Jungian interpretation of *The Hobbit*, explaining that the lack of female characters, the repressed feminine, manifests itself in the feminine traits of various male characters such as Gandalf, who functions as Bilbo's female "anima" or guide figure.

Feminist readings of Tolkien can be identified in various approaches, from Christian feminism, to Jungian interpretations, to literary-historical interpretations generally. Thorough studies from the perspective of feminist and gender theorists such as Hélène Cixous, Julia Kristeva, Judith Butler, or Luce Irigaray would also be valuable (Donovan, 131), as would further examination from a feminist perspective of Tolkien's work on medieval texts for or about women, such as *Ancrene Wisse* and *Juliana*.

ALINE RIPLEY

Further Reading

Crowe, Edith L. "Power in Arda: Sources, Uses and Misuses." In *Proceedings of the J.R.R. Tolkien Centenary Conference 1992*, edited by Patricia Reynolds and Glen H. GoodKnight, 272–77. Milton Keynes, UK, and Altadena, CA: The Tolkien Society / Mythopoeic, 1995.

Donovan, Leslie A. "The Valkyrie Reflex in J.R.R. Tolkien's *The Lord of the Rings*: Galadriel, Shelob, Éowyn, and Arwen." In *Tolkien the Medievalist*, edited by Jane Chance, 106–32. London: Routledge, 2002.

Fenwick, Mac. "Breastplates of Silk: Homeric Women in *The Lord of the Rings*." *Mythlore* 81 (1996): 17–23, 51.

Fredrick, Candice, and Sam McBride. *Women Among the Inklings: Gender, C.S. Lewis, J.R.R. Tolkien, and Charles Williams*. Contributions in Women's Studies, 191. Westport, CT: Greenwood, 2001.

Green, William H. "'Where's Mama?': The Construction of the Feminine in *The Hobbit*." *The Lion and the Unicorn* 22 (1998): 188–95.

Hopkins, Lisa. "Female Authority Figures in the Works of Tolkien, C.S. Lewis and Charles Williams." In *Proceedings of the J.R.R. Tolkien Centenary Conference 1992*, edited by Patricia Reynolds and Glen H. GoodKnight, 364–66. Milton Keynes, UK, and Altadena, CA: The Tolkien Society / Mythopoeic, 1995.

Lewis, Alex, and Elizabeth Currie. *The Uncharted Realms of Tolkien: A Critical Study of Text, Context and Subtext in the Works of J.R.R. Tolkien*. Oswestry: Medea Publishing, 2002.

Myers, Doris T. "Brave New World: The Status of Women According to Tolkien, Lewis, and Charles Williams." *Cimarron Review* 17 (1971): 13–19.

Partridge, Brenda. "No Sex Please—We're Hobbits: The Construction of Female Sexuality in *The Lord of the Rings*." In *J.R.R. Tolkien: This Far Land*, edited by Robert Giddings, 179–97. London: Vision / Barnes & Noble, 1983.

Pretorius, David. "Binary Issues and Feminist Issues in *LOTR*." *Mallorn* 40 (2002): 32–38.

Rawls, Melanie. "The Feminine Principle in Tolkien." *Mythlore* 10 (1984): 5–13.

Richmond, Donald P. "Tolkien's Marian Vision of Middle-earth." *Mallorn* 40 (2002): 13–14.

Stimpson, Catherine. *J.R.R. Tolkien*. New York: Columbia, 1969.

See also **Arwen; Éowyn; Galadriel; Gender in Tolkien's Works; Goldberry;** *Hobbit, The*; **Homer; Inklings;** *Juliana*; *Letters of J.R.R. Tolkien*; *Lord of the Rings*; **Lúthien; Melian; Old Norse Literature; Power in Tolkien's Works; Shelob;** *Silmarillion*; **T.C.B.S. (Tea Club and Barrovian Society); Women in Tolkien's Works**

FICTIONALITY

All works of narrative literary art are fictitious, but some are more fictitious than others. As far as events and the setting of them are concerned, Tolkien's work is clearly fictitious, but it is often categorized further into "fantasy," a mode of writing containing clear contradictions to "consensus reality." Tolkien's views on the fictionality of fairy stories and literary narratives in general can be found in "On Fairy-stories," where his term "secondary world" simply means literary fiction (60–61, 69), and his term "sub-creation" links the making of fictions with the human creative faculty and with the creator-God (75). Fairy stories, he argues, on the one hand relate to a historically evolving complex of stories (the "Pot of Story"), and on the other take their literary fiction seriously enough never to subvert or ironize it (39), letting it stand independent without frame or connection (41–42).

This might seem to contrast with Tolkien's conception of his mythological stories as a connected body of legend he would dedicate to England: this necessitates a connection with England as a real place in "consensus reality." Furthermore, the philological method of reconstruction that Tolkien applied to unsolved English or Norse philological cruxes to offer imaginative "origins" witnessed how reconstruction often slips into construction and thus fiction, a peculiar sort of fictionality that Tom Shippey calls "asterisk-reality" (20–22). Both by the originally proposed frame narratives and by the relationship to the sources in actual literary history, Tolkien's work seems to fall short of his requirements from true fairy stories, since the fictional mediation of the frame always connects the secondary world to the reader's reality and attempts to gloss over that it is a secondary world.

In letters, Tolkien maintained after the publication of *The Lord of the Rings* that Middle-earth is "the objectively real world" as opposed to "imaginary worlds" such as Fairyland (*Letters*, 239), but the story is set to an imaginary period of history. The nature of fictionality of his works thus remains a debated matter, since the only connection the finished works and even the published *Silmarillion* (1977) (as opposed to the variant corpus published in *The History of Middle-earth*) retain to the readers' actual world is the persona of the translator/editor who publishes the English translation of the manuscript. The final indecision on how *The Silmarillion* is to be presented results in *The Lord of the Rings* being (by default) the presentation frame, where the mediator by whom the stories of the Elder Days are collected and shared is Bilbo Baggins, himself a part of the secondary (but not of primary, even by "historical" fiction) reality. Tolkien's use of sources (such as Anglo-Saxon culture and Old English language in Rohan and Norse in Dwarf names) is thus part of the fiction of translation (as explained in the note "On Translation" at the end of *The Lord of the Rings*) and does not function as a connecting device in the sense in which the original conception would have made use of it. The indecision on the presentation frame can mean that Tolkien gradually dissociated his fiction from historical reality and finally let it stand independently. Verlyn Flieger, in treating the evolution of the presentation frame extensively, argues that this simply results from Tolkien's lack of time to offer a finished version of any of the later frames; her interpretation suggests that "The Lost Road" and "The Notion Club Papers" were prospective frames for Tolkien in which he would have been able to present his fiction as connected and even genuinely, "genetically," English (Flieger, 107, 115). As the work remains unfinished and the final presentation of

The Silmarillion (by Christopher Tolkien in 1977) happened without any such frame, the nature of the fictionality of Tolkien's works is differentiated and problematic, not finalized and oscillating.

Tolkien felt that his works were in some sense "true" and not "invented" by him; he often stressed that he did not consciously "make up" anything but had the feeling of "discovering" what was already there, thus reflecting on the problematic fictionality of his Middle-earth.

GERGELY NAGY

Further Reading

Flieger, Verlyn. *Interrupted Music: The Making of Tolkien's Mythology*. Kent, OH: Kent State University Press, 2005.

Shippey, Tom. *The Road to Middle-earth: How J.R.R. Tolkien Created a New Mythology*. Revised and Expanded edition. Boston, MA: Houghton Mifflin, 2003.

Tolkien, J.R.R. "On Fairy-stories." In *The Tolkien Reader*, 31–99. New York: Ballantine, 1966.

See also **Bilbo; Cruces in Medieval Literature; Frame Narrative;** *Lost Road*; *Silmarillion, The*

FILM SCRIPTS, UNUSED

In 1957, Tolkien reviewed and rejected a screen treatment of *The Lord of the Rings* that had been prepared by Morton Grady Zimmerman, Al Brodax, and Forrest J. Ackerman. The treatment and Tolkien's critique of it (now in the Tolkien Collection at Marquette University) are invaluable materials for understanding Tolkien's views on adapting *The Lord of the Rings* for film and provide specific insights into the elements of his story he felt essential to its successful dramatization.

Tolkien considered drama naturally "hostile" to fantasy (*MC*, 140) and *The Lord of the Rings* "unsuitable for dramatization" (*Letters*, 228). But after Ackerman and others visited him in late 1957, he stated that "an abridgement by selection with some good picture-work would be pleasant, and perhaps worth a good deal in publicity" (*Letters*, 260–61).

However, the proposed story line concerned him. He felt his work had been treated "carelessly in general, in places recklessly, and with no evident signs of any appreciation of what it is all about" (*Letters*, 270). There were many misspellings and inaccuracies, such as a glass-windowed room in Rohan and beaked and feathered Orcs (Croft "Three Rings," 2; *Letters*, 274, 276). To Tolkien, this demonstrated a lack of respect for the details of story and an urge to "standardize everything in Middle-earth to suburban norms" (Shippey, "Temptations" 16).

Tolkien would not tolerate alterations that did not suit the tone of *The Lord of the Rings,* such as portraying Lothlórien as a fairy-tale land (*Letters,* 274). He resented character representations "that have little or no reference to the book" (*Letters,* 267), such as giving Saruman hypnotic powers (*Letters,* 276), and lamented the elimination of Galadriel's temptation and "practically everything having moral impact" (*Letters,* 274). He also said changes to the Ring-bearer's journey, with Sam abandoning Frodo to Shelob and going to Mount Doom alone, "murdered" the story and "made no attempt to represent the heart of the tale" (Croft "Three Rings," 2; *Letters,* 271).

The strongest of Tolkien's criticisms were directed at liberties taken with the dialog (Hyde, 20). He insisted his characters speak in the same "style and sentiment" as in the book, stating, "I should resent perversion of the characters . . . even more than the spoiling of the plot and the scenery" (*Letters,* 275).

Tolkien was not totally inflexible, however. He recommended deleting one major battle, the Hornburg (*Letters,* 276), and preferred eliminating minor characters like Goldberry rather than diminishing them (*Letters,* 272). He could accept a "vaguer" time frame for the story, provided its seasonal pattern remained (*Letters,* 271–72), and he suggested leaving Saruman "to the Ents" if his death could not be shown properly (*Letters,* 277). But he did not agree with "unwarranted" additions, such as a "preference for fights" or moments of "irrelevant magic," such as Gandalf turning the Ringwraiths to stone (*Letters,* 271–72; Croft "Three Rings," 2).

Tolkien has been praised for recognizing cinema's ability to suggest scenery and seasons and for realizing how anticipating or exaggerating story elements "flattened out" his tale, which Zimmerman did in ways like overusing the eagles (Rosebury, 205). His disapproval of intercutting his narratives, it is argued, shows that Tolkien "did not think in dramatic terms" (Fuller, 19), and *The Lord of the Rings'* structure has been said to be "antipathetic" to American cinema (Shippey, "From page", 71–72). Films that do not use a single straightforward narrative, however, such as *Pulp Fiction,* have been cited as models for how Tolkien's original structure can succeed (Croft, "Mithril Coats", 70–71).

Tolkien readily admitted his ignorance of filmmaking (*Letters,* 266), and it can be argued that as a narrative author he did not understand the process of adaptation (Croft, "Mithril Coats", 71). Nonetheless, his critique of the 1957 treatment provides direct insight from Tolkien on translating *The Lord of the Rings* to the screen, making it a valuable tool in discussions of completed or attempted adaptations of his works.

PATRICIA TUBBS

Primary Sources

Tolkien, J.R.R. "On Fairy-stories." In *Monsters and the Critics and Other Essays,* edited by Christopher Tolkien, 109–61. Boston, MA: Houghton Mifflin, 1984.

Further Reading

Croft, Janet Brennan. "Three Rings for Hollywood: Scripts for *The Lord of the Rings* by Zimmerman, Boorman and Beagle." Presented at the Popular Culture Association / Southwest-Texas Popular Culture Association Annual Conference, San Antonio, April 2004. http://faculty-staff.ou.edu/C/Janet.B.Croft-1/three_rings_-for_hollywood.htm.
———. "Mithril Coats and Tin Ears: 'Anticipation' and 'Flattening' in Peter Jackson's *The Lord of the Rings* Trilogy." In *Tolkien on Film: Essays on Peter Jackson's "The Lord of the Rings,"* edited by Janet Brennan Croft, 63–80. Altadena, CA: Mythopoeic, 2004.
Fuller, Graham. "Trimming Tolkien." *Sight & Sound* 12, no. 2 (February 2002): 18–20.
Hyde, Paul Nolan. "Gandalf, Please Should Not 'Sputter.'" *Mythlore* 13 (Spring 1987): 20–28.
Rosebury, Brian. *Tolkien: A Cultural Phenomenon.* New York: Palgrave Macmillan, 2003.
Shippey, Tom. "Temptations for All Time." *Times Literary Supplement* (December 21, 2001): 16–17.
———. "From Page to Screen." *World Literature Today* 77, no. 2 (July–September 2003): 69–72.

See also **Bakshi, Ralph; Frame Narrative; Frodo; Galadriel; Gandalf; Goldberry; Jackson, Peter; Lothlórien; "On Fairy-Stories"; Race in Tolkien Films; Rankin/Bass; Rohan; Sam; Saruman; Shelob; Tolkien Scholarship: Since 1980**

FINLAND: LITERARY SOURCES

Tolkien's primary Finnish source was *Kalevala,* the Finnish national epic of oral poetry transcribed by Elias Lönnrot, a Finnish physician and literary scholar who hiked the countryside in the early 1800s listening to rune singers and notating their performances. During his many "walking journeys" into the Finnish countryside, sponsored by the Finnish Literature Society, Lönnrot collected more than sixty-five thousand lines of folk poetry, some of which he published in 1835 under the title *Kalevala* (literally, the land of Kaleva). An expanded version followed in 1849 (organized into fifty *runos* or verses).

The meter of *Kalevala* is trochaic tetrameter: a stressed syllable followed by an unstressed one, performed four times per line. Although Tolkien did not use *Kalevala* meter directly, its musicality and conventions abound in his poetry, such as Bilbo's walking song from *The Fellowship of the Ring* (I, iii, 86–87).

Kalevala poems fall into two categories: (1) creation myths, hero tales, and the warring societies of Kalevala and Pohjola and (2) lyrical poems, wedding songs, magical charms, and proverbs. Major themes include the struggle between the forces of light and those of darkness, the dilemmas of ethics and morality, the joys of love, and the sorrow of death. These themes are acted out by characters who combine superhuman powers with human foibles and can spin magical spells, as well as wield a hunting knife.

Major characters relevant to Tolkien's fiction include Väinämöinen (wizard and sage who seeds the world), Ilmarinen (blacksmith who forges the Vault of Heaven and the mysterious, magical Sampo), Joukahainen (young wizard who becomes Väinämöinen's adversary), Kullervo (tragic youth who unwittingly commits the sin of incest), Ilmatar (goddess of the air, mother of Väinämöinen), and Louhi (witch, dark mistress of Pohjola).

Lönnrot saw common threads in the poems but not a coherent plotline. Deliberately following what he assumed to be the tradition of Homer, he undertook to create that epic for the posterity of the Finnish people, arranging the poems into a story line with his own framing verses. Thus, although *Kalevala* has its origin in the folk poetry of many generations of nomadic Finns, its overall structure is the work of one man.

Tolkien Discovers *Kalevala*

Tolkien first read W.F. Kirby's 1907 translation of *Kalevala* around age twenty, shortly before his enrollment at Oxford. In *J.R.R. Tolkien, A Biography,* Humphrey Carpenter notes how Tolkien enjoyed the odd, rustic world of the early Finns, especially the boisterous, seemingly amoral behavior of the "lowbrow" heroes (1977, 57). In *Tolkien and the Great War,* John Garth explains how the Romantic concept sweeping Europe that "ancient literature expressed the ancestral voice of a people" had immense appeal to young Tolkien on the eve of war in 1914 (2003, 51).

The best source for documenting Tolkien's interest in *Kalevala* is his published letters. From them we learn how his discovery of Charles Eliot's Finnish grammar inspired him to learn Finnish well enough to read the epic in the original. In a 1955 letter to W.H. Auden, Tolkien remarked that he "never learned Finnish well enough to do more than plod through a bit of the original, like a schoolboy with Ovid; being mostly taken up with its effect on 'my language'" (*Letters,* 214).

Influence on Language

Just as *Kalevala* launched the establishment of Finnish as the national language for Finland, it launched Tolkien's invented language Quenya, spoken by High-elves and used by Númenóreans as the language of ritual. Tolkien's letters reveal his appreciation of the sounds of Finnish. Of Quenya, he wrote that it had a Latin base "with two other (main) ingredients that happen to give me 'phonaesthetic' pleasure: Finnish and Greek" (*Letters,* 176). According to Garth, the "stark array of consonants and the chiming inflexional word-endings of Finnish produce a distinctive musicality that Tolkien adapted for Qenya" (*Letters,* 61).

Influence on Storytelling

Kalevala's influence on Tolkien's fiction was both direct and indirect. At first, Tolkien attempted to take an actual character from the epic (Kullervo) and rewrite the story, but he abandoned it unfinished. However, the *Kalevala* world runs like an undercurrent through Tolkien's fiction, from its cosmogonic myth where music creates the world (Ainulindalë) and tales of doomed lovers (Beren and Lúthien, Túrin and Finduilas) to its "landscape of mysterious islands bordered by misty coasts and inland waterways (the topography of Middle-earth and Númenor)" (Petty, 78).

In *The Silmarillion, Kalevala*-character archetypes include Aulë, the smith of the Valar (similar to Ilmarinen, god-like blacksmith and maker of the magical Sampo); Varda, whom the Elves called Elbereth (like Ilmatar, creation goddess and mother of Väinämöinen); Fëanor, tragic leader of the Noldorin Elves (Joukahainen, an ambitious and embittered young wizard); the hero Beren (Lemminkäinen, the reckless adventurer and wooer of maidens); and Túrin Turambar (Kullervo, who committed incest and suicide).

Gandalf, like Väinämöinen, is both sorcerer and sage. Throughout Middle-earth, he is a wise adviser to Elves, Hobbits, and Men, but to the Valar (Tolkien's pantheon) he is known as Olórin, wisest of the race of Wizards. Among female characters, Galadriel has qualities of both Ilmatar (as a semidivine being embodying the Light of creation) and Louhi (as female leader of a mysterious hidden land, with the potential for dark power).

Plot elements inspired by *Kalevala* can be found in both *The Lord of the Rings* and *The Silmarillion*. Väinämöinen's sowing chant suggests *The Silmarillion*'s "Great Music." Ilmarinen's wedding celebration (with beer making, dancing, singing, and storytelling) finds its way into Hobbiton and even Gondor. Tragic Kullervo becomes the doomed hero Túrin Turambar. Theft of a mysterious object forged by magic incites greed and war, a pattern found in both the history of the Silmarils and the One Ring.

Much of Tolkien's poetry has the feel of transcribed oral folk song, in which natural magic is revealed through the power of song. Examples from *The Silmarillion* include Lúthien's songs that conquer the stronghold of Angband and reunite her as a mortal with her lover Beren; Yavanna's singing that creates the Spring of Arda and Two Trees of Valinor; and the singing contest between Sauron and Elven King Finrod Felagund.

For setting and atmosphere, Middle-earth echoes the northern landscape of Kalevala and Pohjola. The running rivers and reed-covered banks; flat, sandy regions and hard rocky scarps; tree-covered hills and knolls dipping into dales and marshes; willows in fenny regions; and the flowering trees and grassy meadows covered in heather all belong to the literary landscape of both Lönnrot and Tolkien.

Lönnrot's framing device—the scribe or bard who shares a body of myths and legends with an audience—can be seen in Tolkien's *Unfinished Tales, The Silmarillion,* and to some extent, *The Lord of the Rings.* Tolkien's fiction gives the illusion of material handed down from Elvish sources and later transcribed as, for example, the "Quenta Silmarillion" in *The Silmarillion* or events recorded by Bilbo and Frodo Baggins in the so-called *Red Book of Westmarch.* This historicity was one means by which Tolkien incorporated the sense of authenticity into Middle-earth, what Tom Shippey refers to as "rootedness" in his article "Tolkien and the Appeal of the Pagan: *Edda* and *Kalevala*" (147–48).

The Kullervo Tale

The story appealed to Tolkien's sense of tragedy and led him to reshape it into a tale that would become part of the "Silmarillion" legends. He wrote to his fiancée Edith Bratt, "I am trying to turn one of the stories—which is really a very great story and most tragic—into a short story somewhat on the lines of Morris's romances with chunks of poetry in between." The Kullervo story he envisioned was never finished, but its tragic implications emerged as "The Children of Húrin," published posthumously in *Unfinished Tales,* and the chapter "Of Túrin Turambar" in *The Silmarillion,* wherein Túrin's unwitting marriage to his sister is the result of Glaurung the Dragon's wicked spell. Tolkien was especially moved by Kullervo's suicide and kept that scene, including the conversation between the sword and its master, in which the sword agrees to slay him swiftly.

The Sampo Legend

The connection between the Sampo legend and Tolkien's work is by inference rather than direct borrowing. The Sampo, forged by Ilmarinen, was never clearly defined in the *runos* Lönnrot collected. As such, this mysterious object remained wide open to interpretation, and the same can be said for Tolkien's use of it. Jonathan Himes's essay, "What Tolkien Really Did with the Sampo," suggests that Fëanor's crafting of the Silmarils from the light of Yavanna's Two Trees is modeled on the Sampo tale.

Other arguments suggest that the Ring is the Sampo of *The Lord of the Rings.* Specifically, the Ring is forged by Sauron using dark magic, a war is fought over it, it is lost, it burns the hands and souls of those who try to use it, and those who destroyed it sail on a ship into the West with a message of hope.

ANNE C. PETTY

Primary Sources

Bosley, Keith, trans. *The Kalevala.* Compiled by Elias Lönnrot, 1849. Oxford: Oxford University Press, 1989.

Friberg, Eino, trans. *The Kalevala: Epic of the Finnish People.* Compiled by Elias Lönnrot, 1849. Helsinki: Otava Publishing, 1988.

Kirby, W.F., trans. *Kalevala: The Land of the Heroes.* Compiled by Elias Lönnrot, 1849. First published in 1907 by J.M. Dent & Sons, 2 vols. Reprint, New York: E.P. Dutton & Co., 1951.

Magoun, Francis Peabody Jr., trans. *The Kalevala or Poems of the Kaleva District.* Compiled by Elias Lönnrot, 1849. Cambridge, MA: Harvard University Press, 1963.

Further Reading

Carpenter, Humphrey. *J.R.R. Tolkien: A Biography.* Boston, MA: Houghton Mifflin, 1977.

Chance, Jane, ed. *Tolkien and the Invention of Myth: A Reader*. Lexington, KY: University Press of Kentucky, 2004.

Flieger, Verlyn, and Carl F. Hostetter, eds. *Tolkien's Legendarium: Essays on "The History of Middle-earth."* Westport, CT: Greenwood, 2000.

Garth, John. *Tolkien and the Great War: The Threshold of Middle-earth.* Boston, MA: Houghton Mifflin, 2003.

Helms, Randel. *Tolkien and the Silmarils: Imagination and Myth in "The Silmarillion."* Boston, MA: Houghton Mifflin, 1981.

Himes, Jonathan B. "What Tolkien Really Did with the Sampo." *Mythlore* 22, no. 4 (2000): 69–85.

Kuusi, Matti, Keith Bosley, and Michael Branch, eds. *Finnish Folk Poetry: Epic.* Helsinki: Finnish Literature Society, 1977.

Pentikainen, Juha Y. *Kalevala Mythology*, translated by Ritva Poom. Bloomington, IN: Indiana University Press, 1989.

Petty, Anne C. "Identifying England's Lönnrot." *Tolkien Studies.* I (2004): 69–84.

Shippey, Tom. "Tolkien and the Appeal of the Pagan: *Edda* and *Kalevala.*" In Chance, ed. *Tolkien and the Invention of Myth: A Reader.* Lexington, KY: University Press of Kentucky. 2004.

See also **Epic Poetry; Finland: Reception of Tolkien; Finnish Language; Frame Narrative; Heroes and Heroism; Languages Invented by Tolkien; Mythology for England; One Ring, The; Oral Tradition; Silmarils; Song Contests; Túrin; Wizards**

FINLAND: RECEPTION OF TOLKIEN

Tolkien's works were first introduced to Finland in their English originals by the active minority of Finns who have a keen interest in English literature and culture. Tolkien's central books reached a wider audience once they started being translated into Finnish. A turning point was 1973 in that it saw the publication of the Finnish versions of both *The Hobbit* (*Lohikäärmevuori*) and *The Fellowship of the Ring* (*Sormuksen ritarit*). *Lohikäärmevuori* was illustrated by Tove Jansson, the Finnish creator of Moomin trolls. Jansson had originally made the illustrations for the Swedish *Hobbit* translation *Bilbo—en hobbits äventyr* in 1962. *The Hobbit, The Lord of the Rings,* and *The Silmarillion* were published in Finnish in the 1970s. More books came out in Finnish in the 1980s, which is when the Tolkien phenomenon started to reach the height of its popularity. The translators who created the Finnish terminology for Tolkien's fantasy world have become well known, Kersti Juva in particular.

The increasing popularity of Tolkien's books created a need for background literature in Finnish. David Day's *A Tolkien Bestiary* (*Tolkienin maailma*) and *Tolkien: The Illustrated Encyclopedia* (*Tolkien:*

tarujen taustaa) were translated in 1990 and 1992, respectively, and Tolkien's biography by Humphrey Carpenter was translated in 1998. Tolkien's books were thus received in Finland in three main stages. At first, they were accessible only in English to those with contacts with the English-speaking world. The second era started with the translation of the major works into Finnish, and the third began when Peter Jackson's films reached Finland and attracted a new audience who had not necessarily been acquainted with the books. In Jackson's films, the English and the Finnish worlds of Tolkien meet: spoken English is translated in the Finnish subtitles, which rely heavily on the vocabulary of the well-established Finnish translations.

Suomen Tolkien-seurary (The Finnish Tolkien Society) serves as a forum for those interested in Tolkien or fantasy literature in general. Particularly, *The Lord of the Rings* and its mythology and language have attracted a lot of scholarly and popular interest: a number of master's theses have been written and articles have been published. Special attention has been paid to the possible Finnish links, the influence of the Finnish language and the Finnish national epic, the *Kalevala,* on the creation of Tolkien's mythology and languages. Tolkien's discovery of Finnish grammar and the *Kalevala* while studying in Oxford have not gone unnoticed. Finnish elements have been looked for and found in Tolkien's mythology (themes and structure, parallels with the *Kalevala*) and his languages (use of Finnish words and Finnish phonology and morphology in Quenyan in particular).

There have been several Finnish theatre productions of *The Hobbit* and *The Lord of the Rings* both for adult and for child audiences, for example, *Taru Sormusten Herrasta* (*The Lord of the Rings*) by Ryhmäteatteri, Helsinki 1989; *Sagan om ringen* (*The Lord of the Rings*) by Svenska teatern (Swedish Theatre), Helsinki 2001; and *Hobitti* (*The Hobbit*) by Kuopion kaupunginteatteri (Kuopio City Theatre). *The Hobbit* has also been produced as a ballet by the Finnish National Opera in 2001 (music by Aulis Sallinen, choreography by Marjo Kuusela).

After Peter Jackson's films, even most Finns without an interest in fantasy literature have at least a vague idea of what *The Lord of the Rings* is about. The popularity of Tolkien's books and of the films based on them, theatre productions in various parts of Finland in both official languages, the Internet (discussion forums, associations, articles, etc.), role-playing games, and various groups and organisations relating to the world created by Tolkien witness that his major works have become part of mainstream Finnish popular culture.

A Chronological List of Tolkien's Works Translated into Finnish

- *Lohikäärmevuori, eli Erään hoppelin matka sinne ja takaisin* (*The Hobbit or There and Back Again,* 1937). Translated by Risto Pitkänen. Helsinki: Tammi, 1973.
- *Sormuksen Ritarit* (*The Fellowship of the Ring,* 1954). Translated by Eila Pennanen and Kersti Juva, poems by Panu Pekkanen. Porvoo: WSOY, 1973.
- *Kaksi tornia* (*Two Towers,* 1954). Translated by Eila Pennanen and Kersti Juva, poems by Panu Pekkanen. Porvoo: WSOY, 1974.
- *Kuninkaan Paluu* (*The Return of the King,* 1955). Translated by Kersti Juva, poems by Panu Pekkanen. Porvoo: WSOY, 1975.
- *Maamies ja Lohikäärme* (*Farmer Giles of Ham,* 1949). Translated by Panu Pekkanen. Porvoo: WSOY, 1978.
- *Silmarillion* (*The Silmarillion,* 1977). Translated by Kersti Juva, poems by Panu Pekkanen. Porvoo: WSOY, 1979.
- *Herra Bliss* (*Mr. Bliss,* 1982). Translated by Panu Pekkanen. Porvoo: WSOY, 1983.
- *Seppä ja Satumaa* (*Smith of Wootton Major,* 1967). Translated by Panu Pekkanen. Porvoo: WSOY, 1983.
- *Hobitti, eli sinne ja takaisin* (*The Hobbit or There and Back Again,* 1937). Translated by Kersti Juva, poems by Panu Pekkanen. Porvoo: WSOY, 1985 (second translation).
- *Keskeneräisten tarujen kirja* (*Unfinished Tales on Númenor and Middle-earth,* 1980). Translated by Kersti Juva, poems by Panu Pekkanen. Porvoo: WSOY, 1986.
- *Roverandom* (*Roverandom,* 1998). Translated by Kersti Juva, poems by Alice Martin. Porvoo: WSOY, 2001.
- *Puu ja lehti* (*Tree and Leaf,* 1964). Translated by Vesa Sisättö and Kersti Juva, poems by Johanna Vainikainen-Uusitalo and Alice Martin. Porvoo: WSOY, 2002.
- *Kirjeitä Joulupukilta* (*The Father Christmas Letters,* 1976). Translated by Kersti Juva, poems by Alice Martin. Porvoo: WSOY, 2004.
- *Bilbon viimeinen laulu* (*Bilbo's Last Song,* 1974). Translated by Jukka Virtanen and Mikael Ahlström. Porvoo: WSOY, 2005.

KANERVA HEIKKINEN

Further Reading

Carpenter, Humphrey. *J.R.R. Tolkien: A Biography.* London: George Allen & Unwin, 1977. (Finnish translation: *J.R.R. Tolkien: Elämäkerta,* translated by Vesa Sisättö, poems by Johanna Vainikainen. Helsinki: Nemo, 1998.)

Day, David. *A Tolkien Bestiary.* London: Mitchell Beazley, 1979. (Finnish translation: *Tolkienin maailma,* translated by Kersti Juva. Porvoo: WSOY, 1990.)

Day, David. *Tolkien: The Illustrated Encyclopedia.* London: Mitchell Beazley, 1991. (Finnish translation: *Tolkien: Tarujen Taustaa,* translated by Tarja Virtanen. Porvoo: WSOY, 1990.)

See also **Finland: Literary Sources; Finnish Language; Jackson, Peter; Languages Invented by Tolkien**

FINN AND HENGEST

Finn and Hengest is based on Tolkien's lecture notes on the so-called Finn Episode in the Old English poem *Beowulf* and an independently transmitted poetic fragment named *The Fight at Finnsburg.* The original manuscript of the latter is no longer extant, and all we have is the transcription of the text, which was published in the first volume of George Hickes's *Linguarum Vett. Septentrionalium Thesaurus* (1705). According to Hickes, the Old English poem was found on a single leaf in a volume of Early Middle English homilies in the Library of Lambeth Palace, the London residence of the Archbishops of Canterbury. Both the Episode and the Fragment deal with the same incident at Finnsburg, which took place sometime in the first half of the fifth century. The basic sequence of events can be reconstructed from the information given in the two texts, and though scholars differ concerning some details, there is general agreement on the main story line, which could be summarised as follows:

- x = Information that immediately precedes the events mentioned in the two texts and that has been reconstructed from hints and details given in the extant texts
- Fragment = Information given by the fragmentary *The Fight at Finnsburg*
- y = Missing information interpolated from the information given in either text
- Finn Episode = Information derived from the Finn Episode in *Beowulf*

[......]	[————————]	[....]	[- - - - - - - - - - - - - - - - - -]
x	Fragment	y	Finn Episode (91 lines)
	(48 lines)		

Hildeburh, a Danish princess and daughter of King Hoc, is given in marriage to Finn, the king of the Frisians. They have a son, who is in his teens at the time the narrative sets in.

- x: Hnaef, a prince of the Danish royal house, visits his sister Hildeburh and his brother-in-law

Finn at their home in Finnsburg. Hnaef's retinue consists of a troop of sixty warriors, among whom is one called Hengest. They are lodged in a building.

- Fragment: Hnaef's retainers see armed warriors advancing in the moonlight. They prepare the defence of the hall. The enemies attack yet cannot overcome the valiant defenders, and many of the attackers are killed, whereas none of Hnaef's men fall during five days.
- y: The fighting continues and Hnaef is killed, as is the (elder?) son of Finn and Hildeburh. Hengest, though most likely not a member of the royal Danish family, takes over the leadership of the defenders.
- Episode: The fight comes to a stalemate, and both sides solemnly swear to an agreement that is to secure Hnaef's retainers a place in Finn's retinue and half a share in the gifts dealt out in the hall. The fallen warriors are burnt on a pyre, and Hildeburh bewails the loss of her brother Hnaef and her son. The surviving men settle in to pass the winter in Frisia. With the arrival of spring, it once more becomes possible to travel by ship. Hengest, who has spent the winter at Finn's court, plots revenge, and Hnaef's retainers attack Finn in his hall, kill him, steal his treasure, and take Hildeburh home to Denmark.

Tolkien knew both texts intimately and, from 1928 to 1937, lectured six times specifically on the story of Finn and Hengest. He did so once again in 1963 when substituting for Charles Leslie Wrenn. In 1966, he offered his lecture notes to Alan Bliss, a scholar of Anglo-Saxon like Tolkien. Yet since Tolkien wanted to bring his notes into order first, but postponed this time and again, the transaction did not take place. It was Christopher Tolkien who, in 1979, encouraged Bliss to undertake the editing of the lecture notes and provided him with the manuscripts. Bliss, after being given the texts, presents the material in five major parts. First, he gives Tolkien's notes on the proper names, which are listed in the sequence they occur in the texts. The second part contains explanatory notes on difficult or interesting words or lines in the Fragment and the Episode. In the third part appear translations of both texts into modern English (the translation of the Fragment is provided by Bliss). Fourth, a reconstruction of the story into a continuous narrative is attempted. Last, three appendices provide material on the Danes, on the dating of Healfdene and Hengest, and on the nationality of Hengest (the last item by Bliss).

As Bliss points out, Tolkien had not only preëmpted many of the insights of later scholars (including Bliss's own) but also uncovered new and hitherto unknown aspects. It is therefore all the more puzzling that *Finn and Hengest* "has had no academic impact at all—no one ever cites it" (Shippey, 267).

Although Tolkien's study of the two texts is primarily of academic relevance, it did have an impact on his creative writing. One of the points made by Tolkien is the identification of Hengest mentioned in the "Finnsburg Fragment" with the Hengest who, together with his brother Horsa, is reported to have led the Germanic tribes in the invasion of Britain (see Bede, I, xv; see also Honegger). The "Finnsburg Fragment" does not give any explicit information as to Hengest's nationality, yet Tolkien builds a strong case for making him a Jutish nobleman. As Michael Drout points out, Tolkien "indulged in the imaginative creation of pseudo-history that [he] himself did not believe to be factually true" (230), yet that helped to solve a number of historical and literary problems. Thus, Tolkien incorporates Hengest within the fictional "historical" framework intended to provide the explanation for the transmission of the legendarium in England. Ælfwine/Ottor/Eriol (also called Angol after the regions of his home), before travelling to Tol Eressëa (the island of the Elves) where he is to be told the legends that make up the legendarium, is married to a woman called Cwén (Old English for "woman" or "wife") and has two sons, Hengest and Horsa. Tolkien now makes Ælfwine an Englishman "avant la lettre" by identifying his home as "Angeln," the region of the Danish peninsula between the Flensburg Fjord and the River Schlei (*Lost Tales I*, 22–24; *Lost Tales II*, 290–91). It is from this area that at least some of the Germanic invaders of Britain came over during the fifth century—presumably under the leadership of the Jutish brothers Hengest and Horsa. Thus, the figure of Hengest links Old English literature (*Beowulf, The Fight at Finnsburg*) not only with Anglo-Saxon history (Bede) but also with Tolkien's legendarium and its transmission in England.

THOMAS HONEGGER

Further Reading

Aurner, Nellie Slayton. *Hengest: A Study in Early English Hero Legend*. University of Iowa Humanistic Studies, 2. Iowa City: University of Iowa, 1921.

Colgrave, Bertiam and R.A.B. Mynors, eds. *Bedés Ecclesiastical History of the English People*. Oxford: Clarendon Press, 1969.

Drout, Michael D.C. "A Mythology for Anglo-Saxon England." In *Tolkien and the Invention of Myth: A Reader*, edited by Jane Chance, 229–47. Lexington, KY: University Press of Kentucky, 2004.

Honegger, Thomas. "Hengest und Finn, Horsa." In *Reallexikon der germanischen Altertumskunde*, 386–91. Vol. 14. Berlin: Walter de Gruyter, 2000.

Shippey, Tom. *J.R.R. Tolkien: Author of the Century*. Boston, MA: Houghton Mifflin, 2001.

See also **"*Beowulf:* The Monsters and the Critics";** **Goths**

FINNISH LANGUAGE

Tolkien's interest in the language of the Finns was sparked by reading W.F. Kirby's English translation of the *Kalevala* (1907), which he found in the library of King Edward's Academy, Birmingham, in approximately 1910. He began studying the language in earnest after discovering *A Finnish Grammar* compiled by Charles Eliot in the library of Exeter College, Oxford, in or around 1912. Late in life, he said that he "never learned Finnish well enough to do more than plod through a bit of the original" (*Letters,* 214). His self-assessments tend to be modest, and other comments indicate he felt he had some grasp of nuances of Finnish such as humor, so it is safe to say only that he was not as proficient as he was in other languages that were his special study (such as Old and Middle English or Old Norse).

Nevertheless, he was strongly influenced by Finnish in devising Quenya, the language of the High-elves. While most of his invented vocabulary is not borrowed directly from another language, he did occasionally borrow words. One example is that Quenya *tie,* meaning "path," clearly comes from the Finnish word for "road," also *tie.* There are other such instances, but a similarity in phonology is more important, and the most pervasive influence is that of Finnish grammar, particularly in morphology (such as the use of multiple suffixes to make a single word rich in meaning). Tom DuBois and Scott Mellor give this example: The English phrase "in my books" is a single word in Finnish and Quenya. Finnish *kirjoissani* has the components *kirja* (the noun "book"), *-i-* (a plural marker), *ssa* (a case ending meaning "in"), and *-ni* (a possessive marker meaning "my"). Tolkien's Quenya word modeled on the Finnish, using a different order for the suffixes, is *parmanyassen,* formed by combining *parma* (the noun "book") with *nya* (the possessive "my"), *sse* (meaning "in"), and *-n* (to indicate the word is plural).

Tolkien was always keenly interested in the intimate relation among language, thought, and story; and his fiction grows out of creating a world in which his invented languages were at home. The Finnish language and the *Kalevala* combined with other linguistic and mythic traditions in his mind to produce such themes as song being a source of supernatural power and the ambivalent hero Kullervo as

the avowed inspiration for his Túrin. Perhaps the greatest single influence was the example of one person, Dr. Elias Lönnrot, compiling a national mythology for Finland, possibly leading to Tolkien's youthful ambition to try to do the same for England.

RICHARD C. WEST

Further Reading

Bosley, Keith, ed. and trans. *The "Kalevala": An Epic Poem after Oral Tradition by Elias Lönnrot*. Oxford: Oxford University Press, 1989.

Carpenter, Humphrey. *J.R.R. Tolkien: A Biography*. London: George Allen & Unwin, 1977. Boston, MA: Houghton Mifflin, 1977.

Chance, Jane, ed. "Tolkien and Finnish." Part V of *Tolkien and the Invention of Myth: A Reader*, 275–304. Lexington, KY: University Press of Kentucky, 2004.

DuBois, Tom, and Scott Mellor. "The Nordic Roots of Tolkien's Middle-earth." *Scandinavian Review* 90, no. 1 (2002): 35–40.

See also **Literary Influences, Nineteenth and Twentieth Century; Mythology for England; Song Contests; Túrin**

FINROD

An Elf of the kindred of the Noldor, Finrod is the brother of Galadriel in *The Silmarillion*. His father is Finarfin, son of Finwë, the high king of the Noldor, by his second wife, Indis of the Vanyar. Finrod's mother is Eärwen of Alqualondë, the daughter of Olwë, the high king of the Teleri and the brother of Thingol. Thus, Finrod is by blood part of all three of the high kindreds of the Elves: Vanyar, Noldor, and Teleri.

Finrod is born in Valinor during the light of the Two Trees and then goes into exile in Middle-earth with the Noldor, where he first founds the citadel of Minas Tirith and then the hidden kingdom of Nargothrond (from which he receives his Dwarvish second name, Felagund, the hewer of caves). His collaboration with the Dwarves leads to the creation of the Nauglamír, the Necklace of the Dwarves, which was composed of jewels brought back from Valinor by Finrod and which eventually housed the Silmaril taken from Thangorodrim by Beren and Lúthien.

Finrod was the first of the High-elves to meet Men, coming upon a camp of the people of Bëor the Old in the north of Ossiriand. The Men named Finrod Nóm (which means "wisdom"), and he taught them much and eventually led them into Beleriand, where they settled. In the battle of Dagor Bragollach, Finrod's life was saved by Barahir, and in recognition of this, Finrod gave to him his ring, which had been made in

Valinor by the Noldor (this ring eventually became an heirloom of the house of Isildur and was inherited by Aragorn).

Finrod's ring passed to Barahir's son Beren, who, on the quest for the Silmaril, called upon Finrod for help. Finrod fulfilled his vow and went with Beren on the quest, but they and their companions were captured by Sauron, who had seized Finrod's tower of Minas Tirith and made it into his citadel. Finrod lost a contest of song with Sauron and was imprisoned in the tower with Beren and their companions. Sauron sent a werewolf to devour each of the companions, intending to leave Finrod for last, but when the werewolf came for Beren, Finrod burst his chains and killed the werewolf, though he was slain in the effort. After the vanquishing of Sauron by Lúthien and Huan the hound of Valinor, they buried Finrod upon the hilltop of that isle, which was now cleansed. But Finrod "walks with Finarfin his father beneath the trees in Eldamar." This was the first specific example of the reincarnation of the Elves published before *The History of Middle-earth*.

Finrod is in some ways the best of the High-elves: he is noble, generous, kind, valiant, mindful of his oaths, and genuinely devoted to Men. In Tolkien's later writings, Finrod represents the Elvish point of view in the "Athrabeth Finrod Ah Andreth," "The Debate of Finrod and Andreth." Andreth is an old, wise woman (human) who had at one point fallen in love with Finrod's younger brother, Aegnor. The two of them discuss the immortality of Elves and the mortality of Men, and Finrod is both kind and firm: he is genuinely moved by the sorrow of Men, but at the same time he strongly asserts his belief in the power and benevolence of Eru, the creator.

The textual history of Finrod is complex. The character who is eventually Finrod Felagund in *The Silmarillion* was originally named Felagoth, then Felagund, then Inglor Felagund. Finrod was originally this character's father (and thus the name of the character who would later become Finarfin). Then the name Finrod replaced the name Inglor, changing Inglor Felagund to Finrod Felagund, and the Finrod character was renamed Finarfin. Gildor Inglorion, the leader of the Elves who meet Frodo in the Shire, says that he is of the house of Finrod, but what this means is not precisely clear, since Finrod had neither wife nor child. Gildor could certainly be of the house of Finarfin, and it is possible that at the time of the writing of *The Lord of the Rings* there was still uncertainty as to the final determination of the name for the head of the house (it is perhaps worth noting that Tolkien named the leader of the wandering Elves Gildor Inglorion in his first version of the scene).

MICHAEL D.C. DROUT

See also **Beren; Elves: Kindreds and Migrations; Elves: Reincarnation; Lúthien; Men of Middle-earth;** *Silmarillion, The*; **Song Contests**

FINWË AND MÍRIEL

Finwë was the first king of the Noldor. One of three Elves chosen to go to Aman as ambassadors when the Valar first find the Elves in Cuiviénen, he journeys into the West and sees the glory of Valinor before the Two Trees are darkened. When he returns to Cuiviénen, he convinces most of the Noldor to accept the Valar's summons. Míriel was Finwë's first wife and the most skilled of all the Noldor at weaving and needlework. In early drafts, she was called Byrde, but in later editions Serindë, "the Broideress." Míriel bears only one son, Curufinwë, who inherits her surpassing skill and becomes the most gifted of mind and body of all the Elves. Míriel gives him the name Fëanor, "Spirit of Fire," by which he is later known.

According to Christopher Tolkien, the story of Finwë and Míriel began only as a rider in the manuscript to the "first phase" revision of chapter 6 of *The Silmarillion,* but later it assumed "extraordinary importance" to J.R.R. Tolkien (*Morgoth,* 205). It is an unusual tale. It is said that "the love of Finwë and Míriel was great and glad, for it began in the Blessed Realm in the Days of Bless." Nonetheless, it is within the house of Finwë that strife first arises in Aman, leading to the oath of Fëanor, the Kinslaying at Alqualondë, and the Doom of the Noldor. Finwë himself is slain before his own doors by Morgoth, becoming the first to have his blood shed in the Blessed Realm. The tragedy begins with Míriel, who in giving birth to Fëanor is "consumed in spirit and body" and loses the desire to live. Before her spirit departs her body, her final words to Finwë indicate foreknowledge of evil to come, for which she desires to be held blameless. Later, against the wishes of Fëanor, Finwë weds Indis. In doing so, he is the only one of the Eldar known to take a second wife after the death of his first. Indis bears him two sons, Fingolfin and Finarfin. (The earliest version records that she also bore three daughters.) The son of Míriel is in constant strife with his two half-brothers, the sons of Indis (*S,* 63–71; *Morgoth,* 207).

The Silmarillion gives no explanation why Míriel would lose the will to live except that she poured into Fëanor strength and life enough for many children. However, Morgoth had already been at work among the Elves in Cuiviénen before the Valar came, and he sowed among them seeds of despair. Míriel's loss of the will to live—even to raise her child—shows a loss of hope, perhaps resulting from Morgoth's deceits.

In the draft of an unsent letter, Tolkien makes reference to the "strange case" of Míriel, who tries to die, wishing "to abandon being, and refus[ing] rebirth." The results of Míriel's actions, he writes, are "disastrous" and lead "to the 'Fall' of the High-elves" (*Letters*, 286). It is also suggested that had Finwë "endured his loss and been content with the fathering of his mighty son . . . a great evil might have been prevented" (*S*, 65). Thus, while it is clear that the Valar hold Fëanor responsible for his actions, neither Finwë nor Míriel is blameless, despite Míriel's request to be held so (*Morgoth*, 242).

MATTHEW DICKERSON

Further Reading

Flieger, Verlyn. *Splintered Light: Logos and Languages in Tolkien's World*. Grand Rapids, MI: Eerdmans, 1983.

See also **Elves: Kindreds and Migrations; Fëanor; *Morgoth's Ring*; Valar**

FOLKLORE

Folklorist Katharine Briggs divided folklore into two basic groups: folk narratives or fiction and folk legends or sagas. The first deals with "beliefs actually held" but is told as a fictional story following a recognizable pattern (using formulas such as "Once upon a time"), whereas the second is presented as a possibly true tale handed down through the ages, incorporating numerous folk motifs and images (Briggs, 6). Tolkien's knowledge and use of folklore includes both groups.

"I have been a lover of fairy-stories since I learned to read," wrote Tolkien in "On Fairy-stories" (*MC*, 108). As a youngster, he drew inspiration from both European and English tales published in magazines and popular collections. Most influential were the German *kunstmärchen* (literary fairy tales) of the Brothers Grimm and Ludwig Tieck (both first appearing around 1812), as well as English collections such as E.H. Knatchbull-Hugessen's *Stories for My Children*, Richard Garnett's *The Twilight of the Gods and Other Tales*, and Edith Nesbit's dragon stories, first published in *Strand Magazine* and collected into *The Book of Dragons*, which included "The Dragon Tamers," a tale of a dragon forced to bargain with humans for its freedom, as does Chrysophylax in *Farmer Giles of Ham*.

Of particular interest are Andrew Lang's color-coded "fairy books" (especially the *Red Fairy Book* containing "The Story of Sigurd"). Lang's retelling of the dragonslayer legend first introduced Tolkien to the Fafnir story, which he would read years later in the original Old Norse and incorporate into Túrin's battle with Glaurung and Bilbo's conversation with Smaug.

As Michael Drout points out, "The great synthesizing works of Jakob and Wilhelm Grimm in German, Elias Lönnrot in Finnish, and N.F.S. Grundtvig in Danish were all well known to Tolkien" (238). The 1853 Danish collections of Svend Grundtvig were translated into English by E.M. Smith-Dampier as *A Book of Danish Ballads* (containing examples of elf–mortal unions). Other collections available to Tolkien during his formative years as student and writer include *English Fairy Tales* by Joseph Jacobs, especially the tale "Childe Rowland" with its "dark tower" motif; *Popular Tales of the Western Highlands* by J.F. Campbell (four volumes); and *English and Scottish Popular Ballads* collected by Francis James Child.

Folk wisdom abounds in Middle-earth, from hobbits, wizards, dwarves, and even men. For example, "dragonlore such as proverbs, maxims, epigrams, and adages ('Every worm has his weak spot'), and old ballads" (Petty 2004, 55) builds up expectation of Smaug in *The Hobbit*. Folklore motifs that surface throughout Tolkien's fiction include riddle contests, a broken sword reforged for a rightful heir, a magic ring that enslaves those who own it, a battle of wits through conversation with a hoard-guarding dragon, a king-in-waiting who goes hidden or disguised for years before revealing himself to claim his throne, a mortal falling in love with an elf or another nonmortal being, a desperate quest with its "road of trials" or tests, and a mission to gain something of great value or save the world in some way.

ANNE C. PETTY

Further Reading

Anderson, Douglas A., ed. *Tales Before Tolkien: The Roots of Modern Fantasy*. New York: Ballantine, 2003.

Briggs, Katharine. *British Folk-Tales and Legends*. London: Routledge, 1977.

Carpenter, Humphrey. *Tolkien: A Biography*. Boston, MA: Houghton Mifflin, 1977.

Drout, Micheal D.C. "A Mythology of Anglo-Saxon England," in Chance, Jane, ed. *Tolkien and the Invention of Myth: A Reader*. Lexington, KY: University Press of Kentucky, 2004, pp. 229–248.

Lindahl, Carl, John McNamara, and John Lindow, eds. *Medieval Folklore*. New York: Oxford University Press, 2002.

Petty, Anne C. *Dragons of Fantasy*. Cold Spring Harbor, NY: Cold Spring Press, 2004.

See also **Dwarves; Elves; Fairies; German Folktale: *Deutsch Mythologie*; Quest Narrative; Riddles; Rings of Power; Towers; Weapons, Named**

FOOD

Food, in various forms, plays an important role in a world as realistically described as Middle-earth. Yet whereas readers are given detailed information about the food production of the Shire (Sarjeant), similarly detailed information for other parts of Middle-earth is missing. We may hear about the vast slave-cultivated fields around Lake Núrnen, which seem to provide most of the provender for Mordor's armies, or about the pleasant valleys of Lossarnach that are likely to furnish their inhabitants with fruit and corn, but this information is given in passing and is not given prominence.

As concerns meals, Tolkien usually avoids going into details, and food is, for example, as at feasts, hardly ever specified and occurs simply as "generic" food. However, he mentions a sufficient number of items for the reader to get a general idea about the eating habits of the Hobbits or the men of Gondor. Despite this general lack of specific information and despite the widespread textual silence about specific meals or recipes, at least one publication has attempted to re-create (mostly imaginatively) some of the dishes (Took).

Those items singled out by Tolkien are familiar food (cheese, cakes, bread, meat, honey, apples, mushrooms, berries, potatoes, wine, beer, tea, etc.) and contribute to the homely atmosphere, or they play an important role in the machinery of the tale (such as *lembas* and *miruvor*). Tolkien furthermore refrains from mentioning glaringly anachronistic food, but he does not feel compelled to keep to a strict historical setting and thus has the Hobbits cultivate the "homely" New World vegetable, the potato.

Next to its function as part and parcel of a world where people have to eat and drink to stay alive, the description of food is often used to further characterise protagonists. Hobbits love, in accordance with their general nature, good, homemade, no-nonsense food, whereas the culinary predilections of the Elves are, with the exception of the Wood-elves' partiality to good wine in *The Hobbit*, hardly ever mentioned; the reference to the wine in this context is motivated by requirements of the narrative rather than by ethnological or culinary interests. Normal Elvish food does not seem to differ much from "human" food, yet it tastes different and seems to affect humans in a positive way. The bread, apples, and drink served to the Hobbits by the wandering Elves in Woody End might indeed be just that, yet their Elvish origin makes them participate in the Elvish "enchantment" of the world so that the Hobbits recover the meaning of these food items "with clear taste-buds," so to speak—a quality shared, to some extent, by the food, and especially the drink, served by Tom Bombadil and Goldberry "down under Hill" (on [re-]enchantment in general, see "On Fairy-stories"). The silence of the text concerning Elvish food production, preparation, or consumption, on the one hand, and the highlighting of the special quality of Elvish food, on the other, both strengthen the overall impression of the Elves' "otherworldliness."

In accordance with their depraved nature, Orcs eat vile food, do not shrink from eating Man- or Orc-flesh, and seem to hate the touch or smell of Elvish food *(lembas)*. Gollum's depravity is likewise highlighted by his diet of raw fish, Orc-flesh, and unspecified slimy creatures, as well as his inability to eat *lembas*. His preference of the "raw" over the "cooked," as shown in the "stewed rabbit" episode, could be seen as an illustration of Claude Lévi-Strauss's anthropological theory. Grima Wormtongue's moral deterioration is likewise illustrated by his (alleged) cannibalism.

The drafts of the Ents, then, fit into the picture and are suited to the "treeish" nature of these creatures, though, as the example of Merry and Pippin shows, they seem also to agree with human digestion.

The descriptions of eating and drinking in Tolkien's fiction, and especially in *The Lord of the Rings*, do occur at strategic places within the narrative and (in most cases) provide moments of relaxation and recovery in an unobtrusive and realistic way.

THOMAS HONEGGER

Further Reading

Burns, Marjorie. "Eating, Devouring, Sacrifice, and Ultimate Desserts (Why Elves Are Vegetarian and the Unrefined Are Not)." In *Perilous Realms: Celtic and Norse in Tolkien's Middle-earth*, edited by Marjorie Burns, 156–71. Toronto: University of Toronto Press, 2005.

Sarjeant, William A.S. "The Shire: Its Bounds, Food and Farming." *Mallorn* 39 (2001): 33–37.

Took, Emerald (Stephanie Simmons). *Regional Cooking from Middle-earth: Recipes of the Third Age*. Oxford: Trafford Publishing, 2003.

See also **Eucharist;** *Lembas*

FORTUNE AND FATE

Like the classical world, Middle-earth is non-Christian. And although Middle-earth's inhabitants are not captive to the whims of gods for success or failure, they are aware of forces beyond their kens. Two of these forces might be called fate and fortune.

Tolkien, as a Medievalist, knew Boethius' *The Consolation of Philosophy*, a work so influential throughout the Middle Ages that it had been translated by both King Alfred the Great and Chaucer. In it Boethius synthesizes classical and Christian thought. Through a dialogue, Lady Philosophy (not Lady Theology) clearly defines the two powers and explains their relationships. For Boethius, the two aspects of "history" are Providence, the timeless and unchanging plan that exists in the mind of God, and Fate, the working out of this plan through time. Thus, there is a changeable Fate governing and revolving all things (Platonism as Boethius found it in fifth-century Proclus) and the "still turning point of the turning world" (Platonism as he found it in Plotinus).

In Anglo-Saxon literature, which Tolkien knew, the place of fate *(wyrd)* is central. Only occasionally is it suggested that the efforts of the hero are determinative. Beowulf, most famously, gives himself up to the powers of *wyrd* before each battle, accepting as fact that the outcome has already been determined. The task of the hero, therefore, was to fight well, to earn a reputation as a great warrior. In this the concept is not that different from the Greek understanding of the role of the gods in determining outcomes. For the audience of the Anglo-Saxon period, however, *wyrd* was a vague power rather than an anthropomorphized human figure.

In this connection, it is worth noting that the Old English *wyrd* is derived from the word for "become" (preterit subjunctive of the verb *wesan,* "to be"). Thus, it literally means "the course of events," "what comes to pass," used with a sense of future: what will happen. "Fate," the word usually used as the translation, derives from the Latin *fatum,* "that which has been spoken," usually that which has been decreed by the Fates: the three Greek, Roman, and Scandinavian goddesses of destiny who predetermined all events from eternity. It also conveys a clear sense of the past. By the later Middle Ages, by which time the term *wyrd* has been lost from the vocabulary, "fate" means simply "that which is destined to happen; one's appointed lot." The association with the three goddesses has disappeared, perhaps with the growth of Christianity.

"Fortune," by contrast, as a word, comes into the English language in the later Middle Ages from the Latin *fortuna* (also a Roman goddess), meaning "that which happens by chance, accident, luck; an adventure, a mishap; a disaster." In late Middle English, it comes to suggest the good or bad luck that befalls a person. Thus, there is an association with "fate," but the lack of a plan is essential. Boethius calls this concept "chance"—as does Tolkien—but Boethius provides as its personification Lady Fortune capriciously spinning her wheel, laughing at the sudden

reversals in the conditions of men: the classic image that pervades the Middle Ages. From Boethius to contemporary times, the meaning of this image has not changed.

In *The Lord of the Rings,* as in Boethius' work, there is no role for chance, but there is a role for fate. And as in the medieval literature Tolkien loved, in the story of Middle-earth the task of the hero is to accept the decisions of that fate and act in a way worthy of a great warrior.

KATHLEEN E. DUBS

See also **Christian Readings of Tolkien; Christianity; Free Will; Theological and Moral Approaches in Tolkien's Works**

"A FOURTEENTH-CENTURY ROMANCE"

This article appeared in *Radio Times,* the BBC's weekly magazine, in connection with the December 1953 broadcast of Tolkien's translation of *Sir Gawain and the Green Knight* on the BBC's Third Programme (which featured programming devoted to culture and the arts). It provides a brief introduction to the poem for a nonspecialist audience, discussing its language, its merits, and its relation to Chaucer. It includes an illustration from the manuscript featuring the Green Knight holding his decapitated head before Arthur's court.

The article begins with an announcement of the broadcast of Tolkien's translation and a quotation from its second stanza (lines 25–36) in which the poet invites the audience to listen; Tolkien's remarks follow in five paragraphs. He begins by repeating the poet's invitation to listen, noting the poem's excellence and concise structure. He expands on the poem's merits as a "well-told tale," identifying it as a fairy story deeply rooted in the pagan past of Ireland and Britain and reshaped in light of fourteenth-century concerns with conduct. In making this identification, he compares the poet's action to that of Shakespeare reworking older inherited material in *King Lear.* Most importantly, Tolkien identifies the poem as a representative of the Alliterative Revival associated with the West Midlands that was overcome by the literary tradition of rhyme represented in Chaucer's works, and he describes the Revival as an attempt to recover an ancestral style and meter, noting the unusual poetic diction featured in such poetry. He asserts Chaucer was aware of the Revival, observing the presence of its vocabulary in Chaucer's works, but again affirms Chaucer's victory over it. Tolkien concludes by emphasizing both the poem's strangeness and its appeal, noting the number of modern translations and then discussing the goals of his own: preservation of the original meter and reproduction of the language "in modern terms," a language he describes as "truly English, and above all courtly, wise, and well bred."

Some themes prominent in Tolkien's work as a whole recur here: He identifies the poem, for example, as both a romance and a fairy story, "but one written in a time when that kind was (happily) not yet associated with children." We see here as well Tolkien's identification with the nobility of fighting a losing battle; he identifies the poem as part of the movement in poetry that "challenged the supremacy of Rhyme— and was defeated." Throughout his discussion of the interaction between the Alliterative Revival and the rhymed poetry represented by Chaucer, Tolkien uses words such as "challenged," "defeated," "rescue," and "vigorous," and he refers to the *Gawain*-poet's and Chaucer's respective positions as those of "the losing" and the "winning side." Though not quite Galadriel's "long defeat" (*FR*, II, vii, 372), there are echoes of the same feeling. Connected with this are Tolkien's regret over the loss of England's native tradition in favor of poetry influenced by continental forms and his natural affinity for the language of the West Midlands as indicated by his description of the language of *Sir Gawain and the Green Knight* as "truly English."

YVETTE KISOR

Primary Sources

Tolkien, J.R.R. "A Fourteenth-Century Romance." *Radio Times* (London), December 4, 1953, 9.

Further Reading

Tolkien, J.R.R., trans. *Sir Gawain and the Green Knight, Pearl, and Sir Orfeo*. Boston, MA: Houghton Mifflin; London: George Allen & Unwin, 1975.
Tolkien, J.R.R., and E.V. Gordon, eds. *Sir Gawain and the Green Knight*. London: Oxford University Press, 1925.

See also **Alliterative Revival; "Chaucer as Philologist: The Reeve's Tale"; "On Fairy-Stories";** *Pearl*: **Edition by E.V. Gordon;** *Sir Gawain and the Green Knight, Pearl, and Sir Orfeo*: **Edited by Christopher Tolkien;** *Sir Gawain and the Green Knight*: **Edition with E.V. Gordon**

FRAME NARRATIVE

The device of frame narrative—a story within a story in which the outside or frame story provides both a context and a history for the inner narrative—is an essential structural element and an authorial conceit in Tolkien's major works: the "Silmarillion" with its multitude of storytellers and poets, *The Hobbit,* and *The Lord of the Rings.*

If we consider these works as autonomous texts, each has its own particular way of being a frame narrative. The interwoven tales that became the "Silmarillion," of which the earliest version is the 1917 notebook called by Tolkien *The Book of Lost Tales,* were presented as told to a specific audience of one. This was Eriol the Mariner, a figure whose name changed over time but whose function remained the same—that of a kind of prehistoric folklorist, a collector who would hear and record for posterity the stories of Creation and of the Elves. The external story of Eriol, what Tolkien later called the "Eriol-Saga," thus encloses and frames the internal tales of the "Silmarillion."

Likewise, *The Hobbit,* although in actual origin began as a sentence idly scribbled on a blank exam page, was presented to the public in what might be called a marginal frame, the literal margins of the top and bottom of the dust jacket decorated with a frieze of runic letters. These are not mere decoration but words spelling out that the book is "the hobbit or there and back again being the record of a year's journey made by bilbo baggins of hobbiton" and noting that it is "compiled from his [Bilbo's] memoirs by J.R.R. Tolkien and published by George Allen and Unwin Ltd." This message was a late epigraph to the actual text, entering only when Tolkien was asked by the publisher in March 1937 to provide a dust jacket design for the book. Nevertheless, although oblique, and certainly more visual than narrative, the runes (for those who trouble to read them) confer on *The Hobbit* the status of a "found" text and on Tolkien the fictive persona of compiler and editor. The message is supported by the maps and the runic superscripture of the introductory note added in 1966. It is not unlikely that the already-existing figure of Eriol the Mariner may have had some influence on Tolkien's insertion of himself as compiler-editor rather than author of the story.

In similar mode, but in different fashion, the prologue to *The Lord of the Rings* provides a pseudo-historical frame to that book. This consists of a long essay on the Shire and hobbits in the voice of an unidentified and equally pseudo editor. It puts the book in the context of its predecessor, *The Hobbit,* but also seats it within another, even earlier, more comprehensive text, "The Red Book of Westmarch". "The Red Book" is both a purely hypothetical construct and an all-enveloping frame, echoing in title and concept a real-account of "The Red Book of Westmarch" given in the "Note on the Shire Records" appended to the prologue in the second edition of *The Lord of the Rings.* Here, Tolkien gives in some detail the history of the composition of the "Red Book", its various addenda, its multiple copies, and their far-flung locations in the libraries of Middle-earth.

Thus, the "Silmarillion" is framed within the Eriol-figure, *The Hobbit* by Tolkien the compiler-editor, and *The Lord of the Rings* by the pseudo-editorial prologue with its references to the "Red Book".

The addition to the picture of the "Red Book" introduces the larger concept of all three works as parts of a whole vision, however accidental the incursion of *The Hobbit* and *The Lord of the Rings* into the already existing world of the "Silmarillion" may have been. In this respect, each text in its own peculiar way becomes a frame for the other two. *The Lord of the Rings,* at first called by its author simply "the new Hobbit," was begun as a sequel to that book and is purported to be the continuation of Bilbo's "memoirs" into the story of the Ring, first by Frodo, then by Sam. Thus, it is framed within the conceit of *The Hobbit* as memoir.

But both *The Hobbit* and *The Lord of the Rings* are folded into the putative "Red Book of Westmarch", which also incorporates Bilbo's "Translations From the Elvish." These are meant to be an account of the First and Second Ages (in a word, the "Silmarillion") written by Bilbo during his stays in Rivendell. However, the circumstance of publishing that brought out the "new Hobbit" before the "Silmarillion," plus the overwhelming response of the public to *The Lord of the Rings,* make that book the de facto frame through which both the others are popularly viewed. The completely hypothetical "Red Book" is therefore the frame for all three actual books, which make up the entirety of its presumed contents.

Such an elaborate and extended conceit of tales within tales has its genesis in Tolkien's original ambition to create an English mythology. He realized almost from the beginning that he had to provide some credible way for his stories of Valinor and Middle-earth to be transmitted from their fictive ancient sources to actual modern readers. If the stories were to be oral in origin, and thus replicate the traditions of real-world mythologies, there had to be some accounting for their preservation as written texts, their eventual presumed translation from the language of origin into modern English, and their actual publication in a modern world. In short, Tolkien had to provide the kind of scholarly apparatus that accompanies the publication of any real-world mythology.

His first strategy for solving this problem was to cast the "Silmarillion" as a series of orally told stories, the aptly named *Book of Lost Tales,* and to frame them as written down by an "outside" author,

Eriol the Mariner. Voyaging west "from the lands to the east of the North Sea" (i.e., continental Europe), Eriol arrived by chance at the Lonely Isle of Tol Eressëa. Welcomed at the Cottage of Lost Play, he there asked about and recorded the stories of the creation of the world, the gods, and the long history of the Elves. Returning east from Tol Eressëa to his homeland, Eriol would bring to what would eventually become the English people these written records, making them available (within the fiction) for transcription, translation, and publication.

Eriol's name was later changed to Ælfwine as being more obviously English (or Old English) and even later changed to Heorrenda. This was coincidentally and not by accident also Tolkien's proposed identity for another Old English mythmaker—the *Beowulf*-poet—thus linking his invented legends to actual English literature and history. By whatever name, this character, originally meant as not just a recorder but a witness to events, subsequently receded in importance, becoming the increasingly shadowy presence behind the stories. But whatever name and identity his creator chose for him, the recording figure never completely disappeared. He is the imaginary writer of the stories in the "Golden Book of Tavrobel" (later the "Golden Book of Heorrenda"), which was to lie unread for many centuries, later to be discovered, transmitted, and published through the efforts of a sequence of equally imaginary redactors, translators, and editors.

The mechanism of the frame would thus provide both a history and a rationale, accounting not just for the existence of the tales but also for their eventual publication. Tolkien considered this frame essential for the validation of his stories as "discovered" mythic material, and while the frame expanded over time and the authorial persona varied, the concept remained unchanged. Christopher Tolkien, who in 1977 edited and published *The Silmarillion,* an unframed and abbreviated version of his father's mythology, belatedly realized the necessity of a frame to validate the stories. His Foreword to the 1984 *Book of Lost Tales* acknowledged his 1977 publication of *The Silmarillion,* "Standing on its own and claiming, as it were, to be self-explanatory. . . . this I now think to have been an error" (*Lost Tales I,* 5).

In the course of Tolkien's many years of work on the project, the frame concept became immensely complicated—more in outline than in execution, which lagged behind and in some respects never came to fruition. As his fictive world expanded and developed, Tolkien added annals, lexicons, poets, translators, and a succession of copyists. The conceit reached its apogee in the contemporary twentieth-century frame he envisioned in his two unfinished time-travel stories, the abortive "Lost Road" (1936) and its successor "The Notion Club Papers" (1945–46). Reconceived and more fully developed than "The Lost Road," "The Notion Club Papers" is presented as the minutes of an informal Oxford club clearly modeled on the Inklings.

The "Papers" were "discovered" in the basement of the Examination Schools at Oxford by "Mr. Howard Green," and after some evaluation by two outside scholars, "Mr. W.W. Wormald" and "Mr. D.N. Borrow," were edited and published by their discoverer. Included among the minutes of the "Papers," chiefly discussions about time and space travel, was a single page in Anglo-Saxon, said to be a "translation" of an earlier account in Adûnaic by Elendil of the Downfall of Númenor. This in turn was derived from the even earlier page from the "book" of Eriol/Ælfwine/Heorrenda. Tolkien thus nested narrative within narrative within narrative within narrative, making each the frame for the one before and the one after it.

The strongest evidence that *The Notion Club Papers* was to be attached to the "Silmarillion" is a fragmentary note jotted at the time of Tolkien's work on the "Papers." It reads, "Do the Atlantis story and abandon Eriol-Saga." Neither term is explained; however, "Eriol-Saga" seems clearly to refer to the stories attached to Eriol the Mariner, the earliest frame figure, and "the Atlantis story" can be identified by comparison with similar phrases in Tolkien's letters as the Drowning of Númenor. If carried out, this strategy of dropping one frame in favor of another would have made a major modification in the frame concept, sending two modern Englishmen time-traveling by way of their ancestral Númenórean identities back to the end of the Second Age of Middle-earth, there to witness the destruction of the island-continent of Númenor and (more important) to bring the story forward into the twentieth century. This complex and involuted scheme was never carried out, but it is testament to the lengths Tolkien was prepared to go to in order to give his invented mythology the semblance, history, and provenance of "real" mythologies.

However, the discrepancy between the internal chronology of the "Silmarillion," *The Hobbit,* and *The Lord of the Rings* and their external publication history is complicated enough and scarcely needs the addition of yet another time and another frame narrative. The entire complex of stories within stories within stories is ingeniously gathered in Sam and Frodo's conversation on the stairs of Cirith Ungol. Here Sam, realizing suddenly that he and Frodo are a part and a continuance of the story of the Silmaril, wonders whether Gollum sees himself as the hero and imagines a "great big book with red and black letters" out of which their story will be read to future generations. This is exactly what "The Red Book of Westmarch" was meant to be and what *The Lord of the Rings* is.

The only other frame structure in Tolkien's work is the pseudo-editor's preface to *The Adventures of Tom Bombadil,* a device for pulling together a number of disparate and separately composed verses in order to publish them as "Hobbit-poems."

VERLYN FLIEGER

Further Reading

Tolkien, J.R.R. *The History of Middle-earth,* edited by Christopher Tolkien. 12 vols. Boston, MA: Houghton Mifflin, 1984–96.

See also **Adventures of Tom Bombadil**; **Ælfwine**; **Book of Lost Tales I**; **Book of Lost Tales II**; **Fictionality**; **Hobbit, The**; **Inklings**; **Lord of the Rings**; **Lost Road**; **Memory**; **Time**; **Time Travel**

FRANCE AND FRENCH CULTURE

Tolkien's antipathy for nearly all things French is well documented. Tolkien had an insular personality and thought of himself as a hobbit; he liked simple things, which may explain the roots of his anti-Gallic sentiment. The actual source of his feelings toward the French is unknown, but tragic and painful personal experiences in France surely reinforced them. His desire to create a mythology for England also expressed an anti-French sentiment. As Humphrey Carpenter has said, the Norman Conquest affected Tolkien almost as if it had occurred during the author's lifetime. His literary creations, as a result, project a past whose future might have been unblemished by the invasion of 1066.

Having learned French from his mother, Tolkien, in 1913, traveled to France as a tutor and escort to two Mexican boys. While there, he visited Paris and Brittany. Tolkien enjoyed Paris very much, but he found the people indecent and vulgar. In Brittany, he experienced France as a tourist. The trip ended suddenly when, accompanied by Tolkien, one of the boys' aunts was run over by a car; she died shortly afterward.

In 1916, Tolkien returned to France to fight in the Battle of the Somme. His close friends, Rob Gilson and Geoffrey Bache Smith, also fought there; both were killed. Tolkien himself fought in the trenches from July 14 to October 27, when he developed symptoms of trench fever. On November 8, 1916, he returned to England. By strange fortune, Tolkien had survived unharmed. He had also witnessed unimaginable suffering and unspeakable horror in the trenches and the fields of France. Sam Gamgee, from *The Lord of the Rings,* is in part a reflection of English soldiers from the Battle of the Somme. Some of the battles and devastation of his text surely also reflect what Tolkien saw in France.

Some of Tolkien's arguments with the French were trivial: he disliked French food and regretted that it was served at high table at Oxford. Of significance was Tolkien's attitude toward the Norman Conquest. At King Edward's Academy, Tolkien expressed strong feelings about the aftermath of 1066 and, by extension, about the French and their language. As Carpenter reports in his biography, in a school debate Tolkien argued that "this House deplores the occurrence of the Norman Conquest" and went on to attack "the influx of polysyllabic barbarities which ousted the more honest if humbler native words" (Carpenter, 40). This may explain the near absence of French references in his creative works. It certainly elucidates the impulse behind *The Silmarillion.* In King Arthur and the Knights of the Round Table, England already had a mythology. The myth of Arthur, however, originated in post-Conquest, Anglo-Norman (i.e., French-speaking) royal courts, and, worse still for Tolkien, it extended the history of the kings of Britain back to ancient Rome. Expressed first in Latin, then in Anglo-Norman, the story of Arthur and his knights spread in textual form in romances written in dialects of Old French and was centuries later adopted in English by Thomas Malory. When Tolkien decided to create languages for his own mythology and to build the foundations of Middle-earth, therefore, it seems that he took inspiration almost exclusively from languages and texts that were not connected to Anglo-Norman and Arthurian tradition, as if, by his own will, he could recreate a world in which the French were absent and the Conquest had never occurred.

GERALD SEAMAN

Further Reading

Carpenter, Humphrey. *Tolkien: A Biography.* Boston, MA: Houghton Mifflin, 1977.

Chance, Jane. *The Lord of the Rings: The Mythology of Power.* Revised edition. Lexington, KY: University Press of Kentucky, 2001.

———. *Tolkien's Art: A Mythology for England.* Revised edition. Lexington, KY: University Press of Kentucky, 2001.

See also **Arthurian Literature; French Language; T.C.B.S. (Tea Club and Barrovian Society); World War I**

FRANCE: RECEPTION OF TOLKIEN

Tolkien's works were first introduced in France through a 1958 article dedicated to *The Lord of the Rings* by Reverend Father Louis Bouyer, from l'Oratoire. Reverend Father Bouyer was to become a personal friend of Tolkien's a couple of years later. Reverend Father Bouyer's theological and fictional works contain several references to Middle-earth (reissued and studied in Devaux 2003). Following a chapter from *Admirations* by Jacques Bergier (1970), *The Lord of the Rings* was to be translated for the publisher Christian Bourgois (1973). The large number of copies of *The Lord of the Rings* that were sold has quite simply enabled this publishing house to survive. Tolkien's works were translated over different periods in time: 1969–82, 1994–99, and since 2001 (Ferré 2004). *The History of Middle-earth* is currently being translated up to volume five under the direction of Vincent Ferré (the third volume was published in May of 2006), who has also had previous translations revised (*Tree and Leaf* and in a near future *The Lord of the Rings*).

A few characteristic features of the publication of Tolkien's works in France and in French deserve to be pointed out. *The Book of Lost Tales* was translated into French by Adam Tolkien (Christopher's son); the first typescript of *Farmer Giles* (still unpublished in England) was translated by Simonne d'Ardenne (1975); and the journal *La Feuille de la Compagnie* published, more recently, previously unreleased texts by Tolkien: a summary of *The Lord of the Rings* (2003) and "Fragments on Elvish Reincarnation" (2006).

Talented French writers have expressed their admiration for Tolkien, Julien Gracq in particular (1995). To the translation into French of Karen Haber's *Meditations on Middle-earth* were added texts from French writers of fantasy (Henri Loevenbruck, Mathieu Gaborit, Fabrice Colin, Laurent Genefort et Ange). The study of Tolkien's relation to *Fantasy,* and more generally to the cycle and series literary genres, was carried out in Anne Besson's thesis published under the title *D'Asimov à Tolkien: Cycles et séries dans la littérature de genre.*

Despite the efforts of Édouard Kloczko from the end of the 1980s, which have been mostly focused on the imaginary languages (1995, 2002), Tolkien's works were hardly studied (most of the studies worthy of interest were put together in his *Tolkien en France*) until Peter Jackson's films, when publishers started issuing introductory books. Two of them deserve to be considered: Vincent Ferré's *Tolkien, sur les rivages de la Terre du Milieu* (on *The Lord of the Rings* and death) and Charles Ridoux's *Tolkien, le chant du monde* (on the whole book).

In-depth studies, which can be compared with what can be found in the criticism in English, and which know of it and go into, for instance, *The History of Middle-earth,* have been published since 2001. As far as themes are concerned, those studies are either literary or theological (as well as philosophical). A closer look at three noteworthy studies reveals themes—death, Gollum, and the Ents—that recur in the work of some writers. Like Vincent Ferré, Michaël Devaux has analysed in a philosophical way the meaning of death in Tolkien from the biblical expression (also present in *Beowulf*) "the shadow of death" in Tolkien. Gollum was studied by Jean-Philippe Qadri ("... un concours avec nous, mon trésor!: étude du tournoi d'énigmes entre Bilbo et Gollum") and by Fabienne Claire Caland ("Sméagol-Gollum ou l'empreinte fantastique dans *The Lord of the Rings*"). Finally, the Ents issue (and trees in Tolkien) was tackled in particular by Sébastien Mallet ("La disparition des Géants," "Le nom du Fangorn: une approche bachelardienne du couple orn et galadh").

Bibliographies of the French studies on Tolkien were published by Édouard Kloczko (1998), Michaël Devaux (2001, 2003, 2006), and Vincent Ferré (who keeps an up-to-date list of academic works, http://pourtolkien.free.fr/recherche.html).

MICHAËL DEVAUX
Translated by DAVID LEDANOIS

Further Reading

Bergier, Jacques. *Admirations.* Paris: Christian Bourgois, 1970. Reprint Paris: L'Œil du Sphinx, 2000.

Besson, Anne. *D'Asimov à Tolkien: Cycles et séries dans la littérature de genre.* Paris: CNRS, 2004.

Caland, Fabienne Claire. "Sméagol-Gollum ou lémpriente Fantastique dans *The Lord of the Rings*." In *Dictionnaire des Mythes du Fantastique,* ed. Pierre Brunel and Juliette Dury, 241–251. Limoges: Presses universitoires de Limoges et du Limousin, 2004.

Devaux, Michaël. "'L'ombre de la mort' chez Tolkien." In *La Feuille de la Compagnie,* edited by Michaël Devaux, 39–63. No. 1. Paris: L'Œil du Sphinx, 2001. (English translation in *2001: A Tolkien Odyssey,* edited by Ron Pirson. Leyde: De Tolkienwinkel, 2002.)

———. "J.R.R. Tolkien & L. Bouyer: une amitié d'écrivains." In *Tolkien, les racines du légendaire* (*La Feuille de la Compagnie,* No. 2), edited by Michaël Devaux, 85–146. Genève: Ad Solem, 2003.

Ferré, Vincent. "La réception de J.R.R. Tolkien en France, 1973–2003: Quelques repères." In *Tolkien, trente ans après (1973–2003),* edited by Vincent Ferré, 17–35. Paris: Christian Bourgois, 2004.

———. *Tolkien, sur les rivages de la Terre du Milieu.* Paris: Christian Bourgois, 2001.

Gracq, Julien. *En lisant en écrivant.* In *Œuvres complètes,* edited by B. Boie, 763. Paris: Gallimard, 1995.

Haber, Karen, ed. *Méditations sur la Terre du Milieu.* Paris: Bragelonne, 2003.

Kloczko, Édouard. *Dictionnaire des langues elfiques.* Vol. 1. Toulon: Tamise, 1995.

———. *Dictionnaire des langues des Hobbits, des Nains, des Orques. . .* Argenteuil: Arda, 2002.

———. *Tolkien en France.* Argenteuil: Arda, 1998.

Mallet, Sébastien. "La disparition des Géants." In *La Feuille de la Compagnie,* edited by Michaël Devaux, 65–88. No. 1. Paris: L'Œil du Sphinx, 2001.

———. "Le nom du Fangorn: une approche bachelardienne du couple orn et galadh." In *Tolkien, l'effigie des elfes* (La Feville de la Compagnie, no. 3), edited by Michaël Devaux. Genève: Ad Solem, 2006.

Qadri, Jean-Philippe. ". . . un concours avec nous, mon trésor!: Étude du tournoi d'énigmes entre Bilbo et Gollum." In *Tolkien, trente ans après (1973–2003),* edited by Vincent Ferré, 49–74. Paris: Christian Bourgois, 2004.

Ridoux, Charles. *Tolkien, le chant du monde.* Paris: Les Belles Lettres, 2004.

Tolkien, J.R.R. "Fragments on Elvish Reincarnation." In *Tolkien, l'effigie des elfes* (La Feuille de la Compagnie, vol. 3), edited by Michaël Devaux. Genève: Ad Solem, 2006.

———. *Le Livre des Contes Perdus.* Édition établie et Avant-propos de Christopher Tolkien, traduit de l'anglais par Adam Tolkien (one-volume edition). Paris: Christian Bourgois, 2001.

———. *Maître Gilles de Ham (première version).* Traduit de l'anglais par Simonne d'Ardenne. Liège: Association des Romanistes de l'Université de Liège, 1975.

———. "Part of a letter to Milton Waldman." In *Tolkien, les racines du légendaire* (La Feuille de la Compagnie, no. 2), edited by Michaël Devaux, 58–78. Genève: Ad Solem, 2003.

See also **French Language**

"FRANCIS THOMPSON": ARTICLE FOR EXETER COLLEGE ESSAY CLUB

The Catholic mystic poet Francis Thompson (b. Preston, Lancashire, 1859; d. London, 1907) had an early impact on Tolkien, who knew his work by 1910 and celebrated him in a talk to Exeter College's Essay Club on March 4, 1914. Tolkien "had felt himself into perfect harmony with the poet," note the minutes (kept in manuscript at Exeter College library and the only available record of his talk). He outlined Thompson's medical career and descent into vagrancy, citing Everard Meynell's *Life of Francis Thompson* as evidence against "misconception and calumny." Tolkien insisted that Thompson used opium purely as a painkiller and wrote only during periods of "conquest and abstinence." The poetry, he added (with characteristic disdain for biography), was the sole guide to the "interior facts" of Thompson's life; the miserable and squalid exterior made his "saintly" charity and yearning for ethereal beauty all the more praiseworthy.

Tolkien praised Thompson's metrical powers but focused on his language and immense imagery. Drawing on liturgical sources, Thompson reunited the Latinate and Anglo-Saxon stock of English vocabulary that had been artificially separated through pedantry, "a most pernicious birth-snobbery of words." Equally intimate with both Elizabethan literature and modern science, Thompson also mended the divide between current and obsolescent English. At the root of Thompson's imagery, in which astronomy and geology were pressed into the service of poetry, Tolkien recognised an intensely Catholic philosophy; he noted that the poet's handling of matters of faith was marked by "the most universally acknowledged characteristic of Catholics": profound awe alternating with familiarity.

Tolkien advocated "an attitude of humility befitting immaturity" to penetrate apparent obscurities in Thompson's work, an idea echoed in his own "Cottage of Lost Play," where the traveller must become child-sized to enter the house of story. Elaborating on this, Tolkien declared, "One must begin with the elfin and delicate and progress to the profound: listen first to the violin and the flute, and then learn to hearken to the organ of being's harmony." The image suggests a model for "The Music of the Ainur" composed some four years later, and the same idea underpins the design of *The Book of Lost Tales,* where cosmogonic myth intertwines with fairy tale.

Thompson's influence may be seen in the Latinate vocabulary and metrical variety of Tolkien's early poems, such as *Kortirion among the Trees* (1915), in which "the seven lampads" derives from *To My Godchild.* Elsewhere, *Southron* (southerner), used in *The Lord of the Rings,* appears in Thompson's *At Lord's.* From *The Mistress of Vision* comes the coinage "Luthany," borrowed by Tolkien briefly for his mythological England, altered to Lúthien and then bestowed on his Elf-heroine Tinúviel. *You and Me and the Cottage of Lost Play* (1915) echoes a phrase from *Daisy* and betrays a Thompsonian weakness for autobiographical nostalgia and sentimentality. One of the Two Trees, Laurelin, was inspired by the laburnum with its "spilth of fire" in *Sister Songs,* which also features a vision of Silvan fairies cited by Humphrey Carpenter as the inspiration for a scene in Tolkien's 1910 poem *Wood-Sunshine* and for his interest in Elves.

JOHN GARTH

Further Reading

Boardman, Brigid M., ed. *The Poems of Francis Thompson.* London: Continuum in association with Boston College, 2001.

———. *Between Heaven and Charing Cross: The Life of Francis Thompson.* New Haven; London: Yale University Press, 1988.

See also **Catholicism, Roman; Literary Influences, Nineteenth and Twentieth Century**

FREE WILL

Tolkien's view of the concept of free will reflects the Judeo-Christian tradition, not surprisingly, given that the author was a practicing Catholic from boyhood to death. The central tenet is that sentient beings have the ability to control and shape their destinies, albeit bounded within a cosmic order. Individuals with intelligence, consciousness, and self-awareness may consider and choose their actions, but they are ultimately subject to the designs of an omnipotent and all-powerful One.

Tolkien's creation account, Ainulindalë, in *The Silmarillion* contains three principles that exhibit what Joseph Pearce has called "the mystical interlinking between Providence and free will" (quoted in "Legacy"): (1) Ilúvatar (which means "All-Father") grants beings the ability to contribute to the "Music" of creation in the universe, according to their "will." (2) If beings attempt to alter the cosmic design, seeking god-like powers, they will be foiled. (3) No matter how much the "rebel" blights creation, some unintended good result will occur. These principles apply to all peoples, which include the angelic Ainur, the immortal Elves, the mortal men, and the humble hobbits.

In all of Tolkien's Middle-earth tales, sentient beings with particular powers are presented with momentous choices, often between good and evil courses of action. In every case, these individuals shape their destinies, affect the lives of others, and influence, sometimes catastrophically, the history and even the geography of the world. Still, these exercises of free will cannot supersede the One's ultimate purposes, even if in the short term the cosmic designs can be altered. In *The Hobbit,* Gandalf remarks to Bilbo that the hobbit's successes were brought about not just for his sole benefit. In *The Lord of the Rings,* Gandalf tells Frodo that the hobbit was "meant" to have the One Ring, and not by its maker, the evil Sauron.

The first instance of this free will/divine order dynamic occurs when Melkor, initially the mightiest of the Ainur, attempted to interweave his own strains into the music of creation in an endeavor to increase his part, which caused a disharmony in the One's plans. Even though Melkor was the offspring of Ilúvatar's thought, he had the free will to oppose his creator's intention. But from this discord, the One begot a new music, which resulted in something glorious: the creation of the world. Melkor (later renamed Morgoth) suffered a fall from grace, in much the same way as Satan, and chose an evil path in his relentless lust for power and domination. However, the One declared that no matter how much Melkor intended to disrupt or blight the world, his actions would only give rise to things more wonderful.

This pattern of existence in Tolkien's tales, although it develops in a multitude of ways, remains constant. In the First Age, there were devastating wars against Morgoth's tyranny that seemed to be endless until the errand of Eärendil, which inspired the Ainur to overthrow Morgoth, though his chief lieutenant Sauron survived. In the Second Age, Sauron seduced King Ar-Pharazôn into invading the Undying Lands and thus avoiding his mortality, which resulted in Ilúvatar intervening to destroy the king's minions in a flood, though the "Faithful" Númenórean Men escaped to Middle-earth. In the Third Age, the One Ring of Sauron is destroyed, which allows the renewal of the land and the restoration of the great line of Númenórean kings.

In short, acts of free will can cause cataclysmic disasters in the temporal and incarnate world, but the One's ultimate purpose remains eternal and inviolable.

DANIEL TIMMONS

Further Reading

Bassham, Gregory, and Eric Bronson, eds. *"The Lord of the Rings" and Philosophy: One Book to Rule Them All.* Popular Culture and Philosophy series, Vol. 5, edited by William Irwin. Peru, IL: Open Court, 2004.

Birzer, Bradley J. *J.R.R. Tolkien's Sanctifying Myth: Understanding Middle-earth.* Wilmington, DE: ISI Books, 2002.

Bruner, Kurt, and Jim Ware. *Finding God in "The Lord of the Rings."* Carol Stream, IL: Tyndale, 2003.

Caldecott, Stratford. *Secret Fire: The Spiritual Vision of J. R. R. Tolkien.* Eastbourne, UK: Gardners Books, 2003.

Dubs, Kathleen E. "Providence, Fate, and Chance: Boethian Philosophy in *The Lord of the Rings.*" In *Tolkien and the Invention of Myth: A Reader*, edited by Jane Chance, 133–44. Lexington, KY: University of Kentucky Press, 2004.

"The Legacy of *The Lord of the Rings.*" Documentary. DVD. Directed by Daniel Timmons. Filmoption International, 2005.

Pearce, Joseph. *Tolkien: Man and Myth.* London: HarperCollins, 1998.

Rutledge, Fleming. *The Battle for Middle-earth: Tolkien's Divine Design in "The Lord of the Rings."* Grand Rapids, MI: Eerdmans, 2004.

Wood, Ralph C. *The Gospel According to Tolkien: Visions of the Kingdom in Middle-earth.* Louisville, KY: Westminster John Knox, 2003.

See also **Christianity; Catholicism, Roman; Theology in** *The Lord of the Rings*

FRENCH LANGUAGE

Tolkien first learned French from his mother. At a young age, he used French in the invention of Nevbosh, a private language. In his creative works, obvious references to the French language are rare but noteworthy. In scholarship, Tolkien's knowledge of French was instrumental to his 1925 edition, with E.V. Gordon, of *Sir Gawain and the Green Knight.* As he noted in his lecture on "English and Welsh," knowledge of French was not only useful but also necessary to the business of being an English philologist.

As an older child, Tolkien, with his cousin Mary Incledon, disguised French, English, and Latin to create Nevbosh, or the New Nonsense, in which they wrote limericks. Tolkien further pursued French at King Edward's Academy in Birmingham and became sufficiently proficient to be hired as a tutor and escort to two Mexican boys during a trip to France in 1913. When the trip ended in a car accident, which killed one of the boys' aunts, Tolkien vowed never to do such work again. Even from the beginning of his studies, Tolkien did not prefer French; it was not a language that brought him pleasure, a sentiment that he did not hesitate to repeat in his later writing and lectures.

Tolkien's creative works contain little obvious French resonance. A slightly obscure and clearly pejorative reference, however, is found in Bag End, the residence of Bilbo and Frodo in *The Hobbit* and *The Lord of the Rings.* As Shippey has noted, Bag End is "a literal translation of the phrase one sees often yet stuck up at the end of little English roads: *cul-de-sac*" (*Road,* 55). In this sense, Bag End erases a known French term and condemns its importation to English language and culture. Such improper use of the language caused French to be associated with snobbishness, and some English people clearly used the French language to reinforce class distinctions, which Tolkien deplored.

An exception to the lack of obvious French references in Tolkien is the name *Rohan.* Tolkien might not have agreed to a strictly French derivation for Rohan; the language and culture of the Rohirrim are, after all, most closely derived from Old English, and the Mark itself harkens back to Anglo-Saxon Mercia. He did acknowledge, however, "the influence of memory of names or words already known, or of 'echoes' in the linguistic memory" (*Letters,* 383) in the creation of the languages of Middle-earth. In that internal linguistic taxonomy, Rohan is a Sindarin name, a "later softened form of *Rochand.* It is derived from Elvish **rokkō* "swift horse for riding + a suffix frequent in names of lands" (*Letters,* 382). External to that taxonomy, Rohan is also an actual place in Brittany; Tolkien had been there, or near there, in 1913, and he later admitted that he found his name for the Riddermark there. As he wrote in a letter: "Rohan is a famous name, from Brittany, borne by an ancient and proud and powerful family. I was aware of this, and liked its shape; but I had also (long before) invented the Elvish horse-word, and saw how Rohan could be accommodated to the linguistic situation as a late Sindarin name of the Mark . . . after its occupation by horsemen" (*Letters*, 383).

Finally, Tolkien's knowledge of French contributed to his edition of *Sir Gawain and the Green Knight.* As Tolkien and Gordon note, the "French element in *Sir Gawain* is . . . extensive. The technical terms used in the description of Gawain's equipment, the castle, and the hunting in the third fitt [*sic*] account for a large proportion of the French loan-words: otherwise, they are mostly domestic terms of the aristocratic household, or abstract nouns. The French forms borrowed are nearly always found to be Anglo-Norman" (Tolkien and Gordon 1925, 128). The editors' presentation of the internal characteristics and history of Anglo-Norman further demonstrates an advanced knowledge of the language's morphology, phonology, and syntax; this also comes to the fore briefly in Tolkien's lecture on "English and Welsh." Without such knowledge, Tolkien and Gordon could not have produced an edition of such quality, and Tolkien's career as a philologist and a novelist would not have been possible. As he implies in a note to a famous lecture, to speak of fairy stories, after all, is to speak with words—*fay, faërie, fairy*—that derive from French.

GERALD SEAMAN

Further Reading

Carpenter, Humphrey. *Tolkien: A Biography.* Boston, MA: Houghton Mifflin, 1977.

Shippey, Tom. *J.R.R. Tolkien: Author of the Century.* Boston, MA: Houghton Mifflin, 2000.

———. *The Road to Middle-earth.* Boston, MA: Houghton Mifflin, 1983.

Tinkler, John. "Old English in Rohan." In *Tolkien and the Critics: Essays on J.R.R. Tolkien's "The Lord of the Rings,"* edited by Neil D. Isaacs and Rose A. Zimbardo, 164–69. Notre Dame, IN: University of Notre Dame Press, 1968.

Tolkien, J.R.R. "English and Welsh." In *The Monsters and the Critics and Other Essays,* edited by Christopher Tolkien, 162–97. Boston, MA: Houghton Mifflin, 1984.

——— "On Fairy-stories." In *The Monsters and the Critics and Other Essays,* edited by Christopher Tolkien, 109–61. Boston, MA: Houghton Mifflin, 1984.

——— "A Secret Vice." In *The Monsters and the Critics and Other Essays,* edited by Christopher Tolkien, 198–223. Boston, MA: Houghton Mifflin, 1984.

Tolkien, J.R.R., and E.V. Gordon, eds. *Sir Gawain and the Green Knight.* Oxford: Clarendon, 1925.

See also **France and French Culture; Languages: Early Introduction and Interest; Nevbosh and Animalic; Rohan;** *Sir Gawain and the Green Knight*

FRODO

Frodo Baggins, distinguished among hobbits as a traveler and Elf-friend, was born on September 22, 2968, Third Age. He was at first brought up at Brandy Hall (where, it was said, he was one of the worst young rascals in Buckland, thanks in part to his insatiable appetite for mushrooms). However, his parents, Drogo and Primula (née Brandybuck) Baggins were drowned in a boating accident when Frodo was twelve, and he was adopted by and went to live with his rich and eccentric older cousin Bilbo Baggins of Bag End, Hobbiton.

As the family trees in Appendix C show, Bilbo and Frodo are cousins and, as Gaffer Gamgee asserts, not just cousins but first *and* second cousins, once removed either way. Twice, though, Tolkien refers to them as uncle and nephew, which is indeed a truer description of their relationship, made up of the respect due to the age difference and the tolerant affection created by blood and proximity.

As Frodo grew to manhood and Bilbo grew to old age, both became noted in the Shire for their friendship with the Elves and for their knowledge of the Elven tongue and other lore well beyond the purview of most hobbits. Since Frodo and Bilbo shared a birthday, the great Party marking Bilbo's eleventy-first birthday also marked, Frodo's coming of age at thirty-three. Bilbo departed soon after to dwell at the house of Elrond in Rivendell, leaving a ring he had found in his earlier travels as an heirloom for Frodo. Clearly, Bilbo meant Frodo to inherit more than just the wretched ring, or even his "jools." Bilbo's sense of adventure and admiration for foreign things like High-elven culture were also part of the heritage.

When Gandalf the Wizard determined that Frodo's ring was the One Ring of great evil power and that its maker Sauron was actively seeking to regain it, Frodo reluctantly undertook to convey the Ring out of the Shire. He left in late September 3018, accompanied by his friend and servant Samwise Gamgee and by his cousins Meriadoc Brandybuck and Peregrin Took. The deeds and dangers of Frodo's journey are chronicled in the three parts of *The Lord of the Rings.* Thanks to Frodo's efforts, the Ring was ultimately destroyed, and Middle-earth was saved; Frodo returned to the Shire in November 3019. But the deep injuries caused by his journey and by long possession of the Ring had made Frodo unable to live at peace in the Shire. He suffered on the anniversaries of his worst injuries, and he suffered greatly from the loss of the Ring, despite its evil. In September 3021, Frodo went to the Grey Havens and embarked with Bilbo and others for the West, where he died an indeterminate time later.

Origin of Frodo as a Character

Frodo's emergence as a chief character in Tolkien's story is itself a convoluted story. *The Return of the Shadow,* Christopher Tolkien's chapter-by-chapter reconstruction of how his father wrote the early parts of *The Lord of the Rings,* shows how the tale changed from its first forms to what we read today. Putting what Christopher Tolkien says into a much condensed form, we see that Frodo emerges thus:

- Bilbo has a party at the end of which he announces he is leaving to marry.
- In early drafts, one Bingo appears as Bilbo's son.
- Quickly, this is changed to Bingo as Bilbo's nephew or cousin.
- The matter of the Ring is brought forward, and a journey to Rivendell seems required. It is undertaken by Bingo as protagonist, accompanied by two hobbit friends, Odo and Frodo.
- After multiple drafts, Frodo becomes the protagonist, with a more fully developed character than the original Bingo, who in effect vanishes. Odo's words and actions are largely taken over by Pippin, Peregrin Took. The process of developing toward what we now have continues; the main piece missing at this stage is Sam Gamgee.

The name *Frodo,* Tolkien explains, "is a real name from the Germanic tradition. Its Old English form was *Fróda* [connected with] the old word *fród* meaning etymologically 'wise by experience'" (*Letters,* 244) (Froda was a king of the Heatho-Bards, mentioned in *Beowulf,* l. 2025).

Frodo's Character

Flanked at one end of the book by his elder cousin Bilbo and at the other by his faithful friend Sam, Frodo is the central character of *The Lord of the Rings.* He is its protagonist and in the eyes of many its hero. Even though he was overpowered at the last moment by the Ring and claimed it for his own rather than destroying it, he had, as Tolkien says, created a situation in which the Ring *could* be destroyed. And it was.

One of the chief traits Tolkien assigns to his hobbits is their potential for growth and change. We rarely see this potential as long as hobbits are living their placid rural and village lives, but it emerges in time of trouble or crisis. There is iron there, and nowhere is it better shown than in Tolkien's exceptional hobbits, Bilbo and Frodo Baggins. Even so unlikely an observer as Saruman notices this when he confronts Frodo at Bag End: "'You have grown, Halfling. . . . Yes, you have grown very much'" (*RK,* VI, viii, 299). (True, but odd that Saruman should say it, since he never met or knew Frodo before the destruction of the Ring. How could he estimate Frodo's growth?)

Frodo was both an unusual and a typical hobbit. He was unusual in having been brought up as an orphan (an only child, rare among hobbit families) in a bachelor household with considerable wealth. Thus, he is independent of the inward-looking, family-centered lives of most hobbits. Worse perhaps, he shares with Bilbo an interest, suspiciously cosmopolitan to many hobbits, in the world beyond the Shire. Intelligent curiosity about such topics as Elves and their languages marked Frodo as strange among his more parochial fellows.

At the same time, he is like most hobbits, including Bilbo, in loving his quiet home and his harmless country, preferring to be left alone, and trying to keep the even tenor of his ways. The difference is that he can rise above these essentially selfish considerations; he may wish, as he says, that evil had not come in his time, but he will do what must be done to combat it.

Frodo becomes an increasingly admirable character as the story proceeds, but he is far from perfect. He can be selfish; he can be impatient; he can act foolishly (especially when prompted by the Ring, as at the Prancing Pony in Bree); he can feel "desperate: lost and witless" when Old Man Willow traps Merry and Pippin (*FR,* I, vi, 125).

Nonetheless, that typical potential for growth appears early in Frodo's journeys. His hobbit courage would be an obvious example: Tolkien tells us that there is a seed of courage hidden, however deeply, in the heart of every hobbit. For Frodo, it takes root and grows as he lies helpless in the Barrow.

Frodo's courage is at the center of a complex of kindred virtues: Qualities like determination, known in some contexts as stubbornness, enable Frodo to continue his journey when all seems hopeless. Qualities like loyalty and its prosaic cousin, keeping one's word, prompt Frodo to choose aright when an array of difficult choices presents itself. And to bring the matter full circle, the power to make difficult choices arises for Frodo from his courage and determination.

Loyalty is perhaps one of Frodo's most important traits, both in the giving and in the inspiring. Frodo does not have many occasions to show loyalty upward (unless loyalty to an ideal or to one's word may be considered such), but loyalty to those beneath him in merit—Gollum primarily—guides his actions throughout the tale. His pity and his pledge to care for Gollum keep the wretched creature alive through all their journeyings east of the river (despite Sam's well-founded misgivings). Sam's unease arises from his own loyalty to Frodo, which is nearly legendary and which both complicates Frodo's life, as in those misgivings about Gollum, and saves it, as in the Tower of Cirith Ungol.

Frodo as a Character

When we consider Frodo's character—the moral structure of his being—we see that his combination of courage, selflessness, and fidelity (to his friends, to his word) make him the ideal bearer and destroyer of the Ring. He is in that regard wholly admirable. When we consider Frodo as a character, an inhabitant of the story, he is not an interesting chap. He is thoughtful and articulate and perceptive, but he is not colorful or highly individualized. He does not have the sturdy down-rightness of a Sam or the antic disposition of a Merry or a Pippin, far less the psychopathology of a Gollum. The maxim that good is less interesting than evil (literarily at least) is borne out in Frodo. Tolkien told his son that "Frodo is not so interesting [as Sam] because he has to be high-minded. . . . Frodo will become too ennobled and rarefied . . . and will pass West with all the great figures" (*Letters,* 105), and Sam will settle down in the Shire and raise childern.

Although Tolkien wrote the preceding words long before *The Lord of the Rings* was completed, something like this happens. With the destruction of the Ring, Frodo's work, like Gandalf's, is done. Frodo steps aside when the time comes to Scour the Shire, and although he says that no hobbits must be killed in the inevitable fighting, his words sound more like a hope or a piece of advice than an order. When Merry addresses him as "my dear Frodo," in a gentle but faintly patronizing tone, and says the battle cannot happen that way, Frodo falls silent (*RK,* VI, viii, 285). Merry both respects Frodo's feelings and underlines how unrealistic his position is. Unlike Merry or Pippin, Frodo has never seen armed combat or the slaughter of actual battle at, say, the Pelennor Fields.

A little later, Frodo can only say, "I wish for no killing" (*RK,* VI, viii, 289). But killing there must be.

It is unusual for a hobbit to become "too ennobled"; good-natured and generous hobbits may be, but they scale few heights. Frodo, however, has lived at the utmost stretch of his being for months; he has literally lived on the edge, and although there is terror there, there is also nobility. No wonder he is willing to give over responsibility on the return to the Shire; it is as he tells Merry: "To me it feels more like falling asleep again" (*RK,* VI, vii, 276).

Frodo has been deeply wounded in various ways, so deeply that he cannot live in the Shire, even as its restoration begins. That is his penalty for having undertaken and completed the Quest to destroy the Ring. As he succinctly puts the story of his journey and his perils, "I am wounded with knife, sting, and tooth. Where shall I find rest?" (*RK,* VI, vii, 268), Two years later, his question is answered, for the very act that brought his wounds also brings his reward. By the generosity of Arwen, Frodo as Ring-bearer is able to pass West and live out his days in a place equivalent if not to Eden then at least to Avalon.

MICHAEL N. STANTON

Further Reading

Auden, W.H. "The Quest Hero." *Texas Quarterly* IV (1962): 81–93. Reprinted in *Tolkien and the Critics: Essays on J.R.R. Tolkien's "The Lord of the Rings,"* edited by Neil D. Isaacs and Rose A. Zimbardo. Notre Dame, IN: University of Notre Dame Press, 1968.

Flieger, Verlyn. "Frodo & Aragorn: The Concept of the Hero." In *Tolkien: New Critical Perspectives,* edited by Neil D. Isaacs and Rose A. Zimbardo. Lexington, KY: University Press of Kentucky, 1982.

Helms, Randel. "Tolkien's World." Chap. 5 in *Tolkien's World.* Boston, MA: Houghton Mifflin, 1974.

Sale, Roger. *Modern Heroism: Essays on D.H. Lawrence, William Empson and J.R.R. Tolkien.* Berkeley, CA: University of California Press, 1973. See esp. chap. 4, "Tolkien and Frodo Baggins." Reprinted in *J.R.R. Tolkien,* edited by Harold Bloom. Philadelphia: Chelsea House, 2000.

Scott, Nan C. "War and Pacifism in *The Lord of the Rings.*" *Mythlore* 15 (1972): 22–29.

See also **Bilbo; Elves; Gandalf; Heroes and Heroism; Hobbiton; Hobbits; Mordor; One Ring, The; Quest Narrative; Sam; Saruman; Weapons, Named**

G

GALADRIEL

The Lord of the Rings has often been criticized for a supposed dearth of strong women, but one need look no further than the character of Galadriel for a counterargument. Sam sums it up nicely when he says, "You could call her perilous, because she's so strong in herself. You, you could dash yourself to pieces on her, like a ship on a rock; or drown yourself, like a hobbit in a river. But neither rock nor river would be to blame" (*TT*, IV, v, 288). Indeed, Galadriel is among Tolkien's strongest and most vividly drawn characters, regardless of gender, and certainly the "greatest of the Elven women" (*RK*, Appendix B, 363). Born during the Bliss of Valinor, she alone among the Elves still living in Middle-earth beheld the unreflected light of the Two Trees. Tolkien affirms that "Galadriel was the greatest of the Noldor, except Fëanor maybe, though she was wiser than he, and her wisdom increased with the long years" (*UT*, 229).

Understating the evolution of Galadriel's personal history, however, is fraught with challenges. During the course of Tolkien's writings, she first appears in *The Lord of the Rings* as something of a "Faerie Queene." And in the first drafts, her original name was not even Galadriel. It changed several times, in fact, before settling into its present form. And its earliest etymology included the Sindarin word, *galað* ("tree")—though Tolkien later changed course on this meaning, declaring it a false cognate with *galad* ("radiance") and altering the meaning of her name to "maiden crowned with a radiant garland" (*S*, 360; *Letters*, 423, 428).

During revision of *The Lord of the Rings*, "the role and importance of Galadriel only emerged slowly, and . . . her story underwent continual refashionings" (*UT*, 228). Tolkien also implanted her into his burgeoning mythology of the Elder Days, as Finarfin's daughter, and wove her into the periphery of those legends—just as he'd woven her into the periphery of *The Lord of the Rings*. Initially, he depicted Galadriel as a willing participant in the Noldor's rebellion against the Valar. She was much like Fëanor—"proud, strong, and selfwilled"—but she disliked and distrusted him. However, she was moved by his entreaties because she "had dreams of far lands and dominions that might be her own to order as she would without tutelage" (*Peoples*, 387). Therefore, Galadriel joined Fëanor in returning to Middle-earth after the theft of the Silmarils, though she never swore the Oath of Fëanor; his revolt was merely convenient to her own ambitions. Nevertheless, by rejecting the Valar, she, too, came under the Doom of Mandos.

Eventually, she came to her own dominion, with Celeborn, in Lothlórien. To preserve its power and refuge, though beleaguered by the forces of Sauron, she wielded one of the hidden Three Rings of the Elves: Nenya, the Ring of Water. During the Great Years, the Fellowship passes into her dominion, bringing with it the One Ring. Frodo, perhaps with the growing keenness of his sight or perhaps out of sheer exhaustion and desperation—or more likely, both—offers Galadriel the Ring. Though, like Gandalf and Elrond, she wishes she might take it, to attempt to turn it to good, she knows she must not. She resists the lure of the Ring, saying, "I pass the test . . . I will diminish, and go into the West and remain Galadriel" (*FR*, II, vii, 381).

In so doing, Galadriel earns the leniency of the Valar. Though under the Ban of the Valar that the exiled Noldor might never return to the West, Tolkien wrote that "her personal ban was lifted, in return for her services against Sauron, and above all for her rejection of the temptation to take the Ring" (*Letters*, 386). Therefore, because of her final "abnegation of pride and trust in her own powers," Galadriel can return from her exile after the fall of Sauron.

Toward the end of his life, Tolkien continued to ruminate on Galadriel, emending her tale in several later writings. It had dawned on him (and to others) that Galadriel had come to reflect a kind of Virgin Mary figure. In several letters, he acknowledges and corroborates this interpretation, agreeing with much of it in principle—for example, *lembas* as a proxy for the Eucharist and the gift of Grace (literally, in the case of Gimli). However, he seems to have been reluctant to accept a total congruence between Galadriel and Mary. As late as 1971, he warned: "I think it is true that I owe much of this character to Christian and Catholic teaching and imagination about Mary, but actually Galadriel was a penitent: in her youth a leader in the rebellion against the Valar (the angelic guardians). At the end of the First Age she proudly refused forgiveness or permission to return. She was pardoned because of her resistance to the final and overwhelming temptation to take the Ring for herself" (*Letters*, 407).

Yet in his very last writings—indeed, in the last month of his life—Tolkien evidently repented this position and more fully embraced the Marian Galadriel. He adumbrated a revision to her story, changing Celeborn into a Telerin prince (not an Elf of Doriath) and offering a radically different explanation for Galadriel's exile. In these sketches, no longer part of Fëanor's rebellion at all, Galadriel and Celeborn proposed to return to Middle-earth on their own—and with the permission of the Valar. At the Kinslaying at Alqualondë, they now actively *fought against* Fëanor, rather than merely declining to fight *for* him. And in that hour, "despairing now for Valinor and horrified by the violence and cruelty of Fëanor," Galadriel and Celeborn took their own ship and sailed to Middle-earth alone and without permission (*UT*, 232). Thus, *independent* of Fëanor, they came under the Ban of the Valar—but wholly differently from the earlier legends. It appears that in his final days, Tolkien may have intended to revise Galadriel into a more deliberately Marian figure after all, and had he lived longer, it seems likely that his vision of her in *The Silmarillion* would have altered considerably. As it is, we're left with a powerful and pivotal character caught in the midst of an unfinished transformation.

JASON FISHER

Further Reading

Bridoux, Denis. "The Tale of Galadriel and Celeborn: An Attempt at an Integrated Reconstruction." *Amon Hen* 104 (July 1990): 19–23.

Caldecott, Stratford. "The Lord and Lady of the Rings: The Hidden Presence of Tolkien's Catholicism in *The Lord of the Rings*." *Touchstone Magazine* 15, no. 1 (January–February 2002).

Goselin, Peter Damien. "Two Faces of Eve: Galadriel and Shelob as Anima Figures." *Mythlore* 6, no 3 (21) (1979): 3–4.

Grant, Patrick. "Tolkien: Archetype and Word." In *Understanding The Lord of the Rings: The Best of Tolkien Criticism*, edited by Rose A. Zimbardo and Neil D. Isaacs. Boston, MA: Houghton Mifflin, 2004.

Helms, Randel. *Tolkien and the Silmarils*. London: Thames & Hudson, 1981.

Johnson, Janice. "The Celeblain of Celeborn and Galadriel." *Mythlore* 9, no. 2 (32) (1982): 11–19.

Kocher, Paul H. *A Reader's Guide to The Silmarillion*. Boston, MA: Houghton Mifflin, 1980.

O'Neill, Timothy R. *The Individuated Hobbit: Jung, Tolkien, and the Archetypes of Middle-earth*. Boston, MA: Houghton Mifflin, 1979.

Ruskin, Laura A. "Three Good Mothers: Galadriel, Psyche, and Sybil Coningsby." In *Mythcon I: Proceedings*, edited by Glen GoodKnight, 12–14. Los Angeles: Mythopoeic Society, 1971.

Startzman, L. Eugene. "Goldberry and Galadriel: The Quality of Joy." *Mythlore* 16, no. 2 (60) (1989): 5–13.

See also **Arwen; Bible; Catholicism, Roman; Christian Readings of Tolkien; Christianity; Eärendil; Elrond; Elves; Exile; Fëanor; Feminist Readings of Tolkien; Gandalf; Gender in Tolkien's Works; Gimli; Jungian Theory; Lothlórien; One Ring, The; Penance; Phial; Rings of Power;** *Road Goes Ever On;* **Sam; Shelob; Silmarils; Two Trees; Women in Tolkien's Works**

GAMING

Fantasy role-playing games (RPGs), like works of fantasy literature, have been influenced, at a fundamental level, by the works of J.R.R. Tolkien. Games of dice and rune tossing have been around for thousands of years, but the term "gaming" has generally been adopted by one specific branch of games: the RPG. In the simplest form, a RPG involves two or more players who assume different persona—or characters—and these characters, in some form, go on adventures, take part in quests, or do battle. These RPGs may use boards and other external features that aid in game play, such as the use of miniatures and figurines, or the players themselves may dress in costume.

Since the nineteenth century, war games, such as *Kriegspiel,* were played on boards or in the sand by military servicemen. The games were utilized by the armed services in developing tactics and predicting enemy maneuvers. RPGs, however, can be traced to famed science fiction author, H.G. Wells. Wells developed games for the amateur, which included sets of miniatures, boards, and dice for war gaming. The efforts of Wells have dubbed him the "grandfather" of RPGs. An RPG differs slightly from the standard war game, in that the game is run by a game master—called a Dungeon Master by fantasy role-players. A game master sets the rules and determines the story for a particular game, or campaign; this includes the setting, characters, and plot for presentation to a group of players. These groups of players then take actions within the world of the game master, that take place within the context of their particular game.

Unlike war games, the fantasy RPG is not limited to the realities or history of our world. In the 1960s, shortly after the launch of the first commercially available war game by the Avalon-Hill Game Company, the second edition of *The Lord of the Rings* was published, creating desire for fantasy RPGs. For gamers, *The Lord of the Rings* provided another avenue of imagination. The trend of reenacting famous battles slowly moved to games that dealt with a medieval-style world complete with orcs, goblins, rings, wizards, and dragons. A war game, styling medieval warfare complete with miniatures and medi-·eval campaigns was soon published, entitled *Chainmail. Chainmail* later included fantasy supplements full of elves, dwarves, and Tolkienesque creatures and settings created by Gary Gygax and his small company, Tactical Studies Rules. As a reader of Tolkien's work, along with a multitude of other fantasy-oriented works, *Chainmail's* designer, Gygax, with friend Dave Arneson, created the first commercially available fantasy RPG in 1974, *Dungeons and Dragons.* From its first publication through to the fifth printing in 1976, *Dungeons and Dragons* featured elements unique to Tolkien, such as Hobbits, Ents, and Balrogs. When Tolkien Enterprises threatened a lawsuit, Gygax changed the names of these creatures to halflings, Treants, and Balor-demons when the sixth printing of the game was published in 1977.

The creators of *Dungeons and Dragons* brought many revisions and editions to the game, which had turned a hobby into a booming industry. *Dungeons and Dragons* was soon followed by many fantasy-based RPGs, such as *Tunnels and Trolls, Chivalry and Sorcery, RuneQuest,* and the science-fiction-oriented game *Traveler.* In 1982, Iron Crown Enterprises (ICE), launched its critically acclaimed, officially licensed, family-oriented adventure game, *Middle-earth Role Playing* game: affectionately called *MERP* by gamers. For gamers, *MERP* provided the essential outlet to role-play in Tolkien's world. It was the only game based on *The Hobbit* and *The Lord of the Rings,* which was also officially licensed by the holders of the merchandising rights, Tolkien Enterprises. The creators of *MERP* provided a detailed system of rules, maps, art, and characters for gamers, which included lists of Tolkien's works to expand the gaming experience. *MERP* was published in over thirteen languages. In 1999, however, ICE ceased producing *MERP*, despite its being the second best-selling RPG of all time.

In the mid-1990s, after the premiere of Richard Garfield's *Magic: The Gathering,* ICE produced a *Middle-earth Collectible Card Game* and adventure board games based on *The Hobbit* and *The Lord of the Rings.* A collectible card game (CCG) gave gamers the opportunity to collect illustrated cards of heroes, villains, and fantasy settings. Statistics and rules appeared upon each card. This new concept of gaming removed the need for books, dice, and the story of RPGs. CCGs could be played anywhere anytime with anyone. The CCG market became as huge a success as the RPG.

As *The Lord of the Rings* films, directed by Peter Jackson, were released, the illustrated, artistic images of Tolkien's world—originally seen in *MERP* and the *Middle-earth CCG*—were replaced by images from the Jackson films These reinterpreted Middle-earth games are produced by Decipher and Games Workshop. As the first installment of *The Lord of the Rings* film was released, Games Workshop, known throughout the 1980s and 1990s for its fantasy strategy battle game *Warhammer*, began producing games that balance both the books and films. Games Workshop has expanded away from the film with *The Lord of the Rings* games based on both *The Hobbit* and *The Lord of the Rings.*

During the 1980s and 1990s, as fantasy RPGs based on Tolkien's work were produced, computer programmers began to bring Middle-earth to other media. *The Hobbit* was produced for the Commodore 64 and other platforms, complete with computer graphic renditions of the story and was a text-based adventure game. This opened the market for Tolkien-inspired computer games. Between 1984 and 1988, fans played fifteen different titles. The developers of these games did not purchase a license, nor did they have copyrights to specific elements from Tolkien. These titles were copies of the events depicted in the *The Hobbit* and *The Lord of the Rings* or were parodies based on National Lampoon's *Bored of the Rings.* The 1990s release of *War of the Ring* by Gameplay and *Lord of the Rings Volume I* by Interplay shifted the game industry from floppy disk to compact disc. The rise of video game platforms such as Nintendo and Playstation increased and expanded the video game play experience. The official licensors of the *The Hobbit* and *The Lord of the Rings*, Tolkien Enterprises, helped develop the *Fellowship of the Ring*, an almost exact rendition of the book. This was followed by video game versions from the Jackson films.

ANTHONY BURDGE

Further Reading

Acaeum: Dungeons and Dragons Knowledge Compendium. http://www.acaeum.com/.

Astinus, Jason. "A History of Role Playing." http://ptgptb.org/index.html.

Iron Crown Enterprises. *Middle-earth Role Playing: The Role Playing Game of JRR Tolkien's World.* Charlottesville, VA.: ICE, 1986.

———. *Middle-earth Role Playing: The Role Playing Game of JRR Tolkien's World Second Edition.* Charlottesville, VA: ICE, 1994.

Mooney, Chris. "Great Escapism: J.R.R. Tolkien's Preindustrial Fantasy Feeds Postindustrial Entertainment." December 2002. http://www.findarticles.com/p/articles/mi_m1568/is_7_34/ai_94775377.

TheOneRing.net. "Interview with Gary Gygax Creator of Dungeons & Dragons." http://www.theonering.net/features/interviews/gary_gygax.html.

Trifkovic, Ranko "Arjuna." "The Lord of the Rings and Video Games." May 2002. http://www.actiontrip.com/features/lordoftheringsandvideogames.phtml.

See also **Fandom; Merchandising**

GANDALF

Character and Background

Gandalf was one of the five Wizards or Istari specifically mentioned as having come to Middle-earth about the year 1000 of the Third Age. (The others were Saruman, Radagast, and the two so-called Blue Wizards, who apparently disappeared into the East and were never heard from again.) Gandalf was one of the Maiar, the servants and helpers of the Valar, and was once known as Olórin "in my youth in the West that is forgotten," as he rather poignantly told Faramir (*TT*, IV, v, 279). When the Valar at last decided to help the peoples of Middle-earth against the evil of Sauron by indirect rather than direct means, they sent the Istari to provide counsel and guidance. Of the five, Gandalf alone remained true to that task.

When Gandalf first arrived in Middle-earth, Círdan the shipwright, master of the Grey Havens, surrendered to him Narya, the Ring of Fire, one of the three great Elven Rings of Power. Gandalf was ever after associated with fire: as he tells the Balrog, he is both the servant and the wielder of fire. His association with fire carries down even to his mastery of those fireworks that so delight the Hobbits.

Like the other wizards, Gandalf came clothed in the form of a venerable old man, white-haired and silver-bearded yet hale and fit, strong and broad-shouldered, dark-eyed under bushy brows. Although he was an emissary from the West, an "angelos" or messenger, in the original Greek acceptation of the word, he lived in Middle-earth as a human being. His physical body was subject to human limitations like weariness and hunger. In his earlier journeys about Middle-earth, he wore a pointed hat and gray robes and thus was often known as the Grey Pilgrim. (As both Humphrey Carpenter and Douglas Anderson note, Tolkien based his image of Gandalf partly on a painting, *Der Berggeist*, "The Mountain Spirit," done in the 1920s by the German artist Josef Madlener [1881–1967].) Gandalf was an inveterate traveler, unlike Radagast and Saruman who established fixed abodes, and thus he knew many peoples (with a special interest in hobbits), knew many languages (he commanded the doors of Moria to open "in every language that had ever been spoken in the West of Middle-earth" [*FR*, II, iv, 321]), and was known by many names, as he once told Faramir: "Mithrandir [Sindarin: "grey pilgrim"] among the Elves, Tharkûn to the Dwarves; Olórin . . . in the West. . . in the South Incánus, in the North Gandalf" (*TT*, IV, v, 279).

Gandalf was the working name Tolkien chose for the wizard, as we see in *The Hobbit*, and like the Dwarves' names there it comes from the Elder Edda. In the very earliest drafts of *The Hobbit*, though, Tolkien called his wizard Bladorthin, and the chief Dwarf was named Gandalf. This soon changed, and Bladorthin became the name of a long-dead king who had ordered spears from the Dwarves' workshops. Besides the names mentioned, Gandalf was also called in Rohan "Greyhame" (grey-cloak), "Stormcrow," and, by Gríma Wormtongue, "Láthspell" (ill news). (Gandalf was not well liked at that moment in Rohan, not least because he had taken the king's finest horse, Shadowfax, and made of him not only a mount but also a friend.)

Like his colleague Saruman, Gandalf possessed vast knowledge; unlike him, Gandalf possessed wisdom also. He possessed self-knowledge, refusing the One Ring when offered it, knowing it would turn his desire to do good with it into a desire to exert sheer power through it. He possessed imagination: he could see or foresee what natures and minds unlike his own might plan or do. He was wise enough to know the limits of wisdom, and could cheerfully acknowledge his own lack of omniscience and his capability for making mistakes. He had a healthy sense of his own identity and purpose and at the same time was totally selfless: although he certainly did not intend to die in Moria, he was willing to risk death to defeat the Balrog.

Gandalf destroyed the Balrog and then, as he says, "passed out of time and thought" and, naked, "was sent back." In his second manifestation, as Gandalf the White, or the White Rider ("Saruman as he should have been" [*TT*, III, v, 98]), Gandalf exerted great moral authority.

Gandalf did not suffer fools gladly, and yet his tenderness toward the merely foolish—the younger hobbits spring at once to mind—is notable. He usually seems more exasperated by than angry at the hapless Peregrin Took and his antics. Part of his wisdom was a well-developed sense of humor and a well-proportioned sense of his own importance. When Treebeard sent the Huorns to the Battle of Helm's Deep and they destroyed the hordes of Orcs, many saw it as an example of Gandalf's power, a suggestion to which he replied, laughing, "that is no deed of mine. It is a thing beyond the counsel of the wise. Better than my design, and better even than my hope the event has proved" (*TT*, III, viii, 148–49).

His Work and Its Significance

It can be said that there are three Gandalfs in Tolkien's Middle-earth, nested one within the other, each successive version greater than the last. The first and least impressive is the Gandalf of *The Hobbit*; the second more powerful one is in *The Fellowship of the Ring*, and the third and most majestic Gandalf appears in the last two parts of *The Lord of the Rings* after his return. A simple contrast: when Gandalf confronts the Wargs or wolves in chapter 6 of *The Hobbit,* he is described as "dreadfully afraid, wizard though he was" (*H*, VI, 148). When Gandalf confronts the Wargs near the foot of Caradhras, he "seemed suddenly to grow: he rose up, a great menacing shape like the monument of some ancient king of stone set upon a hill. Stooping like a cloud, he lifted a burning branch and strode to meet the wolves" (*FR*, II, iv, 312). In each case, Gandalf uses fire to defeat the beasts, but his posture is radically different. After his return from Moria, he seems even more powerful: in Théoden's hall he "raised his staff. There was a roll of thunder. The sunlight was blotted out from the

eastern windows; the whole hall became suddenly dark as night.... There was a flash as if lightning had cloven the roof" (*TT*, III, vi, 118–19), This is the Gandalf of great presence and power. He is still literally "an old man with a staff," as he was in *The Hobbit*, but enormously magnified.

There are several ways of discussing Gandalf's role and significance in Middle-earth. One obvious way is to look at his direct confrontations with evil, as, for instance, when he faces the demonic Balrog on the Bridge of Khazad-dûm or the Captain of the Nazgûl at the gate of Minas Tirith or still later the so-called Mouth of Sauron at the Black Gate of Mordor.

More subtle but equally important is to see when he fulfills his original task, which was to give counsel and guidance to the Free Peoples of the West.

Near the beginning of the Ring's adventures, Gandalf counsels Frodo to remember pity and mercy; the occasions when Frodo does so are all-important. Gandalf does not offer Frodo this counsel because it is expedient, although it is, but because it is morally correct to act according to such feelings.

He counsels Frodo to take the Ring from the Shire in July of 3019 at the latest; that advice does not reach Frodo, but his advice in the same letter to accept the friendship of Aragorn does come in time, barely.

He advises those gathered at the Council of Elrond that the Ring must be destroyed, even though it seems a dangerous and foolhardy course of action; he reminds the Council that "despair is only for those who see the end beyond all doubt" (*FR*, II, ii, 285), which is not only sage but also theologically correct. More immediately important, he counsels the doubtful Elrond to let Merry and Pippin accompany Frodo, a decision that will resonate through the rest of the tale.

Finally, at the Last Debate, Gandalf achieves his finest moment. Having barely beaten back Sauron's might, the captains of the West must decide what to do next. Prudence would dictate a kind of bunker mentality, to paraphrase what Gandalf says. Hunker down and await the outcome. "I said this would be prudent," Gandalf says. "But I do not counsel prudence" (*RK,* V, ix, 155). We must attack Sauron, he says: we must make ourselves the bait, and let him seize us, while the Ring-bearer does what he can.

For the second time, then, Gandalf proposes to sacrifice himself to save Middle-earth, because he sees that as his proper role and duty. "I . . . am a steward," he tells Denethor. "Did you not know?" (*RK,* V, i, 31).

His stewardship of Middle-earth, his care for it in the absence of its lord or proprietor, is the duty that defines and underlies all his other tasks. When the Ring is destroyed and Middle-earth is saved, he can lay down his burden and go home. "The Third Age was my age," he tells Aragorn. "I was the Enemy of Sauron and my work is finished" (*RK,* VI, v, 249).

MICHAEL N. STANTON

Further Reading

Anderson, Douglas A., ed. *The Annotated Hobbit.* 2d ed., rev. Boston, MA: Houghton Mifflin, 2002.

Birzer, Bradley J. *J.R.R. Tolkien's Sanctifying Myth: Understanding Middle-earth.* Wilmington, DE: ISI Books, 2003.

Burns, Marjorie. "Gandalf and Odin." In *Tolkien's "Legendarium,"* edited by Verlyn Flieger and Carl Hostetter. Westport, CT: Greenwood, 2000.

Carpenter, Humphrey. *Tolkien: A Biography.* Boston, MA: Houghton Mifflin, 1977.

Dickerson, Matthew T. *Following Gandalf: Epic Battles and Moral Victory in "The Lord of the Rings."* Grand Rapids, MI: Brazos Press, 2003.

Noel, Ruth. *The Mythology of Middle-earth.* Boston, MA: Houghton Mifflin, 1978.

O'Neill, Timothy R. *The Individuated Hobbit.* Boston, MA: Houghton Mifflin, 1979.

Petty, Anne C. *Tolkien in the Island of Heroes.* Cold Spring Harbor, NY: Cold Spring Press, 2003.

See also **Bilbo; Dwarves; Frodo; Maiar; Saruman; Wizards**

GARM

Garm appears in *Farmer Giles of Ham.* In the story, he is Giles's talking watchdog. The name Garm itself comes from Norse mythology. The mythological Garm was a monstrous four-eyed guard in charge of guarding Helheim, the realm of the dead, and he lived in cave called Gnipa. It was prophesized that Garm's howl would signal the coming of Ragnarok, the final, apocalyptic battle in Norse mythology.

Both Garms serve as watch dogs. The Norse Garm is the guardian of Hell, while Giles's Garm is the guardian of the farm. Also, both signal the coming of an ominous event, the Norse Garm with his howl and Giles's Garm with his speech. While Giles's Garm's cry does not signal a coming apocalypse and the end of the world, it does signal the coming of a giant. This howl that signals the coming of a giant or giants is identical for both Garms. The Norse Garm's howl signals the coming of Ragnarok, at which point the Norse Gods will do battle with the Frost Giants. The other Garm's cry awakens farmer Giles, who then does battle with the giant destroying his fields. Thus, both Garms serve to signal the coming of giants.

Just as it is Garm who finds the giant rampaging in Farmer Giles's field, later on he also encounters the dragon Chrysophylax while out walking. Chrysophylax incinerates large parts of the countryside and wreaks havoc. At Ragnarok, the Norse Garm's howl will also signal that that the Nidhog dragon has gnawed through the root of the world tree Yggdrasil. Thus both Garms herald the destructive power of dragons.

Another link to Norse mythology is a comment made by Farmer Giles: "he had his hands full (he said keeping the wolf at the door." (10) In Norse mythology the greatest of the wolves is Fenrir, who will break his chains at Ragnarok and devour the sun. However, when Fenrir was being chained, he bit off the god Tyr's hand. Hence, having a hand full to keep the wolf at the door is a pun on Ragnarok.

The howls, the giants, the dragons, and the imagery all show the link between the Garms in Norse Mythology and *Farmer Giles of Ham*; the humor in Tolkien's story arises from the enormously diminshed stature of Giles' Garm coupled with the dog's continual arrogance.

JOHN WALSH

See also **Animals in Tolkien's Works;** *Farmer Giles of Ham*; **Farmer Giles; Hell; Old Norse**

GAZE

One of the central metaphors of *The Lord of the Rings* is the Eye of Sauron: lidless, never-sleeping, it seeks out its enemies, pins them down, identifies their thoughts and dominates them. The Eye has a power and potency that is felt by both Frodo and Gollum (*TT,* IV, ii, 238). The Lord of the Nazgûl threatens Éowyn with its gaze: "thy shriveled mind be left naked to the Lidless Eye" (*RK,* V, vi, 116). Even before the Ring has achieved its baleful power in close proximity to its master, Bilbo feels that it is like an eye, looking at him (*FR,* I, i, 43).

In his use of the gaze metaphor, Tolkien turns out to be very consistent with some of the major threads of literary and cultural theory from the later part of the twentieth century. In "Panopticism," Michel Foucault asserts that the ability to see everything about a person, to observe him or her ceaselessly, is a form of power that is used to transform multiplicity into unity, difference into sameness. This is exactly what Sauron's gaze does. As Gergely Nagy has noted, Sauron's gaze turns free individuals into mere bodies, subject to his gaze and thus able to be dominated and controlled, smaller shadows under his great shadow, signifying nothing in themselves, only existing as servants for his greedily expanding power (64–65).

Dragons, too, have the power of the gaze. Bilbo is comparatively safe from Smaug because the dragon cannot see him (or smell him, another form of identification), but, even invisible, he knows to avoid the worm's eyes. In *The Silmarillion*, Glaurung, the father of dragons, is able to daunt, control, and ensnare individuals through his gaze. That one must avoid looking into the eyes of dragons is a traditional maxim in dragon lore, but Tolkien's use and expansion of the trope is consistent with the logic of the gaze in other beings in Middle-earth.

But not only evil creatures are empowered by the gaze in *The Lord of the Rings*. Galadriel tests the members of the Fellowship by gazing upon them, apparently seeing their innermost thoughts and desires and testing them. Sam interprets her gaze in slightly sexualized terms—"I felt as if I hadn't got nothing on" (*FR*, II, vii, 373)—but more important than any sexual discourse is the functioning of the power that allows Galadriel—though not with words—to ask questions and get answers. Fëanor's gaze is so powerful that few are able to withstand it, and he is even able to pierce through Morgoth's veils of secrecy and dissembling to discover that the Dark Lord covets the Silmarils (*S*, 72).

The gaze is thus a metaphor for and an operationalization of power: those who have power have the power of the gaze, the ability to categorize and control the individuals upon whom they are looking. That Tolkien's development of this metaphor—obviously completely separate from Foucault and the other (mostly feminist) critics who have discussed it—is so consistent with Foucaultian cultural theory is a point of great interest, both to Tolkien studies and to literary and cultural scholarship as a whole.

MICHAEL D.C. DROUT

Further Reading

Bryson, Norman. *Vision and Painting: The Logic of the Gaze*. New Haven, CT: Yale University Press, 1983.
Foucault, Michel. "Panopticism." In *The Foucault Reader*, edited by Paul Rabinow, 206–13. New York: Pantheon, 1984.
Nagy, Gergely. "The 'Lost' Subject of Middle-earth: The Constitution of the Subject in the Figure of Gollum in *The Lord of the Rings*." *Tolkien Studies* 3 (2006): 57–59.

See also **Evil; Galadriel; Light; Morgoth and Melkor; Sauron**

GEACH, E.F.A.: "ROMANCE"

The 1918 issue of *Oxford Poetry* included poems by E.F.A. Geach. One poem, "Romance," is a possible source of inspiration for Tolkien and may have been used by him to compose Bilbo's "Road Goes Ever On" song.

Both are short, eight-line poems, and Geach's poem expresses the same themes as Bilbo's song:

adventure awaits the traveler on the road; one never knows what lies around the next bend or corner. Compare, for example:

> Oh who can tell what you may meet
> Round the next corner and in the next street!

And Bilbo:

> Pursuing it with eager feet
> Until it joins some larger way
> Where many paths and errands meet.
> And whither then? I cannot say.

While no words are similar, the similar theme suggests a level of inspiration.

L.J. SWAIN

Further Reading

Earp, T. W., Dorothy L. Sayers, and E.F.A. Geach. *Oxford Poetry, 1918*. Oxford: Blackwell, 1918.

See also **Oxford**

GENDER IN TOLKIEN'S WORKS

In one of his letters, Tolkien explains that part of women's "servient, helpmeet instinct" is "to be receptive, stimulated, fertilized (in many other matters than the physical) by the male" (*Letters*, 49). Here, Tolkien is taking an essentialist view, which sees gender as an inborn characteristic essential to one's sex and not as a set of expected roles determined by one's society. In this letter, Tolkien sees the male as naturally active and superior while the female is passive and subordinate by "instinct." In his fiction, the Valar's genders are an essential part of their natures: they assume male or female forms because "that difference of temper they had even from their beginning" (*S*, 11). The Valar replicate traditional gender norms, with feminine activities including nurturing, gardening, healing, weaving, and mourning, and the masculine qualities being more active and vigorous (Fredrick and McBride, 115). In a discussion of the Elven race, however, Tolkien allows for both nature and nurture in defining masculinity and femininity. In "Laws and Customs among the Eldar," he explains that some gender differences are natural and others occur by "custom" (*Morgoth*, 213). Generally, though, traditional gender norms are reproduced throughout Middle-earth: Aragorn, for example, takes an active masculine role by fighting and leading others, while Arwen remains in the domestic sphere, weaving and waiting.

In Tolkien's cosmography, Eru and his chief representative Manwë are male, thus establishing a gendered hierarchy in which the masculine is dominant. However, even though Manwë is ranked highest of the Valar, his spouse Varda is more widely revered in Middle-earth. The spiritual powers of the Valar are equally divided between males and females (Crowe, 273), and they are usually greater when masculine and feminine powers are combined rather than separated. This "dance" of complementarity (Rawls, 5) extends to Tolkien's other characters. Melanie Rawls identifies masculine and feminine "principles" evident in characters of both sexes and finds that those who either embody both principles or have access to their opposite in a spouse, sibling, or mentor are more successful (Rawls, 5).

Because Tolkien emphasizes the interdependence of masculinity and femininity rather than fixed boundaries between them, some critics see the feminine as highly valued in his works (Crowe, 276). Even women who remain in conventional roles are not weak or passive (Lewis and Currie, 202); sometimes, their femininity is the source of their strength, as in Éowyn's ability to kill the Nazgûl lord (Hopkins, 365). Some critics find that Tolkien's strong female characters challenge stereotypical gender roles. Galadriel, Éowyn, Emeldir the Man-hearted, Haleth, and Idril tend to synthesize masculine and feminine qualities (Armstrong, 250) as they become heroic leaders defending their homes and peoples. Lúthien is a leading character: active, creative, and willing to defy her father in order to save her lover (Lewis and Currie, 196). Others, however, believe that even exceptional women do not escape their gendered roles: Éowyn, for example, after fighting heroically on the battlefield, opts for a traditional feminine life of healing and marriage (Hopkins, 366). Debate over Tolkien's views on femininity often centers on the singular image of Shelob, with some critics reading her as an expression of hostility to the feminine (Stimpson, 19), while others, seeing Shelob in opposition to Galadriel rather than as an enemy of Sam, view this episode as a conflict between an idealized woman and her monstrous female antithesis (Fenwick, 23; Donovan, 112–21).

Although most gender criticism examines Tolkien's representation of femininity and its status, analyses of his male characters have produced interesting insights into Tolkien's critique of traditional masculine roles. Conventional heroism as represented in medieval literature is attractive to Tolkien, but he also creates major characters like Frodo and Sam who embody an internal and spiritual heroism more in keeping with Tolkien's Christian beliefs (Clark, 44). In *The Hobbit*, Bilbo does not lead in battle, kill the dragon, or keep the treasure, as a medieval warrior-hero would (Clark, 41–43). William Green sees Bilbo as an androgynous character and *The Hobbit* as a "focused rejection of traditional masculine values," a throwback to Victorian gender ideology (Green, 194–95). Whatever the impulse behind their creation, Tolkien's male characters enact a number of different roles, from heroic warriors like Boromir to healers and counselors like Elrond and Gandalf, whose characters combine conventional masculine and feminine traits.

It is difficult to pin down a consistent and simple definition of gender roles in Tolkien's life and work. Although he sometimes expresses traditional views of separate masculine and feminine spheres of activity set in a male-dominated universe, his fictional characters often exemplify the complementarity of masculine and feminine qualities and, on occasion, even challenge gender stereotypes.

ANNA SMOL

Further Reading

Anderson, Douglas A., ed. *The Annotated Hobbit*. 2nd ed., rev. Boston, MA: Houghton Mifflin, 2002.

Armstrong, Helen. "Good Guys, Bad Guys, Fantasy and Reality." In *Proceedings of the J.R.R. Tolkien Centenary Conference 1992*, edited by Patricia Reynolds and Glen GoodKnight, 247–52. Milton Keynes and Altadena: Tolkien Society and Mythopoeic Press, 1995.

Clark, George. "J.R.R. Tolkien and the True Hero." In *J.R.R. Tolkien and His Literary Resonances: Views of Middle-earth*, edited by George Clark and Daniel Timmons, 39–51. Westport, CT: Greenwood, 2000.

Crowe, Edith L. "Power in Arda: Sources, Uses and Misuses." In *Proceedings of the J.R.R. Tolkien Centenary Conference 1992*, edited by Patricia Reynolds and Glen GoodKnight, 272–77. Milton Keynes and Altadena: Tolkien Society and Mythopoeic Press, 1995.

Donovan, Leslie A. "The Valkyrie Reflex in J.R.R. Tolkien's *The Lord of the Rings*: Galadriel, Shelob, Éowyn, and Arwen." In *Tolkien the Medievalist*, edited by Jane Chance, 106–32. London and New York: Routledge, 2003.

Fenwick, Mac. "Breastplates of Silk: Homeric Women in *The Lord of the Rings*." *Mythlore* 81 (1996): 17–23, 51.

Fredrick, Candice, and Sam McBride. *Women among the Inklings: Gender, C.S. Lewis, J.R.R. Tolkien, and Charles Williams*. Contributions in Women's Studies 191. Westport, CT: Greenwood, 2001.

Green, William H. "'Where's Mama?': The Construction of the Feminine in *The Hobbit*." *The Lion and The Unicorn* 22 (1998): 188–95.

Hopkins, Lisa. "Female Authority Figures in the Works of Tolkien, C.S. Lewis and Charles Williams." In *Proceedings of the J.R.R. Tolkien Centenary Conference 1992*, edited by Patricia Reynolds and Glen GoodKnight, 364–66. Milton Keynes and Altadena: Tolkien Society and Mythopoeic Press, 1995.

Lewis, Alex, and Elizabeth Currie. *The Uncharted Realms of Tolkien: A Critical Study of Text, Context and Subtext in the Works of J.R.R. Tolkien.* Oswestry, UK: Medea Publishing, 2002.

Rawls, Melanie. "The Feminine Principle in Tolkien." *Mythlore* 10 (1984): 5–13.

Stimpson, Catharine R. *J.R.R. Tolkien.* New York: Columbia University Press, 1969.

Tolkien, J.R.R. "Laws and Customs among the Eldar." In *Morgoth*, 207–54.

See also **Aragorn; Arwen; Bilbo; Elrond; Éowyn; Eru; Feminist Readings of Tolkien's Works; Frodo; Galadriel; Heroes and Heroism;** *Lord of the Rings*; **Lúthien;** *Morgoth's Ring*; **Sam; Shelob;** *Silmarillion*; *Hobbit, The*; **Women in Tolkien's Works; Valar**

GENESIS

The Old English *Genesis* is the first poem in the eleventh-century Junius manuscript (Oxford, Bodleian Library, MS Junius 11). *Genesis* is accompanied by forty-eight illustrations and followed by three other religious/biblical poems: *Exodus*, *Daniel*, and *Christ and Satan*. Given the importance of the name Ælfwine, "elf-friend," to Tolkien, the presence of a small medallion portrait inscribed with the name *ælfwine* beneath the second illustration (God enthroned) is worthy of note. The poem is less a translation in the modern sense than a fairly faithful paraphrase, with various interpolations and omissions. It covers the first part of the biblical book of Genesis (through Abraham's aborted sacrifice of Isaac, Gen. 22:13). *Genesis* is actually two poems; the larger poem is termed *Genesis A*, but lines 235–851, known as *Genesis B*, are an interpolation deriving from an Old Saxon original. There is no question that Tolkien knew the Old English *Genesis*—not only is it a text that all students and scholars of Old English know, but Tolkien himself worked extensively on the *Exodus*, the poem following *Genesis* in the Junius manuscript (his edition, translation, and commentary, compiled from his notes, were published posthumously in 1981).

Genesis A follows the biblical Genesis fairly closely, with two major interpolations and several smaller additions, as well as some omissions, often eliminating repetition or passages of genealogy. In general, the Old English poem tends to graft in Germanic elements and presents the relationship of God to his people, and that of patriarchs to their kin, as that of the *comitatus*: the Germanic war-band. The first major interpolation is the opening (lines 1–102), a brief hymn of praise to God and the nonbiblical story of the Fall of the Angels, presenting the rebellious angels as disloyal thanes who are rightly punished by their king. The second major interpolation recounts the battles in Sodom and Gomorrah in which Abraham rescues a captured Lot as an abbreviated Germanic-heroic battle epic (lines 1960–2095; Gen. 14:1–16).

Genesis B recounts the Fall, and while it occupies the place of Gen. 3:1–7, almost all of it is extra-biblical. It begins with the prohibition, God's command to refrain from eating the fruit of one tree, and then leaves the story of Adam and Eve to narrate the Fall of the Angels, already recounted in lines 1–77 of *Genesis A*. The version in *Genesis B* is longer and more detailed and dramatizes the event, developing the character of Satan and his principal lieutenant—nameless, but it is he, not Satan, who tempts first Adam and then Eve. Some influence on Tolkien's account of the Fall of Melkor, in the Ainulindalë, and perhaps even on Melkor's lieutenant, Sauron, is possible here. Like Melkor the Satan of *Genesis B* is greater than the other angels: "But one He made so great and strong of heart, He let him wield such power in heaven next unto God, so radiant-hued He wrought him, so fair his form in heaven which God had given, that he was like unto the shining stars" (252–56). Tolkien's Melkor is driven by a desire to make things of his own; Satan too desires to exercise his creative power in a manner equal to God: "My hands are strong to work full many a wonder. Power enough have I to rear a goodlier throne" (279–81). Sometimes indicated as a possible influence on Milton's *Paradise Lost*, the Old English *Genesis* may, in its emphasis on Satan's desire to implement his own designs, as well as the elevated role given to his lieutenant, be identified as well as a possible influence on Tolkien's cosmogony.

YVETTE KISOR

Further Reading

Kennedy, Charles W., trans. *The Caedmon Poems.* London: G. Routledge & Sons; New York: E.P. Dutton & Co., 1916. "Genesis (Genesis A and B)." Codex Junius 11. The Online Medieval and Classical Library. Release #14b. 1996. http://sunsite.berkeley.edu/OMACL/Junius/genesis.html.

Krapp, George Philip. *The Junius Manuscript.* The Anglo-Saxon Poetic Records: A Collective Edition 1. New York: Columbia University Press; London: Routledge & Kegan Paul, 1931.

See also **Ælfwine; Angels; Devils; Eru;** *Exodus*, **Edition of; Fall of Man; Heaven; Hell; Morgoth and Melkor; Milton; Paradise; Pride; Publications, Posthumous; Satan and Lucifer; Sauron;** *Silmarillion, The*; **Valar**

GERMAN FOLKTALE: *DEUTSCHE MYTHOLOGIE*

The first two-volume edition of *Kinder- und Hausmärchen* [*Children and Household Tales*], by the German brothers Jacob (1775–1863) and Wilhelm (1786–1859) Grimm, was published between 1812 and 1815, with frequent revisions taking place in the following years. In particular, Wilhelm continued to expand and refine the collection until his death.

The importance of the Grimms' enterprise for the development of historical studies on the fairy-tale tradition in Europe cannot be overstated. Their painstaking search for traditional folktales lasted several years and resulted in a collection that, in its final version, came to include over two hundred stories. It was published seventeen times between 1812 and 1864; the Small Edition, intended specifically for children, was illustrated by Jacob and Wilhelm's younger brother, Ludwig Emil Grimm.

Both Jacob and Wilhelm agreed that fairy tales should be recorded and presented as close as possible to their original version. They were also widely criticized for tampering with the original texts, so that the final result privileged literary quality at the expense of authenticity. Nevertheless, in his essay "On Fairy-Stories," Tolkien expressed his appreciation for "Von dem Machhandelboom" ["The Juniper Tree"], in spite of its horrific aspects, and berated any attempt to "mollify" the Grimms' version in order to spare children's sensibilities.

Besides his seminal work in the field of Germanic philology, Jacob Grimm was also the author of the extensive *Deutsche Mythologie* [*Teutonic Mythology*], first published in 1835. Together with Grundtvig's *Nordens Mytologi* (1808, 1832), it was one of the first attempts to collect and study the ancient beliefs of Germanic peoples in the pre-Christian era. Grimm maintained that the correspondence between fairy tales and ancient texts such as the *Eddas* was not coincidental, but rather stood to prove some "original unity." Christianity and foreign influence had tried to undermine the status of these remnants of Germany's ancient culture by reducing them to mere stories for children and illiterate people. In the light of the time's political climate, it is quite interesting to observe how Jacob Grimm's use of the word *deutsch* (translated into English as the less controversial "Teutonic") appropriated something that was not really German, but of largely Scandinavian origin.

The work of the brothers Grimm led the way for a series of other similar operations, the most relevant of which being Elias Lönnrot's *Kalevala*, another fundamental inspiration for Tolkien's lifetime project of creating a "mythology for England." Therefore, the influence of *Deutsche Mythologie* on Tolkien's legendarium is quite noteworthy, especially as regards Grimm's treatment of some key terms of Tolkien's own mythology. This, for instance, is the case of the word *elf*, which Grimm derived from an original *albs*, connected to Latin *albus* [white]. However, he could not solve the problem posed by the presence of both "light-elves" and "dark-elves" (identified with dwarves) in Old Norse texts; a problem that Tolkien tried to solve by contrasting the two categories while at the same time stating their original identity.

A number of motifs from the Grimms's fairy tales can be recognized in Tolkien's work, especially in *The Hobbit*. As both Shippey and Anderson point out, part of the episode of the three trolls in chapter 2 was inspired by "Der tapfere Schneiderlein" [The Brave Little Tailor], which appeared in the 1812 edition of *Kinder- und Hausmärchen*. Besides, Tolkien probably derived some elements of the Dwarves's character and behavior from the tales of "Schneewittchen" ["Snow-white," also from 1812] and "Schneeweisschen und Rosenrot" ["Snow-white and Rose-red," from the 1837 edition]. The influence of the Grimms' tales can even be seen in *The Silmarillion*, with the episode of Lúthien growing her hair in order to effect her escape echoing the well-known tale of "Rapunzel."

MARIA RAFFAELLA BENVENUTO

Further Reading

Anderson, Douglas A., ed. *The Annotated Hobbit*. Rev. and expanded ed. London: HarperCollins, 2002.

Grimm, Jakob. *Teutonic Mythology*. Translated by James S. Stallybrass. 4 vols. New York: Dover Publications, 2004.

Grimm, Jakob, and Wilhelm Grimm. *The Complete Grimm's Fairy Tales*. London: Routledge & Kegan Paul, 1975.

Hostetter, Carl F., and Arden R. Smith. "A Mythology for England." In *Proceedings of the J.R.R. Tolkien Centenary Conference*, edited by Patricia Reynolds and Glen H. GoodKnight, 281–90. Milton Keynes and Altadena: Tolkien Society and Mythopoeic Society, 1992.

Shippey, Tom. "*Grimm, Grundtvig, Tolkien: Nationalisms and the Invention of Mythologies.*" In *The Ways of Creative Mythologies—Imagined Worlds and Their Makers*, edited by Maria Kuteeva, 7–17. Telford: Tolkien Society, 2000.

———. *J.R.R. Tolkien: Author of the Century*. London: HarperCollins, 2001.

———. "Light-elves, Dark-elves and Others: Tolkien's Elvish Problems." In *Tolkien Studies* edited by Douglas A. Anderson, Michael D.C. Drout, and Verlyn Flieger, 1:1–15. Morgantown, WV: West Virginia University Press, 2004. pp. 1–15.

———. *The Road to Middle-earth*. Rev. and expanded ed. London: HarperCollins, 2005.

———, ed. *The Shadow-Walkers: Jacob Grimm's Mythology of the Monstrous.* Tempe, AZ: Arizona State University Press, 2005.

Tolkien, J.R.R. "On Fairy-Stories." In *MC.*

Zipes, Jack, ed. *The Oxford Companion to Fairy-Tales.* Oxford: Oxford University Press, 2000.

See also **Dwarves; Elves; Finland, Literary Sources; Folklore; German: Modern; Literature and Folktale, Russian; Mythology for England; Mythology, Germanic; Old Norse Literature; "On Fairy-Stories"; Oral Tradition; Ylfe, Alfr, Elf**

GERMAN RACE LAWS

The German Race Laws (*Nürnberger Gesetze*) were enacted on September 15, 1935, at the Nazi Party's national convention in Nuremberg; they were intended to further limit the rights of Germany's Jews following the "protective laws" prohibiting Jews from working in civil service positions (1935). The *Reichsbürgergesetz* (Reich Citizens Law) defined as Jewish anyone with three Jewish grandparents and reduced those so identified to "subjects" (*Staatsangehörige*) rather than "citizens" (*Staatsbürger*); citizens derived their political rights from their ability to demonstrate "Aryan" (i.e., non-Jewish) descent. The *Gesetz zum Schutze des deutschen Blutes und der deutschen Ehre* (Law for the Protection of German Blood and German Honor) outlawed sexual relations between Jews and gentiles. These laws and further measures culminated in the *Reichskristallnacht* of November 9–10, 1938, when the SA (Nazi storm troopers) attacked Jewish businesses, after which Jews began to be placed in *Schutzhaft* ("protective custody"), that is, concentration camps.

That Tolkien was aware of these laws is apparent in two letters of July 25, 1938, sent to Sir Stanley Unwin, who had arranged for the German publication of *The Hobbit* by Rütten & Loening of Potsdam. The German publisher was obligated to inquire after Tolkien's racial heritage prior to publishing his novel. Tolkien's reaction to this request was registered in the cover letter to Unwin; calling the inquiry after his heritage an "impertinence" and the German Race Laws "lunatic" (*Letters,* 37), he sent two possible replies to Unwin, with the request that his publisher decide which the German publisher should receive. The reply that remains in Unwin's files is a strongly worded refusal by Tolkien to provide the requested information. The letter contains the following arguments: (1) that *Aryan* denotes Indo-Iranian (including Gypsy!) speakers, not gentiles, (2) that the inquiry is actually about possible Jewish ancestry and that Tolkien "regret[ed] that [he had] no ancestors of that

gifted people (i.e., the Jews)," (3) that he is of English and German extraction and considers himself an English subject, (4) that he has heretofore viewed his German ancestry with pride, but that such "impertinent and irrelevant inquiries" discourage this feeling, and (5) that while the inquiry is obviously required by German law, it is both improper to apply such laws to citizens of other countries and irrelevant to the quality of *The Hobbit,* which is the basis of the decision to publish it (*Letters,* 37–38). No German translation appeared until 1957.

Tolkien's views on racialism are clear in two other letters written to his son Christopher while the latter was stationed in South Africa in 1944, in which he criticizes Apartheid (*Letters,* 73) and anti-German hysteria (*Letters,* 93). Tolkien's espousal of Germanic mythology, the same sources misappropriated by the Nazis, has led to accusations of fascism (see the articles by Chism, Straubhaar, and Yates, for examples); however, his use of the same sources should not cause him to be identified with those whom he accused of "ruining, perverting, misapplying, and making forever accursed" the sources and their "northern spirit" of courage in adversity, which he so admired (*Letters,* 55).

CAROL A. LEIBIGER

Further Reading

Chism, Christine. "Middle-earth, the Middle Ages, and the Aryan Nation: Myth and History in World War II." In *Tolkien the Medievalist,* edited by Jane Chance, 63–91. New York: Routledge, 2003.

Plank, Robert. "The Scouring of the Shire: Tolkien's View of Fascism." In *A Tolkien Compass,* edited by Jared Lobdell, 107–15. Lasalle, IL: Open Court, 1975.

Straubhaar, Sandra Ballif. "Myth, Late Roman History, and Multiculturalism in Tolkien's Middle-earth." In *Tolkien and the Invention of Myth: A Reader,* edited by Jane Chance, 101–17. Lexington, KY: University Press of Kentucky, 2004.

Yates, Jessica. "Tolkien the Anti-Totalitarian." *Mythlore* 21, no. 2 (1996): 233–44.

See also **Germany; Judaism; Mythology, Germanic; Nazi Party; Northern Courage; Old Norse Literature; Philo-Semitism; World War II; Race and Racism**

GERMAN: MODERN

Tolkien's knowledge of Modern German was excellent. As a matter of fact, his father's ancestors had come to England from Germany in the eighteenth century, although Tolkien always considered himself first and foremost an Englishman. When approached in 1938 by the German publishers Rütten & Loening about a possible translation of *The Hobbit*, Tolkien reacted angrily to their inquiry about his Aryan origins, which disregarded the fact that he was a British subject even though he had a German surname (*Letters*, 29, 30).

In order to prevent further misspelling of his surname as "Tolkein," he explained its origin in a letter to the American publishers Houghton Mifflin (*Letter*, 165). It was the anglicization of *Tollkiehn*, a name originating from Saxony and derived from the German adjective *tollkühn*, meaning "foolhardy." However, in letter 294, written as a commentary on the text of a draft interview, Tolkien firmly refuted any notion that his interest in Germanic languages might have stemmed from his ancestry. In fact, none of the members of his paternal family had any knowledge of German or of any other language but English. It was Tolkien's mother, instead, who had taught the language to him, as well as Latin and French.

Thanks to her tutoring, while still at school Tolkien was able to start reading German books on philology, as Carpenter relates in his *Biography*. He also mentions that Tolkien, when working for the *Oxford English Dictionary* in 1919–20, drew extensively upon his knowledge of numerous ancient and modern languages, including Modern German, for the compilation of his entries. Besides, Shippey points out that Tolkien had certainly read the Grimms' fairy tales in the original and even appreciated the dialectal forms they contained.

Tolkien's thorough knowledge of Modern German is also demonstrated by his practical advice to prospective translators in his "Guide to the Names in *The Lord of the Rings*." As a matter of fact, the "Guide" was mainly written with a view to a German translation of the book, as Tolkien did not presume to offer advice to speakers of non-Germanic languages. Many of the entries of the guide contain suggestions of possible German translations in which Tolkien brings his keen interest for etymology to bear, as in the case of *Alp* (or, more precisely, *Alb*) for "elf"; or in his observations on the word *Gau* as a translation for "shire," which was rendered quite unsuitable by its connection with Nazism.

MARIA RAFFAELLA BENVENUTO

Further Reading

Carpenter, Humphrey. *J.R.R. Tolkien: A Biography*. London: HarperCollins, 1995.

Shippey, Tom. *The Road to Middle-earth*. Rev. and expanded ed. London: HarperCollins, 2005.

Tolkien, J.R.R. "Guide to the Names in The Lord of the Rings." In *A Tolkien Compass*, edited by Jared Lobdell. La Salle, IL: Open Court, 1975.

See also **German Race Laws; Languages, Early Introduction and Interest; German Folktales:** *Deutsche Mythologie*; **Nomenclature of** *The Lord of the Rings*; **Old High German; Tolkien, Mabel**

GERMANY

Tolkien's paternal ancestors came to England in the eighteenth century from Germany, and the name Tolkien is said to derive from the German nickname (or byname) *tollkühn* (rash-bold) by way of *Tollkiehn*. Although Tolkien felt emotionally closer to his mother's family, the Suffields, he never denied the German part of his ancestry.

There are no records of Tolkien having ever visited Germany itself. The only German-speaking country he traveled to was Switzerland, where he spent a hiking holiday in summer 1911 together with his brother Hilary as part of a party organized by the Brookes-Smiths (Carpenter, *Tolkien*, 57). It is not known which route the party took to reach Switzerland, and they may well have come via Germany.

Tolkien's knowledge of the German language, however, is better attested. His mother Mabel Tolkien, who spoke the language, had taught him in his childhood, and he deepened his knowledge during his grammar school days and in the course of his philological studies—not least since many of the books on philology were written in German by German scholars.

Tolkien's service in the British Army brought him to France in 1916 and thus face to face with the German enemy at the Somme. He witnessed the storming of the Schwaben Redoubt, a massive fortification of German trenches, and "he spoke to a captured officer who had been wounded, offering him a drink of water; the officer corrected his German pronunciation" (Carpenter, 92). As Garth (218) points out, "prior to the Somme, Tolkien had written the Germans into his Qenya lexicon as kalimbardi, associated with kalimbo, 'a savaged, uncivilized man, barbarian—giant, monster, troll'." The battlefields of World War I were, of course, not the best place to get to know and appreciate the German people and thus to revise his image of the Germans. But Tolkien soon realized that he was facing a foe with all the hallmarks of humanity and that the use of poison gas and the killing of captives was no prerogative of the enemy. As a consequence, he would later avoid wholesale condemnation of peoples or nations and point out repeatedly that ignorance, cruelty, tyranny, and inhumanity can be found on all sides. This can be seen in those of his published letters that were written immediately before, during, and after World War II. He does not only stress the fact that "Orc-minded" people are to be found also in England, but furthermore that the German people, though misguided by Hitler, possess great virtues.

Tolkien's political views on Germany make up only one part of the picture. For Tolkien, Germany was also the home of philology, this rigorously scientific yet at the same time deeply romantic academic discipline. Joe Wright, one of his teachers at Oxford, had studied *Philologie* in Germany and passed on his enthusiasm for this most German of disciplines to Tolkien. Furthermore, Germany partook in the common "Northern heritage," which Tolkien admired all his life and which he saw perverted and ruined through the misuse of the Northern mythologies by Adolf Hitler (*Letters*, 255–256). Thus, Tolkien's view of and emotional response toward contemporary Germany, German history, and culture were complex and, as Chism and Bachmann and Honegger argue, influenced his view and representation of matters Germanic in his fictional writings.

THOMAS HONEGGER

Further Reading

Bachmann, Dieter, and Thomas Honegger, "Ein Mythos für das 20. Jahrhundert: Blut, Rasse und Erbgedächtnis bei Tolkien." *Hither Shore* 2 (2006), in press.

Carpenter, Humphrey. *J.R.R. Tolkien: A Biography.*, 1977; rpt. London: HarperCollins, 1995.

Chism, Christine. "Middle-earth, the Middle Ages, and the Aryan Nation," In *Tolkien the Medievalist*, edited by Jane Chance, 63–92. London and New York: Routledge, 2003.

Garth, John. *Tolkien and the Great War*. London: Harper-Collins, 2003.

See also **German Language; Gothic Language; Philology**

GERMANY, RECEPTION OF TOLKIEN

The popular reception of Tolkien in (West) Germany has been secured ever since the German versions of *The Hobbit* (*Der kleine Hobbit*, translated 1957 by Walter Scherf; new translation *Der Hobbit* [1998] by Wolfgang Krege) and *The Lord of the Rings* (*Der Herr der Ringe*, translated 1969–70 by Margaret Carroux; new translation 2000 by Wolfgang Krege) have been published. Most of Tolkien's other writings, with the exception of the bulk of *The History of Middle-earth*, have also been translated into German and are thus available to the general audience. The German radio-play adaptations of *The Hobbit* (1999) and *The Lord of the Rings* (1992) as well as a plethora of games

have, next to the dubbed versions of Peter Jackson's movies, anchored the work of Tolkien deep in the public mindset, and at least one original German creative retelling of the story has been published by a major publishing house (Helmut W. Pesch and Horst von Allwörden, *Die Ringe der Macht* [1998]).

The history of the (scholarly) reception of Tolkien's work in Germany, however, is a different matter and has been dominated by two major factors. First, Tolkien's fictional works (*Hobbit, Lord of the Rings, Silmarillion*) have, until recently, been excluded from the official canon of "readable books" at grammar schools and universities. This has been remedied, and teachers (and students) willing to deal with Tolkien's work find helpful critical guides adjusted to the respective level of expertise (e.g., Frank Weinreich, *J.R.R. Tolkien's The Lord of the Rings/Der Herr der Ringe: Inhalt, Hintergrund, Interpretation* [2002]). Second, if an academic were to write about these books, he or she would do so, most likely, in English and address an international, English-reading community. It is therefore not such a surprise to find one of the few European academic publishers (Walking Tree Publishers, founded 1997) dedicated to offering a platform to English-speaking Tolkien scholarship in the German-speaking part of Switzerland.

The first book-length study on Tolkien in German was published by Dieter Petzold in 1980 (*J.R.R. Tolkien: Fantasy Literature als Wunscherfüllung und Weltdeutung*). Also during the eighties and into the nineties, Helmut W. Pesch published numerous articles on Tolkien, most of them with the EDFC (*Erster Deutscher Fantasy Club* = First German Fantasy Club; www.edfc.de). The EDFC (founded in Passau, Germany, in 1978) was probably the first literary society to put at least one focus on Tolkien.

Five years later, in 1983, the Inklings were founded. The Inklings are a scholarly society dedicated to research into the works of the Inklings and the fantastic in literature in general. The annual conferences and the *Inklings Jahrbuch* (Inklings Yearbook; often with contributions in English) became a rallying point for scholars interested in Tolkien. The Inklings clearly aim at addressing an academic public and have remained, due to this, with a limited impact on the larger public.

Between 1980 and 1991, only a handful of monographs in German were published—of which even fewer had found acceptance with an established German publisher. This has changed, not least since an author does no longer need a publisher to print his book and the "books on demand" technology has spawned several micropublishing houses with one or two books to their credit each.

In spite of the fact that Tolkien's work enjoyed great popularity and that there was no other society channelling the enthusiasm of Tolkien readers, it took another fourteen years until the *Deutsche Tolkien Gesellschaft* (DTG; German Tolkien Society) was founded (1997). With over five hundred members and a widespread network of local chapters all over Germany, it soon became the driving force in the German-speaking countries (the Swiss TS, founded in 1986, and the Austrian TS, founded in 2002, have either never gained large-scale membership or are still in the phase of growth). At about the same time, a new generation of scholars, both freelance and in positions of influence in institutionalised academia, turned their attention to the discussion of Tolkien's work. Thus, the DTG was able to organize the first scholarly Tolkien seminar in Cologne in 2004. The series is continuing with Jena (2005) and Mainz (2006). The proceedings of these conferences are published in the peer-reviewed journal *Hither Shore: Interdisciplinary Journal on Modern Fantasy Literature* (Jahrbuch der Deutschen Tolkien Gesellschaft), an annual publication that is also open to contributions on modern fantasy literature in general. Although the contents of the first two volumes are predominantly in German, English contributions are welcome, and it is the aim of the editors to give *Hither Shore* an international profile.

Tolkien scholarship in German to date has been dependent on and in dialogue with the Anglo-Saxon traditions. Shippey's *Author of the Century* (2002, *Autor des Jahrhunderts*, translated by Wolfgang Krege) has been rendered into German, as has Humphrey Carpenter's biography (*Biographie*) and his selection of Tolkien's letters (*Briefe*; both translated by Wolfgang Krege). The German-speaking reader can also fall back upon a revised and adapted German version of Robert Foster's *The Complete Guide to Middle-earth* (2002, *Das große Mittelerde-Lexikon*, translated and revised by Helmut W. Pesch) and translations of several of David Day's encyclopedic books, next to Karen Fonstad's *The Atlas of Middle-earth* (1985, *Historischer Atlas von Mittelerde*, translated by Hans J. Schütz) and Wayne Hammond and Christina Scull's *J.R.R. Tolkien: Artist and Illustrator* (1996, *J.R.R. Tolkien der Künstler*, translated by Hans J. Schütz).

Substantial original contributions to Tolkien scholarship in German have been rare, yet we may mention three exceptions. The first is Friedhelm Schneidewind's *Das große Tolkien-Lexikon* (2002), an extensive encyclopedia with entries covering the entire range of Tolkien's work. The second is *Edition Stein und Baum*, a new series dedicated to scholarly publications on Tolkien (vol. 1, *Eine Grammatik der Ethik* [2005]). And last we must mention Helmut W. Pesch's contribution to Elvish studies in the form of two books on the Elvish languages (*Elbisch: Grammatik, Schrift und Wörterbuch der Elben-Sprache von J.R.R. Tolkien* [2003]; *Elbisch: Lern- und Übungsbuch der Elben-Sprachen von J.R.R. Tolkien* [2004]). They are, in their scope and expertise, unique and a comparable counterpart in the English-speaking world (*pace* David Salo's *Gateway to Sindarin*) is as yet missing.

THOMAS HONEGGER

Further Reading

Eisenach, Jutta von. "Lewis und Tolkien in der DDR." *Inklings-Jahrbuch* 3 (1985): 169–70.

Pesch, Helmut W. "Tolkien 2001. Eine Bestandsaufnahme." In *Das Vermächtnis des Rings*, edited by Stefan Bauer, 453–78. Bergisch Gladbach: Bastei Lübbe, 2001.

www.tolkiengesellschaft.de

Petzold, Dieter. "Zwölf Jahre Tolkien-Rezeption in Deutschland, 1980–1991." *Inklings-Jahrbuch* 10 (1992): 241–55.

GIBBON, EDWARD: *DECLINE AND FALL OF THE ROMAN EMPIRE*

Edward Gibbon, an eighteenth-century English historian and scholar, has been considered the "first modern historian" for his epic achievement *The Decline and Fall of the Roman Empire*. Gibbon's work influenced Tolkien's understanding of the Goths and cultures of the North, and later proved inspirational when creating the Rohirrim and the Battle of the Pelennor Fields.

This work, originally published as *The History of the Decline and Fall of the Roman Empire*, was published in several volumes: the first in 1776, the second in 1781, and the final volume in 1788. Gibbon's undertaking provides a vivid narrative of more than thirteen centuries of the Roman Empire from 180 CE through events ending in 1590 CE. *Decline* offers answers to one of history's greatest questions: why did the Roman Empire fall? Gibbon's theories, with use of primary sources and documents dating back to the Roman Empire, derive from fourth- to fifth-century Roman and Greek historians. These sources include Jordanes's *Gothic History*, which recorded these events and outlined the decisions leading to the decay of the Roman Empire.

Gibbon credited the Gothic tribes with the fall of Rome. It was the Gothic language, the earliest recorded Germanic language, that entranced Tolkien all of his life. An early name attributed to the Goths was "horse-folk/people" (Shippey, 97). When establishing the culture of Rohan, Tolkien utilized Gothic when shaping the forms and names of the early Rohirric ancestors, prior to the dynasty of Eorl. The later Rohirric language and names were shaped after the Anglo-Saxons, The exploits of King of Rohan in *The Two Towers,* Théoden, achieves great glory; however, he emanates much grief during his reign. Théoden, including his being trampled and subsequent death, resembles Gibbon's picture of the Gothic King Theodorid.

ANTHONY S. BURDGE and JESSICA BURKE

Further Reading

Hammond, Wayne G., and Christian Scull. *The Lord of the Rings: A Readers Companion.* Boston, MA: Houghton Mifflin, 2005.

Shippey, Tom, *The Road to Middle-earth.* Boston, MA: Houghton Mifflin, 1983.

Tolkien, Christopher. *The Battle of the Goths and the Huns, Saga-Book.* London: University College, London, for the Viking Society for Northern Research, 1955–56.

See also **Goths; Rohirrim; Rohan; Théoden**

GILSON, ROBERT QUILTER (1893–1916)

Robert Quilter Gilson was Tolkien's school friend and a T.C.B.S. member. His father, Robert Cary Gilson, was headmaster of King Edward's School, Birmingham; his mother died in 1907; his stepmother, Marianne, nurtured his passion for Italian Renaissance painting and his talent for drawing. An eloquent debater and a keen actor, he produced the 1911 school show of Sheridan's *The Rivals* in which Tolkien, just before leaving for Oxford, played Mrs. Malaprop. Gilson then took over as school librarian and wittily edited the school *Chronicle* with Christopher Wiseman. Gilson was affable, intelligent, and gently humorous; though the least close of Tolkien's three dearest school friends, he was an early member of the T.C.B.S. and its linchpin at King Edward's after Tolkien had left. In 1912, he entered Trinity College, Cambridge, as a classical scholar and achieved first-class honors in the second-year Classical Tripos; but he planned to train as an architect.

Tolkien and Wiseman's purge of the T.C.B.S. after the outbreak of war in 1914 was partly aimed at halting Gilson's drift toward pure aestheticism by removing members they considered a bad influence. After the "Council of London" that December,

Gilson enthused about the group's moral and cultural mission. He hoped to contribute a book of designs to the cause.

The first of the T.C.B.S. to enlist, Gilson joined the Eleventh Battalion of the Suffolk Regiment, training mostly in Cambridge, in Yorkshire, and on Salisbury Plain, near G.B. Smith. Meanwhile Gilson was preoccupied with an attempt to win the hand in marriage of Estelle King, daughter of a U.S. consul. The T.C.B.S. did not discuss such matters; Gilson lost touch with Tolkien until late in 1915, and although he read Tolkien's poetry and was impressed by it, for months he failed to comment on it.

In France, in 1916, the Suffolks were posted to the Flanders front line, then moved south to the Somme as the Allies prepared their grand summer offensive. Wiseman feared for his sanity: Gilson was dutiful but hated war and the military mindset. A final letter to Tolkien on June 22 credits "the oasis of TCBSianism" with sustaining him.

Gilson was killed shortly after taking over command of his battalion in No Man's Land on July 1, 1916, the first day of the Battle of the Somme. He is buried at Bécourt Military Cemetery. His death was a great loss to the T.C.B.S.; Tolkien felt (initially at least) that the group could not continue.

One of Gilson's 1913 sketches of a French church was printed on his memorial card, reproduced in Priestman, *Life and Legend.* His trench-digging drill, devised for his own battalion, was incorporated in W.A. Brockington, *Elements of Military Education.* Two poems in memory of Gilson, "For R.Q.G." and "Let Us Tell Stories of Quiet Eyes," were published in *A Spring Harvest* (1918), the posthumous collection of G.B. Smith's poetry edited by Tolkien and Wiseman. His father named his retirement home Quilters after him.

JOHN GARTH

Further Reading

Carpenter, Humphrey, *Tolkien: A Biography.* Boston, MA: Houghton Mifflin, 1977.

Gorth, John, *Tolkien and the Great War: The Threshold of Middle-earth.* Boston, MA: Houghton Mifflin, 2003.

See also **Smith, Geoffrey Bache; T.C.B.S.; Wiseman, Christopher; World War I**

GIMLI

Gimli son of Gloin is a unique character in the *Lord of the Rings.* Four of the principal characters, the hobbits, are "us," the readers, in the sense that not only is the story told mostly from their perspective, but also in the sense that they are indeed every man. The other characters are "high": of long, important, and distinguished lineage, heroic, and somewhat larger than life. Gimli fits both groupings. He is of distinguished lineage and is certainly heroic in every sense of the word. At the same time, when the narrative is no longer focused on the hobbits, it is Gimli's perspective that we share, and it is Gimli who often voices what would have been our reaction to an event in the story.

Along with Boromir and Legolas, Gimli is introduced at the Council of Elrond at Rivendell. The last mention in the narrative is in Chapter 6 of Book VI, "Many Partings," where the fellowship is at long last sundered. It is Gimli who is given the last words and the last farewell at this moment.

Gimli exemplifies the high order of person in Tolkien's world. He is descended from Gloin, one of the Dwarves of *The Hobbit*, himself descended from Durin I, father of one of the houses of the Dwarves and the one mentioned the most often by Tolkien. Like Aragorn and Legolas, Gimli has a noble and long heritage to live up to. Unlike the others mentioned however, Gimli is not an heir to the kingdom or to the head of his house.

Gimli further exemplifies the heroic ideals in his complete loyalty to both lord and companion. His loyalty to his own people and lord is difficult to find in *The Lord of the Rings* since Dain is not a character in the story. At the previously mentioned parting of the fellowship, however, Aragorn asks Gimli and Legolas to return to his kingdom someday, and Gimli replies that he would so return if his lord allows him to.

His loyalty to Aragorn is also a tie that is not easily broken. He unquestionably follows Aragorn after Gandalf's fall. He and Legolas await Aragorn's decision after the sundering of the Fellowship at the end of Book I and continue to follow him though Gimli's feet might fall off in pursuit of the captured hobbits through Book III. His loyalty there is never put to the test. Until Aragorn takes the Paths of the Dead in Book V, Gimli follows this lord without question. Gimli says of himself that the only thing that held him on that road was the very will of Aragorn: "not for any friendship would I have taken the Paths of the Dead" (*RK*, V, ix, 150) (Although Aragorn is only loosely taken as Gimli's "leader," their relationship is certainly to be set against the background of the Germanic comitatus: for example, in *Beowulf* Hrothgar's "shoulder-companion" Æschere, obviously a close friend is also one of Hrothgar's thegns. Other examples from Old English and Norse literature could be used to illustrate this point. Chiefly,

though, one could turn to the Old English poem *The Wanderer*, a poem imitated and adapted by Tolkien in *The Two Towers*. Against this background, then, the conversation of Gimli and Legolas, who follow Aragorn through the Paths of the Dead in part by his will, and in part for love and friendship, is illuminated by these examples. Gimli and Legolas during this time consider Aragorn their lord and friend (as these Old English examples illustrate).

Gimli's loyalty to his comitatus is best illustrated by his attitude toward the hobbits. At the beginning of the Fellowship's journey, Elrond and Gimli exchange a "battle" of proverbs. Elrond has just enjoined the Company that each can only go as far as he wills, as companions on the way to assist the Ring-bearer, but none is charged with remaining with Frodo the whole way to Mount Doom. Gimli is the only one to reply: "Faithless is he that says farewell when the road darkens." Elrond replies, and Gimli again responds: "Yet sworn word may strengthen quaking heart" (*FR*, II, iii, 294). Though Elrond has the last word, this brief exchange illustrates profoundly Gimli's character. It is just this sort of faithfulness to companions that Beowulf's men lack in the eponymous poem and whom Wiglaf roundly condemns for that lack of faith.

One of the more humorous moments in the *The Lord of the Rings* comes in the *The Two Towers* when the sundered companions are reunited at the destroyed gates of Isengard. In the midst of the formalities, Gimli is beside himself and cannot contain himself. He is correct in pointing out, however, that, with Legolas and Aragorn, he has followed the two hobbits Merry and Pippin across the breadth of Rohan, even when all hope was lost. Much later in the work, it is again Gimli who saves Pippin, pulling him by the foot out from under a troll during the final battle. Here, too, friendship and loyalty are Gimli's characteristics, a steadfast Dwarf.

Gimli's heroic prowess in battle needs little comment. Like Aragorn, Eomer, and Legolas, the prowess of the heroes in battle is comparable to the prowess of other such heroes in the epic literature on which Tolkien drew, such as the *Aeneid*, the *Iliad*, the *Odyssey*, *Gilgamesh*, *Beowulf*, and *Song of Roland*.

But Gimli is not simply another example of an epic hero in *The Lord of the Rings*. When the hobbits from whose viewpoint the story is told are absent, it is Gimli's perspective the reader is given. This is largely true of the chapters detailing the pursuit of the Urukhai, and at least at the beginning of the tale of the Paths of the Dead. In these chapters, it is Gimli's fear, his weariness, that dominate the narrative. It is Gimli who professes joy at finding Merry and Pippin at

Isengard, and it is Gimli who is given the final farewell to the others. It seems that when the hobbits are not present, it is Gimli with whom the reader is to bond.

Gimli is often noted for his relationship with Legolas the Elf. During the Second Age of Middle-earth, Dwarves and Elves lived in proximity to one another. The Dwarvish kingdom at Moria had the Elves of Eregion on one side and the Elves of Lothlorien on the other. With the awakening of the Balrog and later the war of the Dwarves and Orcs, relations between the two races soured. As with much in *The Lord of the Rings*, the great friendship between Gimli and Legolas heals age-old sundering of peoples (other examples being Aragorn and Arwen). The friendship, beyond merely being in the same company together, does not seem to develop until Book III when the three hunters pursue the Uruk–Hai and grows from there through the Orc-killing competition at Helm's Deep to the promise to visit wonders together. Eventually, in the Appendices, the reader is informed that Legolas and Gimli depart Middle-earth together, and Tolkien in his *Letters* notes that Gimli was received in Valinor. And so Tolkien healed the brokenness of the races.

Related to this theme is the remarkable relationship of Gimli and Galadriel. The friction between the Elves and Dwarves is illustrated clearly when the Fellowship enters Lothlorien and in order to proceed Gimli alone is singled out to be blindfolded through the land. The reader is not informed as to why this must occur. Gimli naturally protests and is ready to back up his words with his axe. Later, before Galadriel, Gimli poetically praises the lady of Lórien, and on the Fellowship's departure from the land the only gift that Gimli requires are locks of Galadriel's golden hair. Such asexual love is reminiscent of medieval Romance. A small step from Romance is the late medieval development of the love between man and woman in Romance as a spark of the love between the soul and God. In many ways, Gimli's adoration of Galadriel seems inspired and related to this latter expression, and some commentators have noted a parallel between Galadriel and Mary, the mother of Christ in late medieval Catholic devotion. These overtones are certainly present, but the adoration of Galadriel serves to heal as much as anything else in the context of the story.

Gimli further is one of the most passionate of characters. On the one hand, he is ready to defend himself and his beliefs with recourse to his axe frequently, such as the previously mentioned entrance to Lothlórien or again later in the exchange between Gimli and Eomer on the plains of Rohan over "the Lady of the Wood." Gimli, however, is capable not just of anger and speaking with arms. He is also a poet. His words to Galadriel have already been mentioned. After the Battle of Helms Deep, Gimli rhapsodizes about the caves he has found in language so moving that even Legolas says that he would like to see these caves. And it is in the dark of Moria that Gimli begins to chant a tale reminiscent in tone of the Dwarves' song in first chapters of *The Hobbit*, but this chant moves Sam, fascinated by things Elvish, to express a desire to learn Gimli's song.

It is Gimli who, in spite of danger and loss, expresses the beauty of the Mirrormere and takes Frodo to gaze on it. It is Gimli who marvels at the construction of Minas Tirith. It is Gimli who expresses his joy and frustration at finding Merry and Pippin. Throughout, Gimli the warrior is also a passionate Dwarf and poet: fierce in battle, fierce in loyalty to lord and friend, fierce in appreciation of beauty.

L.J. SWAIN

See also **Dwarves**

GLORFINDEL

Late in life, while preparing "The Silmarillion" for publication, Tolkien addressed the issue of whether Glorfindel, Elf-lord of Rivendell in *The Lord of the Rings*, was to be the same character as Glorfindel, chief of the House of the Golden Flower of Gondolin from his earlier stories. He admitted that the issue arose from *The Lord of the Ring*'s "somewhat random use of names found in the older legends." When Tolkien considered the "repetition of so striking a name" to be unlikely within his created world, he concluded that one identity might "actually explain what is said of him [in *LotR*] and improve the story" (*Peoples*, 379–80).

Glorfindel ("golden-haired"), a lieutenant of King Turgon, first appeared in 1917's "Fall of Gondolin," in which he and his people fought valiantly, holding the rear as the survivors, including young Eärendel, retreated from the city. Encountering a Balrog in the mountains, Glorfindel attacked the enemy, plunging them both to their deaths. His body was recovered by the Lord of Eagles, and a stone cairn was erected where afterward grew yellow flowers (*Lost Tales II*, 194). This story, set in Middle-earth's First Age, was retold in multiple narratives throughout Tolkien's life, and a condensed version is given in *The Silmarillion*.

A 1938 *Lord of the Rings* outline, stating that "Glorfindel tells of his ancestry in Gondolin," reveals that Tolkien initially considered reusing the earlier character (*Shadow*, 214). Gandalf's description of the mighty "Elf-lord of a house of princes," whose shining white figure thwarted the Nazgûl, definitely hints at Glorfindel's deeper past and greater powers (*FR*, II, i, 235). He also displays unusual wisdom at the Council of Elrond: hesitating to send the Ring to Bombadil, first suggesting the Ring's destruction, and voicing a willingness to sacrifice the Three Rings to accomplish this end. Further, he is recorded as the Elf-lord who defeated Angmar earlier in the Third Age (*RK*, Appendix A, 331–332). However, the unequivocal death of Glorfindel of Gondolin may possibly have prevented Tolkien from making an explicit connection between the two in the published *Lord of the Rings*.

Tolkien had actually considered Elven reincarnation by the time of *The Lord of the Ring*'s publication (*Letters*, 187) and developed it extensively afterward (*Morgoth*, 207–52): essentially, slain Elf spirits would return to the Halls of Mandos in Valinor to await judgment, and those chosen could readopt bodily form. Flieger suggests that Tolkien's Catholicism initially made this idea theologically problematic, until he realized he could intellectually accept the concept (Flieger, 134–35, 168). Though he admitted reincarnation to be "bad *theology*" and difficult biology, Tolkien described it as "a biological dictum in my imaginary world . . . its purpose largely literary" (*Letters*, 189). Whether Glorfindel's situation influenced this process is unknown, but Tolkien certainly employed it in his late writings devoted to unifying the Elf's identity.

The major obstacle, Tolkien wrote, was Glorfindel's status as a Noldor Exile. He resolved the issue by explaining that Glorfindel, "of high and noble spirit," left Valinor reluctantly because of kinship and allegiance to Turgon, and was blameless in the Kinslaying. Moreover, his sacrifice was deemed "of vital importance to the designs of the Valar." Thus, Glorfindel, purged of any guilt, was granted an exception to the Exiles' ban. He was then restored and allowed to dwell in Valinor, almost an equal of the Maiar, for "his spiritual power had been greatly enhanced." Tolkien speculates that there he became a companion of Olórin/Gandalf (*Peoples*, 380–81).

One mystery left unsolved, however, concerns Glorfindel's return to Middle-earth. Tolkien suggests that he may have come back with Gandalf in the Third Age but stated that it was more probable that Glorfindel returned during the Second Age, since breaching the divide between Valinor and the Circles of the World would make him "of greater power and importance than seems fitting." He therefore proposes SA 1600, when war with Sauron became inevitable and messages were sent to Valinor, as the most likely date (*Peoples*, 377–82).

Since all of this was as yet unpublished when *The Silmarillion* was posthumously released, a real mystery suddenly took hold among readers concerning Glorfindel's death and subsequent "reappearance" in *The Lord of the Rings*, forcing various Tolkien compendiums into speculation (Foster, 212; Tyler, 249). Only with the *History of Middle-earth*'s complete publication is Tolkien's idea of an improved story for Glorfindel possibly realized.

Don N. Anger

Further Reading

Flieger, Verlyn. *A Question of Time: J.R.R. Tolkien's Road to Faërie*. Kent, OH: Kent State University Press, 1997.

Foster, Robert. *The Complete Guide to Middle-earth: From the Hobbit to The Silmarillion*. New York: Ballantine Books, 1978.

Hood, Gwenyth. "The Earthly Paradise in Tolkien's The Lord of the Rings." In *Proceedings of the J.R.R. Tolkien Centenary Conference 1992*, edited by Patricia Reynolds and Glen H. GoodKnight. *Mythlore* 21, no. 2 & Mallorn 30 (1996): 142.

Kocher, Paul H. *Master of Middle-earth*. New York: Ballantine, 1977.

Lewis, Alex. "Historical Bias in the Making of The Silmarillion." *Proceedings of the J.R.R. Tolkien Centenary Conference 1992*, edited by Patricia Reynolds and Glen H. GoodKnight. *Mythlore* 21, no. 2 & Mallorn 30 (1996): 158–59.

Noad, Charles E. "On the Construction of 'The Silmarillion'." In *Tolkien's Legendarium: Essays on The History of Middle-earth*, edited by Verlyn Flieger and Carl F. Hostetter, 62. Westport, CT: Greenwood Press, 2000.

Tyler, J.E.A. *The New Tolkien Companion*. London: Picador, 1979.

See also **Elves; Finwë and Míriel; Gandalf; Maiar; Reincarnation; Rivendell;** *Peoples of Middle-earth, The*; **Sacrifice; Wizards**

GOLDBERRY

The character of Goldberry combines elements of the natural and domestic. She is a woodland goddess, loving wife, and devoted daughter. Her husband, Tom Bombadil, makes reference to her heritage in his first song:

Hey! Come merry dol! Derry dol! My darling!
Light goes the weather-wind and the feathered starling.
Down along under Hill, shining in the sunlight,
Waiting on the doorstep for the cold starlight,
There my pretty lady is, River-woman's daughter,
Slender as the willow-wand, clearer than the water.

(*FR*, I, vi, 130)

Most of what the reader learns about Goldberry is through Tom's songs, but there are a few key moments when we see her appearing to the hobbits as goddess, nurturer, and manager of domestic responsibilities. The hobbits first see her sitting, wearing shimmering clothes as they enter the house with Tom:

> In a chair, at the far side of the room facing the outer door, sat a woman. Her long yellow hair rippled down her shoulders; her gown was green, green as young reeds, shot with silver like beads of dew; and her belt was of gold, shaped like a chain of flag-lilies set with the pale-blue eyes of forget-me-nots. About her feet in wide vessels of green and brown earthenware, white water-lilies were floating, so that she seemed to be enthroned in the midst of a pool. (*FR*, I, vii, 134)

In this first appearance of Goldberry, Tolkien calls to mind a Botticelli-like image of a woman embodied and surrounded by the natural characteristics of her environment. The descriptions of her clothing refer to a peaceful existence within that environment. Her gown is as "green as young reeds"; her gold belt is "shaped like a chain of flag-lilies,' and "earthenware" vessels hold flowers by her feet. These items that, at the time *The Lord of the Rings* was written, were typically man-made or machine-made, using highly industrial processes, are here connected with nature in the passage without the indication that any of Goldberry's fellow creatures were made to sacrifice for her to have them. We get another glimpse into Goldberry's symbiotic relationship with the natural world on the third day the hobbits spent in her home when it began to rain:

> Frodo stood near the open door and watched the white chalky pathy turn into a little river of milk and go bubbling away down into the valley. Tom Bombadil came trotting round the corner of the house waving his arms as if he was warding off the rain—and indeed when he sprang over the threshold he seemed quite dry, except for his boots. These he took off and put in the chimney-corner. Then he sat in the largest chair and called the hobbits to gather round him.
> "This is Goldberry's washing day," he said, "and her autumn-cleaning. Too wet for hobbit folk." (*FR*, II, vii, 140)

This passage makes reference to both Goldberry's domestic nesting and keeping of her home, as well as to her overall position as a goddess-like figure in the natural world of Middle-earth. Both worlds are connected and intertwined: her home and family and the universe for which she is responsible. She achieves a work-life balance that would be envied by women of the Western world in many time periods.

What is quite possibly the most significant point when describing Goldberry as a feminine figure in *The Lord of the Rings* is the cooperative and reciprocal relationship that she shares with her husband Tom Bombadil. They share domestic responsibility in a way that is not seen between men and women anywhere else in Tolkien's work. In the Shire we are introduced to a male-domestic, almost completely free of women. The hobbit men cook, clean, arrange parties, purchase and wrap gifts, write and send correspondence, and, in the case of Bilbo Baggins, adopt and nurture young hobbits. Among the men in *The Lord of the Rings*, we see much clearer separation between the behaviors of men and women, most especially in the character of Éowyn, who must dress as a man in order to participate in the efforts of the soldiers and eventually appears as a cup-bearer, serving the soldiers, in what is an allusion to Queen Waltheow in the work *Beowulf*.

Goldberry and Tom's domestic life is shared equally, mutually appreciated, and enjoyable. The following passage, which describes their setting of the table, enables the reader to make a metaphorical assumption about their entire life together:

> Quickly he returned bearing a large and laden tray. Then Tom and Goldberry set the table; and the hobbits sat half in wonder and half in laughter: so fair was the grace of Goldberry and so merry and odd the caperings of Tom. Yet, in some fashion they seemed to weave a single dance, neither hindering the other, in and out of the room, and round about the table; and with great speed food and vessels and lights were set in order. The boards blazed with candles, white and yellow. Tom bowed to his guests. "Supper is ready," said Goldberry. (*FR*, I, vii, 143)

Goldberry and Tom bear a resemblance to Aule of the Valar and his wife, Yavanna, who are introduced in *The Silmarillion*. Aule is described as having "lordship over all the substances which Arda has made," and overseeing the "gems in the earth and the gold that is fair in the hand," and also the "walls of the mountains and the basins of the sea. This is very similar to Tom being named the master of all the creatures in the Old Forrest and being described as the oldest being in Middle-earth (*S*, 20). Yavanna's description makes her very similar to Goldberry, in that they are both in appearance and behavior so closely related to nature. Yavanna appears as a woman "robed in green" as Goldberry is, but also takes the form of "a tree under heaven, crowned with the Sun." She is called "Queen of the Earth" by the Eldar (*S*, 21). It has been argued that Tom and Goldberry are the very same as Aule and Yavanna, though their names and some characteristics have been morphed and changed as the mythology evolved.

Goldberry, with the smooth and kind way she relates to her odd husband Tom Bombadil and through her elegance, accomplishment, and connection to the natural world, brings much-needed peace to Tolkien's *Lord of the Rings*. She seeks nothing, longs for nothing, yet appreciates and nurtures everything and everyone around her. She is the only female character in *The Lord of the Rings* without a personal agenda. She is not looking to earn battle glory like Eowyn; to satiate her hunger, as Shelob is; to take residence in Bag-End, as Lobelia Sackville-Baggins; to defy her father for the sake of love, like Arwen; and she is in no danger of being influenced by the Ring as Galadriel fears she might be. Goldberry provides a feminine figure who is pure, content, significant to the world around her, and wise.

KATHERINE HESSER

See also **Tom Bombadil**

GOLLUM

This character, one of Tolkien's most interesting and memorable figures, first appeared in chapter 5 of *The Hobbit* ("Riddles in the Dark") and returned to play a crucial role in *The Lord of the Rings*. In *The Hobbit,* Gollum is an uncategorized creature (referred to first simply as "old Gollum") who derives some of his uncanny effect exactly from his unidentified origin. In the writing of *The Lord of the Rings,* however, Tolkien found that as the Ring is used as the main link between *The Hobbit* and its sequel, Gollum had to play some role as well, and a story had to be constructed to explain how he came to possess the Ring. In Book I, chapter 2, "The Shadow of the Past," the new story of Gollum is first told by Gandalf; from this the reader learns that he originally had been a hobbit and lived with his community near the Gladden Fields before the hobbit migrations to the Shire. The possession of the Ring separated him from the community and drove him underground into the caves of the Misty Mountains, where he is found by Bilbo centuries later. Gandalf recounts how Gollum, after he lost the Ring to Bilbo, in search of it and drawn by the power that made it, finally found a way to Mordor, received a mission to find the Ring from Sauron, was eventually captured by Aragorn, and then escaped the captivity of the Elves of Mirkwood. Following the Fellowship of the Ring from Moria, Gollum is confronted and "tamed" by Frodo and Sam in the Emyn Muil, from which point he serves as their guide, first through the Dead Marshes to the Morannon and then through Ithilien up to Cirith Ungol. Here, Sam catches him nearly touching the sleeping Frodo, a gesture motivated by Gollum's affection for his master; Sam misunderstands this and rebukes him. Tolkien reflected in letters that at this point Gollum came very close to repentance, but Sam's action upset the balance, and consequently Gollum carries on with his evil plan and betrays the

Ring-bearer to Shelob (*Letters*, 110). Through Frodo and Sam's journey through Mordor to Mount Doom, Gollum is following them, and finally on the slopes of the volcano confronts them again. Sam is left to deal with him, but seeing the prostrate form, lets him go; Gollum eventually comes to the Sammath Naur, disposes of Sam, and fights Frodo, who has just claimed the Ring and refused to destroy it. Biting off Frodo's finger with the Ring, he accidentally falls to the fire, completing the mission.

Gollum's figure naturally went through considerable transformation from *The Hobbit* to *The Lord of the Rings*, and even between editions of *The Hobbit*. This resulted from the need for different motivations: when *The Hobbit* was written, Tolkien did not envisage the later developments of the history of the Third Age or the importance of the Ring, and therefore in the 1951 edition of *The Hobbit*, he changed a significant part of chapter 5 to bring Gollum in line with the developments. In the original 1937 version, Gollum offers to give Bilbo "a present" if he wins the riddle game; the intended present was the Ring. Realizing how important the Ring was for Gollum, Tolkien could not let this stand, and Gollum's wager is changed to showing the way out. This change is taken up into the fiction itself, reflected on in *The Lord of the Rings* prologue: the 1937 version was Bilbo's original story he told the Dwarves and put into his book, while the 1951 version was the true story. The way Tolkien takes up this change into the story is remarkable and entirely conscious (see *Letters,* 142) and contributes to the emphasis on different versions of texts that is characteristic of his writings.

The character itself was marked out from the beginning by his peculiar use of language (judging from the drafts for the part of *The Lord of the Rings* where he appears, this effect took a long time to achieve), especially his use of "my precious" as a formula to address both himself and others along with the Ring, and his talking nearly always in the third person, avoiding the use of "I." This changes when Frodo takes him into his service and addresses him as Sméagol (his original hobbit name), from which point Gollum often calls himself by this name and uses "I" again, marking a return to the personality underlying the one distorted by the Ring and justifying Gandalf's and Frodo's claim that there is still a chance for his rehabilitation. The peculiarities of his speech and his most important concerns (eating, hiding from uncomfortable circumstances, etc.) suggest that his thinking is most focused on the body and its desires; indeed, the Ring is figured as the object of physical desire for him that has to be satisfied. The idea of a creature degenerated and corrupted by time and a complete lack of morality, fixated on the body, and with a characteristic speech patterns has suggested the figure of Gagool in H. Rider Haggard's *King Solomon's Mines* as a possible source for Gollum; in Tolkien's own writings, a figure somewhat similar (small, slimy creature with shining eyes, hiding in dark caves, and eating fish) is found in an early poem entitled "The Glip," written around 1928 as part of the series "Tales and Songs of Bimble Bay" (*H*, V, 119, n. 6); it might be an interesting coincidence that "golden rings" also appear in this poem (line 20).

Gollum is most frequently interpreted in terms of his degeneration, corruption, generally as a contrast for hobbits (especially Bilbo and Frodo), often called their alter ego or "shadow" in psychologizing readings. A warning about the power of the Ring to corrupt, his function in the narrative is also related to other themes not strictly connected to the hobbits: the concepts of heroism, definitions of moral goodness or evil, the nature and operations of power, and the reflection of such operations in characters' subjects, their uses of language. The importance that bodily, physical, material drives and desires have in the character, and their relation to the Ring, have led to Tom Shippey's now classic reading of Gollum as an "addict," in terms of physical (even pathological) addiction. The role of Gollum in the texture of themes in *The Lord of the Rings* is indeed central, as his centrality for the narrative shows, and this has led to approaches that in addition to seeing him as a contrast to the "good" hobbits Frodo and Sam (their "shadows" or "other selves" they have to learn about and understand in order to battle successfully), define him as the "hero of *The Lord of the Rings*" (Arthur, 19). Gollum's role in the final achievement of Frodo's quest is often the object of speculative interpretation: there have been readings that seek to explain or find motivations for his falling into the fire, but these disregard that Gollum's fall is clearly described to be accidental and that Frodo's use of the Ring to "command" Gollum or even Gollum's own (unconscious) desire to destroy the Ring together with himself would severely impair the eucatastrophic or providential nature of this simple accident.

The character of Gollum is in clear connection with the One Ring that he seeks to regain. The peculiarities of this figure were originally (in the first edition of *The Hobbit*) not attributed to his relationship to the Ring but grew into a very elaborate and subtle examination of that relation in *The Lord of the Rings*. Gollum, in fact, is alive solely because he is fueled by the desire to get back the Ring, and the Ring's influence, ironically, works exactly to deprive him of everything that would make a long life worth living. First, he is driven to murder by the desire of the Ring, then cast out from his community and forced to live in the caves of the Misty Mountains; the mere possession of the Ring, which he uses simply for its power to make invisible, fills his mind totally. In the course of this, his speech assumes the peculiar forms that make Gollum into a most memorable character, and the simple bodily sounds, lacking grammatical distinctions and often proper articulation, mirror his mainly bodily concerns and physical drives, becoming in the end not meaningful linguistic utterances but simple actions (Gollum even gets his new name after one of these utterances, the gulping sound). This process of degeneration, the "loss" of Sméagol's identity, and his turning into the obsessed creature who hunts the Ring through Middle-earth is part of how the Ring asserts the power behind it and, instead of giving effectual power to its possessor, in fact produces a subject for the Lord of the Ring, Sauron. It is the effect and operation of Sauron's power through the Ring that explains Gollum's character and its gradual emptying, as it is the effect of Frodo's suddenly appearing new power (derived partly from the fact that he possesses the Ring, partly from the situation, and partly from his own strength to see the situation) over him that temporarily reverses the process to bring back Sméagol, Gollum's old self.

Gollum's loss of self and identity can be linked up with a concept Tolkien systematically explores in *The Lord of the Rings*: the variety of positions in which subjects can be situated and produce meaning. These subject positions are in most cases linked to communities and traditions as well as to power, but the case of Gollum helps fix one end of Tolkien's presented spectrum of such positions, a (nearly) entirely erased subject who does not produce meaning but reproduces someone else's meanings. Significantly, the most terrible effect of Sauron's power is figured in the subject not being able to function properly in communal contexts of meaning production, an isolation that deprives it of interpretive choices and its own meaning, a powerful comment on the concept of ideology and discourses of power. Tolkien's (and Frodo's) concern about "reconstructing" Gollum illustrates the importance that he attributes to cultural/communal frameworks and the subject's situatedness in these to draw on discourses of tradition in order to become meaningful. Gollum's reentering the normal arena of signification marks his return from empty subjection (in the sense of "a subject of Sauron") to meaningful subjectivity through the actions Frodo's mastery offers him, and certainly his meaning in the story is defined not by reference to his relationship to Sauron, but to Frodo.

Gollum's relationship to the Ring is manifested in his language and actions, but the effects of the Ring's dominance over him are also always figured in physical terms. The degeneracy, the unrecognizability of Gollum's body is often referred to, and the shift between his two selves while in Frodo's service is usually marked by the mention of a different "light" in his eyes (as well as a change in his speech). In this, Gollum is the illustration of the brutally physical nature of Sauron's (and the Ring's) dominating operation (which itself is metaphorized in images of visibility, as Sauron himself is symbolized by the great Eye), and this develops concepts about the nature of power that Tolkien apparently intends to keep in the center.

Gollum's figure is perhaps one of the most complex ones in *The Lord of the Rings*, and his relationships to other characters, most notably to Frodo and Sam, serve to contextualize the problem of his doubleness and comment on the role of different cultural frameworks and technologies of power in constructing subjects and identities. The motivations discernible behind his actions point him out effectively as a central point in Tolkien's examination of morality and responsibility and the idea of service and betrayal, and supply a character whose story can nearly become tragic for the readers.

GERGELY NAGY

Further Reading

Arthur, Elizabeth. "Above All Shadows Rides the Sun: Gollum as Hero." *Mythlore* 18, no. 1 (1991): 19–27.

Chance, Jane. *"The Lord of the Rings": The Mythology of Power*. Rev. ed. Lexington, KY: University Press of Kentucky, 2001.

Christensen, Bonniejean. "Gollum's Character Transformation in *The Hobbit*." In *A Tolkien Compass*, edited by Jared Lobdell. La Salle, IL, 9–28: Open Court, 1975.

Nagy, Gergely. "The 'Lost' Subject of Middle-earth: Elements and Motifs of the Constitution of the Subject in the Figure of Gollum in *The Lord of the Rings*." *Tolkien Studies* 3 (2006): 57–79.

Rogers, William N. III, and Michael R. Underwood. "Gagool and Gollum: Examplars of Degeneration in *King Solomon's Mines* and *The Hobbit*." In *J.R.R. Tolkien and His Literary Resonances: Views of Middle-earth*, edited by George Clark and Daniel Timmons, 121–31. Westport, CT, and London: Greenwood Press, 2000.

Shippey, Tom. *The Road to Middle-earth*. 3rd ed. Boston, MA: Houghton Mifflin, 2004.

See also **Eucatastrophe; *Hobbit, The*; One Ring, The; Semiotics and Subject Theory; Textuality**

GONDOR

Gondor, the longest-lived (3,240 years by the time of the War of the Ring) of the two Númenórean kingdoms in exile, was established between the mountain range of the Ered Nimrais and the mouths of the River Anduin at the end of the Second Age by Elendil the Faithful and his two sons Isildur and Anárion. Gondor's varied geography, featuring vast and fertile farmlands, a long coastline rich in fish, and a number of navigable rivers, including the Great River Anduin with its several harbors, assured its long viability as a prosperous and dominant nation. Gondor's proximity to Mordor on its eastern border, on the other hand, necessitated constant military vigilance and caused its people many sore trials. These were only partly relieved by such alliances as that with Rohan, whose kings maintained a fealty oath to aid Gondor against Mordor from the last third of the Third Age henceforward.

The name Gondor ("Stone-land"; in earlier versions of Tolkien's narrative Ond or Ondor, but with the same meaning) presumably refers to the Númenóreans' unique predilections and skills for building large structures in stone, including the fortified towers of Minas Anor and Minas Ithil (later renamed Minas Tirith and Minas Morgul, respectively); the tower of Orthanc, to guard the Gap of Calenardhon; the fortifications at Helm's Deep; and the two monumental statues of the Argonath, carved in the likenesses of Isildur and Anárion. The Northerners of Wilderland and the Rohirrim, who built chiefly with wood, stood in awe of the monuments of Gondor, which they called "Stoningland," and its chief fortress "Steinborg" or "Stanburg" (Minas Anor/Tirith); similarly, the tribal "Woses" of Drúadan Forest called the Gondorians "Stonehouse-folk."

The onomastics and heraldry of Gondor were stamped early with the marks of Elendil's family, particularly the themes of sun (Anárion), moon (Isildur), and stars (Elendil) embodied in the names of its founders. The fief of Anórien and its fortress of Minas Anor echoed "Anárion"; Ithilien and Minas Ithil, "Isildur"; and the citadel of Osgiliath (Citadel of the Stars), straddling the River Anduin, likewise built within Elendil's lifetime, contain a hidden reference to the founding father by means of an embedded synonym (gil = elen).

The White Tree as a device of Gondor, as well as of the royal lines formed by Elendil's and Isildur's descendants, derives from Isildur's having planted a fruit of Nimloth, the White Tree of Númenor, in the courtyard of Minas Anor. Other treasures brought by Elendil's family to the new land included seven *palantíri*, as the Rhyme of Lore quoted by Gandalf to Peregrin Took enumerates:

Tall ships and tall kings
Three times three
What brought they from the foundered land

Over the flowing sea?
Seven stars and seven stones
And one white tree.
(*TT*, II, xi, 202)

Elendil's reign—in Gondor, as well as in the North-kingdom of Arnor, jointly with his two sons—lasted 121 years, until his death at the siege of Barad-dûr in the War of the Last Alliance of Elves and Men. Anárion also died there, leaving the kingship of Gondor to his son Meneldil. Isildur and his three eldest sons were slain by Orcs two years later at the Battle of the Gladden Fields. Isildur's youngest son, Valandil—left behind in Rivendell—inherited the North-kingdom, establishing a line of descent of kings (and later chieftains) that continued unbroken for some three thousand years, culminating in Aragorn Elessar, who returned to Minas Tirith at long last to reclaim the kingship of both Númenórean exile kingdoms.

Anárion's dynasty continued uninterrupted in Gondor for two thousand years until the War of the Kin-strife, precipitated by King Valacar's marrying of a Northern barbarian (Vidumavi), with the result that the heir to the throne (Eldacar, also called by the Northern name of Vinitharya) was not a pure-blooded Númenórean. (It can be argued that Gondor's intrinsic racial elitism and xenophobia, as evidenced by this episode, are meant to be seen as a major factor in its decline.) This half-blood king, Eldacar, was dethroned by his cousin Castamir, spending afterward ten years in exile in the north gathering followers, and eventually returning to the throne. After this, Eldacar's direct line continued uninterrupted for two hundred years, at which point the Great Plague wiped out the ruling king, Telemnar, and most of his house; the succession then went to a nephew. Another interruption in the line of kings occurred three hundred years after the Plague, when king Ondoher and his three sons were slain by invading Wain-riders from the East. Ondoher was succeeded by only two more kings: Eärnil, a cousin; and Eärnil's son Eärnur, who foolishly rode to Minas Morgul (recently taken and renamed by the Enemy) to answer a challenge to single combat with the Witch-king.

Gondor was from Eärnur's day ruled by the Stewards, holders of an office that had been established early in Gondor's history by king Rómendacil I and had been made hereditary (in the House of Húrin) by king Minardil (the grandson of Eldacar, mentioned above). The descendants of Húrin after Eärnur's departure then became Ruling Stewards, holding Gondor "against the king's return," which they continued to do for almost a thousand years. When Aragorn Elessar became king, he did not dissolve the Steward's office, but confirmed Faramir son of Denethor, Húrin's latest descendant, as Steward—although no longer a ruling steward.

Readers of *The Lord of the Rings* have long been divided on the issue of Gondor's prototypes (if any) in our primary world. Some see the Gondorians as Normans. Like the historical Normans, they came from across the sea to establish a new kingdom along a fertile coast. Like Sir Walter Scott's narrated Normans, they are a darker people to whom blonder, and more primitive, peoples owe fealty. Additional support for the "Norman" theory can be found in one of the few close looks at Gondorian physical culture that Tolkien grants us, namely, Prince Imrahil's "burnished vambrace" (with which he tests Éowyn's breathing), which seems to reflect late-medieval primary-world European armor. However, Tolkien himself directed readers looking for real-world parallels to Byzantium and Egypt (*Letters*), and, indeed, parallels between imperial Gondor and these two empires can be found as well.

Perhaps the most striking similarities, however, can be found with ancient Rome. Gondor's physical location in Middle-earth, just north of the equivalent of the Mediterranean, as well as the location of its capital "at about the latitude of Florence," as Tolkien suggested (*Letters,* 376), might be taken as strong clues; but even clearer parallels can be found between Gondorian and Roman history. For instance, Æneas (*pius Æneas,* as Vergil calls him) and Elendil "the Faithful" both escape the wreck of their homelands (Troy, Númenor) to become founding rulers overseas. Romulus and Remus are, like Isildur and Anárion, dynasty-founding brothers; rivalry between the two houses breaks out early in the Roman case, later in the Númenórean one. Perhaps most obviously, both Rome and Gondor experience decadence and decline. But Gondor, in contrast to Rome, is saved from utter downfall by subcreatorial grace at the penultimate moment, in a eucatastrophical move when, against all reasonable odds, the king does in fact return.

SANDRA BALLIF STRAUBHAAR

Further Reading

Ford, Judy Ann. "The White City: The Lord of the Rings as an Early Medieval Myth of the Restoration of the Roman Empire." *Tolkien Studies* 2 (2005): 53–73.

Straubhaar, Sandra Ballif. "Myth, Late Roman History and Multiculturalism in Tolkien's Middle-earth." In *Tolkien and the Invention of Myth: A Reader,* edited by Jane Chance, 101–18. Lexington, KY: University Press of Kentucky, 2004.

See also **Egyptians; Goths; Huns; Jordanes:** *History of the Goths;* **Norman Conquest; Roman History**

GOOD AND EVIL

Many of Tolkien's writings describe conflicts between good and evil. That they do so with such conviction is one source of their popularity. What they do not describe, however, as his defenders have often pointed out, is conflicts between entirely and unchangeably good and evil sides.

In *The Lord of the Rings*, for example, among the "good" characters Frodo comes close to succumbing to the corrupting power of the Ring, and Boromir actually does so, while Gandalf and Galadriel take precautions against doing so. Denethor and Théoden both give way to despair, from which only the latter recovers. Among the "bad," Saruman has only relatively recently fallen into evil, while Gollum, in spite of his history of murder and cannibalism, is at one point almost redeemed. Even Sauron himself is a fallen angel and was thus originally good. If we consider entire peoples, the Númenóreans have been eminently corruptible in the past—it was from among them that the Ringwraiths were recruited—and in the "Scouring of the Shire" episode, even a few hobbits are found to have "gone over to the other side" (*RK*, VI, viii, 285). The High-Elves may appear serenely virtuous in their closing years in Middle-earth, but their earlier history, glanced at in the appendices of *The Lord of the Rings* and expounded at length in "The Silmarillion," is full of pride, cupidity, and internecine violence.

Underpinning Tolkien's conception of good and evil is the Augustinian theology that is a major strand in Catholic and indeed Christian thought. According to this view, God created all, and all that he created was good. "For nothing is evil in the beginning. Even Sauron was not so" (*FR*, II, ii, 281). Human beings and other intelligent creatures have from God the gift of freedom and so may often freely choose evil. But, as Tolkien's creation myth, Ainulindalë, asserts through the voice of God (Ilúvatar) himself, the struggle with evil ultimately serves to enrich and make morepoignant the joy and glory of the created world.

On this view, evil lacks any independent power to create and is essentially the negation (or corruption or mockery) of good. Even its acts of negation are imperfect, at least in the mortal world. As Tolkien protested in an unpublished essay, "In my story I do not deal in Absolute Evil. I do not think there is such a thing, since that is Zero" (*Letters*, 243). Sauron and his servants are ultimately destined to "nothingness" (*RK*, V, iv, 103), or to the shriveled existence of "a mere spirit of malice that gnaws itself in the shadows, but cannot grow again" (*RK*, V, ii, 155).

Though consistently maintained, the presentation of this vision varies greatly across Tolkien's works.

In the writings which culminated in the published *Silmarillion*, there is a sustained focus on the moral weakness and incontinence of Elves, Dwarves, and Men. The narratives of the First Age, despite some episodes of heroism, show how the repercussions of perfidy and vengeance, and the enslavement of individuals by their own and others' prior misdeeds, perpetuate misery from generation to generation. Among Men, a tragic focus is provided by the complicated misfortunes of Túrin Turambar, whose guileless impulsiveness the tyrannical Morgoth exploits to diabolical effect. But many of the Elves show a far greater capacity for transgression, and with less excuse. The sublime creativity and heroism of Fëanor do not excuse the folly of his rebellion against the Valar or the blasphemous oath that implicates and destroys his descendants.

The realms of the Eldar in Beleriand, being largely founded on this very rebellion by Fëanor and his followers, cannot escape ultimate defeat by Morgoth. The ostensibly positive ending of this epoch, as the immortal Valar finally intervene to dethrone Morgoth after his victory, seems little more than a formality, designed to draw a line under the destruction of Beleriand and to vindicate the official Augustinian theory: it has none of the heart-rending joy of "eucatastrophe" Tolkien was to celebrate in his essay "On Fairy–Stories," written long after he had conceived the history of Beleriand.

The history of Númenor in the Second Age, narrated in the "Akallabêth" (see *The Silmarillion*) is a version of the human Fall, with Sauron in the Satan/tempter role; here again, divine intervention is required to overturn Sauron's threatened triumph, and the price for this is the destruction of Númenor itself.

Some critics, notably Shippey, have detected in Tolkien a "Manichean" view of evil, in tension with the Augustinian view described above. According to this alternative tradition, as Shippey expounds it, we need above all to recognize that evil has effective power. It equips itself with armies and can seize control of large parts of the earth and enslave whole populations. Patient forbearance alone is not a sufficient response. Evil must be resisted, even at the risk of committing harmful deeds oneself (such as Beregond's killing of the porter of the Citadel, an act pardoned but not wholly exculpated).

The Ruling Ring offers a challenge that requires these two alternative responses to evil—passive forbearance and active opposition—to unite. Frodo and his friends must resist the temptation to use the Ring's corrupting power; yet if they attempt to hide it, Sauron will recover it sooner or later. They must both renounce it and actively seek its destruction, using courage and guile to outwit its master.

Shippey plausibly suggests that these complex reflections on evil show Tolkien coming to terms intellectually and emotionally with his personal experience as a survivor of the Great War, and with the twentieth century's horrors of mechanized warfare, totalitarianism, "brainwashing," and mass murder. That Tolkien did come to terms with his personal trauma is suggested by the fundamentally genial tone of his works set in the Third Age, *The Hobbit* and *The Lord of the Rings*. They depict a world that is predominantly happy (or seems so, when viewed through the benignly appreciative consciousness of hobbits) and that survives a life-threatening onslaught by a nihilistic antagonist. In these works, the efflorescent beauty and joyous diversity of Middle-earth become part of their moral as well as their aesthetic power.

BRIAN ROSEBURY

Further Reading

Rosebury, Brian. *Tolkien: A Cultural Phenomenon.* Basingstoke: Palgrave Macmillan, 2003.
Shippey, Tom. *J.R.R. Tolkien: Author of the Century.* London: HarperCollins, 2000.
Tolkien, J.R.R. "On Fairy Stories." In *MC.*

See also **Angband; Augustine of Hippo; Boromir; Christian Readings of Tolkien; Gollum; Heroes and Heroism; Lewis, C.S.; Morgoth and Melkor: Mordor; Northern Courage; Rings of Power; Sacrifice; Saruman; Sauron; Silmarils; Theological and Moral Approaches in Tolkien's Works; One Ring, The; Tyranny; Valinor; Violence; War; Williams, Charles; Theology**

GORDON, E.V. (1896–1938)

Eric Valentine Gordon was born in Salmon Arm, British Columbia, on February 14, 1896, the son of James and Annie McQueen Gordon. He was educated at Victoria College and at McGill University College, both in Victoria, British Columbia. In 1915, he was elected a Rhodes Scholar and went to University College, Oxford. His education was interrupted by World War I, after which he returned to University College, completing his BA in 1920. He was tutored in 1920 by Tolkien, the beginning of their long friendship. After receiving his degree, Gordon remained in Oxford working on a B.Litt., but he never completed it. He was awarded an MA from Oxford (which required no further study) in 1926.

In 1922, he followed Tolkien to Leeds University, where he was appointed Assistant Lecturer in English. In 1923, when Tolkien became ill, Gordon was allowed to take over Tolkien's responsibility for the review chapter on philology for *The Year's Work in English Studies 1922.* This earned Gordon the right to contribute the chapters on Old English and Middle English to the annual in subsequent years. Both Gordon and Tolkien were also active at Leeds, publishing poems and translations in local magazines and anthologies, and as members of the Yorkshire Dialect Society.

Gordon's first book was his collaboration with Tolkien, a critical edition of *Sir Gawain & the Green Knight* (1925). For this edition, Tolkien was primarily responsible for the text and glossary, while Gordon contributed the majority of the notes. They soon began work on further collaborations, including an edition of *Pearl,* but when Tolkien left Leeds for Oxford at the end of 1925, the geographical distance made working together much more difficult. In January 1926, Gordon succeeded Tolkien as the Professor of English Language at Leeds.

In 1927, Gordon published *An Introduction to Old Norse,* which became a standard textbook. It contains a long introduction, a grammar, and a moderate glossary, along with a wide-ranging selection of extracts from the *Elder Edda* and a large number of the sagas. For this work and other services to Icelandic studies, Gordon was awarded a Knighthood of the Royal Icelandic Order of the Falcon by Christian X, the King of Iceland and Denmark, and he was elected an Honorary Fellow of the Icelandic Society of Letters.

On July 30, 1930, Eric Valentine Gordon married one of his students, Ida Lilian Pickles (b. 1907). They had four children, three daughters and one son.

In 1931, Gordon was appointed Smith Professor of English Language and Germanic Philology at the University of Manchester. In the following year, a London publisher began a small series of books, intended as student editions, that would comprise the "Methuen's Old English Library." Gordon and Tolkien were signed up to collaborate on two, *The Wanderer* and *The Seafarer.* These editions were essentially complete by the mid-1930s, but Gordon passed away while the manuscripts awaited reduction and final revision. Only Gordon's work on *The Seafarer* would ever appear in print, under his wife's name, whose edition was published in 1960.

In 1937, Gordon published two books, a translation of Haakon Shetelig's and Hjalmar Falk's *Scandinavian Archaeology,* and his edition of *The Battle of Maldon,* the latter a part of Methuen's Old English Library.

In July 1938, Gordon suffered an attack of gallstones. An operation was successfully performed to remove his gall bladder, after which things went very wrong. Gordon died on July 29, 1938 at the age of forty-two. Gordon's widow was left to raise four children on her own. Her professional philological qualifications fortunately enabled her to take over some of her late husband's teaching duties. She remained a lecturer at the University of Manchester until 1968.

After Gordon's death, Tolkien took over their planned edition of *Pearl*, but he proved unable to finish it. In 1950, it was returned to Mrs. Gordon. Published in 1953 solely under E.V. Gordon's name, it more accurately should have been designated as edited in collaboration with his wife.

Most of Gordon's books contain an acknowledgement of assistance from Tolkien, and it is clear that each of the two scholars was very interested and supportive of the other's professional works. Tolkien's biographer Humphrey Carpenter characterized Gordon as an ideal collaborator for Tolkien, one who could keep him working and get him to surrender materials to the publishers. Unfortunately, a closer examination of their working relationship has shown that Gordon was no better in motivating Tolkien to complete work than any other person.

Gordon's work did have some effect on Tolkien's creative writings. The ink drawing of an Old Norse hall that appears in *An Introduction to Old Norse* provided the model for Tolkien's own illustration of Beorn's Hall as published in *The Hobbit*. And some particular points of Gordon's discussion of *The Battle of Maldon* seem to have been addressed by Tolkien in his verse-drama "The Homecoming of Beorhtnoth," and particularly in its companion essay "Ofermod."

Two other works are closely related to both Tolkien and Gordon. Around 1924, one of their students at Leeds, Stella Marie Mills (1903–89), translated *Hrolf Kraki's Saga* under Gordon's guidance. The character of Bothvar Bjarki in this saga significantly influenced the Beorn character in *The Hobbit*. Mills's translation was published in 1933 under the title *The Saga of Hrolf Kraki*. The volume is dedicated to Gordon, C.T. Onions, and Tolkien, with whom Mills maintained a lifelong friendship. Gordon contributed an enthusiastic introduction to the book.

Also at Leeds, Gordon and Tolkien had formed a Viking Club for undergraduates, which met to drink beer, read the sagas, and sing drinking songs in Old English and Old Norse. A number of these songs were distributed as stenciled sheets. In 1936, their former pupil A.H. Smith (1903–67) set his students at University College, London, the task of printing on their Elizabethan printing press a small edition of the stenciled Leeds sheets under the title *Songs for the Philologists*. Copies were printed up as a book before Smith realized that he had never asked Tolkien or Gordon for their permission, so the most of the copies remained undistributed and were thereafter destroyed in a fire. Many of the poems in *Songs for the Philologists* were by Tolkien, but two were by Gordon, including "When I'm dead don't bury me at all, just pickle my bones in alcohol" (in three versions, Old English, Gothic, and a Scottish dialect) and "Su Klukka Heljar," an Icelandic version of "The Bells of Hell." Gordon probably never knew of the volume's existence, and *Songs for the Philologists* is the greatest rarity among Tolkien's publications.

Douglas A. Anderson

Further Reading

Anderson, Douglas A. "'An Industrious Little Devil': E.V. Gordon as Friend and Collaborator with Tolkien." In *Tolkien the Medievalist*, edited by Jane Chance. London: Routledge, 2002.

Barman, Jean. *Sojourning Sisters: The Lives and Letters of Jessie and Annie McQueen*. Toronto: University of Toronto Press, 2003.

Gordon, E.V., ed. *The Battle of Maldon*. London: Methuen, 1937. Rev. ed., with a supplement by D.G. Scragg. Manchester: Manchester University Press, 1976.

———. *An Introduction to Old Norse*. Oxford: Clarendon Press, 1927. Second edition, revised by A.R. Taylor. Oxford: Clarendon Press, 1957.

———, ed. *Pearl*. Oxford: Clarendon Press, 1953.

Gordon, I.L. *The Seafarer*. London: Methuen, 1960. New ed., with bibliography by Mary Clayton. Exeter: University of Exeter Press, 1996.

Hammond, Wayne G., with the assistance of Douglas A. Anderson. *J.R.R. Tolkien: A Descriptive Bibliography*. Winchester: St. Paul's Bibliographies; New Castle, DE: Oak Knoll Books, 1993.

Mills, Stella M., with an introduction by E.V. Gordon. *The Saga of Hrolf Kraki*. Oxford: Basil Blackwell, 1933.

Shetelig, Haakon, and Hjalmar Falk. *Scandinavian Archaeology*. Translated by E.V. Gordon. Oxford: Clarendon Press, 1937.

Tolkien, J.R.R., and E.V. Gordon, eds. *Sir Gawain & the Green Knight*. Oxford: Clarendon Press, 1925. 2nd ed., revised by Norman Davis. Oxford: Clarendon Press, 1967.

See also **Gordon, Ida; Leeds;** *Leeds University Verse, 1914–24; A Northern Venture*

GORDON, IDA (1907–)

A scholar and critic of medieval literature, Ida Gordon (née Pickles, born 1907) was married to fellow scholar E.V. Gordon and continued much of his scholarly work after his unexpected death in 1938. In many cases this included work E.V. Gordon had begun with Tolkien. Specifically, after their successful edition of *Sir Gawain and the Green Knight* (published 1925), Tolkien and E.V. Gordon were collaborating on two more editions: one of the Middle English poem *Pearl*, presumably by the same author as *Sir Gawain and the Green Knight*, and one of the Anglo-Saxon elegies *The Seafarer* and *The Wanderer*. After E.V. Gordon's death, Tolkien undertook the task of completing the edition of *Pearl*, but never concluded it. In a 1945 letter to Stanley Unwin, Tolkien makes reference to being "in trouble with the widow of Professor E.V. Gordon" for having "failed to do my duty" in this regard; Ida Gordon eventually completed it and published it under her husband's name in 1953, thanking Tolkien for his assistance in the preface. As for the edition of *The Wanderer* and *The Seafarer*, Ida Gordon undertook the completion of that work, with Tolkien's approval. She eventually published an edition of *The Seafarer* alone under her own name in 1960, finding that the work had undergone such substantial change in the intervening years that it was essentially different from the draft her husband and Tolkien had left unfinished; she thanks Tolkien in her preface for notes he had given her. Ida Gordon taught at the University of Manchester until 1968; her other scholarship includes work on *Gísla-saga* and Chaucer's *Troilus and Criseyde*, including a 1970 book *The Double Sorrow of Troilus: A Study of Ambiguities in "Troilus and Criseyde."*

YVETTE KISOR

Further Reading

Gordon, E.V. *Pearl*. Oxford: Clarendon Press, 1953.

Gordon, Ida L. *The Double Sorrow of Troilus: A Study of Ambiguities in "Troilus and Criseyde."* Oxford: Clarendon Press, 1970.

———. *The Seafarer.* Methuen's Old English Library. London: Methuen, 1960.

Tolkien, J.R.R., and E.V. Gordon. *Sir Gawain and the Green Knight.* London: Oxford University Press, 1925.

See also **Gordon, E.V.;** *Pearl:* **Edition by E.V. Gordon; Scholars of Medieval Literature, Influence of;** *Seafarer:* **Ida Gordon Edition**

GOTHIC LANGUAGE

The publication of Joseph Wright's *Grammar of the Gothic Language* in 1910 virtually coincided with Ronald Tolkien's going up to Oxford. For a young man of philological bent, the opportunities presented by Gothic were fascinating, even enchanting, and the presence of Joe Wright at Oxford not only meant that Tolkien's philological bent was fully nourished (and, not incidentally, directed toward the Celtic: "go in for the Celtic boy—there's money in it!") but meant as well that a certain kind of man was enthroned in his imaginative faculty—gruff, self-educated, and of surprising sweetness—a character study for Sam Gamgee.

There is a poem Tolkien wrote in the Gothic language (or, perhaps more accurately, neo-Gothic), to fill the gap left by the ages, for no Gothic poetry has survived. A few Crimean Gothic words were taken down by the Flemish traveler and diplomat Ogier de Busbecq in the sixteenth century; otherwise, there is the Gothic translation of the Septuagint by Ulfilas or Wulfilas (311–82), which of course shows the effects of its Greek origins, and there are a couple of later deeds (in Rome) in what may be a Visigothic form of the language. Jordanes in his *History of the Goths* gives a few words of the language, but the *History* is not written in Gothic. So far as we can tell, there were Ostrogothic (East Gothic) and Visigothic (West Gothic) dialects, and some Spanish names (*Rodrigo*, for example) preserve something of their Visigothic antecedents. Curiously, the story of "The Battle of the Goths and the Huns" that has come down to us is in *Heidrek's Saga*, in Icelandic.

Of his discovery of Gothic in Wright's *Grammar*, Tolkien wrote (letter to W.H. Auden, June 7, 1955), "I discovered in it . . . for the first time the study of a language out of mere love: I mean for the acute aesthetic pleasure derived from a language for its own sake, not only free from being useful but free even from being the 'vehicle of a literature'" (*Letters*, 213). But he reconstructed what might have been a piece of that lost literature in the form of a paean to the white birch tree, "ruler of the mountain" (printed in *Songs for the Philologists*, University of London, 1936).

"Brunaim bairiþ bairka bogum / laubans liubans liudandei, / gilwagroni, glitmujandei, / bagme bloma, blauandei, / fagrafahsa, liþulinþi, / fraujinondei fairguni. // Woþjand windos, wagjand lindos, / lutiþ limam laikandei; / slaihta, raihta, hweitarinda, / razda rodeiþ reirandei, / bandwa bairhta, runa goda, / þiuda meina þiuþjandei. // Andanahti milhmam neipiþ, / liuhteiþ liuhmam lauhmuni; / laubos liubai fliugand lausai, / tulgus, triggwa, standandei. / Bairka baza beidiþ blaika / fraujinondei fairguni."

That is, "The birch bears fine leaves on shining boughs, it grows pale green and glittering, the flower of the trees in bloom, fair-haired and supple-limbed, the ruler of the mountain. // The winds call, they shake gently, she bends her boughs low in sport; smooth, straight, and white-barked, trembling she speaks a language, a bright token, a good mystery, blessing my people. // Evening grows dark with clouds, the lightning flashes, the fine leaves fly free, but firm and faithful the white birch stands bare and waits, ruling the mountain."

The sensibility underlying "Brunaim bairiþ bairka bogum" is presumably Tolkien's own. It is unclear if anything of the Gothic sensibility can be learned from Ulfilas and Joe Wright, though it might be noted that in "The Battle of the Goths and the Huns" there is a reference to *Mirkviùdr*, Mirkwood (from which has been suggested it enters *The Lord of the Rings* and the larger legendarium), which (though West Germanic) suggests that there was a Gothic equivalent for *Mirkviùdr*, extant texts do not in fact provide (albeit the current Project Ulfila indicates) Gothic *Mairqrwidus*. The Neo-Gothic *liþulinþi* in the "brunaim" verses seems to belong by sound and signifier to the Elvish.

The full title-page description of Wright's *Grammar* is *Grammar of the Gothic Language and the Gospel of St Mark, Selections from the Other Gospels and the Second Epistle to Timothy*, with Notes and Glossary by Joseph Wright, Ph.D., D.C.L., LL.D., Litt.D., Fellow of the British Academy, Corpus Christi Professor of Comparative Philology at the University of Oxford. There is nothing about this book to excite the imagination—unless one's imagination is excited by the language itself.

One remark by Professor Wright in his introduction is revealing (iv): "In fact, it is in my opinion a sheer waste of time for a student to attempt to study in detail the phonology of any language before he has acquired a good working knowledge of its vocabulary and inflexions." In other words, before one writes much *about* Gothic, one should write *in* Gothic, which Tolkien did.

The Gothic language as it has survived through Ulfilas is a branch of East Germanic, a set of languages of which there is no current survivor. Even Visigothic (West Gothic) was East Germanic. The Gothic language had only a relatively brief florescence and had largely passed out of use (except in isolated parts of the Crimea) by the later sixth century CE.

JARED LOBDELL

Further Reading

Wright, Joseph. *Grammar of the Gothic Language and the Gospel of St. Mark, Selections from the Other Gospels and the Second Epistle to Timothy*. Edited by O.L. Sayce 2nd ed. Oxford, 1954.

See also **Jordanes; Goths; Philology; Oxford**

GOTHS

The Goths are an East Germanic people first documentable in the Black Sea area in the third century CE, although their own internal legends traced tribal origins to points considerably farther north, perhaps in today's southern Sweden (Götaland; Gotland). In the third century, the Goths of the Black Sea region split into two confederations, the Ostrogoths and the Visigoths, who thereafter expanded into Italy and Iberia, respectively. In heroic legend as well as partially in fact, the Goths were the hereditary enemies of the Huns (q.v.); however, the celebrated defeat of the Hunnish leader Attila ("Little Father" in Gothic) in 451 was in fact accomplished by an alliance of Romans, Burgundians, and Salian Franks with Visigoths.

The Gothic language is the earliest Germanic dialect of which we have record. It is known to us chiefly from the fourth-century Bible translation by the (Arian) bishop Wulfila ("Little Wolf"). Of Wulfila's original, presumably complete Bible, we retain a good portion of the New Testament (gospels and epistles) and a few other fragments.

J.R.R. Tolkien's acquaintance with the Goths would have been first and primarily through their language, for which he conceived an early and strong affection. It goes without saying that Tolkien would have noted how comfortably the Gothic language (despite its antiquity) sits in the mouth of a modern English-speaker; it displays an easily observed kinship with its younger and more widely studied cousins, Old English and Old Norse. *Songs for the Philologists*, written by Tolkien with E.V. Gordon when both were colleagues at Leeds in the early 1920s, includes Tolkien's "Bagme bloma" (Flower of Trees), an original alliterative poem in the Gothic language praising a birch tree as "bandwa bairhta, runa goda, thiuda meina thiuthjandei" (a bright token, a good mystery, blessing my people [trans. T.A. Shippey]).

Enthusiasm for the Goths and their language was rising, not only on the academic horizon in Tolkien's youth (Joseph Wright's *Grammar of the Gothic Language* first appeared in 1910), but also in popular culture, as can be seen in William Morris' 1890 romance *The House of the Wolfings*, a linguistically mixed, mythologized retelling of the defeat of the Roman legions by a coalition of Germanic tribes. Its heroes bear Old Norse names and belong to the "kindreds of the Mark"—a subgroup of the "sons of the Goths," in the story. They speak "the tongue of the Goths," and they fight the Romans in an impassible forest called "Mirkwood," which name Morris (who read Old Norse without difficulty) would have found in the Poetic Edda.

Next after the Gothic language itself in importance to Tolkien's understanding of Goths would have been epic poetry in Old Norse and Old English. From the Old English side, it is no distant leap to identify the "Geats" of the Old English poem *Beowulf* (q.v.), who include the epic's eponymous hero and who come to King Hrothgar's Danish court from across the sea, with the "Götar" of Götaland (southern Sweden), "Gautar" in Old Norse. Although there are some mismatches in the vowel sounds of these varied tribal names, it is not unreasonable to see *Beowulf*'s Geats as one of a number of legendary incarnations of the Goths (or of their close relatives), for all that they have been brought across the North Sea to speak good Old English to the Danes, and to each other, by an English poet knowledgeable in Dano-Swedish heroic lore. (Beowulf and Hrothgar are analogues of Bödhvarr bjarki and Hrólf kraki, respectively, for instance.) And indeed, Tolkien's choice of "Gothland" as a modern English translation for *Beowulf*'s "Geatland" in 1940 indicates that some kind of connection between Geats and Goths made sense to him at the time.

Known just as fully to Tolkien would have been the sense of a lost Gotho-centric world that lies behind much Old Norse epic poetry. (See Edda.) This underlying narrative is related to the heroic legends that lie behind *Beowulf* and can be seen to reflect actual Migration-Age history to some degree, although through a glass darkly. In Old Norse poems such as *Hlödhskvidha* (also called "Battle of the Goths and the Huns") and in the Sigurd-cycle poems of the Codex Regius such as *Atlakvidha* and many others, "Gotar" (Goths; this alternative root-vowel matches the one in "Gotland," a Swedish island) can refer to fine-bred Gothic horses, as well as generic (human, male) warriors; this suggests that the narrators of the original versions of these epics self-identified as Goths (or their close kin) themselves. Similarly, "Gota málmr" (Gothic metal) is what the best mail shirts and edged weapons are made of in these poems, and others like them. "Gotna dróttinn" and "Gotna thjódhann" (Lord of the Goths) are common circumlocutions for Gunnar the western king, although he is simultaneously and elsewhere identified as a Burgundian (as was, in fact, his real-world prototype, Gundaharius [411–37]). The "Gota thjódhir" (Gothic people), as they are named in *Hlödhskvidha*, are ever ready to ride eastward through pathless "Myrkvidhr" (Mirkwood), as it is called in *Hlödhskvidha* and three poems of the Codex Regius (*Atlakvidha, Lokasenna, Völundarkvidha*), to do battle with their Hunnish foemen. In the poems *Gudhrúnarhvöt* and *Hamdhismál*, the body of the unfortunate maiden Svanhildr (whose fate is also recounted in Jordanes's sixth-century *Getica* chronicle; see below) is pulled apart by gray, gait-trained Gothic horses ("grá, gangtöm Gotna hross"). In *Hervararkvidha*, the warrior maid Hervör seeks to wake her dead father armed with "gröfnum geiri . . . Gota málmi . . . hjálmi ok medh brynju" (graven spear, Gothic iron, helmet and mail).

These heroic-age Goths were also celebrated in the prose sections of a number of Old Norse legendary sagas, perhaps most prominently in *Hervarar saga ok Heidhreks konungs* (edited by Christopher Tolkien in 1960), in which the much older poem *Hlödhskvidha*, cited above, is embedded. In these sagas, the Goths are generally said to have lived in "Árheimar" (Homes of Yore) or "Hreidhgotaland" (Land of the Famous Goths, Nest-Goths, or possibly Riding-Goths). Árheimar and Hreidhgotaland are generally said to be bordered on the east, as mentioned above, by the forest of Mirkwood, on the other side of which lurk the enemy Huns. These places are of course impossible to locate on a real-world map, but that has not stopped people from trying to do so. Twelfth-century Icelandic writer Snorri Sturluson, for instance, placed Hreidhgotaland specifically on the Swedish island of Gotland. Other late-medieval Icelanders used "Hreidhgotaland" for Jutland (continental Denmark), as distinct from "Eygotaland" (Island Goth-land), which was used to denote the Danish islands.

Third in importance for Tolkien's understanding of Goths would have been Latinophone chroniclers. Pliny the Elder (first century) and Tacitus (first century) both wrote of northern barbarian tribes with similar names ("Gutones" and "Gothones," respectively). Jordanes (sixth century), who identified himself as a Goth ("Geta"), wrote *De origine actibusque Getarum* (Of the Origin and Deeds of the Goths), also called *Getica* (Of the Goths), which was a condensation of a lost, much longer work written in Ravenna by Cassiodorus for the Ostrogothic king Theodoric the Great (fifth–sixth century). Jordanes (and presumably Cassiodorus also) located his people's origin on the far-northern island of "Scandza" (possibly referring to southern Sweden; its name may match the "Scandia" of Ptolemy's *Geographia* [written in Greek, second century], as well as today's Skåne), from whence they migrated south to "Gothiscandza" (possibly the mouths of the Vistula), and thence to the Black Sea ("Sea of Pontus"). One could also note here that Jordanes's contemporary, Gregory of Tours, wrote in his *Gesta Francorum* (History of the Franks) of a certain pirate king of the "Getae" named "Chochilaicus" who crossed the sea to harry the Lowland coast; the name of this figure can be readily matched with that of Hygelac of the Geats in *Beowulf*.

Linguistic evidence for the origin of the historical Goths (as differentiated from the legendary Goths) in southern Sweden is present but not unequivocal. Swedish place names still in use, such as those of the provinces of Västra Götaland and Östergötland and the island of Gotland, seem to provide corroboration for the idea; as well as for the idea that *some* of the

Gautar/Götar—or Gotar—did *not* migrate south to become the "Getae" of Jordanes, Gregory, and other chroniclers but stayed right where they were. As has been noted, though, the vowels in these names are frustratingly inconsistent; and the debate, as is generally the case when the ethnic origins of living persons are at stake, has been continuous.

Archeological evidences of the Goths of which J.R.R. Tolkien certainly knew include such finds as the fourth-century hoard of Pietroasa (Romania), found in 1837, containing gold and jewels presumed to have been hidden by Goths fearing a Hunnish attack. Among them was a splendid neck ring (damaged, alas, since discovery) with the runic inscription *gutaniowihailag*, possibly meaning "holy possession of the Goths."

A direct use of the Goths and their language by Tolkien can be found in *The Lord of the Rings* in the account of the chieftains of Rhovanion (*RK*, Appendix A, 326–327), whose kin married into the royal line of Gondor, thereby causing the Kin-strife. Just as Tolkien assigned Norse names to the Dwarves, and Old English ones to the Rohirrim, he has given these northern kin of the Rohirrim (and their royal Gondorian descendant) names in the Gothic language: Vidugavia, Vidumavi, and Vinitharya.

SANDRA BALLIF STRAUBHAAR

Further Reading

Chambers, R.W. *Beowulf: An Introduction to the Study of the Poem, with a Discussion of the Stories of Offa and Finn.* Cambridge: Cambridge University Press, 1921.

Goffart, Walter. *The Narrators of Barbarian History.* Princeton, NJ: Princeton University Press, 1988.

Larrington, Carolyne, trans. *The Poetic Edda.* Oxford: Oxford University Press, 1999.

Mierow, Charles Christopher, ed. and trans. *The Gothic History of Jordanes.* Cambridge: Speculum Historiale, 1966.

Neckel, Gustav and Hans Kuhn, eds. *Edda: Die Lieder des Codex Regius nebst verwandten Denkmälern.* Heidelberg: Carl Winters Universitätsverlag, 1968.

Shippey, Tom. *The Road to Middle-earth: Revised and Expanded Edition.* Boston, MA: Houghton Mifflin, 2001.

Tolkien, Christopher, ed. and trans. *The Saga of King Heidrek the Wise.* London: Thomas Nelson & Sons, 1960.

Tolkien, J.R.R. "On Translating *Beowulf.*" In *MC*.

See also **Beowulf**; **Edda**; **Geats**; **Gothic Language**; **Huns**

GRAMMAR

Tolkien's lifelong fascination with language is well documented. As a matter of fact, his preoccupation with grammar and lexicon was a constant feature of both his academic work and his literary production. In letter 163, written in 1955 to the poet W.H. Auden, he declared that linguistic patterns had the power to affect him emotionally; then, in the same letter, he commented on his first encounter with a Finnish grammar, in the library of Exeter College, by comparing it to the discovery of a cellar filled with bottles of heady wine. His 1931 essay "A Secret Vice" illustrates the pleasures of linguistic invention, which are superior to those of mere language learning. In the essay, grammar is described as a more purely intellectual interest than philology, and the ways in which the relations of words are expressed are compared to "skillful bits of machinery."

The first theoretical treatises written by Tolkien for his invented languages date from the 1915–17 period, when he was also working on *The Book of Lost Tales*. These were grammars and lexicons for both Qenya (later to become Quenya) and Gnomish (or Goldogrin), the ancestor of Sindarin. Another important source are the *Etymologies*, a dictionary of Elvish published posthumously in 1987 as part of the fifth volume of *The History of Middle-earth*, *The Lost Road*. However, most of the materials produced by Tolkien are incomplete, and the emphasis seems to be more on words than on purely grammatical structures. In most cases, the evolution of Quenya and Sindarin in their mature form can only be inferred by an analysis of the texts included in Tolkien's works of fiction. Toward the end of his life, though, Tolkien sent to Richard Plotz of the Tolkien Society of America a chart (written in 1966–67) containing the declension of two nouns in "Book Quenya," *cirya* and *lasse*, accompanied by a page of explanatory notes.

However, it is one of Tolkien's shorter works of fiction, 1938's *Farmer Giles of Ham*, that provides the most significant illustration of his views on grammar and language. The story contains a series of subtle jokes that give it a strong allegorical slant. The parson, described as a "grammarian" who can read into the future, is probably a mild caricature of the professional philologist: in fact, when confronted with the inscription on the sword Tailbiter's sheath, he starts using difficult words to conceal his inability to interpret the signs. Linguistic humor is central to the story: Giles, who can hardly read, makes frequent grammar mistakes, which, however, are not as serious as the "folly" of spelling Thame with an *h*.

Even though Shippey points out that most modern readers would miss the connection between grammar and foresight in the parson's character, this was instead much more evident in the Middle Ages. In fact, the word "glamour" was originally a corruption of "grammar," as was *gramarye*, meaning "magic." Indeed, "grammar" and *gramarye* were almost synonymous, meaning that the knowledge of the inner workings of a language and the occult arts were considered in some way related, something that Tolkien found deeply fascinating.

MARIA RAFFAELLA BENVENUTO

Further Reading

Carpenter, Humphrey. *J.R.R. Tolkien: A Biography*. London: HarperCollins, 1995.

Gilson, Christopher, and Patrick Wynne. "The Growth of Grammar in the Elven Tongues." In *Proceedings of the J.R.R. Tolkien Centenary Conference*, edited by Patricia Reynolds and Glen H. GoodKnight, 187–94. Milton Keynes and Altadena: Tolkien Society and Mythopoeic Society, 1995.

Gilson, Christopher. "Gnomish Is Sindarin: The Conceptual Evolution of an Elvish Language." In *Tolkien's Legendarium: Essays on the History of Middle-earth*, edited by Verlyn Flieger, and Carl F. Hostetter, 95–104. Westport, CT: Greenwood Press, 2000.

Shippey, Tom. *J.R.R. Tolkien: Author of the Century*. London: HarperCollins, 2001.

———. *The Road to Middle-earth*. Rev. and expanded ed. London: HarperCollins, 2005.

Tolkien, J.R.R. "A Secret Vice." In *MC*.

———. *Farmer Giles of Ham*. In *Tales from the Perilous Realm*, 1–57. London: HarperCollins, 2002.

See also **Elvish Compositions and Grammars; *Farmer Giles of Ham*; Humor; *I·Lam na·Ngoldathon*; Languages, Early Introduction and Interest; Languages Invented by Tolkien; Language: Theories of; *Qenyaqetsa***

GREAT HAYWOOD

Great Haywood is a village in Staffordshire at the confluence of the Rivers Sow and Trent, five miles east of Stafford. Tolkien was posted to training camps on Cannock Chase south of here from October 1915, so after his marriage in March 1916 his wife, Edith, and her cousin Jennie Grove moved to lodgings in the village to be near him. They stayed here after he was sent to France that June. Tolkien joined them during his convalescence from trench fever, from December 1916 to February 1917, after which he was posted to Yorkshire. Tolkien was stationed again on Cannock Chase in April–June 1918, during which time he was able to live with his family, now including baby John. They had lodgings at Gipsy Green, a house on the Teddesley estate on the west edge of the Chase, about six miles southwest of Great Haywood.

Great Haywood held strong emotional meaning to Tolkien as the site of Edith's residence while he was at war and of his reunion with her. He commemorated this by incorporating the village into the topography of his mythology. A love poem written during his convalescence, "The Grey Bridge at Tavrobel," memorializes their reunion. Tavrobel also appears in *The Book of Lost Tales*, which Tolkien began writing at this time. Like Great Haywood, Tavrobel is located at the confluence of two rivers; the bridge is equivalent to the Essex Bridge, an old packhorse bridge over the Trent. It has been suggested that Tavrobel's House of a Hundred Chimneys was inspired by both Shugborough Hall at Great Haywood (*LR*, 413) and Gipsy Green.

DAVID BRATMAN

Further Reading

Hammad, Wayne, and Christing Scull. *J.R.R. Tolkien: Artist and Illustrator*. Boston, MA: Houghton Miffin, 1997.

See also ***Book of Lost Tales I***

GREECE: RECEPTION OF TOLKIEN

Tolkien's work first became available to the Greek readership through the translation of *The Hobbit* in 1978 as Χόμπιτ, followed by the publication of the three volumes of *The Lord of the Rings* (Ο Άρχοντας των Δαχτυλιδιών: Η Συντροφιά του Δαχτυλιδιού, Οι Δυο Πύργοι, and Η Επιστροφή του Βασιλιά), which were translated between 1985 and 1988. *The Silmarillion* (Το Σιλμαρίλλιον) appeared in the Greek language in 1996, and by 2000 a greater number of Tolkien's works had been translated, namely, *Unfinished Tales* (Ατέλειωτες Ιστορίες) and *Roverandom* (Ροβεράντομ).

Until 2001, Tolkien's work was known to a small but devoted readership in Greece. Mostly they were admirers of the fantasy and science fiction genre as a whole, or fans of role-playing games. After the release of Peter Jackson's film adaptations of *The Lord of the Rings*, interest in Tolkien's work in Greece increased considerably as a wider readership became aware of it. As a result of this, more of Tolkien's works were translated in Greek, including *Smith of Wootton Major* (Ο Σιδεράς του Μεγάλου Δασοχωρίου), *The Father Christmas Letters* (Γράμματα από τον Αη-Βασίλη), as well as *Tree and Leaf* (Το Φύλλο και το Δέντρο: Ιστορίες για Νεράιδες... και Άλλα). *Farmer Giles of Ham* has also been translated and published in two different versions, its title rendered as Ο Γεωργός ο Γίλης απ' το χαμ and Ο Αγρότης ο Τζάιλς από το Χωριό, respectively. Michael Coren's biography of Tolkien has also been translated into Greek, but neither Carpenter's authorized biography nor his collection of Tolkien's letters has been. A few popular introductory books on Tolkien's life and work have been written and published by Greek authors, and there have also been a few more specialized books written on Quenya, Tolkien's invented language which he declared to have classical Greek as one of its main ingredients (*Letters,* 176). Finally, after the success of Peter Jackson's films, Tolkien's works in the original are more readily available to the Greek readership in major bookstores in Greece.

In 2002, the "Cultural and Literary Society of Tolkien's Friends 'The Prancing Pony'" was founded (usually referred to as the Greek Tolkien Society), having as an aim the study of the literary work of Tolkien, its diffusion in Greece, and the encouragement of communication and contact among the interested. The Society consists of both older fans of Tolkien's works and of readers who discovered his work through the films of Peter Jackson. The Greek Tolkien Society is a member of the International Tolkien Fellowship and has represented Greece at international Tolkien fan events, like the Oxonmoot in Oxford, the Ring*Con in Germany, and Tolkien 2005 in Birmingham. It also maintains the website "LordOfTheRings.gr" with information on Tolkien's work, articles (both authored and translated) of fan criticism on Tolkien, as well as information and news coverage on Peter Jackson's films. The Society also provided advice for the Greek subtitling of Peter Jackson's films before they were released to the Greek audience.

DIMITRA FIMI

Further Reading

Carpenter, Humphrey. *Tolkien: A Biography.* London: Allen & Unwin, 1977.
Coren, Michael. *J.R.R. Tolkien: The Man Who Created "The Lord of the Rings."* Toronto: Stoddart, 2001.
"LordOfTheRings.gr." October 2005. *http://www.lordofthe-rings.gr.*

See also **Jackson, Peter; Languages Invented by Tolkien**

GREEK GODS

A disproportionate amount of the source hunting in Tolkien studies has centered around the influence of Scandinavian mythology on his works, but while this influence was undeniable, it is really only part of the story. Depending on which elements of Tolkien's world one examines, Greek mythology made an even greater impact on Tolkien. Tolkien acknowledged this debt to the Greek language and mythology in his letters. In 1956, he wrote to an unidentified Mr. Thompson: "I made the discovery that 'legends' depend on the language to which they belong; but a living language depends equally on the 'legends' which it conveys by tradition. (For example, that the Greek mythology depends far more on the marvellous

aesthetic of its language and so of its nomenclature of persons and places and less on its content than people realize, though of course it depends on both ...). " And in his famous 1951 letter to Milton Waldman, Tolkien wrote that because England "had no stories of its own," he turned to "legends of other lands . . . Greek, and Celtic, and Romance, Germanic, Scandinavian, and Finnish (which greatly affected me)."

In Tolkien's published works, the influence of Greek mythology is nowhere more apparent than in the Valar, which, as Richard Purtill correctly points out, "have a greater resemblance to the Olympian gods than to the Scandinavian gods such as Odin and Thor." There is, in fact, very close congruence between the Olympian pantheon and that of Valinor. For Manwë, lord of the air atop Taniquetil, to whom the eagle is sacred, we find a clear analogue in Zeus. Likewise, Ulmo, lord of waters, corresponds to Poseidon; Aulë, the smith, is Hephaestus; Mandos, master of the underworld, echoes Hades; Yavanna mirrors Demeter; Vána, Persephone. Even Taniquetil itself, the tallest mountain in the world, finds its antecedent in Mount Olympus.

Going beyond the Olympians, one may note that Tolkien borrowed from many other Greek myths and legends also. For the punishment of Prometheus, Hephaestus forges a chain of unbreakable adamantine; Aulë forges a similar chain, Angainor, with which to bind Melkor. Prometheus is chained to the bare face of the mountain, Caucasus, much as Maedhros hangs by his wrist from the face of Thangorodrim. Wayne Hammond and Christina Scull point out that Gandalf's battle with the Balrog in Moria resembles the battle between Zeus and Typhoeus in Hesiod's *Theogony.* The story of Elros and Elrond—with one brother choosing mortality, the other immortality— echoes that of Castor and Pollux. The tale of Theseus and the Minotaur reminds one of Aragorn's arrival at Minas Tirith in the black-sailed ships of the Corsairs. The legend of Beren and Lúthien exhibits many identifiable parallels in the Greek myth of Orpheus and Eurydice. And, in perhaps his crowning allusion to the myths of the Greeks, Tolkien famously recast the Downfall of Númenor as the origin of the legend of Atlantis, to be subsequently recorded by Plato in the dialogues, *Timaeus* and *Critias.*

The Norse pantheon also played a role in seeding Tolkien's fertile imagination; however, the Norse gods bear much less direct correspondence to Tolkien's theogony than do the Greek. Still, one should point out that the Ainur and Valar likely trace their origins (at least, philologically) to the Norse Æsir and Vanir. Even the word *vala* means, in Old Norse, "seeress" and therefore seems to reinforce the foresight of Tolkien's Valar. Too, the Rainbow Bridge that leads to

Asgard must remind one of the Straight Road to the Uttermost West. And Odin sits upon a high seat of his own, Hliðskjálf, which is as much an analogue for Taniquetil as Olympus. Nevertheless, Odin is more Gandalf than Manwë, and the other Valar likewise seem to owe little to any direct Norse counterpart (with some exceptions—for example, Tulkas, as discussed by Tom Shippey).

Interestingly, Tolkien's painstaking construction of an entire mythology, with its feigned connections to bodies of other recorded mythologies and erosions into the first germs of many real legends, may owe something to the work of Euhemerus, a fourth-century BCE Greek mythographer. Euhemerus's central argument was that mythology reflected a kind of divinized account of true, but inadequately remembered, history. By his account, the "gods" had probably once been ordinary human beings, albeit ones who accomplished great deeds. Over time, their successors told and retold the legends of their exploits, rendering them more and more godlike with each generation—in essence, mythologizing them. In the end, the result was a mythology based on "confused history" (to quote C.S. Lewis). Tolkien's approach to mythology (see parts 1 and 2 of *Sauron Defeated*) may find an antecedent in Euhemerism, although more work needs to be done to determine the extent of the connection.

JASON FISHER

Further Reading

Chance, Jane. *Tolkien and the Invention of Myth: A Reader*. Lexington, KY: University Press of Kentucky, 2004.

Day, David. *Tolkien's Ring*. London: HarperCollins, 1994.

Noel, Ruth S. *The Mythology of Middle-earth*. London: Thames & Hudson, 1977.

Pearce, Joseph. *Tolkien: Man and Myth: A Literary Life*. London: HarperCollins, 1998.

Petty, Anne C. *One Ring to Bind Them All: Tolkien's Mythology*. Updated ed. Tuscaloosa: University of Alabama Press, 2002.

Purtill, Richard. *J.R.R. Tolkien: Myth, Morality, and Religion*. New ed. San Francisco: Ignatius Press, 2003.

Shippey, Tom. "Tolkien and Iceland: The Philology of Envy." Delivered at the Sigurður Nordal Institute, September 2002. http://www.nordals.hi.is/shippey.html. Accessed January 2006.

See also **Greek Language; Homer; Mythology, Celtic; Mythology, Germanic; Mythology for England; Old Norse Literature; Plato;** *Sauron Defeated*; **Taniquetil**

GREEN, ROGER LANCELYN (1918–87)

A friend of Tolkien's and scholar both in classics and English who early turned to exploring the tradition of children's literature and becoming an authority in this field. As well as writing his own fiction and poetry, he became much more widely known as a writer of stories from Norse and classical mythology, who also retold European folktales and stories of Robin Hood and King Arthur. He wrote studies of Rudyard Kipling, J.M. Barrie, Andrew Lang, Lewis Carroll, and C.S. Lewis. His Oxford B. Litt. formed the foundation for the first edition of his *Tellers of Tales* (a study of the early generations of British children's writers, from Catherine Sinclair to A.A. Milne), which was expanded in later editions to bring the study up to contemporary times. He studied under both Tolkien (who supervised his B. Litt., "Andrew Lang and the Fairy Tale," and shared his interest in Andrew Lang) and C.S. Lewis, later attending a number of Inklings gatherings in the Eagle and Child public house. With Tolkien's dismissal of Lewis's early chapters of *The Lion, the Witch and the Wardrobe*, and lack of sympathy for the other Narnian chronicles, Green became a substitute for Tolkien so far as commenting on Lewis's children's stories was concerned. He read each book in draft form and commented upon the handwritten scripts. His assessment of *The Lion, the Witch and the Wardrobe* was in total contrast to Tolkien's, his feeling being that it was likely to become a classic of children's literature, on a par with Kenneth Graham's *The Wind in the Willows*—though he was uneasy about the inclusion of Father Christmas, an element that irritated Tolkien and illustrated the contrast between Lewis's eclectic imagination and Tolkien's systematic one. Green admired Tolkien's fiction as much as Lewis's, and said of *Smith of Wootton Major* (a comment much appreciated by Tolkien), "To seek for the meaning is to cut open the ball in search of its bounce." Arguably the character Wilfred Trewin Jeremy, the C.S. Lewis enthusiast in "The Notion Club Papers," owes something to Green.

After completing his B. Litt, Green had a variety of occupations: a period as a professional actor (1942–45), deputy librarian in Merton College Oxford (1945–50), and William Nobel Research Fellow in English Literature at the University of Liverpool (1950–52), and later on its Council. He lived near Liverpool in his ancestral home, Poulton Hall, the family seat since before the Norman Conquest, in Lower Bebington on the Wirral, about which he wrote a history. In its drawing room is a large mirror in a gilted frame above the mantelpiece. Green told Brian Sibley about a childhood incident: "One day after reading *Through the Looking-Glass*, I climbed up onto the mantelpiece and tried to follow Alice into Looking-Glass House!"

Charles Dodgson (Lewis Carroll) was one of his many interests, and Green wrote books and articles about him. His early study, *The Story of Lewis Carroll*

(1949) impressed Dodgson's nieces, who invited him to edit his diary, which came out in 1953. He helped to found the Lewis Carroll Society and aided Morton Cohen in his work of editing Dodgson's collected letters. A similar fervent interest in J.M. Barrie was enhanced by his experiences as an actor in the play of *Peter Pan* (he played Noodler in the 1942 tour). In 1954 he brought out *Fifty Years of Peter Pan*, which chronicles the years from the initial reception of the play through to its later productions. The book was published by Peter Davies, who as a boy was the Peter Llewelyn Davies who provided the name for the central character, Peter, in 1904.

Green's older son Richard, who took up his father's interest in Arthur Conan Doyle and became a world expert on Sherlock Holmes, died in tragic circumstances in May 2004. Roger and June Green had two other children, Priscilla and Scirard.

COLIN DURIEZ

Further Reading

Duriez, Colin. *The C.S. Lewis Chronicles*. New York: Bluebridge, 2005.

Green, Roger Lancelyn. *Into Other Worlds. Space-Flight in Fiction, from Lucian to Lewis*. London and New York: Abelard-Schuman, 1957.

———. *King Arthur and His Knights of the Round Table*. London: Everyman's Library Children's Classics, 1993.

———. Oral history interview. The Wade Center, Wheaton College, IL., 1986

———. *Tellers of Tales: Children's Books and Their Authors from 1800 to 1968*. Rev. ed. London: Kaye & Ward, 1969.

Green, Roger Lancelyn, and Walter Hooper. *C.S. Lewis: A Biography*. Rev. ed. London: HarperCollins, 2002.

See also **Inklings; Lewis, C.S.; Oxford**

GREGORY THE GREAT
(c. 540–604)

Gregory I (known as "the Great) was born into a prestigious and wealthy Roman family in the sixth century CE. He grew up in Rome during its capture by the Goths under Totila, and his writings hint at this early experience in his end of the world descriptions. He was an exemplary student; Gregory of Tours mentions that he was second to none in Rome in the areas of grammar, dialectic, and rhetoric. His religious upbringing by his saintly mother and aunts caused him to give up the office of prefect of Rome in 574 and become a monk. He turned his Sicilian estates into six monasteries, and his home on the Caelian Hill into a monastery devoted to St. Andrew. In 579, Pope Pelagius II sent Gregory to the Byzantine court as his permanent ambassador, where he stayed for six years. When he returned in 585, the famous incident with the English slaves in the Roman marketplace took place. Gregory attempted to undertake a mission to the English himself at this point, but the Roman populace angrily forced Pope Pelagius II to return Gregory to Rome. In 589, a number of disasters swept through Italy, and Pope Pelagius II died in 590. Gregory was then made pope, although unwillingly.

In his remaining fourteen years, Gregory devoted himself to building the power of the Roman papacy (the foundations of which would grow into the Middle Ages), writing extensive sermons and letters to missions and other colleagues, and formulating and standardizing the Roman liturgy and chant. He was so successful with the latter work that the music of the Roman Church afterward came to be known as Gregorian chant. Gregory spent much of his time building relationships with the suburbicarian churches, with the Byzantine Church and Empire, and with the Lombards and Franks. In terms of missionary work, he is best known for his mission to the English, which is amply recorded and survives in a number of sources. He also sent missions to Gaul, Africa, and North Italy and Istria. His writings on monasticism were widely read during the Middle Ages.

Gregory was in ill health for most of his adult life. Despite suffering continually from indigestion, slow fever, and gout, he was able to have a dramatic impact on the Roman papacy during its infancy, and the power base that he established through his numerous writings and missionary work laid the foundation for the primacy of the Roman papacy. He died on March 12, 604. He is known as a Doctor of the Church.

BRADFORD LEE EDEN

References and Further Reading

Attwater, D. *The Penguin Dictionary of Saints*. Baltimore, MD: Penguin Books, 1965.

Hudleston, G. Roger. "Pope St. Gregory I ('the Great')" *New Catholic Encyclopedia* on-line. http://www.newadvent.org/cathen/06780a.htm.

See also **Augustine of Canterbury**

GRÍMA (WORMTONGUE)

Son of Gálmód, known as Wormtongue; chief counselor to King Théoden of Rohan. Described as wizened and twisted, with "a pale wise face" and dark eyes with heavy lids. He was secretly an agent of Saruman, and around 3014 the king's health began to fail under his influence. Gríma manipulated the king by flattering his pride; planting suspicion of his allies and kin; and constantly reminding him of his age, his grief, and the vulnerability of Rohan. Théoden's trusted subordinates resented Gríma's influence but were powerless to displace him.

Gríma was captured in the wilds of Rohan by the Nazgûl on September 20, 3018, two days after Gandalf's escape from Orthanc, and under questioning revealed Saruman's knowledge of the general location of the Shire. It was due to Gríma's advice to Théoden that the victory of the First Battle of the Fords of Isen (February 25, 3019) was not followed up by a strengthened defense, allowing Saruman to invade Rohan several days later. When Gandalf came to the Golden Hall of Meduseld with Aragorn, Legolas, and Gimli, they found that Gríma had ordered that no strangers be admitted and that Éomer be imprisoned. Gríma had long advised "craven counsel," according to Éomer (who had suspected his treachery and his lust for Éowyn), and wanted the king and his forces to remain penned up defensively in Edoras.

After Théoden was healed by Gandalf (March 2, 3019), Gríma was found to have hidden many treasures, including the king's sword, in his chest (and when Aragorn became king and reclaimed Orthanc, many more heirlooms stolen from the House of Eorl were found there as well). When Gandalf exposed Wormtongue's bargain with Saruman, he was given a chance to redeem himself by going to war with the Rohirrim, but he preferred to return to his master at Isengard (March 5). However, he arrived after the Ents had captured the wizard's stronghold, and Treebeard locked him in the tower of Orthanc with Saruman. At the end of Gandalf's confrontation with the renegade wizard, Wormtongue threw Saruman's *palantír* out of an upper window; it was unclear whether he meant to hit Saruman or Gandalf. The Ents were left in charge of guarding Saruman and Wormtongue in Orthanc, but Treebeard eventually let them go in mid-August. The returning Company came across them in the wild, where Gandalf observed that Saruman might still "do some mischief in a small mean way" and offered Wormtongue a chance to leave his hated master. Indeed, when the Hobbits finally returned to the Shire, they found Saruman had taken over their country in late September. When the hobbits came to rout "Sharkey" out of Bag End, Frodo offered Wormtongue shelter in the Shire, but Saruman revealed he had forced Wormtongue into murdering and perhaps even eating Lotho Sackville-Baggins. In a final act of treachery, Wormtongue, himself betrayed by his master, leapt on the wizard and killed him, and in turn was shot down by the Hobbit guards (November 3). The Passing of Saruman is considered the final event in the War of the Ring.

Christopher Tolkien points out that the Old English name-element *grím* means mask, and Gríma is a character who masks his true intents and deeds under a fair cloak of concern for his king's health and peace of mind. He is almost as subtle and powerful with words as his master, but confines his poisonous insinuations primarily to Théoden and Éowyn. His true relationship with Saruman was an uneasy and deceitful mask as well; he never confessed his betrayal of Saruman to the Nazgûl, nearly killed him with the *palantír*, followed him into exile torn between hatred and fear, and finally slit his throat from behind. In earlier drafts, Wormtongue was named Frána, and it is not until later versions of the tale that he assumes the treacherous role seen in the finished work. Sources for Wormtongue may include the king's counselor Unferth in *Beowulf* and Uriah Heep in Dickens's *David Copperfield*. His character arc and tragic end mirror that of Gollum (Rateliff), and the two could be regarded as doubled characters.

JANET BRENNAN CROFT

Further Reading

Rateliff, John. "Gríma the Wormtongue: Tolkien and his Sources." *Mallorn* 25 (September 1988): 15–17.

See also **Doubles; Éowyn; Palantíri; Rohan; Théoden; Saruman**

GROVE, JENNIE (1860–1938)

Mary J. Grove (b. Birmingham, England, c. 1860; d. Birmingham, 1938) was an older cousin of Edith Tolkien née Bratt and a surrogate grandmother to the Tolkien children, who called her "Auntie Ie." Grove helped Edith's mother bring her up in Handsworth, Birmingham. Though an Anglican, in 1913 she set up home in Warwick with Edith, who had been made unwelcome in her Cheltenham lodgings after converting to Catholicism on her engagement to Tolkien.

Grove was Edith's principal companion throughout the First World War, moving with her to Great Haywood after the wedding in March 1916, remaining with her throughout Tolkien's absence on the Western Front that year, and then sharing her peripatetic life as Tolkien moved from camp to hospital to camp; he was only occasionally able to live with them. She returned with the exhausted Edith to

Cheltenham in late 1917 for the birth of John Tolkien. At the end of the war, having shared twenty-two sets of lodgings with Edith since 1916, Grove moved with the Tolkiens to 50 St John's Street, Oxford. However, she did not accompany them to Leeds after Tolkien took up his post at the university there in 1921.

A bricklayer's daughter, Grove was poorly educated, and stood only four feet eight inches tall with a deformed back as a result of an accident in her youth, but the Tolkiens saw her as an indomitable character. Her distant family connection with Sir George Grove, author of the *Dictionary of Music and Musicians* (1878 onward), had been prized by the Bratts. She is buried at St. Mary's, Handsworth.

JOHN GARTH

Further Reading

Carpenter, Humphrey. *J.R.R. Tolkien: A Biography.* London: George Allen & Unwin, 1977.

Hammond, Wayne G., and Christina Scull. *J.R.R. Tolkien: Artist and Illustrator.* London: HarperCollins, 1995.

Tolkien, John, and Priscilla Tolkien. *The Tolkien Family Album.* London: HarperCollins, 1992.

Tolkien, Priscilla. "J.R.R. Tolkien and Edith Tolkien's Stay in Staffordshire, 1916, 1917 and 1918." In *Angerthas in English 3*, edited by Magne Bergland. Bergen, Norway: Arthedain (The Tolkien Society of Norway), 1997.

1881 Census for Aston, Warwickshire.

See also **Great Haywood; Marriage; Warwick**

GUTHLAC, POEM

The manuscript of Old English poetry known as the Exeter Book contains two substantial narrative poems about the Anglo-Saxon saint Guthlac. See Guthlac, saint. Although these poems, known as *Guthlac A* and *Guthlac B*, are composed by separate authors with differing style and diction, they appear consecutively in the Exeter Book and can be read as a single unit. *Guthlac A* describes the hermit's encounters with demons in the borderland fens between Mercia and East Anglia, while *Guthlac B* recounts the saint's deathbed conversation with his follower, Beccel, and Beccel's mourning at Guthlac's death. While *Guthlac B* is clearly based on the Latin version of Guthlac's biography, written by the monk Felix in the early eighth century, the relationship between *Guthlac A* and the Latin text has been difficult to establish, and it is possible that the earliest rendition of *Guthlac A* predates the Latin version.

Tolkien finds in the Guthlac poems "a well-wrought finish, weighty words, [and] lofty converse" comparable with *Beowulf*'s dignity of style. Like other Old English hagiographic verse, both Guthlac poems consist primarily of speeches: *Guthlac A* of adversarial speeches between the hermit and the devils who wish to drive him from his hermitage, and *Guthlac B* of deathbed speeches between the saint and his retainer. In phrasing and theme, both sets of speeches echo the early Germanic heroic culture of *Beowulf*: Guthlac's arguments with demons are reminiscent of the heroic word-battle or *flyting*, and his interaction with Beccel in *Guthlac B* sounds much like a conversation between a dying warlord and loyal retainer, comparable to Beowulf's dying exchange with Wiglaf. The Guthlac poems thus represent a complex blending of heroic and Christian culture.

Because of the ambiguity of the Old English word *beorg*, which can mean both "hill" and "tomb," scholars have debated whether or not the *beorg* which Guthlac inhabits in *Guthlac A* is a pre-Christian burial site. Whether it is a tomb or simply a hill, Guthlac's fenland *beorg* bears an interesting likeness to the tombs of Tolkien's barrow-wights in *The Fellowship of the Ring*. Both are situated in a misty borderland area, and both are occupied by a nebulous demonic presence which is eventually exorcised. Also resonant with *The Return of the King* is the motif of a lord's death in battle; Theoden's death and Merry's attendant grief have parallels not only in *Beowulf* but also in *The Battle of Maldon*, elaborated by Tolkien in *The Homecoming of Beorhtnoth Beorhthelm's Son*. These pieces share with *Guthlac B* the figure of the seasoned war leader (in Guthlac's case, a leader in spiritual warfare against demons) whose fitting and honorable time for death has come, and the response of his followers to his death. Because *Guthlac A* and *Guthlac B* incorporate such themes and represent them in an Anglo-Saxon Christian heroic style, these two poems occupy an important place in the corpus of medieval literature that shaped Tolkien's Middle-earth.

SARAH DOWNEY

See also **Anglo-Saxon Poetry;** *Battle of Maldon*; *Beowulf*; *Beowulf and the Critics*; **Saints**

GUTHLAC, SAINT

Guthlac was an Anglo-Saxon saint who lived as a hermit in the fens of East Anglia around the year 700. His name means "gift of battle" in Old English. The definitive Latin version of his life story was written in the early eighth century by a monk called Felix, who recounts Guthlac's early battles with wilderness-dwelling demons and his later miracles of healing, exorcism, and prophecy. Also extant are two Old English poems, called *Guthlac A* and *Guthlac B*, which use language and motifs from Anglo-Saxon heroic culture to describe Guthlac's demon-fighting and death.

In Felix's account, Guthlac is born to noble parents and enters the military at a young age. Eventually, he becomes disillusioned with his life as an earthly soldier and decides instead to become a *miles Christi*, soldier of Christ. He joins a monastery at Repton for two years before going out in search of a place where he can live alone. The forbidding fenlands (often compared to Grendel's stalking grounds) on the border between Mercia and East Anglia offer Guthlac an ideal territory for spiritual warfare. He establishes his hermitage on an island called Crowland, where he endures various temptations from demons and the devil. The most spectacular of these is an encounter in which flying demons carry Guthlac through the air to the mouth of hell and threaten to throw him in. Guthlac is saved by the appearance of his own patron saint, the apostle Bartholomew, who orders the demons to carry Guthlac home safely. Later in his life, Guthlac becomes known for friendship with various kinds of birds inhabiting Crowland. People begin to come to him for healing and exorcism, and eventually he is ordained to the priesthood by a visiting bishop. Near the end of his life, and later in the form

of an apparition after his own death, Guthlac consoles and advises the exiled Mercian king Æthelbald. True to Guthlac's prophecy, Æthelbald regains his kingdom. After Guthlac's death in 714, his sister Pega arrives to bury him at Crowland, which eventually became the site of a thriving monastery. The present-day Crowland Abbey is a parish church dedicated to St. Guthlac, St. Bartholomew, and St. Mary the Virgin.

In keeping with the conventions of medieval "sacred biography," Guthlac's life story imitates the biographies of well-known saints such as Anthony, Benedict, Martin, Fursey, and Cuthbert. Guthlac's period of demonic temptations in the wilderness recalls that of Anthony; his later, more pastoral miracles echo those of Benedict; his military background is comparable to Martin's; his vision of hell is much like Fursey's; and his death scene is strongly influenced by Cuthbert's death. These parallels suggest that Guthlac's life story was carefully constructed to represent him as a native English saint on equal footing with his eastern and continental predecessors. Guthlac consequently represents a significant Anglo-Saxon appropriation of Christian tradition.

SARAH DOWNEY

See also **Anglo-Saxon Poetry;** *Beowulf and the Critics;* **Devils;** *Guthlac,* **Poem**

H

HAIGH, WALTER E. (1856–1931)

Walter E. Haigh is the author of *An Analytical Outline of English History* (1917) and *A New Glossary of the Dialect of the Huddersfield District* (1928), for which Tolkien wrote a foreword. Haigh was the head of the English and History Department of Huddersfield Technical College for close to three decades and was emeritus lecturer in English there when he wrote the *Glossary*. Haigh became a member of the Yorkshire Dialect Society in 1899–1900 and for the last two years of his life was a member of the Society's council. Tolkien joined the society in 1920–21 and first saw the manuscript for the *Glossary* in 1923. In his foreword, he recalls encouraging Haigh to complete the valuable work of capturing an endangered dialect from a crossroads of English linguistic history before it completely disappeared. Huddersfield was a particularly isolated area of South Yorkshire up until the end of the eighteenth century, and the dialect preserves layers of influence from Scandinavian through Medieval French. Several of the words in the *Glossary* can be found in the Common Speech as spoken by the Hobbits; some are used as place-names like Bree (the brow of a hill), Staddle (a timber stand), and the element Brock- (badger) in Brockenborings; or as family names like Baggins (a meal, particularly a brown-bag lunch). However, several are used in exactly the same way as in the Huddersfield dialect: gæffer (gaffer), a corruption of grandfather, for an old man, vittlz (vittles) for food, nout (nowt) for nothing, or nunkl (nuncle) for uncle.

JANET BRENNAN CROFT

Further Reading

Haigh, Walter Edward. *An Analytical Outline of English History*. London: Oxford University Press, 1917; reprinted 1929.

———. *A New Glossary of the Dialect of the Huddersfield District*. London: Oxford University Press, 1928.

Transactions of the Yorkshire Dialect Society. Ilkley: Yorkshire Dialect Society, 1898.

See also **"Chaucer as Philologist: The Reeve's Tale";** ***New Glossary of Our Dialect of the Huddersfield District***

HAVARD, HUMPHREY (1901–85)

Robert Emlyn Havard was the Tolkien family physician, a family friend, and a member of the Inklings. He received his undergraduate and medical educations at Oxford, served as a researcher and teacher in biochemistry at various hospitals and universities, and received his MD degree and took over a general medical practice in Oxford in 1934. C.S. Lewis was one of Havard's first patients and brought him into the Inklings, where Havard became a regular attendee of evening meetings and pub sessions. He frequently drove his fellow Inklings to outings at country inns and pubs.

Tolkien appreciated that Havard was a Catholic and a sympathetic physician "who thinks of people as people, not as collections of 'works'" (quoted in Carpenter, *Inklings,* 130). Some time around World War II, according to Havard's recollection, Tolkien asked him to become the family doctor (Havard,

"Professor," 61). During the war, Havard served in the Navy as a medical officer; Tolkien helped arrange for him to be stationed in Oxford in 1944 (*Letters*, 68). Between 1953 and 1968, the Tolkien and Havard families were neighbors in Headington. By then Havard was a widower with five children. He regularly met Tolkien and attended mass with him.

Havard attracted various nicknames from the Inklings. He is referred to in Tolkien's published letters as "Honest Humphrey," "the Useless Quack" or "U. Q.," and (when bearded and in naval uniform) "the Red Admiral." In a list attached to *The Notion Club Papers*, Tolkien identifies Havard with the quiet but perceptive character Rupert Dolbear, a research chemist "known to the Club as Ruthless Rufus" (*Sauron,* 150, 159).

DAVID BRATMAN

Further Reading

Carpenter, Humphrey: *The Inklings.*
Havard, R.E. "Professor J.R.R. Tolkien: A Personal Memoir." *Mythlore* 64 (Winter 1990): 61.

See also **Inklings; Lewis, C.S.; Life; Oxford**

HEALTH AND MEDICINE

Tolkien's primary innovation in health and medicine for his Middle-earth tales, particularly *The Lord of the Rings*, was to import the vernacular medicinal sources from early medieval England and invert the role played by Elves from the cause of to the cure for various illnesses. In addition to transforming the role of Elves, Tolkien also returned to the old idea of the power of kings to heal scrofula (sometimes known as the "King's Evil") through their touch.

In "The Houses of Healing" chapter of *The Return of the King*, Tolkien develops the idea that the "hands of the king are the hands of a healer," and in this signifies the political legitimacy of Aragorn. Aragorn seeks an herb called *athelas* (also *kingsfoil* and *asëa aranion*) to heal Faramir, Éowyn, and Merry, which he had previously used to partially heal Frodo's wound from the blade of the Black Rider (*FR*, I, xii, 210–11). The name *athelas* appears related to Old English *æðele*, meaning "noble" or "aristocratic," though among the Old English leechbooks a reference to *æðel-ferðing-wyrt*, or "stitch-wort," can also be found. The doggerel poems and folklore of the people of Gondor suggest that through the use of *athelas* to heal, "so shall the rightful king be known" (*RK*, V, viii, 139).

Tolkien frequently suggests in his Middle-earth stories that older, more powerful methods of healing had been replaced by empty theories. He writes, "For though all lore was in these latter days fallen from its fullness of old, the leechcraft of Gondor was still wise, and skilled in the healing of wound and hurt, and all such sickness as east of the Sea mortal men were subject to" (*RK*, V, viii, 136). The herb-master of the Houses of Healing enters into a debate with Aragorn over the potency of *athelas*, denigrating it as a cure from the old days. Aragorn's power to use the herb is connected to his direct descent from the old line of kings. When Frodo is wounded, he is taken to Elrond, "a master of healing," whose mastery of healing Imrahil attributes to his age when he says, "Would that Elrond were here, for he is the eldest of all our race, and has the greater power" (*RK*, V,viii, 139).

Tolkien also inverts the role that Elves play in illness. Tolkien uses the Old English term "leechcraft" to describe medical craft of all types, whether good or evil, including describing Wormtongue's hold over Théoden (508). The Old English leechbooks and herbaria depict Elves as small, invisible creatures that shoot illness into people and animals. Being "elfshot" was to be ill from some unknown cause. In the Middle-earth books, Elves are skilled healers, not the cause of illness. Elvish medicine, particularly that of Elrond, is depicted as being potent. Elves also demonstrate the power to heal in non-Middle-earth stories, as in *Smith of Wootton Major,* where Nokes, who has become fat, lazy, and sickly, is healed by the King of Faery (55–57).

RICHARD SCOTT NOKES

Further Reading

Cockayne, T.O. *Leechdoms, Wortcunning, and Starcraft of Early England.* London: Rolls Series 35, 1864.
Jolly, Karen. *Popular Religion in Late Saxon England: Elf Charms in Context.* Chapel Hill: University of North Carolina Press, 1996.
Tolkien, J.R.R. *Smith of Wootton Major & Farmer Giles of Ham.* New York: Del Rey, 1986.

See also **Elf–Shot;** *Leechbook* **and** *Herbarium;* **Lord of the Rings;** *Smith of Wootton Major*

HEATHENISM AND PAGANISM

In *The Return of the King*, when Gandalf finds Denethor in the process of trying to burn alive both himself and his son Faramir, the wizard says: "Only the heathen kings, under the domination of the Dark Power, did thus, slaying themselves in pride and despair, murdering their kin to ease their own death" (*RK*,V,vii,129). Tolkien's use of the word "heathen" here is curious, in that it carries with it religious connotations. Tom Shippey, for example, calls the adjective "in a way illogical," for in "Gandalf calling someone else a heathen" the wizard is implying "that he himself is not one"—that is, Gandalf adheres to an established religious belief (177). Though Tolkien viewed *The Lord of the Rings* as deeply religious and fundamentally Christian, he made an effort to "cut out" of it "practically all references to anything like 'religion,'" by which he meant religious practices as they are known in our world (*Letters*, 172). Some scholars have therefore supposed the use of the word "heathen" to be a mistake on Tolkien's part: an accidental usage the author must have overlooked in the revision. This leads to the question of how Tolkien used the word "heathen" and the related word "pagan" and what he thought of heathenism and paganism.

Though the Modern English "heathen" and "pagan" are closely related and sometimes used interchangeably, the words have distinct meanings. "Heathen" comes from OE *hæwen* and means one from the heath (hæw): that is, an uneducated rustic. (See *Beowulf*, lines 852, 986, etc). More specifically, a "heathen" is one who does not know about God, and thus when used in Christian cultures refers to anyone who is not a Christian. Although the OE *hæwen* was used as a translation of the Latin *paganus* (a "country dweller"), the Modern English "pagan" has the more narrow meaning of one who follows the old gods, that is, a polytheist. While a pagan is also a heathen, heathens are not necessarily pagans. Thus, Tolkien could use the words with distinct meanings and yet not be inconsistent when in "The Monsters and the Critics" he refers to "heathen imagination," heathen days, and "heathen ancestors" while describing the myths of "pagan English and Norse imagination" (*MC*, 22–23).

When Gandalf uses the adjective "heathen" to describe Denethor's actions, Tolkien may have had in mind its more literal, nonreligious, and certainly derogatory meaning: Gandalf was simply associating Denethor—who was proud to be the steward of the most literate culture of Men in Middle-earth at that time—with the uneducated traditions of the heath. Yet at the same time, the internal use of the word is consistent—the author would have known the religious connotation that the word held with his readers. Tolkien had a high view of many aspects of pagan Norse heroism and saw them as complementing Christian virtue at many levels. He thus defends the pagan imagination, especially in "The Monsters and the Critics." As Birzer summarizes, "For Tolkien, the *Beowulf* poet beautifully intertwined pagan virtues with Christian theology." And "the Christian should embrace and sanctify the most noble virtues to come out of the northern pagan mind" (35). At the same time, however, Tolkien saw paganism itself as ultimately hopeless and futile: the rejection of Christ that defines heathenism will lead, as in the case of Denethor, to pride, despair, and death.

MATTHEW DICKERSON

Further Reading

Birzer, Bradley. *J.R.R. Tolkien's Sanctifying Myth.* Wilmington, DE: ISI Books, 2002.
Dickerson, Matthew. *Following Gandalf: Epic Battles and Moral Victory in The Lord of the Rings.*
Shippey, Tom, *J.R.R. Tolkein: Author of the Century.* Boston, MA: Houghton Mifflin.

See also **Beowulf; "Beowulf: The Monsters and the Critics"; Denethor**

HEAVEN

The most incisive insights into Tolkien's understanding of Heaven are given in his important poem "Mythopoeia" and in his equally important short story "Leaf by Niggle." Apart from their undoubted literary merit, these two works serve as an exposition of Tolkien's philosophy of myth. Tolkien believed that human creativity was a reflection of Divine Creativity, the former being the image of the latter. Human imagination is God's image in us. Like God, we can create—or, more correctly and as Tolkien stressed, we can subcreate. God creates from Nothing by giving things existence; we subcreate by making new things from other things that already exist through the use of the imagination. In the conclusion of "Mythopoeia," Tolkien asserted his belief that this human creativity will be beatified in Heaven by its being made perfect. Souls in Heaven will still "renew/ from mirrored truth the likeness of the True."

> Salvation changes not, nor yet destroys,
> garden nor gardener, children nor their toys.

Our human creativity is not destroyed in Heaven but perfected, in the absence of evil, into the unfallen splendor that it was meant to be.

> In Paradise they look no more awry;
> and though they make anew, they make no lie.
> Be sure they still will make, not being dead,
> and poets shall have flames upon their head,
> and harps whereon their faultless fingers fall:
> there each shall choose for ever from the All.

This poetic vision of the triumph of True Art in Heaven was re-presented in "Leaf by Niggle," a story that is the nearest Tolkien ever came to writing a formal allegory. The character of Niggle, a thinly disguised allegory of Tolkien himself, has spent his life trying to paint a landscape but has only managed to render individual leaves to his perfectionist satisfaction. When Niggle dies, he stumbles across his imaginary unfinished tree in Heaven. Yet now it is Real. The fruits of his flawed imagination have been perfected and have become incarnate in Paradise. His art shares his crown of Glory.

The third place in which Tolkien's philosophy of myth finds heavenly expression is in the *Ainulindalë*, the Creation Myth at the beginning of *The Silmarillion*. In the Beginning, Eru, the One God, propounds themes of music to the angelic Ainur: "Of the theme that I have declared to you, I will now that ye make in harmony together a Great Music. And since I have kindled you with the Flame Imperishable, ye shall show forth your powers in adorning this theme, each with his own thoughts and devices, if he will. But I will sit and hearken, and be glad that through you great beauty has been wakened into song." God, in the Primal Heaven of his Creation, blesses his creatures with the twin gifts of Freedom and Creativity. As with the Alpha of the *Ainulindalë* before the birth of time, so with the Omega of Niggle's heavenly vision after death. In the beginning and in the end, among angels and mortals alike, the Creator is glorified in the beauty of Creation's creativity.

Whereas the essentially orthodox vision of Heaven described in "Mythopoeia," "Leaf by Niggle," and the *Ainulindalë* can be seen to be the fruits of Tolkien's Catholicism, the pseudo-heavens described elsewhere in his legendarium might appear to be less in harmony with his Christian beliefs. In fact, however, they emerge as being more harmonious with Christian orthodoxy than might perhaps be supposed. The halls of Mandos and the mystic West can be likened to the *limbus patrum*, the limbo of the fathers, which is the mystical place of waiting for all just souls who died before the coming of Christ. In Christian tradition, souls in the *limbus patrum* were in a state of happiness awaiting the Messianic Kingdom to be established upon Christ's Ascension into Heaven. Since Tolkien maintained that Middle-earth is our earth, not some strange planet in outerspace, and since the tales he tells occurred long before the Coming of Christ, the similarities between the description of the halls of Mandos and the mystic West with Christian concepts of the *limbus patrum* resonate with Tolkien's evident desire to conform his legendarium to his religious beliefs.

JOSEPH PEARCE

Further Reading

Birzer, Bradley J. *J.R.R. Tolkien's Sanctifying Myth*. Wilmington, DE: ISI Books, 2002.

Caldecott, Stratford. *Secret Fire: The Spiritual Vision of J.R.R. Tolkien*. London: Darton, Longman & Todd, 2003.

Pearce, Joseph, ed. *Tolkien: A Celebration*. London: HarperCollins, 1999.

———. *Tolkien: Man and Myth*. London: HarperCollins, 1998.

Purtill, Richard. *J.R.R. Tolkien: Myth, Morality and Religion*. San Francisco, CA: Harper & Row, 1984.

See also **Angels; Catholicism, Roman; Christ; Christianity; Fall of Man; Hell; Paradise; Redemption; Resurrection; Saints**

HELL

Hell, as it appears in Tolkien's work, is most noticeable in his description of Mordor. This description of Hell is very in line with Christian and Anglo-Saxon iconography and descriptions.

The traditional description of Hell in Christian mythology is a place of fire, ash, and suffering. Hell is a barren, desolate place from where no good comes. This depiction stems from Sumerian mythology, where the afterlife was described as a place of endless dust and parched clay. The same theme of barren desolation and fire is how Mordor is described. The name of Mordor, the center of Sauron's power in Middle-earth, is likely derived from "morthor," the Anglo-Saxon word for murder. While Tolkien maintained that "mor," meaning dark or black, derives wholly from Elvish, the linguistic coincidence is too interesting to let pass unmentioned.

In Christianity, the sin of murder would result in one being sent to Hell after death. In Norse mythology, Hell was called "Nelheim" and was a cold, mountainous place geographically very similar to Mordor. Frodo and Sam's quest to destroy the One Ring leads them to climb Mount Doom above the Plain of Gorgoroth, mountain terrain that is similar to that of the Norse concept of Hell.

Hell is also the home of devils. In Christian mythology, devils are angels who were corrupted by pride and waged war against God. When the rebellion in Heaven ended, the renegade angels were cast down from Heaven by God to burn in Hell. Similarly, the Orcs who inhabit Mordor were (at least in one explanation) originally Elves who had slain other Elves and then been corrupted by Sauron's power.

While Sauron is the Lord of Mordor, Satan is the Lord of Hell. Satan is always not a personally active force in the world in Christian mythology; he often operates through intermediaries. In Tolkien's work, Sauron is disembodied after the loss of the One Ring and his defeat by Isildur, and he must also work through intermediaries such as Saruman and Wormtongue.

Frodo and Sam travel to Mordor to cast the One Ring into the Cracks of Doom, since it cannot be destroyed by any mortal means. To destroy it, the One Ring must to be cast into the Hellfire from which it was forged. The Cracks of Doom match the Christian description of fire and ash. The "rivers of fire" and "rain of hot ash" are iconographic of Christian Hell.

Frodo and Sam are taken out of Mordor by Gandalf and Gwaihir of the eagles. This rescue, being plucked from the depths of Hell, is very similar to salvation as described in Christianity. Frodo and Sam travel to the deepest, darkest part of Hell and are saved by Gandalf, whom Tolkien, in one of his letters, describes as an angel. Gandalf is a servant of the Valar who were created by Eru, the One who created the world; so Gandalf's station, third removed from the creator figure of Middle-earth, puts him close to that of an angel.

The geographical and environmental similarities of Hell, as described in both Norse and Christian mythology, match up with Mordor. The corrupting influence that Hell shows on the devils and Orcs shows a correlation as well. Both dark lords must work through intermediaries. Gandalf's standing in the mythic hierarchy of Middle-earth parallels that of an angelic being. All these factors show that Hell in Tolkien's writing shares iconographical and geographical similarities to Christian and Norse Hell.

JOHN WALSH

HEROES AND HEROISM

Tolkien's approach to the heroic and heroism is not as straightforward as one might first assume. The literary influences on Tolkien and his use in particular of Germanic models might suggest that his heroes might be similar in many ways. This is true and false at the same time. In essence, Tolkien had the same problem and displays the same kind of problem that writers of Old English and Old Norse literature had once they became Christianized: how to reconcile Christian ethos with the warrior ethos.

Frodo and Bilbo provide the clearest contrast in this regard. Bilbo in many ways seems to be a hero modeled on the Germanic mold. Bilbo is more or less shamed into undertaking his adventure. As he is entertaining his surprise guests, thirteen Dwarves

and a wizard, he overhears one of the Dwarves remark, "As soon as I clapped my eyes on the little fellow bobbing and puffing on the mat, I had my doubts." Bilbo's reaction to this statement is to begin to feel "really fierce." He undertakes the challenge and journey because his reputation has been questioned. Further, he is promised a one-fourteenth share of the dragon's hoard should the quest be successful. Bilbo's acceptance of the terms is taken as a commitment by the Dwarves, Gandalf, and Bilbo, not unlike a vow in the Germanic ethos. The Dwarves themselves seek revenge on the monster for burning and destroying their home, and fame and wealth if they succeed.

This is precisely parallel to *Beowulf*, the *Battle of Maldon,* and other Germanic works. *Beowulf* is described in the last line of the poem as *lofgeornost,* most eager for fame. Part of the motivating factor for the hero is to earn fame and reward. In his initial speech before Hrothgar, Beowulf even states that should he be victorious his deeds will increase the fame of his lord Hygelac. After he defeats Grendel, Beowulf is rewarded with costly gifts; and again after he defeats Grendel's mother he is again given a huge reward. In the third episode, part of the motivation is revenge on the dragon for its depredations on Beowulf's people, but part of the motivation is also the dragon's hoard.

The Hobbit is in some important ways both a recasting of *Beowulf* but also a critique. It is a critique in the sense that Bilbo is not royal or a king as Beowulf is. The kings and rulers in this book do not behave heroically. Thorin is less than heroic until the end, stubbornly even refusing to aid those of Laketown who lost everything to the dragon but also killed Smaug for the Dwarves. The Elven king imprisons the Dwarves. The men of Laketown also help the Dwarves while at the same time plotting to relieve the Dwarves of their treasure when the time came. The only character to have been in a "war of words" is Bilbo. The only character who displays skill is Bilbo. It is this "grocer"-looking Hobbit who displays heroic qualities.

Frodo, though Bilbo's adopted heir and inheritor of his treasure, is the opposite sort of hero. He does not undertake the quest for promised reward nor for reputation. He undertakes the journey for love. At first it is love of the Shire, later love of all good things. Sam, Merry, and Pippin accompany him also out of love, mostly love for Frodo and by extension for Bilbo. Merry becomes a warrior of Rohan for love of Theoden. Frodo does little on the journey, except the one thing that in this novel appears to be the most important. That is, the journey for Frodo is more an interior, spiritual battle resisting the power of the

Ring in contrast to the heroic ethos seemingly espoused by the other characters. The heroism of the Hobbits is motivated by self-sacrifice for those they love. This is the inverse of the Germanic heroic ethos.

Tolkien's clearest critique of the heroic ethos is exemplified by Boromir in *The Lord of the Rings*. His brother describes Boromir as one excellent in arms, desirous of glory (perturbed that the Stewards of Gondor were not kings; "ever anxious for the victory of Minas Tirith and his own glory therein."), heroic in every aspect. It is in fact Boromir's desire for the victory of Minas Tirith and his own glory therein that motivates his own grasp for the ring: the heroic motivations of fame, reward, and revenge (in this case on Sauron). In the context of the story, however, this attempt by Boromir is seen as a great evil, the result of the ring's temptation and its twisting of motivations. Boromir is redeemed in death, a death selflessly protecting the weak, and perhaps most importantly, recognizing his error. In these final acts, Boromir achieves heroism that evaded him before, and he earns both a heroic burial at the hands of his companions and a hagiographical scene later as his brother comes upon his body shining with an otherworldly light as it floats out to sea, a scene reminiscent of the much–praised Scyld Scefing in *Beowulf* and Arthur's death scene in Malory.

Aragorn is a contrast to Boromir. Aragorn has much to gain and much to lose in the War of the Ring. But it is not concern for fame, wealth, or revenge that motivates him. His motivations are choices between good and evil, love and loss. Before we meet him in the story, he chooses to oppose Sauron. He journeys in his youth to lands bordering on Mordor, earns fame, and as his fame reaches a zenith first in Rohan then in Gondor and he is to be richly rewarded for his prowess, he gives it all up, eschewing fame, riches, and even the chance to rule, and disappears. When the reader encounters him in *The Lord of the Rings*, he is keeping the few inhabitants of the North safe from the Enemy and other evils, only to receive ridicule, rejection, and pain from those whom he protects. The reader finds out much later that Aragorn undertakes the quest in part for these selfless reasons, but also to possibly win a kingdom, and by winning his kingdom, to win the hand of the woman he loves. Fame, wealth, and revenge do not form a part of Aragorn's motivational paradigm. As such, the Ring poses no temptation to Aragorn beyond what is expected, and there is no temptation scene as there is for Frodo, Sam, Gandalf, Galadriel, and Boromir. Aragorn rejects certain fame and pursues Merry and Pippin in the hopes of rescue; he rejects fame again and says that Gandalf should lead after

the battle of the Pelennor. He uses his name and lineage to attract Sauron's attention so that Frodo and Sam may have opportunity to complete their task, in the episode of the palantír and again later as the Captains of the West march on Mordor. Thus, while Aragorn is a gifted warrior, deserving of fame, glory, wealth, and a noble wife, he rejects all these and undertakes the quest for love, not fame. In the end, he receives fame, glory, wealth, and the most noble of wives.

Gimli is perhaps the best example of the Germanic hero, providing a foil to Boromir's negative portrayal. But even here certain key elements are missing. While Gimli has prowess in battle, is passionate, ready to right wrongs, he is not motivated by revenge, fame, wealth, or glory. Nor is he motivated by love. His motivation chiefly is loyalty, one of the positive concepts in the Germanic hero from Tolkien's point of view. When faced with a situation of gift-giving by Galadriel, Gimli opts for strands of her hair rather than a more costly gift.

In the same vein, one could point to *Farmer Giles of Ham*. Giles is a reluctant hero who, while the danger is past, enjoys the prestige, but does not undertake any of his adventures with giants, dragons, and kings willingly, certainly not for fame, glory, wealth, or revenge. Giles shoots the giant to save his farm from being trod on. Giles searches for the dragon because he is pressured by the members of his community. Second, he undertakes these adventures through guilt, and all his excuses not to go are countered by the parson and/or the miller. He goes in search of the dragon the second time because the king orders him to. And third, when he defies the king at the bridge in a sort of class warfare, he has developed ideas. It is only here that he begins to think like the hero. Here too, then, Tolkien seems to be engaging in a deliberate reworking of the Germanic ethos into one more akin to what the Germanic peoples were after when they became Christian.

The great problem for Anglo-Saxons and other Germanic peoples was how to accept their Germanic past while maintaining their new faith. One example of this is the well-known poem *Dream of the Rood*. Here, the hero is Christ, who, like a warrior, ascends the cross but, unlike the typical warrior, to battle against sin. He is described in heroic terms doing exactly the opposite of what a hero might do: accepting death without a fight. The poem *Christ and Satan* also depicts Christ's harrowing of hell in heroic terms while inverting those terms to apply to the Christian ethos. One could also point to the other poems of the Junius manuscript that illustrate the same process. The merger, then, of the Germanic hero exemplified in *Beowulf* or the Icelandic sagas and eddas with the Christian hero exemplified in the gospels produces a hero who, while still heroic and recognizable in these contexts, in key places and emphasis is transformed into a Christian hero as well. In medieval literature, this is exemplified by Arthur, as one instance, and in modern literature by Tolkien's heroes in *The Lord of the Rings*.

L.J. SWAIN

Further Reading

Bradley, S.A.J. *Anglo-Saxon Poetry. An Anthology of Old English Poems in Prose Translation*. London: Dent, 1982.
Clark, George. "Tolkien and the True Hero." In *Tolkien and His Literary Resonances*, edited by Clark, George and Daniel Timmons. Westport, CT: Greenwood Press, 2000.
Dronke, Ursula. *The Poetic Edda: The Heroic Poems*. Oxford: Clarendon, 1969.
Klaeber, Fr. *Beowulf*. 3rd. ed. Boston: D.C. Heath, 1950.
Liuzza, R.M. *Beowulf: A New Verse Translation*. Orchard Park, NY: Broadview Press, 2000.
Shippey, Tom. *The Road to Middle-earth*. Hammersmith: Grafton, 1992.

See also **Anglo-Saxon Poetry; Aragorn; Bilbo; Boromir; Dwarves;** *Farmer Giles of Ham;* **Frodo; Gimli;** *Hobbit; Lord of the Rings;* **Old Norse; Thorin**

HIERARCHY

A defining feature of Tolkien's invented universe is its complex hierarchical structure modeled upon that of Christian thought. All beings occupy an appointed place in a vast continuum ranging from the Eru Ilúvatar, the Creator, down to the lowest level in a framework resembling the medieval and Renaissance scheme of cosmic classification known as the "Great Chain of Being" (Lovejoy). Rose A. Zimbardo characterizes Tolkien's chain of being as a *concors discordia* of different creatures bound together into a unity (Zimbardo). The forces of evil seek to oppose this hierarchy by setting up their own corrupt chain of being. Thus, Tolkien's legendarium provides catalogs of interrelated and opposing hierarchies that form the basis for his conception of universal harmony (or disharmony) and social order.

The many versions of the "Silmarillion" legends depict the vast array of heavenly and earthly hierarchies designed to administer and populate Arda. Eru stands at the top followed by the Ainur, "the offspring of his thought" (*S*, 15). The Valaquenta illustrates how the Ainur descend into Arda and fall into

ranks similar to the Seraphim, Cherubim, and others in the Judeo-Christian angelic hierarchy. The fourteen Valar, "The Powers," are the mightiest of the Ainur with the eight Aratar, "The Exalted," occupying the highest echelon. Manwë, "the first of all Kings" (*S*, 26), functions as divinely ordained ruler of the creation. The numerous Maiar serving under them are "of the same order as the Valar but of less degree" (*S*, 30). *The Book of Lost Tales* enumerates a host of other lesser Ainur/spirits that were "born before the world and are older than it" (*Lost Tales I*, 66), but later versions of the "Silmarillon" legends do not name those orders.

Melkor or Morgoth, Manwë's "brother" and most powerful of the Ainur, heads the negative divine hierarchy that stands in opposition to the orders of the Valar and Maiar. Sauron, who later becomes the Dark Lord in the Second and Third Ages, functions as his chief Maia servant, followed by the Balrogs, the other fallen Maiar. Only Ungoliant, the mysterious Ainu-like being who "descended from the darkness about Arda" (*S*, 73), remains an elusive figure in this hierarchy, unclassifiable like her good counterpart, the "oldest and fatherless" Tom Bombadil in *The Lord of the Rings* (*FR*, I, ii, 278).

The Children of Ilúvatar also belong to hierarchically ordered ranks with many subdivisions. The Eldar or Elves are divided into the Caliquendi ("Light Elves") of Valinor—the Vanyar, Noldor, and Teleri—and the lower Moriquendi ("Dark Elves")—the Úmanyar (the Sindar and the Nandor) and the Avari. The various clans of the Eldar have their own hierarchical ruling structures with Ingwë of the Vanyar as the High King in Valinor, and the other kings and princes arrayed under him. In Beleriand, the title of High King of the Noldor is passed from one of the descendents of Finwë to another during the wars with Morgoth. Among the Atani or Men, there are the three houses of the Edain, each with their own ruling hierarchy, and the other lesser Men who come under Morgoth's influence. Aulë's Dwarves were later incorporated into Ilúvatar's design, though their place in the hierarchy is not clear. Orcs form the negative equivalents of the Children of Ilúvatar. Like dragons, Trolls, and other fell beasts Morgoth bred, Orcs are, as Treebeard later explains, but "counterfeits" or perverse imitations made by the Enemy in mockery of creation (*TT*, III, iv, 89).

The Lord of the Rings illustrates how the disparate ranks of beings can unite to form a "chain of love" to oppose the "chain of sin" represented by Sauron and his followers, Morgoth's progeny (Chance, 151). The free peoples of Middle-earth, ranging from the Istari, highest and most ethereal in the chain, to the immortal Elves to mortals and the earth-bound Dwarves, make up a single, well-ordered system, and each tier has its dark counterpart in forces of the Enemy (Sauron or Saruman versus Gandalf, the Nazgûl versus the Dúnedain, Trolls versus Ents, etc.). The bond of the Fellowship, especially that of Legolas and Gimli, demonstrates how all levels can cooperate, the highest to the lowest each playing a role in the workings of providence within Tolkien's universe.

The peoples of Middle-earth during the Third Age are themselves ordered, both in terms of their place within the ranks of their kind and their place within the related social and governing hierarchies, but they are suffering a decline from their heights in the legendary past. The High Elves have largely departed Middle-earth by the end of the Third Age, and no High King followed Gil-galad, but Elven realms still exist in the Third Age ruled by lords of great lineage (Noldor, Sindar, or Teleri) such as Celeborn with Galadriel, Elrond, Círdan, and Thranduil. Men, as Faramir explains to Frodo and Sam, formerly fell into three distinct categories: the Dúnedain, "High or Men of the West"; the "Middle Peoples, Men of the Twilight," such as the Rohirrim; and finally "the Wild, the Men of Darkness" (*TT*, IV, v, 387). Elendil, with his sons Isildur and Anárion, then headed the social pyramid of the exiled Dúnedain in Arnor and Gondor following the destruction of Númenor. Yet by the time of War of the Ring the throne is empty and the Men of the West are waning as they mix with lesser Men, becoming more like the Middle Peoples. The princedoms and fiefdoms of Gondor such as Dol Amroth and Lossarnach have their own lords and ruling structures, but still pay homage to the absent king by showing their loyalty to the Stewards. Indeed, respecting the boundaries among the branches of the peoples and the authority of their rulers is still essential, even in that diminished age. Théoden, for instance, chides Saruman for presuming to extend his rule over "me and mine" (*TT*, III, x, 185)—the king and his proper subjects—though he is but a lesser heir of Eorl and his other great forefathers.

The hobbits, the people forgotten even in the Ents' lists, mirror the divisions in the "Big Folk" though they are "Halflings between kingly nature and animal nature" (Zimbardo, "Moral," 102). Hobbits fall into three branches, with the Fallohides functioning as the de facto rulers over the more numerous but lowlier Harfoots and Stoors. Although the Shire lacks a central authority to govern it as a whole apart from the mayor of Michel Delving, the thain of the Shire originally served as the king's surrogate and the military leader, thereby connecting the hobbit hierarchy to that of Men. The hobbits have their own intricate scheme of social, familial, and other distinctions in their culture, and all play their appointed parts in that system, from the Fallohidish great families (the Tooks and Brandybucks) to the wealthy "gentle-hobbits" (the Bagginses) to the laboring Harfoots and Stoors such as the Gamgees and other rustic hobbits. This interaction among the various ranks of hobbits, from the gardener Samwise to the well-born Frodo, gives their culture stability even as other peoples decline.

The transition from the Third Age to the Fourth witnesses a shift in the hierarchical structure of Middle-earth as Elves give way to Men at the top tier. The last of the High Elves sail to the Undying Lands at the end of the Third Age, leaving only the fading Silvan Elves behind. The Dúnedain, even at their low ebb, thus become the dominant race remaining in the mortal lands. The return of the king and the defeat of Sauron restore the rightful position of Númenóreans in the order of things, even if the line cannot regain all of its former glory. The great chain of being thereby persists into the new age, albeit in a diminished state.

The hierarchies in the legendarium reflect Tolkien's overall attitude toward world order and especially social station. An opponent of democracy and advocate of an "unconstitutional" monarchy, Tolkien believed that all persons were born into a specific "estate" from the monarch down to the common laborer and should respect their role in that system and the rule of their superiors. Humphrey Carpenter quotes Tolkien on the deference one should show to those higher in rank: "Touching your cap to the Squire may be damn bad for the Squire but it's damn good for you" (Carpenter). Thus, Tolkien conceived of hierarchy as both a basis for political practice and a fundamental cosmic organizing principle in this world as well as in his invented universe.

David D. Oberhelman

Further Reading

Carpenter, Humphrey. *Tolkien: A Biography*. Boston, MA: Houghton Mifflin, 1977.

Chance, Jane. *Tolkien's Art: A Mythology for England*. Rev. ed. Lexington, KY: University Press of Kentucky, 2001.

Lovejoy, Arthur O. *The Great Chain of Being: A Study of the History of an Idea*. Cambridge, MA: Harvard University Press, 1936.

Otty, Nick. "A Structuralist's Guide to Middle-earth." In *J.R.R. Tolkien: This Far Land*, edited by Robert Giddings, 154–178. London: Vision Press, Ltd., 1983.

Zimbardo, Rose A. "Moral Vision in The Lord of the Rings." In *Tolkien and the Critics: Essays of J.R.R. Tolkien's The Lord of the Rings*, edited by Neil D. Isaacs and Rose A. Zimbardo, 100–8. Notre Dame, IN: University of Notre Dame Press, 1968.

See also **Angels; Class in Tolkien's Works; Elves, Kindreds and Migrations of; Kingship; Race and Ethnicity in Tolkien's Works; Theological and Moral Approaches in Tolkien's Works**

HISTORY OF MIDDLE-EARTH: OVERVIEW

The History of Middle-earth is a longitudinal study of the development and elaboration of Tolkien's legendarium through his transcribed manuscripts, with textual commentary by the editor, Christopher Tolkien. It consists of twelve volumes, which, with publication dates, are

  1–2: *The Book of Lost Tales* (2 vols., 1983–84)
    3: *The Lays of Beleriand* (1985)
    4: *The Shaping of Middle-earth* (1986)
    5: *The Lost Road and Other Writings* (1987)
    6: *The Return of the Shadow* (1988)
    7: *The Treason of Isengard* (1989)
    8: *The War of the Ring* (1990)
    9: *Sauron Defeated* (1992)
  10: *Morgoth's Ring* (1993)
  11: *The War of the Jewels* (1994)
  12: *The Peoples of Middle-earth* (1996)

Each of these volumes has a separate entry in this encyclopedia. The purpose of this entry is to provide an overview of the whole.

The term "History" in the title *The History of Middle-earth* has two applications: the internal history of the secondary world of the legendarium, from its creation through to the War of the Ring and a little after; and the external history of the author writing about it. The published volumes are organized primarily by the external history, and within individual "phases" by the internal history. The earliest materials in the *History* are ancillary poems attached to *The Book of Lost Tales* dated 1914; the main text of the *Lost Tales* was begun 1916–17. The last works are primarily philosophical and linguistic notes datable to 1972, published in *The Peoples of Middle-earth.*

The History of Middle-earth serves several purposes that evolved in the course of its editor's research and compilation of the volumes. Primarily, it is a history of the more than sixty years' creative work that J.R.R. Tolkien put into his legendarium. By comparing successive drafts and retellings of a story, readers may follow the evolution of Tolkien's literary style and creative approaches. The characteristic strategies he used to develop his stories become clear: enlarging and expanding chronology and geography, changing the nature and significance of events

and characters while leaving surface characteristics unchanged. This presents "The Silmarillion" in its true form of multiple, often contradictory versions in different styles and levels of detail, rather than as a single finished text. This shows that the deep background of history and mythology visible in *The Lord of the Rings* has a real existence. Also, the series presents for the readers' enjoyment various works that, for reasons of stylistic incongruity or internal inconsistency, could not have been incorporated into *The Silmarillion*. Few of the texts presented in the series were ever actually completed: Tolkien would work on some in multiple drafts for long periods but would usually move on to new approaches or other projects, sometimes returning to the older material at a later time, usually reworking it from the beginning rather than attempting to complete older unfinished texts.

At different stages in his creative career, Tolkien concentrated on different portions of the history of his legendarium. When he wrote disparate materials during the same time period, *The History of Middle-earth* places related materials together. The series begins with *The Book of Lost Tales*, a cycle of myths telling the history that would later evolve into "The Silmarillion" as tales recounted within a frame story of a wandering traveler visiting the Elven isle of Tol Eressëa. After not quite finishing *The Book of Lost Tales* about 1920, Tolkien decided to retell some of the major stories of the cycle in verse. During the early 1920s, he composed *The Lay of the Children of Húrin*, and in the later 1920s he composed *The Lay of Leithian*: these two incomplete poems, along with a critique of the later poem written in 1930 by C.S. Lewis make up the greater part of the volume *The Lays of Beleriand*. In the early 1950s, Tolkien began a rewriting of *The Lay of Leithian,* which is also included in this volume.

Meanwhile, in 1926 Tolkien prepared a "sketch of the mythology" as background for a friend reading the earlier lay. Rewritings and rapid expansions of this over the next twelve years produced a series of chronological annals and various texts of a narrative history eventually titled *Quenta Silmarillion*. The narratives followed the general course of *The Book of Lost Tales* but omitted the frame story and greatly changed the tone, literary style, and the details and overall significances of characters and plot events. To these he also attached some ancillary writings, such as the cosmological *Ambarkanta* and a number of linguistic texts including a large dictionary of Elvish etymologies. These works, which together form the earlier texts of what may be referred to collectively as "The Silmarillion," are published in the volumes *The Shaping of Middle-earth* and *The Lost Road and Other Writings.*

The Lost Road itself, the title story of volume 5, arose from an inspiration for an Atlantean myth that Tolkien decided to attach as a sequel to the developing "Silmarillion" legendarium. In 1936–37, he wrote both *The Fall of Númenor*, a brief account of a kingdom of Men postdating the events of the *Quenta* and Annals, and the sketchy beginnings of a novel, *The Lost Road*, depicting mythic or spiritual parallels and relationships between modern men and the men of lost Númenor.

After 1938, Tolkien set aside both existing parts of the legendarium to take up seriously his publisher's suggestion to write a sequel to his children's novel *The Hobbit*. This book, which takes place in an undated distant past, contains casual references to events of the legendarium as having taken place further in its past. In writing the sequel, titled *The Lord of the Rings*, Tolkien clarified and expanded the relationship between *The Hobbit* and the legendarium. Volumes 6–8 and part of volume 9 of *The History of Middle-earth* recount its composition over the years 1937–48, and the four volumes bear the subseries title *The History of The Lord of the Rings*.

Tolkien wrote four "phases," each markedly expanding on and enriching its predecessor, of the opening chapters of *The Lord of the Rings* during 1937–39 before proceeding much further in the story. Texts and commentaries on the first three phases comprise *The Return of the Shadow*; the fourth, along with drafts going as far as Book III of the finished work and written 1939–42, are *The Treason of Isengard*. *The War of the Ring* contains drafts of Books III–V written, 1942–46. Part one of *Sauron Defeated, The End of the Third Age* (also published separately), contains drafts of Book VI written 1946–48. By the time he completed *The Lord of the Rings*, Tolkien had identified it and *The Hobbit* as taking place during a Third Age, after the Elder Days (the pre–Sun Ages and the First Age of the Sun) of "The Silmarillion," and a Second Age including the matter of Númenor.

In 1945–46, before completing *The Lord of the Rings*, Tolkien returned to the matter of Númenor, writing the beginning of a novel, *The Notion Club Papers*, that takes up the ideas of *The Lost Road* with new characters and an evolved conception, with a supplementary text, *The Drowning of Anadûnê*, as a distorted Mannish legend of the fall of Númenor. Texts of these comprise the remainder of the volume *Sauron Defeated*.

After finishing the draft of *The Lord of the Rings* in 1948, Tolkien took up again the Elder Days material. Texts written between then and about 1960 comprise volumes 10–11 of *The History of Middle-earth*, bearing the subseries title *The Later Silmarillion*. These are subdivided not by date of composition but by the portion of the story that they relate to: *Morgoth's Ring* is subtitled *The Legends of Aman*, and *The War of the Jewels* is subtitled *The Legends of Beleriand*. These volumes include recommenced versions of the Annals and the *Quenta Silmarillion*, omitting parts of the latter copied nearly verbatim into the volume *The Silmarillion*. They also include a number of ancillary historical and linguistic texts, as well as the section of *Morgoth's Ring* titled "Myths Transformed," an attempt by the author at a thorough reimagination of the nature and purpose of his legendarium.

The greater part of the volume *The Peoples of Middle-earth* consists of drafts of the prologue and appendices to *The Lord of the Rings*, consideration of which had been omitted from the subseries *The History of The Lord of the Rings*. These date from early in the work's conception in 1938 to just before publication of the third volume in 1955. The volume also includes ancillary writings (historical, linguistic, and philosophical) dating from the 1950s or later that are not specifically attached to the Elder Days and the beginnings of two stories too fragmentary to have been included in *Unfinished Tales*.

Christopher Tolkien's indexes to the twelve volumes have been combined into a single alphabetical arrangement by Helen Armstrong and published as *The History of Middle-earth Index* (2002).

DAVID BRATMAN

See also **Book of Lost Tales I; Book of Lost Tales II; Lays of Beleriand, The; Lost Road, The; Morgoth's Ring; Peoples of Middle-earth; Publications, Posthumous; Return of the Shadow; Sauron Defeated; Shaping of Middle-earth; Tolkien, Christopher;** *Treason of Isengard;* **War of the Ring; War of the Jewels, The**

HISTORY, ANGLO-SAXON

As a philologist and a professor of Anglo-Saxon, Tolkien studied the development of Old English, the language of the Anglo-Saxon people. His academic training enabled him to investigate the historical traces in Anglo-Saxon place names and personal names and to analyze and edit documents from the Anglo-Saxon era. Tolkien's scholarship includes essays and lectures on the Old English epic *Beowulf*, some of which are published in *Beowulf and the Critics* and *Finn and Hengest*, in which Tolkien deals with historical questions about the Germanic tribes on the continent before the Anglo-Saxon settlement. His commentary on *The Battle of Maldon*, a poem commemorating the Anglo-Saxons who died fighting a Viking invasion in 991, was published in the form of a verse drama, with notes, entitled "The Homecoming of Beorhtnoth

Beorhthelm's Son." Here, as in his work on *Beowulf,* Tolkien attempts to understand the perspective of a Christian Anglo-Saxon poet illustrating a pre-Christian heroic ethos. In such scholarly publications, Tolkien was expected to advance knowledge of Anglo-Saxon history based on linguistic evidence. In his fiction, Tolkien engaged in a freer and more imaginative reconstruction of Anglo-Saxon history.

One event in Anglo-Saxon history that recurs prominently in both Tolkien's scholarship and his fiction is the first settlement of Germanic invaders in Britain. According to the eighth-century historian Bede, the brothers Hengest and Horsa arrived in 449 leading three tribes, the Angles, Saxons, and Jutes, who eventually displaced or assimilated the native Britons. After studying the appearance of Hengest in various documents and place names, Tolkien accepted the historical probability of this account (*Finn and Hengest,* 63–72). The Anglo-Saxons, as the various tribes are known today, were illiterate but presumably brought with them a thriving oral poetic tradition; it is likely that a story such as *Beowulf* could have belonged to their store of tales. Christian missionaries in the sixth century gradually introduced literacy to the Anglo-Saxons, who were soon producing manuscripts written in Latin and Old English. Old English texts that Tolkien studied and that influenced his fiction, such as *Beowulf,* "The Battle of Maldon," "Christ," "The Wanderer," and "The Seafarer," were written down in this period, many in the ninth and tenth centuries. Tolkien was an expert in all forms of Old English, but he felt an affinity with the dialect of the Anglo-Saxon kingdom of Mercia in the Midlands, his English home; as Tolkien states repeatedly in his letters, he felt he was a West-midlander "by blood" and most at home in that dialect (*Letters,* 213, 218). The conventional end point of the Anglo-Saxon period, the Norman Conquest in 1066, introduced a French influence that would eventually transform the Old English language; Tolkien made known his dislike of French (*Letters,* 288).

Hobbits and the Rohirrim

Echoes of Anglo-Saxon history appear throughout *The Lord of the Rings,* but some of the more prominent examples occur in descriptions of the hobbits and the Rohirrim. Paralleling the Anglo-Saxon migration to England, three branches of hobbits, the Harfoots, Stoors, and Fallohides, crossed the Brandywine River under the leadership of the brothers Marcho and Blanco to begin the settlement of the

Shire. Tolkien makes the correspondence a linguistic one as well: just as Hengest and Horsa are two names meaning "stallion" and "horse," so too Marcho and Blanco are derived from Old English words for "horse" and "white horse" (Shippey, *Road,* 102). Shippey also compares the places of origin of the hobbits and the Anglo-Saxons: "they come from somewhere else, indeed from the Angle (in Europe between Flensburg Fjord and the Schlei, in Middle-earth between Hoarwell and Loudwater)," and even Shire place names, such as Nobottle and Buckland, derive from Old English and refer to real Oxfordshire places, granting Middle-earth an "air of solidity" (Shippey, *Road,* 102–3). The hobbits' use of a word like "mathom," Old English for "treasure," not only reinforces the Anglo-Saxon connection but also explains their affiliation with the world of humans in terms of a linguistic connection to the Rohirrim.

In *The Lord of the Rings,* it is the Rohirrim who have Old English names, who speak Old English, and who even declaim poetry in the Old English alliterative style. Shippey remarks that, except for the fact that Anglo-Saxon culture did not revolve around horses, "the Riders of Rohan resemble the Anglo-Saxons down to minute details" (Shippey, *Road,* 117). Names such as Théoden and Eorl are Old English common nouns for "prince, king" and a "man of high rank" (Tinkler, 165–66), denoting important positions in Anglo-Saxon society. As Shippey points out, the Riders of Rohan seem to belong in the Anglo-Saxon kingdom of Mercia, home of Tolkien's Birmingham and Oxford; even their Old English dialect is Mercian (Shippey, *Road,* 123).

The Anglo-Saxon epic poem *Beowulf* helps to shape Tolkien's conception of the Rohirrim, especially in "The King of the Golden Hall" chapter in *TT,* which parallels certain scenes in the epic (Shippey, *Road,* 124–26). What is not as evident, however, is the way in which Tolkien's historical work on the poem plays into his fictional choices. For example, Michael Drout outlines one complex scholarly argument about the identity of Beowulf's Swedish tribe, the Geats. Some scholars postulated that the Geats were actually the historical Goths, thus making Beowulf one of the people who were believed to have been ancestors of the Anglo-Saxons. Although Tolkien translated the "Geats" in *Beowulf* as "Goths" at one point, he seems to have dropped the connection in his later academic work, as did most scholars. However, Tolkien did give the Rohirrim, his Middle-earth version of the Anglo-Saxons, Gothic ancestors (*RK,* Appendix A, 326–27, 344–46). The connection between the Rohirrim/Anglo-Saxons and the Goths was "pseudohistory," and Tolkien knew it, according to Drout, who argues that Tolkien's claim that the Rohirrim were not the Anglo-Saxons was made only to avoid scholarly scrutiny of a connection that could not be supported historically (*RK,* Appendix F, 414). The fictional connection, however, did satisfy "the synthesizing impulse of myth" by connecting the Anglo-Saxons to the historical Goths, who were renowned as horse people and who spoke Gothic, the oldest recorded Germanic language and one of Tolkien's favorites (Drout, 236–39).

Tolkien did compare the Rohirrim and the Anglo-Saxons in one respect: they both ruled lands that once belonged to more advanced civilizations (*RK,* Appendix F, 414). The relationship between the people of Rohan and Gondor is reminiscent of the Anglo-Saxons and the Romans, who occupied Britain between 43 and 410 CE. *The Anglo-Saxon Chronicle* attempts to record this pre–migration history as well as contemporary events; Tolkien's Appendix B, "The Tale of Years," adopts the same annalistic form and purpose in outlining significant events in Middle-earth. In fact, Tolkien even might have come across the name Éomer in the *Chronicle,* where it is noted twice (Hammond and Scull, 367–68).

the historical Viking and Norman invasions of England (*Lost Tales II,* 302, 323). In any of these permutations, the Eriol/Ælfwine character serves to connect Tolkien's mythology with Anglo-Saxon history.

Ælfwine later reappears in "The Lost Road" and then "The Notion Club Papers," two unfinished stories from the 1930s and 1940s in which Tolkien experiments with ideas about time travel. Here, the historical connections are more complex, extending into the future and looking back into a mythical and historical past. The recapitulation of various episodes of English history and myth, transmitted through ancestral memories, would have provided a "psychohistory," according to Flieger (*Interrupted,* 102–3), in which Ælfwine of England is a central, mediating character (Flieger, "Do," *Question,* and "Footsteps").

Reconstructing Anglo-Saxon history was part of Tolkien's job as a philologist, and that history formed an integral part of his imaginative conception of Middle-earth. What Tolkien did was to "create a mythology and a pseudohistory that had an interface with the actual history of England"; this interweaving of history, legend, and literature is how "the stories become mythology" (Drout, 241).

ANNA SMOL

Eriol/Ælfwine

Very early in Tolkien's conception of his legendarium, he looked to Anglo-Saxon history as a bridge between historical and mythological worlds. In "The Cottage of Lost Play," Tolkien introduces the Eriol story as a narrative framework for further tales. Christopher Tolkien remarks that one of Eriol's names, Angol, "refers to the ancient homeland of the 'English' before their migration across the North Sea to Britain" (*Lost Tales I,* 24). Tolkien makes Eriol the son of the mythical Eoh (Old English for "horse") and the father of the historical Hengest and Horsa. Eriol also fathers Heorrenda, a legendary poet from the Old English poem "Deor," but also a name that Tolkien sometimes used for the anonymous *Beowulf* poet (*Lost Tales I,* 22–25; *Lost Tales II,* 323). Tolkien locates Eriol's sons in the Midlands: Hengest in Warwick (which is Kortirion in Tolkien's invented etymology), Horsa in Oxford (or Taruithorn), and Heorrenda in the Staffordshire village, Great Haywood (Tavrobel) (*Lost Tales II,* 291–93). The role of the Eriol character is eventually taken up in other drafts by Ælfwine ("Elf-friend" in Old English, also one of the loyal warriors named in "The Battle of Maldon" and "Homecoming"). In some of his notes, Tolkien places Ælfwine in the eleventh-century Anglo-Saxon kingdom of Wessex, and invasions of his homeland reflect

Further Reading

Drout, Michael. "A Mythology for Anglo-Saxon England," in *Tolkien and the Invention of Myth: A Reader,* edited by Jane Chance, 229–47. Lexington, KY: University Press of Kentucky, 2004.

Flieger, Verlyn. *Interrupted Music: The Making of Tolkien's Mythology.* Kent, Ohio, and London: Kent State University Press, 2005.

———."Do the Atlantis Story and Abandon Eriol-Saga." *Tolkien Studies* 1 (2004): 43–68.

———. *A Question of Time: J.R.R. Tolkien's Road to Faërie.* Kent, Ohio. and London: Kent State University Press, 2001.

———. "The Footsteps of Ælfwine." In *Tolkien's Legendarium: Essays on The History of Middle-earth,* edited by Verlyn Flieger and Carl F. Hostetter, 183–98. Contributions to the Study of Science Fiction and Fantasy 86. Westport, CT, and London: Greenwood Press, 2000.

Hammond, Wayne G., and Christina Scull. *The Lord of the Rings: A Reader's Companion.* London: HarperCollins, 2005.

Shippey, Tom. *The Road to Middle-earth: Revised and Expanded Edition.* Boston and New York: Houghton Mifflin, 2003.

Tinkler, John. "Old English in Rohan." In *Tolkien and the Critics: Essays on J.R.R. Tolkien's "The Lord of the Rings,"* edited by Neil D. Isaacs and Rose A. Zimbardo, 164–69. Notre Dame and London: University of Notre Dame Press, 1968.

Tolkien, J.R.R. "Cirion and Eorl and the Friendship of Gondor and Rohan." In *UT,* 373–414.

———. "The Cottage of Lost Play." In *Lost Tales I,* 13–44.

———. *Finn and Hengest: The Fragment and the Episode.* edited by Alan Bliss. London: Allen & Unwin, 1982.

————. "The History of Eriol or Ælfwine and the End of the Tales" and "Ælfwine of England." In *Lost Tales II*, 278–334.

————. "The Homecoming of Beorhtnoth Beorhthelm's Son." In *TL*, 119–50.

————. "The Lost Road." In *Lost Road*, 36–104.

————. "The Notion Club Papers." In *Sauron*, 145–327.

See also **Ælfwine; Alliterative Verse by Tolkien; Augustine of Canterbury;** *Battle of Maldon;* **Bede;** *Beowulf and the Critics;* **"Beowulf: The Monsters and the Critics";** *Beowulf:* **Tolkien's Scholarship;** *Beowulf:* **Translations by Tolkien;** *Book of Lost Tales I; Book of Lost Tales II;* *Christ:* **"Advent Lyrics";** *Deor;* **Epic Poetry; Frame Narratives; French Language; Great Haywood; Gregory the Great; Education;** *Finn and Hengest;* **Gothic Language; Goths; "Homecoming of Beorhtnoth"; Languages: Early Introduction and Interest; Letters of J.R.R. Tolkien;** *Lord of the Rings; Lost Road, The;* **Mythology for England; Norman Conquest; Northern Courage; Old English; Philology; Anglo-Saxon; Oxford; Rohan;** *Sauron Defeated; Seafarer;* **Shire; Tavrobel; Theoden; Time;** *Unfinished Tales;* **Viking Raids;** *Wanderer;* **Warwick; Ylfe, Alfr, Elf**

HOBBIT, THE

Summary

The Hobbit follows Bilbo Baggins from his home, through peril to the lair of the dragon Smaug, and back again.

Bilbo Baggins has lived for fifty comfortable, unremarkable years, when Gandalf arrives with thirteen Dwarves led by Thorin Oakenshield, who seek revenge against Smaug, the destroyer of their ancient home. Bilbo is swept along in the quest as a treasure-finder or "burglar." His journey is marked by encounters with strange beings: the Dwarves, trolls, Elrond and the Elves of Rivendell, goblins, Gollum, talking eagles, Beorn, gigantic spiders, and the Elves of Mirkwood. Along the way, Bilbo and his company gain various items, including the Ring, which in this story functions merely as a device for making the wearer invisible. For much of the adventure, Gandalf parts with the others to attend to a more urgent mission: dealing with the mysterious Necromancer, who plays no other role in this story.

Eventually, the Dwarves and Bilbo arrive at the Mountain. Their arrival angers the dragon and causes him to attack Lake-town, a nearby community of Men. The town is destroyed, but Bard, a descendant of the townsmen's ancient line of kings, slays Smaug.

The Men of Lake-town seek reparations from the Dwarves, who refuse to give them. Negotiations follow, in which Bilbo fulfils his role as burglar; he steals the Arkenstone, the central heirloom of Thorin's family, and presents it to the Men and their allies, the Wood-Elves. This attempt to avoid battle fails, as Thorin's cousin Dain arrives with an army of Dwarves; yet as the battle lines are drawn, an army of goblins and wargs arrives to plunder the Mountain. In the ensuing Battle of Five Armies, Men, Elves, Dwarves, and the recently returned Gandalf are arrayed against goblins and wargs; the arrival of the Eagles and of Beorn turns the tide, and the battle is won by the forces of good, though at the expense of many lives, including Thorin's.

Bilbo returns home with Gandalf just in time to avoid his entire estate being auctioned off. After he resettles, he discovers that while he has gained wealth, as well as renown outside his own land, he has lost his respectability at home.

Discussion/Analysis

The Hobbit was Tolkien's first published work of fiction. The book's subtitle, *There and Back Again*, gives the basic structure of the plot: a quest for hidden treasure across a landscape of perils and discovery, followed by the hero's return. Tolkien combines this basic adventure plot with aspects of *Bildungsroman*, saga, and elements from his already-developed "Silmarillion" mythos to create the first modern fantasy novel.

The Hobbit also introduces five characters central to *The Lord of the Rings*: Bilbo, Gandalf, Gollum, Elrond, and Sauron (known here as the Necromancer). Although the latter two play scant roles in *The Hobbit*, their presence connects the story, originally a tale that Tolkien told his children, to the "Silmarillion" tales. Most crucially, *The Hobbit* introduces the Ring, which functions here as a harmless but useful talisman; its function is to enable the timid Bilbo to rise to the same adventurous level as the battle-hardy Dwarves.

Much of the humor and characterization in *The Hobbit* derives from the contrast between Bilbo's anachronistically modern, bourgeois manners and the ancient world in which the other characters live and act. Many subsequent fantasy novels similarly use anachronism to bridge the gap between their quasi-medieval settings and their readers' modern sensibilities, but seldom with Tolkien's sophistication. Much of the novel's flavor also derives from the voice of the narrator, which contrasts the grandeur of ancient epic with the cozy, even patronizing asides of the Victorian children's tale. Tolkien later regretted this latter feature, yet he never fully edited it out.

"Riddles in the Dark"

The most significant change to the text of *The Hobbit* is to the fifth chapter, "Riddles in the Dark." The first version, published in 1937 in the first edition, greatly differs from the second version, published in 1951 in the second edition and printed in all subsequent editions.

Both versions of the chapter have these points in common: Bilbo is lost under the Misty Mountains; he finds the Ring and puts it in his pocket; he meets Gollum; the two play a riddle game with Bilbo's life as one of the stakes; Bilbo wins, departs, and escapes the Mountains. Yet the characterization of Gollum, the nature of the Ring, and the moral questions raised are quite different.

The change came about because of *The Lord of the Rings*. In the 1937 version, Bilbo's riddle game with Gollum has the following stakes: if Gollum wins, he eats Bilbo; if Bilbo wins, Gollum gives him the Ring. When Bilbo wins and Gollum cannot find the Ring (not knowing that it is in Bilbo's pocket), Bilbo suggests a reward instead: Gollum will show him the way out. Gollum agrees, and the two part on amicable terms.

As Tolkien was writing *The Lord of the Rings*, the nature of the Ring grew and darkened, and Tolkien realized that the original version of the chapter was not in line with the new story. Therefore, for the second edition of *The Hobbit*, Tolkien rewrote the chapter. In the new version, the stakes of the riddle game are as follows: if Gollum wins, he eats Bilbo; if Bilbo wins, Gollum shows him the way out. When Gollum loses, he looks for the Ring, intending to eat Bilbo despite his loss; when he cannot find it, he realizes that Bilbo must have the Ring and chases Bilbo, unwittingly showing Bilbo the way out in the process. The two part with Gollum's enraged cry, "Thief, thief, thief! Baggins! We hates it, we hates it, we hates it for ever!" (134) echoing in Bilbo's ears.

Other changes that Tolkien made to the chapter include the specification that Gollum is small and various indications of his moral and emotional wretchedness. These elements reflect Tolkien's realization that Gollum must himself be an unnaturally long-lived Hobbit, a fact that is entirely absent from the first edition. Additionally, the second version of the chapter introduces the theme of mercy. In the first version, Bilbo and Gollum depart on good terms, their conduct bound by the ancient rules of the riddle game. In the second version, Bilbo has both reason and opportunity to kill Gollum during the final chase but decides not to out of pity for Gollum's wretchedness. Bilbo's mercy sets up a major theme in *The Lord of the Rings*; indeed, it is not wrong to note that it is Bilbo's mercy and its unfolding implications that ultimately tip the balance away from Sauron and in favor of Middle-earth's survival.

Publication and Critical History

The Hobbit was first composed in the early 1930s as an entertainment for Tolkien's children. At the time of its writing, Tolkien had already written much of his "Silmarillion" mythos but had not attempted to publish it. When he began telling the story of Bilbo, he did not at first realize that it was connected to those tales. Tolkien's own famous explanation of how it all started suggests a completely unintentional flash of invention: he was marking exams one day, so he said, and on a page that a student had left blank he wrote, spontaneously, "In a hole in the ground there lived a hobbit." This famous opening line, Tolkien said, came without any indication of what Hobbits were or why they lived in holes—two things that he had to discover for himself.

As he wrote the story, he began to realize that it was set in the "Silmarillion" world, but in a later age. Although he did not finish the initial manuscript, his former student Elaine Griffiths arranged for Susan Dagnall of Allen & Unwin to read it. Dagnall encouraged Tolkien to finish and submit the manuscript for publication, and he did so. Stanley Unwin, the chairman, turned the manuscript over to his seven-year-old son Rayner to review; Rayner's report was positive, and the book was accepted and published in September 1937.

A second edition, substantially revised, appeared in 1951, as Tolkien was working on *The Lord of the Rings*; a third, with further revisions, appeared in 1966, and a fourth in 1978. This posthumous edition, however, contains an unreliable text, which more recent editions attempt to correct. There has never been a designated fifth edition, although Anderson states (*Annotated*, 386) that the 1995 HarperCollins text is technically just that. Further corrections have been made since then. Additionally, however, a number of variations exist even within this account of four (or five) editions; misprints and bibliographic misattributions led to a confusion of designations. There have also been a Folio Society edition, numerous illustrated editions, and translations into dozens of languages.

The Hobbit was for the most part extremely well received in the popular press upon its initial publication and is still considered a children's classic. Even many of those critics who are dubious about *The Lord of the Rings* often acknowledge, if grudgingly, the charms of the earlier book. Yet within the field of Tolkien studies, *The Hobbit* has often remained in the shadow of the later, longer book, and has rarely inspired book-length treatment. Honorable exceptions are Douglas A. Anderson's indispensable edition, *The Annotated Hobbit*, and William Green's *The Hobbit: A Journey into Maturity*, which treats the *Bildungsroman* aspect of the book from a psychological perspective. Important work on *The Hobbit* has also been done as parts of larger studies by Tom Shippey and Jane Chance, whose books are mentioned in the "further reading" section at the end of this article.

Revisions

Tolkien was always a meticulous reviser, even in the proofs stage. For the first edition, Tolkien made substantial changes to the proofs, correcting errors in tone, geography, and consistency. Yet the most substantial revisions Tolkien made to *The Hobbit* occurred long after its publication, in the late 1940s, as he was writing *The Lord of the Rings*.

In addition to rewriting "Riddles in the Dark," Tolkien made other changes that reflect his attentiveness to pseudo-historical verisimilitude: for example, in chapter 1, the first edition lists tomatoes among the contents of Bilbo's larder; the second edition changes this to pickles. Similarly, in chapter 2, the first edition contains the phrase, "Policemen never come so far"; this anachronism was excised in the second edition. Other changes reflect Tolkien's desire to integrate *The Hobbit* into the larger history of Middle-earth as he composed *The Lord of the Rings*: for example, the first edition describes Bilbo's mail coat as "silvered steel"; the second edition adds the phrase "which the elves call *mithril*." Other revisions reflect internal corrections: for example, in the first edition the text did not match the runes on Thor's Map, and some of Thorin's ancestral history was inconsistently told; these details were straightened out. Still other revisions merely reflect improvements of phrase or detail: for example, at the end of chapter 2 Tolkien changes the phrase "practicing burglary" to the alliterative "practicing pinching."

One notable inconsistency that escaped Tolkien's notice and was not corrected until long after his death is the question of the dating of Durin's Day. At the end of chapter 3, the day is dated as "the first day of the last moon of autumn," while at the beginning of chapter 4 the dating is given as the "first moon of autumn." However, in chapter 11, when Durin's Day actually occurs, it is during "the last week of autumn," suggesting that the dating in chapter 2 is the correct one; recent printings of *The Hobbit* have changed the text of chapter 4 to bring it consistently into line with the rest of the book.

The text shows many other small revisions, which are fully collected and explained in Douglas A. Anderson's *The Annotated Hobbit*.

CHESTER N. SCOVILLE

Further Reading

Anderson, Douglas A., ed. *The Annotated Hobbit*. 2nd ed. Boston, MA: Houghton Mifflin, 2002.

Carpenter, Humphrey. *J.R.R. Tolkien: A Biography*. London: Allen & Unwin, 1977.

Chance, Jane. *Tolkien's Art: A Mythology for England*. 2nd ed. Lexington, KY: University Press of Kentucky, 2001.

Shippey, Tom. *J.R.R. Tolkien: Author of the Century*. Boston, MA: Houghton Mifflin, 2000.

———. *The Road to Middle-earth*. Rev. ed. Boston, MA: Houghton Mifflin, 2003.

See also **Arkenstone; Arms and Armor; Beorn; Bilbo; Caves; Children's Literature and Tolkien; Comedy; Criticism of Tolkien, Twentieth Century; Darkness; Death; Descent; Doors and Gates; Dwarves; Elrond; Fortune and Fate; Gandalf; Gollum; Good and Evil; Heroes and Heroism; Hobbiton; Hobbits; Humor; Industrialization; Jewels; Kingship; Lonely Mountain (Erebor);** *Lord of the Rings*; **Magic: Middle-earth; Maps; Mercy; Middle-earth; Mirkwood; Misty Mountains; Mithril; Moria; Mountains; Music in Middle-earth; Nature; "On Fairy-Stories"; The One Ring; Possessiveness; Prophecy; Prose Style; Publishing History; Quest Narrative; Rhyme Schemes and Meter; Riddles; Riddles: Sources; Rings; Rings of Power; Rivendell;** *Roverandom*; **Sacrifice; Sauron; Shire;** *Silmarillion*; **Thorin; Time; Tolkien Scholarship; Treason; Violence; War; Weapons, Named; Wilderland**

HOBBITON

Hobbiton, the home of Bilbo and Frodo Baggins, is one of the principal villages of the Westfarthing in the Shire. It is located north of the Great East Road and just a mile or so northwest of the village of Bywater, where hobbits congregate at the Ivy Bush or the Green Dragon. It is a desirable address, containing some fine hobbit homes, the finest of which may be that built by Bilbo's father and called Bag End. Here Bilbo and Frodo were living at the times their separate adventures began.

On its east-west axis Hobbiton lies along the Bywater Road, south of The Water (a stream that runs into the Brandywine River at the eastern border of the Shire). Its south-north axis is perhaps more notable; it is the subject of Tolkien's painting *The Hill: Hobbiton across the Water*. In the painting, we look north along Hill Lane and first see Sandyman's Mill on the right, on The Water itself. On the left is a lovely row of shade trees, including some fine old chestnuts. Further on, the Old Farm is on the right, and the Old Grange on the left. Still further up the gently curving lane, Bagshot Row branches off to the left; number 3 Bagshot Row is the home of Hamfast (the Gaffer) Gamgee and his son Samwise. The lane continues upward, curving left or west, with the Party Field and the Party Tree within the curve, and goes past the front door and the windowed side of Bag End. Up to the top of the hill it goes and beyond, to the village of Overhill and toward the Northfarthing. The vivid greens and yellows of Tolkien's watercolor, the red roofs of a few buildings and the blue sky above, give a strong sense of rural idyll. All this is what we see of Hobbiton before the War of the Rings, and before Sharkey's underlings, and finally Sharkey himself, the corrupt wizard Saruman, occupied the Shire.

When Frodo and his companions returned, they saw a very different Hobbiton. The Mill had been rebuilt in an ugly graceless style to straddle The Water and was sending its pollutants into the stream; nearby stood a huge chimney or smokestack. The shade trees along the Bywater Road and the trees lining the west side of Hill Lane had all been cut down. The Old Farm had been converted into a workshop, and the Old Grange had disappeared altogether in favor of rows of tarred sheds. Further up, Bagshot Row, including the ancestral Gamgee home, had been dug up for a sand and gravel pit. Tawdry huts lay on the downhill side of the lane opposite Bag End, and worst of all, perhaps (Sam burst into tears at the sight), the Party Tree had been cut down and lay there dead.

But things changed for the better in Hobbiton. After the disembodiment of Saruman and the defeat of his allies, the community of hobbits went to work to restore Hobbiton. The interlopers were driven out, and freedom and order returned. On the physical level, the many shabby brick and wooden structures were dismantled and some of the material recycled. A new version of Bagshot Row was built, and Frodo's house at Bag End was put to rights. Even the Elves were able indirectly to help restore the village and the Shire. With soil from Lothlórien's gardens, Sam nurtured new plantings all around the Shire, including a beautiful mallorn tree to replace the Party Tree, and the gift of Galadriel encouraged plentiful life everywhere.

MICHAEL N. STANTON

Further Reading

Anderson, Douglas A., ed. *The Annotated Hobbit*. 2nd ed., rev. Boston, MA: Houghton Mifflin, 2002.

Burger, Douglas A. "The Shire: A Tolkien Version of Pastoral." In *Aspects of Fantasy: Selected Essays from the Second International Conference on the Fantastic in Literature and Film*, edited by William Coyle. Westport, CT: Greenwood, 1986.

Curry, Patrick. *Defending Middle-earth: Tolkien: Myth and Modernity*. Rev. ed. Boston, MA: Houghton Mifflin, 2004.

Hammond, Wayne G., and Christina Scull. *J.R.R. Tolkien: Artist and Illustrator*. Boston, MA: Houghton Mifflin, 1995.

Stoddard, William H. "Law and Institutions in the Shire." *Mythlore* 70, 18, no. 4 (1992): 4–8.

See also **Art and Illustration by Tolkien; Bilbo; Frodo; Galadriel; Hobbits; Men; Saruman; Shire; Trees**

HOBBITS

Hobbits are a distinctive form of human beings invented by J.R.R. Tolkien and found in the realm called Middle-earth in his fictions *The Hobbit* (1937) and *The Lord of the Rings* (1954–55). Two basic facts, dealt with below, color all of hobbit life: they are small, and, traditionally, they live in holes.

Origin of the Word

"In a hole in the ground there lived a hobbit," says the first sentence of *The Hobbit*, and this was the sentence, according to legend, that Tolkien scribbled on a blank sheet during a boring session of reading exams back around 1930. There are many versions of this anecdote, with several dates, but its essential truth is there: the word came first.

Several possibilities have been canvassed for the origin of the word. Tolkien may have been thinking of an English dialect word "hob," meaning a rustic or country fellow (we find old Hob Hayward, a hobbit, at the Brandywine Bridge when Merry and the others return to the Shire). In an interview, Tolkien suggested the Sinclair Lewis character, the smugly bourgeois Babbit; T.A. Shippey has put forth considerable evidence for linking the word to "rabbit," although Tolkien had earlier disavowed the link. Also, Douglas A. Anderson has cited the word "hobbit" in an 1895 compilation of folkloric terms from the north of England for supernatural beings (*Annotated*, 9).

Hobbits are also called Little People or Little Folk (to distinguish them from ordinary-sized people), Halflings (for similar reasons), *Periannath* (in Sindarin Elvish), *holbytlan* ("hole-dwellers" in Rohirric, actually a Tolkien coinage based on Old English). "Hobbit," as Tolkien notes, is an invention; their own word for themselves was "kuduk" (*RT,* App. F, 415–16, 419–24).

Origins, Kindred, and History of Hobbits

Although hobbits speak only a regional dialect of Westron or the Common Speech of Middle-earth, vestigial elements in it suggest an origin in the North of Middle-earth. Some hobbit populations are associated with the folk of Rohan, the Rohirrim, who also migrated from the North, although considerably later than the hobbits.

Hobbits settled in Eriador in west-central Middle-earth as early as the eleventh century of the Third Age; eventually, they began to call their small district "the Shire." King Argeleb II granted the Fallohide brothers, Marco and Blanco, some 18,000 square miles in 1601 TA to constitute the Shire formally; this grant was twice augmented by areas called the Westmarch and the Eastmarch, so that the Shire's total territory came to be about 21,000 square miles.

Hobbits began to reckon their history from that grant of 1601; thus, the Shire calendar, or Shire Reckoning, is always 1,600 years behind the common calendar of the rest of Middle-earth. Events important in Hobbit history, given in Shire Reckoning, include:

SR 37 The Dark Plague and following years
   of dearth
SR 1147 The Battle of the Greenfields in the
   Northfarthing district of the Shire; invading
   Orcs are defeated
SR 1311 The Fell Winter; invasion of White Wolves
SR 1419 The Battle of Bywater
SR 1420 The year of peace and plenty

The first hobbits to appear in Eriador were the Harfoots, followed by the Fallohides, and last by the Stoors. The Harfoots (archaic English, "hairy-foot") are the most numerous and most "typical" in appearance, being short and brown of skin. The fairer and taller Fallohides (archaic English, "Pale skin") were less numerous but included some distinguished hobbit families: the Brandybucks and the Tooks, among others. Bilbo and Frodo Baggins are of Fallohide stock. The Stoors (early English "large" or "strong") were stouter than other hobbits; they alone grew beards, and unlike most hobbits they liked boating and fishing and tended to concentrate in riverine districts (some ancestral Stoors remigrated east from the Shire into Wilderland; these included Gollum's forebears).

The most important physical attribute of hobbits is their size; they range between two and four feet in height. They tended to be taller in the old days, but few exceeded four feet, except that Merry and Pippin grew considerably after their sojourn in Fangorn subsisting on Treebeard's Ent-drink. Other notable physical traits included curly brown hair as a norm and of course hairy toes on their tough, usually bare, feet. Hobbits tended to be healthy and long-lived (living for a century was no great feat, and Bilbo Baggins set the record at 131 years). Maturation was therefore a slow process, and hobbits were not considered to have reached true adulthood until the age of thirty-three.

Life in the Shire

Originally, hobbits did live in holes, but by the time of Bilbo and Frodo, much residential construction was above ground, and hobbits lived in wood and stone houses. Only the richest and poorest, as Tolkien notes, still lived in holes: the latter because they could afford only simple burrows, the former because they could create large spread-out structures often called *smials*, built on side-hills, many-windowed and many-roomed. Such was Bilbo's Bag End, which even had a cellar.

Because of their inferior size, hobbits tended to prefer an isolated way of life. The borders of the Shire were carefully maintained, both by hobbit officials known as Bounders, and in the later days of the Third Age by the Rangers of the North and other protectors. But hobbits and Big Folk dwelt unconcernedly side by side at the village of Bree near the Shire, "rightly regarding themselves," Tolkien tells us, "as necessary parts of the Bree-folk. Nowhere else in the world was this peculiar (but excellent) arrangement to be found" (*FR,* I, ix, 161–62). Hobbits in the Shire, however, referred to hobbits beyond as Outsiders and considered them unworthy of notice. The reverse of the coin of needful self-protection was xenophobia.

Within the Shire, the great interests of hobbits were land and family. Most hobbits were farmers and fruit-growers or worked in farm-related pursuits like smithery or milling. Important crops of the Shire included tobacco or pipeweed, grapes (for wine), barley (for beer), and mushrooms. Villages like Hobbiton and Bywater were oriented to the rhythms of the seasons and life on the land.

The family was the key unit of hobbit society. Frodo and Bilbo were exceptional in being bachelors; Frodo was doubly exceptional in being an only child. Progeny mattered: Bilbo's mother was one of the Old

Took's twelve children; and after Frodo's faithful companion, Sam, himself one of six, married Rosie Cotton they had thirteen children. These numbers help explain why one of the chief intellectual interests (if that is the right term) among hobbits was the study of genealogy.

Family was not only a key unit; it seemed to be almost the sole unit of communal life, except perhaps the casual society of the tavern for the males. There is no mention of churches as resorts for either worship or community life. Schools at even the elementary level are only obliquely alluded to: not all hobbits are literate (although, among those who are, letter writing is a favorite recreation), and very few pursue any higher scholarship. The one skill or art in which all hobbits are proficient is cooking. To match that proficiency is a universal love of good food and beverage; eating and drinking one's fill as often as possible is an honorable pursuit among hobbits.

Essentially peaceable beings, hobbits did not need much government. There were the Bounders already mentioned, constables called shirriffs in each of the four divisions or farthings of the Shire; a mayor headquartered at the Shire's chief town, Michel Delving; and a Thane or kind of honorary lord, with influence but not much power.

The Character of the Hobbit

"Essentially peaceable" certainly describes one aspect of hobbit makeup; one may say "easy-going" or "good natured" as well. By and large, hobbits are neither ambitious nor introspective, but content to eat hearty farm fare, drink good beer, and raise children. Contentment, however, can edge over into complacency, and satisfaction into smugness, states of mind that made the Shire vulnerable when Saruman began to take an interest in it.

But hobbits have strengths beneath that placid surface. There is a seed of courage hidden deeply in every hobbit heart, Tolkien says, and it grows at need. Bilbo and Frodo were quite exceptional among hobbits, and they therefore found the resources they needed rather quickly. And once awakened, even the hobbits of the Shire can drive out Saruman's ruffians and their quisling helpers.

And in the unfolding of events in the Third Age, Hobbits can play an unguessably important role, as Gandalf the Wizard sensed long ago. His friend Elrond Half-Elven expresses it best at the Council of Elrond when Frodo volunteers to destroy the One Ring: "'This is the hour of the Shire-Folk, when they arise from their quiet fields to shake the towers and counsels of the Great. Who of all the Wise could have foreseen it? Or, if they are wise, why should they expect to know it . . . ?'" (*FR*, II, ii, 284).

Tolkien claimed more than just an affinity with his creations: "I am in fact a *Hobbit* (in all but size)," he once told a correspondent; he favored simple food including mushrooms, unmechanized farmlands, trees, and the occasional colorful waistcoat in his wardrobe. He also liked to imagine that hobbits are still among us, having become extraordinarily adept at self-concealment.

Readers may argue amicably about degree, but certainly Englishness as one quality of hobbits is evident. A settled way of life, an almost unbreachable politeness, modesty combined with courage, powerful use of understatement, all are thought of by the world at large as things traditionally English. They are likewise hobbitish.

Hobbits are conservative in the best sense of the word and resist or at least resent abrupt changes in their lives such as those brought by the War of the Ring. Frodo and his friends may have undertaken their Quest to save the world in an abstract or ideal sense, but when they came home they realized that that truly meant saving the Shire and also restoring as best they could the hobbit way of life.

MICHAEL N. STANTON

Further Reading

Anderson, Douglas A. *The Annotated Hobbit*. 2nd ed., rev. Boston, MA: Houghton Mifflin, 2002.

Chance, Jane. *The Lord of the Rings: the Mythology of Power*. Rev. ed. Lexington, KY: University Press of Kentucky, 2001. Ho, Tisa. "The Childlike Hobbit." *Mythlore* 34, 9, no. 4 (1983): 3–9.

Kocher, Paul. *Master of Middle-earth*. Boston, MA: Houghton Mifflin, 1972.

Miller, David. "Hobbits: Common Lens for Heroic Experience." *Tolkien Journal* 11 / *Orcrist* 3 (1969): 11–15.

O'Brien, Donald. "On the Origin of the Name 'Hobbit.'" *Mythlore* 60, 16, no. 2 (1989): 32–38.

Rogers, Deborah C. "Everyclod and Everyhero: The Image of Man in Tolkien." In *A Tolkien Compass*, edited by Jared Lobdell, 69–76. La Salle, IL.: Open Court, 1975.

Shippey, T.A. *J.R.R. Tolkien: Author of the Century*. Boston, MA: Houghton Mifflin, 2002.

Tolkien, J.R.R. "Guide to the Names in *The Lord of the Rings*." In *A Tolkien Compass*, edited by Jared Lobdell, 153–201. La Salle, IL: Open Court, 1975.

HOLY MAIDEN HOOD BY J. FURNIVAL: REVIEW BY TOLKIEN

On April 26, 1923, the *Times Literary Supplement* ran an unsigned review of F.J. Furnivall's posthumously published Early English Text Society edition of *Hali*

Meidenhad. This review was written by J.R.R. Tolkien. The edition had been published after Furnivall's death, and Tolkien did not think that the state of the edition, which he believed could have been improved without a great deal of extra work, reflected well on the memory of Furnivall: "The translation is probably not to be regarded as such a revision as the founder of the Early English Text Society would himself have sent to press."

But the review is not merely a recitation of the flaws in the edition. Tolkien also explains the significance of the text and prefigures many of the arguments he would later make in "*Ancrene Wisse* and *Hali Meiðhad*" about the consistency and quality of the language, whose "technical excellence is not easy to match from Middle English prose of other regions until a much later period." Tolkien linked this excellence to a close connection to Old English and argues that the language was "no mere survivor of a dying tradition, but was in the closest touch with the living colloquial speech," a point on which he would elaborate in his later article.

Of interest to students of *The Hobbit*, Tolkien notes the derivation of Modern English "gold" from Old Norse "gull," a word Douglas A. Anderson links to the name "Gollum," which, if the Tolkien truly viewed the element "Goll-" as cognate with "gull," might be translated as "gold" or "precious" (*H*, V, 120, n. 8).

MICHAEL D.C. DROUT

Further Reading

[Tolkien, J.R.R.]. "Holy Maidenhood." Review of *Hali Meidenhad: An Alliterative Prose Homily of the Thirteenth Century*, ed. F.J. Furnivall. *Times Literary Supplement*, London, April 26, 1923.

See also **Ancrene Wisse**; MS Bodley 34; D'Ardenne, S.R.T.O.; Katherine Group

HOMECOMING OF BEORHTNOTH

Tolkien's *The Homecoming of Beorhtnoth Beorhthelm's Son* was written before 1945 but first published in the journal *Essays and Studies* in 1953. The work has three sections: two prose pieces ("Beorhtnoth's Death" and "Ofermod") flank an alliterative verse play. A short fragment of an earlier rhyming version of the play has been published posthumously (*Treason*, 106–7).

In "Beorhtnoth's Death," Tolkien gives a brief account of the battle between Vikings and Anglo-Saxons that took place near Maldon, Essex, in 991,

drawing particularly on the Old English poem *The Battle of Maldon.* Vikings landed on a small island joined to the mainland by a causeway. Unable to overcome the defense of this causeway, they asked for permission to cross in order to fight, and Beorhtnoth, the English commander, allowed them to do so: "This act of pride and misplaced chivalry proved fatal." The English were defeated and Beorhtnoth killed. Tolkien quotes two lines in which Beorhtnoth's retainer Beorhtwold encourages his comrades after the death of their lord by declaring that their courage and spirit will be the stronger as their might lessens. Tolkien describes these words as "a summing up of the heroic code" and claims they were probably a traditional expression of "heroic will."

A twelfth-century history of Ely Abbey maintains that its abbot retrieved Beorhtnoth's body from the battlefield, and this is the scenario for Tolkien's dramatic sequel to *The Battle of Maldon*: the abbot and monks have come as far as Maldon but then sent two men to the battlefield to bring back the body. These two fictional characters are Torhthelm, a young minstrel versed in Germanic heroic legend, and Tídwald, an old farmer experienced in the reality of warfare. As they search for Beorhtnoth's body, they reflect on the battle, giving expression to conflicting value systems.

When Torhthelm bemoans Beorhtnoth's decapitation, Tídwald points out that it is the kind of thing that happens in battle: similar atrocities took place, he says, in the battles in which the legendary heroes Fróda and Finn died. Torhthelm performs a lament as they carry Beorhtnoth's body to a cart, but Tídwald associates heroic ethics with pre-Christian beliefs when he remarks that "Beorhtnoth we bear, not Béowulf here: / no pyres for him, nor piling of mounds." The proper way to mourn this man, he suggests, is not in heroic verse, but with the church's liturgy.

At the causeway, Tídwald attributes Beorhtnoth's allowing the Vikings across to "pride." He pointedly explains to Torhthelm that Beorhtnoth allowed the Vikings across the causeway "to give minstrels matter for mighty songs" and describes Beorhnoth's action as "needlessly noble." Torhthelm, however, continues to see matters in the light of heroic legend, alluding in a reference to Hengist and Horsa to the earlier Germanic invasion of Britain by the Anglo-Saxons themselves.

As the cart carrying Beorhtnoth's body moves off, Torhthelm chants lines from a dream: Beorhtwold's words from *The Battle of Maldon* are combined with clearly pre-Christian sentiments. Monks are then heard chanting from the Latin Office for the Dead, before a voice in the dark utters a rhyming couplet in English. The chanting resumes and fades into silence.

As Tolkien indicates, his verse play is written in an alliterative meter like that of *The Battle of Maldon*; the rhyme at the end presages the introduction of new verse forms after the Norman Conquest. Tolkien weaves in allusions to a number of surviving Old English texts, including a reference to the monster Grendel from *Beowulf*. The verse play was broadcast on the radio on December 3, 1954, and repeated the next year.

In the final section of the work, "Ofermod," Tolkien asserts that his poem merits a place in *Essays and Studies* as an "extended comment" on lines 89 and 90 of *The Battle of Maldon*, the lines expressing the poet's disapproval of Beorhtnoth's allowing the Vikings across the causeway. In his version of these two lines, Tolkien translates *ofermod* as "overmastering pride."

Tolkien notes that Beorhtwold's words in *The Battle of Maldon* "have been held to be the finest expression of the northern heroic spirit... the clearest statement of the doctrine of uttermost endurance in the service of indomitable will." But he argues that Beorhtwold is able to give such a clear statement of the heroic ethic only because he is a "subordinate," someone in whom loyalty to his superior is greater than personal pride. A careful analysis follows of the relation between pure heroism and the desire for glory as motivating factors in Northern heroic literature. Pride may lead beyond heroic necessity to excess, something here equated with "chivalry." Tolkien cites as an example Beowulf's going beyond what is necessary in fighting Grendel and later risking defeat against the dragon; in *The Battle of Maldon*, Beorhtnoth provides a "real life" example of the consequences of such pride. His defeat results from a character defect that Tolkien argues would have been nurtured by the aristocratic heroic tradition in which he was educated—the tradition of which Torhthelm is a representative exponent in Tolkien's poem. In such a context, the loyalty of retainers such as Beorhtwold is seen as even more praiseworthy.

Tolkien concludes by associating *The Battle of Maldon* with *Beowulf* and *Sir Gawain and the Green Knight* as poems that study at length "the heroic and the chivalrous": all three evaluate a code of sentiment and conduct, and all three find an aristocratic hero's behavior wanting.

Previous scholars had seen *The Battle of Maldon* as a celebration of the heroic spirit, a view shared by Tolkien's friend E.V. Gordon in his edition of the poem. Tolkien sees it instead as a powerful critique, which he develops in his own sequel to the poem. Tolkien's reading of the poet's stance toward Beorhtnoth's actions has been highly influential, but several scholars have dissented from it: Shippey, for example, argues that Tolkien's interpretation is "tendentious and personal to a marked degree" (Shippey, "Boar," 233; for an overview of the debate, see Cavill).

CARL PHELPSTEAD

Further Reading

Bradley, S.A.J., trans. *Anglo-Saxon Poetry*. London: Dent, 1982.

Cavill, Paul. "Interpretation of *The Battle of Maldon*, lines 84–90: A Review and Reassessment." *Studia Neophilologica* 67 (1995): 149–64.

Gordon, E.V., ed. *The Battle of Maldon*. London: Methuen, 1937.

Nitzsche, Jane Chance. *Tolkien's Art: "A Mythology for England."* London: Macmillan, 1979.

Phelpstead, Carl. "Auden and the Inklings: An Alliterative Revival." *Journal of English and Germanic Philology*. 103 (2004): 433–57.

Shippey, T.A. "Boar and Badger: An Old English Heroic Antithesis?" *Leeds Studies in English*, n.s. 16 (1985): 220–39.

———. *J.R.R. Tolkien: Author of the Century*. London: HarperCollins, 2000; paperback ed. 2001.

Tolkien, J.R.R. "The Homecoming of Beorhtnoth Beorhthelm's Son," In *Essays and Studies by Members of the English Association*, n.s. 6 (1953): 1–18.

See also **Alliterative Verse by Tolkien; *Battle of Maldon*; History, Anglo-Saxon; Northern Courage; Old English**

HOMER

Homer is the early Greek poet traditionally credited with the authorship of *The Iliad* and *The Odyssey*. The historian Herodotus (2.53), writing in the fifth century BCE, claims that Homer lived not more than four hundred years before his time, or circa 850 BCE, but there are no extant records to corroborate his hypothesis. There is no existing biography of Homer, but Greek tradition claims that he was a blind man born in or somewhere near Ionia. Though they share many of the same characters and themes, it is generally believed that the collection of poems known as *The Homeric Hymns* were not written by the same person who may have written *The Iliad* and *The Odyssey*.

Modern scholars and translators such as Richard Latimore and Robert Graves contest that Homer was not the name of an actual person but of a school of poets and rhapsodes who may trace their lineage to a real individual, a mythic personage, a shared location, or an epitaph. The name *Homēros* in the Greek language means "hostage," which may linguistically relate Homer to a society of poets known as the *homeridae*, or "sons of hostages."

In a letter, Tolkien writes: "I was brought up in the Classics, and first discovered the sensation of literary pleasure in Homer." Like all male school children of his era and class, Tolkien quickly became proficient in classical and Homeric Greek and thoroughly versed in Homer's mythology. It was not long, however, before the budding linguist discovered German, Gothic, and Anglo-Saxon, leaving ancient Greek behind. It would not be until Tolkien began writing *The Hobbit* that specifically Homeric motifs would find their way into his work.

In prewar Britain, the classics "had become romantically entangled with Victorian triumphalism" (Garth, 42), and it was at this time that Tolkien began to distance himself from the sun-drenched Greek poetry that had entranced him in his youth, opting instead for the grimmer lays of the northern climes. Once deployed to the trenches of the first world war, both G.B. Smith and Rob Gilson, two of Tolkien's closest friends and founding members of the T.C.B.S., carried with them copies of *The Odyssey* (Garth, 116, 135), but Tolkien characteristically focused his attention on the northern European epic tradition as well as composing the first poems and stories that would later become *The Silmarillion*.

There is much in Tolkien's work that is reminiscent of Homer, but the two are very different artists portraying very different worlds. Tolkien's shape-changing Balrog may be reminiscent of Homer's Proteus; the lighting of the beacons of Gondor may mirror a similar event in *The Iliad,* and Bilbo's barrel riding and name trading may have been inspired by Odysseus' adventures, but there is nothing in Tolkien's correspondence to indicate that he consciously employed Homer's motifs as his own. Rather, the two artists, separated by almost three millennia, speak the common language of myth, a language spoken by every tongue in every age, making it virtually impossible to say anything truly novel.

DUSTIN EATON

Further Reading

Garth, John. *Tolkien and the Great War.* Boston, MA: Houghton Mifflin, 2003.

Hammond, Wayne G., and Christina Scull. *The Lord of the Rings: A Readers Companion.* Boston, MA: Houghton Mifflin, 2005.

See also **Education; Greek Language**

HOMOSEXUALITY

Queer theory questions the heterosexist assumption that human sexuality fits neatly into rigid categories of behavior (the heterosexual norm and the various sexualities that deviate from that norm) and posits that the above assumption belongs to a long-standing but not ahistorical ideology essentially discriminatory to lesbians, gay men, bisexuals, and transgendered individuals.

Evolving out of a critique of the feminist movement's early preoccupation with mostly white heterosexual women's rights, a more pluralist feminism sought the inclusion of lesbians and women of color. Lesbian and gay studies quickly emerged from the chrysalis of women's studies with its attention to sexuality. Coined in 1991, the literary term "queer" signifies an awareness of the dangers of labels and categories, even those behind which lesbian and gay activists historically rallied. "Queer" speaks to the fallacy of ahistorical identities, and queer theory continues to problematize the too convenient categories, easy euphemisms, and ambient cultural behavior designed in part to maintain a sexual status quo.

Michel Foucault's *The History of Sexuality* (1978) argues that sexuality is not conceptualized today as it was in medieval Europe; sex has a history. Categories such as heterosexuality and homosexuality did not nor will they always exist, and the binary they set up is itself a manifestation of a dominant cultural view of sex. In 1980, Adrienne Rich published her essay "Compulsory Heterosexuality and Lesbian Existence" in which she defines the term "lesbian continuum" as a range of female-to-female bonding that reached from a desire for sexual contact to an intense emotional intimacy and sharing. Like Rich, Eve Sedgwick (*Between Men*, 1985) defines a continuum of homosocial desire, this time among men. She maps out activities ranging from sexual genital contact situated at one end of the continuum to men supporting and promoting the interests of men at the other.

Much of the work on sexuality in Tolkien studies concentrates on the intense intimacy exhibited between Frodo and Sam. Their relationship fits neatly into the discourse of friendship expressed by homosexual men until the mid-twentieth century. Frodo is a gentleman, and Sam is a gardener under his employ. During their quest to destroy the Ring, they take on the characteristics of an officer and his batman, an image Tolkien knew through his experiences in World War I and wrote about in his letters. While Frodo is often burdened by spiritual and physical wounds, Sam repeatedly behaves exceedingly tenderly and tactily. While it might be quite easy to pass this behavior off as either an example of the powerful bonds manifest during times of war, to do so without accounting for the discomfort Sam's behavior causes in and outside the novel would be to perpetuate an ongoing cultural disengagement with issues of sex.

A passage within the novel, which critics frequently cite, acknowledges Sam's own discomfort at his tender behavior:

> At that moment there was a knock on the door, and Sam came in. He ran to Frodo and took his left hand, awkwardly and shyly. He stroked it gently and then blushed and turned hastily away.

> "Hullo Sam!" said Frodo.
> "It's warm!" said Sam. "Meaning your hand, Mr. Frodo. It has felt so cold through the long nights."
>
> (FR, II, i, 237)

Sam blushes at his own overt tenderness because it exposes the degree to which he adores his master. His emotional attachment makes him vulnerable, and he turns quickly away. As befits his characterization, the truth of Sam's feelings is pinned to his sleeve for all to see. The gentle stroke of Frodo's hand is not sexual in a genital sense (nor would it have been coded as such during Victorian and Edwardian England); however, Sam's tactile behavior does seem to cross class, gender, and sexual boundaries, particularly as they were constructed after World War II, and offers a potentially significant image to those readers who identify as homosexual.

When actor Dominic Monaghan (Merry) asks Elijah Wood (Frodo) whether or not Frodo and Sam are gay in the extended DVD edition of Peter Jackson's *Return of the King* (2003), the issue of queer behavior in the novel is ushered to the foreground. The Easter-egg skit possesses entertainment value but also speaks to the existence of a male intimacy in the novel/romance not commonly expressed in Western Europe or the United States today.

Exploring the continuum of male intimacy, Brenda Partridge draws on biography to assist in her interpretations. Pointing to the all-male schooling of Tolkien and the rigid social and vocational boundaries set up between men and women in the late nineteenth and early twentieth centuries, Partridge argues that Tolkien's deep emotional investment in his male friendships (influenced by C.S. Lewis's advocacy of warrior-to-warrior love) accounts for Frodo and Sam's striking intimacy and the lack of any real depth in the female characters. Relatively unexplored, however, is the potential for readers to find a queer component in the gender fluidity of Éowyn's character, who despite her marriage toward the novel's denouement presents a powerful image of a woman unrestrained by the will of the father figure and defiantly successful within the male-dominated arena of the battlefield. Tolkien himself first conceived of her as a young troubled amazon warrior likely to die on the battlefield, as David M. Craig points out. Interestingly, her position outside the paradigm of home and marriage left Tolkien with few conceivable options other than death or transformation into a heterosexual women.

Anna Smol continues along Partridge's trajectory in her examination of the tactile intimacy manifest within *The Lord of the Rings* and the large corpus of homoerotic fan fiction it incites, most of which are written by heterosexually identified women. Smol's attention to the continuum of nongenital tactile intimacy between men makes permeable the culturally determined boundaries coding some friendships as heterosexual and others as homosexual.

Regardless of Tolkien's own attitude toward sex and alternative sexualities, his readers will continue to locate their own fantasies (libidinous and otherwise) within the heart of Middle-earth. As Ty Rosenthal remarks, "Tolkien imagined worlds and epics with sex confined to a respectable margin. But the modern world cannot. The libidinal force that Tolkien acknowledged, and tries to negate, is swept in by the reader in the present" (42).

CHRISTOPHER VACCARO

Further Reading

Craig, David M. "'Queer Lodgings': Gender and Sexuality in *The Lord of the Rings.*" *Mallorn: The Journal of the Tolkien Society* 38 (January 2001): 11–18.

Patridge, Brenda. "No Sex Please—We're Hobbits: The Construction of Female Sexuality in *The Lord of the Rings.*" In *J.R.R. Tolkien: This Far Land*, edited by Robert Giddings, 179–97 London & Totowa, NJ: Vision—Barnes & Noble, 1983.

Rich, Adrienne. "Compulsory Heterosexuality and Lesbian Existence." *Signs: Journal of Women in Culture and Society* 5, no. 4 (Summer 1980): 631–60.

Rosenthal, Ty. "Warm Beds Are Good: Sex and Libido in Tolkien's Writing." *Mallorn: The Journal of the Tolkien Society* 42 (August 2004): 35–42.

Roy, Valerie. "On Fairy Stories." *Modern Fiction Studies* 50 no. 4 (Winter 2004): 927–48.

Sedgwick, Eve. *Between Men: English Literature and Homosocial Desire.* New York: Columbia University Press, 1985.

Smol, Anna. "'Oh . . . Oh . . . Frodo!': Readings of Male Intimacy in *The Lord of the Rings.*" *Modern Fiction Studies* 50, no. 4 (Winter 2004): 949–79.

See also **Feminist Readings; Gender; Sexuality**

HOWARD, ROBERT E. (1906–36)

American author of pulp fiction, creator of Conan the Barbarian, and father of the "swords and sorcery" subgenre of modern fantasy. In *Tolkien: A Look behind the Lord of the Rings* (1969), Lin Carter stated that Professor Tolkien "rather enjoys" the Conan stories (32n). Carter apparently based his claim on information communicated to him by his colleague L. Sprague de Camp, who visited Tolkien once, in February 1967. De Camp recalled their conversation at Tolkien's residence, in *Literary Swordsmen and Sorcerers* (1976). De Camp had already sent Tolkien a copy of his 1963 anthology *Swords and Sorcery*, which contains Howard's "Shadows in the Moonlight" as well as stories by Poul Anderson, Lord Dunsany, Fritz Leiber, H.P. Lovecraft, Henry Kuttner, C.L. Moore, and Clark Ashton Smith. "[Tolkien] said he found [the anthology] interesting but did not much like the stories in it," de Camp said (243). However, de Camp added, "[Tolkien] indicated that he 'rather liked' Howard's Conan stories" (244). Since de Camp offers no indication of where Tolkien might have read any Conan stories other than the one included in the 1963 anthology, it appears possible that Tolkien actually read only "Shadows in the Moonlight." On the other hand, since the American publisher Lancer had begun to release paperbacks of Conan stories (with editing by de Camp) by 1966, someone might have shown Tolkien a copy of *Conan the Adventurer* (1966), with its cover blurb promising adventures "more imaginative than *The Lord of the Rings.*" A 1983 letter from de Camp to John Rateliff implies that de Camp would not have been prepared to stand by his earlier suggestion of Tolkien having read multiple Conan stories. Rateliff quotes de Camp: "During our conversation, I said something casual to Tolkien about my involvement with Howard's Conan stories, and he said he 'rather liked them.' That was all; we went on to other subjects. I know he had read *Swords and Sorcery* because I had sent him a copy. I don't know if he had read any other Conan besides 'Shadows in the Moonlight,' but I rather doubt it."

DALE NELSON

Further Reading

Carter, Lin. *Tolkien: A Look Behind "The Lord of the Rings."* New York: Ballantine, 1969.
De Camp, L. Sprague. *Literary Swordsmen and Sorcerers.* Sauk City, WI: Arkham, 1976.
Rateliff, John. Letter. *Beyond Bree*, March 2005, 4.

HUMOR

If for purposes of discussion humor can be divided into situational humor, acts and deeds, and verbal humor, or words, Tolkien's humor falls largely into the verbal category, as might be expected from a writer whose life was language. There are notable situations, especially perhaps in *The Hobbit*—a flustered Bilbo dashing out without a handkerchief, Dwarves floating down river in barrels, encounters with irritable dragons—with humorous content, but when we think of humor in Tolkien, we think mostly of what people say.

Thus, even in *The Hobbit* there is verbal humor, if riddles may be considered humor. They provide amusement for onlookers at the puzzlement of those trying to guess them and at the defeat of conventional expectations. And they are of course a mainstay of the tale.

In *The Lord of the Rings*, situations do not permit much humor, but there are partial exceptions: we think of the running joke or contention between Gimli and Éomer about the beauty of Galadriel. It recurs seldom enough to retain some edge and is used nonhumorously to mark the growing respect between these two warriors. Rather different in tone is the "purely Bywater joke" about New Row's being locally known as Sharkey's End: verbal humor arising out of grim situation.

Throughout Tolkien's work, however, the major modes of humor are two: comic verse and exaggeratedly elevated speech.

Light verse and nonsense verse occur often enough to merit mention. Nonsense verse, of course, is a misnomer: the nonsense is only in repeated syllables or in comic (usually double) rhymes ("Tinbone, thinbone, shinbone"). The collection of verse called *The Adventures of Tom Bombadil* includes comic poems that reappear in *The Lord of the Rings,* such as Sam Gamgee's "Oliphaunt" and "The Stone Troll," a poem that creates an interesting transposition of humorous effects since the Trolls themselves, with their comic accents, appear only in *The Hobbit.*

If riddles can mark the affinities of Tolkien's humor with Old English literature, the cozy whimsicality of this sort of poetry can mark the similarities of his humor to that of Victorian fantasists like Edward Lear.

Tolkien deploys elevated diction and exaggeratedly elaborate rhetoric to comic effect on several occasions. Bilbo's knowing how to address, and flatter, dragons, is a clear example. Less obvious, perhaps, are Merry and Pippin's speeches when other members of the Company find them at Isengard smoking contentedly amid the ruins. Their style of speech is both self-deprecating and meant to provoke.

Tolkien's short work, *Farmer Giles of Ham*, operates on the use of high styles of speech. It features bilingual, macaronic language, both Latin and "the vulgar tongue," English, for things like book titles. One may say that *Farmer Giles* is in part the comic explanation of how various English places got their names.

Repartee or witty retorts are rarely part of Tolkien's humor. But here is a notable exception: on the Hobbits' second day out of Hobbiton, Frodo is munching Elvish leftovers, and Pippin is plaguing him with questions about Gildor. Frodo says sharply,

> "'I don't want to answer a string of questions while I am eating. I want to think!'"
> "'Good heavens!' said Pippin. 'At breakfast?'"

(FR, I, iv, 95)

MICHAEL N. STANTON

Further Reading

Anderson, Douglas A., ed. *The Annotated Hobbit*. 2nd ed., rev. Boston, MA: Houghton Mifflin, 2002.

Helms, Randel. *Tolkien's World*. Boston, MA: Houghton Mifflin, 1974.

Johnson, George Burke. "The Poetry of J.R.R. Tolkien." *Mankato Studies in English* 2 (1967): 63–75.

Nash, Walter. *The Language of Humor: Style and Technique in Comic Discourse*. London: Longmans, 1985.

Robinson, Derek. "The Hasty Stroke Goes Oft Astray: Tolkien and Humor." In *J.R.R. Tolkien: This Far Land*, edited by Robert Giddings. London: Vision Press, 1983.

Stevens, C.D. "High Fantasy and Low Comedy: Humor in J.R.R. Tolkien." *Extrapolation* 21 (1980): 122–29.

Tolkien, J.R.R. *The Tolkien Miscellany*. New York: Quality Paperback Book Club, 2002. Includes *Farmer Giles of Ham* and *The Adventures of Tom Bombadil*.

See also **Adventures of Tom Bombadil; Farmer Giles of Ham; Hobbits; Sam**

HUNGARY: RECEPTION OF TOLKIEN

The following works by Tolkien have been translated into Hungarian: *The Hobbit* (1975, trans. Tibor Szobotka and István Tótfalusi), *The Lord of the Rings* (1981, Árpád Göncz, Ádám Réz, and Dezső Tandori), *Farmer Giles of Ham* (1988, Árpád Göncz), *The Silmarillion* (1991, Judit Gálvölgyi), *Smith of Wooton Major* (1994, Anikó Németh), *Unfinished Tales* (1995, Judit Szántó and Gábor Koltai), *Tree and Leaf* (1996, Anikó Németh), *The Book of Lost Tales* (1996, Dezső Tandori), *Roverandom* (2001, Zsolt Szántai), *The Adventures of Tom Bombadil* (2002, István Tótfalusi and Iván Uhrman), *The Monsters and the Critics* (forthcoming, Gábor Koltai and Gergely Nagy).

Early interest in his works, especially *The Lord of the Rings*, was connected to Péter Kuczka (1923–99), poet and editor of the acclaimed science fiction periodical *Galaktika*, who was the first to mention Tolkien's book. After the translation of *The Hobbit* (in revision now as thought to be too childish), it was the publication (in 1981) of *The Lord of the Rings* that made Tolkien a valued and popular author. Its translation was started by Ádám Réz, who is responsible for the text of the appendices, chapters 1–11 of book 1, and most of the nomenclature. Owing to Réz's death, most of the text was translated by Árpád Göncz (1920–), writer, translator, and future (1990–2000) president of Hungary. The remaining poems were supplied by poet Dezső Tandori, one of the greatest living Hungarian translators of poetry.

The Lord of the Rings, although popular and widely known, usually remained in children's sections in libraries and received the most serious critical appreciation in Göncz's afterword. In this, he emphasized Tolkien's connection to fairy tales and myths, pointing out that Tolkien's folklore and fairy tale material are very different from Hungarian native tales, and he called the book "the longest fairy tale of all time." After the change of political regime in 1989, appreciations started to appear in newly founded role-playing game magazines (as well as in *Galaktika*), and 1990 saw the translation of several important Tolkien texts (most notably *The Silmarillion*). Academic interest was aroused, and in the late 1990s, university instructors started offering courses and undertook to supervise theses on or including Tolkien (e.g., American scholar Donald Morse at the University of Debrecen or György E. Szőnyi at the University of Szeged).

The news of Peter Jackson's films in the making called to life several Hungarian Internet sites dedicated to Tolkien, where people involved (among other things) in academic approaches and commentary gathered. In 2002, one of these communities crystallized into the officially founded Hungarian Tolkien Society (Magyar Tolkien Társaság), which, in addition to popularizing Tolkien, had also taken up into its mission to organize and further scholarly activities. The Society has organized three conferences (2003, 2004, 2005) where all important Hungarian universities were represented by students, doctoral candidates, and faculty members, effectively establishing Tolkien as a legitimate academic subject. Publication of the proceedings is mainly through the Society's Internet site and journal (*Lassi Laurië*), but there are planned volumes to collect the most important papers by scholars like Gergely Nagy, Iván Uhrman, Norbert Gyuris, Zoltán Kelemen, Benedek Tóth, and Pál Regős. A notable theoretical bent is observable in these scholars' approaches (especially Nagy, Gyuris, and Tóth), but readings informed by cultural history are also prominent. The Tolkien Society has also taken part in the translation of secondary works on Tolkien (Lin Carter's *A Look behind the Lord of the*

Rings, Michael Martinez's *Visualizing Middle-earth*, and Bassham and Bronson, eds., *The Lord of the Rings and Philosophy*); and members have served as experts supervising translation of Tolkien texts and the dialogue in Peter Jackson's films.

GERGELY NAGY

HUNS

Huns, an Asiatic equestrian people, first entering Europe in the fourth century, whose hostile encounters with various European tribal groups continued to be reshaped and renarrated in epic poetry up to ten centuries later.

J.R.R. Tolkien would have known of the historical Huns from late-classical historians such as Ammianus Marcellinus (fourth c.), Priscus (fifth c.), Jordanes (sixth c.), and Procopius (sixth c.). He probably also knew of such archeological finds as the deformed Hunnish skulls from Thuringia and Kirghizstan, or the fourth-century hoard of Pietroasa (Romania), found in 1837, containing gold and jewels presumed to have been hidden by Goths (q.v.) fearing Hunnish attack. But surely Tolkien would have best known the Huns in the finest of their legendary incarnations (tenth to thirteenth century): (1) in a handful of Old Norse epic poems, including *Atlakvidha* (*The Lay of Atli* [Attila]; from the second half of the Sigurd cycle) and *Hlödhskvidha* (*The Battle of the Goths and the Huns*) and (2) in the German versions of the Sigurd cycle (e.g., the *Nibelungenlied*).

The Easterlings (q.v.) of Middle-earth, equestrian (and sometimes wain-riding) invaders out of the east, enemies of the Free Peoples in the First and Third Ages, are probably based at least in part on historical and legendary images of the Huns.

Christopher Tolkien occupied himself extensively in the 1950s with the *Hervarar saga*, a late Norse legendary saga in which the much older poem *Hlödhskvidha* is embedded. The interface between history and legend in the poem was of particular interest to him, and he concluded (1956) that although many of the poem's place names could be matched to actual Danube Valley sites, it was probably ill advised to try (as many had tried before) to connect the battle between the Goths and the Huns recounted in the poem with the specific, historical defeat of Attila in 451 at what Jordanes had called the "Catalaunian Plains."

SANDRA BALLIF STRAUBHAAR

Further Reading

Goffart, Walter. *The Narrators of Barbarian History*. Princeton, NJ: Princeton University Press, 1988.

Larrington, Carolyne, trans. *The Poetic Edda*. Oxford: Oxford University Press, 1999.

Mierow, Charles Christopher, ed. and trans. *The Gothic History of Jordanes*. Cambridge: Speculum Historiale, 1966.

Neckel, Gustav, and Hans Kuhn, eds. *Edda: Die Lieder des Codex Regius nebst verwandten Denkmälern*. Heidelberg: Carl Winters Universitätsverlag, 1968.

Tolkien, Christopher. "The Battle of the Goths and the Huns." *Saga-Book of the Viking Society* 14, no. 3 (1955–56): 141–63.

———, ed. and trans. *The Saga of King Heidrek the Wise*. London: Thomas Nelson & Sons, 1960.

See also **Edda; Goths; Men: Easterlings; Old Norse Language**

I

I·LAM NA·NGOLDATHON: THE GRAMMAR AND LEXICON OF THE GNOMISH TONGUE

This title was given by Tolkien to his first (extant) effort at a formal and comprehensive description of Goldogrin, or "Gnomish," the later of his two chief invented Elvish languages—though cross-references to Goldogrin forms are found in the earlier *Qenyaqetsa*, with respect to which *I·Lam na·Ngoldathon* stands in close relation as a complementary work. It was begun in 1917, while Tolkien was convalescing at various camps in England, and was most likely abandoned, with the *Qenyaqetsa*, in or about 1919. Goldogrin is the initial conceptual form of the language that would subsequently become and be called, first, Noldorin, the language of the exiled Noldor and, eventually, not long preceding the publication of *The Lord of the Rings*, Sindarin, the language of the Grey-elves in Beleriand. The title *I·Lam na·Ngoldathon* is itself Goldogrin, meaning "The Tongue of the Gnomes." Like the *Qenyaqetsa*, *I·Lam na·Ngoldathon* comprises (by plan) two main parts, a brief grammar and a large lexicon, though as also with the *Qenyaqetsa* the grammar was left far from complete, here covering only the article, the noun, and the adjective, presenting a detailed if concise description of their morphology, inflection, and syntax.

The vast bulk of the work is thus formed by the "Gnomish Lexicon" (extracts from which were given by Christopher Tolkien in the appendices to his two volume edition of *The Book of Lost Tales*), comprising a large dictionary of Goldogrin words,

organized as (more or less) alphabetic lists of words grouped under their initial letter (though naturally this ordering was in the manuscript only approximate, as Tolkien added words over time within the major sections, but not necessarily in their precise alphabetic slot). Entries often include an etymological cross-reference to Qenya cognates and/or to reconstructed forms in the common parent language illustrating the phonological history of the Goldogrin forms. As with the "Qenya Lexicon" of the *Qenyaqetsa*, this "Gnomish Lexicon" also provides a remarkable insight into Middle-earth as Tolkien then conceived of it, in its terminology and the milieu that is thereby implied by the lexicon for its speakers. In fact, in this regard both the "Gnomish Lexicon" and the "Qenya Lexicon" provide a remarkably rich vocabulary for the invented languages, far richer than that provided for any of the subsequent conceptual stages of these languages by any of Tolkien's later lexical efforts.

Another particularly noteworthy feature of Goldogrin as represented in *I·Lam na·Ngoldathon* is the degree to which it is less fully influenced by the phonology of Welsh than are the later Noldorin and Sindarin stages of the language—lacking, for example, the striking and strongly characteristic *i*-affection plurals of Noldorin, Sindarin, and Welsh (analogous to such English "irregular" plurals as "goose/geese" and "mouse/mice"), which would not enter into Tolkien's conception of this language until at least a year after primary work on the "Gnomish Lexicon" has ceased—and in fact is, as Patrick H. Wynne has shown, intriguingly English-like in its vowel gradations, particularly in those of its past-tense formations, which rather closely model the set of sound changes known as the "Great Vowel Shift" of Middle to Modern English.

The composition of *I·Lam na·Ngoldathon* was quite similar to that of the *Qenyaqetsa*, and again entirely characteristic of Tolkien's description of his languages. It exhibits three distinct layers differentiated by the instrument of writing, with early and partially erased pencil underlying a later ink recapitulation of the work and with the subsequent revision and expansion of this ink layer in crayon and pencil; the whole resulting in essentially three distinct but nonetheless closely related and physically entangled versions of the work within the single manuscript as it was left to stand when Tolkien abandoned it, moving on to another recapitulation and conceptual shift in a fresh set of manuscript (and typescript) descriptions of the altered conceptions of these languages in the early 1920s.

CARL F. HOSTETTER

Further Reading

Garth, John. *Tolkien and the Great War* (London: Harper-Collins, 2003). See in particular chap. 12, *"Tol Withernon* and *Fladweth Amrod,"* which discusses the circumstances in which Tolkien composed *I·Lam na·Ngoldathon.*

Renk, Thorsten. "The Goldogrin Grammar—an Introduction." http://www.phy.duke.edu/~trenk/elvish/goldogrin/grammar.html. n.d.

Tolkien, J.R.R. *I·Lam na·Ngoldathon: The Grammar and Lexicon of the Gnomish Tongue.* Edited by Christopher Gilson, Patrick Wynne, Arden R. Smith, and Carl F. Hostetter. *Parma Eldalamberon* 11 (1995).

———. *Qenyaqetsa: The Qenya Phonology and Lexicon.* Edited by Christopher Gilson, Carl F. Hostetter, Patrick Wynne, and Arden R. Smith. *Parma Eldalamberon* 12 (1998).

Wynne, Patrick H. "Are Goldogrin and Qenya 'Primitive'?" *Tengwestië,* April 2004. http://www.elvish.org/Tengwestie/editorials/20040404.phtml.

———. "The Goldogrin Past Tense." *Tengwestië,* April 2004. http://www.elvish.org/Tengwestie/articles/Wynne/goldpat.phtml.

———. "Goldogrin Pronouns." December 2003. http://www.pa2rick.com/langlab/goldogrin_pronouns.html.

IMMORTALITY

Tolkien has stated that the wish to escape death is one of the most profound human desires expressed in fairy stories and fantasy. Along with death, he claimed immortality to be a dominant theme in *The Lord of the Rings* (*Letters,* 186). Through the juxtaposition of human beings, with their mortality and short life spans, and Elves, who possess the potential of deathlessness, the theme of death pervades the novel structurally. The deathlessness of the Elves, however, is not understood as authentic immortality: the author has referred to it as rather "serial longevity" (*Letters,* 284). Paradoxically, in Tolkien's mythology true immortality is intimated for humans.

Thus, Aragorn's last words to Arwen include the conviction "Behold! We are not bound for ever to the circles of the world, and beyond them is more than memory" (*RK,* Appendix A, 344), while in *The Silmarillion* it is stated that although human beings die, they shall eventually join the angelic Ainur in the "Second Music of the Ainur" at the end of time, when creation will be set aright. Since, among others, for Tolkien Middle-earth is purported to exist in an imaginary period before Christian revelation, such beliefs are likely intended to imply a monotheistic natural theology, where people have an intuition of their ultimate immortality: witness the belief of Theoden upon his death that he will be meeting his ancestors.

While Elves are "naturally" deathless, their life span is connected with the duration of life on earth, and they are not known to be included in the Second Music of the Ainur, thus they are excluded from true immortality. In the post–*The Lord of the Rings* tale "Athrabeth Finrod ah Andreth," set in the First Age, Finrod the High Elf is keenly aware that even death delayed for eons is no less dreaded: "it is not clear that a foreseen doom long delayed is in all ways a lighter burden than one that comes soon" (*Morgoth,* 312). Moreover, life on Middle-earth eventually becomes wearying. Upon leaving Lothlórien, Legolas explains that the necessity of Elves witnessing the fleetingness of all of creation constitutes "a grief to them" (*FR,* II, ix, 405). Only beyond Middle-earth in the undying land of Aman are deathlessness and immortality somewhat conjoined. An alternative for Elves is to marry a mortal: on the one hand, they "truly die;" on the other hand, they may partake of the possibility of the human hope for eternal life in Ilúvatar.

For human beings, however, the deathlessness of the Elves presents a powerful temptation, since it is empirical and not a matter of faith. This theme is the dominant motif of the "Akallabêth," the story of Numenor, posthumously published in *The Silmarillion* and briefly recapped in the appendixes of *The Lord of the Rings.* In the story, the people who helped the High Elves and the Valar in the war against Morgoth at the conclusion of the First Age are bequeathed the island of Númenor, located between Middle-earth on one side and the Undying Lands of Aman on the other. They are rewarded with a near paradise: their life spans are exceedingly long, and there is little sickness. However, they must willingly accept the time of their death, for it is the gift of Ilúvatar. Furthermore, the Númenoreans must not sail in the direction of the Undying Lands: both conditions are obviously correlated. As time goes by, the Númenóreans are disturbed by the temporality of life and complain to the messenger of the Valar: "Why should we not envy the Valar, or even the least of the Deathless? For of us is required a blind trust, and a hope without assurance, knowing not what lies before us in a little while. And yet we also love the Earth and would not lose it" (*S,* 265). Tempted by the subsequently "captured" Sauron, a combined fear of death and pride leads the Númenóreans to assault the stronghold of the Valar in the hope of seizing immortality for the select few. This breach of the Ban of the Valar leads to the catastrophic downfall of Númenor, and the paradise is lost, with only a faithful few escaping to Middle-earth.

One of the signs of the Númenóreans' growing inability to accept death is their increasing practice of "build[ing] great houses for their dead" (*S,* 266). This theme is carried over into *The Lord of the Rings,* where the same practice of their descendants is a sign of the decline of Minas Tirith. Thus, building monuments is considered a kind of impure substitute immortality. The actual conclusion of the story of Numenor, however, takes place in the appendixes of *The Lord of the Rings* when Aragorn accepts the time of his death without rebellion.

If the story of Númenor together with its conclusion in the trilogy indicates the sinfulness of attempting to strive for deathlessness, this does not mean that the desire for immortality is altogether impure for Tolkien. In her dialogue with Finrod, Athrabeth proclaims that, according to the lore of her people, "we knew that we had been born *never to die.* And by that, my lord, we meant: *born to life everlasting, without any shadow of any end*" (*Morgoth,* 314). This posthumously published story is the point where Tolkien's mythology comes closest to evoking his own Christian belief, wherein death is introduced into the world through original sin. As the ensuing dialogue indicates, bemoaning the intervening "darkness" that defiled its true state, the desire of immortality is demonstrated to stem from the intuition of the prelapsarian state of humanity.

Thus, the Middle-earth conviction that death is a "gift of Ilúvatar" and as such must be accepted ultimately stems from the belief that Iluvatar can eventually turn the wrongdoings of humanity toward a greater good. Or as it is put in "The Quenta Silmarillion" regarding the disharmonious actions of people: "These too in their time shall find that all that they do redounds at the end only to the glory of my work" (*S,* 42) The difference between the desire of immortality

as a genuine intuition of humanity's true state and the sinful version subverted by pride is consonant with the strong Augustinian sense of evil as perverted good that pervades Tolkien's mythopoeic writing.

CHRISTOPHER GARBOWSKI

See also **Death; Elves; Fall of Man; Theological and Moral Approaches in Tolkien's Works**

INCARNATION

As a Christian, Tolkien considered the Incarnation to be the center and purpose of human history. It is, therefore, hardly surprising that the incarnational dimension is axiomatic to Tolkien's legendarium in general and to *The Lord of the Rings* in particular.

With customary and characteristic subtlety, Tolkien hides the key to understanding the incarnational aspect of his work in one of the appendices of *The Lord of the Rings.* It is here, tucked away as an apparent afterthought, that he reveals that March 25 is "the date of the downfall of the Barad-dûr," adding that the New Year began on March 25, "in commemoration of the fall of Sauron and the deeds of the Ring-bearers." This date is of singular significance in the Christian calendar. It is the Feast of the Annunciation, the date on which Christians celebrate the Incarnation of Christ. It is traditionally believed to be the date on which Christ's Crucifixion occurred. Annunciation Day, as it was called, was also the start of the New Year in most countries in Christian Europe during the Middle Ages. Taken together, Christ's Incarnation and Crucifixion redeemed humanity from original sin. It can be said to have "unmade" original sin, casting it back into the fires of hell in which it was originally forged. The connection between the Incarnation and the destruction of the One Sin that rules them all and "in the darkness binds them" is clearly at the very heart of *The Lord of the Rings.*

Apart from its subtextual centrality to *The Lord of the Rings,* Tolkien discusses the Incarnation in "Athrabeth Finrod ah Andreth" ("The Debate of Finrod and Andreth") in *Morgoth's Ring,* volume 10 of *The History of Middle-earth.* Described by Christopher Tolkien as a "major and finished work," this debate between the Elven king, Finrod, and the human wise-woman, Andreth, offers many fascinating insights into the Christian theology underpinning the reality of Middle-earth, including a prophetic inkling of the future Incarnation. Referring to what she called the "Old Hope," Andreth explains the belief that "the One will himself enter into Arda, and heal Men and all the Marring from the beginning to the end." She goes on to state that the Old Hope passes her own understanding. "How could Eru enter into the thing that He has made, and than which He is beyond measure greater? Can the singer enter into his tale or the designer into his picture?" "He is already in it, as well as outside," Finrod replies. "But the 'in-dwelling' and the 'out-living' are not in the same mode." Andreth understands these fundamental notions of God's immanence and transcendence but stresses that the Old Hope speaks of something different, something incarnational: "They speak of Eru Himself *entering into Arda*, and that is a thing wholly different." This concept of incarnation is a revelation to Finrod, but he sees instantly why it might be the only answer to the problem of Evil: "I cannot see how else this healing could be achieved. Since Eru will surely not suffer Melkor to turn the world to his own will and to triumph in the end. Yet there is no power conceivable greater than Melkor save Eru only. Therefore Eru, if He will not relinquish His work to Melkor, who must else proceed to mastery, then Eru must come in to conquer him."

JOSEPH PEARCE

Further Reading

Birzer, Bradley J. *J.R.R. Tolkien's Sanctifying Myth.* Wilmington, DE: ISI Books, 2002.
Caldecott, Stratford. *Secret Fire: The Spiritual Vision of J.R.R. Tolkien.* London: Darton, Longman & Todd, 2003.
Pearce, Joseph, ed. *Tolkien: A Celebration.* London: HarperCollins, 1999.
———. *Tolkien: Man and Myth.* London: HarperCollins, 1998.
Purtill, Richard. *J.R.R. Tolkien: Myth, Morality and Religion.* San Francisco, CA: Harper & Row, 1984.

See also **Immortality;** *Morgoth's Ring*; **Reincarnation**

INDUSTRIALIZATION

In his fiction, essays, and letters, Tolkien is clearly hostile to industrialism. This attitude was part of his overall romantic antimodernism, since it also extended to the nation-state and modern techno-science.

Its biographical roots lie in his experience of the effects of the continuing industrial revolution, in terms of increasingly mechanized methods of production and increased urban development, during his youth in the West Midlands. At the age of eight, after four years in the then bucolic hamlet of Sarehole, Tolkien found himself in thoroughly industrialized Birmingham, living alternately with his mother in cramped and poor accommodation and at King Edward's School. Sarehole gradually became a suburb of Birmingham, and when he revisited it in 1933,

he lamented the "violent and peculiarly hideous change" that had taken place (Carpenter, 125). It remained in his memory, however, as an unspoiled paradise; and all true paradises, as Proust once remarked, are ones we have lost. Eventually, the old mill of Sarehole became transformed in Middle-earth into the mill in Hobbiton "modernized" by Ted Sandyman. (Ironically, the "real" mill of Tolkien's childhood, along with its green environs, has survived, thanks to local conservationist efforts.)

Tolkien articulated this outlook in his essay "On Fairy-Stories" when he defended fantasy as "the Escape of the Prisoner" from "the Robot Age, that combines elaboration and ingenuity of means with ugliness, and (often) inferiority of result" (*TL*, 56). It is quite possible, he wrote, to rationally condemn "progressive things like factories, or the machine-guns and bombs that appear to be their most natural and inevitable . . . products" (*TL*, 58). The same applies to "the noise, stench, ruthlessness and extravagance of the internal-combustion engine" (*TL*, 60). The resonance with Tolkien's prescient ecological concerns is obvious.

Excoriating someone overheard defending mass-production factories and traffic as bringing "real life" to Oxford, Tolkien declared that "the notion that motor-cars are more 'alive' than, say, centaurs or dragons is curious; that they are more 'real' than, say, horses is pathetically absurd" (*TL*, 57). (Incidentally, this is one of several points at which Tolkien's antimodernism offers tantalizing purchase for a postmodern antirealism.)

In Tolkien's fictional world, there is a significant description of goblins (i.e., orcs) in *The Hobbit*: "It is not unlikely that they invented some of the machines that have since troubled the world, especially the ingenious devices for killing large numbers of people at once, for wheels and engines and explosions always delighted them . . . but in those days and those wild parts they had not advanced (as it is called) so far" (*H*, IV, 109).

Turning to *The Lord of the Rings*, we have already mentioned Sandyman's mill. Not unconnected is the renegade wizard Saruman who, as Sharkey, was behind the attempt at forced industrialization of the Shire. Earlier, he had passed from being a polite neighbor of Fangorn Forest to its destroyer, cutting down the trees "to feed the fires of Orthanc" and his program of military and industrial domination. Other times they are "just cut down and left to rot—orc-mischief, that" (*TT*, III, iv, 77). As elsewhere in Tolkien's work, industrialism is of a piece with empire; in Treebeard's words, Saruman "is plotting to become a Power. He has a mind of metal and wheels; and he does not care for growing things, except as far as they serve him for the moment" (*TT*, III, iv, 76).

The ultimate epitome of industrialism in Middle-earth, however, is Sauron's Mordor. It is (1) politically totalitarian and completely centralized, (2) the leading military and imperialist power, and (3) highly industrialized, with great mines and forges in the north and slave-worked agricultural fields in the south. Quite intentionally, these attributes are closely connected, and what unites them is the desire for power. It should also be noted that in relation to the modern world, whether they are interpreted in terms of capitalist or state-socialist industrialism is secondary; both the drive and the consequences are the same.

The consequences of Sauron's pathological industrialism are made perfectly plain: at their fullest stretch, the destruction of all difference and independence or, in a word, pluralism. Under threat are all places where peoples (whether hobbits, Dwarves, Elves, or humans) rule themselves, all spiritual values that transcend the cult-worship of Sauron himself, and all natural beauty and integrity.

The latter is made perhaps particularly clear. Approaching the Black Gate of the Morannon, for example, the hobbits encounter a sickening wasteland where "nothing lived, not even the leprous growths that feed on rottenness. . . . They had come to the desolation that lay before Mordor: the lasting monument to the dark labour of its slaves" (*TT*, IV, ii, 239). In Morgul Valley, "Earth, air and water all seem accursed" (*TT*, IV, viii, 320). In striking contrast, those cultures and societies that are least industrial—paradigmatically, Lothlorien—are those where the wonder of Enchantment, not the will of Magic, is the ultimate value. And as John Ruskin and William Morris would have concurred, they are also the most beautiful places in Middle-earth. (In this respect, the Shire is a kind of half-way house of agrarian-domestic labor and enjoyment, poised between the fully lyrical Elves and the fully instrumental servants of Sauron.)

In summary, in Tolkien's view, the machine—and by extension, techno-science—is our modern form of Magic, the use of the will to remake the world and dominate others in order to do so (as distinct from Enchantment and its creation of secondary worlds). Given in addition the consequences of humanity's fallen condition, "we come inevitably from Daedelus and Icarus to the Giant Bomber. It is not an advance on wisdom!" (*Letters*, 88). In today's hypertechnological world, we might also reflect on Tolkien's prophetic observation in a letter to his son toward the end of World War II: "As the servants of the Machines are becoming a privileged class, the Machines are going to be enormously more powerful. What's their next move?" (*Letters*, 111). It is no mere figure of speech for Tolkien to attribute such quasi-autonomy to the mechanical; he was well aware of the dynamic that another shrewd observer of modernity, Max Weber, likened to finding oneself aboard a speeding train while being unsure that the next set of switches is correctly set.

PATRICK CURRY

Further Reading

Curry, Patrick. *Defending Middle-earth: Tolkien, Myth and Modernity*. 2nd ed. Boston, MA: Houghton Mifflin, 2004.

See also **Capitalism; Environmentalism and Eco-Criticism; Nature**

INKLINGS

J.R.R. Tolkien was a main figure in the Inklings, a literary group of friends centered largely around C.S. Lewis. Tolkien described the club in a letter as an "undetermined and unelected circle of friends who gathered around C.S.L[ewis]., and met in his rooms in Magdalen. . . . Our habit was to read aloud compositions of various kinds (and lengths!)."

As Tolkien's description suggests, there is somewhat of a problem of definition. Furthermore, contrary to Tolkien's portrayal, at many meetings no readings took place. The group called the Inklings was so informal and casual that very little common entity at first seems to remain. As Tolkien points out, that "the Inklings had no recorder and C.S. Lewis no Boswell." Glimpses of meetings, however, are seen in the letters of Tolkien, Lewis; another Inkling, Charles Williams; and in the diaries of Lewis's brother, Major Warren Hamilton Lewis, a retired army major. After his brother's death, Warren lamented: "Had I known that I was to have outlived Jack I would have played Boswell on those Thursday evenings, but as it is, I am afraid that my diary contains only the scantiest material for reconstructing an Inklings" (from his unpublished biography of C.S. Lewis). There are also comments in memoirs by Warren Lewis and John Wain, a poet, novelist, and literary critic who attended meetings for a time. Curiously, furthermore, we have a fictional portrayal of the Inklings in Tolkien's unfinished and profound "The Notion Club Papers," in which some of the characters reflect aspects of actual members. Lewis's editorial preface of *Essays Presented to Charles Williams* is also informative, a collection that includes Tolkien's "On Fairy-Stories." This volume, originally intended as a Festschrift to mark Williams' return to London after the ending of the war, was brought out instead after his untimely death.

C.S. Lewis provides a rare window into the Inklings in this preface. He points out that three of the essays in the collection are on literature, and, specifically, one aspect of literature, the "narrative art." That, Lewis says, is natural enough. Charles Williams's *"All Hallows Eve* and my own *Perelandra* (as well as Professor Tolkien's unfinished sequel to *The Hobbit*) had all been read aloud, each chapter as it was written. They owe a good deal to the hard-hitting criticism of the circle. The problems of narrative as such—seldom heard of in modern critical writings—were constantly before our minds."

The Inklings embodied the ideals of life and pleasure of Tolkien and Lewis and centered around an appreciation of the continuing power of myth and romance stories that included glimpses or more of other worlds. Such stories, they believed, were adult fare. Lewis spoke of Inklings' meetings full of "the cut and parry of prolonged, fierce, masculine argument." (Oxford societies of the time were invariably male only.) Both Tolkien and Lewis were clubbable—Tolkien had been in the T.C.B.S. group of school friends and in the Coalbiters (along with Lewis) in previous years. The Inklings was based upon a network of friends and professional acquaintances. The group had an edge to it in that most had experienced combat in World War One. Several had been wounded, such as Lewis and Dyson (the latter so severely that he had an out-of-the-body experience). The reality of war was internalized, especially by Tolkien and Lewis, as a natural image of spiritual battle between good and evil.

The Inklings' most important years were the 1940s, especially the Second World War years when Charles Williams was resident in Oxford and added his distinctive presence to the group. He attended regularly and was often in the company of Tolkien and Lewis outside of Inklings meetings, when sometimes Tolkien would read additional chapters of *The Lord of the Rings* fresh from drafting. According to John Wain, after Charles Williams' death in 1945, the two most active members of the group became Tolkien and Lewis. In his autobiography, *Sprightly Running*, Wain, in broad brush strokes and no doubt with some irony, describes the Inklings as "a circle of instigators" encouraging each other "in the task of redirecting the whole current of contemporary art and life." He writes that "While Lewis attacked on a wide front, with broadcasts, popular-theological books, children's stories, romances, and controversial literary criticism, Tolkien concentrated on the writing of his colossal 'Lord of the Rings' trilogy. His readings of each successive installment were eagerly

received, for 'romance' was a pillar of this whole structure."

Tolkien occasionally refers to the group in his letters. Writing approvingly to his publisher about Lewis's science fiction story *Out of the Silent Planet*, he speaks of it "being read aloud to our local club (which goes in for reading things short and long aloud). It proved an exciting serial, and was highly approved. But of course we are all rather like-minded." It is clear from his letters that the Inklings provided valuable and much-needed encouragement as he struggled to compose *The Lord of the Rings*.

Another member, Colin Hardie, wrote of the Inklings, and its literary character, in 1983, fifty years after its inception: "Oxford saw the informal formation of a select circle of friends, mostly writers or 'scribblers' (reminiscent perhaps of the 18th century Scriblerus Club, whose members were Pope, Swift, Gay, Arbuthnot, author of the *Memoirs of Martinus Scriblerus*, and others . . .)."

As a specifically literary club ("the Inklings proper" according to Warren Lewis), the confraternity lasted from 1933 to 1949, over fifteen years, a little over half of the existence of the Inklings in its one form or the other. The other form, subsidiary to the "proper" Inklings, was that of informal meetings, usually in Oxford pubs. One of the most favored haunts was "The Eagle and Child" public house in St. Giles (known more familiarly as "The Bird and Baby"). Many a discussion or friendly argument was washed down with beer or cider.

In the first years of its life, from 1933, the Inklings was solely a literary gathering in Lewis's college rooms. At around the beginning of the war, the parallel pub gatherings began as an institution, usually on Tuesday mornings, with the literary club normally on Thursday evenings, but occasionally other evenings. The literary group seems to have concluded in the fall of 1949, coinciding with Tolkien's completion of the main writing of *The Lord of the Rings*. During the next thirteen or so years, from the end of 1949 to Lewis's death in November 1963, there were no recorded Thursday night meetings in the college rooms of either Lewis or Tolkien specifically to read work in progress. The pub gatherings continued, however, moving from Tuesday to Monday mornings to accommodate Lewis, when, after 1954, he commuted to Cambridge during term time, leaving Oxford on Tuesdays and returning later in the week. A few days before his death, Lewis in a letter referred to the group in diminished terms: "Once a week I attend a re-union of old friends at one of the Oxford taverns. (*Beer* thank goodness is not on the list of things denied me.)" (Letter to Mrs. Jones, November 16, 1963.)

In view of its predominantly literary character, it is appropriate to ask which of the Inklings were those who actually read to the group (so far as we can tell, from what limited documentation we have). C.S. Lewis read extensively to the Inklings. Tolkien read much of *The Lord of the Rings* to the Inklings and earlier from *The Hobbit* as he reworked it in the thirties. Charles Williams read plays, poetry, and his last novel, *All Hallows Eve,* which benefited greatly from the criticism received. Though Owen Barfield was rarely able to attend, he read to the club while there—he was a close friend of Lewis's whose views on the poetic imagination, metaphor, and language profoundly influenced him and also Tolkien. (In addition, Lewis frequently commented on Barfield's writings-in-progress by letter.) Adam Fox, dean of Divinity at Magdalen College, read poetry. Warren Lewis read from elegant histories of France that he was writing. Dr. R.E. Havard read short pieces, such as an account of mountain climbing and the appendix he wrote at Lewis's invitation for *The Problem of Pain.* Colin Hardie, classics tutor at Magdalen College, read occasionally. Lord David Cecil, biographer and literary critic from New College, also read— Warren Lewis records an occasion in 1947 when he read from his forthcoming book on Thomas Gray. Those documented as attending, permanently, frequently, or occasionally, in addition to those just mentioned, include Christopher Tolkien (who, as the better reader, often read the latest installment from *The Lord of the Rings*); R.B. McCallum, fellow in History at Pembroke College and later master of the college; J.A.W. Bennett, a fellow and tutor like Lewis in English at Magdalen; Nevill Coghill, one of the earliest members of the Inklings; Hugo Dyson, another early member; Charles Wrenn, who succeeded Tolkien as professor of Anglo-Saxon in 1946; Gervase Mathew, a medievalist and writer; John Wain, later a major novelist and poet; James Dundas-Grant, in charge of a resisential home for Roman Catholic students in Oxford; C.E. "Tom" Stevens, a fellow and tutor in ancient history at Magdalen College; and Roger Lancelyn Green, a writer and historian of children's literature and future biographer of C.S. Lewis.

In an early description, in 1936 to Charles Williams, Lewis points out that one element that the Inklings had in common was a Christian faith. He clearly felt that one purpose of the club was its shared beliefs. This fits with the probably exaggerated picture given by John Wain. Lewis and at least some others, so far as Lewis was concerned, stood against the modern world in respect of its post-Christian character. All of them seemed convinced that myth had the ability to generalize without losing contact with the individual character of natural things. This was one of the bases of the argument employed by Tolkien and Hugo Dyson in the fall of 1931 to convince Lewis of the truth of the Christian claims. At a particular point in real history, they reasoned, myth had become fact, fulfilling countless prefigurements in human storytelling and making of myths. The telling of stories and making of myth was high on the agenda of the literary meetings of the Inklings. Evidently, even those who could not spin a story (such as Dyson and Warren Lewis) encouraged those who could (Lewis, Tolkien, Williams, and, when he could attend, Owen Barfield).

The Inklings is to be seen mainly as a very significant literary group. While the other meetings in pubs, which were undoubtedly important, carried on the literary impact informally, they mainly were gatherings of friends with no clearly functional purpose. The members constitute a literary group that is very much part of mainstream twentieth-century literature.

In the Inklings there is a guiding vision of the relationship of imagination and myth to reality and of a Christian worldview in which a pagan spirituality is seen as prefiguring the advent of Christ and the Christian story. In the club, Lewis, Tolkien, Williams, and Barfield are central figures, so much so that the other members, even though important, are defined in relation to one or more of the four as part of the literary movement. There are major and lesser Inklings, defined in terms of attendance or nonattendance at the literary gatherings and by their literary influence or light they shed on Lewis, Tolkien, Williams, or Barfield, or more than one of the four.

Between them, the Inklings produced an impressive array of literature, including fiction, poetry, biography, history, literary criticism, philology, theology, philosophy, and drama. Works of the two most well-known Inklings, Tolkien and Lewis, have been adapted for radio, television, and cinema, reinforcing their impact upon popular culture.

COLIN DURIEZ

Further Reading

Carpenter, Humphrey *The Inklings: C.S. Lewis, J.R.R. Tolkien, Charles Williams and Their Friends.* London: Allen & Unwin, 1978.

Duriez, Colin, and David Porter. *The Inklings Handbook.* London: Azure, 2001.

Inklings-Jahrbuch. Vol. 1, 1983.

Knight, Gareth. *The Magical World of the Inklings.* Longmead: Element Books, 1990.

Lewis, W. H. *Brothers and Friends: The Diaries of Major Warren Hamilton Lewis.* San Francisco: Harper & Row, 1982.

Pavlac, Diana. "The Company They Keep: Assessing the Mutual Influence of C.S. Lewis, J.R.R. Tolkien, and

Charles Williams." Ph.D. thesis, University of Illinois at Chicago, 1993.

Tolkien, J.R.R. "The Notion Club Papers." In *Sauron*.

Wain, John. *Sprightly Running: Part of an Autobiography*. London: Macmillan, 1962.

See also **Barfield, Owen; Bennett, J.A.W.; Dundas-Grant, James; Dyson, Hugo; Hardie, Colin; Havard, R.E.; Lewis, C.S.; Lewis, Warren; Cecil, Lord David; Notion Club Papers; Oxford; Green, Roger Lancelyn; Wain, John; Williams, Charles; Wren, Charles; Tolkien, Christopher**

IRELAND

Between his first visit to Eire in 1949 and his resignation from the National University of Ireland in 1959, Tolkien frequently toured the Isle, made friends, and examined for various colleges, "much to his taste" (Carpenter, 136). Highlights included an August 1952 holiday, captured in his *Summer in Kerry* and other paintings (Hammond and Scull, 32), and his doctorate of letters received from University College Dublin, July 1954. Despite acquiring a fondness for Ireland and "(most of) its people" (*Letters*, 289), Tolkien disliked the Irish Gaelic language, which he admits "heavily defeated" him (*Letters*, 134).

In 1937, Tolkien stated a distaste for things Celtic, and "their fundamental unreason . . . like a broken stained glass window reassembled" (*Letters*, 26). He softened those views by his 1955 O'Donnell lecture, declaring his work to contain "much of what I personally have received from the study of things Celtic" (*MC*, 162). Critics have compared his Elves with the *Tuatha Dé Danann* (People of the Goddess Dana), the fairy-folk of Irish myth, and Valinor with *Tir-nan-Og* (Celtic Paradise). Shippey explores Irish themes of sailing west to "a resolution of hope and prohibition" in Tolkien's poetry, from 1920 to 1955's "extremely private poem" *Imram*, based on the voyages of St. Brendan (Shippey, 252). Flieger analyzes the proposed "Lost Road" and "Notion Club" stories revealing an "Irish strain in Tolkien's work, often overlooked" (Flieger, 155).

Tolkien always regarded Ireland as alien to his senses. In "The Lost Tales," Ossë breaks off the western half of the Lonely Isle, becoming the Isle of Íverin (Ireland in the "Qenya dictionary"), whose "dwellers come not into these tales" (*Lost Tales II,* 312, 344). Completing *The Lord of the Rings*, his visits provided a retreat, an isle in the west. By 1955, he still considered "the air of Ireland wholly alien," but attractive (*Letters*, 219).

DON N. ANGER

Further Reading

Carpenter, Humphrey. *J.R.R. Tolkien: A Biography*. London: Allen & Unwin, 1977.

Carter, Lin. *Tolkien: A Look behind the Lord of the Rings*. New York: Ballantine Books, 1969.

Duriez, Colin. *Tolkien and C.S. Lewis: The Gift of Friendship*. Mahwah, NJ: Hiddenspring, 2003.

Flieger, Verlyn. *A Question of Time: J.R.R. Tolkien's Road to Faërie*. Kent, OH: Kent State University Press, 1997.

Gillespie, Gerald V. "The Irish Mythological Cycle and Tolkien's Eldar." *Mythlore* 30 (Winter 1982): 8–9, 42.

Hammond, Wayne, and Christina Scull. *J.R.R. Tolkien: Artist & Illustrator*. London: HarperCollins, 1995.

Jones, Leslie Ellen. *Myth & Middle-earth: Exploring the Mediaeval Legends behind J.R.R. Tolkien's Lord of the Rings*. New York: Cold Spring Press, 2002.

Kocher, Paul H. *Master of Middle-earth: The Fiction of J.R.R. Tolkien*. New York: Ballantine Books, 1977.

Parker, Douglass. "Hwæt We Holbytla..." *Hudson Review* 9 (Winter 1956–57): 606.

Shippey, Tom. *The Road to Middle-earth*. London: Grafton, 1992.

See also **Celtic Mythology; "English and Welsh"; Report on the Excavation of the Prehistoric, Roman and Post-Roman Site in Lydney Park; Saint Brendan; Welsh Language**

ITALIAN LANGUAGE

Tolkien was exposed to languages for all his life. He was familiar with Italian, although he never studied it at school. This is due above all to his love for Latin and other Romance languages. When he was four years old, his mother began to teach him French and Latin. The latter delighted Tolkien for the sounds and shapes of the words. When he was ten years old, he began learning Spanish. His guardian, Father Francis Xavier Morgan, spoke Spanish fluently, and Tolkien used to borrow Spanish books from his collection and tried to learn the language. The two Tolkien brothers usually served Mass in the Birmingham Oratory before going to school; so Ronald grew up learning also the Oratorian Italian pronunciation of Latin, very different from the strictly "philological" one taught at school in those days. In the summer of 1918, he improved his Spanish and Italian, while suffering from trench fever and lying in bed in a military hospital in Hull. In Oxford, Tolkien and his friend and colleague C.S. Lewis used to read Dante's works to each other. Tolkien for a while was also a member of the "Oxford Dante Society." In August 1955, the professor and his daughter Priscilla went to Italy for a holiday. They spent two weeks in Venice and in Assisi. He recorded his feeling of having "come to the heart of Christendom: my exile from the borders and far provinces returning home, or at least to the home of my fathers." In Venice, among the canals he found himself "almost free of the cursed disease of the internal combustion engine of which all the world is dying"; and he wrote afterward: "Venice seemed incredibly, elvishly lovely—to me like a vision of Old Gondor, or Pelargir of the Numenorean Ships, before the return of the Shadow." In Venice, he visited an exhibition on Giorgione's paintings, and he saw Verdi's *Rigoletto*; he was shocked by the frescoes of Assisi's Cathedral. "I remain in love with Italian," he wrote to his son Christopher in the letter dated August 15, 1955, "and feel quite lorn without a chance of trying to speak it! We must keep it up."

In August 1954, *The Fellowship of the Ring* was published, and on the blurb Lewis wrote: "If Ariosto rivalled it in invention (which in fact he does not), he would still lack its heroic seriousness." Critics displayed an extraordinary personal animosity against Lewis and mocked this comparison. "I don't know Ariosto," Tolkien himself said, "and I'd loathe him if I did."

Tom Shippey points out that Tolkien's success with millions of ordinary readers proved the critics wrong and that comparison with Ariosto was almost right. In *The Lord of the Rings*, Tolkien did produce a narrative of "entrelacement," the ancient and prenovelistic device used in Italian epics about the knights of Charlemagne, Boiardo's *Orlando Innamorato* and Ariosto's *Orlando Furioso*, imitated in English by Spenser's *The Faerie Queene*. According to Shippey, Italy was in Tolkien's mind at least once in *The Lord of the Rings*, when he describes Ithilien as the land of the olive and the tamarisk, but also the land of ancient civilization, where the stream may halt in "an ancient stone basin" with "carven rim."

ROBERTO ARDUINI

Further Reading

Carpenter, Humphrey. *The Inklings: C.S. Lewis, J.R.R. Tolkien, Charles Williams, and Their Friends*. Boston, MA: Houghton Mifflin, 1979.
———. *Tolkien: A Biography*. Boston, MA: Houghton Mifflin, 2000.
Devaux, Michaël. "Le gondole di Gondor: il viaggio di Tolkien a Venezia (1955)." In *I quaderni della Contea*, vol. 3. Società Tolkieniana Italiana, 2005.
Garth, John. *Tolkien and the Great War: The Threshold of Middle-earth*. Boston, MA: Houghton Mifflin, 2003.
Gibaldi, Joseph "Will Ariosto Be the Next Tolkien?" *College Literature* (West Chester State College) 2 (1975): 138–42.
Isaacs, Neil D., and Rose A. Zimbardo. *Tolkien and the Critics*. Notre Dame, IN: University of Notre Dame Press, 1968.
Shippey, Tom. "Preface to the Italian Translation." In *La via per la Terra di Mezzo*. Genoa and Milan: Marietti.
———. *The Road to Middle-earth: Revised and Expanded Edition*. Boston, MA: Houghton Mifflin, 2001.
Spirito, Padre Guglielmo. "Il viaggio di Tolkien ad Assisi." In *I quaderni della Contea*, vol. 1. Società Tolkieniana Italiana, 2005.

See also **Continental Europe; Dante; Italy: Reception of Tolkien**

ITALY: RECEPTION OF TOLKIEN

Tolkien in Italy was a well-known author but his books did not have a typical editorial history. First, because he has been considered a politicized writer for long time; second, although *The Lord of the Rings'* Italian translation may be regarded as very outstanding, it had only a word-of-mouth cult following; Peter Jackson's movies have brought Tolkien's writings into prominence, but this is perhaps, at its peak.

Il Signore degli Anelli was published at the end of 1970s, translated not by a seasoned professional, but rather by a teenaged girl of aristocratic descent, Vicky Alliata di Villafranca. In 1967, publishing house Astrolabio had realized only the first part of her original translation, *La Compagnia dell'Anello* ("The Fellowship of the Ring"). So, three years later, a new right-wing publishing house, Rusconi, published the whole translation, revised by Quirino Principe, a translator and music critic. Tolkien's 1966 "Foreword to the Second Edition" wasn't published, but a well-known right-wing intellectual Elémire Zolla wrote his own foreword. It was one of the cornerstones of Tolkien's gross misunderstanding in Italy, where he was considered a right-wing writer.

In an article, Principe stated that he strongly disagreed with many of the choices made by Alliata, which led him to alter the original translation in a rather heavy-handed way. As far as we know, Principe retranslated all the poems and the appendices, as well as changing many of the proper names present in the book. The motivations for Principe's changes are often rather questionable. He had not read Tolkien's "Guide to the Names in *The Lord of the Rings*" as Alliata had, although it should be pointed out that a number of choices are instead remarkably faithful to Tolkien's guidelines.

In 1973, *Lo Hobbit*, translated by Elena Jeronimidis Conte, was published by *Adelphi*. In 1978, *Rusconi* published *Il Silmarillion*, translated by Francesco Saba Sardi. In his translator's note at the end of the book, he wrote that, rather than turning to the original text, he "trusted to his hears." In 1982, Emilia Lodigiani wrote *Invito alla lettura di Tolkien* ("Tolkien Reading Guide"), published by *Mursia*, the first critical book on Tolkien and almost the only of certain value so far.

In 1994, soon after Tolkien's birth anniversary, the Società Tolkieniana Italiana (STI) was founded in Udine. Since then, it has edited two official fanzines, *Terra di Mezzo* (Middle-earth) and *Minas Tirith*, and organized an annual gathering, Hobbiton.

Since 1999, many Tolkienian communities have been founded: Endòre, which publishes an annual magazine, in Brescia; Eldalië, an association from a Web site community; and Gran Burrone ("Rivendell") association, which takes place in Monza. From 2003 on, many STI local "smials" were created.

In 2003, a "new" revised edition of *The Lord of the Rings* was published by Bompiani, thanks to a team recruited by the STI. Although there are still mistakes, this edition finally provides Tolkien's 1966 foreword.

It is a pity that the STI gives still an "Evolian" point of view on Tolkien (from Julius Evola, a controversial Italian esotericist, "Traditionalist," and politically extreme right-wing writer). In the Act of the Society, in fact, there still a reference to the "Sacred Roots" of the "European Tradition," and in a recent issue of *Minas Tirith* there was an essay en-titled "What Is the Tradition?"

ROBERTO ARDUINI

Further Reading

Arduini, Roberto, and Raffaella Benvenuto. "Place-Names in the Italian Translation of the Lord of the Rings.". In *Tolkien 2005 Conference Proceedings*. Udine: Tolkien Society, forthcoming.

Principe, Quirino. "Note sulla vicenda editoriale di Tolkien in Italia.". *Endòre* (Brescia), no. 5 (September 2002): 60–61.

———. "Editor's Note.". *Il Signore degli Anelli*, 22. Milano: Bompiani, October 2003.

Saba Sardi, Francesco. "Translator's Note." In *Il Silmarillion* Milano: Rusconi, 1978.

See also **Dante; Italian Language**

'IÞÞLEN' IN *SAWLES WARDE*

"'*Iþþlen*' in *Sawles Warde*" is a three-page note in *English Studies*, which Tolkien wrote in collaboration with S.R.T.O. d'Ardenne. The article is an excellent example of how philological techniques for reconstructing word meanings and manuscript relationships led Tolkien to speculate about the literary qualities of medieval texts and the way readers might have responded to them. *Sawles Warde* is a thirteenth-century Middle English homily based on part of Hugh of St. Victor's *De Anima*, in which Wit is the master of the House of the Soul, whose servants who conspire with Will, his housewife, in an attempt to please her. It survives in three manuscripts: Bodley 34, Royal 17 A xxvii, and Cotton Titus D xviii. The text is part of the Katherine group of West Midland texts, the language which Tolkien studied closely for his edition of *Ancrene Riwle*. Tolkien and d'Ardenne analyze a sentence that in the Bodley manuscript contains the unexplained word *iþþlen*: *þah we hit ne here nawt, we mahen iþþlen hare nurhð & hare untohe bere, a þet hit cume forð & ba wið eie & wið luue tuhte ham þe betere.* (The Middle English letters þ "thorn" and ð "eth" are pronounced like modern "th.")

They translate this as "Though we do not hear this (sc. ? the swearing of the conspirators) we can their noise and unruly clamour, until it comes out and with fear and love teach (train) them to do better" (indicates the untranslatable *iþþlen*).

Noting that the Royal and Titus manuscripts read *felen* and *fele*, "feel," respectively, Tolkien and d'Ardenne suggest that this word was left out by the "inattentive" scribe of the Bodley manuscript, who was prone to such omissions. The word *iþþlen*, written above *mahen* and *hare*, is in a different hand, and they conclude that it is an emendation by an ancient reader who attempted to understand the passage and who had no access to a better copy. Tolkien and d'Ardenne point out that the letters rendered *iþþlen* by modern editors most clearly resemble *r þ ? l e n* (the third letter is almost illegible and only resembles *þ* because of the *h* in *hare* below). They dismiss this possibility that the letters may represent the word *riwlen,* "rule" as inappropriate to the context. Instead, they point out that the phrase *hit cume forð*, "it comes out," in the Bodley manuscript differs from the readings of the Cotton and Titus manuscripts, which have *wit cume forð*, "Wit comes out." Hence, the sense of the passage is "Though we do not hear it (sc. the actual voices of the servants, which is only said allegorically), we can in our feelings and emotions experience the clamour, until Wit is aroused." Although they do not give a complete revised translation of the sentence, according to their interpretation it would be "Though we do not hear it, we can feel their noise and unruly clamour, until Wit comes out and with fear and love teaches them to do better." Although the textual disruption in the Bodley manuscript may derive ultimately from the scribe's inattentiveness, Tolkien and d'Ardenne place some of the blame on the original author's interjection about our inability to hear the noise of the conspirators: "Nothing could be more destructive for his allegory, or more confusing, than to introduce *we* at this point, the real persons, who are being allegorically analysed." This statement, they conclude, is "nothing more than a weak apology for his allegory, almost before it has begun, an 'aside' to the reader that it would have been better not to make."

SCOTT KLEINMAN

Further Reading

Eggebroten, Anne. "*Sawles Warde*: A Retelling of *De Anima* for a Female Audience." *Mediaevalia* 10 (1988): 27–47.

Ker, Neil R., ed. *Facsimile of MS Bodley 34: St. Katherine, St. Margaret, St. Juliana, Hali Meiðhad, Sawles Warde.* EETS o.s. 247. London: Oxford University Press, 1960.

Millett, Bella. "*Hali Meiðhad, Sawles Warde*, and the Continuity of English Prose." In *Five Hundred Years of Words and Sounds: Festschrift for Eric Dobson*, Edited by Eric Gerald Stanley and Douglas Gray, 100–8. Cambridge: D.S. Brewer, 1983.

Morris, R., ed. *Old English Homilies & Homiletic Treatises of the Twelfth and Thirteenth Centuries.* EETS o.s. 29, 34. London: Trübner & Co. 68; repr. New York: Greenwood Press, 1969.

Tolkien J.R.R., and S.R.T.O. d'Ardenne. "'*iþþlen*' in *Sawles Warde.*" *English Studies: A Journal of English Letters and Philology* 28 (1947): 168–70.

Wilson, R.M., ed. *Sawles Warde: An Early Middle English Homily. Edited from the Bodley, Royal and Cotton MSS.* Leeds School of English Language Texts and Monographs 3. Leeds: University of Leeds, 1938.

See also **d'Ardenne, S.R.T.O.; Katherine Group; Manuscripts, Medieval; Middle English; Middle English Vocabulary; Scholars of Medieval Literature, Influence of**

J

JACKSON, PETER

The three films of *The Lord of the Rings* appeared largely due to the effort, dedication, and vision of Peter Jackson. He directed, coproduced, and cowrote the films, based on Tolkien's books, *The Fellowship of the Ring* (2001), *The Two Towers* (2002), and *The Return of the King* (2003) for New Line Cinema. There can be (and has been) debate about the relative merits of Jackson's creative choices. Still, Jackson was the key individual who managed the monumental and risky, both artistically and financially, endeavor to bring Tolkien's masterpiece to the screen.

Bio-sketch of Peter Jackson

Some of Jackson's biography before *The Lord of the Rings* films foreshadowed that he would be the guiding force behind the project. According to Rebecca Flint in the *All Movie Guide,* Jackson, born and raised in New Zealand, became interested in filmmaking at age eight when his parents acquired an eight-mm camera. Throughout his teenage years, Jackson continued to make short films with a special emphasis on cheap special effects and blood-and-guts horror. His first break came after four years of working on a comedy/horror movie titled *Bad Taste* (1987); the film was a cult hit. Jackson followed that with another film in the same genre, *Meet the Feebles* (1989), which was about a puppet show that exhibited "graphic debauchery and twisted violence." In 1994, Jackson transcended his obsession with film gore and released

his critically acclaimed *Heavenly Creatures,* which was based on the real case of school girlfriends who murdered the mother of one of the young women. The film, a blend of realism and fantasy, was the screen debut of Kate Winslet. The effort garnered Jackson and his partner Fran Walsh an Academy Award nomination for Best Original Screenplay. Jackson's first "Hollywood" film was *The Frighteners* (1996), starring Michael J. Fox as an investigator of the supernatural, which allowed the director to experiment with special effects. The film was a disappointment in comparison with *Heavenly Creatures.* Then in 1998, Jackson made the surprise announcement that his next project would be a film adaptation of *The Lord of the Rings.*

Background to *The Lord of the Rings* Film Production

The author sold the film rights in 1969, so Jackson did not have to go to the Tolkien Estate for permissions. The holder of the rights is Saul Zaentz, well-known producer of the Oscar-winning films *Amadeus* and *The English Patient.* Zaentz produced an animated *Lord of the Rings,* directed by Ralph Bakshi, in 1979. The film, which only covered *The Fellowship of the Ring* and about half of *The Two Towers,* was deemed a failure, and Zaentz lost all interest in producing the second part. But he agreed to license the rights to Jackson if the director could find a studio to finance the films.

According to the account in the *Fellowship* DVD extra "From Book to Vision," Jackson shopped around the idea, which included his storyboards and working adaptation. Miramax decided to finance the initial preproduction. Jackson developed his script and envisioned two films. When the massive scope and cost of the project became apparent, Miramax executives stated that they would only be willing to finance one film. Jackson believed it was tremendously difficult to pare down Tolkien's epic into two films; one film would be unworkable. Miramax permitted Jackson to look for another studio.

Jackson managed to arrange a meeting with Bob Shaye, film financier and chief executive of New Line Cinema. Jackson made his presentation, hoping Shaye would see the need to finance two films of the three-volume *Lord of the Rings*. Shaye responded, "Since there are three books, there should be three films." With an initial budget of about $300 million, Jackson received the go-ahead to start production.

Production Technique

The documentary material in the DVDs of all three films presents the production techniques for the films. Jackson set up production in his native New Zealand. Not only did this choice help reduce costs, but the entire environment was conducive to his daunting task. He took advantage of the gorgeous and varied landscape of the country to represent the fields, the woods, the rivers, and the mountains of Tolkien's Middle-earth. Jackson even used an abandoned quarry to construct the sets for the sites of the two major battles at Helm's Deep and Minas Tirith. Edoras, the home of the court of Théoden, was entirely built on an open hillside, which enhanced its authenticity. Large production facilities were erected as well. These buildings were used for settings, such as the Dead Marshes, for which Jackson could not find a suitable outdoor location. Large stages also were the backdrops for the digitally created scenes, such as Aragorn's meeting with the Dead Men of Dunharrow.

Jackson surrounded himself with familiar film professionals of New Zealand, which included his own company, Weta Workshops. This firm was responsible for creating all props and sets based on Tolkien's works. Jackson insisted on authenticity in relation to both the descriptions in *The Lord of the Rings* and the materials used, such as real wood, iron, and glass. For art direction, Jackson secured the services of two of the world's most well-known illustrators of Tolkien's work, Alan Lee and John Howe.

Jackson's company was also responsible for the production of the films' special digital effects. Advances in such technology had made Jackson's task more manageable. Still, he had to depict realistically Tolkien's many creatures, such as the Balrog, the Nazgûl's flying beasts, the Trolls, and perhaps most difficult of all, Treebeard and the Ents. Digital effects were also used to create additional horses and people, which could be multiplied and manipulated. The Hobbits were all normal-size actors who appeared small on-screen through the use of clever camerawork and digital editing.

Gollum was a special case. Originally, Jackson intended to create an entirely digital creature. However, he liked the movements of the actor Andy Serkis, who had signed on to do the voice of Gollum. Serkis was fitted with a special suit that digitally captured his motion, and then it was integrated with the animated character. The combination resulted in a character that appeared more realistic than the other purely digital creatures.

Jackson's production schedule was unique for a three-film project. He decided to shoot all three films at the same time over an eighteen-month period. Costs and time requirements were certainly factors. Also, the various schedules of the actors may have posed a problem. But perhaps most important, this grueling schedule allowed Jackson to maintain the momentum of the project, which may have been impeded if the three films were produced over several years.

The Cast

While the selection of actors is rarely the director's sole decision, Jackson gathered an interesting cast, a mixture of distinguished, familiar people and some impressive new faces. The accomplished veterans of the British stage and screen included Ian McKellen as Gandalf, Christopher Lee as Saruman, Cate Blanchett as Galadriel, Sean Bean as Boromir, Ian Holm as Bilbo, Bernard Hill as Théoden, and John Rhys-Davies as Gimli and the voice of Treebeard the Ent. The well-known American actors were Elijah Wood as Frodo, Liv Tyler as Arwen, and Viggo Mortensen as Aragorn. Lesser-known yet notable actors included Hugo Weaving as Elrond, Sean Astin as Sam, Brad Dourif as Wormtongue, Karl Urban as Éomer, David Wenham as Faramir, and John Noble as Denethor.

The major newcomers included Orlando Bloom as Legolas, Miranda Otto as Éowyn, and Andy Serkis, who provided the voice and motion-capture movements for Gollum. Billy Boyd as Pippin and Dominic

Monaghan as Merry rounded out the central cast members.

The Music Score

Jackson's vision was well complemented by the music score of Howard Shore. The composer and conductor provided music with a variety of motifs: medieval, classical, sacred, Celtic, mechanistic (particularly in the themes of evil). Shore employed a traditional orchestra, modern instruments, and choir. During the credits at the end of each film, an original ballad was played. In *Fellowship,* the song was "May it be;" in *Towers,* "Gollum's Song"; in *Return,* "Into the West." The tone and cadence of the score enhanced the impact of Tolkien's subcreations through Jackson's interpretations of the fantasy realms, characters, and story.

The Adaptation

Jackson's most formidable task may have been adapting the massive amount of detail of the books, particularly the history of Tolkien's Middle-earth. Even with the latitude of producing three films, each approximately three hours, Jackson was forced to abridge and compress extensively. In a letter, Tolkien, when he was involved in a proposed animated production of the books, remarked that abridgment is a better option than compression because at least the integrity of material can be maintained (*Letters,* 261). Jackson's adaptation is a problematic blend of abridgment, compression, transformation, and addition.

Abridgment

Jackson retained all material necessary to understand the history of the One Ring, Sauron's threat to Middle-earth, the dangerous quest of Frodo to destroy the Ring, Aragorn's efforts to reclaim his kingship, the machinations of Saruman, the journey and break-up of the Fellowship, the vital role of Gollum, the contributions of Treebeard and the Ents and of Faramir, the major battles at Helm's Deep and Minas Tirith, the encounter with Shelob, Frodo and Sam's escape from Cirith Ungol, their wretched journey toward Mount Doom, the diversionary battle before the Black Gate of Mordor, the destruction of the Ring and death of Gollum, the rescue of Frodo and Sam, the coronation of Aragorn, and the departure of Frodo and the Great Ones at the Grey Havens. Jackson also retained key atmosphere material from the book, such as the depiction of the Shire and Bilbo's birthday party, the threat of the Ringwraiths, the aura of Rivendell, the menace of Moria, the culture of Rohan, the history of the Dead Men of Dunharrow, and much else that was not necessary to the central plot. The major cuts from Tolkien's text were the Tom Bombadil chapters and the return journey of the Hobbits, including "The Scouring of the Shire." Some may argue that these cuts left major gaps in the representation of Tolkien's vision. However, for any adaptation hard decisions have to be made. All things considered, abridgment was the most successful of Jackson's adaptation techniques.

Compression

Prose fiction and film are quite different artistic forms. Compression (or condensation) of the source material is unavoidable. A Hollywood film is usually required to shun a leisurely pace and any material that does not advance the plot or develop character. Even when Jackson retained the core material noted previously, the structure and pace of film forced him to edit and accelerate the presentation. Typical examples include the long conversation between Gandalf and Frodo in the book chapter "The Shadow of the Past"; the search for Merry and Pippin by Aragorn, Gimli, and Legolas; and the journey of Sam and Frodo across the desolated plains of Mordor. These compressions still conveyed the aura of the source text. However, haste weakened the essence of certain scenes, such as the initial meeting between Frodo and Strider, the time in Lothlórien, the fall of Saruman, the tension between Gandalf and Denethor, the blooming of the love between Faramir and Éowyn, Frodo's troubled return to the Shire, and many other incidents. It requires a deft touch to maintain a balance between artistic integrity and the demands of Hollywood producers, a balance that Jackson often failed to strike.

Transformation

If abridgment and compression might misrepresent the spirit of the source material, then transformation can be fraught with pitfalls. Directors must have their own vision and interpretation, so some measure of artistic license is necessary and desirable. Jackson transformed much of the diction and the plot from Tolkien's books. Some changes were relatively minor, such as Gandalf's remarks to Frodo in Moria about

Gollum's pivotal role, rather than in Bag End, where Tolkien placed the dialogue. Most alterations were major, such as Elrond's words about "small hands" doing great deeds, which were rewritten for the film and given to Galadriel. As David Bratman points out, the revision, "even the smallest person can change the course of the future," replaces the literary tone of the original with a contemporary cliché (Croft, 48–49). Occasionally, Jackson retained the poetic quality of inverted word order, such as Boromir's line in the film's Council of Elrond: "By the blood of my people are your lands kept safe." Yet on the whole, Jackson seems to have believed that Tolkien's wordings sound too formal for a modern-day movie audience.

Moreover, Jackson's transformations often seemed designed for cheap thrills or blatant melodrama. For example, Jackson neglected all vestiges of Frodo's self-control and fortitude in favor of a character who constantly looks weak and helpless, such as his virtually comatose demeanor at the Ford of Rivendell. Instead of having Frodo defy the Ringwraiths' call to evil, Jackson gave this act to Arwen, who also summons the flood that overwhelms the Black Riders. Many viewers likely enjoyed, for instance, the sword fight between Aragorn and the Ringwraiths on Weathertop, Gandalf's exorcising Théoden of Saruman's spirit, or Frodo barely hanging on to a precipice above the Cracks of Doom. But such changes to Tolkien's material, as David Bratman argues, neglect the unique literary essence of the book and offer run-of-the-mill "sword-and-sorcery" fantasy (Croft, 30).

Addition

Jackson's additions to the source material are even more controversial than his transformations. Given the massive amount of detail at the director's disposal, it seems a strange and hazardous choice to invent plot and dialogue that might clash with the original. One major addition that did work nicely was Jackson's use of Tolkien's appendix account, "The Tale of Aragorn and Arwen," to provide a secondary plot line that dramatizes the bittersweet love affair between the mortal Man and the immortal Elven princess. Sometimes Jackson develops the feelings of a character and it works, such as having Boromir wax eloquent about the glory of his home city, which enriches Tolkien's explanation of the gruff character's strong desire to bring the Ring to Minas Tirith.

A few additions were either inspired, such as the lighting of the beacons of Gondor, or harmless, such as the Orc chasing Merry and Pippin into Fangorn Forest. But other additions seem less defensible.

Much of the Saruman plot in *Fellowship,* from his telekinesis fight with Gandalf to the Orc-spawning scene, sometimes overshadowed the main story of Frodo's quest. In *Towers,* Jackson inserted a plot line where the transformed and dubious Faramir character forces Frodo and Sam to journey toward Minas Tirith with the intention to give the Ring to Denethor. They stop at the ruined fortress of Osgiliath, where, when under attack by a Nazgûl and his beast, Frodo inexplicably offers the Ring to Sauron's servant; only Sam's violent intervention prevents disaster. And in the final film, Jackson, seemingly more motivated to have melodrama rather than narrative logic, put in a scene where Gollum succeeds in enticing Frodo to distrust and reject Sam—and Sam initially leaves his master's side. These additions do not just misrepresent Tolkien's vision; they are inconsistent with Jackson's plot and character development in other parts of the films.

In summary, the problem with Jackson's adaptation is not that it may stray from the letter and spirit of Tolkien's text but that the director's compressions, transformations, and additions often undermine the cohesiveness and consistency of the films.

Artistic Impression

A film or, in this case, films adapted from a book, even a masterpiece, should not be evaluated strictly on the fidelity to the source material. As Robert Stam has observed, looking for a totally faithful film adaptation may be an impossible ideal, and perhaps a misguided wish (2000, 54). During the transformation from page to screen, even the most earnest desire to reflect the unique essence of the book in the film may prove fruitless. However, we can appraise films on their artistic impression in terms of tone, story, character, and theme. These aspects are not mutually exclusive, but they provide useful benchmarks to judge Jackson's films.

Much of the tone of a film appears in the visuals. This area is probably Jackson's finest achievement. The cinematography, art direction, sets, props, and costumes were spectacular. Jackson reflected the ancient, venerable, and fantastic essence of Tolkien's Middle-earth in its history, artifacts, peoples, countries, culture, and creatures. Jackson paid attention to large and important details, such as Edoras, home of the court of Théoden, in all its Anglo-Saxon essence, and small and peripheral aspects, such as the portraits of Bilbo's parents. The combination of the fabulous New Zealand landscape with superb set design conveyed wonderfully the visual splendor of Tolkien's book.

By comparison, the special effects and computer-generated images seemed less effective. In certain moments of the films, Jackson's use of animation technology was stunning. Gandalf's battles with the Balrog, both at the Bridge of Khazad-dûm and in the subterranean depths of Moria, are perfect examples. Another is the motion-capture technique to make Gollum look like a real character, one with which we can sympathize, rather than the awful computer-generated image of Jar Jar Binks of the second *Star Wars* trilogy. The halls of Moria and the spider Orcs were marvelous. The visual effect to multiply people and horses, in some places, appeared genuine—and saved production costs. However, the monsters, the Trolls, the Nazgûl beasts, the Wargs, and so on, looked like animated figures, especially in the battle at Minas Tirith. The Ents, too, seemed less than realistic, though we should acknowledge the difficulties that Jackson's creative team had in trying to render Tolkien's imaginative beings. In all three films, the epic tone of the set design and props was often diminished by the animated fantasy figures. Particular examples include the fight with the Cave-troll in Moria, the clash against the Warg riders on the plains of Rohan, and the battle before the Black Gates of Mordor. The difference is between high film art, such as the prologue in *Fellowship,* and a B-grade movie feel, such as Éowyn and Merry's ride against the *mûmakil* in *Return.*

This disharmony of tone revealed itself in the plot of the films. As discussed previously, Jackson used several adaptation techniques. This mixture of approaches impinged on the consistency of the story, particularly in its pace. For instance, in *Fellowship,* Jackson spent a great deal of screen time (and even more in the extended DVD) depicting the background history to the story, the hobbits and their lifestyle, and Gandalf discovering of the truth about Bilbo's ring and conveying it to Frodo. Then Frodo and Sam leave Hobbiton and, for the rest of the journey, Jackson minimizes mood development and dialogue and offers seemingly nonstop flights and fights, some from Tolkien's text and others of the director's invention. The significance of Frodo's inner journey becomes submerged in frenetic action. Also, Jackson's added scene of the Dwarf corpses just inside Moria (and Saruman's earlier remarks when showing a picture of the Balrog), as Janet Croft observes, undermines the suspense that Tolkien created with the actual menace and danger only gradually revealed (Croft, 72). When the Company is entering Lothlórien, Frodo hears Galadriel's voice in his head say, "You are the footstep of doom to us"; but

Jackson deleted the explanation for this remark, which is that the destruction of the One Ring will destroy the potency of her Ring of Power that sustains the timeless realm. And the end of the first film is such an orgy of Orc killing that it defies plausibility. There are many fine moments in *Fellowship,* such as when Frodo, amid the squabbling of the Council of Elrond, heroically yet humbly volunteers to bear the Ring. But with too little time spent in the Elven havens of Rivendell and Lothlórien, particularly in the theatrical release of the film, and too much time spent running and hacking, the story structure was unbalanced.

Towers is more tightly and evenly structured, perhaps because it was based on only twelve chapters of Tolkien's book, whereas the first film was based on twenty-three. Even Jackson's added scenes, such as Éomer's banishment at the hands of Wormtongue or Arwen's disagreement with her father over her sorrow-filled relationship with Aragorn, seemed more integrated with the original material. Jackson chose not to reproduce Tolkien's structure of the self-contained plot lines of the two parts of the *Two Towers* book. The intercutting of the various story threads could have caused some audience disorientation, but it added an element of suspense. *Towers* may have contained the greatest moment of all three films, a perfect example of Tolkien's concept of "eucatastrophe," when Gandalf and the Riders of Rohan arrive in the nick of time to succor Helm's Deep. And yet, the second film had possibly the worst scene when Frodo, after being dragged to Osgiliath, offers to give the Ring to the Nazgûl. Not only did it make Frodo look like a witless fool, but given the symbiotic link between Sauron and his servants, the Dark Lord would've known the location of the Ring, thereby ruining the errand of secrecy. This grievous plot addition marred the ending of an essentially consistent story line in the second film.

The story in *Return* presented a challenge because Jackson chose to combine a large amount of material from the *Two Towers* book with that from Tolkien's *The Return of the King.* The director wanted to follow the chronology of the books to maintain the intercutting of the story lines. However, this structure created an imbalance because so much was happening in the subplots of Aragorn and his rise to the kingship, Gandalf and Pippin at the siege of Minas Tirith, and Théoden and Éowyn with the muster of Rohan. The central plot of Frodo, Sam, and Gollum and their journey to Mordor became subordinated. Jackson tried to compensate by adding scenes involving Frodo, Sam, and Gollum, which include physical and verbal fighting. Gollum, in a dual personality dialogue, reveals to the audience and, unintentionally, to Sam that the creature has a plan to kill the hobbits and seize the Ring. Besides undermining the suspense, Jackson has Frodo inexplicably dismiss Sam's warnings about the treacherous Gollum. Later, Gollum uses a ruse to make it look like Sam secretly wants the Ring—and Frodo is easily fooled and casts off his beloved friend. Jackson's desire for melodrama seemed to override the need for narrative logic and consistency.

Not surprisingly, when Jackson stayed close to Tolkien's text the story lines flowed more smoothly and effectively. The scenes in which Aragorn summons the Dead Men of Dunharrow, the sudden arrival of the Riders of Rohan at Minas Tirith, the duel between Éowyn and the Witch-king, and the struggle of Frodo and Sam on the slopes of Mount Doom were particularly well done. Too much of the film centered on fighting, both from incidents in Tolkien's text and Jackson's additions. Still, the destruction of the Ring and Frodo's sad departure from Middle-earth were both visually stunning and dramatically moving. Jackson's films ended, like they began, on a very high note.

In key instances, the most significant departure from Tolkien's text was Jackson's presentation of the characters. Again, the problem is not merely a lack of textual fidelity but rather is internal consistency. Gandalf in the beginning is the recognizable wise and strong counselor and sorcerer. Then he has moments in which he appears skittish and shortsighted—such as telling Elrond that they "cannot ask any more of" the hobbit hero then later stating Frodo was "meant" to have the Ring. In *Towers,* Gandalf the White appears to be powerful and even angelic; then in the final film, Gandalf often acts boorishly and pessimistically, especially in his dealings with Denethor and in his belief that he has sent Frodo "to his death." Aragorn, as the hidden heir to the throne of Gondor, sometimes looks confident and invincible, especially when wielding a sword against multiple foes. At other times, he appears weak and indecisive, needing Arwen and Elrond to encourage him to feel worthy to reclaim his birthright. I have argued that Jackson's Frodo, on the whole, appears imperceptive and weak-willed (Croft, 123–48). Frodo rarely seems to be worthy of divine designation to have the Ring, someone who will "find a way" when no one else could.

Sam was Frodo's constant and loyal companion, right to the triumphant and sorrowful end. Boromir appeared like a tragic hero, flawed by selfishness and impatience yet full of honor and dignity, especially in death. Most of the secondary characters were successful, such as Saruman, Arwen, Legolas, Wormtongue,

Théoden, Éomer, and Éowyn, although each had moments of "soap operaish" behavior. Merry, Pippin, and Gimli, while effective in places, too often were used for juvenile humor. ("Dwarf tossing" is an inside joke because the practice is a pub game in New Zealand.)

The characterization of Elrond, Faramir, and Denethor was so far from Tolkien's text that it's hard to judge their effectiveness in Jackson's portrayals. Still, these three characters most acutely revealed the disharmony of tone as Jackson transformed the subtle emotions of Tolkien's text and presented overt angst.

However, for all of Jackson's transformations and additions, the thematic core of Tolkien's masterpiece is evident in the films. By giving the Ring a subtle and seductive voice, Jackson dramatizes the insidious temptation to evil, which may affect all of us, and the firmness of will needed to resist it. Through the falls of Saruman, Denethor, and Sauron, we see the bitter fruits of the lust for power and its corrupting influence. In the horrific trials of the Hobbits and Aragorn, Jackson presents the importance of steadfast determination combined with humility and self-sacrifice. In the wretched and pathetic portrayal of Gollum, we see the degrading and deadly path of obsessive materialism. Jackson even dramatized Tolkien's religious vision of a divine order (Frodo was "meant" to have the Ring), which works its way through seemingly angelic helpers; the visual imagery around Gandalf the White appeared like celestial light, particularly when he "was sent back" to complete his task after the battle against the Balrog. Along with the visuals, the strong thematic thrust holds the films together, despite the imbalances in the story and disharmonies of tone.

Film Reviews

The fine movie Web site, RottenTomatoes.com, provides two good guides to the collective opinion on a given film. One is the "Tomatometer," which is a percentage of favorable reviews out of the total; and the second is the average rating out of ten. On both these scales, Jackson's *The Lord of the Rings* fared extremely well.

Fellowship scored an impressive 93 percent on the Tomatometer, with an average rating of 8.1/10 based on 181 reviews; *Towers* an astonishing 98 percent, with an 8.5/10 average based on 202 reviews; and *Return* 95 percent, with the highest rating of the three films, 8.7/10, based on 219 reviews. With these numbers, any dissenting movie reviews seem hardly relevant.

Of course, even in generally positive reviews, critics had reservations about Jackson's films. Roger Ebert remarked that the *Fellowship* film is "more of a sword and sorcery epic than a realization of the more naïve and guileless vision of J.R.R. Tolkien" (*Chicago Sun-Times,* December 19, 2001). Elvis Mitchell stated that "*Towers* is like a family oriented E-rated videogame, with no emotional complications other than saving the day" (*New York Times,* December 18, 2002). Kenneth Turan observed that since "*Return* by definition has to showcase battles that would literally end all battles, the brevity of those character beats at times threatens the critical human thread with unraveling" (*Los Angeles Times,* December 16, 2003). Still, overall, Jackson received high praise from the film critics.

Audience Response

There are two main measures of audience response. The first is the reported gross box office figures. Given the financial risk that New Line Cinema took, investing in three films without any guarantee even one would be successful, Jackson, as the saying goes, certainly "delivered the goods." According to the Web site BoxOfficeMojo.com, *Fellowship* brought in approximately $870 million worldwide, *Towers* $925 million, and *Return* $1.1 billion, which made the films among the highest grossing of all time. And these figures do not include the many millions of dollars in video and DVD sales, not to mention merchandise, such as posters and games. By these accounts, the films were widely and enthusiastically embraced.

The second measure of audience response is more elusive yet still suggestive. Hundreds of Web sites sprung up devoted to the films and to Tolkien's work in general. Through online publications and chat rooms, the films have been extensively and passionately discussed. There are lovers and defenders of Jackson and his vision, as well as critical and hostile voices. It's a daunting task to try to gauge the response of people online, though Martin Barker of the University of Wales, Aberystwyth, has made a worthy attempt. In 2003 and 2004, Barker conducted an online study and received a remarkable twenty-five thousand responses in seven languages from twenty countries (MacLeod, August 6, 2005). According to Barker, a major reaction was that the audience believed they were on a "spiritual journey" while viewing the films. Certainly Jackson has detractors, such as members of the literary organization the Mythopoeic Society. Still, the general audience response appears to be mainly appreciative and supportive.

Awards

If critical acclaim and audience enthusiasm were not enough for Jackson, the many awards the films received offered further validation. The Internet Movie Database (http://www.imdb.com) lists award nominations and wins from a host of film associations. *Fellowship* garnered 150 nominations and 74 wins, including the Academy Awards with 13 nominations and 4 Oscars: Best Cinematography, Best Effects & Visual Effects, Best Makeup, and Best Original Music Score. *Towers* had 129 total nominations and 57 wins, including the Academy Awards with 6 nominations and 2 Oscars: Best Effects and Best Sound Editing. Finally, *Return* received an amazing 162 nominations and 68 wins, including a perfect 11 for 11 Academy Awards: Best Art Direction-Set Direction, Best Costume Design, Best Editing, Best Makeup, Best Original Music Score, Best Original Song, Best Sound, Best Visual Effects, Best Adapted Screenplay, Best Director, and Best Picture.

However one feels about the films of *The Lord of the Rings,* Peter Jackson achieved phenomenal success with his adaptations.

DANIEL TIMMONS

Further Reading

Bauer, Erik. "'It's Just a Movie': Erik Bauer Speaks with Peter Jackson." Review of *The Fellowship of the Ring*, directed by Peter Jackson. *Creative Screenwriting* 9, no. 1 (2002): 6–12.

Croft, Janet Brennan, ed. *Tolkien on Film: Essays on Peter Jackson's "The Lord of the Rings."* Altadena, CA: Mythopoeic, 2004.

Dickerson, Matthew T. *Following Gandalf: Epic Battles and Moral Victory in "The Lord of the Rings."* Grand Rapids, MI: Brazos, 2003.

Diehl, Patrick. "*The Lord of the Rings* and the Trials of Adaptation." *West by Northwest.org Online Magazine,* January 9, 2004. http://westbynorthwest.org/artman/publish/article_677.shtml.

Flint, Rebecca. Biography of Peter Jackson. *All Movie Guide,* September 4, 2005. http://www.allmovie.com/cg/avg.dll?p=avg&sql=2:95689.

Jackson, Peter, Fran Walsh, and Philippa Boyens. *The Lord of the Rings: The Fellowship of the Ring.* Theatrical Release DVD. Directed by Peter Jackson. United States: New Line Home Entertainment, 2002.

———. *The Lord of the Rings: The Fellowship of the Ring.* Special Extended DVD Edition. Directed by Peter Jackson. United States: New Line Home Entertainment, 2002.

———. *The Lord of the Rings: The Return of the King.* Theatrical Release DVD. Directed by Peter Jackson. United States, New Line Home Entertainment, 2004.

———. *The Lord of the Rings: The Return of the King.* Special Extended DVD Edition. Directed by Peter Jackson. United States, New Line Home Entertainment, 2004.

———. *The Lord of the Rings: The Two Towers*. Theatrical release DVD. Directed by Peter Jackson. United States: New Line Home Entertainment, 2003.

———. *The Lord of the Rings: The Two Towers*. Special Extended DVD Edition. Directed by Peter Jackson. United States: New Line Home Entertainment, 2003.

"The Legacy of *The Lord of the Rings*." Documentary. DVD. Directed by Daniel Timmons. Montréal: Filmoption International, 2005.

MacLeod, David. "Research Reveals Spiritual Journey of Tolkien Fans." *Guardian Unlimited* August 6, 2005. http://education.guardian.co.uk/higher/research/story/0,9865,1543523,00.html (accessed September 5, 2005).

Porter, Lynette R. *Unsung Heroes of "The Lord of the Rings": From the Page to the Screen*. Westport, CT: Praeger, 2005.

Pryor, Ian. *Peter Jackson: From Prince of Splatter to Lord of the Rings: An Unauthorized Biography*. New York: St. Martin's, 2004.

Shippey, Tom. "Temptations for All Time." Review of *The Fellowship of the Ring*, directed by Peter Jackson. *Times Literary Supplement* (December 21, 2001): 16–17.

———. "Another Road to Middle-earth: Jackson's Movie Trilogy." In *Understanding "The Lord of the Rings": The Best of Tolkien Criticism*, edited by Rose A. Zimbardo and Neil D. Isaacs, 233–54. Boston, MA: Houghton Mifflin, 2004.

Sibley, Brian. *The Making of the Movie Trilogy: The Lord of the Rings*. Boston, MA: Houghton Mifflin, 2002.

Smith, Patricia Burkhart. "Ring Bearer: Patricia Burkhart Smith Talks with Philippa Boyens." *Creative Screenwriting* 8, no. 2 (2001): 4, 6, 8.

Stam, Robert. "Beyond Fidelity: The Dialogics of Adaptation." In *Film Adaptation*, edited by James Naremore, 54–77. Newark: Rutgers University Press, 2000.

Thompson, Kristin. "Fantasy, Franchises, and Frodo Baggins: *The Lord of the Rings* and Modern Hollywood." *The Velvet Light Trap* 52 (2003): 45–63.

Verini, Bob. "Hobbit-Forming: Adapting *The Lord of the Rings*." *Scr(i)pt* (2001): 34–37, 62–63.

Wright, Greg. *Peter Jackson in Perspective: The Power Behind Cinema's "The Lord of the Rings": A Look at Hollywood's Take on Tolkien's Epic Tale*. Hollywood, CA: Jesus Books, 2004.

See also **Bakshi, Ralph; Dramatizations: Stage and Spoken; Fandom; Film Scripts, Unused**

JAPAN: RECEPTION OF TOLKIEN

Although Tolkien's books had been widely available in Japan, until 2001 their readership was rather limited. After Peter Jackson's film *The Fellowship of the Ring* was released, fans increased, and in 2002 there was a boom of publications and Web sites about works by Tolkien. Academic dissertations also increased, and *The Hobbit* and *The Lord of the Rings* began to be taught at university. However, a Japan Tolkien Society does not yet exist.

In 1965, *Hobitto no Bōken*, (Adventure of the Hobbit), translated by Teiji Seta (1916–79) and illustrated by Ryuichi Terashima, was published by Iwanami Shoten. Its tenth impression, in 1983, featured a revised translation by Seta. In 1997, Shiro Yamamoto translated *Hobitto, Yukite Kaerishi Monogatari (The Annotated Hobbit)*, published by Hara Shobo. This translation was the object of sharp criticism: for instance, in *Mythlore* it was defined as "smooth, idiomatic, simple in vocabulary." From 1972 to 1975, *Yubiwa Monogatari (The Lord of the Rings)* translated by Seta, was published by Hyôronsha. In 1992, Akiko Tanaka, Seta's assistant, revised the text, keeping most of the original translation intact. It was published in three-, seven-, and nine-volume editions, and it featured the latter half of the Appendix, which had never been previously translated. In 1982, Tanaka translated *Sirumariru no Monogatari (The Silmarillion, "Tale of Silmaril")*, published by Hyôronsha.

The translation of *The Lord of the Rings* by Seta and Tanaka may be regarded as almost perfect. Teiji Seta was an expert in classical Japanese literature and a *haiku* poet. *Yubiwa Monogatari* is intentionally written in an old-fashioned style, although some problems are due to the linguistic structure of Japanese. Some titles of the books were changed: *The Lord of the Rings* became *Yubiwa Monogatari* (Tale of the Ring), in which the Ring is explicitly named without any mention of Sauron; *The Fellowship of the Ring* became *Tabi no nakama* (The Fellowship of the Journey) because a literal translation, *Yubiwa no nakama*, could be misinterpreted as "The Ring's Friends."

One distinguishing feature of the translation is its emphasis on relationships. Japanese has two speaking styles, polite and normal; Seta added an archaic style to portray these relationships accurately. He faced a difficult challenge translating the proper nouns, because Tolkien's "Guide to the Names in *The Lord of the Rings*" was not at all helpful with Japanese. All names written in English in the original, such as Crickhollow and Staddle, were translated into *kanji* (Chinese-character) names, and other names, as Baggins and Bree, were treated as loanwords (*katakana*, or syllabic letters). Although it is correct according to Tolkien's "Guide," *kanji* names sound too rustic and *katakana* names sound foreign. For instance, Frodo uses a *kanji* pseudonym *Yamanoshita* (Underhill) to conceal his name *Baginzu* which is in *katakana*. Tanaka changed a few place-names: Bree, originally *Kayu no sato* (Porridge Village), became *Burii-mura* (Bree Village).

Shiro No Norite (The White Rider), a Tokyo-based group of fans, was established in 1981. It published the indexes to *The Lord of the Rings* and *The Hobbit*, then, in 2003, *Unfinished Tales*. Peter Jackson's *The Lord of the Rings* film trilogy was the first glimpse of Tolkien's world for most Japanese people.

After the release of *The Fellowship of the Ring,* fans started complaining about the movie's subtitles by Natsuko Toda, a famous translator who had never read the book. They petitioned to change them, and in the next two parts of the trilogy Toda was assisted by Akiko Tanaka.

ROBERTO ARDUINI

Further Reading

Bree. *The Lord of the Rings: Fantasy World.* Tokyo: Art Books Forest, 2002.

Ellwood, Robert. "The Japanese Hobbit." *Mythlore* 1, no. 3 (July 1969): 14–17.

Okunishi, Takashi. "The Japanese Hobbit." In *Translations of "The Hobbit" Reviewed,* 19–20. Quettar Special Publication no. 2. London: Tolkien Society, 1988.

Scull, Christina. "*The Lord of the Rings* in Japanese." *Tolkien Collector,* no. 7 (1994).

———. "*Farmer Giles of Ham, Smith of Wootton Major,* and *Mr. Bliss* in Japan." *Tolkien Collector,* no. 8 (1994).

Takahashi, Makoto. "Impressions of Books by J.R.R. Tolkien published in Japan." http://homepage1.nifty.com/hobbit/english/tolkien/versions.html.

———. Letter of. *Tolkien Collector,* no. 17 (December 1997): 13.

See also **Fandom; Jackson, Peter; Publishing History**

JEWELS

Jewels are a typical motif of traditional tales. An abundance of precious stones or metals can simply create an impression of exoticism, or a hoard of treasure, with its implication of fabulous wealth, can provide a motive for treachery. Jewels can also possess special powers; even today precious stones are bought for the mystical influence that they are believed to have on the wearer, perhaps as that person's "birthstone." All these elements can be found in Tolkien.

The early depictions of Eldamar in *The Book of Lost Tales,* in which the Noldoli (Noldor) first make gems from the elements of nature and distribute them freely to beautify their surroundings, are examples of the first kind, typifying the book's Baroque exuberance. When Eärendil comes to Tirion, his feet are covered with the sparkling diamond dust from the streets.

More often, Tolkien emphasizes the danger of treasures. Attempts to capture or enhance the natural beauties of the primary creation can lead to a selfish, illicit form of subcreation. Although Fëanor makes the Silmarils using the freely available light of the Two Trees, he comes to covet them and will not allow them to be broken for the common good after the Trees have been destroyed. The oath taken by Fëanor's sons to regain them at all costs after they

are stolen by Melkor constantly underlies the tragedy of *The Silmarillion.* The Necklace of the Dwarves, a gem-studded gold carcanet crafted for Finrod Felagund, enhances the beauty of whoever wears it, but strife is renewed when Thingol has the Silmaril mounted in it, leading to the deaths of both Thingol and Dior. In *The Hobbit,* the Arkenstone, the large crystal from the heart of the Lonely Mountain, is so prized by Thorin that he grudgingly ransoms it from Bilbo for his thirteenth share of the treasure; his attempt to avoid paying precipitates the Battle of Five Armies.

The white stone that Arwen gives to Frodo to soothe the pain of his loss clearly belongs to the third group. The green stone worn by Aragorn on his brow when he comes to Minas Tirith, leads people to call him by his prophesied name, Elessar, the Elfstone. It is a symbol of his legitimacy and a tangible link with the past.

Possible sources for some of the jewel motifs can be found in Tolkien's study of medieval texts. The Arkenstone may be seen as a creative explanation of the *eorclanstānas* (usually glossed as "precious stones") in *Beowulf.* The gems of Eldamar recall the bejewelled landscape and city in *Pearl,* which itself derives from the heavenly Jerusalem in Revelation 21. Some resemblance to the Silmarils may be seen in the crown of the King of Faërie in *Sir Orfeo,* which is made of a single gem that shines like the sun, and the fact that his land is lit by precious stones. It is impossible to say what influence, conscious or unconscious, these texts had on Tolkien's creative process.

ALLAN TURNER

Further Reading

Tolkien, J.R.R., trans. *Sir Gawain and the Green Knight, Pearl, and Sir Orfeo.* London: George Allen & Unwin, 1975.

See also **Arkenstone; Elendilmir; Possessiveness; Silmarils**

JONES, GWYN

Gwyn Jones (1907–99) published Tolkien's poem *The Lay of Aotrou and Itroun* in 1948, though he is best known for his translations from Old Norse and medieval Welsh. Jones was also a respected novelist and short story writer and a driving force behind the Anglo-Welsh literary renaissance. Born in Blackwood, Monmouthshire (now Gwent), Wales, Jones was educated at University College Cardiff, University of Wales (BA 1927, MA 1929) and wrote while teaching school. He accepted a lectureship at

University College Cardiff, then in 1940 he moved to University of Wales, Aberystwyth, where he was the Rendel Professor of English Language and Literature. In 1964, he accepted a post at the University of Wales, Cardiff, retiring in 1974 to live in Aberystwyth, where he died. He received an honorary D.Litt. from the University of Wales in 1977.

Jones's M.A. thesis was "Legal Procedure and the Conduct of the Feud in the Icelandic Saga." In 1935, Jones's translation of Old Norse sagas was published as *Four Icelandic Sagas*. In February 1939, Jones and Creighton Griffiths founded the monthly literary journal *Welsh Review;* wartime paper shortages caused Jones to suspend publication of the journal in November 1939. Jones began publication again in 1944, only to cease permanently 1948, but not before publishing Tolkien's poem *The Lay of Aotrou and Itroun.* In 1944, Jones translated *The Vatnsdalers' Saga.* In 1948, he collaborated with Professor Thomas Jones, a Celticist, on a translation of the medieval Welsh collection of tales, the *Mabinogion.* This translation, published by Golden Cockerel Press in 1948, was the edition cited by Tolkien in his O'Donnell lecture "English and Welsh." Jones and Jones later published a revised edition of *The Mabinogion* in the Everyman series, and in 1989 Gwyn Jones and his wife Mair Jones published a revised third edition. The Jones and Jones translation is the first scholarly English translation and still the most frequently cited by scholars. Like Tolkien, Jones had a strong interest in fairy tales and folklore, and he published two illustrated collections of *Welsh Legends and Folk-Tales* and *Scandinavian Legends and Folk-Tales.* He also translated *Egil's Saga;* and his 1964 *The Norse Atlantic Saga: Being the Norse Voyages of Discovery and Settlement to Iceland, Greenland, America,* revised in 1984, is still the standard text. Jones's 1968 *History of the Vikings,* revised in 1984, is a standard introductory text. In 1977, he edited *The Oxford Book of Welsh Verse in English.*

LISA L. SPANGENBERG

Further Reading

Jones, Gwyn. *A History of the Vikings.* Oxford: Oxford University Press 1968. 2nd ed., 1984.

Jones, Gwyn, trans. *Egil's Saga.* Syracuse, NY: American-Scandinavian Foundation and Syracuse University Press, 1960.

———, trans. *Four Icelandic Sagas.* Princeton, NJ: Princeton University Press, 1935. Reprint, University Microfilms, 1972.

———, trans. *Eirik the Red, and Other Icelandic Sagas.* Oxford University Press, 1961. 2nd ed., 1972.

———, trans. *The Norse Atlantic Saga: Being the Norse Voyages of Discovery and Settlement to Iceland, Greenland, America.* Oxford: Oxford University Press, 1964. 2nd ed., 1986.

Jones, Gwyn, with Thomas Jones, trans. *The Golden Cockerel Mabinogion De-luxe Edition.* London: Golden Cockerel Press, 1948. Published as *The Mabinogion.* Everyman's Library, 97. London: J.M. Dent; New York, E.P. Dutton, 1949. Everyman edition revised by Gwyn Jones and Mair Jones, 1974, 1989.

Tolkien, J.R.R. "The Lay of Aotrou and Itroun." *Welsh Review* 4 (December 1945): 245–66.

———. "English and Welsh." In *Angles and Britons: O' Donnell Lectures,* 1–41. Aberystuyth: University of Wales Press, 1963. Reprinted in *The Monsters and the Critics,* edited by Christopher Tolkien. London: George Allen & Unwin, 1984.

See also **Mythology, Celtic; Old Norse Language; Poems by Tolkien in Other Languages; Welsh Language**

JORDANES: *HISTORY OF THE GOTHS*

Jordanes was a sixth-century historian also called Iornandes by subsequent writers. He identified himself as a Goth (Geta) and is known for the chronicle *De origine actibusque Getarum* (Of the Origin and Deeds of the Goths), sometimes also called *Getica* (Of the Goths). Jordanes' book is a condensation of a lost, longer work written in Ravenna by one Cassiodorus for the Ostrogothic King Theodoric the Great (fifth–sixth century). Jordanes (and presumably Cassiodorus) located the origin of the Goths on the far-northern island of "Scandza" (possibly referring to the peninsula of today's southern Sweden; its name may match the "Scandia" of Ptolemy's *Geographia* [written in Greek, second century], as well as today's Skåne), from whence they migrated south to "Gothiscandza" (possibly the mouths of the Vistula), and thence to the Black Sea (Sea of Pontus).

Jordanes' "history" is a loose amalgam of recent Gothic legends and royal histories appliquéd onto an older layer of narrative concerning a tribe called the Getae from 400 BCE (a Dacian or Thracian group), who were almost certainly unrelated to the Goths of Jordanes' own time, despite their similar name. Jordanes' accuracy, always questionable, is presumably strongest closest to his own lifetime; this is borne out by the identifiably Gothic names in the pertinent sections.

It is likely that Tolkien read Jordanes' *Getica* closely. We know that he read a parallel and near-contemporaneous Germanic chronicle, Paul the Deacon's eighth-century Lombard history, because of his use of Lombard names in "The Lost Road" and "The Notion Club Papers." We also know of Tolkien's early fondness for the Gothic language, presumably

Jordanes' own mother tongue. Finally, Jordanes' history includes figures and events featured in literary texts known to Tolkien. *Getica* tells how the Gothic King Ermanaricus sentenced one Sunilda to be pulled apart by horses, after which her brothers Ammius and Sarus took revenge. Parts of this story are found in *Beowulf*, where the king appears as Eormenric, as well as in the Sigurd-cycle of Eddic poems (in *Gudhrúnarhvöt* and *Hamdhismál*), where the tragic figures appear as Jörmunrekkr, Svanhildr, Hamthir, and Sörli.

It has been argued that an episode in Jordanes' chronicle provided the inspiration for the death of Théoden in *The Lord of the Rings*. This may be so, since no less than three kings of the Goths (Theoderidus, Thorismundus, and Valamir in their Latinized forms) are said in *Getica* to have died in battle after being thrown from their horses. It is worth noting that Théoden's own name (in Old English, a language related to Gothic) is similar to the first of these names and that the name of Théodred, Théoden's son (who is also slain in a presumably equestrian battle) is its exact Old English equivalent.

It is also possible that Jordanes' xenophobic descriptions of the Huns (Hunni), the traditional eastern enemies of the Goths, informed Tolkien's construction of the Western Mannish views of eastern enemies in Middle-earth from Easterlings to Orcs:

> [They are] a stunted, foul and puny tribe, scarcely human. . . . Their swarthy aspect [i]s fearful, and they ha[ve] . . . a sort of shapeless lump, not a head, with pinholes rather than eyes. . . . They are short in stature, quick in bodily movement, alert horsemen, broad shouldered, ready in the use of bow and arrow, and have firmset necks which are ever erect in pride. Though they live in the form of Men, they have the cruelty of wild beasts. (Mierow 1966, Book 24)

SANDRA BALLIF STRAUBHAAR

Further Reading

Ford, Judy Ann. "The White City: *The Lord of the Rings* as an Early Medieval Myth of the Restoration of the Roman Empire." *Tolkien Studies* 2 (2005): 53–73.

Goffart, Walter. *The Narrators of Barbarian History*. Princeton, NJ: Princeton University Press, 1988.

Larrington, Carolyne, trans. *The Poetic Edda*. Oxford: Oxford University Press, 1999.

Mierow, Charles Christopher, ed. and trans. *The Gothic History of Jordanes*. Cambridge: Speculum Historiale, 1966.

Neckel, Gustav, and Hans Kuhn, eds. *Edda: Die Lieder des Codex Regius nebst verwandten Denkmälern*. Heidelberg: Carl Winters Universitätsverlag, 1968.

See also **Easterlings; Goths; Lombardic Language; Lost Road**

JOYCE, JAMES (1882–1941)

Irish novelist, poet, and playwright James Joyce is the author of *Chamber Music* (1907), *Dubliners* (1914), *A Portrait of an Artist as a Young Man* (1916), *Exiles* (1918), *Ulysses* (1922), and *Finnegans Wake* (1939).

Tolkien and Joyce make an odd pair. At first glance, the fantasy fiction of Tolkien seems to reside in a different literary universe than the modernist novels of Joyce. There is no strong evidence that either writer read or admired the other's work (though the Bodleian Library houses a manuscript that appears to be Tolkien's notes on the linguistic puzzles in *Finnegans Wake*). Also, the staggering popularity of Tolkien appears almost grotesque when compared to the small number of literary specialists that comprise the readers of Joyce. Yet, ironically, the net effect of Tolkien's popularity and Joyce's critical reception has been the same and has, to some degree, thrown them together as rivals: both *The Lord of the Rings* and *Ulysses* have been voted the greatest novels of the twentieth century, the first by the BBC's *Bookchoice* and the Waterstone's bookshop in 1997, and the second by the Modern Library in 1998.

But there are more compelling reasons for comparing these writers than reader polls and book list competitions. On any given intellectual or literary issue, Tolkien and Joyce appear to be photographic negatives of each other. The question of religion, for example, illustrates their differences of sensibility. Joyce abandoned Catholicism at an early age, yet the church and its symbols dominate much of his fiction. Tolkien remained committed to the Church of Rome his entire life but carefully refrained from overt references to Christian myth in his major works. As artists, Joyce and Tolkien reacted to the twentieth century with two different literary methods. Joyce pursued an avant-garde experimentalism and was rewarded fulsomely by the critical establishment, an establishment that, for the most part, rejected Tolkien for adhering to epic and romance traditions and for writing children's literature and works of fantasy, genres often dismissed as puerile. Joyce's later works move beyond character and plot, but Tolkien's later works succeed partly because both are so well rendered. Joyce's novels and short stories explore a squalid, lower-middle class Dublin suffering the effects of colonialism and an inequitable social order, and Tolkien's novels dramatize the fading beauties of a war-ravaged imaginary world.

But Tolkien and Joyce did not always move in opposite directions. Both were deeply interested in the linguistic and mythological underpinnings of early European literature. Both were inspired by and alluded to existing bodies of myth. Both were experimenters and inventors of languages. Tolkien's Middle-earth was linguistically inspired: he invented the Elvish languages and then created a secondary world where they could be spoken. Joyce's last two novels are complex and dense creations, filled with puns, word games, neologisms, and portmanteau words. Furthermore, both writers achieved an impression that a vast historical and cultural antiquity formed the background for their fiction. Tolkien hoped to create a many-voiced body of myth that he could dedicate to England. Joyce's doppelgänger Stephen Dedalus sought "to forge in the smithy of [his] soul the uncreated conscience of [his] race" *(A Portrait of the Artist as a Young Man).* This conscience would find final expression in *Finnegans Wake,* a vast and dream-like encyclopedia of history, culture, and languages. Paradoxically, it is in Joyce's most avant-garde novel that the similarities between Tolkien and Joyce emerge, for there modernist difficulty meets retrograde romance and academic industry finds commonality with popular readership.

CHARLES H. FISCHER and PAUL EDMUND THOMAS

Further Reading

Attridge, Derek, and Daniel Ferrer, eds. *Post-structuralist Joyce: Essays from the French.* Cambridge: Cambridge University Press, 1984.

Burgess, Anthony. *Here Comes Everybody: An Introduction to James Joyce for the Ordinary Reader.* London: Faber, 1965.

Devlin, Kimberly J., and Marilyn Reizbaum, eds. *Ulysses: En-Gendered Perspectives; Eighteen New Essays on the Episodes.* Columbia: University of South Carolina Press, 1999.

Duffy, James. *The Subaltern "Ulysses."* Minneapolis, MN: University of Minnesota Press, 1994.

Ellmann, Richard. *James Joyce.* New York: Oxford University Press, 1959.

Flieger, Verlyn. *Interrupted Music: The Making of Tolkien's Mythology.* Kent, OH: Kent State University Press, 2005.

Gifford, Don, with Robert J. Seidman. *"Ulysses" Annotated.* Berkeley, CA: University of California Press, 1989.

Hart, Cliff, and David Hayman, eds. *James Joyce's "Ulysses": Critical Essays.* Berkeley, CA: University of California Press, 1974.

Herr, Cheryl. *Joyce's Anatomy of Culture.* Urbana: University of Illinois Press, 1986.

Kenner, Hugh. *Dublin's Joyce.* Reprint New York: Columbia University Press, 1987.

Shippey, Tom. *J.R.R. Tolkien: Author of the Century.* New York: HarperCollins, 2000.

See also **America in the 1960s: Reception of Tolkien; Auden, W.H.: Influence of Tolkien; Catholicism, Roman; Christianity; Criticism of Tolkien, Twentieth Century; Languages Invented by Tolkien; Literature, Twentieth Century: Influence of Tolkien; Mythology for England; Theological and Moral Approaches in Tolkien's Works; Tolkien Scholarship: An Overview; Tolkien Scholarship: First Decades; Tolkien Scholarship: Institutions; Tolkien Scholarship: Since 1980**

JUDAISM

Tolkien says little about Jews, Judaism, or the Hebrew language. In terms of his own "Jewishness," Tolkien replies in Letter no. 30 in 1938 to a query by the German publishers of *The Hobbit* that he is not Jewish: "I appear to have *no* ancestors of that gifted people." Toward the end of the Second World War, Tolkien met Jewish Scholar Cecil Roth, a historian at Oxford during this period. They were both speaking at an event in Cardiff. Tolkien expresses in a letter to his son Christopher how touched he was that Roth lent Tolkien his watch and later woke Tolkien in time to get ready to attend Communion. The impression from Tolkien's writings and letters is that he knew few people of Jewish persuasion and little regarding modern Judaism. His response to the German publishers makes it clear that he did not approve of anti-Semitism.

Tolkien's knowledge of Hebrew and biblical Judaism is another matter, though often an overstated case. In Letter no. 176, in 1955, Tolkien remarks to Naomi Mitchison that he thought of the Dwarves as being like the Hebrew people in the sense that they are exiles from their native land, speaking privately their own language in the lands they now occupy and publicly the languages of those they live among, though with an accent that betrays their origin. The Dwarvish calendar also bears some marks of being inspired by the Jewish calendar: the Dwarvish calendar is essentially a lunar calendar calibrated with the solar calendar by the occasional insertion of extra days and months.

The Hebrew language served as an inspiration or model for Tolkien in other ways as well. Shortly after World War I, Tolkien created the "Alphabet of Rúmil," named after an Elvish sage in his stories. The alphabet was in part based on Hebrew, Greek, and Pitman's shorthand. Tolkien used this alphabet at the time to write in his diary, but he frequently changed the character of the graphs, with the result that later Tolkien could not read parts of his own diary.

Returning to the question of the Dwarves, what little is recorded of their language seems based on Semitic languages, probably Hebrew. Roots of the words recorded in Dwarvish, or Khuzdul, are based on three consonants, and infixes and affixes are attached to affect meaning, part of speech, and so on. Tolkien never developed this, however, and there are only isolated words and a few phrases of the language of the Dwarves.

Others have pointed to the *Jerusalem Bible* as evidence of Tolkien's detailed knowledge of the Hebrew language. At the beginning of the *Jerusalem Bible* translation project headed by Father Anthony Jones, the idea was to quickly provide good English translations of the French text of *La Bible Jerusalem,* completed and published in 1954, but to provide new commentary by English, Roman Catholic scholars and authors. It was in this context that Jones wrote to Tolkien inviting him to be part of the project. Because of time, Tolkien accepted the book of Jonah, which he then seems to have translated from French. Jones then checked it against the Hebrew and Greek and revised it. Jones's initial invitation assures Tolkien more than once that knowledge of the languages was not necessary. The aim of the *Jerusalem Bible* was to have an eye on English style as much as on accurate translation. Jones makes it clear that he was inviting Tolkien onto the board because of Tolkien's expertise in English philology and because Jones was taken with *The Lord of the Rings,* not because of any supposed expertise in Hebrew on Tolkien's part. This was not unusual. There are other members of the *Jerusalem Bible* board who were like Tolkien—not expert in the original languages of the Bible but desirable for their expertise in English and because they were prominent Roman Catholic thinkers or writers in England.

In the end, as Tolkien says, he was able to contribute little, despite writing to his grandson Michael in 1957 that he hoped to take a larger role in the *Jerusalem Bible* and was learning Hebrew a year after he had submitted the translation of Jonah. As he indicates elsewhere he never got far because of the demands of other work. Jones, wanting to keep Tolkien on the board and involved in the project, offered to Tolkien the task of revising some of the translation—not by comparing it with the originals but by making comments on improving the English style of some of the translations. Tolkien received the copy of Job that had been translated by Andrew Keeney, Jones's nephew and a board member. Tolkien held up the work for a long time because he was unable to complete his revisions in part due to other work, in part due to Tolkien's perfectionism. According to Keeney, when he and Jones went to Tolkien's home to discuss the translation, Tolkien proved difficult and intractable on some of the issues of the translation's English expression and forced through the changes. This resulted in yet more delay in publication.

The note from the publisher reproduced in *Amon Hen* in 1977 reporting that Tolkien translated Job and is mistaken. The author conflates Tolkien's tardiness in preparing a revision of the translation of Job with the statement that Tolkien was important, saying Tolkien provided the translation although he did not. Tolkien revised the English translation of Job, but the translation was done by Keeney. There is also a report that Tolkien revised part of the book of Proverbs. Tolkien's name is listed among the board members, but he thought it generous, considering how little he had done.

Having reported all this, however, it should be noted that Tolkien's manuscript of the translation of Jonah has in Tolkien's hand marginalia that in part consists of Hebrew words penciled in. Tolkien apparently compared at least some words of his translation with a Hebrew text and lexicon. This suggests, particularly because so little Dwarvish and Adûnaic survive, that Tolkien had learned enough of the alphabet and the language to work with basic lexical tools but had not advanced much beyond that state. Thus, his knowledge of Jews, Judaism, and Hebrew seems limited.

L.J. SWAIN

Further Reading

Bramlett, Perry C. *I Am In Fact a Hobbit: An Introduction to the Life and Work of J.R.R. Tolkien.* Macon, GA: Mercer University Press, 2002.

Carpenter, Humphrey. *Tolkien: A Biography.* Boston, MA: Houghton Mifflin, 1977.

Jones, Alexander, ed. *The Jerusalem Bible.* London: Darton, Longman & Todd, 1966.

Kenny, Anthony. *A Path From Rome: An Autobiography,* 117. Oxford: Oxford University Press, 1986.

See also **Dwarves; Philo-Semitism**

JULIANA

Juliana is an Old English poem by Cynewulf that was known and studied by Tolkien. It is one of many retellings of a sixth-century Latin martyrology, and depicts a virgin who was tortured, imprisoned, tempted by a demon, and beheaded for refusing to marry a pagan. Cynewulf's version aligns Juliana's suitor with the demon and makes her defeat of evil, through words and courage, the dramatic emphasis of the story (15).

Juliana was written in the Anglian dialect, no later than the middle of the tenth century, in either the Mercian or Northumberland kingdoms (Sisam, 2); this makes it part of the West Midlands language and literature Tolkien studied because of the strong ties he felt to this region (*Letters,* 54, 108, 213, 218).

Tolkien also studied the Middle English homily *Juliene* that is part of the Katherine Group of religious instructional texts for women composed in the West Midlands in the 1200s. Tolkien examined these texts for evidence that some form of English language and tradition had survived the invasions of the French and Norse (Shippey, 31–32).

Tolkien felt that *Juliana* and *Juliene* were lineally connected, as reflected in notes for his landmark *Beowulf* essay (*B&C*, 129). This claim, which is considered controversial, was not included in the final version of the essay (*B&C*, 291).

Juliene is found in MS Bodley 34. It is one of the primary texts edited by Simonne d'Ardenne, one of Tolkien's students and collaborators, for her book *Þe Liflade ant te Passiun of Seinte Juliene*. This book is dedicated to Tolkien and based on the doctoral thesis she prepared under his supervision. E.V. Gordon, another of Tolkien's colleagues, wrote the introduction to the 1936 edition of this book, and both he and d'Ardenne felt that it contained more of Tolkien's insights into early Middle English language than anything he published himself (Anderson, 22).

Some scholars relate the Eddic Valkyrie tradition to Juliana and other women featured in Old English heroic poetry through characteristics such as a sober mind, noble birth, and courage (Damico 1990, 182). Radiance is also a Valkyrie characteristic, used particularly by Cynewulf in reference to Juliana, and Tolkien's association of Galadriel with light has been used to demonstrate her connection with the Valkyrie tradition (Donovan, 114). Éowyn is also described in terms of Valkyrie images of brightness (Donovan, 124), although other English and Icelandic works known to Tolkien have been suggested as alternatives to the Valkyrie model for her character development (Lewis and Currie, 209–10).

Although he translated or adapted many other Old or Middle English legends, and was strongly associated with d'Ardenne's book on St. Juliene, Tolkien did not publish any individual scholarly works focused solely on *Juliana*. In its language, place of origin, and subject matter, however, there is evidence that her legend in its various forms was influential for Tolkien, not just in his scholarly studies and academic collaborations but also in the portrayal of women in his fiction.

PATRICIA TUBBS

Primary Sources

Cynewulf. *Juliana*, edited by Rosemary Woolf. London: Methuen, 1955.

d'Ardenne, Simonne R.T.O., ed. *Te Liflade ant te Passiun of Seinte Juliene*. London: Oxford University Press / Early English Text Society, 1961.

Further Reading

Anderson, Douglas A. "An Industrious Little Devil: E.V. Gordon as a Friend and Collaborator with Tolkien." In *Tolkien the Medievalist*, edited by Jane Chance, 15–25. London: Routledge, 2003.

Damico, Helen. "The Valkyrie Reflex in Old English Literature." In *New Readings on Women in Old English Literature*, edited by Helen Damico and Alexandra Hennesy Olsen, 176–90. Bloomington, IN: Indiana University Press, 1990.

Donovan, Leslie. "The Valkyrie Reflex in J.R.R. Tolkien's *The Lord of the Rings:* Galadriel, Shelob, Éowyn, and Arwen." In *Tolkien the Medievalist*, edited by Jane Chance, 106–32. London: Routledge, 2002.

Lewis, Alex, and Elizabeth Currie. *The Uncharted Realms of Tolkien: A Critical Study of Text, Context and Subtext in the Works of J.R.R. Tolkien*. London: Medea Publishing, 2002.

Shippey, Tom. *The Road to Middle-earth*. Boston, MA: Houghton Mifflin, 1983.

Sisam, Kenneth. *Studies in the History of Old English Literature*. Oxford: Clarendon, 1953.

See also **Beowulf and the Critics; Cynewulf; Éowyn; Epic Poetry; Feminist Readings of Tolkien; Galadriel; Gender in Tolkien's Works; Gordon, E.V.; Heroes and Heroism; History, Anglo-Saxon; Katherine Group; Manuscripts, Medieval; Middle English Vocabulary; Northern Courage; Old English; Old Mercian; Old Norse Literature; Scholars of Medieval Literature, Influence of; Sexuality in Tolkien's Works; Suffield Family; Women in Tolkien's Works**

JUNGIAN THEORY

Carl Gustav Jung (1875–1961) founded the school of analytic psychology, which sought to explain the development of individual personality formations through a complex system of concepts. Jung was a contemporary of Sigmund Freud and shared his interest in dream analysis and free association, though he disagreed with Freud's emphasis on sexuality. Jung argued that personality was formed in relation to the conscious and unconscious realms of the psyche. An individual is aware of conscious thoughts, and unconscious thoughts exist unnoticed. According to Jung, there are two forms of the unconscious, the personal and the collective. The personal unconscious contains unique content belonging to an individual, and the collective unconscious is a reservoir of humanity's experiences passed from one generation to the next. Jung defined those primordial images shared by all humans regardless of history or geography as archetypes. These play a significant role in behavioral development; some examples include the mother, the shadow, the child, the hero, and the wise old man. Archetypes manifest themselves through various symbols, which alter depending on the cultural context. The objective of analytic psychology is to help patients transcend the bifurcation of consciousness and unconsciousness and become more aware of their whole selves, a process Jung called individuation or self-actualization.

Though a recognized school of psychological analysis, Jungian theory is more commonly known for its insights into literature, and in this mode it has been employed by Tolkien scholars. Timothy R. O'Neill demonstrates the ease with which one can fit *The Lord of the Rings* into Jung's model, and Dorothy Matthews illustrates Bilbo's individuation. Experts in the field agree that there is no direct evidence of Jung's influence; however, some acknowledge Tolkien's familiarity with Jung's theory on dreams.

The Misty Mountains provide excellent terrain for Jungian analysis. The roots of the mountains (a symbol of the unconscious) run deep, delving into the darkest regions of the earth where creatures from Middle-earth's history lie. The novel's heroes encounter monstrous representations of their own darker selves, their shadows, repositories of their darkest desires and evil thoughts. Bilbo faces and triumphs over Gollum, a hobbit-like creature twisted by the One Ring. Bilbo's success is more than a minor victory. The experience transforms him and initiates a spurt of psychic growth. Bilbo matures and emerges from the mountains wiser through his meeting with his shadow-self. Likewise, Gandalf becomes self-actualized (becoming Gandalf the White) through his battle with the Balrog of Moria, a semidivine creature like himself. Gandalf, himself a symbol of the wise old man archetype, struggles against his shadow-self, becoming fully self-aware and ready to tackle the challenges presented by Sauron.

CHRISTOPHER VACCARO

Further Reading

Grant, Patrick. "Tolkien: Archetype and Word." In *Understanding "The Lord of the Rings": The Best of Tolkien Criticism*, edited by Rose A. Zimbardo and Neil D. Isaacs, 163–82. Boston, MA: Houghton Mifflin, 2004.

Kotowski, Nathalie. "Frodo, Sam, and Aragorn in the Light of C. G. Jung." *Jahrbuch fur Literatur und Asthetik* 10 (1992): 145–59.

Matthews, Dorothy. "The Psychological Journey of Bilbo Baggins." In *A Tolkien Compass*, edited by Jared Lobdell, 29–42. La Salle, IL: Open Court, 1975.

O'Neill, Timothy R. *The Individuated Hobbit: Jung, Tolkien and the Archetypes of Middle-earth*. Boston, MA: Houghton Mifflin, 1979.

See also **Symbolism in Tolkien's Works**

JUSTICE AND INJUSTICE

Tolkien's writings reflect on the nature of justice and injustice, in terms of both divine justice coming from God or his representatives and justice in the dealings of one being with another. Mercy or pity also figures prominently in these discussions, for Tolkien sees justice as inexorably linked to that important virtue. Using different notions of justice derived from classical heroic, Norse, Anglo-Saxon, and Christian Catholic traditions, Tolkien articulates a theory of cosmic and individual justice that shapes his universe.

Divinity is central to the idea of justice in the traditions from which Tolkien borrowed. Justice in the world of the Homeric epics was predicated upon notions of kingship and divine order: rulers dispense the justice that Zeus has entrusted to them, and their justice must accord with the natural order of things (MacIntyre, 14). This concept appears also in the Norse and Anglo-Saxon worlds in which kings serve as representatives of the heathen gods and later the Christian God, and their dooms are thus sacred (Chaney, 186). The king is justice according to an Old Norse kenning (Vigfusson and Powell, 480). Oaths form an important component of justice dating back to the heroic worlds of the Old English *Beowulf* and the earlier Norse sagas (Holmes 2004). Vengeance and blood feuds were also basic features of Norse legal codes such as the Icelandic *Grágás,* though they faded as Christianity gained ascendancy (Miller, 190).

In the Christian/Catholic tradition, God's justice is closely related to his mercy. God in the Old Testament is exacting, but the New Testament and Catholic doctrine make justice the basis of salvation. For St. Thomas Aquinas, the justice of God is the foundation for ideas of justice among fallen humans, and justice and mercy (which are inseparably linked) are the essential components of God's absolute goodness (Weinandy, 71). Aquinas adds that justice is what one human being owes another and how one should act with another, and he says that acting justly is what all beings owe God (MacIntyre, 199).

Tolkien's letters and writings display the influence of these traditions of justice upon his thinking. In "On Fairy-stories," he notes that justice must be tempered by mercy; he echoes G.K. Chesterton's observation that "children are innocent and love justice; while most of us are wicked and prefer mercy" (*MC,* 137). *Leaf by Niggle* contains a debate over Niggle's penance in the workhouse, with one voice calling for justice, the other for mercy. This dialogue recalls the judgment of souls in medieval morality plays (Kocher, 162). For Tolkien, final judgment is indeed reserved for God. Gandalf's admonition to Frodo about judging Gollum is an axiom: "be not too eager to deal out death in the name of justice, fearing for your own safety" (*TT*, IV, i, 221). In Letter no. 181 Tolkien comments, "Into the ultimate judgment upon Gollum I would not care to enquire. This would investigate 'Goddes privitee,' as the Medievals said" (*Letters*, 234). The pity Frodo shows Gollum is a corollary of the need to leave ultimate questions of justice and punishment in the hands of the higher powers.

Yet Tolkien's characters have an innate sense of right and wrong that gives them a sense of universal justice in their relationships with each other. As Aragorn tells Éomer, "'Good and ill have not changed since yesteryear; nor are they one thing among Elves and Dwarves and another among Men" (*TT*, III, ii, 41). The peaceful Shire with its few Shirriffs is the epitome of a society predicated upon justice, and the breakdown of justice under Sharkey's police state reflects the disharmony introduced into the world by evil. As in Anglo-Saxon society, oaths between individuals and groups form an important basis of justice in Tolkien's mythology. Violators must suffer the consequences of their bad faith to others as Gollum's fate or that of the Oathbreakers demonstrates.

Rulers or the representatives of the divine are entitled to use their heavenly granted wisdom and sense of cosmic order to see that justice is fulfilled. In *The Silmarillion*, Manwë knows the most of Eru's thought and is the ultimate judge in Arda, though he exercises mercy in his judgments (as he does with Melkor). Mandos, in contrast, is a spokesman for "strict justice" rather than compassion (Kocher, 15). The Oath of Fëanor, which sets up a blood feud between his house and the other Elves and Valar, and the subsequent Kinslaying, lead to the just wrath expressed in the Doom of Mandos. Only Eärendil's sacrifice can secure the Valar's mercy in the end.

Aragorn and Faramir in *The Lord of the Rings* become the ideal judge figures in the legendarium. Faramir spares Frodo and Sam and heeds Frodo's pleas for mercy for Gollum even though he has trespassed into the Forbidden Pool. Once he becomes king and passes his judgments, Aragorn becomes the quintessential wielder of divine justice. He pardons the contrite Easterlings and Haradrim and shows mercy to the disobedient but loyal Beregond. Aragorn typifies the model ruler who judges fairly and has the authority to make pronouncements. These quasi-Christian and other views of justice thus structure Tolkien's universe on both the macro- and microcosmic levels.

DAVID D. OBERHELMAN

Further Reading

Chaney, William A. *The Cult of Kingship in Anglo-Saxon England*. Berkeley, CA: University of California Press, 1970.

Holmes, John R. "Oaths and Oath Breaking: Analogues of Old English *Comitatus* in Tolkien's Myth." In *Tolkien and the Invention of Myth: A Reader*, edited by Jane Chance, 249–62. Lexington, KY: University of Kentucky Press, 2004.

Kocher, Paul Harold. *Master of Middle-earth: The Fiction of J.R.R. Tolkien*. Boston, MA: Houghton Mifflin, 1972.

———. *A Reader's Guide to "The Silmarillion."* Boston, MA: Houghton Mifflin, 1980.

MacIntyre, Alasdair. *Whose Justice? Which Rationality?* Notre Dame, IN: University of Notre Dame Press, 1988.

Miller, William Ian. *Bloodtaking and Peacemaking: Feud, Law, and Society in Saga Iceland*. Chicago: University of Chicago Press, 1990.

Vigfusson, Gubrand, and F. York Powell, eds. *The Poetry of the Old Northern Tongue from the Earliest Times to the Thirteenth Century*. Vol. 2. New York: Russell and Russell, 1965.

Weinandy, Thomas G. "Justice of God." In *New Catholic Encyclopedia*. 2nd ed. Vol. 8, pp. 70–73. Detroit: Thomson Gale.

See also **Aquinas, Thomas; Catholicism, Roman; Heathenism and Paganism; Law; Mercy**

K

KATHERINE GROUP

The group of Middle English writings called the Katherine Group usually refers to five early thirteenth-century prose works all found in MS Bodleian Library 34. They are the lives and passions of three virgin martyrs, St. Juliene, St. Katherine, and St. Marharete, a text on virginity called *Hali Meidenhad*, and a treaty on the custody of the soul called *Sawles Warde.*

The five texts, which are all free translations of Latin sources, are usually associated in time, origin, and language with the *Ancrene Wisse.* J.R.R. Tolkien showed in a famous essay called "Ancrene Wisse and Hali Meiðhad" that the scribes of MS Cambridge, Corpus Christi College 402, the Ancrene Wisse (= A), and of MS Bodley 34, the Katherine Group (= B), were written in the same standard literary language from the West Midlands. Tolkien published his essay in *Essays and Studies of the English Association,* 14 (104–26). He called this literary dialect "the AB language." The so-called Wooing Group of texts, represented by *The Wohunge of Ure Lauerd*, is also counted among the AB texts. See further *The Ancrene Wisse* and *The AB Language.*

There are clear signs indicating that literary standards had existed in Old English besides Late West Saxon. This is true of the Mercian type of dialect found in the Vespasian Psalter Gloss from the ninth century. There is an obvious continuity of writing traditions from this westerly part of England in Old English times to the West Midlands of England in the thirteenth century, where the AB language was located.

The connections between the manuscripts of the *Ancrene Wisse* and those of the Katherine Group had been touched on by some previous scholars. It was, however, Tolkien who pointed out the close relationship in language and spelling, almost amounting to identity, between the *Ancrene Wisse* (A) and the Bodleian manuscript of the Katherine Group (B). Nowhere else in Middle English literature do we find two different manuscripts of two different literary works copied by different scribes that show such obvious similarities. It is clear that the two manuscripts must be connected in time and place.

These unique circumstances led Tolkien to suppose either (i) that A or B are both originals, or (ii) that A or B are in whole or part accurate translations, or (iii) that the vanished originals of A and B were in this same language (AB), and so belonged to practically the same period and place as the copies we have. The first possibility can at once be dismissed. Neither A nor B can be originals. Tolkien did not think that an accurate translation is credible.

Tolkien became particularly renowned for his essay on the AB language from 1929 and his edition of the *Ancrene Wisse* from 1962. However, he was also notably involved in research concerning the Katherine Group texts. The edition of *Seinte Juliene* by the Belgian scholar Simonne d'Ardenne was praised by reviewers as the best Middle English text edition so far (1936). Tolkien was d'Ardenne's supervisor at Oxford, and it was a well-known fact that the detailed linguistic observations on the language of the

AB texts were based on Tolkien's ideas concerning the AB language.

Tolkien and d'Ardenne also cooperated for some time on an edition of the *Life of St. Katherine,* but Tolkien's commitments to his fictional writings prevented their joint publication of this text. Later, the edition was completed by E.J. Dobson and published as a joint edition by d'Ardenne and Dobson in 1981. The manuscripts of the Katherine Group, which have all, except *Sawles Warde,* been edited by the Early English Text Society, are listed below:

> Facsimile of MS. Bodley 43: *St Katherine, St Margaret, St Juliana, Hali Mei[ð]had, Sawles Warde.* Introd. N.R. Ker. EETS 247. London: Oxford University Press, 1960.
>
> *Seinte Katerine*: Reedited from MS Bodley 34 and the Other Manuscripts. Ed. S.R.T.O. d'Ardenne and E.J. Dobson. EETS, suppl. ser., 7. London: Oxford University Press, 1981.
>
> *Seinte Marharete the Meiden and Martyr*: Reedited from MS. Bodley 34, Oxford and MS. Royal 17A xxvii, British Museum. Ed. Francis M. Mack. EETS 193. London: Oxford University Press, 1934.
>
> *Þe Liflade ant the Passiun of Seinte Iuliene.* Ed. S.R.T.O. d'Ardenne. EETS 248. London: Oxford University Press, 1961.
>
> *Hali Mei[ð]had.* Ed. Bella Millett. EETS 284. London: Oxford University Press, 1982.
>
> *Sawles Warde: An Early Middle English Homily (Bodley, Royal and Cotton MSS).* Ed. R.M. Wilson. Leeds 1938.
>
> *The Wohunge of Ure Lauerd.* Ed. Meredith Thompson. EETS 241. London: Oxford University Press, 1938.

ARNE ZETTERSTEN

Further Reading

Millett, Bella. "*Hali Meidhad, Sawles Warde,* and the Continuity of English Prose." In *Five Hundred Years of Words and Sounds: Festschrift for Eric Dobson,* edited by Eric Gerald Stanley and Douglas Gray, 100–8. Cambridge: D.S. Brewer, 1983.

———, with the assistance of George B. Jack and Yoko Wada. *Ancrene Wisse, The Katherine Group, and the Wooing Group: Annotated Bibliographies of Old and Middle English Literature.* Vol. 2. Cambridge: D.S. Brewer, 1996.

———. "The *Ancrene Wisse* Group." In *A Compendium to Middle English Prose,* ed. A.S.G. Edwards. Cambridge: D.S. Brewer, 2004.

Stevenson, Lorna, ed. *Concordances to the Katherine Group and the Wooing Group.* Woodbridge, Suffolk: Boydell & Brewer, 2000.

Tolkien, J.R.R., "*Ancrene Wisse* and *Hali Meiðhad*". *Essays and Studies of the English Association* 14 (1929): 104–26.

Wada, Yoko, ed. and trans. *Temptations from* Ancrene Wisse. Vol. 1. Kansai University Institute of Oriental and Occidental Studies Sources and Materials Series 18. Osaka: Kansai University Press, 1994; Cambridge: D.S. Brewer, 1994.

———. *A Companion to* Ancrene Wisse. Cambridge: D.S. Brewer, 2003.

See also **AB Language**; *Ancrene Wisse*; **d'Ardenne, S.T.R.O.; MS Bodley 34**

KING ALFRED

Alfred, the only English monarch to be called "the Great," ruled England from 871 to 899. The epithet stems first from Alfred's military and political accomplishments, uniting Wessex with Mercia (a mixed blessing for Tolkien, who cherished his Mercian heritage) and winning decisive battles against Viking invaders. But a second reason Alfred is "the Great" is his revival of learning in England, brought about by his writers and support of his own writing and translation of works as diverse as Boethius's *Consolation of Philosophy*, Bede's *Ecclesiastical History*, and Gregory's *Pastoral Care*.

While other medievalists, and English cultural historians in general, saw Alfred's support of learning as strictly a neo-Latin affair, Tolkien insisted that the great king had an equal interest in Anglo-Saxon learning. In two early drafts of "*Beowulf*: The Monsters and the Critics," Tolkien inferred that native Old English poems "were loved no less by Alfred the revivalist than the Latin learning which he strove to reestablish" (B & C, 62, 120). In support, Tolkien cited William of Malmsbury's observation that Aldhelm was Alfred's favorite Anglo-Saxon poet—a phrasing that implies a taste that could discriminate among others (B & C, 209–10).

The image of Alfred the military hero Tolkien developed as a fantasy vision of a heroic lay celebrating Alfred's victory at Ashdown in 871, just before he became king. Such a hypothetical heroic poem (which in the published version of "*Beowulf*: The Monsters and the Critics," Tolkien changed to a hypothetical poem on St. Oswald) would still not carry the cultural weight of *Beowulf*, Tolkien argued, because Alfred's enemies were merely human, while *Beowulf*'s were monsters of mythological and supernatural proportions.

JOHN R. HOLMES

Further Reading

Asser. *Life of King Alfred.* Translated by L.C. Jane. London: Chatto & Windus, 1924.

Duckett, Eleanor Shipley. *Alfred the Great*. Chicago, IL: University of Chicago Press, 1956.

Shippey, Tom. *The Road to Middle-earth: Revised and Expanded Edition*. Boston, MA: Houghton Mifflin, 2003.

See also **Kingship; Old English; Vale of the White Horse**

KINGSHIP

Tolkien's enduring interest in the nature and practice of kingship may be traced to his professional study of medieval literary kings like Beowulf, his Christian ideals, and to the growing disillusionment with the institution of monarchy within his own lifetime. In letter 52, perhaps Tolkien's most explicit statement of his political views, Tolkien himself professed to favoring "anarchy" or "unconstitutional monarchy." By "anarchy" he meant a state without a state, the "abolition of control" by some members of society over others, as exemplified by the Shire. "Unconstitutional monarchy," on the other hand, meant the placement of control in the hands of a single person. The kings in Tolkien's writing, along with those who aspire to royalty, serve as an extended meditation on the nature of good rulership by such a figure.

Tolkien's kings, particularly in *The Silmarillion*, frequently face dilemmas typical of medieval kingship. Since medieval kingship involved loyalty to an individual, the transference of authority to the king's successor was uneasy, and disputes over the succession were frequent, especially between relatives with rival claims. So we find Fëanor and Fingolfin, the two half-brothers, vying for the affection of their father King Finwë, and ultimately for the leadership of the Noldor. Further discord is created by a king's lack of moderation; hence, Fëanor's unwillingness to make personal sacrifices for the sake of the Elves' unity brings about the Noldor's exile from Valinor and his own demise. Fingolfin, by contrast, takes the responsibility for the Elves' unity upon himself, and, when that unity is broken, he is driven by despair to challenge Morgoth in single combat and is slain. Another kind of king turns his attention inward, away from his responsibilities in the wider world. Such a king is Thingol, who becomes increasingly reclusive and obsessed with material possessions (including his daughter). In his sense of self-importance, he resembles the parsimonious king of *Farmer Giles of Ham*, whose disdain for the commoners whom he is sworn to protect is all too clear.

The temptation toward hubris is perhaps the most accessible, and troublesome, royal dilemma for a modern audience. In letter 52, Tolkien relates the empires of the Persian King Xerxes and of Alexander the Great to the political dictatorships of his own time, and his story of the pursuit of immortality by the Númenórean king Ar-Pharazôn bears striking resemblances medieval accounts of Alexander the Great, such as the Middle English *Wars of Alexander*. In *The Homecoming of Beorhtnoth Beorhthelm's Son*, Tolkien attaches an essay on *ofermod* (which he translates as excessive chivalry) in the Old English poem *The Battle of Maldon*. There he argues that Beorhtnoth (although not a king, still a leader of men) neglects his duty to his subordinates in pursuit of personal glory, allowing them to be slaughtered by an invading Viking army. In *The Lord of the Rings*, Denethor, the steward of Gondor, similarly models a lordship failed because of excessive personal pride. But *The Lord of the Rings* also showcases two good kings, Théoden and Aragorn, and in many ways the book can be read as mirror for princes, a medieval genre that depicts the ideal king. Théoden's subjects follow him out of personal devotion, following the Germanic models of kingship Tolkien found in such works as *Beowulf* and *The Battle of Maldon*. Aragorn also inspires such devotion, and, as Jane Chance has argued, further embodies a particularly Christian ideal of kingship in his role as healer, as well as warrior.

Ultimately, however, Tolkien wrestles with modern suspicions about kingship as a means of government, manifested in his own lifetime by events such as the Russian Revolution and the abdication of Edward VIII. In the Third Age of Middle-earth, the leaders of the Elves are not generally named as kings or queens (Galadriel explicitly rejects the title), even when they are legitimate heirs to crowns. Service is also an insufficient claim to royalty; hence, the stewards of Gondor (including Denethor) do not claim the crown. By coupling virtue with lineage in the figure of Aragorn, Tolkien ends up endowing the kingship with a mystical quality from which the majority of the population are excluded both by ancestry and by experience. This is both a conservative desire for an older system in which the legitimacy of kingship was based on the personal devotion of his subjects and an acknowledgment that, in a world where the machinery of the State gives leaders the power to command other men, "not one in a million is fit for it" (*Letters*, 64).

SCOTT KLEINMAN

Further Reading

The Battle of Maldon. In *The Anglo-Saxon World*, edited by Crossley-Kevin Holland. Oxford: Oxford University Press, 2000.

Beowulf. Translated by Roy Liuzza. London: Broadview, 2002.

Chance, Jane, *Tolkien's Art*. Lexington, KY: University Press of Kentucky, 2001 [1979].

Duggan, Hoyt N., and Thorlac Turville-Petre, eds. *The Wars of Alexander*. Oxford: Oxford University Press, 1989.

Kleinman, Scott. "Service." In *Reading "The Lord of the Rings,"* edited by Robert Eaglestone. London: Continuum, 2006.

Meyers, Henry Allen. *Medieval Kingship*. Chicago, IL: Nelson Hall, 1982.

Spellman, W.M. *Monarchies 1000–2000*. London: Reaktion, 2001.

See also **Aragorn;** *Battle of Maldon*; **Class in Tolkien's Works; Communism; Denethor;** *Farmer Giles of Ham*; **Fëanor; Finwë and Míriel; Galadriel;** *Homecoming of Bearhtnoth*; **Politics; Power in Tolkien's Works; Théoden; Thingol**

KNOWLEDGE

Tolkien's views on epistemology clearly owe more to Augustine and Christian thought than to more modern scientific theorists. Knowledge, according to Augustinian theory, consists of a "hierarchical structure of reality with God, its creator, at the apex . . . the source of human existence and the goal of human knowledge" (Nash, 5). Rational knowledge, or *scientia*, a means to an end, is differentiated from *sapientia*, intuitive wisdom, which may be defined as "the capacity to discover what is desirable and of value in life" (Maxwell, 66).

In Tolkien's fictional world, there is a similar moral component to this distinction. Knowledge is absolute in Ilúvatar the One God, but was imparted to the Valar, the offspring of his thought, each comprehending that part of his mind from which he came (*S*, 15). To the archangel Melkor went the greatest gifts of power and knowledge, but he sought the Imperishable Flame—perhaps a metaphor for the pursuit of unattainable knowledge—while the other Valar remained true. However, there is another partial exception: Aulë, to whom Eru gave "skill and knowledge scarce less than to Melkor" (*S*, 19). He transgresses by creating the Dwarves, but humbles and redeems himself before Ilúvatar.

Aulë seems to pass down this problematic creative knowledge, as not only both Sauron and Saruman begin as his pupils, but Dwarves and Noldor Elves, both considered his people, tend to waver between benevolent and malevolent acts (*UT*, 328, 508). The Noldor symbolize this dichotomy, as their name means wise, "but wise in the sense of possessing knowledge, not in the sense of possessing sagacity, sound judgment," and they took delight in the hidden knowledge Melkor offered them (*S*, 66, 344). Fëanor

and Celebrimbor create great works, but are corrupted by pride, possessiveness, and eagerness for knowledge. The Noldor, Tolkien states, "were always on the side of 'science and technology'" (*Letters*, no. 153, 190).

In *The Lord of the Rings*, Saruman represents this pursuit of illicit knowledge. Shippey explains Saruman's progression: his goals are first just knowledge, then organization in the service of knowledge, and finally total control of others. He cooperates with forces he knows to be evil, but thinks he can use for his own "admirable purposes, and later suppress or discard" (Shippey, *Author*, 126). Saruman declares this to Gandalf, misrepresenting his "ultimate purpose: Knowledge, Rule, Order" (*FR*, II, ii, 272). Tolkien suggests Saruman's likeness to Sauron made him more susceptible to corruption, especially using the Seeing-stone (*Morgoth*, 396). Critics have compared Saruman and Denethor in this regard. Kocher states that for Denethor, corrupted similarly by Sauron, "false knowledge was worse for him than none" (Kocher, 68).

Yet displayed in Tolkien's world is the use of knowledge for good ends: Círdan masters shipbuilding; Aragorn, botany; Radagast, zoology; and Gandalf consults the libraries of Gondor, piecing together the history of the Ring. Tolkien says that Elves in general—apart from the taint of the Noldor—raise the artistic, aesthetic, as well as scientific "aspects of the Humane nature" by their "love of the physical world, and a desire to observe and understand it for its own sake . . . not as a material for use or as a power-platform" (*Letters*, 236). Aulë's spouse Yavanna, with her beneficial command of growing things, is representative of this Baconian theory that in "acquiring genuine knowledge of Nature, we can enormously enhance our power to act, to do good" (Maxwell, 10).

In Middle-earth, knowledge used and shared with wisdom, according to one's measure, for the greater plan of Ilúvatar is good. Knowledge attained in secrecy, acquired by deception or force, to further one's own power, pride, or possessions, is evil. As Kocher explains, knowledge doesn't "remain neutral on Middle-earth, but is good or ill depending on the use to which it is put" (Kocher, 67). Tolkien's philosophical views may have been ultimately expressed when he responded to Camilla Unwin's query on the meaning of life. He wrote "that requires a *complete* knowledge of God, which is unattainable . . . [but] our ideas of God and ways of expressing them will be largely derived from contemplating the world about us [and] to increase according to our capacity our knowledge of God by all the means we have" (*Letters*, 400).

DON N. ANGER

Further Reading

Canfield, John V., and Franklin H. Donnell, Jr. *Readings in the Theory of Knowledge.* New York: Meredith Publishing, 1964.

Chance, Jane. *The Lord of the Rings: The Mythology of Power.* Lexington, KY: University Press of Kentucky, 2001.

Crowe, Edith L. "Power in Arda: Sources, Uses and Misuses." In *Proceedings of the J.R.R. Tolkien Centenary Conference 1992*, edited by Patricia Reyonolds, and Glen H. GoodKnight. *Mythlore* 21, no. 2 & *Mallorn* 30 (1996): 272–77.

Curry, Patrick. *Defending Middle-earth: Tolkien Myth and Modernity.* Edinburgh: Floris Books, 1997.

Flieger, Verlyn. *Splintered Light: Logos and Language in Tolkien's World.* Kent, OH: Kent State University Press, 2002.

Kocher, Paul. *Master of Middle-earth.* New York: Ballantine Books, 1977.

Maxwell, Nicholas. *From Knowledge to Wisdom: A Revolution in the Aims and Methods of Science.* Oxford: Basil Blackwell, 1987.

Nash, Ronald H. *The Light of the Mind: St. Augustine's Theory of Knowledge.* Lexington, KY: University Press of Kentucky, 1969.

Petty, Anne C. *One Ring to Bind Them All: Tolkien's Mythology.* Tuscaloosa, AL: University of Alabama Press, 2002.

Schweicher, Eric. "Aspects of the Fall in *The Silmarillion*." *Proceedings of the J.R.R. Tolkien Centenary Conference 1992*, edited by Patricia Reyonolds, and Glen H. GoodKnight. *Mythlore* 21, no. 2 & *Mallorn* 30 (1996): 170–71.

Shippey, Tom. *J.R.R. Tolkien: Author of the Century.* Boston, MA: Houghton Mifflin, 2001.

———. *Poems of Wisdom and Learning in Old English.* Cambridge: D.S. Brewer, 1976.

Stock, Brian. *Augustine the Reader: Meditation, Self-Knowledge, and the Ethics of Interpretation.* Cambridge: Harvard University Press, 1996.

See also **Catholicism, Roman; Christian Readings of Tolkien; Christianity; Dwarves; Eru; Fëanor; Good and Evil; Heaven; Hell; Industrialization; Morgoth and Melkor; Nature; Palantíri; Possessiveness; Power in Tolkien's Works; Rings of Power; Saruman; Sauron**

KOIVIË-NÉNI AND CUIVIÉNEN

Cuiviénen, where Tolkien's Elves awoke in Elder Days, is Quenyan for "Waters of Awakening"—*cuivië* "awakening" + *nen* "water . . . used of lakes, pools— or Nen Echui in Sindarin (*S,* 357, 362). Koivië-néni appears (c. 1917) in Tolkien's *Lost Tales,* World-ship map, and Elvish lexicons giving roots Koyo "have life" and Nene "flow" (*Lost Tales I,* 257). Tolkien altered the name to Cuiviénen/Kuiviénen (c.1925; *Lays,* 3, 18).

Despite being variously identified as a bay, lake, pool, and mere, Christopher Tolkien observes consistency in Cuiviénen's description as a wide water in a deep vale, fed by a waterfall, and surrounded by a rocky landscape of flowing waters amidst wild evergreen woods (*Jewels,* 424); and he also suggests consistency in location, on the eastern shore of the Inland Sea of Helcar beneath the Mountains of the East in Middle-earth (*Morgoth,* 76–77). He further notes that Tolkien's *Ambarkanta,* "The Shape of the World," distinctly locating Cuiviénen on map 4, "agrees perfectly" with *The Silmarillion* (*Shaping,* 249, 256).

Cuivienyarna, "Legend of the Awaking of the Quendi," recounts the 144 First Elves who "slept 'in the womb of the Earth," awakening near Cuiviénen, in three Clans led by Elf-fathers (*Jewels,* 421–23). According to *The Silmarillion,* "their eyes beheld first of all things the stars of heaven," which they loved ever after; and to their ears the first sound was "water falling over stone" (*S,* 48–49). Flieger suggests that through Elves, "Tolkien makes real the interdependence of consciousness, language, and myth." With language, history begins, and "in Tolkien's world we see it happen" (Flieger, 72). In *The Silmarillion,* Elf-song attracts the Valar huntsman Oromë, whom the Elves fear, as the Enemy has already been hunting them; and in after-ages the "most ancient [Elf-]songs" would echo a Hunter enslaving Elves about Cuiviénen (*S,* 49–50). Thus, the Valar, fearing Enemy devices, subdue Morgoth and summon the Elves to march West to safety. The first sundering of Elves then occurs at Cuiviénen, between Eldar, who undertake the journey, and Avari, the "Unwilling" who refuse. "Quendi and Eldar" details this break-up of Clans (*Jewels,* 381), which, according to "Annals of Aman," occurs fifty-five Valarian years (approx. 527 Sun years) after the Awakening (*Morgoth,* 58–81).

Hammond and Scull propose that Coleridge's *Kubla Khan* inspired Cuiviénen's imagery, evidenced by Tolkien's 1913 painting *Xanadu* (41). Garth suggests Cuiviénen's concept evolved between Tolkien's 1915 poem "A Song for Aryador," which contains recognizable elements, and his convalescence in 1917 (Garth, 241, 259). Tolkien also alludes to Cuiviénen in *The Lord of the Rings* when Merry and Pippin in Fangorn Forest are likened to Elves long ago in "the Wild Wood . . . at their first Dawn" (*TT,* III, iii, 62), and he patterns the Mirrormere after Cuiviénen's "mirrored stars" (*Treason,* 184).

Cuiviénen's most striking theme, however, seems to be that of a "lost paradise," best expressed by Fëanor's attraction at returning to Middle-earth when he declares that in "Cuiviénen sweet ran the waters under unclouded stars, and wide lands lay about, where a free people might walk. There they lie still and await us who in our folly forsook them" (*S,* 83). Though Fëanor's fate would not allow such a return, the fate of Cuiviénen remains a mystery: "In the changes of the world the shapes of lands and of seas have been broken and remade, rivers have not kept their courses, neither have mountains remained steadfast" (*S*, 48). Foster posits the Drowning of Númenor ending the Second Age as Cuiviénen's demise (Foster, 99); while Fonstad, by her depiction of the Inland Sea's reduction from Helcar to Rhûn, hints at the sinking of Beleriand ending the First Age (Fonstad, 39). Nonetheless, "to Cuiviénen there is no returning" (*S*, 48).

DON N. ANGER

Further Reading

Flieger, Verlyn. *Splintered Light: Logos and Language in Tolkien's World, Revised Edition*. Kent, OH: Kent State University Press, 2002.

Fonstad, Karen Wynn. *The Atlas of Middle-earth, Revised Edition*. London: Grafton, 1992.

Foster, Robert. *The Complete Guide to Middle-earth: From The Hobbit to The Silmarillion*. New York: Ballantine Books, 1979.

Garth, John. *Tolkien and the Great War: The Threshold of Middle-earth*. London: HarperCollins, 2003.

Hammond, Wayne G., and Christina Scull. *J.R.R. Tolkien: Artist and Illustrator*. London: HarperCollins, 1995.

See also **Darkness; East, The; Elves; Elves: Kindreds and Migrations; Genesis; Incarnation; Pilgrimage;** *Shaping of Middle-earth, The*

KOLBÍTAR

Kolbítar in Old Norse means "coalbiter," men who sat close enough around the kitchen fires that they could bite the coals. Considered loutish for occupying a female sphere and forsaking manly tasks, Coalbiters often went on to noble ends after such inauspicious beginnings. Tolkien gave the name to the group he founded at Oxford to read the Eddas and sagas in Old Norse. One can argue that without the *Kolbítar* there might have arisen no friendship with C.S. Lewis, no Inklings, and therefore none of the indispensable encouragement Tolkien needed to produce *The Lord of the Rings*.

After assuming the chair of Anglo-Saxon in 1925, Tolkien founded the *Kolbítar* in 1926. According to Humphrey Carpenter's authorized biography, members continued meeting several times each term until 1933, when they had read all the sagas and both the Poetic and Prose Eddas, a claim some question because of the size of that task.

Not only did the *Kolbítar* afford Tolkien the chance to study carefully the Norse language and myth that so influenced his work, the group also served as a key transitional period in Tolkien's involvement with scholarly societies. Much of the *Kolbítar*'s importance springs from its formative position among the many clubs and societies that attracted Tolkien's involvement. The *Kolbítar* falls between the Viking Club, which he organized for undergraduates with the help of E.V. Gordon while the two taught at Leeds, and the Inklings, which began meeting as the *Kolbítar* wound down.

At Leeds, Tolkien had founded with a colleague the Viking Club for younger students, while men all roughly Tolkien's contemporaries made up the Inklings. In the *Kolbítar,* however, we find a kind of finishing school for Tolkien, for two of his most important mentors participated. George S. Gordon was Tolkien's superior at Leeds before going to Oxford, where he helped Tolkien attain the chair of Anglo-Saxon. Carpenter calls Gordon "a great intriguer and campaigner" for his protégés. When Tolkien joined the staff of the New English Dictionary, C.T. Onions served as an intellectual example to Tolkien in a way similar to how Gordon had mentored Tolkien professionally. He never after repeated this group dynamic, and one might suppose that, having on some level finished his education in the *Kolbítar*, Tolkien was ready to start the society that would encourage his greatest work.

The *Kolbítar* also offered Tolkien a climate of friendship around shared interests, especially with Nevill Coghill and C.S. Lewis. Lewis credits Tolkien with providing him with a mythic view of Christianity that led directly to Lewis's conversion and indirectly to his most popular and mythic works, the *Chronicles of Narnia*. In turn, Tolkien repeatedly acknowledges Lewis's unswerving and effective support, without which Tolkien almost certainly would never have published his own most famous myth, *The Lord of the Rings*. The *Kolbítar* then acted as an indispensable catalyst for the founding of the Inklings and much of the writing that group fostered.

ANDREW CHARLES LAZO

Further Reading

Carpenter, Humphrey. *The Inklings: C.S. Lewis, J.R.R. Tolkien, Charles Williams and Their Friends*. London: HarperCollins, 1997.

Hooper, Walter. *C.S. Lewis: A Companion and Guide*. San Francisco: HarperSanFrancisco, 1996.

Lazo, Andrew. "Gathered Round Northern Fires: The Imaginative Impact of the *Kolbítar*." In *Tolkien and the Invention of Myth: A Reader*, edited by Jane Chance, 191–226.Lexington, KY: University Press of Kentucky, 2004.

Lewis, C.S. *C.S. Lewis: Collected Letters*. Vol. 1, *Family Letters, 1905–1931*, ed. Walter Hooper. London: HarperCollins, 2000.

See also **Coghill, Nevill; Inklings; Leeds; Lewis, C.S.; Literary Context, 20th Century; Mythology, Germanic; Old Norse Literature; Old Norse Translations**

KÔR

Kôr is an Elvish city on a hill, found under that name in *The Book of Lost Tales* and other early works by Tolkien. It may be considered the original, archetypal city in Tolkien's legendarium. All his cities of his later mythology, such as Tirion, Gondolin, and Minas Tirith, draw on it to at least some extent.

Kôr first appears in "Kôr: In a City Lost and Dead," a poem written in 1915 and first published in 1923 (*Lost Tales I,* 136). The meaning of the name in Qenya varies; it is glossed as both *revere* and *round*. Many of Tolkien's earliest Elven names have external linguistic origins, and Kôr is the name of a deserted city in *She* (1887) by H. Rider Haggard. In *The Book of Lost Tales*, Kôr is the city of the Elves on the shore of Eldamar and also the name of the hill it is on. Kôr is deserted when the Elves go out into the world after the theft of Melko and the darkening of Valinor.

Kortirion on Tol Eressëa is named for Kôr and is built in imitation of it and in its memory. In the early versions of the story, in which Tol Eressëa becomes England, Kortirion is associated with Warwick. So as Warwick is considered a later echo of Kortirion, and Kortirion of Kôr, a distant connection may be made between Kôr on its hill and Warwick Castle on its hill.

In later stories, Eldamar is not deserted, but Kôr does inspire the building of Gondolin, largest city of the Exiles. In texts of the 1920s, the name is respelled Cor; later, Kôr is retained as the name of the hill and is used metonymically for Eldamar (and vice versa), while the city becomes Tûn, later Túna, a name derived from Old English *tún* meaning town. In the later "Silmarillion," Túna is the name of the hill, and the city is Tirion or "Great Watch-tower."

Throughout the legendarium, under any name Kôr is depicted as a shining or golden city of great beauty. It is the goal of Earendel's voyage in the earliest poems. Other cities show an inspiration, either internal or external, from Kôr by having similar characteristics.

DAVID BRATMAN

See also **Book of Lost Tales I; Eladamar; *Silmarillion*; Valinor; Warwick**

L

LANGLAND, WILLIAM

Although the two revised states of the alliterative poem *Piers Plowman* vary radically from the first version and from each other, there is general critical agreement that they represent the work of a single author over many years (nothing else is known of William Langland, presumed to be that author). In the original A-text, *Piers* is a dream vision that takes the form of a relatively concise but scathing "Estates Satire," emphasizing the shortcomings of the wealthy and powerful, both in terms of Christian morality and in terms of the implied social contract by which the nobles were presumed to act to defend the common people and the churchmen were presumed to focus on their spiritual and material well-being—a contract Langland does not think is being upheld. The poem may be based on disputes internal to the Franciscan order, as has recently been argued by Lawrence Clopper. The revolutionary economic, religious, and class ferments of later-fourteenth-century England are vividly conveyed, even though the extremely specific veiled references to contemporary personalities and events are often incomprehensible to present-day scholars. *Piers* is also characterized by powerful portrayals of the seven deadly sins, in the form of vividly humanized "concretized abstractions" (the phrase used to describe Chaucer's pilgrims by Jill Mann). The B- and C-texts represent considerable rewriting and elaboration, amounting to double the length of the A-text, and have large additional elements of reference to scripture, doctrinal disputes, and elaborate allegory.

While it is now common to teach *Piers* either as part of an undergraduate survey course or even as a single-topic course at the university level, this canonization process had not entirely taken place when Tolkien was most active in his work (the *Piers* editions by George Kane [A-text, 1960] and Kane and E. Talbot Donaldson [B-text, 1975], along with the heightened interest in class and social issues prevalent in literary studies in recent decades, helped inaugurate the modern era of *Piers* studies). Tolkien's view of the text may have had something in common with that of C.S. Lewis, who reportedly belittled what he saw as the burgeoning "*Piers Plowman* factory, cranking out dissertations at an alarming rate" at a lecture devoted to the topic at Oxford in the late 1950s (Fowler, 64).

At the same time, both Lewis and Tolkien would have been well aware of the large and varied set of surviving manuscripts—attesting to the wide readership and interest the text generated in its time—their enormous range of dialectal variations, and the evident influence of *Piers* on Chaucer (the prologue of the *Canterbury Tales* is considered to have been inspired in part by that of *Piers;* the frequent presence of an apocryphal "Plowman's Tale" in manuscript and print copies of the *Canterbury Tales*, giving a voice to a pilgrim who in Chaucer's more nobility-centric text is completely wordless, may also attest to the influence of *Piers* on the reception of Chaucer's work). More generally, *Piers*, being part of the genre of the medieval dream vision, is situated well within a poetic mainstream containing many other major

English works, such as *Pearl* (considered to be the work of the *Gawain*-poet) and Chaucer's *House of Fame*, as well as the broader context of continental medieval literature, including Dante; *Piers* was familiar to any serious scholar of Middle English for those reasons, along with others. Nevill Coghill's analysis in the Tolkien *festschrift* (a collection presented to honor a retiring, or in this case a seventy-year-old, professor) was devoted to Langland and describes him as "the greatest of English Christian poets" (217)—though one might expect Tolkien to have reserved that honor for the *Beowulf*-poet.

None of Tolkien's published scholarship focused on *Piers* as a primary topic (with the exception of his *Middle English Vocabulary Designed for Use with Sisam's Fourteenth Century Verse & Prose*, originally intended to be, and later published as, the glossary in Kenneth Sisam's anthology; it glosses *Piers*, since that is one of the texts included). But whether it was any source of direct inspiration to Tolkien or not, the focus in *Piers* on the plight of the "little man"— almost unique in either early or later medieval British literature—and the elevation of the lowly peasant not only as someone worthy of a role in governance but also as a figure with inherent nobility and a clear vision of moral right and spiritual guidance express themes that also arise in *The Lord of the Rings*, when the lowly Hobbits and their peasant background are thrust into the councils of the mighty, acquitting themselves honorably as "citizens" of Middle-earth and warriors for the cause of righteousness. When Merry and Pippin, combat veterans elevated to formal knighthood, return to the Shire to set things aright, they exemplify the chivalric ideal of knights defending peaceable commoners against violence and depredation—a duty explicitly laid by Piers at the feet of the knight to whom he appeals in Passus VI (the sixth section of the poem).

JAMES I. MCNELIS III

Further Reading

Clopper, Lawrence M. "*Songes of Rechelesnesse*": *Langland and the Franciscans*. Ann Arbor, MI: University of Michigan Press, 1998.

Coghill, Nevill. "God's Wenches and the Light That Spoke (Some Notes on Langland's Kind of Poetry)." In *English and Medieval Studies Presented to J.R.R. Tolkien on the Occasion of His Seventieth Birthday*, edited by Norman Davis and C.L. Wrenn, 200–218. London: George Allen & Unwin, 1962.

Fowler, David. "*Piers the Plowman* after Forty-Five Years," *Æstel* 2 (1994): 63–76.

Kane, George, ed. *Piers Plowman: The A Version*. London: Athlone, 1960.

Kane, George, and E. Talbot Donaldson, eds. *Piers Plowman: The B Version*. London: Athlone, 1975.

Mann, Jill. *Chaucer and the Medieval Estates Satire: The Literature of Social Classes and the General Prologue to the Canterbury Tales*. London: Cambridge University Press, 1973.

Tolkien, J.R.R. *Middle English Vocabulary Designed for Use with Sisam's Fourteenth Century Verse & Prose*. Oxford: Clarendon Press, 1922.

See also **Brut** by Layamon; "Chaucer as Philologist: The Reeve's Tale"; Middle English Vocabulary

LANGUAGE, THEORIES OF

Comparative Philology

It has long been recognised that Tolkien's academic interests are reflected in his creative writing, for example, by Randel Helms (1974). However, the all-pervasive influence of his concern with language was only made clear by Tom Shippey's book *The Road to Middle-earth*, first published in 1982. The linguistic paradigm that Tolkien adhered to both as student and as teacher was comparative philology. Elaborated mostly in Germany during the nineteenth century, this discipline is based on the principle that languages change over the course of time, not randomly but through the operation of regular sound shifts. These have led to the differentiation of languages and language groups stretching from Portugal to India, descended from a common ancestor that is no longer extant. By comparing related languages, it is possible not only to trace the history of individual words but also to postulate the hypothetical forms of many that no longer exist. At the time, it was an exciting new science that promised to reconstruct the history not only of languages but also of the peoples who spoke them in a period before written documents existed.

The aims of comparative philology were determined by the Romantic philosophy of historicism, which asserts that there is no universal basis for understanding events and ideas but rather that they can be properly comprehended only in their historical context. In contrast to more recent, poststructuralist views of language, in which meaning is not fixed but is negotiated by the reader, who uses the ambiguities inherent in language to "deconstruct" the meaning, philologists (including Tolkien) believed that by patient linguistic and historical research they could achieve an ever greater approximation to the meaning of ancient texts as intended by the author and understood by the original audience.

The relationship between Tolkien's philological work and his fiction is regarded as fundamental to a critical appreciation by Jane Chance (2001) and Shippey (2005), who both offer a detailed analysis. Shippey suggests convincingly that the construction of hypothetical histories lies at the heart of Tolkien's creative processes. However, the comparative method is demonstrated most clearly by his invented languages, in which Quenya and Sindarin, despite their phonological differences, are shown to be derived from a common primitive Elvish ancestor.

The Influence of Barfield

Tolkien acknowledged the influence of his fellow Inkling Owen Barfield, according to C.S. Lewis (in Carpenter, 1978). Barfield's central ideas appear in his book *Poetic Diction*, first published in 1928. Like Tolkien in "On Fairy-stories," he disagrees with Max Müller's theory that myths arise through a misunderstanding of metaphorical expressions of the forces of nature. Giving the example of Latin *spiritus*, Greek *pneuma* and Sanskrit *asu*, which had a similar range of signification, from the concrete sense of "blowing" through "breath" to "principle of life," he argues that meanings existed in early stages of language as broad bundles of concepts. The more abstract, metaphorical meaning was not derived from the concrete one; both existed together from the beginning. Metaphor is therefore not a mere embellishment but an integral part of the way in which human beings conceptualise the world. In insisting on the centrality of metaphor, Barfield adopts a similar position to modern cognitive linguistics. Verlyn Flieger (1983) gives a detailed account of Barfield's theories and the extent of his possible influence on Tolkien's creative writing.

This insight certainly influenced Tolkien in his understanding of the conventional metaphors in Old English and Old Norse known as *kennings*. In "On Translating *Beowulf*," he rejects the traditional wisdom that compounds such as *flæschama*, "flesh-raiment," or *ban-hus*, "bone-house," simply meant "body" to the poem's early audience; rather, those who heard it were likely to picture the frail covering of the soul at the same time as and on an equal level with the more prosaic denotation. It was here that the poetry lay, not in the mechanical juggling of synonyms, and any modern interpretation of the poem must take it into account.

For Tolkien's creative writing, it follows from this that the way in which characters express themselves will be determined by how they conceptualize their world. This is seen most clearly in Letter no. 171, where he justifies his use of archaising language through the example of Théoden's attitude to his possible death in battle if he fulfils his oath of loyalty to Gondor and leads his men himself: "Thus shall I sleep more easily" (*Letters*, 225). A modern person would not normally see life and death in this way, so to make the king speak in a twentieth-century idiom would introduce an insincerity of thought more bogus than the representation of an older style of language.

Translation

Translation underlies much of Tolkien's linguistic thought and was an essential component of his professional linguistic activity. This was recognised publicly by his being asked to contribute to the Jerusalem Bible, even though he maintained (Letter no. 294) that he had played only a small role. His essay "On Translating *Beowulf*," originally written as the preface to a new edition (1940) of the *Beowulf* translation by Clark Hall (1911), contains his most important theoretical statements on translation, in particular the translation of ancient texts for a modern readership. Fundamentally, he regards translation as a necessary evil, since the connotations of words in the source text cannot be adequately conveyed by our modern vocabulary, nor can the concentrated effect of a strict verse form be adequately represented in prose, but not everyone has time to acquire a deep understanding of the original language. He gives the example of *eacen*, which is translated variously as "stalwart," "huge," "broad," and "mighty," although it has the additional connotation of an increased power beyond the natural, something for which modern English has no corresponding concept; in fact, it is like one of Barfield's conceptual bundles. He concludes that Old English epic poetry was never intended to reproduce everyday prose for its original audience, so the best way to capture the flavor for modern readers would be through a moderated archaism, which would avoid on the one hand modern colloquialism and on the other obsolete or obscure expressions: "The words chosen . . . must be words that remain in literary use, especially in the use of verse, among educated people." This principle can also be seen in his representation of archaic societies and characters in his creative writing, as in the case of Théoden.

As with the kennings mentioned previously, Tolkien believed that to translate effectively it was necessary to preserve as many of the formal linguistic features as possible. This included verse forms, even (or especially) if they were unfamiliar to modern readers. His translations of *Sir Gawain, Pearl,* and *Sir Orfeo* are distinguished by their re-creation in modern English of the original, often highly complex, metres and alliterative patterns. This concern for verse form is reflected in his creative writing, where particularly the alliterative verses of Rohan and *The Lay of the Children of Húrin* resulted from his efforts to translate *Beowulf* strictly in the original metre, an example of which is given in his lecture "On Translating *Beowulf.*"

Tolkien's experience of translation, in particular from older languages, also underlies the conceit of *The Lord of the Rings* as a pseudo-translation, in which the Westron of a fictional *Red Book of Westmarch* is translated into English. This justifies the use of Old English, which would otherwise have no place in an imaginary Middle-earth, to represent the language of the Rohirrim, which Merry experiences as related to his Shire dialect but more archaic. Tolkien's arguments in Appendix F for distinguishing between what is familiar and what is exotic to the hobbits, through whose eyes the events are seen, thus correspond to the discussion in modern translation theory of domesticating versus foreignising translation. Similarly, it was his belief in the desirability of maintaining the linguistic distinctions built into his nomenclature that led him to take a strong personal interest in translations of his books and to take the unprecedented step of writing the "Guide to the Names in *The Lord of the Rings*" for translators, with prescriptive rules about what was to be translated and what was to be left as exotic. Tolkien's theories of translation and the influence of his guide on published translations are dealt with in detail by Allan Turner (2005).

Tolkien's "Linguistic Heresy"

For Tolkien, the sound pattern of a language was the source of a special aesthetic pleasure. In his invented languages, he set out to create linguistic forms that would satisfy this personal aesthetic and noted that other people had also found this a source of pleasure, for example, in the many Sindarin names in *The Lord of the Rings*. His theory, although perhaps more subjective than scientific, is found both in his contribution to *The Year's Work in English Studies* in 1926, where he suggests that there might be a branch of language study devoted to language aesthetics, for which he proposes the tautologous name *Lautphonetik*, and in his lecture "English and Welsh" from 1954.

In the lecture, he lists Welsh words that appeal to him because of the combinations of sounds from which they are formed, regardless of their meaning. Similarly, when he claims that "cellar door" is more pleasing than "beautiful," this has nothing to do with its connotations. He suggests that such personal preferences are not necessarily acquired through education but may be based on a hereditary predisposition to a "native language" that is different than the first language a person learnt as a child. So he, as a descendant of West Midland families, even though born in South Africa, felt an immediate affinity for the West Midland dialect of Middle English, which represented for him a partial survival of pre-Conquest purity. This theory can be traced in episodes from *The Lord of the Rings*, such as the meeting with Gildor and the Elves in the Woody End or the hymn to Elbereth at Rivendell, where characters feel that they subliminally understand something of the meaning even when they know little or nothing of the Elvish language.

All of this would contradict the structuralist tenet that meaning is arbitrary: there is no necessary connection between the sounds /b/, /e/, and /d/ and the support that people sleep on; rather, the meaning is created by the relation among the signifier (the combination of sounds), the signified (the abstract idea in the mind), and the referent (the piece of furniture in the concrete world). Therefore, you can understand the meaning only if you have internalised the linguistic system. That is why Shippey calls the idea of an innate language affinity Tolkien's "linguistic heresy." By extension, this theory explains Tolkien's belief, implicit in Appendix F, that readers will feel instinctively the differentiations in his complex nomenclature, appreciating that *Bree* and *Crickhollow*, which contain real-world Celtic elements, are somehow more exotic than *Hobbiton* or *Bywater*, although not alien like *Lothlórien* or *Gondor*.

There are occasional hints in Tolkien's fiction of a state in which meaning really is inherent in words. This is shown particularly by the importance of names, which by their nature are congruent with individual people or places: "I am Gandalf, and Gandalf means me," declares that character when he is first introduced in *The Hobbit*. Treebeard the Ent explains, "Real names tell you the story of the things they belong to in my language," and in the case of Tom Bombadil the propositional content of language seems to have been absorbed into the music of the sounds alone. This is probably not something that Tolkien would have proposed as a serious linguistic theory; rather, it may be seen as an aspect of human desire, like the existence of dragons or communication with animals, that can be realised through fantasy as explained in "On Fairy-Stories." It may have been an idea discussed by the Inklings, because Lewis presents it more explicitly in his novel *That Hideous Strength:* in Old Solar, the universal language from before the Fall, "the meanings were not given to the syllables by chance, or skill, or long tradition, but truly inherent in them."

ALLAN TURNER

Further Reading

Barfield, Owen. *Poetic Diction.* 3rd ed. Middletown, CT: Wesleyan University Press, 1973. First published in 1928.

Carpenter, Humphrey. *The Inklings: C.S. Lewis, J.R.R. Tolkien, Charles Williams, and Their Friends.* London: George Allen & Unwin, 1978.

Chance, Jane. *Tolkien's Art: A Mythology for England.* Revised edition. Lexington, KY: University Press of Kentucky, 2001.

Flieger, Verlyn. *Splintered Light: Logos and Language in Tolkien's World.* Grand Rapids, MI: Eerdmans, 1983.

Helms, Randel. *Tolkien's World.* London: Thames and Hudson, 1974.

Shippey, Tom. *The Road to Middle-earth: How J.R.R. Tolkien Created a New Mythology.* Revised and Expanded edition. London: HarperCollins, 2005.

Turner, Allan. *Translating Tolkien: Philological Elements in "The Lord of the Rings."* Frankfurt: Peter Lang, 2005.

See also **Alliterative Verse by Tolkien; Epic Poetry; Languages Invented by Tolkien; "Nomenclature of *The Lord of the Rings*"; Prose Style**

LANGUAGES: EARLY INTRODUCTION AND INTEREST

The *textus receptus* for the history of Tolkien's developing interest in languages is the June 7, 1955, letter to W.H. Auden (*Letters*, 211–17), in which he briefly tells of his writing (about the age of seven) a story about a "green great dragon" and being told by his mother that he could not say "green great dragon" but had to say "great green dragon"—of which he writes to Auden, "I wondered why, and still do. The fact that I remember this is possibly significant, as I do not think I ever tried to write a story again for many years, and was taken up with language" (*Letters*, 214). It is to be assumed his mother thought of "green dragon" as the species and "great" as the qualifier, as against, for example, a small green dragon. It is to be assumed that the seven-year-old Tolkien thought of the "great dragon" as the species, and "green" as the qualifier, as against, for example, a red great dragon. (Using myself as evidence, I can recall that at age eight I thought of "light dragons" and "dark dragons" as species so

different that one was good and one was evil. The difference from Tolkien is that I neither shared my thoughts with anyone nor went on to consider questions of language, as he so obviously did.) Also, I believe, the contrasting sound of "great green" and "green great" was of major interest.

Tolkien's discovery of Gothic was one (slightly later) strand in his developing interest in language. Earlier was the "fascination that Welsh names had for me [from childhood], even if only seen on coal-trucks" (*Letters*, 213), and another, later than the Welsh names but before the Gothic, was the Spanish: "my guardian was half-Spanish, and in my early teens I used to pinch his books and try to learn it: the only Romance language that gives me the particular pleasure of which I am speaking—it is not quite the same thing as the perception of beauty . . . it is more like the appetite for a needed food" (*Letters*, 213–14). To Welsh, Gothic, and Spanish was later added Finnish, with his discovery of a Finnish grammar at Exeter College—but that is long past his early life. In all of these there is a concern with the relationship between sound and sense.

The curious thing about Tolkien's childhood and boyhood interest in languages is that, after the "green great dragon," he was interested in language as language ("sound and sense") and not for use. In his essay "A Secret Vice," he notes the phenomenon of nursery-languages or schoolboy-languages: "I can still remember my surprise after acquiring with assiduous practice great fluency in one of these 'languages' my horror at overhearing two strange boys conversing in it. This is a very interesting matter—connected with cant, argot, jargon, and all kinds of human undergrowth, and also with games and many other things" (*MC*, 201). But "the argot-group are not primarily concerned with the relations of sound and sense"—with which Tolkien was primarily concerned and which opened him to the effect made by Joseph Wright's *Grammar of the Gothic Language.*

JARED LOBDELL

Further Reading

Carpenter, Humphrey. *J.R.R. Tolkien: A Biography.* London: George Allen & Unwin, 1977.

Shippey, Tom. *J.R.R. Tolkien: Author of the Century.* London: HarperCollins, 2000.

Tolkien, J.R.R. "A Secret Vice." In *The Monsters and the Critics and Other Essays,* edited by Christopher Tolkien, 198–223. Boston, MA: Houghton Mifflin, 1984.

See also **Childhood of Tolkien; Morgan, Father Francis; Gothic Language; Languages Invented by Tolkien; "A Secret Vice"; Spanish Language; Tolkien, Mabel**

LANGUAGES INVENTED BY TOLKIEN

Introduction

As Tolkien details in his essay "A Secret Vice," he was from his childhood both a language aesthete and a language inventor. From "A Secret Vice" and certain of his letters, we see that already before the age of twenty Tolkien had invented or participated in the invention of at least four languages, from the coded form of English called Animalic (for its simple substitution of the names of animals for English words); through Nevbosh ("new nonsense," in that tongue), in which entered the invention of new forms (inspired by but not merely reusing elements from English, Latin, and French vocabulary); to the more grammatically sophisticated and more lexically innovative Naffarin (though still inspired by Latin and, here, Spanish vocabulary); to the invention of an "'unrecorded' Germanic language" early in his college years (*Letters*, 214), no doubt inspired by his first encounter with Gothic and the concomitant discovery of historical philology within the pages of Joseph Wright's *Primer of the Gothic Language* at King Edward's School in 1908–1909. It was in this encounter that Tolkien discovered and pursued "for the first time the study of a language out of mere love," by which he meant: "for the acute aesthetic pleasure derived from a language for its own sake, not only free from being useful but free even from being the 'vehicle of a literature'" (*Letters*, 213, 357; see also *Parma Eldalamberon* 12, x–xi).

Even from just the few surviving scraps of these earliest creations, and by Tolkien's own account, we see in this progression of invention a number of crucial trends, all moving toward what would become the hallmark characteristics of Tolkien's later invented languages:

1. From creative reuse of words in existing languages to the creation of words within an invented phonological and grammatical system, thus distinguishing Tolkien's languages from the sorts of simplistic language invention most often found among children;

2. From simple coding of English grammar and syntax toward languages with their own invented grammar and syntax, thus aligning Tolkien's languages with such well-known invented languages as Esperanto;

3. From the creation of languages for utility, "intended in theory for speaking" (*MC*, 207), to a purely aesthetic endeavor in which the chief interest lay "in word-form, and in word-form in relation to meaning (so-called phonetic fitness) than in any other department" of language (*MC*, 211), thus distinguishing Tolkien's languages from such languages as Esperanto that are chiefly and deliberately designed to serve as auxiliary languages;

4. From language creation as a shared endeavor representing "the *highest common linguistic capacity* of a small group, not the best that could be produced by its best member" (*MC*, 207–8) to glossopoeia done purely for one's own intellectual and aesthetic pleasure and consideration: that is, as an art in which the individual artist is free to pursue the heights of his own excellence in accord with his own tastes, without practical consideration or constraint, again distinguishing Tolkien's languages from such languages as Esperanto (which is not to say that intellectual and aesthetic pleasure play no role in either the creation or the appeal of Esperanto, only that such pleasure was a secondary concern to the auxiliary nature of Esperanto, whereas with Tolkien's languages this pleasure came to be essentially the only concern);

5. From the creation of isolated, static languages devoid of historical context or internal development to families of related languages, each designed to appear to have undergone characteristic internal development and all sprung from a common prehistoric source language through long years of gradual, systematic changes of sound over time, thus again distinguishing Tolkien's languages from auxiliary languages such as Esperanto and indeed from most (if not all) invented languages both before and after Tolkien's own were made known publicly.

In short, we see a movement from language creation as a utilitarian and thus shared endeavor toward glossopoeia that is at once strongly abstract and artistic in pursuing and expressing a private and personal linguistic aesthetic and that is rigorously historical and systematic, susceptible within the fictive construct to the scientific tools of historical philology: an aspect of language creation nearly if not entirely unique to Tolkien.

All of these trends converged during Tolkien's undergraduate career at Exeter College through the catalyst of two further language encounters that set in motion the two chief courses of language invention that Tolkien would follow for the rest of his life. The first of these was his discovery, in the Exeter College Library late in 1911, of a copy of C.N.E. Eliot's *Finnish Grammar*, which Tolkien compared to "discovering a complete wine-cellar filled with bottles of an amazing wine of a kind and flavour never tasted before. It quite intoxicated me; and I gave up the attempt to invent an 'unrecorded' Germanic language, and my 'own language'—or series of invented languages—became heavily Finnicized in phonetic pattern and structure" (*Letters*, 214). By his "'own language'—or series of invented languages," Tolkien means the earliest-invented (extant) Elvish language, Quenya, the first recorded form of which, found in the grammar and lexicon in the *Qenyaqetsa*, dates from early 1915 but which he continued to develop and change in successive versions throughout his life in accordance with changes in his linguistic aesthetic. The second catalytic encounter came in 1914 with Tolkien's purchase of John Morris-Jones's *Welsh Grammar: Historical and Comparative.* Although he had discovered Welsh as a youth in names seen on railway coal-trucks and station-signs, which he described as "a flash of strange spelling and a hint of a language old and yet alive [that] pierced my linguistic heart" (*MC*, 192), Tolkien had also discovered that at that time it was "easier to find books to instruct one in any far alien tongue of Africa or India than in the language that still clung to the western mountains and the shores that look out to Iwerddon [the Welsh name of Ireland]"; consequently, he was unable to study Welsh until he matriculated at Oxford, where, upon winning the Skeat Prize for English at Exeter College, he shocked his college by spending it on Morris-Jones's *Welsh Grammar* (Tolkien's heavily annotated copy of which is in the English Faculty Library of Oxford University). In Welsh Tolkien found "an abiding linguistic-aesthetic satisfaction" that profoundly influenced the phonology and grammar of the later of his two chief Elvish languages, Sindarin, the first recorded form of which, called Goldogrin or Gnomish, is found in the grammar and lexicon in *I·Lam na·Ngoldathon*, dating from 1917. As with Quenya, Tolkien would continue to develop and change Goldogrin throughout his life, elaborating it most fully in the later 1930s, by which time it had been renamed Noldorin, a name it retained until just a few years before the publication of *The Lord of the Rings*, when the language was revised and renamed again, in accordance with the vastly increased length of its fictional history that arose with the introduction of the Second and Third Ages of Middle-earth into Tolkien's legendarium during the drafting of *The Lord of the Rings*, and with a profound change in its place of origin from Valinor to Beleriand arising with Tolkien's return to work on the legendarium after the completion of the drafting of *The Lord of the Rings*.

The Historical Nature of the Languages

As noted previously, one of the unique aspects of Tolkien's language invention is its *historical* nature. What is meant by this is that Tolkien crafted his languages to appear to be related to one another, just as, for example, English, Icelandic, Gothic, and German are historically related to one another, having sprung from a common Germanic source language (now no longer spoken and never recorded in writing), and more remotely to such widespread languages as Welsh, Latin, Greek, Russian, and Sanskrit, all ultimately descended, through many centuries of systematic but divergent sound change, from a common Indo-European parent language (likewise now nowhere spoken and never recorded). And just as historical linguists, through comparison of these related languages with one another and with their own earlier forms (as, for example, of Old, Middle, and Modern English), have been able to discern the underlying system of sound changes that gave rise to the rich diversity of the Indo-European languages, and thereby even to recover what earlier, unrecorded forms of words must have been in the vanished parent languages, so too can cognate forms among Tolkien's invented languages be compared to one another, an underlying system of sound changes be discerned for each language, and earlier forms be recovered. It is plain from such key works as the *Qenyaqetsa* and "The Etymologies" that Tolkien's process of invention was chiefly conducted in an historical manner: that is, the starting point was a set of abstract roots or bases, each expressing some core meaning or concept that Tolkien found suitable, within and according to his linguistic aesthetic, to the sound of that basic element. From this root or base, Tolkien derived a set of primitive (i.e., within the framework of the fictional history, ancient and unrecorded) words by systematic elaborations of the base—as, for example, by the addition of a primitive suffix or by some internal modification. From such primitive forms, Tolkien derived words for the recorded forms of his languages (again, within the framework of the fictional history) by applying the particular set of abstract and systematic changes of sound that he selected as desirable for and characteristic of each language.

As an example of this historical nature of Tolkien's languages, consider the Eldarin base KWET-, which is listed in "The Etymologies" with the verbal meaning "say" and in later sources with the additional glosses "speak, utter words." From this base Tolkien derived the concrete Eldarin noun *kwetta* (which he marked with an asterisk to indicate that the word is, within the fictional framework, an unrecorded form that can nonetheless be theoretically assumed to have existed on the basis of comparison of recorded cognate forms in the descendant languages). In turn, from this original ancient form is derived, as though by natural phonological development over millennia within the fictional history (in this case, including the regular development of original *kw to p and of *tt to th), the Sindarin noun peth, "word" (which is found in a grammatically marked form beth in Gandalf's spell before the West-gate of Moria in The Lord of the Rings). Similarly, from another ancient derivative of KWET-, the noun *kwentā, "tale," arose both Quenya quenta, "tale, history" (seen for example in the title Quenta Silmarillion, "The History of the Silmarils"), and its Sindarin cognate pennas, "history" (again, through the regular development of original *kw to p and of original *-nt- to -nn-; the ending -s is apparently due to an original abstract nominal ending *-ssē seen in many other forms, which in Sindarin came to be shortened to -s). Still other derivatives of KWET- in the recorded languages include the Quenya aorist verb quete, "say, speak"; its exact Telerin and Sindarin cognates pete and pêd, respectively (both showing the change of original *kw to p shared by these two languages); and the Sindarin imperative verb pedo, "say, speak," seen in the inscription on the West-gate of Moria (the latter two Sindarin forms arising in part from the regular voicing of original intervocalic *t to d, a change, however, that is not found in Telerin). Therefore, as these examples show, neither the individual words in Tolkien's languages nor the languages themselves stand in isolation but instead are in systematic relation to one another through an underlying set of abstract correspondences and sound changes determined ultimately by Tolkien's own aesthetic choices for the particular character and fictional history of the various languages. It is in making these choices that the influence of such languages as Finnish and Welsh on Tolkien's own languages chiefly lies (the specific changes highlighted previously for Sindarin, namely, *kw > p, *-t- > d, *tt > th, and loss of all final vowels are all characteristic of the development of Welsh from the ancient Indo-European common language, as seen, for example, in Welsh pedwar, "four," versus Latin quattuor < Indo-European *kwetwer-, "four," and in Welsh saeth, "arrow," versus Latin sagitta). It is in variations in the particular choices made by Tolkien at any one time in the conceptual history of these languages, in accordance with changes in his linguistic aesthetic, that the conceptual changes exhibited throughout the long external history of these languages arose.

The Two Histories

It is thus important to bear in mind that each of Tolkien's languages has essentially two histories: first, the history that it has through its position within the nearly six-decades-long course of Tolkien's conceptual development of his languages and of its relation to preceding and following conceptual forms of that language, which may be called its external history; and second, the fictive history of phonological and lexical divergence and development that Tolkien invented for each of his languages within Middle-earth, and at each stage in their external history, which may be called its internal history. As a consequence of this dual-historical nature, it should further be noted that when speaking of, say, Quenya or Sindarin, other than informally, we must specify which Quenya and Sindarin we mean: that is, do we mean (as usually in informal discussion) Quenya as exemplified in The Lord of the Rings? If so, it must be borne in mind that this is a different form of Quenya (as a "strain" or "flavor" of language invention), that is, at a different conceptual stage in its primary-world history and thus in Tolkien's ever-shifting linguistic aesthetic, than is exemplified in earlier writings, such as the Qenya of "The Etymologies," which itself is not the same as the Qenya of the Qenyaqetsa. Similarly, Sindarin as exemplified in The Lord of the Rings is not the same as the Noldorin of "The Etymologies" (nor is it simply Noldorin renamed), which itself is not the same as earlier forms of the language called Noldorin, which in turn is not the same as the Goldogrin of I·Lam na·Ngoldathon.

Nonetheless, each successive stage reflects Tolkien's changing conception of that language within its broad flavor and thus his particular aesthetic with respect to that flavor at that particular time in his life (and it is in this sense—and only in this sense—of a broad flavor of language exemplified by the commonalities of character shared by each successive stage that we can speak formally of Quenya and Sindarin without further qualification). It must also be emphasized that it is not the case that the later conceptual forms of Tolkien's languages are (necessarily) any more developed, detailed, or "perfected" than any earlier form: each stage, each conceptual form, is a distinct language in its own right, with its own particular character and specific set of phonological and grammatical features and details (albeit with considerable affinity of character and detail with both preceding and following forms). It is in recognition of this fact that Tolkien in 1955 qualified a reference to his "Finnicized" language—that is, Quenya—as being a "series of invented languages" (Letters, 214). Indeed, Tolkien wrote that the "process of invention" of his languages, which continued until nearly the end of his life, had its purpose in "giving expression to my personal linguistic 'aesthetic' or taste *and its fluctuations*" (*Letters*, 380, emphasis mine in both places). That is, rather than indicating flaws or deficiencies in the earlier forms of the languages as compared with later forms, this succession of conceptual forms of Tolkien's invented languages reflects, and arose *to express*, his changing linguistic ideas and aesthetic over time.

The Influence of Other Languages

It is fairly well known and often repeated that Tolkien's two chief Elvish languages, Quenya and Sindarin, are "based" on Finnish and Welsh, respectively. The complex and abstract nature of this influence is, however, usually poorly understood. This influence is found, in varying degree, in four main aspects of Tolkien's invented languages (themselves fundamental and characteristic aspects of any "real" language). In decreasing order both of abstractness and, not coincidentally, of importance as influencing Tolkien's inventions, these aspects can be listed as follows: (1) *structural*, that is, pertaining to the constrained set of permissible phonetic patterns within the underlying (often prehistoric and theoretical) root forms of a language, and of the limited and systematic means by which these root forms could be varied to express different meanings and functions and thus to give rise to different grammatical categories; (2) *phonological*, that is, in the constrained and selective systems of regular sound changes that occurred within a language over the course of its history of change from earlier forms and ultimately of divergence from some common parent form shared with other, related languages (by which is meant languages that likewise diverged and descended from that parent language through their own characteristic systems of regular phonological change over time); (3) *phonetic*, that is, in the limited set of permissible sounds and combinations of sounds at any particular stage of a language's phonological development that give each language its particular character at any given time (and largely by which readers and listeners are able to identify and discern the difference between even languages the vocabulary of which they have little or no knowledge); and (4) *lexical*, that is, in the pairing of particular phonetic forms with particular meanings—words—and the borrowing of those particular (or similar) forms paired with those particular (or similar) meanings into another language.

While many people who know or hear that Quenya is "based on" Finnish and that Sindarin is "based on" Welsh probably think that this indicates *lexical* influence, that is, the actual "borrowing" and reuse of words from these languages in Quenya and Sindarin, this is the least aspect of influence in Tolkien's languages (though it is present: for example, the form *tie* has the meaning "road, path" in both Quenya and Finnish). Instead, the influence of "real" languages on Tolkien's own is overwhelmingly structural, phonological, and phonetic in nature, and the sets of the particular characteristics within these aspects found among Tolkien's invented languages in many ways reflect the sets of such characteristics found among the languages of Europe and the Near East—that is, of those very regions of which Tolkien's Middle-earth is intended to represent a fictive past configuration and history. We thus find languages that have a structurally Semitic character (e.g., Khuzdul and Adûnaic) against those that are structurally Indo-European (e.g., the Eldarin tongues), and we find languages phonologically and phonetically similar not just to Finnish (Quenya) and to Welsh (Sindarin) but also to various members of the Germanic language family, such as Old English (Danian/Nandorin) and Gothic (Taliska). These influences will be identified (briefly and where discernible with confidence) for each of the chief languages of Arda discussed in the next section.

The Languages of Arda

What follows is, by intent, neither an exhaustive list nor a complete discussion of all languages named and/or cited by Tolkien as being spoken in Arda but instead is a general thematic and (internal) historical survey of those languages invented by Tolkien for which more than just a name, a few example forms, or both are attested and that illustrate something about the range and character of Tolkien's linguistic aesthetic. It is further selective in presenting the set and form of the languages attested and described in Tolkien's later writings, namely, from the publication of *The Lord of the Rings*, as having the form and history already encountered by readers of that work and of *The Silmarillion*. (In particular, it should be noted that the internal historical viewpoint adopted here is that of "Quendi and Eldar" and the later "Silmarillion" writings, in which the Elves invent a language for themselves *ab initio* and the exiled Ñoldor speak Quenya on their return to Middle-earth but then adopt the already-present Sindarin as their daily language, as opposed to that of "The *Lhammas*," "The Etymologies," and the earlier "Silmarillion" writings, in which the Elves are taught their first language by Oromë and the exiled Noldor arrive in Middle-earth already speaking a Sindarin-like language greatly changed from Qenya and in many ways like the languages that had in the meantime developed in Beleriand.)

Primitive Quendian and Common Eldarin

The Elves that awoke at Cuiviénen, in the far east of Middle-earth, began immediately to make a language for themselves, long before their first encounter with any other speaking beings, which at that remote time included only the Valar and Maiar in Aman, far to the west of Middle-earth beyond the Great Sea. This original language of all the first Elves is called *Primitive Quendian*, indicating that it was an ancient, aboriginal, and unrecorded language spoken by all original speakers (in Quenya, *quendi*) in Middle-earth. The first division of this language began with the separation of the Elves, which occurred at the start of the Great March west to Aman, into those who set out on the March, who were called in Quenya the *Eldar* (which can be interpreted as both "the people of the stars" and "those who departed"), and those who chose to remain behind, called in Quenya the *Avari* (the refusers, the unwilling). From this point, the originally shared language of each of these two divisions of the Elves underwent separate development and change, resulting in the latter case in the Avarin languages—a vast but almost completely unattested family of descendant languages and dialects in Middle-earth for which Tolkien provides only a handful of example words and about which no more need be said here—and in the former case the Eldarin languages, from which are descended most languages featured in Tolkien's legendarium, including, ultimately, his two chief invented languages, Quenya and Sindarin.

The form of the language spoken by all the Eldar when they separated into further independent divisions (and independent courses of language development), and thus the latest stage of the Primitive Quendian language common to all the Eldar, is called *Common Eldarin*. Note that within the internal history of the fictional framework, both Primitive Quendian and Common Eldarin are unrecorded languages (having ceased to be spoken by any Elf long before the Elves developed any writing systems), so all forms in these languages given by Tolkien are marked by him with an asterisk (*) in accordance with a convention of linguistics denoting that a form is not actually attested in the historical records but is a theoretical reconstruction that can be assumed to have existed on the evidence of recorded cognate forms in the descendant languages.

Structurally and phonetically, both Primitive Quendian and Common Eldarin, and thus all Elvish languages descended from them, exhibit a strongly Indo-European character. Most words are formed from bases (roots) that exhibit two or, far less often, three consonants (and these chiefly extensions of a related two-consonant base) and a characteristic vowel that distinguishes a base from others having the same sequence of consonants but a different characteristic vowel (thus MAT-, "eat," but MET-, "end"). There is in addition a small set of words arising (or seeming to arise) from bases having only one consonant, and these typically have basic meanings, such as the pronouns or various prepositional senses. Most of the words "reconstructed" by Tolkien for both Primitive Quendian and Common Eldarin thus have either two or three syllables, though in the case of words having only one root consonant there is a small set of one-syllable words. The permissible set of consonants among and the patterns of consonants within Quendian bases are similar to those posited for Indo-European (especially as these were posited during the early part of the twentieth century, a rather radical restructuring of Indo-European phonological theory now having intervened), with both voiced and unvoiced series of unaspirated stops (e.g., voiced *b, d, g* and voiceless *p, t, k*), a voiceless series of aspirated stops *(ph, th, kh)*, nasals *(m, n, ñ)*, liquids *(l, r)*, a labiovelar *(w)*, and so forth. The vowels are the usual set of five cardinals *(a, e, i, o, u)*, with their usual European values in both long and short quantities. Also, like Indo-European, the main stress or accent in Primitive Quendian and Common Eldarin words was *free;* that is, the main stress could occur on any syllable of a word, not necessarily on a root syllable, and could even occur on the final syllable or be absent entirely in words of one syllable (which typically had both stressed and unstressed forms).

Grammatically, not much is known about Primitive Quendian and Common Eldarin, though from certain statements and by comparison of forms in Quenya, Telerin, and Sindarin it can be deduced that they were in this regard also of an Indo-European type, with the notable exception of having no categories corresponding to grammatical gender (which may have been a development within Indo-European not found in its most primitive state).

As the March continued, further separations of the Eldar and thus of their languages occurred as various groups of the *Teleri* (Q., "those at the end of the line, the hindmost") abandoned the March: first the *Nandor* (Q., "those who went back") balked at crossing the Misty Mountains, then the *Sindar* (Q., "Grey-elves") remained with Thingol in Beleriand, and finally the remaining Teleri balked at crossing the Great Sea and remained on the shores of Middle-earth. As a result, the Eldarin languages came to be widely distributed geographically into two chief groups: those spoken by the Eldar that came at last to Aman and those spoken by the Teleri that remained in Middle-earth.

The Languages of Aman

Valarin

The Eldar coming to Aman did not find it a silent land, because the Valar, who lived there, had made a spoken language for themselves, called in Quenya Valarin. Tolkien provides only a handful of actual Valarin words, but from these it is evident that Valarin is intended to have seemed quite alien to the Eldar, both structurally and phonetically. Attested Valarin words chiefly include the names of the Valar and words of law, theology, and ceremony adapted into Quenya forms more pleasing to the Elves of Aman; thus Valarin *Mānawenūz*, "Blessed One, One (closest) in accord with Eru," became Quenya *Manwë*, and Valarin *akašān*, "He [Eru] says," became Quenya *axan*, "law, rule, commandment."

Quenya

The Eldar arriving in Aman spoke a language much changed from Common Eldarin and in their language called *Quendya* (in the Ñoldorin dialect *Quenya*), meaning simply "Quendian, belonging to the Quendi," that is, "the language of the Quendi." Of particular note among the many phonological changes from Primitive Quendian resulting in Quenya are the following:

1. The fronting of the originally free Eldarin main stress to become fixed in most (unprefixed) words on the first syllable.
2. The main stress in words of three or more syllables was retracted to either the penultimate syllable, where that is long (i.e., has an original long vowel or has a short vowel followed by two or more consonants), or the antepenultimate syllable.
3. As a result, original final vowels (which most Common Eldarin words had) were, if originally long, shortened (and subsequently the newly short final *-i* and *-u* were lowered to *-e* and *-o*) and, if originally short, lost entirely.
4. All now-final consonant clusters were reduced to a single consonant. These and all other now-final single consonants were *dentalized* so that in Quenya only *t, n, l, r,* and *s* occur in word-final position.
5. Original *b, d,* and *g,* where not in contact with a nasal consonant, were weakened, lost, or both so that in Quenya these sounds occur only in the combinations *mb, nd,* and *ng.*
6. In certain circumstances, *syncope* or loss of an unstressed vowel occurred in the second of two adjacent syllables having the same vowel.

Thus, for example (in accordance with one etymology offered by Tolkien, though characteristically not with those preceding and following), original *galata-rīg-elle*, "lady *(elle)* with a garland *(rīg)* of sunlight *(galata)*," became in Quenya *Altariel* by loss of the original *g* (in two places), syncope of the second (unstressed) *a*, loss of the original final short *-e*, and reduction of the then-final *-ll* to *-l*. (In Middle-earth this name and its derivation were subsequently remodeled in accordance with Sindarin phonology and phonetics to produce *Galadriel.*)

It is chiefly in certain aspects of its phonological development and especially in the position of the main stress that Quenya exhibits the influence of Latin and, to a lesser extent, in its phonology the influence of Greek. Quenya phonetics strongly shows the influence of Finnish, which also does not permit voiced stops *(b, d, g)* in isolation: like Quenya, Finnish does not have *g* except in combination with *n* and Finnish does not have *b* or *d* at all except in loanwords. Furthermore, the restriction of permissible word-final consonants to simple dentals mirrors that of Finnish. It should be noted, however, that Quenya and Finnish also have some marked differences in phonetics and in stress: for example, Finnish has a larger set of vowels that includes many distinctive sounds not found in Quenya, such as *ä* (the sound of *a* in *cat*), *ö* (as in German), and *y* (the German *ü*); the main stress in Finnish is fixed on the first syllable; and the distinctive Finnish system of coordinated vocalic qualities known as *vowel harmony* is absent from Quenya, with the result that the effect of Quenya on the ear is quite distinct from Finnish and more like Latin.

Grammatically, Quenya resembles both Latin and Finnish in having a rich set of inflectional classes in both the noun and the verb and in having verbs inflected for both person and number, in addition to tense and perfective aspect. (It even shares with Finnish some pronominal endings, such as *-n* for first person singular "I," *-t* for [one form of] second person singular "you," and at an earlier stage in the external history of Quenya -*mme* for [one form of] first person plural "we.") But Quenya most closely resembles Finnish in the following ways:

1. It lacks grammatical gender entirely.
2. It has a set of adverbial cases of the noun (in form further inspired by the frequent presence of *geminate*, or doubled, consonants in the corresponding set of Finnish cases) used to express position, movement, or both with respect to the noun, whereas Latin (like English) chiefly expresses this with a preposition: thus, for example, allative *kiryanna*, "to(ward) a ship"; locative *kiryasse*, "in/(up)on a ship"; ablative *kiryallo*, "from a ship," which can be compared with Finnish allative *vedelle*, "to(ward) water"; inessive *vedessä*, "in water"; and ablative *vedeltä*, "from water" (though Quenya has only three such cases, and Finnish has upward of ten).
3. It distinguishes inflectionally between a *general* and a *partitive* noun, that is, roughly corresponding to the difference in the indicated membership between "apples are red" and "some apples are green" in English (though the actual mechanisms and application are rather different than those in Finnish).

Under the general name Quenya in Aman are grouped two dialects, namely, Vanyarin, the more conservative dialect spoken by the Vanyar; and Ñoldorin, the more innovative dialect spoken by the Ñoldor. Few specifically Vanyarin forms are attested, so little is known about its distinct nature, save the remarkable fact, recounted in "The Shibboleth of Fëanor," that the deliberate Ñoldorin alteration of *þ* to *s* in the dialect became caught in the political and familial strife between the Ñoldor and the Vanyar preceding the exile and actually contributed to that strife (*Peoples*, 331–66).

Telerin

Eventually, a portion of the Teleri that had stopped on the shores of Middle-earth came to Tol Eressëa and to Aman and settled in both places. Their language naturally continued to develop, independently of the Telerin spoken by their kin who remained in Middle-earth and under the influence of the contact with Quenya (upon which this form of Telerin likewise exerted some influence). Little is known, however, of the precise ways in which the Telerin spoken in Aman came to differ from the Telerin spoken in Middle-earth, so for present purposes the development and character of Telerin can be treated in the next section as a language of Middle-earth.

The Languages of Middle-earth

The Eldarin Languages

Telerin   The earliest separation from the Common Eldarin tongue to occur in Middle-earth was between the form of the language as spoken by the Vanyar and the Ñoldor, which would eventually result in Quenya in Aman, and that spoken by the Teleri, those of the Eldar that remained in Middle-earth after the Vanyar and Ñoldor departed to Aman. The first separation of Teleri from the March occurred when the Nandor balked at crossing the Misty Mountains and instead settled in those environs (though some of the Nandor eventually passed over the mountains and some of these came at last into Beleriand and settled in Ossiriand), giving rise to Nandorin, of which Silvan Elvish and Nandorin (proper) as spoken in Ossiriand are descendants. The form of the Eldarin language that developed among the Teleri of (at least) Beleriand, before they still further separated geographically and linguistically, is called Common Telerin, which is the (in the internal history, unrecorded) common ancestor both of Telerin (proper), the language of those of the Eldar who settled on the shores of Beleriand (and thus of the form of Telerin subsequently brought to and developed in Tol Eressëa and Aman), and of Sindarin, the predominant language of Beleriand spoken by those of the Eldar who remained with Thingol in Doriath and in most of the rest of Beleriand and eventually by the exiled Ñoldor. A particularly noteworthy development of Common Telerin from Common Eldarin is the change of original **kw* to *p*, which is also characteristic of the development of Welsh from Indo-European (whereas in Latin as in Quenya the sound remained and became *qu*). (It is unclear whether, at the stage of the external history considered here, the Nandor separated before or after the development of Common Eldarin, that is, whether the Nandorin language participated in the sound changes that characterize Common Telerin in distinction to Common Eldarin, such as **kw > p*).

Telerin (proper) arose from Common Telerin and developed independently after the separation of the Sindar, though judging by the (relatively small) number of attested Telerin forms its further development was quite conservative compared to that undergone by Sindarin (and is in some respects even more conservative of Common Eldarin features than was Quenya). Both Common Telerin and Telerin proper are cited by Tolkien chiefly to illuminate certain otherwise puzzling or opaque correspondences between Quenya and Sindarin (a role in which it is somewhat reminiscent of Italo-Celtic, a posited though hotly debated common ancestor of both the Italic and the Celtic subfamilies of Indo-European from which Latin and Welsh, respectively, are descended—all the more so given the influence of Latin and Welsh on Quenya and Sindarin, respectively). Something of this relationship can be glimpsed from comparing the (only) three attested examples of Telerin sentences with the parallel sentences in Quenya and Sindarin with which they are cited: (1) *ēl sīla lūmena vomentienguo*, corresponding to Frodo's Quenya greeting, *elen síla lúmenn' omentielvo*, meaning "A star shines upon the hour of the meeting of our ways"; (2) *abá care!* "don't do it!" corresponding to Q. *ava kare!* and S. *avo garo!*; and (3) *orē nia pete nin*, "my heart *(orē)* tells me," corresponding to Q. *órenya quete nin* and S. *guren bêd enni*.

Nandorin Little is known of Nandorin proper (even, as mentioned previously, whether it is descended from Common Telerin), but if at least some of the (also scant) evidence of its earlier form in the external history of this language, called Danian in "The Etymologies," is counted as belonging still to the later form, Nandorin (and Danian in any event) is nonetheless noteworthy here as exhibiting a pronounced influence from Old English, particularly in the phonological phenomenon known as *breaking*, by which certain original short unitary vowels became diphthongs when immediately followed by original *h* or (in certain circumstances) by *l* or *r* (though the details differ at least slightly in Danian/Nandorin): for example, Danian (Nandorin?) *beorn*, "man," < *bernō* < BER-; *ealc*, "swan," < *alkwā* < ÁLAK-; and *meord*, "fine rain," < *mirde* < MIZD-.

Silvan Elvish Although it was apparently spoken widely in the lands of Middle-earth east of the Blue Mountains, even less is attested or known concerning the phonological or grammatical features of Silvan Elvish, save that its speakers, called in Sindarin *Tawarwaith*, "the Forest-folk," were descendants of the Nandor, the portion of the Teleri that balked at crossing the Misty Mountains during the Great March, and that it was chief among the languages spoken by the Elves of Lórien and of Mirkwood. It appears to be cited by Tolkien mostly to explain forms of names in the legendarium that, in the external history of the languages, arose in the Sindarin-like form of Noldorin of "The Etymologies" or in (again, externally) still earlier forms of this language but that could not be explained (at least not readily) in terms of the altered internal phonological history that arose with the conceptual change from Noldorin to Sindarin.

Silvan Elvish is also referred to as the "woodland tongue."

Sindarin Sindarin (which for present purposes can be discussed as a unitary language, though numerous dialects are named or implied by Tolkien) is the language of the *Sindar* (Quenya for "Grey ones [Elves]"), namely, of all those of the Eldar that remained in Beleriand excepting the Teleri and the Nandor, arising first and most properly with those followers of Thingol who abandoned the March to remain with him in Doriath and its environs, but (in various dialectal forms) afterward spread throughout most of Beleriand and eventually adopted by the exiled Ñoldor. It alone of all the Eldarin tongues of Beleriand persisted as a spoken language into the Third Age, where it was spoken still in a few Eldarin strongholds such as Rivendell, as well as among the remaining Dúnedain, chiefly in Gondor.

As has already been noted, Sindarin (from its external inception as Goldogrin and even more so in its external development into Noldorin and then into Sindarin) is profoundly influenced by Welsh in its phonology and (as a shared consequence of their phonological development) in its grammar. Like Welsh (and, it should be noted, in some of these respects like English), Sindarin is strongly characterized in its phonology most notably by (1) the voicing of original intervocalic voiceless stops (e.g., $p > b$, $t > d$, $k > g$); (2) the spirantizing of original intervocalic voiced stops (e.g., $b > v$, $d > ð$, $g > ʒ$, which was subsequently lost entirely) and of original *m* ($>v$); (3) the mutation or *affection* of susceptible vowels when preceding a syllable containing certain sounds (e.g., *ī, *ā, and *yā, all of which were frequent final elements in Common Eldarin words, such as the plural ending *-ī of nouns); and (4) the loss of all original final vowels (as a consequence of the weakening caused by the fronting of the main stress) in Common Eldarin words of two or more syllables.

From these characteristic changes arose as a consequence three particularly noteworthy grammatical features of Sindarin, likewise shared with Welsh:

1. The *ī*-affection plurals, such as *adan* "man," plural *edain* < *atanī, and *orod*, "mountain," and plural *eryd* (later *ered*) < *orotī (though the proportion of such plurals in Sindarin is much greater than that for Welsh, which further and frequently employs a rich set of plural endings instead of or in addition to internal mutation).
2. The *grammatical mutation* of initial consonants (as in Welsh often informally called *lenition* [< Latin *lenis*, "soft"], though not all such

mutations resulted in a soft, i.e., voiced, consonant), arising from, *inter alia*, the application of the various intervocalic consonant changes cited previously to the initial consonant of words immediately following a word with which it was felt by the speakers to stand in close syntactic relationship. This could, for example, be of a noun following a definite article (thus *Baranduin*, "Brandywine," but *i Varanduiniant*, "the Brandywine Bridge"); of the object of an imperative verb when immediately following that verb (thus *lasto beth lammen*, "listen to the word of my tongue," where the object *beth* of *lasto*, "listen!" is the lenited form of *peth*, "word," but *lacho calad*, "flame, light!" where the subject *calad*, "light," of *lacho*, "flame!" is unlenited); or (less regularly) of an adjective following the noun it modifies (thus *morn*, "dark," but *Eryn Vorn*, "Dark Woods").

3. A drastic reduction in the use and number of inflectional endings in the language, particularly in the noun, due to the weakening and then loss of all original final vowels—itself caused by the fronting of the main stress. This led to the selection and then generalization of other means to convey grammatical relationships and functions, such as the use of word order (e.g., showing possession by juxtaposition of two nouns, such as *Ennyn Durin*, "the Doors of Durin," and *Aran Moria*, "Lord of Moria") and adverbial prepositions (note that increased reliance in English on prepositions and on word order arose from essentially the same mechanism and root cause).

For all the phonological similarities of Sindarin to Welsh, it should be noted that the effect of Welsh on the ear is nonetheless quite different than that of Sindarin, largely because of the presence in Welsh words of *schwa*—ə, the "uh" sound of many unstressed vowels in English, as in the word *phonology*, "fuh-NAH-luh-gee"—which in Welsh is spelt *y*. This sound occurs frequently in Welsh words in both stressed and unstressed positions but is lacking in Sindarin. Another frequent and characteristic Welsh sound is spelt *ll* and pronounced (approximately) by holding the tongue in the *l* position and blowing air through the mouth around the tongue, without voicing. This sound does occur in Sindarin, where it is usually spelt *lh* (though in certain cases in *The Lord of the Rings* it is spelt *ll* just as in Welsh, most notably in the tree-name *mallorn*), but it is encountered less frequently in Sindarin words than in Welsh.

Sindarin is one of only a few of Tolkien's invented languages that he developed sufficiently for use in poetry or even in more than the briefest declarative prose. The principal examples of such Sindarin compositions include Bilbo's song in Rivendell (*A Elbereth Gilthoniel. . .*), Gandalf's spell before the West-gate of Moria (*Annon edhellen. . .*) and the inscription on the gate (*Ennyn Durin Aran Moria. . .*), and the "King's Letter" from Aragorn to Sam in the original (unused) epilogue to *The Lord of the Rings* (see *Sauron*). Something further of the character of Sindarin can be shown here from Tolkien's Sindarin translation of the Lord's Prayer, which begins *Ae Adar nín i vi Menel, no aer i eneth lín. Tolo i arnad lín; caro den i innas lin, bo Ceven sui vi Menel* (*Vinyar Tengwar* 44).

Under the general name Sindarin are grouped numerous regional dialects—Doriathrin (i.e., as spoken in Doriath), of Hithlum, of Mithrim, and so on—each differing (chiefly) in some detail of phonological development or of grammar but apparently remaining quite close in most particulars and certainly mutually intelligible.

Sindarin is also referred to as "Grey-elven."

Quenya For the general character of Quenya and influences upon it, see the preceding discussion under "The Languages of Aman."

The exiled Ñoldor returned to Middle-earth speaking Quenya, as they did in Aman. But for both political and practical reasons (i.e., the ban by Thingol against speaking Quenya anywhere within his realm and the predominance of Sindarin in Beleriand), they soon ceased using Quenya as a daily tongue. After this, Quenya (all but) ceased to be spoken and thus (all but) ceased to change, so eventually, and long before the Third Age, Quenya could only be learned as a dead language, and its use was confined to poetry, song, and scholarly or ceremonial texts and pronouncements (and then chiefly only by the remaining Ñoldorin exiles and, among Men, the descendants of the Faithful Númenóreans); it is in these senses specifically that Tolkien refers to Quenya as an "Elf-latin."

Like Sindarin, Quenya is one of only a few of his invented languages that Tolkien developed sufficiently for use in poetry or more than the briefest declarative prose. The principal examples of such Quenya compositions include Frodo's greeting of Gildor (*Elen síla. . .*), Galadriel's lament (*Ai! laurië lantar lassi súrinen. . .*), Aragorn's coronation oath (*Et Eärello Endorenna. . .*), Cirion's oath in *Unfinished Tales* (*Vanda sina termaruva. . .*), and the long poem *Oilima Markirya, The Last Ark*, in the essay "A Secret Vice" (*Men kenúva fane kirya. . .*). Something further of the character of Quenya can be shown here from Tolkien's Quenya translation of the Lord's Prayer, which begins *Átaremma i ëa han ëa, na aire esselya. Aranielya na tuluva; na care indómelya cemende tambe Erumande* (*Vinyar Tengwar* 43).

In Middle-earth, Quenya is also referred to as "Valinorean," "High-elven," the "High tongue," the "noble tongue," the "Elder tongue," the "Ancient tongue," and the "Ancient Speech."

Khuzdul

All languages discussed previously ultimately derive from a single ancient root language, namely, Primitive Quendian, the language that the Elves first made for themselves after waking at Cuiviénen. But the Elves were just one of the speaking races of Middle-earth, and Primitive Quendian was not the only root language (although its descendants certainly exerted considerable influence on most other chief languages of Middle-earth). Like Primitive Quendian, *Khuzdul*, the language of the Dwarves (the name means "Dwarvish" in that tongue), was an aboriginal language, used anciently by the first-awakened ancestors of the race. However, unlike the first Elves and Primitive Quendian, these first Dwarves did not create Khuzdul but instead received it from the Vala Aulë, who created both the language and the Dwarves. (Not surprisingly, the phonetics of Khuzdul appears to have some affinities with that of Valarin, though there is too little material in both languages to make more than general and conjectural observations on this.) The Dwarves closely guarded this language, both from change and from the eyes and ears of the other races of Middle-earth. As a result, little is known of Khuzdul even by the Ñoldorin linguistic loremasters beyond a small set of words, chiefly place-names associated with Dwarvish strongholds and their environs, such as *Khazad-dûm*, "mansion of the Dwarves."

Where, as he said, Tolkien created Primitive Quendian to have an essentially Indo-European root structure and phonetics, it is likewise clear, as Tolkien also stated, that he constructed Khuzdul on a Semitic structural and phonetic basis. This can readily be seen by examining the attested words of Khuzdul and those bases cited by Tolkien, from which it is clear that Khuzdul is, like the Semitic languages, characterized by *triconsonantal roots*, that is, roots (bases) formed by a set of three consonants and differentiated from one another solely by those consonants (unlike the Eldarin bases, which are characterized by their consonants together with a characteristic vowel). The various grammatical forms associated with a root meaning are derived by variation in the quality of vowels occupying (or absent from) one or more of the interconsonantal positions of the base and in some cases further by the addition of suffixes to the elaborated base. For example, by comparing the (apparent) adjective *Khuzdul*, "Dwarvish," and the plural noun *Khazâd*, "Dwarves," we can see that both are derived from a base KhZD-, "Dwarf," and that their individual elaborated meanings are indicated by (1) the particular vowels used in the interconsonantal positions; (2) the presence or absence of a vowel in each of these interconsonantal positions; and (3) in *Khuzdul*, the addition of an apparent adjectival suffix *-ul*.

Khuzdul is also referred to as "Dwarvish."

The Languages of Men

Taliska

Although it is unclear whether Taliska continued as part of the internal history of the languages of Middle-earth in the external historical stage presented here, it bears notice because it shows that Tolkien's interest in creating an "'unrecorded' Germanic language" continued well past the point at which he began work on Q(u)enya and the other Elvish languages.

Taliska arose as the earliest language (both internally and externally) of those Men who first came into Beleriand long ages after the awakening of their ancestors in the east of Middle-earth. It is said to have been influenced before the arrival in Beleriand, first by Khuzdul (a fact particularly significant in light of the Khuzdul/Semitic structure of Adûnaic, its successor language, though Taliska itself is firmly Eldarin/Indo-European in its root structure) and subsequently by the language of the Green-elves, that is, (in terms of the later external history) by Nandorin. As noted previously, Nandorin (perhaps) shows a marked influence of Old English in its phonology; it is not surprising, then, that Taliska also shows in its phonology the clear influence of another early Germanic language of keen interest to Tolkien, namely Gothic (though apparently in a form predating that of the few surviving Gothic manuscripts, which are themselves somewhat influenced by Greek vocabulary and syntax). Remarkably, the influence of Gothic and early Germanic extends beyond phonology into the lexicon itself, as shown by such Taliskan words as *widris*, "wisdom" (cf. Old Norse *vitr*, "wise," ultimately derived from Indo-European *weid-, wid-*, "to see"), and *skirditaila*, "runic series" (cf. Old Norse *skera*, "cut, carve," and Old English *tæl*, "number, reckoning, series"). But these forms can also be related to Eldarin bases and words of intriguingly similar form and meaning, such as Noldorin *idhren*, "pondering, wise, thoughtful," < ID-, Sindarin *cirth*, "runes," < KIRIS-, "cut," and Quenya *taile*, "lengthening, extension," < TAY-, "extend, make long(er)." Indeed, Taliska seems to be a close amalgamation of both Gothic/early Germanic and Eldarin features and bases and to have been intended to serve as a sort of bridge, within the fiction, between the ancient languages of Middle-earth, in particular the Elvish tongues, and the Indo-European tongues of history.

Adûnaic

At the ruinous end of the First Age, those houses of Men that had remained faithful to the Elves in the wars against Morgoth were rewarded by the Valar with the gift of a new home, *Númenor* (Quenya, "Western Land"), an island raised up for them amid the Great Sea and to which they removed. The Númenóreans brought with them their ancestral language, *Adûnaic* (apparently an anglicized name derived from *Adûnâim*, "Men of the West," thus "language of Western Men"), which had already been greatly influenced through long ages of contact with Khuzdul and by the various Elvish languages and dialects of Middle-earth, including eventually by Sindarin in Beleriand, and now came under further Elvish influence from the increased congress with the Elves of Tol Eressëa.

Like Khuzdul, Adûnaic has a strongly Semitic structure, characterized by triconsonantal bases; but unlike Khuzdul, it has, accompanying and underlying these, a large number of old biconsonantal bases, reflecting an original stratum of ancient Quendian derivation of and/or influence on the language. Furthermore, unlike Khuzdul but like the Eldarin languages, all Adûnaic bases have a *characteristic vowel* by which they are distinguished from other bases having the same consonantal pattern but unrelated meaning: thus, for example, the base KALAB, "fall," is distinct from and unrelated to KULUB, "root, edible vegetable that is a root." Again like Khuzdul, grammatical forms and their associated, elaborated meanings are derived from a base by variation in the quality of vowels occupying (or absent from) one or more of the interconsonantal positions of the base. Yet they are (apparently) unlike Khuzdul in that this elaboration can also involve modification of one of the basic consonants and in that vowel variations are not so free as in Khuzdul, since the characteristic vowel must appear in at least one of the interconsonantal positions of an elaborated base (though it can appear in lengthened or diphthongized form): thus *kalab*, "fall (down)"; past tense *kallab*,

"fell"; and *Akallabêth*, "She-that-is-fallen" (a name of Númenor), are all < KALAB, "fall," and *zîr*, "love, desire," and *zâir*, "yearning," are both < ZIR, "love, desire."

Further unlike Khuzdul, Adûnaic shows a heavy influence in its lexicon from words of Eldarin origin, though these are phonetically adapted to (or, depending on the age of the inheritance or borrowing, phonologically developed in accordance with) the Adûnaic system: thus, for example, Adûnaic MINIL and Eldarin MENEL, both meaning "heaven, sky," and Adûnaic *lômi* and Quenya *lóme*, both meaning "night."

Adûnaic is also referred to as "Númenórean."

Sōval Phāre

Sōval Phāre (meaning "Common Speech" in that language) developed from the mingling of Adûnaic with the kindred languages of those Men who remained in Middle-earth about the coastal harbors and havens maintained by the Númenóreans in the Second Age, becoming the common speech of trade and government among both peoples. After the Downfall of Númenor at the end of the Second Age, the surviving faithful Númenóreans who returned to Middle-earth eventually adopted this Common Speech in daily use, which thereby came under further and stronger influence from Adûnaic and through it from the Elvish languages. Sōval Phāre became in the Third Age the native language of all peoples in the Númenórean kingdoms of Arnor and Gondor, including the Men of Rohan and the Hobbits, save for the Elves and Dwarves, who maintained their own languages but who also used the Common Speech in their dealings with the other peoples of western Middle-earth.

These various peoples had their own dialects of Sōval Phāre, differing to lesser or greater degree from the more formal standard as used by the Gondorians, to which the dialect of the Hobbits nearly approached. As Tolkien explains in Appendix F to *The Lord of the Rings*, Modern English is used in the novel to represent or "translate" this standard form, and the other dialectal forms are represented according to a scheme in which a language having an historical and linguistic relationship with Modern English similar to that of the dialect with the standard form is used to "translate" that dialect. As a result, the somewhat rustic dialect of Sōval Phāre spoken by the Hobbits is represented by a similarly rustic form of Modern English, and the archaic northern dialect of the Common Speech spoken among the Dwarves and their neighbors is represented by a partially anglicized form of Old Norse, mostly seen in personal names such as *Durin, Gimli,* and *Thráin.* The similarly ancient but more southern dialect of the Common Speech spoken by the Men of Rohan is represented by a form of Old English, mostly seen in personal names and place-names such as *Théoden, Éomer,* and *Edoras.*

Tolkien actually invented and recorded only a handful of authentic Sōval Phāre forms, apparently solely for use in the appendices to convey some flavor of the actual Common Speech of Middle-earth and more particularly of that dialect spoken by the Hobbits and of the related but more archaic dialect of the Rohirrim: thus, for example, the word "hobbit" translates *kuduk* in Sōval Phāre as spoken by the Hobbits, which is a worn-down form of the word *kûd-dûkan,* "hole-dweller," in the older but closely related dialect of Rohan. Little can be said about the character of Sōval Phāre from the few examples Tolkien recorded, save that it was clearly intended to resemble Adûnaic in structure and phonetics.

Sōval Phāre is also referred to as "Westron," the "Common Speech," the "Common Language," and the "Common Tongue."

The Black Speech

In a perverse antiparallel with Aulë's creation of Khuzdul for the Dwarves, the children of his craft to whom Ilúvatar gave life, Sauron (who, it is noted, was a Maia formerly devoted to Aulë) created the Black Speech to serve as the common language of his minions and slaves, the Orcs, and of all those whom he subjugated. In the event he failed even to impose this language on the Orcs, who used it if at all only in a debased form, instead primarily speaking a similarly debased form of the Common Speech, though punctuated with words and jargon taken and twisted both from the Black Speech and from other languages of Middle-earth.

From the few words of the Black Speech and the debased form of it spoken by the Orcs of Mordor, it is clear that it was constructed (by Tolkien and as by Sauron) to be a harsh and guttural language, characterized by such sounds as *sh, gh, zg;* indeed, establishing this effect, as well as the bits of grammar needed to lend the Ring-inscription linguistic verisimilitude, seems to have been about the extent of Tolkien's work on this language. Further suggesting this, for the only other (debased) Black Speech utterance Tolkien wrote, the curse of the Mordor-orc, Tolkien at different times provided three different translations that cannot be fully reconciled with one another. Certain possible correspondences in the (apparent) grammar of the Ring-inscription and its vocabulary with Quenya, Khuzdul, Adûnaic, and Valarin have been

suggested, and its phonetics certainly invites comparison with the latter three languages; but although these are intriguing proposals, they cannot be confirmed from Tolkien's own writings.

The Black Speech is also referred to as the "language of Mordor."

CARL F. HOSTETTER

Chief Sources

Tolkien, J.R.R. "Appendix E." In *The Lord of the Rings.*
———. "Appendix F." In *The Lord of the Rings.*
———. "Dangweth Pengoloð." In *The Peoples of Middle-earth.*
———. "Drafts for a Letter to 'Mr. Rang.'" In *The Letters of J.R.R. Tolkien,* edited by Humphrey Carpenter, 379–87. Boston: Houghton Mifflin, 1981.
———. "The Early Qenya Grammar." *Parma Eldalamberon* 14 (2003): 35–86.
———. "The Etymologies." In *The Lost Road and Other Writings: Language and Legend before "The Lord of the Rings,"* edited by Christopher Tolkien. New York: Ballantine, 1996.
———. "From 'Quendi and Eldar,' Appendix D." *Vinyar Tengwar* 39 (July 1998): 4–20.
———. "From 'The *Shibboleth* of Fëanor.'" *Vinyar Tengwar* 41 (July 2000): 7–10.
———. "The *Lhammas.*" In *The Lost Road and Other Writings: Language and Legend before "The Lord of the Rings,"* edited by Christopher Tolkien. New York: Ballantine, 1996.
———. "Lowdham's Report on the Adûnaic Language." In *Sauron Defeated,* edited by Christopher Tolkien, 413–40. Boston, MA: Houghton Mifflin, 1992.
———. "*Notes on Óre.*" *Vinyar Tengwar* 41 (July 2000): 11–19.
———. "*Ósanwe-kenta*: Enquiry into the Communication of Thought." *Vinyar Tengwar* 39 (July 1998): 21–34.
———. "The Problem of *Ros.*" In *The Peoples of Middle-earth.*
———. "*Qenyaqetsa*: The Qenya Phonology and Lexicon." *Parma Eldalamberon* 12 (2003): x–xi.
———. "Quendi and Eldar." In *The War of the Jewels,* edited by Christopher Tolkien. Boston, MA: Houghton Mifflin, 1994.
———. *The Road Goes Ever On.*
———. "A Secret Vice." In *J.R.R. Tolkien: The Monsters and the Critics,* edited by Christopher Tolkien, 198–223. Boston, MA: Houghton Mifflin, 1984.
———. "The *Shibboleth* of Fëanor." In *The Peoples of Middle-earth.*
———. "To Richard Jeffery." In *The Letters of J.R.R. Tolkien,* edited by Humphrey Carpenter, 424–28. Boston, MA: Houghton Mifflin, 1981.

Further Reading

Allan, Jim, ed. *An Introduction to Elvish.* Somerset: Bran's Head, 1978.
Eliot, C.N.E. *Finnish Grammar.* Oxford: Clarendon Press, 1890.
Gilson, Christopher. "Gnomish Is Sindarin." In *Tolkien's Legendarium: Essays on the History of Middle-earth,*

edited by Verlyn Flieger and Carl F. Hostetter, 95–104. Westport, CT: Greenwood, 2000.

Hostetter, Carl. "Elvish as She Is Spoke." In *The Lord of the Rings, 1954–2004: Scholarship in Honor of Richard E. Blackwelder*, edited by Wayne Hammond and Christina Scull. Milwaukee, WI: Marquette University Press, 2005.

———. "Resources for Tolkienian Linguistics." http://www.elvish.org/resources.html.

Morris-Jones, John. *Welsh Grammar: Historical and Comparative*. Oxford: Clarendon Press, 1913.

Parma Eldalamberon. A journal of the Elvish Linguistic Fellowship, a special interest group of the Mythopoeic Society. http://www.eldalamberon.com/parma15.html.

Quettar. Tolkien Society's linguistic bulletin. http://tolklang.quettar.org/quetinfo.

Salo, David. *A Gateway to Sindarin*. Salt Lake City, UT: University of Utah Press, 2004.

Tengwestië. The online journal of the Elvish Linguistic Fellowship. Edited by Carl F. Hostetter and Patrick H. Wynne. http://www.elvish.org/Tengwestie/.

Vinyar Tengwar. A journal of the Elvish Linguistic Fellowship. Edited by Carl F. Hostetter. http://www.elvish.org/VT/.

Welden, Bill. "Negation in Quenya." *Vinyar Tengwar* 42 (July 2001): 32–34.

Wright, Joseph. *Primer of the Gothic Language*. Oxford: Clarendon Press, 1892.

LATIN LANGUAGE

Tolkien's Knowledge of and Familiarity with Latin

Tolkien first encountered Latin in his childhood as the language of worship and prayer for the Catholic faith in which his mother had raised him (*Letters*, 66, 395; cf. *Letters*, 340, 354). His early experiences with these Tridentine "words of joy" led him to associate Latin with the sacred, the august, and the joyous (*Letters*, 66; *Sauron*, 24). Tolkien started formally to study Latin and Greek at age eleven, in King Edward's School in Birmingham, where he spent most of his time learning both classical languages (Carpenter, 27, 34; cf. *Letters*, 213). He was "brought up in the Classics" (*Letters*, 172), although he preferred Latin to Greek (*Letters*, 419). His command of Latin allowed him to translate English poetry into Latin verse at a young age (*Letters*, 213), as well as to debate and write reports in Latin for the school's periodical (*Acta Senatus*, published in 1911). He was awarded an Open Classical Exhibition at Exeter College, at Oxford, where he started to read for classics (Carpenter, 48–49), although he formally abandoned Greek and Latin in 1913 to read for English and its kindred in 1913 (Carpenter, 63). Tolkien's linguistic taste changed and oscillated between poles (*Letters*, 214; cf. *Lost Road*, 38–39, 43), but Tolkien always confessed to having a "particular love for the Latin language" (*Letters*, 376; cf. *Lost Road*, 41–42). For Tolkien's "phonaesthetic" tastes, Latin supplied the standard of "normalcy" against which all other languages came to be measured (*Letters*, 419; *MC*, 191). Tolkien appeared to regard himself as a man placed in the intersection between Latin and the Germanic languages (*Letters*, 213, 376; cf. *Lost Road*, 38–39, 41–43). Some of the poems he wrote in Old English bear a Latin title, such as *Enigmata Saxonica Nuper Inventa Duo* (1923) and *Natura Apis: Morali Ricardi Eremite* (1936). Tolkien's use of Latin was on occasion as mischievously humorous as it was creative: revered Virgilian lines were altered to make a learned pun (e. g., *Letters*, 24, "sic hobbitur ad astra"); pig-Latin was included in the full title of his short tale *Farmer Giles of Ham* (1949) for satirical purposes, and homely Hobbit nomenclature was to be translated by jokingly grandiose Latin names—an idea Tolkien soon abandoned (*Peoples*, 46–47, 102–3).

Use and Influence of Latin in Tolkien's Literature

A flawless command of Latin was required for Tolkien's philological research interests (Anderson, 230–34). Tolkien's professional concern with the interrelation of British Celtic (primarily Welsh), Latin, and Anglo-Saxon, shown in his 1955 O'Donnell Lecture "English and Welsh" (*MC*, 162–97), played also a fundamental part not only in Tolkien's "secret vice" of inventing new languages (according to *Letters*, 219, Sindarin was made to have a relation to Quenya similar to that existing between British Celtic and Latin) but in his fiction as well (as shown in *Farmer Giles of Ham*).

Latin is a clearly discernible element in two of Tolkien's early invented languages, Nevbosh and Naffarin. Part of the vocabulary of the former was based on Latin (*MC*, 205), and the latter showed traces of Latin and Latin-derived languages in its sound choices, combinations, and general word-form (*MC*, 209). Latin was also one of the three linguistic bases on which High-elven or Quenya was modelled, as Tolkien was at some pains to explain: Quenya was conceived as "a kind of Elven-latin" and thus transcribed into a spelling "closely resembling that of Latin" so that the similarity to Latin may be "increased ocularly" (*Letters*, 176). Tolkien's character Aurry Lowdham ("The Notion Club Papers") calls Avallonian (an early form of Quenya) "the Elven-latin" by virtue of its "simpler and more euphonious phonetic style" and its "more august . . . more ancient and . . . sacred and liturgical" character (*Sauron*, 241; cf. *Lost Road*, 43). The status of Latin as a tongue that, although no longer spoken as a birth-language, continued to be a language of culture and civilization, a *lingua franca* or common speech for the learned, and a vehicle of converse with the Divine, left its mark on the conception and function of Quenya in Tolkien's legendarium as well: In Valinor, the Gods used Quenya to communicate with the Elves. In their turn, Elves of different kindred, who no longer spoke the same language, had the "Elven-latin" as their *lingua franca* (*RK*, Appendix F, 406). The High-elven was also the tongue "chiefly used in inscriptions or in writings of wisdom or poetry." Thus "the Elf-latin" (*RK*, Appendix F, 406) became fixed "as a language of high speech and writing, and as a common speech of all Elves," which "all the folk of Valinor learned and knew" (*Lost Road*, 172) Like Latin, although it was no longer a cradle-tongue, Quenya maintained its sacred character in that "the names of the Gods were preserved by the Eldar and chiefly used only in Quenya form" (*Lost Road*, 172; on the term "Elven-latin" see also *The History of Middle-earth*, Index, 126, s.v. "Elf-latin," and *Letters*, 425). Accordingly, Tolkien devised a system whereby "as English replaces the Shire-speech so Latin and Greek replace the High-elven tongue" (*Letters*, 343). The logical outcome of the close association of Quenya and Latin in Tolkien's mind was his translation of the Lord's Prayer, the Hail Mary, the Gloria Patri, and the litanies of Loreto from Latin into Quenya (Wynne, Smith, and Hostetter, 5–38).

The "phonaesthetic pleasure" afforded by Latin (*Letters*, 176) also played an important part in the creation of Tolkien's core mythology. For Tolkien, his literary work was fundamentally linguistic in inspiration: the stories were made "to provide a world for the languages" (*Letters*, 219). Two of the central strands that helped shape Tolkien's legendarium, the Drowning of Númenor and Ælfwine's voyage to the Lonely Isle (*Lost Road*, 77, 98), were partially inspired by the sound of medieval Latin names and words found in such works as Paul the Deacon's *Historia gentis Langobardorum* (*Lost Road*, 37–38, 53–55; *Letters*, 257), dated to the eighth century CE, and the anonymous *Navigatio sancti Brendani abbatis* (*Lost Road*, 81–82; *Sauron*, 265), from the eleventh century CE.

MIRYAM LIBRÁN MORENO

Primary Sources

Diaconus, Paulus. *Historia gentis Langobardorum*. Monumenta Germaniae Historica. Scriptores rerum Langobardicarum et Italicarum saec. VI–IX. Herausgegeben von Georg Waitz. Hannover: Hahnsche Verlagsbuchhandlung, 1878.

Selmer, C., ed. *Navigatio Sancti Brendani Abbatis from Early Latin Manuscripts*. Notre Dame, IN: University of Notre Dame, 1959.

Tolkien, J.R.R. "Acta Senatus." *King Edward's School Chronicle*. 186 (1911): 26–27.

———. "English and Welsh," In *The Monsters and the Critics and Other Essays*, edited by Christopher Tolkien, 198–223. London: HarperCollins, 1997.

———. "Enigmata Saxonica Nuper Inventa Duo." In *A Northern Venture: Verses by Members of the University of Leeds*. Leeds: Swan Press, 1923.

———. *Farmer Giles of Ham: Aegidii Ahenobarbi Julii Agricole de Hammo, Domini de Domito, Aule Draconarie Comitis, Regni Minimi Regis et Basilei mora facinora et mirabilis exortus, or in the Vulgar Tongue, The Rise and Wonderful Adventures of Farmer Giles, Lord of Tame, Count of Worminghall and the King of the Little Kingdom*. London: George Allen & Unwin, 1949.

———. "Natura Apis: Morali Ricardi Eremite." In *Songs for the Philologists*. London: Department of English at University College, 1936.

———. "A Secret Vice." In *The Monsters and the Critics and Other Essays*, edited by Christopher Tolkien, 162–97. London: HarperCollins, 1997.

Further Reading

Anderson, Douglas A. "J.R.R. Tolkien and W. Rhys Robert's 'Gerald of Wales on the Survival of Welsh.'" *Tolkien Studies* 2 (2005): 230–34.

Bertenstam, Åke. "A Chronological Bibliography of the Writings of J.R.R. Tolkien." http://www.forodrim.org/arda/tbchron.html (accessed September 2005).

Carpenter, Humphrey. *J.R.R. Tolkien: A Biography*. Boston: George Allen & Unwin, 1977.

Librán Moreno, Miryam. "Parallel Lives: The Sons of Denethor and the Sons of Telamon." *Tolkien Studies* 2 (2005):15–52.

Morse, Robert E. *The Evocation of Virgil in Tolkien's Art: Geritol for the Classics*. Oak Park, IL: Bolchazy-Carducci, 1986.

Wynne, Patrick, Arden R. Smith, and Carl E. Hostetter. "Words of Joy: Five Catholic Prayers in Quenya (Part One)." *Vinyar Tengwar* 43 (2002): 5–39.

See also **Aragorn; Augustine of Hippo; Languages Invented by Tolkien; Latin Literature; Virgil**

LATIN LITERATURE

One aspect of Tolkien's imagination is the influence of Latin literature on his subsequent work. Even before they entered school, Tolkien's mother Mabel gave her sons a rudimentary foundation in Latin, Greek, French, and other subjects. Later, Tolkien received at King Edward's School a traditional, Edwardian period education, which at that time meant a strong foundation in

Latin and Greek languages and literatures. His teachers at King Edward's encouraged students to examine classical linguistics, not simply read the text, and this was already Tolkien's inclination. His career as a philologist began by comparing Greek and Latin. While at the school, Tolkien debated in Latin, as was the custom, in addition to other languages, and he wrote Debating Society reports in Latin.

By the time he went to Exeter College, Oxford, to take a degree in classics, he was thoroughly versed in Latin and Greek. He had, however, become bored with them and had become far more excited and interested in Germanic languages. This boredom was reinforced by the fact that Exeter had no resident tutor in classics during Tolkien's first two terms there. The great Joseph Wright, however, was Tolkien's tutor for his special subject, comparative philology. When Tolkien took his master's degree, this special area was the only one in which he achieved a First. Based on this, he was encouraged to take his advanced degree in English and study philology, which he did.

The most obvious influences of Latin literature and language on Tolkien are in terms of his invention of languages and his professional life. Latin influenced the development of Tolkien's invented languages, in terms of phonology and morphology. Furthermore, approximately while Tolkien was continuing work on his languages, he was working on the *Oxford English Dictionary*, where his knowledge of languages, Latin included, stood him in good stead.

Specifically though, certain Latin texts may be said to be Tolkien's inspiration at various points. For example, Virgil and *The Aeneid* seem to be a particular source for the Paths of the Dead. The entrance to the Underworld in *The Aeneid* is a multi-caverned place suggesting a mountain; its entrance is described as a maw with jaws twice, and Aeneas is afraid to enter and grabs his sword just as Gimli is afraid and reaches for his axe. Also informing this episode in Tolkien is the medieval tradition of the "exercitus mortuorum," the army of the dead that first begins to appear in Latin texts in the twelfth century with *Orderic Vitalis* and others writing in medieval Latin.

There are also a number of important parallels between Aragorn and Aeneas as heroes and kings, not least the journey to an underworld and the oathbreakers. Both men are of high lineage, are exiled kings with the hope, even the promise, of recovering their kingdoms elsewhere. Each is promised that if successful he will marry a queen, start a new line, and renew the kingdom of his ancestors. Both face a challenger to his throne who in his moments of death recognizes the right to kingship of the hero. Both meet a young, beautiful, strong, and heroic woman who falls in love with the hero, and each hero must reject that love to achieve his own destiny. Each woman seeks death, although only one succeeds. Both men begin their role as leader at the death of an older man and fatherly figure. The list of parallels could be continued.

In addition to these parallels in plot, however, there is something more important in the makeup of the characters. Both Aeneas and Aragorn seem to be driven by *pietas*. For Aeneas this is the most important quality indicating his faithfulness to the gods, particularly Venus; his family; even his unborn progeny; and the founding of the dynasty that would result in Rome and eventually in Augustus Caesar. Similarly, Aragorn is driven by *pietas:* faithfulness to his call, his ancestors, and the gods in the person of Gandalf. His willingness to follow Frodo into Mordor even at the expense of his own desires demonstrates faithfulness to a higher goal, the "higher powers" of the Valar, and the Elves; and his ancestors and all that they fought for. Both men secure their kingdom before they marry, thus showing that the order of their *pietas* is the higher goal or mission.

St. Augustine of Hippo is also an obvious influence on Tolkien. In particular, Augustine's notion of evil as privation and twisted good, and that even the most evil may choose good, is one obvious influence on Tolkien. Furthermore, Augustine's explication of creation in his commentary *De Genese* is certainly a key to understanding Tolkien's creation myth.

Paulinus of Nola, who in the fourth century CE, wrote a number of poems may have influenced Tolkien as well. Paulinus wrote several letters to his mentor and friend Ausonius; the emotions and dedication each man expresses to the other may have provided a literary affirmation reinforcing Tolkien's real-life experiences with his friends and so providing a model for the friendships and male camaraderie depicted in Tolkien's works. Paulinus' contemporary Prudentius wrote the *Psychomachia*, an allegorical struggle between seven virtues and seven vices. Tolkien may owe some of his depiction of good and evil, particularly the overall character of the Orcs or pride as an inspiration for Sauron or Morgoth, to this influential work. Much discussion has been carried out in comparing Boethius' understanding of evil in the influential *Consolation of Philosophy* with Tolkien's depiction of evil, particularly in reference to the Ring and its effects. Other Latin authors who may have inspired or influenced Tolkien include Jordanes, Bede, various chronicles and annals, Ovid, Horace, and Jerome. Tolkien, like the medieval languages and literatures he studied, is a skein of multiple crosscurrents of Germanic, biblical, and classical allusions, inspirations, and influences.

L.J. SWAIN

Further Reading

Carpenter, Humphrey. *Tolkien: A Biography*. Boston, MA: Houghton Mifflin, 1977.

See also **Augustine of Hippo; Bede; Heroes and Heroism; Latin Language**

LAW

Tolkien wrote that all stories are ultimately about the fall from grace. Specifically, he wrote that myths and fairy stories should contain elements of moral and religious truth, but not in an explicit form. It is this theory that explains the absence of religion from *The Silmarillion* and *The Lord of the Rings*. Tolkien "absorbed" the religious element into the story and its symbolism. His characters were forced to make difficult decisions that they encountered during moral struggles. In Tolkien's own words, the moral of the tale is "that without the high and noble the simple and vulgar is utterly mean; and without the simple and ordinary the noble and heroic is meaningless" (*Letters*, 160). This theme is recurrent but begins in the First Age of Middle-earth with the story of Ilúvatar and the Valar who symbolize divine law.

Ilúvatar, "The One," is the creator of; and the Valar, or gods of Middle-earth, were exposed to the will of Ilúvatar and bound to obey his will. Divine law is apparent in the all-encompassing knowledge, limitless power, and absolute free will exercised by Ilúvatar. He showed the Valar a vision of Middle-earth and sent them as emissaries there. The Valar realized that Middle-earth did not resemble the vision and that it was their employ to create the vision in preparation for the arrival of the Children of Ilúvatar—Elves, blessed with immortality, and Men, blessed with mortality. The Valar's power stemmed from their knowledge of Ilúvatar's vision. They exercised delegated authority from Ilúvatar to subcreate his vision.

Before Elves and Men arrived on Middle-earth, one of the Valar, Yavanna, created Ents. Ents were symbols of rational thought and the theory of natural law propounded by St. Thomas Aquinas, which holds that law is innate, can be derived from nature, and is binding upon society in the absence of positive or created law. Ents are the oldest living rational beings on Middle-earth. They separate themselves from the struggles of other Middle-earth creatures and do not have a positive law system or government. They are free of the dominion of Elves or Men and do not bother themselves with their concerns. However, when the forests and trees are threatened, Ents become angered and act violently in defense of the natural world.

This is in direct opposition to the positive law system of the other races in Middle-earth that rely on hierarchy and negotiated law. The history and politics of Men and Elves were intertwined, "the Elder Children, doomed to fade before the Followers (Men), and to live ultimately only by the thin line of their blood that was mingled with that of Men, among whom it was the only real claim to 'nobility'" (*Letters*, 176).

The claim to nobility can be traced through the story of Fëanor, one of the High-elves who dwelt among the Valar. He created the Silmarils, the fairest gems ever created, and when darkness came over Valinor, he was asked by the Valar to break them to release the light they contained. He refused. Darkness swept over Valinor, and the Silmarils were stripped from Fëanor's possession. He departed Valinor with his seven sons and other kinfolk. Before departing, Fëanor cursed Morgoth, who had stolen the gems, and with his sons swore an unbreakable oath, "vowing to pursue with vengeance and hatred to the ends of the World Vala, Demon, Elf, or Man as yet unborn, or any creature great or small, good or evil, that time should bring forth unto the end of days, whoso should hold or take or keep a Silmaril from their possession" (*S*, 83). During the flight from Valinor, Fëanor and his kin murdered their kinsman and stole their ships. This was the first Kinslaying, and Fëanor and his house were cursed by the Valar. Fëanor renounced the curse (or the Doom of Mandos), renewed the vow, and continued on with his sons.

The legal import of the Doom of Mandos came many years after it was first incurred, when Beren, a Man whose father allied with an Elf, descended from kinsman slaughtered by Fëanor fell in love with Lúthien, daughter of Thingol, brother to Olwë, king of the slaughtered. Thingol manipulated Beren into swearing an oath to retrieve one of the Silmarils from Morgoth's crown, before he would be allowed to take the hand of Lúthien. Beren set out, and Lúthien escaped her father's prison to pursue Beren. She was waylaid by Celegorm, Fëanor's son, whom she told of the oath sworn by Beren. Mention of the Silmarils sent Celegorm into a rage, and he vowed to kill Beren before allowing him to have possession of the Silmaril.

Fëanor's oath and the Doom of Mandos extended beyond the positive law systems established in Middle-earth. It was a blood oath that could not be broken and was doomed to cause suffering among kin. Beren did die pursuing the Silmaril, but Lúthien interceded with Mandos, sacrificed her immortality and returned to Middle-earth with Beren to live and die together.

Aragorn is a direct descendant of Beren and Lúthien. He further intertwined the Elvish and

Human bloodlines by marrying Arwen Evenstar, descendant of both the house of the Elves slaughtered by Fëanor, through her mother, and the marriage of Beren and Lúthien, through her father. Arwen too was forced to give up her claim to immortality in order to marry Aragorn. Aragorn's birthright to the throne came from the noble blood of the Elves.

However, the Stewards, whose duty it was to protect the throne from being overtaken during the absence of the King, had no legitimate blood-right to the throne. Tolkien said that Denethor "was tainted with mere politics." He did not have claim to the throne and turned from his duty of protecting throne to that of "keeping" the throne (*Letters*, 241). Similar to the situation in Shakespeare's *Macbeth*, Denethor, like Lady Macbeth, was driven to madness when he realized that he had no right to the throne and would be unable to keep it. After his death, Faramir, his son, took over the position of Steward for the King.

At the end of the story, Aragorn pronounced judgments against participants of the War of the Ring. Aragorn changed the law of governance by naming Faramir Prince of Ithilien, instead of disclaiming his nobility as without birthright. This is a subtle legal development, shifting from focusing on inheritance to focus on the individual achievement. Although there was a king still, the right to govern was now based on personal achievement, not solely the family tree, which in turn opens the possibility of replacing rulers who have a birthright but are poor governors with those without "nobility" but who will be reliable rulers.

JENIFFER G. HARGROVES

Further Reading

The Columbia Electronic Encyclopedia. 6th ed. New York: Columbia University Press, 2003. s.v. "natural law." http://www.answers.com/topic/natural-law (accessed September 17, 2005).

Posner, Richard A. *Law and Literature*. Cambridge: Harvard University Press, 1998.

Shakespeare, William. "Macbeth." In *The Complete Works of William Shakespeare*. New York: Gramercy Books, 1997.

Shippey, Tom. *J.R.R. Tolkien: Author of the Century*. Boston, MA: Houghton-Mifflin, 2001.

Tolkien, J.R.R. "On Fairy-stories." In *The Tolkien Reader*, 33–99. New York: Ballantine Books, 1966.

See also **Aquinas, Thomas; Aragorn; Arwen; Astronomy and Cosmology, Middle-earth; Christian Readings of Tolkien; Denethor; Elves; Ents; Eru; Fall of Man; Free Will; Hierarchy; Justice and Injustice; Kingship; Law; Power in Tolkien's Works; Shakespeare; Theological and Moral Approaches in Tolkien's Works; Treebeard; Two Trees; Valar**

LAYS OF BELERIAND, THE

This third volume of *The History of Middle-earth* series consists of Tolkien's long narrative poems about the First Age, chiefly the stories of Túrin and of Beren and Lúthien that are central to his legendarium, plus a few fragments.

The Lay of the Children of Húrin dates from 1920 to 1925 and exists in two versions, both found in manuscript and typescript. The first version opens with the capture of Túrin's father Húrin after the Battle of Unnumbered Tears. When Húrin refuses to betray his friends and allies, Morgoth curses his wife and children and places an enchantment on Húrin whereby he will witness his family's evil fate without being able to help them. Túrin's mother, Morwen, sends the child to be fostered by Thingol, King of the Elves of Doriath, a forested land protected from Morgoth by the power of Queen Melian that Túrin is able to reach, thanks to meeting and being guided by Beleg the great bowman. Túrin grows into a redoubtable warrior with Beleg as his constant companion in arms, but, when by mischance he slays an Elf (here called Orgof, but Saeros in later versions), he flees and (this element makes its first appearance in the story in this version) gathers a band of rough outlaws about him. Beleg joins him and they turn the band into a guerilla force against Morgoth, but one of the outlaws betrays them (in later versions the traitor is instead Mîm the Dwarf), and all are killed by Orcs, save Beleg, who is left for dead, and Túrin, who is taken prisoner. After being healed by Queen Melian, Beleg tracks down the Orcs. On the way, he meets another Elf (here called Flinding, but Gwindor in later versions), who is himself escaping from Morgoth's dungeons, and together they locate their quarry and carry an unconscious Túrin away from his captors. Túrin, awaking in the dark, mistakes his rescuers for Orcs and rashly kills Beleg. He is horrified upon discovering this but is brought back to his senses by the magical waters of the springs of Ivrin (this part of the story has its fullest treatment in this version). Flinding returns to his own land, Nargothrond, bringing Túrin with him, and again Túrin becomes a leader of Elves in the war against Morgoth, winning the love of the Elf princess Finduilas (also called Failivrin). Here the poem breaks off.

The second version of this *Lay* begins again, using many passages unchanged from the first version but also expanding it greatly, especially in the scenes where an increasingly angry Morgoth tries and fails to corrupt Húrin. It continues through Túrin's fostering in Doriath but breaks off just before Orgof would have been introduced to insult Túrin's mother and precipitate their fatal quarrel.

The saga of Túrin is grim in mood in all versions, but this *Lay* is particularly so at many points, as in the sudden savagery of the flung drinking-horn that kills Orgof (in later versions this is not lethal, though it starts a feud that leads to the Elf's death) and the outlaw band that initially will attack anyone until Beleg (rather than Túrin alone, as in later versions) transforms it into a foe only of the evil. The major themes of the story are the tension between fate and free will and the virtues and defects of the heroic ethos that Túrin embodies. Such a world is appropriate for Old English alliterative verse, and both versions of this *Lay* use the traditional metrical types familiar to Tolkien from his scholarly studies. He emulates the half-lines joined by alliteration that he admired in medieval poems like *Beowulf*, also employing standard features such as an occasional "Lo!" where an Anglo-Saxon poet would have said *hwæt* to command attention.

Some fragmentary verses included in this volume are also in the tradition of alliterative verse: one is a lay describing the flight of the Elves from Valinor to Middle-earth; another is apparently background to the story of Eärendil the Mariner, and one is on the fall of the kingdom of Gondolin. A chart by Tolkien is included that analyzes the Old English metrical types in several lines of the first fragment.

Most of the remainder of the volume is devoted to *The Lay of Leithian*, a title that Tolkien translated as "Release from Bondage" without explaining precisely what that meant to him. It was composed (and much revised) from about 1925 to 1931. In 1929, C.S. Lewis read what was then available, and, probably in the following year, he wrote a mock-scholarly analysis (included in this volume), treating it as an anonymous old text in variant manuscripts, a device allowing him both to censure and to praise it diplomatically.

This lay opens with a description of King Thingol and his daughter Lúthien in Doriath. To the north, Barahir and a small band of Men resist Morgoth but are betrayed, and all are slain by Orcs except Barahir's son Beren, who avenges his father before fleeing to Doriath. Beren and Lúthien meet and fall in love, and, to win her hand, Beren embarks on a quest to regain one of the Silmarils stolen by Morgoth. He obtains the aid of Felagund, king of the Elves of Nargothrond, but their party is captured by Thû (called Sauron in later versions) and killed one by one. Lúthien magically escapes from her father's guards then is waylaid by the sons of Fëanor, who also seek to recover the Silmarils their father had made. But, with the help of Huan, the hound of Valinor, she escapes them also, and she and Huan rescue Beren from Thû. Since Beren is honor-bound to keep his vow, the reunited lovers go on to Morgoth's

fortress, where Lúthien puts the Dark Lord and his court into an enchanted sleep. As they flee with a Silmaril, they are confronted by the great wolf Carcharoth, and the lay breaks off as the wolf's jaws close on Beren's hand. Tolkien did not take the story any further when, in about 1949–50, he began a revision published in this volume as *The Lay of Leithian Recommenced*, but he expanded the story of how Barahir was betrayed and improved many of the verses.

Leithian is a quest story that makes excellent use of traditional motifs such as the bride-price, magical objects like cloaks of invisibility and jewels of power, and magical animal helpers. It deals with themes of truth and lies, keeping or breaking oaths, and the power of love. The prominence of as strong a female character as Lúthien is an unusual feature in a genre normally dominated by male heroes.

Tolkien chose to use octosyllabic couplets for the story of Beren and Lúthien, a verse form associated with medieval romance and thus more appropriate than alliterative meter to a tale of love overcoming great obstacles. This form has an inherent danger of monotony, which he avoids to a large degree (if not entirely) by such means as ending a sentence within a line (and sometimes then beginning a new paragraph) so that the rhymes are not stressed and rhyming English with Elvish words so that the rhymes are not overly familiar. Too often, he uses *do* and *doth* for scansion rather than for emphasis, and many of his revisions are to correct this. He loves to use old words, so Christopher Tolkien provides a glossary to help the nonspecialist.

Christopher Tolkien's editorial work is considerable. He sets forth the evidence for dating the texts; notes newly added story elements, as well as changes from earlier versions and changes made in later ones; discusses variant readings; and quotes from his father's outlines and sketches of the stories. His love for and his intimate knowledge of his father's writing make him a useful guide.

The lays both of Beren and Lúthien and of Túrin are examples of Tolkien's penchant for paying homage to older literature by writing modern works in the same tradition. Most critics do not consider his poetry to be as successful as his prose, but he shows much skill in developing complicated plots and characters and in describing natural scenery, and he achieves some passages of lyrical beauty and some of mythic power.

RICHARD C. WEST

Further Reading

Shippey, Tom. *The Road to Middle-earth: How J.R.R. Tolkien Created a New Mythology*. Revised and Expanded edition. Boston, MA: Houghton Mifflin, 2001.

West, Richard C. "Real-World Myth in a Secondary World: Mythological Aspects in the Story of Beren and Lúthien." In *Tolkien the Medievalist*, edited by Jane Chance, 259–67. London: Routledge, 2003.

See also **Beren; Eärendil; Lúthien; Melian; Thingol, Elwë, Elu Singollo; Túrin**

LEECHBOOK AND *HERBARIUM*

The major medical works surviving in Old English are the *Læceboc*, generally known as Bald's *Leechbook* (ca. 950) and the *Old English Herbarium*. Bald's *Leechbook* (London BL Royal 12.D, xvii) consists of three books, the first two largely drawn from Latin texts and the third featuring more native English material, including more charms and other "magical" remedies. The *Old English Herbarium* exists in four manuscripts, one with illustrations, and falls into two parts. The first, focusing on herbal remedies, is a translation of the *Herbarium of Pseudo-Apuleius*, as well as other Latin sources; the second is a translation of the *Medicina de Quadrupedibus* attributed to Sextus Placitus and focuses on remedies derived from animals. The first part is divided into 185 chapters, each entry giving the various names for the plant, usually Latin and Old English; sometimes its habitat and appearance; and finally its medical uses. The second part is arranged in 14 chapters and gives the disease or ailment first, followed by the animal-derived remedy thought to be efficacious. In addition to Bald's *Leechbook* and the *Old English Herbarium*, two other texts should be mentioned, the *Lacnunga* Manuscript (London BL Harley 585), an eleventh-century, rather haphazard, collection of remedies (*lacnunga* means "healings" or "cures") that features a significant number of charms and magical remedies, and the *Peri Didaxeon* "Concerning Schools of Medicine" (London BL Harley 6,258), ca. 1200.

Tolkien's familiarity with these texts is likely, given the existence of Thomas Cockayne's edition (1864–66) and Tolkien's general familiarity with the entire Old English corpus. In addition, Tolkien's interest in names is well known, and in a 1944 letter discussing *foxglove* he notes that a form of the Anglo-Saxon name occurs "in old herbals" (it occurs in both the *Lacnunga* and the *Old English Herbarium*, in two forms); the discussion betrays a general interest in and familiarity with English plant names and references as well his own practice of invention (*Letters*, 106). Tolkien's preface to *The Fellowship of the Ring*, "Concerning Pipe-weed," recalls such "old herbals," and his herb-master in *The Return of the King* betrays knowledge of the format of the *Old English Herbarium* in his insistence on answering Aragorn's request for *kingsfoil* by listing the various names by which the herb is known; Aragorn interrupts him by supplying yet another name, this one in Quenya. Furthermore, Tolkien's description, in a 1954 letter, of Aragorn's healing as possibly "magical" is accompanied by a definition in line with the medicomagical practices evident in the Old English sources: "a blend of magic with pharmacy and 'hypnotic' processes" (*Letters*, 200). The name *kingsfoil* itself recalls various plant names compounded on *-foil* (*cinquefoil, milfoil*), as well as *kingspear*, or *asphodel*. In the *Old English Herbarium*, *kingspear* is known as *wudurofe* or *wuduhrofe* (woodruff), or *astularegia* (Latin), and is noted for its aroma and its usefulness on wounds to promote healing. Also noteworthy, given Tolkien's designation of *lembas* as the "way bread of the elves," is *wegbræde* (way-bread), which appears throughout the *Lacnunga* (most famously in the *Nine Herbs Charm*), the *Herbarium*, and Bald's *Leechbook*, noted for its power and resilience. Lastly, the *Lacnunga* mentions a recipe for a salve to cure headache and limb ailments that must be stirred by a spoon made of *cwicbeam* (Quickbeam).

YVETTE KISOR

Further Reading

Cockayne, Thomas Oswald, ed. *Leechdoms, Wortcunning and Starcraft of Early England*. 3 vols. Rerum Britannicarum Medii Ævi Scriptores 35. London: Longman, Green, Longman, Roberts, and Green, 1864–66.

DeVriend, Hubert Jan, ed. *The Old English Herbarium and Medicina de Quadrupedibus*. Early English Text Society, o.s., 286. London: Oxford University Press, 1984.

Pollington, Stephen. *Leechcraft: Early English Charms, Plant Lore, and Healing*. Norfolk, UK: Anglo-Saxon Books, 2000.

See also **Charms; Elf-Shot; Folklore;** *Lembas*; **Magic in Middle-earth; Nature; Plants; Trees**

LEEDS

Leeds is an industrial town in Yorkshire and home of Leeds University. Tolkien taught at Leeds from 1920 through 1926, first as Reader then as Professor of English Language.

Tolkien's initial task at Leeds, under Professor of English George Gordon, was to organize the Anglo-Saxon and Middle English syllabus into a scheme that would be popular and philologically sound. The result was an English program divided into what Tolkien called "A and B" schemes: the A-scheme for students of modern literature, the B-scheme for philologists. Years later, Tolkien was to suggest renaming the Oxford curriculum thus, without success. The A and B schemes remained the basis for the Leeds English syllabus for decades after Tolkien departed. Tolkien codified into teaching practice at Leeds the belief that he always held, that philology and literature were and should be inseparable.

Tolkien taught busily and successfully at Leeds; the B, or philology, scheme that he supervised grew from about 5 percent of all English students to nearly a third during his time there. Tolkien taught courses in Old English, Middle English, Germanic philology, Gothic, Old Norse, and Medieval Welsh. In addition, partly to attract students and partly for their own enjoyment, Tolkien and E.V. Gordon formed an undergraduate Viking Club, which met to drink beer and to read Old English and Old Norse texts—some authentic and some invented.

In 1922, George Gordon left Leeds University and was replaced by Lascelles Abercrombie. In 1924, Tolkien was appointed professor of English language, a new post created just for him. In 1925, however, he applied and was accepted to the Rawlinson and Bosworth Professorship of Anglo-Saxon at Oxford. His early departure from the Leeds professorship was somewhat awkward and meant that he continued to lecture at Leeds through 1926, during the same year that he was also beginning his duties at Oxford.

Tolkien's time at Leeds was one of his most energetic and prolific, and he remembered the experience fondly—although he recalled later in life that he had neglected his religion while there. Although it is sometimes alleged that the industrial surroundings and working-class Yorkshire students must have been disagreeable to Tolkien, there is no evidence from Tolkien's letters or writings to support this contention; indeed, he always wrote and spoke well of his Leeds students in his reminiscences later in life.

It was during his time at Leeds that Tolkien published his *Middle English Vocabulary* (1922) and that Tolkien and E.V. Gordon published their edition of *Sir Gawain and the Green Knight* (1925). Tolkien also published, in local and university journals, "The Cat and the Fiddle" (1923), an early version of the song that Frodo sings in the Prancing Pony (*FR*, I, ix, 170–71), and "Light as Leaf on Lindentree" (1925), an early version of Strider's song about Lúthien (*FR*, I, xi, 204–05). He also worked on *The Book of Lost Tales* and began to put into verse the tales of Túrin and Beren.

CHESTER N. SCOVILLE

Further Reading

Carpenter, Humphrey. *J.R.R. Tolkien: A Biography*. London: George Allen & Unwin, 1977.

Shippey, Tom. *The Road to Middle-earth: How J.R.R. Tolkien Created a New Mythology*. Revised and Expanded edition. Boston, MA: Houghton Mifflin, 2003.

See also **Book of Lost Tales I; Book of Lost Tales II; Gordon, E.V.; Lays of Beleriand; Leeds University Verse 1914–24; Middle English Vocabulary**

LEEDS UNIVERSITY VERSE 1914–24

A more ambitious follow-up to *A Northern Venture* (1923), *Leeds University Verse 1914–24*, compiled and edited by the English School Association at Leeds, builds on the success of the earlier volume, expanding the scope to include verse written by members of Leeds University during the previous ten years. It was published in May 1924 in an edition of five hundred copies.

Like its predecessor, *Leeds University Verse 1914–24* is arranged alphabetically by author, but the new book is significantly larger, containing fifty-two poems by thirty-four poets. Contributors include Tolkien (three poems) and his colleagues and friends Lascelles Abercrombie (two poems), Wilfred Rowland Childe (three poems), and G.H. Cowling, E.V. Gordon, and A.H. Smith (one poem each). Other contributors include William Fryer Harvey, Storm Jameson, Herbert Read, and the publisher, Sydney Matthewman.

Tolkien's contributions are "An Evening in Tavrobel," "The Lonely Isle," and "The Princess Ni." All are published here for the first time. "An Evening in Tavrobel" remains unreprinted, and "The Lonely Isle" is reprinted in John Garth's Tolkien and the Great War (145). "The Princess Ni" was expanded and rewritten as "Princess Mee" in *The Adventures of Tom Bombadil*. The original version has not been reprinted.

Lascelles Abercrombie (1881–1938) was probably the most well-known contributor to the book, as a poet and as a literary critic. He was appointed professor of English literature at Leeds in 1922. His two poems were chronologically outside the described period of the book, having appeared in *Interludes and Poems* (1908).

Wilfred Rowland Childe's three poems are representative of his ecclesiastical Gothic style. Both of the poems by G.H. Cowling (1881–1946) and A.H. Smith (1903–67) are written in Yorkshire dialect. Smith's poem "The Country and the Town," is revised from its publication in Smith's booklet, *The Merry Shire* (1923).

E.V. Gordon's "A Ballad of Tristram" is the longest poem in the book. It is adapted from an unspecified Scandinavian version. In Gordon's version,

Tristram lays dying and seeks to see Isoult. His messengers are sent with instructions that, when returning, blue sails will signal that his lady comes. But the ship bringing Isoult bears black sails, and Tristram dies on learning this news. Isoult, arriving later, dies at his feet.

Of the other contributors, William Fryer Harvey (1885–1937) is remembered as a distinguished Quaker and a writer of ghost stories. His poems center on death and are reprinted from his rare collection *Laughter and Ghosts* (1919). Jameson (1891–1986) would later become well known as a novelist. Read (1893–1968) had already published a few books of poems and would soon become known as a distinguished literary and social critic.

A review appeared in the *Times Literary Supplement* on May 29, 1924, giving some details of the contents, but Tolkien's contributions are not mentioned.

Tolkien published in one other collection associated with the Swan Press of Leeds, a slim volume, *Realities: An Anthology of Verse* (1927), done to benefit the Queen's Hospital for Children, Hackney. It was edited by Gwendoline Sybel Tancred (1869–?) and copublished with Gay and Hancock of London. Tolkien's contribution was "The Nameless Land."

DOUGLAS A. ANDERSON

Further Reading

Garth, John. *Tolkien and the Great War: The Threshold of Middle-earth*. London: HarperCollins, 2003.

Hammond, Wayne G., with the assistance of Douglas A. Anderson. *J.R.R. Tolkien: A Descriptive Bibliography*. Winchester, UK: St. Paul's Bibliographies; New Castle, DE: Oak Knoll Books, 1993.

Tomkinson, Geoffrey Stewart. *A Select Bibliography of the Principal Modern Presses Public and Private in Great Britain and Ireland*. London: First Edition Club, 1928.

See also **Adventures of Tom Bombadil (Collection); Gordon, E.V.; Northern Venture, A; Poems by Tolkien: The History of Middle-earth; Poems by Tolkien in Other Languages**

LEGOLAS

The Elf Legolas, son of Thranduil, King of the Elves of Northern Mirkwood, is a major character in *The Lord of the Rings*. Translated as "Greenleaf" in the Common Speech of Middle-earth, his name is a dialect variant spelling of the Sindarin word *laegolas*, which is a compound of words meaning a fresh and green collection of leaves (*Letters*, 282, 382).

Legolas first appears in "The Council of Elrond" chapter, where he tells of Gollum's escape from captivity in Mirkwood (*FR*, II, ii, 268–69). Elrond chooses Legolas to represent the Elves as one of the nine members of the Fellowship of the Ring. Legolas accompanies Frodo on the journey toward Mordor until the events at Amon Hen split up the Fellowship. Legolas thereafter accompanies Aragorn and Gimli until the end of the War of the Ring. With them, he helps track the Orcs that capture Merry and Pippin at Amon Hen; he goes to Edoras where Gandalf rouses Théoden to action; he fights at Helm's Deep under siege from the Orcs of Isengard; he witnesses the dismissal of Saruman from the White Council; he rides the Paths of the Dead beneath the Dwimorberg, and he fights for Gondor at the Battle of the Pelennor Fields.

Legolas has many strengths. He has remarkable endurance: he shows little fatigue while pursuing the Uruk-hai on foot from Amon Hen into Rohan (*TT*, II, ii, 31), and he alone among the Fellowship is unaffected by the blizzard on Caradhras, where he treads lightly over the drifts while others toil through them (*FR*, II, ii, 305–6). An expert with the bow, Legolas can kill with precision: he slays the Warg captain in Hollin with an arrow through its throat and two Orcs in Moria in the same manner during the fight in the Chamber of Mazarbul in Moria (*FR*, II, iii, 305–06). With a bow of the Galadhrim, a gift from Lady Galadriel, he slays the winged steed of a Nazgûl flying at a great height with a single shot by moonlight (*FR*, II, ix, 403). This last deed emphasizes his powerful eyesight: Legolas's vision is of great use during the pursuit of the Orcs into Rohan; Gandalf calls upon his far-seeing eyes more than once, and from Edoras he can even see, more than four hundred miles away, the glowing crater of Mount Doom (*TT*, III, vi, 121). Legolas is also a skillful horseman who easily tames the Rohan steed Arod (*LotR*, II, 42). Tolkien wrote, in an undated note quoted by Christopher Tolkien, that Legolas was "tall as a young tree, lithe, immensely strong, able swiftly to draw a great war-bow and shoot down a Nazgûl, endowed with the tremendous vitality of Elvish bodies, so hard and resistant to hurt that he went only in light shoes over rock or through snow, the most tireless of all the Fellowship" (*Lost Tales II*, 327).

These many strengths and abilities are founded on Legolas's steadfastness and courage: he can endure the heart-penetrating gaze of Galadriel (*FR*, II, vii, 372), and he shows no fear either during the battles at Helm's Deep and Pelennor Fields or in riding the Paths of the Dead (*RK*, V, ii, 59). Notably, the only moment in which Legolas's courage appears to falter occurs when he, first of all the company, sees and names the Balrog in Moria (*FR*, II, v, 343–44).

Legolas knows many songs and tales of the Mirkwood Elves. Through them, he knows the nature of Lórien and its history. He knows some of the song of Amroth and Nimrodel, both in the Elvish of Mirkwood and in the Westron Speech (*FR*, II, vi, 353–55). Yet Legolas is apparently not a loremaster: he does not assist Gandalf (though the text does not say he cannot assist him) in guessing the Elvish password that opens the Moria Gates, and he does not have the skill to translate for the hobbits the songs sung in tribute to Gandalf in Lórien (*FR*, II, vii, 374). However, when Tolkien makes him one of the singers of the dirge for Boromir, it appears as though Legolas has a poetic gift for spontaneous composition of verse in rhymed couplets of iambic heptameter (*TT*, III, i, 20).

Through their shared experiences, Legolas and Gimli form a fast friendship exceedingly rare among Elves and Dwarves. Their affection first begins to appear when Legolas persuades the Elves of Lórien to admit Gimli within their borders (*FR*, II, vi, 358). However, it does not develop immediately: Legolas grows angry when Gimli refuses to accept a blindfold in Lórien unless everyone in the Fellowship is also blindfolded (*FR*, II, vi, 362). Later, Legolas supports Gimli when Éomer threatens him (*TT*, III, ii, 35). Their friendship grows at the Battle of Helm's Deep, where they compete in killing Orcs. They also fight together at the Pelennor Fields. And, they ride together upon Legolas's horse, Arod. After the end of the War of the Ring, they visit the Glittering Caves at Helm's Deep and then journey together into Fangorn Forest. Gimli is later named Elf-friend because of his friendship with Legolas.

Galadriel rightly predicts that Legolas will long for the West when he hears the cries of gulls near the sea. Though this longing awakens in him during the story, Legolas does not act upon it immediately. Instead, he remains in Middle-earth for 122 years after the destruction of the One Ring. Then Legolas builds a ship in Ithilien and sails into the West, and, for the sake of their friendship, Gimli goes with him (*RK*, Appendix A, 362; Appendix B, 378).

Tolkien first used the name Legolas in approximately 1920 in "The Fall of Gondolin" for a Gondothlim Elf who, gifted with keen night vision, helps lead the survivors of Gondolin's destruction over the plain of Tumladin. Tolkien made an "Appendix on Names" for the tale in which he states that this early Legolas "liveth still in Tol Eressëa." Because Tolkien did not emend this statement later to connect the Legolas of *The Lord of the Rings* to this earlier Legolas, we can infer that he chose to keep the two characters distinct (*Lost Tales II*, 189, 217).

PAUL EDMUND THOMAS

See also **Aragorn;** *Book of Lost Tales II*; **Boromir; Elrond; Elves; Elves: Kindreds and Migrations; Éomer; Éowyn; Frodo; Galadriel; Gandalf; Gimli; Gollum;** *Lord of the Rings*; **Merry; Mirkwood; Pippin; Sam; Saruman; Théoden**

LEMBAS

(Sindarin, derived from older *lenn-mbass*, "journey-bread"; Quenya *coimas*, "life-bread"; stem MBAS, "knead"; Quenya *masta*, Noldorin *bast*, "bread.")

Lembas, or the waybread of the Elves, is known to the readers of *The Lord of the Rings* as the cakes that Galadriel presents the members of the Fellowship at their departure from Lórien. Like some of the other gifts (e.g., the cloaks or the rope), it partakes of the power of the Eldar without being "magical" in the narrower sense of the meaning and is only to be used by those friendly towards the Eldar. Thus, the Orcs despoiling Frodo's gear would not touch it, and Gollum seems to be unable to eat it. The Elf Beleg, in the "Narn i Hîn Húrin" (*UT*, 195ff.), refuses to let the Dwarf Mîm eat from the *lembas* he had been given by Melian.

As Tolkien stated in one of his letters (*Letters*, no. 210, p. 274), an analysis in a laboratory would discover no "chemical properties of *lembas* that made it superior to other cakes of wheat-meal" (*Letters*, 274). And yet "one will keep a traveller on his feet for a day of long labour, even if he be one of the tall Men of Minas Tirith" (*FR*, II, viii, 386). As such, it serves as a device for making credible the long marches with little provisions.

The Human members of the Fellowship are not the first mortals to receive *lembas* from an Elven queen. Túrin, upon departing from Doriath, receives the sword Anglachel from Thingol and *lembas* from the Maia Melian (*S*, 243). It will not only provide indispensable nourishment but also prove an efficacious medicine to treat the sick and exhausted.

There is, however, another, even more significant, side to *lembas*. Tolkien hints at the "religious" quality of *lembas* and does not reject a critic's equation of the waybread with the viaticum (i.e., the host) (*Letters*, 288).

This religious dimension, which has been only implicit in *The Lord of the Rings* or hinted at in *The Silmarillion*, is rendered explicit in a short text by Tolkien titled "Of *Lembas*" (*Peoples*, 403–5). It is dated by Christopher Tolkien to the time between 1951 and 1960—and thus seems to be contemporary with the writing of "Of Tuor and his Coming to Gondolin" and the "Narn i Hîn Húrin." *Lembas*, or and the waybread of the Elves, respectively, is mentioned in the former (*UT*, 44) and plays a more prominent role in the latter.

The information given in "Of *Lembas*" is presumably based on Pengoloth's answer to Ælfwine's question, "What is the *coimas* of the Eldar?" The origin of *lembas* is traced to the Vala Yavanna, who prepared it from the corn that grew in the fields of Aman and who gave it to the Eldar to sustain them on the Great Journey. The growing, harvesting, and grinding of the corn in the lands of Middle-earth were the responsibility of the Yavannildi, Elven-women who had the privilege of handling the corn and the flour. Ever since, it has been traditionally the prerogative of the highest women among the Elves to keep and to give away the *lembas*, which is why they were called *massánie* or *besain*; that is, the Lady or breadgiver. Tolkien alludes to the etymology of English "lady" < Old English hlǣfdīge, that is, "bread" (OE hlāf) and "knead" (OE *dīg(an)).

Since the corn from which *lembas* flour is ground retains the strong life of Aman, it is said that mortals who often eat from *lembas* become weary of their mortality and begin to long for the Undying Lands. The Eldar have therefore been commanded not to let mortals partake of it except in special cases—of which Túrin and the Fellowship seem to have been the only ones we know about.

THOMAS HONEGGER

Further Reading

Tolkien, J.R.R. "Of *Lembas*." *Peoples*, 403–5.

See also **Food**

LETTERS OF J.R.R. TOLKIEN, THE

For scholars of Tolkien's stories, as even early reviewers recognized, *The Letters of J.R.R. Tolkien* "is a trove worthy of protection by one of his dragons" (Bruckner, 7).

Before *Letters* was published in 1981, more than 40 of Tolkien's letters had appeared in books, newspapers, fan magazines, and, increasingly after Tolkien's death, in auction catalogues (Hammond, 1992, 353–61). Some of these are republished in *Letters*, but most of the collection was previously unknown. Humphrey Carpenter, assisted by Christopher Tolkien, selected 354 letters from thousands he had read while researching Tolkien's biography (Anderson, 219). Tolkien's publishers at George Allen & Unwin and his sons, Christopher and Michael, provide the greatest number of letters in the collection, almost all

of which date from 1937 to 1973, with eight letters for 1914–26.

Despite frustration with critics' attempts to connect his life and fiction—"I do not really belong *inside* my invented history" (*Letters*, 398)—Tolkien frequently invokes Orcs, Hobbits, and other figures from his stories when discussing his experiences and opinions, as *Letters* illuminates both Tolkien's life and tales. While Carpenter's selection of letters emphasizes the best-known works, there are "fresh insights into everything Tolkien ever wrote" (Johnson 1986, 134–35). Many of these insights are achieved by Tolkien himself, commenting on his intentions, his methods, and even his mistakes.

The Lord of the Rings receives the fullest analysis in *Letters*, but Tolkien considers several other works at length, including *The Hobbit*, "Leaf by Niggle," and *The Adventures of Tom Bombadil*. Tolkien feels that *The Hobbit* contains his "favorite 'motifs' and characters" and ponders its debt to *Beowulf*, the *Eldar Edda*, and the "Silmarillion" (*Letters*, 29, 31). "Leaf by Niggle," he says, is partly "explicable in biographical terms," with *LotR* as the story's Tree, but it is "mythical" not allegorical (320–21). Concerning *The Adventures of Tom Bombadil*, Tolkien identifies medieval allusions in "Bombadil Goes Boating," and expresses gratitude for W.H. Auden's praise of "The Sea-bell" (318–19, 379).

Tolkien discusses *LotR* from its inception through his last year. The value of *Letters* to studies of *LotR*'s creation is shown by frequent citation of the collection in Volumes VI–IX of *The History of Middle-earth*. Beyond that, *Letters* suggests connections between the story and Tolkien's experiences, including an awareness of the "darkness of the present days" coloring *LotR* as early as 1938, though he later notes that "it is precisely against the darkness of the world that comedy arises, and is best when that is not hidden" (41, 120).

Another feature of *LotR*'s development that *Letters* shows is Tolkien's sense of discovering rather than creating. He writes of Faramir, for example, "I am sure I did not invent him, I did not even want him" (79). Such "discoveries" continue after *LotR* is published, as readers' questions lead Tolkien to invent Wizards who fail as "missionaries to 'enemy-occupied' lands," and to a role for Ents in the "Silmarillion," where previously they had not appeared (280, 344). He even explores alternative storylines for *LotR:* what if Gandalf had claimed the Ring, or if Sam had not spoiled Gollum's repentance in the story's "most tragic moment" (329–32)?

Here are two further examples of Tolkien's exhaustive examination of his creation: Responding to a query about the apparent absence of religion from

Middle-earth, Tolkien outlines a history in which monotheism becomes a kind of "negative truth" (203–7). And answering a charge of archaism in *LotR*'s language, he rewrites a passage to show how modern idioms would fail the story (225–26).

Looming in the background, beginning with the collection's first letter, is *The Silmarillion*, which comes to the fore in a long letter of 1951 to a potential publisher, summarizing the story of the entire legendarium of *The Silmarillion* and *LotR* together (several pages of this letter omitted from the collection have since been published [Tolkien 2005, 742–49]). Here, Tolkien relates how his love of language and fairy stories inspired him to create a collection of legends possessed of "fair elusive beauty," how *The Hobbit* was the mythology's "mode of descent to earth" that led to *LotR*, and how the whole "is mainly concerned with Fall, Mortality and the Machine" (143–61).

However, that a story concerns mortality means just that it is "written by a Man" (*Letters*, 262). In its glimpses of the life of the man behind Middle-earth, *Letters* reveals some provocative opinions on marriage, government, and religion, though Tom Shippey ("A Philologist," 975) argues that Tolkien's biases "were cohesive, and cogent, and . . . accessible to reason." Certainly Tolkien's reason leads him in surprising directions, such as to sympathy for the "anti-regimentation and anti-drabness" of the 1960s youth movement (*Letters*, 393).

Letters is "vital to understanding Tolkien's creativity" (Bratman, 74–75) and is even more useful following a fourfold expansion of its index in 1999. However, there are several reasons the collection must be consulted with care. There is a difficulty in being sure of to what Tolkien is responding: The letters of his correspondents are not included, and only a few items, like Auden's review of *The Return of the King*, are available for comparison with their synopses in *Letters* (238). Shippey (Road, xviii) identifies a further danger of misunderstanding Tolkien's obliquely critical style, the "politeness-language of Old Western Man." Even where the meaning is unmistakable, there may be contradictions among different letters or between *Letters* and Tolkien's other works, as Verlyn Flieger (147–58) observes of Tolkien's oft-quoted assertion, "In all my works I take the part of trees as against all their enemies" (*Letters*, 419).

Finally, there is a need for fuller publication of Tolkien's letters. First, many of the published letters were edited for length or to omit private matters or were even from drafts that may represent ideas rejected by Tolkien. Second, the selection of letters forces scholars to work with secondhand material: Stenström (310), for example, shows how one phrase

regularly attributed to Tolkien, "a mythology for England," never appears in *Letters* but seems to have been coined in Carpenter's biography. That work and Carpenter's *The Inklings*, though they predate *Letters*, were the first studies to use its rich material, but for all their care and intelligence, they represent only one view of Tolkien. He himself doubted the value of his biography to literary scholarship "in any form less than . . . I alone could write" (*Letters*, 257). Until more of his private papers are released, *Letters* is the best substitute for a Tolkien autobiography.

MERLIN DeTARDO

Primary Sources

Tolkien, J.R.R. "Extracts from a Letter by J.R.R. Tolkien to Milton Waldman, Late 1951, on *The Lord of the Rings*." In *The Lord of the Rings: A Reader's Companion*, edited by Wayne G. Hammond and Christina Scull, 742–49. Boston, MA: Houghton Mifflin, 2005.

Further Reading

Anderson, Douglas A. "Obituary: Humphrey Carpenter." *Tolkien Studies* 2 (2005), 217–24.
Auden, W.H. "At the End of the Quest, Victory." In *A Tolkien Treasury*, edited by Alida Becker, 44–48. Philadelphia: Running Press, 2000.
Bratman, David. "The Literary Value of *The History of Middle-earth*." In *Tolkien's Legendarium: Essays on "The History of Middle-earth*," edited by Verlyn Flieger and Carl F. Hostetter, 69–91. Westport, CT: Greenwood, 2000.
Bruckner, D.J.R. Review of *The Letters of J.R.R. Tolkien*, edited by Humphrey Carpenter. *The New York Times Book Review*, November 15, 1981, 7, 26–27.
Carpenter, Humphrey. *Tolkien: A Biography*. Boston, MA: Houghton Mifflin, 1977.
———. *The Inklings: C.S. Lewis, J.R.R. Tolkien, Charles Williams, and Their Friends*. Boston, MA: Houghton Mifflin, 1979.
Flieger, Verlyn. "Taking the Part of Trees: Eco-Conflict in Middle-earth." In *J.R.R. Tolkien and His Literary Resonances: Views of Middle-earth*, edited by George Clark and Daniel Timmons, 147–58. Contributions to the Study of Science Fiction and Fantasy, 89. Westport, CT: Greenwood, 2000.
Hammond, Wayne G., with the assistance of Douglas A. Anderson. *J.R.R. Tolkien: A Descriptive Bibliography*. New Castle, DE: Oak Knoll Books, 1993.
Johnson, Judith A. *J.R.R. Tolkien: Six Decades of Criticism*. Westport, CT: Greenwood, 1986.
Scull, Christina, and Wayne G. Hammond. "Corrigenda to the Index to *Letters of J.R.R. Tolkien* (1999)." http://bcn.net/~whammond/addenda/letters.html.
Shippey, Tom. "A Philologist in Purgatory." *Times Literary Supplement*, August 28, 1981, 975–76.
———. *The Road to Middle-earth: How J.R.R. Tolkien Created a New Mythology*. Revised and Expanded edition. Boston, MA: Houghton Mifflin, 2003.

Stenström, Anders. "A Mythology? For England?" In *Proceedings of the J.R.R. Tolkien Centenary Conference 1992*, edited by Patricia Reynolds and Glen H. GoodKnight, 310–14. Milton Keynes, UK, and Altadena, CA: Tolkien Society / Mythopoeic, 1995.

See also **Adventures of Tom Bombadil** (Collection); **Allegory; Death;** *Farmer Giles of Ham*; **Free Will; Frodo; Gandalf; Gollum; Good and Evil;** *Hobbit, The*; **Hobbits; Humor; Immortality; Industrialization;** *Lord of the Rings*; *Lord of the Rings:* **Success of; Mythology for England; Politics; Prose Style; Publishing History; Sam;** *Silmarillion*; *Smith of Wootton Major*; **Tolkien, Christopher; Tolkien, Michael; Tolkien Scholarship: Since 1980; Trees**

LEWIS, C.S. (1898–1963)

Lewis and Tolkien met for the first time on May 11, 1926. Both men were newly appointed members of the English faculty at Oxford University, but their roles were, and were to remain, rather different. Tolkien had been appointed the previous year to the Rawlinson and Bosworth Chair (i.e., professorship) of Anglo-Saxon, and Lewis had been made a Tutorial Fellow in English of Magdalen College. Lewis's main responsibility was to direct the education of the small number of undergraduates who happened to be reading English in that one college. There were then probably no more than ten or fifteen of them at any one time, but the main method of teaching at Oxford then (and for many years after) was the one-on-one tutorial, typically lasting an hour, once a week. To this, conscientious tutors, like Lewis, would add classes on particular topics for students in any one year. Lewis was also bound to give two lecture courses a year, each of seven lectures, to the undergraduates of all colleges; attendance at these was optional, and often small, though Lewis soon attracted large numbers. Tolkien, by contrast, as a professor, had no tutorial responsibilities to undergraduates, even in his own college of Pembroke, but had to give five lecture courses a year and organize the supervision of graduate students, often supervising them himself. Lewis did more teaching than Tolkien for many years, but less administration. Lewis's main responsibility was to his college, Tolkien's to the University School of English.

There were other possible sources of tension between the two men. Tolkien was an English Catholic, Lewis a Northern Irish Protestant. Although both were medievalists, Tolkien's interests were primarily linguistic, Lewis's firmly literary; Tolkien was also oriented towards the earliest periods of English literary record, Lewis towards the later Middle Ages.

Although both men were more than competent in Latin, Greek, and Old and Middle English and Lewis knew at least some Old Norse, in which Tolkien was expert, Lewis was the more convinced classicist, Tolkien much the better Germanist. They might not necessarily take the same side in faculty and syllabus politics.

On the other hand, and more significantly, both men were former infantry officers and combat veterans of the First World War. Both were hostile to and repelled by the new mood of irony, cynicism, and rejection of authority common in British intellectual circles after the trauma of the war. While they might have different views about what to teach from the Middle Ages, both were entirely convinced that it was more important to teach the Middle Ages than contemporary novels, plays, and poetry. They were both, in an entirely literal sense, "reactionaries" against "modernism" in all its forms. Lewis would eventually call himself a "dinosaur," left over from a past age. The two men became friends and remained so until Lewis died. Though the tensions did not entirely go away—notably over the issue of Roman Catholicism—each in his own way supported and stimulated the other. One may well believe that Tolkien would never have completed *The Lord of the Rings* if it had not been for Lewis's continuing enthusiasm and encouragement over more than fifteen years.

There are several biographies of Lewis, some of them eccentric or unreliable, but the basic facts of his life are well known and need be repeated only briefly here. Clive Staples Lewis was born in Belfast on November 29, 1898, second son of Albert Lewis, a police-court solicitor. His mother Flora died when he was nine, and his father sent him and his elder brother to a succession of boarding schools in England and Ireland. His experiences in these, especially the first, were appalling and have been described in his autobiography *Surprised by Joy*. Lewis went on to a private tutor, the much-respected William T. Kirkpatrick, and gained entrance to Oxford as an undergraduate in 1917. As an Irishman, he was exempt from conscription but volunteered to fight in World War I. At this time, he made an agreement with another officer, "Paddy" Moore, that if either survived he would care for the other's dependants, and when Lewis indeed survived his friend (killed in 1918), he assumed responsibility for Moore's mother, Janie. When, after the war, he went back to Oxford as an undergraduate, he set her and her daughter up in a house in Oxford, unknown to his tutors and entirely contrary to normal practice. They continued to live together for many years, till she died in January 1951. This unorthodox *ménage* was later increased by Lewis's elder brother Warren (1895–1973), who retired from the

Army and came to live with them in 1932, thereafter acting also as his younger brother's diarist and amanuensis. Lewis meanwhile graduated in "Greats" (classics, philosophy, ancient history) in 1922, took a further degree in English in 1923, and was elected to his tutorial fellowship in Magdalen in 1925. He remained there, without promotion to a professorship, until in 1954 he accepted the new Chair of Medieval and Renaissance Literature at the University of Cambridge. He continued to live in Oxford and commute to Cambridge, but travel problems and new responsibilities caused some estrangement from Tolkien, as did his late marriage to an American divorcée, Joy Davidman. Lewis died on the same day as American President John F. Kennedy, November 22, 1963.

During his time as professor at Leeds University, Tolkien had set up a small group known as the *Kolbítar*, or "Coal-biters," to read Old Norse sagas in the original language. At Oxford he did this again, and Lewis was invited to join the group. Another unofficial reading group, at University College, was known as "the Inklings." Neither group lasted long, and around 1933 Lewis borrowed the name "Inklings" to describe a loose circle of friends, including several *Kolbítar*, for whom he acted as unofficial convenor. For many years thereafter, Lewis, his brother, Tolkien, and a number of others met frequently if irregularly to talk and exchange ideas and gossip, getting into the habit of meeting either on Thursday evenings at Lewis's college or on Tuesday mornings in the back bar of the Eagle and Child pub on St. Giles. They also often read one another samples of "work in progress." Late in 1929, for instance, Tolkien showed Lewis his unpublished poem *The Gest of Beren and Lúthien*, and Tolkien later read to him parts of the still-developing *Silmarillion*.

Even more momentous was a conversation between the two men on September 19, 1931. Lewis, already moving away from his earlier atheism, explained his reasons for lack of faith to Tolkien, who replied with an argument based on the truth of myth. Tolkien eventually put this into poetic form as *Mythopoeia*, which is addressed "To one [i.e., Lewis] who said that myths were lies and therefore worthless." Tolkien's argument was that all imaginative creations (including his own) must come from God and that the faculty of creating myths is itself in origin divine. Lewis later wrote that the conversation "had a good deal to do" with his final conversion to Christianity a few days later, something that further cemented the bond between the two men.

Another momentous conversation took place at some time in 1936. At this point, both men had strong reasons for feeling anxious or unfulfilled. Both had

committed immense time and effort to writing poetry. Tolkien had sent a collection of poems called *The Trumpets of Faerie* to the publishing firm of Sidgwick and Jackson in 1916 but had had them rejected; since then he had written thousands of lines of his poems on Beren and Túrin, but there was little hope of them ever being published (they appeared posthumously as *The Lays of Beleriand* in 1985). Lewis had had two volumes of poetry published, *Spirits in Bondage* in 1919 and *Dymer* in 1926, but neither had achieved any great sale or reputation. Tolkien had produced little since his coedited work on *Sir Gawain* in 1925, and Lewis only his "allegorical apology for Christianity," *The Pilgrim's Regress* in 1933. It would be no surprise if their Oxford colleagues were beginning to refer to both as "under-published." It is true that Tolkien's essay on "*Beowulf:* The Monsters and the Critics" was about to appear, as was Lewis's extensive academic book *The Allegory of Love*, which introduced the notion of "courtly love" to the academic curriculum and immediately made Lewis a groundbreaking and controversial figure. *The Hobbit* was also close to acceptance. But both men were, as John Rateliff has said, at this date "largely frustrated authors" (Rateliff, 200). What kept them writing was each other.

About this time, as Tolkien repeatedly recorded, he and Lewis made an agreement that each should write "an excursionary 'Thriller': a Space-journey and a Time-journey . . . each discovering myth." Lewis's "Space-journey" appeared in 1938 as *Out of the Silent Planet*, the first volume in his inaccurately named "space-fiction" trilogy—the other two are *Perelandra* (1942) and *That Hideous Strength* (1945). Tolkien's "Time-journey," never completed, was *The Lost Road*, published posthumously in 1987. All four of Lewis's adult novels indeed follow Tolkien's brief account of their agreement in one respect at least, which is that they are all about "discovering myth": in each of them, the hero or heroine discovers that something he or she thought to be "mythical," that is, false, is literally true. In *Silent Planet*, the hero Ransom—generally agreed to be based on Tolkien—discovers the truth of the myth of the Fall of the Angels: Earth is "the Silent Planet," cut off from the rest of the Solar System, because its demiurge or presiding spirit has fallen or been cast out from heaven. Earth is the dominion of Satan. *Perelandra*, meanwhile, reenacts on Venus the myth of the Fall of Man, and in *That Hideous Strength* Merlin, the magician of Arthurian myth, is brought back to life. Lewis's fourth novel for adults, *Till We Have Faces* (1956), is subtitled *A Myth Retold* and indeed retells the Greek myth of Cupid and Psyche, set in a forgotten barbarian kingdom in pre-Christian times.

Tolkien's *The Lost Road* was based more loosely on the myth of Atlantis, with other mythical elements added from Old English legend, but it failed to take off as a narrative.

One major difference between Lewis's successful "Space-journey" and Tolkien's abortive "Time-journey" is pace. Five thousand words into *The Lost Road* and Tolkien's characters are still ruminating on dreams and the history of languages; five thousand words into *Silent Planet*, and Ransom has been kidnapped, bundled into a spaceship, and is on his way to Mars to be sacrificed to unknown powers. It is possible that Lewis made this sudden breakthrough to "thrillerdom" as a result of the influence of Charles Williams (1886–1945), who would become a member of the Inklings in 1939, when his employer, Oxford University Press, moved him to Oxford. In 1936, Williams and Lewis read and admired each other's books almost simultaneously, Williams reading the proofs of *The Allegory of Love* in the course of business, and Lewis reading Williams's occult thriller *The Place of the Lion* (1931) on the recommendation of a friend. The start of *The Place of the Lion* is quite similar to the start of *Silent Planet*, but what Williams seems to have shown Lewis was that intellectual and even academic ideas could be conveyed with the techniques of pulp fiction. From Williams, Lewis learned to popularize.

The success of *Silent Planet* seems to have stimulated in Lewis a sudden and almost prodigious outpouring of writings. His short book *The Problem of Pain* came out in 1940. *The Screwtape Letters* was published serially in 1941 and collected in book form in 1942. At much the same time, Lewis gave a series of lectures on Milton that became *A Preface to Paradise Lost* (1942); the academic work is paralleled in the fiction *Perelandra*. His readiness to give talks to servicemen on RAF stations in the second year of the war led to a request from the BBC to give a series of broadcast talks on "The Christian Faith," and these too became a sequence of three books: *Broadcast Talks* (1942), *Christian Behaviour* (1943), and *Beyond Personality* (1944). Also, 1944 brought the publication of another series of lectures, *The Abolition of Man*, the theme of which was again to be repeated in fictional form in Lewis's dystopian *That Hideous Strength* (1945). *The Great Divorce*, Lewis's "Descent into Hell," also appeared in 1945, followed in 1947 by *Miracles* and in 1952 by *Mere Christianity*. These works, written mostly in the decade 1936–45, established Lewis as probably the most popular lay theologian in the Christian world, whether he was writing theology or fiction, or—as with *The Screwtape Letters* and *The Great Divorce*—something between the two.

It would be only human if Tolkien—at this time, as clear from "Leaf by Niggle" and "The Notion Club Papers," prey to doubts and anxieties about the future of his unfinished works—had felt a certain jealousy at his younger friend's sudden blaze of success, especially as he had in a way been responsible for the start of it all, recommending *Silent Planet* to Stanley Unwin, publisher of *The Hobbit*, when it had failed to find another publisher. Lewis seems to have wished whole-heartedly for Tolkien to repeat his own success. At the end of *Silent Planet*, he drops a hint that any sequel will have to be a time-travel story, as if trying to open a door for Tolkien's projected tale. At the start of *That Hideous Strength*, he again refers to possible further tales of "Numinor" [*sic*] from "my friend, Professor J.R.R. Tolkien," though in both cases he was probably thinking not of *The Lord of the Rings*, begun in late 1937, but of *The Lost Road*, the result of their agreement of 1936. Nevertheless, throughout the war years, Tolkien continued to work on *The Lord of the Rings*, continued to read it in sections to Lewis and the other Inklings, and found in Lewis constant approval and enthusiasm, the value of which cannot even be estimated.

Both men, however, reached their major successes in the 1950s. Tolkien had effectively finished *The Lord of the Rings* by 1949, though complex negotiations with publishers meant that it did not appear till 1954–55. It was then immediately reviewed with great appreciation by Lewis in *Time and Tide* (and with a good deal less appreciation or understanding by critics and journalists elsewhere); despite the hostile or uncomprehending reviews, it immediately started to sell unexpectedly well, a process that has since accelerated beyond anyone's imagination. As his friend finished one major fantasy, Lewis began to write another, *The Chronicles of Narnia*, with all his accustomed speed. *The Lion, the Witch and the Wardrobe* seems indeed to have been begun in 1939 but was left unfinished until ten years later. Lewis then resumed and finished it, and he followed it with the other six volumes of the series, all written by early 1953, though published at annual intervals from 1950 to 1956. Lewis's Narnia books and Tolkien's Hobbit cycle have been (along with J.K. Rowling's Harry Potter series) the most popular fantasies of the English-speaking world and among the most popular works of all time—something that no one, in 1936, could ever have predicted for the works of two obscure and apparently unproductive Oxford academics.

It is known that Tolkien did not have a high opinion of the Narnia books, and from his point of view one can see why. They lack a kind of intellectual rigor. What is a Victorian English lamppost doing in the middle of the Narnian forest? Even more strangely, how can a world without Christ have a Father Christmas? And how is it that all the Narnians speak English? In the sixth book of the series, *The Magician's Nephew*, Lewis provided answers to some of these questions: the Narnians speak English because some of them are the descendants of a London cabdriver and his wife, brought into the world by magic long ago; the lamppost grew from a metal fragment dropped in the skirmish when the White Witch found her way in with him. But this retrospective solution only raises further questions. What about the Calormenes? Why has Narnian English gone through a medieval phase? These points do not matter to Lewis's intended child audience, or indeed to the modern mass movie-audience, but they did to Tolkien, always meticulous over matters of consistency, especially in language. Such differences of attitude and opinion may have reinforced the latent tensions between the two writers indicated previously.

Narnia's virtues, conversely, are easy to point out. The main one is Lewis's unceasing power of invention and assimilation. To the dwarves, giants, and dragons of Northern mythology, Lewis added the centaurs, fauns, and dryads of the classical world. A toned-down Bacchus and Silenus appear in *Prince Caspian*, and the witch of *The Silver Chair* is a lamia. Then there are the creatures of Lewis's own invention: the Marshwiggles of *Silver Chair*, the Dufflepuds of *The Voyage of the Dawn Treader*, and the many talking beasts, headed by Reepicheep the Mouse, the Narnian D'Artagnan. The tone of the books, moreover, is often comic, with Chaucer's "Parliament of Fowls" replaced by a "Parliament of Owls," and even satirical, as in the comments on Eustace Scrubb's parents, "Experiment House," and the bureaucrats of Narrowhaven in *Dawn Treader*. Child-audiences also respond well to the rivalries within the Pevensie family.

However, another point of contention between Tolkien and Lewis was likely to be the overtly Christian message of the Narnia books. Tolkien deliberately excluded all but the slightest open allusions to religion from *The Hobbit* and *The Lord of the Rings*, but—however one phrases it—the lion Aslan of Narnia is a clear Christ analogue. His self-sacrifice, death, and resurrection in *The Lion, the Witch and the Wardrobe* closely parallel the Passion (though there are also significant differences). Lucy's experiences in *Prince Caspian* look like a disguised homily on faith; serious points are made about the nature of sin in *Silver Chair* and *Dawn Treader*; and *The Last Battle* puts forward an old, but now quite unfamiliar, theory about salvation. In doing all this, Lewis was behaving in character. For years, he had been explaining elementary Christian doctrine to a culture that had largely forgotten it; since *The Screwtape Letters*, he

had also been preoccupied with the roots of sin and the nature of temptation, even in apparently innocent minds, like those of children. He had also, and probably as a result of his interaction with Tolkien, done his best in *Mere Christianity* to concentrate on the many points where all Christians were in agreement and not on the few where Catholics and Protestants, for instance, disagreed.

Tolkien was less tolerant, or more committed, than Lewis. He did not approve, for instance, of cremation (which Lewis had shown being used in *Silent Planet*). He was firmly opposed to divorce, as one can see from a letter he wrote to Lewis, but did not deliver, in 1943 (*Letters*, 59–62). In 1948, Tolkien seems to have expressed his annoyance at a draft section of Lewis's book on the sixteenth century (described here later) so firmly that he felt obliged to explain himself in writing (*Letters*, 125–29). We do not know what the disagreement was about, but it may have been about the many vexed sectarian issues of the Reformation. Late in life, Tolkien wrote a commentary on Lewis called "The Ulsterior Motive," in which he suggested that Lewis was reverting to the militant Irish Protestantism of his Belfast birth. Finally, Tolkien may well have been shocked by Lewis's marriage (in a registry office, not in church) to the divorcée Joy Davidman on April 23, 1956. One motive of this was to allow Davidman, a U.S. citizen, to remain in Britain. She was soon diagnosed as suffering from cancer, and in March 1957 her condition was pronounced beyond hope; a second, religious marriage was solemnized in the Churchill Hospital in Oxford. Amazingly, however, even miraculously, she then recovered, and she and Lewis had three happy years together till she relapsed, dying on July 14, 1960.

Much of Lewis's writing after Narnia was inspired by his wife. *Till We Have Faces* (1956) was dedicated to her; *Surprised by Joy* (1955) puns on her name; *A Grief Observed* (1961) remembers her. Other major works from the last decade of his life include the magisterial, if forbiddingly titled, *English Literature in the Sixteenth Century Excluding Drama* (1954). This is above all a reference work in the Oxford History of English Literature series, but it is engagingly-written and shows signs of Inkling influence, especially in the opening pages, which discuss the notion of "magic" and argue for serious changes— and not for the better—between a more natural medieval *magia* and a more learned and malevolent Renaissance *goeteia*. Lewis may have picked up the latter term from Williams, with his contacts in occultist circles, and Tolkien seems to be thinking of it when he has Galadriel, for instance, talking to Sam Gamgee, distinguish what she does from "the deceits of the Enemy." Another important work, published posthumously, was *The Discarded Image* (1964), in which

Lewis explained the late classical or learned medieval world view: though this had been in his mind and his writing at least from the time of *Silent Planet*, where one of the great shocks Ransom experiences is the replacement of his modern tellurocentric view—the Earth is the source of life, space cold and dead—with a view Lewis presents as at once pre- and postmodern, in which space is filled with life and light and Earth is the cold, dark margin. The Chronicles of Narnia also end with what could be called a neo-Platonic vision.

Furthermore, from the 1940s on, Lewis had been an indefatigable giver of papers and lectures. After he died, many more of these were collected and published or republished. Among the most valuable collections are *Studies in Medieval and Renaissance Literature* (1966), *Of Other Worlds: Essays and Stories* (1966), *Selected Literary Essays* (1969), and *The Dark Tower and Other Stories* (1975), all edited by Walter Hooper. The last collection contains what remains of a fifth, unfinished novel, again seemingly "discovering myth."

Summing up a man as generous, and an author as prolific, as Lewis can never be satisfactory. Among his qualities, though, were deep and wide learning in several languages and literatures; an unusual ability to empathize with the sentiments and attitudes of apparently superseded cultures or "discarded images," including pagan ones; and, quite unconnected with the two virtues just mentioned, unusual insight into the psychology of everyday life, especially into petty vices and domestic temptations, which one might call the roots of sin. All these qualities were shared with Tolkien, though Lewis's learning and Tolkien's were often complementary rather than the same. Lewis also shared with Tolkien a deep interest in language and language change, expressed in Lewis's case in his late work *Studies in Words* (1960), and in both cases to some extent affected by the writings of another Inkling, Owen Barfield (1898–1997), author of *Poetic Diction* (1928). In this area as in others, however, Tolkien felt that Lewis was slapdash and unprofessional; he may have been a "philologist" in the old sense, a "lover of words," but unlike Tolkien he was not a proper "comparative philologist," aware of linguistic change from the earliest records and beyond. Finally, both men had something that is incalculable and beyond learning: the gift of narrative invention. Both men, furthermore, used that gift to argue for the truth of myth and against many of the ruling orthodoxies of their time. It is these latter that now seem dated.

TOM SHIPPEY

Further Reading

Carpenter, Humphrey. *The Inklings: C.S. Lewis, J.R.R. Tolkien, Charles Williams and Their Friends.* London: George Allen & Unwin, 1978.

Duriez, Colin. *Tolkien and C.S. Lewis: The Gift of Friendship.* Mahwah, NJ: Hidden Spring, 2003.
Green, Roger Lancelyn, and Hooper, Walter. *C.S. Lewis: A Biography.* New York: Harcourt Brace Jovanovich, 1974.
Hutton, Ronald. "The Inklings and the Gods." In *Witches, Druids and King Arthur,* edited by Ronald Hutton, 215–37. London: Hambledon and London, 2003.
Rateliff, John D. "'The Lost Road,' 'The Dark Tower,' and 'The Notion Club Papers': Tolkien and Lewis's Time-Travel Triad." In *Tolkien's Legendarium: Essays on "The History of Middle-earth,"* edited by Verlyn Flieger and Carl F. Hostetter, 199–218. Westport, CT: Greenwood, 2000.
Wilson, A.N. *C.S. Lewis: A Biography.* New York: W. W. Norton, 1990.

See also **Barfield, Owen; Catholicism, Roman; Christianity; Church of England; Devils; Heathenism and Paganism; Heaven; Hell; Inklings; Lewis, Warren Hamilton; Literary Context, Twentieth Century; Mythology, Germanic; Oxford; Satan and Lucifer**

LEWIS, WARREN HAMILTON (1895–1973)

Warren Hamilton Lewis, nicknamed Warnie, was born in Belfast, Northern Ireland, the elder brother and only sibling of C.S. Lewis. He was educated at Malvern College in England and by private tutoring from William T. Kirkpatrick, as was his brother after him. Unlike his brother, he entered the Royal Military Academy at Sandhurst in February 1914, having won a prize cadetship. Due to the exigencies of World War I, his officer training was accelerated to nine months instead of the usual two years, and he served with the British Expeditionary Force in France. After the war, he had postings in England, Sierra Leone in West Africa, and Kowloon and Shanghai in China. He retired with the rank of captain in 1932 and joined his brother's household, The Kilns, in Headington. He was recalled to duty in September 1939 and sent to France, and he was promoted to major the next year. In May 1940, he was evacuated with his unit from Dunkirk. Thereafter, he served in the Home Guard in and around Oxford, during the summers in the "floating Home Guard" on his motorboat, the *Bosphorus.* He retired again from his military career after World War II and devoted himself to assisting his brother and to his own extensive historical research.

The Lewis brothers remained close friends throughout their lives, living under the same roof most of the time. As children, they created imaginary worlds together. They returned to the Church of England independently but almost at the same time, and Warnie served as his brother's secretary from about

1943 on (he estimated that he typed at least twelve thousand letters for C.S. Lewis). Beginning about 1912 (with occasional gaps), he kept a diary that is a vibrant social history of his time and a prime source of information about the doings of his brother and the other Oxford Inklings, at whose meetings Warnie was a regular participant. (His long entry for November 12, 1949, for instance, reflects on his reading *The Lord of the Rings* in manuscript.) He also published several books on seventeenth- and early-eighteenth-century French history (about which Tolkien noted that, though he himself had little interest in the court of Louis XIV, Warnie's witty and learned writing made the subject engaging). Warnie's overview of the period in *The Splendid Century* (1953) is the best known of these histories, but all of his books are well done.

Plagued by alcoholism for the latter half of his life, he fought the disease successfully most of the time. John Wain called him "a man who stays in my memory as the most courteous I have ever met—not with mere politeness, but with a genial, self-forgetful considerateness that was as instinctive to him as breathing."

RICHARD C. WEST

Further Reading

Kilby, Clyde S., and Marjorie Lamp Mead, eds. *Brothers and Friends: The Diaries of Major Warren Hamilton Lewis.* San Francisco: Harper and Row, 1982.

Lewis, Warren Hamilton. *Assault on Olympus: The Rise of the House of Gramont Between 1604 and 1678.* London: Andre Deutsch; New York: Harcourt Brace, 1958.

————. "The Galleys of France." In *Essays Presented to Charles Williams*, edited by C.S. Lewis, 136–45. :Oxford University Press, 1947. Reprinted as "The Galleys," chap. 10 in *The Splendid Century: Life in the France of Louis XIV.* London: Eyre and Spottiswoode; New York: William Sloane, 1953.

————, ed. *Letters of C.S. Lewis.* With a memoir by Warren Hamilton Lewis. London: Geoffrey Bles; New York: Harcourt, Brace and World, 1966. Revised and enlarged edition edited by Walter Hooper. London: Collins, 1988; San Diego: Harcourt Brace, 1993.

————. *Levantine Adventurer: The Travels and Missions of the Chevalier d'Arvieux, 1653–1697.* London: Andre Deutsch, 1962; New York: Harcourt, Brace and World, 1963.

————. *Louis XIV: An Informal Portrait.* London: Andre Deutsch; New York: Harcourt, Brace, 1959.

————. "Malvern in My Time." *The Beacon* [the magazine of Malvern College], 1953. Reprinted in *CSL: The Bulletin of the New York C.S. Lewis Society* 12, no. 8, whole no. 140 (June 1981): 1–3. [Written at the suggestion of George Sayer.]

————, ed. *Memoirs of the Duc de Saint-Simon.* Translated and abridged from the French by Bayle St. John. London: B. T. Batsford; New York: Macmillan, 1964. This translation was originally published as *The Memoirs of the Duke of Saint Simon.* London: Chapman & Hall, 1857.

————. *The Scandalous Regent: A Life of Philippe, Duc d'Orleans, 1674–1723, and of His Family.* London: Andre Deutsch; New York: Harcourt, Brace and World, 1961.

————. *The Splendid Century: Life in the France of Louis XIV.* London: Eyre and Spottiswoode; New York: William Sloane, 1953. New York: Doubleday Anchor Books, 1953, 1957. [Written in 1942.]

————. *The Sunset of the Splendid Century: The Life and Times of Louis Auguste de Bourbon, Duc de Maine, 1670–1736.* London: Eyre and Spottiswoode; New York: William Sloane Associates, 1955. Garden City, NY: Anchor Books, 1963.

Wain, John. *Sprightly Running: Part of an Autobiography*, 184. London: Macmillan; New York: St. Martin's, 1965.

West, Richard C. "W.H. Lewis: Historian of the Inklings and of Seventeenth-Century France." *Seven* 14 (1997): 75–86. Photograph of Warren Hamilton Lewis on p. 74.

Wrong, Charles. "W.H. Lewis: Popular Historian," *Canadian C.S. Lewis Journal*, no. 86 (Autumn 1994): 33–40. Frontispiece is photograph.

See also **Inklings; Lewis, C.S.; Oxford; Wain, John; World War I**

LIBRARY, PERSONAL

Like most scholars, Tolkien is known to have accumulated a fairly large personal library. And as with most working libraries, Tolkien's collection was fluid within his lifetime, with books both coming in and going out. The content of his library covered many areas of his professional expertise and personal interest, including Old English, Middle English, and Old Norse languages and literatures; Celtic, Finnish, and Semitic languages; books on general philology, place-names, and dialects; dictionaries, classical literature, and postmedieval English literature. Tolkien frequently signed his name on the flyleaf of books that he acquired, often adding the year and sometimes the full date.

After Tolkien's death in 1973, his library passed to his third son and literary executor, Christopher Tolkien, who worked as a scholar in the same field as his father and who merged the bulk of his father's library with his own. A few years later, before moving to France, Christopher disposed of a portion of his father's library while retaining the majority. Some books were donated to Oxford libraries, and others were weeded out and entered the used book market.

Around three hundred volumes were donated to the English Faculty Library. These books were of the subject areas of Germanic languages and linguistics and Celtic languages and literature.

A large number of books and scholarly offprints were disposed of through a local bookseller, who added a small sticker to many items stating that it was "From the Library of J.R.R. Tolkien." It is from these discards that comes the majority of books from Tolkien's library that circulate in the rare books market.

A small number of books, around forty-five, were also deposited in the Bodleian Library with Tolkien's papers. These include several books he owned as a schoolboy and as an undergraduate.

DOUGLAS A. ANDERSON

LIGHT

Light is the primary reality, controlling metaphor, and guiding symbol in Tolkien's cosmology. Over the course of the story, light changes in intensity, color, and meaning, becoming ever dimmer and more remote.

In his poem "Mythopoeia" Tolkien pictured light as "a single White" refracted through the prism of human consciousness, splintered "to many hues" and recombined in "endless shapes that move from mind to mind." Here, light is the metaphor for inspiration from the primary Creator, God, filtered through and by human creativity. The metaphor becomes literal in his invented world, where the white light is broken into colors, set into jewels, dimmed by distance, countered by darkness, and shaded to gray. This extended process mirrors the separation of language and peoples from light as the Elves of Middle-earth fragment into disparate, sometimes conflicting communities speaking different languages.

The first light in Middle-earth shines continuously so that there is no night. Two Lamps on mountainous pillars, one in the North and one in the South, burn with brilliant white light. When they are overturned by the rebellious demigod Melkor, the spilled light is so intense that it scorches what it touches. The milder second light, removed from Middle-earth to Valinor, the realm of the gods, comes from the Two Trees, gold Laurelin and silver Telperion. The White Light is broken into colors. Each Tree glows with its own hue, one dimming as the other brightens, and this waxing and waning alternation creates Time. Not just illumination, this light is a physical substance that drips as dew from the Trees and is caught in vats at the base of each trunk. It can be touched, handled, shaped.

With this physical light, the great Elven craftsman Fëanor creates the Silmarils. When Melkor and Ungoliant destroy the Trees, the Silmarils hold the last of the light. Hidden by Fëanor, stolen by Morgoth, their attainment by various forces comprises much of the rest of the story. The jewels eventually find their "long homes," one in the earth, one in the sea, and one in the sky, still visible as the star Eärendil. This star light finds its ultimate repository in the Phial of Galadriel, where, as "a light when all other lights go out," it sustains Frodo and Sam on their journey in Mordor.

Light is the generating force behind Tolkien's Elven languages, Quenya and Sindarin, and the created worlds for which they were the impetus. These languages were developed on the Indo-European model of a protolanguage whose primal expressions embodied whole perceptions from which ever smaller and more precise meanings or words split off and diversified. The resultant variations are as complex and numerous as the societies that express them, shifting and changing over time, always retaining, however distantly, some relationship to light. A few examples must stand for many. The primal word, *ele*, "behold!" is generated by light when the awakening Elves first see the stars (made from the light of the Silver Tree). From *ele* derive *êl* and *elen*, "star," and *elda* and *elena*, "of the stars." From their first utterance, the Elves name themselves *Quendi*, "Those That Speak With Voices," and the Valar name them *Eldar*, "People of the Stars."

Other light-related words and concepts, such as Quenya *kal*, "shine," and light's opposite, *mor*, "dark," are also reflected in peoples. Elves who go to Valinor, the place of the light, are Calaquendi, "Elves of Light" (literally "Shining Elves" or "Shining Speakers"), and their language, Quenya, reflects this. Elves who refuse to go or turn back are Avari (Unwilling) or Úmanyar (Not of Aman) but are given yet another name by the Light-elves, who call them Moriquendi, "Dark-elves." Thus, light and language create each other, and from this earliest, most light-responsive speech differing perceptions of identity develop.

Although these groups subdivide into many more than there is room to describe here, one particular group, the Sindar, deserves notice. Technically, they are Dark-elves, but they are called Grey-elves because their leader, Thingol, is one who, though he chose to stay in Middle-earth, has seen the light of the Trees. Thus, his people are neither light nor dark but a mixture of both. Their language, Sindarin or "Grey-elven," becomes the major Elvish tongue of Middle-earth; and Quenya, the language of light, recedes to a formal language of lore, what Tolkien later called "Elven-latin."

Light, language, and the peoples of Middle-earth are mirrors of one another, each of them dimming, splintering, yet always reflecting the other two.

VERLYN FLIEGER

Further Reading

Flieger, Verlyn. *Splintered Light: Logos and Language in Tolkien's World*. 2nd ed. Kent, OH: Kent State University Press, 2002.

Helms, Randel. *Tolkien and the Silmarils: Imagination and Myth in "The Silmarillion."* Boston, MA: Houghton Mifflin, 1981.

Kilby, Clyde S. *Tolkien & the Silmarillion.* Wheaton, IL: Harold Shaw Publishers, 1976.

Shippey, Tom. "Light-elves, Dark-elves and Others: Tolkien's Elvish Problem." *Tolkien Studies* 1 (2004): 1–15.

See also **Astronomy and Cosmology, Middle-earth; Elves: Kindreds and Migrations; Languages, Invented; Two Trees; Ylfe, Alfar, Elves**

LITERARY CONTEXT, TWENTIETH CENTURY

Writers and critics of twentieth-century British literature have typically relegated Tolkien to a minor footnote, with *The Lord of the Rings (LotR)* "fated to become only an intricate Period Piece," according to critic Harold Bloom in 2000. W.H. Auden's early championing of both *LotR* and Tolkien's poetry was unusual and much appreciated by Tolkien, who wrote Robert H. Boyer on August 25, 1971, that Auden "was, in fact, sneered at for it" (*Letters*, 412). More characteristic were the attacks on *LotR* by central figures within the post-1945 English literary world like Edwin Muir, Philip Toynbee, and Anthony Burgess, although it is important to recognize that other notable novelists such as Iris Murdoch and Naomi Mitchison admired the book. Criticism of Tolkien's fantasy literature tends to hinge on the belief that it is peripheral to the literary movements and cultural trends of the twentieth century and thereby premodern. Even his early biographer Humphrey Carpenter argues, "He could scarcely be called a modern writer" (1977, 157). As a result, serious Tolkien scholars like Tom Shippey and Brian Rosebury argue for his modernity, but in doing so, they often find themselves enmeshed in definitions of the modern produced by the very writers and critics to whom Tolkien seemed a peripheral figure.

A revisionist approach to twentieth-century English culture and to the history of modernism in recent years offers new possibilities for Tolkien scholarship. Recent scholarship has rid us of a number of myths about how we understand literary modernism and its influence during the first half of the twentieth century. Modernists such as Ezra Pound, T.S. Eliot, and Wyndham Lewis were themselves effective publicists for their aesthetic priorities. *Blast, Egoist, The Criterion*, and other literary magazines, directly produced or indirectly controlled by the major names of Anglo-American high modernism, consciously worked to redefine the forms and subject matter of quality literature during the teens and twenties.

An antirealist formal aesthetic, the refusal to separate the domains of art and life, and the focus on a "subjective" reality became hallmarks of mainstream modernist writing. By the 1950s, when *LotR* appeared, these criteria for literary value dominated the academy in both Britain and the United States, thanks to a generation of critics whose interests, tastes, and procedures had been formed by high modernism. In the United States in particular, modernism's dominance rested on the triumph of New Criticism. Alan Tate, Cleanth Brooks, and John Crowe Ransom had successfully grounded critical practice in a radical formalism, with poetic language as its object of analysis. Their aim was to defend high culture against the profound transformation of literature in the context of new forms of mass culture, such as Hollywood film. The dismissal of *LotR* as "juvenile taste" by the late modernist novelist and critic Edmund Wilson belongs within such a framework.

The seventies and eighties saw challenges to a modernism exclusively defined by the practice of a small group of Anglo-American writers termed high modernists. Research into modernism's close engagement with both popular culture and the literary marketplace has dislodged the emphasis on a self-referential and autonomous domain for modernist aesthetics. An emphasis on modernism's connections to the fin-de-siecle Victorian moment has likewise brought into question the central claim of modernists like Pound and Wyndham Lewis to break with the past. Feminist critics in particular have sought to understand "a turn-of-the-twentieth-century cultural landscape" in terms that emphasize a various and lively debate over aesthetic values that had not yet been resolved in favor of modernism. Most significant for any consideration of Tolkien must be the way in which "thick" descriptions of early twentieth-century literature bring to the center a significantly expanded range of genres and thematic concerns, both within the practices of modernists and in the writing of modernism's so-called others, middlebrow writers such as H.G. Wells, John Buchan, Radclyffe Hall, Ivy Compton Burnett, and John Galsworthy, whose thematic, generic, and stylistic preferences fell outside traditional definitions of modernism.

Tolkien critics have been quick to point to the continuity between many of his central interests and those of his modernist contemporaries, principal among which would have to be that of language. Tolkien's invention of the Middle-earth languages, and his polyglot linguistic world in *LotR* and *The Silmarillion*, has rightly been compared to modernist writing by Shippey and other critics. And although alienation and decentering are not part of Tolkien's design, his incorporation of fragments of Dwarvish and Elvish scripts, etymologies, and other textual traces of linguistic materiality are consonant with major modernist texts like *The Wasteland, Ulysses,* and *Trilogy,* as well as less-often-cited examples such as David Jones's *In Parenthesis.* Cultural materialist critic Raymond Williams, in "Language and the Avant-Garde," teaches us to understand Tolkien alongside a broad set of avant-garde European aesthetic movements in a context of twentieth-century theories of literary language. Williams criticizes the tendency to conflate approaches as diametrically opposed as the formalist "resurrection of the word," characteristic of James Joyce, and the symbolist "poetic word," found throughout William Butler Yeats's verse. Vastly different aesthetic theories and practices are lumped with modernism and treated as unprecedented. The emphasis on the materiality of language, for example, is as much a feature of the rules of earlier poetics, "from the Welsh *cynghanedd* to medieval alliterative verse" as it is of modernism. Tolkien only appears peripheral to the twentieth-century interest in language when high modernism is used as the starting point.

A shared preoccupation with temporality also links Tolkien to modernist writers, although this has most often been used to differentiate them. Well-known modernists such as Eliot, Pound, Wyndham Lewis, Virginia Woolf, Dorothy Richardson, Rebecca West, and D.H. Lawrence emphasized the distinctive modernity and newness of the moment in which they wrote, while acknowledging that moment's entanglement in the past. This may be apocalyptic and dystopian, as in Eliot's "The Wasteland," or euphoric, as in Woolf's aesthetic layering of past and present in the consciousness of Clarissa in *Mrs. Dalloway.* These interests are indebted to major trends in nineteenth-century thought, whether to Georg Wilhelm Friedrich Hegel's dialectical model of history; Darwinian theories of evolutionary development in the natural sciences, anthropological, and sociological applications of Charles Darwin's ideas to human society; or the emergence of a psychology of human perception and consciousness.

By the beginning of the twentieth century, these earlier paradigms were being recast in ways that stressed "uneven or competing temporalities" over a single unfolding development. Albert Einstein's theory of relativity, William James's and Henri Bergson's interest in the perception of time, and Sigmund Freud's theory of a psychic reality that constantly interrupts the rationally organized chronology of daily life are all obvious examples of this recasting. These larger trends translated into such thematic interests as cultural fragmentation, consciousness as a mode of apprehension in time, and art as a form of

consciousness, as well as the formal experimentation associated with literary modernism. More recently, the field of modernist studies has added the reconsideration of historical time to the list.

In this context, Tolkien's extraordinary epic vision, with his invention of an entire history of Middle-earth, seems at odds with modernism, only because of the overly exclusive emphasis on Pound's call to break with a moribund past and "make it new." Modernists persistently grappled with how to represent the present in relationship to the past, within an understanding of history as discontinuous rather than progressive and linear. The work of Thirties writers like Rebecca West, and Sylvia Townsend Warner are particularly important here—and closer than might at first appear to Tolkien, who also offers an alternative model to the evolutionary narratives of nineteenth-century realist fiction. His narratives of Middle-earth are mythically, linguistically, and historically layered in ways that reconceptualize time and history just as much as an Eliot or a Joyce.

Other of Tolkien's themes have less to do with modernism but are nonetheless shared with many of his contemporaries. His portrait of the Shire in *LotR* has often been judged as a conservative recourse to a nostalgic paradigm of idealized rural Englishness. The Shire, and elements like Tom Bombadil and the Ents, find a context in the continuation of a tradition of English rural writing in the twentieth century. The predominantly urban and cosmopolitan profile of modernism has tended to obscure the importance of this tradition, even within English modernism, with the exception of Lawrence's detailed evocation of rural Nottinghamshire in *Sons and Lovers* and *The Rainbow.* The largely middlebrow status of rural and regional fiction in the twentieth century has not helped the reputation of ruralists; neither has its characteristic reliance on an elegiac image of a vanished or vanishing English countryside. In recent years, a more nuanced account has emerged that pays attention to the multiple forms and purposes of writers in this tradition. Thanks to postcolonial theory and cultural geography, writing about localized rural communities does not have to be seen as inherently collusive with British imperialism. Tolkien's careful delineation of the Shire as having its own history and lore can be seen to defend "place against placelessness, home against empire, the local and particular against bland megalopolitan uniformity" (Ludwig, 74).

The rural novel in the twentieth century took a variety of forms: documentary realism, fictional naturalism, fable, romance, and fantasy. John Cowper Powys borrows Thomas Hardy's Wessex focus in novels like *Wolf Solent* (1929), *A Glastonbury Romance* (1932), and *Maiden Castle* (1936) but makes religion and the supernatural important, as well as the relationship between human and natural worlds. Some writers, like Eden Phillpotts and T.F. Powys, create isolated and distinct localities emphasizing a primitivist vision of the rural Englander. Others like Henry Williamson and Llewelyn Powys, treat nature and the countryside as a source of expressive intensity dependent on a Wordsworthian spiritual affinity between man and nature. Their writing tends necessarily toward nostalgia. Mary Webb, whose novel *Precious Bane* won the Prix Femina Vie Heureuse in 1924, represents a kind of nature-mysticism, defining the natural world as holding "Life—the unknown quantity, the guarded secret" (134). By contrast, other novelists explore the human social world through naturalism, whether as outsiders like Sheila Kaye Smith and Constance Holme or as documentary realists in the case of the farmer novelists of the nineteen thirties, such as H.W. Freeman and A.G. Street, whose writing replaces the picturesque with an intimate absorption in the purpose and function of the landscape.

The rural life of Tolkien's Hobbits may perhaps be linked most fruitfully to the range of writing that uses the countryside as an occasion rather than an object for fantasy (Cavaliero, 35). The children's novel *Wind in the Willows* (1908) is an obvious and well-known Edwardian example, but the tradition is fully alive in writing for both children and adults in the nineteen twenties and thirties and even later in Richard Adams's *Watership Down* (1972). Warner combines the rural novel with fantasy as a way of avoiding both the sentimental and the primitivistic, to spectacular effect in her portrait of an urban spinster turned witch in *Lolly Willows* (1926). T.H. White directly addressed the changing nature of rural experience in his early novel *Farewell Victoria* (1933) and the autobiographical *England Have my Bones* (1936). But when he turns to fantasy in his most enduringly successful work, *The Sword in the Stone* (1939), he grounds the Arthur stories in a carefully particularized natural world, most famously in Arthur's transformations into fish, hawk, snake, and badger. Fantasy, as Glen Cavaliero notes, is about making not only "an idyllic world" of the countryside "but also a gateway into worlds greater than itself" (34–35). In the context of the twentieth-century English rural tradition in literature, Tolkien's insistence on the Hobbits' attachment to the rural Shire may be a mechanism well suited to the exploration of major questions of the century.

In the early twentieth century, poets had to contend with rural England's place in the later moment of British imperialism as an emblem for the pure heart of England and its empire—enduring, unchanging, and innocent of colonial rapaciousness. In the context of late Victorian militarism and jingoism, Hardy's poetry best registers the pressures on a literary tradition in which relationship to place is central. Always skeptical of nostalgic idealizations of rural life, Hardy's poetry explores the countryside of rural Wessex as a changing and often haunted landscape, layered with human existence and imaginings that contrive to alienate rather than root the speakers. Hardy's poetry was incorporated into the Georgian movement, the group of writers who aimed to modernize English verse in the prewar years, combining established forms with naturalism in, for example, the poems of Edward Thomas and W.H. Davies.

The pastoral became a pervasive motif in First World War poetry by combatants and civilians alike. Many well-known soldier poets—Rupert Brooke, Wilfred Owen, Siegfried Sassoon, Edward Blunden, Charles Sorley, Ivor Gurney, and Edward Thomas— were also associated with the Georgians. In Brooke's work, the pastoral famously continued the Victorian tradition of domestic patriotism, in which the soldier's death in a foreign land makes affective and organic links between the English homeland and the "foreign field[s]" of empire where "a dust whom England bore" transforms the alien soil into an eternal England. For Thomas, who died in 1917, two years after Brooke, war deaths and rural life are entwined, with minutely observed details of the countryside providing a measure of what is of value and what is irretrievably damaged. Yet it would be hard to argue that Thomas's rural world is emblematic of a larger Englishness; if anything, the precisely localized world resists such patriotic simplifications, as does Ivor Gurney, who brings unobtrusive life to the soldier's link to locale in, for example, the "infinite lovely chatter of Bucks accent," silenced by death except in the poet's memory. Most characteristic of war poetry is the evocation of natural images to highlight the unnatural horror of the war, in, for example, Owen's antielegy "Anthem for Doomed Youth," which revises Thomas Gray's "Elegy in a Country Churchyard," "What passing-bells for these who die as cattle?" or Edmund Blunden's twist to Keats's line "'And all her silken flanks with garlands drest'—/ But we are coming to the sacrifice" in "Vlamertinghe: Passing the Chateau, July 1917." Blunden brings a painful conclusion to the antipastoral strand in war poetry in his postwar poem "1916 seen from 1921," where the speaker finds himself permanently separated from the English countryside by the memories of the war-dead. Blunden's postwar elegy helps us understand how the elegiac and pacifist strand in *LotR* entitles Tolkien to a central place in the twentieth-century tradition of war writing, even though his poems and fiction are outside the typical genres of war writing: memoirs rooted in combatant experience, first-person, quasi-autobiographical fiction, and the soldier-poet's lyric verse.

LotR's publication in 1954 linked it in critical and popular thought to World War II and the writers of the 1940s and 1950s who confronted a half century of war, the rise of modern totalitarianism, the massive genocide of the Holocaust, and the dropping of nuclear bombs on Japan. Despite Tolkien's resistance to simplistic allegorical readings of his work, *LotR* compares with works by writers who grapple with the relationship among political power, state aggression, and violence. This work begins in the thirties, when Tolkien was already working on *LotR*, with writers such as George Orwell, Stevie Smith, W.H. Auden, Rebecca West, and Christopher Isherwood, as well as those who are more concerned, like the Catholic Tolkien, with the religious and moral dimensions of good and evil, for example, C.S. Lewis and Graham Greene. During the Forties and Fifties, the events of the war era and the emergent nuclear age inevitably fuelled the vision of a dystopian century. Allegory and fantasy provided useful vehicles for engagement with postwar issues for prewar writers such as Orwell, C.S. Lewis, and Wyndham Lewis, as well as a new generation, notably William Golding, Doris Lessing, and Mervyn Peake.

Many writers, such as Rosamond Lehmann, Elizabeth Bowen, L.P. Hartley, Joyce Carey, and Evelyn Waugh, chose to look back to the early years of the century, as well as their main characters' youth, in an effort to understand the history of events. This was an era, too, of major novel sequences tracking the histories of families, individuals, and English society, among them C.P. Snow's eleven-volume *Strangers and Brothers* (1940–70), Henry Williamson's fifteen-volume *A Chronicle of Ancient Sunlight* (1951–69), Anthony Powell's twelve-volume *Dance to the Music of Time* (1951–75), and Olivia Manning's six-novel sequence *The Balkan Trilogy* and *The Levant Trilogy* (1960–80). These so-called sagas parallel in naturalistic form Tolkien's urge toward historical writing.

At the end of the century, critics understand the effects of England's decline as an empire on the nation's self-imagining as essential features of English literature from Joseph Conrad's *Heart of Darkness* in 1902 to the rich output of novels and poetry produced by postcolonial writers living in postwar Britain, such as John Agard, Grace Nichols, V.S. Naipaul, Salman Rushdie, and Samuel Selvon. Whether or not Tolkien aimed to produce a new national mythology for England, as is sometimes claimed, is a matter of critical dispute. However, there are important ways in which his work can be seen as part of an effort to

grapple with the condition of modern British society evident in writers as different as modernists such as Lawrence, Woolf, and Warner; post-1945 poets such as Ted Hughes, Basil Bunting, Philip Larkin, Donald Davie, and Tony Harrison; and the generation of novelists who have flourished since Tolkien's death, such as Monica Ali, Peter Ackroyd, Martin Amis, A.S. Byatt, Ian McEwen, Sadie Smith, Graham Swift, and Rose Tremain, who all investigate and reimagine contemporary Englishness.

Tolkien's relationship to the twentieth century, as Shippey convincingly argues, is best understood through his invention of the heroic fantasy novel. At the century's end, Tolkien appears as an innovator whose grasp on the potential of the fantastic as a medium for fiction compares with twentieth-century writers, both British and American, whose centrality is already assured. Yet Tolkien's claim to be a modern writer is not just a result of his influence on a whole genre: it rests on the degree to which his fiction and poetry stand amid rather than apart from the main preoccupations of English literature in the last century.

CLAIRE BUCK

Further Reading

Ardis, Ann L. *Modernism and Cultural Conflict, 1880–1922.* Cambridge: Cambridge University Press, 2002.

Armstrong, Tim. *Modernism.* Cambridge: Polity Press, 2005.

Carpenter, Humphrey. *J.R.R. Tolkien: A Biography.* London: George Allen & Unwin, 1977.

Cavaliero, Glen. *The Rural Tradition in the English Novel, 1900–1939.* Totowa, NJ: Rowman and Littlefield, 1977.

Ludwig, Hans-Werner, and Lothar Fietz, eds. *Poetry in the British Isles: Non-Metropolitan Perspectives.* Cardiff: University of Wales Press, 1995.

Stevenson, Randall. *A Reader's Guide to the Twentieth-Century Novel in Britain.* Lexington, KY: University Press of Kentucky, 1993.

Webb, Mary. *Precious Bane.* London; Jonathan Cape, 1924.

Williams, Raymond. *The Politics of Modernism: Against the New Conformism.* Edited by Tony Pinkney. London; Verso, 1989.

See also **Auden, W.H.: Influence of Tolkien; Joyce, James;** *Lord of the Rings:* **Success of; World War I; World War II**

LITERARY INFLUENCES, NINETEENTH AND TWENTIETH CENTURIES

The twenty-four British authors and one American author discussed here were all born in the nineteenth century. Authors are listed in alphabetical order by last name rather than by date of birth. Henry Rider

Haggard and H.G. Wells are treated as nineteenth-century authors even though they published new works in the twentieth century. Fourteen authors are considered twentieth-century writers because their work of interest to Tolkien appeared after 1901.

Nineteenth Century

Tolkien claimed to "loathe" the *Pied Piper* of Robert Browning (1812–89) (*Letters*, 311). Imagery and thematic material in Browning's *Childe Roland to the Dark Tower Came*, however, seem likely to have contributed to *The Lord of the Rings*. The Dark Tower is a name for Sauron's fortress of Barad-dûr. Phrases describing the poem's wasteland strongly suggest the approaches to the Dark Land and the ash-smirched leagues of Mordor: "grey plain," grass that grows "scant as hair / In leprosy," "Bog, clay and rubble, sand and stark black dearth," "blotches rankling," and "two hills. . . . Crouched like two bulls locked horn and horn in fight" (Browning 2000); "Hard and cruel and bitter was the land that met his gaze," "tormented earth," the Tower of Cirith Ungol having a "horn," and so on. While a "red eye" glares across Sauron's domain, in Browning's poem the setting sun "shot one grim / Red leer" across the landscape. The weary narrator of Browning's poem cannot recall anything pure and good, and Frodo loses the ability to remember the Shire and professes to have no hope left (*RK*, VI, iii, 215). The Dead Marshes, so often associated with Tolkien's experiences in the trenches of the Great War, may also have been suggested by a shallow river in Browning's poem; when the narrator fords it, he fears that he will "set my foot upon a dead man's cheek" and that, as he tests the depth with his spear, his weapon will catch in a corpse's tangled hair.

Tolkien's posthumous *Roverandom* appears to allude to *Sylvie and Bruno* (1889) by Lewis Carroll (1832–98), and its extravagant playfulness may owe something to the Alice books. Tolkien rules out the latter as works of fantasy, in his sense of the term, in "On Fairy-stories."

In *The Black Douglas* (1899), S.R. Crockett (1859–1914), tells how William, eighteen-year-old Earl of Douglas, one of the most powerful men in Scotland in 1440, is captivated by *la Joyeuse*, the Lady Sibylla, who is under the spell of Gilles de Retz and a pawn in a scheme of French and Scottish lords. The Lady Sibylla at first seems almost to be a fay-woman. The "Black Douglas" proclaims his love and faith in the lady, who comes truly to love him, even to the moment when his enemies take his and his brother's lives. A subplot concerns Sholto McKim, a master armorer,

who though youthful speedily rises to knighthood, and his infatuation with Maud Lindesay, companion of Margaret, the earl's little sister. These two are kidnapped and taken to France, where they are captives of the satanist Marshal Gilles de Retz. De Retz is aided by the werewolf-witch, le Meffraye, and a pack of savage, uncanny wolves. His hidden charnel-house, containing the tumbled remains of many child-victims, is described with a gruesomeness avoided by Tolkien. The Lady Sibylla, however, turns against the Marshal, and with her help Sholto, who has become a true hero; Laurence; and their father rescue Maud and Margaret. There is much description of characters' clothes and other medieval props, in the manner of Sir Walter Scott in his inferior works, in the first half of the novel. However, after the murder of the Black Douglas, the pace is brisker, and tension and a sense of the weird deepen.

Jared Lobdell, in *The World of the Rings*, asserts more than is justified by the evidence of the Tolkien letter he cites (no. 306) in claiming not only that the battle with the werewolves in chapter 49 contributed to the fight with the Wargs in *The Hobbit* (*H*, VI, 149) but also that Tolkien acknowledged that Gilles de Retz was "the source of his creation of Sauron" (Lobdell 2004, 6). However, although Tolkien doesn't say so, he might have modeled Sauron on the novel's satanist in a few details. Both agents of wickedness command armies of wolves or even werewolves; both torture victims in their high towers. Whereas Sauron seeks to enslave the free peoples of Middle-earth, however, Gilles de Retz desires renewed youthfulness. (He is a prematurely aged man in his mid-thirties when he is put to death.) The mail-coat that Sholto's mother gives him in chapter 39 "will lie soft as silk, concealed and unsuspected under the rags of a beggar," and "No sword can cut through these links" (Crockett 1901, 281): it is possible that Frodo's hidden *mithril*-coat owes something to this. Although Lobdell suggests that Tolkien's style was influenced by Crockett's, Tolkien's assertion that he had not looked at *The Black Douglas* since he was a boy (*Letters*, 391), added to the inconclusiveness of the evidence Lobdell presents, undercuts this suggestion.

Characters and scenes from the novels of Charles Dickens (1812–70) were part of the culture in which Tolkien grew up. Despite a claim never to have been able to enjoy *The Pickwick Papers* (*Letters*, 349), Tolkien was bound to know something of Dickens, if only indirectly. There seem to be traces of Dickens in several places in Tolkien's writings. A comparison of the speech-making in chapter 1 of *Pickwick* (1837) with Bilbo's after-dinner speech in the first chapter of *The Fellowship of the Ring* suggests tongue-in-cheek allusion. Frodo's flight, in the company of Gollum, across blighted landscapes may have owed something to Dickens's account, in *The Old Curiosity Shop* (1841), of Little Nell, accompanied by her untrustworthy grandfather, fleeing from the wicked Quilp and venturing into ghastly industrial wastelands. Councillor Tompkins, in Tolkien's tale "Leaf by Niggle," is represented satirically, by his way of speaking like the schoolmaster Thomas Gradgrind in Dickens's *Hard Times* (1854); Gradgrind's best pupils learn to think of a horse as a "Quadruped," "Gramnivorous," and so on, while Tompkins shows his contempt for Niggle's love of flowers, and his thorough materialism, by asking, "What, digestive and genital organs of plants?" Niggle's acquisition of love of his neighbor may well have been influenced by Dickens's parable of Scrooge's spiritual renewal, *A Christmas Carol* (1843).

A patter song, "I Am the Very Model of a Modern Major-General," from *The Pirates of Penzance* (1879), the words by W.S. Gilbert (1836–1911) with music by Arthur Sullivan (1842–1900), evidently inspired "Errantry" in *The Adventures of Tom Bombadil*. Donald Swann's musical setting of the poem, for *The Road Goes Ever On*, is obviously a *pastiche* of Sullivan's musical style.

Several elements in *King Solomon's Mines* by Henry Rider Haggard (1856–1925) may have contributed to Tolkien's creative works. As a quest for ancient wealth that takes an amusingly varied little band across forbidding territory, the 1885 romance recalls the central situation of *The Hobbit*. The device of the old and damaged map, reproduced for the reader's consultation, occurs in both books, and in both books the travelers agree upon terms before setting out. Although narrator Allan Quatermain is a wily big-game hunter, rather than a respectable Hobbit, he mediates between the reader and the more heroic characters, such as the modern-day Viking Henry Curtis or his Kukuana counterpart, Ignosi, in a fashion close to that by which Bilbo mediates between the reader and Thorin, Bard, and others.

It has been suggested that Tolkien's Gollum owes something to the wizened, treacherous, gloating figure of Gagool, an ancient, hideous crone, who guides Quatermain and his companions Curtis and Good through the tunnels of the Mines, somewhat as Gollum guides Bilbo out of the deep places of the Misty Mountains into which he has strayed in *The Hobbit*. When first seen, the hag crawls on all fours, as Gollum sometimes does in *The Lord of the Rings*. The plot element whereby the noble Ignosi assumes the rule of the Kukuanas, after years of exile under an assumed name, somewhat recalls Aragorn's assumption of his throne at last. In both cases, the king's return is celebrated with quasi-Psalms of victory

(Haggard 1989, chap. 14). The hiddenness of the realm of the Kukuanas, surrounded by mountains, may remind readers of the secret Elf-realm of Gondolin in the midst of the Encircling Mountains in *The Silmarillion*, one of the earliest elements of Tolkien's legendarium (*Lost Tales II*, 166).

Battle scenes in the two books have similar qualities, such as a simplified presentation of tactics, an emphasis on the role of one or a few heroes wielding fearsome weapons (Haggard's Curtis and his battle-axe), restraint in the depiction of suffering, and minimal interest in the details of postcombat activities (e.g., disposal of enormous numbers of corpses). Cunningly wrought armor saves Frodo from injury, except for bruises, in the battle in Moria, and John Good recovers after a similar experience (*Mines*, chap. 15). Quatermain is struck senseless during the great combat (chap. 13), and Pippin passes out when a Troll collapses upon him. The strange beauty of the caves in *King Solomon's Mines* (chap. 16) may have had a little to do with the account of the Caves of Aglarond in *The Lord of the Rings*, and the heroes of Haggard's novel face a difficult choice about which way to turn, underground, in chapter 18, as Gandalf does in Moria.

Deeply read in Anglo-Saxon literature, Tolkien would have appreciated the similarity between the figurative language used by King Alfred the Great and that used by Ignosi (still known as Umbopa) in chapter 5 of *King Solomon's Mines*: "What is life? . . . Out of the dark we came, into the dark we go. Like a storm-driven bird at night we fly out of the Nowhere; for a moment our wings are seen in the light of the fire, and, lo, we are gone again into the Nowhere" (68).

Published a year after *King Solomon's Mines*, "Long Odds" (1886) is an Allan Quatermain anecdote. Quatermain recalls being severely wounded in the thigh by a lion-bite in March 1869, about twenty years ago. He says that, to the present day, "in the month of March the wound always troubles me a great deal." In *The Lord of the Rings*, Frodo is poisoned by Shelob on March 13, 1319; on the anniversary of the injury in 3020 and 3021, he takes ill (*RK*, Appendix B, 377). The coincidence would not seem worth noticing except for the frequency of other Haggard–Tolkien parallels.

In 1966, interviewer Henry Resnik asked Tolkien to name two or three of his favorite books. The only particular work Tolkien mentioned was Haggard's *She: A History of Adventure* (1887). Early in the book, the heroes study an ancient potsherd covered with inscriptions in Greek, Latin, and so on, which are reproduced over several pages. The device of the inscribed potsherd appealed to Tolkien, whose invented alphabets and documentary sources for *The Lord of the Rings* have an obvious affinity with it. In *Tolkien and the Great War*, John Garth discusses Tolkien's use of the name Kôr, the immense, deserted city in Haggard's novel, in his own early legendarium (78ff.). Jared Lobdell compares the description of Ayesha's death, in *She*, with that of Saruman in *The Lord of the Rings* (5). It is possible that Haggard's conception of Ayesha's earthbound immortality contributed to Tolkien's development of Elvish immortality, as Mark Hooker argues in a paper not yet published as of this writing; also, Sam's rustic suspicion of foreigners may owe something to that of the manservant, Job, in *She*.

In Tolkien's opinion, Haggard's *Eric Brighteyes* (1891) was "as good as most sagas and as heroic," according to a remark reported by Douglas Anderson in *Tales Before Tolkien* (430). The extensive passages of emotive dialogue and the romantic interest in the individual contrast with the terse and objective style of the genuine Icelandic sagas and their attention to matters of reputation and property. The medieval works give more prominence to the genealogies of their numerous actors, and Haggard's tale has an elaborate plot centered on the scheming of the witch-daughter Swanhild; Eric and his true love, Gudruda, more often than not just react to situations shaped by Swanhild and men who have succumbed to her allure. Haggard's plot often depends on accidental misunderstandings, which is not typical of the sagas. Tolkien was bound to recognize these differences.

Among Tolkien's writings, perhaps the "Narn i Hîn Húrin" (in *Unfinished Tales*) is most like *Eric Brighteyes* in plot and style. In both fictions, a generally virtuous warrior-hero becomes an outlaw and unwittingly transgresses sexually due to a supernatural agency: in Haggard's tale, Swanhild slips Eric a love potion and he lies with her—in Tolkien's narrative, the dragon Glaurung deprives Nienor of the memory of her parents so that, Túrin having parted from his mother before Nienor's birth, unknowingly commits incest by marrying her. Túrin takes several names, and Eric Brighteyes is renamed Eric the Unlucky (chap. 20); the interest of both stories largely depends on the revelation of how the anticipated doom of the hero comes about. Haggard and Tolkien include uncanny portents in their stories, and both have their heroes referred to as *fey*. The name of one of Haggard's evil characters, Gizur, may have contributed to one of Sauron's names, Zigûr, in "The Notion Club Papers."

Haggard's *Ayesha: The Return of She* (1905) is much inferior to *She*; however, if Tolkien read it, which, given his enjoyment of *She*, is likely, he might have been impressed by a few descriptive passages. A landscape in chapter 8 may have contributed to Tolkien's vision of Mordor:

> Now as the light faded the wreaths of smoke which hung over the distant Fire-mountain began to glow luridly. Redder and more angry did they become while the darkness gathered, till at length they seemed to be charged with pulsing sheets of flame propelled from the womb of the volcano, which threw piercing beams of light through the eye of the giant loop [a formation in the shape of an *ankh*] that crowned its brow. Far, far fled those beams, making a bright path across the land, and striking the white crests of the bordering wall of mountains. (Haggard, *Ayesha*, 118)

In the first chapter of *Heu-Heu or The Monster* (1923), Haggard's Allan Quatermain describes a thunderstorm in language that may have influenced Tolkien's thunderstorm in chapter 4 of *The Hobbit*. The dangerous weather "seemed to come upon us from two quarters of the sky, the fact being that it was a twin storm of which the component parts were travelling towards each other." Soon, around "the peaks of the mountains lightnings were already playing." Quatermain's native servant, Hans, anxiously says: "Two storms. . . . And when they meet they will begin to fight and there will be plenty of spears flying about in the sky, and then both these clouds will weep rain or perhaps hail." He urges that they take shelter in "a big cave yonder."

Quatermain and Hans seek refuge while lightning flashes around them; the violence of the storm is "beyond description." "Lightnings, everywhere lightnings . . . one of them . . . looked like a crown of fire encircling the brow of a giant cloud." A "continuous roar of thunder" adds to the terror. While Hans and Allan huddle in the cave, hail and "torrential rain" descend. They decide to stay in the cave until the storm and the darkness of night have passed. Quatermain puffs his pipe and talks with Hans. He also explores the cave and discovers a weird painting that figures in the subsequent development of the story. When they eventually emerge, they find that some of their cattle have died in the tempest.

The episode as described by Haggard may have contributed to a key chapter in *The Hobbit*. In the Misty Mountains, Gandalf, the Dwarves, and Bilbo meet "a thunderstorm—more than a thunderstorm, a thunder-battle. You know how terrible a really big thunderstorm can be . . . especially at times when two great thunderstorms meet and clash." Bilbo and the others see "stone-giants" that are "out" "hurling rocks at one another for a game" (cf. Quatermain's reference to the lightnings "playing"). Rain, wind, and hail force the companions to seek shelter, with their ponies, in a nearby cave. The Dwarves light their pipes and talk copiously. Once asleep, though, they are captured by Goblins. When Gandalf reappears, to frighten and confuse the Goblins, the result, Tolkien writes, is "beyond description," the same phrase Haggard's Quatermain had used to characterize the storm. While separated from the Dwarves, Bilbo acquires Gollum's Ring. At last all of the travelers escape, though their pack animals are gone.

Published posthumously, Haggard's *The Treasure of the Lake* (1926) is yet another Quatermain romance. A woman called White-Mouse urges the hunter and Hans to help her to rescue Kaneke, a warrior imprisoned at the top of a precipice. White-Mouse plans that they will use a long, "very steep" tunnel leading to a trapdoor through which they may be able to reach Kaneke. The tunnel proves to be an almost perpendicular tube wide enough to admit them and furnished with "a kind of ladder with little landing-places at intervals." There are three of these landing places. When they reach the third, Quatermain estimates that they are "quite two hundred feet above the spot where the actual tunnel sprang from the cleft." White-Mouse opens the trapdoor and, just before the moment of supreme danger, Quatermain sees "a star shining in the sky [that] gave me comfort, though I did not know why it should." In the rescue of Kaneke, White-Mouse, in her white garments, frightens the guards, who evidently take her for a ghost and stabs one of them with her knife.

Similarly, in *The Lord of the Rings* Tolkien tells that Frodo, poisoned by Shelob but alive, is taken to the top of the Tower of Cirith Ungol and must be rescued by Sam. Sam climbs the "steep," winding stairs of the three-tiered Tower, losing count of the steps after two hundred. He takes advantage of a startled Orc's confusion, crying, "Yes! The Elf-warrior is loose!" Sam is miserable about the odds he faces but is cheered when he recalls the sights of western lands and the sight of stars. He attacks an Orc and cuts its hand from its arm with his blade, Bilbo's small old sword Sting (*RK*, VI, i, 186). To reach Frodo, Sam passes through a trapdoor. The coincidence of Haggard's and Tolkien's conceptions—the steep ascent, the ladders, the threefold construction, the significance of two hundred, the encouragement provided by stars, the impersonation of a frightening being, the trapdoor, the rescue itself, the rescuer's blow struck by a blade—suggests that *The Treasure of the Lake* was one of the Haggard volumes that Tolkien read.

The adducing of so much material from this and other books by Haggard is not intended here to suggest that Tolkien drew, consciously and copiously, from the earlier writer. However, the evidence suggests that when Tolkien was writing *The Lord of the Rings*, he conceived himself to be writing something in the manner of Haggard, although he never said as much, and that his having read Haggard was of great importance to Tolkien in the "invention" of the plot of *The Hobbit* and *The Lord of the Rings*. Academic critics read Haggard as a relic of imperialism or as a case study in Jungian psychology, but Tolkien was evidently spontaneously moved by mythopoeic and straightforward adventure romance as found in the older writer's books.

In *The Fellowship of the Ring*, Frodo and his companions are endangered by trees in the Old Forest: "The countless years had filled them with pride and rooted wisdom, and with malice. But none were more dangerous than the Great Willow; and his heart was rotten, but his strength was green" (*FR*, I, vii, 141). If Tolkien read *Wood Magic* (1881) by Richard Jefferies (1848–87), he may have been unconsciously echoing what is said in chapter 6 about a "malicious," "wicked," "treacherous" elm who waits for the opportunity to drop a crushing limb on humans or cattle. "That elm across there is quite rotten inside—there is a hold inside so big you could stand up" (79–80). Perhaps this passage suggested the episode in *The Lord of the Rings* in which the Willow imprisons Merry and Pippin within itself (116).

Late in his life, Tolkien recalled a modern fairy tale, "Puss-Cat Mew," by E.H. Knatchbull-Hugessen (1829–93), as a favorite from boyhood. Douglas A. Anderson, reprinting the story in *Tales Before Tolkien*, suggests that the story adumbrates Tolkien's conceit of giving the truth behind a nursery rhyme (cf. the *Man in the Moon* poems in *The Adventures of Tom Bombadil*).

A 1964 letter shows that Tolkien had read *John Inglesant* (1881) by Joseph Henry Shorthouse (1834–1903) with interest; he characterized this religious romance of the seventeenth century as "queer, exciting, and debatable" (*Letters*, 348). Tolkien recollected having lived in the same Edgbaston, Birmingham, neighborhood where his fellow-"amateur" author predecessor had lived. An article by Norman Power records Tolkien's gift of a collection of essays that included a paper on Shorthouse and his most famous book; however, Power's suggestion that Inglesant's renunciation of vengeance for the killing of his brother influenced the theme of *The Lord of the Rings* is unconvincing.

In early writings, Tolkien conceived of Luthany as "the only land where Men and Elves once dwelt an age in peace and love." This name was replaced by Lúthien, a name that would finally be given to one of his principal heroines (*Lost Tales II*, 304, 329). Luthany occurs in *The Mistress of Vision* by the poet Francis Thompson (1859–1907), whose *Collected Poems*, Christopher Tolkien reports, his father secured in 1913–14 (*Lost Tales II*, 329). Christopher suggests that Tolkien's poem *You & Me and the Cottage of Lost Play* contains an echo of a couple of lines from Thompson's *Daisy* (*Lost Tales I*, 29). He also records that his father recognized an influence from a description, in Thompson's *The Sister Songs*, of a laburnum, upon the conception of the Tree Laurelin, from which yellow light dripped (*Morgoth*, 157–58). More generally, John Garth states that, as a young man, Tolkien strongly approved of Thompson's poetic skills, as well as his Catholic faith, and may have been influenced by his fairy themes (13–14).

Tolkien refers to *The Time Machine* (1895) by H.G. Wells (1855–1946) in "On Fairy-Stories" (*Reader*, 41, 67). He contends that the Eloi and Morlocks in Wells's novel are closer kin to the denizens of a fairy story than Swift's Lilliputians because they "live far away in an abyss of time so deep as to work an enchantment upon them." Because "the magic of Faërie" operates upon the human desire "to survey the depths of space and time," *The Time Machine* has some claim to "right of entry" into, at least, "the borders of fairy-story," although the Machine itself is "preposterous and incredible." Guildford, in Tolkien's "Notion Club Papers," objects in like manner to the Machine, though finding the tale itself "remarkable" (*Sauron*, 165).

Wells's Traveller journeys more than thirty million years into the future, although his principal adventure occurs in the year 802,701. It may be that Tolkien's own conception of the several ages of Middle-earth, encompassing thousands of years, was encouraged by the example of Wells.

Wells theorizes that, lacking difficulties requiring intellectual and physical effort, human beings would decline; both the androgynous, surface-dwelling Eloi and the Morlocks are diminutive and apparently have no art or science of their own (the Morlocks seem to tend machines that are mostly automatic). Wells sees society as determined by materialistic forces. Tolkien's various annals of the Númenóreans show them becoming decadent at the time of their greatest worldly power. His analysis of Númenórean society is based on morality. Both Tolkien and Wells, though, certainly are intrigued by the imaginative possibilities of tracing social-cultural trajectories.

Tolkien may be specifically indebted to Wells for the description of Gollum. Wells's Morlocks are the stunted and hideous descendants of humans alive today. Upon his first good look at a Morlock, the Traveller notes its "dull white" skin, "strange large grayish-red eyes," and its posture when running ("I cannot even say whether it ran on all fours, or only

with its forearms held very low"), and he says it was "like a human spider." The Morlocks have developed this way due to generations lived in the darkness underground. "In the first place, there was the bleached look common in most animals that live largely in the dark—the white fish of the Kentucky caves, for instance. Then, those large eyes, with that capacity for reflecting light, are common of nocturnal things. . . . And . . . that evident confusion in the sunshine" (Wells, 39–40). Tolkien describes Gollum (who lives on a rock in a lake inside a cave) thus in *The Hobbit:* "small slimy creature," "big round pale eyes," and so on (*H*, V, 118, 119). In *The Lord of the Rings*, Gollum is said to have "gleaming" eyes, "a clinging grip, soft but horribly strong," and "bone-white" arms and legs. When he falls, Gollum "curled his arms and legs up around him, like a spider whose descending thread is snapped." Prowling for food, Gollum is seen by Sam "crawling away on all fours." Gollum was originally a hobbit or of some similar type but has come to have his present form due to his relationship with the Ring and, evidently, his many years of life underground. The Morlocks blink painfully in the light (Wells, 47), and Gollum flinches from sunlight and curses the sun as the "White Face." The Morlocks eat the Eloi (Wells, 52); when he dwelled under the Misty Mountains, Gollum ate Goblins (*H*, V, 119).

If Tolkien read Wells's gruesome short novel *The Island of Dr. Moreau* (1896), he may have recalled it when he pondered the origin of Orcs. Frodo, here surely speaking for the author, says, "The Shadow that bred [Orcs] can only mock, it cannot make: not real new things of its own" (*RK*, VI, i, 190) and Tolkien states, in Appendix F, that the Orcs "were first bred [not "created"] by the Dark Power of the North," that is, Morgoth, "in the Elder Days" (*RK*, Appendix F, 409). Treebeard teaches that the Trolls "are only counterfeits, made by the Enemy in the Great Darkness, in mockery of Ents, and Orcs were of Elves" (*TT*, III, iv, 89), but Tolkien's Letter no. 153 (to Mr. Hastings, September 1954) advises that this does not necessarily mean Treebeard thought that Morgoth *created* them—and, in any event, Tolkien adds, Treebeard is not to be taken as infallible (*Letters*, 190). Tolkien ruled out the idea that Sauron or Morgoth created the Orcs *ex nihilo;* they must, then, in some way be the result of wicked tampering, like the Trolls, with some "stock" (*RK*, Appendix F, 410). That conception may be derived from Wells's novel. *Moreau*'s Beast-Folk were "manufactured" through vivisection, transfusions, skin grafts, and so on, performed upon existing animals. Dr. Moreau discovered that the "plasticity of living forms" is such that numerous grotesque creatures, some of them composed of body parts from more than one species, may be devised (Wells, 131). They are hypnotized in some manner not shown in the narrative (132) and fear and worship Moreau, somewhat as the Orcs are swayed by Sauron's will (so that, when the Dark Tower falls, the Orc-horde is instantly bewildered.

In years after publication of *The Lord of the Rings*, Tolkien speculated about the origin of the Orcs, noting that they could not have been developed from human "stock" since they fought with the Elves in the primordial past before the appearance of Men and gingerly wondered about how corrupted Elves might have been used in some way: "It remains therefore terribly possible there was an Elvish strain in the Orcs. These may then even have been mated with beasts (sterile!)—and later Men" (*Morgoth*, 411). Tolkien evidently conceived of Morgoth and Sauron, and Saruman in his development of the Uruk-hai, as proceeding somewhat as Wells's Moreau does. Treebeard says, with grim understatement, "he [Saruman] has been doing something to them" (the Orcs) (*LotR*, 462)—apparently something like what Moreau was doing to animals.

In folklore, magical devices conferring invisibility may help heroes perform worthy deeds. The first account of the Ring, in *The Hobbit* emphasizes how its power is used by Gollum to enable him to live a squalid, quasi-cannibalistic life in the depths of the Misty Mountains (*H*, V, 127–28). Before Tolkien's composition of *The Hobbit*, Wells's novel *The Invisible Man* (1897) related how Griffin of University College sought and found the scientific secret of invisibility because he was bitter about his life as "a shabby, poverty-struck, hemmed-in demonstrator, teaching fools in a provincial college" and believed that invisibility would make it possible for him to gain "the things a man reckons desirable." Eventually, he decides to begin a "Reign of Terror [in which] all who disobey his orders he must kill." Before this, his father dies when the Invisible Man steals money from him; the Invisible Man claims to feel no sorrow for him. Perhaps Tolkien's exploration of the corrupting effects of the Ring was suggested, in part, by the example of Wells's account.

Wells's *The First Men in the Moon* (1901) is a combination of pioneering straightforward science fiction adventure and satire. C.S. Lewis praised its chapter "Mr. Bedford Alone," for its quality of the sublime, in his essay "On Stories" (9). When Tolkien and Lewis agreed that each would write a book of the sort they liked and of which there was a quantity insufficient to suit them (Carpenter, 170), the book that Lewis wrote for his part of the bargain, *Out of the Silent Planet*, was obviously intended as both homage

and rejoinder to this novel of Wells's (Tolkien's effort was the unfinished *Lost Road*).

Tolkien's account of Moria and the creature in the pool at its Gate perhaps owes something to *First Men*: the lunar fishermen accidentally catch a "many-tentacled evil-eyed black thing, ferociously active" (Wells, 592). Tolkien's tentacled creature is in a deep pool outside the subsurface habitations of the Dwarves. Before Cavor and Bedford begin their journey among the Selenites, they hear alarming sounds: "Boom . . . Boom . . . Boom" (Wells, 507); compare the drumbeats in Orc-infested Moria: "Doom, doom." Bedford and Cavor escape from the inner world of the moon, their emergence (Wells, 556) vaguely suggesting the emergence from Moria of the surviving members of the Fellowship.

Tolkien's knowledge of Wells's novel is evident in the discussion of the gravity-repelling compound Cavorite in "The Notion Club Papers" (*Sauron*, 165–66); the substance is said there to be unconvincing.

Twentieth Century

Humphrey Carpenter's biography reports that Tolkien saw a production of *Peter Pan* by J.M. Barrie (1860–1937) in April 1910 (47). This would have had Pauline Chase as Peter and Frederick Annerley as Captain Hook (Green, 223). The production was "indescribable," Tolkien wrote in his diary, "but [one that I] shall never forget as long as I live" (Carpenter, 47). *Peter Pan* may have contributed to the idea of children in a fairy realm in Tolkien's early (approximately 1916) and unfinished *Book of Lost Tales*. Inventions such as "Tombo, the Gong of the Children," "the Room of the Log Fire for the telling of tales," children playing freely in a magical realm, and the enchanted land of the poem *You & Me and the Cottage of Lost Play* sound like they could have been things influenced by *Peter Pan*. But Christopher Tolkien states that "the entire conception of the Children who went to Valinor was to be abandoned almost without further trace" (*Lost Tales I*, 27). The play's "pattern of intricate role-playing, especially the interchange of pretences between child and adult, adult and child" (Barrie, note by Peter Hollindale to p. 89) or its "comic fantasy" mixing "sexual comedy and tensely exposed innocence" (note to p. 113) had nothing of lasting value to contribute to the development of Tolkien's legendarium.

Tolkien pondered Barrie's drama *Mary Rose* (first performed in 1920; Tolkien saw a theatrical performance at some time and read the play, first published in 1928). In the published form of "On Fairy-stories,"

Tolkien focused on Barrie's "cruelly tormented" humans who have lost someone they love to the fairies, who are never seen (*Reader*, 96). It is true that Mary Rose's parents, husband, and son have grieved over their loss, and that Mary's husband has been a harsh father to his motherless son, but in the play the bereft humans discover that their lives have continued and their hearts have *not* broken, not quite (*Mary Rose*, Act 3, lines 138–40, 180, 220). Also, Mary was allowed to return from Faërie twice: the first return permitted her to grow as a girl at home with her parents and to become a wife and mother, although the second return, after an absence of many years, evokes the father's unanswered question: "Do you think she should have come back?" (Act 3, line 402). Moreover, the conclusion of the play suggests the idea that the faithfulness of Mary's son is what enables her spirit to depart from this world and Faërie, and, before she does, she is permitted to tell Harry that the Other World where she had sojourned was "Lovely, lovely, lovely" (Act 3, line 547), though she had retained no memory of it when she returned alive to mortal fields. Tolkien believed that Barrie was unwilling to develop adequately the dark implications of the story. His unpublished notes to "On Fairy-stories" contain the phrase "entangled in 'Faerie'" (Flieger, 53), and even though he may not have settled the matter of Barrie's play to his own satisfaction, it is likely that it contributed to the seriousness with which he developed his own theme of mortal–elf entanglements in the accounts of, for example, Lórien and the sojourner of "The Sea-Bell" (98, 213), as well as the predicament faced by the Elf-woman Arwen in her love for Aragorn, a mortal.

That Tolkien had read some work by Algernon Blackwood (1869–1951) is certain based on "Notes on the Nomenclature of *The Lord of the Rings*" in its original, but not its published, version. Tolkien says, in the original "Notes," that the phrase "crack of doom" derives from an unnamed story by Blackwood (Lobdell, 9). This story by Blackwood has not been traced, however. Lobdell finds that "the treachery of natural things in an animate world," in Blackwood's "The Willows" and "The Glamour of the Snow," is evident in Tolkien's Old Man Willow and the snowstorm on Mount Caradhras in *The Fellowship of the Ring*.

Whatever else Tolkien may have read by Blackwood, he probably did read "The Willows" and "The Wendigo," which are often cited as the best of Blackwood's many tales. Passages in the chapter of *The Fellowship of the Ring* called "The Old Forest" seem to recall "The Willows"; a reader of the Blackwood story should compare Tolkien's description of "a dark river of brown water, bordered with ancient willows, blocked with fallen willows, and flecked with thousands of faded willow-leaves" (*FR*, I, vi, 126). Blackwood's evocation of landscape, as with Tolkien's, is unusually convincing. And perhaps "The Wendigo," with its dreadful aerial entity and the wailing cries from above that cause panic in hearers, contributed to one of the most important sources of terror to be found in *LotR*, the airborne Nazgûl.

One of the first American reviews of *The Fellowship of the Ring*, that of W.H. Auden, praised Tolkien's book as an adventure story "at least as good" as *The Thirty-Nine Steps*, the classic thriller by John Buchan (1875–1940). Tolkien was a confirmed reader of Buchan (Carpenter, 165). Buchan's "The Far Islands" from *The Watcher by the Threshold* (1902) is a tale rich in Tolkienian suggestions. Colin Raden is descendant of ancient Scottish chiefs. According to legend, "mad western voyages" are the "weird" of the family down through the generations, and "more than one sailed straight out of the ken of mortals" (97). From boyhood, Colin has recurrent fancies, dreams, and reveries. He broods over a "white road" by which he might walk west from the mainland, and as he matures he dreams of sailing toward the sea-fog and beyond, to hidden shores where he will find a well of sweet water and from whence he smells the scent of apple-blossom. He is outwardly successful in school and in business. Eventually he finds himself remembering scraps of "a kind of Latin," which a scholarly friend translates for him; the phrases refer to a land "far out in the Western Ocean, beyond the Utmost Islands." But Colin becomes a soldier, and in these last days of his life, "fragments of the Other world" impinge upon his awareness of the desert around him. Close to the end of the story, feverish in his tent, Colin begins to be haunted with a sense that the visionary "Rim of the Mist," ahead of him in his "fancies," is vaguely dreadful. The island is called "the forbidden shore," but when he receives a fatal bullet-wound, his soul escapes to the land of heart's desire, although his body is carried back to camp (111–12, 115–17).

Tolkien could have seen the story in editions of the collection *The Watcher at the Threshold* or other anthologies, or even perhaps its initial publication in an 1899 issue of *Blackwood's*. Buchan's story is remarkably similar both in atmosphere and in some details to Tolkien's unfinished stories "The Lost Road" and "The Notion Club Papers." Alboin in "The Lost Road," as a boy, is like Colin in being of uncertain health. Alboin's dreams bring him not only visions of some unknown land but also patches of language. In "The Notion Club Papers," to the element of recurrent dreams and memories of phrases is added the impingement of the other world upon the waking world. The cataclysm that Lowdham "remembers" breaks into his own time in "The Notion Club Papers"—the irruption in modern time of the destruction of Númenor that followed upon its armada's approach to the forbidden shore of the realm of the Lords of the West. Buchan's story begins with reference to the mythological world of Bran the Blessed (from the *Mabinogion*) and subsequently refers to "legend" (96), before arriving at the modern era, the world of Buchan's own youthful days and the school-story that occupies some pages of "The Far Islands." A similar progression is apparent when Jeremy, in "The Notion Club Papers," supposes that "if one could go back, one would find not myth dissolving into history, but rather the reverse: real history becoming more mythical" (*Sauron*, 227).

In Buchan's *The Power-House* (1913; book publication 1916), narrator Edward Leithen is menaced in the streets of London by members of a conspiratorial ring. The tense plot would have appealed to Tolkien, as would the theme of the insecurity of humane civilization. Leithen is told: "You think that a wall as solid as the earth separates civilisation from barbarism. I tell you the division is a thread, a sheet of glass" (64–65). In *The Lord of the Rings*, the power of Sauron's ring is so great that unless it is destroyed, all that is good and fair in Middle-earth will remain terribly vulnerable.

Buchan's *Greenmantle* (1916) is a story of desperate chances and plentiful good luck, of cross-country pursuit and massive battles. As with *The Lord of the Rings*, the focus is on the heroism of a handful of men, who sometimes act by themselves; events are so arranged that the heroes are not compelled to kill any of their enemies in cold blood. Frodo and others have precognitive dreams in *The Lord of the Rings*, and Hannay, in *Greenmantle*, dreams of a moment of supreme danger that arrives in the penultimate chapter. It occurs as a last stand on a fortified slope. There at last, the mission undertaken by Hannay and his friends has succeeded, though they expect to die at any moment, so Hannay muses: "It's the job that matters, not the men that do it. And our job's done. . . . After all, we never expected to come out of this thing with our lives" (263)—language similar to that of Frodo on the side of Mount Doom, after the Ring's destruction (*RK*, VI, iii, 224–25).

Buchan's *Mr. Standfast* (1919) is a novel of the Great War, Tolkien's war. It provides plenty of Buchan's customary cross-country flights (the sort of thing that Tolkien wrote in the early chapters of *The Fellowship of the Ring*) and escapes, highlighting individual heroism, as well as a sustained account of a frontline campaign. Eighteen-year-old Mary

Lamington insists on a dangerous, if noncombatant, role in the struggle. Like Éowyn, she has "had to wait and endure," although "women aren't the brittle things men used to think them" but supple and tough like whipcord (217).

A fifty-five-year-old, short, well-fed, and prosperous grocer on holiday, Dickson McCunn joins in the defense of an exiled Russian princess and a fortune in jewels in Buchan's *Huntingtower* (1922). If Tolkien read it, he might have been influenced in his conception of some elements of *The Hobbit*. "See here," McCunn complains to one of the princess's protectors, "You can't expect me to be going about burgling houses. . . . I'm a respectable man. . . . And I've no call to be mixing myself up in strangers' affairs." But he goes along on the "preposterous adventure," though he has to talk himself into behaving bravely more than once, like Bilbo. It falls to the lot of other characters in the novel, however, to bewilder a pack of ruffians with unexpected voices from unseen places (197; cf. Bilbo and the spiders of Mirkwood). McCunn grows in the esteem of the princess and her aristocratic fiancé—"He is what they call the middle class, which we who were foolish used to laugh at" (206)—and Bilbo eventually earns the approval of the lordly Thorin Oakenshield. The swift pace and high spirits of *Huntingtower* also align it with *The Hobbit*. Lobdell is right, in *The World of the Rings*, to suggest that Tolkien might have stolen a little time from writing for the journal *Essays and Studies* to read Buchan's yarn (17).

Interesting similarities exist between the rhyme that guides Sir Richard Hannay's quest to save the lives of three kidnapping victims in Buchan's *The Four Hostages* (1924) and the verse prophecy, recited by Boromir at the Council of Elrond, that alludes to the two chief events of the War of the Ring, namely, the assumption by a true King of the throne of Gondor and the fate of the Ring. For both poems, the context is a crisis in which time is severely limited and action must be taken soon. Both begin with "seek." Objects are named in riddling fashion: for example, in Buchan's verse "the sacred tree" means Gospel Oak, a London site, and in Tolkien's "Isildur's Bane" is Sauron's Ring. The meter of both poems is irregular, and each uses alliteration.

Seek where under midnight's sun / Laggard crops are hardly won;—/ Where the sower casts his seed in / Furrows of the fields of Eden;—/ Where beside the sacred tree / Spins the seer who cannot see. (Buchan 1955, 26)

The poem—called "doggerel" by Hannay (27)—rhymes AABBCC: the first two lines seven syllables, middle two lines eight syllables, and final two lines seven and eight syllables per line.

While the *Hostages* poem was sent, tauntingly, by the kidnappers but connects with an obscure memory of Dr. Greenslade, Hannay's friend, the prophecy came to Faramir and Boromir in their dreams; in either case, there is something preternatural about the poem's origin.

The *LotR* poem has a complicated rhyme scheme: ABCBADCD. The first two lines have, respectively, eight and six syllables, and the final two lines have eight and seven; the middle four lines have eight, six, eight, and six syllables. It is as if Tolkien liked the idea of a riddling quest-poem associated with elusive mental states (incomplete memory, dream) but was determined to write something more impressive than "doggerel."

Tolkien's interest in time-travel through use of faculties of the mind may have been prompted in part by Buchan's *The Gap in the Curtain* (1932), although he might not have been impressed by the working-out of the idea in the stories of six men and a woman who agree to participate in Professor Moe's experiment. The book's first part (of six) provides the theory, which is probably indebted to J.W. Dunne, author of *An Experiment with Time*, which Tolkien read with much interest (Flieger, 47). Through a regime of mental training and diet, and at the last the administration of a drug, the patients will, for a moment, glimpse something one year in the future, peeping through the "curtain" that normally prevents perception of the future. (The professor says that sometimes people do this in their dreams.) At the critical moment, the woman faints, and the book's narrator, Edward Leithen, rebels against Moe's psychic influence. The other five men see newspaper headlines indicating political developments or even their own deaths. *The Gap in the Curtain* has plenty of discursive dialogue, like Tolkien's "Notion Club Papers," but Buchan's book tends to have a worldly tone and lacks enchantment. Where Tolkien's dreamers sought knowledge of a mythic past, Buchan's dreamers deal in matters such as personal neurosis, political schemes, an "April–August" romance, and speculation in business shares.

The Warlord of Mars (1919) completes the trilogy, begun by *A Princess of Mars* and continued by *The Gods of Mars*, that launches the eleven-volume Martian cycle of Edgar Rice Burroughs (1875–1950). In *Warlord* chapter 5, narrator John Carter describes a sith, encountered in a jungle, thus: "a bald-faced hornet grown to the size of a Hereford bull. . . . Frightful jaws in front and mighty, poisoned sting behind . . . myriad facet eyes . . . six powerful legs," and so on. The sith attacks Carter's faithful calot (a sort of large Martian dog) so that "it might bring its sting beneath and pierce the body." Richard Lupoff asked Tolkien about siths and the apt, described in chapter 8 as "a huge, white-furred creature with six limbs" with a head like that of a hippopotamus. Tolkien acknowledged that he "did read many of Edgar Rice Burroughs' earlier works" but said he didn't remember these Martian monsters and said that he came to dislike the character of Tarzan (Lupoff, 246–47).

By 1937, Tolkien had read widely enough in the literary fantasies of Lord Dunsany (1878–1957) to feel competent to judge his nomenclature unfavorably (*Letters*, 26). In a 1972 letter, he alluded to Dunsany's tale of the rival idols Chu-Bu and Sheemish (*Letters*, 418). Tolkien's poem *The Mewlips* may be a recasting of the plot of Dunsany's "Hoard of the Gibbelins." Lyon Sprague de Camp records, in *Literary Swordsmen and Sorcerers* (243), that Tolkien referred disparagingly to Dunsany's "Distressing Tale of Thangobrind." The three stories are found in the collection *The Book of Wonder* (1912). There is little reason to suspect that Dunsany influenced Tolkien appreciably. Dunsany proffered many of his fictions as "dreams," even titling a typical collection of them *A Dreamer's Tales*, but Tolkien debarred stories with a dream explanation from Faërie ("On Fairy-stories" in *Reader*, 42) and never referred to Dunsany publicly. In a sense, Dunsany is an anti-Tolkien. Where Tolkien esteemed the "Elvish craft" (*Reader*, 70) that creates a convincing secondary world, Dunsany's pervasive irony and unreality suggest skepticism even about the value of the "primary world."

Tolkien commended *The Wind in the Willows* (1908) by Kenneth Grahame (1859–1932) as an "excellent book" in an aside in "On Fairy-stories" (*Reader*, 91). Its polarity, with underground coziness at one point and outdoors adventures at the other, may have contributed to *The Hobbit*. When Tolkien learned of the publication of *First Whispers of the Wind in the Willows*, a book with "stories (about Toad and Mole, etc.) that [Graham] wrote in letters to his son," in 1944, he was eager to acquire a copy (*Letters*, 90).

Although C.S. Lewis had read *The Night Land* (1912), there seems to be no certain evidence that Tolkien read it or any other works by William Hope Hodgson (1877–1918). If Tolkien were able to tolerate the pseudo-archaic style of the book, its episodes of a warrior's hazardous quest for his beloved, through weird landscapes of earth's remote, sunless future, could have appealed to him. It is possible that his conception of the Eye of Sauron, peering, as it were, from Mordor, owes something to the vast, immobile Watchers. The first few pages of "The Stairs of Cirith Ungol" (*TT*, IV, viii), describing Minas Morgul, the city of the Ringwraiths, might have been influenced by Hodgson.

C.S. Lewis's 1948 essay, "Kipling's World," suggests that Rudyard Kipling's strange stories may be his best (Lewis *Selected Essays*, 249). Among those cited by Lewis is "Wireless" (1902), in which a commonplace drugstore employee unknowingly begins to "tune in" on the consciousness of John Keats as the poet is/was writing "The Eve of St. Agnes." The idea of fragmentary mental connection across time appears in Tolkien's "Notion Club Papers," and the story by Kipling (1865–1936) is one of the possible sources from which Tolkien might have derived the idea.

Tolkien surely would have appreciated the feeling for England's past that comes across in the poem "Puck's Song" about "Merlin's Isle of Gramarye" at the beginning of *Puck of Pook's Hill* (1906). The first story, "Weland's Sword," establishes Puck, the only "Old Thing" left in the region, as mediator between the modern children Una and Dan and the lore of the fairies and English legendry. Supernatural Puck's deep voice, laughter, and lore, and his affinity for trees—"By Oak, Ash, and Thorn!"—make him kin to Bombadil and Treebeard. Weland, worshiped as a god, became Wayland the wonderful Smith and made a rune-marked sword. The penultimate story, "Dymchurch Flit," reveals how the fairies, or Pharisees as the country folk called them, left England at the time of the Reformation. The fairies are imagined as "knee-high" to an adult human and as having wings. The theme of the departure of the fairies/elves was crucial for Tolkien, and in his early legendarium he struggled to find a satisfactory way of integrating this with the heritage of England.

Lewis described *A Voyage to Arcturus* (1920), the only book by David Lindsay (1876–1945) that is at all well known, as "a passionate spiritual journey" in the guise of a science fiction romance, finding it "shattering, intolerable, and irresistible" (Lewis *On Stories*, 19, 71). As the hero, Maskull, explores the planet Tormance, encountering inhabitants such as Joiwind, Panawe, Oceaxe, and Spadevil, Lindsay's allegory is elaborated, its central thesis being that the phenomenal world is a sham and matter is a prison and the real world (Muspel) transcends all images and even life. The Tormantians embody various states of the soul, such as altruism, assertion of the will, love, and aesthetic ecstasy—none of which is the way to Muspel. *Voyage* abounds in people and scenes that should have been illustrated by Hannes Bok. Tolkien read the book "with avidity" as a "thriller" that required attention to its philosophical and religious themes (letter to Stanley Unwin, March 4, 1938; *Letters*, 26), though Tolkien would have disagreed with Lindsay's ideas: for example, Maskull says, "I'm aware I am on a strange planet where all sorts of unheard

of things may happen, and where the very laws of morality may be different" (Lindsay, 91), and Aragorn says, "Good and ill have not changed since yesteryear; nor are they one thing among Elves and Dwarves and another among Men. It is a man's part to discern them, as much in the Golden Wood as in his own house" (*TT*, III, ii, 41). Tolkien also regretted Lindsay's apparatus of "back-rays" and a "crystal torpedo" rocket ship; in his "Notion Club Papers" he has Guildford censure such "contraptions."

According to John Garth (79), Tolkien donated a copy of *The Lost Explorers* (1907) by Alexander MacDonald (1878–1939) to the King Edward's School in Birmingham in 1912. One should not assume that the gesture betokens great enthusiasm on Tolkien's part for this "lost race" romance; it's possible that he did not want to keep his copy and thought other readers might like it more than he had. A story for boys that is largely about gold-digging in the Australian desert, the book eventually features pursuit inside a mountain by warriors pattering after the heroes. There could be a faint echo of this sequence in the pursuit of the Fellowship by Orcs in Moria. That a "Mystic Mountain" is prominent in *The Lost Explorers'* search for hidden wealth could have meant something to the author of *The Hobbit*.

Early in his writing of *Roverandom* (begun ca. 1925; published posthumously in 1998), Tolkien called the character Psamathos a *Psammead*, using the word for a sand-goblin from *Five Children and It* (1902) by Edith Nesbit (1858–1924). Tolkien settled on *Psamathists* as the name for the sand-sorcerers. Nesbit's fantasy is largely concerned with humorous episodes in the real world that occur when the Psammead grants wishes to four English children, and Tolkien's book is about a dog's adventures in fantastic undersea and lunar realms.

Writing to Stanley Unwin to recommend publication of C.S. Lewis's *Out of the Silent Planet* in 1938, Tolkien referred to his great fondness for supposedly true accounts of journeys in strange lands of the imagination, "even" to the point of "having read *Land Under England* with some pleasure (thought it was a weak example, and distasteful to me in many points" (*Letters*, 33).

Perhaps Tolkien enjoyed most the first five chapters of this 1935 book by Joseph O'Neill (1886–1953), which precedes the description, cumbered with redundancies, of a subterranean, totalitarian civilization, descended from ancient British Romans. The narrator's quest for the hidden entrance to the underworld, and the description of his descent, possess imaginative power. The inscribed slab in chapter 3 might have contributed to the account, in *The Fellowship of the Ring*, of the tomb of Balin in Moria, on which runes have been carved (*FR*, II, iv, 334). The protagonist of *Land Under England* is endangered by creatures that have whip-like appendages; Frodo and his companions are attacked by a tentacled monster on the doorstep of Moria. O'Neill's protagonist, so long deprived of sunlight, "the barking of dogs," and other concomitants of life on the Earth's surface, remembers them with desire when his clothes are returned to him (O'Neill 1985, 189), suggesting the experience of renewed love of the commonplace that Tolkien identifies as one of the blessings provided by fairy stories (*Reader*, 77).

Tolkien was interested in the writings of Beatrix Potter (1866–1943) and knew enough about the author to refer sympathetically to her giving her translators hell (*Letters*, 251). Of her books, *The Tailor of Gloucester* comes closest to the borders of Faërie, and *The Tale of Mrs. Tiggy-Winkle* would "come as near" if not for the suggestion of a dream explanation, Tolkien avers in "On Fairy-stories" (*Reader*, 43). He approves of the moral dimension of these stories and sees *The Tale of Peter Rabbit* as hinting at the biblical account of Paradise lost (57).

Tolkien's combination of verbal and visual storytelling in *Mr. Bliss* (which is not a Faerian tale) may owe something to the example of Potter.

In "The Notion Club Papers," Ramer refers to "the telepathic notion" as one possible way by which human beings might "visit" other worlds (*Sauron*, 175). Ramer guesses that this idea is found in *Last Men in London* (1932) by Olaf Stapledon (1886–1950), a book that science fiction critic Sam Moskowitz has described as "at best a dull work" and a disappointment after the better-known *Last and First Men* (1930), first of Stapledon's fictional books (Moskowitz, 41). Much of *Last Men in London* is about the World War I experiences of "Paul," as evaluated by the consciousness of someone from the far future. It may be that Tolkien read some, but not all, of this book.

Conclusion

C.S. Lewis thought it was just possible that "our age" might one day be "known to posterity not as that of Eliot and Auden but as that of Buchan and Wodehouse" ("High and Low Brows," Lewis, *On Stories*, 273). Tolkien's rejoinder, to reviewers who found *The Lord of the Rings* "boring, absurd, or contemptible," was to state that he had similar views of their works or those they presumably liked; conversely, he freely enjoyed, and was influenced by, writings that such critics would have disapproved of.

He saw himself, at least as regards *The Lord of the Rings*, as being, like Buchan—and Haggard and others discussed—first and foremost a teller of tales (*LotR*, xvi).

DALE NELSON

Further Reading

Anderson, Douglas A., ed. *Tales Before Tolkien: The Roots of Modern Fantasy*. New York: Ballantine, 2003.

Auden, W.H. "The Hero Is a Hobbit." *New York Times Book Review*, October 31, 1955, 37.

Barrie, J.M. *Peter Pan, and Other Plays*. Edited by Peter Hollindale. Oxford: World's Classics, 1995.

Blackwood, Algernon. *Best Ghost Stories*. Edited by E.F. Bleiler. New York: Dover, 1973.

Browning, Robert. *Childe Roland to the Dark Tower Came*. In *The Norton Anthology of English Literature*. 7th ed. Vol. 2, Edited by M.H. Abrams et al. New York: Norton, 2000.

Buchan, John. *The Far Islands and Other Tales of Fantasy*. Edited by John Bell. West Kingston: Donald M. Grant, 1984. ["The Far Islands" was published in 1899.]

———. *The Four Hostages*. Harmondsworth: Penguin, 1955. [First published in 1924.]

———. *The Gap in the Curtain*. Project Gutenberg of Australia E-text, 2003. [First published in 1932.]

———. *Greenmantle*. edited by Kate MacDonald. Oxford: Oxford University Press World's Classics, 1993. [First published in 1916.]

———. *Huntingtower*. edited by Ann F. Stonehouse. Oxford: Oxford University Press, World's Classics, 1996. [First published 1922.]

———. *Mr. Standfast*. edited by William Buchan. Oxford: Oxford University Press, World's Classics, 1993. [First published in 1919.]

———. *The Power-House*. Edinburgh: Blackwood, 1916.

Burroughs, Edgar Rice. *The Warlord of Mars* (1919). Text available online at Project Gutenberg. http://www.gutenberg.org/etext/68.

Carpenter, Humphrey. *Tolkien: A Biography*. Boston: Houghton Mifflin, 1977.

Crockett, S.R. *The Black Douglas*. New York: Doubleday and McClure, 1901.

de Camp, Lyon Sprague. *Literary Swordsmen and Sorcerers*. Sauk City, WI: Arkham, 1976.

Dickens, Charles. *A Christmas Carol*. New York: Pocket Books, 1958. [First published 1843.]

———. *Hard Times*. New York: Books, Inc. [n.d.] [First published 1854.]

———. *The Old Curiosity Shop*. New York: Books, Inc. [n.d.] [First published in 1841.]

———. *The Pickwick Papers*. edited by Mark Wormald. Harmondsworth: Penguin, 1999. [First published in 1837.]

Dunsany, Lord. *Gods, Men and Ghosts*. edited by E.F. Bleiler. New York: Dover, 1972.

Flieger, Verlyn. *A Question of Time: J.R.R. Tolkien's Road to Faërie*. Kent, OH: Kent State University Press, 1997.

Garth, John. *Tolkien and the Great War: The Threshold of Middle-earth*. London: HarperCollins, 2003.

Gilbert, W.S., and Arthur Sullivan. *The Pirates of Penzance*. New York: Schirmer, [n.d.].

Green, Roger Lancelyn. *Fifty Years of Peter Pan*. London: Peter Davies, 1954.

Haggard, H. Rider. *Ayesha: The Return of She*. New York: Grosset and Dunlap, 1905.

————. *Eric Brighteyes*. Hollywood: Newcastle, 1974. [First published in 1891.]

————. *Heu-Heu or The Monster* (1923). Available online at Project Gutenberg.

————. *King Solomon's Mines*. Edited by Dennis Butts. Oxford: Oxford University Press World's Classics, 1989. [First published in 1885.]

————. "Long Odds" (1886). Available online at Project Gutenberg. http://www.gutenberg.org/etext/2730.

————. *She: A History of Adventure*. edited by Daniel Karlin. Oxford: Oxford University Press World's Classics, 1991. [First published in 1887.]

————. *The Treasure of the Lake* (1926).

Hodgson, William Hope. *The Night Land*. 2 vols. New York: Ballantine, 1972. [First published in 1912.]

Jefferies, Richard. *Wood Magic*. New York: Third Press, 1974. [First published in 1881.]

Kipling, Rudyard. *A Choice of Kipling's Prose*. edited by Craig Raine. London: Faber, 1987. [Contains "Wireless."]

————. *Kipling: A Selection of His Stories and Poems*. Vol. 1, edited by John Beecroft. New York: Doubleday, [n.d.]. [Contains "Puck's Song," "Weland's Sword," and "Dymchurch Flit."]

Lewis, C.S. *On Stories and Other Essays on Literature*. Edited by Walter Hooper. San Diego: Harcourt Brace Jovanovich, 1982.

————. *Selected Literary Essays*. edited by Walter Hooper. Cambridge: Cambridge University Press, 1969. [Contains "Kipling's World" and "High and Low Brows."]

Lindsay, David. *A Voyage to Arcturus*. New York: Ballantine, 1973. [First published in 1920.]

Lobdell, Jared. *The World of the Rings: Language, Religion and Adventure in Tolkien*. Chicago: Open Court, 2004.

Lupoff, Richard. *Edgar Rice Burroughs: Master of Adventure*. New York: Canaveral, 1965.

MacDonald, Alexander. *The Lost Explorers*. London: Blackie, 1907.

Moskowitz, Sam. *Far Future Calling: Uncollected Science Fiction and Fantasies of Olaf Stapledon*. Philadelphia: Train, 1979.

Nelson, Dale. "Haggard's *Heu-Heu* and *The Hobbit*." *Beyond Bree* (December 2005): 2.

————. "Haggard's *The Treasure of the Lake* and Tolkien's 'Tower of Cirith Ungol' Episode." *Beyond Bree* (January 2006): 8.

————. "Little Nell and Frodo the Halfling." *Tolkien Studies* 2 (2005): 245–48.

————. "Possible Echoes of Blackwood and Dunsany in Tolkien's Fantasy." *Tolkien Studies* 1 (2004): 177–81.

————. "'Queer, Exciting, and Debatable': Tolkien and Shorthouse's *John Inglesant*." *Beyond Bree* (January 2006): 4–5.

O'Neill, Joseph. *Land Under England*. Woodstock: Overlook, 1985.

Power, Norman. "Ring of Doom." *The Tablet* (December 20/27, 1975): 1,247–48. [On Tolkien's interest in J. H. Shorthouse.]

Resnik, Henry. "An Interview with Tolkien." *Niekas* 18 (Spring 1967): 37–47.

Shorthouse, J.H. *John Inglesant: A Romance*. New York: Macmillan, 1889.

Stapledon, Olaf. *"Last and First Men" and "Last Men in London"* (one volume). Harmondsworth: Penguin, 1973. [*Last Men in London* originally published in 1932.]

Thompson, Francis. "Daisy." Text online at Bartleby.com. http://www.bartleby.com/103/26.html.

————. "The Mistress of Vision." In *New Poems*. Classic Books Online from Emotionalliteracyeducation.com, 2005. [First published in 1897.]

————. *The Sister Songs*. Available online at Project Gutenberg. http://www.gutenberg.org/etext/1731. [First published in 1895.]

Tolkien, J.R.R. *Roverandom*. Boston: Houghton Mifflin, 1998.

————. *The Tolkien Reader*. New York: Ballantine/Del Rey, 63rd printing.

Tolkien, J.R.R., and Donald Swann. *The Road Goes Ever On: A Song Cycle*. 3rd ed. London: HarperCollins, 2002.

Wells, H.G. *Seven Science Fiction Novels of H.G. Wells*. New York: Dover, [n.d.].

LITERATURE, TWENTIETH CENTURY: INFLUENCE OF TOLKIEN

The simplest claim one can make for Tolkien's influence on the literature of the twentieth century is to say that he established the genre of serious heroic fantasy. That flat statement immediately requires some qualification. Heroic fantasy existed before Tolkien, sometimes on an ambitious scale, as in the works of the Englishman E.R. Eddison (1882–1945), author most notably of *The Worm Ourobouros* (1922) and *A Fish Dinner in Memison* (1941); or in those of the American James Branch Cabell (1879–1958), whose slightly risqué series set in the realm of Poictesme includes *The Cream of the Jest* (1917) and *Jurgen* (1919) and was offered for favorable comparison with Tolkien by the critic Edmund Wilson (1895–1972). Shorter fantasies had also sometimes been successful, especially those of Lord Dunsany (1878–1957), as described later.

In America, two schools of writers centered on rival, or complementary, pulp fiction magazines, *Weird Tales* and *Unknown*. Among the major contributors to *Weird Tales* were H.P. Lovecraft (1890–1937) and Robert E. Howard (1906–36). Both the horror stories of the former, with their hints of a lost mythology, and the sword-and-sorcery tales of the latter, with their elaborately detailed geography, resembled Tolkien in creating generations of imitators and would-be continuators. *Unknown*'s contributors tended toward a more comic style and included Fritz Leiber (1910–92), Lyon Sprague de Camp (1907–2000), and Fletcher Pratt (1897–1956). A slightly younger generation, writing in similar style, included Jack Vance (1916–) and Poul Anderson (1926–2001). Most of this group had extraordinarily long and productive careers. Leiber's Lankhmar series ran in the end to six collected volumes; de Camp's writing career in fantasy, science fiction, and "alternative history" spanned almost sixty years from the 1930s to the 1990s; and Vance kept up an astonishingly high level of quality in his fantasy from *The Dying Earth* in 1950 to his Lyonesse sequence of 1983–89, as did Anderson, whose work receives further comment later. Pratt produced two extended heroic fantasies in *The Well of the Unicorn* (1948) and *The Blue Star* (1952) and is known also for his Incomplete Enchanter series with de Camp.

Fantasy would have flourished, then, without Tolkien. Yet Tolkien made a serious and lasting difference. For one thing, *The Lord of the Rings* was unprecedentedly successful commercially. The rise of "the Tolkien cult" is often thought to date from the 1960s, with the pirated Ace paperback edition of 1965, the immediate and unexpected anger of fans and writers that forced Ace to make terms, and the authorized American paperback brought out by Ballantine the same year. It should be noted, though, that the first hardback edition of *The Lord of the Rings* went through at least nine impressions before 1960, most of them selling in the United Kingdom at twenty-five shillings a volume at a time when a working man's wage might be some five or six shillings an hour. The books were imposingly printed and finished as well, with elaborate covers, foldout maps, and a slip case for the three volumes. This was clearly neither "pulp fiction" nor "coterie fiction." Publishers, including Tolkien's own publisher, George Allen & Unwin, took note of a surprising success and scented a new market.

Another significant factor was that no sequel emerged. It was rumored early on that Tolkien had another work in progress, *The Silmarillion*, which many assumed would be a sequel, and there was great interest in its appearance. But as the years went by and nothing emerged, publishers sensed a growing hunger, only increased when, in 1977, *The Silmarillion* did finally make its appearance but proved to be neither a sequel nor a work similar to *The Lord of the Rings*.

A further factor has been well expressed by Diana Wynne Jones (1934–), herself a prolific and successful author of many fantasies. In her highly un-Tolkienian fantasy *Fire and Hemlock* (1984)—a retelling in a modern urban setting of the old ballad of "Tam Lin"—she shows her schoolgirl heroine reading *The Lord of the Rings*. Polly is bowled over by it. She reads it four times through and then immediately writes her own adventure, of "Tan Coul and Hero, and how they hunted the Obah Cypt in the Caves of Doom . . . it was clear to her that the Obah Cypt was really a ring

which was very dangerous and had to be destroyed." She posts the manuscript off to her mentor Mr. Lynn, but he replies discouragingly: "No, it's not a ring. You stole that from Tolkien. Use your own ideas."

No one can say that Jones does not use her own ideas, but she notes a phenomenon: Middle-earth is such a powerful universe that many readers—as one can see from the flood of "fan fiction" posted on the Internet—felt and feel an immediate urge to write their own story in it or alongside it. In *Meditations on Middle-earth*, a set of reflections on Tolkien collected by Karen Haber and written by many of the most prominent contemporary writers of fantasy and science fiction, the "Polly phenomenon" is repeatedly corroborated. Harry Turtledove (1949–) records that he wrote a sequel to *Lord of the Rings* as an eighteen-year-old undergraduate. It was never published, but it formed the basis for his first published novel twelve years later. He notes that he was neither of the two people mentioned in the letter dated December 12, 1966 (*Letters*, 292), who sent Tolkien outlines for a sequel; the same idea occurred independently to several, perhaps to many, aspiring writers. In the same volume Robin Hobb (1952–) mentions her despair at finishing *Lord of the Rings:* "I feared I'd never find anything again that would satisfy me as it had." Could she write something like that herself? One thing she knew was that "the bar had been raised." Any fantasy author now would have to do what Tolkien had done—the phrase this time comes from the introduction to the volume by George R.R. Martin (1948–)— "create a fully realized secondary universe."

By the early 1970s, there was therefore strong reader interest in stories like Tolkien's and publisher awareness of an immense potential new market, one result of which was the launching, by Ballantine Books, of an Adult Fantasy series edited by Lin Carter. This republished successfully a number of forgotten fantasies, including three volumes of stories by Lord Dunsany and his novel *The King of Elfland's Daughter* (1924). There was meanwhile an unknown number of ambitious writer-followers, all of them trying, one might say, to be like Tolkien but not like Jones's heroine Polly. Tolkien's example was inspiring, but it could also be crushing. The problem was to find one's own voice.

The clearest example of a work from this period dominated by Tolkien is *The Sword of Shannara* by Terry Brooks (1944–), published in 1977, again by Ballantine, with the deliberate aim of satisfying the Tolkien-fan market. The book was an immediate success and has generated many successors in the Shannara series. The 1977 volume is, however, in many respects a point-for-point copy of *Lord of the*

Rings. Evil is rising again after an earlier defeat to menace Men, Elves, and Dwarves. It is centered in the Skull Kingdom, ruled by the Warlock Lord (Mordor, Sauron). There is a talisman that can be used against him, but this must be wielded by Shea from Shady Vale, accompanied by Flick (Frodo and Sam from the Shire). They are informed by Allanon the Wizard, and their company is joined by Balinor and Menion Leah (respectively, repeats of Gandalf, Boromir, and Aragorn). The Skull Bearers who hunt them correspond to Ringwraiths, the Black Oaks to the Old Forest, the Mist Wraith to the Watcher in the Water, the Druid Council to the White Council, and so on. Even the names are similar, or simply taken over: Brooks has an Elf called Durin and an Elven banner of the house of Elessedil (Elessar/Elendil?). Brooks's Gollum-equivalent is the Gnome Orl Fane: he is found clutching the Sword of Shannara in the climactic scene and is killed because he "would not give up his precious possession" to Shea. The continuing appetite of a large readership indicates that Brooks has succeeded at some level in creating his own "secondary universe." But to begin with, at least, it is so derivative from Tolkien as perhaps to deserve the term "tertiary universe."

This is not the case with another sequence begun in the same year, 1977, when Stephen Donaldson (1947–) brought out the first volume of his Chronicles of Thomas Covenant, *Lord Foul's Bane.* Similarities are almost as pronounced as in Brooks's work. The character Berek Halfhand is bound to recall Beren One-handed; the Plains of Ra are like the Riddermark of Rohan; "ur-viles" are Orcs, Ravers correspond to Ringwraiths, the sylvan city of Soaring Woodhelven resembles the Wood-elven land of Lothlórien. Perhaps most obviously, Foamfollower the Giant is a close match to Treebeard the Ent, sharing both his strange, slow language and his racial childlessness. However, Donaldson's world, theme, and plot are all strikingly different than Tolkien's. It could be argued that Frodo and even more Bilbo function as "mediators" between the ancient world of Middle-earth and the world of modern readers, for in most respects they resemble modern if by now old-fashioned Englishmen. Donaldson's hero Thomas Covenant, though, does not resemble a modern American: he is one, transported into the fantasy world. He is also a most abnormal American in being a leper, and he is unlike any Tolkienian hero in committing a rape shortly after his arrival in the fantasy world. Where Tolkien is concerned above all with corruption, one might say, Donaldson's theme is healing, of the hero and the land. The debt (and this applies to many if not most of Tolkien's followers) is on the level of setting, not theme or even style.

Donaldson's case raises a further issue. What is one to make of the many fantasy authors, usually English (Moorcock, Pullman, Garner), who reject and even attack Tolkien, for essentially political reasons? Alan Garner (1934–) has denied any influence from Tolkien, and this seems entirely true of his later works. Yet his early children's novel, *The Weirdstone of Brisingamen* (1960), looks Tolkienian in just the same way as the two discussed previously. Deep in the mine of Fundindelve, the Dwarf Fenodyree tells the children Colin and Susan, "so deep did men delve that they touched upon the secret places of the earth, known only to a few . . . and they are places of dread, even for dwarves." Even in phrasing this is too like the Mines of Moria to be coincidence. Garner might respond, however, by pointing to his title. "Brisingamen" is clearly taken from the famous necklace of Old Norse and Old English legend, the *Brisinga mén,* which is also the model for the Nauglafring in *The Silmarillion.* Just as Tolkien drew inspiration from ancient myths, so Garner could do the same. Some similarities could derive from a common source, not from direct one-to-one borrowing— though many would never have been drawn to the common source without Tolkien's example.

An analogous point may be made by looking at the works of Terry Pratchett (1948–), who apart from J.K. Rowling (discussed later) is probably the most commercially successful fantasy author now writing. Pratchett's Discworld, with its dwarves, trolls, wizards, dragons, and elves (these latter admittedly rarely encountered), seems heavily dependent on Tolkien, and in-jokes scattered through the series make it certain that Pratchett has read Tolkien with care and attention and assumes that his readers have, too. Nevertheless, the first work in the series, *The Colour of Magic* (1983), consists of four sections, each a parody of a different fantasy author or authors: in sequence, Leiber, Howard/Lovecraft, Anne McCaffrey (1926–), and de Camp, four of them certainly independent of Tolkien, as noted earlier, and McCaffrey likely so. Just as Garner shows that a debt to Tolkien may also be a debt to mythology, so Pratchett's case shows that a debt to Tolkien may be mingled with a debt to fantasy in general.

Three final individual cases one might consider are those of C.S. Lewis (1898–1963), J.K. Rowling (1965–), and Philip Pullman (1946–). How much do *The Chronicles of Narnia* owe to Middle-earth? They were published between 1950 and 1956, but are known to have been written in a shorter period from 1948 on. At this time, Lewis was in regular if not quite daily contact with Tolkien, and he had, for more than a decade, been present at meeting of the Inklings, at which Tolkien often read sections of his developing work, *The Lord of the Rings*. Lewis's influence on Tolkien was indeed great, if only as encouragement. One has every reason to expect the reverse to be true. Yet the Narnia books are in some respects un-Tolkienian, and it is known that Tolkien was unimpressed by them. Lewis never sorted out the linguistic history of his imaginary world; he allows violent anachronisms and illogicalities, like the appearance of Father Christmas in a world that does not know Christ; and an element of Christian allegory is often strongly present. Yet there are perhaps deeper similarities: the idea of a world containing many different intelligent species, all with their own concerns, and the strong sense of sinfulness, even in child-heroes and heroines. Most undeniably, the very success of Tolkien's work, that he could finish something as aberrant in the postwar world as a romantic epic and find a publisher and a readership for it, must have had some effect on Lewis, if only again as encouragement. Tolkien had brought fairy tale and myth back into the world and made them respectable. This unlikely achievement should never be underestimated.

What of Rowling's Harry Potter stories? Even in setting these seem to owe nothing to Tolkien. They take place in the contemporary world and in England, even if in them there is a magical world side by side with the mundane one of the "muggles." Rowling's unmatched creative flow of names, spells, games, and objects betrays no Tolkien borrowings. In the most general terms, there is a kind of similarity of plot outline: in both authors there is a Dark Lord who aims to take over the world, is opposed by a small group of heroes and heroines, and is abetted by non-human groups and human traitors. Harry Potter is a little like Frodo in being a parentless child thrust suddenly into universal conflict, with enormous responsibilities. In his wisdom, benevolence, and great but limited power, as in his dress and appearance, Rowling's Dumbledore resembles Tolkien's Gandalf. But wizards and the good fortune of orphans are both standard elements of fairy tale, going back long before either author. Meanwhile, Philip Pullman has made his dislike of Tolkien, and even more of Lewis, perfectly clear. He thinks both were essentially reactionary authors, trying to bring back an older conservative and hierarchical system that he had hoped would be eradicated. Pullman's *His Dark Materials* trilogy (1995–2000) owes nothing to Tolkien in setting, theme, or style. Just the same, if Pullman had approached a publisher in any pre- or non-Tolkienian universe with a proposal for a long and ambitious trilogy, set in a world of witches, talking bears, and animal-daemons, one feels his chances of success would have been low.

The point is made in a personal way by Poul Anderson in the volume of *Meditations* already mentioned. Anderson made his name and career as an author primarily of science fiction, but he also had ambitions to write mythological fantasy. He wrote such a work in 1948 and saw it published as *The Broken Sword* in 1954, to little interest. When he offered to revise and reissue it in 1971, the response was very different, and Anderson is in no doubt that this was because of Tolkien. Other authors in the volume—besides those already mentioned, there are contributions from Raymond Feist, Michael Swanwick, Terry Pratchett, Ursula K. Le Guin, Orson Scott Card, Charles de Lint, Terri Windling, and others, all prominent and successful fantasy writers or anthologists—continue the theme of deep, personal indebtedness. Martin Greenberg's anthology *After the King: Stories in Honor of J.R.R. Tolkien* (1992) contains stories by six of the authors mentioned already (Donaldson, Pratchett, Anderson, Turtledove, de Lint, and Haber) and thirteen more, including authors more familiar in science fiction. And behind these there lie an almost incalculable number of other imitators, followers, rivals, and competitors, their motives and results as varied as themselves. One can see the Tolkien influence, often from titles alone. Clifford D. Simak's *The Fellowship of the Talisman* (1978) changes only one word of its title from Tolkien's first volume. R.A. Salvatore's *The Halfling's Gem* (1990) uses a word all but lost from the language before Tolkien, and it was followed by the Dark Elf trilogy (1990–91). David Eddings's Malloreon sequence, begun by *Guardians of the West* (1987), has *The Silmarillion* behind it. Guy Gavriel Kay got his start by helping Christopher Tolkien to edit the same work. *The Elfin Ship* (1982), by James Blaylock (1950–), was followed by *The Disappearing Dwarf* (1983). Mike Scott Rohan's name (1951–) is genuine coincidence, but his *Winter of the World* trilogy (1986–88) is Tolkienian at least in original impulse. Any visit to a contemporary bookstore will disclose, first, a section labeled "Fantasy and Science Fiction" (the majority of it fantasy) and, second, literally scores of works showing an evident debt to Tolkien, in title, personnel, setting, and even layout—all authors now know that an essential part of creating the "fully realized secondary universe" is the creation of a map. The phenomenon was so marked as to provoke Diana Wynne Jones, again, to publish her satirical *Tough Guide to Fantasyland* in 1996.

Tolkien revitalized fantasy; he made it respectable; he created an appetite for it in both readers and publishers; he brought fairy tale and myth back from the literary margins; he "raised the bar" for fantasy writers. His influence has been so powerful and so pervasive that for many authors the problem has been not to follow him but to disengage from him, to find their own voices, something often achieved only at length, by steadily writing the Tolkien influence out of their systems. The world of Middle-earth, like the world of *Grimms' Fairy Tales* in the previous century, has become part of the Western world's mental furniture. All these claims seem undeniably true. Yet one might also consider the question of Tolkien's influence on the shared culture of Europe and America, even outside literature.

The critique of Tolkien mounted by Michael Moorcock (and many others) could be summed up by saying that in creating the idyllic preindustrial landscape of the Shire and its Hobbit inhabitants, a society saved in the end by a revived monarchy and the return of its ancestral lords, Tolkien was promoting a characteristically English nostalgia for the past, a rejection of the issues of the present and future. There are several possible responses to this, including the counterclaim that Tolkien was confronting the most serious issues of his time (power and its abuses) and the demonstration that his work has proved immensely popular well beyond its original English target audience. However, one may agree that Tolkien has become a major figure in what are often called "the culture wars."

His position is rather strange but not by any means unfamiliar. Tolkien shows no great feeling for democracy, but his work has popular appeal; by contrast, the works promoted by theoretically democratic, or even Marxist critics, are often clearly designed for a literary elite. Tolkien's world is a masculine one, Éowyn, Arwen, and Galadriel apart; but he appeals as much to one gender as to the other. He is often accused of "racism," but a glance at Richard Blackwelder's *Tolkien Thesaurus* (1990) shows that in *The Lord of the Rings* he rarely uses the word "race" and never in the modern sense used by official bureaucracies (Caucasian, Asian, Hispanic, etc.). In Tolkien's English, the word means either "species" (the hobbits are "a remarkable race") or more often family bloodline ("the race of Elendil"). His personal record in opposing Nazi anti-Semitism cannot be faulted, which is more than one can say for many literary icons of his time.

What these apparent contradictions collectively suggest is that many of the issues that perturb the academic and political worlds were of little interest to Tolkien and remain so to millions of readers. Tolkien has proved a powerful reinforcement for conservative or traditional values, not least in his creation of a newly heroic style, immune to the pervasive irony, or cynicism, of the educated literary world. It would be a mistake to label this as "right-wing." If he

were voting today, Tolkien would certainly vote for the Green Party; in the 1960s and 1970s, he was very much part of the American "counterculture," and he remains immensely popular with demonstrators and protest groups, not least in Eastern Europe. Nevertheless, one of his major roles has been to provide ideological support, largely unconscious, for many readers who have not become disenchanted with "Western civilization" or "liberal humanism," despite all efforts of educators, critics, and other professional elites. When one adds to his own impact that of the uncountable numbers of his followers, Tolkien becomes one of the few writers in world literature who may be thought to have made a difference, perceptible though beyond estimation, on the wider world beyond literature. Finally, his influence, literary and cultural, has grown steadily for more than fifty years and shows no sign of slackening.

TOM SHIPPEY

Further Reading

Anderson, Douglas A., ed. *Tales Before Tolkien: The Roots of Modern Fantasy*. New York: Ballantine, 2003.

Clute, John, and John Grant, eds. *The Encyclopedia of Fantasy*. New York: St Martin's, 1997.

Haber, Karen, ed. *Meditations on Middle-earth*. New York: St Martin's, 2001.

Jones, Diana Wynne. *The Tough Guide to Fantasyland*. London: Vista, 1996.

Le Guin, Ursula K. *The Language of the Night: Essays on Fantasy and Science Fiction*. Revised edition. London: Women's Press, 1989.

Magill, Frank N., ed. *Survey of Modern Fantasy Literature*. 5 vols. Englewood Cliffs, NJ: Salem Press, 1983.

Senior, William A. "Donaldson and Tolkien." Chap. 3 in *Stephen R. Donaldson's "The Chronicles of Thomas Covenant": Variations on the Fantasy Tradition*, 62–97. Kent, OH: Kent State University Press, 1995.

Shippey, Tom, ed. *The Oxford Book of Fantasy Stories*. London: Oxford University Press, 1994.

See also **America in the 1960s: Reception of Tolkien; Auden, W.H.: Influence of Tolkien; Environmentalism and Eco-Criticism; Literary Context, Twentieth Century; Marxist Readings of Tolkien; Philo-Semitism; Politics; Race and Ethnicity in Tolkien's Works; Racism, Charges of; Russia: Reception of Tolkien**

LOMBARDIC LANGUAGE

Lombardic has been considered by some a cognate of Old High German (which is a West Germanic tongue) but more often an Ingaevonian (or North-Sea German) tongue, cognate with English and Frisian (and thus from a different branch of West Germanic). Paul the Deacon (eighth century) tells us the Langobardi were ultimately of Scandinavian origin, pausing at the Elbe for some time before coming into Italy. Tacitus *(Germania)* puts them among the *Suevi.* Their alphabet seems essentially that of the Goths, with *-h-* having the *-kh-* value of Gothic but with a grapheme representing *[s]*, as well as *-s-* and *-ts- (z).*

However, Gothic was an East Germanic tongue (with Vandalic, Burgundian, Rugian, Herulian, Scirian, and Bastarnae), and some language trees show Lombardic with these. Lombardic inscriptions are mostly in the Elder Futhark (the oldest form of the runic alphabet, from the second to the seventh century), which suggests a North Germanic origin, closer to West Germanic than to East. (Note that the current "Lombard" language in the region of the Italo-Swiss border is descended from the Italic of Roman times, not from Latin, though a good bit of Latin is intermixed. This "Lombard" has nothing to do with "Lombardic.")

Paul the Deacon tells the story of Audoin and Alboin. In the great battle between the Lombards and the Gepids, Alboin son of Audoin slew Thurismod, son of the Gepid King Thurisind, in single combat. When the Lombards returned home after their victory, they asked Audoin to give his son the rank of a companion of his table, since it was by his valour that they had won the day. But this Audoin would not do, for, he said, "It is not the custom amongst us that the king's son should sit down with his father before he has first received weapons from the king of some other people."

When Alboin heard this, he went with forty young men of the Lombards to King Thurisind to ask this honour from him. Thurisind welcomed him, invited him to the feast, and seated him at his right hand, where his dead son Thurismod used to sit. "But as the feast went on Thurisind began to think of his son's death, and seeing Alboin his slayer in his very place his grief burst forth in words: 'Very pleasant to me is the seat,' he said, 'but hard is it to look upon him who sits in it.' Roused by these words the king's second son Cunimund began to revile the Lombard guests; insults were uttered on both sides, and swords were grasped. But on the brink Thurisind leapt from the table, thrust himself between the Gepids and the Lombards, and threatened to punish the first man who began the fight. Thus he allayed the quarrel; and taking the arms of his dead son he gave them to Alboin and sent him back in safety to his father's kingdom" (quoted in *Lost Road*, 54).

This passage, as Tolkien writes it from Paul the Deacon, strongly suggests that the Gepids could converse easily with the Lombards. As the Gepids are believed to have spoken a kind of Gothic (though separate from East and West Gothic), the implication is that Lombardic was close to Gothic and thus an

East Germanic language. There are some hints, in "The Notion Club Papers" and especially in "The Lost Road," that Tolkien (at least for inventive purposes) regarded the Lombardic language as having some kind of special place among the languages of *our* Middle-earth. Indeed, it seems that the story of Alboin and Audoin in Paul the Deacon's *Historia Langobardorum*, and the whole story of the "Longbeards," as well as their language (or because of it), had a special significance. In "The Lost Road," the father is Alboin Errol (introduced at the beginning with *his* father Oswin Errol), and the son is Audoin Errol. The Lombardic names are unmistakable.

In his school days, Alboin Errol asked his father (37), "Why am I called Alboin?" and when his father gives him an answer that is not truly an answer, he responds, "But it is a *real* name, isn't it? . . . I mean, it means something, and *men* have been called it? It isn't just invented?" One wonders if Alboin Errol, Audoin Errol, and Oswin Errol are a kind of Tolkienian answer to Cedric Errol (Lord Fauntleroy in Frances Hodgson Burnett, *Little Lord Fauntleroy*), whose "English" name was not a real name but a miswriting of Cerdic (itself Brythonic), which in its miswritten form was thereby fastened on thousands of children in the years after 1886, though so far as we know no man had been called by it earlier.

Alboin, his father assures him, is a real name: Oswin tells Alboin "the tale of Alboin son of Audoin, the Lombard king, and the great battle of the Lombards and the Gepids, remembered as terrible even in the grim sixth century." And he asks him, when Alboin suggests a preference for Thurisind and Thurismod, "Would you rather have been called Elf-friend? For that is what the name means." And Alboin answers doubtfully, "I like names to mean something, not to say something."

In Part II of "The Notion Club Papers" is the following passage (Arry Lowdham speaking):

> Seven sons he begat, sire of princes, men great of mood, mighty-handed and high-hearted. From his house cometh the seed of kings, as songs tell us, fathers of the fathers, who before the change in the Elder Years the earth governed, Northern kingdoms named and founded, shields of their people: Sheave begat them: Sea-danes and Goths, Swedes and Northmen, Franks and Frisians, folk of the islands, Swordmen and Saxons, Swabians, Angles, and the Longobards, who long ago beyond Mircwudu [=Mirkwood] a mighty realm and wealth won them in the Welsh countries, where Ælfwine, Eadwine's son in Italy was king. All that has passed! (*Sauron*, 276)

In Part II of "The Notion Club Papers," Alwin Arundel (Arry) Lowdham is the son of Edwin Lowdham, who disappears in his yacht, the *Earendil,* at sea. As Alwin (Ælfwine = Alboin) is the son and Edwin (Eadwine = Audoin) the father, we are here matching the generations in Paul the Deacon, not the case with the generations Oswin-Alboin-Audoin in *The Lost Road*. Lowdham suggests it is only in Anglo-Saxon that the ancient languages of Westernesse are recalled, but the implication of Alboin and Audoin is that the earlier Langobardic (Lombardic) recalls the same languages. And the pattern Audoin/Eadwine-Alboin/Ælfwine carries down through the ages, even to England after World War I, making possible a kind of time-travel by identification.

JARED LOBDELL

Further Reading

Flieger, Verlyn. "The Footsteps of Ælfwine." In *Tolkien's Legendarium: Essays on "The History of Middle-earth,"* edited by Verlyn Flieger and Carl F. Hostetter. Westport, CT: Greenwood, 2000.

Rateliff, John. "'The Lost Road,' 'The Dark Tower,' and 'The Notion Club Papers': Tolkien and Lewis's Time Travel Triad." In *Tolkien's Legendarium: Essays on "The History of Middle-earth,"* edited by Verlyn Flieger and Carl F. Hostetter. Westport, CT: Greenwood, 2000.

See also **Ælfwine; Gothic Language;** *Lost Road, The*; *Sauron Defeated*

LONELY MOUNTAIN (EREBOR)

Erebor is the Elvish (Sindarin) name for the mountain that figures prominently in the tale of *The Hobbit*. In Westron, the Common Tongue, the site is more often referred to as the Lonely Mountain or simply the Mountain.

The Lonely Mountain is located in the northern part of Middle-earth just east of the forest of Mirkwood, about 50 miles south of the Grey Mountains and about 125 miles west of the Iron Hills. It is of strategic importance in Middle-earth due to its proximity to both the habitation of the Wood-elves and the settlement of Men in Dale. Two important battles in Middle-earth are fought on its slopes: the Battle of the Five Armies, recorded in *The Hobbit*, and the Battle of Dale, fought during the War of the Ring.

The history of the Lonely Mountain, like most Dwarvish history, is fraught with stories of beauty gained and lives lost. According to Appendix A of *The Lord of the Rings*, Erebor was first settled in 1999 of the Third Age of Middle-earth. At that time, Thráin I founded the kingdom of Erebor with a group of Durin's Folk who had fled from their defeat by the Balrog of Moria. Thráin became the first King Under the Mountain and later discovered the famed Arkenstone, the Heart of the Mountain.

In 2210, Thorin I, Thráin's son, chose to leave Erebor and took the Dwarves north to the Grey Mountains, where the remnants of Durin's Folk were gathered. There, in the rich-veined mountains, they established a thriving settlement until the dragons of the northern wastelands made war against the Dwarves and plundered their treasures. This war ended in the death of Dáin I, who ruled the Grey Mountains and, again, the Dwarves were forced to abandon their home.

As a result, Thrór, the heir to the throne of the King Under the Mountain, returned to Erebor in 2590 with a band of Dwarves, bringing the Arkenstone with him. He and his folk prospered in the Lonely Mountain for many years, fashioning works of beauty and creating swords and armory highly prized by Men and Elves. In *The Hobbit*, Thorin Oakenshield, the grandson of Thrór, recounts tales of these glory days of the Kingdom of Erebor.

However, in 2770 disaster again struck the Dwarves. Smaug the Golden, greatest of the northern dragons, heard rumors of their wealth and assaulted Erebor, laying waste Dale and forcing the Dwarves to again flee from their home. Thrór and his son Thráin II, fled through a secret door in the Lonely Mountain, and his young grandson, Thorin II (later known as Thorin Oakenshield), escaped the wrath of Smaug.

After the sack of the Lonely Mountain, the Dwarves of Erebor wandered homeless for many years. Thrór passed the last of the Seven Rings to his son Thráin and, with only one companion, unwisely sought to enter again into the Mines of Moria, where he was beheaded by an Orc-chieftain named Azog. This began the War of the Dwarves and the Orcs, which ended at the gates of Moria when Dáin Ironfoot slew Azog. However, many of the Dwarves were lost in the battle, and Moria was not regained, for the Balrog remained.

Thráin, his son Thorin Oakenshield, and many of the Dwarves of Erebor then established a home in exile in the mountains of Ered Luin, just beyond the Shire. In 2841, Thráin, unknown to Thorin Oakenshield, left with a small group of Dwarves on a quest to reclaim Erebor. However, they were waylaid under the eaves of Mirkwood. Thráin was captured and brought to Dol Guldur, where he was tortured by Sauron and stripped of his Ring.

Meanwhile, Smaug remained in possession of the Lonely Mountain for many long years. The Wizard Gandalf became concerned about the strategic importance of the Lonely Mountain and was fearful that Sauron, who was regaining power, would use Smaug for his own ends to invade the north. In 2941, Gandalf and Thorin Oakenshield met "by chance" in Bree and agreed to work together to try to defeat

Smaug and reclaim the Lonely Mountain. More details about the Gandalf's role in the story are provided in "The Quest of Erebor," found in *Unfinished Tales.*

Thorin Oakenshield had grown restless in exile after his father had disappeared and became obsessed with the idea of reclaiming Erebor. On Gandalf's advice, he returned to the Mountain with a band of twelve Dwarves and one Hobbit, Bilbo Baggins. It was on the journey to Erebor that Bilbo found the One Ring, which he used to aid in the defeat of Smaug and the winning of the Lonely Mountain.

The events in *The Hobbit* relate the details of the reclamation of Erebor. In the course of exploring Smaug's lair, Bilbo Baggins discovered the Arkenstone, which he attempted to use an object of reconciliation among Dwarves, Men, and Elves. Despite his efforts at peace, the War of the Five Armies was fought at gate of the Lonely Mountain, and Thorin Oakenshield lost his life in the conflict. He was buried under the Mountain with the Arkenstone on his breast.

Dáin Ironfoot, the hero of Moria, arrived with a band of Dwarves from the Iron Hills and established a colony in Erebor with Dáin as the new King Under the Mountain. Under Dáin's leadership, the Dwarves of Erebor prospered. However, the Shadow fell even on the Lonely Mountain, and Dáin was killed at last as his people and the Men of Dale fought the forces of Sauron before the Gate of Erebor during the course of the War of the Ring. After his death, Erebor was ruled by his son Thorin III Stonehelm.

Another well-known Dwarf of Erebor was Gimli, the son of Gloin. In 3018, he sought Bilbo in Rivendell to warn him that Sauron's representatives had come to Erebor seeking information about Bilbo and the Ring. While in Rivendell, Gimli joined the Fellowship of the Ring and played an important role in the defeat of Sauron. After the War of the Ring was ended, Gimli took a group of Dwarves from Erebor and established a new Dwarvish realm in the Glittering Caves. Both Erebor and the Glittering Caves were established as independent realms but were allied with the Reunited Kingdom.

AMELIA HARPER

Further Reading

Foster, Robert. *The Complete Guide to Middle-earth.* New York: Del Rey, 1971.

Sibley, Brian, and John Howe. *The Maps of Tolkien's Middle-earth.* Boston: Houghton Mifflin, 1994.

See also **Arkenstone; Bilbo; Dwarves;** *Hobbit, The*; **Thorin;** *Unfinished Tales*

LORD OF THE RINGS, THE

Publication History

The Lord of the Rings was not a book Tolkien intended to write. When *The Hobbit*, first published in 1937, met with positive reactions from critics and readers, however, Rayner Unwin of George Allen & Unwin asked Tolkien for a sequel. Tolkien submitted excerpts of poetry and prose about the First Age of Middle-earth, writings he already had been working on for two decades, which would later become part of *The Silmarillion.* These were rejected, and the request for a sequel—something with more Hobbits—was repeated. And so, without an outline or clear plan, Tolkien began writing *The Lord of the Rings* in December 1937.

The text continued to grow as Tolkien developed his tale. As he wrote, he shared installments with his son Christopher, as well as with his literary group of friends at Oxford, the Inklings, most notably C.S. Lewis. Because of the way Tolkien linked the basic premise of *The Lord of the Rings* to prior action in *The Hobbit*, one chapter in *The Hobbit* required substantial revision. This Tolkien accomplished as he wrote *The Lord of the Rings*, and the 1951 reprint of *The Hobbit* became the first edition to include this revised chapter. While writing *The Lord of the Rings*, Tolkien also wrote two shorter works of fiction, "Leaf by Niggle" and *Farmer Giles of Ham.*

Eventually, the story was divided by the publishers into three separate books, *The Fellowship of the Ring, The Two Towers*, and *The Return of the King*, which were printed in 1954–55. Publisher Stanley Unwin, who had supported and encouraged Tolkien over the sixteen-plus years the volumes were under construction, fully expected to lose money on the books. George Allen & Unwin even arranged a profit-sharing agreement with Tolkien under which the author would earn no royalties until the books made money.

This they quickly did. Mixed reviews of the trilogy immediately appeared. Some, from critics such as C.S. Lewis and W.H. Auden, were unreservedly enthusiastic about the resonating power and vision of the epic; others, such as those from critics Edmund Wilson and Philip Toynbee, were quite brutal about what they considered to be juvenile rubbish. Such vehement reactions drew public attention to the works, as did a 1956 BBC radio adaptation of the novels. Sales of the hardback volumes soared to the point Tolkien regretted that he had not chosen to take early retirement from his position at Oxford University.

Then, in 1965, unauthorized editions of the trilogy appeared in the United States from Ace Books. Thanks to a copyright loophole, Ace did not have to compensate Tolkien or his previous publishers for the sales of these new versions, which it printed at 150,000 copies per volume. This put the books in the hands of new readers, and the resulting copyright dispute drew even more attention to the works, making *The Lord of the Rings* an international phenomenon. Eventually, Ace agreed to pay royalties and cease printing the novels.

Some errors had appeared in the original George Allen & Unwin versions of the books, however, and even more existed in the Ace versions. Tolkien revised his three works, correcting errors, adding a new introduction and index and extending the prologue. These new editions meant more accurate texts and a secure copyright for Tolkien. The corrected versions were published by Ballantine Books in 1965, and further revised texts, the "second editions," were published in Great Britain in 1966 and the United States in 1967. Subsequent versions have been published since then, incorporating changes specified by Tolkien and, after his death in 1973, his son Christopher, as well as translating the texts into dozens of different languages.

Summary

The Lord of the Rings is divided into eight parts. In the format of its original publication, the first three, the Prologue and Books I and II, form *The Fellowship of the Ring*. Books III and IV together are *The Two Towers*. Books V and VI, as well as the six Appendices, comprise *The Return of the King*.

The first part of *The Fellowship of the Ring* is the Prologue. In its first section, "Concerning Hobbits," Tolkien introduces the reader to the history, lifestyle, and temperament of the pastoral and parochial hobbits, the short-bodied and hairy-footed inhabitants of the Shire. Here is found the first mention of the great hobbit families such as the Bagginses, Tooks, and Brandybucks. The second section, "Concerning Pipeweed," explains the hobbit fascination with cultivating and smoking various varieties of pipeweed. "Of the Ordering of the Shire," the third section, notes how the Shire is subdivided into four Farthings and how they are administered.

The fourth section of the Prologue, "On the Finding of the Ring," essentially revisits the relevant portions of Tolkien's previous book, *The Hobbit*. Bilbo Baggins, a hobbit of the Shire, goes with Gandalf the Grey, a Wizard, and the company of Thorin Oakenshield, made up of Dwarves, on a dangerous quest for the great treasure hoard of the Kings Under the Mountain, which is guarded by the dragon Smaug. As the group's adventures unfold, Bilbo is separated from the others in the deep tunnels of the goblins. As Bilbo searches for a way out, he stumbles upon a ring lying abandoned in a tunnel, and he takes it with him. Then he finds a horrible creature who engages him in a riddle game. It becomes apparent to Bilbo that the ring belongs to the creature, named Gollum, who wishes nothing more than to kill and eat Bilbo. In his escape, Bilbo discovers that the ring has the magical ability to render him invisible. Bilbo escapes by using the ring, and eventually he helps the company thwart the dragon, seize the hoard, and make peace with its allies. He returns to his home a wealthier and worldlier hobbit, still in possession of the ring.

The final section of the Prologue, "Note on the Shire Records," identifies key volumes through which history has been passed down among the Shire-folk. It implies that *The Hobbit* and *The Lord of the Rings* are excerpts of a text known as *The Red Book of Westmarch*, which was begun by Bilbo Baggins and expanded and annotated by Frodo Baggins and the descendants of Samwise Gamgee. All of these hobbit characters play key roles in the story of *The Lord of the Rings*.

Book I opens sixty years after the adventures described in *The Hobbit*. Bilbo Baggins prepares to celebrate his eleventy-first birthday, also the thirty-third birthday of his cousin and adopted heir Frodo Baggins, with a great party, to which nearly all the hobbits in the Shire are invited. At the feast on the night of the party, Bilbo disappears from the gathering with the help of his magic ring and then, reluctantly leaving the ring behind for Frodo, departs the Shire in secret to pursue a quiet retirement at the home of his friend Elrond in the Elvish refuge of Rivendell. Seventeen years pass. Gandalf visits Frodo in the Shire and explains that the ring Bilbo left him is not any magic ring but the One Ring forged by the evil Sauron to amplify his strength and control the lesser magical rings belonging to Elves, Men, and Dwarves. Sauron now is seeking the Ring, a fact that puts Frodo personally and the Shire in general in great danger. Frodo follows his advice and takes flight, bringing with him his loyal servant Samwise Gamgee and two of his cousins and best friends who demand to share his danger, Merry Brandybuck and Pippin Took.

The four soon learn they are being followed by Black Riders, servants of Sauron. Though they expect Gandalf to join them, they are forced to continue on when he does not appear. They flee through Buckland and the Old Forest, encounter Tom Bombadil and his wife, Goldberry, the River-Daughter, who help them. After capture and escape in the Barrow-Downs, they arrive in Bree, a crossroads town of Men and Hobbits. There they meet Strider, a mysterious Ranger, who claims friendship with Gandalf and offers to lead them to Rivendell. As the four hobbits and Strider continue, they are pursued by Black Riders. Frodo is attacked and wounded by one. The Elf Glorfindel, sent by Elrond from Rivendell to look for the travelers, finds them, and a dramatic chase ensues as the companions and their guide attempt to reach Rivendell.

Book II opens with the healing of Frodo and a reunion with Gandalf in Rivendell. Frodo learns how Gandalf was held prisoner by his fellow Wizard Saruman, who is making his own bid for power in Middle-earth. Elrond then holds a council, which is attended by Gandalf and representatives of the Elves, Men, Dwarves, and Hobbits. The attendees recount the long history of the Ring and discern its immediate threat. They determine the Ring must be returned to Sauron's evil land of Mordor in the south and destroyed in the fires that made it before Sauron can regain it and enslave the Free Peoples of Middle-earth. Frodo volunteers for the task. He leaves on his quest accompanied by the three other hobbits, Gandalf, Strider (now identified as Aragorn, heir to the throne of Gondor), Boromir (son of the Steward of Gondor), Gimli (son of the Dwarf Gloin, once of Bilbo's company in his earlier adventure), and Legolas (of the Woodland Elves). The group, now the Fellowship of the Ring, encounters first Orcs when they pass through the Dwarvish Mines of Moria and then a Balrog. Gandalf falls while fighting the Balrog, and the others escape to the Elvish land of Lothlórien, where they are given hospitality by its lord and lady, Celeborn and Galadriel. When the Fellowship members continue south via the Great River, they come to the Falls of Rauros, where Boromir, who is tempted by the Ring, tries to take it from Frodo. He fails, however, and the company is scattered by an Orc attack.

In Book III, the first half of *The Two Towers*, Orcs mortally wound Boromir as he attempts to defend Merry and Pippin. The Orcs take the two Hobbits and leave Boromir to die; before he does, he confesses to Aragorn that he tried to take the Ring, and Aragorn comforts him. While Frodo and Sam continue on their own toward Mordor, Aragorn, Gimli, and Legolas follow the Orcs who captured Merry and Pippin. These two hobbits escape from their captors, however, and meet the Ent Treebeard. The Ents, after hearing of all that has transpired, make war on Saruman's stronghold of Isengard. Meanwhile, Aragorn, Gimli, and Legolas discover that Gandalf has returned to Middle-earth as Gandalf the White, and together they seek Théoden, king of Rohan, the ally

of Gondor. They find the king greatly diminished and weakened by the deception of his adviser Gríma Wormtongue, who is secretly in league with Saruman. Gandalf releases the king and restores him to vitality, and Théoden and company fight to defend Rohan from Orc armies at the Battle of Helm's Deep. After achieving victory, Théoden, Gandalf, Aragorn, Gimli, and Legolas travel on to Isengard, where they reunite with Merry and Pippin.

Book IV follows the parallel story of Frodo and Sam as they make their way to Mordor. Gollum, the owner of the Ring before Bilbo, has been shadowing Frodo in the hopes of again taking possession of the Ring, and he reluctantly becomes their guide. The three pass through the Dead Marshes and arrive at the Black Gate, but at Gollum's suggestion they decide to follow an alternate route to their ultimate destination in Mordor, Mount Doom. As they travel, they meet Faramir, brother of the late Boromir, who tells them of his brother's fate and withstands the temptation of the Ring. Gollum proves treacherous as they continue: he leads the two hobbits into the lair of a giant spider named Shelob. She attacks Frodo and stings him unconscious. Sam kills Shelob but, thinking Frodo dead, takes the Ring to continue the quest to destroy it. Only when Orcs carry Frodo away does Sam realize his mistake. He follows them into the Tower of Cirith Ungol in the hopes of liberating his wounded master.

Book V begins *The Return of the King*. Gandalf and Pippin go to the heart of Gondor, Minas Tirith, where Pippin meets the Steward of Gondor, Denethor, and pledges himself to the Steward's service. Aragorn, Legolas, and Gimli take the Paths of the Dead to muster additional forces for the defense of Gondor. Merry rides with Théoden, to whom he has sworn allegiance, and the muster of Rohan, including Théoden's nephew and heir, Éomer, and Théoden's niece, Éowyn, disguised as the rider Dernhelm. In Minas Tirith, Sauron's forces lay siege to Gondor. Denethor, believing his wounded son Faramir to be dying, commits suicide. Rohan comes to its ally's defense. At the Battle of Pelennor Fields, Théoden dies and Éowyn and Merry slay the Witch-king of Angmar, the leader of the Black Riders. Aragorn heals the wounded Faramir, Éowyn, and Merry and leads the last of the forces to the Black Gate in the slim hope of distracting Sauron and giving Frodo and Sam the chance to destroy the Ring.

In Book VI, Sam liberates Frodo from Cirith Ungol, and they continue to Mount Doom. Sam is attacked by Gollum, and Frodo, at the limit of his endurance, at last succumbs to the Ring and claims it for his own. Gollum fights Frodo for the Ring and bites off Frodo's finger to get it; in the process, both

Gollum and the Ring plunge into the fire and are destroyed. All of Mordor disintegrates as the Ring's destruction breaks Sauron's power. Frodo and Sam are saved by eagles and brought to the Field of Cormallen, where all surviving members of the Fellowship are reunited. Aragorn is crowned King of Gondor. The four hobbits return to the Shire, which they find in the grips of tyranny and corruption. They lead their neighbors in rebellion against the forces of Sharkey, who is in fact Saruman, and liberate the Shire. Gríma Wormtongue kills Saruman. Samwise, Merry, and Pippin assume roles of leadership in the Shire, but Frodo finds no healing from the internal and external wounds left by his quest. At last, he joins Bilbo, Gandalf, Elrond, and Galadriel in sailing West to the Undying Lands.

The Appendices begin with the "Annals of the Kings and Rulers," which offers a chronology of the Númenórean Kings and the rulers of Gondor and Rohan, as well as the leaders of Durin's Folk, the Dwarves. This section also recounts the extended story of the courtship, marriage, and later lives of Aragorn and Arwen. Appendix B, "The Tale of Years," provides a chronology of the Westland, with brief accounts of the First and Second Age, and an extended timeline of the Third Age. It ends with "Later Events Concerning the Members of the Fellowship of the Ring." Here is told of the beginning of the Fourth Age and how the three remaining hobbits rise to preeminence in the Shire: Samwise as a repeatedly reelected Mayor, Merry (the Magnificent) as Master of Buckland, and Pippin as Took and Thain. All three become the royal Counsellors of the North-kingdom to King Elessar, or Aragorn. Eventually, Samwise apparently follows Frodo over the Sea. Merry and Pippin leave the Shire and visit King Éomer of Rohan before his death then travel to Minas Tirith, where they stay until their own deaths. After Aragorn dies, Legolas takes Gimli over the Sea to the Undying Lands.

Appendix C contains family trees representing the following hobbit clans: Baggins of Hobbiton, the Took of Great Smials, Brandybuck of Buckland, and the Longfather-Tree of Master Samwise. The last Appendices include information about the Shire calendar, writing, and spelling and the languages and peoples of the Third Age of Middle-earth, including Elves, Men, and Hobbits.

Themes

In a letter to Milton Waldman written perhaps in 1951, Tolkien explains that his Middle-earth works are mainly "concerned with Fall, Mortality, and the Machine." The repeated theme of the Fall appears throughout *The Lord of the Rings*. The characters inherit a world already tainted by Sauron (and, before him, the master he serves, Morgoth, or Melkor), who has tempted others through the lesser Rings of Power and played on the weaknesses of different races to create allies. Gollum has been twisted by the One Ring until he is almost unrecognizable. Saruman represents a fall from wisdom into vanity, greed, and ambition. Evil in Middle-earth cannot create, but it can bend and defile that which has already been created: thus Orcs, for example, represent the corruption of probably Elves.

And yet, despite the Fall, there is redemption. Boromir erases his betrayal by his later contrition and valor. Bilbo's great mercy in sparing Gollum returns to make that terrible creature in the end the agent of the Ring's destruction and the salvation of Middle-earth. And Frodo, wounded beyond healing, at last finds rest over the Sea. Moreover, Tolkien brings together the peoples of Middle-earth who have been sundered by past abuses and forces them to build new unity and sometimes even friendship together: Elves and Dwarves, Men and Hobbits, Rohirrim and Wild Men.

Mortality is a second theme that repeatedly appears in *The Lord of the Rings*. The ages of Middle-earth reflect an ebb and flow of realms and peoples. The War of the Ring provides an opportunity for hobbits to play a central role, even as the power of the Elves is waning and the era of Men is born. Just as each people have a period of ascendancy, so too will they diminish and fade.

Moreover, willing sacrifice purchases victory. The deaths of Gandalf, Boromir, and Théoden, and the wounding of Frodo, are reminders of the cost paid in the fight of good against evil. Elrond and Galadriel support the strategy of destroying the Ring, even though this means irreparable damage to their own realms, which rely on the magic of lesser Rings of Power. And in a story of particularly personal importance to Tolkien, the Elvish Arwen chooses mortality over endless life to marry Aragorn and be with her love—and provide an heir and future for Gondor.

The Machine, the symbol for Tolkien of industrialism over agriculture and war over peace, wears several faces in *The Lord of the Rings*. The powers of evil are known for mechanized destruction on a grand scale, as the wasteland of Mordor and the devastation of Isengard prove. When the Shire falls under the control of Sharkey, or Saruman, it transforms from a green countryside to something akin to a blackened factory. Likewise, lands at peace thrive, but with the organized warfare of the Orcs, who love producing weapons and devising new ways to kill, lands become empty ruins. Many scholars see Tolkien's concerns about the vanishing English countryside during an era of industrialization and urbanization, and his experiences with warfare personally in World War I and through his son in World War II, reflected in his conception of the Machine.

Furthermore, in *The Lord of the Rings*, Tolkien intentionally allows the meek and small, rather than the powerful and wise, to perform the necessary acts of courage and dedication to save and restore Middle-earth. The tree-like Ents destroy the evil Isengard, a maiden and a hobbit slay a Witch-king, and, most importantly, two hobbits journey into the heart of evil, destroying the One Ring. The "joyous turn"— or eucatastrophe, as Tolkien calls it—of the text involves the triumph of the simple hobbits and the restoration of the pastoral Shire, which regains its natural beauty and is made a Free Land.

Style

The Lord of the Rings is unique for many reasons: its pervasive sense of epic history, its many invented languages for its various fictional races, its frequent employment of verse—as well as prose—as a storytelling device, its roots in Tolkien's understanding of philology, religion, and world mythology. Yet another reason the work is noteworthy is that it follows a medieval writing style known as interlace structure. Rather than unfolding the plot in a linear way, as he does with *The Hobbit*, Tolkien weaves together multiple plotlines, separating and dividing them and winding between them to develop his tale in a tapestry-like fashion. Scholars date this style as early as Ovid's *Metamorphoses* in the ninth century and as late as Spenser's *Faerie Queene* in the sixteenth century, but its high point came in the medieval Arthurian romances such as the *Prose Lancelot* of the early thirteenth century.

This style is apparent in *The Lord of the Rings* in several ways. First, once the main characters are united as members of the Fellowship of the Ring, they are then split, first divided in half, and then in three, and followed in separate, parallel sections of the text as the action becomes increasingly complex. Second, even these fractured stories are not told in a purely linear fashion. There are jumps in time, as dream sequences foreshadow the future, remember the past, or see real-time events in a different place. Retellings of past actions also form part of Tolkien's technique, as do using ancient examples to explain the present. The structure allows Tolkien to develop

an intricate plot while underscoring the frequent bewilderment and disorientation of his characters— especially the hobbits, through whose eyes the reader encounters the action.

What some critics see as meandering, other scholars find intricate. Although Tolkien incorporates twentieth-century issues such as large-scale industrialization and warfare into his work, the literary structure he employs has caused some to consider *The Lord of the Rings* the last great work of medieval literature.

Adaptations

Critics over the decades remain divided over *The Lord of the Rings*, as some continue to see it as an epic masterpiece of timeless relevance and others perceive it as an adolescent adventure with delusions of grandeur. Certainly the story has made a lasting impact on the literary genre of fantasy, as many authors who have followed Tolkien publicly recognize his work as an influence and inspiration. The worldwide public clearly remains interested in the tale. *The Lord of the Rings* has been translated into dozens of languages; visual artists in various media continue to interpret its scenes and characters, and musicians from Argentina to Italy and Russia to Canada have made albums devoted to exploring the story in song.

The first adaptation of *The Lord of the Rings* was a thirteen-part BBC radio dramatization in 1956. The United States' NPR produced its own radio adaptation in 1979. The most critically acclaimed version came with the 1981 BBC drama, produced in twenty-six installments of thirty minutes, and starring Ian Holm as Frodo Baggins, the same actor who portrays Bilbo Baggins in Peter Jackson's film trilogy.

Apparently, both the Beatles and the celebrated director Stanley Kubrick considered adapting *The Lord of the Rings* for film, but the first *Lord of the Rings* movie did not debut until 1978. Directed by Ralph Bakshi, this United Artists picture features an unusual technique in which animation is placed over live-action sequences to create a surreal and heightened visual effect. Other scenes are thoroughly animated. This adaptation covers the complete story of *The Fellowship of the Ring* and ends amid the action of *The Two Towers*. Rankin-Bass Studios produced a fully animated version of *The Return of the King* for television two years later.

Miramax Films developed Peter Jackson's film trilogy of *The Lord of the Rings*, whose parts debuted in 2001, 2002, and 2003. Filmed with a combination of live actors and computer-generated images, the films appealed more to an adult audience than the previous movies, and the final of the three, *The Return of the King*, won eleven Academy Awards. The success of the films no doubt influenced sales and heightened awareness of Tolkien's *The Lord of the Rings*.

But even before Jackson's cinematic success, *The Lord of the Rings* possessed an impressive track record, remaining in print continuously since its first publication, repeated appearing on lists of most influential and loved literature, and providing the subject of university courses for decades. Although it was not the work Tolkien intended to write, *The Lord of the Rings* remains the epic with which he is forever linked.

AMY H. STURGIS

Primary Sources

Tolkien, J.R.R. "Letter to Milton Waldman, date unknown (1951?)." In *The Letters of J.R.R. Tolkien*, edited by Humphrey Carpenter, no. 131, pp. 143–61. Boston, MA: Houghton Mifflin, 2000.
———. "On Fairy-stories." In *The Tolkien Reader*, 33–99. New York: Ballantine Books, 1966.

Further Reading

Auden, W.H. "The Hero is a Hobbit" and "At the End of the Quest, Victory." In *A Reader's Companion to* The Hobbit *and* The Lord of the Rings. New York: Quality Paperback Book Club, 1995.
Carpenter, Humphrey. *Tolkien: A Biography*. Boston, MA: Houghton Mifflin, 1977.
Clute, John, and John Grant, eds. *The Encyclopedia of Fantasy*. New York: St. Martin's, 1997.
Duriez, Colin. *Tolkien and "The Lord of the Rings": A Guide to Middle-earth*. Mahwah, NJ: Hidden Spring, 2001.
Garth, John. *Tolkien and the Great War: The Threshold of Middle-earth*. Boston, MA: Houghton Mifflin, 2003.
Lewis, C.S. "The Gods Return to Earth" and "The Dethronement of Power." In *A Reader's Companion to* The Hobbit *and* The Lord of the Rings. 31–42. New York: Quality Paperback Book Club, 1995.
Shippey, Tom. *J.R.R. Tolkien: Author of the Century*. Boston, MA: Houghton Mifflin, 2000.
———. *The Road to Middle-earth: How J.R.R. Tolkien Created a New Mythology*. Revised and Expanded edition. Boston, MA: Houghton Mifflin, 2003.
West, Richard C. "The Interlace Structure of *The Lord of the Rings*." In *A Tolkien Compass*, edited by Jared Lobdell, 82–102. New York: Ballantine Books, 1975.
Wilson, Edmund. "Oo, Those Awful Orcs!" In *A Reader's Companion to* The Hobbit *and* The Lord of the Rings. New York: Quality Paperback Book Club, 1995.
Zimbardo, Rose A. and Neil D. Isaacs, eds. *Understanding* The Lord of the Rings: *The Best in Tolkien Criticism*. Boston, MA: Houghton Mifflin, 2004.

See also **Aragorn; Arthurian Literature; Arwen; Bakshi, Ralph; Bilbo; Boromir; Death; Denethor; Dreams; Dwarves; Elrond; Éomer; Éowyn; Elves; Ents; Eucatastrophe; Fall of Man; Faramir;** *Farmer Giles of Ham***; Free Will; Frodo; Galadriel; Gandalf; Gimli; Glorfindel; Goldberry; Gondor; Good and Evil; Grima Wormtongue;** *Hobbit, The***; Hobbits; Industrialization; Inklings; Jackson, Peter; Legolas; Lewis, C.S.; Lothlórien; Men of Middle-earth; Mercy; Merry; Middle-earth; Mordor; Morgoth and Melkor; Moria; One Ring, The; Pippin; Redemption; Rings of Power; Rivendell; Rohan; Sam; Saruman; Sauron; Shelob; Shire; Spenser; Théoden; Tolkien, Christopher; Tom Bombadil; Treebeard; War; Wizards**

LORD OF THE RINGS, THE: SUCCESS OF

This section includes coverage of financial success and the effect of success on Tolkien, but not the influence of *The Lord of the Rings* on other authors, which would be a different (and in the end, possibly more interesting) measure of success than the financial. The stories of the events after the book's "success" are well known: Tolkien and his wife leaving Oxford and 76 Sandfield Road for Bournemouth (or Poole). The classic view is that Tolkien neither desired nor expected his success. That he did not care for some of the side effects of that success is clear (midnight phone calls from American "fans" who did not think of the time difference were a particular nuisance and worse), but that is not to say he neither desired nor expected his success.

The abortive attempt to transfer *The Lord of the Rings* to Collins, involving the long and indispensable letter to Milton Waldman (in *Letters*, 143–61) and all his long work to make his creations publishable, left incomplete at his death, argue for both a desire and expectation of success. Not the financial success he eventually enjoyed, but he, like John Buchan a little earlier, wanted a good and comfortable life. It would have been strange (given his friendship with Lewis and his knowledge of Buchan) if he had not seen his books in that light—"I am myself a hobbit," he said, liking the comfortable life, and he did not like being poor. The "hem-touchers" among the fans eventually interfered with that good and comfortable life, not only because of their interruption but also because, as he said in an unsent 1954 letter to Hugh Brogan, "I do not naturally breathe an air of undiluted incense" (*Letters*, 225). He also said to Brogan that the success of *The Lord of the Rings* was unexpected—but that success lay in readers liking what he had written (*Letters*, 232). His letter to Michael Straight in early 1956 makes it clear what kind of success interested him and casts a light on the kind of success he was seeking (after all, no one undertakes a project like *The Lord of the Rings* without hoping for some kind of success): "I hope that you *enjoyed The Lord of the Rings. Enjoyed* is the key word. For it was written to *amuse* (in the highest sense): to be readable (*Letters*, 232)."

While he might have meant financial success, the letter to Brogan was written in December 1955, long before the pirated Ace edition, the Ballantine edition, and the worldwide success of *The Lord of the Rings*. In 1955, it was a *succes d'éstime*, perhaps a critical success, not yet the eventual great financial success, that was "v. unexpected." Not long thereafter, however, by 1957, Tolkien was beginning to feel the effects of financial success and wondering if he should have moved his retirement up two years if he had known just how big the cheque from George Allen & Unwin would be: "I'm afraid I cannot help feeling that there is a lot to be said for 'the grosser forms of literary success' as a sneering critic recently called it (not mine but a 'grosser' case)" (*Letters*, 256).

After American science fiction and fantasy fan Forry Ackerman visited Tolkien in September 1957 with plans for a film of *The Lord of the Rings*, Tolkien remarked that he and Sir Stanley Unwin had come to a conclusion on the matter: "art or cash"—"either very profitable terms indeed; or absolute author's veto on objectionable features or alterations" (*Letters*, 261). But that was written in bemusement after he received the International Fantasy Award, "a massive 'model' of an upended Space-rocket (combined with a Ronson lighter)," and before he was able to ask for both. One remarkable letter to Aunt Jane Neave (July 18, 1962) urges her to spend the cheque he has sent her (she was trying to give it back to him so he could spend it on Edith) and remarks, "I have never been able to give before. . . . I receive as a septuagenarian a retirement pension, of which I feel it proper to give away at least what the tax collectors leave in my hands." He then goes on to say, "I gather that he [Sir Stanley Unwin] told Edmund Fuller that my books were the most important, and also the most profitable thing that he had published in a long life, and that they would certainly remain so after his time and his sons' time" (*Letters*, 315–16).

When the unauthorized Ace paperback edition of *The Lord of the Rings* appeared in the United States in 1965 (copies of the three paperback volumes now sell for above $200 for the three), Ballantine Books brought out an "authorized" paperback edition that bore on the covers of all three volumes Tolkien's statement that "This paperback edition, and no other, has been published with my consent and cooperation. Those who approve of courtesy (at least) to living authors will purchase it, and no other." The cooperation (and consent) did not extend to the design of the original Ballantine cover, with a lion and emus and a thing in the foreground with pink bulbs. When Tolkien remarked on the inappropriateness of the cover, over the phone, to a woman representing Ballantine, "her voice rose several tones and she cried, 'But the man hadn't TIME to read the book' . . . with regard to the pink bulbs she said as to one of complete obtusity, 'they are meant to suggest a Christmas tree.' Why is such a woman let loose? I begin to feel that I am shut up in a madhouse." At that point he told Rayner Unwin, to whom the letter was written, that he would shortly go "into purdah (to commune with my creative soul), the veil of which only you have authority to lift" (*Letters*, 362–63).

He did not, but clearly the madhouse of the modern world did not appeal, and by 1968—though not because of the emus and pink bulbs—he and Edith were living in the suburbs of Bournemouth (actually Poole in Dorset), where they lived until Edith's death November 29, 1971 (it would have been C.S. Lewis's seventy-third birthday). Only Rayner Unwin could lift the veil (and, of course, John and Michael and Christopher and Priscilla, and a few old friends, but I do not think they ever did). He returned to Oxford in 1972, to Merton College, and tried to finish *The Silmarillion*—not for any monetary reward but simply not to leave it unfinished. One of his letters after his return to Oxford harks back to one of Lord Dunsany's tales in his youth. "Being a cult figure in one's own lifetime I am afraid is not at all pleasant. . . . But even the nose of a very modest idol (younger than Chu-Bu and not much older than Sheemish) cannot remain entirely untickled by the sweet smell of incense" (*Letters*, 432). But he did not say "by the sweet smell of success." He was intrigued to be famous, happy to be well off after a lifetime as a scholar without much in the way of funds: when he and Edith celebrated their silver wedding anniversary in 1941, it was with a modest supper party including C.S. Lewis and Hugo Dyson at home at 20 Northmoor Road. The effects of the financial success enabled him to mitigate the effects of the fame.

Priscilla recalls a "somewhat poignant memory" of her father opening an envelope from George Allen & Unwin after the publication of *The Hobbit* and passing the enclosed cheque for fifty pounds to Edith so that she could pay an outstanding and previously unpayable doctor's bill with it (71). She also recalls the splendid party for the golden wedding anniversary—what a difference a book makes!—with the bouquet of fifty golden roses from Sir Stanley Unwin (81). But it was not until they bought the bungalow outside Bournemouth at 19 Lakeside Road, in 1968, that

Ronald and Edith Tolkien had central heating and a bathroom each (83)—and Edith was delighted by her up-to-date kitchen. By 1969, when Tolkien sold the subsidiary rights to *The Lord of the Rings* for what has been reported as a mere $10,000, total book sales of the three volumes had reached three million copies. The figure now stands at more than one hundred million, eleven million in the United States alone in the year after the movie of *The Return of the King* was issued. Tolkien had sold the manuscripts of *The Lord of the Rings* (and *The Hobbit* and the unpublished *Mr. Bliss*) to Marquette University in Milwaukee for a similar sum back in the 1950s. As his remark on art or cash to Sir Stanley Unwin suggests, Tolkien never expected the huge success that would make it possible for him to have both, and he thought of subsidiary rights as he thought of the sale of the MSS of the work that went into *The Lord of the Rings*, as a kind of extra benefit—in the American vernacular, "gravy."

JARED LOBDELL

Further Reading

Tolkien, John, and Priscilla Tolkien. *The Tolkien Family Album*. Boston, MA: Houghton Mifflin, 1992.

See also **Bournemouth; England, Twentieth Century; Fandom; Oxford**

LOST ROAD, THE

The Lost Road and Other Writings: Language and Legend before "The Lord of the Rings" is the fifth volume in *The History of Middle-earth* series edited by Christopher Tolkien. It is a pivotal addition to the series for several reasons. As the subtitle indicates, it brings the history of the legendarium to the end of 1937, the time at which Tolkien turned from this project to start on the "new Hobbit" that became *The Lord of the Rings*. It thus marks a turning point in Tolkien's creative work. In addition, the story that gives the volume its title, "The Lost Road," introduces two related concepts—reincarnation and inherited memory—that came to affect Tolkien's ideas for the fictive transmission of his mythology. The major elements of this unfinished story, time-travel and dream, added materially to the portrayal of Frodo's inner life and added a parapsychological aspect to *The Lord of the Rings*.

While all the selections in the volume were composed during the same span of years, roughly the 1930s, this overarching time frame is their chief commonality. The contents include two related narratives entirely new to the mythology, "The Fall of

Númenor" and "The Lost Road"; revised versions of the Annals of Valinor and Beleriand; a version of the "Quenta Silmarillion"; and a good deal of hitherto-unpublished linguistic material. All are concerned in one way or another with the matter of Middle-earth; however, the second half of the title, *and Other Writings*, signals the nature of the volume as an *omnium gatherum*, lacking the coherence of theme and subject matter that marked the earlier volumes in the series.

These disparities notwithstanding, the book is of great significance on three major counts. First, it presents the earliest appearance of Númenor, a cultural and geographic element that became an integral part of the mythology and contributed important elements to the fictive historical background of *The Lord of the Rings*. Second, it contains the earliest version of Tolkien's first and only attempt at science fiction, the time-travel story that gives its name to the entire volume. Third, it contains valuable information on the formation of Tolkien's languages, material unavailable until this publication.

The volume is arranged in three major segments and an appendix. Part I, "The Fall of Númenor and The Lost Road," is itself divided into three parts, the first being "The Early History of the Legend"; the second "The Fall of Númenor" proper, containing the original outline, the two subsequent versions, and discussion of "The Further Development"; and the third presenting the text and outline notes for "The Lost Road," the time-travel story precursor to the later and more successful "The Notion Club Papers." Part II, the longest of the three sections, encompasses writings on "Valinor and Middle-earth Before *The Lord of the Rings*" with subdivisions on "The Texts and Their Relations," The Later Annals of Valinor," "The Later Annals of Beleriand," a late version of the "Ainulindalë," "The Lhammas" (Account of Tongues), and a text of the "Quenta Silmarillion" intermediate between the "Quenta Noldorwina" of Volume IV and the version published in *The Silmarillion* in 1977. Part III is given entirely to "The Etymologies" and is largely a list of words with their roots and derivations in dictionary format. The appendix contains "The Genealogies," a brief list of characters and their descendants, a "List of Names" and their definitions, and sectional reproduction covering four book pages of "The Second 'Silmarillion' Map."

Comprising the only entirely new material, "The Fall of Númenor" and its companion narrative, "The Lost Road," with their accompanying notes and sketches, are in this respect the most noteworthy elements in the volume. "The Fall of Númenor" accounts for the shift from a flat earth to the world made round in the cataclysm of the Destruction of Númenor, which ushers in the Second Age, and "The Lost Road" comprises Tolkien's first attempt to expand the scope of the mythology by connecting it to the presumed Fourth Age of his own time. "The Lost Road" was also Tolkien's first venture into the new (for him) genre of science fiction, a departure occasioned by his bargain with C.S. Lewis that since there was too little of the sort of reading they liked (i.e., science fiction), they should write it themselves, Lewis taking space-travel and Tolkien time-travel.

Precisely where the idea of Númenor and its destruction connects to this story and to the mythology itself is a vexed question. The name itself occurs only once before "The Lost Road," in a reference in the "Ambarkanta" (a text dating from the mid-1930s) to the "assault of the Númenóreans" on Valinor. Though Tolkien later wrote as if "the Fall of Númenor" was already an established entity when he began "The Lost Road," Christopher Tolkien's "Early History of the Legend" concludes from the available evidence that the two narratives arose together as interconnected entities in or about 1936. It seems probable, therefore, that the concept of Númenor was only fully realized in association with the time-travel story.

After the account of "The Early History of the Legend," Part I moves to an outline and two brief versions with notes and commentary of "The Fall of Númenor." Neither version is as long as the later "Akallabêth" in *The Silmarillion* or "The Drowning of Anadûne" appended to "The Notion Club Papers," both of which describe the same event. "The Fall of Númenor" is directly followed by "The Lost Road," which begins in Tolkien's contemporary England. Here Alboin and Audoin, a modern English father and son surnamed Errol (cf. Eriol the Mariner from *The Book of Lost Tales*) travel by means of their dreams through recessive ancestral identities. These were to participate in a sequence of episodes from early English history, prehistory, and myth, arriving finally at Númenor in time to witness its destruction in the fictive prehistory of Tolkien's mythology. Though most of the historical chapters were never written, the names in each were to be forms of *Alboin* and *Audoin*, translated as "Elf-friend" and "Bliss-friend," culminating in the Númenórean identities Elendil and Herendil (the names retain the same meanings). These names, together with a sentence to be uttered in each chapter about the eagles of the Lords of the West, were to provide the thread linking the episodes.

As it stands, "The Lost Road" consists of four chapters, the first two in present-day England and the third and fourth in Númenor but breaking off before the projected cataclysm. Appended to the story as published are Tolkien's rapidly jotted ideas for the chapters, envisioned but never realized, intervening between modern England and Númenor. These include a "Lombard story," a "Norse story," an "English story," a "Tuatha-de-Danaan story," a story concerning "painted caves," one on "the Ice Age" and one "Before the Ice Age," and a "post-Beleriand story," as well as a begun but uncompleted story of Ælfwine, followed by both a prose and a verse form of the story of King Sheave, concluding with two versions of an early poem, one titled *The Nameless Land* and the other *The Song of Ælfwine.*

Part II, "Valinor and Middle-earth before *The Lord of the Rings,*" begins with a brief introduction by Christopher Tolkien concerned largely with the dating of materials. Entirely separate from Part I, and the least thematically coherent of the sections, it collects as elements of the history proper: "The Later Annals of Valinor" and "The Later Annals of Beleriand"; a text of the "Ainulindalë" intermediate between the early version given in *The Book of Lost Tales* and the later account in *The Silmarillion;* a full (albeit composite) text of the "Quenta Silmarillion"; and "The Lhammas" (Account of Tongues).

Of the two sets of "Annals," it need only be noted that they are slightly but not materially revised or emended from earlier versions. "The Lhammas" is philological in nature, comprising detailed charts and commentaries on the increasingly complex and complicated history of the languages and dialects of Middle-earth and their connection to the divisions and subdivisions, migrations and wanderings of the Elven peoples. In addition to several family trees of the proliferating Elven cultures, it includes two hand-drawn charts of Elven language families, modeled on similar charts of actual Indo-European language families. "The Lhammas" might as easily have been grouped with Part III, which is also philological in nature, but since it involves some history of the peoples involved, Christopher Tolkien has assigned it to Part II.

The text of the "Quenta Silmarillion" here presented is a composite. The first five chapters, marked as I-3(c), are taken from a typescript of revisions made to the manuscript of the "Quenta Noldorwina" (published in *Shaping*) when it was returned to Tolkien by George Allen & Unwin in December 1937. These chapters are supplemented with commentary by Christopher Tolkien on developments from the original. The ensuing chapters present the manuscript text as it existed before the revisions and the making of the typescript. The version as a whole has not the narrative expansion and detail of the version published in *The Silmarillion*, being noticeably briefer and more compressed.

Part III is entirely devoted to an extensive etymological dictionary titled "The Etymologies." This gives the proto-Eldarin roots of a large number of words and names in Quenya and Sindarin and a number of lesser languages, including Danian, Doriathrin, Ilkorin, Noldorin, Lindarin, Ossiriandeb, and Telerin. The importance of this material to the linguistic side of Tolkien's mythology cannot be overestimated. Aside from *The Silmarillion*'s Index of Names and the appendix on word elements, information on Tolkien's etymological material had heretofore been confined to what could be gleaned from scattered references in *The Lord of the Rings*. Such gleanings were sparse, often conjectural, and of necessity patched together using incomplete and insufficient data. "The Etymologies" is invaluable not only as the first extensive Tolkien-authored offering on the languages and a primary source for the words themselves but also for better understanding of (1) the fluidity of the languages in their development and (2) the relationship of the languages to the invented world. It should be noted that an important "Addenda and Corrigenda to the Etymologies," based on a close study of Tolkien's manuscript by Carl F. Hostetter and Patrick H. Wynne, was subsequently published in two parts in *Vinyar Tengwar*, a journal of Tolkien linguistics, nos. 45 (November 2003) and 46 (July 2004).

Rounding out *The Lost Road* is what its editor calls "the inevitable Appendix." This includes "The Genealogies," additions to the genealogical tables given in *The Shaping of Middle-earth;* "The List of Names," a brief selection from a longer and much-added-to list of names concerned with the legends of the Elder Days; and the second "Silmarillion" map, a reproduction of this much altered and added to map as it was originally drawn, here printed in sections on four successive book pages.

As always, Christopher Tolkien's extensive commentaries and notes in each section provide a chronological and creative context for all material, offering variant readings and noting major revisions from earlier texts.

VERLYN FLIEGER

Further Reading

Bratman, David. "The Literary Value of *The History of Middle-earth*." In *Tolkien's Legendarium: Essays on "The History of Middle-earth,"* edited by Verlyn Flieger and Carl F. Hostetter. Westport, CT: Greenwood, 2000.

Flieger, Verlyn. "The Footsteps of Ælfwine." In *Tolkien's Legendarium: Essays on "The History of Middle-earth,"* edited by Verlyn Flieger and Carl F. Hostetter. Westport, CT: Greenwood, 2000.

Noad, Charles. "On the Construction of *The Silmarillion.*" In *Tolkien's Legendarium: Essays on "The History of Middle-earth,"* edited by Verlyn Flieger and Carl F. Hostetter. Westport, CT: Greenwood, 2000.

Rateliff, John. "'The Lost Road,' 'The Dark Tower,' and 'The Notion Club Papers': Tolkien and Lewis's Time-Travel Triad." In *Tolkien's Legendarium: Essays on "The History of Middle-earth,"* edited by Verlyn Flieger and Carl F. Hostetter. Westport, CT: Greenwood, 2000.

Scull, Christina. "The Development of Tolkien's Legendarium: Some Threads in the Tapestry of Middle-earth." In *Tolkien's Legendarium: Essays on "The History of Middle-earth,"* edited by Verlyn Flieger and Carl F. Hostetter. Westport, CT: Greenwood, 2000.

See also **Ælfwine;** *Book of Lost Tales I; Book of Lost Tales II; Lays of Beleriand;* **Memory;** *Return of the Shadow;* **Sauron Defeated; Shaping of Middle-earth; Time; Time-Travel;** *Treason of Isengard; War of the Ring*

LOTHLÓRIEN

Lothlórien is also called Lórien, the Golden Wood, the Hidden Land, and in Rohan Dwimordene. Originally known as Laurelindórinan ("Land of the Valley of Singing Gold," says Treebeard), but renamed after Lórien in Valinor, the garden of the Vala Irmo, Lothlórien (Dreamflower) is the heart of Elvendom in Middle-earth. In Rivendell, the Elves remember the Blessed Realm; in Lothlórien they preserve a fragment of it, as Frodo thinks on first coming there:

> As soon as he set foot upon the far bank of Silverlode . . . it seemed to him that he had stepped over a bridge of time into a corner of the Elder Days, and was now walking in a world that was no more. In Rivendell there was memory of ancient things; in Lórien the ancient things still lived on in the waking world. (*FR*, II, vi, 364)

Lothlórien is an irregularly shaped region of more than two thousand square miles, bounded on the west by the River Celebrant or Silverlode, which once joined by the Nimrodel turns south then east to form also the southern boundary of the land. On the east, Lothlórien is bounded by the Great River (Anduin) and on the north by the edges of its own native forests, the Northern Fences as they are called. The central area of Lothlórien is called the Naith or Gore; it contains the knoll of Cerin Amroth. Further southeast in the Naith, within the area of the Angle between the Silverlode and the Anduin, is Egladil, the region where the Tree-City of Caras Galadhon is located.

The Elf-lady Galadriel, who rules Lothlórien with her consort Celeborn, has long dwelt there. The biography of Galadriel seemed to evolve constantly in Tolkien's mind (he was revising her history in the last month of his life), but she told Frodo that she had crossed the mountains from Beleriand before the fall of Nargothrond (i.e., before ca. 500 of the First Age). She and Celeborn did not come to Lothlórien until considerably later, but Galadriel has been able to preserve it as an Elven realm unsullied because she possesses one of the Three Rings of Power, Nenya, the Ring of Adamant.

Its native forests make Lothlórien uniquely beautiful among all beautiful places in Middle-earth, for they consist of the *mellyrn* or mallorn trees that, with a single notable exception, will be found nowhere else east of the Sea. The trunks of these great beech-like trees are silver. Their foliage turns gold in the autumn but does not fall until spring, when new green foliage and yellow blossoms appear. The forest canopy is then green and silver and gold, and the floor below is golden. Looking at it as they come to Lothlórien in January, the hobbits can see the forest "like a sea of fallow gold tossing gently in the breeze" (*FR*, II, vi, 360).

Some authorities trace the origin of these remarkable trees to Númenor, whose king long ago gave their seeds or acorns to Gil-galad of Lindon, who in turn gave them to Galadriel. Less certainly, mallorns might be traced back to Aman itself. At any rate, the hobbits and their friends spend their first night in Lothlórien's forest on a *flet* or *talan*, a tree-platform, which is typically the dwelling of Galadriel's Tree-people, the Galadhrim or Silvan Elves.

As the Company proceeds eastward through Lothlórien, its members come first to the great knoll of Cerin Amroth, a spot that forms the background of two love stories. Cerin Amroth is ringed by a double circle of trees, the inmost of which consists of mallorns. The grass is carpeted with the yellow *elanor* and the white *niphredil*, which flower there in winter. The place is named for an Elven prince, Amroth, who once dwelt there and who, a millennium and more ago, was lost in the Sea when he would not forsake his love, Nimrodel. It is also the spot where more recently Aragorn and Arwen Evenstar (who is Galadriel's granddaughter) pledged their troth. Here his heart ever dwells, Aragorn tells Frodo.

On the evening of the second day of marching, the Company comes to the mightiest of all groves of mallorns, Caras Galadhon, the home of Galadriel and Celeborn. The Tree City lies in a green shade, a place of lamplight and music. In the mightiest of its trees is a flet on which stands a great house, as large as a hall of Men. Here, the two Elvish rulers welcome and converse with the eight members of the Company.

The hobbits, and the others, learn much in Lothlórien. They learn that time seems to flow differently in the world of the Elves: Sam can remember but a few days there, yet a whole month has apparently passed. They learn something about Elven craft, in the making of rope, boats, *lembas* or waybread, and even cloaks, which seem to be "magic" cloaks, but only in the eyes of those who do not understand nature in the way Elves do. Each of the Company receives a gift that will be useful in the shorter or the longer term. They learn that the Elves are doomed, however Frodo's mission turns out.

After the unmaking of the One Ring, the Ring Nenya loses its power to protect and preserve. A few days later, Galadriel and Celeborn cross the Anduin and destroy Sauron's old stronghold of Dol Guldur in Mirkwood. Galadriel leaves Middle-earth with Elrond, Frodo, and the others in 3021, and Celeborn remains, eventually removing to Rivendell and dwelling with Elrond's sons. Lothlórien is now empty, and Caras Galadhon is silent.

And yet, Lothlórien and its lovely mallorns are not forgotten. Part of Galadriel's gift to Sam Gamgee created the notable exception mentioned previously: the acorn of a mallorn, which Sam planted in the Shire to replace the Party Tree. It was the only mallorn in the west of Middle-earth and grew to be one of the most beautiful anywhere.

MICHAEL N. STANTON

Primary Sources

Fonstad, Karen Wynn. *An Atlas of Middle-earth*. Revised edition. Boston, MA: Houghton Mifflin, 1998.

Strachey, Barbara. *Journeys of Frodo*. London: HarperCollins, 1998.

Further Reading

Brice, Lynn. "The Use of Christian Iconography in Selected Marginalia of J.R.R. Tolkien's Lothlórien Chapters." *Extrapolation* 5 (1984): 51–59.

Giddings, Robert, and Elizabeth Holland. "Lothlórien and the Lost Horizon." Chap. 5 in *J.R.R. Tolkien: The Shores of Middle-earth*. Frederick, MD: University Publishers of America, 1982.

Hood, Gwenwyth. "The Earthly Paradise in Tolkien's *The Lord of the Rings*." Proceedings of the J.R.R. Tolkien Centenary Conference 1992. *Mythlore* 21, no. 2, whole no. 80 (1996): 139–44.

Kocher, Paul Harold. "The Free Peoples. Part 1: Elves." Chap. 5 in *Master of Middle-earth: The Fiction of J.R.R. Tolkien*. Boston, MA: Houghton Mifflin, 1972.

Pitts, Mary Ellen. "The Motif of the Garden in the Novels of J.R.R. Tolkien, Charles Williams, and C.S. Lewis." *Mythlore* 8 no., 4 whole no. 30 (1982): 3–6, 42.

See also **Elves: Kindreds and Migrations; Finrod; Galadriel; Melian**

LÚTHIEN

Lúthien is figuratively the mother of Middle-earth. Daughter of King Thingol and Melian (a Maia), Lúthien and her husband Beren are the main characters in the core story of Tolkien's *Silmarillion*, "Of Beren and Lúthien," which derives from *The Lay of Leithian: Release from Bondage*. Their union, the first joining of the Eldar and the Edain, gives a genealogical basis to Tolkien's mythology and makes *The Lord of the Rings* cohere on a cosmological and historical level. Elrond, Half-elven, his daughter Arwen, and Aragorn are all descended from lines that can be traced to Lúthien. Their lives, their choices, and their fates are all intertwined with hers, the first of the Eldar to choose a mortal life. With gray eyes and dark hair, Lúthien is unsurpassed in beauty; Arwen is Lúthien's likeness in the Third Age. More than lovely, Lúthien is also a hero with great power. She contends with evil and defeats it, and she heals grievous wounds. Inspired by a vision of his wife Edith, Lúthien is the character about whom Tolkien cared most deeply and personally. The name "Lúthien" is engraved on Edith's tombstone.

In *The Silmarillion*, Tolkien insists that it is love for Beren that binds Lúthien to his fate. Knowing this, Beren attempts to leave her and to pursue the quest for the Silmaril on his own. Lúthien prohibits this, saying, "I shall go with you, and our doom shall be alike" (*S*, 177). Huan, "chief of the wolfhounds that followed Celegorm"(*S*, 172), speaking for the second of three times, then foreshadows Lúthien's end to Beren: "From the shadow of death you can no longer save Lúthien, for by her love she is now subject to it" (*S*, 179). When Beren is killed by Carcharoth, the Wolf of Angband and servant of Morgoth, Lúthien is left to confront her solitude. Imploring Mandos with "the song most fair that ever in words was woven, and the song most sorrowful that ever the world shall hear" (*S*, 186–87), Lúthien earns his pity. So moved, Mandos intercedes with Manwë, Lord of the Valar, who ultimately presents Lúthien with her choice: to go to Valimar and dwell among the Valar without Beren or to become mortal and return to Middle-earth, in which case the Valar would restore Beren to life, but both Beren and Lúthien would eventually die. Lúthien chooses the latter and thus, as the subtitle to *The Lay of Leithian* suggests, is released from what would have been an imprisoning immortality. In her union with the resurrected Beren, Lúthien joins the two kindreds of Elves and Men and founds the line of the Númenórean Kings in whom Tolkien invests the hope and the future of Middle-earth.

Tolkien considered the Beren and Lúthien tale a fundamental link in the story cycle that begins with *The Silmarillion* and concludes with *The Lord of the Rings*. Each contains a marriage of Man and Elf—Beren and Lúthien, Aragorn and Arwen—and depicts a love story with two crucial parallels between the female Elven characters: their beauty and their choice of the mortal life. As Tolkien relates Aragorn's first vision of Arwen, in the appendices to *The Lord of the Rings*, he explicitly references the lay and overlays the Beren and Lúthien story onto the setting, the woods, and the description of Arwen: "For Aragorn had been singing a part of the Lay of Lúthien which tells of the meeting of Lúthien and Beren in the forest of Neldoreth. And behold! there Lúthien walked before his eyes in Rivendell, clad in a mantle of silver and blue, fair as the twilight in Elven-home; her dark hair strayed in a sudden wind, and her brows were bound with gems like stars" (*RK*, Appendix A, 338). Arwen's choice, to marry Aragorn and to forego immortality, is also partially equivalent to Lúthien's; but, in making departure with the Elves a gift to Frodo, Arwen's gesture is also dramatically different. As she says to him: "A gift I will give you. For I am the daughter of Elrond. I shall not go with him when he departs to the Havens; for mine is the choice of Lúthien, and as she so have I chosen, both the sweet and the bitter. But in my stead you shall go, Ring-bearer, when the time comes, and if you desire it" (*RK*, VI , vi, 252–53).

Like her father Elrond, Arwen is Half-elven. For this entire race, the choice of Lúthien is perpetuated: to return to the Blessed Realm with the Elves or to live and die as Men do in Middle-earth. The circumstances of this choice, however, are materially different than those that originally faced Lúthien. For the Half-elven, to choose between the fates of Man and Elf is a choice between one side and another of one's nature. Lúthien had no such other side; hers was a decision against her kin, to abandon the Eldar and forever to leave their world. Different from Arwen, Lúthien is the sole member of the Eldalië ever to have died. While her descendants preserve the choice to return to the Eldar, she never could. Hence the profound sense of regret that pervades the Elvish songs of Lúthien. Similar to Lúthien, Arwen chooses a mortal life out of love for a Man and sacrifices herself in a way that changes another's fate. Lúthien chooses death so that Beren may return to life; immortality is bestowed upon their children, but only if they choose differently from their mother.

The choice of Lúthien is essential to Tolkien's mythology. No less essential is Lúthien's status as a female hero. Though the quest for the Silmaril belongs to Beren, credit for its accomplishment is due to Lúthien. It was not Beren but Lúthien who overcame Sauron, Morgoth's lieutenant, daring "that which the sons of

Fëanor had not dared to do" (*S*, 176). She commanded Carcharoth to sleep, cast Morgoth's entire court into slumber, placed a blindness on Morgoth's eyes, and "set upon him a dream, dark as the Outer Void where once he walked alone" (*S*, 181). From this Morgoth fell, and the iron crown with the Silmarils "rolled echoing from his head" (*S*, 181). Next, Lúthien roused Beren, who had been as a dead beast on the ground, to achieve his quest and cut a Silmaril from the crown. This was not the first or the last time Lúthien aided or restored Beren. With a forest herb, her own arts, and her love, she healed Beren's wound from the arrow shot by Curufin. And she drew the venom of Carcharoth out of him and staunched the wound left by the bite that took Beren's hand.

Tolkien gave his tale of Beren and Lúthien various titles and related it in verse and prose, reworking it throughout his lifetime. In the history of Middle-earth, *The Lay of Leithian: Release from Bondage* is the fairest and one of the longest songs of the Elves. "Of Beren and Lúthien" is a shorter prose version of the same tale, "told in fewer words and without song" (*S*, 162). This same verse-prose dichotomy recurs in *The Lord of the Rings* when Aragorn, on Weathertop, softly chants nine stanzas of the song and afterward recounts the rest of the tale to the hobbits in prose narrative. Later, Tolkien tells us that the hobbits in Rivendell "heard told in full the lay of Beren and Lúthien and the winning of the Great Jewel" (*FR*, II, iii, 290). As the *Gest of Beren and Lúthien*, the story was once offered (and rejected) as a potential successor to *The Hobbit*. In a letter to Stanley Unwin, Tolkien conceded that the verse-form *Gest* "in spite of certain virtuous passages has grave defects" (*Letters*, 26). Tolkien wrote often in verse and enjoyed doing so, but his success as a lyricist was limited. Most illuminating, however, is Tolkien's subsequent remark to Unwin that "[the *Gest*] is only for me the rough material" (*Letters*, 26). The substance of the Beren and Lúthien story was of greater significance than its form.

GERALD SEAMAN

Further Reading

Carpenter, Humphrey. *Tolkien: A Biography*. Boston, MA: Houghton Mifflin, 1977.

Chance, Jane. *The Lord of the Rings: The Mythology of Power*. Revised edition. Lexington: University Press of Kentucky, 2001.

———. *Tolkien's Art: A Mythology for England*. Revised edition. Lexington, KY: University Press of Kentucky, 2001.

Chism, Christine. "Middle-earth, the Middle Ages, and the Aryan Nation: Myth and History in World War II." In *Tolkien the Medievalist*, edited by Jane Chance, 63–92. New York: Routledge, 2003.

Eden, Bradford Lee. "The 'Music of the Spheres': Relationships Between Tolkien's *The Silmarillion* and Medieval Cosmological and Religious Theory." In *Tolkien the Medievalist*, edited by Jane Chance. New York: Routledge, 2003.

Flieger, Verlyn. *Splintered Light: Logos and Language in Tolkien's World*. Grand Rapids, MI: Eerdmans, 1983.

Noel, Ruth S. *The Mythology of Middle-earth*. Boston, MA: Houghton Mifflin, 1977.

Schlobin, Roger C. "The Monsters are Talismans and Transgressions: Tolkien and *Sir Gawain and the Green Knight*." In *J.R.R. Tolkien and His Literary Resonances: Views of Middle-earth*, edited by George Clark and Daniel Timmons, 71–81. Contributions to the Study of Science Fiction and Fantasy, 89. Westport, CT: Greenwood, 2000.

Shippey, Tom. *J.R.R. Tolkien: Author of the Century*. Boston, MA: Houghton Mifflin, 2000.

———. *The Road to Middle-earth*. Boston, MA: Houghton Mifflin, 1983.

West, Richard C. "Real-World Myth in a Secondary World: Mythological Aspects in the Story of Beren and Lúthien." In *Tolkien the Medievalist*, edited by Jane Chance. London: Routledge, 2003.

See also **Aragorn; Arwen; Beren; Elrond; Elves; Immortality;** *Lays of Beleriand*; **Marriage; Melian; Morgoth and Melkor; Sauron;** *Silmarillion*; **Silmarils; Thingol; Valar; Women in Tolkien's Works**

LYME REGIS

Lyme Regis is a coastal town in Dorset, a county in the west of England. It is small; even today the population is around four thousand, and a significant number of its residents are retired people.

Known as "The Pearl of Dorset," it was a major British port in the thirteenth century but declined as a working town in the last century. It is famous for what is known as "The Cobb," a magnificent harbor wall that featured in various novels by Jane Austen, who at one time lived in Lyme Regis.

It is historically significant as the place where the Duke of Monmouth landed and began his ill-fated rebellion in 1685. But the history of the town is genuinely ancient, being a centre for dinosaur fossils and prehistoric remains.

Tolkien became familiar with Lyme Regis after his mother's death, when Father Morgan took him and his brother there for summer holidays. They stayed at the Three Cups Hotel. The Tolkien boys had various friends in the area and spent time visiting them and touring the local attractions. They also spent hours hiking around the town and along the cliffs that are only a short walk from the town center.

The scenic beauty of those cliffs and the neighboring sea gave Tolkien the opportunity to sketch and paint. On one occasion, he found a prehistoric jawbone and immediately imagined that it was it was part of some ancient dragon.

The beauty of the town and the childhood pleasure he enjoyed within it remained with him for the rest of his life.

MICHAEL COREN

See also **Art and Illustrations by Tolkien**

LYRIC POETRY

By "lyrical poetry," if one is a traditionalist, one means poems—usually short poems—that have been or could be set to music (like ancient Greek poems sung with lyre accompaniment); more generally, the term refers to any poems that emphasize personal moods, whether of the author or of a fictional speaker. Tolkien wrote lyrical poems in both of these senses.

Songs for the Philologists (1936) contains, *inter alia*, thirteen poems by Tolkien; the traditional tunes of these are noted by name in Hammond's *Descriptive Bibliography*. For example, one was "The Root of the Boot," an early version of "The Stone Troll," sung to the folk tune "The Fox Went Out." Tom Shippey's *Road to Middle-earth*, Appendix B, reprints, by Tolkien, a poem in Gothic and three in Old English from this songbook.

Tolkien's best known poems come from *The Hobbit* and *The Lord of the Rings*, sometimes suggested there as songs, sometimes as recitative pieces. Donald Swann's setting of six of these appeared in *The Road Goes Ever On: A Song Cycle* (along with "Errantry" from *The Adventures of Tom Bombadil* and the separately published "Bilbo's Last Song"—the latter added to Swann's second edition). Tolkien himself suggested to Swann the Gregorian chant approach to "Namárië." Some of these poems—such as Swann's titular choice—are plain in their English and occasionally have drawn complaints that the imagery is not richer; but music, whether mental or actual, adds the richness, and Shippey (188–92) finds, for example, thematic significance in the words of the two walking songs in *The Lord of the Rings*.

About seventy-five poems (thirty-five not collected elsewhere) appear in *The History of Middle-earth*, edited by Christopher Tolkien. The present writer discusses four of the seventy-five in "Tolkien's Lyric Poetry" (Christopher).

Tolkien writes in a variety of verse forms, including the alliterative meter. Three original examples from *The Adventures of Tom Bombadil* are as follows: (1) The titular poem and "Bombadil Goes Boating" are written in couplets with the lines having seven stresses each—four in the first half of each line, three in the latter half (in accentual groupings, not in a regular meter); (2) "Errantry" can be read as built on iambic tetrameter quatrains (rhyming ABCB), but Tolkien's recorded reading shows each line intended to be two second-class pæons (each pæon equivalent to an iamb and a pyrrhus) and further, an extra rhyme (or near rhyme) connects the final pæon of the A or C lines with the following first pæon of the B lines; and (3) "The Mewlips" twice has the pattern of three stanzas of common meter and then a stanza of six-stress lines rhyming AABB (mainly iambic in rhythm, but with one line beginning with a spondee and a bacchius). Tolkien also invented three names of verse forms for poems in Sindarin—*ann-themmath, Minlamad thent/estent*, and *linnod* (Wynne and Hostetter).

JOE R. CHRISTOPHER

Further Reading

Christopher, Joe R. "Tolkien's Lyric Poetry." In *Tolkien's Legendarium: Essays on "The History of Middle-earth,"* edited by Verlyn Flieger and Carl F. Hostetter. Westport, CT: Greenwood, 2000.

Shippey, Tom. *J.R.R. Tolkien: Author of the Century*. London: HarperCollins, 2000.

Wynne, Patrick, and Carl F. Hostetter. "Three Elvish Verse Modes." In *Tolkien's Legendarium: Essays on "The History of Middle-earth,"* edited by Verlyn Flieger and Carl F. Hostetter. Westport, CT: Greenwood, 2000.

M

MACDONALD, GEORGE (1824–1905)

George MacDonald was born in Huntly, Scotland, into a family and culture that was deeply rooted in the Christian faith and the stories of scripture. While MacDonald questioned some of the harsher forms of Calvinism that he experienced in his youth, he remained deeply committed to his Christian heritage, and his stories give witness to his unwavering belief in a loving and gracious God. His higher education included classical literature, natural sciences, and theology. A careful reading of MacDonald's stories reveals his exposure and indebtedness to a wide range of the Western literary tradition such as Dante, Milton, Goethe, and Shakespeare. While his intention was to become a minister, MacDonald started writing at a young age, and literature would become MacDonald's primary way of expressing his faith.

MacDonald was deeply impressed by early German Romanticism and the German *Kunstmärchen* (artistic fairy tales), and of the writers working in this genre, Novalis was the most influential. Novalis's emphasis on the recovery of the poet as priest had a deep impact on MacDonald. The fairy tale *The Golden Key* is based on an idea by Novalis, while his adult fantasies *Phantastes* and *Lilith* reveal MacDonald's debt to Novalis most profoundly. When asked, "What is a fairy tale," MacDonald simply responded, "Read Undine," a fairy tale by the German Romantic writer De La Motte-Fouqué.

MacDonald developed his fantasy writing in the context of other Victorian writers with whom he shared a deep concern for social justice in light of human exploitation in Victorian Britain. MacDonald's profound Christian faith, enhanced by a Romantic outlook on creation and creativity, became embodied in his imaginative fairy tales. It is this interplay between faith and imaginative writing that made MacDonald such a unique writer. It is not surprising that he is often referred to as the "grandfather" of the Inklings, as he had such a strong impact not only on C.S. Lewis and J.R.R. Tolkien but also on G.K. Chesterton, W.H. Auden, and Charles Williams. While C.S. Lewis was rather outspoken about his admiration of George MacDonald, Tolkien's praise is more guarded and his debt to MacDonald less explicit.

The influence of MacDonald on Tolkien began at an early age. Carpenter, in his biography, tells us that the stories of George MacDonald were Tolkien's "childhood favourites," especially the "Curdie books." In a letter, Tolkien acknowledges his debt to MacDonald's *The Princess and the Goblin* for the creation of Orcs, and as one reads MacDonald's and Tolkien's stories alongside one another, one will find a number of parallels. However, MacDonald influenced Tolkien on a much deeper level than just ideas for various characters and episodes. A careful reading of Tolkien's essay "On Fairy-Stories" alongside MacDonald's essays on the imagination show how deeply Tolkien's thinking about fairy stories was shaped by MacDonald, especially in regard to the relationships among faith, imagination, and fantastic writing.

According to Tolkien, a fairy tale usually has three faces: the Mystical toward the Supernatural; the

Magical toward Nature; and the Mirror of scorn and pity toward man. In relation to the Mystical, Tolkien singles out MacDonald as someone who sought to make the fairy tale into a "vehicle of Mystery," and he lists *The Golden Key* and *Lilith* as two examples.

Tolkien's understanding of the imagination and its function closely resembles that of MacDonald, who firmly established human creativity in the context of God as the creator. Humanity is made in the image of God and therefore has the ability to create what MacDonald calls "little worlds" and Tolkien calls "subcreations." MacDonald emphasized that while a writer might be free to create a new world with its own set of laws, one must never meddle with moral laws as they must stay the same. Works of the imagination should always embody old truths, which are anchored for MacDonald in his Christian worldview. Tolkien, in his epilogue to "On Fairy-Stories," affirms this conviction even more strongly. For Tolkien, the "eucatastrophic" tale is the true form of a fairy tale, and it is its highest function. The highest and truest "eucatastrophe" is found, according to Tolkien, in the "evangelium." The Gospel stories contain "the greatest and most complete conceivable eucatastrophe," the good news of Jesus Christ.

Faith and fairy tales are not opposites, but rather faith hallows fairy tales and can make them into a vehicle of divine grace, hope, and joy. MacDonald was certainly an important inspiration for Tolkien in this regard, and it is therefore justified to call MacDonald the true founder of modern fantasy.

GISELA KREGLINGER

Further Reading

Lewis, C.S. *George MacDonald: An Anthology*. New York: HarperCollins, 2001.
———. "The Fantastic Imagination." In *Dish of Orts*. Whitehorn: Johannesen, 1996.
———. "The Golden Key." In *George MacDonald The Complete Fairytales*. New York: Penguin Books, 1999.
———. "The Imagination: Its Function And Its Culture." In *Dish of Orts*. Whitehorn: Johannesen, 1996.
———. *Lilith*. Grand Rapids, 2000.
———. *Phantastes*. Grand Rapids, Mich.: Eerdmans, 2000.
———. *The Princess and Curdie*. New York: Penguin, 1996.
———. *The Princess and the Goblins*. New York: Penguin, 1996.
Tolkien, J.R.R. "On Fairy-Stories." In *TL*.

MAGIC: MIDDLE-EARTH

Tolkien briefly explained magic at the end of "The Mirror of Galadriel" (*FR*, II, vii, 376–77). Frodo and Sam are discussing Elf-magic, when Galadriel appears and takes them to the Mirror. She tells them the Mirror is what hobbits (and perhaps humans) call magic, a term Elves find confusing, because it uses "the same word for the deceits of the Enemy."

A never-sent draft in *The Letters of J.R.R. Tolkien*, letter 155, explains what lay behind Galadriel's remark. Within his tale, Tolkien wrote, there is a "latent distinction" between two forms of magic: *magia* (ordinary magic) and *goeteia* (witchcraft, perhaps using spirits). In Middle-earth, neither is good or bad, "but only by motive or purpose or use." (Writing to a fellow Catholic in letter 153, Tolkien argued that "sub-creation" permitted an "imaginary world" with different rules from our own.)

Magia involves mechanism. Say the proper words at the west gate of Moria, and the door opens. *Magia*, Tolkien explained in letter 155, has "real effects in the physical world. . . . like fire in a wet faggot." Elves and Gandalf "sparingly" use *magia* "for specific beneficent purposes." In contrast, Sauron uses *magia* "to bulldoze both people and things." Tolkien gave no example, but the darkness beginning on March 10 is an illustration.

Goeteia has to do with perception and will. The *goeteia* of Elves is "entirely artistic and not intended to deceive." In letter 131, Tolkien said that "their 'magic' is Art" and that magic allowed them to create beauty effortlessly. (Tolkien must have envied that gift.) For the Elves, magic was linked to beauty in the same sense that for Sauron it meant power and domination. Unfortunately, as Tolkien pointed out in that letter, the Elves also used their magic to embalm beauty. Letter 154 says such misuse "has its own punishments."

Without using the term, Tolkien gave another aspect of *goeteia* in letter 210, where *lembas*, the waybread of the Elves, is described as having a power "superior to other cakes" that "no analysis in any laboratory would discover." (*Magia* would have altered its chemistry.) In "Mount Doom" (*RK*, VI, iii, 213), Tolkien wrote that *lembas* "had a virtue. . . . It fed the will, and it gave strength to endure." In letter 213, Tolkien mentioned parallels to *lembas* in Catholic doctrines such as the viaticum, the last rites for the dying.

In letter 155, Tolkien stressed that Sauron uses *goeteia* "to terrify and subjugate" as well as to deceive. In letter 210, he mentioned that the Black Riders' power was "almost entirely due to the unreasoning *fear* that they inspire," since they "have no great physical power against the fearless."

In contrast, Gandalf strictly limited his power to bend others to his will. The four hobbits who defy Sauron's *goeteia* also play a critical role. As Tolkien wrote near the end of letter 131, his grand theme is the "unforeseen and unforeseeable acts of will, and deeds of virtue" of the "small, ungreat, forgotten." Magic can be defeated by virtue. At the Crack of Doom, Frodo's pity for Gollum defeats the Ring's power to enslave.

Although Tolkien did not get specific, we might say that the *goeteia* of *lembas* was good, strengthening Frodo and Sam's wills. The *goeteia* of the *palantírs* was less certain. Aragorn was strong enough to bend a *palantír* to his will, while Denethor's mind was deceived and his will broken by one. Finally, the *goeteia* of the One Ring was so great that the will of all who used it would turn to evil—which explains why the Ring cannot be used to fight Sauron.

Because *magia* is good or evil, depending on its purpose, Tolkien drew little distinction between *magia* and technology—both were simply means to manipulate the world. In letter 155, he noted that "both sides" in the struggle "live mainly by 'ordinary' means." The same motives that drive "The Enemy" to use *magia* also turn it to machinery. Both reduce "to a minimum . . . the gap between the idea or desire and the result or effect." He goes on to note that because *magia* "may not be easy to come by," slaves and machinery can serve in its place—hence the vast armies of Saruman and Sauron.

In letter 155, Tolkien also said that in Middle-earth, magic was not something that anyone could practice simply by becoming learned in the proper lore or spells. It was an "inherent power not possessed or attainable by Men as such," with hobbits probably included with Men.

Dwarves, Elves, and wizards could work magic. In *The Hobbit*, the Dwarves place spells over troll-cave gold. In *The Lord of the Rings*, Elrond places a spell on the Ford of Bruinen, and later, when Gandalf places a spell on a door in Moria, he finds his "inherent power" to do so challenged by a powerful counterspell. The two exceptions Tolkien noted were Aragorn as a healer (but he is not a "pure Man") and the Númenóreans, a gifted race of men who used spells with their swords. Beorn's ability to change into a bear also seems magical.

Men and hobbits, however, could use magical objects made by others. Bilbo and Frodo use the One Ring's power to make themselves invisible, and both Frodo and Sam draw light from the Phial of Galadriel. There are also suggestions that, although lacking magical power in themselves, men could become sorcerers, using or being used by evil spirits. In the Ithilien cave, Faramir tells Frodo and Sam that the "Men of Númenor . . . fell into evil. . . . and the black arts" (*TT*, IV, v, 286).

Since magic in Middle-earth was closely linked to Dwarves, Elves, and wizards, their disappearance, and the arrival of what Gandalf would call the "Dominion of Man," meant that magic would fade from Middle-earth. In fact, during the War of the Ring, the great instruments of magic are mostly ancient artifacts, and both Saruman and Sauron are fought mostly by "ordinary means."

MICHAEL W. PERRY

See also **Devils; Enchantment; Faërie; Heathenism and Paganism**

MAIAR

An order of semidivine spirits created to assist the Valar in protecting and preserving the ongoing creation and refinement of the world. Of the same order as the Valar, "but of less degree," *The Silmarillion* says their exact number is unknown, and few are named. Their cosmological role is similar to that of the Valar: each Maia has a function closely associated with one of the Valar. Their perpetual importance in the cosmic order is suggested in a statement that says their joy "is as an air that they breathe in all their days, whose thought flows in a tide untroubled from the heights to the deeps" (*S*, 95).

Ilmarë, a handmaid of Varda (Elbereth), is thus associated with stars. Eönwë, "mightiest in arms," is a banner-bearer of Manwë, lord of the winds and chief of the Valar. Ossë is a servant of Ulmo, master of the seas; he also serves Manwë and is associated with wind and tempests. Ossë's spouse Uinen, a female Maia, is the "lady of the seas"; she restrains Ossë's wildness. Uinen, beloved of the Númenóreans, loves all creatures of the "salt streams," in particular the seaweed. Her hair spreads through all the waters of the world. Like Ossë, the Maia named Salmar is also associated with Ulmo; he made the Ulumúri, great horns of white shell that create an indelible sea-longing in those who hear them.

Two of the Maiar are central to the myth of the Sun and Moon. Arien, a spirit of fire, is said to have tended the golden flowers in the gardens nourished by Vána, watering them with the dew of Laurelin, one of the Two Trees of Valinor. Tilion, a huntsman in the company of Oromë, sometimes sought rest from hunting in the gardens of Lórien. By the pools of Estë he would lie dreaming under the silver beams of Telperion. Upon the Two Trees' death, Tilion asked to tend forever the last flower of Laurelin, which is the source of the moon's light. Arien is chosen for the task, Ambiguously, Arien seems to be both a guide for the sun and the sun itself. She is unhurt by the heat of Laurelin, brighter of the Two Trees; upon leaving Valinor she becomes "as a naked flame, terrible in her splendour." Her eyes are so bright that Eldar cannot look upon them. Tilion, a lover of silver, guides the moon in its courses.

Melian, one of the more important Maiar, is devoted to both Vána, "the weaver" and Estë, "the healer." Before entering Middle-earth, she lived in Valinor in the gardens of Lórien and is associated with nightingales. In Middle-earth, she is married to Thingol, king of the Noldor in Beleriand. Their daughter Lúthien is thus half Elven and half divine. Through Dior, son of Beren and Luthien, she is an ancestor of the Númenorean kings and thus an ancient foremother of Aragorn. The ruling house of Gondor, then, is especially significant in having a divine strain, however faint, descended from Melian.

The Istari, apparently a special suborder of the Maiar, are an unspecified number including those named Olórin, Curunír, Aiwendil, Alatar, and Pallando. These five become the Wizards of Third-Age Middle-earth. In Valinor, Olórin—the wisest among the Maiar—lived in Lórien and went often to house of Nienna, the Vala of grief and mourning, where he learned pity and patience. In Middle-earth, Olórin comes to be known as Gandalf. Likewise, Curunír becomes Saruman, whose interest in forging and artifice, as well as his eventual affinities with Sauron, suggests an original association with Aulë. Aiwendil, or "bird-friend," becomes Radagast and seems to have been a servant of Yavanna. Alatar and Pallando go to the east but otherwise are not mentioned in the canon of writing on Middle-earth. Sauron, servant of Melkor, was originally associated with Aulë the smith, a relationship echoed vestigially in his friendship with the Elven-smiths of Eregion and his skill as the artificer of the Rings of Power.

JONATHAN EVANS

Further Reading

Crowe, Edith L. "Power in Arda: Sources, Uses and Misuses." In *Proceedings of the J.R.R. Tolkien Centenary Conference*, edited by Patricia Reynolds and Glen H. GoodKnight, 272–77. Milton Keynes and Altadena: Tolkien Society/Mythopoeia, 1995.

Houghton, John. "Augustine in the Cottage of Lost Play: The Ainulindalë as Asterisk Cosmology." In *Tolkien the Medievalist*, edited by Jane Chance, 172–93. London and New York: Routledge, 2003.

See also **Angels; Astronomy and Cosmology, Middle-earth; Gandalf; Luthien; Melian; Saruman; Sauron; Wizards; Valar; Valinor**

MANDOS

The halls of Mandos are the dwelling place in Valinor of the Vala Namo the elder (often called Mandos himself). They are also known as the Houses of the Dead since Namo brings the spirits of the dead to Mandos. In this purgatory, the spirits of Elves wait for reincarnation. After the Kinslaying of Aqualonde, the guilty Elves were subjected to the Prophesy of Mandos, including the curse that in Middle-earth they can be killed and their spirits shall go to Mandos and that the "kinslayers" were to stay there longer: "[In Mandos] long shall ye abide and yearn for your bodies, and find little pity though all ye have slain entreat for you" (*S*, 88).

In the later writings, it is evident that Mandos does not hinder the free will of its residents; it even seems essential to the purification of the spirits of the Elves. A case in point occurs when Finwe volunteers to remain in Mandos so that his first wife Miriel's spirit could leave. Namo proclaims: "It is well that thou . . . hast made this offer, to deprive thyself, of thy free will, and out of pity for another" (*Morgoth*, 249).

The fate of humans after death is more of a mystery. Even though it is suggested their spirits might likewise visit Mandos, they do not stay there long. This is made most explicit in the case of Beren. Thus, through joining Beren's fate upon relinquishing her immortality, Luthein "died indeed," that is, her spirit went beyond Mandos after death.

CHRISTOPHER GARBOWSKI

See also **Beren and Lúthien; Death; Elves: Reincarnation of; Middle-earth; Valar; Valinor**

MANUSCRIPTS BY TOLKIEN

Tolkien's writing habits and his "archivist's soul" (Hammond and Scull, *Artist*, 7), while perhaps a great frustration to his publishers, would prove invaluable to countless future scholars and enthusiasts. In addition to an extraordinarily meticulous process of writing, revising, and rewriting, both backward and forward, Tolkien himself typed the bulk of his holographic manuscripts. As he put it in his foreword to the second edition of *The Lord of the Rings*, "it had to be typed, and re-typed: by me; the cost of professional typing by the ten-fingered was beyond my means." And we are very lucky this was the case, as it became Tolkien's pattern to emend (one might almost say obsessively) his typescripts with all manner of illuminating marginalia. Incredibly, in some cases, he wrote and typed as many as eighteen drafts of a single chapter. And as far as we know, he saved all of it.

Today, the greater part of Tolkien's manuscripts (as well as his notes, jottings, letters, typescripts, and galley proofs) are preserved by two institutions: the Special Collections and Archives Department of Marquette University, in Milwaukee, Wisconsin, and the Department of Western Manuscripts at the Bodleian Library in Oxford, Great Britain. Additional manuscripts do exist—these are predominantly in the hands of private collectors or smaller collections (such as the Pierpont Morgan Library, the archives of the Oxford English Dictionary, and the collections of unpublished letters at HarperCollins and at Reading University)—but the majority of Tolkien's important works and private papers are divided between Marquette and the Bodleian. The Bodleian Library, among the oldest research libraries in Europe, houses the manuscripts for *The Silmarillion*, *The Father Christmas Letters*, *Roverandom*, *The Adventures of Tom Bombadil*, "Smith of Wootton Major," "Leaf by Niggle," and other minor works. And the Bodleian has continued to acquire new material, such as the collection of Tolkien papers formerly housed at the University of Liege in Belgium. The Bodleian also keeps the vast majority of Tolkien's academic writings, notes, as well as unpublished criticism and translations—including drafts of his landmark lecture, "*Beowulf*: The Monsters and the Critics"; his work on the Old English *Exodus*; his edition and translations of *Sir Gawain and the Green Knight*, *Pearl*, and *Sir Orfeo*; and his work on the *Ancrene Wisse*, just to name a few of the better known. Perhaps the most legendary among the academic holdings at the Bodleian are Tolkien's as yet unpublished translations of *Beowulf*. All of the preceding material, subject to special permission, may be viewed and studied by scholars; however, the Bodleian also contains a large collection of unpublished family papers, diaries, and letters, and (with a few notable exceptions, such as for Humphrey Carpenter's biography of Tolkien) these have generally not been made available to scholars. Certain of these have been displayed, discussed, and reproduced in exhibitions and their accompanying publications (of which perhaps the most notable is *J.R.R. Tolkien: Life and Legend*).

On the other side of the Atlantic, Marquette University preserves the holographic manuscripts, typescripts, galley proofs, and other related material for some of Tolkien's most beloved works. These include *The Hobbit*, *The Lord of the Rings*, *Farmer Giles of Ham*, and *Mr. Bliss*. The manuscripts reached the unlikely final resting place of Milwaukee, Wisconsin, because of the foresight and diligence of William B. Ready, directory of Marquette's libraries from 1956 to 1963. Distinguishing *The Lord of the Rings* very early on as the masterpiece it would come to be seen as, Ready contracted the services of Bertram Rota, an antiquarian book dealer in Great Britain, as intermediary in negotiations between Marquette and Tolkien. In early 1957, Ready and Tolkien finalized their agreement, settling on a very modest purchase price of £1,250 (this total is given by Carpenter; however, the sum of £1,500 has also been widely reported). Over the course of 1957–58, the bulk of the material was transferred to Marquette; however, in the years since Tolkien's death, Christopher Tolkien has continued to unearth new matter covered by the terms of the sale, and the Marquette collection has grown as a result. In addition to these manuscripts of Tolkien's most well-known works, Marquette also houses a collection of other papers, including letters and unpublished linguistic material on Tolkien's invented languages. With special arrangement, scholars can visit Marquette and view the entire collection, which was microfilmed for study in 1983; for the obvious reasons of their age and fragility, the original documents are only rarely handled. In addition, a complete online inventory of the material is available at the Marquette University Libraries Web site.

Much of what we know about the manuscripts and about Tolkien's creative process has come to us through the posthumous publication of *The Silmarillion*, *Unfinished Tales of Númenor and Middle-earth*, and the twelve-volume *History of Middle-earth*. These published works expose much of Tolkien's early conception of Middle-earth, its mythology, and its denizens. In addition, Christopher Tolkien has provided valuable insight into the timing and development of the work through his collation of the material and his uniquely insightful observations and inferences. Indeed, his work may be thought of as the map to the manuscripts, without which all but the most dedicated and intrepid scholars would quickly find themselves hopelessly lost. In addition to these invaluable works, there is an ongoing process, still underway today, to collate, edit, and publish the large body of Tolkien's unpublished linguistic writings. This project, headed up by Christopher Gilson, with the assistance of such Tolkien linguistic scholars as Carl F. Hostetter, Arden R. Smith, and Patrick Wynne, has already resulted in the addition of considerable new material to the published canon (in the forms of the journals *Parma Eldalamberon* and *Vinyar Tengwar*). Yet the amount of material Tolkien produced was so voluminous that the pages of these journals will probably be occupied with this work for years to come.

JASON FISHER

Further Reading

Carpenter, Humphrey. *J.R.R. Tolkien: A Biography*. London: Allen & Unwin, 1977.

Carter, Curtis L. *The Invented Worlds of J.R.R. Tolkien: Drawings and Manuscripts from the Marquette University Collection*. Milwaukee, WI: Marquette University, 2004.

———. *J.R.R. Tolkien: "The Hobbit": Drawings, Watercolors, and Manuscripts*. Milwaukee: Marquette University, 1987.

Hammond, Wayne G., and Christina Scull. *J.R.R. Tolkien: Artist & Illustrator*. London: HarperCollins, 1995.

———. *The Lord of the Rings: A Reader's Companion*. Boston, MA: Houghton Mifflin, 2005.

J.R.R. Tolkien Collection at Marquette University. http://www.marquette.edu/library/collections/archives/tolkien.html (January 2006).

Priestman, Judith. *J.R.R. Tolkien: Life and Legend. An Exhibition to Commemorate the Centenary of the Birth of J.R.R. Tolkien (1892–1973)*. Oxford: Bodleian Library, 1992.

Tolkien, John, and Priscilla Tolkien. *The Tolkien Family Album*. Boston, MA: Houghton Mifflin, 1992.

See also **"*Beowulf*: The Monsters and the Critics"; *Beowulf*: Translations by Tolkien; Bodleian Library, Oxford; *Exodus*, Edition of; *Sir Gawain and the Green Knight***

MANUSCRIPTS, MEDIEVAL

J.R.R. Tolkien's scholarship on Old and Middle English required him to read texts whose original forms are manuscripts, texts that are handwritten on tanned animal hide (the skin of sheep or cows). All we know of medieval literary culture is preserved in manuscripts, and the majority of important English literary manuscripts are held in three libraries in England: London's British Library, Corpus Christi College Library at Cambridge, and the Bodleian Library at Oxford.

Because manuscripts are each unique (even a copy of a known manuscript will have different errors, letter forms, and spacing than the original), they are cataloged by shelf mark, a system that varies from library to library and even within some ancient libraries (such as those listed above). Thus, the manuscript that contains *Beowulf* is labeled London, British Library, Cotton Vitellius A. xv. The encoding is mostly straightforward. The city, institution (in Tolkien's time "British Museum" was used instead of "British Library"), the individual collection in the library, and the location within that collection are usually listed in a shelfmark. In this case, "Cotton" refers to the library of Sir Thomas Cotton, eighteenth-century antiquarian. Cotton organized his library by putting the busts of Roman emperors atop each of its bookcases (hence the "Vitellius"). "A"

refers to the first shelf and "xv" to the fifteenth manuscript.

Although Cotton Vitellius A. xv. was of special interest to Tolkien, it is not clear if he ever handled the *Beowulf* manuscript or saw it personally (in unpublished lecture notes dating from the 1920s or 1930s he states that he has not seen the manuscript itself but has instead relied on the facsimile edition edited by Julius Zuptiza). But Tolkien did work very closely with at least one Oxford manuscript: Oxford, Bodleian Library, Bodley 34, a small, thirteenth-century manuscript that contains the Middle English Lives of Saints Katherine, Margaret, and Juliana; *Hali Meiðhad* ("Holy Maidenhood," a discourse on virginity); and *Sawles Warde* (an allegory about the care of the soul). These texts are all related to the practice of anchoritism—they are inspirations and guides for nuns. Tolkien and his student S.R.T.O. d'Ardenne worked closely with the texts in the manuscript and with the manuscript itself, transcribing and editing it. They also, in "MS. Bodley 34: A Recollation of a Collation," harshly criticized the article "A Collation of the *Katherine Group* (MS Bodley 34)" by Ragnar Furuskog. Later scholarship has shown that Tolkien and d'Ardenne, although somewhat abrasive in their criticism, were correct in their reading of the scribe's close and somewhat difficult handwriting (see entry on "MS. Bodley 34: A Recollation of a Collation"). D'Ardenne's edition of *St. Juliana* (*þe Liflade ant te Passiun of Seinte Iuliene*) also owes a great deal to Tolkien's and her work with the manuscript, and Tolkien also influenced (though not to the same degree) her edition of St. Katherine (*Seinte Katerine*).

Tolkien also worked closely with Cambridge, Corpus Christi College 402, the manuscript of *Ancrene Wisse*, which he edited for the Early English Text Society. And either Tolkien or his collaborator, E.V. Gordon, would have consulted the manuscript London, British Library, Cotton Nero A. x., which contains *Sir Gawain and the Green Knight*.

Medieval manuscripts also influenced Tolkien's imaginative creations. The most famous manuscripts so created are the pages of the Book of Mazarbul which Tolkien intended to include in *The Lord of the Rings*. These manuscript pages are likely to have been influenced by two different medieval manuscripts: the above-mentioned *Beowulf* manuscript and the Ragyndrudis Codex (Fulda, Dombibliothek, Bonifatianus 2). In 1731, the *Beowulf* manuscript was housed along with the rest of the Cotton Library in the aptly named Ashburnham House, which caught fire on October 23. Many manuscripts were destroyed, and *Beowulf* was damaged, being charred around the edges. The Book of Mazarbul's burned state may owe something to the *Beowulf* manuscript. Its slashed condition links it with the Ragyndrudis Codex. This manuscript was, according to legend, used by St. Boniface to shield himself from the blows of his attackers before he was eventually martyred. The book does indeed bear long slashes, similar to those Tolkien describes in the Book of Mazarbul.

A final manuscript that may have influenced Tolkien is the Codex Argenteus, the so-called Silver Bible, held in the Uppsala University Library in Sweden. This manuscript contains sections of each of the four Gospels written in Gothic and thus was certainly familiar to Tolkien (most likely from the facsimile edition of 1927). Tolkien would also have known the texts from Joseph Wright's *Grammar of the Gothic Language*. The letter forms in the Codex Argenteus are strikingly similar to some of those of the Goblin Alphabet that Tolkien discussed in his 1932 and 1936 letters from Father Christmas to his children.

Using alphabets and languages of his own invention, Tolkien also created additional beautiful manuscripts of his own compositions, ornamenting them in styles that, while they owed much to the traditions of the Middle Ages, were also his own. But as much as he might have been influenced by medieval manuscripts, Tolkien's own creations often surpassed even these marvelous artifacts in beauty and originality.

MICHAEL D.C. DROUT

Further Reading

Ardenne, S.R.T.O. d', ed. *Þ Liflade ant te Passiun of Seinte Iuliene*. EETS 248. London, New York, and Toronto: Oxford University Press, 1961 (for 1960). [Reproduced, with a list of corrigenda on p. xiii, from *An Edition of Þ Liflade ant te Passiun of Seinte Iuliene*. Bibliothèque de la Faculté de Philosophie et Lettres de l'Université de Liège, fasc. LXIV. Liège: Faculté de Philosophie et Lettres; Paris: Droz, 1936.]

———— [initials misprinted S. T. R. O.], ed. *The Katherine Group: Edited from MS. Bodley 34*. Bibliothèque de la Faculté de Philosophie et Lettres de l'Université de Liège, fasc. CCXV. Paris: Les Belles Lettres, 1977.

Ardenne, S.R.T.O. d', and E.J. Dobson, eds. *Seinte Katerine: Re-Edited from MS Bodley 34 and the Other Manuscripts*. EETS S.S. 7. Oxford: Oxford University Press, 1981.

Becht-Jördens, Gereon. "Heiliger und Buch: Überlegungen zur Tradition des Bonifacius-Martyriums Anläßlich der Teilfaksimilierung des Ragyndrudis-Codex." *Hessisches Jahrbuch für Landesgeschichte* 46 (1996): 1–30.

Colborn, A.F., ed. *Hali Meiðhad: Edited from MS. Bodley 34 and MS. Cotton Titus D. xviii*. Copenhagen: Einar Munksgaard, 1940.

Furuskog, Ragnar. "A Collation of the *Katherine Group* (MS Bodley 34)." *Studia Neophilologica*. 19, no.1–2 (1947 [for 1946–47]): 119–66.

Gollancz, Israel, ed. *Pearl, Cleanness, Patience, and Sir Gawain: Reproduced in Facsimile from the Unique MS.*

Cotton Nero A. x. in the British Museum. EETS O.S. 162. Oxford: Early English Text Society, 1923.

Ker, N.R., ed. *Facsimile of MS. Bodley 34: St. Katherine, St. Margaret, St. Juliana, Hali Meiðhad, Sawles Warde*. EETS O.S. 247. Oxford: Early English Text Society, 1960.

Munkhammar, Lars. *Silverbibeln: Theoderiks bok*. Stockholm: Carlsson, 1998.

Von Padberg, Lutz. *Studien zur Bonifatiusverehrung: Zur Geschichte des Codex Ragyndrudis und der Fuldaer Reliquien des Bonifatius*. Fuldaer Hochschulschriften 25. Frankfurt am Main: Josef Knecht, 1996.

Von Padberg, Lutz, and Hans-Walter Stork. *Der Ragyndrudis-Codex des Hl. Bonifatius* Paderborn: Bonifatius; Fulda: Parzeller.

Zupitza, Julius. *Beowulf Reproduced in Facsimile from the Unique Manuscript, British Museum Ms. Cotton Vitellius A. XV*. 2nd ed. rev. Edited by Norman Davis. EETS 245. London: Early English Text Society, 1959.

See also **Alphabets by Tolkien;** *Ancrene Wisse;* **Beowulf; Boniface; d'Ardenne, S.R.T.O.;** *Father Christmas Letters;* **Katherine Group; Manuscripts by J.R.R. Tolkien; MS Bodley 34**

MAPS

"Those days, the Third Age of Middle-earth, are now long past, and the shape of all lands has been changed" (*FR*, prologue, 2). The maps in J.R.R. Tolkien's fiction show the shape of Middle-earth, and in turn they helped shape the writing of the stories. Two maps were published with *The Hobbit;* three in *The Lord of the Rings,* and two were made for the "Silmarillion." Tolkien wrote, "I wisely started with a map, and made the story fit" (*Letters,* 144, 177). The lovingly detailed maps are the glue that helps stick the story together into a believable whole.

Tolkien's maps do not have an authentic medieval style, despite their "archaic air" (*Treason,* 299). Although Tolkien was doubtless familiar with medieval maps, he chose a cleaner, more modern style. In the eighteenth century, blank places on a map became a symbol of rigorous standards and lent authority to all on the map that was unblank (Turchi, *Maps,* 37). Tolkien's hand-drawn maps follow William Morris's Arts and Crafts style; they are functional, but with an eye to grace and beauty. The long, flowing lines, rhythmic patterning, and graceful curves blur the line between the craft of cartography and the art of illustration. But the maps were not intended to be decorative only; they were integral parts of the written work and were intended to be accurate representations of the text.

Tolkien based the lands of the "Silmarillion" and *The Lord of the Rings* on England and Western Europe, but not with any strict equivalency. "If Hobbiton and Rivendell are taken (as intended) to be at about the latitude of Oxford, then Minas Tirith, 600 miles south, is at about the latitude of Florence. The Mouths of Anduin and the ancient city of Pelargir are at about the latitude of ancient Troy" (*Letters*, 376). A reasonable fit can be made spatially to Europe (Montiero, Moehn). But Tolkien's geography was imagined and developed for his stories. He combined places where he had traveled, in England and Europe, with places from literature, history, and his imagination. "And though I have not attempted to relate the shape of the mountains and land-masses to what geologists may say or surmise about the nearer past, imaginatively this 'history' is supposed to take place in a period of the actual Old World of this planet" (*Letters*, 220). Tolkien identified some of the sources for his geography: "I left the view of Jungfrau with deep regret: eternal snow, etched as it seemed against eternal sunshine, and the Silberhorn sharp against dark blue: the Silvertine (Celebdil) of my dreams" (*Letters*, 392). Others can only be guessed at: Dullatur bog, the location of the Battle of Kilsyth, may have provided the inspiration for the Dead Marshes; during construction of a canal in the 1800s, it yielded up the preserved bodies of several soldiers, one still seated on a horse (http://www.waterscape.com/servicesdirectory/D/Dulllatur_Bog.html).

The maps were an integral part of Tolkien's writing process, and were intended to be spatially accurate. He carefully coordinated the story timelines with distances and positions on his working sketch map by overlaying *The Lord of the Rings* map with a one-hundred-mile square grid to aid in calculating distances for each daily journey of ten to seventeen miles (*Treason*, 300). He did not, however, allow for the curvature of the earth. Near Oxford, each degree of longitude is forty-two miles wide, near Florence, Italy, fifty miles wide. As the Company traveled south, Gondor's east-west distances by his map would be 20 percent longer than Eriador's. However, he notes that the "stars are strange" in the southern regions (*FR*, II, ii, 261), so he obviously intended that the world was round. He may have felt the difference was unimportant to the story.

Tolkien began work on *The Hobbit* with Thror's map between 1930 and 1932 (redrawn for publication 1937) (*Letters*, 177). Thror's map is a treasure map, with clues to the location of the secret door to the treasure written in moon-letters. Tolkien intended the moon-letters to be printed in reverse on the back of the map so they would be seen when held up to light, but publishing costs eliminated this feature. Paperback and modern hardback editions print these sections in gray or outline. The writing on the map is in English (referred to as the Common speech within the story), some in a style of calligraphy resembling the Irish half-uncials, and some in an English rune alphabet (*H*, 3rd ed., preface). This device suggests that it was drawn by Dwarves, later annotated by a hobbit. The runes can be translated into phonetic English. Unlike all the other maps, Thror's depends heavily on its text, as the drawing lacks a scale and detail that would make it useful as a road guide.

The *Annotated Hobbit* shows the original idea for the map (Anderson, 29). North was at the top, and the compass-rose had symbols for north (the Big Dipper), south (a sun), east (sun rising from Door of Night), and west (Pélori of Valinor). Allen & Unwin asked Tolkien to turn the map so it could be used as an endpaper. Thus, the final map is oriented with east at the top, seemingly like many medieval maps, because that was the direction of the Garden of Eden from Europe. Tolkien later claimed that this was "typical of Dwarf-maps" (*H*, 3rd ed., preface). However, in *The Lord of the Rings*, he maintained that the Elves oriented their maps to the west, the direction of Valinor, and his published maps were reoriented to the north only for the convenience of modern readers (*RK*, Appendix E, 401).

The label "Thror's Map" signifies that this is an illustration of the original map and not the real map itself. Tolkien's second draft of the map included the note, "copied by Bilbo Baggins" (Anderson, *Annotated*, 29), but it was deleted from the final map, possibly because it was redundant. The note is consistent with Tolkien's experience with medieval manuscripts, which were often rewritten, copied, annotated, or expurgated. After *The Hobbit* went to press, a discrepancy was found between the map and the text regarding Thrain. Instead of changing the map to fit the text, he changed the text to include a king named Thrain I (*H*, all editions, preface) and later invented a complicated genealogy to account for it (*RK*, Appendix A, III, 352).

Tolkien prepared the map of Wilderland for the endpapers of the first edition of *The Hobbit* in 1936. Christopher Tolkien, whose monogram is on the corner of the map, redrew Tolkien's sketch. Tolkien's preliminary map, like many other of his sketch maps, showed topographic contours (a modern device invented in 1584 but uncommon before 1900 [http://www.homepage.mac.com/awakelate/.Public/TopographicMapping_UAA.doc]). The final version is more decorative, with rhythmic patterns of mountains and trees dotted with spider webs and towns. The colored original was re-rendered in simple black, with cross-hatching, but like Thror's map, is sometimes printed with red highlights. One interesting and unusual feature of both this and Thror's map is the vertical margin line along the right-hand side, called "the boundary of the wild." The first "Silmarillion" map in the *Shaping of Middle-earth* (*Shaping*, following 232) shows the reason for this line: it was drawn on three-hole school paper with a printed margin on the right (and a printed admonition "Do not write in this margin," which was overwritten). Hammond and Scull, however, attribute this to "design considerations" (95).

The "Silmarillion" map of Beleriand and the Lands to the North was begun in 1926, had two major versions, and was continually revised during Tolkien's lifetime. It was redrawn and finally published in 1977. The map of Beleriand illustrates chapter 14 of the "Silmarillion," "Of Beleriand and Its Realms." Beleriand's geography resembles parts of the British Isles. One feature, the Andram cliffs, through which the River Sirion flowed, matches the abrupt line of hills on the boundary of Dorset and Somerset, extending two hundred miles to Yorkshire, marked by a sudden, steep line of cliffs and hills, which forms one of the most recognizable features in Britain. The willow-meads of Tasarinan and the bird-filled lakes at Nevrast are based on Oxfordshire, Warwickshire, and the fen country; and the blighted lands around Angband are based on the northern iron and coal country with mine waste fires and pollution. The use of characteristic English landforms for the large-scale features of Beleriand, and later for the small-scale features of the Shire, is consistent with both Tolkien's dream to create a mythology for England, and with his use of recognizable place descriptions to strengthen the story's illusion of reality.

Christopher Tolkien notes that the "Silmarillion" maps do not show the Dwarf-road mentioned often in the text (*Jewels*, 336). "But none of the Noldor went over Ered Lindon, while their realm lasted" (*S*, chap. 14). The road is missing because none of the Noldor ever went east of the Blue Mountains or took the Dwarf-road. On a map made by Elves, a lack of information is itself information.

The map of the West of Middle-earth, probably the best known of the maps, was begun in 1942, redrafted for publication by Christopher Tolkien, and published in 1954 in *The Fellowship of the Ring*. Christopher Tolkien describes the history of *The Lord of the Rings* maps in *The Treason of Isengard* (295 et seq.). *The Lord of the Rings* map grew by extension from the Wilderland map of *The Hobbit,* and was in four sections, assembled with some overlap. This and the other *Lord of the Rings* maps have less decoration than those in *The Hobbit,* more detailed geography, and more complex culture. The draft map was a living, working document, and shows signs of repeated modifications and heavy wear. Forests and waters were color-coded, and much is in pencil, allowing for adjustments during the writing process. Because the tale "grew in the telling" (*FR*, foreword, 1), some of *The Hobbit* geography does not match the later *Lord of the Rings* maps in small details, and Tolkien never reconciled them. Fonstad notes that the route described in *The Hobbit* from the Bag End to Rivendell varies from *The Lord of the Rings* map in many details. The Misty Mountains were extended to the northwest, and the rivers Hoarwell and Loudwater were redirected to the south (*Atlas*, 97).

"A Map of Part of the Shire" faces the first page of *The Fellowship of the Ring* and was first sketched in 1939 and published in 1953. "If we drop the 'fiction' of long ago, 'The Shire' is based on rural England and not any other country on the world. . . . After all, the book is English, and by an Englishman" (*Letters*, 250). The map of the Shire is the only map showing political boundaries, which suggests that they were only important to Hobbits. The Shire is based on the rural Warwickshire area where Tolkien grew up. The places Bindbole Wood, Rushock Bog, Nobottle, and Pincup never appear in the text, but their presence invites the imagination into a wider world of the Shire.

Because of the complicated plotline at the climax of the story, many close-up maps of the Rohan/Gondor/Mordor region were prepared (1940–53). They were much revised as the story evolved, as shown by surviving detail sketches (*Treason*, 315 et seq.). The final map, which was drawn by C. Tolkien, was published in *The Return of the King* in 1955. Because it was more difficult to change the map than the text, earlier spellings such as "Kirith Ungol" survive. The contour lines, beacon hills, battle sites, and passes lend the map a military theme and a distinctly more modern look.

Tolkien's last map, of the island of Numenor, was sketched in 1960 and drafted and published 1980 (*UT*, preface). It accompanies the text description of the realm of Númenor (*UT*, 173). The five-pointed star shape of the island may be a graphic pun on its name, "The Land of the Star." Numenor, about the size of Ireland, has a central plain surrounded more or less by mountains, with a high central mountain called Meneltarma. The map lacks the geographic detail of the Beleriand and Middle-earth maps. It has relatively few place names, lakes, roads, and cities, and not a single bog, perhaps because so few stories occur on Númenor.

Tolkien paid great attention to the lettering on his maps. His lifelong interest in calligraphy derived from his mother, Mabel, who came from a family of engravers. Tolkien used an upright "foundational hand," preferably with a steel nib and ink bottle (Garth), which produces letters with thick and thin strokes typical of medieval manuscripts. Tolkien's maps often have capitals decorated with double descenders (see Thror's map), while Christopher's maps have capitals with thicker single descenders, indicating he used a very fine but flexible steel nib. Tolkien varied the lettering style on Thror's map according to the culture represented: rounder uncials for Elvish maps, thinner Roman letters for hobbits and men, and runes for Dwarves. Bilbo, we are told, wrote with a thin, spidery hand, which is seen on early versions of Thror's map (*H*, I, 51), but this subtlety is lost in the professionally illustrated versions. Tolkien uses parallel contour lines to denote the water in lakes and oceans. This is called waterlining and was developed in France in the seventeenth century. Allen & Unwin asked Tolkien to use waterlining instead of color to help reduce publication costs of the maps (Hammond and Scull, 91).

Successive generations of redrafted maps in current popular editions of Tolkien's works, such as the paperbacks, have lost some of the fine detail of Tolkien's originals, because professional illustrators, not cartographers, reproduced the maps. Illustrators tend to straighten rivers, tidy swamps, square-up mountains, and simplify coastlines, which erodes a map's credibility as a representation of natural landforms. The Númenor map in the Ballantine paperback of *Unfinished Tales* (1980) is an illustration without much stylistic consistency with Tolkien's maps. Like the unfortunate cover artist for the 1960s Ballantine paperbacks, the illustrator has not spent enough time studying either the previous maps or the story. In particular, the leaping dolphins are a jarring note and have no obvious connection with the story. The last "200" in the scale should read "300"; and the off-axis compass rose goes against most standards of cartography.

HarperCollins commissioned a redrafting of the maps for a new edition of *The Lord of the Rings* (http://www.tolkienmaps.com/tollkienmapsstory. html). The resulting Rohan/Gondor/Mordor map has large, dark, practically unreadable realm names that detract from the map's clarity. The scale is missing initial and final numbers. The charming hand lettering of the original maps, which maintained the illusion of Bilbo's own fair copies of older maps and which suggested a culture without printing presses or engraving, has been "improved" to bland, modern, professional illustrations of maps. The overall result is an unintentional reversion to decorative but technically inaccurate medieval-style maps. These modern redrawings are on the wrong track, for this is one area where Tolkien desired accuracy more than decoration.

Tolkien's maps and text work together to create a fictional world. *The Lord of the Rings* storyline traces a great circle clockwise through the map. While the story unfolds line by line over hours of reading, the map allows the entire story to be recalled at a glance, producing a rich tapestry of associations. While a word may automatically activate a mental image of an object, the map automatically recalls the story's whole physical and emotional space. The success of the maps, and their continuing popularity as even posters on walls, results from the extraordinary amount of detail they contain, their skilled integration with the story, and their graphic excellence. Because the maps are referenced within the story, and the fiction is maintained that the maps are fair copies of Bilbo's maps, which are fair copies of the Elves' maps, the antique style of the maps themselves adds another level of historicity connecting the past with the present. The maps invite the viewer to adventure, which pulls him or her instantly into the world of the story just as Thror's map pulled Bilbo from his comfortable parlor on a spring day in an earlier age of the world.

ALICE CAMPBELL

Further Reading

Anderson, Douglas A., ed. *The Annotated Hobbit*. By J.R.R. Tolkien. Rev. and expanded ed. Boston, MA: Houghton Mifflin, 2002.

Fonstad, Karen Wynn. *The Atlas of Middle-earth*. Rev. ed. Boston, MA: Houghton Mifflin, 1991.

Garth, John. *Tolkien and the Great War*. Boston, MA: Houghton Mifflin, 2003.

Hammond, Wayne G., and Scull, Christina. *J.R.R. Tolkien: Artist & Illustrator*. Boston, MA: Houghton Mifflin, 1995.

Moehn, Andreas. http://rover.wiesbaden.netsurf.de/~lalaith/Tolkien/Grid.html.

Montiero, Alberto. http://www.geocities.com/area51/corridor/8611/megrid1.gif (n.d.)

Turchi, Peter. *Maps of the Imagination: The Writer as Geographer*. Trinity University Press, 2004.

See also **Alphabets, Invented; Artists and Illustrators' Influence on Tolkien; Mythology for England; Treason of Isengard;** *Unfinished Tales***; Wilderland**

MARRIAGE

Tolkien had a Roman Catholic, sacramental view of marriage. He believed it to be a God-given institution and one of the central, foundational elements of the church and of a stable and civilized society. He did not believe in divorce, took the marriage vows extremely seriously, and told his friends and family to do the same.

He considered the subject of marriage thoroughly and in 1941 wrote that, "This is a fallen world. The dislocation of sex-instinct is one of the chief symptoms of the Fall. The world has been 'going to the bad' all down the ages. The various social forms shift, and each new mode has its special dangers: but the 'hard spirit of concupiscence' has walked down every street, and sat leering in every house, since Adam fell."

He continued, "The devil is endlessly ingenious, and sex is his favorite subject. He is as good every bit at catching you through generous romantic or tender motives, as through baser or more animal ones" (*Letters*, 48).

He was convinced that his motives were beyond question when he met Edith Mary Bratt. She was born in Gloucester in 1889 and had lived for most of her life in Handsworth in Birmingham. She was extremely pretty, slim and petite, with dark hair cut short and piercing gray eyes. Her mother had died when Edith was just fourteen, and her father some time before that. She had been sent away to boarding school, where she received a first-class musical education. She was also illegitimate. After finishing school, her guardian, the family lawyer Stephen Gateley, had found her rooms with a local woman renowned for holding musical evenings.

In fact, as a talented musician she was supposed to become a music teacher, but this career never materialized. Instead, she performed at her landlady's soirees, and it was at one such event that she and Tolkien first met. He was sixteen, Edith three years older. The attraction was immediate, and it soon deepened into love. The couple were anxious to become engaged but Father Francis Morgan, who was Tolkien's guardian, cautioned the couple to take more time about such a lifelong commitment. Edith was removed to the home of two family friends in far away Cheltenham.

Tolkien was heartbroken but threw himself into his studies and waited. He would later explain that on the very stroke of midnight, as he turned twenty-one, he wrote to Edith to propose marriage, only to be told that she had become engaged to another man. This was George Field, the brother of one of Edith's school friends. Tolkien immediately took the train to Cheltenham and managed to persuade Edith to change her mind. They went for a walk together into the countryside and sat under a railway bridge and talked. By the end of the evening, Edith had agreed to marry Tolkien and returned her engagement ring to a distraught George Field.

The only remaining obstacle was that Edith was not a Roman Catholic, and Tolkien was absolute in his faith. She converted from Anglicanism to Roman Catholicism on January 8, 1914, and her family responded by ordering her out of the house. She went to live in Warwick, where she and Tolkien were married on March 22, 1916, at the Church of St. Mary Immaculate. They enjoyed a short honeymoon in Somerset in the west of the country and then found a house in Staffordshire.

Once again, their romance was interrupted when, after only a few months, Tolkien sailed for France and the Battle of the Somme. He saw action but, along with many other men serving in the front lines, contracted trench fever. This sent him home and enabled him and Edith to spend more time together while he recuperated.

This was an intensely happy period, when Edith would sing and dance for her husband and play the piano as he rested or wrote. It was to inspire a scene in "The Silmarillion," with the tale of a mortal man who falls for an Elven, immortal maid after watching her dance in the forest. It was also at this time that Edith copied out *The Fall of Gondolin* in a large exercise book.

They conceived their first child in early 1917 during Tolkien's convalescence, and John Francis Reuel was born on November 16, 1917. But as Tolkien was fully recovered his regiment wanted him back, just as the war was at a particularly bloody stage. Yet he became ill once again—there is no hint of malingering—and escaped the carnage.

After the war, the family settled down and grew. Michael Hilary Reuel was born in 1920. They lived in a small apartment and then at 11 St. Mark's Terrace, close to Oxford University. Their third child, Christopher Reuel, was born in 1924 and their daughter, Priscilla, in 1929.

Theirs was generally an extremely joyous marriage and, to the surprise and disappointment of those who look for scandal or sensation in the lives of authors, quite wonderfully ordinary. They were committed as husband and wife and committed as parents. Some critics have argued that Edith made Tolkien more "suburban" than he desired, but there is no genuine evidence that he was in any way dissatisfied with his marriage or with his situation.

Nor was this partnership lacking in passion and physical intimacy. Tolkien wrote to C.S. Lewis that "Christian marriage is not a prohibition of sexual intercourse, but the correct way of sexual temperance—in fact probably the best way of getting the most satisfying sexual pleasure."

Edith did not, however, particularly enjoy Oxford's parties and social life. Nor was she especially comfortable with her husband's increasing fame, but then neither was Tolkien himself.

Edith did not share her husband's devotion to Roman Catholicism. Though a convert, she still held on to aspects of the anti-Catholicism of her family. At one point, she appeared to abandon the church completely and resented Tolkien's regular confession and attendance at Mass. There were heated arguments, and this was probably the only serious division in the Tolkien marriage. It could have become more damaging, but there was a partial resolution. While she was never a dedicated Catholic, Edith did support her husband and her children in their faith and showed an interest in the church.

They were genuinely fond of one another and deeply in love, and this was demonstrated vividly when either of them was in need. They grew old in harmony and balance. Tolkien's biographer Humphrey Carpenter visited the couple in 1967 and remembered Edith as "smaller than her husband, a neat old lady with white hair bound close to her head, and dark eyebrows." They were a unit, a being, a couple.

Edith's health began to decline in middle age, and she suffered greatly from arthritis. This made it difficult for her to walk very far and was one of the reasons why the couple moved Bournemouth, on the south coast. There was sea air, beautiful scenery, and the quiet of retirement living.

This was certainly a sacrifice for Tolkien, as he loved Oxford and his Oxford friends. But he felt that he owed Edith the time and the companionship. She had always been proud of his work and encouraged him in his writing. She always supported him, and he would now do likewise for her.

Sadly, they did not have enough of that time left. In 1971, Edith was taken seriously ill with an inflamed gall bladder and taken to hospital. On November 29, she died, and Tolkien wrote tenderly and movingly that the pain was so great that he could not "lift up his heart."

She was buried in Wolvercote Cemetery in Oxford. Tolkien decided that the inscription on Edith's grave should be simple: "Edith Mary Tolkien 1889–1971. Luthien." His Luthien was the most beautiful maiden ever to walk in Middle-earth, the pure and innocent girl who had danced for him so many years ago and inspired everything.

Joseph Pearce in a book on Tolkien writes that "friends of the Tolkiens remembered the deep affection between them which was visible in the care with which they chose and wrapped each other's birthday presents and the great concern they showed for each other's health."

Tolkien would live on for less than two years and never quite got over the loss of his wife. He returned to Oxford, but told friends that he was often lonely. He decided to visit Bournemouth, where Edith had been so happy and where she had breathed her last. And in this same town he, too, would die. He was buried in the same grave as his wife, and the inscription now reads, "Edith Mary Tolkien, Luthien, 1889–1971, John Ronald Reuel Tolkien, Beren, 1892–1973."

MICHAEL COREN

See also **Oxford**

MARXIST READINGS OF TOLKIEN

Marxist critics have often vilified Tolkien for his conservative political, social, and economic views, some resorting to extreme hyperbole in their attacks. In general, Marxist readings focus upon two interrelated thematic strains: the politics and veiled geopolitics in Tolkien's books themselves and the role of *The Lord of the Rings* and other works as cultural phenomena with political implications. Central to these readings is the premise that Sauron's Mordor and Sharkey's dictatorship in the Shire are parodies of Soviet Communism or British postwar Socialism, even though Tolkien insisted "such allegory is entirely foreign to my thought" (*Letters*, 307). The noted leftist historian E.P. Thompson sums up this view when he blames "too much early reading of *The Lord of the Rings*" for the cold warrior mentality (Thompson, 70). Thus, Tolkien's work serves as battleground for critics determined to see him as a mere mouthpiece for the right wing and his works as escapist literature for the bourgeois class.

Marxist interpretations of Tolkien appear prominently in the criticism of the early 1980s. The now somewhat disparaged 1983 compilation *J.R.R. Tolkien: This Far Land*, edited by Robert Giddings, contains a number of essays lambasting Tolkien's social conservatism and writing off his works as ideological tools. Giddings refers to *The Lord of the Rings* as an economic commodity that can only exist in the age of modern capitalism, "a product of the age of the mass production of books" (Giddings, "Introduction," 12). He also comments on the fixed class relationships in the book with the "lower orders" always deferring to their superiors (Giddings, "Introduction," 12). Fred Inglis picks up on the notion that Tolkien's epic promotes the ideals of English class system. In another study, he characterizes Tolkien's beliefs as a "non-historical, romantic Fascism" (Inglis, *Promise,* 197) and argues that *The Lord of the Rings* gives readers "a pre-Romantic, motiveless heroism which consoled a large section of the bookish classes for their powerlessness in the modern world" (Inglis, *Promise,* 200). In the 1983 essay, Inglis modifies his earlier accusation that Tolkien was a fascist but still maintains that the novel is an escapist "political fantasy" for middle-class readers seeking an outlet in the modern capitalist world (Inglis, "Gentility," 1983). Roger King's essay also describes Tolkien's fiction as an escape from modern technology made possible by the rise of postwar cultural consumption and Nigel Walmseley suggests that *The Lord of the Rings* appealed to the primitivist strain in rebellious youth culture in the mid-1960s, but the upheavals of 1967–68 pushed them in the direction of true leftist political engagement.

Nick Otty's essay in the Giddings volume sharply denounces Tolkien's supposed views on class and politics. Otty sees the Mordor as a crude caricature of the "evil" Communist East, and wonders what motivates its inhabitants "to get out of bed in the morning" (Otty, 162). He sees the Shire as an unreal agricultural utopia and calls Samwise's subservience the "idyllic face of class warfare" (Otty, "Structuralist's," 173). His statements, along with those of the others in the volume, demonstrate the extremes to which some Marxist readings of Tolkien can go and have been taken to task by later critics for their lack of subtlety and misunderstanding of the text (Drout and Wynne).

Other Marxist readings date from the 1980s and early 1990s and often echo the contentions in the Giddings volume. Roger Griffin examines Tolkien in relation to Italian neofascist thinkers in a 1985 study, once again suggesting that the author is an ideological brother of the radical right. For Michael Moorcock, *The Lord of the Rings* is a "pernicious confirmation of the values of a morally bankrupt middle class." Jessica Yates takes on such critics in her 1996 *Mythlore* article, which challenges naive assertions that Tolkien is a fascist. She points out the fallacies in these and earlier studies as well as the absurdities that result from equating Tolkien's universe with modern totalitarian thought.

The new millennium has ushered in some new theoretical Marxian or nontraditional Marxist readings of Tolkien. Ishay Landa uses Frederic Jameson's theory of the "political unconscious" of literary texts—how they play out and try to resolve conflicts within capitalist society—to examine the accumulation and renunciation of property in Tolkien's books. Ben Watson seeks to develop a new historical materialistic definition of fantasy, though he only makes passing reference to Tolkien's fantasy genre fiction. In the first issue of *Tolkien Studies*, Olga Markova gives a detailed account of the political and cultural reception of *The Lord of the Rings* in Russia during the Soviet era and the post-Communist period. These studies could perhaps lead to more sophisticated political and class-based explorations of the legendarium than those found in earlier Marxist analyses.

DAVID D. OBERHELMAN

Further Reading

Drout, Michael D.C., and Hilary Wynne. "Tom Shippey's *J.R.R. Tolkien: Author of the Century* and a Look Back at Tolkien Criticism since 1992." *Envoi* 9, no. 2 (Fall 2000): 101–67.

Giddings, Robert. "Introduction." In *J.R.R. Tolkien: This Far Land*, edited by Robert Giddings, 1–24. London: Vision Press, 1983.

Griffin, Roger. "Revolts against the Modern World: The Blend of Literary and Historical Fantasy in the Italian New Right." *Literature & History* 11, no. 1 (1985): 101–23.

Inglis, Fred. "Gentility and Powerlessness: In *J.R.R. Tolkien: This Far Land*, edited by Robert Giddings, 25–41. London: Vision Press, 1983.

———. *The Promise of Happiness: Value and Meaning in Children's Fiction.* Cambridge: Cambridge University Press, 1981.

Landa, Ishay. "Slaves of the Ring: Tolkien's Political Unconscious." *Historical Materialism* 10, no. 4 (2002): 113–33.

King, Roger. "Recovery, Escape, Consolation: Middle-earth and the English Fairy Tale." In *J.R.R. Tolkien: This Far Land*, edited by Robert Giddings, 42–55. London: Vision Press, 1983.

Markova, Olga. "When Philology Becomes Ideology: The Russian Perspective of J.R.R. Tolkien." *Tolkien Studies* 1, no. 1 (2004): 163–70.

Moorcock. Michael. *Wizardry and Wild Romance.* London: Victor Gollancz, 1987.

Otty, Nick. "A Structuralist's Guide to Middle-earth." In *J.R.R. Tolkien: This Far Land*, edited by Robert Giddings, 154–78. London: Vision Press, 1983.

Thompson, E.P. "America's Europe: A Hobbit among Gandalfs." *Nation*, January 24, 1981, 68–72.

Walmsley, Nigel. "Tolkien and the '60s." In *J.R.R. Tolkien: This Far Land*, edited by Robert Giddings, 73–86. London: Vision Press, 1983.

Watson, Ben. "Fantasy and Judgement: Adorno, Tolkien, Burroughs." *Historical Materialism* 10, no. 4 (2002): 213–38.

Yates, Jessica. "Tolkien the Anti-totalitarian." *Mythlore* 21; 33, no. 2 (December 1996): 233–45.

See also **Class in Tolkien's Works; Communism; Criticism of Tolkien, Twentieth Century; Hierarchy; Russia: Reception of Tolkien**

MATHEW, FR. ANTHONY GERVASE (1905–76)

Gervase Mathew lectured in history, patristics, and English at Oxford University beginning in about 1937 and was University Lecturer in Byzantine Studies from 1947–71. He took the name "Gervase" when he joined the Dominican friars in 1928. He was ordained a priest in 1934. He had a special interest in the art of Byzantium on which he gave illustrated lectures; his books on the subject are well regarded by art historians. He was noted for his work on the history of fourteenth-century England, such as *The*

Court of Richard II (1968). Among his many essays are contributions to the Festschriften for Charles Williams and for C.S. Lewis. He also published on the archaeology of Africa and the Middle East, where he took part in many surveys.

Humphrey Carpenter says that he invited himself to the Inklings meetings but was not unwelcome (*Inklings*, 186). He attended from at least 1946 on, possibly earlier. Certainly, he knew members of the group well enough that, a few days after the death of Charles Williams in 1945, he celebrated a memorial Mass for his friend, at which Tolkien served. W.H. Lewis called him "the universal Aunt" because he was a rich source of local news and especially because of his penchant for putting people in touch with others who might be of help. It was Father Mathew who introduced Tolkien to publisher Milton Waldman, to whom the author sent a sketch of his legendarium (*Letters,* 143–61).

RICHARD C. WEST

See also **Inklings; Oxford; Williams, Charles**

MCCALLUM, RONALD BUCHANAN (1898–1973)

Ronald Buchanan McCallum was an Oxford academic and member of the Inklings. Born in Scotland, he was elected a tutor in history and Fellow of Pembroke College, Oxford, in 1925. He became acquainted with Tolkien, who was attached to the same college until 1945. Humphrey Carpenter describes McCallum as one of Tolkien's few friends at the college (*Tolkien,* 119). McCallum favorably reviewed *The Hobbit* in the *Pembroke College Record* for 1937–38 and included a linguistic comment by Tolkien in his study *Public Opinion and the Last Peace* (1944). He is recorded as having attended Inklings evening meetings and pub sessions after about 1945. W.H. Lewis's diaries, in Carpenter's words, describe McCallum's "manner [as] too formally 'donnish' to make him an entirely congenial member of the group" (*Inklings,* 186). However, McCallum continued to attend until the pub meetings ceased about 1964.

McCallum was active in college and university administration. He served as master of Pembroke, head of the college, from 1955 until his retirement in 1967. Like Tolkien, McCallum wrote for the *Oxford Magazine*. He also edited the journal on several occasions.

McCallum's scholarly writings are primarily on modern British political history. He is credited with founding and naming the field of psephology, the academic study of elections. His tutorial pupils included Tolkien's son Michael as well as a number of future major political figures.

Alexander Cameron, a historian who is a minor figure in Tolkien's *The Notion Club Papers*, has been identified with McCallum by some scholars.

DAVID BRATMAN

See also **Inklings;** *Notion Club Papers*; **Oxford; Tolkien, Michael**

MELIAN

Melian is a Maia who serves and helps the Valar in their endeavors. For a time, her mission was to care for the fruiting trees in Lórien. She is defined by her beauty and her connection to the natural world. Melian is known for foresight, wisdom, compassion, and most of all for her angelic and haunting singing. With this singing, she is able to charm Elwe in much the same way that the Sirens charmed Odysseus and his men in Homer's *Odyssey:* "And it chanced on a time that he came alone to the starlit wood of Nan Elmoth, and there suddenly he heard the song of nightingales. Then an enchantment fell on him, and he stood still; and afar off beyond the voices of the lomelindi Elwë heard the voice of Melian, and it filled all his heard with wonder and desire. He forgot then utterly all his people and all the purposes of his mind" (*S*). Melian's ability to enchant proves useful for Elwë, (later called King Thingol) on several occasions, beginning with their first meeting when she keeps him away from his people for long enough—years and years—that his friends and followers eventually stop looking for him. Melion "spoke no word; but being filled with love Elwë came to her and took her hand, and straightway a spell was laid on him, so that they stood thus while long years were measured by the wheeling stars above them; and the trees of Nan Elmoth grew tall and dark before they spoke any word" (*S,* 55).

In this passage, we see that Melian did not need to convince Elwë to stay with her or even speak to him, but her enchanting powers, being "filled with love," drew him to her and fixed him with the desire to spend the rest of his years with her. "Thus Elwë's folk who sought him found him not, and Olwë took the kingship of the Teleri and departed and is told hereafter. Elwë Singollo came never again across the sea to Valinor so long as he lived, and Melian returned not thither while their realm together lasted; but of her there came among both Elves and Men a strain of the Ainur who were with Ilúvatar before Eä" (*S,* 56). Here again, we see Melian's enchantment and ability to draw others to her benefiting Elwë and his hierarchical standing. When they emerge into society, Men and Elves are drawn to Melian and then become Elwë's subjects. "In after days he became a king renowned, and his people were all the Eldar of Beleriand; the Sindar they were named, the Grey-elves, the Elves of the Twilight, and King Greymantle was he, Elu Thingol in the tongue of that land. And Melian was his Queen, wiser than any child of Middle-earth; and their hidden halls were in Menegroth, the Thousand Caves, in Doriath. Great power Melian lent to Thingol, who was himself great among the Eldar" (*S,* 56). Once Melian becomes queen, she turns her powers toward protection and education of her people, the Sindar, who she teaches to be the "fairest and the most wise and skilful of all the Elves of Middle-earth" (*S,* 91). It was Melian's instinct to protect her people, her husband, and child, Lúthien, that led to her greatest contribution in the "Silmarillion"—the Girdle of Melian. In a time of turmoil, when the Orc-host threatened the safety of Doriath, Melian created an invisible fortress to protect all of Elwë's lands and people.

> And when Thingol came again to Menegroth he learned that the Orc-host in the west was victorious, and had driven Círdan to the rim of the sea. Therefore he withdrew all his people that his summons could reach within the fastness of the Neldoreth and Region, and Melian put forth her power and fenced all that dominion round about with an unseen wall of shadow and bewilderment: the Girdle of Melian, that none thereafter could pass against her will or the will of King Thingol unless one should come with a power greater than that of Melian the Maia. (*S,* 96–97).

Through what may have appeared as a capturing, Melian sets off a series of events for Elwë that result in good fortune and security. Her singing drew him to her; her love enticed him to stay with her; her magnetism gained him a kingdom; her wisdom made them the most skilful Elves in Middle-earth, and her unique powers and will protected them. Though Melian could have sought power for herself, she devoted her life and talents to Elwë, creating for him a better life than the one for which he set out himself.

KATHERINE HESSER

MEMORY

The idea of memory is of central importance in Tolkien's invented world and functions in several ways. Memory is the connector between past and present through the recall of long-lived creatures such as Elrond, who recalls the Second Age and the Last Alliance, or Treebeard, whose eyes, as Pippin describes them, are "filled up with ages of memory"

that go back to the earliest days. Imaginary books such as Bilbo's memoirs, "The Red Book of Westmarch," or the much earlier "Golden Book of Tavrobel" are mnemonic preservations of the history and lore that is the fictive context for *The Hobbit* and *The Lord of the Rings.* Even more important are the oral traditions of the cultures of Middle-earth, the stories, poems, lists, and sayings that keep memories of the past alive in the present. Gandalf's explanation to Frodo that Gollum and Bilbo shared memories of riddles establishes the kinship of these most dissimilar hobbits (*FR,* I, ii, 63–64). The lament of Treebeard for the Entwives and his telling of "their beautiful names" bring them to life not just for the reader but for Merry and Pippin as well (*TT,* III, iv, 80).

Readers are reminded of the importance of old tales, songs, and sayings through two interdependent techniques. The first technique is negative, setting up as straw arguments the patently nearsighted statements of skeptics. The short-term memories of the men of Laketown have nearly eradicated the old songs and prophecies. A Rider of Rohan dismisses Halflings as "only a little people in old songs and children's tales." The intellectually snobbish herb master in the Houses of Healing disparages as "doggerel . . . garbled in the memory of old wives" the mnemonic folk-rhyme about *athelas* (*RK,* V, viii, 141).

The second technique is positive, as one by one these naysayers are confounded and memory of the past asserts its claim over the present—and the future. The "old wife" Ioreth's proverb about the healing hands of the king jogs Gandalf's memory to bring Aragorn to heal Faramir and Merry (*RK,* V, viii, 138–139). Aragorn's defense of the green earth as "a mighty matter of legend," his declaration that "not we but those who come after us will make the legends of our time" rebukes the Rider's cynicism (*TT,* III, ii, 37). Thorin Oakenshield's confident introduction of himself, his heritage, and his return astonishes the unprepared men of Laketown. The herb master's intellectual snobbery is laid low, and Ioreth's memory and reliance on old lore are validated by Aragorn's laying on of hands and his use of athelas in the healing of Faramir and Merry.

Tolkien's most untraditional treatment of memory, however, is also his most idiosyncratic and esoteric. This is his concept of inherited memory as a direct channel to the past, not through song or story or proverb but through the operations of the unconscious mind in dreams. Tolkien uses memory as the psychic or psychological connection between characters of the narrative present and their inherited or ancestral past. In *The Lost Road* and *The Notion Club Papers,* his two unfinished time-travel stories, modern-day Englishmen travel back to Númenor at the time of its downfall via their own ancestral pasts, experiencing or inhabiting the memories of a succession of forebears. In both stories, the memories are embedded in words from Tolkien's invented languages that are "remembered" in dreams.

It is in the matter of inherited memory particularly that Tolkien transferred two elements of personal experience into his fiction. The first element concerns his time-traveling Englishmen, who witness (in dreams) the drowning of Númenor in a great wave that overwhelms that land. This derived directly from what Tolkien called his "Atlantis haunting," his own recurrent dream of the "Great Wave" towering above him, from which he said he awoke" gasping out of deep water" (*Letters,* 213, 347). The second element, also shared by the time travelers, is inherited memory of language. This is cited in his O'Donnell lecture, "English and Welsh," delivered in 1955, where Tolkien makes a distinction between one's "native language," or inherent linguistic predilection, and one's "cradle-tongue," the first-*learned* language of custom ("Angles and Britons," 36). Both *The Lost Road*'s Alboin Errol and *The Notion Club Papers*' Arry Lowdham experience direct memory of languages they could not have known in waking life (*Lost Road,* 41; *Sauron Defeated,* 139). Indeed, in an explicitly autobiographical reference, Tolkien had Lowdham replicate his own experience by reporting knowledge of a real world language, Anglo-Saxon, before he learned it from books. This unambiguously replicates Tolkien's statement in a letter to W.H. Auden that he "took" to west midland Middle English as a "known tongue" as soon as he saw it (213). In the same letter, he made the notable suggestion that linguistic tastes might be as good a test of ancestry as blood groups (214).

A strikingly contemporary treatment of memory comes in Tolkien's use of flashback. This is not as the ordinary literary device in which the reader is switched from the narrative present to the narrative past. Rather, it is a remarkably authentic treatment of the psychological phenomenon of actual re-living of an incident, such as is frequently experienced by those who have undergone violent trauma. In the climactic scene of *The Notion Club Papers,* which takes place in Tolkien's fictively future but actually contemporary Oxford, the protagonists Lowdham and Jeremy are invaded by inherited memories from the destruction of Númenor that erupt violently into and change their present experience. For a brief space of time, in a college room in Oxford they become their Númenorean selves, address one another by their Númenorean names, and have the physical experience of being aboard a ship in a violent storm.

So powerful is this flashback that the reality of ancient Númenor temporarily possesses modern-day Oxford, and the same storm sweeps over both locations. This is memory with a vengeance and stands as Tolkien's most explicit treatment of both psychological flashback and reincarnation, for unlike modern trauma victims, the memories that repossess Lowdham and Jeremy are not their personal ones, but those of their most remote ancestors.

A less explicit, less immediately apparent, but equally parapsychological memory overtakes Merry at the barrow in *The Lord of the Rings.* Awakening to find himself crowned with gold, he undergoes a sudden, unexpected flashback into the memory of some unnamed, long-ago combatant and re-experiences that man's death as the spear goes into his heart. When the flashback passes, Merry, now returned to his own present, feels he must have been dreaming. The parallels between his experience and that of Lowdham and Jeremy are unmistakable, though the incident bears little relationship to anything else in Tolkien's depiction of Merry.

VERLYN FLIEGER

Further Reading

Dunne, J.W. *An Experiment with Time.* London: A. & C. Black, Ltd., 1927.

Flieger, Verlyn. *Interrupted Music.* Kent, OH: Kent State University Press, 2005.

———. *A Question of Time.* Kent, OH: Kent State University Press, 1997.

Rateliff, John. "The Lost Road, The Dark Tower, and The Notion Club Papers: Tolkien and Lewis's Time-Travel Triad." In *Tolkien's Legendarium: Essays on* the history of Middle-earth, ed. Verlyn Flieger and Carl Hostetter. Westport, CT: Greenwood Press, 2000.

See also **Lost Road, The**; **Notion Club Papers**; **Time**; **Time Travel**

MEN, MIDDLE-EARTH

"Men" is used throughout Tolkien's narratives to mean "human beings, male or female." This designation sounds odd and short-sighted to twenty-first-century ears but mirrors the use of "man" (as in "places where man had never set foot") common in English usage throughout Tolkien's lifetime. It is also perhaps meant to echo the conventional use of "men" in Old Icelandic saga prose ("ok that segja menn," "Men say that"), in keeping with the archaic diction of many of Tolkien's narratives.

In Middle-earth Men are said to be the "Younger Children" of Ilúvatar, or the Atani (Second People).

Like their predecessors the Elves or Eldar (the "Elder Children"), the earliest Men awoke to self-knowledge in eastern Middle-earth, but soon turned their faces and their steps in the direction of the Undying Lands to the west, specifically following, in the case of Men, the newly launched vessel of the sun.

The Eldar seem to have been to some degree baffled by these newcomers, to whom Ilúvatar had granted the Gift of Men, namely, death. This meant that unlike Elves, Men died in fact— leaving "the circles of the world" permanently, going to a place unknown even to most of the Valar—when afflicted by grievous illness, mortal wounds, or old age. Not surprisingly, many of the early names given to Men by the Eldar were pejorative: Hildor (Followers; the name echoes or anticipates the name of the place where Men began, Hildórien), Apanónar (Afterborn), Engwar (Sickly), and Fírimar (Mortals); also the Usurpers, the Strangers, the Inscrutable, and the Self-Cursed. These last few are doubtless meant to echo the obscure tragedy of Men's blighted origin— presumably the fall of Adam in our primary world as constructed in Tolkien's own Christian worldview. As the patriarch Bëor is said in the *Silmarillion* to have told Finrod Felagund, the Noldo Elf who had taught his people speech and music, "A darkness lies behind us . . . and we have turned our backs upon it, and we do not desire to return thither even in thought. Westwards our hearts have been turned, and we believe that there shall we find Light." Men's flawed nature is similarly suggested in the following passage from the *Silmarillion*: "To Hildórien came no Vala to guide Men, or to summon them to dwell in Valinor; and men have feared the Valar, rather than loved them, and have not understood the purposes of the Powers, being at variance with them, and at strife with the world" (*S*, 103).

Thinking to take advantage of this fear, the fallen Ainu Melkor (Morgoth) attempted from early in the First Age to make Men the foes of the Eldar. This ploy failed in general (although sometimes succeeding in specific), particularly with the Three Houses of the Edain. "Edain" is simply the Sindarin version of the Quenya name "Atani," meaning "Second People" and therefore "Men" in general; but both of these terms were later narrowed to refer specifically to the Three Houses of the Edain—the Houses of Bëor, Hador and Haleth—who formed many close alliances and ties with the Eldar against Morgoth, up to and including marriage in two early cases (Beren of the house of Bëor with Lúthien, and Tuor of the house of Hador with Idril).

Early in the Second Age, the Valar gave to the families of these faithful Edain, as a reward for their part in the defeat of Morgoth, the newly raised island kingdom of Númenor in the western ocean. Thereafter their descendants were called Dúnedain (Men of the West). Númenor's first king was Elros Half-elven, a descendant of both Beren and Tuor, who chose to accept the Gift of Men; his brother Elrond, who chose to remain with the Elves, remained in Middle-earth until the end of the Third Age.

Númenor remained a mighty seafaring kingdom for over three thousand years, under twenty-two kings and three ruling queens. These rulers sent ships back to Middle-earth to visit and aid their Eldar allies in their campaigns against Sauron, Morgoth's former servant, to build cities and harbors, and to colonize human populations not of the Three Houses. Some few stayed behind in Middle-earth and joined the cause of Sauron; they became called the Black Númenóreans, settling the Havens of Umbar in the south. Sailing westward to the Undying Lands was forbidden to Númenóreans, which became a sore point for many as time wore on. Although the Númenórean lifespan was longer than that generally allotted to Men later, for many it became not long enough; estrangement from, and resentment of, the Eldar became commonplace. Finally, seduced by Sauron, Númenor's last king, Ar-Pharazôn the Golden (whose lack of piety can be seen by his use of an Adûnaic or Mannish name; his Quenya coronation name would have been Tar-Calion), sailed west to Valinor to wrest the power of immortal life from its keepers. As punishment for this king's hubris, the island of Númenor sank beneath the ocean under the onslaught of a great wave. Those few Númenóreans who had remained faithful to the Valar, led by Elendil the Tall and his two sons Isildur and Anárion, were able to flee by ship to Middle-earth, where they founded the Dúnedain kingdoms in exile, Gondor and Arnor.

Elendil reigned as king in Gondor and Arnor, jointly with his two sons, for 121 years, until his death at the siege of Sauron's fortress of Barad-dûr in the War of the Last Alliance of Elves and Men that marked the end of the Second Age. Anárion also died there, leaving the kingship of Gondor to his son Meneldil.

Isildur and his three eldest sons were slain by Orcs two years later at the Battle of the Gladden Fields. Isildur's youngest son, Valandil—left behind in Imladris in the care of Elrond Half-elven—inherited the North-kingdom of Arnor. Valandil's descendants established a line of kings (and later clan chieftains) that continued unbroken for some three thousand years, although the kingdom itself did not; it fragmented into bits rather in the manner of the early Frankish kingdoms in our primary world. Isildur's and Valandil's most famous descendant, of course, was Aragorn son of Arathorn, titled chieftain of the Dúnedain of Arnor like all of his recent ancestors; he came to Minas Tirith at long last to claim the kingship of both Númenórean exile kingdoms under the name of Elessar Telcontar (Elfstone of the house of Strider).

Anárion's dynasty continued uninterrupted in Gondor for two thousand years until the War of the Kin-strife, precipitated by King Valacar's marrying of a northern barbarian (Vidumavi), with the result that the heir to the throne (Eldacar, also called by the northern name of Vinitharya, was not a pure-blooded Númenórean. (It can be argued that Gondor's intrinsic racial elitism and xenophobia, as evidenced by this episode, are meant to be seen as major factors in its subsequent decline.) This half-blood king, Eldacar, was dethroned by his cousin Castamir, spending afterward ten years in exile in the north gathering followers, and eventually returning to the throne. Castamir's followers fled south to the Havens of Umbar, there joining the Black Númenóreans; their descendants were those Corsair pirates who continually harried Gondor in the centuries to come. After Eldacar's restoration, his direct line ruled uninterrupted for two hundred years, at which point the Great Plague wiped out the ruling king, Telemnar, and most of his house; the succession then went to a nephew. Another interruption in the line of kings occurred three hundred years after the Plague, when King Ondoher and his three sons were slain by invading Wain-riders from the East. Ondoher was succeeded by only two more kings: Eärnil, a cousin; and Eärnil's son Eärnur, who foolishly rode to Minas Morgul (recently taken and renamed by the Enemy) to answer a challenge to single combat with the Witch-king.

Gondor was from Eärnur's day ruled by the Stewards, holders of an office that had been established early in Gondor's history by King Rómendacil I and had been made hereditary (in the House of Húrin, whose founder may have been named after, but is not to be confused with the First Age hero of the Edain) by King Minardil (the grandson of Eldacar, mentioned above). The descendants of Húrin after Eärnur's departure then became Ruling Stewards, holding Gondor "against the king's return," which they continued to do for almost a thousand years. When Aragorn Elessar became king, he did not dissolve the Steward's office, but confirmed Faramir son of Denethor, Húrin's latest descendant, as Steward—although no longer a ruling steward.

It is in fact a speech of that same Faramir, prior to his succession as Steward, that gives us the clearest picture of the attitudes of Third Age Númenórean—descended Men with regard to the taxonomy of Men in general. It is an arrogant picture, and one that Faramir was to have cause to repent within a year of articulating it. Men, said Faramir to Frodo at Henneth Annûn, came in three types: High (Men of the West, Númenóreans), Middle (Men of the Twilight), and Wild (Men of the Darkness, generally in service to Sauron) (*TT*, IV, v, 287). High Men, then, would be the Three Houses of the Edain who went to Númenor and their descendants. Middle Men would be those of the Edain (but not the Three Houses) who remained in Middle-earth, forming such barbarian nations as the chieftains of Rhovanion, the people of Dale (and perhaps of Bree?), the Beornings, and the Rohirrim. (Faramir admitted a begrudging, if patronizing, admiration for these Middle Men; and a good thing too, since he was destined to marry one.) Wild Men would presumably include all other tribes and nations, those whose ancestors never allied with the Eldar. (The origins of these Wild Men are problematic; are we meant to conclude that they descended from some branch of the original Edain, or that they had an independent creation?)

The first Wild Men that had dealings with the Edain in the First Age were the Easterlings, whose very name hints that unlike the Three Houses of the Edain, they did not feel a yearning towards the Sun or the West. In contrast to the "Free Peoples," then, the Easterlings were infidels. In fact, the most prominent Easterlings of the First Age, Ulfang and Bór, and later Brodda, allied themselves with Morgoth or with various sons of Fëanor—or both, in turns. Morgoth made Brodda lord of Hithlum after its capture, after which Brodda took Aerin of the house of Hador by force to wife. Whether these First Age enemy Easterlings are related to those equestrian (and sometimes wain-riding) "Easterling" invaders (including Sauron's sometime liege people the Balchoth) who harried Gondor in the Third Age is unknown, but likely.

Not all foreign tribespeople encountered by the Edain were hostile, however. The Lossoth, the Snow-Men of the Ice Bay of Forochel, befriended the last king of the North-kingdom, Arvedui, in his flight from the forces of Angmar. The Drúedain, the "Woses" or wild men of the forest, aided the Edain against Morgoth in the First Age and were granted passage to Númenor in the Second Age; their chieftain, Ghân-buri-Ghân, helped the Rohirrim in the War of the Ring in the Third Age. Perhaps these two groups, by virtue of their not serving Darkness, fall outside Faramir's taxonomy and are therefore not classifiable as Wild Men.

It is unclear whether the Haradrim, Gondor's ancient enemies to the south and allies with Sauron in the War of the Ring, are intended to be construed as Wild Men or not. They seem to have a culture at least the equal of that of the Rohirrim; their ornaments are finely made, and their fearsome war elephants, the *mûmakil*, are well trained. They are pictured as ethnic others but not as ugly, except perhaps those of "Far Harad," who are said to have seemed (to the eyes of Gondorians) "black men like half-trolls with white eyes and red tongues." If the Haradrim have a didactic purpose in the narrative, it is to awaken empathy; Samwise Gamgee's thoughts upon having a close encounter with a newly dead warrior of Harad are largely of charity and regret.

In contrast to the Haradrim, the lesser-known Variags of Khand, who are seen as vassals of Mordor at the Battle of the Pelennor Fields, can perhaps be construed as Wild Men. "Variag" is a word from our primary world—it is simply the Russian word for "Varangian," designating those Nordic and Germanic warriors who took service with the Byzantine emperors. Tolkien may have chosen the term because of common (southeastern) geography, or perhaps to suggest foreign mercenaries in the service of a lord more culturally advanced than they. If "Variag" is meant to suggest "Nordic," though, it is possible that we are meant to see them as fallen Men of "Middle" or "Twilight" descent, akin to the northern chieftains or the folk of Dale—if in fact Faramir's taxonomy is meant to be taken at face value, which it most likely is not.

At the end of the War of the Ring, Gandalf tells the new king Aragorn Elessar that "the time comes of the Dominion of Men, and the Elder Kindred shall fade or depart. . . . The burden must lie now upon you and your kindred" (*RK*, VI, v, 249) The Elder Children of Ilúvatar must then give way to the Younger; but the Eldar are not entirely lost, for their blood runs in Men, and will continue to, through Aragorn's alliance in marriage with Arwen daughter of Elrond. Significantly, Aragorn is one of the few Men who is specifically said to have gracefully accepted the Gift of Men when the time came, to have gone into death on his own initiative; another was his distant ancestor Bëor, who "relinquished his life willingly and passed into peace."

Tolkien explored many philosophical, sociological, and religious issues through his multifaceted portraits of the family of Men. Men are flawed from the beginning, but redeemable. Ilúvatar loves them— maybe even above his other children, for he has given them the Gift; they *may* even rest in his presence after their death, since none (except perhaps Manwë and Mandos) know where that unknown place is whither they go. Like Túrin son of Húrin in the First Age, Men can be proud, arrogant, willful, and wrong and paradoxically not cease to be heroic. As happened with the Nazgûl, the Nine Ringwraiths, who began life as mortal Men, Men's desire for power and riches can

ruin them; so can the desire for immortality, which similarly ruined Ar-Pharazôn, the last king of Númenor. Like many of the Dúnedain in the Second and Third Ages, Tolkien's Men can display racial elitism and xenophobia; but this does not remotely mean that Tolkien promoted such attitudes or excused them in our primary world. Men, as Tolkien depicted them, are created beings endowed with free will, carrying a near-unlimited potential for good or evil. Men can descend into Orc-like disregard for one another and the natural world or rise to unselfish kingship, incorporating empathy for ethnic and cultural Others and defense of the weak. The applications to humankind's estate as we know it in our primary world are both inspiring and sobering.

SANDRA BALLIF STRAUBHAAR

Further Reading

Hoiem, Elizabeth Massa. "World Creation as Colonization: British Imperialism in 'Aldarion and Erendis.'" *Tolkien Studies* 2 (2005): 75–92.
Rearick, Anderson. "Why Is the Only Good Orc a Dead Orc? The Dark Face of Racism Examined in Tolkien's World." *Modern Fiction Studies* 50, no. 4 (2004): 861–74.
Straubhaar, Sandra Ballif. "Myth, Late Roman History and Multiculturalism in Tolkien's Middle-earth." In *Tolkien and the Invention of Myth: A Reader*, edited by Jane Chance, 101–18. Lexington, KY: University Press of Kentucky, 2004.
Tolkien, J.R.R. "Tal-Elmar." In *Peoples*, 422–38.

MERCHANDISING

The rights to the works of J.R.R. Tolkien have since 1969 been divided in two groups: his literary estate, represented by the Tolkien Estate, headed by Christopher Tolkien, and the publishing house of HarperCollins, based in London; and certain exclusive film, stage, and merchandising rights of *The Hobbit* and *The Lord of the Rings*, first acquired by United Artists and now in the hands of Tolkien Enterprises, headed by Saul Zaentz.

According to the *Guardian*, only in December 2001 was it made public that J.R.R. Tolkien had sold these rights at the cost of $250,000 (approximately £1.7m in 2001). It was made clear that Tolkien's heirs had no claim in the film rights licensed to New Line Cinema. These were directly related to Tolkien Enterprises. The company had acquired the rights in 1976 to produce the first *The Lord of the Rings* film directed by Ralph Bakshi. Tolkien Enterprises states on its Web site that it owns the rights to "titles, names of characters, places, scenes things and events appearing in the works as well as short phrases and sayings from these two books" (tolkien-ent.com).

Tolkien himself had made his position quite clear already in 1957 when the first attempt at bringing *The Lord of the Rings* to the movie screen was brought to his attention. "Stanley U[nwin]. & I have agreed on our policy: *Art or Cash*. Either very profitable terms indeed; or absolute author's veto on objectionable features or alterations" (*Letters*, 261) After a first script was sent to him, he tore it apart in a lengthy and detailed criticism in 1958 with the finishing words: "*The Lord of the Rings* cannot be garbled like that" (*Letters*, 277).

Why Tolkien eventually decided to sell the rights seemingly without any further restrictions is not quite clear. However, the move of J.R.R. and Edith Tolkien to Bournemouth in 1969 and their consequent need for funds may be directly related to this. Humphrey Carpenter argues in his biography that Tolkien made the move to please Edith, who in old age felt much more comfortable with the seaside resort than with Oxford (*Tolkien*, 247–52). Tolkien also may have sold the film and merchandise rights in order to avoid (or to have funds to pay for) inheritance taxes. He did not at the time link the move with the sale of the film rights, but Carpenter makes abundantly clear that the financial demands on the Tolkiens were sizable, and, although the royalties for his publications were quickly accumulating, the costs for a house in Bournemouth and their prolonged stays at the Miramar Hotel had to be taken care of. Presumably, this need for money made Tolkien decide to sell the rights mentioned above.

Tolkien-related merchandise has been extremely visible in the wake of the Peter Jackson *Lord of the Rings* films, with everything from action figures to clothing to replica artifacts being made for sale. Even those enthusiasts who have not been completely happy with the Jackson films have often been attracted to the high quality of some of the merchandise.

MARCEL R. BÜLLES

Further Reading

Carpenter, Humphrey. *J.R.R. Tolkien: A Biography*. Boston, MA: Houghton Mifflin, 1977.
http://books.guardian.co.uk/tolkien/story/0,11168,618713,00.html. Accessed February 20 2006.
http://www.tolkien-ent.com Accessed February 20, 2006.

See also **Fan art; Film Scripts—Unused**

MERCY

Mercy, and the related concept of Pity, are key virtues in Tolkien's theology. In a letter, Tolkien defines Mercy as "the supreme value and efficacy of Pity and forgiveness of injury" (*Letters*, 252). Mercy operates throughout Tolkien's fiction as a form of divine grace. He writes that "in its highest exercise it belongs to God" (*Letters*, 326). Here, he is using OED sense 1, "Forbearance and compassion shown by one person to another who is in his power and who has no claim to receive kindness," and specifically sense 1b, "God's pitiful forbearance towards His creatures and forgiveness of their offenses." Pity to Tolkien is the human expression of the same forgiveness and is to Tolkien a word "of moral and imaginative worth" (*Letters*, 191).

The key example of this virtue in Tolkien's work is the divine mercy shown to Frodo at Mount Doom, as a result of the pity he and Bilbo showed to Gollum. The "sudden understanding, a pity mixed with horror," that "welled up in Bilbo's heart" on realizing Gollum's wretchedness first appears in the 1951 second edition of *The Hobbit* (*H*, V, 133), but Gandalf and Frodo's conversation about it is present in its essentials from the earliest drafts of *The Lord of the Rings*. In the final text, Frodo says, "What a pity that Bilbo did not stab that vile creature, when he had a chance!" Gandalf replies, "Pity? It was Pity that stayed his hand. Pity, and Mercy: not to strike without need." Gandalf adds that Bilbo's moral state on taking possession of the Ring has caused his taking so little hurt from its possession, and he concludes, "My heart tells me that [Gollum] has some part to play yet, for good or ill, before the end; and when that comes, the pity of Bilbo may rule the fate of many – yours not least" (*FR*, I, ii, 68–69). Frodo remembers this conversation when he meets Gollum and spares him through the pity that he now feels. The text never makes this explicit, but Tolkien repeatedly emphasizes in letters that the pity shown by Frodo on this occasion leads to the success of his mission after he is unable to surrender the Ring: "his exercise of patience and mercy towards Gollum granted him Mercy: his failure was redressed" (*Letters*, 326; see also 191, 234, 252, 253).

Another prominent example of mercy in Tolkien's fiction is "the mercy of Eru to Aulë in the matter of the Dwarves," as he puts it in a letter (335). In *The Silmarillion*, Eru Ilúvatar refrains from destroying the Dwarves or punishing Aulë for his presumption in making them. The only use of the word in this story, however, occurs where the Dwarves themselves "begged for mercy" from Aulë (*S*, 44). Here, as frequently in his work, Tolkien uses the word "mercy" in the nontheological meaning, to refer to legal authority refraining from just punishment, OED senses 5a and 5b. In this sense, for example, Aragorn shows mercy to Beregond in *The Lord of the Rings*; and in his late work on Orcs, Tolkien states that mercy must be shown even to Orcs who ask for it (*Morgoth,* 419). The importance of mercy and pity are shown by their appearance at other critical points elsewhere in *The Silmarillion*: Lúthien pleading before Mandos for Beren, and Eärendil pleading before the Valar for the Noldor, are both asking for mercy by those authorized to grant it to those not owed it. Refusal to show mercy is stigmatized: Morgoth feigns mercy as a form of additional cruelty, and Finrod fears that the sons of Fëanor will show to Beren "neither love nor mercy" (*S*, 169).

Tolkien strictly distinguishes mercy and pity from prudence and simple lack of wanton cruelty: "Pity must restrain one from doing something immediately desirable and seemingly advantageous" (*Letters,* 191).

Tolkien also uses the word "ruth" to mean pity or compassion (*Lays,* 371).

DAVID BRATMAN

MERRY

Meriadoc Brandybuck, hobbit, one of Frodo's companions in *The Lord of the Rings*, is the only recorded child of Saradoc "Scattergold" Brandybuck and Esmeralda Took. Born in 1382 SR, he was thirty-six years old—in hobbit years, a young adult just recently come of age—when he joined Frodo on the journey from the Shire to Rivendell. There, Elrond formally appointed him a member of the Company. At Parth Galen, Merry and his friend Pippin were captured by Orcs from Isengard, but escaped into Fangorn Forest and met Treebeard, the Ent. The hobbits accompanied the Ents to the siege of Isengard, where they rejoined several other members of the Company. After Gandalf took Pippin to Gondor, Merry swore allegiance to Théoden, king of Rohan. Against Théoden's orders, Merry secretly joined the Rohirrim riding to the relief of Gondor. Merry was at the king's side when Théoden was slain at the Battle of the Pelennor Fields, and the hobbit wounded the Witch-king, enabling Éowyn to kill him. When the hobbits returned to the occupied Shire, Merry organized the rebellion that evicted Sharkey's ruffians from the land.

Merry, nicknamed "the Magnificent," succeeded his father as master of Buckland in 1432. He married Estella Bolger and left a son when he and Pippin rode off to spend their last years in Gondor and Rohan. He died sometime after 1484, and his body lies next to that of King Elessar in Minas Tirith.

It took Tolkien a long time to settle on the names, personalities, and ancestry of the hobbits in *The Lord of the Rings*. Merry, surprisingly, is the first to acquire his final name, even before Frodo, in the first draft of the Tom Bombadil chapter in the earliest phase of the writing. Before this, he was called Marmaduke, but he is from the start a Brandybuck with a Took mother ("a lively blend") and exhibits many of the same personality traits seen in the completed work.

The casual reader may think of Merry and Pippin as one indistinguishable unit because of their shared adventures and deep friendship, and the early drafts even attribute some of Pippin's later actions and speeches to Merry. But by the time the book was finished, Tolkien actually portrayed two quite distinct individuals, as he often did with paired characters. Merry and Pippin are together almost constantly from the time the "conspirators" assemble at Crickhollow until Gandalf takes Pippin to Minas Tirith, and during this time Pippin's effervescence tends to overshadow the more retiring Merry. While they are separated and pursue their independent but parallel adventures, it is easier to get a sense of their differing personalities.

At the start of the story, Merry is already an adult hobbit with a place in society as the master of Buckland's heir. While Pippin may seem the quicker thinker, Merry is by no means slow and promptly picks up his cues in their attempt to escape the Orcs. Merry is sometimes solitary and thoughtful, for example, preferring a walk in the night air of Bree to the smoky, noisy common room of the Prancing Pony. He is also emotionally sensitive; witness the poignant moment where he turns away in sympathetic shame while Pippin is questioned about the *palantír* (though this ambiguous moment can be read differently [Bradley]), the pity and wonder at Éowyn's courage that turn his paralyzing fear into determined action, and his grief over Théoden's death in the Houses of Healing.

As Gandalf implies, part of the reason Merry and Pippin were chosen by fate as members of the Fellowship was to make them fit leaders of their people—settling the affairs of their homeland and putting things right is "what you have been trained for," as he tells them on their return to the Shire (*RK*, VI, vii, 175). If Merry has any faults that must be corrected during this 'course of honor,' they are subtle and perhaps the opposite of Pippin's—a lack of assertiveness, a repression of impulsive instincts, and a tendency to feel his losses so keenly that action is inhibited. Merry must learn to trust his strengths, step forward, and take his place in society.

The parallel motifs of first swearing fealty to a king figure, then witnessing his death, bring two major pairs of contrasting characters together: Merry and Pippin, and Théoden and Denethor. Merry, overcome by Théoden's courtesy and kindness after he is separated from Pippin, impulsively offers his service to the king out of love and respect. He looks on Théoden as a father figure and yearns to serve him in battle for his own sake. The hobbits are more than simply witnesses to the differing deaths of one ruler restored to his right mind and one fast retreating from sanity; by disobeying direct orders, they offer a commentary on the value of independent thought even in wartime.

Merry, like many only children, is steadfast, independent, pragmatic, and capable, as well as self-contained, an organizer, and a secret-keeper. It was Merry who first observed Bilbo using the Ring and teased out its secrets from Sam. Merry organized the conspiracy of friends that helped with Frodo's counterfeit move to Crickhollow, down to the detail of sufficient bathtubs in Frodo's new house. Merry had a scholarly turn of mind as well and can be characterized as a "knowledgeable hero" (Porter)—he read Bilbo's book, studied the maps in Rivendell during the Company's stay (and later visited to consult other works), maintained a large library at Brandy Hall, and wrote *Herblore of the Shire*, *Reckoning of Years*, and *Old Words and Names in the Shire*, among other books. His accumulated knowledge proves useful many times during his adventures.

The leadership ability Merry has been steadily but quietly developing during the story comes to the fore during the Scouring of the Shire. Merry steps forward as spokesman during the first encounter with gate wardens, takes charge of escorting the sheriffs to Bywater, and parleys with the men at the Green Dragon. It is Merry who tells Frodo that he cannot save the Shire by being shocked and sad, and he determines the rebellion's strategy, blowing the Horn of Rohan and ordering barriers put up. He defers to Frodo's moral authority but takes over all the practical planning and leadership. Merry leads both the confrontations at Bywater and kills the leader of the ruffians himself.

The personality of Meriadoc Brandybuck is one of the subtle delights that repay a close and attentive reading of *The Lord of the Rings*. Tolkien's skill in developing character is evident in the portrait of this quiet, level-headed, dependable hobbit, often overshadowed by his brash cousin, who matures into assertiveness and leadership ability.

JANET BRENNAN CROFT

Further Reading

Bradley, Marion Zimmer. "Men, Halflings, and Hero Worship." In *Tolkien and the Critics: Essays on J.R.R. Tolkien's the Lord of the Rings*, edited by Neil D. Isaacs and Rose A. Zimbardo, 109–27. Notre Dame, IN: University of Notre Dame Press, 1968.

Croft, Janet Brennan. *War and the Works of J.R.R. Tolkien*. Contributions to the Study of Science Fiction and Fantasy. Westport, CT: Praeger, 2004.

Fader, Shanti. "A Fool's Hope." *Parabola* (Fall 2001): 48–52.

Longstaff, Hilary. "Merry in Focus: On Ring Fever . . . and Being Overlooked." *Mallorn* 43 (July 2005): 43–48.

Porter, Lynnette R. *Unsung Heroes of the Lord of the Rings: From the Page to the Screen*. Westport, CT: Praeger, 2005.

Rutledge, Fleming. *The Battle for Middle-earth: Tolkien's Divine Design in the Lord of the Rings*. Grand Rapids, MI: Eerdmans, 2004.

See also **Doubles; Frodo; Pippin; Shire; Théoden; Treebeard**

"MIDDLE ENGLISH 'LOSENGER:' A SKETCH OF AN ETYMOLOGICAL AND SEMANTIC INQUIRY"

The academic year 1950–51 marked the fiftieth anniversary of Germanic philology and Romance philology as subject disciplines in the Faculté de Philosophie et Lettres de l'Université de Liège. To celebrate the occasion, a committee of scholars put together two conferences of papers celebrating aspects of these areas of study. Tolkien participated in the second of these conferences in 1951, and the proceedings were finally published in 1953.

Tolkien felt uncomfortable in French apparently, as his is the only English paper in the volume. His contribution was titled "Middle English 'Losenger': Sketch of an Etymological and Semantic Enquiry." Tolkien's article claims to be no more than "a footnote" but if correct is the call to additional areas of study in philology and the linguistic interplay of the early middle ages.

Losenger is a Middle English word of French origin that appears in Chaucer among other authors. Interestingly enough to students of Tolkien, Tolkien reports that he first encountered the word when at King Edward's School. He came across the word when reading Chaucer with the same teacher who introduced him to Germanic philology. The word is usually defined as "flatterer," and Tolkien suggests rather stronger language in saying that the contexts suggest "slanderer, backbiter, liar."

Other than these comments, Tolkien leaves Middle English and delves into Old French, Latin, and Germanic languages. In Old French is found *losengar*, the related verb *losengier*, and *lozenge*, the product of one who *losengier*. He notes that the Old French semantic range leans more toward the side of "lying" rather than "flattery" although the range extends from "praise" in the sense of exaggerated or inappropriate praise to flattery with an evil intent to simply lying.

Tolkien next discusses the roots of this word, suggesting that it is the product of some semantic and orthographic/phonological conflation. On the one hand are the Latin roots *laudare, laudes,* and so on, meaning praise. These come into northern Old French as *laudemia,* which would produce *loenge* (compare Provençal *lauzemia*), *laudenja.* On the other hand is the Germanic root *lausing-,* which entered the dialects of Northern Gaul as *lauzenga* f. "lying." The phonetic similarity added to the fact that both words dealt with some form of speech about another being and so often appeared in the same context aided a conflation of the words. Thus, the Germanic word, the foreign one, developed a semantic range from "lying" in origin to "false adulation" or "false praise." To this point Tolkien is reiterating and affirming previous work on the question by previous scholars.

Not satisfied merely to affirm this work, however, Tolkien presses onward. The Germanic root is not only Germanic but specifically a borrowing into early Old French from Old English. Tolkien remarks that this may have been the first *perfidia anglosaxonica* exported to Gaul, with the caveat that he is neither specifying that the word may not have been borrowed from England per se, but rather *Anglo-Saxon* (Tolkien's preferred term for Old English) stands in for a range of Germanic dialects and that this linguistic event occurred far enough back in history to effect the whole subsequent history of the *laus* word family.

Tolkien's argument regarding the Old English source of the French word rests first on the form. Only Old English uses *–ung* or *–ing* as a feminine ending forming verbal abstract nouns, such as Old English *leasung,* "lying." Not only is word formation indicative but so is the semantic range of the French and borrowed Germanic words. Similar words in other Germanic languages do not have the sense required to account for the Old French term, and Tolkien is careful to examine words in Gothic, Old Saxon, and Old Norse, excluding them from possible consideration as the source of the borrowing. Thus, the Old English development of the word is unique and different than the other Germanic languages' use of the same proto-Germanic root.

One further consideration is that it is also only Old English that possesses the verb *leasian<lauson, lausingo,* "to tell lies," and so develops the noun *leasung/ing<lausungo,* "lying." Thus, Old English is the only possible source for the Old French speakers to borrow *lausing-* in the sense of "lie" to conflate with the Romance word to produce *losenger.* Tolkien makes the added comment that Old and early Middle English speakers recognized the word as a "relation" when encountered in French, for they translated it

with the native equivalent. When Middle English borrowed the word from French, it was only the verb form *losengier* and the courtly term *losengeour,* the flatterer. The terms, however, are not recorded beyond the early sixteenth century.

Tolkien's study of this word seems to have made little impact. In part, this is because of the article's place of publication. *Essais de Philologie Moderne* is a respected publication but not a widely available one. In discussions of Tolkien's work, this essay is seldom mentioned. In fact, in Bramlett's overview of Tolkien's work (see the bibliography to the *Old English Exodus*), the essay is not mentioned or included in the bibliography of Tolkien's works. Nor did Humphrey Carpenter include it in his bibliography of Tolkien's works (see Carpenter). Beyond the world of Tolkien studies, the essay again seems to have made little impact. The *Middle English Dictionary* reports the word family's etymology as simply from Old French, as does the second edition of the *Oxford English Dictionary.* Wider publicity for this article might encourage reconsideration of the history of *losenger.*

L.J. SWAIN

Further Reading

Bramlett, Perry C. *I Am In Fact a Hobbit: An Introduction to the Life and Work of J.R.R. Tolkien.* Macon, GA: Mercer University Press, 2002.
Carpenter, Humphery. *J.R.R. Tolkien: A Biography.* Boston, MA: Houghton Mifflin, 1977.
Tolkien, J.R.R. "The Middle English *Losenger.*" *Essais De Philologie Modern* (1951). Paris: Société d'édition "Les Belles Lettres," 1953.

See also **Chaucer; Middle English; Philology**

MIDDLE ENGLISH VOCABULARY, A (1922)

Tolkien's first published book comprises a concise etymological glossary of the Middle English (q.v.) texts included in its companion work, Kenneth Sisam's (q.v.) *Fourteenth Century Verse and Prose* (1921). As Tolkien states in his introductory "Note" to the work, it is neither a complete glossary of those texts nor is its concern only or primarily with difficult or obscure forms; instead, its focus is on those forms and idioms that Tolkien called "the backbone of the language," by which he meant a vocabulary that would provide the student with a "familiarity with the ordinary machinery of expression" in Middle English (considered broadly) of the fourteenth century. As such, the selection of forms in this glossary, and the fullness with which those forms are treated, while naturally owing much to the selection of texts by Sisam for his reader, also is due to and exhibits Tolkien's own views of the essential character of the language of those texts.

The "Glossary" proper comprises some 4,700 entries, providing for each word its part of speech, an English gloss, a list of the principle occurrences of the word in Sisam's reader (by text and line number), and a concise etymological note, (naturally) most frequently a reference to an Old English, Old Norse, Old French, or Medieval Latin cognate form, where one is clear or can be reasonably surmised, that illustrates its phonological development. Where an idiomatic phrase in the text hinges on the word, the phrase is given together with an English paraphrase rendering the idiom's (nonliteral) meaning. To aid the student, chief variant forms and spellings of words (with which Middle English texts are notoriously replete) are called out in separate entries, but cross-referenced to the main entry where the principal form is treated in full. A list of "Principal Variations of Form or Spelling" preceding the "Glossary" also aids in this regard. Per the usual practice, proper names are not treated in the "Glossary," but their occurrences in the texts are listed in the "Index of Names" that ends the work. (The first printings of the work also appended a brief list of "Corrigenda to Sisam's *Fourteenth Century Verse and Prose*," most likely discovered by Tolkien in the course of finishing his work for publication. All of these were soon incorporated into a revision of the reader, after which the "Corrigenda" was naturally dropped from the glossary.)

The history of the publication of Tolkien's first book would also establish *ab initio* a clear trend in Tolkien's publishing habits, that of long delay. The glossary and Sisam's reader were intended to be published together, and indeed Tolkien's protracted completion of the glossary also long delayed the reader's publication (see *Letters*, 11); so much so that in the event Sisam's reader was finally published, in October 1921, as a separate work from the glossary, with only a brief note indicating that Tolkien's glossary was in preparation. The *Middle English Glossary* was then itself published, in May 1922, as a separate volume (Hammond A1), and both works continued to be published separately for some time, even after the two works were finally joined together in a single volume (Hammond B3) in June 1922.

Although no revisions to the text of the glossary are noted in its publication indicia, at least one small set of changes was made in a few entries after its first publication, probably in 1945 and certainly by the 1946 impression, presumably by Tolkien himself,

and apparently arising from his work on a Middle English version of *Sir Orfeo* (q.v.).

CARL F. HOSTETTER

Further Reading

Carpenter, Humphrey, ed., with the assistance of Christopher Tolkien. *The Letters of J.R.R. Tolkien*. Boston, MA: Houghton Mifflin, 1981.

Hammond, Wayne G., with the assistance of Douglas A. Anderson. *J.R.R. Tolkien: A Descriptive Bibliography*. New Castle, DE: Oak Knoll Books, 1993.

Hostetter, Carl F., ed. "*Sir Orfeo*: A Middle English Version by J.R.R. Tolkien." In *Tolkien Studies: An Annual Scholarly Review*, 1:85–123. Morgantown, WV: West Virginia University Press, 2004.

Sisam, Kenneth. *Fourteenth Century Verse and Prose*. Oxford: Clarendon Press, 1921.

Tolkien, J.R.R. *A Middle English Vocabulary*. Oxford: Clarendon Press, 1922. Reference is also made to the slightly revised imprint of 1945.

See also **Oxford; Philology**

MIDDLE-EARTH

Middle-earth exists on two interrelated planes. One, more general, refers to the entire imaginary world in which Tolkien's best-known fiction is set: *The Lord of the Rings*, *The Hobbit*, and *The Silmarillion*. The other refers to the specific meaning it carries within that world. The earliest published reference to Middle-earth comes from *Lord of the Rings*. It is in response to a letter regarding the novel that Tolkien explains his conceit that "*Middle-earth* is not an imaginary world. The name is the modern form . . . of *midde-erd > middle-erd*, an ancient name for *oikoumenë*, the abiding place of *Men*" (*Letters*, 239). He provides further explanation in another letter: "I have, I suppose, constructed an imaginary *time*, but kept my feet on mother-earth for *place*. I prefer that to the contemporary mode of seeking remote globes in 'space'" (*Letters*, 283). Essentially, in constructing his world, Tolkien is distancing himself both from science fiction and pure fantasy worlds, or "Neverlands." Elves, Dwarves, hobbits, and so on, may be imaginary; however, in Middle-earth they are to have an abode as closely related to our own and as credible as Tolkien can construct it. For this purpose, Middle-earth requires both depth and presence. That he was fairly successful in achieving both goes some way toward explaining the critical opinion that "the imaginary world and its contents are highly affectively charged. The point may be expressed aphoristically by saying that Middle-earth, rather than any of its characters, is the hero of *The Lord of the Rings*" (Rosebury, 34).

Depth is conveyed, among other methods, through the layers of history that Middle-earth accrues in Tolkien's mythopoeic writings. Any geography of the author's world is essentially a historical geography, or, rather, a socio-historical geography. The Elves of *The Lord of the Rings*, for instance, have their own history, of which Tolkien's major opus only gives the vaguest idea, and Middle-earth is quite a different place when it ensues. Obviously, the concreteness of Middle-earth and the concreteness of its "peoples" are interrelated, the Elves merely being among the most prominent of the world's "humane" beings.

Tolkien essentially presents Middle-earth as a kind of dynamic proscenium for his legendarium. As such, to some extent its properties alter according to narrative need. It is "middle," he insists, "because thought of as vaguely set amidst the encircling Seas and (in the Northern-imagination) between ice of the North and fire of the South" (*Letters*, 283). Herein he discloses the closest sources of his created world. In the Norse *Poetic Edda*, there are several mentions of *Miðgarð*, which fit this description. Tolkien readily admits to this source of influence, adding the above-mentioned Anglo-Saxon term. These sources, among others, likewise influence the narratives that take place in the world (Chance).

Another source that cannot be omitted is the Bible, especially the *Book of Genesis*. Middle-earth is created by Eru Ilúvatar, the monotheistic godhead of Tolkien's mythology, but, somewhat confusing in this regard, with the assistance of angelic beings, the Valar and Maiar. These beings metaphorically roll up their sleeves and enter Middle-earth to prepare it for the habitation of the "Children of Ilúvatar," that is, Elves and Men, its dominant natural sentient beings. However, one of their members has earlier defected, and thus the preparatory phase resembles a tug of war. Considering the author's known religiosity, it is interesting that Tolkien at times "corrects" biblical creation in line with modern evolutionary thinking. And so it is that after one of the initial conflicts with Melkor/Morgoth the Springtime of Arda comes to an end, and consequently carnivorousness is introduced to Middle-earth eons before the arrival of Elves and people, which in *Genesis* occurs after the Flood.

These sources indicate, among others, that in creating his imaginary world Tolkien was consciously working within, but in a creative relationship to, a vast store of tradition, which bestows upon Middle-earth a sense of both freshness and familiarity, and constitutes another ingredient in its depth and substance. The fact that Middle-earth is set in an imaginary past seems not to create a barrier between it and many contemporary readers; as Aragorn puts

it: "Good and ill have not changed since yesteryear; nor are they one thing among Elves and Dwarves and another among Men" (*TT*, III, ii, 41) At the deepest level, the "ethics of Elfland," to use Chesterton's expression, that permeate Middle-earth also evoke familiarity, whether the reader agrees with them or not.

Levels of Representation in Middle-earth

At the time that Tolkien wrote the above-cited letters stressing the strong relationship of Middle-earth with our own world, he had already published *The Lord of the Rings,* wherein his world appears with great verisimilitude heightening its sense of reality. In his essay "On Fairy-Stories," the author claims that Faërie, "the realm or state in which fairies have their being" alongside imaginary creatures and beings, "holds the seas, the sun, the moon, the sky; and the earth, and all things that are in it: tree and bird, water and stone, wine and bread, and ourselves, mortal men" (*TL* 113). Thus, to a large extent the imaginary world, especially as it is developed in Tolkien's later work, intentionally contains many primal elements from our world; in the case of vegetation, for instance, excluding the imaginary flora, Patrick Curry counts sixty-four noncultivated plants mentioned in *The Lord of the Rings* (62).

The tangibility of the world is heightened by the naturalistic prose, creating, among others, almost palpable landscapes, which captivate the reader with their overabundance: "The circumstantial expansiveness of Middle-earth itself is central to *The Lord of the Rings'* aesthetic power" (Rosebury, 12–13). This has the consequence that although certain roads are chosen by the characters, there is the naturalistic sense that there exist horizons unexplored; therefore, the Middle-earth landscape is not deterministic.

In contrast, the Middle-earth landscapes preceding Tolkien's novel, likewise placed earlier in its chronology, render a different sense. They are stripped down, adequate to the purpose of a more fundamental, mythic narrative, where, as C.S. Lewis says of mythical heroes, "we do not project ourselves strongly into the characters. They are like shapes moving in another world" (quoted in Purtill, 9). The primal landscapes of, for instance, "The Quenta" or "Quenta Silmarillion" of the 1930s add to this perception.

The texts written after *The Lord of the Rings* generally continue its simulated naturalism in their depiction of Middle-earth. One need only compare the starkness of the version of Tuor's journey to Gondolin from the published version of *The Silmarillion* with the sensuality of the later "Of Tuor and His Coming to Gondolin" found in *Unfinished Tales* to see the radically different presentation of Middle-earth. Nonetheless, even at that late period Tolkien had not given up treating Middle-earth as a tableau when the narrative requires it. This is illustrated in the scene where the haggard First Age hero Húrin, released from imprisonment after the fulfillment of Morgoth's curse on his family, arrives at the spot where the passageway to the hidden Elven city of Gondolin once was. One of Manwë's eagles sends news of this to Turgon within the hidden city, much to the latter's disbelief. Feeling this must mean Húrin is now in league with Morgoth, Turgon refuses to send help, only to belatedly regret his decision, sending his eagles once again with aid:

But it was too late . . .

> For Húrin stood at last in despair before the stern silence of the Echoriad, and the westering sun, piercing the clouds, stained his white hair with red. Then he cried aloud in the wilderness, heedless of any ears, and he cursed the pitiless land: "Hard as the hearts of Elves and Men." (*Jewels*, 272)

Although the passage was written after *The Lord of the Rings* and stylistically resembles its prose, it provides an altogether different impression of Middle-earth than in the trilogy. The vast geographical distance between Húrin and Turgon is traversed at virtually the speed of thought. And "the 'long' and thoughtful delay of Turgon seems to take no time at all" (Shippey, 223). Logically, Húrin should have remained on the spot for an appropriate length of time for some communication between himself and the Elven-king via the eagles before uttering any accusation, which follows. Long distances can be traversed quickly in the trilogy, by Gandalf, for instance, but always at some explainable speed. Tom Shippey aptly calls the above scene a "posed tableau" centering on "an outcry of spontaneous passion" (223).

One striking element that binds Middle-earth at different levels of representation is the importance of nomenclature, whether for personal names or geographical. There are approximately eight hundred names mentioned in *The Silmarillion* alone. Besides demonstrating Tolkien's proclivity toward philological exploration, "true names," to use Treebeard's term, crucial to the "'chain of causality' between language and things in *The Lord of the Rings* [are] forged by the Christian-Neoplatonic principles presented in Tolkien's *Silmarillion* as underlying Middle-earth's creation" (Zimmer, 50).

An obstacle for a reader gaining a clearer perception of Middle-earth outside of *The Lord of the Rings* stems from the fact that there exists a welter of texts that present it, most of which were not published during the author's lifetime. The relatively polished *Silmarillion* is a posthumously edited version of these texts. A truer extent of these writings is painstakingly presented in *Unfinished Tales of Númenor and Middle-earth* and the twelve-volume *The History of Middle-earth* series. (*Unfinished Tales* and *History* volumes are edited by Christopher Tolkien.) For those who take the trouble of studying them, and a surprising number of readers do, out of the maze of texts of Middle-earth mythology arise at once an alternative world and one that is hauntingly like our own. A new geography and imaginary history unfold with practically each version. Studied chronologically in accordance with Tolkien's authorship, over the years Middle-earth undergoes a growth in quite diverse fields of human thought and perception: linguistic, geographical, historical, philosophical, and aesthetic. Significantly, the number of genres that are explored by Tolkien to convey this world (novel, lay, fictional essay, etc.—and a children's story to boot!) simply cannot contain it.

Thus, although none of the above posthumous texts have "canonic" status, and occasionally they contradict themselves, through them Middle-earth has taken on an existence extending beyond that created in the few works Tolkien managed to see through to publication. Opinions vary, but the general consensus is that with the posthumous texts the texture of that mythological world has been enhanced, or at least not harmed, even though the literary value of the writings themselves, not to mention their level of completion, varies radically.

If any greater controversy exists, it is over a major conceptual modification that Tolkien was contemplating: that of changing his originally flat-earth imaginary world into a round-earth one. In the thirties, the story of Númenor acts as a transition myth. Through the Númenoreans breaking the ban of the Valar, the initially flat earth is transformed into a round one through the intervention of Iluvatar. Thus, the shift from a flat-earth into a round-earth is given a moral explanatory fable that Tolkien has called his Atlantis myth. At that point, the imaginary world combines both a flat and round earth related through the intervening catastrophe.

That Tolkien was unsatisfied with this solution might account for his new version of his creation story from 1948, labeled the "Round Arda" version. In it there is the evocative line that makes its way into the published *Silmarillion*: "and [the Valar] saw a new World made visible before them, and it was globed amid the Void, and it was sustained therein, but was not of it" (17). In contradistinction to his earlier mythology, there are also lines that suggest that the sun and moon were created coterminous or even earlier than the earth. Quite telling, as Douglas Anderson points out, is the change of a sentence from the originally published *Hobbit*: "In the Wide World the Wood-elves lingered in the twilight before the raising of the Sun and Moon." The revised version of 1966 is "In the Wide World the Wood-elves lingered in the twilight of our Sun and Moon, but loved best the stars" (*H*, 218–19 n23). Tolkien explains this change in conception in a letter as inevitable "to a modern 'mythmaker' with a mind subjected to the same 'appearances' as ancient men, and partly fed on their myths, but taught that the Earth was round from the earliest years" (*Letters*, 197).

Be that as it may, in his commentary to his father's pertinent writings, Christopher Tolkien, also his literary executor, expressed alarm "in the face of such a dismantling and reconstitution" of beautiful myths (*Morgoth*, 369); Wayne Hammond concurs that if Tolkien had continued, "it would have had a deadly effect on the whole of the mythology" ("Continuing," 27). Michał Leśniewski, however, points out that with the current state of multiple available texts and a number of implied "modes of transition," the reader does not have to choose, and a different version could easily coexist with the familiar ones. The "Round Arda" even possesses an advantage: "For us, modern readers with our inevitable ballast of scientific knowledge, it is the next element which makes Tolkien's secondary reality even more convincing" (116). Regardless of how one responds to the question of the "Round" or "Flat Arda," it further illustrates Tolkien's intention of Middle-earth becoming more a part of our own world at the around the time of *The Lord of the Rings*, if not earlier.

A pertinent matter is likewise the transition device from the Middle-earth legendarium to our world. The solution presented in *The Lord of the Rings*, that of the existence of a body of manuscripts—most notably the Red Book of the Shire—was a late device. The original solution, a sailor from Anglo-Saxon times named Ælfwine discovering the Elf-inhabited island of Kôr and gaining a body of lore, became problematic after the mythology developed. As in a number of other matters, Tolkien developed no definitive solution.

The Historical Geography of Middle-earth

If Middle-earth is "our own world" in an imaginary time, it is hardly surprising the reader finds much in it that is familiar. The presented landforms vary from mountains, hills, and plateaus to plains and undulating lowlands; the continental expansiveness provides occasion for a variety of climactic conditions and vegetation; while the population densities, though unspecified, are imaginable, and the welter of languages have an air of credibility. In contrast to his various "Annals" focusing on Middle-earth's chronology, few of Tolkien's writings are dedicated solely to the geography of Middle-earth: there is the several-page-long sketch in the "Ambarkanta" of the 1930s, the essay "The Rivers and Beacon-hills of Gondor," a few maps, and whatever can be gleaned in the various Middle-earth texts themselves, albeit the last source is quite rich. Its most familiar version exists in *The Lord of the Rings*, wherein the narrator locates the imaginary world as follows: "Those days, the Third Age of Middle-earth, are now long past, and the shape of all lands has been changed; but the regions in which Hobbits then lived were doubtless the same as those in which they still linger: the North-West of the Old World, east of the Sea" (*FR*, Prologue, 11).

This intimation of Europe, or even England, and the vast geographical canvas has led to speculation that Middle-earth is largely influenced by Europe's geography. Despite "the shape of all lands" having been "changed," some resemblances are clear; however, Karen Wynn Fonstad is of the opinion that "Tolkien's landscape [has primarily] resulted from vivid mental images based on specific areas with which he was familiar"(xi).

Regardless of the sources, the landforms within the chronology change enormously. In *The Lord of the Rings*, Treebeard chants a poem of his youthful ramblings among "the willow-meads of Tasarinan," the "elm-woods of Ossiriand," the "beeches of Neldoreth," and the "pine-trees upon the highland of Dorthonion." But he concludes the verses about the past with the line: "And now all those lands lie under the wave" (*LotR*, 458). Treebeard is talking about the First Age of millennia earlier, and the geographical names come from Beleriand in its North-East. Nonetheless, a historical geography of Middle-earth would have to go back even further in time. For the sake of simplicity, in describing this geography the best-known synthesized version largely consistent with the published *Silmarillion* and earlier works will be delineated. Moreover, a strictly round-earth geography to replace it was never developed, thus it remained largely hypothetical.

As mentioned above, the Valar and Maiar entered Middle-earth in order to prepare it for the Children of Ilúvatar. This primordial flat world is lit by two lamps, Illuin and Ormal, which are set on huge pillars. that will eventually become the sun and moon. Melkor assails these lamps, and in the ensuing chaos the Springtime of Arda comes to an end. The most important aspect of this phase of Middle-earth's history is that the angelic Valar remove themselves from Middle-earth to Aman, where they establish Valinor with their separate courts. Thus, the world is split into Middle-earth and the sacred realm of the Valar, which is removed from the "Hither Lands," where humans and Elves will dwell, by the Belegaer, the Sundering Sea. Only the evil Vala Melkor/Morgoth remains in the thus impoverished Middle-earth in his northern strongholds of Utumno, and later Angband, in the North, while the benign Ulmo visits its waters, which are his domain, and through which he can influence matters. Water is also the element through which, however slightly, the Music of the Ainur continues to resonate in Middle-earth, that is, the force behind the creation of Arda.

At this early stage, after the War of the Gods, the huge landmass of Middle-earth has an enormous Inland Sea of Helcar close to the borders of which the Elves "awaken" by the bay of Cuivienen. Since the Valar have raised a precipitous mountain range for protection, the light from the luminous Two Trees in Aman that have replaced the lamps does not reach the "First Born," thus solely the stars illuminate Middle-earth. They have been provided by Varda, called Elbereth by the Elves, with the Elves in mind: "The sign of the sickle Varda hung above the North as a threat to Morgoth and as an omen of his fall. At its first shining the Elder Children of Ilúvatar awoke in the midmost of Middle-earth. They are the Elves. Hence they are called the children of the stars" (*Lost Road*, 111).

A large (although by no means complete) party of Elves journeys to Aman at the invitation of the Valar, only to return in two separate groups under highly strained circumstances. These are the Noldor, who settle in Beleriand in order to attempt to reclaim the Silmarils from Morgoth, who stole them from Fëanor in Valinor. From this juncture until the end of the First Age of the Sun, the physical geography of Middle-earth remains remarkably constant. The Elven kingdoms are established in Beleriand, later to be joined by Men, who assist the former in the siege of Angband, which, unsuccessful, becomes a retreat until the Valar are forced to intervene in the War of Wrath. The major change in Middle-earth during that period is astrophysical, that is, the creation of the moon and sun, in that order, after which measured time and humans enter the imaginary world. The astral bodies bear a symbolism concerning the "Children of Ilúvatar": "Men, the Younger Children of Ilúvatar, awoke in the East of the world at the first Sunrise; hence they are also called the Children of the Sun. For the Sun was set as a sign of the waning of the Elves, but the Moon cherisheth their memory" (*Lost Road*, 118).

A geographical connection between the First Age and the Second Age of the Sun is the mountain range of Ered Luin, the Blue Mountains. However, until that juncture, the settlement of the High Elves, those that had resided for a time in Valinor, has been to the east of the mountain range. The War of Wrath that closed the period resulted in huge portions of the landmass falling away "under the wave." In a poignant later story, Tolkien adds that "still the Tol Morwen stands alone in the water beyond the new coasts that were made in the days of the wrath of the Valar" (*Jewels*, 296). The island commemorates the tragedy of Túrin Turambar's mother: proof that in the imaginary world geography and story are closely intertwined, even down to the level of individual fates. The major significance of the changes is that the distance between Middle-earth and Aman grows, symbolizing the fact that the influence of the Valar becomes less direct.

In the Second Age, there is only an insignificant territory east of Eréd Luin, which constitutes a remnant of Beleriand. The Gulf of Lune breaks through the mountain range, where the Grey Havens are situated. Middle-earth is obviously a different place. Angband is broken, and Morgoth removed from Middle-earth, while Sauron his servant eventually sets up a realm, with various fortunes, in Mordor. The human allies of Elves and the Valar are rewarded with the island of Númenor situated between Middle-earth and Aman in the Sea of Belegaer.

However, in the Second and Third Ages, the geography of Middle-earth proper changes far less in fact than in principle. Toward the end of the Second Age, the Númenóreans attempt their disastrous assault of Valinor, with the subsequent sinking of their island and the removal of the straight way to the country of the Valar. The World becomes "bent," or round, and the lands are filled in on the other side of the globe, but these are insignificant to any of the related histories of the legendarium. Thus, all this occurs without any essential changes to the Middle-earth geography where the "history" that is ultimately recounted in *The Lord of the Rings* takes place. The main changes are in the social geography: whereas in the Second Age the High Elves still play a major role, as well as the Númenóreans with whom they are allied, in the Third Age the remaining Elves are in the process of slowly taking their leave of Middle-earth; and the realms of ordinary people, however problematically, slowly come to the fore.

In the flat earth version, Middle-earth is bounded in all directions. In the East of the world are the Walls of the Sun, and next to them are the Burnt Lands of the Sun. Similarly, there are the Mountains of Valinor and the land of Aman in the West, where the Doors of the Night are located. These are connected with the movement of the sun and the moon through *Ekkaia*, the Encircling Sea. Beyond this is the Void.

Prophecies and the End of Middle-earth

The participation of Melkor/Morgoth in the creation of the world signifies that "Arda is Marred." It is within Ilúvatar's love of the earth that its ultimate hope lies in the Middle-earth mythology. There are a number of prophecies to this effect. At the end of the first complete sketch of the "Silmarillion" mythology, there is an account of what is known as the Second Prophecy of Mandos. When the Valar are tired of the world, Morgoth and his host shall return through the Door of the Night, where he will be met on the plain of Valinor. Interestingly, Túrin, Tolkien's most tragic hero, shall "slay Morgoth." Remembering the case of Denethor, it would seem a character who had committed suicide would not be fit for such a role in Tolkien's mythology, but *The Book of Lost Tales* relates how Túrin becomes purified through his entry into "Fos'Almir, the bath of flame"(*Lost Tales II*, 115–16), symbolic of Ilúvatar's love washing away his sin. After a successful battle, the Silmarils are regained, allowing for the Two Trees to be relit, and "the Mountains of Valinor shall be levelled so that it goes out over the world" (*Shaping*, 41). This suggests a restoration of the unity of the sacred land of Valinor and Middle-earth.

This Ragnarok-like apocalypse is complicated somewhat in *The Lord of the Rings*, where the Second Age has been incorporated into the as yet unpublished "Silmarillion" mythology. Since the trilogy refers to these matters in a less systematic manner than the later writings, there are only the eschatological insinuations of some of the characters. When Treebeard parts with the high Elves Celeborn and Galadriel and bemoans the unlikelihood of their ever meeting again, the latter prophesies: "Not in Middle-earth, nor until the lands that lie under the wave are lifted up again. Then in the willow-meads of Tasarinan we may meet in the Spring" (*RK*, VI, vi, 259).

What this refers to is a restoration of the earlier geography of Middle-earth. It can be inferred that the leveling of the Mountains of Valinor previously mentioned is incorporated in Galadriel's prophesy, but the new element is the lifting up of "the lands that lie under the wave." In a sense, both are connected. The mountains are what the Valar erected to separate themselves from the cares of the world, while the previously flat Middle-earth was made round to separate the Númenóreans, that is, Men, from the Undying Lands and their impossible dreams of overcoming the limitations of mortality.

A less obvious prophecy that is effectively fulfilled within the Middle-earth mythology, and that simultaneously points beyond it, is connected with the fact that "the Sun was set as a sign of the waning of the Elves" (*S*, 103). Significantly, at the conclusion of *The Lord of the Rings,* the sullied Minas Morgul, formerly Minas Ithil, the Tower of the Moon, is razed to the ground rather than restored. This leaves Minas Tirith, originally Minas Anor, the Tower of the Sun, as the dominant city, and the solar myth reigns supreme in Middle-earth. In a sense, this is among the strongest symbolic indications that the imaginary world is now under the Age of Men. Lionel Basney notes that "one of Middle-earth's cosmic concerns is the growth of legend into history" (16). The preeminence of the solar myth reinforces this process, since it is related to a major Indo-European myth (about which Tolkien actually had ambivalent feelings: cf. *Letters*, 148) that eventually made its way into Christian symbolism, toward which Tolkien subtly directs Middle-earth. Significantly, when Frodo's Fellowship of the Ring moves out from Rivendell on its near-hopeless quest, as we learn in "The Tale of Years" in Appendix B, it is December 25, the date of Christmas, which is connected with its portent of the ascendancy of the sun as a sign of hope. The defeat of Sauron on March 25, with its participation in both solar myth and Christian tradition, reinforces this symbolism. As Tom Shippey points out: "By mentioning the date Tolkien was presenting his 'eucatastrophe' as a forerunner or 'type' of the greater one of Christian myth" (181).

On the one hand, Tolkien's positioning Middle-earth toward our own world, with its "Primary Myths," serves a dramatic function. The whole legendarium becomes a kind of explanatory fable, providing an imaginary rationale for why there are no longer Elves or wondrous creatures in our world. However, Middle-earth's significance is more profound, connected with that of recovery, which Tolkien named as one of the primary functions of fantasy as an art. Middle-earth's closest relationship with our own world lies in the evidence it gives of the author's conviction that, as he has Aragorn exclaim: "The green earth . . . is a mighty matter of legend, though [we] tread it under the light of day" (*TT*, III, ii, 37). Above all, Middle-earth beckons us to look with renewed wonder at our own world.

CHRISTOPHER GARBOWSKI

Further Reading

Anderson, Douglas A. *The Annotated Hobbit*. By J.R.R. Tolkien. Boston, MA: Houghton Mifflin, 2002.

Basney, Lionel. "Myth, History and Time in *The Lord of the Rings*." In *Tolkien—New Critical Perspectives*, edited by Neil D. Isaacs and Rose A. Zimbardo. Lexington, KY: University Press of Kentucky, 1981.

Chance, Jane, ed. *Tolkien and the Invention of Myth. A Reader*. Lexington, KY: University of Kentucky Press, 2004.

Curry, Patrick. *Defending Middle-earth: Tolkien, Myth and Modernity*. Edinburg: Floris Books, 1997.

Flieger, Verlyn, and Carl F. Hostetter, eds. *Tolkien's Legendarium: Essays on the History of Middle-earth*. Westport, CT: Greenwood Press, 2000.

Fonstad, Karen Wyn. *The Atlas of Middle-earth*. Rev. ed. London: Grafton, 1992.

Garbowski, Christopher. *Recovery and Transcendence for the Contemporary Mythmaker: The Spiritual Dimension in the Works of JRR Tolkien*. 2nd ed. Zurich and Berne: Walking Tree Publishers, 2004.

Hammond, Wayne. "A Continuing and Evolving Creation: Distractions in the Later History of Middle-earth." In *Tolkien's Legendarium: Essays on the History of Middle-earth*, edited by Verlyn Flieger and Carl F. Hostetter, 19–29. Westport, CT: Greenwood Press, 2000.

Leśniewski, Michał. "The Question of the 'Round Arda': An Abandoned Idea, or Another Perspective on Tolkien's Legendarium." *Aiglos: Tolkienistic Almanac*, Special Issue (Summer 2005): 101–17.

Purtill, Richard. *J.R.R. Tolkien: Myth, Morality and Religion*. San Francisco, CA: Harper & Row, 1984.

Rosebury, Brian. *Tolkien: A Cultural Phenomenon*. Hampshire: Palgrave MacMillan, 2003.

Shippey, Tom. *The Road to Middle-earth*. London: Grafton, 1992.

Tolkien, J.R.R. "On Fairy-Stories," in *MC*, 109–61.

———. "The Rivers and Beacon-hills of Gondor," ed. Carl F. Hostetter, *Vinyar Tengwar* no. 42 (July 2001): 18–23.

Zimmer, Mary. "Creating and Re-Creating Worlds with Words: The Religion and Magic of Language in *The Lord of the Rings*," in Chance, ed. *Tolkien and the Invention of Myth. A Reader...*, pp. 49–60.

See also **Ælfwine; Angband; Arda; Astronomy and Cosmology, Middle-earth; Calendars; Dwarves; East, The; Elves: Ents; Eru; Eucatastrophe; Koivië-néni and Cuiviénen; Kôr; Maiar; Maps; Men, Middle-earth; Monsters, Middle-earth; South, The; Theological and Moral Approaches in Tolkien's Work; Tol Eressea; Valar; Valinor**

MILTON

At first consideration, John Milton might seem the last English poet to resonate with Tolkien, either poetically or philologically. With Shakespeare and Spenser, he represents the epitome of "southern" (Greek and Roman) European notions of literature: his impulse was epic to Tolkien's elegiac and Calvinist (interior) to Tolkien's Catholic (sacramental); where Milton condemned the paganism of pre-Christian England, Tolkien looked for common ground. Still, as the Romantics knew quite well, there is no English writer after 1700 who does not write in Milton's shadow, and Tolkien's art gains more than it loses by that shade. When Tolkien wrote in his 1936 *Beowulf* lecture that Milton "might have done worse" than retell Jack and the Beanstalk in heroic verse, he was not, as many readers have supposed, taking a swipe at Milton.

Tolkien's mythology in *The Silmarillion* shows the most obvious Miltonic touches, particularly in the character of his fallen angel, Melkor. Critics may have overemphasized Tolkien's debt to *Paradise Lost*'s Satan in his conception of Melkor, particularly since Milton himself may have known the Old English poetic versions of *Genesis*, which Tolkien knew more intimately. But there is nothing in the Old English *Genesis* like the Miltonic motif of Christ reverting the Satanic inversion of good and evil, God ever bringing good out of Satan's evil. In Tolkien's *Ainulindalë*, Melkor attempts to compose music for his own glory out of Ilúvatar's themes: the resultant discord Ilúvatar easily works into a harmony again.

Critics will surely continue to find the most surprisingly fruitful Miltonisms. Jane Chance likens the Elvish exodus from Lórien to Adam and Eve's expulsion from the garden that ends *Paradise Lost*. Debbie Sly finds Milton's characters Sin and Death, despite their allegorical nature, an expression of the same tendency Tolkien found in *Beowulf*'s monsters: an embodiment of evil threatening to destroy all good.

Though there is much in Milton's *History of Britain* (1670) to offend both Tolkien's "Northernism" and his Catholicism, his celebration of the English character in Anglo-Saxon times harmonizes with Tolkien's thought. If he opens the book by rejecting the truth of the earliest oral tradition (thereby privileging Latin over Germanic, literary over philological), he concludes that very rejection by insisting that they be scrupulously preserved, "be it for nothing else but in favour of our English Poets and Rhetoricians." Later editions include a "Digression" (an editorial title, not Milton's) on the English Civil War, but in its original form the history concludes with the Norman conquest—a focus with which Tolkien would certainly have no quarrel.

Stylistically, one of the most striking qualities in Tolkien's prose is one that he shares with Milton: a heightened etymological awareness to the diction. This quality in Milton is often falsely characterized as "inkhornism," a learned Latinism that stultifies his verse. It is, on the contrary, as playful and natural as Tolkien's Anglo-Saxonisms. In Book IX of *Paradise Lost*, when Eve tastes of the Tree of the Knowledge of

Good and Evil, Milton does not use the Anglo-Saxon word "knowledge," but the uncommon Latinism "sapience." But the choice is not dictated by linguistic chauvinism, but rather poetic economy: Milton knows that the etymon of "sapience" is the verb *sapere*, to taste, which connects in a sensual, concrete way to the fruit. Of the hundreds of examples of similar poetic equivocations in Tolkien, one must suffice: "doom" in *The Lord of the Rings* sometimes has its modern meaning of "disaster," sometimes its etymological sense of "judgment," sometimes its onomatopoetic force of a drum beat, and sometimes a dual-language pun on the Dwarvish *Dûm*, "excavation." Tolkien's multilayered etymological diction is positively Miltonic and sometimes includes Latinate words like "precious" or "conspiracy."

JOHN R. HOLMES

Further Reading

Chance, Jane. *Tolkien's Art: A Mythology for England.* Rev. ed. Lexington, KY: University Press of Kentucky, 2001.
Duriez, Colin. "Sub-creation and Tolkien's Theology of Story." In *Scholarship and Fantasy: Proceedings of the Tolkien Phenomenon, May 1992, Turku, Finland*, edited by Keith J. Battarbee, 133–50. Anglicana Turkuensia 12. Turku: University of Turku, 1993.
Sly, Debbie. "Weaving Nets of Gloom: 'Darkness Profound' in Tolkien and Milton." In *J.R.R. Tolkien and His Literary Resonances: Views of Middle-earth*, George Clark and Daniel Patrick Timmons, 109–19. Westport, CT: Greenwood, 2000.
Tolkien, J.R.R. "*Beowulf*: The Monsters and the Critics." In *MC*, 5–48.

See also **Latin Language; Light; Satan and Lucifer**

MIRKWOOD

A forest east of the Misty Mountains in Rhovanion, or Wilderland, some four or five hundred miles in length and two hundred miles at its widest. Mirkwood is the largest of the forests surviving into the Third Age from the primeval forest said to have covered most of western Middle-earth. The names applied to Mirkwood provide a glimpse of its long history. First named in Sindarin as Eryn Galen, "Greenwood the Great," in the early Third Age it was called Taur-e-Ndaedelos, "the forest of the great fear," owing to the evil presence of Sauron at Dol Guldur in the southern portion of the wood (*RK*, Appendix F, 412). Alternately, it bore the name Taur-nu-Fuin, "forest under night," of which the name "Mirkwood" is said by Tolkien to be a "translation" (*UT*, 281). Christopher Tolkien remarks that his father's use of this Sindarin name, also used in *The Silmarillion* for the forest of Dorthonion in northern Beleriand, is

noteworthy, given the similarity between depictions of them in *Pictures by J.R.R. Tolkien* (1979). *Lord of the Rings* Appendix B adds that after the War of the Ring Mirkwood was renamed again as Eryn Lasgalen, "the Wood of the Greenleaves." In *The Return of the King*, chapter 9, Legolas calls it simply "the Great Wood" (*RK*, V, ix, 154).

Outside the main narratives, Tolkien's sketch of the history of western Middle-earth suggests Mirkwood's importance as an early settlement area for both the Hobbits and the Men of Rohan. The "Prologue" to *The Lord of the Rings* says the hobbits' earliest tales indicate they lived for a while at the edge of Greenwood between the forest and the Misty Mountains. Though the reason for their eventual crossing of the Misty Mountains is "no longer certain," it is guessed that this arduous migration was motivated in part by the growth of Sauron's evil influence, "a shadow that fell on the forest," whence its subsequent, darker name. Similarly, the ancient homes of the Northmen, ancestors of the Rohirrim or Éothéod, are said to have lain along the eastern edge of the forest. The great eastern indentation, visible on maps near the forest's southern end, is called the "East Bight," said to have been made by the Northmen's extensive felling of trees (*UT*, 288 ff.). Sauron's reclamation of Dol Guldur seems to explain their migrations north and west before their ultimate settlement further south in Rohan.

The arboreal vegetation of northern Mirkwood near Thranduil's realm consists of dense stands of oak and beech, with dark firs at the southern end, seemingly the only significant coniferous forest in Middle-earth besides Dorthonion (Fonstad, 184). However, Tolkien notes that the Emyn Duir, "dark mountains" comprising the Mountains of Mirkwood, are so named owing to "dense fir-woods" growing on their slopes.

Though it is referenced only in passing in *The Lord of the Rings*, Mirkwood contributes both to the plot and to the fairy-tale atmosphere of *The Hobbit*. The narrator's description of it as a gloomy place strangled with ivy, lichen, and blackened leaves evokes a sense of foreboding which is stereotypical of haunted forests in folklore, including fairy-tales set in the German Schwarzwald, the Black Forest of Baden-Württemberg. Bilbo and the Dwarves perceive Mirkwood's tangled boughs, matted twigs, and the sound of unseen scuttlings, grunts, and scufflings in the undergrowth. The wood is said to be everlastingly still, dark, and stuffy, full of cobwebs, and pitch-dark at night. Tolkien's descriptions of other forests—Fangorn, the Old Forest, and several of the forests of Beleriand—similarly evoke an atmosphere of suspicion, hostility, and enmity between people and the wilderness environments in which they are unwelcome intruders.

Tolkien's conception of Mirkwood is illustrative of his imaginative use of philological reconstruction for literary purposes. The name derives from poems in the Old Norse *Poetic Edda*, where the compound *Myrkviðr* is cognate with English "murk(y)" plus *viðr* "wood," referring to a mythical forest. *Atlakviða*, for example, speaks of *hrís þat it mæra, er meðr Myrkvið kalla*, "the great forest which men call Mirkwood," described also in *Oddrúnnargrátr* as *Myrkvið inn ókunna*, "untracked Mirkwood," through which Atli sends spies to murder Gunnar. *Atlakviða* also mentions *Myrkheim*, "home of darkness," possibly a synonym for *Myrkviðr*. Other eddic poems similarly refer to *Myrkviðr* as separating the human world and the supernatural world of the gods; in the prose *Herverar saga*, the army of the Hunnish king Hlǫðr rides through *skóg þann er Myrkviðr heitir, er skilr Húnaland ok Gotaland*, "the forest called Mirkwood, which divides Hunnish land from the land of the Goths." Though Old English contains no cognates of the ON term, in *Beowulf*, the path between Hrothgar's hall and Grendel's mere leads *ofer myrcan mor*, "a gloomy moor" through a *wynleasne wudu* "joyless wood" in a landscape where *mistige moras* "misty moors" separate the human from the monstrous world.

Shippey shows how the romantically inspired philological interpretations of *Myrkviðr* by Grimm, Tolkien, and others have contributed to the imaginative—though sometimes faulty—reconstruction of lost or imaginary cultures. Jacob Grimm hypothesized that since ON *mark* means "boundary" and *mǫrk* means "forest," the two words must derive from an earlier form meaning "wood": presumably, forests often marked the boundaries of kingdoms or wooded territory surrounding areas of domestic settlement. The ON literary references to *Myrkviðr* seem to suggest cultural memory of contested woodlands or disputed territory claimed by both the Goths and the Huns (Shippey, "Goths"). In some ways anticipating Tolkien, in *The Roots of the Mountains* (1889) William Morris used the place name "Mirkwood," drawing similar surmises without the elaborate philological machinery. Two separate proto Indo-European roots for these two ON terms and their English cognates have been reconstructed since Grimm, however: *mer-*, "to flicker," with derivatives indicating dim states of illumination, and *merg-*, "boundary, mark, border." Tolkien's recreation of the name's mythic associations makes perhaps the best use of the scant material left to the linguistic imagination.

JONATHAN EVANS

Further Reading

Dickerson, Matthew, and Jonathan Evans. *Ents, Elves, and Eriador: J.R.R. Tolkien's Environmental Vision.* Lexington, KY: University Press of Kentucky, 2006.

Fonstad, Karen Wynn. *The Atlas of Middle-earth.* Rev. ed. Boston, MA: Houghton Mifflin, 1991.

Shippey, T.A. "Goths and Huns: The Rediscovery of the Northern Cultures in the Nineteenth Century." In *The Medieval Legacy: A Symposium*, edited by Andreas Haarder, Iorn Pio, Preben Meulengracht Sorensen, and Reinhold Schroder, 51–69. Odense: Odense University Press, 1982.

———. *The Road to Middle-earth: Revised and Expanded Edition.* Boston, MA: Houghton Mifflin, 2001.

See also **Art and Illustrations by Tolkien;** *Beowulf***; Environmentalist Readings; Goths; Hobbits; Huns; Maps; Middle-earth; Misty Mountains; Mythology, Germanic; Old English; Old Norse Language; Old Norse Literature; Trees; Wilderland**

MISSIONS FROM ANGLO-SAXON ENGLAND

Soon after Ethelbert of Kent allowed St. Augustine of Canterbury and his monks to come to Britain in 597, a number of monasteries were established in southern Britain, and early attempts to convert other British kingdoms were made. Ethelbert's death in 616 resulted in a number of British kingdoms reverting back to paganism. St. Paulinus, a Roman monk of St. Augustine's, was able to convert King Eadwine of Northumbria in 627, and he established the church of St. Peter in York in northern Britain. Felix, a Burgundian monk from Canterbury, gained access to the king in East Anglia; and Birinus worked on converting the people of Wessex in 634. All of these conversion attempts were influenced by the Roman mission; in 634, Irish missionaries from Iona established a monastery on the island of Lindisfarne in northeastern Britain. St. Wilfrid (634–709), abbot of Ripon, championed the Roman versus the Celtic customs in Britain after a trip to Rome around 654 AD. Tension between the Roman and Celtic branches of Christianity in Britain often resulted in different celebrations of the Easter festival, eventually resulting in the Synod of Whitby in 664, where the Northumbrian King Oswiu decided in favor of the Roman practice rather than the Celtic. St. Wilfrid also spent a brief period of time evangelizing in Friesland on the Continent in 678–79, as a precursor to the many English missions to the Germanic peoples, and he preached and converted many of the South Saxon peoples from 680–86.

Both British Roman and Celtic Christian missions to the Continent were extensive in the eighth century.

St. Columbanus (543–615) was the first and most celebrated of the Irish monks to visit central and western Europe, and he established many monasteries there, including Luxeuil and Bobbio. The West Saxon monk Winfrith, better known as St. Boniface, was the first of many Anglo-Saxon missionaries to the Continent. Born around 675, into a noble family, he early on decided on a monastic life. Establishing success as a preacher, he decided that his mission was to bring the Gospel to the Saxons in Germany. In 716, he set out for Frisia, following the efforts by the Northumbrian St. Willibrord (d. 739), who was made archbishop of the Frisians soon after Boniface arrived. In 718, Boniface went to Rome to receive his authority from the pope. Working with a number of Northumbrian missionaries, Boniface received the support of Charles Martel, who assisted in his enormous success in converting the people of Hesse. Boniface then went on to Thuringia, where he recruited more missionaries, was made an archbishop, created new dioceses, founded many monasteries, established the church hierarchy in Bavaria, and reformed the Frankish church. In 740, he was assisted in his work by St. Willibald (d. 786), his cousin, who was also the first known Englishman to visit the Holy Land. Willibald was made bishop of Eichstatt, and helped to found the monastery of Heidenheim. In 754, Boniface resigned from his see to spend the last years of his life trying to convert his first audience, the Frisians. He and a large number of companions were murdered by some Frisians in 754, thus assuring Boniface his permanent fame and the title "apostle of Germany."

The Anglo-Saxons continued to send missions to the Continent well into the ninth century. Many of these missionaries were women as well as men, including Saints Walburg, Tecla, and Lioba. The northern lands of Denmark and Scandinavia, as well as Norway and Sweden, were all influenced by missions from Britain throughout the early medieval period, and one can find many references to Anglo-Saxon saints in their calendars and celebrations.

BRADFORD LEE EDEN

Further Reading

Attwater, D. *The Penguin Dictionary of Saints*. Baltimore, MD: Penguin Books, 1965.

Mershman, Francis. "St. Boniface." *New Catholic Encyclopedia* online. Available at http://www.newadvent.org/cathen/02656a.htm.

Thurston, Herbert. "The Anglo-Saxon Church." *New Catholic Encyclopedia* online. Available at http://www.newadvent.org/cathen/01505a.htm.

See also **Augustine of Canterbury**

MISTY MOUNTAINS

A range of mountains some nine hundred miles in length curving eastward then west again on a north-south axis from the Northern Waste to the Gap of Rohan. The Misty Mountains are "undoubtedly one of the most important features in Middle-earth" (Fonstad, 79). The map in *The Hobbit* equates them closely with the western edge of Wilderland. Also called the Hithaeglir, "Towers of Mist," their name—a descriptive epithet—may have been inspired by the phrase *úrig fill* ("wet/rainy mountains") in the Old Norse *Skírnisml*. Grendel's refuge in the *mistige moras* ("misty moors," *Beowulf,* 1.1. 162, 710) may also have contributed. Meteorological and geographic details suggest similarities with the Swiss Alps, which Tolkien hiked in the summer of 1911, presumably providing later inspiration and geological/geographic verisimilitude. At heights approaching twelve thousand feet, the Misty Mountains would block the flow of atmospheric moisture, creating the cloudy conditions and precipitation from which the name derives. The orogenic processes explaining the uplift are unspecified, but they are expressed mythically in the titanic geological upheavals in the wars of the Valar against Melkor in the First Age. The tectonic forces creating this range may be part of a global mountain-building pattern that includes the Ered Luin in the northwest and the Orocarni far to the east. Glacial events shaping its valleys and escarpments are suggested by the recurrence of "horn" and "trough" in names and descriptions of the mountains' formations.

Both as barriers and as strongholds, they are strategically and narratively significant to many of the characters and events in the Middle-earth canon. In *The Silmarillion*, we learn these mountains were raised originally in the First Age by Melkor to waylay Oromë the hunter in his journeys. Subsequently, they hinder the westward migrations of Elves, Men, Dwarves, and Hobbits. During the wars in the Northern Kingdom of Arnor, King Arvedui of Arthedain hides briefly in "tunnels of old dwarf-mines" near the northern end of the range, whose northern-most point at Carn Dûm serves also as a defensive refuge for the Witch King of Angmar. At the southern-most point north of the Gap of Rohan, the valley of Nan Curunír is important to Rohan and Gondor as a natural fortress and as the site of Orthanc/Isengard. Though their height suggests that geologically the Misty Mountains are still relatively young, extensive detritus below the northwestern slopes has created the tumbled piedmont landscape of the Trollshaws and Ettenmoors, whose names indicate oral traditions concerning habitation by giants ("Ettins") and trolls.

At the eastern edge of Eregion, Celebdil, Fanuid-hol, and Caradhras comprise the formation called Thrihyrn, or "the Three Peaks." During the Second Age, beneath Caradhras, the tallest of the three, Dwarves from Ered Luin discover the only vein of mithril found in Middle-earth and subsequently excavate the vast mines and subterranean mansions of Khazâd-dûm, later the Orkish stronghold of Moria. In the Third Age, Gollum makes his way furtively beneath the Misty Mountains into Moria seeking respite from the sun. In *The Hobbit*, their "lonely peaks and valleys" waylay Bilbo and the Dwarves in their Quest for Erebor. Forced to seek shelter in a cave, Bilbo is captured by goblins and taken deep into the mines, where he discovers the One Ring, an event of monumental importance in the subsequent history of Middle-earth. Similarly, in *The Lord of the Rings,* the ascent of Caradhras by Frodo and the Company of the Ring is halted as the peak is rendered impassable by an alpine blizzard.

JONATHAN EVANS

Further Reading

Fonstad, Karen Wynn. *The Atlas of Middle-earth*. Rev. ed. Boston, MA: Houghton Mifflin, 1991.

Sarjeant, William Antony Swithin. "The Geology of Middle-earth." In *Proceedings of the J.R.R. Tolkien Centenary Conference*, edited by Patricia Reynolds and Glen H. GoodKnight, 334–39. Milton Keynes and Altadena: Tolkien Society/Mythopoeic Press, 1995.

Shippey, Tom. *The Road to Middle-earth: Revised and Expanded Edition*. Boston, MA: Houghton Mifflin, 2001.

See also **Caves; Gollum; Mountains; Moria; Wilderland**

MITHRIL

Mithril, also known as true-silver, Moria-silver, or silver-steel, is found only in the farthest reaches of Khazad-dûm—in the mines of Moria. Because of its scarcity, *mithril* grew from a much-admired and highly valued metal to a metal that was without price. *Mithril* was likened to silver in appearance, but its strength and beauty far surpassed simple silver. *Mithril* was lightweight and was stronger than steel. It was easily worked, and when wrought and polished, it would not lessen in strength. Unlike silver, *mithril* would not tarnish. *Mithril* was used not only for its beauty and therefore was widely employed in the crafting of jewellery and the setting of gems. It was also practical and could be used in place of steel.

Mithril was valued by all the races of Middle-earth, but especially by the Dwarves, and it could be argued that Mithril occasioned the rift that ran between Dwarves and Elves. *Mithril* roused the Balrog in the Mines of Moria. In the Third Age, during the reign of Durin VI (c. 1980), with the power of Sauron growing, the Dwarves of Moria dug ever deeper for *mithril,* which was becoming even more scarce. While delving beneath Barazinbar, the great peak of the Misty Mountains known to Men as the Redhorn and to the Elves as Caradhras, the Dwarves discovered a mother lode of *mithril* (*RK*, Appendix A, 353). The Dwarves' joy at discovering the precious metal they sought was short-lived, for their efforts awoke a Balrog, one of the mightiest of the servants of Morgoth.

The Elves also prized *mithril* highly. The Noldor settled Eregion in the Second Age to be closer to the lodes of *mithril* found in Khazad-dûm. The Elves used *mithril* to make another substance, *ithildin* (*Shadow*, 463; *FR*, II, iv, 318). *Ithildin*, which means "starmoon" in Sindarin, was developed in the Second Age by Noldorin smiths (*RK*, Appendix B, 363; *Lost Road*, 361). This reveals a potential inspiration for Tolkien's *mithril:* silver classically is associated with the moon in many cultures, from Greco-Romans to Norse. *Ithildin* was used as an adornment, especially on stonework, and was particularly useful for hiding markings in that it would not shine unless illuminated by rays of star or moon in conjunction with the correct words of opening or spells of unlocking. The hidden Doors of Moria were embellished with *ithildin* (*FR*, II, iv, 318).

Mithril was also held in the highest reverence by the Númenóreans. The fifteenth ruler, Tar-Telemmaitë, was called the "silver-handed" because of his love of silver and, especially, of *mithril*. His servants ever sought the precious metal throughout Middle-earth (*UT*, 221, 284).

Some of the more notable objects made from *mithril* in the works of Tolkien include:

- Bilbo's corselet of Moria-silver given to him by Thorin in appreciation and as a first payment for the Hobbit's burgling of Smaug. In original drafts of the tale and in the original publication, the corselet was made of silver, but Tolkien changed it to a specialized material, far greater in strength and value: *mithril* (*H*, XIII, 295).
- *Nenya*, the Ring of Adamant, one of the Three Elven Rings of Power, given by Celebrimbor to the Lady Galadriel (*S*, 357, 370). *Nenya* was a slender band of *mithril* set with a white Elven gem.
- The *Elendilmir*, or the Star of Elendil, was the crown of Arnor, a single band of *mithril* set with a white diamond. The *Elendilmir* was a great symbol of Númenórean kingship outside the Sceptre of Annúminas and the Silver Crown.

Thought lost, the *Elendilmir* was discovered in the Third Age, after the crowning of King Elessar and the restructuring of his kingdom. It was rescued from Saruman's hoard in Orthanc by Aragorn himself.

- The boat of the mariner Eärendil was crafted of *mithril* and Elven glass (*FR*, II, i, 248).
- The gates of Gondor broken by the Witch-king were replaced with mighty gates crafted of *mithril* and steel (*RK*, Appendix A, 360).

JESSICA BURKE

Further Reading

Helms, Randel. *Tolkien's World*. Boston, MA: Houghton Mifflin 1974.

See also **Bilbo; Dwarves; Eärendil; Elendilmir; Elves; Gondor; Misty Mountains; Moria; Rings of Power; Thorin**

MONSTERS

Besides Elves, Men, Dwarves, and hobbits—the so-called speaking peoples of Middle-earth—Tolkien's imaginary world includes creatures of another order—monsters. In the same way that Tolkien based most of his imagined races—excepting hobbits—on pre-existing archetypes in European folklore and mythology, his monsters by and large have counterparts in literary tradition predating his work. Medieval and Renaissance literature reveals a long-standing fascination with monstrous races: in the Anglo-Saxon period, the *Liber Monstrorum*, *The Wonders of the East*, and the *Letter of Alexander to Aristotle* give evidence of this perennial interest. *Beowulf*, a source crucial to Tolkien's literary inventions, includes two types of monster: the troll-like Grendel and his mother, and the dragons slain by Sigemund and Beowulf. Additionally, it mentions Orcs (*orcneas*; see below) and giants in Grendel's monstrous ancestry. Tolkien considered the monsters central to the plot and theme of *Beowulf* and not, as earlier scholarship held, marginal. The manuscript in which the poem appears also contains the latter two monster texts mentioned above, and the manuscript as a whole has been regarded as a compendium on the theme of monstrosity. The fifteenth-century work *Mandeville's Travels* is in the same tradition. Swift's *Gulliver's Travels* (1726) suggests this genre remained popular into the early modern period. Monsters generally are purported to exist in reality but almost always in distant corners of the world. Echoing this, characters in both *The Hobbit* and *The Lord of the Rings* initially doubt the veracity of

monster tales; in these novels, the Shire is the psychological center of known and knowable reality, and there are no monsters there. As a result of their adventures in the wider world, however, the Hobbits are forced to accept them as real.

The term "monster" derives from Latin *mnstrum*, "that which is shown, portent, marvel, prodigy" and *mnstrre*, "to show, exhibit," perhaps with the added sense of "to marvel (at)." Many of the marvels reported in European monster literature are of humanoid physiognomy or hybrids of human and animal; others appear as less humanoid, hybrid, or gigantic animal forms. Similarly, Tolkien's monsters are of two types: (1) forms similar to the "people" of Middle-earth but distorted or otherwise anomalous and (2) beings modeled on creatures from the natural world but of enormous size. Monsters of both types possess rudimentary emotive psychology, and many of them are endowed with speech; but neither type seems to exhibit the moral and spiritual faculties associated with full personhood. None are included in Treebeard's song of the "living creatures."

Trolls, Orcs, and Balrogs fit into the first category. Orcs are perverted versions of Elves and synonymous with *goblins*, which appear in *The Hobbit* and are reinterpreted later as Orcs. Tolkien borrowed goblins from earlier writers including probably Andrew Lang and George MacDonald, while the term "orc" derives from *orcneas*, "demon-corpses," and *orcþyrs*, "orc-giant," in OE literature. Trolls were made by Melkor in mockery of Ents; they are mentioned in the Old Norse mythic poem *Völuspá* but play a greater role in later medieval Icelandic literature and Scandinavian folklore. Balrogs are spirits of fire—originally Maiar, corrupted by Melkor—incarnate in Middle-earth as demonic giants. The Balrog that Gandalf fights in the tunnels beneath Moria, its fire quenched, becomes "a thing of slime stronger than a strangling snake." Not much is said concerning the rock-throwing stone-giants encountered by Bilbo in the Misty Mountains (*H*, IV, 104); Shippey regards them as ineffective, redolent of nature myth, and thus "too allegorical." Nor are the giants that are suggested in the geographical name Ettenmoors north of Rivendell explained or even purported as real (cp. OE *eoten*, ME *ettin*, ON *jötunn*, "giant").

The second group of monsters in Tolkien's work comprises all other extraordinary life forms regarded generally as malevolent and anomalous in the natural order. These include wolflike Wargs, with origins in OE *wearh* and ON *vargr*, combining underlying meanings in "wolf" and (later) "outlaw, exile." Ungoliant, a giant spider appearing in *The Silmarillion*, poisons and destroys the mythically central Two Trees of Valinor. She breeds with other primordial creatures of spider form before devouring them; Shelob, one of her many offspring, stings Frodo almost fatally in Cirith Ungol and is mortally wounded by Sam. Shelob too has offspring, "lesser broods, bastards of [her] miserable mates," among them, presumably, the spiders of Mirkwood that waylay the Dwarves in their quest of Erebor.

Other monsters include the vague Watcher in the Water, a many-tentacled creature in the lake outside the West Gate of Moria. Gandalf says it crept or was driven from the dark waters under the Misty Mountains; he alludes to "older and fouler things than Orcs" in the deep places of the world. Echoing this later, he says "the world is gnawed by nameless things" older than Sauron and unknown even to him in the deepest mines beneath Khazad-dûm. Bilbo alludes to the "wild Were-worms of the Last Desert" (*H*, I, 49), about which nothing more is said. Vaguer still—perhaps not even living creatures—are the "monstrous Watchers" at the gate of Cirith Ungol. These are hybrid figures with three joined bodies "human and bestial," seated on thrones, "corrupt and loathsome," each with three vulture-faces, their clawlike hands laid upon their knees. Though seemingly carved from stone, they are inhabited with "some dreadful spirit of evil vigilance" and have some form of awareness: they "knew an enemy" and forbid entry or escape from the Tower (*RK*, VI, i, 178).

Dragons, an especially important monstrous type, are treated in a separate entry; in *The Return of the King*, the winged creature on which the chief Nazgûl is mounted seems related to them. This monster is described as birdlike but featherless, with wings of hide between horned claws. A survivor from "an older world, maybe" bred in hideous eyries "in forgotten mountains cold beneath the Moon . . . apt to evil," it is taken by Sauron and nursed "with fell meats" to become greater than any other flying creature (*RK*, V, vi, 115).

JONATHAN EVANS

Further Reading

Orchard, Andy. *Pride and Prodigies: Studies in the Monsters of the Beowulf-manuscript*. Cambridge: D.S. Brewer, 1995.

Shippey, Tom. *The Road to Middle-earth: Revised and Expanded Edition*. Boston, MA: Houghton Mifflin, 2001.

———, ed. *The Shadow-Walkers: Jacob Grimm's Mythology of the Monstrous*. Tempe: Arizona Center for Medieval and Renaissance Studies, 2005.

Verner, Lisa Ruth. *The Epistemology of the Monstrous in the Middle Ages*. New York: Routledge, 2005.

See also **"*Beowulf*: The Monsters and the Critics"; Dragons; Maiar; Manuscripts, Medieval; Mirkwood; Misty Mountains; Moria; Shire**

MORDOR

Mordor is Sauron's stronghold at the end of the Third Age, the Black Lands in the East of Middle-earth. (for detail, see Fonstad's *Atlas*, but note, that her inference that the Sea of Helcar originally overlay Mordor and its surrounding areas was invalidated by the subsequent publication of *The Peoples of Middle-earth*). It lay north and east of the mountains of the Ephel Dúath (Mountains of Shadow) and south of the Ered Lithui (Ash Mountains). Most of its land area was characterized by wide lifeless plains of volcanic waste and barrenness. Major features at the time of *The Lord of the Rings* included:

1. Morannon, The Black Gate, built by Sauron to secure the Udûn valley in the northwest, the only natural gap in the mountain circuit by which Mordor was defended. The rear (southeast) entry to the valley was through the Isenmouth. The battle-plain of Dagorlad lay in front (that is, to the north-northwest) of the gate.
2. Mount Doom (Amon Amarth, or Orodruin), a volcano; Sauron's forge where the Ring was made and ultimately unmade.
3. Plateau of Gorgoroth, the northwestern plain.
4. The tower of Barad-dûr, Sauron's Dark Tower, built toward the end of the Second Age.
5. Minas Morgul, originally Minas Ithil, built by Gondor.
6. Cirith Ungol (cirith = cleft), the fortress of the Black Captain, the leader of the Nazgûl, who had been the witch-king of Angmar in the Second Age.
7. Another stronghold was Durthang in the Ephel Dúath.
8. The plain of Lithlad, to the east of Barad-dûr.
9. In the southern plain, Nurn, vast fields worked by armies of slaves provided food for Sauron's empire; included the inland sea, Núrnen. The area was granted to the slaves, and to Gondor's defeated enemies, at the end of the War of the Ring.

JAMES MCNELIS

MORGAN, FATHER FRANCIS

Father Francis Xavier Morgan was one of the most significant figures in Tolkien's early life. "He was more than a father to me," Tolkien wrote. "I first learned charity and forgiveness from him."

Born in Spain on January 18, 1857, Father Francis was of Welsh and Anglo-Spanish heritage. His father was a wine merchant based in Puerta Santa Maria. From 1868 until 1874, he was educated at the Oratory School in Edgbaston and then in London and at the University of Louvain in Belgium. He joined the community of the Birmingham Oratory in 1877 and was ordained a priest on March 4, 1883.

He worked as church treasurer, sang in the choir, and heard confessions for both the local English- and Spanish-speaking congregants. But his main work was in parish life and with the local mission schools. He was a natural teacher and won the respect and affection of the boys he taught.

Although charismatic and clever, he was no intellectual and is remembered at the Birmingham Oratory today for his "many deeds of generous charity, for the brightness and kindness of his disposition and for his talent as a mimic."

It was while working with members of the parish that he encountered the Tolkien family and became a close and trusted friend of Mabel Tolkien. Life would have been far more difficult, if not impossible, for this widowed woman and her two young sons without his moral, emotional, and financial support.

In April 1904, Mabel was hospitalized with diabetes, and Tolkien and his brother Hilary were sent away to relatives. Father Francis arranged that Mabel and her sons live in small cottage on property owned by the oratory in the nearby countryside. Father Francis was a regular visitor, delighting the boys with his stories and with his pipe smoking. This may well have been the beginning of Tolkien's love affair with the pipe.

After Mabel's death, Father Francis became the Tolkien boys' legal guardian. He was a loving and generous man, helping them financially with income from the family sherry business. He found them accommodation, but they spent much of their time at the oratory, serving at Mass, taking meals, enjoying the company of Father Francis and the other priests.

Father Francis gave Tolkien the run of his library, including his books in Spanish. These, and the Welsh language knowledge of Father Francis, had a major influence on Tolkien's love of linguistics. He also took the boys on an annual vacation to Lyme Regis.

It was in a house found by Father Francis that Tolkien met and fell in love with Edith Bratt, yet once he found out about his ward's relationship with a girl three years his senior, living in the same house, he ordered Tolkien and Edith to break up and moved the boys to another home.

In 1913, however, when Tolkien told Father Francis that he now intended to marry Edith, the understanding priest gave his full blessing. The couple named their first child John Francis Reuel, after Father Francis, who also baptized the baby.

Father Francis died on June 11, 1935. In his will, he left one thousand pounds each to Tolkien and to Tolkien's brother Hilary.

MICHAEL COREN

Further Reading

Carpenter, Humphrey. *J.R.R. Tolkien: A Biography*. London: George Allen & Unwin, 1977.

See also **Education; Spanish Language; Tolkien, Arthur; Tolkien, Hilary; Tolkien, Mabel**

MORGOTH AND MELKOR

In *The Road to Middle-earth*, T.A. Shippey describes "the history of Genesis" as the "most obvious fact about the design of *The Silmarillion*." Shippey compares Tolkien's Creation myth with "a summary list of doctrines of the Fall of Man common to Milton, to St Augustine, and to the Church as a whole." Satan is, of course, a central figure in the story of the Fall of Man in *Genesis*.

Melkor, later known as Morgoth, is Middle-earth's equivalent of Lucifer, or Satan. Melkor is described by Tolkien as "the greatest of the Ainur" as Lucifer was the greatest of the archangels. Like Lucifer, Melkor is the embodiment of, and the primal perpetrator of, the sin of pride; like Lucifer he is intent on corrupting humanity for his own purposes. Melkor desired "to subdue to his will both Elves and Men, envying the gifts with which Ilúvatar promised to endow them; and he wished himself to have subjects and servants, and to be called Lord, and to be master over other wills" (*S*, 18).

The biblical parallels become even more obvious when Tolkien describes the war between Melkor and Manwë, the latter of whom is clearly cast in the role of Lucifer's adversary, the archangel Michael. Manwë is "the brother of Melkor in the mind of Ilúvatar" and was "the chief instrument of the second theme that Ilúvatar had raised up against the discord of Melkor" (*S*, 21).

The link between Melkor and Lucifer is made most apparent in the linguistic connection between them. As a philologist, Tolkien employs language to synthesize his own Satan with his biblical archetype. The original spelling of Melkor, in the earliest drafts of the mythology, is Melko, which means "the Mighty One"; Melkor means "He who arises in Might"—"But that name he has forfeited; and the Noldor, who among the Elves suffered most from his malice, will not utter it, and they name him Morgoth, the Dark Enemy of the World" (*S*, 31). Similarly, Lucifer, brightest of the angels, means "Light Bringer," whereas the Jews named him Satan, which means "Enemy" in Hebrew. Linguistically, therefore, "Morgoth," "Satan," and "Enemy" share the same meaning. They are the same word in three different languages. "Morgoth" and "Satan" clearly represent the same primal "Enemy" of humanity. Tolkien's intention, both as a Christian and as a philologist, in identifying Melkor with Lucifer is plain enough.

In the earlier drafts of the mythology that predate the publication of *The Lord of the Rings*, Melko's role parallels that of the biblical Satan. He is the primal bringer of discord into Ilúvatar's Design, and he harbors a desire to have dominion in the world contrary to the will of Ilúvatar. In the later versions of the myth, the role of Melko, now known as Melkor, becomes more complex, itself a reflection of Tolkien's increasing concern with theological intricacy, yet Melko-Melkor-Morgoth always remains essentially a depiction of Satan.

Taking his inspiration, perhaps, from the Book of Isaiah ("Thy pomp is brought down to the grave, and the noise of thy viols: the worm is spread under thee, and the worms cover thee. How art thou fallen from heaven, O Lucifer, son of the morning"; Isa. 14:11–12), Tolkien says of Melkor: "From splendour he fell through arrogance to contempt for all things save himself, a spirit wasteful and pitiless ... He began with the desire of Light, but when he could not possess it for himself alone, he descended through fire and wrath into a great burning, down into Darkness" (*S*, 31).

Shortly after this description of Melkor, Tolkien introduces Sauron, the Enemy in *The Lord of the Rings*. Sauron is described as a "spirit" and as the "greatest" of Melkor's, alias Morgoth's, servants: "But in after years he rose like a shadow of Morgoth and a ghost of his malice, and walked behind him on the same ruinous path down into the Void" (*S*, 32). This brief depiction of Sauron in *The Silmarillion* unveils the evil power in *The Lord of the Rings* as being directly connected to Tolkien's Satan, rendering implausible a nontheistic interpretation of the book's deepest moral meaning.

In *Morgoth's Ring*, volume 10 of *The History of Middle-earth*, Tolkien is preoccupied with the figure of Melkor-Morgoth. "Above all," wrote Christopher Tolkien in his foreword to *Morgoth's Ring*, "the power and significance of Melkor-Morgoth ... was enlarged to become the ground and source of the corruption of Arda" (*Morgoth*, viii-ix). Whereas Sauron's infernal power was concentrated in the One Ring, Morgoth's far greater diabolic power was dispersed into the very matter of Arda itself: "the whole of Middle-earth was *Morgoth's Ring*" (*Morgoth*, ix). The pride of Melkor-Morgoth had "marred" the whole of material Creation just as, according to the Christian doctrine of the Fall, the pride of Lucifer-Satan had marred the very fabric of the world.

If, however, the Shadow of Morgoth had fallen across the face of Middle-earth, marring it terribly, Tolkien asserts with Christian hope that the final victory would never belong to Morgoth. "Above all shadows rides the Sun," Samwise Gamgee had affirmed in the Tower of Cirith Ungol, (*RK*, VI, i, 185) and Tolkien uses the childlike wisdom of the hobbit to express deep theological truths. The sun is a metaphor for Ilúvatar, the All-Father, God Himself, and the shadows a metaphor for evil. The final triumph of Good, that is, God, and the ultimate defeat of Evil, was spelled out by Ilúvatar himself in the Ainulindalë, at the very beginning of Creation. Referring to Melkor's introduction of disharmony into the Music of the Ainur, Ilúvatar warned his Enemy of the ultimate futility of his rebellion: "And thou, Melkor, shalt see that no theme may be played that hath not its uttermost source in me, nor can any alter the music in my despite. For he that attempteth this shall prove but mine instrument in the devising of things more wonderful, which he himself had not imagined" (*S*, 17). Eventually, even the evil will of Melkor will understand that all its evil actions have been the unwitting servant of unimaginable Providence. "And thou, Melkor, wilt discover all the secret thoughts of thy mind, and wilt perceive that they are but a part of the whole and tributary to its glory" (*S*, 17). Sauron is mighty, and Melkor is mightier still, but, as Frodo exclaimed at the Cross-roads, "They cannot conquer forever!" (*TT*, IV, vii, 311)

JOSEPH PEARCE

Further Reading

Birzer, Bradley J. *J.R.R. Tolkien's Sanctifying Myth*. Wilmington, DE: ISI Books, 2002.

Caldecott, Stratford. *Secret Fire: The Spiritual Vision of J.R.R. Tolkien*. London: Darton, Longman & Todd, 2003.

Pearce, Joseph. *Tolkien: Man and Myth*. London: HarperCollins, 1998.

———, ed. *Tolkien: A Celebration*. London: HarperCollins, 1999.

Purtill, Richard. *J.R.R. Tolkien: Myth, Morality and Religion*. San Francisco, CA: Harper & Row, 1984.

See also **Angels; Fall of Man; Hell; Incarnation; Redemption**

MORGOTH'S RING

Morgoth's Ring, volume 10 of the *History of Middle-earth*, forms, with *The War of the Jewels*, a subset entitled "The Later Silmarillion" containing Tolkien's last, unfinished narrative work on his mythological cycle. The texts in *Morgoth* date from between 1948 and 1959 and deal primarily with the early chronology of the Elves and Valar before the exile of the Noldor to Middle-earth. The title was chosen by Christopher Tolkien (CT) as representative of the daring revisions his father considered during this period, one of which was to drastically increase the power and reach of Morgoth's evil (*Morgoth*, ix, 400).

Morgoth is divided into five parts: the last drafts of the "Ainulindalë" creation myth; "The Annals of Aman," which "speak of the coming of the Valar to Arda" (*Morgoth*, 48); the first half of the post–*Lord of the Rings* "Later Silmarillion" drafts; a key dialogue entitled "Athrabeth Finrod ah Andreth"; and a collection of informal philosophical, theological, and cosmological essays gathered by CT under the heading "Myths Transformed."

The "Annals" and the "Quenta" are by far the longest and most detailed works in the book. CT highlights their "curious relationship" (*Morgoth*, ix, 290), showing that in places entire passages were lifted almost word-for-word from the "Annals" and used in the "Quenta." Notable introductions from *The Lord of the Rings* include the presence of Galadriel as a "tall and valiant" leader of the Noldor (*Morgoth*, 112) and the usage of names such as "Eriador" and the "Anduin," which originate in *The Lord of the Rings*. The "Later Quenta Silmarillion" was a major source for the published *Silmarillion* and resembles it closely, though CT was forced to use other texts (including the "Annals of Aman") where the "Quenta" was lacking in sufficient detail. Only the first half of the "Quenta" revisions are included in *Morgoth's Rings*; the second part can be found in *The War of the Jewels*.

"The Annals of Aman" record that the Orcs (or, as Tolkien later decided to spell it, "orkor") were corrupted Elves, twisted by Morgoth into grotesque parodies of their kin (*Morgoth*, 72–74, 78). Tolkien, a devout Catholic, later found difficulty with the idea of irredeemably corrupt Elves, and an essay in "Myths Transformed" argues that, since only Eru has the power and authority to create wholly new life, the Orcs must in fact have been "beasts of humanized shape" made to speak by Morgoth (*Morgoth*, 410). Characteristically, Tolkien approaches the matter as if he were an outside observer, sifting the evidence and alternately formulating and dismissing theories—though he reaches no final conclusion. Another essay in "Myths Transformed" shows the clear influence of *The Lord of the Rings*. The author compares Morgoth and Sauron, explaining that while the former was "the greatest power under Eru" (*Morgoth*, 390), the latter was "wiser" in that his plans were more focused and less brutal. In a passage

linking their natures, the author tells us that "the whole of Middle-earth was Morgoth's Ring"; as Sauron concentrated his malice into his own Ring, so Morgoth disseminated his into the whole world—thereby weakening himself and marring the Earth forever (*Morgoth*, ix, 400).

"Laws and Customs among the Eldar" provide information about gender roles and domestic practices among the Elves, from child-naming rituals to marriage ceremonies. Tolkien also comments on the nature of Elvish immortality, describing the "fading" of the Elves in latter days as the gradual "consumption" of the Elvish "hröa" or body by the "fëa" or spirit, until the former becomes "a mere memory" held by the latter (*Morgoth*, 219). Finally, "Laws and Customs" expands upon the story of Finwë and his wife Miriel, describing the debate among the Valar over whether Finwë should be permitted to remarry after her death. The question is complicated by the Elvish ability to reincarnate, and the resulting dialogue offers a unique insight into some of the thornier practicalities of immortality in Tolkien's universe.

The "Athrabeth Finrod ah Andreth," called "one of the great conversations in Tolkien's work" (Bratman, 77), is an emotional exchange between Beren's great-aunt and the Elvish king Finrod Felagund. Through the voice of the wise woman Andreth, Tolkien explores the myths held by Men in his universe. Key among these is the belief that they were once "immortal" like the Elves and became short-lived "through the malice of the Lord of Darkness whom they do not name" (*Morgoth*, 309). An appended story, "The Tale of Adanel," describes a version of the Fall of Men set in the earliest times "before any yet had died" (*Morgoth*, 345). This is clearly Tolkien's myth of Original Sin, only hinted at elsewhere in his works, describing how Men were corrupted into the worship of Morgoth and thereby tainted forever.

At some point during the writing of *The Lord of the Rings,* Tolkien became unsatisfied with his "Ainulindalë" creation myth, considering its "flat earth" mythology—with the sun as a faded remnant of the light of the mythic Trees—too unscientific to be credible in the modern age. In an experimental revision of 1948, therefore, he wrote a draft featuring a sun that predates the Trees, a moon that resembles our own, and an earth that was always round and never "bent" into its current form. Yet much of the "Silmarillion" was rooted in the older cosmology; even the race name "Eldar" translates as "Star-folk," a reference to the first awakening of the Elves before the moon was made (*Jewels*, 360). An alteration to the mythology would demand a revision of not only the Elvish histories, but the whole Elvish lexicon. Tolkien worked on a number of rationalizations and revisions (*Morgoth*, 385–86), but ultimately the "devastating surgery" (*Morgoth*, 383) required to make the mythology conform to real world physics was simply too damaging to its beauty and power. In a letter of 1951 to a potential publisher, Tolkien mentions only the earlier myth (*Letters*, 143), and even though he later maintained that "you can't expect people to believe in a flat earth any more" (Hammond, 27), it was the more beautiful and coherent, if less credible, "flat world" cosmology that his son chose to include in the *Silmarillion*.

Morgoth's Ring is a key volume of the *History of Middle-earth*. More than just the final drafts and notes for the first half of the *Silmarillion*, it contains some of Tolkien's most daring and speculative work. While much of this material was eventually rejected, either by Tolkien himself or during the compilation of the *Silmarillion*, *Morgoth's Ring* remains both an intriguing glimpse into just how different the *Silmarillion* may have been had Tolkien managed to complete it during his lifetime, and a unique lesson in the difficulties of creating a coherent secondary world.

MATTHEW FENSOME

Further Reading

Bratman, David. "The Literary Value of The History of Middle-earth." In *Tolkien's Legendarium: Essays on the History of Middle-earth*, edited by Verlyn Flieger and Carl F. Hostetter. Westport, CT: Greenwood Press, 2000.

Hammond, Wayne G., "'A Continuing and Evolving Creation': Distractions in the Later History of Middle-earth." In *Tolkien's Legendarium: Essays on the History of Middle-earth*, edited by Verlyn Flieger and Carl F. Hostetter. Westport, CT: Greenwood Press: 2000.

See also **Astronomy and Cosmology, Middle-earth; Elves; Elves: Reincarnation of; Finwë and Miriel; Good and Evil;** *History of Middle-earth*: **Overview; Immortality;** *Lembas*; **Maiar; Morgoth and Melkor; Resurrection; Tolkien, Christopher; Valar; War of the Jewels**

MORIA

Moria (Sindarin for "black chasm") was the Elvish name of Khazad-dûm, also called the Dwarrowdelf: a vast underground realm beneath the Misty Mountains. Founded in the First Age by Durin, eldest of the Seven Fathers of the Dwarves, Moria became the most famous of all Dwarf kingdoms. It endured through the Dark Years and throughout the Second Age was "the major realm of the Dwarves" (*Letters*, 152). Though it held countless valuable gems and veins of precious ore, the foundation of its wealth was *mithril*. Also known as Moria-silver, or true-silver, mithril had ten times the value of gold and could only be found in Moria.

The realm of Moria was the most significant place in Middle-earth where Dwarves and Elves enjoyed lasting peace. Its western gates at Hollin were marked with the emblem of Durin as well as the Tree of the High Elves and the Star of the House of Fëanor. The doors were designed to allow Elves to enter Moria during "happier days, when there was still close friendship at times between folk of different races" (*FR*, II, iv, 316). They were usually left open, and when closed, Elves needed only speak the word "friend" in their own tongue to open them. In SA 1697, Elrond was nearly overwhelmed in Sauron's assault on Eriador, and was rescued by the Dwarves of Khazad-dûm who assaulted Sauron's army from the rear (*UT*, 238).

By the end of the Third Age, however, Khazad-dûm had become Moria, the Black Pit: a legendary place of great dread. Durin's kingdom had long ago been destroyed. Thus, Boromir speaks of it as "a name of ill omen" and "to the hobbits it was a legend of vague fear" (*FR*, II, iv, 309). When, as an alternative to crossing Caradhras, Gandalf refers to a "dark and secret way" (later revealed to be Moria), even Aragorn is "filled with dismay" and begs Gandalf not even to speak of it with the others (*FR*, II, iii, 300); Aragorn's memory of the place is "very evil" (*FR*, II, iv, 310).

Though the rumors associated with Moria had become dark and malevolent, the reason for the dread was not fully known even to Gandalf until the Fellowship encountered its source. Moria had become inhabited by a Balrog of Morgoth, one of the Valaraukar: an ancient demon that was one of the fiercest and most fell enemies of the Elves; one of the "older and fouler things . . . in the deep places of the world" that Gandalf guessed at (*FR*, II, iv, 323). Buried in the roots of the mountains and released by the delving of the Dwarves in the middle of the Third Age, the Balrog destroyed Khazad-dûm and earned the title Durin's Bane. Durin's line never failed, and he was said to be Deathless. "Five times an heir was born in his House so like to his Forefather that he received the name of Durin." The Durin slain by the Balrog was the sixth of that name, but would have been held by many Dwarves to be the same person (*RK*, Appendix A, 353–54).

The first reference to Moria in Tolkien's published works is in the opening chapter of *The Hobbit*, when Thorin speaks of paying back the goblins of Moria. At the time, Tolkien himself had no idea what the Mines of Moria were, other than a name that he borrowed from a Scandinavian tale translated by Dasent; though he didn't like the tale itself, he liked the "sound-sequence" and the fact that Moria alliterated with mines (*Letters*, 384). The reader learns nothing else about Moria until *The Lord of the Rings*. At the Council of Elrond, the name appears when Glóin speaks longingly of "the mighty works of our fathers that are called in our own tongue Khazad-dûm." The sense of something wonderful is further heightened when the Dwarf adds with a sigh, "Moria! Moria! Wonder of the Northern world!" A moment later, however, the wonder associated with the name is mediated when Glóin speaks of the "nameless fear" that was awakened there by the overly deep delving of his people. Gimli explains that "of old it was not darksome, but full of light and splendour" (*FR*, II, iv, 329). For Dwarves, then, the name Moria awakens simultaneously both "dread" and "longing" (*FR*, II, ii, 253).

Thus, as with the tragic tales of Fëanor or the Steward Denethor, the beauty, peace, and grandeur of the ancient kingdom of Moria make later history, and especially its downfall due to the lust of the Dwarves, all the more tragic and poignant. As Gandalf explains, mithril was not only the foundation for the wealth of Moria, but "so also it was their destruction; they delved too greedily and too deep" (*FR*, II, iv, 331). That greed would resurface at the end of the Third Age when Balin "listened to whispers" (initiated perhaps from Sauron), and against the will of King Dain returned to Moria and died in his attempt to reestablish the kingdom (*FR*, II, ii, 254).

A final note should be made regarding the symbolic importance of Moria. It has been noted by various scholars that Tolkien's work is full of caves, tunnels, and underground kingdoms, and that many significant events occur in these places. These include the barrows, the Paths of the Dead, the tunnels of Gollum, the Glittering Caves of Aglarond, Menegroth, Nargothrond, Angband, and Henneth Annûn to name only a few. They can be either tombs or wombs: symbols of death or of fertility and life.

A good case can be made that Moria is the most significant of them all and may function as a symbol of both womb and tomb. It is in Moria that Gandalf falls. Yet it is from out of Moria that Gandalf returns to life with his power greatly enhanced. It is also in Moria that Aragorn comes into his own as leader of the company. Tolkien also begins and ends the journey through Moria in *The Fellowship of the Rings* with significant bodies of water representing death and life. As Hugh Keenan notes: In the "journey through the tunnels of Moria . . . we find two contrasting lakes. The one before the entrance is dark, loathsome, and artificial, a product of the evil within.

. . . On the other side of Moria lies a beautiful, natural, life-giving lake of Mirrormere." This water imagery suggests that for the fellowship, the experience in Moria is a baptism—the central Christian symbol of passage through death to life.

MATTHEW DICKERSON

Further Reading

Keenan, Hugh T. "The Appeal of *The Lord of the Rings*: A Struggle for Life." In *J.R.R. Tolkien's The Lord of the Rings: Modern Critical Interpretations*, edited by Harold Bloom, 3–15. Philadelphia: Chelsea House Publishers, 2000.

See also **Dwarves; Gandalf; Gimli;** *Mithril*

MORRIS, WILLIAM

The breadth of William Morris's (1834–96) art is amazing. He designed stained glass, wallpaper, and typographic fonts. He wrote poetry and epics, translated Icelandic sagas, and founded Kelmscott Press. His edition of *The Canterbury Tales* is considered one of the most beautiful books ever printed. And like Tolkien, he studied at Exeter College, Oxford.

Although Tolkien might not have appreciated Morris's role in the early socialist movement, in the arts the two had much in common. Morris was active in the British Arts and Crafts movement, restoring the role of craftsman in architecture, decorative arts, and cabinetmaking. Furniture was to be individually built, rather than by factory workers making only a small part of a table or chair. You see that same craftsmanship in how the Elves of Middle-earth work precious metals, how the Dwarves shape stone, and even in the love hobbits have for their locally brewed beer. Morris and Tolkien agreed that we are on this earth to create beauty.

It was through his writings, however, that Morris had his greatest impact on Tolkien, who acknowledged that debt in letters that span forty-four years. The first letter in *The Letters of J.R.R. Tolkien* mentions Morris's influence. Writing in October 1914 to his wife-to-be, Tolkien said, "Amongst other work I am trying to turn one of the stories [of the Finnish *Kalevala*]—which is really a great story and most tragic—into a short story somewhat on the lines of Morris' romances with chunks of poetry in between."

Tolkien never completed that rewrite of the *Kalevala*'s "The Story of Kullervo," although it resembles *The Silmarillion*'s tale of Túrin Turambar. The latter involves a quest in which Turambar sets out, despite great peril, to "seek the dragon on the borders of the land." The are also quests in Morris'

The Wood Beyond the World and *The Well at the World's End.*

Tolkien recognized the link between that early tale and all that followed. In a June 7, 1955, letter to W.H. Auden, he (grudgingly) adopted Auden's own term for *The Lord of the Rings,* "trilogy," and wrote, "But the beginning of the legendarium, of which the Trilogy is a part (the conclusion), was an attempt to reorganize some of the *Kalevala,* especially the tale of Kullervo the hapless, into a form of my own." Tolkien's Middle-earth corpus thus began with a Morris-like reworking the *Kalevala,* turning an ancient epic into a story more like a modern novel. (Although Tolkien preferred to call it a "heroic romance," in an October 1971 letter.)

The first of such tales to get a public hearing was "The Fall of Gondolin," which, Tolkien told Auden, he "had the cheek to read to the Exeter College Essay Club in 1918." An endnote in *Letters* dates that reading to March 10, 1920. The club minutes note that Tolkien had written "in the manner of such typical romantics as William Morris, George Macdonald, de la Motte Fouqué, etc."

Forty years later, in a letter written to L.W. Forster at the end of 1960, Tolkien was specific about his debt to Morris. He noted that the Second World War had not influenced the basic plot of *The Lord of the Rings.* Turning to the First World War, he limited the influence to his own experiences after the Battle of the Somme on the imagery of the Dead Marshes and the blasted landscape around Morannon. In contrast to two real wars, the book's plot and unfolding, he wrote, "owe more to William Morris and his Huns and Romans, as in *The House of the Wolfings* or *The Roots of the Mountains.*"

To understand how Morris's style influenced Tolkien, we can turn to an essay on Morris that C.S. Lewis wrote for *Rehabilitations* (1939). The attacks Lewis saw literary circles making on Morris, a "false medievalism," a "poetry of escape," and stories that are "mere tapestries," are not that different from present-day attacks on Tolkien. Yet Lewis noted that "even the sternest theories of literature cannot permanently suppress an author who is so obstinately pleasurable."

Tolkien invented languages for his imaginary world. So did Morris, although his was a dialect of English that, Lewis notes, "has never at any period been spoken in England." There is also the "matter-of-factness" of both as they describe scenery. What Lewis said of Morris applies equally well to Tolkien: "Other stories have only scenery: his have geography. He is not concerned with 'painting' landscapes; he tells you the lie of the land, and then you paint the landscapes for yourself."

There's also the longing both felt for immortality. In Morris, Lewis wrote, it "is as wild, as piercing, as orgiastic and heart-breaking as his presentations of sexual love are simple, sensuous and unimpassioned." Yet that feeling was balanced by a contrary one, "that such desire is not wholly innocent, that the world of mortality is more than enough for our allegiance." Compare that to the draft of a 1956 Tolkien letter to Joanna de Bortadano. "Death and Immortality," he wrote, was the real theme of *The Lord of the Rings,* "the mystery of the love of the world in the hearts of a race 'doomed' to leave and seemingly lose it; the anguish in the hearts of a race 'doomed' not to leave it, until its whole evil-aroused story is complete."

In their depictions of romantic love, however, the two could not be more different. "Morris," Lewis wrote, "does not deal much in world-without-end fidelities, and his heroes are seldom so enamoured with one damsel that they are quite indifferent to the beauty of others." Indeed, in many of his tales, Morris heroes often seem so smitten with fair damsels they have difficulty focusing on great deeds and noble quests. Contrast that to Tolkien's Aragorn, who waited sixty-eight years to marry Arwen. One reason for the oft-mentioned lack of romance in *The Lord of the Rings* may have been Tolkien's desire to distance himself of Morris in that area.

The House of the Wolfings

At the Council of Elrond, to save Middle-earth Frodo must choose to take the Ring to Mordor, even though that may mean his death. In Morris's *The House of the Wolfings* (1888), Thiodolf must make a similar choice about a magical hauberk (chain mail coat). In both, the plot hinges on making the right choice about a powerful magical object.

In a 1988 letter, Morris noted that his tale of "Gothic tribes on their way through Middle Europe, and their first meeting with the Romans in war," was intended to "illustrate the melting of the individual into the society of tribes." Like the evil in Tolkien's Ring that makes dangerous its full use, Thiodofl concluded that a curse on the hauberk meant "either for the sake of the folk I will not wear the gift and the curse, and I shall die in great glory . . . or else for thy sake [the beautiful goddess Wood-Sun] I shall bear it and live, and the House may live or die as may be."

There is a forest in Morris's tale called Mirkwood, although it's not as dark and mysterious as Tolkien's, and a coat of Dwarf-made mail more powerful than that Bilbo gave Frodo. In chapter 2, a messenger brings the Wolfings a war arrow as a sign of impending war.

The Roots of the Mountains

The Roots of the Mountains (1889) involves the same Germanic tribe as *The House of the Wolfings* but is set hundreds of years later in the foothills of a great mountain chain. This time the foe is not the civilized Romans but the cruel and Orc-like Dusky Men (Huns). As in the former tale, there is a conflict between the desires of an individual, the handsome Gold-mane, and the needs of his people. Like Aragorn, Gold-mane is wooed by two women, the unfortunately named Bride, a member of his tribe, and the mysterious Sun-beam, who has been chosen to seduce Gold-mane into protecting her tiny tribe against the Dusky Men. Imagine Tolkien writing of an Éowyn who attempts to win a peaceable Aragron away from Arwen and into war with Sauron.

The Wood beyond the World

Quests are stories of people who set out, often through mysterious forests and lofty mountains, to reach an exotic locale and achieve a great goal. In *The Hobbit*, Bilbo and the Dwarves bound for the Lonely Mountain and dragon gold. In *The Lord of the Rings*, Frodo must journey to Mount Doom and destroy the Ring.

In Morris's *The Wood Beyond the World* (1894), Walter, the son of a wealthy merchant, flees an unhappy marriage, and while traveling repeatedly sees a stately woman, a Dwarf, and a pretty slave maiden. The Maid, who is a captive in the Wood Beyond the World, is the focus of his quest.

The Well at the World's End

The Well at the World's End (1896) is the best-known of Morris's fantasy tales. Ralph, one of four princes in a small kingdom, leaves home looking for adventure and ends up seeking the Well at the World's End, said to bestow good fortune and a long life, with a pretty maiden. The story has geography as rich as that of Tolkien and deals with the same question that haunts Tolkien's Elves, is a much-prolonged life a blessing or a curse?

The similarities to *The Lord of the Rings* do not seem accidental. There is a horse named Silverfax, although less important than Shadowfax. There is a major character named Gandolf, although he is the evil Lord of Utterbol, rather than Gandalf the good wizard. And finally, some shepherds hold a folkmoot to decide on war plans much like Tolkien's Ents at their Entmoot.

Michael W. Perry

Further Reading

Lewis, C.S. *Rehabilitations*. Oxford: Oxford University Press, 1939.

Morris, William. Among the works that influenced Tolkien are *The House of the Wolfings* (1888), *The Roots of the Mountains* (1889), *The Wood Beyond the World* (1894), and *The World at the Well's End* (1896). For understanding Morris, *The Collected Works of William Morris*, edited by his daughter May Morris, is useful. For reading, any modern edition will do.

See also **Literary Influences, Nineteenth and Twentieth Century; Mythology for England; Northern Courage; Quest Narrative**

MOUNTAINS

Without any doubt, mountains are a major motif in Tolkien's fictional world. As well as being a very prominent physical feature of the geography of Middle-earth, they often have a strong symbolic connotation. Mountains can perform different functions: like walls, they defend and hide places as different as the Elvish city of Gondolin and Mordor; they act as barriers that must be crossed in order to reach a destination; or, as in the case of the Lonely Mountain in *The Hobbit* and Mount Doom in *The Lord of the Rings*, they may themselves be the final aim of a quest. In several instances, mountains appear as the instruments of a sort of "rite of passage," which does not leave any of the characters unchanged.

Among the numerous mountain ranges of Middle-earth, the Misty Mountains surely take pride of place. As Anderson points out, they were inspired by Tolkien's 1911 trip to Switzerland, which he related to his son Michael (*Letters*, 391–92). In both *The Hobbit* and *The Lord of the Rings*, the attempts of the two companies to cross this formidable barrier bring about a series of events that are crucial to the development of both stories: Bilbo finds the Ring in an underground cave, while Gandalf sacrifices his life in his fight with the Balrog in order to save the rest of the Fellowship.

There are also isolated mountain peaks that are of paramount importance in Tolkien's subcreation. Not only are the Lonely Mountain and Mount Doom reached through a long and difficult journey, but they are extremely dangerous in themselves. As a matter of fact, the greatest dangers are often posed by the creatures that dwell inside or beneath the mountains, such as Gollum, Smaug, the Balrog, Shelob, and the Dead Men of Dunharrow. Moreover, as do every other natural feature in Tolkien's world, mountains often give the impression of having a life of their own; indeed, in at least one remarkable case a mountain acts as a sentient being: Caradhras becomes a manifestation of Wrathful nature, which, according to Brisbois, does not distinguish between the good and the bad, therefore reacting violently to the Fellowship's attempted crossing.

Mountains can also have definite religious implications, as demonstrated by their role in many of the world's mythologies. In *The Silmarillion*, the peak of Taniquetil, strongly reminiscent of the Greek Mount Olympus, is the abode of the two highest Valar, Manwë and his spouse Varda. Similarly, the mountain of Meneltarma, in the center of the island of Númenor, is a hallowed place, the only one in Middle-earth that is explicitly associated with some sort of religious ritual.

Mountains play an essential role even in one of Tolkien's shorter works of fiction, "Leaf by Niggle." They first appear as the background of the protagonist's unfinished painting of a Tree, which he must complete before he is left free to reach the mountains. Here, as Kocher maintains, the mountains represent a higher stage of spiritual growth, an image of Paradise that Niggle cannot attain before having spent a period of penance in Purgatory.

MARIA RAFFAELLA BENVENUTO

Further Reading

Anderson, Douglas E, ed. *The Annotated Hobbit*. Rev. and expanded ed. London: HarperCollins, 2002.

Brisbois, Michael J. "Tolkien's Imaginary Nature: An Analysis of the Structure of Middle-earth." In *Tolkien Studies*, 2 (2005): 197–216.

Burns, Marjorie. *Perilous Realms: Celtic and Norse in Tolkien's Middle-earth*. Toronto: University of Toronto Press, 2005.

Fonstadt, Karen Wynn. *The Atlas of Middle-earth*. Boston, MA: Houghton Mifflin, 1991.

Kocher, Paul. *Master of Middle-earth: The Achievement of J.R.R. Tolkien*. London: Pimlico, 2002.

Tolkien, J.R.R. "Leaf by Niggle." In *Tales from the Perilous Realm*, 119–44. London, HarperCollins, 2002.

See also **Lonely Mountain (Erebor); Middle-earth; Misty Mountains; Mordor; Nature; Paradise; Taniquetil; "Tree and Leaf"**

MR. BLISS

As the sole publication of *Mr. Bliss* (1982) is in effect a facsimile of the MS at Marquette (which was purchased with the MSS of *The Hobbit*, *The Lord of the Rings*, and *Farmer Giles*), it should be one of the best known of Tolkien's MSS. Nevertheless, it may be worth noting that the MS is comprised of four signatures, the size of the unfolded leaves being 39.6 cm by 12.2 cm, making each individual page approximately 19.4 cm by 12.2 cm. The wrapper (front and back covers) was once a single piece measuring 41 cm by 13 cm, heavy stock dark green papers. The title is written in the center of the front cover in white water-color and surrounded by a fancy gilded design (now faded).

Christopher Tolkien believes that the handwriting of the MS suggests a date in the 1930s, but the story as we have it likely has its origins in 1928 (before Priscilla was born) in a toy car belonging to Christopher—as *Roverandom* owes its origin to Michael's toy dog. The three bears in *Mr. Bliss* are the three bears belonging to John, Michael, and Christopher, the names—Archie, Teddy, and Bruno—being those given by the boys to their bears.

Mr. Bliss was one of the three stories (with *Farmer Giles* and *Roverandom*) originally to have been published as a kind of sequel to *The Hobbit*—before *The Hobbit* (so to speak) "took off" and there was a premium on the next book's being a genuine sequel (as with *The Lord of the Rings*). The book originally was to have been printed in Austria, but the Anschluss in 1938 would have rendered that impracticable, even if the projected cost had not in fact been prohibitive. In the 1970s, the Tolkien family was apparently unaware that the MS of *Mr. Bliss* had been sold to Marquette. A proposal from an independent scholar to publish from the MS called their attention to it, and the facsimile edition was duly published in 1984 by Allen & Unwin and Houghton Mifflin.

"Mr. Bliss's first outing in his new motor car, shared with several friends, bears, dogs, and a donkey, though not the Girabbit, proves to be unconventional, though not inexpensive" (summary of *Mr. Bliss* on the reverse of the title page). This introduces one of Tolkien's great humorous creations, the Girabbit "(which he kept in the garden but its head often looked in at the bedroom windows)." The name more or less explains itself—rabbit's head and cotton tail, but giraffe's body and hooves (on rabbit legs) and especially neck—though it does not itself tell us (as Tolkien does) that "all days were fine to him for his skin was made of mackintosh, and he had made a deep deep hole in the ground, and he was blind, so he never knew whether the sun was shining or not."

When Mr. Bliss buys his bright yellow car for five shillings, with giant red wheels six pence more, he leaves his bicycle as a deposit (it has no pedals being used only for riding downhill), goes to visit the Dorkinses, and on the way runs into Mr. Day and his wheelbarrow of cabbages and Mrs. Knight and her donkey cart full of bananas. He loads the car with the bananas and cabbages and Mr. Day and Mrs. Knight, with the pony tied on behind, and sets off on the road through the forest.

In the forest, they are stopped by the three bears—two of whom take the bananas and cabbages off to their house (on the donkey's back)—and when they come back (with the donkey), they all get in the car, except the donkey, which is tied back on behind. On the way up the hill, all goes well (though slowly), but on the way down Mr. Bliss is so crowded he cannot work the brakes; the car plows into the Dorkinses' garden wall at the bottom of the hill; the donkey somersaults into the car, and the bears and Mr. Bliss and Day and Knight go over the wall and into the Dorkinses' garden, where the four fat Dorkinses are just sitting down to eat on a lovely carpet.

The bears eat up almost everything in the Dorkinses' garden; the Dorkinses set the dogs on them; they go back to their wood; the Dorkinses and Mr. Bliss and Day and Knight follow them in the car (drawn by the Dorkinses's ponies and Mrs. Knight's donkey), and after stopping at the Cross Roads Inn for tea (charged to Mr. Bliss's account) they arrive at Three Bears Wood after dark (and now the illustrations begin to take on the characteristic Tolkienian look we know from his illustrations to *The Hobbit*). The bears came out in the gloom, painted with phosphorescent paint, and Mr. Bliss "ran all night till morning." Everyone else had a wonderful time at the bears' house.

Meanwhile, Mr. Bliss ran all night without knowing where he was running to, picked up his silver bicycle from Mr. Binks (but still without paying for the car), hurried home to find the Girabbit (who hadn't been fed) having eaten its way through the dining-room ceiling into the best bedroom, and the bedroom ceiling into the attic, and up the attic chimney. The next day, the bears and Mr. Binks and Sgt. Boffin and Day and Knight come by for the money they say Mr. Bliss owes them. They see the Girabbit, and (in a scene very like one in Farmer Giles with Chrysophylax Dives) they are not nearly so brave after as before. But everything is sorted out (though the Girabbit runs away); Mr. Bliss gives the car to Knight and Day when they get married; he drives a donkey cart thereafter; the Girabbit comes back after having eaten the absent bears and Dorkinses out of house and home in their absence at the wedding; and everyone apparently lives more or less happily ever after. It may be worth noting that one of the crowd in the village when the bears and Dorkinses and Day and Knight come back with Mr. Bliss's car is Gaffer Gamgee.

JARED LOBDELL

Further Reading

Lobdell, Jared. "Mr. Bliss: Notes on the Manuscript and Story." In *Selections from the Marquette J.R.R. Tolkien Collection*. Milwaukee: Marquette University Library 1987.
Wayne Hammond, and Christina Scull. *J.R.R. Tolkien: Artist and Illustrator*. Boston, 1995.

See also **Children's Literature;** *Hobbit, The*; **Manuscripts by Tolkien**

"MS BODLEY 34: A RE-COLLATION OF A COLLATION"

Volume XIX of *Studia Neophilologica*, appearing in 1947, contained an article bound to catch Tolkien's interest: "A Collation of the *Katherine Group* (MS Bodley 34)" by Ragnar Furuskog, a postgraduate student in Stockholm.

Furuskog had briefly corresponded with Tolkien about plans for a thesis on the AB-language described in Tolkien's seminal "*Ancrene Wisse* and *Hali Meið-had*." For his article, Furuskog had compared editions of the Katherine Group (the five texts in the manuscript known as B, MS Bodley 34) with photostats of the original, remarking on 1,371 points. Notes mentioned Tolkien's above-mentioned study and "Some Contributions to Middle-English Lexicography." And the collated edition of the middle text, *Juliene* (or *Seinte Iuliene*), was that from 1936 by Simonne d'Ardenne, who had Tolkien as academic supervisor.

"MS. Bodley 34: A Re-collation of a Collation," in *Studia Neophilologica* the following year, is written by d'Ardenne and Tolkien together in response to Furuskog. (Tolkien also had personal exchange with him; he was at Oxford in 1948 and later.) They find his interpretation of letter-forms too mechanical and many times wrong: the variant shapes of letters in B "require not only attention but familiarity; they have led editors and collators into many misjudgments. In these respects Mr. Furuskog hardly seems to have improved on his predecessors." They list thirty examples of errors (one from Colborn's edition of *Hali Meiðhad* spuriously included) and in the course of their article mention sixteen more; they estimate that his genuine corrections are about as many as the cited mistakes.

"But with regard to *Juliene*, it has for some time been desirable to publish a list of corrigenda to the edition of Professor d'Ardenne"; they therefore cite fifteen correct observations among Furuskog's 157 remarks on that text (of which five are cited as errors). When the edition was republished in 1961 with ninety-six listed corrigenda, fifty-five accorded with Furuskog.

In the last part of their article, d'Ardenne and Tolkien themselves offer some corrections to previous readings of B. In *Sawles Warde*, where editors had read *ipþlen* and Furuskog *iwelen*, they read *rw?len* (agreeing, thus, with him that the second letter was a wyn); their separate article on this is announced.

Notably, they finally announce their own edition of the Katherine Group: "This edition begun long ago was interrupted in 1938–1945, when we were otherwise engaged. It is now, however, nearly completed on the basis of a careful review of the manuscript itself, and will, we hope, shortly be in print." That was saying too much. An edition of *Seinte Katerine*, the first of the texts, by d'Ardenne in collaboration with Eric Dobson appeared in 1981. Its preface explains that she "had hoped to have the collaboration of J.R.R. Tolkien, . . . but in the event (initially because of the war of 1939–45) he took no part in it." Her transcript of B had been published a few years earlier, in 1977 (in *Juliene*, validating 106 of Furuskog's 157 remarks), dedicated to the memory of Professor J.R.R. Tolkien.

BEREGOND, ANDERS STENSTRÖM

Further Reading

Colborn, A.F., ed. *Hali Meiðhad: Edited from MS. Bodley 34 and MS. Cotton Titus D. xviii.* Copenhagen: Einar Munksgaard, 1940.

d'Ardenne, S.R.T.O., and J.R.R. Tolkien. "MS. Bodley 34: A Re-collation of a Collation." *Studia Neophilologica.* 20, no. 1–2 (1948 [for 1947–48]): [65]–72.

d'Ardenne, S.R.T.O., ed. *Þe Liflade ant te Passiun of Seinte Iuliene.* EETS 248. London, New York, and Toronto: Oxford University Press, 1961 (for 1960). [Reproduced, with a list of corrigenda on p. xiii, from: *An Edition of Þe Liflade ant te Passiun of Seinte Iuliene.* Bibliothèque de la Faculté de Philosophie et Lettres de l'Université de Liège, fasc. LXIV. Liège: Faculté de Philosophie et Lettres; Paris: Droz, 1936.]

——— [initials printed as S.R.T.O.], ed. *The Katherine Group: Edited from MS. Bodley 34.* Bibliothèque de la Faculté de Philosophie et Lettres de l'Université de Liège, fasc. CCXV. Paris: Les Belles Lettres, 1977.

d'Ardenne, S.R.T.O., and E.J. Dobson, eds. *Seinte Katerine: Re-Edited from MS Bodley 34 and the Other Manuscripts.* EETS S.S. 7. Oxford: Oxford University Press, 1981.

Furuskog, Ragnar. "A Collation of the *Katherine Group* (MS Bodley 34)." *Studia Neophilologica* 19, no. 1–2 (1947 [for 1946–47]): [119]–66.

See also **AB Language;** *Ancrene Wisse*; **d'Ardenne, S.T.R.O.;** **"'*Ipþlen*' in** *Sawles Warde*"; **Katherine Group; Manuscripts, Medieval; Middle English**

MUSIC IN MIDDLE-EARTH

Tolkien's medieval educational background and Catholic religious knowledge would have exposed him to the importance of music as creational material in many of the existing world mythologies. Indeed, the concept of the "music of the spheres" was founded in ancient and classical philosophy by Plato and Aristotle, discussed and debated through early Christian writers up to the third-century pagan philosopher Plotinus and the neoclassical tradition, and finally codified and standardized by Boethius (c. AD 480–524) in the early sixth century. In his treatise *De institutione musica*, Boethius divided music into three specific kinds, in order of priority and importance: the music of the universe, human music (vocal), and instrumental music. The music of the universe can be seen in the harmony of the four elements, the four seasons, and in the movement of the celestial bodies (for a fuller explanation of the "music of the spheres" as a medieval concept and its conscious/subconscious use by Tolkien, see Eden).

In his early writings related to the construction of *The Silmarillion*, Tolkien incorporated a strong musical creational thread throughout his construction of Middle-earth. Not only does the *Ainulindalë* as the creation story for Middle-earth illustrate this, but the entire history of Middle-earth, from its creation all the way through *The Lord of the Rings* in the Third Age, follows the decay and descent of musical power that closely parallels Boethius's model of medieval cosmological music theory. In addition, *Ainulindalë* in particular brings to the fore Plotinus's neoclassical mindset in the idea of the One and the concepts related to thinking, being, and creating matter in the neoclassical tradition.

In his authorized biography of Tolkien, Humphrey Carpenter goes to great lengths to document the musical threads throughout Tolkien's early life. Tolkien's grandfather was a maker of pianos in Victorian England; his mother had musical talent and tried to pass it on to her sons; his wife was planning on a career as a classical pianist before their marriage, and even stayed with cousin Jenny Grove (related to Sir George Grove of *Grove's Dictionary of Music and Musicians* fame) in Warwick before Tolkien proposed to her; and Tolkien in his *Letters* stated that musical talent ran in his family, although those genes had not surfaced in him. It is indeed interesting that, despite Tolkien's absence of talent in music performance, that he so thoroughly and at some level of depth and substance, incorporated so many allusions to music and its power in his writings.

This is evident in no small part in his great creation story of Middle-earth, the *Ainulindalë,* or "Music of the Ainur," in *The Silmarillion.* Christopher Tolkien, in *The Book of Lost Tales,* volume 1, states that his father wrote "Music of the Ainur" between 1918–20, that it went through at least two major revisions and numerous rewrites, and that it is one of the few writings of his father's for which there is a surviving manuscript transmission from earliest draft to its final version. At first, Tolkien attributed the writing of *Ainulindalë* to the Elf musician Rumil, his earliest story known as the "Cottage of Lost Play" that would eventually transform into the *Silmarillion* material. In the final version of *Ainulindalë* that Christopher Tolkien provided in *The Silmarillion*, Ilúvatar and the Ainur are highly musical deities that learn and then compose music as part of their divine nature. Iluvatar then proposes themes of music to the Ainur, who then expound upon and improvise on the One's themes (both for good and for ill). In the end, the One shows the Ainur not only the vision of their musical improvisation, a world shaped by their melodies and harmonies, but is able to go even further by speaking the word of power and making the vision a reality, Eä, the World that Is. So Tolkien not only writes one of the greatest musical creation stories in human mythology in the *Ainulindalë*, but brings up even more questions regarding the One in his mythology and the One described in Plotinus's Neoplatonic theses; the concepts surrounding predestination, as well as good and evil, that this musical world creation ultimately bring into question; and the musical structure and indeed focus of the entire history of Middle-earth related to its basis and grounding in medieval cosmological musical theory.

Taking these points even further, the history of Middle-earth can be likened to a huge mythological parable of Boethius's three types of music. The power of the Elves in the First Age, both before and after their sojourn in Valinor, is based on their closeness and even creation through one of the major musical themes expounded by the Ainur at the creation of Middle-earth. The Elves themselves are musical beings, who awake in Middle-earth hearing the sound of water flowing, and thus are always and forever linked to water and the sea throughout their history. The power of song and music in Tolkien's mythology can be seen not only in the Elves, but in his references to musical power in earlier versions of *The Silmarillion*. *The Book of Lost Tales* material contains numerous references to music as a powerful historical and dramatic device that Tolkien incorporates to perfection, only some of which passes on into *The Silmarillion*. Almost all of these musical references are related to the Elves or the Ainur who descended to live on Middle-earth. These references include Tinfang Warble, the greatest minstrel on Middle-earth; earlier emanations of Dairon, an antagonist in the Beren and Luthien story, whose musical power is even more apparent in Tolkien's earlier writings related to this character; and names of songs that never appear in *The Silmarillion* (but do as occasional references in *The Hobbit* and *The Lord of the Rings*),

such as "Song of the Valar," "Song of Aryador," "Song of Light," "Song of the Sleeper," "Flight of the Gnomes," "Song of the Sun and Moon," "The Siege of Angband," "The Bowman's Friendship," "Song of the Great Bow," "the Song of Tuor for Ëarendel" (which is in three versions and five different texts), and "Light as Leaf on Linden Tree" (which Aragorn quotes from and sings on Weathertop).

These are only a few of the musical allusions that Tolkien appeared to use early in his writing career, either consciously or unconsciously, in the creation both figuratively and literally of Middle-earth. There is plenty of room for research in this area, especially examination of the decay and decline of the power of music, and thus of the Elves, as time and space move further away from Middle-earth's creation. Even in *The Hobbit* and *The Lord of the Rings*, this decline and decay can be seen as the Elves are still able to show glimpses of their ancient musical power throughout the dramas, though nothing compared to their earlier histories.

BRADFORD LEE EDEN

Further Reading

Eden, Brad. "The Music of the Spheres: Relationships between Tolkien's *Silmarillion* and Medieval Cosmological and Religious Theory." In *Tolkien the Medievalist*, edited by Jane Chance. New York: Routledge, 2003.

See also **Book of Lost Tales I**; **Eru**; *Silmarillion*; **Valar**

'MYTHOLOGY FOR ENGLAND'

Birth of the Term

A "mythology for England"—this must surely be the most-often cited quotation that Tolkien never actually said (at least, it is nowhere recorded that he ever said it). The genesis of the term occurs in Humphrey Carpenter's biography of Tolkien, where he refers explicitly to Tolkien's "desire to create a mythology *for England*" (italics in original). Carpenter goes on to say that Tolkien "had hinted of this during his undergraduate days when he wrote of the Finnish *Kalevala*: 'I would that we had more of it left—something of the same sort that belonged to the English.'" But how did Carpenter's term become the Tolkien misquote that it is today? Anders Stenström lays out a convincing reconstruction of how it may have happened, the key point being the misapplication of single quotation marks to the term in the biography's index (whether Carpenter's or the publisher's doing, we do not know). Because the term was shown in quotation marks, like the one other (legitimate) Tolkien quote referenced in the index, it was subsequently accepted by many as a bona fide quotation and not an invention.

But while Tolkien may never have put down this exact phrase, we can be relatively certain he would have accepted it, just as we can be sure that the creation of a so-called mythology for England was indeed one of his early goals. In 1956, he wrote to an unidentified Mr. Thompson,

> "having set myself a task . . . to restore to the English an epic tradition and present them with a mythology of their own." Even earlier, in his famous letter to Milton Waldman, penned in 1951, Tolkien wrote: "Do not laugh! But once upon a time (my crest has long since fallen) I had a mind to make a body of more or less connected legend, ranging from the large and cosmogonic, to the level of romantic fairy-story—the larger founded on the lesser in contact with the earth, the lesser drawing splendour from the vast backcloths—which I could dedicate simply to: to England; to my country."

Tales "Lost" and Found

Wishing to "restore to the English . . . a mythology of their own," then, how did Tolkien proceed? This is a complex and convoluted chronicle of borrowings, manipulations, tales (and languages) begun, abandoned, and often recommenced, which we cannot fully explore here. Interested readers are referred to the many worthwhile works at the close of this entry, where Tolkien's notion of a "mythology for England" is taken up as a critical commonplace by many of the foremost scholars writing today.

Though we cannot do full justice to the topic, we may at least revisit the major points in Tolkien's early efforts. It should be pointed out that Tolkien was not the first to attempt such a thing—that is, to assemble an integrated collection of legends with a distinctly nationalist identity; as Tom Shippey has explained, he was preceded by the German, Jacob Grimm, and the Norwegian Dane Nikolai Grundtvig, in the century prior to his own. And let us not forget the work of Elias Lönnrot, the father of the Finnish *Kalevala*, which had a profound impact on Tolkien at a highly formative time in his life (Carpenter indicates that Tolkien probably first read the *Kalevala* at nineteen).

Tolkien's desire to perform a service for England like the one that Lönnrot performed for Finland is a topic explored in detail by Anne C. Petty in her article, "Identifying England's Lönnrot." Here, let us just point out that "the *Kalevala* and the mythology of Middle-earth were both compiled and invented by their authors, each of whom created a fictional framework upon which to hang their tales." Tolkien himself acknowledges the influence the *Kalevala* had on him in several places, including the Waldman letter previously cited, where he explained, "I was from early days grieved by the poverty of my own beloved country: it had no stories of its own (bound up with its tongue and soil), not of the quality that I sought, and found (as an ingredient) in legends of other lands. There was Greek, and Celtic, and Romance, Germanic, Scandinavian, *and Finnish (which greatly affected me)*; but nothing English" (italics mine).

In addition to his impetus to follow in the footsteps of Lönnrot, Grimm, and Grundtvig, Tolkien drew on other sources besides the *Kalevala*. Perhaps most prominent among these, as Tom Shippey points out in his essay "Tolkien and Iceland: The Philology of Envy," is the Old Norse literary and mythological tradition. As Shippey writes, "Tolkien wanted English myths . . . and these did not exist. He refused to borrow from Celtic tradition, which he regarded as alien. What was he going to do? The answer is, of course, that he was going to borrow from Old Norse, which, for philological reasons, he did NOT regard as alien." Above and beyond the purely philological (and geographical) connections between England and Scandinavia, the Old Norse legends echoed what, for Tolkien, was a fundamental tenor of his own mythopoeic efforts: that "it is deeply sad, almost without hope." For Tolkien, this ingredient was essential in his construction of a pre-Christian world, steeped in nostalgia, doomed to pass away.

Informed by these two examples, the Old Norse and the Finnish mythic traditions, Tolkien set out to create his own "body of more or less connected legend" through which to fill in the myths and legends he supposed had genuinely been lost following the Norman conquest. Thus, his earliest tales, aptly called "the Lost Tales," establish a mythic framework in which England itself, physically, is the center. At the same time, he struggled to develop philological and structural links between his feigned mythology and the "genuine" mythologies of Europe. One of the best-known examples, of course, is the ingenious connection between Númenor (in his mythology) and Atlantis (in the Greek tradition). Verlyn Flieger, Carl Hostetter and Arden Smith, and Anne Petty have done excellent work in untangling the matter of the early tales, their relationship to Tolkien's later writings, and their role as the underpinnings of the so-called mythology for England.

The Critical Milieu

The question of whether Tolkien's attempts to create a mythology for England have been successful is a particularly thorny one. Michael D.C. Drout and Hilary Wynne sum up the nature of the problem very well when they point out that

> "Not only must critics analyze Tolkien's text, but they have to define what 'England' they are talking about (for which people, in what time period, for what level of generality, and so on) and this sociological problem itself is enormous. Furthermore, there is no agreed-upon definition of what 'mythology' means. For those who follow Tolkien's explicitly stated views it is one thing; but for, say, orthodox Marxists, it is entirely another. Critics thus end up arguing past each other, since one's mythologizing is positive and the other's negative."

Indeed, before one can answer whether Tolkien successfully constructed a mythology for England, one must confront other questions: why would Tolkien, a devout Roman Catholic, wish to construct a *mythology* at all? Why did Tolkien abandon his early attempts to center the mythology, literally, on the *real* island of England? And of course, how can we make sense of the tangled and inconsistent mythopoeisis left unresolved in the wake of Tolkien's death in 1973? His son and literary executor, Christopher Tolkien, has made a valiant effort to collate and comment on his father's previously unpublished papers, and other scholars have taken the work further, but there is still much work to be done before a critical consensus can assert final success or failure on this point—if indeed, the answer can ever be a final one.

JASON FISHER

Further Reading

Chance, Jane. *Tolkien and the Invention of Myth: A Reader.* Lexington: University Press of Kentucky, 2004.

———. *Tolkien's Art: A Mythology for England.* 2nd ed, rev. and expanded. Lexington, KY: University Press of Kentucky, 2001.

Curry, Patrick. *Defending Middle-earth: Tolkien: Myth and Modernity.* Edinburgh: Floris, 1997.

Day, David. *Tolkien's Ring.* London: HarperCollins, 1994.

Drout, Michael D.C., and Hilary Wynne. "Tom Shippey's J.R.R. Tolkien: Author of the Century and a Look Back at Tolkien Criticism since 1982." *Envoi* 9, no. 2 (Fall 2000): 111–13.

Fairburn, Elwin. "J.R.R. Tolkien: A Mythology for England." In *Tolkien: A Celebration: Collected Writings on a Literary Legacy*, edited by Joseph Pearce, 73–85. San Francisco, CA: Ignatius Press, 1999.

Flieger, Verlyn. "Do the Atlantis Story and Abandon Eriol-Saga." *Tolkien Studies* 1 (2004): 43–68.

———. *Interrupted Music: Tolkien's Making of a Mythology.* Kent, OH: Kent State University Press, 2005.

———. *Splintered Light: Logos and Language in Tolkien's World.* Kent, OH: Kent State University Press, 2002.

———. "The Footsteps of Ælfwine." In *Tolkien's Legendarium*, edited by Verlyn Flieger and Carl F. Hostetter, 183–98. Westport, CT: Greenwood, 2000.

Hostetter, Carl J., and Arden R. Smith. "A Mythology for England." In *Proceedings of the Tolkien Centenary Conference 1992 (Mallorn 33 / Mythlore 80)*, edited by Patricia Reynolds and Glen H. GoodKnight, 281–290.

Pearce, Joseph. *Tolkien: Man and Myth: A Literary Life.* London: HarperCollins, 1998.

Petty, Anne C. "Identifying England's Lönnrot." *Tolkien Studies* 1 (2004): 69–84.

———. *One Ring to Bind Them All: Tolkien's Mythology.* Updated ed. Tuscaloosa, AL: University of Alabama Press, 2002.

Purtill, Richard. *J.R.R. Tolkien: Myth, Morality, and Religion.* New ed. San Francisco, CA: Ignatius Press, 2003.

Scull, Christina. "The Development of Tolkien's Legendarium: Some Threads in the Tapestry of Middle-earth." In *Tolkien's Legendarium*, edited by Verlyn Flieger and Carl F. Hostetter, 7–18. Westport, CT: Greenwood, 2000.

Shippey, Tom. *Author of the Century.* London: HarperCollins: 2000.

———. "Grimm, Grundtvig, Tolkien: Nationalisms and the Invention of Mythologies." In *The Ways of Creative Mythologies: Imagined Worlds and Their Makers*, edited by Maria Kuteeva. Vol. 1. Telford: Tolkien Society, 2000.

———. *The Road to Middle-earth.* 3rd rev. ed. Boston, MA: Houghton Mifflin, 2003.

———. "Tolkien and Iceland: The Philology of Envy." Delivered at the Sigurður Nordal Institute, September 2002. http://www.nordals.hi.is/shippey.html. (Accessed January 2006.)

Stenström, Anders. "A Mythology? For England?" In *Proceedings of the Tolkien Centenary Conference 1992 (Mallorn 33 / Mythlore 80)*, edited by Patricia Reynolds and Glen H. GoodKnight, 310–14.

Wainwright, Edmund. *Tolkien's Mythology for England: A Middle-earth Companion.* Middlesex: Anglo-Saxon Books, 2004.

See also Ælfwine; Arthurian Literature; *Book of Lost Tales I*; *Book of Lost Tales II*; Eärendil; Finland: Literary Sources; Greek Gods; History, Anglo-Saxon; *History of Middle-earth:* Overview; Kôr; Mythology, Celtic; Mythology, Germanic; Old English; Old Norse Literature; Tavrobel

MYTHOLOGY, CELTIC

In a letter responding to an Allen & Unwin reader's description of an early draft of "Silmarillion" as "Celtic," Tolkien writes that "Silmarillion" is not Celtic; he adds that he knows Celtic things in Irish and Welsh, and he feels a certain "distaste" for them, finding them lacking in reason and design (*Letters*, 26). Tolkien's fondness for the Welsh language is well documented. He was less fond of medieval Irish, calling Old Irish "difficult" (*Letters,* 385), but he was not incapable of reading it. His references to etymology and Celtic mythology in "The Name 'Nodenns'" imply greater expertise and access to references than his modest statements suggest. Ability, however, is not the same as liking.

In "The Cottage of Lost Play," Tolkien describes a cottage that appears tiny until Eriol enters, is capacious and full of light, and where he is fed and entertained (*Lost Tales I,* 14). The episode is similar both to a Celtic motif of the otherworldly feast, and to a small house in the medieval Irish tale, the "*Compert Con Culainn*" or "Birth of Cú Chulainn." Whether or not Tolkien had the tale in mind is a different question. It is wise to remember that a Celtic motif may occur in a Celtic text, as well as in Old French or Middle English text, since all draw upon the common pool, and many motifs are part of a shared Indo-European heritage. *The Motif-Index of Early Irish Literature* may be of some use in determining the Celticity of a given motif.

There are indications that Tolkien knew some of the medieval Irish myths about the semidivine Tuatha De Dannan. These immortal beings dwell under and inside the hills, that is, the *síd* of Ireland, and are often referred to as the *Sídhe*, the people of the hills, or in English, fairies. In *The Lost Road*, in an early outline for a projected historically episodic work, Tolkien has a note listing possible episodes (*Lost Road,* 36–104). He lists the Tuatha De Dannan, Fintan the "oldest man," Irish saints Brendan and Maelduin, and various otherworld Irish paradises, including *Tír nan Óg*, the "Land of Youth," or "Land of the Ever Young." Tolkien glosses the Irish name Finntan as *Narkill*, with the etymology "white fire." A note refers to Maclean's *The Literature of the Celts*, a summary of medieval Irish and Welsh literature. Christopher Tolkien supplies the passage in question (*Lost Road,* 80–83). Finntan derives from Proto-Celtic *vindotenos* "White fire," or possibly *vendos-senos*, "white ancient," indicating again that Tolkien senior knew his Celtic etymology. It's perhaps worth noting as well that H. Rider Haggard used the name "white fire" as a sword-name in *Eric Brighteyes*, a novel Tolkien read.

In the Breton *lay* poem "Aotrou and Itroun," a husband and wife want a child, and the husband makes a rash promise to the Corrigan for her magical assistance. Like his Breton *lay* models, Chaucer's *Franklin's Tale*, *Sir Orfeo*, and the *Lais of Marie de France*, Tolkien uses Celtic folklore. The *korrigan* is a Breton fairy with a fondness for springs, fountains, and liaisons with mortal men. See Jessica Yate's article for Tolkien's probable sources.

In many Celtic texts, an otherworld animal, typically a white deer, dog, or boar, leads the hero into the woods and the otherworld. In Tolkien's "Aotrou and Itroun," the *korrigan* changes into a white hart and leads the hero into the forest and an enchanted spring. In *The Hobbit*, a white deer with fawns appears, and the Dwarves spend their arrows without hitting the deer (*H,* 200). Tolkien uses the word "glimmering" to describe the snow-white deer, reminiscent of the brilliant glittering of the white dogs with red ears Pwyll encounters while hunting in the first branch of the Welsh *Mabinogi*. This episode from the *Mabinogi* is one Tolkien quotes in "English and Welsh."

Tolkien reworked part of the unfinished *The Lost Road* into an episode in *The Notion Club Papers*, part of which he published, extensively revised, as the poem "Imram" (*Sauron,* 295–99). An *immram* is a medieval Irish tale genre. *Immram* literally means "rowing about" but is usually translated "voyage." As Dumville explains, the *immram* is a frame tale, allowing for various adventures in the course of a voyage. Tolkien's poem, while personal, is also inspired in part by the life of Saint Brendan the Navigator. During Saint Brendan's voyage, he encounters an enchanted stream that puts those who drink from it into a deep sleep, much like the stream encountered by Bilbo and the Dwarves in *The Hobbit,* as noted by Douglas Anderson (*H*, VIII, 198). Paul Kocher in *Master of Middle-earth,* Verlyn Flieger in *A Question of Time: J.R.R. Tolkien's Road to Faërie,* and Tom Shippey *The Road to Middle-earth* have explored the Irish antecedents of "Imram."

It is quite likely, as Leslie Jones and others have noted, that the march of the Ents (*TT,* III iv) is inspired by both Macbeth (*Letters,* 211–12) and by the Old Welsh poem "Cad Goddeu" from *The Book of Taliesin.* "Cad Goddeu" means "army" or "battle" of trees, and the poem depicts such an army.

Perhaps the most striking connection between *The Lord of the Rings* and Celtic mythology is one of form; Irish medieval stories mix verse and prose, with songs and poetry interspersed in the prose narrative. Finally, the idea that time in the otherworld or in *faërie* functions on a different scale than it does in the mortal world, as when Sam attempts to count the days the companions pass in Lothlorien (*FR,* II, ix, 404–05), is a motif common in both Irish myth and fairy folklore, ably explored by Verlyn Flieger in *A Question of Time: J.R.R. Tolkien's Road to Faërie* and in *Interrupted Music: The Making of Tolkien's Mythology.* Flieger also does an admirable job of discussing the Celtic versions of the Atlantis myth and Tolkien's use of the myth.

Lisa L. Spangenberg

Further Reading

"Cad Goddeu." In *The Book of Taliesin*, edited by J. Gwenogvryn Evans, 23.09–27.12. Llanbedrog, Wales, 1910. Translated in "Appendix: Cad Goddeu." In *The Mabinogi and Other Medieval Welsh Tales*, 183–87. Berkeley: University of California Press, 1977.

"Compert Con Culainn." In *Compert Con Culainn and Other Stories*, edited by A.G. Van Hame. Dublin: Dublin Institute of Advanced Studies, 1933. Translated by Peete Cross and Clark Harris Slover in *Ancient Irish Tales*, 134–36. New York: Henry Holt, 1936; reprinted New York: Barnes & Noble, 1988.

Cross, Tom Peete. *Motif-index of Early Irish Literature*. Bloomington, IN: Indiana University Press, 1952.

Dumville, David N. "*Echtrae* and *Immram*: Some Problems of Definition." *Ériu* 27 (1976): 73–94.

Flieger, Verlyn. *Interrupted Music: The Making of Tolkien's Mythology*. Kent, OH: Kent State University Press, 2005.

———. *A Question of Time: J.R.R. Tolkien's Road to Faërie*. Kent, Ohio: Kent State University Press, 1997.

Jones, Leslie Ellen. *Myth & Middle-earth*. Cold Spring Harbor, NY: Cold Spring Press, 2002.

MacLean, Magnus. *The Literature of the Celts*. London: Blackie and Son, 1902.

Shippey, Tom. *The Road to Middle-earth: Revised and Expanded Edition*. Boston, MA: Houghton Mifflin, 2001.

Tolkien, J.R.R. "Imram." *Time and Tide*, 1955.

———. "The Lay of Aotrou and Itroun." *Welsh Review* 4 (December, 1945): 245–66.

———. "The Name 'Nodens'." In " Appendix I" to *Report on the Excavation in Lydney Park, Gloucestershire*, 132–37. Reports of the Research Committee of the Society of Antiquaries, no. 9. London: Oxford University Press, 1932.

Yates, Jessica. "The Source of 'The Lay of Aotrou and Itroun.'" In *Leaves from the Tree: J.R.R. Tolkien's Shorter Fiction*, edited by Alex Lewis, 63–71. London: Tolkien Society, 1991.

See also **Arthurian Literature;** *Book of Lost Tales I*; **Druids; "English and Welsh"; Folklore; Jones, Gwyn; "On Fairy-Stories";** *Orfeo, Sir*; **Romances: Middle English and French; Saint Brendan;** *Sir Gawain and the Green Knight*; **Time Travel; Welsh Language**

MYTHOLOGY, GERMANIC

The study of myth was profoundly altered from the seventeenth century on by the rediscovery of pagan Scandinavian mythology in two related works, the *Elder* or *Poetic Edda*, a set of heroic and mythical poems in Old Norse, mostly recovered from a single manuscript, and the later *Prose Edda* of Snorri Sturluson, written about 1220 CE. Snorri knew and quoted from the poems of the *Elder Edda* but added to them a great deal of further material, including stories of the gods Odin, Thor, and Loki. The new material slowly became available to scholars and general readers, attracting attention perhaps because it was so markedly different from the familiar biblical and classical mythologies. The Norse gods were more limited, more human, often more cruel, and at once harsher and funnier than the Greek and Latin pantheons. The stories about them offered an insight into a quite different worldview.

Was this purely Norse? German, and to a lesser extent English, scholars were reluctant to think so, for they were well aware that the name Odin was paralleled by (in England) Woden, in Germany Wotan, the former, like the names of the gods Tyr/Tiw and Thor/Thunor, remembered in the English names for days of the week. Surely the English and the Germans had once had a similarly developed mythology, since unfortunately lost. This thought led to a series of attempts to gather together such fragments of old belief as might still exist and fit them together, such as N.F.S. Grundtvig's *Nordens Mytologi* (1808, 2nd version 1832), Jacob Grimm's *Deutsche Mythologie* (1835) and the English translation of Grimm's much-expanded fourth edition, and J. S. Stallybrass's *Teutonic Mythology* (1883–84). All three, and many others, were writing about the same phenomenon, but their titles either claim national ownership of it, or implicitly deny other modern national claims to ownership.

Tolkien fits perfectly into this context. His regret for the lost imaginary world of early England, and his ambition to "present [his countrymen] with a mythology of their own" is well attested (see *Letters*, 144, 231). Several of his early academic essays, notably the two on *Sigelwara land*, are exercises in fitting fragments together to retrieve a lost concept, in this case that of something like fire-giants (or Balrogs). In his fiction, the Ents, Orcs, and woses all derive from very slight clues in Old or Middle English poems, though in the last case—again entirely characteristically—these clues are interpreted in the light of words and names surviving into the present day. "Middle-earth" itself shows similar linguistic reconstruction: the Old Norse term was *Mithgarthr*, closely paralleled by Old English *middan-geard*, though Old English tradition has nothing to say of the nine worlds centered on the human one in the Norse system. As the word *geard*, pronounced "yard," narrowed its meaning over time, Middle English writers began to use the term "medill-erde," and this, once again modernized, is Tolkien's Middle-earth. Tolkien's Elves and Dwarves also combine features found, for instance, in Snorri, with elements of later and even contemporary folktale. Tolkien's interest in fairy tale was once again prefigured by the brothers Grimm. All the early mythographers were fascinated by "survivor-genres," such as fairy tale, riddle, oral ballad, and nursery rhyme. There was a chance, they thought, that from these childish or low-class forms skilled investigators might recover traces of pre-Christian belief. Tolkien went beyond his predecessors, though, in turning such investigations into fiction.

An important question, especially for committed Christian scholars like all those so far mentioned, was what to think of the pagan gods and goddesses, the Norse/English/German pantheon headed by Odin and detailed in the two *Eddas*. The Eddic mythology was strongly unlike the Christian one in being (as detailed by Snorri, a Christian himself, but with some corroboration elsewhere) in essence hopeless. As Tolkien pointed out in his 1936 lecture on *Beowulf*, in this mythology, gods and men would fight giants and monsters in a last climactic battle—but the side of good would be defeated. That defeat had already in a sense been prefigured by the death of Balder, Odin's son, most beautiful of the gods, and by Odin's inability to bring him back from Hel. In this mythology, the fate of the soul after death remained unclear: the custom of ship-burial suggested a belief in travel to another world, as did the provision of "Hel-shoes" for the dead, but other Norsemen seem to have believed they would be reunited with their ancestors, perhaps within a mountain, that they might live on within their funeral barrows, or that they might be reincarnated in their descendants. Snorri indicates that there are different homes for the dead, presided over by different deities, including Odin's Valhöll, "the halls of the slain," where dead warriors go to fight and feast till the last battle, Vídbláin, "wide-dark," where the light-elves live, and Nástrandir, "the corpse-beaches," where the wicked are tormented.

Tolkien remembered and used much of this material, as well as concepts from the similarly recovered mythologies of Finland and Ireland, in his presentation of the Valar. These are subject to Ilúvatar, the One, and so capable of being seen within a Christian monotheistic framework, but they resemble pagan gods in their relative independence, differing natures and fields of action, and the limitations on their power. Uncertainty about human and even Elvish fate after death, and the possibility of exceptions being made, as for Beren, also connect Tolkien's mythology with the Norse one. The idea of a fallen and disobedient Vala, Melkor, is more reminiscent of the Christian myth of Lucifer, but Norse mythology too has its renegade deity connected with the monster-world in Loki, a figure more profoundly ambiguous than any in Tolkien.

As time went by, Tolkien seems to have toned down the aggressive strain in (some of) the Valar, derived from their pagan models, and also become more critical of the Northern "theory of courage," which he had once seen as derived from the conviction that both gods and men were doomed: "The Homecoming of Beorhtnoth" in 1953 shows a less sympathetic attitude than the 1936 lecture on *Beowulf* to "heathenish" views and to the Vikings, "hell's children." Nevertheless, Tolkien's understanding of and admiration for the lost world of pagan Germanic mythology formed a major part of his creative inspiration.

TOM SHIPPEY

Further Reading

Auden, W.H., and Paul B. Taylor, trans. *Norse Poems.* London: Athlone Press, 1981.

Burns, Marjorie. *Perilous Realms: Celtic and Norse in Tolkien's Middle-earth.* Toronto: University of Toronto Press, 2005.

Chance, Jane, ed. *Tolkien and the Invention of Myth: A Reader.* Lexington, KY: University Press of Kentucky, 2004.

Davidson, H.R. Ellis. *Gods and Myths of Northern Europe.* Harmondsworth: Penguin, 1964.

Hutton, Ronald. "The Inklings and the Gods." In *Witches, Druids and King Arthur*, edited by Ronald Hutton, 215–37. London and New York: Hambledon & London 2003.

Orchard, Andy. *Dictionary of Norse Myth and Legend.* London: Cassell, 1997.

Shippey, Tom, ed. *The Shadow-Walkers: Jacob Grimm's Mythology of the Monstrous.* Tempe, AZ: Arizona State University Press, 2005.

———. "Tolkien and 'The Homecoming of Beorhtnoth'." In *Leaves from the Tree : J.R.R. Tolkien's Shorter Fiction*, 5–16. London: Tolkien Society, 1991.

Sturluson, Snorri. *Edda, Prologue and Gylfaginning.* Translated by Anthony Faulkes. Oxford: Clarendon Press, 1982.

See also **"*Beowulf*: The Monsters and the Critics"; Finland: Literary Sources; Heathenism and Paganism; *Homecoming of Beorhtnoth*; Mythology for England; Mythology, Celtic; Northern Courage; Old Norse Literature**

"MYTHOPOEIA"

On the night of Saturday, September 19, 1931, Tolkien took an evening stroll along Holywell Stream in Magdalen Grove, one of the most arboreal areas of Oxford, with Hugo Dyson and C.S. Lewis. In his biography of Tolkien, Humphrey Carpenter attempted to reconstruct that night's conversation, but Tolkien's own distillation of it is his 148-line poem "Mythopoeia," much of which was written within weeks of the event. Tolkien's only composition in heroic couplets, "Mythopoeia" is one of his most clearly articulated expositions of his theory of mythmaking (which is what "Mythopoeia" means).

Tolkien recast that night's conversation as a dialogue between Philomythus ("Myth nature of language. Lover," Tolkien himself) and Misomythus ("Myth Hater," Lewis). From Lewis's letters to Arthur Greeves Carpenter (and later Christopher Tolkien, in his introduction to the second edition of *Tree and Leaf*) abstracted Lewis's position as an inability to see the mythic function of Christ's death and resurrection. Yet, Dyson and Tolkien countered, Lewis admitted an emotional appreciation of the Norse myth of Balder, a similar "dying god" story. But that is a myth, Lewis objected, a lie, even if it be a lie "breathed through silver." It is at that point in the conversation that Tolkien's poem opens.

Tolkien's choice of heroic couplets for this poem could hardly be accidental. Alexander Pope had shown it to be admirably suited for discursive poetry, and Pope's *Essay on Man* and *Essay on Criticism* modeled precisely the versified philosophy Tolkien was attempting in "Mythopoeia." Tolkien divides the poem into twelve "verse paragraphs" of varying lengths, each separated by a blank space. In the first, though the speaker is Philomythus, he is expressing Misomythus's rationalist, materialist vision of the universe, so that he can rebut it in the rest of the poem:

> You look at trees and label them just so,
> (for trees are "trees", and growing is "to grow")

To the Lucretian, Newtonian Misomythus, language is just taxonomy, each word a tag for the thing it names. Any connection between the real trees (without quotation marks) and the word "trees" (with quotation marks) is arbitrary.

But in the second verse paragraph, Philomythus presents a rival perspective, in which the universe of things bends "at bidding of a Will":

> God made the petreous rocks, the arboreal trees,
> tellurian earth, and stellar stars, and these
> homuncular men, who walk upon the ground
> with nerves that tingle touched by light and sound.

In these five adjective-noun pairs, Tolkien illustrates the abstraction process that he calls in his later essay "On Fairy–Stories" "the invention of the adjective." The nouns, since they are mere names, are closer to the things they name: they are all Anglo-Saxon words (rocks, trees, earth, stars, men). But the adjectives (all Latinate or Greek: petreous, arboreal, tellurian, stellar, homuncular) are further removed from the things they describe.

The tingling "touched by light" suggests sight, of course—apprehending the thing itself by eye. But the "sound" includes not only the auditory phenomena of nature but also the words for the things themselves. When we see a thing, we are imprinted with a sensory "image" of the thing; when we say its name, we are likewise imprinted, as Tolkien suggests in the third section.

> Yet trees are not "trees", until so named and seen
> and never were so named, till those had been
> who speech's involuted breath unfurled,
> faint echo and dim picture of the world

This naming process is not a reduction for Tolkien: the word, we see in section four, is a means of recreating the primal experience of the wonder of creation:

> He sees no stars who does not see them first
> of living silver made that sudden burst
> to flame like flowers beneath an ancient song

The ancient song recalls the myth that Tolkien says in his "Fairy–Stories" essay is "coeval" with language, and in the rest of this verse paragraph he suggests that the mythic images of the sky as a tent or earth as a mother's womb are more real than the Lucretian materialist's "cold Inane" (a phrase borrowed from Tennyson's "Lucretius") or "minor globes of Space."

The reason myth is truer than materialism, Tolkien continues in section 5, is that man the mythopoet echoes God's creative urge, becoming "sub-creator" (the word appeared in this poem years before the "Fairy–Stories" essay). The rest of the poem is a celebration of the creative power by which we imitate God, making the artist scorn the "progressive apes" of scientific materialism.

JOHN R. HOLMES

Further Reading

Carpenter, Humphrey. *Tolkien: A Biography*. London: Allen & Unwin, 1977.

Duriez, Colin. "Sub-creation and Tolkien's Theology of Story." In *Scholarship and Fantasy: Proceedings of the Tolkien Phenomenon, May 1992, Turku, Finland*, edited by Keith J. Batterbee, 133–50. Turku: University of Turku, 1993.

Tolkien, Christopher. "Introduction." In *TL*, 6–8.

See also **Language: Theories of; "On Fairy–Stories"; Subject Theory and Semiotics**

N

NATURE

Nature is an integral dimension in all of Tolkien's work. Patrick Curry has suggested that it is symbolised by Middle-earth itself and coexists, in a complex relationship, with the cultural, social, and political (principally the Shire) and with the spiritual and ethical (the Sea). Be that as it may, it cannot be doubted that the natural world was of intense interest and concern to Tolkien; the high value that he placed on it, or found in it, is clearly evident in his biography and his letters. Unsurprisingly, it also shines forth in his fiction. One of the latter's most distinctive marks is the extent to which its natural places are so individual, varied, and fully realised. Furthermore—and this is a key point—they are never mere settings for the human drama; rather, they participate in and help determine the narrative. The various places of Middle-earth could themselves be said to figure as characters in the stories of *The Hobbit* and *The Lord of the Rings.*

In Tolkien's stories, no aspect of the natural world—geology, flora, fauna, weather, and the stars and Moon—is wholly neglected, and most receive respectful, even loving attention at some point. Nature is never abstract but rather as we actually experience it, sensuous and particular. Thus, the power of place is paramount, just as it was in aboriginally mythic and enchanted nature—and still is, in so far as such a sensibility survives. Indeed, it is plausible to suggest that Tolkien's fiction is an instance of its contemporary cultural resuscitation.

The places of Middle-earth are thus never generic. Each forest, each river, each mountain range is distinctive, and *a fortiori,* more precise places (such as Caras Galadhon, Rauros, and Moria) each has its own personality. Another characteristic is that every natural place has a cultural dimension, and vice versa. Thus, the Elves (at least while in Middle-earth) are unimaginable without the forests, the Dwarves without the mountains, the hobbits without the domesticated nature of the Shire. And it would be impossible to say which or who came first. The only exceptions, in the first case, are the Old Forest, where the only humanoid culture-bearer to whom it is home is Tom Bombadil (together with Goldberry, who is more or less a nature spirit), and Fangorn. But as Goldberry says to Frodo, Tom doesn't own the forest, and its inhabitants: they "belong each to themselves" (*FR,* I, vii, 172). And in Fangorn Forest, the Ents are trees become conscious: an autochthonous nonhuman culture. Tolkien thus rejects any sharp divide between cultural "legends" and "the green earth" of nature—and explicitly so, in Aragorn's riposte to the cynical Rider of Rohan: "That is a mighty matter of legend, though you tread it under the light of day!" (*TT,* III, ii, 39).

A related and still more striking aspect of nature in Middle-earth is its agency. Examples abound: the mountain Caradhras does not want to be crossed by the Company of the Ring and sends snow to block its way (*FR,* II, iii); when the herb *athelas* is crushed, the air ("the air itself," as Tolkien writes to emphasise the point) awakes and sparkles with joy (*RK,* V, viii, 168); when Frodo laughs "a long clear laugh from his heart" on the stairs of Cirith Ungol, the stones listen (*TT,* IV, viii, 404); the sky weeps "grey tears" for

Théoden and Éowyn (*RK,* V, vi, 142). It would be a serious mistake to dismiss these as mere poetic license; the words mean exactly what they say, which is also how they are experienced by the characters.

Tolkien's portrayal of nature can thus be characterised as (1) respectful of qualitative local distinctiveness, (2) disrespectful of any foundational distinction between "nature" and "culture," and (3) cognisant of its agency and subjectivity, as well as its materiality and objectivity. This attitude had precise and positive literary effects in terms of the compelling reality of his narrative. Its more general significance, however, is that in all three respects, Tolkien broke with the modernist ideology (with Platonic, Christian and Cartesian roots), that extols a disenchanted world where subjectivity and agency are confined to humanity alone, and the desacralisation and commodification of nature are licensed as part of Progress. His work reconnects readers to a natural world that is still enchanted, that is alive in all its parts, and that can be meaningfully said to have concerns—concerns that (as Treebeard says [*TT,* III, iv, 89]) are not necessarily identical with ours. The appropriate mode of relationship in and with such a world is fundamentally one between equals, not one between master and slave. The chief exemplar of the latter mode in Middle-earth, not coincidentally, is Sauron, "the Lord of magic and machines" who, as Tolkien remarked, "goes in for 'machinery'...because 'magicians'...would do so (do do so)" (*Letters,* 146, 200). (These issues are perceptively explored in Max Horkheimer and Theodor Adorno's *The Dialectic of Enlightenment* (1944)—a book Tolkien almost certainly never read!)

Humanity last lived in such a world when the dominant "religion" was pagan animism. Yet it feels somehow familiar to many of Tolkien's readers, probably because its collective cultural memory, despite the best efforts of modernity, survives. The effect upon his readers is not necessarily purely nostalgic, however; there is evidence that it can also reawaken awareness of the enchanted nature of the "real" world here and now. His work thus also has interesting resonances with contemporary environmental and ecological movements such as Deep Ecology.

It should be added that Tolkien does not romanticise nature in the pejorative sense. The places of Middle-earth are often dangerous, sometimes fatally so. By the same token, conflict between nonhuman natural interests and those of humanity (more or less) are certainly possible, the uneasy truce between the Old Forest and the Hobbits of Buckland being a case in point. Ultimately, as in any ongoing relationship, between humanity and nonhuman nature is one in which outcomes are not reliably predictable,

uncertainty is ineliminable, and respectful attention is the most promising way forward.

PATRICK CURRY

Further Reading

Curry, Patrick. *Defending Middle-earth: Tolkien, Myth and Modernity.* 2nd ed. Boston, MA: Houghton Mifflin, 2004.

See also **Capitalism; Environmentalism and Eco-Criticism; Heathenism and Paganism; Industrialization**

NAZI PARTY

While sharing his contemporaries' hatred for Adolf Hitler, Tolkien had his own "burning private grudge" against the Nazi leader for hijacking the "'Germanic' ideal" embodied in the ancient Germanic literatures, the philosophy of "Northern courage." "I was much attracted by it as an undergraduate (when Hitler was, I suppose, dabbling in paint, and had not heard of it)," Tolkien said in 1941. Scorning him as "that ruddy little ignoramus" and "a vulgar and ignorant little cad," Tolkien accused him of "ruining, perverting, misapplying, and making for ever accursed, that noble northern spirit, a supreme contribution to Europe, which I have ever loved, and tried to present in a true light."

Hitler and Tolkien were both indebted to the nineteenth-century fusion of nationalism and romanticism that had brought a European revival of interest in indigenous literatures and pre-Christian cultures. It produced the Finnish *Kalevala,* Lady Charlotte Guest's *Mabinogion,* and *Grimms' Fairy Tales,* and such works of fiction as William Morris's *The House of the Wolfings,* all of great interest to Tolkien. But in Germany it also fostered tendencies that Hitler was able to exploit politically: youth movements made icons of the hammer of Thor and the swastika, an ancient sun symbol, and some rural communes took up a neo-paganism justified on largely spurious historical and philological grounds.

Tolkien's "private grudge," though, was against the Nazi use of the Germanic ideal as a flag of convenience to excuse military expansionism and the "wholly pernicious and unscientific race-doctrine" under which European Jews were persecuted. Furious in 1938 when the prospective German publisher of a translation of *The Hobbit* sought confirmation of his "Aryan" extraction, he later cautioned against calling his work "Nordic," a word he associated with "racialist theories."

To Tolkien, the Germanic ideal was more appropriately deployed, no doubt, in *The House of the*

Wolfings, in which the Germans (Goths) are not Reich-builders like Hitler but resistance fighters opposing a land-grabbing imperium (Rome). Tolkien defined his own brand of nationalism (cultural and linguistic self-rule, including Home Rule in Ireland) in 1914 in direct opposition to the German military imperialism that Hitler later came to represent, declaring, "I don't defend 'Deutschland über alles' but certainly do in Norwegian 'Alt for Norge' [All for Norway]."

Tolkien's approval for Hitler's nationalist allies in Spain may seem to contradict this principle, but it was largely or wholly inspired by their defence of the Roman Catholic Church during the Spanish Civil War; it is unclear what else Tolkien thought of General Franco and his fascists. As a self-proclaimed philosophical anarchist or "unconstitutional monarchist," however, he condemned the Nazi Party's exercise of brute state power. Hitler misused the native strengths of the Germans, as Tolkien saw them (having witnessed them firsthand in the trenches). In 1941, he felt Germany to be "under the curse of God" and saw the Führer as "a man inspired by a mad, whirlwind, devil: a typhoon, a passion: that makes the poor old Kaiser look like an old woman knitting."

In his foreword to the second (1966) edition of *The Lord of the Rings,* Tolkien claimed that readings of the book as an "allegory" of the Second World War were unfounded because the chapter revealing the threat to Middle-earth was written "long before the foreshadow of 1939 had yet become a threat of inevitable disaster." In fact, it cannot have been written earlier than March 1938, the month that Hitler annexed Austria, and indeed Tolkien admitted in October 1938 that "the darkness of the present days" (a month after Britain had appeased Hitler at Munich) had had some effect on his story. In 1944, he demonstrated its applicability to the contemporary situation when he wrote, "we are attempting to conquer Sauron with the Ring," meaning with modern military force.

The foreword is more successful in showing that no point-for-point correlation between the book and the war is sustainable. Tom Shippey has demonstrated the limits of an equation between the Sauron of *The Lord of the Rings* and Hitler, instancing the Vichy-like terms offered to the Captains of the West at the Black Gate. A closer likeness exists between Hitler and the Sauron of the unfinished 1936 time-travel story "The Lost Road," a tyrant who combines militarisation and industrialisation with a programme to crush freedom of thought among the Númenóreans. The likeness, however, extends also to Stalin. Certainly in the run-up to the Second World War, Tolkien was more wary of the Soviet Union, writing: "One fancies

that Russia is probably ultimately far more responsible for the present crisis and choice of moment than Hitler."

JOHN GARTH

Further Reading

Shippey, Tom. *J.R.R. Tolkien: Author of the Century,* London: HarperCollins, 2000.

See also **Allegory; German Race Laws; Germany; Judaism;** *Lost Road;* **Northern Courage; Philo-Semitism; Race and Ethnicity in Tolkien's Works; Racism, Charges of; Tyranny**

NEAVE, JANE (1872–1963)

Born Jane Suffield, Jane Neave was the younger sister of Mabel, Tolkien's mother. She supplemented the tuition Mabel gave Tolkien as a young child, teaching him geometry. She married Edwin Neave, an insurance clerk. In 1904, when Mabel was seriously ill with diabetes, Tolkien was sent to Hove to stay with the Neaves. In 1911, Jane Neave, now widowed, took a summer walking holiday with Tolkien, his brother Hilary, and others in Switzerland, starting out from Interlaken. No doubt her presence gave some comfort to the orphaned brothers. Late in September 1914, Tolkien stayed with Hilary at his aunt's Phoenix Farm, in Gedling, Nottinghamshire. This was a significant moment in Tolkien's life. Here, he decided to defer enlisting—he told Aunt Jane that he intended to complete his Oxford studies first. While he was at Phoenix Farm, he was reading the old English poem, *Christ,* coming across the lines that inspired the genesis of his mythology—Eärendil the Mariner, the earliest element of *The Silmarillion.* On September 24, he began writing: "Éarendel sprang up from the Ocean's cup / In the gloom of the mid-world's rim." Neave later took a farm in Dormston, Worcestershire, called "Bag End," which Tolkien visited from time to time. "Bag End" was, in his words, "an old tumbledown manor house at the end of an untidy lane that led nowhere else" (unpublished letter to Ken Jackson, January 29, 1968). In her eighties, still alert, Neave suggested that Tolkien should create a book around the character Tom Bombadil. Tolkien was glad that he "cheered and amused" her by consulting her over poems he selected and composed for the book. Three of Tolkien's letters to his aunt are preserved in *The Letters of J.R.R. Tolkien* (numbers 234, 238, 241).

COLIN DURIEZ

See also **Marriage; Tolkien, Hilary; Tolkien, Mabel**

NETHERLANDS: RECEPTION OF TOLKIEN

The first article on Tolkien that appeared in the Netherlands was a review of *The Fellowship of the Ring* in the *Algemeen Handelsblad* (a quality newspaper) on November 20, 1954. Under the title "A Fantastic Epic," Guus Sötemann wrote an enthusiastic review: "In a majestic way Tolkien has managed to write a divers story. He has succeeded in letting adults forget their prejudices and have them listen, like a child, to a story without any deliberate allegory or symbolism." Because he was acquainted with the editor of Het Spectrum, it was also Professor Sötemann who was responsible for the fact that the Dutch translation of *The Lord of the Rings,* titled *In de Ban van de Ring,* appeared so quickly after the English original.

In October 1956, the Dutch translation of *The Fellowship of the Ring* was published, and over the period 1956–58 about one hundred reviews appeared, the vast majority favourable. It is clear that most reviewers were not sure in which category the book fit. Fantasy as a genre did not exist yet (Tolkien created that), so most compared it with mythologies like *The Iliad,* the *Edda*s, and King Arthur. The Dutch publisher Het Spectrum stimulated this by an advertising campaign, emphasising the "modern myth" angle: "What Columbus did for America, J.R.R. Tolkien does for the imagination: he brings a whole new world to light."

It was mentioned in a review that the first hundred pages or so were rather rough going. These are in style more like *The Hobbit,* but the odd situation in Holland was that there was no Dutch translation of *The Hobbit.* That was corrected in 1960. A common criticism was the lack of sex and gender as a theme in the book. Some reviewers remarked that it was peculiar that a book so rich with the psychological journey of the main characters lacks this vital part of life. This leads to the familiar criticism in the few hostile reviews that *The Lord of the Rings* was juvenile thrash, a pretentious children's book, an overgrown fairy story. One reviewer saw no character development and was annoyed with the stereotypical depictions: "the Men are too heroic, the Elves too noble, the Dwarves too stout, the Ents too vague and the Hobbits too cool."

But these were the exception. Most praised Tolkien for his powerful imagination and his great style. One remarked that Tolkien had a talent of making landscapes come to life. That the story was compelling and had outgrown the level of fairy story made the book suitable for children and adults alike. That the book did not fit the known literary labels did not bother the reviewers; compellingly new and original, back to pure imagination and the essential human experiences, was the phrase used. Often also the translator, Max Schuchart, is praised for his excellent translation, especially of the poems, which pleased Schuchart, who was a published poet. In 1959, his translation won a prestigious Dutch literary prize.

The book was hailed as a great work of literature about the vital battle against all evil, in which friendship, sacrifice, and determination are of crucial importance. No doubt in the back of the minds of these reviewers was the Cold War. Some went a step further and made the Mordor–Soviet Union, Sauron–Stalin connection, an allegorical interpretation so hated by Tolkien.

Some were puzzled when they learned that this massive epic, this almost believable imaginary world, was invented by just one man. It must have been difficult to construct such a complex plot with so many strands of story line. For one reviewer, Tolkien went too far with this; the book is too convoluted because of the inability of the author to separate the main topics from the details.

Despite all the good publicity Tolkien received, sales were poor. That Tolkien was an unknown author, writing in a new genre, and the lack of a Dutch translation of *The Hobbit* are factors in explaining this. Also, the books were expensive. Like George Allen & Unwin, Het Spectrum had opted for a three-volume, de luxe hardback set of just three thousand copies, costing 37.50 guilders for the whole set; a single hardback in those days retailed for about 7 guilders. But Tolkien was already gathering a loyal following in Holland, as he discovered when he visited the country in March 1958. As he wrote to Rayner Unwin, apparently well over two hundred (largely ordinary people) had paid to be present at the Hobbit Maaltijd (the Hobbit Meal) in Rotterdam, where Tolkien was the guest of honour. He found the Dutch "almost intoxicated with hobbits. It was almost entirely of hobbits that they spoke." It was also in Rotterdam in 1958 that the Dutch fans first organised themselves and held meetings, being in the vanguard of the international Tolkien fandom.

Just like in the rest of the Western world, Tolkien reached a mass audience when the first cheap paperback editions of *The Lord of the Rings* appeared in 1965. Forty years later, Tolkien is still one of the best-known and well-read authors in Holland. His death was featured in the main evening TV news. In a nationwide opinion poll in the late seventies, *The Lord of the Rings* was voted the most popular work of literature not written in Dutch. All his books (not including *The History of Middle-earth*) have been translated into Dutch and are almost all still in print. There is both a Tolkien museum and a flourishing Tolkien society in the Netherlands.

RENÉ VAN ROSSENBERG

Further Reading

van Rossenberg, René. *Hobbits in Holland.* Koninklijke Bibliotheek: Den Haag, 1992.
Vanhecke, Johan. *In de Ban van de Hobbit.* Houtekiet: Antwerpen, 2005.

See also **Dutch Language;** *Lord of the Rings:* **Success of**

NEW GLOSSARY OF THE DIALECT OF THE HUDDERSFIELD DISTRICT, A

Walter Edward Haigh (1856–1930) taught English at the Technical College in Huddersfield, West Yorkshire, and was Lecturer Emeritus there at the time of publication of his *Glossary* (1928). He probably first met Tolkien in January 1922, when Tolkien gave a lecture at Leeds University to the Yorkshire Dialect Society, of which Haigh was one of the leaders. In his preface to the *Glossary,* Haigh notes that Tolkien had "almost from the first shown his warm approval of the work," and Tolkien further contributed a six-page foreword to it.

What Haigh did, between 1922 and 1928, was collect some four thousand dialect words and list them, with their pronunciation, meaning, suggested etymology, and illustrative examples collected from local speech. It is likely that Tolkien influenced the collection, as well as encouraging it, for Haigh's use of illustrative examples, though oral rather than literary, follows the practice of the *Oxford English Dictionary (OED),* on which Tolkien had given his 1922 lecture; in addition, the layout of the suggested etymologies is similar to that in Tolkien and E.V. Gordon's 1925 edition of *Sir Gawain and the Green Knight.*

Tolkien mentions this poem several times in his foreword and was charmed by the way in which words familiar to him only from the medieval poem reappeared in modern dialect speech. He gives more than a dozen examples, including the dialect verb *dloppen,* in Huddersfield "to frighten, surprise, amaze, disgust," in *Sir Gawain* a noun with identical meaning—Morgan le Fay sent the Green Knight to Camelot to upset Guinevere by *glopnyng* at the supernatural beheading. Tolkien notes also that the medieval poet and modern mill-hands used both *ænt* and *nont* for "aunt," though the former word was now considered affected, and that both fourteenth-century manuscript and twentieth-century speech wobbled between the forms *foch* and *fech* for "fetch," a warning

to editors not to overcorrect. Haigh claimed that his local dialect was not "the haphazard invention of country folk" but "of ancient origin . . . of as worthy lineage as standard English itself," and Tolkien would have agreed with him. Tolkien also noted, however, that it was as important to record the way in which learned words were adopted as to look for old survivals, picking out among others the dialectal use of "auction" to mean "any untidy room," as illustrated by the comment "on a slatternly woman," "Shu'z nout but e slut; er ees ez e feer *okshen.*"

Possibly, Tolkien remembered this in the final scenes of *The Hobbit,* where Bilbo finds Bag End "a fair auction" in both senses, and there are other indications of Haigh's influence on Tolkien, as well as the reverse. The *OED,* for instance, has no explanation of Sam Gamgee's word "Noodles!" But Haigh records *nuidl* as a diminutive form of *noddi,* a simpleton, one who is half asleep. He derives *sæmmi,* with the same meaning, from Old English *sám-wís,* which Tolkien gave as the original of Sam's full name, Samwise. Haigh may also have given a hint for Barliman Butterbur, for he records several local names beginning with Butter—as possibly deriving from Old English *botel,* "a dwelling." Tolkien derived "hobbit" from Old English *hol-bytla,* in which case he may have thought of Butterbur as coming from Old English **botel-(ge)búr,* "one who lives in, or is a neighbor of, a (hobbit-)dwelling," which would seem especially apt for a human native of Bree. Tolkien was always interested in survivals from the past to the present, especially if these were natural and colloquial rather than scholarly and antiquarian. Haigh's *Glossary* gave him many such examples and much food for future thought.

TOM SHIPPEY

See also **Cruces in Medieval Literature; Oral Tradition;** *Sir Gawain and the Green Knight:* **Edition with E.V. Gordon**

"NOMENCLATURE OF *THE LORD OF THE RINGS*"

"Notes on the Nomenclature of *The Lord of the Rings*" was Tolkien's title for notes he provided to would-be translators of *The Lord of the Rings* after the Dutch and Swedish translations. In a conversation at the Elizabethan Club at Yale in 1972, Jules Wright, then of the University of Guelph, told Jared Lobdell about the "Notes"—an Italian friend of Professor Wright being the intended translator of *The Lord of the Rings* into Italian. Neither Tolkien nor (after his death) his son Christopher could see why it was thought the "Notes" would make a welcome addition to the book *A Tolkien Compass,* then being assembled from papers delivered at the First (1969) and Second (1971) Conference on Middle-earth, but permission to publish was duly given to Open Court, the publisher of *A Tolkien Compass.*

Unfortunately, the Open Court compositors had trouble with the typescript, and Christopher Tolkien's special efforts were needed to put a workable version into print by the time of planned publication. In the editor's recollection, the printed version differs from the translation in only one important way, the omission of a reference to a story by Algernon Blackwood as part of the origin of the name "the Crack of Doom" for Orodruin (Lobdell 2004, 8–9), which in turn conceals a clue that Tolkien read Blackwood.

The "Notes" were published under the title "Guide to the Names in *The Lord of the Rings*" in the first Open Court edition of *A Tolkien Compass,* with the subsidiary title "Nomenclature of *The Lord of the Rings*" on p. 155. The heading "Names of Persons and Places" is on p. 159, but pp. 160–75 cover only personal names. The heading on p. 177 is "Place-Names" and these are covered on pp. 178–96. Finally, p. 197 prints the heading "Things" with entries on pp. 198–201, including the entry for the Púkel-men (200)—images and therefore "Things" rather than "Persons." In the Ballantine paperback edition (New York 1980), the "Guide" appears on pp. 168–216, without a separate page for each subtitle. The text otherwise does not differ.

When the new edition of *A Tolkien Compass* appeared from Open Court in 2003, the Tolkien Estate withdrew Tolkien's permission to publish the "Notes," citing the problems in preparing the text for the first edition. Unauthorized versions of the "Notes" have appeared on various Web sites: it is to be hoped that the authorized version will be brought back into hard-copy print, though of course its value is less in the twenty-first century than at the beginning of Tolkien scholarship. The "Notes" generally tell the prospective translator (and those reading, as it were, over his or her shoulder) what names are to be fully translated (Bag End), translated in part (for "Chetwood," retain *chet* and translate *wood*), left as is (i.e., retained, as "Dunlending"), or translated or retained depending on the language of translation ("Isengard," where translation into Germanic tongues is recommended). Generally, Elvish names and Rohan names are to be retained, though there are cases in question.

The "Notes," though more important thirty years ago for their incidental information than they are in 2005, are still valuable—an example would be (under "The Firstborn," 1975 edition, 166) the throwaway remark, "Hobbits are of course meant to be a special variety of the human race." Or the entry under "Yule" (201), where Tolkien says that "December 25 (setting out) and March 25 (accomplishment of the quest) were deliberately chosen by me"—the significance of December 25 may be obvious, but it may be necessary to remind ourselves of the belief that the world would end on that March 25 (Lady Day), which was also Good Friday (as in 1066). Moreover, the insight given by the "Notes" into the recommended principles of translation has not been superseded. Looking at the "Notes" in connection with a reexamination of Tolkien's neglected 1934 essay on "Chaucer as Philologist" *(Transactions of the Philological Society)* suggests why Tolkien found this particular aspect of Chaucer's creation especially sympathetic. The reminder (Tolkien 1975, 200) that "*Tale* in *Tale of Years* means 'counting,' 'reckoning'" first made possible an appreciation of what some have called the "Tolkienian pun"—exact usage that most readers take as colloquial (see also a possible converse example with "Sayce" and "Waugh" in the entry for "Welsh Language").

JARED LOBDELL

Further Reading

Lobdell, Jared. *The World of the Rings: Language, Religion and Adventure in Tolkien.* La Salle, IL: Open Court, 2004.

Tolkien, J.R.R. "Guide to the Names in *The Lord of the Rings.*" In *A Tolkien Compass,* edited by Jared Lobdell, 153–201. La Salle, IL: Open Court, 1975.

See also **Estate**

NORMAN CONQUEST

The Norman Conquest, one of the most significant events in English history, began in 1066, when William, Duke of Normandy, invaded England and fought and defeated King Harold Godwinson and the Anglo-Saxon army at the Battle of Hastings. Over the next century, as Norman governance transformed both the language and the sociopolitical face of England, the previous Anglo-Saxon culture disappeared almost completely. At the turn of the twentieth century, English scholarship held two opposing views about the Conquest. One side considered Norman rule and the social changes it brought the beginning of actual civilization in England and found within this period the roots of modern British culture and its attendant accomplishments. For this view, Anglo-Saxon England represented the "Dark Ages" of barbarity, much in need of Norman reform. The other school of thought, proponents of the so-called Norman Yoke, believed that the Norman rule had not improved the English state but had brutally oppressed it and through domination had eradicated much of the earlier, purer English identity.

Perhaps because of his childhood fascination with surviving forms of pre-Conquest languages, Tolkien from his earliest days subscribed to the Norman Yoke view—while a schoolchild in Birmingham, he once argued in debate for the negative impact of the Conquest upon English society. As his medieval studies progressed, Tolkien's fascination with Old and Middle English languages, coupled with a growing dislike of all things Gallic (intensified, no doubt, by a disastrous trip while a student tutor at Oxford to Brittany in 1913 and then World War I service on the French front lines), only increased his disdain for the effects of the Conquest. Moreover, as Tolkien began to perceive what he saw as the devastating effects of industrialization and modernity upon English landscape and culture, the Conquest came to represent the first step in the globalizing, centralizing, and bureaucratically minded "progress" that threatened the social fabric of his beloved England.

In no small part, the nostalgic, mythic contours of Tolkien's writings derive from this historical bias. For Tolkien, the Norman Conquest prevented the survival of a distinctively English language and corrupted the ideal of English life. Indeed, the very lexicon Tolkien uses in his own fiction seeks to moderate the linguistic impact of the Conquest; throughout his work, he employs primarily words of Germanic (i.e., Old English) derivation over ones of more recent French or Latin origins. Furthermore, Tolkien saw the Conquest as ultimately suppressing the essence of English myth, and his works of Middle-earth may be viewed as a response this perceived deficiency, drawing as they do upon Old English vocabulary and texts to fashion a mythic surrogate. In sum, the pre-Conquest linguistic and literary elements of Tolkien's fiction contribute heavily to their central nature, a nature in no small part inspired by imagining what English myth could have been were it not for the reality of the Norman Conquest and the changes it wrought.

MARTIN K. FOYS

Further Reading

Chibnall, Marjorie. *The Debate on the Norman Conquest.* Manchester, UK: Manchester University Press, 1999.

Curry, Patrick. *Defending Middle-earth: Tolkien; Myth and Modernity.* 2nd ed. New York: Houghton Mifflin, 2004.

Garth, John. *Tolkien and the Great War: the Threshold of Middle-earth.* London: HarperCollins, 2003.

See also **England, Twentieth Century; France and French Culture; History, Anglo-Saxon; Mythology for England**

NORTHERN VENTURE, A

A small booklet bound in green wrappers, *A Northern Venture: Verses by Members of the Leeds University English School Association* was published in an edition of 170 copies in June 1923 by The Swan Press, a small press in Leeds. A second edition of 200 copies appeared in July.

No editor is listed, but it was presumably compiled by Sydney Matthewman (1902–70), a Leeds University alumnus and poet who ran The Swan Press and who acted as a kind of focal point for Leeds poets. *A Northern Venture* contains twenty-three poems by ten poets, arranged alphabetically by author. Contributors include Tolkien (three poems), his friends and colleagues (two poems each) Wilfred Rowland Childe and E.V. Gordon, and his student A.H. Smith (two poems).

Tolkien's contributions are *Tha Eadigan Saelidan: The Happy Mariners, Why the Man in the Moon Came Down Too Soon,* and *Enigmata Saxonica Nuper Inventa Duo.* The first poem is slightly revised from the version titled *The Happy Mariners* and published in *The Stapledon Magazine,* June 1920. It is reprinted in *Lost Tales II* (273–74). The second poem was published in *A Northern Venture* for the first time. It would later be much revised and published in *The Adventures of Tom Bombadil and Other Verses from The Red Book* (1963) as *The Man in the Moon Came Down Too Soon* (34–38). Another version has been published in *The Book of Lost Tales: Part I* (204–6). *Enigmata Saxonica Nuper Inventa Duo* is actual two poems in Anglo-Saxon, which the Latin title describes as *Two Saxon Riddles Recently Discovered.* Both are reprinted with translations in *The Annotated Hobbit: Revised and Enlarged Edition* (124–25).

Wilfred Rowland Childe (1890–1952) was at the time of publication the most recognized name among the contributors, though he is now barely remembered as a minor Georgian poet. As a fellow Catholic, he was close with Tolkien, and he was godfather to Tolkien's third son, Christopher. Childe's contributions to *A Northern Venture* are typical of his work: formal and flowery.

More interesting to Tolkien scholars is one of the two contributions by E.V. Gordon, *A Skald's Imprompu,* which is a twelfth-century Old Norse verse composed by Skuli, Earl of the Orkneys, edited and translated into skaldic metre by Gordon. (Gordon's other contribution is an English rendering of an Ibsen poem.)

Albert Hugh Smith (1903–67) was one of Tolkien's and Gordon's most distinguished student at Leeds. Smith contributed two poems written in Yorkshire dialect, one of which, *Spring,* appeared in a revised form in his interestingly titled collection *The Merry Shire: Poems in the Yorkshire Dialect* (1923), also published by The Swan Press.

A brief review in the *Times Literary Supplement* of July 12, 1923, assesses the collection as follows: "The pictures, brightly tinted, of Mr. W.R. Childe's fancy, the dialect verses of Mr. A.H. Smith, who knows his Yorkshire, and a couple of riddles in Saxon by Mr. J.R.R. Tolkien are perhaps the outstanding things in this unpretentious anthology" (474).

DOUGLAS A. ANDERSON

Further Reading

Hammond, Wayne G., with the assistance of Douglas A. Anderson. *J.R.R. Tolkien: A Descriptive Bibliography.* Winchester, UK: St. Paul's Bibliographies; New Castle, DE: Oak Knoll Books, 1993.

Tomkinson, Geoffrey Stewart. *A Select Bibliography of the Principal Modern Presses Public and Private in Great Britain and Ireland.* London: First Edition Club, 1928.

See also **Adventures of Tom Bombadil** (Collection); **Gordon, E.V.;** *Leeds University Verse 1914–24;* **Poems by Tolkien:** *The History of Middle-earth;* **Poems by Tolkien in Other Languages**

NORTH POLAR BEAR

North Polar Bear is one of Tolkien's most vividly drawn characters. His role in *The Father Christmas Letters* is that of a helper, but he consistently upstages all other characters in the letters, including Father Christmas himself. North Polar Bear's personal name is Karhu, meaning "bear" in Finnish, and his high-spirited nephews are also given Finnish names: Paksu (fat) and Valkotukka (white-hair). As with many of Tolkien's other characters, Polar Bear displays some of the talents and interests of a philologist, especially in the creation of a goblin alphabet from cave art found under Father Christmas's house.

As a fierce, goblin-fighting warrior bear, the closest parallel character is probably the shape-shifting Beorn in *The Hobbit.* Like Beorn, North Polar Bear is frequently bad-tempered, is implacable in his hatred of goblins, and has a similar preference for sweet foods. Unlike Beorn, however, North Polar Bear is also frequently a figure of fun. While he is a hero, he is also very like a child: he demands attention; he is

often destructive, and he is unable to think about the consequences of his actions. Even his accidents occur on a heroic scale, often while North Polar Bear is unsupervised or attempting tasks beyond his skill. Particular incidents such as charring the North Pole black when he turns on all the Northern Lights for five years (using a small tap in the style of a garden tap) and thoughtlessly opening a window while Father Christmas compiles his lists of gifts for children and allowing the wind to blow the lists everywhere are typical of the bear's interaction with his environment.

North Polar Bear shares that strong characteristic of small children: wanting to help. Perhaps reassuringly to Tolkien's audience of his own children, Polar Bear's help is indispensable to Father Christmas. Even when Polar Bear's mistakes result in chaos, his supernatural strength and enthusiastic willingness ensure that presents are packed and distributed every year, even in the most extremely challenging situations. In many ways, he both represents how a child is seen as dangerous, uncontrolled, and without discipline and portrays the positives of the same behaviors, strong, committed, and enthusiastic.

In the last letter, Father Christmas describes him as "rather a hero (I hope he does not think so himself)," which sums up the way North Polar Bear is described throughout the work; there is plenty of emphasis on his misdemeanors to ensure he does not develop an inflated idea of himself. North Polar Bear, then, functions as a role model, a warning, and a consolation to an ordinary child. Wayne Hammond and Christina Scull (1995, 69) suggest that the Tolkien children all had much-loved stuffed bears and that the prominence of North Polar Bear reflects this. Hammond and Scull also highlight the fondness with which Polar Bear is illustrated.

But, above all, North Polar Bear is funny. His pratfalls, enthusiasms, and wild, clumsy excesses are a contrast to the Elf Ilbereth's fussiness, Father Christmas's slightly world-weary tone, and the evil threat of the goblins. Whether blowing up the North Pole or flooding Father Christmas's "English Delivery Room," North Polar Bear keeps everyone laughing.

PENELOPE DAVIE

Further Reading

Croft, Jane Brennan. "Beyond *The Hobbit:* J.R.R. Tolkien's Other Works for Children." *World Literature Today* (January–April 2004): 67–70.

Hammond, Wayne G., and Christina Scull. *J.R.R. Tolkien: Artist and Illustrator.* London: HarperCollins, 1995.

Hyde, Paul Nolan. "A Philologist at the North Pole: J.R.R. Tolkien and *The Father Christmas Letters.*" *Mythlore* vol. 15, no. 1, whole no. 55 (1988): 23–27.

Tolkien, J.R.R. *The Father Christmas Letters*, edited by Baillie Tolkien. London: Unwin Paperbacks, 1990.

———. *Letters from Father Christmas*, edited by Baillie Tolkien. London: Collins Children's Books, 1995.

———. *Letters from Father Christmas*. London: HarperCollins, 2004.

See also **Animals in Tolkien's Works; Art and Illustrations by Tolkien; Father Christmas; *Father Christmas Letters*; Humor**

NORTHERN COURAGE

In his essay "*Beowulf*: The Monsters and the Critics," and in an earlier version published posthumously in *Beowulf and the Critics,* Tolkien uses the term "Northern courage" to refer to a kind of heroism that found expression in Old English and Old Norse texts from Anglo-Saxon England and medieval Iceland. Tolkien's discussion draws on the accounts of heroism in Old Norse literature found in W.P. Ker's *The Dark Ages* (1904, 57–58) and in E.V. Gordon's *Introduction to Old Norse* (1927, xxix–xxx). Tolkien uses "Northern" to refer to the peoples speaking Germanic languages in England, Scandinavia, and Iceland; in one of his letters, he expresses a dislike of the term "Nordic" because of its association with racialist theories, stating that "geographically, *Northern* is usually better" (*Letters,* 375).

In "*Beowulf*: The Monsters and the Critics," Tolkien describes the fusion of cultures that took place when the Anglo-Saxons converted to Christianity. He writes that "one of the most potent elements in that fusion is the Northern courage: the theory of courage, which is the great contribution of early Northern literature" (*MC,* 20). He goes on to write of "the central position the creed of unyielding will holds in the North" in the early Middle Ages (*MC,* 21). Tolkien relates this characteristically "Northern" kind of courage to pre-Christian beliefs; since there is almost no surviving evidence for pre-Christian English mythology, Tolkien turns to Norse mythology as it is preserved in Icelandic sources (he shows an awareness of the need for care in doing so). In Norse mythology, the gods are finally defeated at Ragnarök, a battle against the forces of Chaos and Unreason. The gods fight in the knowledge that they will be overwhelmed, but they refuse to accept that their inevitable defeat proves them wrong. Tolkien claims that the pre-Christian English shared this vision of the final defeat of what is right and good.

For Anglo-Saxons after the conversion to Christianity, Tolkien argues, the fight against evil goes on, and it continues to lead to inevitable defeat and death in this world, but the Christian revelation promises a final victory of good over evil. This means that although "the tragedy of the great temporal defeat remains for a while poignant" (*MC,* 22), it eventually has little significance beside the ultimate victory of good at the end of this world. Tolkien argues that the *Beowulf*-poet still feels the poignancy of the temporal defeat and celebrates the courage of the hero who fights on in the face of such inevitable failure. In *Beowulf* the "northern mythological imagination" puts the forces of chaos and evil, the monsters, at the centre and gives them the victory; the poem presents "naked will and courage" as the proper response to this situation, and Tolkien claims such indomitable courage in the face of defeat has the power "to revive its spirit even in our own times" (*MC,* 26).

In another Anglo-Saxon poem, *The Battle of Maldon,* a retainer called Byrhtwold gives memorable expression to this Northern theory of courage, and Tolkien speculates that other short heroic lays in Old English, which no longer survive, might also have dealt with the actions of heroes in hopeless circumstances and provided further examples of "the exaltation of undefeated will" (*MC,* 18). Of the surviving poems, however, it is only in *Beowulf* that this theme is treated at length.

In "*Beowulf*: The Monsters and the Critics," Tolkien celebrates Northern courage as the outstanding contribution of the early northern Europeans to humanity. In later works, he prefers to stress the tension between Christian and heroic values and acknowledges that Anglo-Saxon poets themselves grappled with this tension. This shift in emphasis may be connected to Tolkien's realisation that Nazi Germany revealed the dangers in a distorted version of the "Northern" theory of courage. In a letter of 1941, Tolkien speaks of Hitler's corruption of "that noble northern spirit, a supreme contribution to Europe, which I have ever loved and tried to present in its true light" (*Letters,* 55–56).

Jane Chance Nitzsche writes that "in the medieval parodies published during the years 1945 to 1955 . . . [Tolkien] focuses primarily on the failure of Germanic values" (80). Among these "medieval parodies" is Tolkien's verse-play "The Homecoming of Beorhtnoth, Beorhthelm's Son," a sequel to the Anglo-Saxon poem *The Battle of Maldon* (1953, but begun in the 1930s). Tom Shippey has written that in this verse-play Tolkien can be seen grappling with an incompatibility between his Christian faith and the despair and "heathen ferocity" at the root of the theory of courage he admired (Shippey, 140–41). Elsewhere, Shippey argues that in "The Homecoming" Tolkien counsels Christians against embracing the theory of courage that had led to and was defeated in World War II. This is seen particularly clearly,

Shippey suggests, in the way Tolkien transfers Byrhtwold's famous expression of the heroic spirit in *The Battle of Maldon* to a dream in which his words are combined with obviously pre-Christian beliefs (Shippey, *Author*, 294–96).

Tolkien also probes the ambiguities of heroism in his various versions of the story of Túrin Turambar. Richard West argues that these texts show Tolkien exploring the "tension between bravery and foolhardiness" and speculating on the "limits of heroism" (236, 244).

Within the pre-Christian world of Tolkien's Middle-earth, as in pre-Christian England and Scandinavia, Northern courage is the best and most appropriate response to the forces of evil. In *The Lord of the Rings,* there are many heroes who fight on although they expect to die or be defeated, and some give memorable expression to their courage. Treebeard's words before the Ents' attack on Isengard are a notable example of such a speech: He declares that it is "likely enough that we are going to *our* doom: the last march of the Ents. But if we stayed at home and did nothing, doom would find us anyway, sooner or later" (*LotR,* III, iv, 90). In *The Lord of the Rings,* Tolkien's heroes operate within a pre-Christian (and often pessimistic) worldview, but as a Christian Tolkien believed that right would be victorious in the end, as it is in the book (if only partially and temporarily).

CARL PHELPSTEAD

Further Reading

Gordon, E.V. *An Introduction to Old Norse.* Oxford: Clarendon, 1927.

Ker, W.P. *The Dark Ages.* London: Blackwood and Sons, 1904.

Nitzsche, Jane Chance. *Tolkien's Art: A Mythology for England.* London: Macmillan, 1979.

Shippey, Tom. *J.R.R. Tolkien: Author of the Century.* London: HarperCollins, 2000. Paperback edition, 2001.

———. *The Road to Middle-earth.* 2nd ed. London: HarperCollins, 1992.

Tolkien, J.R.R. "*Beowulf:* The Monsters and the Critics." *Proceedings of the British Academy* 22 (1936): 245–95. Reprinted in *The Monsters and the Critics and Other Essays*, edited by Christopher Tolkien, 5–48. London: Allen & Unwin, 1983. Paperback edition, London: HarperCollins, 1997.

———. "The Homecoming of Beorhtnoth, Beorhthelm's Son." *Essays and Studies by Members of the English Association*, new ser. 6 (1953): 1–18.

West, Richard C. "Túrin's *Ofermod:* An Old English Theme in the Development of the Story of Túrin." In *Tolkien's Legendarium: Essays on "The History of Middle-earth,"* edited by Verlyn Flieger and Carl F. Hostetter, 233–45. London: Greenwood, 2000.

See also **Battle of Maldon; Beowulf and the Critics;** **"Beowulf: The Monsters and the Critics"; Beowulf:**

Tolkien's Scholarship; *Homecoming of Beorhtnoth*; Old Norse Literature

NORWAY: RECEPTION OF TOLKIEN

Tolkien's books came relatively late to Norway. The first Tolkien text known to have been translated into Norwegian was a part of the chapter "The Old Forest" from *The Fellowship of the Ring,* which appeared in the science fiction anthology *Østenfor sol* in 1969 (edited by Jon Bing and Tor Åge Bringsværd. Oslo: Den norske bokklubben). A translation of *The Hobbit* followed in 1972 (*Hobbiten.* Oslo: Tiden Norsk Forlag), and of *The Lord of the Rings* in 1973–75 (*Krigen om Ringen.* Oslo: Tiden Norsk Forlag). Both these were, however, marred by many grave errors and inconsistencies. A deluge of complaints from Tolkien enthusiasts resulted in the 1980–81 publication of a completely new translation of *The Lord of the Rings* (*Ringenes Herre.* Oslo: Tiden Norsk Forlag. Revised edition 1999). Two translations of such a large work in less than ten years constituted a considerable outlay for the publisher, but the second translation sold well and gradually established Tolkien in the public consciousness. Whereas few Norwegians had heard of Tolkien in the early 1970s, he had become a well-known author by the late 1980s and a truly famous one ten years later, before the media attention accorded to Peter Jackson's *The Lord of the Rings* films made his name universally recognized. However, *The Silmarillion* did not appear in translation until 1994 (*Silmarillion.* Oslo: Tiden Norsk Forlag), and the unsatisfactory *Hobbit* translation was not superseded until 1997 (*Hobbiten.* Oslo: Tiden Norsk Forlag), the year in which a translation of *Unfinished Tales* appeared (*Ufullendte fortellinger.* Oslo: Tiden Norsk Forlag). By then, the readership was deemed large enough to justify translations of *Tree and Leaf* (*Trær og blader.* Oslo: Tiden Norsk Forlag, 1995), *Smith of Wootton Major* (*Volund Smed fra Store Skauby.* Oslo: Tiden Norsk Forlag, 1995), *The Father Christmas Letters* (*Brev fra Julenissen.* Oslo: Tiden Norsk Forlag, 1997), and even *Roverandom* (*Rundtomrask.* Oslo: Tiden Norsk Forlag, 1999). *Farmer Giles of Ham* had already been translated in 1980 (*Eigil Bonde fra Heim.* Oslo: Tiden Norsk Forlag). It is estimated that almost 270,000 copies of the translated *Lord of the Rings* and more than 140,000 copies of *The Hobbit* had been sold by 2005, to a population of 4.6 million (2005). To this must be added large sales of English-language editions.

Parallel to the widening dissemination of his books, the public perception of Tolkien has shifted. He was originally firmly associated with hippie culture and escapism and seen mainly as a juvenile, lowbrow author, hardly worthy of serious literary or academic attention. Over the years, the verdict has become more nuanced. In particular, Tolkien's use of Old Norse myths and sagas, and of well-known folk traditions and fairy tales, has attracted attention (including musical attention from "metal" bands). Nevertheless, there have been relatively few academic works—almost exclusively theses or dissertations—written on Tolkien, and they have often suffered from lack of in-depth knowledge of work done elsewhere.

The Tolkien Society of Norway, dedicated to the "furtherance of the interest in, and knowledge of" Tolkien and his works, was founded in 1981. Although its main activities have been publishing the journal *Angerthas* (in Norwegian, with occasional material in English) and arranging member meetings, it has also organized or co-organized several international scholarly seminars.

Apart from the publications of this society, Norwegian Tolkien readers had few sources of information about the author until 2000, when a translation of Humphrey Carpenter's biography appeared. The following years saw the publication of several other translated biographies and introductions, as well as a number of books related to Jackson's films. The first research-based book about Tolkien and his writings to be written in Norwegian was published in 2003.

NILS IVAR AGØY

See also **Norwegian Language; Old Norse Literature**

NORWEGIAN LANGUAGE

Both Tolkien's youthful attraction to sagas, and other things northern, and his later professional interests dictated that he should familiarize himself with Norway—its language, history, and culture. He acquired an intimate knowledge of Old Norse literature and its historical and cultural contexts (spanning the eighth to the thirteenth century), but he was also familiar with Norwegian archaeological finds and rock carvings dating from prehistoric periods and with at least some of the folk traditions and fairy tales collected during the early and mid nineteenth century. He was able to read modern Norwegian but probably not to speak it. He was a member of The Viking Society for Northern Research.

Tolkien's knowledge of Norwegian matters is apparent in his philological work in too many ways to enumerate here (and be aware that it is sometimes difficult—and not always meaningful—to distinguish sharply between Norwegian, Danish, Icelandic, and Swedish culture in the Early Middle Ages, although

the poems of the *Elder Edda,* the single most important source to Norse mythology, are usually regarded as predominantly Icelandic, Norwegian, or both). Tolkien shows familiarity with the work of some nineteenth- and early twentieth-century comparative philologists from Norway: the famous runologist and *Edda* expert Sophus Bugge and the etymologist Alf Torp. In "On Fairy-Stories," he refers to the traditional Norwegian fairy tales collected by Peter Christen Asbjørnsen and Jørgen Moe (in George W. Dasent's English translation; one of these fairy tales is faintly echoed in Tolkien's use of the name "Moria").

The Old Norse language, mythology, literature, and culture constituted a main point of departure for Tolkien's legendarium. Because they were so closely related to their Old English counterparts, they could be used to "fill" gaps where the Old English traditions that Tolkien primarily wished to build on and revive were lost or only partially preserved (see especially "*Beowulf:* The Monsters and the Critics" for his views on the defensibility and utility of using the one to throw light on the other). Intriguingly, Tolkien appears to have been aware of Bugge's controversial theory that "the oldest, and, indeed, the great majority of both the mythological and heroic poems [of the *Elder Edda*] were composed by Norwegians *in the British Isles*" (Bugge 1899, emphasis mine), under crucial influence from the Christianized English and Irish culture there. Bugge thus postulated a profound link between the Anglo-Saxon culture, with which Tolkien so strongly identified himself, and the *Elder Edda,* which he admired and from which he drew much of the background for Middle-earth.

Direct references to Norway in Tolkien's fiction are scarce. They occur in "The Notion Club Papers" and, more numerously, in *Letters from Father Christmas* (where we learn that Father Christmas's Christmas Tree is felled in Norway, that one of his friends is the Norwegian wood-cutter Olaf, and that a few of the real old families of Red Gnomes were still to be found in that country in the 1930s). In addition, Vikings appear under several other names in the story of Ælfwine in *The Book of Lost Tales,* and there is an allusion to Snorri Sturluson's "King Olaf Trygvason's saga" in *Roverandom.*

NILS IVAR AGØY

Further Reading

Bugge, Sophus. *The Home of the Eddic Poems with Especial Reference to the Helgi-Lays.* London: David Nutt, 1899.

See also **Old Norse Language; Old Norse Literature; Old Norse Translations;** *Roverandom*

OBITUARY FOR HENRY BRADLEY

Henry Bradley (1845–1923) was a prominent scholar of the English language and one of the early editors of the *Oxford English Dictionary*. Tolkien was an assistant to Bradley at the *OED* from 1919 to 1920, working on entries for words beginning with the letter *W*. Upon Bradley's death in 1923, Tolkien wrote an obituary that appeared in the *Bulletin of the Modern Humanities Research Association*. In the obituary, Tolkien describes Bradley as one of the most important scholars of his time, citing not only his work on the *OED* but also his widely used text on the history of the English language, *The Making of English*. The bulk of the obituary, however, focuses on Tolkien's personal recollections of Bradley, whom he portrays in largely avuncular terms. Tolkien recalls the great pleasure Bradley took in investigating obscure points of language and in sharing his discoveries with others, and praises Bradley for his kindness and enthusiasm in encouraging young scholars, presumably including Tolkien.

Tolkien's fondness for Bradley is clear throughout the obituary, especially in his descriptions of the scholar at work in the Dictionary Room of the Old Ashmolean Building at Oxford. Near the end of the obituary, Tolkien describes in warm terms the familiar figure of Bradley walking across the campus at Oxford, lost in contemplation of some particularly difficult point of language. His death would, according to Tolkien, be felt by all members of the Oxford community.

The obituary ends with an original thirteen-line poem in Old English in which Tolkien praises Bradley's achievements and kindness. The poem concludes by describing Bradley, in lines reminiscent of the ending of *Beowulf,* as *léodwita lípost ond lárgeornost / démena gedéfost ond déophýdgost* (mildest of intelligent men and most eager for learning, kindest of thinkers and most thoughtful).

WILLIAM SMITH

Further Reading

Tolkien, J.R.R. "Henry Bradley: 3 Dec., 1845–23 May, 1923." *Bulletin of the Modern Humanities Research Association* 20 (October 1923): 4–5.

See also **Oxford**

OLD ENGLISH

Learning and Teaching

Old English is the language of the Anglo-Saxons, documented in writing in England between the late seventh and the early twelfth centuries. Tolkien's preoccupation with Old English lasted almost as long as his life. When one of his teachers at King Edward's lent him an Anglo-Saxon primer, Tolkien began to study the language "as a boyish hobby when [I was] supposed to be learning Greek and Latin" (*Letters,* 381). Soon he recited excerpts from *Beowulf* to his friends in the Tea Club and Barrovian Society (TCBS) and spoke Old English at a Latin-language meeting of the school Debating Society (Carpenter, 34–35, 46).

His scholarly engagement with the language began at Oxford, in the summer term of 1913, when he abandoned his initial study program (classics) and entered the Honour School of English Language and Literature. There he specialized in linguistic studies, for which he had shown exceptional aptitude, with Kenneth Sisam as his tutor (62–63).

The study of Old English dominated Tolkien's professional life. During his work at the *Oxford English Dictionary* (1919–20), the editor in chief, Dr. Henry Bradley, praised him for his "unusually thorough mastery of Anglo-Saxon" (101). As reader and later professor of English language at the University of Leeds (1920–24), he organized a syllabus for students interested in Old and Middle English and in philology (*Letters*, 12). As Rawlinson and Bosworth Professor of Anglo-Saxon at Oxford (1925–45), he delivered, as part of his substantial teaching duties, popular lectures on *Beowulf* (117, 132–33). As Merton Professor of English Language and Literature at Oxford (1945–59), he relinquished the teaching of Old English to the next professor of Anglo-Saxon, Charles Wrenn (*Letters*, 117). However, as his valedictory address shows, he still championed the study of "so-called Anglo-Saxon" literature as not merely a root but a flower of English literature, as important and worthy of study as the literature of later periods (*MC*, 230). In 1962, in Wrenn's absence, Tolkien emerged from retirement to deliver lectures on *Beowulf* published posthumously as *Finn and Hengest: The Fragment and the Episode* (vi).

Tolkien's Scholarship

In 1936, Tolkien read "*Beowulf:* The Monsters and the Critics," the Israel Gollancz Memorial Lecture, to the British Academy. The lecture asserts the intrinsic poetic merit of *Beowulf,* defending its focus on the monsters and investigating the poem's structure and its use of the legendary past. Summarizing critical opinion of the past half-century, Andy Orchard describes Tolkien's "ground-breaking" lecture as the most significant impetus for the "continuing attempt to assess *Beowulf* as a work of literature" (7), and Michael D.C. Drout calls it "the single most important critical essay ever written about *Beowulf*" (*B&C*, 1).

Most of Tolkien's Old English scholarly studies demonstrate his preoccupation with language. "Sigelwara Land" investigates the etymology of the

Old English word denoting Ethiopians, and the "Prefatory Remarks on Prose Translation of *Beowulf*" focuses on the poetic language of *Beowulf,* discussing *Beowulf*'s diction and its proper rendering into modern English, as well as the structure and effect of the poem's meter and alliteration. *The Old English Exodus* and *Finn and Hengest: The Fragment and the Episode,* posthumously published collections of lecture notes, both demonstrate the same minute attention to the words of each text. The first contains Tolkien's edition of the Old English poem, his translation, and his textual commentary; the second, a group of lectures on *Beowulf,* attempts to reconstruct the background and implications of the battle at Finnsburg, a legendary incident narrated allusively in the poem. "The Homecoming of Beorhtnoth, Beorhthelm's Son" is a hybrid of fiction and scholarship concerning another Old English poem, *The Battle of Maldon.* The poem recounts the tenth-century defeat of an English defense force led by Beorhtnoth at the hands of the invading Vikings. "The Homecoming" consists of three parts: an introduction about the poem's historical context; a play in alliterative verse, set in the immediate aftermath of the battle of Maldon; and (as its main scholarly component) a detailed discussion of the word *ofermod* in relation to the poem's treatment of heroism. Tolkien translates the word as "overmastering pride" (19) and interprets it as the poet's indictment of Beorhtnoth's morally culpable desire for personal glory.

Tolkien's Fiction

As early as 1938 (a year after *The Hobbit* was first published), readers suggested Old English literature as a source of inspiration for Tolkien's fiction. Asked if Bilbo's theft of Smaug's cup was "based on" the theft of the dragon's cup in *Beowulf,* Tolkien played down the connection but nevertheless called *Beowulf* one of his most valued sources (*Letters,* 31). In other letters, too, he acknowledged his use of Old English material in his writing (150, 208, 212, 220, 283, 385). Often his sources of inspiration were single obscure words and their ramifications (Shippey, 338). An invocation of "Earendel" in the Old English poem *Crist,* for instance, is the origin of a great hero of Tolkien's mythology, Eärendil. The expression *eald enta geweorc* ("the ancient work of giants," usually denoting a great work of the past) contributed to Tolkien's creation of the Ents, who "grew rather out of their name, than the other way about" (*Letters,* 208). The most pervasive influence of Old English appears in the culture of Rohan (Shippey, 124–25). The language and the names of Rohan are Old English; the poetry of Rohan is alliterative, like

Old English poetry. The protagonists' arrival at Théoden's court strongly resembles the arrival of Beowulf and his retainers at Hrothgar's court. Besides containing clear verbal echoes of the Old English poem, the episode in *The Lord of the Rings* parallels the poem in the detailed ceremonial process through which the protagonists approach their respective kings.

Tolkien's fiction also echoes the themes of Old English poetry. Tom Shippey notes that Aragorn's song of Rohan (*TT*, III, vi, 112), a lament of transience, closely resembles a passage in the Old English elegy *The Wanderer* (Shippey, 126). Miranda Wilcox demonstrates echoes of another Old English elegy, *The Seafarer*. Versions of *The Seafarer* appear in Tolkien's unfinished works "The Lost Road" and "The Notion Club Papers." *The Lord of the Rings* itself, a work so preoccupied with transience and exile, recalls the concerns of the poem—especially in the Elves' seafaring to their eternal home. Jane Chance traces how Tolkien develops in his fiction ideas about lordship and heroism that he analyzed in his scholarly studies of Old English literature.

In addition to verbal echoes and similarities of content, Tolkien's fiction often parallels Old English works in themes and narrative structure, especially *Beowulf*. Especially in its deployment of Bilbo's adversaries, Gollum and Smaug, *The Hobbit* parallels the bipartite structure that Tolkien traces in *Beowulf* (Chance, *Tolkien's Art*, 48–52). *The Lord of the Rings* uses allusions to the legendary past to create the same sense of historical "rootedness" and mythical resonance as Tolkien himself praised in *Beowulf* (Shippey, 229–30, 308–18; Nagy, 239–58). In *The Lord of the Rings,* the inset narratives from the legendary past also echo or gloss the central narrative, much as they do in *Beowulf* (Jones 94; Bolintineanu 263–73), so that present and past enhance each other's significance.

The very world in which Tolkien sets his stories is deliberately rooted in Old English matters, from Tolkien's adoption of Middle-earth as its name (*Letters*, 283) to his creation of "a mythology and a pseudo-history that had an interface with the actual history of [Anglo-Saxon] England" (Drout, 241). But Tolkien did try to separate the two realms of his engagement with Old English: he is skeptical about the usefulness of tracing Old English (and other) influences in his fiction (*Letters*, 380–83), and upon publication of *The Lord of the Rings,* he attempted to disconnect his invented history of Anglo-Saxon England from its real history, especially through his appendices to *The Lord of the Rings* (Drout, 229–48). Nevertheless, Tolkien's fiction draws constant inspiration from the words, narrative techniques, and visions of the world with

which he became so closely acquainted through his scholarly work in Old English.

ALEXANDRA BOLINTINEANU

Primary Sources

Tolkien, J.R.R. *Finn and Hengest: The Fragment and the Episode*. Edited by Alan Bliss. London: George Allen & Unwin, 1982.
———. "The Homecoming of Beorhtnoth, Beorhthelm's Son." In *The Tolkien Reader*, 3–24. New York: Ballantine, 1966.
———. *The Old English Exodus*. Text, translation, and commentary by J.R.R. Tolkien. Edited by Joan Turville-Petre, 33–36. Oxford: Clarendon, 1981.
———. "Sigelwara Land" [1]. *Medium Aevum* 1, no. 3 (1932): 183–196.
———. "Sigelwara Land" [2]. *Medium Aevum* 3, no. 2 (1934): 95–111.

Further Reading

Bolintineanu, Alexandra. "'On the Borders of Old Stories': Enacting the Past in *Beowulf* and *The Lord of the Rings*." In *Tolkien and the Invention of Myth*, edited by Jane Chance, 263–73. Lexington, KY: University Press of Kentucky, 2004.
Carpenter, Humphrey. *Tolkien: A Biography*. Boston, MA: Houghton Mifflin, 1977.
Chance, Jane, ed. *Tolkien and the Invention of Myth: A Reader*. Lexington: University Press of Kentucky, 2004.
———. *Tolkien's Art: A Mythology for England*. Lexington, KY: University Press of Kentucky, 2001.
Drout, Michael D.C. "A Mythology for Anglo-Saxon England." In *Tolkien and the Invention of Myth: A Reader*, edited by Jane Chance, 229–48. Lexington, KY: University Press of Kentucky, 2004.
Jones, Diana Wynne. "The Shape of the Narrative in *The Lord of the Rings*." In *J.R.R. Tolkien: This Far Land*, edited by Robert Giddings, 87–107. London: Vision Press, 1983; Totowa, NJ: Barnes & Noble Books, 1984.
Nagy, Gergely. "The Great Chain of Reading." In *Tolkien the Medievalist*, edited by Jane Chance, 239–58. London: Routledge, 2003.
Orchard, Andy. *A Critical Companion to "Beowulf."* Cambridge, UK: D.S. Brewer, 2003.
Shippey, Tom. *The Road to Middle-earth: How J.R.R. Tolkien Created a New Mythology*. Revised and expanded edition. Boston, MA: Houghton Mifflin, 2001.
Wilcox, Miranda. "Exilic Imagination in *The Seafarer* and *The Lord of the Rings*. In *Tolkien the Medievalist*, edited by Jane Chance, 133–154. London: Routledge, 2003.

See also **Alliterative Verse by Tolkien;** *Battle of Maldon;* **Beowulf and the Critics; "Beowulf: The Monsters and the Critics";** *Beowulf:* **Tolkien's Scholarship;** *Beowulf:* **Translations by Tolkien; Cædmon;** *Christ:* **"Advent Lyrics"; Cynewulf;** *Deor;* **Eärendil; Education;** *Exodus,* **Edition of;** *Finn and Hengest; Genesis;* **History, Anglo-Saxon;** *Homecoming of Beorhtnoth, Beorhthelm's Son;*

Leeds; "On Translating *Beowulf*"; Oxford; Riddles: Sources; Runes; *Seafarer; Solomon and Saturn*; TCBS (Tea Club and Barrovian Society); *Wanderer*

OLD ENGLISH *APOLLONIUS OF TYRE,* EDITED BY TOLKIEN

Apollonius of Tyre is an Old English translation of a Latin text but was originally composed in Greek in the second century BCE. The genre "Greek Romance" contains tales that involve love as a motivating factor in the hero's near-fatal misfortune. He is saved by improbable escapes and miraculous and shocking reunions involving journey, pirates, and shipwrecks; and every woman's morality is tested (not unlike much female hagiography). All examples of this genre end happily. This particular tale was popular in late antiquity and the medieval period.

The Old English poem is preserved in a single eleventh-century manuscript that includes a number of works of Wulfstan. In contrast to the Latin sources, the hero is less emotional in the Old English version, and he is more restrained; in fact, he becomes more the Germanic hero in the Old English recasting of the story.

Peter Goolden produced an edition of the work in 1958 for the Oxford Monograph Series. Tolkien was a general editor of the series from 1940 until his retirement in 1959. He contributed an introductory preface to the *Apollonius of Tyre* volume, a short paragraph justifying the edition and apologizing for delays in production. In his introduction, Goolden thanks Tolkien for the many corrections and suggestions that Tolkien had made to Goolden during the editorial stage.

L.J. Swain

Further Reading

Goolden, Peter, ed. *Apollonius of Tyre.* Oxford Monograph Series. Oxford: Oxford University Press, 1958.

See also **Old English; Oxford**

OLD FRENCH LITERATURE

A medieval scholar, editor, and translator of *Sir Gawain and the Green Knight,* where borrowings from Anglo-Norman are substantial, Tolkien had read widely and was professionally familiar with Old French literature. As a philologist, he was knowledgeable of Old French language. His creative works, moreover, evince structural patterns, characters, themes, and conventions that are common to Old French literature, especially the eleventh-century *Song of Roland* and the twelfth-century Arthurian romances of Chrétien de Troyes, which were continued by others in centuries beyond. Following Breton minstrels, Tolkien also wrote *lays,* for example, *The Lays of Beleriand, The Lay of Eärendil,* and *The Lay of Aotrou and Itroun,* and he at least imagined *The Lay of Leithian,* whence the story of Beren and Lúthien, in *The Silmarillion,* is supposedly derived. His translation of *Sir Orfeo* (ca. 1300), which claims to be a Breton *lai,* connects his scholarship and his fiction to Marie de France, another twelfth-century French author who composed *lais* for the English court of Henry II Plantagenet.

As scholars have noted, Tolkien's *Lord of the Rings* employs, adopts, and controls—"by a map and an extremely tight chronology of days and dates" (Shippey, *Road,* 121)—the medieval interlace structure in the assembly of its complex, overlapping narrative. *Interlace,* or, in French, *entrelacement,* does not originally apply, however, to narrative. Rather, it depicts the interwoven patterns of ornamentation and illustration common to initials found in medieval manuscripts. By analogy, the French critic Eugène Vinaver, following Ferdinand Lot, argued that these patterns also describe a variety of medieval narratives, saying that "the interlace proper consists of threads superimposed upon one another in such a way as to make it impossible to separate them" (78).

Such interlace patterns exist in *Beowulf,* which Tolkien knew well and studied closely, though scholarship on this specific topic postdates the publication of *The Lord of the Rings* by more than a decade. Interlace is also, and perhaps most significantly, prevalent in Arthurian literature in Old French. De Troyes's five Arthurian romances are all built using the interlace structure. Thirteenth-century continuations of Arthurian material—for example, the prose *Lancelot,* Robert de Boron's *L'Estoire dou Graal,* the *Queste del Saint Graal,* and *La Mort le Roi Artu*—all rely on interlace. Not inconsequentially, these Old French romances provide the essential substance, and sometimes the exact text, for the eventual English-language story of King Arthur: Thomas Malory's fifteenth-century *Le Morte d'Arthur.* Tolkien's most obvious point of connection with Old French literature, therefore, is in the construction of *The Lord of the Rings* by interlace, a form common to medieval French romance, apparent in *Beowulf,* and adopted in English by Malory, Edmund Spenser, and others.

Beyond romance and interlace, there are connections to Old French epic that bear noting in Tolkien. The eponymous hero of France's most famous epic, *The Song of Roland,* is in some ways an archetype for *The Lord of the Rings'* Boromir: each carries and blows an ivory horn; each is his lord's "right arm," unmatched on the battlefield and thus the key to securing and defending the power of the sovereign; both share pride as a flaw; and each dies in a similarly tragic fashion: away from home, in the wilderness, defending his company against overwhelming enemy force and numbers, and, in the moment before death, sounding his horn as a final sign of defiance and fealty. As with Boromir, the death of Roland is an apparent precursor to the failure of his lord's rule. It seems to presage the last days of Charlemagne and the collapse of the Christian empire in the face of the invading Saracens. Likewise, the death of Boromir, at least for Denethor, seems to forecast the fall of Gondor to the army of Sauron.

The Lord of the Rings is also linked to *The Song of Roland* through its other story of a degenerate lord, King Théoden of Rohan, who faces defeat and the end of his royal lineage after the loss of his son Théodred, who is described as the king's "right-hand." What unites these stories, however, is not simply the death of the heroic warrior and the threat of sovereign collapse. Rather, it is the depiction of the aged and decrepit king who has been misled into ruin by his evil counselor. The parallels are not perfect, but Théoden, with his long white hair and his beard "like snow upon his knees" (*TT,* III, vi, 116), recalls uncannily the old, white-bearded Charlemagne from *The Song of Roland.* That each was remarkable for his height is another striking similarity. As Tolkien describes Théoden, "bent though he was, he was still tall and must in youth have been high and proud indeed" (*TT,* III, vi, 117); Charlemagne (Charles the Great), as his name suggests, was renowned for his size. Finally, just as Grima Wormtongue deceived Théoden, and thus created the conditions for Théodred's demise, so did Ganelon deceive Charlemagne, convincing him to leave Roland in charge of the rearguard even as he plotted the Saracen ambush that would eventually destroy the king's greatest knight.

GERALD SEAMAN

Primary Sources

De Troyes, Chrétien. *Oeuvres Complètes.* Paris: Gallimard, 1994.

Rychner, Jean, ed. *Les Lais de Marie de France.* Paris: Champion, 1983.

Short, Ian, ed. *La Chanson de Roland.* Paris: Librairie Générale Française, 1990.

Tolkien, J.R.R., trans. *Sir Gawain and the Green Knight, Pearl, and Sir Orfeo.* Boston, MA: Houghton Mifflin, 1975.

Tolkien, J.R.R. and E.V. Gordon, eds. *Sir Gawain and the Green Knight.* Oxford: Clarendon, 1925.

Further Reading

Brewer, Derek S. "*The Lord of the Rings* as Romance." In *J.R.R. Tolkien, Scholar and Storyteller: Essays in Memoriam,* edited by Mary Salu and Robert T. Farrell, 249–64. Ithaca, NY: Cornell University Press, 1979.

Bruckner, Matilda Tomaryn. "Marie de France." In *Literature of the French and Occitan Middle Ages: Eleventh to Fifteenth Centuries,* edited by Deborah Sinnreich-Levi and Ian S. Laurie, 199–208. Dictionary of Literary Biography 208. Detroit, MI: Bruccoli, Clark, Layman, 1999.

Leyerle, John. "The Interlace Structure of *Beowulf,*" *University of Toronto Quarterly* 37 no. 1 (October 1967): 1–17.

Shippey, Tom. *J.R.R. Tolkien: Author of the Century.* Boston, MA: Houghton Mifflin, 2000.

———. *The Road to Middle-earth.* Boston, MA: Houghton Mifflin, 1983.

Vinaver, Eugène. *The Rise of Romance.* Oxford: Clarendon, 1971.

West, Richard C. "The Interlace Structure of *The Lord of the Rings.*" In *A Tolkien Compass,* edited by Jared Lobdell, 77–94. La Salle, IL: Open Court, 1975.

See also **Arthurian Literature; Carolingians;** *Sir Gawain and the Green Knight:* **Edition with E.V. Gordon**

OLD HIGH GERMAN

Old High German *(Althochdeutsch)* was spoken from approximately 500 to 1050. Old High German evolved from West Germanic, from which it is divided by the Second Sound Shift or Old High German Consonant Shift. This sound shift also makes the Old High German consonant system significantly different from that of the Low German languages (including English).

It is not known if Tolkien read Old High German fluently, although given Tolkien's knowledge of many other Germanic languages and his mastery of the sound changes in Germanic, it is certainly likely that he could understand Old High German if the necessity occurred. Tolkien did work with Old High German when producing etymologies for the *Oxford English Dictionary,* and in later work on Middle English words he often cites cognates in Old High German.

In *Beowulf and the Critics* Tolkien refers to the Old High German *Wessobrunner Gebet (Wessobrunn Prayer),* an eighth- to early-ninth-century poem written in a Bavarian dialect of Old High German found in or near the monastery of Wessobrunn. The poem, which consists of nine lines of alliterative verse, tells a creation story similar to that found in stanzas three to five of the Old Norse *Völuspá.* Tolkien relates these texts to the "creation hymn" in *Beowulf* that enrages Grendel (*B&C,* 137–38). Tolkien may have been especially interested in the *Wessobrunner Gebet* because it is thought to show evidence of Anglo-Saxon influence. In the context of the argument in which he cites it, however, he also may have simply been taking up part of W.P. Ker's argument in *The Dark Ages*

(Ker also compares the *Wessobrunner Gebet* to the opening lines of *Völuspá*).

In *Beowulf and the Critics,* Tolkien also refers to the Old Low German *Heliand,* an epic verse retelling of the life of Christ, in the context of discussing the Old English word *Metod,* which can mean "The Measurer," in *Beowulf.* Tolkien notes that in the *Heliand* it is said that John the Baptist never will touch wine, *so habed im uurd giscapu metod gemarcod endi maht godes* ("this is the way the works of fate made him, time formed him, and the power of God as well," G. Ronald Murphy's translation).

MICHAEL D.C. DROUT

Further Reading

Bostock, John Knight. *A Handbook on Old High German Literature.* Oxford: Clarendon, 1955. 2nd ed., revised by K.C. King and D.R. McLintock, 1976.

Murphy, G. Ronald, trans. *The Heliand: The Saxon Gospel.* New York: Oxford University Press, 1992.

Ker, W.P. *The Dark Ages.* London: Blackwood and Sons, 1904.

Sievers, Eduard, ed. *Heliand.* Halle: Verlag der Buchhandlung des Waisenhauses, 1878.

See also **Beowulf and the Critics**

OLD HIGH GERMAN LITERATURE

Given Tolkien's level of expertise in the field of Germanic philology, he would have been familiar with a variety of literary works written in the various dialects of Old High German. Few of these, however, are explicitly mentioned in Tolkien's published works.

The extant corpus of Old High German, like those of Gothic and Old English, is primarily ecclesiastical in nature. One text of this sort that was certainly known by Tolkien is the *Wessobrunner Gebet* (Bavarian dialect, ca. 800), consisting of a prayer in prose preceded by nine lines in alliterative verse. The verse portion, which tells of the Chaos before the Creation, bears similarity to a passage in the Old Norse *Völuspá.* Tolkien comments on this similarity in the B-text of *Beowulf and the Critics* (138, 298–99).

Most ecclesiastical literature in Old High German, however, consists of glosses, translations, and adaptations of Latin texts. Some of the most significant of these are the translation of Tatian's *Diatessaron,* a Gospel harmony telling the life of Jesus in prose (East Franconian dialect, ca. 830); the *Evangelienbuch* of Otfrid of Weissenburg, which presents the life of Christ in more than seven thousand lines of rhyming verse (South Rhenish Franconian dialect, completed between 863 and 871); and various works translated

into Alemannic dialect by Notker III of St. Gallen (d. 1022). Though these works are not mentioned in any of Tolkien's published writings, he likely would have been aware of them.

Tolkien does mention similar texts written in Old Saxon, a Low German dialect. In his review of "Philology: General Works" in *The Year's Work in English Studies* (1925, 57), Tolkien praises Edward H. Sehrt's dictionary of the language of the *Hêliand* and *Genesis.* Tolkien would have been familiar with the fragmentary Old Saxon *Genesis,* which was the source of a portion of the Old English *Genesis B.* The *Hêliand,* the other literary monument of Old Saxon, is an epic poem in 5,983 lines of alliterative verse on the life of Christ, probably written between 822 and 840. Tolkien quotes from this poem in the A- and B-texts of *Beowulf and the Critics* (72, 135, 246–47) and mentions it in his article on "Middle English 'Losenger'" (70).

The heroic poetry of Old High German has been lost, apart from the two surviving leaves of the *Hildebrandslied,* a text with which Tolkien was undoubtedly familiar. Tolkien certainly knew the heroic poetry of the Middle High German period, especially the *Nibelungenlied* (ca. 1200), an epic poem in thirty-nine cantos of rhyming verse, telling of the exploits of Siegfried and the fall of the Burgundians. Tolkien refers to the poem in *Finn and Hengest* (27, 35, 51–53), where he also mentions another Middle High German epic, *Kudrun* (ca. 1230). In "Middle English 'Losenger'" (Tolkien 1951, 66), he demonstrates an even broader knowledge of Middle High German poetry, referencing Hartmann von Aue's *Iwein,* Gottfried von Strassburg's *Tristan,* Konrad von Würzburg's *Trojan War,* and Wernher the Gardener's *Meier Helmbrecht.*

ARDEN R. SMITH

Primary Sources

Braune, Wilhelm, ed. *Althochdeutsches Lesebuch.* 16th ed., revised by Ernst A. Ebbinghaus. Tübingen: Max Niemeyer Verlag, 1979.

Tolkien, J.R.R. *Finn and Hengest: The Fragment and the Episode.* Edited by Alan Bliss. Boston, MA: Houghton Mifflin, 1983.

———. "Middle English 'Losenger': Sketch of an Etymological and Semantic Enquiry." *Essais de Philologie Moderne* (1951): 63–76.

———. "Philology: General Works." *The Year's Work in English Studies* 6 (1925): 32–66.

Further Reading

Bostock, John Knight. *A Handbook on Old High German Literature.* 2nd ed., revised by K.C. King and D.R. McLintock. Oxford: Clarendon, 1976.

Hatto, A.T., trans. *The Nibelungenlied*. Harmondsworth: Penguin, 1969.

Murphy, G. Ronald, trans. *The Heliand: The Saxon Gospel*. New York: Oxford University Press, 1992.

Walshe, Maurice. *Medieval German Literature: A Survey*. Cambridge, MA: Harvard University Press, 1962.

See also **Carolingians; Genesis; Mythology, Germanic; Old High German; Old Norse Literature**

OLD MAN WILLOW

In a draft of a letter written in 1958, Tolkien explains that in his myth of the Fall, all things and all inhabitants of Eä are affected by corruption, and even "trees may 'go bad'" (*Letters,* 287). Old Man Willow is a prime example of this. Old Man Willow first appears as a villainous tree called Willowman in the poem *The Adventures of Tom Bombadil* (published in the *Oxford Magazine* in 1934). In both the 1934 and the 1962 versions of the poem, Willowman is one of four hostile forces (along with the River-woman's Daughter, the Badger-brock, and the Barrow-wight) who appear as potential threats to Tom Bombadil, each in their turn trying to imprison him. As with the other three, Old Man Willow is effortlessly dismissed by Bombadil through the singing of a song.

Later, when Tolkien was searching for a story line for *The Lord of the Rings* and needed to provide for the four Hobbits some sort of "an 'adventure' on the way," he inserted the "already 'invented'" Tom Bombadil character, and with him came some version of Willowman, the Barrow-wight, and the River-woman's Daughter—though not the Badger-brock (*Letters,* 192). In *The Lord of the Rings,* however, Old Man Willow takes a more sinister role than in *The Adventures of Tom Bombadil,* appearing as a powerful malevolent will—"a grey thirsty spirit"—exerting an influence over nearly all of the Old Forest. His goal is to draw other creatures to himself and to consume them. Bombadil says of him that he has "a hatred of things that go free upon the earth" and that "his heart was rotten, but his strength was green" (*FR,* I, vii, 141). Early in *The Fellowship of the Ring,* he nearly succeeds with the four Hobbits—Pippin is swallowed completely, and only Merry's legs lie outside the trunk—before Tom Bombadil appears (by accident it seems) and rescues the hobbits, forcing Old Man Willow to release them.

As to the nature of Old Man Willow's evil, in a letter of 1955 Tolkien dismissed (with two exclamations!) the idea that "Willowman was an ally of Mordor" (*Letters,* 228), echoing a comment by Aragorn that "there are many evil and unfriendly things in the world . . . not in league with Sauron" (*FR,* II, iii, 302). (A parallel could be drawn, for example, with

Shelob.) Randel Helms suggests that "the directing will of the forest is, as it were, an objectification of the hobbits' own lack of will" while they are still overly timid (86). Tom Shippey, however, referring to *Unfinished Tales* (348), points out that "in later years Tolkien was to toy with the idea that . . . Willow-man, the Barrow-wight, and the elementals who send the storm on Caradhras, were all operating under the command of the chief Ringwraith" (Shippey, 67). In any case, Old Man Willow, along with the bad-hearted huorns of Fangorn Forest, illustrates that, despite Tolkien's famous affiliation with and love of trees in the legendarium, trees are not unambiguously good. Like sentient beings, they are susceptible to some form of corruption and the Fall.

MATTHEW DICKERSON

Further Reading

Helms, Randel. *Tolkien's World*. Boston, MA: Houghton Mifflin, 1974.

Shippey, Tom. *J.R.R. Tolkien: Author of the Century*. London: HarperCollins, 2000.

See also **Goldberry; Tom Bombadil; Treebeard; Trees**

OLD MERCIAN

Old Mercian is one of the four dialects spoken and written in the Anglo-Saxon period (roughly 500–1066). Mercia was the "middle" kingdom in the sense that it lay north of Wessex, west of Essex, and south of Northumbria and was bordered on the west by Wales. During the eighth and early ninth centuries, Mercia was in the ascendant among the four strong Anglo-Saxon kingdoms.

The geographic area of Mercia is Tolkien's homeland and the area of England in which he spent almost all his life. It was outside Birmingham that he lived his early years with his mother; he spent his formative years in Birmingham at King Edward's School and later went up to Oxford. All these locations are within the kingdom of Mercia.

Tolkien expressed himself as enamored of the dialect of his homeland and roots. Undoubtedly, some of the emotional attachment to the dialect stems from his association of the land and people with his youth and his mother. In any case, Tolkien expressed himself as desiring to speak Mercian all the time if he could and seemed to give it a special status in his created world.

The influence of the Mercian dialect is seen most clearly in the Tolkien's depiction of the Rohirrim. These people call their land the "Mark." This name is from an Old English word, *mearc,* and the name of

Mercia in West Saxon is *Myrce*. In Mercian it would have been something like *Mearc* or, without the West Saxon diphthong, **Mark*. Names also take a Mercian form: Saruman from *searo- man*, a compound and name meaning "crafty man, man of skill." Other names are given in the Mercian form, including Eorl and Hasufel. Places from Mercia also appear in Tolkien's work: for example, Bree < Brill (Bree Hill) and the Barrow-downs in *The Lord of the Rings* and Thame, Worminghall, and Oakley in *Farmer Giles of Ham*.

L.J. SWAIN

Further Reading

Shippey, Tom. *J.R.R. Tolkien: Author of the Century*. London: HarperCollins, 2000.

See also **Old English**

OLD NORSE LANGUAGE

For a linguistic specialist, "Old Norse" carries several possible meanings. It can mean the language of the Scandinavian countries during the Viking age, roughly AD 750–1050; this is preserved largely through short runic inscriptions carved on stone. Dialect differences were already present at this period, with "East Norse" in Sweden and Denmark marked off from "West Norse" in Norway. "Norse" and "Norseman" are also sometimes used to indicate "Norwegian" in particular. Meanwhile, from the ninth century onward, Iceland was settled by colonists, most of whom spoke a Norwegian dialect. In that remote island, there was little linguistic contact or linguistic change, so the language of the Viking Age has remained surprisingly little altered to the present day. Furthermore, the culturally conservative Icelanders began, from the twelfth century, to preserve a great deal of earlier myth and legend in writing, creating a substantial corpus of Eddic and skaldic poetry, as well as scores of sagas and shorter prose narratives, all of them in their own language. The standardized form of this language is most often meant by "Old Norse," as in the still-influential *Introduction to Old Norse* published by Tolkien's friend and collaborator E.V. Gordon in 1927. Modern scholars prefer to use the catch-all term "Old Norse-Icelandic."

Old Norse (used in its widest sense) was important to Tolkien for several reasons. It was closely related in its origins to Old English; during the Viking Age and after, it continued to be spoken in the Danish-Norwegian colonies in Britain; and it left a heavy imprint even on modern English. The Middle English poem *Sir Gawain and the Green Knight*, edited by Tolkien and Gordon in 1925, showed marked influence from Norse in its vocabulary, much of which survived into the modern day in English dialects such as that studied in Walter Haigh's *New Glossary of the Dialect of the Huddersfield District*, to which Tolkien contributed a foreword in 1928. In addition, the better-preserved records of Old Norse allowed one at least to imagine what the pagan mythology and terminology of Old English would have been like if these had survived.

In *The Hobbit*, Tolkien gave Norse names from a genuine Eddic poem to all the Dwarves (except one, Balin), and to Gandalf. Smaug's name is also a Norse form of a word found only in Old English, and the sword names Glamdring and Orcrist look like a combination of Old Norse and Old English. Logically, it was impossible that any form of Old Norse could have been spoken in the far past of the Third Age (it is not old enough). Tolkien eventually rationalized this by saying, first, that the Dwarves had names in their own language that they did not reveal but used names from the language of their human neighbors and, second, that that human language, spoken east of Mirkwood, was related to the language of the Riders of Rohan and to the Common Speech in much the same way as Old Norse was related to, respectively, Old English and modern English. It was therefore appropriate for him to "translate" Dwarf names into Old Norse.

Finally, as with Smaug and Glamdring, Tolkien from an early period showed a tendency to merge Old English and Old Norse as if to recover genuine early English tradition by imaginative reconstruction from Norse. The nickname of his hero Ottor "Wæfre" (*Lost Tales I*, 23–24) is good Old English (see modern English "waver"), but Ottor is neither quite Old English *(Ohthere)* nor quite Old Norse *(Óttarr)*. His sons Hengest and Horsa are the legendary founders of England, but legend also insists that they were Jutes, from Jutland in Denmark. Tolkien viewed Old Norse as a great and valuable resource for the recovery of English tradition, but he remained well aware of its increasing separation over time and the continuing paganism of its cultural tradition; his ambiguous feelings toward the language and the culture are well expressed in the figure of Orm, Ælfwine's master (*Lost Tales II*, 318).

TOM SHIPPEY

Further Reading

Gordon. E.V., ed. *Introduction to Old Norse*. London: Oxford University Press, 1927. Second edition revised by A.R. Taylor, 1957.

Haugen, Einar. *The Scandinavian Languages: An Introduction to their History*. Cambridge, MA: Harvard University Press, 1976.

Jansson, Sven B.F. *The Runes of Sweden*. Translated by Peter G. Foote. New York: Bedminster, 1962.

Moltke, Erik. *Runes and their Origins: Denamrk and Elsewhere.* Translated by Peter G. Foote. Copenhagen: Nationalmuseets Forlag, 1985.

Shippey, Tom. "Tolkien and Iceland: The Philology of Envy." http://www.nordals.hi.is/Apps/WebObjects/HI.woa/wa/dp?detail=1004508&name=nordals_en_greinar_og_erindi.

See also **Mythology for England; Mythology, Germanic; Old English; Old Norse Literature**

OLD NORSE LITERATURE

(Norse names that are commonly anglicized have been kept in anglicized form.)

Tolkien's attraction to Old Norse literature began in his boyhood as part of that "pre-eminently desirable" fascination he felt for the "nameless North of Sigurd of the Völsungs" (*TC*, 40). The consistency of Tolkien's interest is easily measured by preferences and choices made during his school and university years and during his early teaching career. He began studying Old Norse (also called Old Icelandic) and translating passages on his own while he was still at King Edward's School in Birmingham. As a student at Oxford, he used part of the five pounds that came with his Skeat Prize for English to purchase William Morris's translation of the *Völsunga Saga*. In his first teaching position at Leeds, he and E.V. Gordon formed a saga-reading Viking Club among their undergraduate students, and in 1926, shortly after his return to Oxford, Tolkien founded yet another club, the *Kolbítar,* this one composed of fellow dons who met in the evenings to read and translate Icelandic sagas.

Throughout Tolkien's life, Old Norse literature continued to play a significant role in both his academic and his creative career—so much so that even a philological article such as "Sigelwara Land," an article on the single Anglo-Saxon word, *sigelwara,* relates this word back to Múspell, the fire realm of Old Norse belief. Still, it is not true that Tolkien idealized all aspects of the Viking world; he was too aware of the "evil side of heroic life," but he emphasized and promoted England's own connections to the Scandinavian North, praising its "theory of courage" and its "creed of unyielding will" and claiming that the early English were like the early Norse in their belief that men are the "chosen allies" of the gods in the war against chaos and monsters (*MC*, 17, 20–21).

In Tolkien's fiction, influence from Norse mythology—especially from the two *Eddas,* the *Elder* (or *Poetic) Edda* and Snorri Sturluson's thirteenth-century *Prose Edda*—is strongly evident. Shortly after the publication of *The Hobbit* in 1937, readers began recognizing the influence of Norse mythology, noting

first that Tolkien's Dwarf names (and even Gandalf's name) came from *Dvergatal,* a catalogue of dwarves that appears both in *Völuspá,* a prophetic poem within the *Elder Edda,* and in *Gylfaginning* of the *Prose Edda.* (See *Letters,* 21, 31, 175, 382, and 383, for Tolkien's commentary.) Another *Elder Edda* poem, *Fáfnismál,* gave Tolkien a model for Bilbo's conversation with Smaug (*Letters,* 134). And still another poem, *Reginsmál,* gave him an Old Norse example of enmity caused by gold. Various Eddic tales of questions and answers exchanged with inhabitants of the underworld—or with giants in their halls—gave Tolkien a model for Bilbo and Gollum's riddle contest (as did *The Saga of King Heidrek the Wise*). The term *mirkwood* appears throughout the *Elder Edda,* and Gandalf's trick for turning Trolls to stone comes from yet another *Elder Edda* poem, *Alvíssmál,* where Thor plays the same trick on a dwarf.

The god who most consistently influenced Gandalf, however, is not Thor but Odin, the Allfather of Norse mythology. Odin wanders the Middle-earth of Norse belief in the guise of a gray-bearded old man; Gandalf the Grey is a version of "the Odinic wanderer" (*Letters,* 119). Like Odin, Gandalf is a visitor from a higher realm who travels through Middle-earth in the likeness of an old, bearded, and yet vigorous man. Several of the traditional epithets or bynames attached to Odin and listed in *Grímnismál* of the *Elder Edda*—as well as in *Gylfaginning* of the *Prose Edda*—help confirm the relationship: Broad-hat, Long-beard, Greybeard, Bearer of the (Magic) Wand, Wayweary, Wayfarer, and Wanderer. Both Odin and Gandalf not only wear broad-brimmed hats and carry staffs (or a wands or spears) but also associate with the three primary beasts of battle in Norse mythology: ravens, eagles, and wolves. Odin has his two news-bringing ravens, Hugin and Munin (Thought and Memory); a wolf hangs over the gate in Odin's hall, and an eagle hovers on high (mostly likely decorative forms); and though Odin is ultimately devoured by the giant wolf Fenrir, he also keeps two pet wolves (Geri and Freki) and feeds them from his hand. In the Eddic tale of how Odin acquired the mead of poetry (from *Skáldskaparmál* in the *Prose Edda*), Odin uses a shape-shifter trick common in Norse mythology and takes on the form of an eagle to escape Sutting, a giant.

Echoes of these Norse battle animals appear throughout Tolkien's literature; in one way or another, all are associated with Gandalf or his cause. In *The Hobbit,* the ancient raven Roäc and others of his race demonstrate the same war-savvy, news-bearing traits as Hugin and Munin. Eagles repeatedly serve as last-minute rescuers of Gandalf and his associates, and Gandalf takes the lead role in attacking or defying wolves, much as Odin takes the lead role in battling

Fenrir during Ragnarök (the final battle of the gods). Both Odin and Gandalf have otherworldly horses that serve in similar ways. Odin's eight-legged Sleipnir can move above the earth; Shadowfax has a "flying" pace and is repeatedly compared to the wind. Whereas Sleipnir is associated with death and journeys to the world of the dead, Shadowfax is described as a "shade" or "shadow." At Minas Tirith, he is the only horse untroubled by the Nazgûl horror and remains as "steadfast as a graven image" in the street of tombs (*RK*, V, iv, 103). He is last seen racing (with Gandalf on his back) toward the mists of the Barrow-downs.

Odin, however, is not a simple or consistent figure. His epithets also include Deceiver, Raven God, Battle-Wolf, Father of the Battle-Slain, and Stirrer of Strife. (For a complete list of Odin's epithets, see *Cassell's Dictionary of Norse Myth and Legend.*) On the plain of Middle-earth, Gandalf is the one who manifests Odin's favorable qualities as a seeker of truth and a defender of good. In *The Lord of the Rings,* Odin's negative traits (those that mark him as a promoter of war, death, and deception) are allotted to both Sauron and Saruman. Of the two villains, Saruman is the one most closely associated with Odin's ravaging wolves and carrion birds; he is also the one who travels (as do Gandalf and Odin) through Middle-earth in the guise of an old man, hooded and cloaked. Though Sauron has less physical presence, his single fiery eye suggests Odin's titles of One-Eyed or Fire-Eye. Like Odin, Sauron has a ring of power. Odin's ring, Draupnir (an arm ring), produces eight more rings every nine nights; Sauron's One Ring has the ability to dominate the three, seven, and nine lesser Rings.

In *The Silmarillion,* Odin's positive traits are manifested in Manwë, Tolkien's ruling Vala. From his throne on the pinnacle of Taniquetil, "highest of the mountains," Manwë looks outward over creation, much as Odin does from his high seat on the Norse Hliðskjálf. (Sauron, as a negative version of Odin, looks outward from the mountains of Mordor, from the fortress of Barad-dûr.) Both Manwë and Odin keep birds in their service (hawks and eagles for Manwë, ravens for Odin). Both Manwë and Odin are associated with the sky or air and appropriately dress in blue—as Gandalf also does at the end of *The Return of the King* (*RK*, VI, vii, 274). And again Odin's less favorable traits are given to the villains, to Morgoth and Sauron (who is Morgoth's servant and imitator in *The Silmarillion*). Both Morgoth and Sauron work through deceit; both create unrest; both keep wolves. Sauron, like Odin, is a shifter of shapes.

Other gods (or god-associated figures) from Norse mythology also left their mark. Tulkas, the Vala "greatest in strength and deeds of prowess," resembles the giant-bashing, half-comic Thor—though another

Vala, Oromë, a "hunter of monsters," shares elements of Thor. Aulë, "a smith and a master of all crafts," is the Vala who created the Dwarves; in temperament and talent, Aulë resembles both the Dwarves he created and the dwarves of Norse mythology. Ossë and his spouse, Uinen, echo the Norse demigods Ægir and Rán in their power over the seas. Melkor, the fallen Vala, is much like Loki. Estë, "healer of hurts," is a version of the Norse healing goddess Eir. Yavanna, Giver of Fruits, suggests the goddess Idun (keeper of Asgard's apples). Nienna, the Vala who weeps for all the world's grievances, is a version of the weeping goddess figure seen in both Freya and Frigg. Nessa, Tolkien's "fleetfooted" Vala, is a version of the huntress goddess, represented in Norse mythology by Skadi, a giantess who marries a god. Vairë, the Vala who "weaves all things" into her "storied webs," plays a similar role to Urðr, Verðandi, and Skuld (Past, Present, and Future), the three Norse Norns, who are sometimes described as weaving the world's destiny. (For a full description of Vala roles, see *S,* 25–29.) And like Asgard's gods, who are divided into the Æsir and the Vanir, Tolkien divides his "Powers" into the Ainur and the Valar, echoing the Norse by the initial use of an *A* or *V* and by plurals formed through an *r.* Even Tolkien's Elves of the Light and Elves of Darkness come from the *Prose Edda,* from the briefly mentioned, god-befriending "light-elves," who live in Álfheim, and from the less appealing "dark elves," who live beneath the earth (*S,* 53).

Incidents and settings in *The Silmarillion* typically show Eddic influence as well. Beren's loss of a hand to the wolf Carcharoth in the tale "Of Beren and Lúthien" echoes Tyr's loss of a hand to Loki's wolf son, Fenrir. Frodo's approach to Mordor (with its bridge, gates, and guardians, its darkness and chill) echoes Hermod's approach to the Norse underworld in a *Prose Edda* account, and Tolkien's conception of a Middle-earth surrounded by an "Outer Sea" (or "Encircling Sea" or "Ekkaia") also comes from Norse mythology (*Letters,* 238). The fire-wielding Balrog and the collapse of Moria's bridge echo the battle of Ragnarök, where Surt, a fire demon or giant, causes Asgard's bridge to be destroyed. In both accounts, a horn is sounded before the battle begins. Like Loki (the traitor god of Asgard), Melkor (who becomes Morgoth) is captured and bound by his fellow "gods"; like Loki, Melkor ultimately becomes free.

Sigurd's adventures (the Norse version of the Germanic Siegfried legend) include a reforged sword, a treasure-guarding dragon, and a "helmet of terror," all of which appear in the story "Of Túrin Turambar" in *The Silmarillion.* The sword Túrin uses to kill Glaurung, "the father of dragons," is a reforged weapon, as is the sword Sigurd uses to kill the dragon

Fafnir. (Aragorn's "renewed" blade in *The Lord of the Rings* should also come to mind.) Like Glaurung in *The Silmarillion* (and Smaug in *The Hobbit*), Fafnir is malicious and cunning, and he creates a paralyzing spell. In Norse legend, Fafnir's "helmet of terror" is claimed by Sigurd after Fafnir's death; in Tolkien's story, Túrin Turambar owns a helmet called the Dragon-helm of Dor-lómin. In both accounts, the dragon is killed by a sword thrust from below; in both accounts, the dying dragon predicts an evil future or reveals an evil truth.

In *The Silmarillion,* Nauglamir, the "renowned" Necklace of the Dwarves, is made greater yet by the inclusion of a Silmaril, but desire to possess the necklace and its accompanying treasure—plus a curse from a dying Dwarf—brings dissention and death (*S,* 114, 231–32, 235–36). In the legend of Sigurd (best told in the *Elder Edda* and the *Völsunga Saga*), a coveted magical ring is similarly cursed by a dwarf; and in various Eddic accounts, a dwarf-made, strife-causing necklace, the Necklace of the Brísings, is owned by the Norse goddess Freya. (See "The Tale of Hogni and Hedinn" for the story of this necklace.)

Over time, Tolkien softened and reduced his dependence on Norse mythology. What appears within the published *Silmarillion* is impressive enough, but early renditions of Tolkien's mythology (in *Unfinished Tales* and the twelve volumes of *The History of Middle-earth*) reveal far more. *The Book of Lost Tales: Part I* and *The Book of Lost Tales: Part II* (the first two volumes of *The History of Middle-earth*) contain what Christopher Tolkien calls his father's "first substantial work of imaginative literature" (*Lost Tales I,* 1). These early representations of Tolkien's mythology are particularly rich in Eddic imitation. In a piece written around 1918 and titled "The Music of the Ainur," Tolkien borrows directly from the *Gylfaginning* of Snorri Sturluson's *Prose Edda*. In a close echo *Gylfaginning,* Tolkien frames his explanation of the Valar "gods" through questions a traveler, Eriol (hiding his true name), poses to his magical hosts, questions about the Valar and whether they are "the Gods" (*Lost Tales I,* 45). In the *Prose Edda,* Gylfi (King of Sweden) travels to Asgard, receives lodging for the night under a false name, and begins his series of questions by asking, "Who is foremost, or oldest of all the gods?"

Tolkien's original concepts of a Great End are also closely based on Norse mythology. Much as the Norse gods anticipate Ragnarök from the beginning of creation, Tolkien's Valar are aware that the world will not always endure. In *The Silmarillion,* the "world's end" is alluded to only in passing. In early versions, however, references to the "Great End" or "Great Wrack" occur repeatedly and show a clearer dependence on

Ragnarök. In "The Hiding of Valinor" (a section in *The Book of Lost Tales*), the Valar, like the Norse gods, not only know there will be an end to the world but also know that they can lose their youth and vitality and that they, too, will be destroyed during the Great End, just as all the world—both good and bad—will ultimately be destroyed and ultimately "rolled away" (*Lost Tales I,* 219).

Other Ragnarök touches appear in other *History of Middle-earth* drafts. In "The Earliest 'Silmarillion'" from *The Shaping of Middle-earth,* Tolkien refers to the "Last Battle" the Valar will fight "when the world is much older, and the Gods weary" (40). At this time, Morgoth will return through the Door of Night to battle against the Valar, just as Loki, in Eddic tradition, is freed from his fetters and joins the final battle against the Asgard gods. During Tolkien's "last battle of all," Fionwë (called the son of Manwë in this account) will fight Morgoth on the plain of Valinor in a close parallel to the Norse, where Odin's son Vídar fights Fenrir (Loki's wolf son) on the plain of Vígríðr. Still another version of Tolkien's Last Battle appears in the "Quenta Silmarillion" of *The Lost Road and Other Writings*. Here Tolkien uses the term "doom of the Gods," a phrase commonly applied to the Norse Ragnarök; and here Morgoth will destroy the Sun and the Moon in an echo of the Eddic wolves that ultimately swallow and destroy both the sun and the moon (*Lost Road,* 332–33; *Shaping,* 165). And just as the world begins again after Ragnarök and a few of the gods survive, Tolkien's world will be renewed and his "Gods will grow young again" (*Lost Road,* 333).

Early accounts of the chaining of Melkor come closer to the Norse binding of Loki. In the *Prose Edda,* Loki is bound to three flat stones with entrails that turn to iron. He remains bound, venom dripping onto his face, until the doom of the gods. In *The Silmarillion,* little is told about Melkor's imprisonment; we know only that he is placed in the "fastness of Mandos" and "chained." In *The Book of Lost Tales,* however, we learn that Melko (Melkor) is chained by each wrist and ankle with specially created manacles and fetters and that these bands are never again "loosened from his hands and feet" (*Lost Tales I,* 104). Like Loki, Melko's punishment marks his face; his lip has been split and his face permanently contorted.

Tolkien also makes greater early use of Bifrost, the three-stranded rainbow bridge made by the Norse gods (and sometimes called a bridge of flame). In "The Hiding of Valinor" from *The Book of Lost Tales,* Tolkien describes how Oromë creates a magical bridge called "the Rainbow" by Men and "Ilweran the Bridge of Heaven" by the fairies (who later become the Elves). Just as Bifrost allows the gods access to the middle world, Oromë's slender bridge allows the Valar to "wander in the Great Lands" (*Lost Tales I,* 212–13). After *The Book of Lost Tales,* Tolkien's rainbow bridge disappears from his mythology—though mention of Bifrost (and Tolkien's appreciation of the Old Norse over the modern) appears again in "On Fairy-Stories" (*TL,* 57).

In "The Coming of the Valar and the Building of Valinor" *(Lost Tales I),* Tolkien includes two highly Norse Valar that later disappear from his mythology. These are Makar (a warrior host much like Odin in his role as Victory Father or Father of the Slain) and Makar's "fierce sister" Meássë, who resembles the Norse Valkyries (those battle maidens who are Choosers of the Slain as well as servers in Odin's hall). Where Makar's name is based on words meaning "slay," "slaughter," "great sword," or "battle," his spear-bearing sister's name means "gore," a name appropriately close to ones among the Valkyries, who are known by such names as Spear-Bearer, Raging, Shrieking, Axe-Time, and Screaming. In the hall shared with her brother, Meássë moves about, urging warriors to come to blows. Those who grow faint she revives with wine. Battle ceases only when there are feasts, and then "fierce songs of victory, of sack and harrying," are sung (*Lost Tales I,* 77–78; see also 89, 259–60.) Idealized renditions of Valkyrie women also appear in Tolkien's literature—from Aredhel in *The Silmarillion* to Éowyn in *The Lord of the Rings.* In *Unfinished Tales,* Galadriel is presented in a similar light, as "strong of body, mind, and will, a match for both the lore-masters and athletes of the Eldar." She is noted as a fierce fighter, and the secondary name her mother gives her is "man-maiden" (227).

In *The Lay of Leithian,* from *The Lays of Beleriand,* Morgoth feeds his wolf Carcharoth on the "flesh of Elves and Men" (288). This is a harsher and more pointed image than the "living flesh" of the published *Silmarillion,* and it links Morgoth even more closely to Odin, who feeds his wolves, Geri and Freki, on a flesh that has been interpreted (by Lee Hollander, for one) to mean the flesh of the battle fallen. Like Geri and Freki (whose names mean Ravener and Greedy), Carcharoth is the Red Maw. Other names given to Carcharoth suggest the same voracity: Carcharas (Knife-fang), Borosaith (Everhungry), and Anfauglin or Anfauglir (Jaws of Thirst) (*S,* 180; *Shaping,* 112, 115). In *The Lay of Leithian,* Sauron (here called Thû) also feeds Draugluin, a wolf or werewolf, on "flesh of Man and Elf" (*Lays,* 252). In the "Quenta," from *The Shaping of Middle-earth,* Thû is called "lord of wolves" (106), and Ilúvatar, like Odin, is called Allfather (78), all of which further link Tolkien's best and worst characters to the best and the worst in Odin.

(See *Lost Road, Sauron,* and *Morgoth* for further references to Ilúvatar as the Allfather.)

Early accounts of Nienna, Tolkien's Vala of lamentation, are also clearly dependent on Eddic tradition. In the published *Silmarillion,* Nienna is a sympathetic figure; but in *The Book of Lost Tales,* she is more closely related to Hel, Loki's monster daughter who presides over one of the Norse worlds of the dead. In the section called "The Coming of the Valar and the Building of Valinor," Nienna (or Fui Nienna) has a number of additional titles and names, among them *Qalmë-Tári,* "the mistress of death" (*Lost Tales I,* 66). Just as Hel's realm is also called Hel, Fui Nienna's hall is called Fui, after its mistress's name. Like Hel, Nienna decides the fate of dead men, and the brazier in her hall has only a single "flickering" coal (*Lost Tales I,* 77), a good match for Hel's hall, which is noted for its damp and chill.

Middle-earth's stars show another Old Norse connection. In *The Silmarillion,* we learn that Varda created certain of the stars from the "silver dews" of the vats of Telperion (48). In "The Coming of the Elves" and "The Tale of the Sun and the Moon," however, Varda is inspired by sparks struck from Aulë's hammer and uses these sparks (and other forms of light) to create fixed and wandering stars (*Lost Tales I,* 113, 133, 181–82). This use of sparks brings her star-making considerably closer to the Norse, where Odin and his brothers use sparks from the fire realm, Múspell, to create stars that wander and stars that are free to move.

In still another section from *The Book of Lost Tales,* Tolkien writes that eating a dragon's heart gives one the ability to "know all tongues of Gods or Men, of birds or beasts" (*Lost Tales II,* 85, 125), a clear link to Sigurd, who understands the speech of birds after tasting Fafnir's roasted heart. In this same volume, Tolkien openly connects two of his Valar to the Norse gods by claiming that the fairies identified Manwë with *Wóden* and Tulkas with *Þunor,* the Old English names for Odin and Thor (*Lost Tales II,* 290). He also mentions the Norse idea that dwarves fear the sun (*Lost Tales II,* 236), and he briefly refers to Ulmo (the Vala of the sea) as Neorth, a clear reference to Njord (or Njörth), the Norse god of ships and the sea (*Lost Tales II,* 331–32; see also *Lost Road,* 97). A further connection with Njord occurs in Tolkien's tale "Aldarion and Erendis: The Mariner's Wife," found in *Unfinished Tales.* In the *Prose Edda,* Njord, the sea-loving god, marries Skadi, a giant's daughter. Njord will never be happy away from the sea, nor will Skadi be content away from the mountains. Like Erendis, who prefers the bleating of sheep to the "mewing of gulls" (*UT,* 185), Skadi is disturbed by the cry of sea birds.

The sagas influenced Tolkien nearly as much as the *Eddas*. It is typical of Old Norse sagas to introduce and define characters through a few short, telling lines. In *Aldarion and Erendis*, Aldarion is introduced in typical saga fashion. We are told right off that he is "a man of great stature, strong and vigorous in mind and body, golden-haired as his mother, ready to mirth and generous, but prouder than his father and ever more bent on his own will" (*UT*, 166). Similar saga-influenced sketches appear throughout *The Silmarillion*, particularly in the story of the ill-fated Túrin and his sister, Nienor—a tale that Tolkien referred to as a "saga" and even titled "Túrins Saga" or the "Saga of Túrin" in early drafts (*Jewels*, 244, 314, 321, 352).

More than one saga contributed to the berserker, shape-shifting Beorn. In the *Völsunga Saga*, Sigurd's father puts on a wolf skin that gives him wolfish traits and wolfish abilities. In the *Hrólfs Saga Kraka*, Bjarki (Little Bear) takes on the form of a massive bear to fight in the Danish king's army. In the saga of Egil Skallagrímsson, Kveld-Úlfr (Evening-wolf) is not only rumored to be a shape-changer but also produces descendants of mixed natures (as Beorn does). Kveld-Úlfr also has a half-troll in his family background (a common saga conception), and a half-troll appears in *The War of the Ring*, where Tolkien temporarily introduces black "half-trolls" (369). Tolkien's half-orc, mixed-breed monsters in *The Lord of the Rings* were no doubt influenced by this same Norse conception.

Accounts of the magical effects that come from eating a dragon's heart appear not only in the *Völsunga Saga* and Eddic versions of Sigurd but in other sagas as well, sagas where drinking the blood or eating the heart of a dragon (or wolf or bear) is a means of gaining the powers and strength of the conquered beast. The idea of werewolves devouring bound men one by one over a period of days appears both in *The Silmarillion* (171–72, 174) and in the *Völsunga Saga*, where a wolf, thought to be a shape-shifting woman, eats nine men on nine consecutive nights. This Norse emphasis on the number nine is itself borrowed by Tolkien. To list a few other examples: there are nine worlds in Norse mythology, nine nights during which Odin hangs from the World Tree, nine magic songs learned from a giant, nine mothers for Heimdall (the watchman god), and nine nights in Hermod's journey to the underworld. Tolkien follows suit with his nine members of the Fellowship (who are balanced against the nine Ringwraiths), the nine years Túrin lives in Thingol's halls, and the nine rings made "for Mortal Men." In "The Earliest Annals of Valinor," Tolkien limits his Valinor "Powers" to nine (*Shaping*, 263); and in the published *Silmarillion* (before the fall of Melkor), there are nine Aratar, the High Ones of Arda.

Saga treasures are commonly guarded by the restless, vampire-like *draugar*, who leave their burial mounds to attack living beings. More than one uneasy spirit does so in *Grettir's Saga*, a tale full of berserkers, a half-troll, a troll-wife, and battles with the undead. Tolkien's Barrow-wight, with its hostility toward the living, comes easily to mind. (Rumors of Gollum as blood-drinking "ghost" suggest the *draugar* as well.) From such barrows, however, come superior weapons that serve the heroes well. For Grettir there is an excellent short sword (he had "never seen a better one") claimed from the mound of a revenant, and Merry's short sword, taken from the Barrow-wight's hoard, serves him well against the Nazgûl lord.

Not all Old Norse barrow encounters are threatening. Some mounds are sources of inspiration or insight, and Tolkien borrows from this tradition as well. Lothlórien's mound of Cerin Amroth is not specified as a burial mound; it is, however, clearly associated with those who have passed away, with lost worlds and lost races, and here Frodo is lifted to a new level of perception and hears the sound of "great seas" and "sea birds" long gone from the Earth.

This is not yet the full picture. There are other Old Norse themes and other Norse stories Tolkien drew from. In *The Lost Road*, Christopher Tolkien explains the connections that link his father's legend of Sheaf with Freyr, a Norse god, and Fróthi, a Danish king (96–97). King Fróthi, whose tale is told both by Snorri Sturluson in the *Prose Edda* and by Saxo Grammaticus in *Gesta Danorum*, was noted for his keeping of the peace, and Tolkien's Frodo, who increasingly avoids violence and "does not wish for any sword" (*RK*, VI, iv, 233) takes both his name and something of his character from this Danish king.

Tolkien's use of prophecy and second sight shows still another Old Norse touch. *The Silmarillion* includes "The Prophecy of the North" and the "Doom of the Noldor," spoken (some believe) by Mandos, the Vala who keeps the Houses of the Dead and "knows all things that shall be" (87, 28); and there are other *Silmarillion* figures, such as Lúthien's mother, Melian, who has "much foresight, after the manner of the Maiar" (92). In *The Lord of the Rings*, Elrond sees something of the future, as does Galadriel. In "Athrabeth Finrod ah Andreth," from *Morgoth's Ring*, Tolkien most closely imitates Old Norse patterns by having his "wise woman," Andreth, speak through a series of responses the way seeresses do in both *Völuspá* and *Baldrs Draumar* in the *Elder Edda*.

Even Tolkien's directional prejudices are indicative. In Norse mythology, danger lies eastward and north. Hel, with its darkness and chill, lies in the north; giants are found both in the east and north. This same sense of directional danger is true of Tolkien's world. In *The Silmarillion,* Morgoth builds his stronghold in the north. In *The Hobbit,* trolls and dragons come from the north and wild Were-worms (so Bilbo claims) are found in "the East of East" (*H,* I, 49). In *The Lord of the Rings,* Mordor appears somewhat to the south on maps but is consistently spoken of as belonging to the east.

More should be said about wolves. In Old Norse literature, wolves are favorite mounts of witches and trolls. In *Hyndluljóð* from the *Elder Edda,* Freya invites the wise giantess Hyndla to mount a wolf and ride with her to Valhalla, and in *Helgakviða Hjörvarþssonar* a troll woman is seen riding a wolf. In *The Two Towers,* Saruman takes Wolf-riders into his service, and these Wolf-riders are seen by scouts before the battle at Helm's Deep. Similar references to Wolf-riders appear in *Lost Tales II, Lays, Treason, War.*

Tolkien also borrowed from the Norse habit of naming weapons and from the Norse idea of everlasting battles where dead men rise to fight again. In saga accounts, Sigurd's dragon-slaying sword is Gram (Troll); in the *Eddas,* Thor's dwarf-made hammer is Mjöllnir (possibly "The Crusher"). In Tolkien, literature, Túrin's sword is Gurthang (Iron of Death); Aragorn's sword is Andúril (Flame of the West), and even Bilbo has his Sting. And in both Tolkien and Old Norse literature, the dead fight again. In the *Prose Edda,* fallen heroes who are taken to Valhalla spend their days in battle. Those who are once more killed rise to fight on the following day. In still other Eddic and saga accounts, dead warriors—magically rendered indestructible—maintain an endless war. Some of these battles take place in burial mounds. Tolkien, in *The Return of the King,* makes his version of the fighting dead less unsavory by allowing the ghosts of oath-breakers a final redeeming battle that at last earns them peace.

It may initially seem that Tolkien does little with the giants of Norse mythology (Hill Giants, Frost Giants, and Fire Giants). As traditional, flesh-and-blood figures, giants appear only in *The Hobbit,* where Stone-giants (echoing a scene from the Eddic *Grottasöngr*) hurl "rocks at one another for a game" (*H,* IV, 104). At one point, however, Tolkien did intend to add a "Giant" to *The Lord of the Rings* (*Letters,* 42n.). This promised giant does not appear, but rejected drafts published in *The Return of the Shadow* give an idea of what Tolkien had in mind. Here, Sam talks about giants said to be as big as trees, a statement subtly but significantly reversed in *The Lord of the Rings,* where "Tree-men" are compared to giants. More remarkable, however, are references to

the malevolent "Giant Treebeard" who deceives Frodo and who holds Gandalf captive for "many weary days" (*Shadow,* 254, 384, 363).

But even in the absence of actual giants, something of the Norse giants' elemental nature still exists in *The Lord of the Rings* in the stony consciousness given to Tolkien's mountains and hills (with their "shoulders," "heads," "arms," "limbs," "knees," and "feet") and especially to Caradhras, the "Red-Peak" or the "Cruel," who seems to combine both Hill and Frost Giant features in a single entity. The Norse Fire Giant role (Surt's role) is also filled by Tolkien through the Balrogs, those "scourges of fire" who appear throughout *The Silmarillion* but who are described with greater detail in *The Lord of the Rings* and *The History of Middle-earth.* In *The Fellowship of the Ring,* the Balrog (the Flame of Udûn) draws "itself up to a great height," its wings spreading "from wall to wall" (*FR,* II, 345). Flames roar up to greet and encircle it. In a close echo of Surt's blazing sword, called "singer-of-twigs" (i.e., "fire"), the Balrog's sword is like "a tongue of fire" (*FR,* II, v, 344). In an earlier version from *The Treason of Isengard* (Vol. VII of *The History of Middle-earth*), the Balrog's sword turns to "flame" (197). (See *The History of Middle-earth: Index,* compiled by Christopher Tolkien, for a full listing of Balrog references.)

From Tolkien's letters come further Eddic and saga references. In a 1938 letter to Stanley Unwin, Tolkien mentions working on an Old Norse project, probably the *Víga-Glúms Saga* (*Letters,* 36, 436); and in a 1962 letter, this time to Rayner Unwin, Tolkien refers to an "echo of the Norse Niblung matter (the otter's whisker)," which he slipped into a poem on Tom Bombadil (*Letters,* 315, 449; see also 319). In a 1967 letter to W.H. Auden, Tolkien mentions an unpublished poem, *Völsungakviða En Nyja,* which he wrote in the late 1920s or early 1930s and had hoped would "unify the lays about the Völsungs from the Elder Edda." In this same letter, Tolkien thanks Auden for sending him a translation of *The Song of the Sibyl* (*Letters,* 379, 452). This translation and others from the *Elder Edda* were later published by W.H. Auden and Paul B. Taylor under the title *The Elder Edda: A Selection.* Their book is dedicated to Tolkien, an honor he well deserves.

MARJORIE BURNS

Further Reading

Burns, Marjorie. "Gandalf and Odin." In *Tolkien's Legendarium: Essays on "The History of Middle-earth,"* edited by Verlyn Flieger and Carl F. Hostetter, 219–31. Westport, CT: Greenwood, 2000.

———. "Norse and Christian Gods: The Integrative Theology of J.R.R. Tolkien." In *Tolkien and the Invention of*

Myth, edited by Jane Chance, 163–78. Lexington, KY: University Press of Kentucky, 2004.

———. *Perilous Realms: Celtic and Norse in Tolkien's Middle-earth*. Toronto: University of Toronto Press, 2005.

Hollander, Lee M., trans. *The Poetic Edda*. Austin, TX: University of Texas Press, 1928.

Fox, Denton, and Hermann Pálsson, trans. *Grettir's Saga*. Toronto: University of Toronto Press, 1974.

Grammaticus, Saxo. *Gesta Danorum*. Translated by Lord Oliver Elton. London: Folklore Society, 1894.

Jones, Gwyn, trans. *Hrólfs Saga Kraka*. In *Eirik the Red and other Icelandic Sagas*. London: World Classics, 1961.

Magnússon, Eiríkr, and William Morris, trans. "The Tale of Hogni and Hedinn." Translated from *Flateyjarbók*. In Vol. 10 of *The Collected Works of William Morris*, 127–39. New York: Russell and Russell, 1966.

Morris, William, trans. *The Völsunga Saga*. In Vol. 7 of *The Collected Works of William Morris*. New York: Russell and Russell, 1966.

Orchard, Andy, ed. *Cassell's Dictionary of Norse Myth and Legend*. London: Cassell, 1997.

Pálsson, Hermann, and Paul Edwards, trans. *Egil's Saga*. Hamondsworth, UK: Penguin, 1976.

Shippey, Tom. *The Road to Middle-earth*. 2nd ed. London: Grafton, 1992.

St. Clair, Glorianna. "*The Lord of the Rings* as Saga." *Mythlore* 6, no. 2 (Spring 1979): 11–16.

Sturluson, Snorri. *Edda*. Translated by Anthony Faulkes. Everyman's Library. London: J.M. Dent & Sons, 1987.

———. *The Prose Edda*. Translated by Arthur Gilchrist Brodeur. New York: The American-Scandinavian Foundation; London: Humphrey Milford; Oxford: Oxford University Press, 1923.

Taylor, Paul, and W.H. Auden, trans. *The Elder Edda*. London: Faber and Faber, 1969.

Tolkien, Christopher, trans. and ed. *The Saga of King Heidrek the Wise*. London: Thomas Nelson and Sons, 1960.

Tolkien, J.R.R. "On Fairy-stories." In *Tree and Leaf*, 9–73. London: George Allen & Unwin, 1964; London: Unwin Hyman, 1988; Boston, MA: Houghton Mifflin, 1989.

———. "Sigelwara Land" [2]. *Medium Aevum* 3 (June 1934), 95–111.

OLD NORSE TRANSLATIONS

Little is known about Tolkien's unpublished Norse poem cycle, *Völsungakviî a en Nyja [New Lay of the Völsungs]*. The cycle is briefly cited by Humphrey Carpenter, and Tolkien mentioned it in a letter to W.H. Auden, explaining that the poems were his attempt to organize the Eddic songs about Sigurð and Gunnar, written in fornyrðislag 8-line stanza, a medieval Icelandic verse form. A note to his letter places composition at some time in the late 1920s or early 1930s. The "attempt to organize" probably refers to the fact that the primary texts are corrupt and incomplete and must be supplemented by other sources to make a coherent story.

The legend that the texts recount is as follows. Sigurð, the legendary "prince of heroes of the North" slew the dragon Fafnir. Carrying off the dragon's gold, Sigurð then plighted troth with Brynhild, one of Oðin's Valkyries (or a mortal woman—here the sources disagree), whom he found sleeping on a rock, surrounded by magic flames. He rescued her, but for unspecified reasons he left her and married Guðrun, the daughter of Gjuki, later returning to Brynhild's rock disguised as Guðrun's brother Gunnar to win her for Gunnar as his bride. The resultant rivalry between the two women led to the killing of Sigurð, leaving the hapless Guðrun to be married again. Her second husband was Atli (Atilla) the Hun, who, coveting their dragon's gold, lured her brothers to his stronghold and murdered them. Guðrun in turn killed Atli and set fire to his hall.

A definite Norse/Icelandic influence is recognizable in Tolkien's work, most explicitly in his Dwarf names and characteristics but also in his reuse of Sigurð's dragon-slaying in the story of Túrin Turambar. In his essay "*Beowulf:* The Monsters and the Critics," he makes specific mention of Sigurð's killing of Fafnir. It is to be hoped that the Völsung poems, his most direct use of Norse material, will at some future date be published to round out our understanding of his debt to Northern literature.

VERLYN FLIEGER

Further Reading

Byock, Jesse L., trans. *The Saga of the Völsungs*. Middlesex: Hisarlik Press, 1993.

Carpenter, Humphrey. *Tolkien: A Biography*. Boston, MA: Houghton Mifflin, 1977.

Hollander, Lee M., trans. *The Poetic Edda*. 2nd ed. Austin, TX: University of Texas Press, 1962.

Sturluson, Snorri. *Edda*. Translated by Anthony Faulkes. Everyman's Library. London: J.M. Dent & Sons, 1987.

See also **Old Norse Literature; Poems by Tolkien**

"ON FAIRY-STORIES"

When the University of St. Andrews invited Tolkien to give the annual Andrew Lang Lecture on March 8, 1939, Tolkien presented "On Fairy-Stories." Tolkien revised and expanded the lecture as an essay for the 1947 memorial volume *Essays Presented to Charles Williams*. Tolkien further expanded the essay for republication in *Tree and Leaf* in 1964. The 1964 text is the version discussed here.

After calling himself "overbold" for presuming to speak on fairy stories without possessing scholarly expertise in the field, Tolkien proposes to address three questions: What are fairy stories? What is their origin? What is their purpose and/or value? (*MC,* 109).

Fairy Stories

Tolkien finds the *Oxford English Dictionary*'s definition of "fairy-story," "a tale about fairies," too narrow when taken with the definition of "fairy," which says, in part, that fairies are "supernatural beings of diminutive size." He denies that fairies are supernatural and says the tradition of smallness is modern and not characteristic of all fairies. Tolkien then disagrees with the *OED*'s recording of a 1493 quotation from John Gower's *Confessio Amatis* as "as he were a faierie," by correcting it to "as he were of faierie." Using this distinction, Tolkien asserts that "fairy" refers to a place, "the realm or state in which fairies have their being," and that "fairy-stories" are stories about that place: "a 'fairy-story' is one which touches on or uses Faërie, whatever its own main purpose may be: satire, adventure, morality, fantasy" (*MC*, 114).

Applying this definition, Tolkien lists types of stories that should not be called fairy stories. He excludes "travelers' tales:" Jonathan Swift's *Gulliver's Travels,* the stories of the adventures of Baron Munchausen, and H.G. Wells's *The First Men in the Moon* and *The Time Machine.* He also excludes stories in which Faërie is reached through dreams, such as Lewis Carroll's *Alice* books. "Beast-fables" also do not qualify: "The Monkey's Heart," "Reynard the Fox," Geoffrey Chaucer's "Nun's Priest's Tale," the Br'er Rabbit stories, "The Three Little Pigs," Beatrix Potter's animal stories, and Kenneth Grahame's *The Wind in the Willows.* Tolkien does not offer a list of successful fairy stories. Instead, he moves abruptly into his second question.

Origins

Tolkien declares he "shall pass lightly over the question of origins" because, borrowing a "soup" metaphor from G.W. Dasent, he believes that it is more valuable to study "the story as it is served up by its author" rather than trying to look at the "bones" from which the soup-stock was formed (120). He uses the metaphor to attack the view that myths and folklore are hierarchical: "the Pot of Soup, the Cauldron of Story, has always been boiling, and to it have continually been added new bits, dainty and undainty" all together (125). He uses King Arthur, King Hrothgar, Bertha Broadfoot, and Ingeld and Freawaru as examples to assert that the most important aspect of the ancient motifs in fairy stories is "the effect produced *now* by these old things in the stories as they are" (128).

Tolkien also advances his own theory that stories and language have a common and simultaneous origin: "To ask what is the origin of stories (however qualified) is to ask what is the origin of language and of the mind" (119). The human mind, observing "grass," also observed that it was "green." "How powerful," declares Tolkien, "was the invention of the adjective: no spell or incantation in Faërie is more potent." The human mind also has the power to rearrange words and ideas, to "make heavy things light," and to "turn grey lead into yellow gold"; when we do so, "we have already an enchanter's power" because in this act of "fantasy" we create new things that dwell on the plane of imagination: "new form is made; Faërie begins; Man becomes a sub-creator" (122).

Emphasizing his belief in the antiquity of subcreation and of its simultaneous birth with language and thought, Tolkien asserts that "the incarnate mind, the tongue, and the tale are in our world coeval" (122). To illustrate his belief and attack the hierarchical theory that nature myths about the gods are forebears first of localized stories in which gods were humanized and then of folktales, Tolkien uses the Norse god Thórr, who "looks like a clear case of Olympian nature myth" because his name means "thunder." However, Tolkien finds it meaningless to try to determine "which came first, nature-allegories about personalized thunder" or stories about Thórr. Tolkien asserts that "if we could go backwards in time . . . there would always be a 'fairy-tale' as long as there was any Thórr." When the fairy story ceased to exist (i.e., if we then went forward many centuries in time), "there would be just thunder, which no human ear had yet heard" (124). In Tolkien's theory of language, as in that articulated by his friend Owen Barfield in *Poetic Diction,* the conscious discerning of literal from metaphoric meanings of words was a modern development in the evolution of European languages.

Children

Tolkien addresses his third point (what are the purposes of fairy stories, and what value do they have for us?) in the context of children's literary tastes. He does not believe that the value of fairy stories emerges by considering children in particular because "only some children, and some adults, have any special taste" for fairy-stories, so it is an error to assume that "there is a natural connection between the minds of children and fairy-stories" (130). Tolkien then attacks Andrew Lang for making that assumption. He sharply criticizes Lang's statements about children's tastes being like those of their "naked ancestors" of long ago (133–34). In so doing, Tolkien recalls the reading experiences of his boyhood years. Lewis Carroll's Alice books only amused him. *Treasure Island* left him "cool." Stories of "Red Indians" were good because of the "strange languages, and glimpses of an archaic mode of life, and above all, forests in such stories." Arthurian stories were better. "Best of all" was "the nameless North of Sigurd of the Völsungs." He believed "fairy-stories were . . . concerned with . . . desirability" and "if they awakened desire, satisfying it while often whetting it unbearably, they succeeded." He liked the *Völsunga Saga* best because he "desired dragons with a profound desire," and it contained "the prince of all dragons." In his young imagination, "the world that contained even the imagination of Fafnir was richer and more beautiful, at whatever cost of peril," than anything else he had yet experienced, in life or in books (134–35).

Tolkien also discusses "literary belief" and further develops his theory of subcreation by disagreeing with Samuel Taylor Coleridge's assertion, in chapter 14 of *Biographia Literaria,* that readers engage in a "willing suspension of disbelief." Instead of suspending disbelief while we read fiction, if the fiction is well wrought, we believe: "what really happens is that the story-maker proves a successful 'sub-creator' because, through art, "he makes a Secondary World which your mind can enter" and "inside it, what he relates is 'true': it accords with the laws of that world"; "you therefore believe it, while you are, as it were, inside" (132).

Closing this section, Tolkien says fairy-stories are valuable because they offer "Fantasy, Recovery, Escape, [and] Consolation" (138).

Fantasy

Tolkien defines fantasy as expression, through the sub-creative art of story-making, that gives an "inner consistency of reality" and the qualities of "strangeness and wonder" to the story-maker's conceived mental images (which Tolkien calls imagination) and that therefore induces secondary belief (i.e., literary belief) in the story-maker's secondary world. He believes that fantasy is a high form of art, "indeed the most nearly pure form, and so (when achieved) the most potent" (138–39). Fantasy "is a thing best left to words, to true literature" rather than to painting, which is less "progenitive" than literature because it presents particular images rather than allowing the viewer to conceive his own, or to drama "which is naturally hostile to Fantasy" (159, 140).

Recovery, Escape, and Consolation

Fairy stories give us recovery, which is "a regaining of a clear view" by freeing us from "the drab blur of triteness or familiarity," and they allow us to see things "as we are (or were) meant to see them" (146).

Fairy stories also allow us to escape from things like "the Morlockian horror of factories" and "the roar of self-obstructive mechanical traffic" to things that are more permanent and beautiful (149–50). Tolkien does not accept "the tone of scorn or pity with which "escape" is used by literary critics because they confuse escape from modern ugliness with "desertion," and "they would seem to prefer the acquiescence of the 'quisling' to the resistance of the patriot" (148).

Our "oldest and deepest desire" for escape, the "Great Escape: the Escape from Death" leads into consolation, in particular, the "Consolation of the Happy Ending." Tolkien coins a term for this: "eucatastrophe," a "good catastrophe, the sudden joyous turn." This, says Tolkien, is "one of the things which fairy stories can produce supremely well," and in so doing, they can console us with "a fleeting glimpse of Joy, Joy beyond the walls of the world, poignant as grief" (153).

Epilogue

Tolkien concludes by discussing the fairy story of the Christian Gospels. Acknowledging that it is "presumptuous . . . to touch upon such a theme," he hopes that "by grace" what he says will have some "validity." He then asserts that "the Birth of Christ is the eucatastrophe of Man's history" and "the Resurrection is the eucatastrophe of the story of the Incarnation." Of all fairy stories, "there is no tale ever told that men would rather find was true, and none which so many sceptical men have accepted as true on its own merits" (155–56).

Tolkien believes that "every sub-creator wishes in some measure to be a real maker," and so, because "Redeemed Man is still man, story, fantasy, still go on, and should go on." Man has been redeemed through Christ, and "so great is the bounty with which he has been treated that he may now, perhaps, fairly dare to guess that in Fantasy he may actually assist in the effoliation and multiple enrichment of creation" (155–56).

Commentary

When Tolkien gave his "On Fairy-Stories" lecture, he was a famous author already, and he had been at work on the "sequel" to *The Hobbit* for more than a year. While the essay is many things—from a definition of fairy stories, to an attack on folklore studies, to a theory of language, to a personal statement of the role of the Christian storyteller—most scholars have also seen the essay as Tolkien's artistic manifesto for writing the kind of fiction that interested him most. Humphrey Carpenter reads the end of the essay as Tolkien's assertion "that there is no higher function for man than the 'sub-creation' of a Secondary World such as he was already making in *The Lord of the Rings*" (191). However, scholars have also noted the essay's faults. Carpenter asserts that Tolkien made too many points "for an entirely cogent argument" (191). Tom Shippey regards the essay as "Tolkien's least successful if most discussed piece of argumentative prose" because it lacks "a philological core" (38). Although these remarks are justified, the essay should not be seen primarily as a persuasive argument. Verlyn Flieger rightly places the essay among the "long line of critical works on the uses of the literary imagination" (147). Some of the most notable works in that line, for example, the essays (both titled "A Defence of Poetry") by Sir Philip Sydney and Percy Bysshe Shelley, are not chiefly valued for their cogency or their success as pieces of persuasive writing, though they possess both qualities in some measure. "On Fairy-Stories" should be seen in the same way. The essay's value does not depend on whether it is convincing to us. The essay is valuable because it was convincing to Tolkien.

PAUL EDMUND THOMAS

Further Reading

Barfield, Owen. *Poetic Diction: A Study in Meaning*. London: Faber & Gwyer, 1928.

Carpenter, Humphrey. *Tolkien: A Biography*. Boston, MA: Houghton Mifflin, 1977.

Flieger, Verlyn. *Interrupted Music: The Making of Tolkien's Mythology*. Kent, OH: Kent State University Press, 2005.

Flieger, Verlyn. *Splintered Light: Logos and Language in Tolkien's World*. Grand Rapids, MI: Eerdmans, 1983.

Shippey, Tom. *The Road to Middle-earth*. Boston, MA: Houghton Mifflin, 1983.

See also **Allegory; Catholicism, Roman; Children's Literature and Tolkien; Christ; Christian Readings of Tolkien; Christianity; Criticism of Tolkien, Twentieth Century; Eucatastrophe; Fall of Man; Incarnation; Language, Theories of; Literary Influences, Nineteenth and Twentieth Century; Literature, Twentieth Century: Influence of Tolkien; MacDonald, George; Mythology for England; Redemption; Resurrection; Theological and Moral Approaches in Tolkien's Works; Tolkien Scholarship: An Overview; Tolkien Scholarship: First Decades; Tolkien Scholarship: Institutions; Tolkien Scholarship: Since 1980; *Essays Presented to Charles Williams***

"ON TRANSLATING *BEOWULF*"

Tolkien's "On Translating *Beowulf*" was originally published in 1940 as "Prefatory Remarks" to a revised edition of John R. Clark Hall's prose translation of the Anglo-Saxon poem *Beowulf*. The essay aims to convey a sense of what the reader is missing by relying on a translation, and it concentrates on formal features of the original and their appropriate translation rather than attempting analysis of the content of the poem.

Tolkien begins by arguing that the proper use of a prose translation is as an aid to study rather than a substitute for the original poem. This is carefully distinguished from the use of a translation as a "crib"; later in the essay Tolkien writes that the most important function of a translation used by students "is to provide not a model for imitation, but an exercise for correction" (*MC*, 53).

Tolkien points out that it is not always possible to translate a single Old English word with a single modern equivalent and that the connotations of Old English words must often be lost in translation. He explains that because Old English poetry used a specifically poetic vocabulary—but also because the surviving texts are only a portion of those that once existed—many Old English words are found only in verse, and some only in *Beowulf*. The difficulties of translating the poetic compounds employed in Old English verse are then illustrated: *swan-rad,* for example, literally means "swan's-riding" but is translated by Clark Hall as "swan's-road" and is a poetic term for "sea." Such diction is said to give to Old English verse "something of the air of a conundrum," but by compressing much meaning into few words it also achieves a powerful brevity.

Tolkien proceeds to justify the revision of Clark Hall's translation, arguing that whereas Clark Hall's original version conveyed meaning accurately enough, it was less successful in finding an appropriate diction. In particular, Tolkien criticises its excessive use of colloquialisms and its air of "false modernity." The revised text rectifies these deficiencies, partly by adopting some archaic diction. Tolkien argues that the use of archaisms in translating *Beowulf* is appropriate, indeed desirable, because in its own time the language of *Beowulf* was itself already archaic and artificial: the poem was not composed in the language of everyday discourse, and certain of its poetic effects are attributable to this. Tolkien goes as far as to argue that to "eschew the traditional literary and poetic diction which we now possess in favour of the current and trivial" would be to "misrepresent the first and most salient characteristic of the style and flavour of the author" (MC, 55): a "high" style is appropriate, indeed essential, for the expression of serious and moving themes. This defence of archaisms sheds light on Tolkien's own use of them in his poetry and fiction. He maintains, however, that archaism is not to be indulged in without reason and any archaic words used should be familiar to readers, not words resurrected from the past solely for the occasion. In addition, etymology is not always a guide to the most appropriate translation: a descendant of a word may not always be its most appropriate translation. Attention is also drawn to the relative poverty of modern English compared with Old English when it comes to synonyms for frequently recurring concepts such as "man": the translator must be content with less variety. Although he criticized Clark Hall's "false modernity," Tolkien defends the use of chivalric terms (such as "knight") in translating *Beowulf*.

The translation of the poetic compounds so characteristic of Old English verse is considered next, and Tolkien maintains that, although each case must be considered on its own merits, it is usually preferable to "resolve" the translation rather than give a possibly meaningless literal version: hence, for example, *gomenwudu,* literally "play-wood," becomes "harp." He makes an exception for descriptive compound metaphors (kennings) that have become a part of poetic language and are not the poet's own creation.

The second section of the essay is devoted to an explication of the alliterative metre of Old English verse, with special reference to *Beowulf* and with the needs of those unfamiliar with the language particularly in mind. Tolkien adopts what he calls a novel procedure by using modern English to illustrate how the metre works (his friend C.S. Lewis had already published an account of alliterative metre adopting the same tactic). In a letter written in March 1940. Tolkien describes the "metrical appendix" as "the most original part" of his preface (*Letters*, 46). His account of the four-stress line employed in all Old English poetry, with its central pause or caesura and its use of alliteration as a structural device to link the two halves of each line, remains one of the most frequently recommended brief introductions to the subject for students. The exposition is illustrated with a translation of lines 210–28 of *Beowulf* in the metre of the original poem (this is one of the passages in the essay where Tolkien recycles, in more polished form, material from his then-unpublished *Beowulf* translation, a small part of which was published in *Beowulf and the Critics;* see *B&C,* 5, 430). Detailed accounts are provided of metrical variations and the various alliterative patterns encountered. The original text of the lines translated is then given, together with a literal word-for-word translation in which words used only or mainly in poetry are underlined.

This essay sheds light not only on Tolkien's understanding of the artistry of the *Beowulf*-poet but also on his reasons for employing archaisms in his own poetry and fiction; it also provides an account in his own words of the alliterative metre of Old English verse that he appreciated so much and in which he composed a number of original poems.

CARL PHELPSTEAD

Primary Sources

Tolkien, J.R.R. "Prefatory Remarks on Prose Translation of *Beowulf*." In *"Beowulf" and the Finnesburg Fragment: A Translation into Modern English Prose,* edited by Charles L. Wrenn and translated by John R. Clark Hall, viii–xii. London: George Allen & Unwin, 1940. Reprinted as "On Translating *Beowulf*." In *The Monsters and the Critics and Other Essays,* edited by Christopher Tolkien, 49–71. London: George Allen & Unwin, 1983. Paperback edition, London: HarperCollins, 1997.
Lewis, C.S. "A Metrical Suggestion." *Lysistrata* 2 (1935): 13–24. Reprinted as "The Alliterative Metre." In *Rehabilitations and Other Essays,* 117–32. London: Oxford University Press, 1939.
Phelpstead, Carl. "Auden and the Inklings: An Alliterative Revival." *Journal of English and Germanic Philology* 103 (2004): 433–57.

See also **Beowulf and the Critics**; **Beowulf: Tolkien's Scholarship; Beowulf: Tolkien's Translations of; Old English**

ONE RING, THE

Three Rings for the Elven-kings under the sky,
    Seven for the Dwarf-lords in their halls of stone,
Nine for Mortal Men doomed to die,
    One for the Dark Lord on his dark throne
In the Land of Mordor where the Shadows lie.
    One Ring to rule them all, One Ring to find them,
One Ring to bring them all and in the darkness bind
      them
    In the Land of Mordor where the Shadows lie.

The One Ring, also known as the Ruling Ring, was created by Sauron during the Second Age of Middle-earth, about 1600. Feigning friendship with the Noldor in craftsmen of Eregion, Sauron aided them in their creation of Rings of Power, all the while planning to betray them by creating in secret a Ruling Ring forged in the fires of Orodruin, or Mount Doom, and pouring into it much of his own power and will.

Celebrimbor, a grandson of Fëanor, realized Sauron's plot and hid the three Elven Rings from him, and war broke out between Sauron and Elves, Dwarves, and Men. During the Last Alliance of Elves and Men, Sauron was overthrown (3441), ending the Second Age, and the Ring was taken by Isildur, who was slain in the river Anduin during an ambush by Orcs several years later.

The Ring remained in the river until found by Sméagol, who murdered his friend Déagol to get it (ca. 2463 Third Age), and then hid for many years in the Misty Mountains with it until Bilbo the Hobbit stumbled upon it and took it (2941 Third Age). Sixty years later, he bequeathed it to his nephew Frodo, the first time the Ring had been relinquished willingly by its bearer. Shortly thereafter, Gandalf discovered it to be the One Ring, and Frodo with eight companions set out from Rivendell to cast it back into Orodruin and destroy it, which happened on March 25, 3019, when Gollum bit off Frodo's finger and fell into the Cracks of Doom.

The One Ring has three chief traits: as an extension of Sauron, it appears to have a power and sentience of its own; it embodies and enacts the absolute corruption of its master upon any other bearer of the Ring; and it consequently betrays any other wearer. Inscribed within it in the language of Mordor are the sixth and seventh lines from the ancient poem cited previously, which articulate its essence: the Ring is an extension of Sauron's will to eradicate any resistance and to assert ultimate dominion over all peoples and other creatures. It is not a weapon of war or of mass destruction per se, thus weakening the interpretation that it is Tolkien's symbolic representation of the atomic bomb. Instead, it is a tool of absolute control able to give power to its wearer according to the power of the wearer but equally capable of submerging that person within its own corruption.

For creatures like hobbits—Gollum, Bilbo, Frodo, and Samwise—its chief seeming benefits are the abilities to make the wearer invisible, to heighten his senses, and to extend his life unnaturally. However, others of much greater power, like Elrond, Gandalf, and Galadriel, wearers of the three Elven Rings, fear and reject it because of the enormous maleficent force it contains, a force that would increase their own powers but ultimately devour them as it did Sauron's chief servants, the Ringwraiths, or Nazgûl, the nine mortal men to whom Rings of Power were given (sometime after 1800 Second Age) but who then came under the dominion of the One Ring. With the destruction of the One Ring, Sauron's fortress of Barad-dûr, whose foundations were laid through the power of the Ring, fell; the Nazgûl were no more; the Three Elven Rings failed; and the Third Age came to an end.

WILLIAM SENIOR

See also **Bilbo; Dwarves; Elrond; Elves; Fëanor; Frodo; Galadriel; Gandalf; Gollum; Hobbits; Misty Mountains; Mordor; Power in Tolkien's Works; Ring-Giving; Rings; Sam; Sauron; Towers**

ORAL TRADITION

Tolkien's expertise in Anglo-Saxon, Old Norse, and even Finnish sagas and alliterative verse shaped the poetic forms and depiction of oral cultures found in his legendarium. The oral-formulaic theory or oral theory of poetry, first articulated in the late 1920s by Milman Parry in his studies of Homeric epics and later developed by Albert Lord in his field work in Yugoslavia, established the basic tenets of a poetics shaped by the circumstances and constraints of oral performance. Later, these theories were applied to the study of Old English and other related national traditions (Parry 1928/1971; Lord 1960; Magoun 1953). Later theorists further outlined the differences and interconnections between oral and chirographic (or writing-based) cultures (Ong 1982). According to these critics, technical aspects of traditional compositions such as alliteration, epithets, formulae, meter, or even narrative structure were intimately related to the manner in which the poets created their works in the process of performing them, though the nature of those oral performances, whether they were spoken or sung, remained hotly debated. Tolkien's writings testify to the influence these academic discussions of oral theory and oral performance theory had on his critical and creative output.

His literary essays lay out some of the principles of Old English oral poetry and the traditions that shaped it. In his landmark 1936 lecture "*Beowulf:* The Monsters and the Critics," Tolkien notes that lines of alliterative verse are based on balance and are "more like masonry than music" (*MC,* 30)—made to be recited or chanted but not sung. "On Translating *Beowulf,*" a preface Tolkien wrote in the 1940s, contains detailed analysis of kennings, alliteration, meter, and other technical aspects of Old English poetry and how they are related to their ultimate origin in oral performance. Oral poetic theories even inform his discussions of tale-telling in "On Fairy-stories"; he regards the practices of oral narrators mixing different narrative elements either instinctively or purposefully as vital to the formation of that "Cauldron of Story" that makes up a fairy-story (*MC,* 129).

The scattered references to poetic technique in the various iterations of the legendarium indicate that Tolkien sought to connect his invented literary traditions to the known oral poetic forms and practices of the Anglo-Saxons and Norse. He provides his own reconstruction of the conditions of oral poetic composition through his brief analyses of Elven poetic forms and his references to *scops* or minstrels performing before audiences, particularly the figure of Ælfwine from the unfinished texts in *The History of Middle-earth* series. As Verlyn Flieger observes, the English mariner Eriol or Ælfwine (Elf-friend), as he is known in some incarnations, serves as a transmitter of lost poetic traditions and legends like his counterpart in Snorri Sturluson's *Prose Edda* and thereby allows Tolkien to reflect on oral poetic practice and to make parallels between his mythic world and the Anglo-Saxon world. In "Ælfwine and Dírhaval," an unused introduction to "Narn i Chîn Húrin," Ælfwine appears as the recorder of the Húrin and Túrin Turambar story that originally existed as a Mannish oral lay attributed to the poet/*scop* figure Dírhaval: "His lay was composed of that mode of verse which is called *Minlamad thent / estent.* Though this verse was not wholly unlike the verse known to Ælfwine, he translated it into prose . . . for he was not himself skilled in the making of verse" (*Jewels,* 311–12). Patrick Wynne and Carl F. Hostetter have commented extensively on the *Minlamad thent / estent* verse form, concluding that it is probably a Sindarin equivalent to Old English alliterative verse based on half-lines with a medial caesura (Wynne and Hostetter, 121–22). Tolkien's gloss on the term *narn*—that it signifies to the Elves "a tale that is told in verse to be spoken and not sung" (*Jewels,* 313)—further demonstrates how the poetics of the early Elves and Men anticipates that of later generations, furthering the conceit Tolkien developed that he is writing a forgotten prehistory of Western civilization.

Ælfwine accordingly appears in the capacity of a minstrel in Tolkien's unfinished time-travel narratives, "The Lost Road" and "The Notion Club Papers." Tolkien uses these examples of Ælfwine's minstrelsy or that of his friend Tréowine to further his views on the performance practices of oral poets, and Wynne and Hostetter discuss at length the extent to which Tolkien here tacitly defends the view that oral poetry was chanted, even with the accompaniment of a harp, rather than spoken (126–30 passim). Although these portrayals of an Old English *scop* are fairly sketchy, they do suggest that Tolkien regarded oral poetic forms and performance as narrative devices for linking the past to the present in English history (the modern Arundel Lowdham dream-traveling back in time to become the tenth-century minstrel) and ultimately as a means for bridging the gap between early medieval English history and the distant imaginative history legendarium, the fall of Númenor. To that end, oral poetics functions as a vehicle for time travel in Tolkien's work.

The conventions of oral poetry and their relationship to the themes of time and nostalgia for past appear prominently in his published works, such as *The Lord of the Rings* and *The Hobbit.* The Hall of Fire in Rivendell is a center for traditional poetry and song, as well as a locus of memory in Middle-earth. The Rohirrim, whom Aragorn characterizes "wise but unlearned, writing no books but singing many songs" (*TT,* III, ii, 33), are modeled heavily upon the Anglo-Saxons and embody many of the ancient traditions of oral culture. Even the very narrative structure of Tolkien's books mimics the conventions of oral composition, grounding his work in that, for Martin Ball, Tolkien is writing a "threnody to the lost culture of oral traditions" in his mournful descriptions of the few remaining oral cultures at the end of the Third Age. In examining Tolkien's tendency to use aspects of oral poetry in his prose fiction, C.W. Sullivan III suggests that "Tolkien committed a traditionally patterned oral narrative to paper" (11) and points out how closely the structure of the narratives resembles that of Icelandic sagas, also originally oral works. Anne C. Petty examines the structure of the "Silmarillion" texts in terms of Lönnrot's reconstruction of the oral Kalevala. These studies all demonstrate that Tolkien sought to re-create oral poetic forms in the twentieth-century genre of the novel, commemorating that almost-forgotten tradition in the era of the printing press.

Tolkien himself even briefly impersonated an Anglo-Saxon *scop* in a recording he made of his poem "The Homecoming of Beorhtnoth, Beorhthelm's Son," a modern English text inspired by the Old English fragment, *The Battle of Maldon.* Chanting some translated lines from that ancient text, Tolkien brought oral tradition to life in the modern age, albeit momentarily. His academic studies of oral poetry and his references to such literary forms in England, Beleriand, and Middle-earth illustrate the extent to which the roots of Tolkien's imagination lay in his fascination with the living art of oral poetic performance.

DAVID D. OBERHELMAN

Further Reading

Ball, Martin. "Cultural Values and Cultural Death in *The Lord of the Rings.*" *Australian Humanities Review*, no. 28 (January–March 2003). http://www.lib.latrobe.edu.au/AHR/archive/Issue-Jan-2003/ball.html.

Flieger, Verlyn. "The Footsteps of Ælfwine." In *Tolkien's Legendarium: Essays on "The History of Middle-earth,"* edited by Verlyn Flieger and Carl F. Hostetter, 183–97. Westport, CT: Greenwood, 2000.

Lord, Albert B. *The Singer of Tales.* Harvard Studies in Comparative Literature, 24. Cambridge, MA: Harvard University Press, 1960.

Magoun, Francis Peabody. "The Oral Formulaic Character of Anglo-Saxon Narrative Poetry." *Speculum* 28 (1953): 446–67.

Ong, Walter. *Orality and Literacy: The Technologizing of the Word.* London: Methuen, 1982.

Parry, Milman. *L'Epithéte traditionelle dans Homère* (1928). In *The Making of Homeric Verse: The Collected Papers of Milman Parry,* edited by Adam Parry. Reprint. Oxford: Oxford University Press, 1971.

Petty, Anne C. "Identifying England's Lönnrot." *Tolkien Studies* 1, no. 1 (2004): 69–84.

Sullivan, C.W., III. "Tolkien the Bard: His Tale Grew in the Telling." In *J.R.R. Tolkien and His Literary Resonances: Views of Middle-earth,* edited by George Clark and Daniel Timmons, 11–20. Westport, CT: Greenwood, 2000.

Wynne, Patrick, and Carl F. Hostetter. "Three Elvish Verse Modes: *Ann-thennath, Minlamad thent/estent,* and *Linnod.*" In *Tolkien's Legendarium: Essays on "The History of Middle-earth,"* edited by Verlyn Flieger and Carl F. Hostetter, 113–39. Westport, CT: Greenwood, 2000.

See also **Ælfwine; Alliteration; Alliterative Verse by Tolkien;** *Battle of Maldon;* **Beowulf and the Critics;** **"Beowulf: The Monsters and the Critics";** *Beowulf:* **Tolkien's Scholarship;** *Beowulf:* **Translations by Tolkien; Finland: Literary Sources; Languages, Invented; Old English; Old Norse Language; Old Norse Literature; "On Translating** *Beowulf***"; Orality; Rhyme Schemes and Meter**

ORALITY

With Tolkien's intention to create a "connected body of legend" and present it in the form in which his models, some of the world's primary mythologies, are available, he needed to create a network of texts and stories that suggest the cultural complexity behind such bodies of story. His philologist training told him that although myths and legends are available to the researcher in numerous written versions, it is usually a primary oral phase that underlies these texts. To make his fiction convincing, or at least to make it suggest this complexity, he needed to include the oral phase implicitly.

The cultures of Tolkien's Middle-earth all have some use of orality and the oral way of preserving information. The earliest of his conceptions for the frame inside which his stories were to be told, the "Lost Tales," rely nearly entirely on oral storytelling, and the long, paratactic sentences (coordinated clauses connected regularly with "and") recall the real accumulative nature of oral performance (this style survives into the published *Silmarillion* in the "high style" of, for example, the "Ainulindalë"). But as orality is most notably characterized by mnemotechnical devices present in poetry, it is in his poetry and the uses his prose makes of poetry that this suggestion of an

underlying orality is most prominent. In *The Silmarillion,* it is said that both Elves and Men knew writing and used it to preserve culturally important information; however, both in the ruin of Doriath and in Elrond's house we are told about "living" sources or spoken narratives. Elvish orality is a special case, since cultural memory is a special function for a people who in the normal course of events do not die (the transmission of information is necessary for education and instruction only, since the original witnesses of any story can still be available). But for Men, the technology of orality is vital.

Tolkien's poetry, especially his alliterative verse, makes extensive use of stylistic devices that can function to suggest oral origin (clearly his reliance on the vocabulary and diction of Old English poetry, itself for some extent rooted in orality, is one reason for this, but this is taken into his consistent depiction of cultural origins). Often, however, Tolkien's prose integrates elements (stylistic or in some cases actual textual units or poetic phrases and images) from his poetry, suggesting successfully an underlying poetic tradition. The use of formula-like phrases or fixed alliterating epithets (Curufin the Crafty) work to suggest storytelling and character-building conventions, as well as an actual (fictitious) tradition of composition behind even texts that had originally been written in prose. The reliance on long accumulative periods in sentences, often punctuated by smaller but regularly repeated units of parallel or contrast ("and they built lands and Melkor destroyed them; valleys they delved and Melkor raised them up," etc.), also imply conventions of rhetoric, rhythm, and poetic meter that are fictionalized into the imagined world and are available only through their "transcriptions" or fictitious adaptations.

The short, concise style of many proverbial expressions in *The Silmarillion* that are especially connected with the culture of Men point to this culture as one of the most important users of orality in Tolkien's Middle-earth. The country of Rohan is said to be relying exclusively on this technique of transmitting culturally important information, and as there are several fragments of Rohirric poetry instanced in *The Lord of the Rings* text (in alliterative meter, using a poetic vocabulary close to that of Old English poetry), orality plays an important role in this work as well. Improvisation and some genres of orally composed and performed poems figure in this work (e.g., the lament for Boromir) and in *The Silmarillion* (e.g., Túrin's song at Lake Ivrin lamenting his accidental killing of his friend Beleg).

Tolkien's integration of the cultural framework of orality, not merely in theory but also in its actual details and elements, adds much to the "depth" effect of his works and functions as a device authenticating traditions and the very processes Tolkien is describing (in fact, creating) in his text. The stylistic or textual details suggesting the underlying orality are therefore an integral part of Tolkien's presentation of culture.

GERGELY NAGY

Further Reading

Flieger, Verlyn. *Interrupted Music: The Making of Tolkien's Mythology.* Kent, OH: Kent State University Press, 2005.

Nagy, Gergely. "The Adapted Text: The Lost Poetry of Beleriand." *Tolkien Studies* 1 (2004): 21–41.

See also **Alliterative Verse by Tolkien; Oral Tradition; Rohan**

ORFEO, SIR

Sir Orfeo is a Middle English rhyming poem, probably composed (or, more likely, translated from an Old French original, now lost) in the latter half of thirteenth century and extant now only in three manuscripts, the best and earliest (Auchinleck) dating probably from ca. 1330 and the other two, later and more corrupt but providing a beginning lost from the earlier, dating from the fifteenth century. *Sir Orfeo* is essentially a Middle English retelling and medieval reimagining, through the genre of the Breton lay, of the ancient Greek myth of Orpheus and Eurydice, in which the semidivine Orpheus, a poet and peerless harper whose music charms man, beast, and god alike, travels to the underworld to free his love, Eurydice, who had been seized by Hades (Pluto), winning her a grant of release from Hades with the beauty of his harping.

In the Middle English retelling, Sir Orfeo remains a peerless harper and is even stated to be descended from Pluto on his father's side and Juno on his mother's. He is king of Thrace (Traciens)—which, however, is here transported to England and identified as the ancient name of Winchester. Finally, his queen, Dame Heurodis, fairest of ladies, is seized not by Hades but first by madness and then by the King of Faërie, who magics her away from amid a thousand knights. In his grief at her loss, Orfeo renounces his crown, handing his kingdom over to a steward, and wanders for ten years in the forests and moors as a beggar, becoming unrecognizable, even to his former subjects. He keeps only his harp, and in the forest his music draws and charms the birds and beasts. There he often sees the King of Faërie and his company, hunting in the woods with his hounds (though never slaying any beast), marching in the hundreds under banner as knights with drawn swords, or reveling with their ladies, dancing

and singing. On one such day, Orfeo sees Heurodis among a passing company of mounted ladies, and grabbing his harp, he runs after them, following as they pass magically through miles of rock and then out into the green, level, and luminous land of Faërie, which glows even at night with its precious stones bright as the sun, and so to the spectacular, hundred-towered palace of the King of Faërie. Orfeo is allowed entry as a minstrel and brought to the King, passing on the way a contorted host of the dead, mutilated, and mad, near which others, including Dame Heurodis, lie by sleeping peacefully and who had been likewise seized there from mortal lands by fairy magic. Coming before the King, Orfeo sits on the ground and plays his harp so sweetly that all the palace inhabitants come and sit at his feet to hear his playing. The King is so moved as to grant Orfeo whatever reward he asks. Orfeo asks for Heurodis but is at first denied her by the King, on the grounds that Orfeo is too dirty, rough, and lean to be with so fair a lady. Orfeo replies that it would be a worse thing for the King to be a liar, and so chastened the King grants his wish, and they depart. Retracing his steps, he comes back to mortal lands and returns with Heurodis to Winchester. Still in his tattered beggar's garb, he walks disheveled and unrecognized through the town, to the scandal of his former subjects, until he meets his own steward. Presenting himself as a wandering harper from heathen lands, he is invited by the steward, for the sake of his harper lord Sir Orfeo, to a feast at Orfeo's castle. There he again charms the palace with his harping, and when asked by the steward how he, a beggar, had come to own such a harp, Orfeo replies that he had come upon it in the wilderness, next to a man who had been torn asunder by wolves. The steward, thinking that this means that Orfeo is dead, swoons in grief and despair. Seeing by this that his steward had been loyal to him through all the years of his absence, Sir Orfeo reveals his identity and his rescue of Heurodis, to the great joy of the steward and of his subjects. With Dame Heurodis, he resumes his crown and the rule of England.

The reader of *The Silmarillion* and *The Lord of the Rings* will readily notice in *Sir Orfeo* many familiar echoes: perhaps most readily in Lúthien's beguiling of Morgoth before his throne with her song in the netherworld fortress of Angband, thereby gaining the release of Beren (though here both Tolkien and *Sir Orfeo* draw ultimately on the Greek myth); in the winning by Beren of the hand of Lúthien from King Thingol as a promised reward (though this motif too is hardly unique to *Sir Orfeo*); and in the return of the King to Gondor ending a long stewardship (though again Greek myth lies beneath them both, namely, the return of Odysseus, unrecognized after many years of wandering, to the rule of Ithaca). Perhaps less obviously, but if anything more significantly and directly influential, is the poem's depiction of the land and inhabitants of Faërie. Tom Shippey is surely correct to suggest that "the 'master-text' for Tolkien's portrayal of the elves is the description of the hunting king in *Sir Orfeo*" (62; cf. 63–64, 259). Among English sources and traditions, the glimpses of the martial prowess and majesty of the inhabitants of Faërie provided in *Sir Orfeo* are remarkable: the Elves of Middle-earth are certainly far more reminiscent of the fairies of *Sir Orfeo* than they are of those in Shakespeare or Spenser. Also noteworthy are the depiction of the King of Faërie's castle as set amid a smooth, level, green plain (line 353) reached only after a long passage underground through rock, which is perhaps echoed in Tolkien's depiction of the hidden Elvish city-kingdom of Gondolin, and the long tunnel that is its sole entrance passage; the detail of Faërie's luminous stones shining at night like the noonday Sun (lines 369–72), reminiscent of the Silmarils; and the poem's swift but lavish descriptions of the bright jewels, dazzling crystals, precious metals, and other adornments of the lands and dwellings of Faërie (see especially lines 355–76), with which *The Silmarillion* in particular is replete.

In addition to the influences of *Sir Orfeo* on his legendarium, the poem attracted Tolkien's special interest in his professional academic career. In 1944, Tolkien prepared, as a small mimeograph booklet (Hammond B18) for use in the naval cadet's course at Oxford (Hammond 1993, 300), a Middle English version of the poem: that is, neither a translation nor an edition but rather a thorough emendation of the Middle English text, as Tolkien states, "in accordance with the grammar of earlier Southern English" to free it from much of "the corruptions of error and forgetfulness [that] have infected it with the forms of later language and different dialect" (Hostetter 104). Shortly thereafter, he also prepared a metrical translation of the poem (published posthumously). Tolkien's greatest influence on the scholarship of the poem, however, was (as so often) achieved indirectly, through the work of his students: the inspiration of Tolkien's tutorial scholarship is the first debt acknowledged in what remains the standard edition of *Sir Orfeo*, that of his erstwhile student, Alan J. Bliss, first published in 1954 (vi). This edition offers a fuller description of the textual history, sources, and linguistic features of the Middle English poem.

CARL F. HOSTETTER

Further Reading

Bliss, Alan J., ed. *Sir Orfeo*. 2nd ed. London: Oxford University Press, 1966. First published in 1954.

Hammond, Wayne G., with the assistance of Douglas A. Anderson. *J.R.R. Tolkien: A Descriptive Bibliography*. New Castle, DE: Oak Knoll Books, 1993.

Hostetter, Carl F., ed. "*Sir Orfeo*: A Middle English Version by J.R.R. Tolkien." *Tolkien Studies* 1 (2004): 85–123.

Shippey, Tom. *The Road to Middle-earth: How J.R.R. Tolkien Created a New Mythology*. Revised and expanded edition. Boston, MA: Houghton Mifflin, 2002.

Tolkien, J.R.R., trans. *Sir Gawain and the Green Knight, Pearl, and Sir Orfeo*. Introduction by J.R.R. Tolkien. Edited with a preface by Christopher Tolkien. Boston, MA: Houghton Mifflin, 1975.

———, ed. *Sir Orfeo*. Oxford: Academic Copying Office, 1944.

See also **Beren; Elves; Faërie; Lúthien;** *Pearl:* **Edition by E.V. Gordon; Thingol, Elwë, Elu Singollo**

OWL AND THE NIGHTINGALE, THE

The Owl and the Nightingale is a poem of some 1,800 lines, written in rhyming couplets in a dialect of early Middle English. Internal evidence indicates that it was written about CE 1200, though the two manuscripts in which it survives date from later in the thirteenth century. It is a debate poem, in which the two named birds argue and abuse each other, the nightingale accusing the owl of being ugly, singing badly, and eating small birds and the owl charging the nightingale with frivolity and immorality. Though the poem is similar in date, and in dialect, to the *Ancrene Riwle,* on which Tolkien worked for so long, it is different in cultural background. It is written in rhyme, not the native poetic mode of alliteration, and the author was familiar with French poetry and the growing cult of romantic love.

The poem is anonymous, but it names a "Maister Nichole of Guildeforde," whom many have thought must be the author. What happens is that the two birds agree near the start that they must have a judge; the nightingale proposes Master Nicholas of Guildford, and the owl agrees, saying that she trusts him to judge fairly, although she knows that once upon a time he was fond of nightingales and "other slim and gentle creatures." The birds then continue arguing without him, but at the end they decide to fly off and find him. But where is he? The thrush says that he is at Portesham in Dorset, in the southwest of England, which is a shame; he ought to be brought home and given advancement. Reading very much between the lines, it sounds as if Master Nicholas is a priest, who has been sent from urban Guildford to rural Dorset for some sexual misconduct. The poem could be seen as a self-advertisement to show off his rhetorical skills and indicate that he has learned his lesson; he can be witty and up-to-date but also serious and judicious. It is philologically interesting that although there are strong indications that the poem was originally composed in a southeastern dialect, perhaps that of Guildford, both surviving manuscripts are in a southwestern one. Possibly Master Nicholas never did come home.

This tale of exile and oblivion may account for Tolkien's wry allusions to the poem in "The Notion Club Papers." The title page of this says, "The author identifies himself with the character called in the narrative Nicholas Guildford; but Titmouse has shown that this is a pseudonym, and is taken from a medieval dialogue, at one time read in the Schools of Oxford" (*Sauron,* 149). The whole framework of the "Papers" indicates that they have been found long after they were written and that no one in the imagined future knows anything of the author, or the Notion Club itself. At the time they were in fact written, 1944–45, Tolkien may well have feared that his life's work would never be published and that, like the medieval Master Nicholas, he would soon be forgotten, leaving behind only a dusty bundle of anonymous manuscript.

TOM SHIPPEY

Primary Sources

Hume, Kathryn. *The Owl and the Nightingale: The Poem and Its Critics.* Toronto: University of Toronto Press, 1975.

Stanley, E.G., ed. *The Owl and the Nightingale.* London: Nelson, 1960.

Stone, Brian, trans. *The Owl and the Nightingale, Cleanness, and St. Erkenwald.* 2nd ed., Harmondsworth, UK: Penguin, 1988.

See also **Lost Road, The**

OXFORD

Explaining the University of Oxford to outsiders is not an easy task; it has many ancient and archaic traditions, but the basic facts are that the university comprises thirty-nine individual colleges and seven permanent private halls, which are private corporations. Each one provides a home to its undergraduates. The university's formal head is the chancellor, who occupies the position for life; the executive head is the vice-chancellor, who is elected for a seven-year period and usually comes from one of the colleges. The university conducts examinations and awards degrees. Two examinations are necessary to gain a bachelor's degree: the preliminary examination, Honour Moderations, is taken at the end of the first or second year of study; the second examination, the Honour School, is held at the end of the undergraduate course. Successful candidates are awarded First, Second, or Third Class honours, depending on their performance at their examinations.

The heads of the different colleges are known by various titles, including provost, warden, principal, president, or master; teaching members of the colleges are collectively known as dons. In addition to residential and dining facilities, each college also offers social, cultural, and recreational activities to its members.

The Undergraduate

Tolkien began his first term at Oxford in 1911, and, despite the unattractive look of the George Gilbert Scott frontage of Exeter College and the rather tasteless chapel, he felt that he could honour Oxford and hold it dear. The trees in the Fellows' Garden were tall and flourishing, and it was the first real home he had known since the death of his mother six years earlier. Tolkien threw himself into university life, joining the rugby team, the college Essay Club, the college debating society, and the Dialectical Society. He also began a club devoted to self-indulgence; the Apolausticks held debates and discussions, read papers, and enjoyed expensive dinners. The Tea Club and Barrovian Society (TCBS) had been only slightly less sophisticated (although rather less indulgent), but both groups were typical of Tolkien's preference for a group of male friends with whom he could smoke, talk, and eat.

At Oxford, Tolkien was reading classics; he was expected to attend regular tutorials (often one-on-one) and lectures. However, during his first two terms, Exeter lacked a resident classics tutor; by the time one was appointed, Tolkien had already become bored with Greek and Roman authors and was taking an interest in Germanic literature. Instead of attending the required lectures on Demosthenes and Cicero, he was sitting in his college rooms working on his invented languages. There was only one area of the syllabus in which he showed any interest: comparative philology, which was taught by Joseph Wright. Wright, a formerly penniless mill-worker, was a passionate and exacting tutor, just what Tolkien needed to shake him out of his superiority towards his fellow classicists. Wright was the author of the Gothic grammar text that Tolkien had purchased from a fellow pupil in Birmingham; when he learnt of Tolkien's burgeoning interest in Welsh, he encouraged Tolkien to follow this interest. Tolkien took his advice, although not quite in the manner Wright had meant. Acquiring some books of medieval Welsh, Tolkien began to read them and found his expectations of the beauty of Welsh were met. Unfortunately,

Tolkien's passionate interest in languages was not duplicated elsewhere in his studies; he developed lazy habits, sitting up late to talk and smoke, doing little work, and even failing to attend Mass because rising early seemed impossible after a late night talking with friends. He needed something to steady him, but he was still forbidden to see or write to Edith Bratt, who might have exerted a positive influence.

At school, Tolkien had read the *Kalevala* in an English translation, and it had awakened in him a desire to learn Finnish; then one day he found a Finnish grammar text in the library of Exeter College, which he used to teach himself the language in which the *Kalevala* was originally written. Although he never learnt Finnish well, Tolkien found the language as intoxicating as wine, and it had an enormous effect on his private languages. He abandoned Neo-Gothic, on which he had been working since his school days, to begin creating a language heavily influenced by Finnish; eventually this language developed into *Quenya,* the High-elven language of his mythology. While working on his private language, Tolkien wrote and read a paper on the *Kalevala,* in particular on the importance of its mythology, to the Essay Club.

During his undergraduate days, Tolkien also developed his painting, drawing, and calligraphy skills, becoming accomplished in many manuscript styles and at sketching landscapes. During the summer vacation of 1912, Tolkien went on a walking holiday in Berkshire during which he climbed the downs and sketched the villages. He maintained an interest in painting, drawing, and calligraphy throughout his life and used it to great effect in his stories.

Five days after his twenty-first birthday, Tolkien was reunited with Edith, and they became unofficially engaged, being uncertain of how Edith's family would react. However, Tolkien returned to Oxford for the start of the spring term full of happiness and determined to concentrate on Honour Moderations, the first of the two examinations he needed to earn his classics degree. Making an attempt to cram four terms of work into the six weeks that remained until the examinations, Tolkien struggled, since he found he could not break his habit of talking until late with his friends, which meant rising early was almost impossible. By the time Honour Moderations began at the end of February, Tolkien was still ill prepared for most of his papers. Although he was relieved to achieve a Second Class, he knew that he ought to have earned a First. Whilst a First in "Mods" was by no means easily achieved, it ought to have been possible for someone as capable as Tolkien, if he had devoted himself to his studies. Fortunately he had achieved a "pure alpha" (an almost perfect paper) in comparative philology, and knowing that Tolkien was interested in Old and Middle English, and other Germanic languages, the rector of Exeter College suggested that Tolkien switch to the English School and become a philologist. Tolkien was aware that the college was disappointed that he had failed to achieve a First, not least because he held an award, so he agreed to Dr. Farnell's suggestion. When the summer term of 1913 started, he began to read English instead of classics.

When Tolkien joined the Honour School of English Language and Literature, it was still a relatively new one, and it was divided in two: the medievalists and philologists on the language side believed that post-Chaucerian literature was not challenging enough for a degree-level syllabus, and the literature enthusiasts believed that philology and the study of Old and Middle English were a waste of time. Tolkien was on the side of the medievalists and philologists and would have preferred to ignore anything written after Chaucer.

Tolkien's tutor was Kenneth Sisam, a young man from New Zealand who was assisting Professor A.S. Napier, who held the chair in English language and literature. Tolkien met Sisam, a quietly spoken man only four years senior to him, looked at the syllabus, then wondered how it could possibly occupy him for the next two years and a term. He was already familiar with many of the set texts, and he had even learned some Old Norse. However, Tolkien grew to like and respect Sisam, despite the latter's quiet demeanour, and he found himself at his desk more often than he had whilst he was reading classics. He quickly discovered that it was not as easy as he had anticipated, particularly because the Oxford English School had high standards. Tolkien began to write long, complex essays on philology topics, to expand his knowledge of the West Midlands dialect of Middle English, and to read Old English works that were new to him. One such text was the *Crist* of Cynewulf, a group of Anglo-Saxon religious poems, two lines of which forcibly struck Tolkien when he saw them:

> *Eala Earendel engla beorhtast*
> *Ofer middangeard monnum sended*
> [Hail Earendel, brightest of Angels
> above the Middle-earth sent unto men]

Whilst Earendel is interpreted by the Anglo-Saxon dictionary as "a shining light, a ray," Tolkien believed that Earendel was originally the name of Venus, the dawn star. He recorded feeling a "curious thrill" when he encountered the name, which he found moving and beautiful yet strange and remote.

He found even more to stir his imagination in his specialist subject of Old Norse. Tolkien already had some familiarity with Norse, but now he began to study its literature in depth. He read the *Poetic (Elder) Edda, the Prose (Younger) Edda,* and the sagas, finding the Völuspa (Prophecy of the Seeress) especially appealing to his imagination, although all Norse literature that he read would have an effect on his mythology, some of it in profound ways.

At the start of the 1913 academic year, Tolkien's friend Geoffrey B. Smith arrived in Oxford, with the result that the TCBS was now represented equally at Oxford and Cambridge since Robert Q. Gilson and Christopher Wiseman were already at Cambridge. Tolkien's secret engagement to Edith would end soon with Edith's reception into the Roman Catholic Church. Tolkien had told his guardian, Father Francis Morgan, about his reunion with Edith, but as yet he had not told his friends. He wrote to Wiseman and Gilson and spoke to Smith; all three of his friends congratulated him, although Gilson perceptively commented that it seemed unlikely that Tolkien's engagement would prevent him from remaining a TCBS-ite. Edith was received into the Roman Catholic Church on January 8, 1914, the first anniversary of their reunion, but she never felt as comfortable in the Roman Catholic Church as she had at the Anglican Church in Cheltenham, and in later life this caused some friction between Edith and Tolkien.

Tolkien began another club, the Chequers, with his friend Colin Cullis; he was elected president of the influential Stapledon Club, Exeter's debating society; he played tennis and went punting; and by the spring of 1914 he had worked hard enough to win the Skeat Prize for English. He used the five-pound prize money to buy several William Morris works and some books of medieval Welsh. Although Morris was a former Exeter man, Tolkien had not read any of his imaginative works before. Tolkien's knowledge of modern literature was limited because he belonged to the language side of the English School. For him, all the stimulus his imagination craved came from the early literature of Iceland and the poetry of the Old and Middle English period. However, Morris's view of literature coincided with Tolkien's, and he found Morris's prose-and-verse romance *The House of the Wolfings* absorbing. Many of its elements impressed Tolkien: the highly idiosyncratic style, the attempt to re-create the aura of ancient legend, and Morris's ability to describe in great detail the landscape he had imagined. All of this can clearly be seen to have influenced Tolkien when he came to write his own mythological stories.

During the summer vacation of 1914, Tolkien visited Edith, then Cornwall, before going to stay with his Aunt Jane in Nottinghamshire. Whilst he was there, he wrote *The Voyage of Earendel the Evening Star,* a poem inspired by the lines from the *Crist* of Cynewulf and the starting point for his mythology. By the time Tolkien wrote the poem, England had declared war on Germany, and young men were rushing to enlist in Horatio Kitchener's new army. Tolkien's brother, Hilary, had already enlisted as a bugler, and his aunts and uncles clearly expected him to follow his brother's example. However, Tolkien wanted to complete his degree first; he hoped to earn a First, a necessity if he was going to be able to pursue the academic career he desired. Initially, he was uncertain whether he would be able to study once he returned to Oxford, but he discovered that a scheme existed that would allow him to train for the army whilst completing his studies; this meant he could defer his call-up until after he received his degree. He immediately signed up for the scheme and then felt he could concentrate on his university career. He and Colin Cullis, who could not enlist owing to poor health, took "digs" in St. John's Street, and Tolkien began to drill with the Officers' Training Corps in the University Parks; although it was necessary to combine his training with his usual college activities, he found he was enjoying himself and that he did not suffer from the usual "Oxford sleepies." Tolkien also began writing a prose-and-verse tale, adapting the story of Kullervo from the *Kalevala,* and whilst it was little better than a Morris pastiche, it was not his last attempt at writing a prose-and-verse legend.

Following a TCBS meeting in London during the Christmas vacation of 1914, Tolkien started to write poetry, but he felt that his poems needed a connecting theme, and early in 1915 he turned back to his Earendel verses and began to work them into a larger story. He had shown his original poem, *The Voyage of Earendel,* to Smith, who had expressed a liking for his Earendel verses, then asked Tolkien what they meant. Tolkien replied that he did not know, but he would try to find out, rather than invent a meaning; as a result of his private language invention, he saw himself as discovering legends, not inventing stories. Tolkien had been working on his language Quenya for some time, and it was now sufficiently advanced for him to write poems in it. But he felt the language needed a history to support it since, as far as Tolkien was concerned, it was impossible to have a language without people to speak it. During 1915, he decided that Quenya was spoken by the Elves or fairies whom Earendel had encountered during his voyage, and Tolkien began writing *The Lay of Earendel,* a series of linked poems that would describe the journeys made by Earendel the Mariner before his ship was turned into a star.

Whilst the germs of his mythology were occupying Tolkien's mind, he was also preparing for Honour School, his final examination in English language and literature. It began in June 1915, and Tolkien succeeded in achieving First Class honours, which meant that he could be fairly certain of academic employment, assuming he could survive the war. Before he went overseas, he and Edith were married, feeling that they had waited long enough to be together. The wedding was on March 22, 1916, and they spent their weeklong honeymoon in Somerset.

Postwar, Pre-Leeds

Tolkien did survive the war, largely as a consequence of suffering badly from trench fever, and by the time he was discharged from hospital in October 1918, the end of the war seemed to be in sight, so he travelled to Oxford in an attempt to find an academic job. Initially, his prospects were not promising; many of the university's buildings had been commandeered by the military for use as hospitals or accommodation for soldiers, and few lectures were being held. No one appeared to know what would happen when the war ended, but when Tolkien visited William Craigie, his former tutor, he was given more promising news; Craigie was a member of the *New English Dictionary*'s staff since the dictionary was still being compiled at Oxford, and he suggested that Tolkien could work as an assistant lexicographer. After the war ended November 11, 1918, Tolkien contacted the army authorities and asked permission to be stationed in Oxford so that he could complete his education, since he had not yet been demobilised. They gave him permission, and Tolkien found some rooms in St. John's Street, close to his old student digs. In late November 1918, he, Edith, and baby John (who had been born in 1917) settled in Oxford.

Throughout his army career, Tolkien had dreamed of returning to Oxford; he had longed to return to his friends, his college, and his Oxford way of life, so he was delighted to be working at the Dictionary in the workroom in the Old Ashmolean building in Broad Street. He liked his colleagues, particularly C.T. Onions, and he soon found himself researching the etymology of various words that included *winter, water,* and *wasp.* The skill that such work demanded is evident from the entry for *wasp;* this word is not difficult, but its entry cites comparative words from thirteen languages. It is not surprising that Tolkien found such work taught him far more about languages than even his degree had done. Once, in later years, he said that he learnt more in his two years at the *New English Dictionary* than in any other two-year period of his life. Dr. Henry Bradley, the dictionary's editor, commented that Tolkien had a far

better grasp of Anglo-Saxon and of the grammar of the Germanic languages than anyone else Tolkien's age. Given the high standards of the Dictionary, this was great praise.

When he was not working at the *New English Dictionary,* Tolkien supplemented his income by teaching at the university. Having informed the colleges that he was available to teach, they began to send him pupils, especially the women's colleges such as St. Hugh's and Lady Margaret Hall, who had no one available to teach Anglo-Saxon. Since Tolkien was married, a chaperone for their young women was unnecessary, which gave Tolkien an advantage over other potential tutors. Tolkien and Edith soon realised that they could afford to rent a small house, so they moved around the corner into Alfred Street (now Pusey Street). They moved late in the summer of 1919; Edith was able to employ a cook-housemaid and to retrieve her piano from storage. Because she was pregnant again, Edith was particularly relieved that they now had a home of their own; she looked forward to having the baby in her own home. By the spring of 1920, Tolkien was earning enough from teaching to give up his job at the Dictionary; he continued to work on *The Book of Lost Tales,* which he had begun during his war service. One evening, he read aloud "The Fall of Gondolin" to the Exeter College Essay Club, where the undergraduates received it well. Amongst the undergraduates were Hugo Dyson and Nevil Coghill, who were to become regular listeners at Tolkien's readings from his mythology in later years.

In 1920, Tolkien applied for a post at the University of Leeds; he hardly expected to be accepted as reader in English language, but he was offered and accepted the job, moving to Leeds in October 1920. Just four years later, he was made a professor, and when he heard early in 1925 that William Craigie was shortly going to America, leaving the Rawlinson and Bosworth Chair of Anglo-Saxon at Oxford vacant, he applied. In theory, he did not stand much chance of receiving the job since there were three other candidates for the post, all of whom had greater experience than Tolkien. However, Allen Mawer chose not to apply; R.W. Chambers refused the post, and it came down to a battle between Tolkien and his former tutor, Kenneth Sisam. By this time, Sisam was in a senior post at Clarendon Press and, whilst he was not engaged in full-time scholarship, his reputation at Oxford was good, so he had a lot of support. However, Tolkien was also supported by a number of people, including George Gordon, who had been responsible for employing Tolkien at Leeds and who was now back in Oxford as professor of English literature. At the election, the voting was split equally between Tolkien and Sisam, and the vice-chancellor,

Joseph Wells, who had the deciding vote, chose to vote for Tolkien.

Scholar

At the beginning of 1926, the Tolkien family—Tolkien, Edith, John, Michael (who was born in 1920), and Christopher (who was born in 1924)—travelled to Oxford from Leeds and moved in to a new house in Northmoor Road. A fellowship at Pembroke College went with the Rawlinson and Bosworth Chair in Anglo-Saxon, so Pembroke became Tolkien's home. At the same time that Tolkien became professor of Anglo-Saxon, C.S. Lewis was elected a Fellow of Magdalen College as a tutor in English language and literature. The two men met for the first time at an English School meeting at Merton College in May 1926. Initially, Lewis was unimpressed by Tolkien, partly because Tolkien was more interested in languages than Lewis, but the two became good friends and worked hard to integrate the literature and language sides of the Oxford English School.

Tolkien proved to be a good teacher, although he was never at his best in a lecture room, where his quick, indistinct speech meant that his students had to concentrate hard to hear and understand him. Nor was he always good at clearly explaining his ideas; he often found it difficult to recall that not everyone was as knowledgeable as he about his subject. However, Tolkien brought his subject to life and showed that it was important to him, which encouraged his students to take an interest in it. Among his students, the best remembered instance of his passion for Anglo-Saxon was the opening of his *Beowulf* lecture series. W.H. Auden recalled that Tolkien would silently enter the lecture room, fix his attention on his students, and then declaim in resounding tones, the opening lines of *Beowulf,* beginning with "*Hwaet!,* which many students took to be "Quiet!" It was less of a recitation than a dramatic performance, and J.I.M. Stewart said that with Tolkien there, the lecture room became a mead hall in which Tolkien was the bard. His effectiveness as a teacher was enhanced because he was a poet and writer, as well as a philologist. He not only found poetry in the sounds of words but also had a poet's understanding of the use of language, which meant that he could not only show students what words meant but also explain why a particular form of expression had been used by an author and how it fitted his or her image scheme. In this way, Tolkien encouraged his students to see early texts as literature that deserved serious study and appreciation in its own right, not merely as examples of a developing language.

In practical terms, what it meant to be the professor of Anglo-Saxon at Oxford was that Tolkien had to give a minimum of 36 lectures or classes a year. But Tolkien did not feel this was a sufficient number to cover his subject, and during the second year after his election, he gave 136 lectures and classes. In part, this was a result of the war; there were too few other tutors available to lecture in Middle English and Anglo-Saxon. After Charles Wrenn was appointed to assist him, Tolkien was able to cut back on his lectures, but he still regularly gave more than twice the expected minimum number of classes and lectures each year during the 1930s. Preparing and giving lectures took up a large proportion of his time, and sometimes Tolkien found he had too little time to prepare a course of lectures, so he cancelled it. This earned him the reputation around the university of being ill prepared for his lectures, but almost the reverse was true since Tolkien was so committed to his subject that he was not ready to tackle it in anything less than an exhaustive manner. This often resulted in him being sidetracked into considering the less important details so that he was unable to finish treating the main subject.

Another time-consuming part of his job was administration. Unlike professors at other universities, Oxford professors do not, by virtue of their office, necessarily have any power over the staff in their faculty. The tutors who make up the majority of faculty staff are appointed by their colleges (as Lewis was), and they do not answer to the professor. This meant that if Tolkien wanted to make any policy changes (such as when he wished to integrate the language and literature sides of the English School), he had to persuade his staff to agree with him rather than instruct them to do as he wanted.

As professor he was also required to supervise postgraduate students and to examine students within the university. Since he had four children by 1930, he also undertook a lot of "freelance" work as an examiner at other universities and marking School Certificate examination papers (this examination was taken at the age of sixteen by British schoolchildren). This annual chore was tedious and dull, but it allowed Tolkien to supplement his income whilst his own children were small. He could have spent his time better in writing or doing research, but he needed the money. Tolkien, like any professor, was expected to devote much of his time to research, and his contemporaries had high hopes of him in this area since his glossary to Sisam's book of Middle English extracts (produced whilst Tolkien was at Leeds), his coediting (with E.V. Gordon) of *Sir Gawain and the*

Green Knight, and his article on the *Ancrene Wisse* manuscripts had demonstrated that he possessed a mastery of the West Midlands dialect of early Middle English that was without equal. Everyone in the Oxford English School confidently expected Tolkien to continue contributing important work in this area—and Tolkien had every intention of doing so, promising an edition of the Cambridge manuscript of the *Ancrene Wisse* to the Early English Text Society. He did a lot of research into this branch of early medieval English, which he loved, but the promised edition was not completed for many years, and the largest part of his research was never published.

One reason for this was Tolkien's lack of time, since he had chosen to devote such a large part of his working life to teaching, which left him little time to spare for original research. His time was also taken up by family life, and then there was the problem of Tolkien's perfectionism, which was a consequence of his emotional commitment to his writing. This meant that he was incapable of treating it in anything other than a deeply serious manner; therefore, everything he wrote (whether philological or fictional) had to be revised, reconsidered, and refined before it could be published. However, what Tolkien did publish during the 1930s proved to be a major contribution to scholarship: his paper on the dialects of Geoffrey Chaucer's "The Reeve's Tale" and his lecture "*Beowulf:* The Monsters and the Critics" were both significant. He planned to produce an edition of *Exodus,* an Anglo-Saxon poem, a task he almost completed, but he was dissatisfied with it. He also intended to collaborate again with E.V. Gordon on new editions of the Anglo-Saxon elegies, *The Seafarer* and *The Wanderer,* and on *Pearl,* which would have complemented their work on *Gawain,* but the geographical distance (more than 120 miles) between the two men made such collaboration difficult once Gordon had moved from Leeds, where he had succeeded Tolkien, to Manchester University in 1931. Then, in the summer of 1938, aged just forty-two, Gordon, after undergoing gall-bladder surgery, died from a hitherto undiagnosed kidney disorder of the suprarenal glands. His death robbed Tolkien not only of a close friend but also of an ideal collaborator. Tolkien did meet another philologist who was a good collaborator; Simone d'Ardenne was a Belgian graduate who had completed a B.Litt. at Oxford, studying Middle English with Tolkien in the early 1930s. Tolkien contributed a great deal to her edition of *The Life and Passion of St. Julienne,* a medieval religious work written in the same dialect as the *Ancrene Wisse.* D'Ardenne went on to become a professor at Liège, and she and Tolkien planned to collaborate on an edition of *Katerine,* another Western Middle English text of the same group, but the outbreak of the Second World War made communication impossible for them for many years.

On November 25, 1936, Tolkien gave a lecture to the British Academy in London. Titled "*Beowulf:* The Monsters and the Critics;" it is one of Tolkien's best-known scholarly papers. Published in the following year, it was a defence of the artistic unity of the early English tale, *Beowulf.* Like Tolkien's later lecture, "On Fairy-stories," the lecture on *Beowulf* provides a key to his work both as a writer of fiction and as a scholar. To Tolkien it was clear that the *Beowulf*-poet had created an illusion of historical truth using his art, or to put it another way, the poet used his instinctive historical sense for poetic and artistic ends. Tolkien went on to talk of the "mythical mode of imagination," something he used as a poet and as the author of *The Hobbit, The Lord of the Rings,* and *The Silmarillion.* Tolkien, like the *Beowulf*-poet, created in his fiction the impression of real history, a sense of the depth of the past. Also like the *Beowulf*-poet, he was influenced by Northern legends.

Tolkien developed these ideas further in his Andrew Lang lecture of 1939, given at St. Andrews University. Titled "On Fairy-Stories," it sets out Tolkien's basic ideas concerning fantasy, imagination, and what he called subcreation. It was Tolkien's intention to rehabilitate the idea of the fairy-story, which had been relegated to the nursery for children's entertainment, for adult reading. He felt that the tendency of adults to regard fairy-stories as trivial and suitable only for children was a mistake because it failed to do justice to either fairy stories or children. It was his aim to show that fairy tales were worthy of serious study because they allow readers or listeners to move from their limited experience to see the depths of both time and space. Tolkien explained that a successful fairy story was a "sub-creation," the highest art and the ultimate achievement of fantasy, which derived power from human language. He explained that a successful writer of fairy-stories creates a secondary world entered by the mind of the reader, and once inside it, whatever is revealed there is true since it is in accord with the laws of the secondary world.

In 1945, Tolkien accepted the Merton Chair of English Language and Literature, after twenty years as professor of Anglo-Saxon. The Merton Chair gave him responsibility for Middle English up to AD 1500, and the move was a reflection of his wider interests, in particular the language and literature of the West Midlands. The new chair allowed him to move from Pembroke College to Merton College as a Fellow, although he had no responsibility to tutor undergraduates as Lewis did at Magdalen College.

Throughout the 1950s, Tolkien continued to teach and explore the literature of the West Midlands in the

Middle English period. He delivered the W.P. Ker Memorial Lecture on April 15. 1953, at the University of Glasgow, where his subject was *Sir Gawain and the Green Knight,* and in December 1953 his translation of the tale was broadcast in dramatic form by the BBC. In 1955, his poem *Imram,* which originally formed a part of "The Notion Club Papers," was published in *Time and Tide.* The poem took the story of St. Brendan's early medieval voyage and fitted the story into Tolkien's invented mythology.

Clubs and Societies

Shortly before his first meeting with Lewis, Tolkien formed a club called the Coal-biters (taken from the Icelandic *Kolbítar,* one who sits so close to the fire in winter that they seem to bite the coal). The club met regularly to read Icelandic myths and sagas. Initially, its membership was limited to dons with a fairly good knowledge of Icelandic. After a while, however, enthusiastic beginners started to join, one of whom was Lewis. It was within the context of this club that the most important friendship of Tolkien's life in Oxford began. Early in December 1929, Tolkien and Lewis sat up until the early hours of the morning discussing Norse gods, giants, and Asgard—a conversation both men enjoyed. A few days later, Tolkien gave Lewis his poem about Beren and Lúthien. Lewis's reaction was favourable, and he promptly wrote to Tolkien expressing his delight in the poem and commenting in particular on its mythical value and the sense of reality it had. Tolkien was delighted to have such a sympathetic and appreciative audience, and soon afterwards he began to read aloud to Lewis from "The Silmarillion" as it then stood. Years later, he called Lewis's encouragement an "unpayable debt."

In the early 1930s, the Kolbítars finished reading all of the key Icelandic sagas, but Tolkien and Lewis continued to meet regularly, together with Lewis's brother Warren "Warnie" Lewis, Hugo Dyson (who was now an English lecturer at Reading University), Lewis's friend Owen Barfield (when he could get away from his job in London as a solicitor), and R.E. "Humphrey" Havard (who was Tolkien's and Lewis's doctor). Others also became regular or semiregular members of the group, which appropriated the name of a now-defunct undergraduate club, the Inklings. As a general rule, the group met twice a week, usually on a Tuesday morning at the Eagle and Child pub in St. Giles and on a Thursday evening in Lewis's rooms at Magdalen College. The Thursday evening meetings tended to involve one or more of the group members reading aloud from a story, poem, or chapter he had written, after which all would join in a critical discussion of the piece. There would then be a general discussion on almost any subject.

In 1945, Tolkien was elected a member of The Dante Society, which met once a term at various colleges, each meeting being hosted by a different member of the society. Lewis had been elected a member in 1937, and when an opening came up—new members joined only when current members died or resigned—in late 1944, Lewis put Tolkien's name forward. Tolkien was elected on February 20, 1945, and attended his first meeting in November 1945. He remained a member until February 1955, although he only hosted a meeting occasionally and presented a paper only once.

The reading meetings of the Inklings ended in 1949, and shortly after *The Lord of the Rings* was published, Tolkien and Lewis's friendship began to wane. This was partly the consequence of Lewis accepting a chair at Cambridge University, after much persuasion from Tolkien, who was upset that Oxford University had refused to offer Lewis a chair; Lewis spent part of the week in Cambridge and weekends in Oxford. Lewis's relationship with, and eventual marriage to, Joy Davidman, a divorced New Yorker, also caused Tolkien and Lewis's friendship to suffer. Tolkien, as a Catholic, did not agree with divorce, a fact the two men had discussed previously. Tolkien was also uneasy with Lewis's role as a popular theologian, feeling that theology should be the preserve of churchmen, not laymen.

Husband, Father, and Storyteller

While Tolkien and Edith originally had little in common, their shared love for their children was a strong bond between them, and it was clear to family and friends that they cared deeply about each other. They each worried about the other's health to an almost ridiculous degree, and they chose and wrapped presents for each other with a great deal of care and attention. Their care for each other was also clear in Edith's pride in Tolkien's later fame as an author and in Tolkien's decision to move to Bournemouth for Edith's sake after he retired from the University of Oxford. Tolkien was an immensely kind and understanding father who showed no embarrassment about kissing his sons in public, even when they were adults.

The children remembered spending long hours one summer digging up the old tennis court at 20 Northmoor Road to enlarge the vegetable plot. Their father supervised this project, for he, like Edith, was a keen gardener, although he preferred to concentrate most of his energies on the lawn and roses, leaving the tree pruning and vegetable cultivation to John. The family also enjoyed visits to the theatre, although Tolkien declared (somewhat mysteriously, given his boyish enthusiasm for acting) that he did not approve of drama. The children would cycle with their father to early Mass at St. Gregory's, St Aloysius's, or the nearby Carmelite Convent. They recalled that Tolkien kept a barrel of beer in the coal hole behind the kitchen; it often dripped, making the house smell like a brewery, or so Edith said. Afternoons in July and August were often spent boating on the nearby River Cherwell or floating in a punt, which the family hired for the summer, down past University Parks to Magdalen Bridge. Even better, though, were the occasions when they poled upriver towards Water Eaton and Islip, where they would enjoy a picnic tea on the riverbank. They would walk across the fields to Wood Eaton, looking for butterflies, and on the way back Michael would hide in the old cracked willow tree. It seemed to the children that their father had an endless store of information about the plants and trees they saw on their walks. After Tolkien acquired a car, they would go for a drive on autumn afternoons, out to the villages of East Oxfordshire such as Brill, Charlton-on-Otmoor, or Worminghall, or they would drive west into Berkshire and up onto White Horse Hill to see Wayland's Smithy, the ancient long-barrow near Uffington.

The children also recalled the stories their father told them, many of which later made their way into print. One such story was *Roverandom* about a small toy dog Michael lost on the beach during a family holiday in Filey. Another toy of Michael's, a Dutch doll named Tom Bombadil, which John hated and once stuffed down the toilet, became the hero of a poem called *The Adventures of Tom Bombadil,* which appeared in the *Oxford Magazine* in 1934. Another story, *Mr. Bliss,* evolved from Tolkien's purchase of, and subsequent misadventures whilst driving, a Morris Cowley car in 1932. Tolkien lavishly illustrated the story in coloured pencils and ink, and he wrote out the tale in a beautiful manuscript style.

The lavish nature of Tolkien's illustrations for *Mr. Bliss,* which is essentially a picture book, demonstrated just how seriously Tolkien took the business of painting and drawing, a skill that he had enjoyed as a child and continued to develop as an adult. His storytelling and illustrating talents were also combined in an annual letter from Father Christmas; beginning in 1920, when John was just three years old and the family was about to move to Leeds, Tolkien wrote a letter in shaky handwriting signed "Yr loving Fr Chr." Although Tolkien began simply enough, he soon expanded his annual Father Christmas letter until a host of other characters were included, such

as Polar Bear, an Elf named Ilbereth, the Snow Man, gnomes, snow elves, and even a horde of goblins who lived in caves beneath Father Christmas's house. Tolkien would write an account of recent events at the North Pole, often at the last minute before Christmas; the letters were written in Father Christmas's shaky handwriting, Ilbereth's flowing script, or the rune-like capitals of Polar Bear. Tolkien would then add drawings, address the envelope (often adding "By gnome-carrier. Immediate haste!" to the envelope), paint and cut out a realistic North Pole stamp, then deliver it. The simplest way of delivering it was by leaving it in the fireplace—he would make various odd noises in the early morning and leave a snowy footprint on the carpet to "prove" the letter had been left by Father Christmas. Later, he involved the local postman as his accomplice, and the latter would deliver the letter with the rest of family mail. Each of Tolkien's children went on believing the letters were genuine until they reached adolescence and found out, through deduction or by accident, that their father wrote the letters, but nothing was ever said so that the younger children could continue believing the letters were real.

The early Inklings meetings listened to at least part of *The Hobbit* being read aloud. Tolkien had begun this tale one day whilst marking School Certificate examination papers. An examinee had left a blank page in the paper, and on it Tolkien wrote, "In a hole in the ground there lived a hobbit." The story developed from there, and Tolkien's eldest sons, John and Michael, remembered being told the story in an oral form initially, like so many of Tolkien's other stories that eventually found their way into print. When *The Hobbit* was published on September 21, 1937 (complete with Tolkien's own illustrations), it had a print run of 1,500 copies; it sold well, and his publisher, Stanley Unwin of George Allen & Unwin, promptly requested a sequel. In the spring of the previous year, Tolkien and Lewis had agreed that there was a need for more stories like *The Hobbit,* and they arranged that Lewis would write a space story whilst Tolkien wrote a time-travel story. Tolkien began a story called "The Lost Road," in which a special father-and-son relationship is repeated throughout history, with the pair being linked to Númenor, the Atlantis-like island of Middle-earth that was destroyed and whose survivors went on to found Gondor and Arnor. Tolkien abandoned the story after just four chapters, although he had shown them to Unwin before abandoning them, offering the story as a possible sequel to *The Hobbit.* The early chapters were almost certainly read aloud to the Inklings since Lewis misspells Númenor as Numinor in his own stories *Perelandra* and *That Hideous Strength.* About the same time that he was writing "The Lost Road,"

Tolkien also wrote the "Ainulindalë," which is called "The Music of the Ainur" in *The Silmarillion* volume. In it Morgoth is one of the Valar rebels against Ilúvatar, but his rebellion is incorporated into the conception and creation of Middle-earth.

By December 1937, Tolkien had begun to write the sequel to *The Hobbit,* although *The Lord of the Rings* took another seventeen years to write and publish. *The Lord of the Rings* is, to a greater extent than *The Hobbit,* intimately related to Tolkien's work teaching Old and Middle English. As a philologist, Tolkien was engaged in constructing earlier forms of English words and in linking them to modern forms. In a similar manner, Tolkien created Quenya and Sindarin, the two Elvish languages. He felt that a language needed a people to speak it, and he began to link the languages to the poems he had already written, such as *The Voyage of Earendel the Evening Star,* and the poem about Beren and Lúthien. Out of them developed the "Silmarillion" material that told of the earlier ages of Middle-earth and led to the development of the tale published as *The Lord of the Rings.*

Whilst Tolkien was writing the early chapters of *The Lord of the Rings,* he read a new story, *Farmer Giles of Ham,* rather than his promised academic paper on fairy stories (which was not complete), to an undergraduate society at Worcester College. Whilst *Farmer Giles of Ham* is suitable for children, it feels like an adult story, which is probably why Tolkien considered it an adequate substitute for the unfinished academic paper. *Farmer Giles of Ham* was not published until 1949 because Unwin did not originally consider it to be long enough to publish on its own, and Tolkien had nothing to go with it that was also written for adults. The tale is fairly light hearted and was received well by the Lovelace Society. It is subtitled "The Rise and Wonderful Adventures of Farmer Giles, Lord of Tame, Count of Worminghall and King of the Little Kingdom" and begins with a pseudo-scholarly foreword about its alleged authorship, its translation from the Latin, and an explanation of the extent of the "Little Kingdom," in the dark period before the days of King Arthur, in the valley of the Thames.

This story, though superficially different from the tales of Middle-earth, is characteristically Tolkienian in its themes. The inspiration for the story was linguistic—it provides a spoof explanation of the name of an east Oxfordshire village, Worminghall, which Tolkien used to visit with his family when they owned a car. There are similarities between the Little Kingdom of Farmer Giles and the Shire, particularly in Giles's sheltered, homely life. He is like a complacent hobbit, though, like Bilbo and Frodo, he has unexpected qualities. The humorous tone, together with the pseudo-scholarship, is echoed in *The Adventures of Tom Bombadil,* which was not published until 1962.

As Tolkien laboured through the weary years of the Second World War, worrying about his sons Michael and Christopher, who were serving overseas, and struggling to manage on the meagre rations imposed on Britain, he occasionally found his progress on *The Lord of the Rings* halted. During one such hiatus, he wrote an incredibly personal story; unusually, he wrote it as an allegory. Published in the January 1945 issue of the *Dublin Review,* "Leaf by Niggle" is the tale of the painter, Niggle, who must make a journey, and it suggests a link between reality and artistic endeavour. It also suggests that even in Heaven there will be opportunities for the artist to add a touch to the created world. Niggle the painter represents Tolkien the perfectionist, who niggled away at his work, revising and polishing it to the extent that he was often reluctant to allow it to be published. The tale can apply to any artist who procrastinates over work. Once *Leaf by Niggle* was written, however, Tolkien returned to working on *The Lord of the Rings,* further aided by the encouragement of Lewis.

There was another hiatus in the writing of *The Lord of the Rings* in 1946; the story had stalled at the end of what would become *The Two Towers.* Tolkien used the pause to begin writing another time-travel story, "The Notion Club Papers," which had the following light-hearted title:

Beyond Lewis
or
Out of the Talkative Planet
Being a fragment of an apocryphal Inklings' saga,
made some by some imitator at some time in the 1980s

Christopher Tolkien, in *Sauron Defeated,* suggests that the story was intended as a mock commentary on Lewis's work, much as Lewis himself had produced a mock commentary on *The Lay of Leithian* many years earlier. Unsurprisingly, "The Notion Club Papers," which used material from the unfinished story, "The Lost Road," was never finished, as Tolkien went back to working on *The Lord of the Rings.* Unfortunately, Tolkien's reading of chapters of *The Lord of the Rings* to the Inklings came to an end in the spring of 1947, when Hugo Dyson began to veto further readings. Tolkien was, therefore, obliged to put it aside if Dyson was at a meeting or meet separately with Lewis (and occasionally his brother Warren, Charles Williams, or both) to continue the readings.

The Lord of the Rings was completed by the autumn of 1949, with much of the final writing and revision being completed whilst Tolkien was staying at the Oratory School in Berkshire in the summer of

1949. Tolkien had revised it to ensure it was internally consistent, and he typed it out in a fair copy; all that remained to be done at that time was to complete the appendices on languages, history, calendars, peoples, and so on. However, the publication of the tale was delayed repeatedly, partly because Tolkien wanted George Allen & Unwin to publish the "Silmarillion" at the same time as *The Lord of the Rings,* which the publisher was reluctant to do. Late in 1949, Tolkien offered both the "Silmarillion" and *The Lord of the Rings* to Milton Waldman at William Collins. Initially enthusiastic, executives at Collins changed their minds about publishing the two books when they discovered the full extent of the text. Eventually, in June 1952, Tolkien offered *The Lord of the Rings* back to George Allen & Unwin unconditionally, accepting that they did not wish to publish the "Silmarillion" at that point and that to have something published was better than to have nothing published. They decided to split the tale into three volumes, partly for economic reasons because paper was still rationed and partly because they were uncertain how well it would sell. This latter concern led them to offer Tolkien a contract that gave him a share in the profits, rather than the usual percentage royalty payment. Neither party knew at the time that such a contract would be far more financially beneficial to Tolkien. The three volumes of *The Lord of the Rings* were published in July and November 1954 and October 1955; the final volume was delayed by Tolkien's struggle to produce the promised appendices. The book was astonishingly successful, despite the critical mauling it received from reviewers, many of whom preferred to lampoon Lewis's dust jacket endorsement instead of discussing the book itself.

In 1959, at the age of sixty-seven, Tolkien retired from his university duties. Since he had never given the traditional inaugural lecture as Merton Chair of English Language and Literature, he delivered instead a valedictory address on June 5, 1959. In it he mentioned how much he disliked the separation of language and literature. Tolkien went back to working on the "Silmarillion" material, and in the 1960s he was aided by Clyde S. Kilby, an American scholar who had befriended both Tolkien and Lewis. Kilby spent the summer of 1966 helping Tolkien arrange the "Silmarillion" material, although it remained incomplete. Aware of the possibility that he would never finish it, Tolkien arranged with his third son, Christopher, that he would deal with it if Tolkien died with it still incomplete.

In 1967, Tolkien wrote his last short story published during his lifetime: *Smith of Wootton Major.* This short story traces the relationship between the primary world and the world of Faery and, as a result, com-

plements Tolkien's 1939 lecture "On Fairy-Stories." At first, *Smith of Wootton Major* appears deceptively simple, but whilst children can enjoy it, it is not intended as a children's story. Tolkien described it as the book of an old man already weighed down by omens of bereavement. The story, and Tolkien's comments, seems to indicate that he expected his imagination to dry up and his ideas to run out. *Smith of Wootton Major,* like *Farmer Giles of Ham,* has an undefined medieval setting, and the villages of Wootton Minor and Major appear to have been transplanted directly from the Shire, although they are representative of the Oxfordshire and Berkshire villages through which Tolkien and his family used to drive when the children were small.

In 1968, partly in an attempt to escape the attentions of increasing numbers of fans of *The Lord of the Rings* and partly to make life easier for Edith, who was by now suffering from severe arthritis, Tolkien and Edith moved to Bournemouth, where she had enjoyed taking holidays in the past. They only lived in Bournemouth for three years, however, as Edith's health suddenly failed; she was hospitalised in November 1971 with an inflamed gall bladder and died a few days later. Tolkien was then offered an honorary fellowship at Merton College and rooms in a house owned by the college. He gratefully moved back to Oxford, and during the final two years of his life he enjoyed travelling to see friends and family and taking holidays. He was awarded the CBE (Commandor of the British Empire) in the spring of 1972, in which year Oxford University awarded him an honorary doctorate of letters for his contribution to philology, not for *The Lord of the Rings,* as they made quite clear. In June 1973, he was awarded an honorary degree by the University of Edinburgh, and he was invited to a number of American universities to receive doctorates, but he preferred not to make such a long journey at his age. In August 1973, he travelled down to Bournemouth to stay with his friends Denis and Jocelyn Tolhurst. During the past year he had been suffering from severe indigestion and had been required to follow a restricted diet. Two days after arriving at the Tolhursts' home, he began to suffer from pain and was taken to a nearby private hospital, where an acute bleeding gastric ulcer was diagnosed. Initially, reports were optimistic, but on September 1 he developed a chest infection and died early on September 2, 1973, at the age of eighty-one. Both Tolkien and Edith are buried at Wolvercote Cemetery, north of Oxford, where Edith's tombstone bears the name "Lúthien" and Tolkien's bears the name "Beren."

Whilst it seems likely that Tolkien would have continued to create his private mythology whether he had moved to Oxford or not, it seems equally likely that his fiction would not have been published without the influence of Oxford and in particular C.S. Lewis.

MICHELE FRY

Further Reading

Carpenter, Humphrey. *J.R.R. Tolkien: A Biography*. London: Grafton, 1992.

Duriez, Colin. *J.R.R. Tolkien and C.S. Lewis: The Story of their Friendship*. Stroud: Sutton Publishing, 2003.

Duriez, Colin, and David Porter. *The Inklings Handbook*. London: Azure, 2001.

———. "The Notion Club Papers." In *Sauron Defeated*, edited by Christopher Tolkien. London: HarperCollins, 1992.

The Dante Society: Minutes 1876–1968 MS 8°It.20.

See also Adventures of Tom Bombadil (Collection); **Art and Illustrations by Tolkien; Auden, W.H.: Influence of Tolkien; Barfield, Owen; "*Beowulf:* The Monsters and the Critics"; Beren; Bilbo;** *Book of Lost Tales I; Book of Lost Tales II;* **Bournemouth; "Chaucer as Philologist: The Reeve's Tale"; Cynewulf; Dante; Dyson, Hugo; Eärendil; Farmer Giles;** *Farmer Giles of Ham;* **Father Christmas;** *Father Christmas Letters;* **Finland: Literary Sources; Finnish Language; Frodo; Gondor; Gordon, E.V.; Grove, Jennie; Gothic Language; Havard, Humphrey;** *Hobbit, The;* **Inklings; Kolbítar; Languages, Invented; Leeds;** *Letters of J.R.R. Tolkien;* **Lewis, C.S.; Lewis, Warren Hamilton;** *Lord of the Rings; Lord of the Rings:* **Success of;** *Lost Road;* **Lúthien; Marriage; Middle-earth; Middle English Vocabulary; Morgoth and Melkor;** *Mr. Bliss;* **North Polar Bear; Old English; Old Norse Language; Old Norse Literature; "On Fairy-Stories";** *Roverandom;* **Saint Brendan;** *Sauron Defeated; Seafarer;* **Shire;** *Silmarillion; Sir Gawain and the Green Knight:* **Edition with E.V. Gordon;** *Smith of Wootton Major;* **Tolkien, Christopher; Tolkien, Hilary; Tolkien, John; Tolkien, Michael; Tolkien, Priscilla; Tom Bombadil;** *Tree and Leaf;* **Valar; Vale of the White Horse;** *Wanderer;* **Welsh Language; Williams, Charles; Wolvercote Cemetery; World War I; World War II**

P

PALANTÍRI

Before the first rising of the Moon, Fëanor walked in Valinor, creating many marvelous things. Among these—perhaps a prelude to his greatest works, the Silmarils—were "other crystals . . . wherein things far away could be seen small but clear." These must certainly have been the *palantíri* (or their progenitors); indeed, Gandalf later says that "the *palantíri* came from beyond Westernesse from Eldamar. The Noldor made them. Fëanor himself, maybe, wrought them, in days so long ago that the time cannot be measured in years" (*TT*, III, xi, 203). These crystals would eventually fulfill a significant destiny, one that Fëanor could never have predicted. Some might argue their role was as important as that of the Silmarils, though more subtle and less dramatic.

A *palantír* was a seeing-stone in which far-off things and places could be glimpsed. Many of the *palantíri* could communicate with their fellows; in some instances, two *palantíri* were specially paired and could not be turned from their appointed partners except by an act of the will by an extraordinarily powerful entity. In other cases, certain *palantíri* were designated "master-stones," capable of governing or contacting lesser stones. All were smooth, perfectly round globes of some unknown crystalline substance. Further details of their design, use, and capabilities are provided in "The Palantíri" in *Unfinished Tales.*

The word *palantír* consists of two Quenya elements: *palan,* "far and wide," and *tir,* "watch, watch over." The word *palantír* is variously translated as "that which looks far away," "a far-seeing stone," and

simply, "far-seer." The word also has an unexpected connection to the Elven chant *A Elbereth Gilthoniel—* specifically, in the lines *Na-chaered palan-díriel / o galadhremmin ennorath.* As Tolkien explains in *The Road Goes Ever On,* "The Elves in Rivendell could only be said to 'gaze afar' in yearning. But actually the form used in the hymn is *palandíriel* (past part.), 'having gazed afar.' This is a reference to the *palantír* upon the Tower Hills (the 'Stone of Elendil'). . . . This alone of the *palantíri* was so made as to look out only west over the Sea" (65).

The total number of *palantíri* is not known. During the waning of Númenor, the Eldar gave certain of the *palantíri* to Amandil, Elendil's father, so that those still faithful to the West might communicate with their sundered friends, and with one another, during the oppression of Ar-Pharazôn, under the dark tutelage of Sauron. Seven of these *palantíri* were saved from the Downfall of Númenor by Elendil; of these, Elendil took three and his sons, Isildur and Anárion, each kept two.

The three stones of Elendil were kept in Arnor. The master-stone of the north was kept in the Watchtower of Amon Sûl, later known as Weathertop. Another was kept in the city of Annúminas. The third, Elendil's private stone, remained in Elostirion in the Tower Hills. It looked toward Mithlond and beyond, along the Straight Road, to "the Tower of Avallónë upon Eressëa, where the Master-stone abode, and yet abides" (*UT,* 414; *RK,* Appendix A, 322). This master-stone probably governed all *palantíri* wherever they were; therefore, it is tempting to wonder whether the

Eldar might have eavesdropped on the events of the War of the Ring through it.

Of the four *palantíri* that Elendil's sons took into the south, one was kept in Orthanc and would later come under Saruman's power. Another was kept in Minas Anor, the city of Anárion. The third Isildur took with him to Minas Ithil. And the fourth, the "chief and master of these was under the Dome of Stars at Osgiliath before its ruin" (*TT*, xi, 203). By the waning days of the Third Age, three of the seven seeing-stones had already been lost. The *palantír* of Osgiliath had fallen into Anduin when that city was destroyed during the Kin-strife in Gondor. Two others, the stones of Annúminas and Amon Sûl, were lost in the shipwreck of Arvedui, last of the northern kings.

Of the remaining four, Elendil's *palantír* was useless for communicating with any other or for looking in any direction other than west. Another fell into Sauron's hands and was removed to Barad-dûr after the Nazgûl took Minas Ithil. Through this stone, Sauron eventually made contact with the other two remaining *palantíri,* at Orthanc and Minas Anor (Tirith). Saruman he bent entirely to his will; Denethor, rightful steward of the Anor-stone and possessed of a powerful will, Sauron could only mislead. However, in both cases the temptation to use the *palantíri* brought about the undoing of their keepers.

After the overthrow of Saruman, Pippin succumbs to the same dangerous temptation, inadvertently contacting the Ithil-stone in Barad-dûr. Subsequently, Gandalf delivers the *palantír* into the keeping of its rightful owner, Aragorn, who reveals himself to Sauron and wrenches the stone to his own will. This greatly increases Sauron's uncertainty and anxiety, and he responds by striking Minas Tirith prematurely—failing to notice two small Hobbits struggling into his own lands. Thus, in essence, the *palantír* plays a small but critical role in eliciting Sauron's eventual downfall.

By the end of the Third Age, Denethor's despair and suicide have all but permanently ruined the Anor-stone. It is to be presumed that the Ithil-stone perished in the fall of Barad-dûr, though it may have endured. Aragorn keeps the Orthanc-stone into the Fourth Age, using it to survey the Reunited Kingdom. But the *palantír* of Elendil returns to the West with the Ring-bearers when they depart from Middle-earth forever (*RK*, Appendix A, 322).

JASON FISHER

Further Reading

Tolkien, J.R.R. *The Road Goes Ever On: A Song Cycle.* Poems by J.R.R. Tolkien. Music by Donald Swann. Boston, MA: Houghton Mifflin, 1967.

See also **Denethor; Fëanor; Gríma (Wormtongue); Jewels; Saruman**

PARADISE

Visions of paradise lurk on the periphery of nearly all of Tolkien's tales and play a particularly important role in the Middle-earth legendarium. Tolkien gives glimpses both of Edenic paradises (pointing backward to the Garden of Eden before its fall) and of heavenly paradises (pointing forward to a life after death and to the biblical notion of a heavenly Jerusalem.)

In the Middle-earth legendarium, Valinor, land of the Valar, initially serves as an Edenic paradise. It is called the Guarded Realm and is part of the Blessed Land of Aman. When the Elves first come to Valinor, it is a land of bliss, free from evil, where the Elves sit at the feet of the gods: the Valar. On numerous occasions, Tolkien refers to "*Valinor* the land of the *Valar*" as an "earthly Elvish paradise" (*Letters,* 198; see also, for example, *Letters,* 156). In most interpretations, the biblical Eden was famous for two trees: the Tree of Life and the Tree of the Knowledge of Good and Evil. So too was Valinor famous for its Two Trees. Eden is most often described as a garden, and Valinor's most holy places are its garden of Lórien and the mound of Ezellohar where grew the Two Trees.

Valinor also bears resemblance to the future heavenly paradise: the new Jerusalem. Unlike the Garden of Eden, Valinor has a city: Valimar of many bells (also called Valmar). Galadriel even speaks of Valimar as equivalent with Valinor, thus associating paradise with a city (*FR*, II, viii, 394). Also like the heavenly Jerusalem, which is associated with Mount Zion, Valinor is associated with Taniquetil, "tallest of all the mountains upon Earth" (*S,* 26). The connection with the heavenly (as opposed to Edenic) paradise becomes more pronounced after the Fall of the Elves: Valinor becomes a place to which Elves can *return* after a life on Middle-earth—either through the long voyage from the Grey Havens or through death when their spirits return to Lórien and are given new bodies. At the end of the Second Age, Valinor is even physically separated from Middle-earth. (It must be noted that for mortal Men Valinor is never a paradise—heavenly or Edenic. It is more of a purgatory; Men, and Hobbits, could only dwell there at most a limited time, for healing, before going to a different, unknown paradise outside of Arda.)

Visions of paradise also appear in some of Tolkien's shorter stories. In *Smith of Wootton Major,* both the Vale of Evermorn and the dwelling place of the Queen of Faërie and her hosts offer a brief glimpse of an Edenic garden. In "Leaf by Niggle" there is an even clearer connection between mountains at the edge of Niggle's picture and heavenly paradise. This being the case, the concluding comments about Niggle's painting being the best introduction to the mountains may be from Tolkien a suggestion that fantasy literature may point its readers toward paradise.

MATTHEW DICKERSON

Further Reading

Birzer, Bradley J. *J.R.R. Tolkien's Sanctifying Myth: Understanding Middle-earth*. Wilmington, DE: ISI Books, 2002.

Dickerson, Matthew T. *Following Gandalf: Epic Battles and Moral Victory in "The Lord of the Rings."* Grand Rapids, MI: Brazos, 2003.

Flieger, Verlyn. *Splintered Light: Logos and Language in Tolkien's World*. Grand Rapids, MI: Eerdmans, 1983.

Purtill, Richard. *J.R.R. Tolkien: Myth, Morality, and Religion*. San Francisco, CA: Harper & Row, 1981.

Wood, Ralph C. *The Gospel According to Tolkien: Visions of the Kingdom in Middle-earth*. Louisville, KY: Westminster John Knox, 2003.

See also **Finwë and Míriel; Heaven; Maiar; Silmarils; Theological and Moral Approaches in Tolkien's Works; Tol Eressëa; Valar**

PARODIES

Any renowned or best-selling author will inevitably attract a corps of parodists, and Tolkien has had a share, particularly since the release of the Peter Jackson films of *The Lord of the Rings*. But while Tolkien's literary style lends itself easily to serious pastiche, it appears to be resistant to comic parody. Brief attempts at direct parodic exaggeration of Tolkien's style, occasionally appearing in such venues as newspaper reader contests, are generally considered to miss the mark conspicuously. The most widely noted and generally appreciated humorous adaptations of Tolkien are not so much parodies as comic pastiches or lampoons: they do not attempt to exaggerate Tolkien's style so much as to use his distinctive content and setting as a line on which to hang a satiric version of general fantasy plots or a parody of another author's style.

The first commercially released Tolkien parody was *Bored of the Rings* by Henry N. Beard and Douglas C. Kenney, then affiliated with *Harvard Lampoon* magazine (1969). This begins as a close and detailed lampoon of the prologue and general map to *The Lord of the Rings* but quickly evolves into a highly abbreviated satiric plot summary. The humor emphasizes slapstick and the incongruous use of American commercial brand names.

Critic and novelist Adam Roberts has written two full-length parodies under the byline "A.R.R.R. Roberts." His *The Soddit* (2003) and *The Sellamillion* (2004) take off on *The Hobbit* and *The Silmarillion*, respectively, but follow their own internal plot logic to frequently serious ends. Specific parodies of Tolkien's style and plot are intermittent. Character names and modern-world references resemble the style of those in *Bored of the Rings*, but much of the humor lies in comically outsized digressions. The main text of *The Sellamillion* is framed by sections of invented documents and editorial commentary lampooning Tolkien's relationships with C.S. Lewis and George Allen & Unwin and introducing parodic cross-fertilizations of Tolkien with other authors.

Other works in book form include *The Roadkill of Middle-earth* by John Carnell (2001), a brief illustrated *Lord of the Rings* parody, and *The Sillymarillion* by D.R. Lloyd (2004), parodying *The Silmarillion* with particular attention to exaggeration of the original's formal prose. Some homages to Tolkien, ranging from *There and Back Again* by Pat Murphy (1999) to the Iron Tower Trilogy by Dennis McKiernan (1984), track their inspirations (*The Hobbit* and *The Lord of the Rings,* respectively) so closely in plot that they may be read as parodies that omit comic intent.

Gentle affectionate parodies of Tolkien's works have always been a staple of Tolkien fandom. Some of these were published in fanzines, and others exist in the oral tradition only. One early prose example, "The Picnic" by Paulette Carroll (1967), was reprinted in *The Tolkien Scrapbook* edited by Alida Becker (1978). Fandom-originated works also include parody songs, known as *filksongs* in science fiction fandom, of which one well-known Tolkien example from the 1960s–1970s was "The Orcs' Marching Song" to the tune of "The Ballad of Jesse James." Many contributors added to its ever-increasing number of verses. A brief selection of these also appeared in *The Tolkien Scrapbook*. The humor in fandom-originated Tolkien parodies often concentrates on creative anachronisms and on picking minute holes in the subcreation.

The World Wide Web has afforded the opportunity for the wide distribution of Tolkien parodies, often by many authors collected onto one Web page. The composition of short excerpts from Tolkien's works as they might have been rendered by other authors with highly distinctive literary styles, such as P.G. Wodehouse or Ernest Hemingway, has been a particularly fertile field. A large collection of these is hosted by *The Straight Dope Message Board* Web site. Also well known on the Web are *The Tolkien Sarcasm*

Page, notable for a deliberately inaccurate Cliffs Notes-style plot summary of *The Lord of the Rings* that has actually misled some newspaper reporters looking for a quick reference source, and *The Very Secret Diaries* series by Cassandra Claire, narcissistic first-person entries by characters from the Jackson films. Repeated lines in the Legolas and Aragorn diaries, "Still the prettiest" and "Still not King," respectively, became catchphrases among readers.

Tolkien scholars and fans are divided in their opinion of parodies: some cherish them as affectionately humorous takes on loved books, and others consider them unfunny and even contemptible. Both opinions are found among serious scholars, as well as casual readers.

DAVID BRATMAN

See also **Jackson, Peter; Literature, Twentieth Century: Influence of Tolkien**

PEARL: EDITION BY E.V. GORDON

E.V. Gordon's 1953 edition of the Middle English poem *Pearl,* published years after his death, was begun in collaboration with Tolkien and retains evidence of Tolkien's lifelong interest in the West Midlands author of *Pearl* and *Sir Gawain and the Green Knight.*

Gordon and Tolkien, colleagues at University of Leeds starting in 1922, began work on *Pearl* following the 1925 publication of their acclaimed edition of *Gawain* (Anderson, 18). When Tolkien departed for Oxford later that year, the work fell largely to Gordon, who nearly completed it on his own before his death in 1938 (Shippey "Gawain-poet," 213). Tolkien then took it up, but he returned it unfinished to Gordon's widow, Ida, in about 1949 (Anderson, 20). Ida Gordon, also a philologist, heavily revised the work for publication (Gordon, iii–iv). Gordon's *Pearl* edition, the first in thirty-two years, was, like Tolkien and Gordon's *Gawain,* long recognized as a standard text (Vantuono, xi).

Ida Gordon acknowledges Tolkien's assistance with "valuable notes and corrections" in her preface (Gordon, iii). Christopher Tolkien identifies the "Form and Purpose" section of Gordon's introduction as his father's primary contribution; this essay was reprinted with Tolkien's translations of *Sir Gawain and the Green Knight, Pearl, and Sir Orfeo.* (8). In the essay, Tolkien responds to then-popular allegorical interpretations of *Pearl* (Savage, 126), arguing that the dream vision it relates arises directly from the grief of "real" sorrow (Gordon, xi–xix), and the edition was praised for refusing to "twist and torture"

the poem into other meanings (Savage, 126). It was also said to reveal "genuine appreciation for the poet's artistry" (Robertson, 107), a hallmark of Tolkien's *Beowulf* essay.

Tolkien's other contributions to the edition can only be inferred. William Cooke finds the glossary's etymology "virtually identical" to that in Simonne d'Ardenne's 1936 edition of *The Life and the Passion of St. Juliene* (Cooke, 21), a text coedited, uncredited, by Tolkien (Carpenter, 140; Anderson, 22). Comparisons of Gordon's edition with Tolkien's comments about *Pearl* elsewhere show where the scholars differ, such as on whether the poem's meter is alliterative or French (Gordon, 90–91; J.R.R. Tolkien, *Sir Gawain,* 208) and whether an extra stanza was intended or accidental (*Letters,* 317–18; Gordon, 88). Finally, Tom Shippey calls some of the edition's notes "resonantly Tolkienian" ("Gawain-poet," 213; *Author,* 204–5), particularly one ascribing to the word *stroþemen* (literally "woodsmen") the meaning of "men of this world" and the suggestion of "the dark, low earth onto which the high stars look down" (Vantuono, 109; Gordon, 52). While the philological point could be attributed either to the Gordons or to Tolkien, the image speaks to "life in Middle-earth" (Shippey, "Gawain-poet," 218).

Many of Tolkien's scholarly projects did not reach print, and Ida Gordon, for one, lamented that Tolkien did not contribute more works to medieval studies (Barman, 233). Nonetheless, Tolkien's contributions to Gordon's *Pearl* and other academic works that did not appear under his name should not be overlooked as sources of insight into his scholarly studies, as influences on his work, and as having a lasting professional impact on his field.

PATRICIA TUBBS

Primary Sources

Gordon, E.V., ed. *Pearl.* Oxford: Oxford University Press, 1953.

Tolkien, J.R.R. "Appendix on Verse-forms." In *Sir Gawain and the Green Knight, Pearl, and Sir Orfeo,* translated by J.R.R. Tolkien, 142–48. Boston, MA: Houghton Mifflin, 1975.

Further Reading

Anderson, Douglas A. "'An Industrious Little Devil': E.V. Gordon as a Friend and Collaborator with Tolkien." In *Tolkien the Medievalist,* edited by Jane Chance, 15–25. London: Routledge, 2003.

Barman, Jean. *Sojourning Sisters: The Lives and Letters of Jessie and Annie McQueen.* Toronto: University of Toronto Press, 2003.

Carpenter, Humphrey. *Tolkien: A Biography*. Boston, MA: Houghton Mifflin, 1977.

Cooke, William. "Me Haterly/Heterly: Origin and Meaning." *English Studies* 1 (2004): 17–21.

Robertson, D.W., Jr. "Review of Gordon's edition of *Pearl*." *Speculum* 30, no. 1 (January 1955): 107–8.

Savage, H.L. "Review of Gordon's edition of *Pearl*." *Modern Language Notes* 71, no. 2 (February 1956): 124–29.

Shippey, Tom. *J.R.R. Tolkien: Author of the Century*. Boston, MA: Houghton Mifflin, 2001.

——. "Tolkien and the *Gawain*-poet." In *Proceedings of the J.R.R. Tolkien Centenary Conference 1992*, edited by Patricia Reynolds and Glen GoodKnight, 213–19. Milton Keynes: Tolkien Society, 1996.

Tolkien. Christopher. "Preface." In *Sir Gawain and the Green Knight, Pearl, and Sir Orfeo*. Translated by J.R.R. Tolkien, 7–9. Boston, MA: Houghton Mifflin, 1975.

Vantuono, William, ed. and trans. *Pearl: An Edition with Verse Translation*. Notre Dame, IN: University of Notre Dame, 1995.

See also **Allegory; Alliterative Revival; "*Beowulf:* The Monsters and the Critics"; Bible; "Chaucer as Philologist: The Reeve's Tale"; Colors; Cruces in Medieval Literature; Dante; Death; Denethor; Despair (Wanhope); Gordon, E.V.; Heaven; Jewels; *Juliana;* Langland, William; Leeds; Manuscripts, Medieval; Middle English Vocabulary; Oxford; Paradise; Publications, Posthumous; Resurrection; Scholars of Medieval Literature, Influence of; *Sir Gawain and the Green Knight, Pearl, and Sir Orfeo:* Edited by Christopher Tolkien; *Sir Gawain and the Green Knight:* Edition with E.V. Gordon; *Wanderer***

PENANCE

Technically, penance is a sacrament of the Roman Catholic Church in which, after confessing sins, feeling remorse and possibly undergoing punishment for those sins, an individual is granted forgiveness. Penance is a multipart process, beginning with *contrition* (sorrow for having sinned), followed by *confession* (explicit verbal acknowledgment of sin), continuing with *satisfaction* (making amends for sin or voluntarily suffering punishment), and concluding with *absolution* (when the confessor pronounces the penitent now to be forgiven for sin and reconciled with the church). Penitential practice was monastic in origin but eventually spread throughout the church. The Fourth Lateran Council of 1215 made yearly confession a requirement for all Christians, but penance had become a common practice for laymen, as well as for monks, even before the Anglo-Saxon period.

In a broader sense, any situation in which a person suffers for some failing can be read as a form of penance, metaphorically connected to the sacrament of the church but symbolically applicable to individuals of all religions (and no religion) in a variety of circumstances. Penance is one of the controlling metaphors of western civilization, and it is linked with ideas of purity, cleansing, and healing throughout western culture.

As there are (deliberately) no explicit references to religion in Tolkien's works, we should not be surprised to find no specific references to penance. But there are penitential motifs found throughout *The Lord of the Rings* and *The Silmarillion,* and elements of "Leaf by Niggle" may be seen as penitential. To recognize these motifs, however, it is important to note that the main focus of penance, for a Roman Catholic, is *not* on physical suffering and punishment but on the feelings of separation and alienation generated by sin and then in the joy caused by the reconciliation of the individual after the successful performance of penance. Thus penance is not mere suffering but is suffering structured as part of the process of contrition, confession, satisfaction, and absolution. So although it is possible to see Frodo's physical suffering throughout his journey as penitential (but what was his sin?), it is more useful to see the development of the penitential motif in the death of Boromir, in the eventual reconciliation of the Elves with the Valar after the voyage of Eärendil, and in Niggle's sojourn at the Workhouse before eventually being allowed to go to Niggle's Parish.

Boromir's sin is obvious: he succumbs to temptation and attempts to take the Ring from Frodo. His remorse for this sin, the first stage in penance, arises not out of specific "fear of God" (which is not relevant to characters in *The Lord of the Rings* but rather out of Boromir's recognition that he has failed to live up to standards of conduct (his own and those of others). Boromir suffers physically from the arrows of the Orcs before he confesses to Aragorn, "I tried to take the Ring from Frodo. I am sorry. I have paid." Boromir's later apparition to Faramir, where he seems to be at peace, suggests that his penance and confession were successful and that Boromir in death is absolved of his sin.

The reconciliation of the exiled Noldor with the Valar in *The Silmarillion* is a less straightforward case. Although Eärendil asks the Valar for "pardon," there is no clear confession of fault from the Noldor, although they have obviously suffered greatly in their wars against Morgoth. But in the end the Elves of Beleriand are summoned to depart from Middle-earth and are reconciled with the Valar: even though they dwell in Tol Eressëa they are permitted to come to Valinor and "were admitted again to the love of Manwë and the pardon of the Valar; and the Teleri forgave their ancient grief, and the curse was laid to rest" (*S*, 254).

In "Leaf by Niggle" (written c. 1942, published in 1947), his short, personal allegory of subcreation, Tolkien has the painter Niggle end up spending a great deal of time in the "Workhouse," where he has to work hard at tedious tasks. During this time, Niggle comes to wish he had helped his neighbor Parish earlier than he had, but there is never any explicit confession of fault. Eventually, after much service in the Workhouse, Niggle receives the gift of seeing his Tree made real, and he is even happier when Parish joins him in the country that has grown up around the Tree. It is important to note, however, that Niggle may be, as Tom Shippey has argued, more eschatological than penitential: that is, the Workhouse is likely meant to indicate Purgatory, just at Niggle's Journey is meant to indicate the afterlife. If this is the case, the penitential motif is complicated by its relationship with the doctrine of Purgatory.

Penitential practice structures the creation of narratives through the requirement that one tell a true story about oneself, a true story focused on sin and its amendment. Contrition, suffering, and the joy of reconciliation provide emotional power to a narrative thus structured, and the underlying penitential motifs in Tolkien's works may contribute to the strong effects they have upon the emotions of many readers. Recognizing the ways in which suffering brings about reconciliation and is not just suffering for its own sake (or even for the sake of a narrative) is the most coherent benefit of viewing Tolkien's works through the interpretive filter of penance.

MICHAEL D.C. DROUT

Further Reading

Bernasconi, Robert. "The Infinite Task of Confession: A Contribution to the History of Ethics." *Acta Institutionis Philosophiae et Aestheticae 6* (1988): 75–92.

Birzer, Bradley J. *J.R.R. Tolkien's Sanctifying Myth: Understanding Middle-earth*. Wilmington, DE: ISI Books, 2002.

Flieger, Verlyn. *Splintered Light: Logos and Language in Tolkien's World*. 2nd ed. Kent, OH: Kent State University Press, 2002.

Frantzen, Allen J. *The Literature of Penance in Anglo-Saxon England*. New Brunswick, NJ: Rutgers University Press, 1983.

McNeill, John T., and Helena M. Gamer. *Medieval Handbooks of Penance*. New York: Columbia University Press, 1938. Reprinted in 1965.

Shippey, Tom. *The Road to Middle-earth: How J.R.R. Tolkien Created a New Mythology*. Revised and expanded edition. Boston, MA: Houghton Mifflin, 2003.

See also **Boromir; Catholicism, Roman; Eärendil; Sin; Theology in *The Lord of the Rings*; Valar**

PEOPLES OF MIDDLE-EARTH

The Peoples of Middle-earth is the twelfth and final volume of *The History of Middle-earth (HoMe)*. It consists of writings, other than those concerned specifically with the Elder Days, composed after the completion of *The Lord of the Rings,* plus Christopher Tolkien's editorial commentary. The title, applied by the editor, refers to the book's concentration on historical and ethnographic study of Middle-earth during the Second and Third Ages. *Peoples* contains much less fictional narrative than other volumes of *HoMe.* Most of its contents are expository works too broad in scope to be limited to any one period of the mythology's internal history. The long narratives composed during Tolkien's later years had already been published in *Unfinished Tales,* which should be read in conjunction with Parts II and IV of *Peoples.*

Peoples consists of four parts. Part I, which occupies two-thirds of the text, is a survey of the drafting of the prologue and appendices to *The Lord of the Rings,* postponed from the volumes in the *History of The Lord of the Rings* subseries (volumes of HoMe). Early drafts of the Prologue were composed in 1938–39, but most of this work was written between the completion of the novel's main text in 1948 and the publication of the third volume in 1955. Appendix A had a particularly complex history, being cut down for space and then built up again. In the process it spun off some supplementary texts whose origin is discussed here: "Akallabêth" (published in *The Silmarillion*), "The Quest of Erebor" (published in *Unfinished Tales*), and a chronology of kings titled "The Heirs of Elendil," printed in chapter 7 of the present book. Drafts and material cut from final versions of the other appendices—the Tale of Years, family trees, calendars, and linguistic materials—are also reproduced here.

Part II, "Late Writings," includes linguistic and historical essays and notes datable from 1967 or later that were not published in *Unfinished Tales.* "Of Dwarves and Men," the longest essay, discusses the ethnography and languages of these two peoples, expounding on the kindreds of the Dwarves, the concept of Westron (the Common Speech), and the use of an English mode for some of the runic and Tengwar texts in *The Lord of the Rings.* "The Shibboleth of Fëanor" discusses Elvish pronunciation and naming customs. "The Problem of Ros" is an abandoned attempt at establishing an etymology for names that predated the systematic development of the Elvish languages. "Last Writings" are a few small notes dated about 1972 concerning the circumstances of the return of the resurrected Glorfindel to Middle-earth, what the two other Wizards may actually have accomplished for good in the distant East, and the significance of Círdan the Shipwright.

Part III, "Teachings of Pengolod," consists of two brief texts attributed to the Elvish scholar Pengolod the Wise of Gondolin, written by Tolkien in the 1950s. "Dangweth Pengoloð" addresses the question of how immortal Elves can have a language that changes and develops; "Of *Lembas*" discusses the growing of the grain from which Elven waybread is made.

Part IV, "Unfinished Tales," contains two fragmentary story-openings that Tolkien drafted in the 1950s and possibly reviewed or revised in the 1960s. "The New Shadow" is a sequel to *The Lord of the Rings* set a century later, in which two Men discuss rumors of the rise of a cult of evil in Gondor. "Tal-Elmar" is the story of a young Wild Man of Middle-earth in the Second Age, capable of being moved by Elven-derived civilization though he does not know what he is longing for, viewing the first arrival of Númenórean ships to his land.

DAVID BRATMAN

See also **History of Middle-earth: Overview; Publications, Posthumous**

PHIAL

Galadriel presents a gift to each member of the Fellowship at their departure from Lothlórien. To Frodo she gives "a small crystal phial" in which the light of Eärendil's star—the last surviving Silmaril—glimmers amid waters from her fountain. She prays that it might "be a light to you in dark places, when all other lights go out," as indeed it proves. Near Minas Morgul, Frodo clutches the phial and, with its strength, turns aside the groping thought of the Nazgûl lord. The phial, too, is central to the Hobbits' defeat of Shelob in the passes above Mordor. Soon after, aided by the phial, Sam overcomes the Watchers of the Tower of Cirith Ungol. Finally, however, on the threshold of the Crack of Doom, "the phial of Galadriel . . . was pale and cold in his trembling hand and threw no light into that stifling dark. He was come to the heart of the realm of Sauron and . . . all other powers were here subdued" (*RK*, VI, iii, 222).

A full treatment of this multifaceted symbol would require a much lengthier article, but a few points are worth making. Tolkien acknowledged that Galadriel epitomizes (at least, partly) the Catholic Virgin Mary; by extension, then, the phial may correlate with the religious ritual of baptism (as *lembas* may typify the Eucharist). Such interpretations liken the phial to early Christian *charismata* (spiritual gifts), pointing to Christ's words in Revelations: "He who conquers and who keeps my works until the end . . . I will give him the morning star." Within Tolkien's legendarium, Eärendil's Silmaril *is* the Morning Star. Other critical approaches to the phial see it as a foil for Shelob or the Ring, and for still others it embodies or reflects aspects of Frodo or of Galadriel. Verlyn Flieger sees the phial and the Ring as the two physical artifacts that "define and bracket Frodo. He must succumb to the one before he can have the hope of becoming like the other" (2002). At its most fundamental, the phial's pure, holy light contrasts the evil darkness of Sauron, against which it is pitted in a final, inexorable struggle.

More narrowly, within the context of Tolkien's mythology, the light of Eärendil's star, the Silmaril, connects the War of the Ring to the earliest legends of the Elder Days—indeed, Galadriel is a living bridge. Its light—starlight—associates the phial with Varda, who made the stars in the remote past. Varda, too, hallowed the Silmarils, of which Eärendil's star is the last. It is thus fitting that Frodo and Sam, moved by the phial to utter words they don't understand, should call upon Elbereth—as the Elves' name Varda—to aid them in the darkness.

Tolkien's choice of "phial" is itself interesting. The word entered Middle English around 1300 from the Old French *fiole*, attested some one hundred years earlier. But although "phial" existed in English from this early time (recorded in Walter Skeat's dictionary of Middle English, though not in Tolkien's 1922 glossary), the word appears to have been relatively uncommon until it experienced something of a heyday during the Victorian period. It seems reasonably likely that Tolkien encountered the word in Joseph Jacobs's collection, *English Fairy Tales*, published in 1892—coincidentally, the year of Tolkien's birth—in the tale, "Childe Rowland":

> "I agree," said the Elfin King, and rising up he went to a chest from which he took a phial filled with a blood-red liquor. With this he anointed the ears, eyelids, nostrils, lips, and finger-tips, of the two brothers, and they sprang at once into life, and declared that their souls had been away, but had now returned.

Childe Rowland was the nephew of Charlemagne, memorialized in the Old French epic, *The Song of Roland*. And though the word *fiole* doesn't occur in *Roland*, it is first recorded not more than a century later. Tolkien would also have come across a variant of the word, and a similar use of it, in Thomas Malory's *Le Morte d'Arthur*: "And pryamus toke fro his page a vyolle ful of the four waters that came oute of paradys / and with certayne baume enoynted theyr woundes / and wesshe them with that water / &

within an houre after / they were both as hole as euer they were."

I will close with a last reference, one a little closer to Tolkien. It is rather an interesting curiosity to find the word in a 1947 poem by Tolkien's friend and fellow Inkling, C.S. Lewis. In *The End of the Wine,* "A phial hangs from his neck, / Holding the last of a golden cordial, subtle and sweet." This sounds rather like *miruvor,* the cordial of Imladris. As a footnote, in "The Disaster of the Gladden Fields," Tolkien would write, years later, a remarkably similar description: "Each of the Dúnedain carried in a sealed wallet on his belt a small phial of cordial and wafers of a way-bread that would sustain life in him for many days." But while it may be amusing to speculate, it really is not possible to know whether Lewis's use of "phial" influenced Tolkien, Tolkien's use influenced Lewis, or their mutual use is mere coincidence.

JASON FISHER

Further Reading

Caldecott, Stratford. "The Lord and Lady of the Rings: The Hidden Presence of Tolkien's Catholicism in *The Lord of the Rings.*" *Touchstone Magazine* 15, no. 1 (January–February 2002).

Flieger, Verlyn. *Splintered Light: Logos and Language in Tolkien's World.* 2nd ed. Kent,OH: Kent State University Press, 2002.

Goselin, Peter Damien. "Two Faces of Eve: Galadriel and Shelob as Anima Figures." *Mythlore* 6, no. 3, whole no. 21 (1979): 3–4.

O'Neill, Timothy R. *The Individuated Hobbit: Jung, Tolkien, and the Archetypes of Middle-earth.* Boston, MA: Houghton Mifflin, 1979.

Rutledge, Fleming. *The Battle for Middle-earth: Tolkien's Divine Design in "The Lord of the Rings."* Grand Rapids, MI: Eerdmans, 2004.

See also **Carolingians; Catholicism, Roman; Eärendil; Feminist Readings of Tolkien; Frodo; Galadriel; Jungian Theory;** *Lembas;* **Light; Literary Influences, Nineteenth and Twentieth Century; Old French Literature; One Ring, The; Sam; Shakespeare; Shelob; Silmarils; Symbolism in Tolkien's Works; Theological and Moral Approaches in Tolkien's Works**

PHILATELY

Tolkien, who enjoyed a characteristically British appreciation of matters postal, saw a functioning mail system as a key component of civic life in the Shire. In "On the Ordering of the Shire" in the prologue to *The Fellowship of the Ring,* he describes how postmaster duties fell to the mayor, who managed both the watch and the messenger service. "These were the only Shire-services," Tolkien explains, "and the Messengers were the most numerous, and much the busier of the two. By no means all hobbits were lettered, but those who were wrote constantly to all their friends (and a selection of their relations) who lived further off than an afternoon's walk." In chapter 1, "A Long-Expected Party," Tolkien documents the strain of Bilbo's famous birthday party on the postal system of the Shire: "Before long the invitations began pouring out, and the Hobbiton post-office was blocked, and the Bywater post-office was snowed under, and voluntary assistant postmen were called for."

In 1992, Royal Mail commemorated the centenary of Tolkien's birth with an eight-page prestige booklet featuring artwork and selected quotes. The booklet, which sold for six pounds, included twenty-six definitive stamps depicting Queen Elizabeth II but no stamps commemorating or depicting Tolkien. In 1998, Royal Mail honored *The Hobbit* on one of five "Magical World of Children's Literature" stamps with an illustration of Bilbo Baggins and the dragon Smaug.

As a result of *The Lord of the Rings* movies directed by New Zealander Peter Jackson and filmed primarily in his native country, New Zealand Post issued three different sets of six stamps in a variety of formats to coincide with the release of each film. To mark the 2003 release of *The Return of the King,* the Isle of Man also issued eight stamps and souvenir sheets. The New Zealand and Manx stamps all featured still photographs of Tolkien's characters as depicted in the films.

In 2004, Royal Mail issued ten first-class commemoratives to mark the fiftieth anniversary of the publication of *The Lord of the Rings.* Nine of the stamps featured Tolkien's own artwork from the archive at the Bodleian Library in Oxford: the valley of Rivendell; Fangorn Forest, Lothlórien in spring; the tower of Orthanc; the city of Minas Tirith; the walls of Barad-dûr; the Doors of Durin; the interior of Bag-End; and Tolkien's original cover concept for *The Fellowship of the Ring.* A tenth stamp featured a map of Middle-earth drawn in the style of Tolkien by his son Christopher.

Tolkien created his own North Pole stamps for use on holiday mail sent to his children from "Father Christmas," as collected in the volume *Letters from Father Christmas.* Likewise, his readers have indulged their imaginations by creating unofficial stamps, typically called "cinderellas" by philatelists. After the success of *The Lord of the Rings* movies, a series of film-related photographic stamps were issued in the name of Karelia, a region divided between Finland and Russia that has no independent postal authority.

By far, the most elaborate Tolkien-related philatelic project began during the late 1980s, when American fan Tom Maringer created a series of postage stamps for the Shire and later imagined an elaborate mail system and postal history. In 1999, Maringer began to display his stamps, postal markings, and coin designs at ShirePost.com, a Web site that as of 2005 also served as a forum for more than four hundred like-minded fans. Maringer also created the invitation envelopes for the Tolkien Centenary Conference held at Oxford in 1992.

JEFF SYPECK

Further Reading

Royal Mail Special Stamps 21: The Stories Behind the 2004 Stamps. London: Royal Mail, 2004.
Tolkien: The Centenary 1892–1992. Royal Mail prestige booklet, 1992.
Tolkien, J.R.R. *Letters from Father Christmas.* Revised edition. New York: Houghton Mifflin, 1999.

See also **Art and Illustrations by Tolkien; Bodleian Library, Oxford; Doors and Gates;** *Father Christmas Letters;* **Finland: Literary Sources; Finland: Reception of Tolkien;** *Hobbit, The;* **Hobbiton; Jackson, Peter;** *Lord of the Rings;* **Lothlórien; Maps; Merchandising; Rivendell; Shire; Tolkien, Christopher; Towers**

PHILO-SEMITISM

Tolkien came to maturity at a time when a casual if not aggressive anti-Semitism was largely acceptable within British society. While organized fascism and political racism never attracted more than a fringe, implicit suspicion of Jews as relative outsiders was far from uncommon.

Within educated and literary circles there was a poignant ambivalence. Traces of anti-Semitism can be found in the writings and comments of, for example, G.K. Chesterton, Hilaire Belloc, and T.S. Eliot. Not so, however, with Tolkien.

On one particular occasion, he was asked in a radio interview if any of his characters possessed any racial traits. Tolkien replied that the Dwarves perhaps demonstrated certain Jewish qualities. In that his Dwarves were brave, loyal, tenacious, and tough, this cannot be interpreted as being anything other than a statement supportive of the Jewish people.

It has been assumed by some critics that Tolkien's conservative Catholicism would have led to a certain degree of anti-Semitism. This reveals a misunderstanding of conservative Catholicism and of anti-Semitism.

It is true that Tolkien exhibited implicit support for General Franco and the Nationalists during the Spanish Civil War, but it must be remembered that fascist elements formed a relatively small part of Franco's coalition and that anti-Semitism was largely irrelevant within the Spanish equation.

The war was seen by many Catholics, and by many outside of the church, as a battle against Communism and those who would destroy Roman Catholicism. Whether this was an accurate perception or not, it hardly infers the evil of anti-Semitism onto a nominal supporter of Franco.

Tolkien was an anti-Nazi before it was altogether respectable to be so, and indeed when many on the political left were still ambivalent about Adolf Hitler and National Socialism. Respected British writers of the political left such as H.G. Wells and George Bernard Shaw took far longer to publicly condemn Nazism than did Tolkien.

Shortly before the Second World War, a German publisher wrote to Tolkien and inquired about buying the rights to some of his works. In so doing, the publisher asked if he was an Aryan. He replied that the word made no linguistic or ethnic sense. But, he added, if they were asking him if he had any Jewish blood he regretted that this was not the case, because he would like to have some connection with such a gifted people.

He concluded by explaining to the writer of the letter that the company would never be allowed to publish him and that the Nazis were destroying German culture and the beauty of the northern spirit. Tolkien explained that he spoke for the genuine Nordic spirit, not in the name of some bizarre and racist nonsense.

Some have argued that Tolkien's partial separation from his close friend C.S. Lewis was because of Lewis's wife Joy Davidman, a Jewish convert to Christianity. While it may be true that Joy was a factor, it had nothing to do with her Jewishness. Despite her many qualities, she could be brash and slightly jarring to the British reserve of the time. Edith Tolkien certainly found her a difficult woman.

MICHAEL COREN

See also **Dwarves; German Race Laws; Judaism; Nazi Party**

PILGRIMAGE

Gandalf is the "Grey Pilgrim" (in the Elizabethan or Jacobean sense, "traveller"), and it could be said that the Nine Walkers take part in his pilgrimage. But there is a difference between pilgrimage and quest, and if *The Lord of the Rings* is closer to either, it would seem closer to quest. The sequel to the *Principal Navigations, Voyages, Traffiques and Discoveries* of Hakluyt is *Hakluytus Posthumus, or Purchas His Pilgrims,* which preserves the Jacobean sense of traveller and sometimes more exactly of traveller into the wilderness. That, certainly, can be applied to Frodo and Sam.

Pilgrimage in English literature had three principal incarnations before the English Renaissance, by which it entered into the seventeenth-century exemplar and the English common mind. The three incarnations are (1) the framework (though not the tales) of Geoffrey Chaucer's *Canterbury Tales,* (2) John Lydgate's *Pilgrimage of the Lyfe of Man* (which is partly or mostly Guillaume de Deguileville's *Pèlèrinage de la Vie Humaine*), and (3) William Langland's *Piers Plowman.* These are, of course, three different poems, with three different uses of pilgrimage. Chaucer takes advantage of the fourteenth-century longing "to goon on pilgrimages" as a *motif* and linkage for his *Canterbury Tales.* But the pilgrimage is prologue and framework. Lydgate's pilgrimage is an allegory of the human soul or life of the soul: it descends from the ancient tradition of the *psychomachia,* and it is peopled with abstractions. It was tremendously popular. But it is not the only one of the three to be peopled with abstractions—yet how concrete are the abstractions in the fair field full of folk, and how marvellous: "Ac on a Mai mornynge on Malverne hulles / Me bifel a ferly of faery me thoghte / I was wery forwandred and went me to reste / On a brode banke bi a bornes syde." And from Langland in the fourteenth century comes John Bunyan in the seventeenth (who may well have read Langland in the 1561 edition and certainly read the contemporary stories of Bevis of Southampton).

In Bunyan, the *pèlèrinage de la vie humaine* is the engine (so to speak) driving Christian's adventures, but it is the characters of the fellow pilgrims (as with Chaucer) and of those in the fair field full of folk, "allegorical" or not (as with Langland), that give them life. There is a ferly "of faery" in Bunyan also. Remember the Enchanted Ground (in Book II of *Pilgrim's Progress*). Remember the opening: "As I walked through the wilderness of this world, I lighted on a certain place where was a den, and I laid me down in that place to sleep, and as I slept I dreamed a dream." (I walked through the wilderness of this world, and was weary for wandering and went me to rest.)

But the idea of pilgrimage and quest (which is here a kind of pilgrimage) does not come to Tolkien directly from Bunyan. As Sir Walter Scott's *Waverley*

novels were still appearing in Great Britain, there appeared in New York, in 1826, the first great American novel, which has been called a Waverley in warpaint, Fenimore Cooper's *The Last of the Mohicans.* As *Waverley* was a Narrative of 1745, so this was a Narrative of 1757. The open Christian faith of Hawk-eye, the supporting of Colonel Munro rather like the supporting of Mr. Feeble-mind, the band of disparate pilgrims searching for Cora, and the ending in triumphant death have more than a faint reminiscence of the Hill Difficulty, the Slough of Despond, and the Valley of the Shadow of Death. Far more than the Picwicaresques of Charles Dickens, Cooper's *The Last of the Mohicans* brings the Pilgrimage into the Novel, as the Novel descends from Scott and the Pilgrimage from Bunyan. After all, one does not live in the Wilderness—one is perpetually journeying through it. Even Chingachgook and Le Rénard are wayfarers.

Quest and pilgrimage have in common the adventures through an inhospitable countryside, and both have the sense about them of signs and wonders. Both have a goal. Moreover, it might be argued that the origin of the Band of Brothers lies in the Knights of the Table Round (on *quest* rather than *pilgrimage*), and I suppose in a sense it does, perhaps indeed through *Bevis of Southampton.* But it was Bunyan who calls it a pilgrim's progress, through the signs and wonders, and it is from Bunyan (through Cooper) that the line descends to modern times and Tolkien. It is worth noting that the one indubitable quest in pastoral England that has endured to the present day, the hunt, finds an echo in Tolkien only in a brief comment on damage wrought by the king's hounds in *Farmer Giles*—even though his edition of *Gawain* shows Tolkien an expert on the medieval hunt, the most important quest of the English Middle Ages.

The text for Tolkien's understanding of this quest is in the notes to his edition (with E.V. Gordon) of *Sir Gawain and the Green Knight* (1925); the original passages in *Gawain* are line 1,421, "Sone þay calle of a quest in a ker syde," and line 1,150, "At þe fyrste quethe of þe quest quaked þe wylde." These refer, respectively, to the searching of hounds for the game and the baying of hounds on scenting or viewing the game. The word is from the Old French *queste* with the same meaning. Line 1,150 refers to the hunting of the deer by braches (smallish beagle-like hounds), and line 1,421 refers to boar-hunting by raches (any scenting-hound) and bloodhounds or lymers. The third quest in *Gawain* ("þrid tyme þrowe best" is quoted in line 1,680) is after the fox. Tolkien's notes on the threefold quest (deer, boar, and fox) are on pp. 100–110 of the 1925 edition corrected to 1955. It has been suggested that there is a symbolism in these three quests, with the deer representing youth, the fighting boar representing manhood, and the fox representing older age ("then witty as foxes till threescore and ten" in the seventeenth-century song).

JARED LOBDELL

Further Reading

Tolkien, J.R.R., and E.V. Gordon, eds. *Sir Gawain and the Green Knight*. London: Oxford University Press, 1925.

See also **Asceticism; Sacrifice;** *Seafarer*; *Wanderer*

PIPPIN

Peregrin Took, hobbit, is one of Frodo's companions in *The Lord of the Rings*. Pippin is the fourth recorded child and first son of Paladin II Took and Eglantine Banks. Born in 1390 (Shire Reckoning), he was twenty-eight at the time of the events in *The Lord of the Rings*—the youngest hobbit in the group, still in his "irresponsible tweens" and not yet come of age. Pippin joined Frodo on the journey from Hobbiton to Rivendell, where Elrond chose him to be a member of the Company. At Parth Galen, Pippin and his friend Merry were captured by Orcs from Isengard, but they escaped into Fangorn Forest and met Treebeard, the Ent. The two hobbits accompanied the Ents to the siege of Isengard and there rejoined several other members of the Company. After Gandalf's confrontation with Saruman, Pippin looked into the renegade Wizard's *palantír* and was questioned by Sauron; Gandalf took Pippin with him to Minas Tirith for his own protection. There Pippin swore fealty to Denethor, Steward of Gondor, and served him as page before and during the Battle of the Pelennor Fields. When Denethor in his madness tried to immolate himself and his dying son Faramir, Pippin sought Gandalf's help and saved Faramir's life. Pippin represented the Shire during the battle at the Black Gate and killed a Hill-troll during the first charge of the hosts of Mordor; he was wounded and was rescued by Gimli the Dwarf. When the hobbits returned to the Shire, Pippin was instrumental in evicting Sharkey's ruffians from the land. He was the first to draw a sword in the revolt, threatening the Men who had taken over the Green Dragon. While Merry prepared Bywater for the expected final assault of the ruffians, Pippin raised an army from Tuckborough that tilted the balance of the battle in their favor. With Merry, he was much honored in the Shire.

Pippin succeeded his father as The Took and Thain in 1434. He married Diamond of Long Cleve in 1427, and they had at least one son, Faramir (b. 1430), who married Sam's daughter Goldilocks in 1463 and became Took and Thain in his turn. Merry and Pippin left the Shire in 1484 to spend their last years in Rohan and Gondor. Pippin's body lies next to that of King Elessar in Minas Tirith.

Tolkien took quite a long time to decide on the names, characters, ancestry, and even number of hobbits on the expedition to Mordor, and Pippin was the last hobbit to take final form. In the earliest drafts, a hobbit named Odo (first Took, then Bolger) is most like Pippin in character, and one called Frodo (later Folco) Took possesses Pippin's ancestry as heir to The Took. Peregrin Boffin was the name originally used for the hobbit Trotter, who evolved into the Man Strider. By the end of the first draft of the Rivendell chapters, Tolkien realized he had too many hobbits involved in the story, especially after adding Sam, who shared some character traits with Folco. He considered dropping Odo altogether, or at least from the group of hobbits traveling from Crickhollow to Rivendell. About the time of the second-phase revision of "Many Meetings," Odo's personality and Folco's genealogy had been merged into one hobbit, renamed Faramond. But it was not until the fourth phase of revisions that Odo Took (and a subplot in which he is captured at Crickhollow by Black Riders and rescued by Gandalf) is completely dropped and Peregrin Took gains his final name and unmistakable personality.

Pippin is youthful, hasty, impertinent, inquisitive, and impulsive; possibly an indulged (but not necessarily spoiled) youngest child of a wealthy family; and eager to prove himself more mature than he is but sometimes betrayed by his impetuousness and pride. He is outgoing and a merry companion on the road. He can be a quick thinker in a tight spot. During the time Merry and Pippin were prisoners of the Orcs, Pippin seized a chance to cut his bonds yet quickly knotted the cords together again so that he could stay with Merry and bide his time to escape. When he had the chance to break away and leave a clue for Aragorn, he took it without a moment's hesitation. And Pippin was quick to take advantage of Grishnákh's treacherous greed, tempting him to steal them away from the Orc camp. Pippin made friends easily across generational lines, as shown by his relationships with Frodo, Gandalf, Treebeard, Beregond, and Bergil, but he was also capable of depth of feeling. Pippin's care for the injured Merry during the siege of Minas Tirith, where roles are reversed and Pippin has to be the sensible, level-headed one, is a sensitively handled portrayal of deep male friendship.

As Gandalf implies, part of the reason Merry and Pippin were chosen by fate as members of the Fellowship was to subject them to a "course of honor" designed to make them fit leaders of their people—settling the affairs of their homeland and putting things right is "what you have been trained for," as he tells them on their return to the Shire. Pippin's task is to learn to control and channel the impulsiveness that leads him to do such things as drop a pebble in the well in Moria or look into Saruman's *palantír*. Instead, he must learn to follow the impulses that help others and ignore those that arise solely from his curiosity.

Tolkien often portrayed contrasting pairs of characters who face similar temptations or go through similar experiences. Merry and Pippin are a case in point. They are together from the time Frodo reaches Crickhollow until Gandalf takes Pippin to Gondor, and while separated, their paths still run in parallel, bringing two major sets of doubles together—Merry and Pippin, Théoden and Denethor. Both hobbits swear fealty to a powerful ruler, experience the trauma of battle, change the course of events through a eucatastrophic act of disobedience, and witness their lord's death. Pippin's version of this arc starts when his pride is stung by Denethor's cold scorn of Halflings and his sense of debt to Boromir; when he impetuously swears fealty to Denethor, his motivation is to prove himself and Hobbitkind worthy of Denethor's respect. Pippin must learn to accept the consequences of his impulsive behavior, which lacks the generosity of spirit of Merry's similar action, and humble his hobbit sense of independence to serve Denethor as his page. Yet Pippin also discovers, when he refuses to accept Denethor's dismissal among the tombs of the dead Stewards, that strict obedience to orders is not necessarily the right or honorable action in all circumstances; independent thought is required for maturity and leadership.

Peregrin Took's irrepressible cheerfulness, endearing flaws, and gift for friendship make him one of Tolkien's most memorable characters and a favorite of many readers. Gandalf's relationship with Pippin, and the Wizard's frequent fond exasperation with the Hobbit, is one of the greatest delights of *The Lord of the Rings*.

JANET BRENNAN CROFT

Further Reading

Bradley, Marion Zimmer. "Men, Halflings, and Hero Worship." In *Tolkien and the Critics: Essays on J.R.R. Tolkien's "The Lord of the Rings,"* edited by Neil D. Isaacs and Rose A. Zimbardo, 109–27. Notre Dame, IN: University of Notre Dame Press, 1968.

Croft, Janet Brennan. *War and the Works of J.R.R. Tolkien.* Contributions to the Study of Science Fiction and Fantasy. Westport, CT: Praeger, 2004.

Fader, Shanti. "A Fool's Hope." *Parabola* (Fall 2001): 48–52.

Porter, Lynnette R. *Unsung Heroes of "The Lord of the Rings": From the Page to the Screen.* Westport, CT: Praeger, 2005.

Rutledge, Fleming. *The Battle for Middle-earth: Tolkien's Divine Design in "The Lord of the Rings."* Grand Rapids, MI: Eerdmans, 2004.

See also **Aragorn; Denethor; Doubles; Frodo; Merry; Shire; Treebeard**

PLANTS

Tolkien once noted in a letter that "I am (obviously) much in love with plants and above all trees, and always have been; and I find human maltreatment of them as hard to bear as some find ill-treatment of animals" (*Letters,* 220). The crowning glory of Middle-earth's flora are its forests, woods, and trees. These were not the sole objects of Tolkien's attention and affection, however. *The Lord of the Rings* contains references to at least sixty-four kinds of noncultivated plants. We can add to these the crops grown in the Shire, with the mushrooms and pipeweed beloved of Hobbits in cultural pride of place.

It is no secret that, both personally and literarily, Tolkien favoured the cool, clear air of "the North-West of the Old World" (*FR,* Prologue, 19). Nonetheless, the breadth of his botany is shown in the account of Frodo and Sam's journey through Ithilien, which includes lovingly detailed descriptions of its distinctly Mediterranean flora.

There are some extraordinary plants only to be found in Tolkien's Middle-earth. *Mallorn* or *mellyrn* is a kind of tree unique to Lothlórien. With silver bark and golden leaves that only fell with the arrival of new leaves in the spring, the mallorn must have recalled Laurelin the Golden of Valinor to the Elves who made their homes in the oldest and tallest of them. And at the end of *The Lord of the Rings,* a mallorn appears in the heart of the Shire, the gift of Galadriel to Sam.

Athelas came to Middle-earth with the Númenóreans at the beginning of the Second Age. By the time Aragorn uses it to bring back Faramir, Éowyn, and Merry from the brink of death, its extraordinary healing properties had been forgotten in Gondor except in folk memory.

Elanor, meaning "sun-star," is a small, golden, star-shaped flower blossoming in the winter in Lothlórien, perhaps particularly on the hill of Cerin Amroth. Sam and Rosie Gamgee borrowed it, at Frodo's suggestion, for the name of their beautiful first daughter. Diane Duane suggests it was inspired by the occasional "sport" version of *Crocus alpinus,* which Tolkien may have seen in the Alps (117–28).

Of the others, *simbelmynë,* meaning "ever-mind," is small white flower in Rohan, growing thickly on the burial mounds of the kings of the Mark. *Lebethron* is a kind of tree with dark wood prized by the woodwrights of Gondor; it was the kind of wood used for the staves given by Faramir to Frodo and Sam. *Niphredil* is a small, pale, winter-blooming flower growing in Lothlórien, often in the company of *elanor.* We do not know the name of the noisome pale flowers of Morgul Vale.

PATRICK CURRY

Further Reading

Curry, Patrick. *Defending Middle-earth: Tolkien, Myth and Modernity.* 2nd ed. Boston, MA: Houghton Mifflin, 2004.

Duane, Diane. "The Longest Sunday." In *Meditations on Middle-earth,* edited by Karen Haber, 117–28. New York: St. Martin's, 2001.

See also **Environmentalism and Eco-Criticism; Nature; Trees; Two Trees**

PLATO

The Athenian Plato (427–347 BCE) developed the philosophy of "Forms" (perfect and independently existing entities underlying and determining worldly phenomena), which is the basis for Western idealism. Tolkien certainly knew Plato's works and possibly read some in the original Greek. Some general and some motivic parallels can be seen between Tolkien's and Plato's works.

Plato, like Tolkien, draws heavily on traditional myths, also including his own "myths" (nowhere else attested and probably written by him) in his dialogues. This can parallel Tolkien's mythopoeic enterprise in its being a reaction to a tradition (to philosophically use myth and the literary traditions of Germanic languages, which serve as Tolkien's inspiration and sources), in its method (to create, in writing, stories that historically should belong to an earlier, primarily oral context and that determine ways of thought and textual manifestations as a background, then to use these as authenticating devices for the whole complex—both essentially reconstructive

processes working from surface toward deeper structures, from historical present toward the past), and in its ultimate aim (to show "truth," in Plato always expressed in mythic scenes and language, and to, in Tolkien, reveal the fictitious past to emphasize its continuity with the present and that the truth is accessible only through a process of learning about the past). Philosophical truth (in Plato) and the history of the world (in Tolkien) are available as "templates" in visions (of the place above the sky, *Phaedrus,* and the Vision in the Ainulindalë). For both Plato and Tolkien, myth is connected to a network of stories and meanings and has close connections with orality and the concept of authority. Although not necessarily an "influence" on Tolkien, Plato's mythopoeic practice similarly problematizes writing, the cultural use of stories, and the communities for which stories function as myths and certain meanings as mythic.

In Plato's *Republic* (2.359c–360b), the story is told of one Gyges who finds a ring of invisibility and then is corrupted by the power this confers upon him; as a parallel to Tolkien's One Ring, this is, however, rather superficial, since Gyges' ring only works to make him invisible and his evil is achieved by the power offered in the knowledge he thus gains.

The imagery of light in Tolkien (especially in *The Silmarillion*), where light is a metaphor for a creating force and ultimately the meaning that the creator implants in the world, is somewhat similar to how Plato (in the simile of the Sun, *Republic* 6.508b–509c) uses light as a metaphor for the Form of the Good lending existence to things. Light as a Neoplatonic symbol of existence, emanating from the One, might also be relevant.

Concerning the hierarchy of the world, Plato's Demiurge (the person shaping the world with an eye on the Forms) and Tolkien's Valar (whose primary action is also said to be "shaping") show similarities. The gradation of created forms from the creator through Valar and Elves to Men and Hobbits also recalls the later Neoplatonist-based "great chain of being."

GERGELY NAGY

Further Reading

Cox, John. "Tolkien's Platonic Fantasy." *Seven* 5 (1984): 53–69.

De Armas, Frederick A. "Gyges' Ring: Invisibility in Plato, Tolkien, and Lope de Vega." *Journal of the Fantastic in the Arts* 3, no. 4 (1994): 120–38.

Flieger, Verlyn. "Naming the Unnamable: The Neoplatonic 'One' in Tolkien's *Silmarillion.*" In *Diakonia: Studies in Honor of Robert T. Meyer,* edited by Thomas Halton and Joseph P. Willimer, 127–32. Washington, DC: Catholic University of America Press, 1986.

Morse, Robert E. "Rings of Power in Plato and Tolkien." *Mythlore* 7, no. 3 (1980): 38.

Nagy, Gergely. "Saving the Myths: The Recreation of Mythology in Plato and Tolkien." In *J.R.R. Tolkien and the Invention of Myth: A Reader*, edited by Jane Chance, 81–100. Lexington, KY: University Press of Kentucky, 2004.

See also **Light; One Ring, The**

POEMS BY TOLKIEN IN OTHER LANGUAGES

Eleven poems by Tolkien, and five fragments, survive in languages other than modern English and Elvish. Nine of the poems and all five fragments are in Old English (OE), or Anglo-Saxon; one poem is in a Chaucerian dialect of Middle English; and one is in Gothic. The first two OE poems are the *Enigmata Saxonica Nuper Inventa Duo (Two Recently Discovered Saxon Riddles),* which Tolkien published in *A Northern Venture* in 1923. They were not, of course, "recently discovered" but recently composed. Tolkien's pretence of having discovered them is a joke, but it contains a serious proposition. There are several genres surviving mostly only among children, riddle, fairy tale, and nursery rhyme among them. It is possible, though, that these were not always confined to children and that the modern rhymes or tales had more elevated ancestors in the ancient world, now irrevocably lost. The same is true of much of the vocabulary of modern languages: they must descend from ancient words, but we do not know what these ancient words were. Historical linguists have long been accustomed to "reconstructing" such words from their modern descendants, conventionally putting an asterisk in front of them to indicate that they were never actually recorded. If, however, linguists are justified in creating "asterisk-words," and if some kinds of traditional poem may have been passed on in the same way as words, then why not create "asterisk-poems"?

Tolkien's two Anglo-Saxon riddles, "egg" and "candle," thus appear as the lost ancestors of modern riddles surviving only as nursery rhymes (*H,* 123–25). In the same year Tolkien also published two extended versions of nursery rhymes, *The Cat and the Fiddle* and *Why the Man in the Moon Came Down Too Soon,* though these are in modern English.

The collection *Songs for the Philologists,* privately published in 1936 and stated as being by "J.R.R. Tolkien, E.V. Gordon and Others," contains twenty-nine poems. Eleven are in Old Norse or Icelandic, six in OE, seven in modern English, one in Latin, one in Gothic, and three in a mixture of languages including Old Norse, OE, Latin, Middle Scots, and Swedish.

Tolkien is known to have written the one Gothic poem, six of the modern English ones, and six of the seven OE pieces (the exception is *Hwan Ic Béo Déad*). The status of the Gothic and the OE poems varies somewhat.

Thus, the Gothic poem, *Bagme Bloma (Flower of the Trees),* is an original work, written in praise of the birch—the emblem of the philological course at the University of Leeds English Department, as oak was the emblem of the literature course. Therefore, it is not an "asterisk-poem," though it could be said to be in an "asterisk-language," largely reconstructed from limited data. One of the OE poems, *Éadig Béo Þu,* also praises the birch and deprecates the oak and likewise has no known ancestor. What, however, are we to make of *Ofer Wídne Gársecg* and *Ides Ælfscýne?* The former is, in Tolkien's own words, "An OE version of [the ballad]: 'Twas in the broad Atlantic, mid the equinoctial gales. . . ." Both the modern English ballad and Tolkien's "OE version" tell of a sailor who falls overboard, is rescued (or trapped) by a mermaid, and turns his back on humanity, a markedly nonmodern theme. Should we see Tolkien's poem, then, as a translation? Or should we see it as another reconstruction of a vanished ancestor, an "asterisk-poem"? In the same way, *Ides Ælfscýne* can be seen as the kind of poem that would have been the ancestor of several modern ballads about lovers abandoned by their elf-mistresses, of which Keats's *La Belle Dame Sans Merci* is the most famous literary example.

Of the remaining three OE poems in the collection, *La, Húru (Lo, Indeed)* is a drinking song with no close parallels. *Ruddoc Hana* is a version of the nursery rhyme *Who Killed Cock Robin?* After an opening stanza of mourning, eleven further stanzas begin with the question "who?" answered successively by the sparrow, who killed him; the peacock, who saw the deed; the fish, who caught his blood; the woodpecker, who will work the shroud; and so on to the ox or heifer, who will toll the knell. Mere translation, or feigned unknown ancestor? The same question can be asked of *Syx Mynet,* at once a translation of *I've Got Sixpence* and possibly the "asterisk-poem" that might have been its original. Finally, in 1967 Tolkien wrote a relatively long, twenty-seven-line poem in OE in praise of W.H. Auden, titled *For W.H.A.* The poem is modeled on the OE poem *The Gifts of Men,* lists several talents, flatteringly suggests that Auden has them all, and remarks that his first name, Wystan, is an honorable one (Weohstan or Wihstan) borne by two heroes of the Anglo-Saxon past. Tolkien also gave a modern English translation in alliterative verse. Tolkien seems to have begun a similar poem in praise of the Inklings, "Hwæt we Inclinga. . . ," but it is only a four-line fragment (Carpenter, 176–77).

The one Middle English poem known to be by Tolkien is *The Clerkes Compleinte,* published in *The Gryphon* in 1922, discovered in 1984 by Anders Stenström, and confirmed as genuine by Christopher Tolkien. It describes the process of registration at University of Leeds at the beginning of the academic year, a comic confusion that ends with the would-be student or "clerke" being ejected; but it is also a complaint about the growing numbers of "vocational" studies and the decreasing level of language skills among university students.

To the preceding list should be added four fragments of OE verse to be found in "The Lost Road" or in "The Notion Club Papers." One of these consists of seven lines, mostly taken from the OE poem *The Seafarer,* expressing the desire of an Anglo-Saxon poet, Ælfwine, to seek out "the land of strangers" or, in Tolkien's later versions, the "Elf-friends island" (*Lost Road,* 84; *Sauron,* 243, 272). Ælfwine also speaks five original lines in OE describing the "homeland of the Elves" (*Lost Road,* 44; *Sauron,* 244) when he meant to declaim a praise-poem on King Edward the Elder, of which we are given the first four lines (*Sauron,* 271–72). On the next page we are also given six lines in OE of a poem by Tréowine on "King Sheave." All four of these fragments relate to genuine OE poems such as *The Seafarer, Widsith, Brunanburh,* or *Beowulf* but also to Tolkien's modern English poems *The Nameless Land* and *King Sheave.* Genuine OE, invented OE, and modern English are presented as parts of one linguistic/literary continuum.

Tolkien was not the only scholar to write "asterisk-poems" as defined previously. Axel Olrik (1864–1917), for instance, composed the lost *Bjarkamál* in Old Norse on the basis of two surviving stanzas and a Latin epitome. Another famous missing text is the Sigurd-lay thought to have been in the pages lost from the middle of the major manuscript of Eddic poetry. It is possible that the as-yet-unpublished poem (or poems) by Tolkien, the *Völsungakviða En Nyja (New Lay of the Völsungs)* mentioned in *Letters* (379 and note), is an attempt to recreate this: such an attempt would be highly characteristic of him and of his profession.

TOM SHIPPEY

Further Reading

Carpenter, Humphrey. *The Inklings: C.S. Lewis, J.R.R. Tolkien, Charles Williams and Their Friends.* London: George Allen & Unwin, 1978.

Shippey, Tom. "Four 'Asterisk' Poems." Appendix B in *The Road to Middle-earth: How J.R.R. Tolkien Created a New Mythology,* 353–61. Revised and expanded edition. Boston, MA: Houghton Mifflin, 2003.

Stenström, Anders. "'The Clerkes Compleinte': Text, Commentary and Translation." *Arda* 4 (1984): 1–11.

———. "'The Clerkes Compleinte' Revisited." *Arda* 6 (1986): 1–13.

See also **Alliterative Verse by Tolkien; Auden, W.H.: Influence of Tolkien; Gothic Language; Old English; Old Mercian; Riddles: Sources**

POEMS BY TOLKIEN: *THE ADVENTURES OF TOM BOMBADIL*

In 1961 Tolkien's aunt Jane Neave, his mother's younger sister, asked him to "get out a small book with Tom Bombadil at the heart of it." The result was *The Adventures of Tom Bombadil and Other Verses from The Red Book,* published the following year and illustrated by Pauline Baynes, who had earlier illustrated *Farmer Giles of Ham. Adventures* is a collection of sixteen poems. Each poem has its own history, often a complex one, but most were reprints, usually significantly or greatly revised, of poems previously published in limited-circulation journals or anthologies between 1923 and 1937. Three of them had furthermore appeared in *The Lord of the Rings:* versions of nos. 5, 7, and 10, respectively, *The Man in the Moon Stayed Up Too Late, The Stone Troll,* and *Oliphaunt,* are sung or recited by Frodo in the *Prancing Pony,* by Sam between Weathertop and Rivendell, and by Sam again in Ithilien.

These last connections explain the collection's subtitle, and the preface, in which Tolkien adopts the pose of a scholarly editor (and adds another untitled seven-line poem). The preface declares that all the poems come from *The Red Book of Westmarch,* feigned to be the main source of *The Lord of the Rings.* Some form part of the narrative of the latter, but others have been added on loose leaves or written in "margins and blank spaces." They are all, then, Hobbit-poems, but they come (the Editor declares) from different times and places. No. 3, *Errantry,* is said in the *Red Book* to be by Bilbo but must have been composed relatively early in life, after he had met Elves and learned something of Elvish tradition but before he knew much of Elvish names or languages: Tolkien-as-Editor notes its relationship to Bilbo's Rivendell *Song of Eärendil,* like *Errantry* in meter and outline but more elevated in tone and subject. *The Stone Troll* is similarly said to be by Sam Gamgee, and nos. 8 and 11, *Perry-the-Winkle* and *Fastitocalon,* also in the *Red Book,* bear his initials (though the preface, as the result of a printing complexity and poem-order shift, gives the latter wrongly as no. 12 and in the first paragraph, again wrongly, lists *Cat* as no. 11). No. 10, *Oliphaunt,* though identical with Sam's rhyme in *The Two Towers,* is not by him; as Sam says there, it is just "a rhyme we have in the Shire." By contrast, the Editor argues, nos. 1 and 2, both "Tom Bombadil" poems, must come from the Buckland, and the note of fear in the second one suggests that it was written later and after reports of the visit of Frodo and his companions to Bombadil had become known. Other poems are said to show the wider horizons opened to the Shire by the events at the end of the Third Age. The truth is that Tolkien had written all these poems before *The Lord of the Rings* and sometimes even before *The Hobbit* had been conceived and that the quasi-Elvish or Númenórean names in some of them are not garbled echoes but early experiments. The preface allows him to construct a fiction that integrates them with his later published work.

The title poem was first published in the *Oxford Magazine* for 1934 and was reprinted in 1962 with little change, other than four added lines containing the two references to the River Withywindle. It tells how Tom is trapped or ambushed by Goldberry, the River-woman's daughter; by Old Man Willow; by the badger-folk; and by the Barrow-wight. Tom escapes easily from all of them and then goes back to catch Goldberry in her turn and marry her, undisturbed by threats and bogies. In *Bombadil Goes Boating,* not previously published, Tom rows down the Withywindle to the Buckland, exchanging amiable insults with a wren, a kingfisher, an otter, a swan, and finally the Hobbits before he joins a festivity at Farmer Maggot's. In the morning Tom has vanished, but the otter and the birds come to retrieve his boat, leaving only the oars behind.

Nos. 5 and 6 form another poem pair, *The Man in the Moon Stayed Up Too Late* and *The Man in the Moon Came Down Too Soon.* The first is a version of *The Cat and the Fiddle: A Nursery Rhyme Undone and Its Scandalous Secret Unlocked,* published in *Yorkshire Poetry* in 1923; the second appeared, with the same title as in *Adventures,* in *A Northern Venture* the same year. Both poems relate to familiar nursery rhymes but make a consecutive (if fantastic) narrative out of what in the nursery rhyme is amusing nonsense. Frodo's version of *Too Late* in *The Prancing Pony* adds five lines to the 1923 original and is then little altered in *Adventures.* The *Adventures* version of *Too Soon* adds sixteen lines to the 1923 version and replaces the East Anglian place-names of the original (based on the nursery rhyme reference to Norwich) with names more suitable to Middle-earth.

Nos. 7 and 8 are narrative poems about Trolls and Men. In *The Stone Troll,* first published in *Songs for the Philologists* in 1936, a confident youth called Tom—who surely cannot be Bombadil—clashes unsuccessfully with a Troll gnawing human bones. Sam Gamgee's version added an extra stanza (no. 5) and is again retained little altered in *Adventures.* In *Perry-the-Winkle,* by contrast, another of the poems in the collection not previously published, Perry befriends "the Lonely Troll" and learns from him how to be a master baker. Under an earlier title, *The Bumpus,* it was one of a set of six *Tales and Songs of Bimble Bay;* two more of these were published separately by Tolkien, and a fourth, *Glip,* appeared in *The Annotated Hobbit* (119). A third pair is formed by nos. 10 and 11, *Oliphaunt* and *Fastitocalon.* Tolkien had previously published two poems called *Fastitocalon* and *Iumbo, or ye Kinde of ye Oliphaunt,* in the *Stapledon Magazine* in 1927. They were signed there "Fisiologus," indicating their debt to the Old English bestiary poems, and their tone was mock-moralistic. *Adventures* no. 11 is similar to, but much shorter than the 1927 poem; *Adventures* no. 10, identical with the Sam Gamgee version, has nothing in common with *Iumbo* other than the word of the subtitle. No. 12, *Cat,* was previously unpublished and is known to have been written in 1956 for Tolkien's granddaughter, Joan Anne; in it a domestic cat dreams not of mice but of lions, pards, and man-eaters.

Four other poems prove less easy to group. *Errantry,* first published in the *Oxford Magazine* for 1933, seems to be just the kind of fairy poetry Tolkien would later abjure. In it an unnamed but tiny fairy-knight marries a butterfly but then leaves her to battle dragonflies and honeybees. It is slightly strange that Tolkien decided to reprint it in 1962, with four lines added and many altered, but he may have been proud of its extraordinarily complex meter, used also in Bilbo's *Song of Eärendil.* Nos. 4, 9, and 13, *Princess Mee, The Mewlips,* and *The Shadow-Bride,* are given little or no connection with Middle-earth. *Princess Mee* has an ancestor in *Princess Ni* in *Leeds University Verse 1914–1924* but is three times as long, with pure description turned into a simple narrative; an elf-princess dances with her shadow. *The Mewlips* was originally titled *Knocking at the Door: lines induced by sensations when waiting for an answer at the door of an Exalted Academic Person* and has only some nine of its thirty-two lines significantly altered from its original appearance in the *Oxford Magazine* for 1937; the original title gives a good idea of the poem's mood, fear, and gloom without revealing who was "exalted" enough to induce such sensations in a Rawlinson and Bosworth Professor of twelve years seniority. *The Shadow-Bride* tells a quasi-mythical story of a man who, like Beren or Tom Bombadil, catches and holds a twilight-lady; unlike Beren and Tom he draws her down into a kind of underworld from which they are released once a year to dance together. A version of it is thought to have been published in the early 1930s, but this has never been located (*H*, III, 92).

The most striking and heavily reworked poems in the collection, however, are the last three, *The Hoard, The Sea-Bell,* and *The Last Ship. The Hoard* began its career in a University of Leeds journal, *The Gryphon,* in 1923, with the title *Iúmonna Gold Galdre Bewunden,* which means "the gold of men of old, wound round with spell," and is line 3,052 of the Old English poem *Beowulf.* In 1937 Tolkien reprinted it in the *Oxford Magazine* with many changes, and eight lines longer, but with the same title. It was this version that was reprinted with few changes as *The Hoard* in *Adventures* and again in a 1970 anthology. In each version a treasure passes from elf to dwarf to dragon to man, always proving destructive and morally corrupting. The poem's different versions show Tolkien developing his ideas on editorial cruxes in *Beowulf* and on the "dragon-sickness" of greed. *The Sea-Bell* and *The Last Ship* may be seen as companion pieces. In the former, based on the 1934 poem *Looney* from the *Oxford Magazine,* a human male voyages to a strange land beyond the sea and returns to find himself shut out. In the latter, based on another 1934 poem, *Firiel,* published in the *Chronicle* of a convent of nuns in Roehampton, a human female refuses an offer to travel to the undying lands of the Elves and stays in Middle-earth. Both poems are significantly darker in their 1962 versions than in 1934. There is a stronger sense in *The Sea-Bell* than in *Looney* that the speaker's sense of alienation and bereavement may be his own fault. *Firiel* ends with the girl, whose name means "mortal maiden," sitting down to tea, returning to a contented life; in *The Last Ship* there is a much stronger sense that by staying in Middle-earth she has opted for death. In his preface Tolkien says that, in the *Red Book, The Sea-Bell* is also titled *Frodos Dreme* and has accordingly been associated, by some unknown Hobbit scholar, with Frodo's feelings of pain and grief before departure to the Grey Havens.

Tolkien-as-Editor remarks on the "metrical tricks" of the collection, which he affects to see as signs of the Hobbits' lack of sophistication. Tolkien-as-Poet was no doubt prouder of his own skill: each poem is in a different meter, rhyme scheme, or stanza form, with the exceptions of nos. 1 and 2, the "Bombadil" poems, and nos. 8, 13, and (with a variation) 16, all in a form of ballad meter. Some of the others, especially *Errantry,* are extraordinarily complex. Though they are presented as fragments of the lost poetic tradition of the Hobbits and the Shire, they also indicate something of what Tolkien thought of the lost poetic traditions of England and his native West Midlands.

Original or alternative versions of the poems in the collection, or other information about them, may be found in the following major works (listed by number in *Adventures*): (1) *Shadow,* 115–16; (3) *Treason,* 81–109; (5) *Shadow,* 145–47; (6) *Lost Tales I,* 204–6; (7) *H,* II, 73–75; (7) *Shadow,* 142–45; (7) *Treason,* 59–61; and (14) *H,* XVII, 335–38.

TOM SHIPPEY

Primary Sources

Tolkien, J.R.R. *Poems and Songs of Middle-earth.* New York: Caedmon Records, 1967.

Further Reading

Auden, W.H. Sleeve notes to *Poems and Songs of Middle-earth.* New York: Caedmon Records, 1967.

Hammond, Wayne G., with the assistance of Douglas A. Anderson. *J.R.R. Tolkien: A Descriptive Bibliography.* Winchester, UK: St Paul's Bibliographies; New Castle, DE: Oak Knoll Books, 1993.

Rateliff, John D., and Wayne G. Hammond, "'Fastitocalon' and 'Cat': A Problem in Sequencing." *Beyond Bree* (August 1987): 1–2.

Shippey, Tom. *The Road to Middle-earth: How J.R.R. Tolkien Created a New Mythology.* Revised and expanded edition. Boston, MA: Houghton Mifflin, 2003.

———. "The Versions of 'The Hoard.'" *Lembas* 100 (2000/ 2001): 3–7.

Tolkien, J.R.R. "The Cat and the Fiddle: A Nursery Rhyme Undone and its Scandalous Secret Unlocked." *Yorkshire Poetry* 19 (1923).

See also **Alliterative Verse by Tolkien; Cruces in Medieval Literature; Rhyme Schemes and Meter**

POEMS BY TOLKIEN: *THE HISTORY OF MIDDLE-EARTH*

Tolkien's Middle-earth began as poetry. Many of these early poems are collected in *The History of Middle-earth (HoMe)* by Christopher Tolkien and are often published in their final variant accompanied by annotations regarding extant revisions. The earliest drafts of Middle-earth poems date roughly from 1914 to 1917 and appear in *The Book of Lost Tales.* The poems found in *The Lays of Beleriand* were written during Tolkien's tenure at the University of Leeds from 1920 until approximately the summer of 1925. *King Sheave* and *The Song of Ælfwine* from *The Lost Road and Other Writings* and *The Death St. Brendan* and *Imram* from *Sauron Defeated* are closely related in that all four result from his experimental time-travel stories, "The Lost Road" (1937) and "The Notion Club Papers" (1946). These works represent a sample of the poetic foundation for Tolkien's Middle-earth and the mythology of *The Silmarillion*.

The Lost Tales

Arguably the most notable among these *HoMe* poems is *Éalá Éarendel Engla Beorthast (Lost Tales II)*. While an undergraduate at Oxford, Tolkien wrote four poems between September 1914 and July 1915 that deal with the mariner Eärendil (Lover of the Sea), the first developed character in his mythology. Tolkien says (*Letters,* 385–87) the title and character of *Éalá Éarendel* comes from Cynewulf's Anglo-Saxon poem *Crist* and the particular line *éalá éarendel // engla beorthast / ofer middangeard // monnum sended* (Hail, Eärendel, brightest of angels, above the Middle-earth sent unto men). Written as forty-eight lines of rhyming couplets, the poem represents the first expression of a "strange" and "stirring" myth being awakened from slumber (*Letters,* 64; Carpenter 1977, 71; *Lost Tales II,* 271; Shippey, *Author,* 247).

Tolkien's next poem to chronicle the developing character Eärendel, *The Bidding of the Minstrel*, was written in the winter of 1914 at his Oxford undergraduate housing at 59 St. John's Street (*Lost Tales II,* 271–73): "Sing us yet more of Eärendel the wandering." *The Bidding* is an attempt to further recover the "strange" and distant Eärendel. The poem is thirty-five lines of simple ABAB rhyming couplets and includes Tolkien morphing the spelling from Éarendel to Eärendel—a trend to continue until the final variation of Eärendil in *The Silmarillion*. *The Shores of Faëry* (July 1915) continued Tolkien's fascination with the Eärendel tale by connecting it to his private Elvish languages. Humphrey Carpenter believed the poem to be important enough to Tolkien's imaginative development that he quotes an early version of the poem in its entirety. Significantly, the poem introduces elements—such as Valinor and the Two Trees of the Sun and the Moon—into his personal mythology, which continue into the final form of *The Silmarillion* (Carpenter, 76–77).

Tom Shippey suggests *The Happy Mariners* (July 1915, published 1923) reflects a shift in Tolkien's early work toward themes of "mortality" and "immortality" and may be a result of Tolkien's preoccupation with war (Carpenter 1977, 278). During this period, Tolkien began training with the thirteenth regiment at Bedford (July 24, 1915) and regularly visited his future wife Edith Bratt in Warwick—a town that becomes part of his developing legendarium. In an attempt to see the land and the myth as one, Tolkien bases Kortirion (Kôr) on the town of Warwick.

Among the other poems Tolkien wrote in 1915 developing this theme are *Kortirion Among the Trees, The Trees of Kortirion,* and *Kôr: In a City Lost and Dead,* which are included in *The Book of Lost Tales: Part I.* Another poem, *The Song of Aryador* (September 12, 1915), reflects a darker theme in "the coming of the Elves" narrative. Aryador (the land of shadow) is the early tale of the lost Elves, or "the shadow folk," who are lost in the shadow of the Iron Mountains of Melko (later Melkor/Morgoth) during what will later become the Elvish march of the First Age from Cuiviénen to the Western Sea (*Lost Tales I,* 112–19; *S,* 48ff.). *Habbanan beneath the Stars* (December 1915 at Brocton Camp in Staffordshire or June 1916) is written in four stanzas with a short prose introduction. Habbanan, which according to Christopher Tolkien could possibly mean "nigh the Valar" (*Lost Tales I,* 91), is about the gift of death for humanity and waiting in a blessed state of faërie "purgatory."

The tale of Eriol (later changed to Ælfwine or "Elf-friend"), the central character in *The Book of Lost Tales,* was written in verse in March 1916 and later rewritten in November 1916. The poem includes a twenty-line prelude in two parts: *The Town of Dreams* (based on the city Warwick) and *The City of Present Sorrow* (based on Oxford). Christopher Tolkien is unclear as to whether this was intended to be a single poem in three parts or three separate and distinct poems, but the only extant version—*The Town of Dreams and the City of Present Sorrow*—contains all three. There is also *The Song of Eriol* written in two parts, the first part being the same twenty lines from the prelude.

Tolkien returned from the war in France (November 1916) suffering the ill effects of "trench fever," and by the winter 1916–17 he had begun work on *The Book of Lost Tales.* The prose version—with the grandiloquent title "The Cottage of Lost Play, which introduceth [the] Book of Lost Tales"—draws from a previous poem *You & Me and the Cottage of Lost Play* (April 27–28, 1915), which became *The Little House of Lost Play: Mar Vanwa Tyaliéva* in a final, undated revision (*Lost Tales I,* 27–31). At the heart of the story was the Elvish city Kortirion (named after the lost city of Kôr in Valinor) on the faerie island Tol Eressëa (the Lonely Island, England?) dragged to the western shores by Ulmo. Tolkien wrote the first poetic mention of Kôr several days after *You & Me* on April 30, 1915. The poem is a simple fourteen-line rhyming couplet (the first eight lines follow ABAB and the last six AAB AAB) titled *Kôr: In a City Lost and Dead;* Christopher Tolkien believes the poem is a reference to the city of Kôr after the exodus of the Elves (*Lost Tales I,* 36). Tolkien's major treatment of Kortirion, the ambitious 140-line

Kortirion Among the Trees, was written while he was on a week of leave to Warwick in late November 1915. *The Book of Lost Tales: Part I* includes three extant versions of the poem (1915, 1937, and 1962?) containing substantial revisions; the final version Tolkien submitted for inclusion in *The Adventures of Tom Bombadil* (*Lost Tales I,* 33–43).

Tolkien wrote *The Horns of Ylmir* (Ylmir is Gnomish for Ulmo) in the spring of 1917. This seventy-five-line rhyming poem, which exists in three extant versions, is the final revision of a developing idea Tolkien had unsuccessfully worked on since December 1914 (*The Sea Chant of an Elder Day,* Carpenter 1977, 73–74). The poem is the song of Tuor, as referenced in the "Quenta Silmarillion," and brings together the tales of "The Fall of Gondolin" and Eärendel (*Shaping,* 142, 213–18; *S,* 238–45).

In 1923, Tolkien published (along with *The Happy Mariners*) the eighty-line "asterisk-poem" *Why the Man in the Moon Came Down Too Soon* in *A Northern Venture: Verses by Members of the Leeds University English School Association.* The poem is a nursery rhyme that connects the children's rhyme to Uolë Kúvion in *The Tale of the Sun and Moon* (*Lost Tales I,* 174ff.). The poem was later greatly changed and published in *The Adventures of Tom Bombadil* (1962). The 1962 version has less to do with Tolkien's legendarium but still represents a philologist's attempt to connect a contemporary nursery rhyme to a time past when "foolish" ditties were adult concerns (Carpenter 1977, xv, 25–26). Similarly, the playful *Tinfang Warble* and *Over Old Hills and Far Away* are also nursery rhymes but are directly tied to the lore of the Elves through their main character, Tinfang or Timpinen (*Lost Tales I,* 96–110). The former poem was originally written in 1914, rewritten 1920–23, and published in Leeds 1927 (*I.U.M[agazine]*). The later exists in five extant versions, the earliest written in December 1915 at Brocton Camp and the final at Oxford in 1927.

Of Leeds and Beleriand

Vol. III of *The History of Middle-earth, The Lays of Beleriand,* examines two of Tolkien's major poems, *The Lay of the Children of Húrin* and *The Lay of Leithian.* Each of these poems—dating from Tolkien's tenure at the University of Leeds—are dealt with at length in other entries. There are, however, several smaller alliterative-verse poems of interest included in *The Lays of Beleriand.* There are three poems associated with *The Children of Húrin* all dating 1924–25. The first untitled poem ("the high summer / waned to

autumn, // and western gales . . .") was probably the basis for lines 2,082–2,113 in *The Children of Húrin* (*Lays,* 128). The second poem, *Winter Comes to Nargothrond,* is based on an extant revision of a previously untitled poem called *Storm over Narog.* Finally, there is another untitled twenty-six-line poem ("with the seething sea // Sirion's waters") based on lines 1,554–70.

Christopher Tolkien devotes a brief chapter in *The Lays of Beleriand* to several significant but abandoned alliterative poems. *The Flight of the Noldoli From Valinor* is a 145-line poem about Fëanor, the saga of the Silmarils, and the fateful oath of Fëanor's sons to recover the Silmarils at all cost. According to Christopher Tolkien, this represents Tolkien's poetry at the height of his alliterative skill (*Lays,* 136–41). Tolkien also produced a metrical analysis of the first twenty (plus seven select) lines, the analysis of which can be found in his essay "On Translating *Beowulf*" (*MC,* 61–71). The fragment of the *Alliterative Lay of Eärendel* (thirty-eight lines) continues Tolkien's treatment of the mysterious Eärendel. A new element of Eärendel lore is introduced in lines 7 and 8: "But Wade of the Helsings // wearyhearted / Tûr the earthborn // was tired in battle" is a reference to an Old English character who travels on his boat *Guingelot,* certainly the source of Eärendel's Wingelot (*Lays,* 143–44; *Lost Tales II,* 252ff.).

Time Travel and Seafarers

Tolkien made two attempts at stories of time travel—"The Lost Road" and "The Notion Club Papers"—which were ultimately abandoned for the simple reason that Tolkien was more interested in where the characters had gone rather than how they went. In November 1937, Tolkien submitted the incomplete manuscript of "The Lost Road," about a father and son who witness the end of Atlantis, to Rayner Unwin. Christopher Tolkien believes this story is significant to the history of Middle-earth because in it Tolkien's Númenor (the Land to the West) and the tale of Elendil come of age (*Lost Road,* 8–10). However, Humphrey Carpenter believes Tolkien composed the tale of Númenor a decade earlier (170–72).

Two poems of great importance in this volume are *King Sheave* and the two versions of *The Song of Ælfwine;* both poems involve the tale of Eriol's, or Ælfwine's (Elf-friend), voyage to Tol Eressëa from *The Book of Lost Tales.* The former is an abandoned fragment of prose and 153 lines of alliterative verse. Tolkien has Ælfwine retell the legend of King Sheave (Sceaf, King of the Lombards, alluded to in the first lines of *Beowulf*), who later appears in "The Notion

Club Papers" (*Sauron,* 236ff., 294n.; *Lost Road,* 91–96). The latter poem continues the tale of Ælfwine, which Tolkien began in *The Book of Lost Tales,* who came upon Tol Eressëa while sailing the Western sea. Christopher Tolkien says there are "many" versions of the poem, which are difficult to date (*Lost Road,* 100). Two final copies are included in "The Lost Road" and titled *The Song of Ælfwine (on seeing the uprising of Eärendel);* the final version (written around the time of "The Notion Club Papers" in 1945) omits an entire stanza and is accompanied by a prose note not included in *The Lost Road and Other Writings* (*HoMe,* Vol. V).

Tolkien's "The Notion Club Papers" was an attempt to revisit the abandoned time-travel narrative and sea narratives. Drawing from the *Navigatio Sancti Brendani (The Voyage of St. Brendan)* ca. 900 CE, *The Death of St. Brendan* is a 140-line poem of an aged St. Brendan who is only able to recall three memories from his travels: "a Cloud, a Tree, a Star." Tolkien later published a revision of the poem under the name *Imram* in the December 3, 1955, edition of *Time & Tide,* which can also be found Volume IX of *The History of Middle-earth* (*Sauron,* 261–99).

RENO E. LAURO

Further Reading

Carpenter, Humphrey. *J.R.R. Tolkien: A Biography.* London: George Allen & Unwin, 1977.

Duriez, Colin. *The J.R.R. Tolkien Handbook: A Concise Guide to His Life, Writings, and World of Middle-earth.* Grand Rapids, MI: Baker Books, 2004.

Shippey, Tom. *The Road to Middle-earth.* London: George Allen & Unwin, 1982.

———. *J.R.R. Tolkien: Author of the Century.* London: HarperCollins, 2000.

See also **Adventures of Tom Bombadil** (Collection); **Alliterative Revival; Alliterative Verse by Tolkien; Kôr;** *Leeds University Verse 1914–24;* **"On Translating Beowulf"; Poems by Tolkien; Poems by Tolkien in Other Languages; Poems by Tolkien: Uncollected; Riddles; Rhyme Schemes and Meter; Saint Brendan; Tol Eressëa**

POEMS BY TOLKIEN: *THE HOBBIT*

Not counting the eight rhyming riddles of chapter 5, most of which are not poems per se and all of which have sources or analogues in existing traditional material, *The Hobbit* contains sixteen original poems fairly evenly spaced throughout the book. All are untitled, and they vary in length from as much as ten stanzas to a scant four lines. Listed by first line, they are in order of appearance as follows:

- "Chip the glasses and crack the plates!" (I, 42)
- "Far over the misty mountains cold" (I, 44–45)
- "O! What are you doing" (III, 91)
- "Clap! Snap! the black crack!" (IV, 107)
- "Fifteen birds in five firtrees" (VI, 151)
- "Burn, burn tree and fern!" (III, 152)
- "The wind was on the withered heath" (VII, 177–78)
- "Old fat spider spinning in a tree!" (VIII, 211)
- "Lazy Lob and crazy Cob" (VIII, 212)
- "Roll—roll—roll—roll" (IX, 234)
- "Down the swift dark stream you go" (IX, 235)
- "The King beneath the mountains" (X, 251)
- "Under the Mountain dark and tall" (XV, 321–22)
- "The dragon is withered" (XIX, 355–56)
- "Sing all ye joyful, now sing all together!" (XIX, 357)
- "Roads go ever ever on" (XIX, 359)

They may be roughly catalogued by genre such as oral history, satire, working or marching song, lullaby, lament, or elegy. They may also be grouped according to those who perform them, five being sung by the Elves (three by the Elves of Rivendell and two by the Elves of Mirkwood), four by the Dwarves, three by the Goblins, three by Bilbo, and one by the people of Lake-town.

Although a writing tradition is implied by Bilbo's morning letters, the note left on his mantelpiece by the Dwarves, and the runic writing on Thror's map, it is nevertheless clear from the context in which each poem appears that none is a written "poem" in the conventional sense of that term. Rather, all are orally composed and with one exception performed as songs. Their orality may derive in part from the book's genesis as a tale first *told* to Tolkien's children and only in later stages *read* to them from manuscript. The fact that each song has a narrative function, paralleling or in some way supporting a particular action during the course of the story, supports Douglas A. Anderson's statement that "virtually all of the poems in *The Hobbit* were apparently written in sequence with the manuscript of the book" (*H,* III, 92).

The songs employ various patterns of end-rhyme, including rhyming couplets AABB, and so on, as in "Fifteen birds," "Under the Mountain dark and tall," "Down the swift dark stream," and "Sing all ye joyful"; the variation AABBA of "Old fat spider"; ABAB in "O! What are you doing," "The dragon is withered," "Lazy Lob," "The King beneath the mountains," and "Roads go ever ever on"; and AABA in, "Far over the misty mountains" and "The wind was on the withered heath." Two that have meter are the Goblins' marching song "Clap! Snap! the black crack!" and "Burn, burn tree and fern!" Indeed, the former, with its heavy beats and preponderance of one-syllable metrical units to which the Goblins keep time "with the flap of their flat feet," might more properly be described as chant than song.

It is worth notice that though Tolkien was known to be professionally familiar with and fond of alliterative verse, none of the poems in *The Hobbit* is in that form. This is in sharp contrast to some of the songs and chants in *The Lord of the Rings,* especially those in *The Two Towers* and *The Return of the King,* many of which are in the Anglo-Saxon mode of the Rohirrim. Although even outside *The Lord of the Rings* alliterative verse was a form in which Tolkien is known to have composed (the early alliterative *Túrin* and the unpublished "The Fall of Arthur" are examples), it seems probable that in writing *The Hobbit* he used end-rhyme as more suitable and accessible for verses in a story to be read to or by children.

Several of *The Hobbit*'s songs are not just oral but spontaneous, generated extempore during specific occasions and addressed to particular circumstances. The Dwarves' wickedly destructive washing-up song, "Chip the glasses and crack the plates!" is of this type, a satiric and deliberately provocative response to Bilbo's concern for housekeeping and the dire consequences of unexpected hospitality. Also occasional, though considerably less pointed, is the Rivendell Elves' "O! What are you doing / And where are you going?" From its teasing references to ponies needing shoeing, "beards all a-wagging," and "Mister Baggins," this appears to be tailored to the Dwarves' immediate arrival in the valley, one of those useful choruses that can be adapted to fit any circumstance.

Worth noting in this context is the narrator's comment that after this light-hearted greeting, the Elves then "went into another song as ridiculous as the one I have written down in full" (*H,* III, 49). Although this other song is not included in the published text, Anderson's *The Annotated Hobbit* notes a hitherto-unpublished poem labeled "Elvish Song in Rivendell," which seems to date from "the very early 1930s, and [is] thus contemporaneous with the writing of *The Hobbit*" (*A,* III, 92). However, if the poem Anderson cites, which begins "Come home, come home, ye merry folk! / The sun is sinking and the oak / In gloom has wrapped his feet" (*A,* III, 92) was intended as the "other song," its romantic lyricism, more complex rhyme scheme, and more formal diction make it seem notably unridiculous and certainly contradict the narrator's description.

Another song performed extempore is the Goblins' jeering "Fifteen birds in five firtrees," a taunt aimed at the Dwarf party marooned in the trees. Even though the following "Burn, burn tree and fern!" is different

in meter and form, the narrator's comment that the Goblins "went on singing" suggests that these verses could be read as a continuation of "Fifteen birds." Both can be seen as the Goblin version of the poetic invective so often a feature of Celtic battle stories like the *Táin,* wherein opposing warriors hurl elaborate insults at each other to work themselves up to battle pitch. It is of a piece with the Goblins' battle heroics that the taunts are not directed at equals but at treed victims with no apparent escape. In contrast to this savagery, Bilbo's hobbit versions, "Old fat spider" and "Lazy Lob," his taunts as he prepares to fight the spiders of Mirkwood, seem fairly mild. The humor of incongruity is probably intended in these last, as Bilbo's opponents are not warriors but creepy-crawlies. All these ditties are generated on the spot and sung by their composer(s).

Songs to accompany repeated activities, variations on the traditional genre of the work song, include "Clap! Snap! the black crack!" the Goblins' marching song in the tunnels of the mountain, (although in this case the "work" consists of whipping the prisoners to set them running), and the Mirkwood Elves' "Roll—roll—roll—roll," as they tilt the barrels into the river. Their following song in rhymed couplets, "Down the swift dark stream you go," is not a work song but a lyrical Elven description of the barrels' journey down the river on their way to Lake-town.

Equally lyrical though considerably more serious are the Dwarves' songs of their own past. "Far over the misty mountains cold" is in a bardic tradition of orally preserved history that tells of the dragon's coming and the doom of the Dwarves. We may suppose this to be a song passed from generation to generation for centuries, reminding the Dwarves of their ancient past and their identity, as well as their lost gold. In this context especially, another Dwarf song, "Under the mountain dark and tall / the King has come unto his hall!" establishes (at least in the Dwarves' eyes) their historic right to the treasure and flings down a challenge to their foes. As a corollary, Tolkien goes as far as to imply that although the modern Men of Lake-town do not all believe the old songs, all know them and have heard them. In this respect, "The King beneath the mountains," though sung by the Men of Lake-town rather than the Dwarves, is both history and prophecy, linking the Dwarves' distant past to the prophecy that their King will return and restore their kingdom.

The Dwarves' songs frequently establish or enhance a mood or atmosphere contributory to that portion of the story. "Far over the misty mountains cold" is sung in Bilbo's cheery Hobbit-hole when dark begins to fill the fire-lit room and Bilbo feels moving through him "the desire of the hearts of dwarves"

(*H,* I, 22). Even more effective is the later tone poem sung by the Dwarves in Beorn's hall after his departure, "The wind was on the withered heath." This lyric, with its images of "dark things" creeping, and the "whistling voices" of a cold wind, enhances the fearsome effect on the Dwarves and Bilbo of the dark and dangerous night outside where Beorn prowls.

The Elves' elegy-cum-celebration near the end of the book, "The dragon is withered," is in the same meter as their first song, "O! What are you doing." Here, however, the striking change in mood wrought by difference in subject matter and diction suggests an alteration in the Elves' sensibilities, as well as in their poetic gifts. Whether intended as such or not, the later poem comments on the frivolity of the earlier version. The Elven lullaby that keeps Bilbo awake on his return to Rivendell, "Sing all ye joyful, "shows the same late sensibility, and like most lullabies is clearly traditional.

The one verse that is spoken rather than sung is Bilbo's final poem, "Roads go ever ever on," a meditation on travel and homecoming. Though not originally intended as such, this verse functions as a bridge from *The Hobbit* to *The Lord of the Rings,* where with some differences from version to version it is spoken by first Bilbo, then Frodo, then Bilbo again. These repetitions with variation make it a kind of leitmotif that thematically reiterates Bilbo's notion of "the road" as a never-ending way joined or branched off by other paths—a metaphor for Frodo's (and Tolkien's) concept of story.

VERLYN FLIEGER

POEMS BY TOLKIEN: *THE LORD OF THE RINGS*

Depending on whether you count variations as fresh poems, and how you parse the songs of Tom Bombadil, there are close to seventy-five poems in *The Lord of the Rings,* a sliding total that encompasses a remarkably varied range of forms, meters, and styles. Some poems are folk songs, some are folk history, some are chants or incantations, some are eulogies, some are praise poems, some might be described as hymns, several have no identified source or authorship and so fall in the category of "traditional," and some are nonce verses generated on the spot for a particular occasion. Many are rhymed, a few are unrhymed, some are in the short Old English alliterative two-part line, some are as brief as a ballad stanza, and some extend to twelve or fourteen or even sixteen syllables per line. Of all these, a little over half—about thirty-eight, again depending on how you count—appear in Volume I, *The Fellowship of the Ring.* The

remainder are divided nearly evenly between Volumes II and III, with eighteen in *The Two Towers* and seventeen in *The Return of the King.* Of the roughly thirty-eight in *The Fellowship of the Ring,* twenty-six occur in Book I and twelve in Book II. Of those in *The Two Towers,* fourteen are in Book III and four in Book IV. In *The Return of the King,* nine are in Book V and eight in Book VI. The pattern is clear: a volume-to-volume decrease in number, with most poems occurring west of the Anduin and before the story line breaks into crosscutting time-parallel sequences.

The Fellowship of the Ring

Of the poems in *The Fellowship of the Ring,* fourteen are by Hobbits, nine are Elvish in origin, between six and ten are sung by Tom Bombadil, one by Goldberry, one is chanted by the Barrow-wight, one is Dwarvish, and two are unattributed—the Ring verse and "Seek for the Sword that was broken." Of the remainder, one, the Ring verse coda in the Black Speech, is a translation; another, Gandalf's incantation at the Doors of Moria, scarcely qualifies as a poem except that it rhymes. With four exceptions—in *The Two Towers* Gollum's complaint "The cold hard lands," his fish riddle "Alive without breath," and Sam's "Grey as a mouse" and in *The Return of the King* Sam's "In western lands beneath the sun"—all Hobbit-originated poems occur in *The Fellowship of the Ring,* with "The Road goes ever on" and "Upon the hearth the fire is red" (as "Still round the corner") reprised in *The Return of the King.*

Book I

- "Three Rings for the Elven-kings," front matter, (ii, 59–60; II, ii, 267)
- "The Road goes ever on and on," (i, 44; iii, 82–83; *RK,* VI, vi, 266)
- "Upon the hearth the fire is red," (iii, 86–87; *RK,* VI, ix, 308)
- "Snow-white! Snow-white! O Lady clear!" (iii, 88–89)
- "Ho! Ho! Ho! to the bottle I go," (iv, 99)
- "Sing hey! for the bath," (v, 111)
- "Farewell we call to hearth and hall," (v, 116)
- "O! Wanderers in the shadowed land," (vi, 123)
- "Hey dol! merry dol! ring a dong dillo!" (vi, 130)
- "Hop along, my little friends, up the Withywindle!" (vi, 132)

- "Hey! Come derry dol! Hop along, my heart-ies!" (vi, 133)
- "Now let the song begin! Let us sing together," (vi, 133)
- "O slender as a willow-wand!" (vii, 135)
- "Old Tom Bombadil is a merry fellow," (vii, 145; viii, 153)
- "I had an errand there: gathering water-lilies," (vii, 137)
- "Ho! Tom Bombadil, Tom Bombadillo!" (vii, 145; viii, 153)
- "Cold be hand and heart and bone," (viii, 152)
- "Get out, you old Wight!" (viii, 153–54)
- "Wake now my merry lads!" (viii, 154)
- "Hey! now! Come hoy now!" (viii, 155)
- "Tom's country ends here: he will not pass the borders" (viii, 159)
- "There is an inn, a merry old inn" *(The Man in the Moon)* (ix, 170–72)
- "All that is gold does not glitter," (x, 182; II, ii, 260–61)
- "Gil-galad was an Elven-king," (xi, 197–98)
- "The leaves were long" (Tale of Tinúviel), (xi, 204–05)
- "Troll sat alone," (xii, 219–20)

Two poems epitomize the story as a whole, one at and one near the beginning of Book I. The first is the Ring verse, "Three Rings for the Elven-kings," the book's signature poem that appears in its entirety only twice, one as the epigraph after the title page of the whole book and once spoken by Gandalf in Chapter 2, "The Shadow of the Past." While Gandalf there quotes it as "a verse long known in Elven-lore," he implies later at the Council of Elrond that the last three lines, which comprise the Ring inscription, were actually spoken by Sauron in "the Black Years" and heard by the Elven-smiths of Eregion. The first five lines, referring impersonally to "the Dark Lord on his dark throne," would seem to be the "Elven-lore" referred to by Gandalf, and the three-line tag, "One Ring to rule them all," with its active verbs "rule" and "bring" and the pronoun "them" as their object, sounds like the voice of Sauron.

Second to the Ring verse in appearance but equal in importance is the Road poem. While the Ring verse is the signature, the poem that most fully epitomizes the story is Bilbo's verse, "The Road goes ever on and on." This is a carryover with some revision from *The Hobbit,* where it rounds off the story. First spoken in *The Lord of the Rings* by Bilbo as he leaves Bag End, it is repeated by Frodo on the way to Crickhollow and repeated again with a farewell variation by Bilbo in his room at Rivendell. The verse reprises the circular structure of *The Hobbit* and foreshadows that of *The*

Lord of the Rings, sets the stage for Frodo's greater journey, and brings him and the story There and bittersweetly Back Again. The poem is the first in Donald Swann's song cycle, *The Road Goes Ever On,* a setting of some of Tolkien's poems to music, and gives its title to the entire volume.

The homely quality of the earliest hobbit songs lends Book I much of its character and does a great deal to make it the least doom-laden part of the story. The songs exemplify what Tolkien liked best about his hobbits, their curiosity and eagerness for adventure coupled with their contrary yearning for home and hearth at the end of the day. "Upon the hearth the fire is red," sung by Frodo, Sam, and Pippin on their first night out from Hobbiton, replicates the Road verse in meter and end-rhyme (adding a four-line coda at the end of every verse). It also echoes the sentiment, combining into one poem the adventurousness and retirement that the Road verse takes the whole book and several variations to wrap up. The concrete images of tree, standing stone, secret gate, hill, and water lead outward, and the equally concrete but far more homely fire, lamp, meat, and bread bring the poem and the hobbits back to where they started. It was also included in the Swann song cycle.

The comfortable mood established by this is abruptly broken by the almost immediate appearance of a Black Rider, foreshadowing trouble to come. The next song, the Elven "Snow-white! Snow-white! O Lady clear!" brings a change in tone from hobbit adventurousness and creature comforts to what is essentially an Elven hymn. The version given is "as Frodo heard it," which suggests that he is translating into English what he hears as Elvish (cf. *A Elbereth Gilthoniel* from Book II). This occasion for the meeting between Frodo and Gildor is the first direct intrusion into the story of material from the "Silmarillion," introducing the "far land beyond the sea," which is Valinor, and Elbereth, who is the "Snow-white" of the invocation.

The story returns to hobbit jollity with "Ho! Ho! Ho! to the bottle I go," a more specific celebration of creature comforts than "Upon the hearth" but like it cut short by a Black Rider. "Sing hey! for the bath" is perhaps the most sensuous of the hobbit poems, with its celebration of hot water, drink poured down the throat, and the joys of splashing in the bath. It is also the last commemoration of freedom from care and danger on the hobbits' one night at Crickhollow. The next song, "Farewell we call to hearth and hall!" containing lines such as "With foes ahead, behind us dread," already signals their awareness of the increasing darkness and danger of the journey as they prepare to enter the Old Forest. This is made even more immediate when they experience the Forest's hostility.

Frodo's "O! Wanderers in the shadowed land," is an effort to counter the increasing menace of the trees. His concluding statement that "east or west all woods must fail" brings the crash of a branch falling just behind the hobbits and a warning by Merry not to provoke "them."

The poetry of Tom Bombadil presents a peculiar problem. All of Tom's speech is in cadence, two-stress phrases with two phrases each to a syntactically divided unrhyming line. One way to read Tom's verses is as a single, continuous flow occasionally broken into discrete units by indentation, line breaks, and italic. Another is to see each as distinct by virtue of its content. Either choice seems arbitrary. "Hey dol! merry dol! ring a dong dillo!" could easily be the opening, interrupted by prose, to the longer "Hey! Come merry dol! derry dol! My darling!" which continues on the next page. All of Tom's subsequent dialogue with the hobbits is in the same rhythm now presented as speech, condensing into song again with "Hop along, my little friends, up the Withywindle!" and reprised as "Hey! Come derry dol! Hop along, my hearties!" at the hobbit's view up the hill to Tom's open door. Goldberry's "Now let the song begin! Let us sing together," in the same meter brings them to the threshold, and Frodo echoes the rhythm and diction with "O slender as a willow-wand!" at the sight of her. Tom's "I had an errand there: gathering water-lilies, . . . And that proved well for you" tells the hobbits how timely their encounter has been and how narrowly he might have missed them. "Old Tom Bombadil is a merry fellow" is his signature refrain, repeated with variation in the next chapter in response to the rescue-charm, "Ho! Tom Bombadil, Tom Bombadillo!"

A different kind of incantation is the Barrow-wight's "Cold be hand and heart and bone." Its weighted one-syllable words, varied in eight lines only by "never," "stony," and "withered," drop like stones into a cold pool. Their spondees are untypically echoed in the welcome appearance of Tom, whose emphatic exorcism, "Get out, you old Wight!" is followed by his command to the hobbits, "Wake now my merry lads!" and his round-up of the ponies, "Hey! now! Come hoy now!" Tom's farewell to the Hobbits, "Tom's country ends here: he will not pass the borders," is also a farewell to the reader and signals his disappearance from the story, as well as the scene.

The next poem is one of several previously written and inserted ready-made into *The Lord of the Rings.* "There is an inn, a merry old inn" is a revision of Tolkien's much earlier *The Cat and the Fiddle: A Nursery Rhyme Undone and Its Scandalous Secret Unlocked,* first published in *Yorkshire Poetry* in October–November 1923 and reprinted in its present form as *The Man in the Moon Stayed Up Too Late* in *The Adventures of Tom Bombadil* in 1962. An obvious variation with embellishment on the traditional nursery rhyme, it has no relation to either theme or plot, nor does it arise out of circumstances such as walking, drinking, or taking a bath. It may have been introduced to lighten the already-darkening atmosphere before the intrusion of the Black Riders. At thirteen stanzas it is the longest poem in the book so far, and the galloping rhythm and tumbling ABCCB rhyme create a headlong pace that propels the reader or hearer from line to line and verse to verse.

"All that is gold does not glitter" makes its first appearance in Gandalf's letter to Frodo at The Prancing Pony, and the unwary reader may suppose that Gandalf is the author. At this point in the story, Strider's statement that "I am Aragorn, and those verses go with that name," means little to anyone but himself and Gandalf and certainly has no significance for the reader until the Council of Elrond near the beginning of Book II. It is here that the poet is revealed as Bilbo, first by his impatient repetition of the poem, then more explicitly in his aside to Frodo about having written it himself. If so, he revised it, for versions in earlier drafts diverge from the published verse in content and form after the first line, which is always the same. In *The Treason of Isengard,* Christopher Tolkien notes that the early drafts are written in four long lines rather than the eight shorter ones of the printed verse. When Bilbo recites the verse it is printed as two separate stanzas rather than one. Bilbo's claim of authorship notwithstanding, the verse appears to be a thematic companion to "Seek for the Sword that was broken," which employs the same meter and rhyme scheme and is cast in much the same gnomic mode.

The journey to Weathertop is the occasion for two poems that bring more Elven history into the narrative present. Aragorn's mention of Gil-galad and the Last Alliance triggers Sam's unexpected recitation of "Gil-galad was an Elven-king," which must qualify as both a hobbit and an Elvish poem, since it is Elvish in origin but repeated by Sam and taught to him by Bilbo. Asked for more, Sam admits that the three verses are all he knows of what is clearly meant to be understood as a longer poem. This Strider identifies as *The Fall of Gil-galad,* a lay in "an ancient tongue." No such longer poem exists, although one is implied in Strider's suggestion that the hobbits may hear the tale "told in full" in Rivendell. The original workings of the fragment that Sam delivers were apparently composed when Tolkien had reached this point in the narrative. The form is ballad stanza, quatrains with end-rhyme AABB / CCDD. The mode is eulogy.

In contrast, the next poem, "The leaves were long," has a considerable history that antedates *The Lord of the Rings.* First as "Light as Leaf on Lind," then "As Light as Leaf on Lindentree" (emended to Linden-tree), and finally "Light as Leaf on Linden," the song was inserted into Part II of the second version of *The Lay of the Children of Húrin,* composed during 1919–25 when Tolkien was at University of Leeds. As "Light as Leaf on Lindentree" it was published in June 1925 in the University of Leeds magazine *The Gryphon.* The phrase is apparently traditional, occurring in the envoy to Geoffrey Chaucer's "Clerk's Tale" as advice to wives to "Be ay of chiere as light as leef on lynde," and in William Langland's *Piers Plowman,* where love," when it hadd of this fold flesh and blood taken [been incarnated], / Was nevere leef upon Lynde lighter thereafter."

Responding to Sam's request for a "tale of the old days . . . a tale about the Elves before the fading time," Strider chants the poem at Weathertop as "the tale of Tinúviel." Since no other allusion to Elven fading occurs in *The Lord of the Rings,* it is clear that Sam knows a surprising amount of Elvish history. More direct reference to Elvish fading can be found in Volumes IV, V, and X of *The History of Middle-earth.* The tale of Tinúviel marks the entry into *The Lord of the Rings* of the story closest to Tolkien's heart of all his writings, that of Beren and Lúthien, included in *The Lays of Beleriand* as *The Lay of Leithian* in the octosyllabic rhymed couplets of medieval romance. "The leaves were long" is an eight-line doubled ballad stanza with end-rhyme ABACBABC. While Tolkien has Strider explain that this is a "rough echo" of the original, said to be cast in a traditional Elvish poetic mode called *ann-thennath* (a Sindarin term meaning roughly "long-shorts"), no such Sindarin poem is known to exist.

The last poem in Book I, "Troll sat alone," is composed and sung by Sam. Originally intended as Frodo's song at The Prancing Pony, this was moved to companion the Troll episode. As with "There is an inn," its composition predates *The Lord of the Rings.* A similar poem written in 1926 titled *Pero and Podex (Boot and Bottom)* was privately printed in 1936 as *The Root of the Boot* in the now-rare booklet *Songs for the Philologists,* and reprinted in Douglas A. Anderson's second edition of *The Annotated Hobbit* in 2002. The "old tune" to which Sam sings his version is an actual English folk song, "The Fox Went Out on a Winter's Night." Sam's version was later included as "The Stone Troll" in *The Adventures of Tom Bombadil.* Its seven stanzas are in an unusual seven-line form rhyming AABCCAC with a constantly changing refrain in the fifth line of each stanza.

Book II

- "Eärendil was a mariner" (i, 246–49)
- *A Elbereth Gilthoniel* (i, 250; *TT,* IV, x, 338–39; *RK,* VI, ix, 308)
- "Seek for the Sword that was broken" (ii, 259)
- *Ash nazg durbatulûk* (ii, 267)
- "When winter first begins to bite" (iii, 286)
- "I sit beside the fire and think" (iii, 291–92)
- *Annon edhellen, edro hi amen!* (iv, 320)
- "The world was young, the mountains green" (iv, 329–330)
- "An Elven-maid there was of old" (vi, 354–55)
- "When evening in the Shire was grey" (vii, 374–75)
- "I sang of leaves" (viii, 388–89)
- *Ai! laurië lantar lassi súrinen* (viii, 394)

The first and at 124 lines the longest poem in Book II, Bilbo's "Eärendil was a mariner" at Rivendell, provides an opportunity to introduce more Middle-earth history. Like "There is an inn" and "Troll sat alone," the song has history that extends both before and after its appearance in *The Lord of the Rings.* (For a full explication, see Christopher Tolkien's lengthy discussion in *The Treason of Isengard.*) An early version was published as "Errantry" in the *Oxford Magazine* in November 1933. The name Eärendel (*sic*), which Tolkien had featured as early as his 1914 poem "The Voyage of Eärendel," appeared in the present poem some time after 1944, suggesting that even while working on *The Lord of the Rings* Tolkien not only found time for the "Silmarillion" but also found a way to bring it into *The Lord of the Rings.* While he described the early "Errantry" as "a piece of verbal acrobatics and metrical high-jinks" with complex interior rhymes in "a metre [he] invented," it is in fact octosyllabic rhymed couplets with feminine endings on the model of the rapidly moving patter-songs in Gilbert and Sullivan. "Errantry" was published as poem no. 3 in *The Adventures of Tom Bombadil* in 1962. In brisk 4/8 time, it was set to music in Donald Swann's Tolkien song cycle in 1967. As the subject matter altered from adventuring for its own sake to Eärendil's purposeful journey to Valinor, however, the acrobatics were subdued, the interior and end-rhymes reduced, and the diction elevated, resulting in "Eärendil was a mariner," a more serious poem with a commensurate slowing of pace.

Comparable in tone and content to the English "Snow-white! Snow-white!" of Book I, *A Elbereth Gilthoniel* is the Sindarin version of the same hymn. It is also the longest passage to be found in *The Lord of the Rings* in the language that Tolkien based on the phonology and structure of Welsh. The Sindarin version does not follow the English word for word, but it preserves the figure of Elbereth and the sense of exile. Bilbo's reference to it as a song "of the Blessed Realm" may mean either that it is from or that it is about Valinor.

Through its form, rhyme scheme, and eight-line length, as well as its gnomic character, the verse of Boromir's dream, "Seek for the Sword that was broken," acts as a companion piece to "All that is gold does not glitter," and their appearance on facing pages furthers the association. However, the specific references in Boromir's verse to the Sword that was broken, Imladris, Isildur's Bane, and the Halfling are more specific and more pointed than the cryptic, aphoristic images of its companion poem.

Aside from what Tolkien called the "debased form" spoken by Grishnákh to Ugluk in chapter 3 of *The Two Towers,* Gandalf's quotation of the Ring inscription, *Ash nazg durbatulûk,* is the best example in the book of the Black Speech. The effect on hearers when Gandalf quotes the verse at the Council of Elrond is visible, with a shadow seeming to pass over the sun and a corresponding darkening of the scene. The nearly word-for-word correspondence to the English version, "One Ring to rule them all," is evidence of the holophrastic nature of the Black Speech. The two words *ash nazg* correspond to "One Ring," but the following word, *durbatulûk,* contains an entire phrase, "to rule them all." This is, as well, an apt illustration of Tolkien's principle that sound and meaning work best when they work together. This he described in "A Secret Vice" as phonetic fitness, "the relation between sound and notion." Certainly, the harsh vowels and jagged consonants and consonant clusters lend themselves to rough and rasping pronunciation, a fitting evocation of the voices of Orcs.

Bilbo's little quatrain "When winter first begins to bite" has the oral flavor of a traditional or anonymous verse. The proverbial opening, "When," followed by a list of evocative events—winter begins to bite, stones crack with frost, pools are black, trees bare—resulting in the conclusion that "'tis evil in the Wild to fare," inevitably recalls Shakespeare's song from *Love's Labours Lost.* "When icicles hang by the wall / And Dick the shepherd blows his nail / And Tom bears logs into the hall, / And milk comes frozen home in pail, / When Blood is nipped and ways be foul, / Then nightly sings the staring owl." In both verses, what appears to be artless and ingenuous is, in fact, carefully crafted. It looks and sounds like folk poetry, but it is the product of conscious and deliberate skill.

The far more pensive and wistful "I sit beside the fire and think," at Bilbo's farewell meeting with Frodo at Rivendell, is not the first entry of nostalgic melancholy into the story: recall Frodo looking back at Hobbiton from the Green Hill Country and wondering if he will ever see it again. It does, however, strike the first explicitly mournful note. The poem sounds the first tone in the theme of transience that increasingly pervades the narrative. The six quatrains are suffused with longing, both for what the old Hobbit has seen and what he will not live to see. The final image of listening for the sound of returning feet is a particularly poignant detail, pertaining to which Christopher Tolkien notes in *The Treason of Isengard* that the word "Verses?" was written on the manuscript, though the poem is not included in that draft. In the rough workings for the poem, however, the last verse is accompanied by Tolkien's observation that Bilbo is thinking about Frodo. The poem was set to music in Swann's song cycle.

Annon edhellen, edro hi amen! / Fennas nogothrim, lasto beth lammen! is Gandalf's spell of opening at the Doors of Moria. Like this one, spells or charms are traditionally cast in verse. In printed literature they appear frequently in medieval ballads, where a charm or curse often propels the action. An example is the Breton "Aotrou Nann Hag Ar Gorrigan" in Hersart de la Villemarqué's *Barzas Breiz,* of which Tolkien had a copy. "Aotrou Nann Hag Ar Gorrigan" is put into English in Tom Taylor's *Ballads and Songs of Brittany* as "The Lord Nann and the Fairy." Here, the Corrigaun or fairy puts a spell on the Lord, "Either thou straight shall wed with me / Or pine for four long years and three; / Or dead in three days space shall be." Tolkien's "Aotrou and Itroun," in form and substance a medieval ballad, has a similar subject and spell. He was, as well, familiar with more positive charms and spells such as those in the Finnish *Kalevala,* where the songs frequently include charms for healing or finding. Though Gandalf tries any number of spells, Tolkien's peculiar spin on the tradition is that in this instance the charm does not work since no spell is needed.

"The world was young, the mountains green" is a rare view of Gimli's little-seen poetic side. It is also a fine representation of Tolkien's poetic skills. The second verse in particular shows his facility with enjambment, not a poetic technique for beginners. While it is clear that the poem is not of Gimli's own composition, it is equally clear that it is an important part of Dwarvish oral history—their creation myth and downfall combined. This song of loss chanted in Moria, the scene of the Dwarves' defeat, is enhanced by the ruined grandeur the Company sees around them. It intensifies the melancholy mood of Bilbo's

"I sit beside the fire" and deepens the sense of passing that emerges in Volumes II and III as a major theme of the story.

This sense of passing and loss continues with the next poem. Legolas's "An Elven-maid there was of old" tells the love story of Nimrodel and Amroth. It is in ballad form—four-line stanzas rhyming ABABCDCD. At thirteen verses the poem is a fragment, for Legolas breaks off at the disappearance of Amroth, commenting that the song is "long and sad" and that he can sing no more. Like Strider's tale of Tinúviel, this is the presumed English version, what Legolas calls Westron Speech, of a poem originally in the woodland tongue of the Sylvan Elves. Much like Gimli's chant about Durin, Legolas's story of the loss of Nimrodel and the disappearance of her lover, Amroth, foreshadows the increasing sadness that overtakes the story.

The note of sadness continues in "When evening in the Shire was grey," Frodo's mourning song for Gandalf in Lórien. Its ballad stanza, rhyming ABAB / CDCD, presents a more poignant picture of Gandalf than we have heretofore seen, contrasting his deadly sword with his healing hand, his trumpet-voice and burning brand with the image of a bent-backed, weary pilgrim in a battered hat. Such sadness intensifies further in Galadriel's "I sang of leaves" on the last day of the Company's visit. "I sang of leaves" is in rhymed couplets using the extra-long medieval poetic line of fourteen syllables in iambic measure.

Even more moving is her song *Ai! laurië lantar lassi súrinen,* familiarly known as *Namárië (Farewell),* the last the Company knows of her as the river carries them away. *Namárië* is the longest example in the entire book of Quenya, the language Tolkien based on the sound and structure of Finnish as he read it in *Kalevala* when he was nineteen. Like Finnish, Quenya is a quantitative language, meaning that vowels can have a temporally long or short pronunciation. Tolkien described the meter of *Namárië* as iambic in lines of five or six feet, shifting in the second part of the poem to all lines of six feet. The text provides an English, or "Westron," translation of *Namárië* to represent the words as later interpreted by Frodo. Tolkien gives a more literal translation in the Swann song cycle, which in addition to setting the poem to music boasts a calligraphic transcription by Tolkien in Fëanorian Tengwar, the most beautiful of his invented scripts. His translation prints the English word directly beneath its Elven equivalent, showing among other things the differences in word order between the two languages. This also shows Frodo's own translation to have considerably smoothed the syntax.

In his foreword to *The Road Goes Ever On,* Swann wrote that Tolkien had approved most of his musical settings for the poems but not the one for *Namárië,* which Tolkien said did not match the melody he heard in his mind. Instead he hummed for Swann a Gregorian chant. Swann made a note of it and transcribed it as the setting for the poem in his song cycle. Swann's melody is almost identical to the one Tolkien sings in the informal recordings he made on his friend George Sayer's tape recorder in 1952, later issued as a long-playing record and more recently as a CD.

The Two Towers

Of the fourteen poems in Book III, five are sung by Ents: three by Treebeard, one by Bregalad, and one, their marching song, by all Ents. One poem is sung by Aragorn and Legolas in alternating stanzas. One is sung by Aragorn alone. Three have no clearly identifiable source or authorship: the catalogue poem "Learn now the lore of Living Creatures!" the folk verse "Ere iron was found or tree was hewn," and "Tall ships and tall kings." While heretofore the poetry has used end-rhyme, Book III marks the entrance into the story of alliteration, especially in the poetry of Rohan in *Beowulf*ian meter that Tolkien knew well and at which he excelled as a poet. Book IV, the journey of Frodo Sam and Gollum, has only four poems: two by Gollum (and one of those a riddle) and two by Sam.

Book III

- "Through Rohan over fen and field" (Lament for Boromir) (i, 19–20)
- "Gondor! Gondor, between the Mountains and the Sea!" (ii, 25)
- "Learn now the lore of Living Creatures!" (iv, 67)
- "In the willow meads of Tasarinan" (iv, 72)
- "When Spring unfolds the beechen leaf" (iv, 80–81)
- *O Orofarnë, Lassemista, Carnamirië!* (iv, 87)
- "We come, we come with roll of drum" (iv, 88–89; ix, 170)
- "Where now are the Dúnedain, Elessar, Elessar?" (v, 106)
- "Legolas Greenleaf long under tree" (v, 106)
- "Where now the horse and the rider?" (vi, 112)

- "In Dwimordene, in Lórien" (vi, 118)
- "Arise now, arise, Riders of Théoden!" (vi, 122; *RK*, V, v, 112)
- "Ere iron was found or tree was hewn" (viii, 149)
- "Tall ships and tall kings" (xi, 202)

The first poem in *The Two Towers* is the formal yet plaintive Lament for Boromir, "Through Rohan over fen and field," sung in alternating stanzas by Aragorn and Legolas. In its earliest version this was titled, "Lament of Denethor for Boromir," which suggests that Tolkien intended it to be used at a later point in the story, perhaps when the narrative had arrived at Gondor. Over against this is a line in a page of rough workings ascribed to "Trotter" (Aragorn), indicating that Tolkien intended the Lament to be inserted at this point in the narrative. The early version differs only slightly from the published poem, though in *The Treason of Isengard* Christopher Tolkien cites a draft written in short (presumably half) lines and a page of "Alternatives to Song of Boromir" that were not used. The drafts appear to be more metrically regular than the published poem, where the poetic line is long and the meter irregular.

No standard poetic form or category quite fits Aragorn's six-line "Gondor! Gondor, between the Mountains and the Sea!" With some minor adjustment in one or two lines the meter can pass as alexandrine with six iambic feet, but the prosody is not perfect and some syllables have to be fudged to fit. While it is not quite a lament, the poem comes out of Aragorn's expressed longing for his country as he turns from it to follow the captured hobbits. It may be best simply to call it nostalgic and then, as Aragorn does, go on to other things.

Treebeard's meeting with Merry and Pippin in Fangorn Forest is the occasion for "Learn now the lore of Living Creatures!" the first of a number of alliterative poems that appear in the later parts of the book. The old Ent tells the hobbits of the "lists" that he learned when he was young. His comment that "they" may have made new lists suggests the Elves as the source for this mnemonic catalogue of species. The strictness of the meter links it to the oldest Old English poetry and does much to give it the archaic feel that Tolkien was aiming for. Nevertheless, Treebeard subsequently inserts a verse about hobbits, implying that new creatures can be added whenever necessary as long as the meter and alliteration are kept. Such catalogues are a traditional oral method of preserving history. The main Old English model is surely the poem known as *Maxims II,* but other examples abound, from Homer's Catalogue of Ships in the *Iliad* to the list of Arthur's warriors in the

medieval Welsh poem *Pa gur* and the even longer list in the Welsh prose tale *Culhwch and Olwen* to the genealogies of West African griots.

More typically Entish are the long lines of the next four poems, "In the willow-meads of Tasarinan," "When spring unfolds the beechen leaf" (Entwife song), *O Orofarnë, Lassemista, Carnimirië!* and the marching song "We come, we come with roll of drum." "In the willow-meads" is irregular in line length and meter, separated only by short-line interjections at uneven intervals. It is included in the Swann song cycle. The many place-names mentioned in it are a mix of Quenya and Sindarin, with *Tasarinan, Nan-Tasarion, Ambaróna, Tauremorna, Aldalómë,* and *Tauremornalómë* being Quenya and *Ossiriand, Ossir, Neldoreth, Taur-na-neldor, Dorthonion,* and *Orod-na-Thôn* being Sindarin. While Treebeard calls "When spring unfolds" an Elvish song—he notes that it would have been longer in Entish—its fourteen-syllable iambics seem more characteristic of Ents than of Elves. In form and content the song is both a duet and an unresolved argument, with the voices singing together at the end and looking forward to reunion in some distant and better future. Bregalad's elegy for the rowan-trees opens with three Quenya descriptive names for the rowan, *Orofarnë* (mountain-dwelling), *Lassemista* (leaf-gray), and *Carnimirië* (with adornment of red jewels). The marching-song is a chorus of Ent voices supplying the "roll of drum" by beating time on their own trunks. In a sixteen-syllable iambic line, it is the longest poem and presumably, therefore, the most Entish.

Two messages from Galadriel, one to Aragorn and one to Legolas, are given poetic form. "Where now are the Dúnedain, Elessar, Elessar?" is her reminder to Aragorn about the Paths of the Dead. Its six lines rhyme AABBCC but are uneven in meter. "Legolas Greenleaf long under tree," her four-line warning to Legolas about the sea-longing that haunts the Elves, is largely a continuation of the adjacent message to Aragorn. Both poems are irregular in meter but rhyming AABB.

"Where now the horse and the rider?" is Aragorn's Common Speech translation of a long-dead Rohan poet's mourning for his nation's past. The poem is in the medieval Latin tradition of *ubi sunt,* "where are . . . ?" a meditation on loss and the transitory nature of all things, of which the best-known modern example is François Villon's "Where are the snows of yesteryear?" in the Rossetti translation. The Old English poem *The Wanderer* is an early medieval example and, as Christopher Tolkien has pointed out in *The Treason of Isengard,* was probably the model for Tolkien's verse:

*Hwær còm mearh? Hwær còm magu? Hwær còm
    maîum-giefa?*
Hwær còm symbla gesetu? Hwær sindon sele-dreamas?
Éa-là beorht bune! Éa-là byrn-wiga!
Éa-là þèodnes þrymm!
(Where is the horse? Where the warrior? Where has
    gone the treasure-giver?
Where are the feast-benches? Where be the hall-joys?
Alas for the bright drinking-cup! Alas for the mailed
    warrior!
Alas for the lords' power!)

Like *The Wanderer,* Tolkien's poem opens with
"Where," a word that occurs twice in the first line
and is repeated as the opening in the following three.
Tolkien also gives a nod here, in mood if not in
precise content, to lines 2,247–66 in the second half
of *Beowulf,* a discrete segment known as "The Lay of
the Last Survivor." A similar meditation on loss, it
begins *Heald þù nù, hrùse, nù hæleð no mostan, / eorla
æhte!* (Hold thou now earth, now heroes may not, /
the possession of princes) and mourns many of the
same losses as does Tolkien's poem—the helmet, the
war coat, the harp.

The ten-line iambic tetrameter "In Dwimordene, in
Lórien" has no perceivable function in the story and,
other than halting the belligerent Gimli from starting
a fight with Gríma Wormtongue, seems to be merely
an interruption in the exchanges between Gandalf
and Théoden's treacherous counselor. No source is
identified for what is essentially a praise poem for
Galadriel, Gandalf's counterattack against Wormtongue's insulting words about her.

The entry of the Riders of Rohan into the story
gave Tolkien the opportunity to work in a mode with
which he was both familiar and comfortable, the
alliterative, stressed Old English meter of *Beowulf.*
The first of seven poems in the Old English meter
appears in Book III, with the rest in Book V to be
discussed in turn. The language, customs, and poetic
tradition of Rohan reflect clearly the Old English
literature and culture from which they were derived.
Théoden's battle cry, "Arise now, arise, Riders of
Théoden!" follows closely the Old English balanced
half-lines, and the subject matter could have come
straight out of the *Fight at Finnsburg* or any one of
a number of other Old English heroic poems. In this
poem and those like it that come later, Tolkien shows
himself to be a poet of extraordinary skill and power
in an archaic poetic mode, writing modern English in
the Old English meter and style.

Metrically, Old English poetry consists of short
lines containing two discrete but related word groups
or phrases of approximately equal weight with a built-
in pause between them, with at least one stress in each

half-line and with agreement of sound (whether vowel
or consonant) in the stressed syllables. Analysis of
Théoden's short verse will serve as a guide for the
other poems in this mode. In the first line the stress
falls: "A*rise* now a*rise,* *Ri*ders of Théoden!" The second line has a slightly different rhythm: two stresses
in a row, "*Dire deeds* awake," and another stress
directly after the break, "*dark* is it eastward." The
third line has one stress in each half line: "Let *horse*
be bridled, *horn* be sounded!"

As with "In Dwimordene, in Lórien," there is no
apparent source for "Ere iron was found." Gandalf
chants it like folklore and Théoden calls it a riddle,
but if it is one, the clues are sparse to nonexistent. The
poem seems like a fragment, a mere four lines in
octosyllabic rhymed couplets. Its function seems
chiefly to increase immeasurably the ancientness of
the Ents and to attest to their existence long before
the entry into the world of technology, greed, and lust
for dominance.

The last poem in Book III, "Tall ships and tall
kings," is almost as short and nearly as allusive.
Gandalf calls it one of the Rhymes of Lore and
remarks that Hobbits have probably forgotten even
those they knew. Pippin's response is that hobbits
have their own such lore, suggesting that such rhymes
were in general possession. The poem has cadence but
no regular meter and mainly provokes Pippin's curiosity, giving Gandalf the opportunity to explain and
give the history of the *palantíri.*

Book IV

- "The cold hard lands" (ii, 227)
- "Alive without breath" (ii, 228)
- "Grey as a mouse" (iii, 254–55)
- *A Elbereth Gilthoniel* (x, 339)

It should come as no surprise to readers of *The Hobbit*
that of the four poems in Book IV two are by Gollum.
His facility with poetry is demonstrated in the earlier
book by the conceptually complex rhyming braintea-
sers he poses in his Riddle Game with Bilbo. Gollum's
complaint, "The cold hard lands," with its monosyllabic words, primitive grammar, and AAB rhyme,
has the look and sound of a nursery rhyme and underscores his psychological split—one personality childish and simple and the other immeasurably old and
cunning. It is the second personality that generates
his next, more metaphorically and prosodically complex poem. "Alive without breath" is the extension
of a riddle Gollum asks in *The Hobbit* and a surprisingly sophisticated evocation of a fish. The last

three lines link to and continue the last line of the previous poem.

Sam's Oliphaunt poem, "Grey as a mouse," is a riddle that solves its own puzzle in the last two lines. The verse is almost as monosyllabic as Gollum's complaint; there are only five two-syllable words and one three-syllable word in twenty-two lines, and the three-syllable word is the answer to the riddle. The poem is to be read as traditional, described by Sam as a rhyme they have in the Shire. It is a simplified version of "Iumbo, or ye Kinde of ye Oliphaunt," a poem written by Tolkien some time in the 1920s and published in the *Stapledon Magazine* of Exeter College for June 1927. *Oliphaunt* appeared as poem no. 10 in *The Adventures of Tom Bombadil* and in the same year (1962) was published by Calico Books as a separate small volume for children with illustrations by Hank Hinton.

A Elbereth Gilthoniel, which seems to begin as a repeat of the Elven song at Rivendell in *The Fellowship of the Ring,* diverges from it in several respects. Although it is the same in style and meter, after the first line the words are quite different. Moreover, the Elven song is a hymn, and Sam's shorter verse was described by Tolkien as an "invocation." The language is Sindarin, and the English translation given by Tolkien in *Letters* (278) makes it clear that Sam is praying to Elbereth for help.

The Return of the King

Of the seventeen poems in *The Return of the King,* five are songs of the Rohirrim, the heroic *Beowulf*ian culture of Rohan. All five are in Book V, where they comprise just over half the total of nine. Of the others, one is a prophecy, one that is an epitaph, one a folk poem, and one that is Legolas's chant for Lebennin. The eight poems in Book VI include four that are reprises of verses in Book I, one that is sung by Sam at the Tower of Cirith Ungol, one that is sung by Legolas of his sea-longing, and one that is a celebration.

Book V

- "Over the land there lies a long shadow" (ii, 54)
- "From dark Dunharrow in the dim morning" (iii, 76–77)
- "Arise, arise, Riders of Théoden!" (v, 112)
- "Mourn not overmuch! Mighty was the fallen" (vi, 119)
- "Faithful servant yet master's bane" (vi, 120)
- "Out of doubt, out of dark to the day's rising" (vi, 122)

- "We heard of the horns in the hills ringing" (vi, 124–25)
- "When the black breath blows" (viii, 141)
- "Silver flow the streams from Celos to Erui" (ix, 151)

"Over the land there lies a long shadow," is the ancient prophecy of Malbeth the Seer about the Paths of the Dead that Aragorn quotes to Legolas and Gimli at the Hornburg. Having neither rhyme nor meter, without alliteration, and with lines of irregular length, it hardly seems a poem. The term "free verse" best describes the form, making it qualify as the least traditional and most "modern" of Tolkien's poems.

With "From dark Dunharrow in the dim morning" Tolkien returns to the poetic tradition in which he worked best, the balanced, alliterative half-line of *Beowulf.* The surrounding text makes clear that this account of the Ride of the Rohirrim is sung much later than the action it describes, as if Tolkien were quoting the words of a future poet looking back at a past that is the story's present. This double perspective of time is a technique he learned from the *Beowulf*-poet, who occasionally looks beyond the time of his poem to events in its future, which is still his past, thus creating an illusion of a past with an even deeper, often darker past behind it. "Doom drove them on. Darkness took them . . . so the songs tell us."

"Arise, arise, Riders of Théoden!" is a reprise and extension of the king's earlier battle cry in *The Two Towers.* Though just as abrupt, it is fuller and fiercer than its earlier version, replacing "dire" deeds with "fell" deeds, eastward darkness with fire and slaughter, and horse and horn with spear and shield. Since Théoden is riding to his final battle and very likely to his death, the phrases "sword-day" and "red day, ere the sun rises" seem intended to recall similar phrases in stanza 45 of the Old Icelandic *Völuspá.* This ninth-century poem describes the onset of *Ragnarøk,* the Doom of the Gods, as *skeggjöld, skálmöld, vindöld, vargöld, áir veröld steypiz* (axe-age, sword-age, wind-age, wolf-age, ere the world falls).

Éomer's terse battlefield elegy for the fallen Théoden, "Mourn not overmuch!" is a brilliant and moving example of compression and expression. In three lines, two of them alliterating on the same mournful *m* sound, Éomer combines grief, expediency, and good counsel, reminding the weeping knights of the household that Théoden died in a manner that matched his might and that the formalities when "women" shall weep must be deferred while the battle summons them.

The epitaph for Théoden's horse, "Faithful servant yet master's bane," wraps up the paradox of

Snowmane in a two wry lines, four noun phrases that capture his dual role as steed and killer and cite both his genealogy and his speed.

The word Tolkien uses for Éomer's battle quatrain, "Out of doubt, out of dark to the day's rising," is *staves,* a deliberately archaic word for lines of verse. Yet it captures the medieval spirit—fey, battle-crazy, almost berserk—that has possessed Éomer since Théoden died and that returns in force as the black sails come up the river. Éomer laughs as he looks defeat in the face, ready for wrath and ruin and a "red nightfall" to match the day's rising.

Like "From dark Dunharrow," the Rohan maker's song of the Mounds of Mundburg takes a multiple view of time, a backward look from the story's future (still in the narrative past) at a deeper past that is the story's present. The first line, "We heard of the horns in the hills ringing" echoes the opening of *Beowulf,* "Lo! We have heard of the glory of the Spear-Danes." Both evidence an oral culture in which the poet or storyteller relates what has been heard from others. While in form it is a prime example of Tolkien's skill at Old English meter, in content it evokes an early and much longer heroic elegy, the sixth-century Welsh poem *Y Gododdin,* a grim celebration of three hundred warriors and their deaths in an otherwise forgotten battle: "Warriors went to Catraeth . . . after the cry of jubilation there was silence. . . . The certain meeting with death came to them." Each man is listed by name and given a verse describing his deeds. Tolkien's poem likewise is a lamentation for fallen warriors and a catalogue of their names. Starting with Théoden, each one is named and his country given: "Long now they sleep / under grass in Gondor."

The six-line "When the black breath blows" about *athelas* is clearly folklore, dismissed as "doggerel" by the herb-master of Minas Tirith, who scorns it as something "garbled in the memory of old wives." In addition to its value in describing and prescribing the herb, the poem in the context of the herb-master's disparagement makes a point of real importance to Tolkien, the value of old songs and tales as repositories of forgotten wisdom. Gondor's herb-master may be compared to *The Hobbit*'s Men of Lake-town, who dismiss legends and songs about dragons and Dwarves until Thorin Oakenshield arrives out of ancient history and announces his return.

Legolas's unrhymed, unmetered "Silver flow the streams" is notable chiefly for its contrast with his description of the green fields of Lebennin as dark gray wastes, the flowers and tall grass trampled by Aragorn's army. His repetition of the phrase "wind from the sea" marks the fulfillment of Galadriel's warning about the sea-longing of the Elves.

Book VI

- "In western lands beneath the sun" (i, 185)
- "Long live the Halflings!" (iv, 231)
- "To the Sea, to the Sea! The white gulls are crying" (iv, 234–35)
- "Sing now, ye people of the Tower of Anor" (v, 241)
- "Out of doubt, out of dark" (vi, 254–55)
- "The Road goes ever on" (vi, 266)
- "Still round the corner" ("Upon the hearth the fire is red") (ix, 308)
- *A! Elbereth Gilthoniel!* (ix, 308)

Of the eight poems in Book VI, the final four, "Out of doubt, out of dark," "The Road goes ever on," "Still round the corner," and *A! Elbereth Gilthoniel!* are reprises with some variation of earlier songs, each made more moving by its conscious evocation of the earlier appearance. Sam's defiant "In western lands beneath the sun" is sung to an "old childish" tune from the Shire. It is in ballad stanza iambic tetrameter, with the fourth, eighth, twelfth, and sixteenth trimeter lines a foot short and the rhyme scheme ABAB / CDCD. It is no accident that song pulls Sam out of his grief and defeat. The function of song throughout the story has been both to express moods and to alter them.

There is no one singer for "Long live the Halflings!" which is more paean than poem, a spontaneous outpouring of praise for the deeds of the Hobbits. Its irregular lines say roughly the same things in multiple voices and three different languages—Common Speech, Quenya, and Sindarin. Christopher Tolkien notes in *Sauron Defeated* that in all preliminary texts Tolkien had included lines in the Old English of the Riders of Rohan. No reason is given for the excision. It seems odd that, having gone to the trouble of creating so faithfully *Beowulf*ian a culture and poetic tradition, Tolkien should have chosen to omit it from what his letter to Milton Waldman called the final eucatastrophe (Hammond and Scull 2005).

Legolas's "To the Sea, to the Sea!" with its lines about days ending and years failing, echoes Galadriel's allusions in Lórien to the fate of the Elves, to their westward movements and their long return to Valinor. The poem thus connects the book's closing with its opening, linking back to Sam's early remarks about Elves sailing West and to the first appearance of Gildor's folk in the Woody End. What unity the poem has comes from this theme and the feminine end-rhymes that pair the couplets, since the poem's lines are of uneven length and the meter is somewhat irregular.

"Sing now, ye people of the Tower of Anor" is the only poem in the book sung by one of Tolkien's beloved eagles—indeed the only one sung by any animal. In both *The Hobbit* and *The Lord of the Rings* the eagles have acted as rescuers, the closest to *deus ex machina* that Tolkien ever comes. Since this one brings news from the Lords of the West his role is clear. Eagles have spoken before (the only animals in the book to do so except the aberrant fox at the beginning of *The Fellowship of the Ring*), but they have never been known to sing, and this eagle's appearance in the role of an announcing angel is one of the few moments in the book that strains credibility. The poem itself, as Tom Shippey points out in *The Road to Middle-earth,* is modeled stylistically on the Bible and particularly the Psalms, and it contains the most archaic language of any of the poems.

The reprise of Éomer's "Out of doubt, out of dark," is among the most moving recurrences in the book. Attributed now to the king's minstrel Gléowine ("Glee-friend" or "Music-friend," but *gléo* can mean both the art of music and the joy it brings), the verse is sung by Théoden's Riders as they circle his burial mound. The scene is an explicit borrowing from the end of *Beowulf,* where Beowulf's thanes ride around the barrow they have built for the dead king on the headland. As they ride, they sing a dirge for their lord that Tolkien found to be among the most moving poems ever written. As Tolkien describes his own poem, the Riders' song for Théoden is long and stirring and full of Rohan's history. Only the ending is given in the text, a variation on Éomer's battlefield elegy that becomes even more moving with its gesture toward this earlier moment.

Fittingly, that heralds the end of the grand, heroic aspects of the book, which now turns to hobbit ordinariness and the doings of little people. The next reprise, Bilbo's variation on "The Road goes ever on and on," replaces "eager feet" with "weary feet" and evokes hobbit longing for rest after adventure and comfort after stress. In Frodo's reprise of the walking song from his first journey out from Hobbiton, the narrative comments that the words are not quite the same. Among other changes, the earlier version's carefree "pass them by" is replaced with the regretful "have passed them by," but the next lines also look ahead to when the singer will take the hidden paths "West of the Moon, East of the Sun." With the reprise of "*A! Elbereth Gilthoniel!*" at the meeting of Frodo and Sam with Gildor, and their reunion with Galadriel, Elrond, and Bilbo in the Woody End, the book has come full circle. Frodo will follow the hidden paths, and the story and the poems will have no more to say.

VERLYN FLIEGER

Further Reading

Aneirin. *Y Gododdin.* Edited and translated by A.O.H. Jarman. Llandysul, Dyfed: Gomer Press, 1988.

Chickering, Howell D., trans. *Beowulf.* Dual language edition. New York: Doubleday, 1977.

Hammond, Wayne G., and Christina Scull, eds. *The Lord of the Rings: A Reader's Companion.* Boston, MA: Houghton Mifflin, 2005.

Hostetter, Carl F. "Ugluk to the Dung-pit." *Vinyar Tengwar* 26 (November 1992).

Pope, John C., ed. *Seven Old English Poems.* Indianapolis, IN: Bobbs-Merrill, 1966.

Russom, Geoffrey. "Tolkien's Versecraft in *The Hobbit* and *The Lord of the Rings.*" In *J.R.R. Tolkien and his Literary Resonances,* edited by George Clark and Daniel Timmons. Westport, CT: Greenwood, 2000.

Shippey, Tom. *The Road to Middle-earth.* 2nd ed. London: Grafton, 1992.

Tolkien, J.R.R. "Prefatory Remarks on Prose Translation of *Beowulf.*" In *"Beowulf" and the Finnesburg Fragment: A Translation into Modern English Prose,* translated by John R. Clark Hall and revised by Charles L. Wrenn. London: George Allen & Unwin, 1940.

———. *The Road Goes Ever On: A Song Cycle.* Poems by J.R.R. Tolkien. Music by Donald Swann. Boston, MA: Houghton Mifflin, 1967.

Yates, Jessica. "The Source of *The Lay of Aotrou and Itroun.*" In *Leaves from the Tree: J.R.R. Tolkien's Shorter Fiction.* 4th Tolkien Society Workshop. London: The Tolkien Society, 1991.

See also **Alliterative Verse by Tolkien; Languages, Invented by Tolkien; Poems by Tolkien:** *Adventures of Tom Bombadil*; **Poems by Tolkien:** *Hobbit, The;* **Poems by Tolkien:** *The History of Middle-earth*; **Poems by Tolkien: Uncollected; Poems by Tolkien in Other Languages**

POEMS BY TOLKIEN: UNCOLLECTED

Tolkien began to write poetry before he embarked on prose fiction, and he kept up the practice all his life. Most of the poems published separately during the 1920s and 1930s were incorporated into *The Lord of the Rings,* reprinted (often much revised) in *The Adventures of Tom Bombadil,* or reprinted (sometimes with variant versions) in successive volumes of *The History of Middle-earth;* these are treated in those entries. Others are discussed under the headings of "Alliterative Verse by Tolkien" or "Poems by Tolkien in Other Languages." A small body of poetry remains, mostly from Tolkien's earlier years.

Tolkien's first poem to be published was *The Battle of the Eastern Field* in the *King Edward's School Chronicle* (1911). In mock-heroic language it describes a house rugby match, played on the school playing-fields on Eastern Road, a few miles from the old school in the city center but close to its present site. The stylistic model is Lord Macaulay's *Lays of Ancient Rome*

(1842). In these Macaulay feigned to recreate the old oral ballads that he thought must have been the sources for later, literate Roman historians. The relationship between the "lays" and the historians is similar to the one Tolkien feigns as the relationship between his later *Lays of Beleriand* and the various versions of the "Silmarillion": Tolkien was interested already in "lost tales" and lost ballads.

Most of his poems in the next few years may be classified as landscapes, cityscapes, or "fairy poems." A six-line fragment published in the *Stapledon Magazine* for 1913, and beginning "From the many-willow'd margin," was originally titled *From Iffley* and consisted of two stanzas rather than one, but the magazine's editor lost both title and second stanza. The poem describes Oxford but could well read as a description of Gondor. Something similar might be said of *City of the Gods,* published in *Microcosm* and reprinted as *Kôr* (*Lost Tales I,* 136): it describes the deserted Elvish city of Kôr but relates also to the poem *Kortirion among the Trees* (*Lost Tales I,* 33–44), where Kortirion is based on Warwick. At this period of his life—both poems were written or begun in 1915—Tolkien was still attempting to identify England with fairyland.

His best-known poem from this period is *Goblin Feet,* published in *Oxford Poetry 1915,* reprinted in several later anthologies, and again in *The Annotated Hobbit* (IV, 113). Part of a manuscript version was printed in Humphrey Carpenter's 1977 biography, regrettably corrupted in the 1987 revision. Tolkien later expressed fervent dislike of the poem: it is in the Victorian tradition of fairy tininess and delicacy that he was soon to abjure. The same is true of *An Evening in Tavrobel,* published in *Leeds University Verse 1914–1924.* It describes tiny fairies dancing and drinking on a late spring day and then under moonlight. Characteristically, Tolkien identified the elvish town of Tavrobel with the English village of Great Haywood, where he spent his convalescence in 1917. In the same publication *The Lonely Isle* is a description and leavetaking of England, written when Tolkien crossed the Channel to the war in France in 1916; in different manuscripts, however, the poem is titled both *Tol Eressëa,* the land of the Elves, and *Seo Unwemmede Ieg,* Old English for "the unstained isle." There are connections between the last six poems mentioned, all dating from 1913 to 1917, and the descriptive poems *The Happy Mariners,* written in July 1915 and printed in 1920 and 1923 (see also *Lost Tales II,* 273–76), and *The Nameless Land,* printed in 1927 (see also *Lost Road,* 98–104).

Tolkien returned to comic poetry with two poems published together in the *Stapledon Magazine* under the title "Adventures in Unnatural History and Medieval Metres, being the Freaks of Fisiologus: (i) *Fastitocalon,* (ii) *Iumbo, or ye Kinde of ye Oliphaunt.*" The poems imitate medieval bestiaries, especially the poems *The Panther* and *The Whale* in the Old English collection *The Exeter Book.* Both Tolkien's poems and the Old English ones tell fantastic tales of real animals and draw morals from them, the Old English poems in all gravity but Tolkien jokingly. The whale "Fastitocalon," writes Tolkien, is a deceiver: as he floats on the sea, unwary people take him for an island, land, dance, and picnic. Then he submerges and they perish. The moral is to avoid dancing, jazz, and excess. The elephant, by contrast, betrays himself. His fault is that he avoids alcohol, drinks tea, but takes the drug mandragora, which allows hunters to trap him. The moral is that one should drink wine and avoid drugs. There is some overlap between the 1927 version of *Fastitocalon* and the much shorter poem of the same title printed in *The Adventures of Tom Bombadil,* but *Iumbo,* apart from its topic, is entirely different from Sam Gamgee's rhyme in *The Two Towers,* printed as *Oliphaunt* in *Adventures.*

Tolkien continued his theme of the unpleasantness of modern pleasures in a set of six poems called *Tales and Songs of Bimble Bay,* probably written in 1928, of which four have now been published. *Progress in Bimble Town* appeared in the *Oxford Magazine.* Bimble Town is said to be based on Filey, a seaside resort in East Yorkshire. Tolkien pictures it as a place disfigured by shops, trippers, and litter: the poem ends with an ironic advertising slogan. In *The Dragon's Visit,* a dragon visits Bimble. Initially friendly, he is provoked by the inhabitants and their fire-engine, eats several, and flies away, lamenting modern degeneracy. The poem was reprinted in two later anthologies, in 1965 and in 1969, with a different ending in which Miss Biggins regretfully stabs the dragon to the heart. A third poem in this group, initially titled *The Bumpus,* appeared in revised form as *Perry-the-Winkle* in *Adventures.* A fourth, *Glip,* describes a Gollum-like creature living in the rocks in Bimble Bay. It was first printed in *The Annotated Hobbit* (V, 119); *Progress* and *Visit* appear in the same volume, with the revised ending of the latter, on pp. 254 and 309–12, respectively.

Also comic in tone are six poems from the collection *Songs for the Philologists,* originally made by Tolkien and his friend and successor E.V. Gordon in Leeds between 1921 and 1926 but printed by students at University College, London, some ten years later. (Tolkien also contributed to the collection six poems in Old English, and one on Gothic, for which see the entry on "Poems by Tolkien in Other Languages.") Of the English poems, one appeared in revised form as Sam's rhyme of the Troll in *The Fellowship of the Ring,* reprinted in *Adventures.* The other five have not been reprinted. *From One to Five* is a counting song: allusions to Leeds were altered in the printed version so that "Loidis" became "London," "maids of Roundhay" (a Leeds suburb) became "Middlesex maidens," and so on. *I Sat Upon a Bench* is a drinking song. *Natura Apis,* which means "the nature of the bee," is a poem in praise of the industrious, cleanly, and war-like bee. In his copy, Tolkien corrected the printed subtitle to "Morali[tas] Ricardi Eremite," "the Moral of Richard the Hermit." The poem indeed has a moral, for in praising the bee Tolkien also alludes to the "B-scheme" of the Leeds English School, which specialized in language and philology, unlike the "A-scheme," which emphasized literary criticism. The sign of the B-scheme was the Anglo-Saxon B-rune, which stands also for *beorc,* the birch tree. Tolkien wrote a runic **B** at the top of the two "birch-poems" in his copy of this collection (see "Poems by Tolkien in Other Languages"), and the last stanza of *Natura Apis,* omitted from the London printed version but again written in by Tolkien, connects birch and bee as implied totems or models for the philologists. The poem "Lit. and Lang.," listed on the contents page as *Two Little Schemes,* develops this theme more aggressively, praising the philological scheme and denigrating the idle and doomed critics. *Frenchmen Froth* extends the aggression by praising England, the English language, and those who study the language at the expense of those who merely follow educational trends. The whole collection, and especially Tolkien's contributions, has a strong element of "office politics," in which, it has to be said, Tolkien's predictions were mostly wrong: his side almost always lost the campus wars.

Much graver in tone is Tolkien's longest uncollected poem, *The Lay of Aotrou and Itroun,* published in the *Welsh Review.* The word "lay" in the title here has different connotations from those in *Lays of Ancient Rome* or *The Lays of Beleriand.* Rather than "lost ballad," it indicates connection with the *Lais* of Marie de France, a collection of poems written in the twelfth century in Norman French. Marie declares that her poems derive from Breton tradition, and eight Middle English "Breton lays" also survive, one of them translated in full by Tolkien, *Sir Orfeo.* Marie's *lais,* and several of the Middle English ones, are tales of love and the supernatural, containing fairy mistresses and hunters, werewolves and enchanted deer, magic herbs and potions. Most of them have happy endings, but Tolkien's does not. Tolkien's immediate source has been shown by Jessica Yates (1991) to have been the Breton ballad allegedly collected in the nineteenth century by the French

scholar Hersart de la Villemarqué—though he has a bad reputation for falsifying his sources—and published as *Aotrou Nann Hag Ar Gorrigan* or *Lord Nann and the Gorrigan* in his collection *Barsaz-Breis: chants populaires de la Bretagne.* Villemarqué's work was translated into English by Tom Taylor (1865), and the "Lord Nann" ballad was also translated by Thomas Keightley in his *Fairy Mythology* (third edition, 1878), but Tolkien owned the 1846 edition of the original. The names *Aotrou* and *Itroun* mean "lord" and "lady," and both are used with that sense in the Villemarqué poem. In Tolkien's version—more than five hundred lines long as published, probably much revised from an original version of 1930—Aotrou and Itroun are childless. Aotrou meets a Corrigan, a witch or fairy, in the forest, who offers him a fertility potion. He gives this to Itroun, and she conceives and bears twins. She then asks for water from the forest; Aotrou returns to it, led by a white doe, and encounters the Corrigan again, who tells him the price of the potion is that he should become her lover. He refuses, is cursed, and dies, and Itroun dies also, of grief. The moral of the poem is one of resignation: take what God sends, do not use or invoke other powers. The main addition Tolkien has made to the story of the Villemarqué ballad is the motif of the fertility potion, which as Yates notes makes Aotrou—but not Itroun—a culpable party.

Another late, serious, and substantial poem is *Imram,* published in the December 3, 1955, edition of *Time and Tide.* It is reprinted in *Sauron Defeated* (296–99), and there is an earlier version of it in "The Notion Club Papers" (*Sauron,* 261–64). The poem tells the story of the voyage into the Far West of St Brendan the Navigator, extant in several medieval texts; it returns to the theme of early poems such as *The Happy Mariners, The Nameless Land,* and *Looney* (for the latter see the entry under *Adventures of Tom Bombadil* [Collection]). Its tone is, however, again sad and resigned.

Finally, *Once Upon a Time* was printed in *Winter's Tales for Children* (1965) and reanthologized in 1969. It brings back Goldberry and Tom Bombadil; Tom meets the mysterious "lintips." And *Bilbo's Last Song* continues the elegiac mood of Tolkien's later years. It is feigned to be Bilbo's farewell as he sails into the West, unlike St. Brendan, never to return, and was originally released as a poster in 1974.

TOM SHIPPEY

Further Reading

Hammond, Wayne G., with the assistance of Douglas A. Anderson. *J.R.R. Tolkien: A Descriptive Bibliography.* Winchester, UK: St Paul's Bibliographies; New Castle, DE: Oak Knoll Books, 1993.

Shippey, Tom. *J.R.R. Tolkien: Author of the Century*, 233–36, 293–94. Boston, MA: Houghton Mifflin, 2000.

Tolkien, J.R.R. "Adventures in Unnatural History and Medieval Metres, being the Freaks of Fisiologus: (i) *Fastitocalon*, (ii) *Iumbo, or ye Kinde of ye Oliphaunt.*" *Stapledon Magazine* no. 40 (June 1927).

———. "The Battle of the Eastern Field." *King Edward's School Chronicle* no. 188 (July 1911).

———. "City of the Gods." *Microcosm* 8, no. 1 (1923).

———. "The Dragon's Visit." *Oxford Magazine* 55, no. 11 (February 4, 1937).

———. "The Lay of Aotrou and Itroun." *Welsh Review* 4, no. 4 (December 1945).

———. "Progress in Bimble Town." *Oxford Magazine* 50, no. 1 (October 15, 1931).

Yates, Jessica. "Macaulay and 'The Battle of the Eastern Field.'" *Mallorn* 13 (1979): 3–5.

———. "The Source of *The Lay of Aotrou and Itroun*." In *Leaves from the Tree: J.R.R. Tolkien's Shorter Fiction*, 63–71. London: Tolkien Society, 1991.

See also **Alliterative Verse by Tolkien; Cruces in Medieval Literature; Poems by Tolkien in Other Languages; Rhyme Schemes and Meter**

POLAND: RECEPTION OF TOLKIEN

The Hobbit was the first book by Tolkien translated into Polish. It was published in 1960, more than twenty years after the first English edition. In the next three years (1961–63) *The Lord of the Rings* was published; after Dutch and Swedish, it was the third translation of the book in the world, and it was the first in the communist block. Both *The Hobbit* and *The Lord of the Rings* were translated at that time by Maria Skibniewska. (In a letter written in 1959, Tolkien mentions Skibniewska's questions concerning the translation of the proper names of people and places.) Her translation is quite faithful to the original and successfully renders Tolkien's style and language, though it contains some mistakes and omissions. Some of them were due to the censorship, and others were the translator's choice: for example, she decided to omit Appendices D and E, explaining that the calendars and alphabets would be quite incomprehensible to the Polish reader. In 1981 a slightly revised edition was reissued, and only in 1996 were major changes introduced; for example, passages and appendices omitted in previous editions were inserted and some proper names were changed to be more faithful to the original.

Published in 1996–97 was a new translation of *The Lord of the Rings* by Jerzy Łoziński. He replaced the Westron proper names with their Polish equivalents, often awkwardly; for example, Sam Gamgee became Sam *Gaduła* (literally, "windbag"). There were also some mistakes, mainly in the appendices. His translation was heavily criticised by most Polish Tolkienists for openly neglecting Tolkien's instructions and intentions.

A new translation of *The Lord of the Rings* appeared in 2001, this time made by several translators: Maria and Cezary Frąc, Aleksandra Januszewska, and Aleksandra Jagiełowicz.

Meanwhile, new translations of *The Hobbit* were published, by Paulina Braiter (1997) and Andrzej Polkowski (2002). In the 1980s and 1990s other of Tolkien's books appeared in Polish from different translators: *The Silmarillion* (1985), *Unfinished Tales* (1994), *The Book of Lost Tales: Parts I and II* (1995–96), and minor works (*Tree and Leaf, Farmer Giles,* etc.) along with Tolkien's *Letters* and *The Monsters and the Critics* (both in 2000). Only *The History of Middle-earth* has not yet been translated into Polish. Humphrey Carpenter's biography and several critical works, by Tom Shippey, L. Carter, and Paul Harold Kocher, have also been published in Polish.

After the publication of *The Lord of the Rings,* an interest in Tolkien's fiction emerged among Polish literary and scholarly circles. In the 1980s influential articles were written by Andrzej Zgorzelski, A. Wicher, and Adam Ziółkowski, some of them reissued abroad. In the following years several books on Tolkien were published by Polish scholars, among them Michał Błażejewski's first Polish biography of Tolkien: *J.R.R. Tolkien: Powiernik pieśni (The Songbearer)* (1993). The subjects treated by the Polish scholars are quite diverse: they range from literary criticism (Christopher Garbowski, Jakub Lichański), to theology (Tadeusz Olszański), to anthropology and history of religion (Andrzej Szyjewski). Tolkien's work has also been the subject of study at Polish universities, mainly in Warsaw, Cracow, Gdańsk, and Wrocław.

Among many groups of fans in Poland the largest and most active is the Polish Tolkien Society (a section of the Silesian Science-Fiction Club), started by Andrzej Kowalski in 1985. Its most active members include Agnieszka Sylwanowicz (translator of Tolkien's *Letters*), Ryszard Derdziński (creator of a Web site devoted to Elvish languages), and Arkadiusz Kubala (author of *Przewodnik po nazwach miejscowych Śródziemia [The Guide to Middle-earth Place Names]*). The Society consists of dozens of subscribed members, is present on the Web, and has published several fanzines, like *Gwaihir* and *Simbelmynë*. The Silesian Science-Fiction Club publishes also *Aiglos,* a Tolkienist semiannual almanac.

There are other, more or less formal, Tolkienist organisations in Poland. Their activities include conventions and festivals, like TolkFolk or ARDA meetings. Many of those groups exist over the Internet where hundreds of Web sites devoted to Tolkien can be found, especially after the boom of Peter Jackson's films. The oldest Polish Tolkienian Web site was created by Gwidon Naskrent in 1996.

Tolkien's fiction has inspired several talented Polish illustrators, including K.K. Chmiel, M. Wygnański, A. Grzechnik, and K. Stopa-Olszańska. Their works are published in fanzines and on Tolkien-related Web sites.

MARCIN MORAWSKI

Further Reading

Błażejewski, Michał. *J.R.R. Tolkien. Powiernik Pieśni* (J.R.R. Tolkien. The Song-bearer). Gdańsk: Phantom Press, 1993.

Dąbkowska, Anna. "Polish Tolkien Fandom." *Aiglos* Special issue (Summer 2005): 25–31.

Garbowski, Christopher. *Recovery and Transcendence for the Contemporary Mythmaker: The Spiritual Dimension in the Works of J.R.R. Tolkien.* Lublin: Wydawnictwo Uniwersytetu M. Curie-Skłodowskiej, 2000.

Kubala, Arkadiusz. *Przewodnik po nazwach miejscowych Śródziemia* (The Guide to Middle-earth Place Names). Warszawa: Amber, 2003.

Lichański, Jakub Z. Bibliography of Polish reception of Tolkien http://www.bilp.uw.edu.pl/pliki/tol.htm.

———, ed. *J.R.R. Tolkien: Recepcja polska* (J.R.R. Tolkien: Polish Reception). Warszawa: Wydawnictwa Uniwersytetu Warszawskiego, 1996.

———. *Opowiadania o . . . krawędzi epok i czasów J.R.R. Tolkiena* (Stories About . . . the Edges of Epochs and J.R.R. Tolkien's Times). Warszawa: Wydawnictwo DiG, 2003.

Niezapominka. Web site of the Polish Tolkien Society (in Polish). http://home.agh.edu.pl/~evermind.

Olszański, Tadeusz A. *Zarys teologii Śródziemia i inne szkice tolkienowskie* (The Theology of Middle-earth and Other Tolkienistic Essays). Gdańsk: Gdański Klub Fantastyki, 2000.

———. "The Polish History of *The Lord of the Rings:* Three Translations, Many Editions." In *Aiglos* Special issue (Summer 2005): 4–24.

Szyjewski, Andrzej. *Od Valinoru do Mordoru: Świat mitu a religia w dziele Tolkiena* (From Valinor to Mordor: The World of Myth and Religion in Tolkien's Works). Kraków: Wydawnictwo M, 2004.

Wicher, A. "The Artificial Mythology of *The Silmarillion* by J.R.R. Tolkien." *Kwartalnik Neofilologiczny* 3/4 (1981): 399–405.

Zgorzelski, Andrzej. "Time Setting in J.R.R. Tolkien's *The Lord of the Rings.*" *Zagadnienia Rodzajów Literackich* 2, no. 25 (1971): 91–100.

Ziółkowski, Adam. "Tolkien oder das rehabilitierte Märchen." *Inklings* 3 (1985): 141–47.

POLITICS

Tolkien wrote in November 1943 that "my political opinions lean more and more towards Anarchy (philosophically understood, meaning abolition of control not whiskered men with bombs)—or to 'unconstitutional' Monarchy" (*Letters*, 63–64).

There is no indication that he ever departed much from this, and the good societies in his fiction tend to be either minimally governed, like the Shire and Bree, or benevolent monarchies, like Gondor, Rohan, and the Elvish and Dwarvish kingdoms (the Shire and Bree are isolated remnants of the old North Kingdom of Arnor).

He went on in the same letter to express himself more forcibly: "I would arrest anybody who uses the word State (in any sense other than the inanimate realm of England and its inhabitants, a thing that has neither power, rights or mind) and after a chance of recantation, execute them if they remained obstinate!"

Tolkien at times used the word "politics" in the sense of power politics, as distinct from competing ideologies or value systems. Thus he wrote that it seemed to him wrong to describe Frodo's quest as having a "political" motive, although part of its intended result was the overthrow of an evil empire. He wrote: "It seems clear to me that Frodo's duty was humane, not political. He naturally thought first of the Shire, since his roots were there, but the quest had as its objective not the preserving of this or that polity, such as the half-republic half-aristocracy of the Shire, but the liberation from an evil tyranny of all the 'humane.' . . . Denethor *was* tainted with mere politics . . . it had become for him a prime motive to preserve the polity of Gondor, as it was, against another potentate, who had made himself stronger and was to be feared and opposed for that reason rather than because he was ruthless and wicked" (*Letters*, 240–41).

Political intrigue concerned with power rather than morality, and consequent in-fighting and civil war, had, at the time of the War of the Ring, desperately weakened Gondor and the West, as it previously helped destroy the Elf-realms in *The Silmarillion* (and as it helped destroy the Roman Empire and innumerable other real-world polities). Meanwhile, the "unconstitutional monarchy" to which he referred was presumably necessary for quick and enforceable decision-making, such as ordering the Muster of Rohan. Monarchical splendour, in good kings like Aragorn/Elessar and Théoden, provides a link with the Numinous, the noble, chivalrous, and splendid, giving such good kings a role beyond just providing leadership, justice, and command and generally setting a good example. The restoration of the Kingdom of Gondor is part of the best outcome possible.

Monarchs in Middle-earth do use councillors (though Denethor, probably a sign of his growing megalomania, apparently does not). However, the only thing we see like a Parliament is the Entmoot, and that has some disadvantages since the lengthy discussions (this is emphasised more in the Peter Jackson film than the book) prevent the Ents from acting until nearly too late.

Tolkien did not appear to respect politicians much. He wrote in World War II: "If people were in the habit of referring to 'King George's council, Winston and his gang,' it would go a long way to clearing thought, and reducing the frightful landslide into Theyocracy" (*Letters*, 63). His tales were set in an ancient world before parliamentary democracy had evolved anyway. In December 1943, while allied propaganda extolled Stalin as kindly "Uncle Joe," Tolkien referred to him at the Teheran conference of allied leaders as "that bloodthirsty old murderer Josef Stalin inviting all nations to join a happy family of folks devoted to the abolition of tyranny and intolerance! But I must also admit that in the photographs our little cherub W.S.C. [Winston Churchill] actually looked the biggest ruffian present. Humph" (*Letters*, 65).

Metapolitics

"Politics" also has the "metapolitical" sense of competing ideologies with competing eschatological claims. Mordor is a totalitarian state, with Sauron demanding the honours of a god. For Tolkien this meant inevitably that the resultant order would be evil, even if Sauron had begun by meaning well. Tolkien wrote in 1956: "Even if in desperation 'The West' had bred or hired hordes of Orcs and had cruelly ravaged the lands of other Men as allies of Sauron, or merely to prevent them from aiding him, their cause would still have been indefeasibly right. As does the cause of those who now oppose the State-God and Marshal This or That as its High Priest" (*Letters*, 243–44). Although *The Lord of the Rings* is not a direct allegory about the assault mounted on the West by totalitarianism in the twentieth century, what Tolkien called the applicability of its values to that situation is obvious.

However, despite Tolkien's denial of direct allegory, the Shire under the control of Saruman's bullies, who initially called themselves "gatherers" and "sharers," may well remind some of the drab, bureaucratic Britain under the first postwar Labor Government with food rationing, power strikes, and uncleared bomb sites, known variously as the Age of Austerity and (by Evelyn Waugh) as The Attlee Terror.

The good side in *The Lord of the Rings* does not hope to build a perfect future, as Karl Marx looked to a perfect society when communism had been achieved and the state had withered away, or as Adolf Hitler looked to the Millennium Reich: if

Sauron is defeated, new evils will certainly come, and moral issues will not change. Also, the good people have faults: the Elves are caught in hopeless nostalgia for the vanished past and are abandoning Middle-earth anyway; the Dwarves can fall prey to "grudge and greed." Gondor is slowly fading, and Aragorn/ Elessar's descendants as rulers will become mere "politicians" like Denethor. There is no Utopia to be made on Middle-earth, and even the desire for it is not good.

The Shire is not a model of a perfect society. Though the inhabitants are essentially good people, they are insular, dangerously ignorant of the outside world, complacent, and often dull, losing the memory of the "high and perilous." Religious consciousness by the time of the War of the Ring has become distant and abstract, though the remnants of it are a saving grace (or, it might be said, religion and politics have come together, generally a sign of dire times).

The Temptations of "Order" and "Power"

Saruman, when trying to suborn Gandalf, evokes values of "knowledge, rule, order." (Similarly, in *Star Wars,* Darth Vader when trying to suborn Luke Skywalker, promises: "Together we can end this destructive conflict and bring order to the Galaxy.") The Ring tempts good people with visions of power to do good and bring "order." Such temptations are the first steps on the slippery slope to Totalitarian tyranny, which soon comes to see all dissent from the tyrant's vision as evil. In Christian terms, the attempt to set up a rival good to God leads straight to the rejection of God, with literally hellish consequences.

Tolkien said of life in postwar Oxford: "I am not a 'socialist' in any sense—being adverse to 'planning' (as must be plain) most of all because the 'planners,' when they acquire power, become so bad—but I would not say we had to suffer the malice of Sharkey and his Ruffians here. Though the spirit of 'Isengard,' if not of Mordor, is always cropping up. The present design of destroying Oxford to accommodate motor-cars is a case. But our chief adversary is a member of a 'Tory' Government. But you could apply it anywhere these days" (*Letters*, 235).

Tolkien's understanding of politics was also illustrated when, on more than one occasion during World War II, he expressed compassion for individual, innocent Germans caught up in the war and denounced collective hatred. In a letter to Christopher Tolkien of January 30, 1945, he expressed pity for the German refugees pouring west to escape the Russians and was horrified that people in England were gloating at their plight: "There seem no bowels of mercy or compassion, no imagination, in this dark diabolic hour." He went on "Well, well—you and I can do nothing about it. And that shd. be a measure of the amount of guilt that can justly be assumed to attach to any member of a country who is not a member of its actual government" (*Letters*, 111). Tolkien was opposed to the totalitarian notion of collective guilt in an enemy. In *The Two Towers* he has Sam contemplate a dead enemy warrior and wonder if he was really evil at heart or if he had been forced to march against Gondor by threats and lies, an important scene reproduced in the Peter Jackson film.

The English political philosopher with whom Tolkien was most in harmony was probably Edmund Burke, a Whig (i.e., "Liberal" in the old sense that included minimal government, not the modern American sense of left-wing and state-interventionist). Burke saw society as an organic whole, whose liberties and rights were to be cherished and whose faults were to be remedied with the utmost care, not a machine that could be torn down and rejigged by radical social engineering (Burke compared this latter to attempting to cure the wounds of one's father by chopping the old man to pieces and throwing the pieces into a magician's cauldron). Burke was horrified by the totalitarian nature of the French Revolution, which he predicted would end in terror and dictatorship, but he regarded rebellion against tyranny as an ancient "right." (The Orcs in *The Lord of the Rings* refer to the free people as "cursed rebels," which is presumably what Sauron had told them.) Like Tolkien, Burke rejected the doctrine of "collective guilt," stating he knew no way of drawing up an indictment against a whole people.

Coercive systems based on false premises about the nature of existence pointed straight to evil and disaster. When Pope John Paul II said in *Centesimus Annus,* "Not only is it wrong from an ethical point of view to disregard human nature, which is made for freedom, but in the long run it is impossible to do so," he might have been speaking for Tolkien, as well as for Burke and Adam Smith.

Tolkien did not see any secular social system as answering all Man's needs on Earth, because Man was not ultimately created for Earth.

HAL G.P. COLEBATCH

Further Reading

Colebatch, Hal G.P. *Return of the Heroes: "The Lord of the Rings," "Star Wars," "Harry Potter" and Social Conflict*. Christchurch, NZ: Cybereditions, 2003.

See also **Capitalism; Communism; Kingship**

POPULAR MUSIC

Popular music is another medium through which Tolkien's works have influenced popular culture.

In a 1951 letter to Milton Waldman, Tolkien discussed his desire to create a linked mythology. Such a mythology would be open to the contribution of many authors and artists, in much the same fashion that any cultural mythology has been receptive to the involvement of many different hands and minds. In this letter, Tolkien notes that he left his tales in two forms: in great fulfillment of their goals or moderately sketched as mere cycles (*Letters,* 144–45). This was done to leave space for others to contribute. In Tolkien's great mythology the Music of the Ainur can be found as a running motif of many beings working toward a harmonic whole, producing in song a creative space, a symphonic end result. An example of this in today's modern world is the many genres of music inspired by Tolkien's work.

From the New Age genre to classically inspired symphonies, from orchestral compositions to progressive rock and even to heavy metal, musicians in various forms of the art have been inspired by Tolkien and taken their inspirations into popular culture. A primary well for such inspirations, or a musicians' muse, can be seen in *The Hobbit* and *The Lord of the Rings;* others glean their work from the pages of *The Silmarillion* and *Unfinished Tales.* The number of musicians and bands that derive their names from Tolkien's work is astronomical. The birthplace of Tolkien-inspired music was alongside other outlets of fan appreciation—fan art, fanzines, fan fiction, and fan societies. Whether original compositions or reworkings of Tolkien's poetry set to originally scored music, Tolkien-inspired music arose in the mid to late 1960s but was fostered by Tolkien himself almost a decade earlier.

In August 1952, while visiting friends in Worcestershire, George Sayer—a close friend of both Tolkien and C.S. Lewis and an avid supporter of *LotR*—tape-recorded Tolkien reading "Riddles in the Dark," the fifth chapter from *The Hobbit,* along with selections of poetry from *LotR.* In this recording, the musical resonance of Tolkien's words is brought out—particularly in the readings *A Elbereth Gilthoniel* and "Old Troll." Tolkien did not write musical accompaniment for any of his works; however, in the 1960s Tolkien was approached by two musicians in regard to musical compositions based on his work. Tolkien received a letter from Carey Blyton in 1964, which asked permission to compose the *Hobbit Overture.* The overture would be based on Tolkien's book. Tolkien said he was honored, granting permission for her to create the work. The following year, in 1965, Tolkien began to collaborate with composer Donald Swann who wanted to set Tolkien's poem *Namarië* to music as part of a Tolkien song cycle. Swann wrote in *The Road Goes Ever On* that Tolkien had sung *Namarië* to a Gregorian chant. A series of seven songs from *LotR,* set to music with vocal and piano accompaniment and titled *The Road Goes Ever On,* was released in 1967. The first U.K. edition of *The Road Goes Ever On* included Elvish calligraphy by Tolkien, who had corrected the Sindarin verses of Swann's cycle. Swann later added several more songs to the cycle from Tolkien's work. Tolkien approved of this contribution to his great mythological structure. In 1966, the year before public release, Swann performed the song cycle for Tolkien, his family, and his wife Edith. The occasion was to celebrate the Tolkiens' golden wedding anniversary (Carpenter, 247).

Shortly thereafter, in 1968, Leonard Nimoy, best known perhaps for his role as Spock in *Star Trek,* sang a hippiesque folk-style song titled "The Ballad of Bilbo Baggins." The dreadfully "catchy" ditty had mixed reception from fans and critics. Before the 1960s ended, *LotR* exploded onto the college scene, becoming immensely popular in the so-called countercultural movement. During the Woodstock Music Festival, many a Tolkien fan could be seen traversing the countryside dressed as hobbits, Elves, and even Gandalf.

Each particular interpretation of Tolkien's works can widely differ from the others depending on the musical styles employed by the artist. The music of Johan de Meij (The de Meij Symphony) and the Tolkien Ensemble bring to life *LotR* in varying orchestral compositions. Johan de Meij studied at the Royal Conservatory of Music at The Hague, and his first symphony illustrates in several movements the journey of Gandalf, Frodo, and the Fellowship. The de Meij compositions trace the journey of the Fellowship throughout *LotR,* from the Mines of Moria to Lothlórien, allowing listeners to experience Galadriel's mirror and Gandalf's fight with the Balrog in bold brass and ethereal wind instruments. The symphony ends with Gandalf and Frodo sailing away on the white ship. The de Meij Symphony won the prestigious Sudler International Wind Band Award in 1989 and was premiered by the Rotterdam Philharmonic Orchestra in 2001.

The Tolkien Ensemble, formed in 1995 and whose members studied at the Royal Danish Academy of Music, has performed at numerous venues, notably its first concert in England being at Tolkien's own college: Exeter (September 1999). As of this writing, the Tolkien Ensemble, with permission from the Tolkien Estate, has produced three of four expected albums, with the theme of Rivendell as part of its title. The order of the group's Middle-earth releases to date are as follows: *An Evening in Rivendell, A Night in Rivendell,* and *At Dawn in Rivendell.* The third album, *At Dawn in Rivendell,* featured guest performer Christopher Lee. Lee is perhaps best known for his many roles in Hammer Studio's horror films throughout the 1950s and 1960s, but he has been reacquainted with Tolkien fans for his role as Saruman in Peter Jackson's film treatment of *The Lord of the Rings.* Lee, an avid Tolkien fan, sings and speaks the role of Treebeard on the album. The album booklet contains illustrations greatly admired by Tolkien. These illustrations were drawings by Eric Fraser based on original illustrations submitted to Tolkien by "Ingahild Grathmer"—Her Majesty Margethe II of Denmark.

The Italian flautist and musician Guiseppe Festa and his band Lingalad find Tolkien's work to be a great influence upon their life and music. Lingalad's multilayered songs highlight the adventures of Tom Bombadil, Bilbo, Gandalf, and the Fellowship. Their songs include original compositions, along with verses from Tolkien's work, using a mixture of cello, violin, mandolin, flute, and bongo. The band has toured throughout Italy and premiered in North America at Toronto's The Gathering of the Fellowship 2003 and New York's Ringbearer's Day 2005, Tolkien events hosted by The Gathering of the Fellowship and The North East Tolkien Society, respectively. Lingalad's organic feel blends sounds of nature and birds, reflecting Tolkien's vision of the environment, that are fundamental to Festa's storytelling. After Lingalad charmed Tolkien's daughter Priscilla and evoking the same emotions as her father's writing, she endorsed the band.

The New Age genre has borne many fruits inspired by Tolkien, from Brocialande's *The Starlit Jewel* (songs from *The Hobbit* and *LotR*) with music by Marion Zimmer Bradley (author of *The Mists of Avalon*) to Sweden's keyboardist/guitarist Bo Hansson, whose most successful album was his 1972 *The Lord of the Rings.* A band from Chicago, Shadowfax, performed from 1972 till 1995, when they disbanded. The jazz-fusion band used numerous percussion, keyboard, and string instruments to highlight their New Age sound. Since 1987, the multi-instrumental efforts of David Arkenstone have explored heroism, cultural myths, and celestial enlightenment, and he captured the spirits of listeners and fans of Tolkien with his 2001 release of *Music Inspired by Middle-earth.* The album is a collaborative effort with Diane Arkenstone and the Elbereth Orchestra, featuring instruments from various music genres, ocarinas, guitars, bells, keyboards, drums, and string and wind instruments.

Each group elaborates on Tolkien's themes, allowing the listener to picture the events of Middle-earth, using illustration via instrument, narration, and song. A listener need not read along from the text or have visual aids. This was a concern of many critics of Howard Shore's score of Peter Jackson's film interpretation of *LotR;* they felt that without the films the score would not have the same effect. The Howard Shore Symphony toured worldwide performing excerpts from or the entire score of the films. Scenes from the film or the illustrations of Alan Lee and John Howe highlighted every piece. While legions of Jackson film fans flocked to performances, many reviewers of the Howard Shore concerts felt that the score was very long and ultimately should not be taken for something it was never meant to be: a stand-alone symphony.

As symphonic and New Age music simulates the peaks and valleys, the emotion and vivacity, of Tolkien, thereby mirroring the events of his books, so do the forceful, hard-edged tones of progressive rock and heavy metal. Throughout the 1960s and 1970s fans enjoyed the lyrical allusions to Tolkien's work in the music of Led Zeppelin, Rush, and Rick Wakemen of the group Yes. The songs of Led Zepplin's Robert Plant and Jimmy Page illustrate an admitted infatuation with Tolkien's Middle-earth, including "Ramble On," "Misty Mountain Hop," and "The Battle of Evermore," all with direct references to Gollum, Mordor, the Ringwraiths, and events described in *The Silmarillion* and *LotR.* Tolkien had such an effect on Plant that he named his dog Strider. Geddy Lee and Rush honored Tolkien with songs such as "Fly by Night," "Rivendell," and "The Necromancer." These songs highlighted Bilbo's journey, the lush ethereal sanctity of Elrond's Elven home, and the stirrings of Sauron in Mordor. These influential bands gave personal tribute to Tolkien by using direct references to his work in their classic songs.

The progressive rock scene continued with Glass Hammer in the 1990s, which lead the genre with such releases as *The Middle-earth Album* (2001) and *The Journey of the Dunadan,* which began their foray into Tolkien-inspired work. The songs of Glass Hammer, with references to writings of C.S. Lewis as well as those of Tolkien, are original works that stand alone, furthering the tapestry wrought by the publications of both authors.

From Germany comes Blind Guardian, whose innovative power metal sounds have dominated heavy metal music inspired by Tolkien. The band has produced many albums with numerous songs oriented to Middle-earth, as well as subjects from the ancient North that inspired Tolkien himself. Blind Guardian has a full-fledged album centered on the events of *The Silmarillion.* The album, titled *Nightfall in Middle-earth* (1998), includes narrative interludes concerning the battle with Morgoth, the Darkening of Valinor, the fallen Noldor, Nom the Wise, and Fëanor's creation of the Silmarils. These unique songs serve as a bridge to other albums like *Tales from the Twilight World* (1999) which include songs based on events of *The Hobbit* and *LotR.*

The Finnish *Kalevala* and its language played a great role in Tolkien's Elvish languages, in addition to being an inspiration for "The Story of Kullervo." Now the people of Finland have found equal inspiration in Tolkien through the heavy metal band Nightwish, with Bilbo and the Hobbits featuring as a basis for their goth metal-styled songs. The Austrian thrash metal band Summoning brings more of *The Silmarillion* into the genre than most bands. The albums include direct readings from *The Silmarillion* by Tolkien, combined with other recorded efforts. From 1995 to 2001 Summoning released albums titled *Dol Guldur, Minas Morgul, Lost Tales,* and *Lugburz,* detailing their own interpretation of each Middle-earth cycle written by Tolkien.

The creative musical cycles of Tolkien's world give a comparative look into our primary world's inspired musical endeavors. Each genre reflects a note within the Music of the Ainur, from the soothing ethereal to the discord of Melkor.

ANTHONY BURDGE and JESSICA BURKE

Further Reading

Carpenter, Humphrey. *J.R.R. Tolkien: A Biography*. Boston, MA: Houghton Mifflin, 2000.

Seeman, Christopher. "The Tolkien Music List." http://www.tolkien-music.com.

Sturgis, Amy H. "Lord of the Rings, Rock On! A Music Consideration of *The Lord of the Rings.*" http://www.popthought.com/display_column.asp?DAID=282.

See also **America in the 1960s: Reception of Tolkien; Fandom; Lyric Poetry; Music in Middle-earth; Rhyme Schemes and Meter**

POSSESSIVENESS

The dangers of possessiveness or the desire to accumulate and hoard is a theme that runs throughout Tolkien's work. In accordance with Catholic doctrine, he views avarice as a capital sin and as a temptation against which all beings must struggle. His 1945 poem

The Lay of Aotrou and Itroun shows how "greed of ownership" can threaten the soul (Kocher, *Master,* 170). In the legendarium Tolkien examines characters consumed by lust for a "hoard" or powerful talismanic objects such as the Silmarils, the Arkenstone, or the One Ring. The story of the Sampo in the Finnish *Kalevala,* the sacred artifact that is ultimately destroyed in the battle to claim it, provides the creative inspiration for Tolkien's reflections on the evil effects of possessiveness (Himes 2000). Redemption only comes from renouncing the objects of power or material wealth.

In *The Silmarillion,* the desire to possess is bound up with the "restless desire to *make*" or subcreate (Shippey 2003, 241). Tolkien notes in Letter no. 131 that this desire "may become possessive, clinging to the things made as 'its own,'" the subcreator attempting to become "Lord and God of his private creation" (*Letters,* 145). Fëanor regards the Silmarils he fashioned (subcreated) as his own, and the oath he and his sons take brings great suffering to their family and the exiled Noldor. Morgoth epitomizes the sin of possessiveness by trying to seize the creative force of the Flame Imperishable and later by stealing the jewels for his crown. The Silmarils infect all with the desire to possess them, as the conflict between Thingol and the Dwarves illustrates (Kocher 1980). Eärendil's surrendering of a Silmaril wins mercy from the Valar, but the loss the two remaining Jewels and the sad fates Fëanor's surviving sons after the War of Wrath demonstrate the ruinous consequences of possessiveness.

The infectious nature of greed figures prominently in *The Hobbit* as well. There Tolkien draws upon the sagas of Beowulf and Sigurd, legends in which dragon hoards "lead only to destruction and death" (Flieger 2002, 110). Thorin's lust for treasure, particularly the Arkenstone, makes him resemble Smaug. The desire for wealth spreads to others, such as the Elven-king, the Master of Lake-town, Bard, and even Bilbo. Only after the Battle of the Five Armies do the combatants overcome their dragon fever and share the treasure fairly. Thorin's dying words convey the basic lesson of *The Hobbit:* "If more of us valued food and cheer and song above hoarded gold, it would be a merrier world" (*H,* XVIII, 348).

The Lord of the Rings offers Tolkien's most complex meditations on the nefarious effects of possessiveness. The One Ring inspires desire in those who come in contact with it and comes to possess them utterly. Sméagol commits murder to keep his "Precious," becoming forever divided from himself by his insatiable desire for the Ring. Saruman, greatest of the Istari, falls prey to the urge to possess it and attempts to rival the Dark Lord, only to fall to an ignominious death in the Shire. Some succumb to other forms of possessiveness, such as the desire to hold onto power or to the past; Denethor, for instance, desperately tries to cling to his authority and dies clutching the *palantír* in his burning hands. Frodo's struggles with the Ring, and his inability to destroy it of his own volition at Orodruin (Mount Doom) reflects the terrible damage temptation can inflict upon the soul. Bilbo and Sam, however, succeed in giving up the Ring and overcoming their possessive impulses. Their examples demonstrate how resisting the desire to possess can lead to happiness and salvation.

DAVID D. OBERHELMAN

Further Reading

Flieger, Verlyn. *Splintered Light: Logos and Language in Tolkien's World.* Revised edition. Kent, OH: Kent State University Press, 2002.

Himes, Jonathan B. "What Tolkien Really Did with the Sampo." *Mythlore* 22, no. 4 (2000): 69–85.

Kocher, Paul Harold. *Master of Middle-earth: The Fiction of J.R.R. Tolkien.* Boston, MA: Houghton Mifflin, 1972.

———. *A Reader's Guide to "The Silmarillion."* Boston, MA: Houghton Mifflin, 1980.

Shippey, Tom. *The Road to Middle-earth: How J.R.R. Tolkien Created a New Mythology.* Revised and expanded edition. Boston, MA: Houghton Mifflin, 2003.

See also **Arkenstone; Good and Evil; Rings of Power; Silmarils; Sin; Theological and Moral Approaches in Tolkien's Works**

POWER IN TOLKIEN'S WORKS

Power is central to Tolkien's work and to *The Lord of the Rings* in particular. However, in contrast to many (lesser) fantasy writers, the actual content of this power remains opaque: for example, apart from making one invisible, what does the Ring actually do to convey its terrible power?

If it is hard to define the core of power in Tolkien, its effects seem to be visible in three forms. First, there is power that stems from people's rank or ability: Denethor, for example, has power as Steward of Gondor; the Orc commanders have power through brute strength. Then there is a sense of power, or charisma, that stems from the person, such as Frodo. In the best cases—Aragorn, Gandalf—these two combine.

Finally, power comes from knowledge about things. It is noticeable that in Tolkien's work, and in *The Lord of the Rings* especially, a great deal of time is spent acquiring knowledge, from lore, from poetry, or from observation: this is part of the point of the many poetic inserts in the text and the tales within tales. While many critics have noted the way the characters grow in self-knowledge in the novel—as in a bildungsroman—it is rarely pointed out that they obtain less metaphorical forms of knowledge too: Pippin, for example, after a tutorial on the *palantíri,* tells Gandalf he wants to know the "names of all the stars, and of all living things, and the whole history of Middle-earth and Over-heaven and the Sundering Seas. . . . Of course! What less?" (*TT,* III, xi, 249–50). This is important because knowledge for Tolkien is not simply about how to achieve ends (e.g., the best way through Moria) but also about defining the world and so shaping the actions of the characters—and this is true of the evil and of the good. That is, knowledge and power are intimately related: Sauron's incarnation as an all-seeing eye is a direct symbol for bringing together power and knowledge.

This sense of power, which is neither rank nor charisma, links Tolkien's vision to the thought of Michel Foucault (1926–84) (Jane Chance draws this parallel in relation to surveillance only). Foucault was perhaps the twentieth-century thinker most concerned with power and its effects. However, in contrast to Marxists (who see power as embedded in class structures) or conservatives (who see it as inherent in our Hobbisian struggle for survival), Foucault found the "core" of power elusive and notoriously refused to define it. However, he did analyse its shifting and changing effects, especially in relation to the ways in which knowledge helps structure or shape power. His argument was that the categories through which we perceive the world create knowledge and that these categories and the resultant knowledge are not neutral. For example, a man might have sex with another man, but it is not until the creation of a whole discipline of "sexology," which has an intention other than simple description, that this person becomes wholly defined as a "homosexual" and so a figure on which power (say, laws forbidding homosexuality) can be exercised. Likewise, the categories of knowledge in Tolkien—principally of race, history, and heritage and of good and evil—shape the knowledge of the world and so direct people's actions in it. This is obvious in simple situations (e.g., choosing the right way) but is also evident in more complex situations, where the knowledge characters acquire of other's history and traditions, and of themselves, shapes their actions and so is interwoven with power and its effects. One example of this is Frodo's manipulation of Gollum, which is only possible because Frodo knows about his history. Another (negative) example is Sauron's blindness to the strategy of the West in

sending Frodo to his likely death: Sauron, as evil, has no knowledge, indeed, cannot even imagine, noble actions like self-sacrifice, so he overlooks this strategy. Knowledge is power in Tolkien's work, and if these two are bought together in the figure of the "all-seeing" eye, they are also bought together in the figure of the Gandalf the Wizard, whose power stems first from his knowledge.

ROBERT EAGLESTONE

Further Reading

Chance, Jane. *Tolkien's Art: A Mythology for England.* Revised edition. Lexington, KY: University Press of Kentucky, 2001.

PREHISTORY: "CAVEMEN"

There is not a surviving prehistory of England. However, Tolkien, in the *Father Christmas Letters,* most noticeably in the letter of 1932, examines the prehistoric Cave-dwellers. The caves near the North Pole, before they held the Goblin armies that routinely assault Father Christmas's workshop, were home to Cave-bears and before that, cavemen. These cavemen left a series of pictographs showing dragons and mammoths that were similar to Neolithic cave drawings. The imagines in the 1932 letter also depict have a pair of Elvish symbols drawn on the wall. Also, according to the letter the drawings were created by cavemen "long ago, when the North Pole was somewhere else." This prehistory of cavemen and Goblins shows an interesting connection to Middle-earth, especially with the two Elvish characters and the idea of caves that were once elsewhere.

While Rome and Greece have mythologies and tales that began with the creation of their societies and cities, the prehistory of England is sparse at best, with such pieces as *Beowulf* and *Ancrene Wisse.* While Layamon's *Brut* attempted to create a British history, it was a Romanized version of Britain's founding. Tolkien's attempt at creating a British mythology aimed to incorporate its Northern roots, not its Latin ones. Tolkien's focus on this mythology sought to emphasize the values of the British individual as inherited from the Northern heroes, such as Beowulf and Sigurd.

The entire history of Middle-earth is documented from the moment, Eru, the One, created the World, and every major event is dutifully recorded. Tolkien's prehistory is complete and robust, unlike the scant prehistory of Britain. In weaving this mythos Tolkien incorporates elements of British and Northern folklore: goblins, dwarves, magical swords, dragons and their hoards, and epic battles, all with a focus on "an unobtrusive but very ancient people" (*FR,* I, Prologue, 10).

The Men and Hobbits of Middle-earth are the inheritors of this prehistory. Even the rise of evil in the world is documented. Melkor, the first evil in the world, has his actions chronicled from start to finish, and the actions of his scion, Sauron, are a matter of record. Tolkien established a cohesive and complete chronicle of history for Middle-earth.

JOHN WALSH

PRIDE

Pride is the chief of the vices and traditionally the first of "the Seven Deadly Sins." Reflecting medieval tradition, Geoffrey Chaucer's Parson calls Pride (Superbia) "the general roote of alle harmes." In ecclesiastical and literary culture, synonyms for pride include *superbia, orgule,* and *hubris.* In Anglo-Saxon heroic literature, terms for pride denote arrogance in war. Tolkien's criticism explores the tragic irony of noble characters' self-defeat through errors in judgment attributable to pride; characters in his fiction exemplify the theme of pride as excessive confidence, often accompanied by rash or self-centered behavior, usually with tragic consequences. Characters in *The Hobbit, The Lord of the Rings,* and *The Silmarillion* exhibit this vice in varying forms and degrees. Tolkien's views combine ideas from Greek philosophy, biblical doctrine, and medieval and renaissance literature.

In the *Poetics,* Aristotle defines pride as *hubris,* a flaw of tragic heroes, noble characters whose downfall results from errors in judgment through arrogance or overconfidence. In the *Nichomachean Ethics, hubris* is associated with courage, a cardinal virtue essential to the other, lesser virtues but taken to excess. Biblical proverbs include the memorable "Pride goeth before destruction, and an haughty spirit before a fall" (Prov. 16:18). Medieval exegesis saw the New Testament coinage "the lust of the flesh, and the lust of the eyes, and the pride of life" (I Jn. 2:16) as a formula expressing a threefold motivation for Adam and Eve's sin in Eden and for worldly temptations afflicting the devout. In *The Faerie Queene,* Book I, Edmund Spenser personifies pride allegorically in the giant Orgoglio, guardian of the House of Pride. In John Milton's *Paradise Lost,* Satan's exile from Heaven is ascribed similarly to his prideful desire to "set himself in glory above his peers."

Germanic heroic literature valued boasts of prowess in battle but saw overgenerous self-assessment as a character flaw of tragic proportions. Commenting on the Old English poem *The Battle of Maldon,* Tolkien describes Beorhtnoth—leader of the Anglo-Saxons against a Viking attack—as "powerful, fearless, proud." The poet captures his strategic error in *ofermod,* an Old English word Tolkien interprets as a touchstone of the poem's tragic theme. Translatable simply as "pride," many critics argue that the term denotes more fully "arrogant overconfidence"; in Tolkien's view, *ofermod* is a term of "*severe* criticism." Because of his arrogant overconfidence, says the poet, Beorhtnoth "yielded too much ground to the hated foe." As a result, Beorhtnoth is slain, many of the defenders retreat, and the valiant remnant are tragically slaughtered. Tolkien says the poem shows how the desire for heroic glory and honor—otherwise admirable within the limits of loyalty and love—"tends to grow, to become a chief motive," leading to forms of excess especially tempting to men of war. In *Beowulf,* Hrothgar warns the Geatish hero, *ofer-hyda ne gym* (17606: "do not give in to pride"). In both terms, the first element *ofer-* suggests excess, paralleling Aristotelian insights. The word *surfet,* "surfeit, excess," also suggests the idea. Sir Gawain blames himself with *surfet* after his chivalric failure in Hautdesert. In his translation, Tolkien renders *surfet* as "pride."

Many of Tolkien's tragic characters are destroyed by pride and possessiveness, ideas closely associated in Tolkien's works (Shippey, 179ff.). *The Hobbit* describes Thorin Oakenshield—Dwarvish king of Erebor (the Lonely Mountain)—as "very haughty," in his self-estimate "an enormously important Dwarf" (*H,* I, 40–41). Thorin's flaw surfaces throughout the novel, culminating in his refusal to reward or parley with the Men of Lake-town. In the resulting battle, Thorin is fatally wounded; though he dies repentant, he appears as a tragic figure brought down by pride. The oath Thorin swears concerning the Arkenstone—"That stone of all treasure I name unto myself, and I will be avenged on anyone who finds it and withholds it" (*H,* XVI, 326)—echoes the Oath of Fëanor, a member of the Noldor in *The Silmarillion* similarly flawed, and ultimately destroyed, by possessive pride. After making the Silmarils, Fëanor begins elevating himself above the other Noldor as their spokesman and fomenting a rebellion resulting in exile from Valinor. Fëanor's vow of vengeance on any who "hold or take or keep a Silmaril" from his family's possession proves tragic for himself and all the Noldor (*S,* 83).

Men, however, seem particularly susceptible to the sin of pride and its tragic consequences (Nelson 2000, 84). The "Akallabêth" in *The Silmarillion* shows the gradual demise of the Dúnedain in the fair island of Númenor as its rulers grow more prideful.

Desiring sole dominion and unbounded power, and besotted by ideas of death, Ar-Pharazôn—the last and proudest of Númenor's monarchs—rules a realm grown fiercely war-like, indolent, and haughty with wealth. In the end, mastered by his pride, he leads an armada to Valinor and, violating the Ban of the Valar, strides arrogantly ashore. Númenor is swallowed into the sea, and the Blessed Realm of Valinor is removed forever from the world. In *The Lord of the Rings*, pride takes the form of excessive desire for power in Boromir and his father Denethor, descendants of Númenóreans in Middle-earth. Boromir is introduced as "tall and proud" in Rivendell, and his first words in the Council of Elrond speak of the valor, dignity, and pride of the House of Stewards (*FR*, II, ii, 258–59). Further remarks thinly veil his quiet arrogance—he seeks no allies and does not wish to "beg any boon," he says proudly. He justifies his violent attempt to seize the Ring later based on his own and his father's military aspirations, Gondor's past glory, and the superiority of his lineage. He thus falls—literally and figuratively—shortly before his death. Similarly, the valor and nobility of Denethor, Boromir's father, are undermined by pride leading to suicidal madness. Upon first meeting him, Pippin is struck by "his carven face with its proud bones and skin like ivory" (*RK*, V, i, 27); Denethor proves to be selfishly preoccupied with his role in history, jealous for his sons' prospects for political stature and military success, resentful over his need for Rohan's aid, and suspicious of Gandalf's offers of counsel.

Perhaps the most tragic human figure in the whole corpus is Túrin Turambar in *The Silmarillion*, whose repeated rash deeds and heedless rejection of advice, warning, pardon, and prophecy result from character flaws centering upon prideful arrogance. In "the pride of his heart" he refuses Thingol's pardon for the death of Saeros; renowned in war later in Nargothrond, he favors "brave strokes and battle in the open," becoming in time "proud and stern" and heedless of counsel. In his dying words, his Elvish friend Gwindor attributes his own demise to Túrin's "prowess and . . . pride" (*S*, 213). Attempting to purge himself of his cursed fate after slaying Brodda, he calls himself Turambar, "Master of Doom"—an ambiguously hopeful yet overconfident self-description (*S*, 217). His decision to fight the dragon Glaurung alone, seemingly a valiant and selfless choice, climaxes in the dragon's death; but in a gloating speech he taunts the dying dragon, whose subsequent revelation of Túrin's unwitting incest leads to his sister Níniel's death, yet another malicious murder, and finally his own suicide.

JONATHAN EVANS

Further Reading

Bloomfield, Morton W. *The Seven Deadly Sins: An Introduction to the History of a Religious Concept*. East Lansing, MI: Michigan State College Press, 1952.

Chance, Jane. *The Lord of the Rings: The Mythology of Power*. Revised edition. Lexington, KY: University Press of Kentucky, 2001.

Evans, Jonathan. "The Anthropology of Arda: Creation, Theology, and the Race of Men." In *Tolkien the Medievalist*, edited by Jane Chance, 194–224. London: Routledge, 2003.

Nelson, Charles. "The Sins of Middle-earth: Tolkien's Use of Medieval Allegory." In *J.R.R. Tolkien and His Literary Resonances: Views of Middle-earth*, edited by George Clark and Daniel Timmons, 83–94. Westport, CT: Greenwood, 2000.

Shippey, Tom. *The Road to Middle-earth: How J.R.R. Tolkien Created a New Mythology*. Revised and expanded edition. Boston, MA: Houghton Mifflin, 2001.

Tolkien, J.R.R. "The Homecoming of Beorhtnoth, Beorhthelm's Son," *Essays and Studies* 6 (1953): 1–18.

———. "*Beowulf*: The Monsters and the Critics." *Proceedings of the British Academy* 22 (1936): 245–95.

See also **Arkenstone; *Battle of Maldon*; *Beowulf*: Tolkien's Scholarship; Bible; Boromir; "Chaucer as Philologist: The Reeve's Tale"; Christian Readings of Tolkien; Denethor; Fall of Man; Fëanor; Heroes and Heroism; *Homecoming of Beorhtnoth, Beorhthelm's Son*; Men of Middle-earth; Milton; Northern Courage; Possessiveness; Power in Tolkien's Works; Satan and Lucifer; Silmarils; Sin; *Sir Gawain and the Green Knight*: Edition with E.V. Gordon; Spenser; Suicide; Theological and Moral Approaches in Tolkien's Works; Thorin; Túrin**

PROPHECY

Prophecy plays a prominent part in Tolkien's stories. Its role is tied to his Catholic beliefs, the prophecies in the Bible, and his source material of various Norse myths and legends.

In Tolkien's Middle-earth cosmology, prophecy, as far as it is explained, is based on characters' understanding or glimpses of the Music of the Ainur, the heavenly plan for the creation and history of Arda (*S*, 3–10). The Valar and Maiar, as Ainur embodied within Eä, have the greatest understanding of the Music as a result of their participation in the Music before the world was—like Merlin, they remember the future. Where the Music is unclear to the Valar—particularly in the role Elves and Men play within Middle-earth, as their theme was sung by Ilúvatar alone—they are unable to see the future clearly (*S*, 43–44). Prophecies within Middle-earth fall into three major categories: direct prophecies of the future, by the Valar and Maiar or by seers; prophecy through the "eyes of death"; and forebodings of the heart.

Seers of Elves and Men prophecy through undefined means—possibly by a connection to the Music or by some gift Ilúvatar has bestowed upon His Children. Their foretellings, generally vague, are open to interpretation or misinterpretation, much like the prophecies of the Oracle at Delphi. Malbeth's prophecy, that Arvedui would be the last king of Arnor unless the Dúnedain chose the "less hopeful" of two paths, did not specify that this choice would fall to Gondor's Dúnedain (*RK,* Appendix A, 330). Glorfindel's prophecy that the Witch-king should not fall "by the hand of man" (*RK,* Appendix A, 332) was not construed by the Witch-king to mean that he would be killed by a woman and a hobbit. Prophecies by the Valar or Maiar are generally less ambiguous. Thus, Mandos prophesies clearly that the Noldor will fail in their attempt to overthrow Morgoth and regain the Silmarils (*S,* 98–99), and Saruman correctly foretells that Frodo will have neither health nor happiness in the Shire (*RK,* VI, viii, 299). One special instance of direct prophecy involves the Dagor Dagorath (*Shaping,* 89), the battle at the end of the world, which has similarities with the biblical Armageddon and with the Norse Ragnarok.

Sometimes, characters on the verge of death see some aspect of the future and pass that foreknowledge on as a prophecy. As Fëanor lies mortally wounded by Balrogs, he foresees that no power of Elves or Men will overthrow Angband (*S,* 125). Huor, preparing a last stand in the Fifth Battle to guard the retreat of Turgon, prophecies "with the eyes of death" of the coming of Eärendil, "a new star" rising from his line and Turgon's (*S,* 237). Some power related to crossing over into death gives these characters the ability to prophecy.

The vaguest of Tolkien's prophecies are forebodings of the heart, in which true pronouncements describe events without means or specifics. Aragorn's heart forebodes danger for Gandalf in Moria, yet no thought of the Balrog or Gandalf's fall from the bridge is part of that foreboding (*FR,* II, iv, 310). Similarly, Gandalf's heart tells him that Gollum has a role to play in Frodo's quest, but that role is unknown to him and only becomes clear at the moment it occurs (*FR,* I, ii, 69; *RK,* VI, iii, 225).

JULAIRE ANDELIN

Further Reading

Shippey, Tom. *The Road to Middle-earth; How J.R.R. Tolkien Created a New Mythology.* Revised and expanded edition, New York: Houghton Mifflin, 2003.

See also **Arthurian Literature; Bible; Finland: Literary Sources; Gandalf; Genesis; Glorfindel; "On Fairy-Stories"; Mythology for England; Saruman;** *Silmarillion, The*

PROSE STYLE

Tolkien's highly individual prose style was clearly felt to be unusual when *The Lord of the Rings* was first published; Tom Shippey quotes early reviewers who described it as "Brewer's Biblical" and "Boy's Own." Even well-disposed critics have considered him a mediocre stylist. Some have singled out supposed "purple patches" for criticism, and others have objected to the archaising language of some passages. Catharine Stimpson claims that "shunning ordinary diction, he also wrenches syntax," inventing phrases like "To an eyot they came" in parody of his typical fronting of adverbials. However, such opinions have seldom been reinforced by close textual analysis. Perhaps critics more familiar with the unified style and plot of the realistic novel did not appreciate the diversity of what Tolkien was trying to achieve and therefore confused their reaction against his design with their assessment of how skilfully he chose the language to realise it.

Brian Rosebury rejects Stimpson's claims of strained syntax and asserts that, on the contrary, large parts of *The Lord of the Rings* are written in a straightforward descriptive style using familiar sentence structures and vocabulary; even the familiar phrasal verbs "have on" and "get off" are preferred to the slightly more literary "wear" and "dismount." He gives a detailed stylistic analysis of the passage in which Frodo and his companions arrive in Bree to demonstrate how the leisurely pace of the narrative and the circumstantial detail underline the tangible quality of the invented world.

Nevertheless, the use in other parts of the narrative of an archaising, high style is important for Tolkien's overall linguistic concept. Shippey demonstrates how the prose style is highly differentiated to characterise not only individuals but whole peoples. The hobbits, who as the characters closest to modern people act as mediators for the reader in the exploration of an archaic world with its different ethos, are usually depicted in the everyday idiom described by Rosebury. Elves, Dwarves, and the human societies of the south, particularly the Rohirrim, who are clearly based on the Anglo-Saxons, are distinguished by a more stately language using archaising vocabulary ("board" for "table") and grammar. Typical features are verb forms without the auxiliary "do" (e.g., "Speak not so"), atypical positioning of adverbs (e.g., "the dead come seldom forth"), and a preference for parataxis, that is, a chain of loosely connected main clauses rather than grammatical subordination. This style is found throughout *The Silmarillion.*

The stylistic contrast is already a clear feature in *The Hobbit,* where the Dwarves who unexpectedly enter Bilbo's Hobbit-hole and turn his life upside down are immediately characterised by their formal, rather antiquated language. In the earlier book this is often exploited as a source of humor, although when the tale builds towards its climax the grim earnestness of the archaic mode becomes recognizable as Thorin and the Dwarves achieve heroic status. As Shippey notes, by the time the action is resolved, even the two linguistic styles are "invulnerable to each other's ironies."

In *The Lord of the Rings* this stylistic contrast, both in speech and in narrative, is fundamental to the texture of the tale, distinguishing "familiar" and "heroic" characters and scenes. The book is constructed in the form of an asymmetrical stylistic arch, beginning with the everyday language of the Shire and building through Books III and V to the climax of the Battle of the Pelennor Fields, which uses biblical-sounding parataxis and ends with a long section of alliterative verse. A second high point is reached with the coronation and wedding of King Elessar, although here the language creates an effect not so much of heroic literature as of a fairy tale or a mythical apotheosis. The return to the Shire finally brings the stylistic level back to the everyday. However, there are many variations within this pattern. The heroic sections are broken up by the journey of Frodo and Sam in Books IV and VI, which is no less climactic, but the dramatic tension is generally achieved through the use of familiar vocabulary and syntax. The younger hobbits Merry and Pippin provide light-hearted contrast, as in their scene with the more archaic Théoden at Isengard, and even the sublimity of the coronation is punctuated by the old nurse Ioreth's comments to her cousin.

Undoubtedly Tolkien's experience as a historical linguist convinced him of the need to reflect premodern modes of thought by something other than everyday language. In Letter no. 171 he defends his use of moderated archaism by showing that Théoden's attitude towards death in battle is different from that of a modern person, so it would be a misrepresentation to let him voice his thoughts in a modern colloquial form. The laconic style of the Dwarves, as in Dáin's exchanges with the messenger from Moria, is reminiscent of Old Norse sagas, as Shippey points out.

Two studies use detailed textual analysis to show how some aspects of Tolkien's prose style create an intertextual link with real-world medieval literary practices. Fronting, the syntactic inversion parodied by Stimpson, is examined by Allan Turner ("Fronting"), writing in the context of translation. This style of verbal patterning, in conjunction with alliteration, parallelism, and chiasmus, is seen in Tolkien's narrative of the chapter "The King of the Golden Hall" to characterise the archaic society of Rohan by echoing some of the formal patterns of Old English epic poetry. Gergely Nagy (2004) performs a similar analysis on parts of *The Silmarillion,* likening the verbal patterning in this prose text to the traces of the alliterative *Morte Arthure* in Thomas Malory.

Michael Drout (2004) and Shippey both find references to Shakespeare (*King Lear* and *Macbeth,* respectively) in Tolkien's choices of phrase. Shippey also juxtaposes one of Bilbo's songs from *The Lord of the Rings* with Shakespeare's "When icicles hang by the wall" to demonstrate how a timeless effect can be created by using only words that would have been recognisable in English from the Old English period to the present day. Although these examples are of verse, the timelessness of Tolkien's prose is also achieved by consciously avoiding modern vocabulary and concepts, as shown by Turner ("Translation").

ALLAN TURNER

Further Reading

Drout, Michael D.C. "Tolkien's Prose Style and its Literary and Rhetorical Effects." *Tolkien Studies* 1 (2004).

Nagy, Gergely. "The Adapted Text: The Lost Poetry of Beleriand." *Tolkien Studies* 1 (2004).

Rosebury, Brian. *Tolkien: A Cultural Phenomenon.* Basingstoke: Palgrave Macmillan, 2003.

Shippey, Tom. *The Road to Middle-earth: How J.R.R. Tolkien Created a New Mythology.* Revised and expanded edition. London: HarperCollins, 2005.

Stimpson, Catharine. *J.R.R. Tolkien.* New York: Columbia University Press, 1969.

Turner, Allan. "Fronting in Tolkien's Archaising Style and Its Translation." In *English Core Linguistics: Essays in honour of D.J. Allerton*, edited by Cornelia Tschichold. Berne: Peter Lang, 2003.

———. "Translation and Criticism: The Stylistic Mirror." *Yearbook of English Studies* 36 (2006).

See also **Alliteration; Arthurian Literature; Epic Poetry; Rhetoric; Shakespeare**

PSEUDONYM: BAGPUIZE, K.

On October 15, 1931, the *Oxford Magazine* published Tolkien's satiric poem *Progress in Bimble Town* under the pseudonym "K. Bagpuize," a name derived from the village of Kingston Bagpuize, a few miles west of Oxford University, in Oxfordshire, England. *Progress in Bimble Town* is part of an unpublished series of

Tales and Songs of Bimble Bay. Progress in Bimble Town is dedicated "To the Mayor and Corporation," a possible allusion to Robert Browning's 1842 poem *The Pied Piper of Hamelin,* which refers to the "Mayor and Corporation." Browning's poem was a work Tolkien disliked intensely, according to a November 22, 1961, letter to his aunt Jane Neave (*Letters,* 311). Douglas Anderson in *The Annotated Hobbit,* like Humphrey Carpenter in his biography of Tolkien, suggests that *Progress in Bimble Town* may have been inspired by the Tolkien family summer holidays in Filey, Yorkshire, in 1922 and 1923. Carpenter quotes Tolkien describing Filey as an unpleasant and suburban seaside resort.

LISA L. SPANGENBERG

Further Reading

Bagpuize, K. [pseud. J.R.R. Tolkien]. "Progress in Bimble Town." *Oxford Magazine* 50, no. 1 (October 15, 1931). Reprinted in *The Annotated Hobbit,* 2nd ed, p. 253–54; 1st ed., p. 212.

Carpenter, Humphrey. *J.R.R. Tolkien: A Biography.* London: George Allen & Unwin, 1977.

See also **Poems by Tolkien: Uncollected**

PUBLICATIONS, POSTHUMOUS

Tolkien's literary oeuvre has been compared to an iceberg: most of it lies below the surface. As both a scholar and a fiction writer he published little during his lifetime. After his death it became clear that this was not due to low productivity. Tolkien wrote a great deal, but various factors—a diligent desire to investigate all possible ramifications of a subject, a stringent perfectionism, a reluctance to let go of creative projects, a preference for rewriting an incomplete work from the beginning rather than finishing an older draft as it stood, and a restless curiosity that often moved on to other things—kept him from finishing much of what he wrote or considering his completed work to be publishable. As a result, Tolkien left behind many unpublished papers, a large number of which have been published posthumously and which loom large in his output. Approximately one-third of his scholarly work and more than three-quarters of his creative work published to date has only appeared since his death. This work ranges from finished and polished texts, lacking only the author's imprimatur, to the most fragmentary and illegible of handwritten sketches. Lengthy annotation and commentary by editors may be found in most of Tolkien's posthumous material.

This article gives a brief overview of Tolkien's posthumous works by category. Dates in parentheses are publication dates. For more detailed information, see the articles on individual books.

Scholarship

The Monsters and the Critics and Other Essays (1983) contains seven major essays on language and literature, all relatively nontechnical. Of these, only "On Fairy-stories" had previously appeared in a book by Tolkien, but three others had been published in his lifetime. The three remaining essays were talks: the "Valedictory Address to the University of Oxford" that Tolkien gave on retiring from his professorship in 1959 (first published in a variant text in 1979); "Sir Gawain and the Green Knight," the W.P. Ker Memorial Lecture in the University of Glasgow, given in 1953 (closely related to a radio talk used as the introduction to the volume of translations); and "A Secret Vice," probably first given in 1931.

The Monsters and the Critics also includes the title essay, "*Beowulf:* The Monsters and the Critics," dating from 1936 and previously published. Two variant texts of this essay have appeared posthumously in the volume *Beowulf and the Critics* (2001).

Two more technical posthumous scholarly volumes are based on Tolkien's notes for lectures that he gave at Oxford on several occasions. *The Old English Exodus* (1981) and *Finn and Hengest: The Fragment and the Episode* (1982) both contain Tolkien's edited texts and prose translations of the Old English works studied, as well as his detailed textual commentaries.

Closely related to these is the earliest of Tolkien posthumous volumes, his verse translations of *Sir Gawain and the Green Knight, Pearl, and Sir Orfeo* (1975), prepared in the 1940s and 1950s. Only the lack of definitive introductions and commentaries from the author prevented these from being published at that time.

Fiction

The greatest quantity of Tolkien's posthumous work is in the volumes of material from his legendarium, all of which are edited by Christopher Tolkien. *The Silmarillion* (1977) is the first of these: it is a reader's edition of the latest versions of the stories of the mythology, selected and edited to be as consistent as possible in approach and in secondary-world facts and to require no editorial apparatus. The texts are from the 1930s and later dates. *Unfinished Tales of Númenor and Middle-earth* (1980) contains some of the more polished narratives of Tolkien's later years, from the 1950s and 1960s, covering all periods of the secondary-world history. *The History of Middle-earth* (1983–96) is a twelve-volume series containing stories, poems, and essays from the earliest period of the legendarium in the 1910s through final jottings and notes of the 1970s.

Posthumous works pendant to this canon are *Bilbo's Last Song,* a short poem first published on a poster in 1974 and in book form in 1990; "Nomenclature of *The Lord of the Rings*" (also titled "Guide to the Names in *The Lord of the Rings*"), an essay written about 1960 as a guide for translators and first published 1975; and volumes of letters and linguistic materials discussed later.

Tolkien wrote three completed children's books unconnected, or only tangentially connected, with his legendarium, that have been posthumously published: *The Father Christmas Letters* (1976), letters purportedly from Father Christmas written annually to the Tolkien children between 1920 and 1943 (later expanded as *Letters from Father Christmas*); *Mr. Bliss* (1982), a short picture book written approximately 1930; and *Roverandom* (1998), a full-length children's novel written in the late 1920s. All three books are illustrated by the author.

An early draft and a fragmentary sequel to *Farmer Giles of Ham,* both written in the 1930s, were first published in the original book's fiftieth anniversary edition, edited by Christina Scull and Wayne G. Hammond (1999). Drafts for and supplementary texts attached to *Smith of Wootton Major,* written 1964–66, were first published in the book's expanded edition edited by Verlyn Flieger (2005).

Linguistics

The creation and elaboration of imaginary languages and alphabets were constant activities of Tolkien's throughout his creative life. Only the minutest percentage of this work appeared during his lifetime, mostly in Appendices E and F of *The Lord of the Rings* and in *The Road Goes Ever On.* A considerable body of technical linguistic material appeared in some volumes of *The History of Middle-earth,* but the greater part is being published in small-press editions edited by members of the Elvish Linguistic Fellowship. Several essays, short poems, and other linguistic texts have appeared in the journal *Vinyar Tengwar* (edited by Carl F. Hostetter) since the early 1990s. Longer linguistic materials, especially vocabularies, have been published as issues of the journal *Parma Eldalamberon* (edited by Christopher Gilson) beginning in 1995, roughly in the order of their composition by

Tolkien. Five volumes have been published as of this writing: *I Lam na Ngoldathon* (1995); *Qenyaqetsa* (1998); *The Alphabet of Rúmil & Early Noldorin Fragments* (2001); *Early Qenya & Valmaric* (2003); and *Si Qente Feanor and Other Elvish Writings* (2004). All of these materials contain extensive commentaries and analysis by various editors.

Other Posthumous Works

The Letters of J.R.R. Tolkien is a brief selection of letters but an important primary source. The long poem *Mythopoeia* has appeared in editions of *Tree and Leaf* since 1988. Many previously unpublished paintings and drawings by Tolkien appear in *J.R.R. Tolkien: Artist & Illustrator,* edited by Hammond and Scull (1995). Excerpts from unpublished Tolkien writings, including letters, diaries, and some creative works, appear in many books about him, including *J.R.R. Tolkien: A Biography,* by Humphrey Carpenter (1977); *The Inklings,* also by Carpenter (1978); *A Question of Time,* by Flieger (1997); *Tolkien and the Great War,* by John Garth (2003); and *The Lord of the Rings: A Reader's Companion* by Hammond and Scull (2005).

Many works by Tolkien remain unpublished as of the date of writing. These include further linguistic materials, many additional letters, draft texts of *The Hobbit,* an incomplete Arthurian romance and other fictions, and translations of *Beowulf.* Some of these works are expected to be published at a future date.

DAVID BRATMAN

Further Reading

Tolkien, J.R.R. *Farmer Giles of Ham: The Rise and Wonderful Adventures of Farmer Giles, Lord of Tame, Count of Worminghall, and King of the Little Kingdom.* Edited by Christina Scull and Wayne G. Hammond. Boston, MA: Houghton Mifflin, 1999.
———. *The Father Christmas Letters.* Edited by Baillie Tolkien. London: George Allen & Unwin, 1976.
———. *Finn and Hengest: The Fragment and the Episode.* Edited by Alan Bliss. London: George Allen & Unwin, 1982.
———. *The Old English Exodus.* Text, translation, and commentary by J.R.R. Tolkien. Edited by Joan Turville-Petre. Oxford: Clarendon, 1981.
———. *Roverandom.* Edited by Christina Scull and Wayne G. Hammond. Boston, MA: Houghton Mifflin, 1998.
———, trans. *Sir Gawain and the Green Knight, Pearl, and Sir Orfeo.* Introduction by J.R.R. Tolkien. Edited with a preface by Christopher Tolkien. London: George Allen & Unwin, 1975.
———. *Smith of Wootton Major.* Edited by Verlyn Flieger. Expanded edition. London: HarperCollins, 2005.

PUBLISHING HISTORY

Probably the most striking fact of Tolkien's publishing history is how little he sought publication for his creative writings. His earliest appearances in print were poems in school magazines at King Edward's School, Birmingham, and at Oxford. Before he was sent to France in World War I, Tolkien did attempt to place with a publisher a collection of poems, titled *The Trumpets of Faerie*. The London publisher Sidgwick & Jackson turned it down in March 1916, and Tolkien did not seek publication elsewhere at that time. When at Leeds in the early 1920s, some of his poems appeared in small publications by the local Swan Press, done in association with the English School Association at Leeds, of which Tolkien was a member. Through this contact with Swan Press, Tolkien apparently offered his poetry collection to this publisher and was again turned down. To a friend in 1925 he complained in a letter that he could not find anyone interested in publishing a collection of his verse, but he made one further attempt, and in the spring of 1926 the Oxford publisher Basil Blackwell turned it down.

Meanwhile, the prose writings of his invented mythology, then called "The Book of Lost Tales," on which he had worked since around 1916, never approached completion. But in the early 1920s Tolkien did begin stories for his children, and a number of these were completed. *Roverandom* (published 1998) was begun in 1925 and apparently completed a few years later. *Mr. Bliss* (published 1982) dates from around 1928, and most significantly, *The Hobbit* was written over two to three years spanning summer 1930 through January 1933. At the time of their writing, Tolkien did not seek publication for any of these works, and it was only through a strange circumstance that *The Hobbit* came to the attention of a publisher.

In 1936, Susan Dagnall, a representative of the London firm George Allen & Unwin, came to Oxford to see Tolkien's student Elaine Griffiths about a project she was working on. Griffiths had not finished the work, but told Dagnall to go to Professor Tolkien and borrow his manuscript of *The Hobbit,* because Griffiths thought it "frightfully good" and that it should be published. Thereby *The Hobbit* came to be published in 1937 by Allen & Unwin, beginning Tolkien's lifelong association with the firm, its publisher Stanley Unwin (1884–1968), and in particular his son, Rayner Unwin (1925–2000). Allen & Unwin quickly found an American publisher, Houghton Mifflin of Boston, which brought out *The Hobbit* in 1938. Houghton Mifflin, like Allen & Unwin, maintained a long tradition of publishing Tolkien's works.

The relationship between Tolkien and Allen & Unwin was special from the beginning. Virtually all dialogue between author and publisher was conducted by correspondence, and Rayner Unwin has noted in his memoir of publishing, *George Allen & Unwin: A Remembrancer,* that "the time and patience that his publishers devoted to what should have been a straightforward typesetting job is astonishing. I doubt whether any author today, however famous, would get such scrupulous attention." Quite unusually Allen & Unwin used the author's illustrations to the story and even solicited a dust jacket design from Tolkien.

After the success of *The Hobbit,* Tolkien showed Allen & Unwin a number of his writings, including *Mr. Bliss* and some of his mythological stories and poems, but all were found to be too unlike *The Hobbit* when what was desired was a successor to it. Thus, in December 1937, Tolkien began writing a sequel, eventually titled *The Lord of the Rings.* Over the next years and throughout the Second World War, Stanley Unwin occasionally prodded Tolkien about the progress of the sequel, and in the meantime he published *Farmer Giles of Ham* in 1949. Tolkien nearly took *The Lord of the Rings* to another publisher in the early 1950s, when through friends he became acquainted with Milton Waldman of the publishing firm Collins. But as his hope to publish one huge volume containing both the "Silmarillion" and *The Lord of the Rings* broke down, he soon came back to Allen & Unwin, which accepted the manuscript of the latter on an unusual profit-sharing agreement (Tolkien would receive no payments until sales of the books had covered its costs, but afterwards he would share equally any profit with his publisher). *The Lord of the Rings* finally saw publication in three volumes in 1954–55.

After the success of *The Lord of the Rings,* Allen & Unwin was basically willing to publish anything that Tolkien would let them, and to the end of his life occasional things did appear in print, including the verse collection (whose idea was suggested by Tolkien's aunt Jane Neave) *The Adventures of Tom Bombadil and Other Verse from The Red Book* (1962); an essay combined with a short story, *Tree and Leaf* (1964); and even a short story, *Smith of Wootton Major* (1967), published as a small book.

The publication of most other individual items by Tolkien, throughout his life, seems to have come about through friends or invitations. Tolkien contributed poems to the *Oxford Magazine* in the 1930s when his colleague Russell Meiggs (1902–89) was the editor. His short story "Leaf by Niggle," collected in *Tree and Leaf,* originally appeared in the *Dublin Review* in January 1945 simply because its editor, T.S. Gregory, wrote to Tolkien and requested a contribution. Tolkien's poem *The Lay of Aotrou and Itroun* appeared in the *Welsh Review* in December of the same year because his friend and colleague Gwyn Jones edited the magazine. A few of his poems later appeared in the anthology *Winter's Tale for Children 1* (1965), edited by Caroline Hillier. Hillier had written to Tolkien, requesting a contribution. Tolkien also wrote a poem in Anglo-Saxon (with a modern English translation) for a special issue of *Shenandoah: The Washington and Lee University Review* (Winter 1967), done as a tribute to his friend W.H. Auden. There were many other similar requests and solicitations that Tolkien turned down.

After his death in 1973, both Allen & Unwin and Houghton Mifflin continued their friendly publishing arrangement with the Tolkien Estate. The long-awaited publication of *The Silmarillion* in September 1977 was an international event. But despite a success like *The Silmarillion,* and to a lesser extent that of *Unfinished Tales* (1980), both edited by Christopher Tolkien, the changes in the publishing trade were making it difficult for smaller firms like Allen & Unwin to survive. In 1986, Allen & Unwin merged with Hyman & Bell to become Unwin Hyman. In 1990 HarperCollins bought out Unwin Hyman and has been the publisher for Tolkien in the United Kingdom ever since.

The publishing history for two of Tolkien's works in particular is especially complicated. The first of these, *The Hobbit,* was originally published in 1937, and in writing the sequel Tolkien found it desirable to alter chapter 5 of the original book to bring it in line with the developing follow-up. In 1947 he sent a revised version of this chapter to Allen & Unwin for comments and consideration and was surprised to learn in 1950 that it was to be put in the next reprint of the book. Tolkien vacillated about the changes he had proposed and then abandoned, but in the end he did accept them, and the second edition was published in 1951. In 1966, he revised the book throughout, albeit lightly (with the revisions complicatedly entering into the various editions then being published) to bring the story more in line with *The Lord of the Rings.* Full details of the revisions Tolkien made at various times to the text of *The Hobbit* can be found in the second edition of *The Annotated Hobbit* (2002).

The publishing history of the second work, *The Lord of the Rings,* is a vast and complex web. To understand it in detail one must delve into copyright history, production problems, printer's errors, and Tolkien's corrections to various editions and their often chaotic implementation, as well as explore questions of Tolkien's original intent (and readings found in his various manuscripts) versus mistakes that may

have entered the text but which he tacitly approved or to which he at least never expressly objected. The question of copyright history involves an interpretation of U.S. copyright law under which one paperback publisher, Ace Books, claimed that the U.S. copyright to *The Lord of the Rings* had been irrevocably lost and even issued a pirated edition in 1965. The copyright status of the work in the United States remained in an uncertain status for nearly three decades, when finally in 1992 a U.S. District Court judge ruled that the original copyrights for *The Lord of the Rings* remain valid. (The case was *Eisen, Durwood & Company, Inc., d/b/a Ariel Books v. Christopher R. Tolkien, et al.* United States District Court, Southern District of New York, April 6, 1992, *West's Federal Supplement,* vol. 794, pp. 85–88.)

There are two main editions of the three volumes of *The Lord of the Rings* that Tolkien himself oversaw through production: the first edition published in the United Kingdom in 1954–55 and in the United States in 1954–56 and the second edition published in the United States in paperback in 1965 (and in hardcover in 1967) and in the United Kingdom in 1966, for which the text in each format was subsequently corrected and revised separately, thereby leaving no single uniform text. A more detailed overview of this publication history can be found in Douglas A. Anderson's "Note on the Text," published in U.S. editions of *The Lord of the Rings* since 1987 and in U.K. editions since 1994. There are four iterations of this "Note on the Text," dated October 1986, April 1993, April 2002, and May 2004, each published with a progressively updated version of the text. Further resources valuable for an understanding of the complicated publishing history of *The Lord of the Rings* are the two chapters on "Publishing Tolkien" by Rayner Unwin in *George Allen & Unwin: A Remembrancer;* the coverage given to editions of *The Lord of the Rings* in *J.R.R. Tolkien: A Descriptive Bibliography;* and the section called "A Brief History of *The Lord of the Rings*" in *The Lord of the Rings: A Reader's Companion* edited by Wayne G. Hammond and Christina Scull.

DOUGLAS A. ANDERSON

Further Reading

Hammond, Wayne G., with the assistance of Douglas A. Anderson. *J.R.R. Tolkien: A Descriptive Bibliography.* Winchester, UK: St. Paul's Bibliographies; New Castle, DE: Oak Knoll Books, 1993.

Hammond, Wayne G., and Christina Scull, eds. *The Lord of the Rings: A Reader's Companion.* London: HarperCollins, 2005.

Unwin, Rayner. *George Allen & Unwin: A Remembrancer.* Ludlow, UK: Merlin Unwin Books, 1999.

Q

QENYAQETSA: THE QUENYA PHONOLOGY AND LEXICON

This title was given by Tolkien to his earliest effort (begun in 1915 and abandoned c. 1919) at a formal and comprehensive description of Qenya, the earlier of his two chief invented Elvish languages. The title is itself a Qenya word, of uncertain meaning, but most likely "The Qenya Language" or "Qenya Grammar." The first of the two main (extant) parts of the *Qenya-qetsa* begins with a brief historical sketch of Qenya's position within the family of Elvish languages, and of the growth and divergence of those languages from their original, common form as the various tribes of Elves themselves separated geographically. The bulk of this first part is a detailed (but incomplete) discussion of the phonology of Qenya, that is, a formal description of the constituent sounds of the language and, in particular, of their systematic development over time from their corresponding constituent sounds in the prehistoric common parent of all the Elvish languages, as well as of the changes in the placement and mode of the stresses or accents in words at the various stages in the history of the Elvish languages and in Qenya itself.

The second and by far the largest part of the *Qenyaqetsa* is the "Qenya Lexicon" (extracts from which were given by Christopher Tolkien in the appendices to his two-volume edition of *The Book of Lost Tales*). This comprises a large dictionary of Qenya, organized as lists of words grouped under and sharing common abstract root forms, or basic elements of meaning, of which the grouped words themselves represent concrete elaborations in form and sense. Thus, for example, under the root "aya," bearing the core sense of "honour, revere," we find such actual Qenya word-forms as the nouns *ainu* (m.), "pagan god," and *aini* (f.), "pagan goddess"; also *aimo* (m.) and *aire* (f.), "saint," and *aimaktu* (m.) and *aimaksin* (f.), "martyr"; the adjective *aina*, "holy, revered"; the abstract noun *aistale*, "worship"; and the name *Ainatar*, "God" (literally "Holy Father"), a by-name of Ilúvatar.

As can further be glimpsed even from this one example, the "Qenya Lexicon" is important not only as a remarkable record of Tolkien's earliest linguistic invention and description, but also as the earliest record—in fact for most elements the very place of origin—of Tolkien's mythology: for in and from the "Qenya Lexicon" can be found or inferred much about the nature of Middle-earth, its peoples, cultures, history, religions, and metaphysics in the form in which Tolkien first conceived of and elaborated them, predating by as much as two years the earliest narrative form of the legendarium in the *Lost Tales*. Thus in this example entry alone we see that Tolkien's mythology was from the beginning monotheistic (*Ainatar/Ilúvatar* is "God," not "[a] god") while yet also containing an order of beings (wrongly) thought to be gods by some peoples; that there was some manner of worship, that is, formal honor or reverence, of God; that there was a moral order among its peoples (hence both saints and martyrs); and so on. (John Garth provides a concise overview and illustration of this mythological, cultural, and historical element of both the "Qenya" and the "Gnomish Lexicon" in *Tolkien and the Great War*, 125–27.) Indeed, in this respect, this earliest lexicon, together with its later companion, "Gnomish Lexicon" (see *I·Lam na·Ngoldathon*), is a far more elaborate and wide-ranging source, not only of the languages but also of the elements of the subcreation, than any of Tolkien's subsequent lexicons. And it is to precisely this gestational nature and aspect of the "Qenya Lexicon" in particular that Tolkien referred many decades later, in the foreword to *The Lord of the Rings*, when he described his mythology as "primarily linguistic in inspiration" and "begun in order to provide the necessary background of 'history' for Elvish tongues."

The composition of the *Qenyaqetsa* would prove characteristic of much of Tolkien's subsequent work on his languages (and to a lesser extent even of his narrative writing). The initial composition was in pencil, often clearly done rapidly with the flow of initial conception. Subsequently, the work was recapitulated in ink, overlaying the original pencil, which was itself erased (sometimes incompletely) as the ink layer progressed, both refining and incorporating revisions and additions to the pencil composition in the process. As reconsiderations or elaborations to the ink layer arose in the course of its writing, it was supplemented with additional pages inserted at the appropriate places in the original manuscript. And of course all of this was itself later subject to still further revisions and additions, as yet another layer of writing on the manuscript (sometimes in a different color of ink or pencil), before the work was eventually abandoned as the linguistic conception continued shifting and the whole process of description was begun anew in a new manuscript. The result is that the *Qenyaqetsa* (as with most of Tolkien's subsequent work on the languages and the legendarium both) is, in the state in which it was left to stand when Tolkien ceased work on it, neither among its parts nor even within individual sections always or entirely self-consistent in its details or systematics; instead, it is a set of (usually) closely related but nonetheless differing strata spanning several years of conceptual invention and change.

CARL F. HOSTETTER

Further Reading

Garth, John. *Tolkien and the Great War*. London: HarperCollins, 2003.
Tolkien, J.R.R. *Qenyaqetsa: The Qenya Phonology and Lexicon*. Edited by Christopher Gilson, Carl F. Hostetter, Patrick Wynne, and Arden R. Smith. *Parma Eldalamberon* (Cupertino, Calif.)12 (1998).

See also **I·Lam Na·Ngoldathon**; **Languages Invented by Tolkien**; **Quenya**

QUEST NARRATIVE

Campbell has identified the "standard path of the mythological adventure of the hero" as consisting of separation, initiation, and return (30), a pattern echoed in fairy tales, albeit on the level of Frye's low mimesis (34). While *The Hobbit* relates the story of Bilbo and the Dwarves' single quest for the gold of the Lonely Mountain, *The Lord of the Rings* comprises two quests, that of Aragorn and that of Frodo (Flieger, 125).

Aragorn is a high mimetic hero, and his quest is a mythic one paralleling that of medieval romance. He follows the trajectory of the quest hero as described by Propp, Lord Raglan, and Campbell (Noel, 70–71; Flieger, 43–49; Potts, 5–6, 10–11) and fulfills Auden's six essential elements of a typical quest (83). Seeking the kingship of Gondor and Arwen as his bride, Aragorn, heir of the Númenórean kings, already possesses the heroic qualities of breeding and character necessary to achieve his quest (Webb, 163–64). He is of immortal ancestry, owns a weapon with a pedigree, and has the ability to heal and renew ("The hands of the king are the hands of a healer" [*RK*, V, viii, 139]). He arises out of obscurity to lead the Fellowship and then Gondor, and as he nears his goal, he becomes increasingly youthful and kingly in his appearance and bearing. With the help of a magical helper (Gandalf), he overcomes a figure of evil to achieve his crown and wed an immortal woman. His journey moves from darkness to light (Flieger, 125), and his victory over evil ushers in peace and prosperity for Middle-earth.

Bilbo's and Frodo's stories seem to be fairy tales because of their low mimetic heroes, with whom the audience can identify (Frye, 34). Like the typical fairy tale hero, they seem unexceptional, but they possess the necessary characteristics to succeed in their quests (their Tookish blood and Hobbitish resilience). Upon leaving home, both participate in adventures that reveal their exceptional characters, with aid from magical helpers (e.g., Gandalf and Galadriel). However, Bilbo engages in a true quest, since his goal is to overcome the dragon Smaug and gain his treasure; additionally, he obtains the One Ring.

Frodo's story is, however, a mythic antiquest or negative quest, since he engages in an adventure of cosmic, even apocalyptic significance, traveling a great distance not to gain, but to lose, the One Ring (Rosebury, Shippey, 324). Frodo struggles less against enemies than against the evil influence of the Ring itself (Webb, 170), which in the end defeats him. He is saved by grace, the reward for his endurance throughout the journey to Mount Doom and especially for his repeated acts of mercy toward Gollum (*Letters,* 326–27). When Frodo succumbs to the Ring, Gollum intervenes to steal it and thus completes the quest for him, providing the eucatastrophe in Frodo's tale. He emerges from his adventure wounded in both body and spirit, and his story ends when he leaves Middle-earth to be healed before he dies (*Letters,* 328).

CAROL A. LEIBIGER

Further Reading

Auden, W.H. "The Quest Hero." *Texas Quarterly* 4, no. 4 (1961): 81–93.

Campbell, Joseph. *The Hero with a Thousand Faces.* Bollingen Series, 17. Princeton, NJ: Princeton University Press, 1949.

Davenport, John J. "Happy Endings and Religious Hope: *The Lord of the Rings* as an Epic Fairy Tale." In *The Lord of the Rings and Philosophy: One Book to Rule Them All,* edited by Gregory Bassham and Eric Bronson, 204–18. Chicago: Open Court, 2003.

Flieger, Verlyn. "Frodo and Aragorn: The Concept of the Hero." In *Understanding* The Lord of the Rings: *The Best of Tolkien Criticism,* edited by Rose A. Zimbardo and Neil D. Isaacs, 122–46. Boston, MA: Houghton Mifflin, 2004.

Frye, Northrup. *Anatomy of Criticism.* Princeton, NJ: Princeton University Press, 1957.

Noel, Ruth. *The Mythology of Middle-earth.* Boston, MA: Houghton Mifflin, 1978.

Persoleo, Paula M. "Frodo: The Modern Medieval Hero." In *The Image of the Hero: Selected Papers of the Society for the Interdisciplinary Study of Social Imagery,* 464–68. Pueblo, CO: Society for the Interdisciplinary Study of Social Imagery, 2004.

Potts, Stephen. "The Many Faces of the Hero in *the Lord of the Rings.*" *Mythlore* 17, no. 4 (66) (1991): 4–11.

Reilly, R.J. "Tolkien and the Fairy Story." *Thought* 38, no. 148 (1963): 89–106.

Rosebury, Brian. *Tolkien: A Cultural Phenomenon.* New York: Palgrave Macmillan, 2004.

Ryan, J.S. "Folktale, Fairy Tale, and the Creation of a Story." In *Tolkien: New Critical Perspectives,* edited by Neil D. Isaacs and Rose a Zimbardo, 19–39. Lexington, KY: University Press of Kentucky, 1981.

Shippey, T.A. *The Road to Middle-earth.* Rev. ed. Boston, MA: Houghton Mifflin, 2003.

Tolkien, J.R.R. "On Fairy–Stories." In *The Tolkien Reader,* 3–84. New York: Ballantine Books, 1966.

Webb, Janeen. "The Quests for Middle-earth." *Inklings-Jahrbuch* 10 (1992): 161–74.

Wright, J. Lenore. "Sam and Frodo's Excellent Adventure: Tolkien's Journey Motif." In *The Lord of the Rings and Philosophy: One Book to Rule Them All,* edited by Gregory Bassham and Eric Bronson, 192–203. Chicago, IL: Open Court, 2003.

See also **Aragorn; Arthurian Literature; Arwen; Bilbo; Eucatastrophe; Frodo; Galadriel; Gandalf; German Folktale; Jungian Theory; Mythology, Germanic; "On Fairy-Stories"; Romances: Middle English and French**

R

RACE AND ETHNICITY IN TOLKIEN'S WORKS

Tolkien, born in South Africa and relocated to England at the age of three, was fascinated by cultural difference and haunted by the exotic, far-flung, and lost. He once wrote that he preferred to read literature written in a foreign language or in forms of English so ancient as to feel foreign, and he declared repeatedly that the most improper study for mankind was man. In "On Fairy-Stories," he defined "the desire to converse with other living things" (152) as one of the great allurements of fantasy. It comes as no surprise, then, that he fills his imagined worlds with a plethora of intelligent nonhuman races and exotic ethnicities, all changing over time: Elves, Dwarves, Men, hobbits, Ents, Trolls, Orcs, Wild Men, talking beasts, and embodied spirits from Balrogs to Istari, and each race is internally divided into different tribes, clans, and ethnicities, each with their own languages and traditions.

There are two approaches to this plethora of races and ethnicities in Tolkien's works. The first treats Middle-earth as an autonomous diagetic space and asks how each race or ethnicity functions within its total cosmography. The second treats Tolkien's works as literary inventions through which he investigated issues important to him—creativity, morality, friendship, heroism, art, history, language, and death—and asks what questions his use of invented races allows him to explore.

In the first approach, within Middle-earth, Tolkien's interest in the evolution of cultural difference over time has a double-edge. On the one hand, generalizations abound about the differences between races; but, on the other, each race shows such internal variation that generalization itself becomes questionable. For instance, hobbits pursue comfort while Númenóreans pursue adventure, but among hobbits, Bagginses pursue comfort while Tooks pursue adventure, and eventually we learn that there is a seed of courage in the heart of the fattest hobbit. Elves are tall, noble, and spiritual, while Dwarves are short, blunt, and materialistic, yet in the First Age, the Elf Fëanor and his people incite the ravaging of Middle-earth in pursuit of three stolen jewels, while in the Third Age Gimli prizes three strands of Galadriel's hair, worthless in themselves, above all gold. Orcs are nasty, but one can still distinguish between the short-sighted Mountain-Orcs, the treacherous Mordor-Orcs, and the chest-thumping Uruk-hai. Ents and tree-creatures can be as grandfatherly as Treebeard or as treacherous as Old Man Willow. Men run the gamut from aboriginal Wild Men to overbred Númenóreans, but nobility and corruption are equally possible all along the line.

The racial generalizations, however nuanced, have incited charges of racism against Tolkien. In particular, critics point out that all the races enlisted by Sauron (Orcs, Southrons, and Haradrim) are dark-skinned and, not incidentally, "evil," while the races arrayed against them are generally light-skinned and, not incidentally, "good." An inherent racialism also dogs Tolkien's characterization of the Númenóreans, inherently longer-lived, more masterly, and more far-seeing than common men. Tolkien's defenders reply that these charges do not account for the internal variation that problematizes moral generalizations such as "good" and "evil": the madness of Denethor and corruptibility of Boromir; the disastrous pride that repeatedly overtook the Númenóreans and their descendants; the treachery of Saruman who, appearance-wise, is virtually indistinguishable from Gandalf; the detachment and occasional arrogance of Elves; the greed of hobbits. If each individual in the Fellowship represents a race, it is nonetheless clear that those who remain faithful do so not because of their intrinsic natures, but they all struggle to persevere in a day-to-day, hard-fought resistance against weakness and fear. Tolkien created a world where darkness exerts a gravitational force to which every race and individual is susceptible.

Tolkien also shows how historic feuds, such as those between the Elves and the Dwarves, or those between the Southrons and the men of Gondor influence present behavior; the Southrons and the Corsairs of Umbar ally with Sauron against Gondor in revenge for Gondor's former expansionist attacks on their kingdoms, not because they are "evil."

However, Tolkien himself was troubled by the Orcs, a race so corrupted it has become irremediably and genetically evil. Unlike the members of the other races, although Orcs exhibit the speech and independence that marks them as sentient creatures, they do not seem to have free will; they are born to corruption. In later essays reconceiving his mythology, Tolkien struggles with the dilemma of Orkish origins. Were they originally Elves Morgoth corrupted, and if so, could his power have been so vast that their corruption became heritable? Could they possibly derive from men—although their appearance predates the awakening of the first men? Were they actually not sentient at all, but beasts imprinted by Morgoth's will? If Morgoth had actually imposed a corruption so powerful as to damn an entire race permanently, why did not Eru, Tolkien's God-figure, intervene? Tolkien seems to have concluded that indeed, Morgoth was that powerful, and Eru would not have interfered, and analogizes the corruption of Orcs to the brainwashing and breaking of men in twentieth-century warfare, which God also does not prevent (*Morgoth*, 408–24).

However, if we abandon questions of internal consistency within the world of Middle-earth and consider how race works as a literary device for investigating important issues, a different set of ideas emerges. Here, race operates analogously to character "types" in medieval works. It helps Tolkien isolate certain characteristics for scrutiny, and it also allow him to play out general predispositions against individual choices, investigating the interplay of determinism and free will. Just as Chaucer's pilgrims—the Miller or the Wife of Bath—are both social functionaries and self-articulating individuals who respond innovatively to their historical situations, characters such as Bilbo, Frodo, Eowyn, and Faramir are born to certain predispositions that they find themselves impelled to abandon.

However, the idea that racial predispositions can work as literary themes presents interesting problems. Tolkien wrote that Dwarves reminded him of Jews and he employed Semitic phonemes in constructing their language. This comparison would whiff of anti-Semitism if Tolkien had not specified that it was rooted in the experience of exile: He saw Jews and Dwarves alike as essentially diasporic, simultaneously at home and foreign. He was fascinated by Dwarves in exile, driven from or attempting to return to ancestral homes or laboring though an unwelcoming world against which their secrecy is a defense. Hobbits investigate issues of home, homeliness, escape, loneliness, and return. Elves incite explorations of artistic creativity, the allure of beauty, and the fragile immortality of art in a changing world. Ents and Huorns speak for nature against the depredations of the other races and are a fitting nemesis for the industrialism of Saruman. Orcs expand on the consequences of tyranny: the mass production of hatred and the squelching of individual choice. Men are the most variable of Tolkien's races; through them he investigates love, weakness, and, above all, mortality.

By refracting these issues through different races, Tolkien, like medieval writers, risks flattening his characters into types—even stereotypes—and many twentieth-century critics decry his lack of psychological depth in its familiar novelistic interiorized forms. However, it can equally be said that Tolkien's fascination with racial and cultural difference allows him to explore both the difficulty and exhilaration of understanding across cultural difference and the need for mutual respect. The monocultural dominion of Morgoth and Sauron is counterposed by the diversity of those who join together against all odds to resist them.

CHRISTINE CHISM

Further Reading

Carpenter, Humphrey. *J.R.R. Tolkien: A Biography*. Boston and New York: Houghton Mifflin, 2000.

Chance, Jane. *"The Lord of the Rings": The Mythology of Power*. New York: Twayne; Toronto: Maxwell Macmillan, 1992.

———, ed. *Tolkien the Medievalist*. New York: Routledge, 2002.

See also **Dwarves; Elves; Ents; Hobbits; Men, Middle-earth; Monsters, Middle-earth; Racism, Charges of**

RACE IN TOLKIEN FILMS

Though adapted for film by an American (Ralph Bakshi, 1978) and a New Zealander (Peter Jackson, 2001–3), *The Lord of the Rings* is a Eurocentric work, its setting "the North-West of the Old World, East of the Sea" (*FR*, Prologue, II). This sea is not the Atlantic, but its "calque," or imagined equivalent. It represents both the material limit of the westward migration of peoples across Middle-earth, and the threshold between romance and myth: beyond it lies the holy mystery of the immortal lands of the West.

As Tolkien acknowledged, the historical situation of the Númenórean settlement in the West of Middle-earth resembles that of the later Roman Empire. It is vulnerable at its eastern borders: to pestilence, to invading warrior hordes ("the Wainriders"), and to the imperialistic despotism of Mordor; and it needs good neighbors like the Rohirrim to replenish its failing strength.

It follows that while the far West is revered, the regions beyond the southern and eastern margins of the *Lord of the Rings* map will be perceived mainly as sources of threat and may take on monstrous connotations. The "wild Easterlings [and] cruel Haradrim" (*TT*, IV, v, 286) are realistically conceived as warlike human peoples, easily drawn into servitude to Sauron's policy of conquest and plunder. But Sauron also produces "out of far Harad black men like half-trolls with white eyes and red tongues" (*RK*, V, v, 121). The echo of racial insult is unsettling to a contemporary reader, notwithstanding Tolkien's dismissal in 1938 of "the wholly pernicious and unscientific race-doctrine" (*Letters*, 37). There is no moral polarization of Men in Middle-earth, however. Not only are many Númenóreans corruptible, but in a crucial passage in *The Two Towers*, Sam Gamgee doubts the evil motives of a slain warrior of the Haradrim, wondering instead "what lies or threats had led him on the long march from his home" (*TT*, IV, 269).

Jackson's comprehensive movie version follows, and occasionally modifies, this Eurocentric vision, unembarrassed by elements that might attract "antiracist" criticism; indeed he arguably courts it by risking the word "race" twice in the prologue, in the sense of species, or what Tolkien more usually called "a people." Given his fidelity to the original, Jackson cannot be blamed for the fact that his heroes, as well as some of his villains, are white. Sam's thoughts about the dead warrior are retained in the film of *The Two Towers*, though transferred to Faramir, and the director's commentary at this point shows that Jackson recognized their moral and political significance. The movie also retains the book's generous emphasis on the need for mutual respect and cooperation among the various peoples who coexist in Middle-earth and whose diverse cultures are threatened by the nihilism of Mordor.

The special problem for the filmmaker lies in the necessity of visualizing precisely both the physiological and the cultural attributes of the various peoples: inevitably, this will lead to reminiscences of actual peoples, who may seem to be negatively represented. The declared strategy of Jackson's team was to avoid leaning too heavily on existing cultures: in practice, this often means blending elements which are near-yet-exotic to a European (North African cultures) with the equivalents for a New Zealander of European heritage such as Jackson himself (Maori, Pacific Island, and Japanese images). Both Easterlings and Haradrim show this composite character. They are plainly not Western Europeans, at any rate.

In the case of the Orcs, some care has been taken to diversify any "human" suggestions in their appearance; and Jackson's are more nearly human, and often more European, in appearance than the black, prognathous, red-eyed beasts and ghouls of Bakshi's incomplete animated version. Skin colors tend to avoid human equivalents, with a predominance of gray-white, dark grey, pale green, or greenish yellow. Individual Orc characters such as Grishnákh and Gorbag have hideous, but often unmistakably Caucasian, features. Jackson's Uruk-hai have attracted the greatest suspicion of racist stereotyping, with their dark purple flesh, dreadlocks, and face-paint suggestive of Maori warriors.

Critics of Tolkien and Jackson sometimes conflate their expressive imagery of light against darkness with a supposed racial privileging of white over black. This is to hold the artists responsible for the critics' confusions. Nevertheless, some may feel that at the start of the twenty-first century, any Eurocentric modeling of peoples in conflict is unacceptable or imprudent. The price of renouncing it, however, presumably in favor of some multiethnic composition of all populations, would have been to undo entirely the quasi-historical coherence of Tolkien's vision.

BRIAN ROSEBURY

Further Reading

Curry, Patrick. *Defending Middle-earth.* London: HarperCollins, 1998.

Kim, Sue. "Beyond Black and White: Race and Postmodernism in The *Lord of the Rings* Films." *Modern Fiction Studies* 50, no. 4 (Winter 2004): 875–905.

Rearick, Anderson. "Why Is the Only Good Orc a Dead Orc? The Dark Face of Racism Examined in Tolkien's World." *Modern Fiction Studies* 50, no. 4 (Winter 2004): 861–874.

See also **Jackson, Peter; Race and Ethnicity in Tolkien Works; Racism, Charges of**

RACISM, CHARGES OF

Critics who accuse Tolkien of racism fall into three camps: those who see him as intentionally racist; those who see him as having passively absorbed the racism or Eurocentrism of his time; and those who, tracing an evolution in his writing, see him becoming aware of a racism/Eurocentrism implicit in his early works and taking care to counter it in his later ones.

Those who see Tolkien as completely racist point out the dark-skinned composition of Sauron's armies of Orcs, Southrons, Easterlings, and Haradrim, and see Tolkien as equating them with "evil," while most of the allies who join against Sauron seem to be white-skinned and equated with "good." As John Yatt wrote in *The Guardian* on December 2, 2002, "White men are good, 'dark' men are bad, orcs are worst of all." In this view, racism is structural to *The Lord of the Rings*' basic conflict, defined as the battle between good and evil; and race ultimately determines morality. In this view, the fantasy genre allows Tolkien to make bigotry acceptable and even heroic. Several neo-Nazi and neo-fascist groups apparently agree; the neo-Nazi British National party have embraced the trilogy, and the national director of Aryan Nation, Charles John Juba, extolled the Peter Jackson movies as "entertaining to the average Aryan citizen" (Leanne Potts, *Albuquerque Journal*, January 26, 2003).

Those who see Tolkien as either passively expressing the racism of his time or coming to question it agree with the general accusation but also point out the inconsistencies that problematize generalizations about "good" and "evil" races in the books. The Rohirrim and men of Gondor may be European-looking but there are notable traitors and villains among them. However, the Orcs remain problematic; they seem to be a dark-skinned race devoted irremediably to destruction. Tolkien himself worried that the Orcs did not fit the mythos he had created, because they seem inherently evil in a world where the importance of individual choice and free will are crucial. To him, they came to signify the terrifying dominion that the great Enemies could exert. Morgoth, Sauron, and Saruman each find ways of corrupting Elves and Men and breeding them into Orcs, which are then dominated, brainwashed, and whipped into serving their needs. However, this does not really answer the accusation of racism; but rather moves it from genetic to equally powerful environmental determinants.

These accusations flared to new life with the release of Peter Jackson's films between 2001 and 2003, lighting especially upon representations of the enemy armies in *The Two Towers* (2002). On December 17, 2002, David Shapiro, a lecturer at the University of Warwick, argued that Tolkien had portrayed "the encounter with racial and cultural others as an event of terror and apocalyptic threat. For today's film fans, this older racial anxiety fuses with a current fear and hatred of Islam that supports a crusading war in the Middle East" (*Black Information Link*, December 17, 2002). David Ibata of the *Chicago Tribune* pointed out on January 12, 2003, that with the second film, the Fellowship faced not only dreadlock-wearing dark-skinned Uruks but also, for the first time, human combatants, the slant-eyed, turbaned, Saracen-evoking Haradrim, and the Easterlings whose portrayal hints at "an Asian influence." In the post-9/11 climate with the American war in Afghanistan heating up, these were "pernicious images." The third film's climactic rallying of the "Men of the West" against the hordes of Mordor, the South, and the East, fed further criticism, especially after the controversial 2003 U.S. invasion of Iraq. In general, critics of racism see both Tolkien's written works and the Peter Jackson movies as dangerously encouraging those racist tendencies they see as most pressing within contemporary society, whether aimed at blacks, Asians, or Arabs.

CHRISTINE CHISM

Further Reading

Goldberg, Jonah. "Movies and Metaphors: Man and the Universe." http://www.nationalreview.com/goldberg/goldber010303.asp (January 3, 2003).

Ibata, David. "'Lord' of Racism? Critics View Trilogy as Discriminatory." http://www.theonering.net/perl/newsview/8/1042475537 (January 12, 2003).

Moorcock, Michael. "Moorcock Weekly Miscellany." http://wwwmultiverse.org/article2181.html (December 19, 2002).

Murray, Jennifer. "*Lord of the Rings* Promotes Racism, Says University Lecturer." http://www.blink.org.uk (December 17, 2002).

Potts, Leanne. "'Lord of the Rings' Unleashes Debate on Racism." http://www.abqjournal.com/shock/827891fun01-26-03.htm (January 26, 2003).

Smith, Don. "An Essay on *The Lord of the Rings*." http://www.tollbooth.org/2005/features/rings.html (May 2005).

Winegar, Astrid. "Aspects of Orientalism in J.R.R. Tolkien's *The Lord of the Rings*." *Grey Book* 1 (2005): 1–10.

Yatt, John. "Wraiths and Race." http://film.guardian.co.uk/lordoftherings/news/0,11016,852217,00.html (December 2, 2002).

See also **Race and Ethnicity in Tolkien's Works**

RANKIN/BASS PRODUCTIONS, INC.

Arthur Rankin, Jr., and Jules Bass began working together on children's television projects in the early 1960s, using stop-motion and traditional hand-drawn animation techniques. Their first major success was *Rudolph the Red-Nosed Reindeer* in 1964, and they are best known for their holiday specials, which include *Frosty the Snowman* and *The Year Without a Santa Claus*. They continued to produce television specials, series, and theatrical releases through the late 1980s.

On November 27, 1977, NBC premiered their ninety-minute animated version of *The Hobbit*. It was at the time the most expensive television cartoon ever produced, taking five years to create and employing over two hundred artists in the United States and Japan to produce 110,000 animated cels. The film won the Peabody Award and Christopher Award in 1977.

The musical numbers are cheery but fairly pedestrian, even when using Tolkien's own words. In spite of the garish cover illustration on the current DVD edition, the Rackhamesque background watercolors are beautifully rendered, but the characters are flatly drawn and somewhat unattractive. Special effects of flame, shadows, and water are very well handled. The voices are well cast for the most part, but John Huston's Gandalf has a folksy Western American delivery that is out of place among the British accents of most of the other characters.

On the whole, the film succeeds fairly well in staying close to the text and telling the story in a condensed but intelligible way, considering the constraints of television writing. For example, the "unexpected party" is shortened to fit into the time allotted before the first commercial break. The introduction of Thrain's map is therefore delayed until after the Troll incident, which is disconcerting but not a fundamental change to plot or character development. The fact that Bilbo finds the Ring by the light of Sting rather than by putting his hand on it in the dark may be considered a matter of cinematic necessity—the audience must somehow be able to see what is happening—though it does detract from the providential nature of the event. The film cuts straight from the Elvenking's prison to the barrels floating down the river; when Bilbo speaks to the other barrels, it adds a nice element of surprise. It is obvious that some cuts were made late in production; when the Dwarves are captured by the Wood-elves, they refer to the Dwarves disturbing their feast, as in the book, but this is never shown on the screen. Beorn and the Mayor of Lake–town are among the characters left out of the story, but the plot does not suffer much from these cuts.

However, the film does not convey some of Tolkien's deeper themes as clearly. For example, the theme song "The Greatest Adventure Is What Lies Ahead" devalues thinking and dreaming in favor of action, but for Tolkien, what made Bilbo special was that he did think and dream more than other hobbits, and therefore was more open to adventure when it came his way. The film also takes an uncompromising antiwar stance, which misrepresents Tolkien's more nuanced attitude toward conflict as undesirable but sometimes necessary; in the book, Bilbo takes his stand near the Elves and is proud of his actions in later years, rather than sitting above the fray and decrying it.

Perhaps a more serious departure from Tolkien's deepest themes is Bilbo's attitude toward Gollum. The film lacks the key moment where Bilbo spares the creature's life out of pity and compassion, a motif repeated frequently in *The Lord of the Rings* and essential to the final resolution at Mount Doom. Bilbo's attitude is flippant and unsympathetic: "my, how he does go on," when Gollum realizes his loss; "how convenient," when he finds out he can become invisible. But worst is how he taunts Gollum at the last by leaping over his head with a gloating "Ta-ta!" as he escapes the caves. The subtle pity and horror of Tolkien's moment is lost.

Henry N. Abrams published an oversized book including the original text accompanied by stills, sketches, character studies, and storyboards from the film. The book includes illustrations for incidents that were not included in the final film, such as Beorn's house and the Arkenstone. A clear acetate dust jacket resembling an animation cel shows Smaug overlaid against backgrounds from the movie. The soundtrack was released in an elaborate boxed set including a book, poster, and iron-on decals.

After the commercial failure of Ralph Bakshi's 1978 adult theatrical cartoon *The Lord of the Rings*, which took the story up through the Battle of Helm's Deep, Rankin/Bass continued the story with a two-hour animated movie made for television. *The Return of the King* was first shown on ABC on May 11, 1980. Viewers were disappointed to find that the story did not pick up exactly where Bakshi left off, and while some may have been grateful that Rankin/Bass did not try to duplicate Bakshi's unique visual style, the film is aimed at a younger audience and is jarringly different in tone. It is obvious, viewing the Rankin/Bass films back to back, that this production was somewhat rushed and not as much care was taken with all aspects of the work, in spite of many of the same artists working on both projects.

The animation is not as polished as that in *The Hobbit*, with static and less detailed backgrounds, more use of limited animation and the same animation sequences repeated against different backgrounds, and much clumsier handling of special effects such as fire and smoke. The songs are also far more intrusive and out of place than those in *The Hobbit*. The actors' voices are gratingly inconsistent; for example, among the hobbits, Frodo, Sam, and Bilbo have British accents, while Merry and Pippin have what can only be described as classic American sitcom voices (in fact, Casey Kasem, who played Merry, provided the voice of Shaggy for the *Scooby-Doo* television cartoon series). There is also an inconsistency in tone showing a lack of understanding of Tolkien's carefully modulated style; in one scene, Denethor's formal language, straight from the book, is juxtaposed with Pippin saying, "He's gone loony, I tell you!" and Sam's interior monologues are an odd mixture of colloquial and sophisticated vocabulary.

The script would be nearly incomprehensible to anyone not already familiar with the plot of the book. In part this is due to the severe compression of trying to fit all of *The Return of the King* and summaries of *The Hobbit*, *The Fellowship of the Ring*, and *The Two Towers* into ninety-seven minutes. However, a great deal of unnecessary time is devoted to a frame story involving a 129th birthday party for Bilbo in Rivendell and to a number of musical interludes that interrupt rather than advance the plot. Perhaps in an attempt to soothe the fears of parents watching the film with their children, the opening party makes it obvious that all four hobbits and Gandalf survive their adventures more or less intact, but reduces the tension of the plot. In the same spirit, the Witch-king is given a withered old man's voice rather than an appropriately terrifying one, and Théoden's battle speech to his troops is cleansed of any reference to fire and slaughter or the joy of battle.

The story proper begins in media res with Frodo already a prisoner of the Orcs in Cirith Ungol. In this version, Frodo simply lost the Ring, Sting, and his "hero's cloak" in the struggle, leaving them for Sam to find—Sam never thinks that Frodo is dead. This gives an entirely different cast to his decision to carry on the quest, which he decides to do only after he can't get into Cirith Ungol. In the film, Sam turns back for Frodo as a result of his temptation by the Ring; in the book, his decision that he could not handle the Quest by himself was made before his temptation. This long and rather incoherent section includes an extended dream sequence with Sam leading an army into Mordor, which fills with blossoming trees as the Orcs turn into small furry animals,

followed immediately by a song featuring hobbit children frolicking in the Shire. Other plot changes include Merry being sent from Minas Tirith to Théoden with the Red Arrow, Merry and Pippin fighting side by side at the Battle of the Pelennor Fields, Snowmane throwing Théoden out of madness rather than injury, Sam searching inside Mount Doom for Frodo for many days, Aragorn planning to march into Mordor the whole way to Barad-dûr, and the elimination of Arwen and Faramir, among other characters.

The story skips from the coronation (at which the hobbits are mere spectators rather than honored guests and participants) directly back to the birthday party. As with other adaptations, the Scouring of the Shire is cut from the story; there is thus no indication in the film that evil still exists and must be fought unendingly even after the Ring is destroyed. When Gandalf announces that he, Elrond, and Bilbo are sailing into the west, Frodo suddenly says he is weary of the world and wants to go along. And Gandalf's parting speech speculates that since hobbits are getting taller with each generation, they will soon become part of the human race; quite the opposite of Tolkien's dwindling species who, like the Elves, are disappearing from our world.

Even worse than the mangling of the plot is a fundamental misunderstanding of Tolkien's work, characters, and philosophy. The movie is given an epic voice-over introduction echoing *The Iliad* or *Henry V*, at odds with Tolkien's deliberately anti-epic, Hobbit-centric opening focusing on the small and homely doings of the Shire. In the same way that Peter Jackson tied Arwen's life to the destruction of the Ring, this film asserts that Aragorn cannot be crowned till the Ring is destroyed and adds that Minas Tirith must be made safe for him to enter.

One of the most tone-deaf changes is the repeated introduction of Judeo-Christian religious references into the dialogue. Characters pray, and prayers are answered; they exclaim in God's name, call Grond the arm of the devil and the Sammath Naur Hell itself. Tolkien quite intentionally and rightly kept all such specific references out of his book, and the book is stronger for it; like Gandalf's discussion of the afterlife with Pippin in Peter Jackson's film, these references detract from a story in keeping with the "Northern theory of courage," where man is on his own to do what is right with no prompting or help from supernatural sources or hope of a reward in the afterlife. Throughout the film the writers exhibit a deep-seated misconception of this underlying theme; characters repeatedly have to be pushed by each other or pray for help rather than finding strength within.

The song "It's So Easy Not to Try," used as a theme in moments where despair threatens the quest, emphasizes making emotional connections rather than inner strength (the "straight road" mentioned in this song predates the publication of *The Silmarillion* and does not refer to Middle-earth's theology). Sam begs for rest in Mordor and Frodo pushes him on, or vice versa; Gandalf is hopeless and despairing instead of a veiled power and a hidden fountain of mirth; and as with Jackson, we never see Denethor in his prime but only after his spirit has been broken. This devaluing of inner strength and self-motivation reduces the sympathetic characters to the level of the Orcs, goaded on by their overseers in their marching "jody," "Where There's a Whip, There's a Way."

While *The Hobbit* is a decent (though shallow) introduction to the works of Tolkien and would be suitable for a child's first exposure to the story, *The Return of the King* mangles the plot, misinterprets the themes, and seems unsure of its intended audience and purpose throughout. With its uninspired songs and inferior animation, it is best avoided and would not make a good introduction to Tolkien or substitute for reading the book.

JANET BRENNAN CROFT

Further Reading

Bernhardt, Peter. "Theatre of the Fantastic." Review of *The Last Unicorn*, dir. Arthur Rankin, Jr., and Jules Bass. *Riverside Quarterly* 8, no. 2 (1988): 115–17.

Goldschmidt, Rick. *The Enchanted World of Rankin/Bass*. Issaquah, WA: Tiger Mountain Press, 1997.

Hammond, Wayne G. *J.R.R. Tolkien: A Descriptive Bibliography*. Winchester: St. Paul's Bibliographies, 1993.

Hardy, Gene. "More than a Magic Ring." Review of *The Hobbit*, dir. Arthur Rankin, Jr., and Jules Bass. In *Children's Novels and the Movies*, edited by Douglas Street, 131–40. New York: Ungar, 1983.

The Hobbit. The Big Cartoon Database. Available: http://www.bdcd.com/cartoon/27844-The_Hobbit.html (November 1, 2005).

The Hobbit (1977) (TV). Internet Movie Database. http://www.imdb.com/title/tt0077687/ (October 19, 2005).

Lawing, John V. Jr. "One Man's Bilbo." Review of *The Hobbit*, dir. Arthur Rankin, Jr., and Jules Bass. *Christianity Today* 22 (1978): 28–29.

Louie, K.F. *Z's Ranting on Rankin/Bass' "Return of the King."* ZMOQ. 2003. http://pw1.netcom.com/~zmoq/pages/ROTK_RB.htm (October 19, 2005).

Rankin/Bass. Wikipedia. 2005. http://en.wikipedia.org/wiki/Rankin-Bass (October 19, 2005).

Reed, A.K. "The Greatest Adventure Is What Lies Ahead—Problems in Media and Mythology—an Analysis of the Rankin-Bass Production of Tolkien the 'Hobbit'." *Journal of Popular Culture* 17, no. 4 (1984): 138–46.

"The Return of the King." Review of *The Return of the King*, dir. Arthur Rankin, Jr., and Jules Bass. *TV Guide*, May 10, 1980, A-32.

The Return of the King. 2005. Big Cartoon Database. http://www.bcdb.com/cartoon/27851-The_Return_of_the_King.html (November 1, 2005).

The Return of the King (1980)(TV). Internet Movie Database. 2005. http://www.imdb.com/title/tt0079802/ (October 19, 2005).

"A Tolkien Fantasy." Review of *The Hobbit*, dir. Arthur Rankin, Jr., and Jules Bass. *TV Guide*, November 26, 1977, A-27.

Wright, Greg. *Peter Jackson vs. Rankin/Bass*. Hollywood Jesus. 2005. http://www.hollywoodjesus.com/lord_of_the_rings_feature_05.htm (October 19, 2005).

See also **Bakshi, Ralph; Christianity; Despair (Wanhope); Dramatizations: Stage and Spoken; Jackson, Peter; Mercy; Northern Courage; War**

RANSOME, ARTHUR

Arthur Ransome was born in Leeds, Yorkshire, on January 18, 1884, and was educated at Rugby School and what would later become Leeds University. As a small boy he spent many happy holidays in the Lake District, where he learned to sail. He became friends with the artist W.G. Collingwood, who was secretary to the British writer and thinker John Ruskin.

Ransome worked as a newspaper journalist and was sent to report on the Russian Revolution. He met Lenin and other Bolshevik leaders and became friendly with Eugenia Petrovna Shelepina, who had been Trostky's secretary. The couple married and set up home in Ransome's beloved Lake District.

In 1929 he began writing what would be twelve novels for children, including *Swallows and Amazons*, *Swallowdale*, *Peter Duck*, *Winter Club*, and *Coot Club*. They were not immediately successful but would become bestsellers. His lyrical accounts of childhood adventures, the delights of nature and beautiful countryside have delighted young people for generations. He died on June 3, 1967.

His fans included Tolkien's children, who read and enjoyed his books and told their father so. In a charming literary circle of chance events, Ransome was himself an admirer of their father and wrote to Tolkien. He described himself as "a humble hobbit fancier" and then gently took Tolkien to task for having Gandalf describe Bilbo as an "excitable little man" and for using the words "man" and "men" when writing of goblins or Dwarves. The two authors had enormous respect for one another.

MICHAEL COREN

See also **Children's Literature**

REDEMPTION

The Redemption—the redeeming of humanity from the slavery of original sin through the Life, Death, and Resurrection of Christ—was central and axiomatic to Tolkien's very understanding of the nature of reality. It is, therefore, not surprising that the Redemption serves as an omnipresent, if largely concealed, ingredient in Tolkien's legendarium.

Tolkien wrote in "On Fairy-Stories" that "successful Fantasy" offered "a sudden glimpse of the underlying reality or truth . . . a brief vision . . . a far-off gleam of *evangelium* in the real world" (*MC*, 155). Tolkien, in his own work, offers his readers this sudden glimpse, this brief vision, this far-off gleam of the underlying reality or truth of the Gospel in a multitude of ways, multifarious and subtle. Such is his genius that his work bears most fruit when it is read in much the same way that Christians read the Old Testament, as a story that prefigures the truth that will be revealed in the New Testament. In much the same way that Old Testament stories point to the Redemption still to come so Tolkien's legendarium points in the same way to Christian truths still to be revealed.

In the appendix to *The Lord of the Rings* Tolkien reveals that the Ring is destroyed on March 25, a date that is so significant to Christians that it could be called the date of the Redemption itself. Christians believe that the Annunciation and the Crucifixion took place on this day, the two events that, alongside the Resurrection, constitute Christ's Redemption of fallen humanity. As such, the Quest at the center of *The Lord of the Rings* can be seen as a metaphor for the Redemption, most particularly with regard to Christ's dying for our sin. The Ring-bearer takes up his burden (his Cross) and walks through Mordor (Death) to Mount Doom (Golgotha, the place of the Skull) where the power of the Ring (Sin) to enslave the people of Middle-earth (humanity) to the will of the Dark Lord (Satan) is destroyed.

The necessity of the Incarnation to the Redemption of fallen humanity was central to "The Debate of Finrod and Andreth" (*Athrabeth Finrod ah Andreth*) in *Morgoth's Ring*, volume 10 of *The History of Middle-earth*. In this story, Andreth tells of the "Old Hope" that Eru (God) would enter into Arda in person to save Middle-earth from Melkor (Satan). Finrod understands instantly why such an Incarnation will be essential to the Redemption of the people of Middle-earth from Melkor's evil grip. Melkor-Morgoth's "marring" of Middle-earth can only be rectified by the physical intervention of God Himself. "I cannot see how else this healing could be achieved.

Since Eru will surely not suffer Melkor to turn the world to his own will and to triumph in the end. Yet there is no power conceivable greater than Melkor save Eru only. Therefore Eru, if He will not relinquish His work to Melkor, who must else proceed to mastery, then Eru must come in to conquer him" (*Morgoth*, 322).

Morgoth's Ring was written after Tolkien had finished *The Lord of the Rings* and some of these finer theological points are not evident in the earlier work. Nonetheless it is clear that Tolkien had the Fall and the Redemption very much in mind at the time he was writing *The Lord of the Rings*. Since, for example, original sin is the One Sin to rule them all and in the darkness bind them, the connection between the One Ring and the One Sin is evident and obvious. It is also made manifest, albeit enigmatically, in the character of Tom Bombadil. "Eldest, that's what I am," says Tom, adding that he "knew the dark under the stars when it was fearless—before the Dark Lord came from Outside" (*FR*, I, vii, 142). Tom is older than the Fall. He remembers when the world was innocent, before fear marred its happiness after the coming of the Dark Lord. Tom is prelapsarian. He predates the Fall. It is, therefore, no surprise that he and presumably Goldberry, his wife, are the only creatures in Middle-earth over whom the One Ring (original sin) has no power. Clearly, Tom Bombadil and Goldberry represent Unfallen Creation; they show the way things could have been if the Marring of Melkor (the Fall) had not happened. The fact that Tom and Goldberry represent primal Innocence and that Tom only has jurisdiction over his Garden remind us insistently of Adam and Eve, prior to the Fall.

Ultimately, Tolkien shows the effect of redeeming grace through the development of his characters. Those who cooperate with the grace grow in virtue, becoming Christ-like; those who refuse to cooperate with the grace wither into pathetic parodies of the people they were meant to be. Gandalf the Grey lays down his life for his friends and is resurrected and transfigured as Gandalf the White. Strider passes the self-sacrificial tests of kingship and ascends the throne as Aragorn. Such is the reward of those who accept the gift of redemption and who respond heroically to the sacrifices demanded of them. On the other hand, those who deny the gift and defy the call to heroic self-sacrifice diminish into grotesque shadows of their former selves. Saruman withers into Sharkey; Gríma slithers into Wormtongue; and, perhaps most tragically of all, Sméagol fades into Gollum.

JOSEPH PEARCE

Further Reading

Birzer, Bradley J. *J.R.R. Tolkien's Sanctifying Myth.* Wilmington, DE: ISI Books, 2002.

Caldecott, Stratford. *Secret Fire: The Spiritual Vision of J.R.R. Tolkien.* London: Darton, Longman & Todd, 2003.

Pearce, Joseph, ed. *Tolkien: A Celebration.* Pearce, Joseph, Editor. London: HarperCollins, 1999.

————. *Tolkien: Man and Myth.* London: HarperCollins, 1998.

Purtill, Richard. *J.R.R. Tolkien: Myth, Morality and Religion.* San Francisco: Harper & Row, 1984.

See also **Christ; Christianity; Fall of Man; Incarnation; Morgoth and Melkor; Resurrection**

REPORT ON THE EXCAVATION OF THE PREHISTORIC, ROMAN AND POST-ROMAN SITE IN LYDNEY PARK, GLOUCESTERSHIRE

An early essay by Tolkien remained in obscurity for a half-century until Tom Shippey identified it as a pivotal influence upon Tolkien's creative process. The essay arose from a project that briefly employed Tolkien as a consulting philologist. Recruited by archaeologists Sir Mortimer and Tessa Wheeler in 1928, he was to explore the origin of a unique name—*deo Nudente/Nodenti/Nodonti*—inscribed on plates of bronze and lead, discovered at the site of a fourth-century Romano-British temple unearthed on a hilltop in Gloucestershire. The result was a detailed essay entitled "The Name 'Nodens'" included as an appendix in Wheeler's 1932 report to the Society of Antiquaries of London.

The excavation of 1928–29 was the second such project initiated by the Bathurst family, owners of Lydney Park since 1719 (Lyons, 56). This dig, unlike that of 1805 when the initial discoveries were made, was to adhere to the latest scientific theories of archaeology, with input from other social sciences including philology. A contemporary review of the report considered it a work of "modern revolution in the technique of archaeology . . . an almost ideal format for publishing major excavations," and cited the appendix that "Prof. J.R. [*sic*] Tolkien writes with learning and skill" (Hawkes, 488–89).

The report traces the occupation of the site from a prehistoric earthwork, through two distinct Roman phases and a post-Roman period, before abandonment to the Anglo-Saxons who nicknamed the site Dwarf's Hill. The first Roman phase (c. 50–350 CE) is distinguished by the existence of an iron mine discovered intact beneath the hill, now "honeycombed

with the hollows which represent blocked mine-shafts" (Wheeler, 22). The second Roman phase is signified by the temple built 364–67 CE, followed by a bathhouse complex and precinct-wall by the end of the century. Although more recent excavations in 1980–81 challenge this chronology, pointing to a late third-century religious presence with a fourth-century "refurbishment" previously thought to be post-Roman (Casey, 81), it is this flourish of the site as a religious centre that presented the mystery. One of Wheeler's stated objectives was to "examine the particular nature of the Lydney cult as witnessed . . . by the name of the presiding deity" (Wheeler, 39).

Tolkien concluded that Nodens is a form of the Irish god/hero *Núada Argat-lam* (Núada of the Silver-Hand), king of the *Túatha dé Danann* (People of the Goddess Dana) the fairy-folk of Irish myth. He then links this to Welsh legendary figures *Lludd Llaw Ereint* (also Silver-Hand) and *Gwynn vab Nudd*, Cordelia's captor in an earlier story of King Lear. Tolkien further traces the stem to Celtic *noud-/neud-*, likely a derivative of *neutan*, a verb common to Indo-European languages, meaning "acquire, have the use of," as in the Gothic *ga-niutan* "to catch, entrap (as a hunter)," and the Old Norse *naut-r* "any piece of valuable personal property, a sword, a ring" (Wheeler, 136). From this, Tolkien loosely hypothesizes an antecedent deity of questionable disposition known as the Snarer, Catcher, or Hunter.

Helen Armstrong, after visiting the site, suggests that exposure to this project may have been a source of inspiration for Celebrimbor and the fallen realms of Moria and Eregion (Armstrong, 13). She mentions the names of Silver-Hand and Dwarf's Hill, as well as small axes found inside the mine's trapdoor, and an inscription translated by Tolkien that reads "To the god Nodens, Silvianus has lost a ring . . . do not allow health until he brings it to the temple of Nodens" (Wheeler, 100). Professor Hinton also includes this site in his overview of Anglo-Saxon archaeology possibly influencing *The Lord of the Rings*, regretting that Tolkien did not reveal more about the process of his involvement in the Lydney project, or his general knowledge of archaeology. Further, in a chapter devoted to this site in his travelogue of Tolkien's England, Mathew Lyons notes the Hobbit-like appearance of the hill's mine-shaft holes, and quotes Lydney curator Sylvia Jones as saying that Tolkien "was very interested in the folklore that surrounded Dwarf's Hill" when he stayed there (Lyons, 63).

More generally, Shippey describes Tolkien's essay as a clear example of "the interaction of poetry with philology" that helped thicken the "brew that was to become his fiction" (Shippey, 32). He discusses the influence it may have had in shaping Tolkien's ideas regarding the nature of stories over time, valuing most in literature the "hints at something deeper further on" (Shippey, 49). Tolkien's essay on Nodens shows how he could illuminate a lost mythology with a single word, and he concludes it with "Even in the dimmed memories of Welsh legend in *llaw erient* we hear still an echo of the ancient fame of the magic hand of Nodens the Catcher" (Wheeler, 137).

DON N. ANGER

Further Reading

Armstrong, Helen. "And Have an Eye to That Dwarf ..." *Amon Hen: The Bulletin of the Tolkien Society* 145 (May 1997):13–14.

Blagg, T.F.C. "Two Decorative Relief Carvings at Lydney Park, Gloucestershire." *Antiquaries Journal* 63 (1983): 355–59, 362.

Boon, G.C. "Lydney Park, Roman Temple, etc." *Archaeological Journal* 122 (1965):223–25.

Casey, P.J., B. Hoffmann, and J. Dore. "Excavations at the Roman Temple in Lydney Park, Gloucestershire, 1980 and 1981." *Antiquaries Journal* 79 (1999): 81–143.

Hawkes, Christopher. "Reviews." *Antiquity: A Quarterly Review of Archaeology* 6 (1932): 488–90.

Hellyer, Arthur. "A Secret Woodland Garden, Lydney Park, Gloucestershire." *Country Life* 169 (June 4, 1981): 1585–86, 1588.

Hinton, David. "Lord of the Hrungs." *British Archaeology* 65 (June 2002), http://www.britarch.ac.uk/ba/ba65/feat4.shtml.

Lyons, Mathew. *There and Back Again: In the Footsteps of J.R.R. Tolkien.* London: Cadogan Guides, 2004.

Shippey, T.A. *The Road to Middle-earth.* London: Grafton, 1992.

Wheeler, R.E.M, and T.V. Wheeler. "Report on the Excavation of the Prehistoric, Roman and Post-Roman Site in Lydney Park, Gloucestershire." *Reports of the Research Committee of the Society of Antiquaries of London* 9 (1932): 1–137.

See also **Mythology, Celtic; Mythology, Germanic; Gothic Language; Ireland; Philology; Roman History; Welsh Language**

RESURRECTION

In his writings, Tolkien divided the incarnate being into two parts: *fëa* (spirit) and *hröa* (bodily form). The Elves and Men are biologically equal, at least in the beginning of each being. Their spirits, however, are radically different. While men have been given the gift of mortality and death, the Elves are tied to the world, at least as long as Arda exists in time. Elves, therefore, if killed, can be reborn or reincarnated, if they so choose to be. Therefore, while their

bodies may be killed, their spirits may not. When reincarnated, though, the Elvish *fëa* grows in strength, and it can shape and form the body to its will in ways impossible for men. Even before death, the Elvish will is much stronger than that of men. The Elvish *hröa*, following the will of the *fëa*, can resist most illnesses and diseases and can heal rapidly. Men refer to this process undergone by the Elves as "fading," for the Elvish body seems to be merely a "memory held by the *fëa*."

The Elves understood little of this in their earlier days, and their awareness or consciousness of the power of their *fëa* and the possibility of reincarnation grew slowly. Much of their ignorance regarding their fate came from the shadow of Morgoth and its evil influence. For, as the Elves assumed, when they died, they became either nothing (annihilation) or entered a realm of darkness.

Eventually, though, many of the Elves learned the truth. From Manwë, they first learned that their *fëas* must stay with Arda until its end. All souls originate with Eru and from Eru alone. When killed, their souls are summoned by Námo, Lord of Mandos. After accepting the summons, the soul waits in the Halls of Mandos, healing. In consultation with Namo, it decides when to be born again. Once born again, "The *fëa* re-born becomes a child indeed, enjoying once more all the wonder and newness of childhood; but slowly, and only after it had acquired a knowledge of the world and mastery of itself, its memory would awake; until, when the re-born elf was full-grown, it recalled all its former life, and then the old life, and the 'waiting,' and the new life became one ordered history and identity" (*Morgoth*, 221). Rarely did anyone experience rebirth more than once.

Some Elves refuse the summons of Námo. Some of these are prideful, others are outright evil. Those who refuse the summons, more often than not, inhabit and haunt places familiar to it as well as attempt to corrupt the fully incarnate. Even the best of those who refuse the summons are "tainted" in some way, and they "remain in regret and self-pity." Sometimes, they attempt to possess an incarnate being, either sharing his body or replacing the original soul altogether.

Tolkien wrestled with the concept of Elvish resurrection and reincarnation during the writing of his entire legendarium. When a Catholic friend and publisher accused Tolkien of overstepping his theological bounds in 1954 by inserting the idea of Elvish reincarnation, Tolkien at first rejected the necessity of being theologically consistent for the legendarium is merely "a tale, a piece of literature, intended to have literary effect, and not real history." Further, he responded,

"Reincarnation" may be bad *theology* (that surely, rather than metaphysics) as applied to Humanity; and my *legendarium*, especially the "Downfall of Numenor" which lies immediately behind *The Lord of the Rings*, is based on my view: that Men are essentially mortal and must not try to become "immortal" in the flesh. But I do not see how even in the Primary World any theologian or philosopher, unless very much better informed about the relation of the spirit and body than I believe anyone to be, could deny the *possibility* of re-incarnation as a mode of existence, prescribed for certain kinds of rational incarnate creatures (*Letters*, 189).

As *The Lord of the Rings* grew in popularity and the possibility of the development of a new cultus seemed probable, Tolkien demanded theological consistency. As Christopher Tolkien noted, his father found the rendering of the legendarium theologically consistent very difficult, adding to the delay in the publication of *The Silmarillion*. Tolkien, though, never abandoned the idea of Elvish reincarnation, as one can readily see in several writings published in *Morgoth's Ring*. The discussion of the Valar and the Elves in these later writings revolve around the decision of Fëanor's mother, Míriel, not to accept reincarnation and indeed rejected all being, as she had spent her life in giving birth to her son. The understandings and judgments of the Valar come from a time prior to the corruption of the world, before all purposes and natures had been made crooked.

The laws, however, remain, perhaps anticipating the end of all time and the creation of Arda into New Arda or Arda Healed. Tolkien speculated that since the nature of the Elves is tied to the nature of Arda itself, "New Arda or Arda Unmarred (Healed) would imply a continuance, beyond the End (or Competition)." New Arda will embody the good, the beautiful, and joy, and, the Elves suppose, Eru intends for them to play a role in its recreation. They are, after all, made by Him directly, and He makes nothing in vain. As Finrod noted in his conversation with Andreth, "For that Arda Healed shall not be Arda Unmarred, but a third thing and a greater, and yet the same." And, as Manwë stated, "To speak according to Time in which they have their being, the Arda Healed, which shall be greater and more fair than the first, because of the Marring: this is the Hope that sustaineth. It cometh not only from the yearning for the Will of Ilúvatar the Begetter (which by itself may lead those within Time to no more than regret), but also from trust in Eru the Lord everlasting, that he is good, and that his works shall all end in good" (*Morgoth*, 245).

BRADLEY J. BIRZER

See also **Elves: Reincarnation;** *Morgoth's Ring*

RETURN OF THE SHADOW

The Return of the Shadow, volume six in the *History of Middle-earth* series, is the first of four works Christopher Tolkien devotes to documenting his father's composition of *The Lord of the Rings*. In addition to drafts, revisions, and notes from the first two years of the novel's creation, Christopher provides extensive commentary to clarify the evolving storyline and characters. He also traces the major shift in tone and genre that ultimately turned the novel into something more than a sequel to *The Hobbit*. The volume opens with the earliest version of the first chapter written in December 1937, three months after the publication of *The Hobbit*, and moves through drafts up to 1939 when, having brought his characters to Balin's tomb in Moria, Tolkien took an almost year-long break from the narrative. The book's name comes from a title abandoned by Tolkien for *The Fellowship of the Ring*.

Although a unifying title and cleanly typeset pages give the illusion of orderly composition, the drafts reveal a labyrinthine process. The opening chapter was begun six separate times during this first two years, and no part of the novel received more attention than the narrative between Hobbiton and Rivendell. As Christopher explains, "My father bestowed immense pains on the creation of *The Lord of the Rings*, and my intention has been that this record of his first years of work on it should reflect those pains. . . . The doubts, indecisions, unpickings, restructurings, and false starts have been described. The result is necessarily extremely intricate" (*Shadow*, 5). A reader's familiarity with *The Fellowship of the Ring* is assumed throughout.

Tolkien struggled with the new work for many reasons. Unlike the creation of earlier works, the impetus for a sequel to *The Hobbit* came from his publisher. Stanley Unwin wanted to take advantage of Tolkien's immediate success as a children's author, and no existing manuscripts, including *Mr. Bliss* or *The Silmarillion* narratives, filled the same niche. Tolkien felt he had already provided closure on Bilbo's happy ending and wished to spend time with the Elvish tales, his first love. He agreed to try, however, and composed the narrative up to Rivendell over three "phases." These make up the bulk of the volume and reveal Tolkien's reluctance, like his protagonists', to leave the Shire. He preferred niggling over hobbit names and genealogies. The final three chapters of the volume, "The Story Continued," move the story south of Rivendell into territory not previously described in *The Hobbit*.

A birthday celebration is fully conceived in the earliest draft, but a replacement for Bilbo as protagonist does not emerge easily. At first Bilbo announces plans to be married, and the story is to be about one of his ancestors. In a later draft, the story is about Bingo, Bilbo's son, who eventually is made nephew of an unmarried Bilbo. The ring provides a natural link to the sequel, but Tolkien ponders its importance in notes: "*The Ring*: whence its origin. Necromancer? Not very dangerous, when used for good purpose. But it exacts its penalty. You must either lose it, or *yourself*" (*Shadow*, 42). As the significance of the ring grows, the tone darkens. The narrator stops being parental, as in *The Hobbit*, but still maintains a hobbit perspective. A unique style thus emerges for *The Lord of the Rings*, balanced somewhere between the levity of *The Hobbit* and the solemnity of *The Silmarillion*. At this stage Tolkien begins integrating characters created years earlier, such as the Willow-man, Barrow-wights, and Tom Bombadil.

One of the most dramatic examples of the tale taking a darker turn is when the hobbits hide from a sniffing figure on horseback. In the original draft this figure is Gandalf, but Tolkien abandons the plot point immediately for a Dark Rider: "Round a turn came a white [>black] horse, and on it sat . . . a small [>short] man wrapped entirely in a great [*added:* black] cloak" (*Shadow*, 48). In the early drafts, the ring is occasionally used for comic effect: Bingo frightens Farmer Maggot with a floating mug of beer. All frivolous uses of the ring are soon excised from the story. As the ring's history grows, Tolkien debates with how to reveal the details, whether in conversation with Gandalf, conversation with the Elf Gildor, or in a prologue. Tolkien also revised the number of hobbit companions accompanying Bingo. As he created, deleted, and renamed characters, he occasionally edited in colored ink. This allowed him to delay a final decision; depending on whom he kept, he could follow one or another set of revisions.

An equally surprising moment in the tale comes when the hobbits arrive in Bree and meet a dark stranger, a hobbit named Trotter. This Ranger, who in a later volume becomes Aragorn, has traveled to Mordor and has wooden feet. Like Aragorn, he aids the hobbits in getting to Rivendell, but his help is minimal once the travelers reach Caradras (later Caradhras). In this volume Tolkien considers making the Rangers human, but has not yet conceived of a returning king. By the time the company sets out from Rivendell, Tolkien has introduced Boromir (a warrior from the Land of Ond, later Gondor), but neither Gimli nor Legolas exists. Bingo's name has been changed to Frodo, and the underlying goal of the narrative has been suggested in an outline: "When Bingo [*written above:* Frodo] at last reaches Crack and Fiery Mountain *he cannot make himself throw*

the Ring away. . . . Gollum *takes Ring* and falls into the Crack" (*Shadow*, 380).

As with every volume in the *History of Middle-earth* series, the editor's work is paramount. Christopher Tolkien had to make sense of manuscripts that were undated, covered with multiple levels of revision, and penned with varying levels of haste and legibility. *The Lord of the Rings* manuscripts provided additional challenges, however, because the documents were split between two locations. Tolkien sold *The Lord of the Rings* drafts to Marquette University, soon after the book's publication (along with drafts of other works), but some were mistakenly left behind when materials began being sent in July 1957. These passed to Christopher Tolkien upon his father's death, and reuniting them was crucial for shaping a coherent picture of composition. The entire collection now resides in Milwaukee.

Along with a color reproduction of the earliest known Shire map, the 1988 volume includes seven other black and white manuscript pages. The presentation of *The Lord of the Rings* manuscripts continues in volumes seven through nine in the *History of Middle-earth* series, *The Treason of Isengard*, *The War of the Ring*, and *Sauron Defeated*.

STEPHEN YANDELL

Further Reading

Carpenter, Humphrey. *Tolkien: A Biography*. Boston, MA: Houghton Mifflin, 1977.
Fonstad, Karen Wynn. *The Atlas of Middle-earth*. Rev. ed. Boston, MA: Houghton Mifflin, 1991.
Miller, David M. "Narrative Pattern in *The Fellowship of the Ring*." In *A Tolkien Compass*, edited by Jared Lobdell, 95–106. La Salle, IL: Open Court, 1975.
Strachey, Barbara. *Journeys of Frodo: An Atlas of J.R.R. Tolkien's "The Lord of the Rings."* New York: Ballantine, 1981.
West, Richard. "The Interlace Structure of *The Lord of the Rings*." In *A Tolkien Compass*, edited by Jared Lobdell, 77–94. La Salle, IL: Open Court, 1975.

See also **History of Middle-earth: Overview; *Letters of J.R.R. Tolkien*; *Lord of the Rings*; *Sauron Defeated*; Tolkien, Christopher; *Treason of Isengard*; *War of the Ring***

REYNOLDS, R.W. (1867–1948)

Richard Williams Reynolds was born in Liverpool and educated at King Edward's School, Birmingham, from 1879–86, and at Balliol College, Oxford (BA 1890). He was intensely interested in politics, journalism, and literature, and initially worked as a barrister, but frequented the circle of W.E. Henley and other writers for the *National Observer*. Through the Fabian Society, he came to know Hubert Bland and his wife, the popular writer E. Nesbit, eventually becoming one of her lovers and living with them in Well Hall at Eltham. Reynolds is the co-dedicatee of Nesbit's novel *The Incomplete Amorist* (1906). His affections transferred to Nesbit's niece, the novelist Dorothea Deakin (1876–1924), whom Reynolds married on December 21, 1910. They had three daughters.

Reynolds had returned to King Edward's School as a temporary assistant master in 1900 and was appointed full master in 1901. He stayed until 1922, when for reasons of his wife's health he and his family left England, settling eventually at Anacapri, on the island of Capri in the Bay of Naples off the coast of Italy. There Reynolds joined the literary community including Norman Douglas, Axel Munthe, and Francis Brett Young. He and his daughters also came to know D.H. Lawrence on his visits to the island. Reynolds translated one chapter of the English version of Edwin Cerio's *That Capri Air* (1929), and the novel *Jim Redlake* (1930) by Francis Brett Young is dedicated to Reynolds, who read and commented on the book as it was written. Reynolds also translated a small book by a German girl, *Myrtles and Mice: Leaves from the Italian Diary of Cordelia Gundolf* (1935). He remarried in 1935, but lost his second wife a year later. Reynolds moved to Chicago in 1939, but returned to Anacapri in 1947, dying there in January 1948.

Reynolds instructed Tolkien and his friends in the T.C.B.S., presiding over the Literary and Debating Societies in addition to teaching history, classics, and English literature. He drove Tolkien in his own motor car (then a novelty) to attend his first term at Oxford in October 1911. Tolkien, despite privately expressing misgivings about certain attitudes of "Dickie" Reynolds, kept in touch with his former teacher. He approached Reynolds for advice on his own early verse, and sought aid from Reynolds in finding a publisher for *A Spring Harvest* (1918), the memorial volume of poems by Geoffrey Bache Smith. Most significantly, Tolkien also wrote out his "Sketch of the Mythology with especial reference to 'The Children of Húrin'"—technically the first prose version of *The Silmarillion*—for his old teacher, sending it to him in Anacapri in 1926, along with many of his poems, including the alliterative verse version of the Túrin story, for Reynolds's comments.

Douglas A. Anderson

Further Reading

Briggs, Julia. *A Woman of Passion: The Life of E. Nesbit 1858–1924*. London: Hutchinson, 1987.

"Obituary," *Old Edwardians Gazette* (1948).
"Retirement," *King Edward's School Chronicle* (November–December 1922).

See also **Silmarillion, The**; **T.C.B.S.**

RHETORIC

Rhetoric may be defined loosely as the art of effective public language. It was practised extensively in the classical civilisation of Greece and Rome, so Tolkien no doubt became familiar with rhetorical styles from his study of classical literature. His own literary rhetoric may be characterized by the qualities that he assigns in his *Beowulf* lecture to the best Old English poetry, "well-wrought language, weighty words, lofty sentiment" (*MC*, 14), although his linguistically most complex work, *The Lord of the Rings*, displays a wide range of personal and ethnic styles.

The hobbits, who according to Shippey (*Road*) are closest in outlook to the modern world and act as mediators for the contemporary reader, normally use a direct conversational style without rhetoric. They have a formal register (Merry tells the intruding Sackville-Bagginses that Frodo is "indisposed") that goes together with their legal niceties such as seven signatures of witnesses in red ink on a will, but it appears that public speaking other than at birthday parties is not part of their culture. Frodo, who has been educated by Bilbo, shows the most skill in varying his speech according to the company (e.g., Galadriel or Faramir, who are both representatives of a long cultural history), while Sam's style remains resolutely rustic. For most other characters, their rhetoric can be understood as a formal style, frequently combined with some archaism of vocabulary or syntax, which was Tolkien's device for distinguishing the archaic, heroic world of Elves, Dwarves, Rohirrim, and so on, from the more modern hobbits. Rosebury complains that there is not sufficient differentiation between minor heroic characters such as Legolas and Gimli, just a generalized archaizing, but that is perhaps an unavoidable side effect of the basic distinction.

Gandalf displays perhaps the widest range of speech. His tone is often familiar when speaking to the hobbits, although he frequently shows the difference of status by bursts of irascibility or riddling. With other characters he uses a more rhetorical style. The exchanges between him and Denethor are constructed particularly tautly, with the antagonists echoing one another's words ("an old man's folly," "the rule of Gondor," "unless the king should come again") and turning them to another significance. In his speech at the Council of Elrond, analysed in detail by Shippey (*Author*), Gandalf represents in addition the voices of Saruman, Radagast, Isildur, and others. Aragorn displays a range almost approaching that of Gandalf, from his affecting of the local rustic style at Bree to the incisive balance of the choice he places before Éomer: "Here is the Sword that was Broken and is forged again! Will you aid me or thwart me? Choose swiftly!" (*TT*, III, ii, 36).

In the case of Saruman, the effect of his negative rhetoric on listeners is commented on explicitly in the text: "All that [he] said seemed wise and reasonable, and desire awoke in them by swift agreement to seem wise themselves" (*TT*, III, x, 183). Within the text-world the effect is imputed to the supernormal power of the voice itself. However, Shippey (*Road*) offers an analysis which shows that Saruman's speech balances incompatible ideas against one another so as to deprive the words of their meaning; so the adjective "real" in "There need not be . . . any real change" opens up the interpretation that there will in fact be a substantial change. Thus, Shippey suggests that Saruman is made to sound like a modern politician. This is reminiscent of Father Simon in Charles Williams's novel *All Hallows' Eve* (1945), who achieves his incantation by "removing meaning itself from the words," or even Newspeak in Orwell's *1984* (1948). It would be interesting to know whether Tolkien saw his other tempters of mankind, Morgoth and Sauron, also neutralizing meaning. However, the extremely compressed style of *The Silmarillion* with its avoidance of direct speech does not provide sufficient data to give a clear picture.

In *The Hobbit* there is frequent play between different linguistic styles. Touches of humor are introduced by drawing attention to rhetorical formulations and explaining the difference between form and content. For example, "But who are you that sit in the plain as foes before defended walls?" is glossed as "You have no business here. We are going on, so make way or we shall fight you!". This is consistent with the narrator's asides to the supposed younger readership.

An ornate, rhetorical style is not restricted to Tolkien's literary works. A number of his academic publications, notably the *Beowulf* article, were originally presented as lectures and display characteristics of public speaking. The style is frequently allusive, and the audience are expected to understand literary allusions and extended metaphors such as the "jabberwocks of historical and antiquarian research." Like the rhetorical style of *The Lord of the Rings*, it is a reminder of a time when a homogeneous cultural background was assumed, and the distinction between formal and informal styles was more thoroughly observed than is usual today.

ALLAN TURNER

Further Reading

Rosebury, Brian. *Tolkien: A Cultural Phenomenon*. Basingstoke: Palgrave Macmillan, 2003.

Shippey, Thomas A. *J.R.R. Tolkien: Author of the Century*. London: HarperCollins, 2000.

———. *The Road to Middle-earth*. Rev. and expanded ed. London: HarperCollins, 2005.

See also **Aristotle; Epic Poetry; Language: Theories of; Prose Style; Tertullian**

RIDDLES

In considering riddles and their place in Tolkien's Middle-earth, the most obvious point at which to begin is with the riddle game in *The Hobbit*. Here, Bilbo Baggins, and Gollum exchange a series of progressively more difficult riddles—with terribly serious consequences for the loser. In Bilbo's case, his very life is at stake. Indeed, it's probably only because of the Elvish knife, Sting, that Gollum bothers with the pretense of the riddle game at all.

And yet, the riddle game is much more than mere embellishment to the storyline of *The Hobbit*. Later, in *The Lord of the Rings*, it serves to explain Gollum's common ancestry with the earliest hobbits. As Gandalf says to Frodo, Bilbo, and Gollum "understood one another remarkably well, very much better than a hobbit would understand, say, a Dwarf, or an Orc, or even an Elf. Think of the riddles they both knew, for one thing." And indeed, riddles are evident in the cultural history of our own world as well. Though Tolkien calls the riddles in *The Hobbit*, "all my own work . . . though their style and method is that of old literary (but not 'folk-lore') riddles," he acknowledges that "there is work to be done here on the sources and analogues" (*Letters*, 32). In fact, it's possible to trace many of them to antecedents outside Middle-earth. In *The Annotated Hobbit*, Douglas Anderson identifies many possible precedent sources, including the Old Norse *Saga of King Heidrek the Wise*, the Old English *Second Dialog of Solomon and Saturn*, Jón Árnason's *Ízlenkzar Gátur*, and common British nursery rhymes—all of which Tolkien probably knew very well. It is worth a passing note that, true to Gollum's shadowy origins, his riddles tend to be modeled on sources in ancient myth and legend, while Bilbo's tend to be comparatively more "modern"—which is to say, more quaint and Victorian.

The riddle contest itself has a venerable history in mythological literature as well, including exemplars like *The Second Dialog of Solomon and Saturn*; *Vafrúnismál*, a poem in the Old Norse *Poetic Edda*; Samson's riddle to the Philistines in the Bible; and Wagner's opera, *Der Ring des Nibelungen*, to name a few. And then there is perhaps the prototype of riddling for one's life, the famous riddle of the Sphinx, which Oedipus answers successfully, and which perhaps finds a loose echo in Bilbo's "No Legs" riddle.

Although the riddles posed between Bilbo and Gollum are the principal examples of bona fide riddles in Tolkien, there are many other passages in *The Hobbit* and *The Lord of the Rings* which might loosely be termed riddles. In *The Hobbit*, for example, there are the Moon Letters on Thrór's map: "Stand by the grey stone when the thrush knocks, . . . and the setting sun with the last light of Durin's Day will shine upon the key-hole" (*H*, III, 96). And a more dramatic example—no riddle at all for readers, but quite a puzzling one for Smaug—is Bilbo's elaborate self-portrait: "I come from under the hill, and under hills and over the hills my paths led. And through the air, I am he that walks unseen . . . I am the clue-finder, the web-cutter, the stinging fly. I was chosen for the lucky number . . . I am he that buries his friends alive and drowns them and draws them alive again from the water. I came from the end of a bag, but no bag went over me . . . I am the friend of bears and the guest of eagles. I am Ringwinner and Luckwearer; and I am Barrel-rider" (*H*, XII, 279).

In *The Lord of the Rings*, we find riddles of a different sort, often linked to prophecy. Though some critics debate whether these are true riddles, such hair-splitting is hardly necessary, since Tolkien himself uses the term often. A prime example is Boromir's riddle, urging him to "seek for the sword that was broken" and warning that "Isildur's Bane shall waken" (*FR*, II, ii, 259)—the answer to this riddle is, of course, the One Ring. Another example, from the same chapter, is Bilbo's verse describing Aragorn. As he admonishes, "All that is gold does not glitter / Not all those who wander are lost ... Renewed shall be blade that was broken / The crownless again shall be king" (*FR*, II, iii, 260–61).

We also have several less ominous and prophetic riddles. The inscription above the West-Gate of Moria, a lighthearted verbal puzzle, challenges even Gandalf until he realizes the trick—at which point it becomes "absurdly simple, like most riddles when you see the answer." One merely has to "say 'friend' and enter" (*FR*, II, iv, 321–22). Gandalf later offers Théoden a riddle of his own, one very much in the style of Bilbo or Gollum (*TT*, III, viii, 149). Its answer—Ents—would have been no challenge for Merry or Pippin, but for the men of Rohan, this riddle is hardly one of Gollum's chestnuts. And Gollum himself offers a lengthier version of his fish riddle (first encountered in *The Hobbit*) while on the trackless journey through the Dead Marshes.

One final example—though "The Authorities" might disallow it as a bona fide riddle—is worth pondering because, like Bilbo's Dúnadan verse, it poses a riddle whose answer can only be understood in the hindsight of a prophecy fulfilled. It is Glorfindel's warning concerning the Witch-King of Angmar: "Do not pursue him! He will not return to this land. Far off yet is his doom, and not by the hand of man will he fall" (*RK*, Appendix A, 332). These words closely echo the pronouncement from Shakespeare's *Macbeth*: "laugh to scorn / The power of man, for none of woman born / Shall harm Macbeth"—a source Tolkien knew quite well indeed. As we know, Macduff, "from his mother's womb untimely ripp'd," was the architect of Macbeth's doom. The fate of the Nazgûl Lord took much longer to find him; however, Éowyn's words on the Pelennor represent a different answer to the same riddle: "But no living man am I! You look upon a woman . . . Begone, if you be not deathless! For living or dark undead, I will smite you, if you touch him" (*RK*, V, vi, 116) Well answered!

JASON FISHER

Further Reading

Anderson, Douglas A., ed. *The Annotated Hobbit: Revised and Expanded Edition*. Boston, MA: Houghton Mifflin, 2002.

Boswell, George W. "Tolkien's Riddles in *The Lord of the Rings*." *Tennessee Folklore Society Bulletin* 35 (1969): 44–49.

Crashaw, Richard. "Gollum and the Riddle-Game." *Amon Hen* 109 (May 1991): 14–15.

Edwards, Owen Dudley. "Gollum, Frodo and the Catholic Novel." *Chesterton Review: The Journal of the Chesterton Society* 28 (2002): 57–71.

Jones, Leslie Ellen. *Myth and Middle-earth*. Cold Spring Harbor, NY: Cold Spring Harbor Press, 2002.

Shippey, Tom. *Author of the Century*. London: HarperCollins: 2000.

———. *The Road to Middle-earth*. 3rd rev. ed. Boston, MA: Houghton Mifflin, 2003.

See also **Bible; Bilbo; Boromir; Éowyn; Folklore; Glorfindel; Gollum; Mythology, Germanic; Old Norse Literature; Prophecy; Poems by Tolkien; Riddles: Sources; Shakespeare;** *Solomon and Saturn*

RIDDLES: SOURCES

Tolkien was somewhat ambiguous on the question of sources for the riddles featured in Bilbo and Gollum's riddle game, in one letter rather playfully challenging readers to find sources and analogues, noting that "I should not be at all surprised to learn that both the hobbit and Gollum will find their claim to have invented any of them disallowed" (*Letters*, 32), while in another rather grumpily asserting that "they are 'all my own work'" (*Letters*, 123). Tolkien excepted only "Thirty White Horses" and "No-legs" as traditional and the "egg-riddle" as a shortened nursery rhyme; he wrote a version of the longer form in Old English. As for the rest of the riddles, he asserted that they have no direct models, but that their "style and method is that of old literary (but not 'folk-lore') riddles" (*Letters*, 123).

The "old literary" riddles Tolkien had in mind are most likely the Old English riddles found in the Exeter Book, dialogues such as *Solomon and Saturn II*, and the riddle contest found in Old Norse tradition, primarily in the *Elder Edda* and *Heidrek's Saga* (later edited and translated by Tolkien's son, Christopher). The ninety-odd riddles found in the late tenth-century Exeter Book are poems of varied length in which the speaker often challenges the reader to guess its identity; almost all riddles are without solutions. The riddles range in subject from the domestic sphere to the heroic world, from natural phenomena to the learned realm, from the frankly sexual to the Christian. Behind the Old English riddles lies a tradition of eighth-century Anglo-Latin riddles and fourth or fifth-century Latin riddles. These tend to be less varied and more learned, and some turn on etymology; this may have been in Tolkien's mind as he composed Bilbo's "sun on the daisies" riddle, which expresses the etymology of "daisy" as "day's eye" (*dæges eage*).

Related to these riddles are a variety of poetic dialogues featuring riddling questions, in particular the tenth-century *Solomon and Saturn II* (MS Cambridge, Corpus Christi College 422), which features a riddle contest between the biblical king Solomon (representing Christian wisdom) and a Chaldean prince, Saturn (representing pagan wisdom). Not only the idea of a contest but at least one of the riddles, posed by Saturn, may have influenced Tolkien: its solution is "old age," but it corresponds to the "time" riddle posed by Gollum; Gollum's "dark" riddle may have an analogue here as well, though the answer is "shadow." The riddle contest is particularly vibrant in Old Norse tradition; it is featured in both *Heidreks Saga* and the Old Norse "Vafthrúdismal" (The Lay of Vafthrúdnir) in the *Elder Edda* (the *Edda* also contains the "Fáfnismál" featuring an antecedent to Smaug's riddling talk). Both these riddle contests feature Odin, and both end with a nonriddle—a question, in fact. Odin asks what Odin whispered in the ear of Baldur before Baldur was killed—a question that only he knows the answer to, just as only Bilbo knows what he has in his pocket.

YVETTE KISOR

Further Reading

Anderson, Douglas A., ed. "Riddles in the Dark." In *The Annotated Hobbit*, 115–36. Rev. ed. Boston and New York: Houghton Mifflin, 2002.

Couch, Christopher L. "From under Mountains to Beyond Stars: The Process of Riddling in Leofric's *The Exeter Book* and *The Hobbit*." *Mythlore* 14, no. 1 (whole no. 51; Autumn 1987): 9–13, 55.

Larrington, Carolyne, trans. *The Poetic Edda*. Oxford: Oxford University Press, 1996.

Shippey, T.A. "*The Hobbit*: Re-Inventing Middle-earth." In *J.R.R. Tolkien: Author of the Century*. London: HarperCollins, 2000.

———. *Poems of Wisdom and Learning in Old English*. Cambridge: D.S. Brewer; Totowa, NJ: Rowman & Littlefield, 1976.

Tolkien, Christopher, trans. *The Saga of King Heidrek the Wise*. Icelandic Texts. London and New York: Nelson, 1960.

Tolkien, J.R.R. "Enigmata Saxonica Nuper Inventa Duo." [Two Saxon Riddles Recently Discovered]. In *A Northern Venture: Verses by Members of the Leeds University English School Association*, 20. Leeds: Swan Press, 1923.

Williamson, Craig. *A Feast of Creatures: Anglo-Saxon Riddle Songs*. Philadelphia, PA: University of Pennsylvania Press, 1982.

See also **Old Norse Literature; Riddles;** *Solomon and Saturn*

RING-GIVING

The motif of ring-giving is central to the Anglo-Saxon concept of the *comitatus*—the Germanic warrior band. The term *comitatus* (from the Latin *comites* meaning "companions") comes from Tacitus's *Germania* (c. 98) and refers to the relationship between a leader and his men. The relationship was one of mutual obligation and the bonds of the *comitatus* were cemented through oaths of loyalty on the part of the thanes, and ring-giving on the part of the lord or king. A ring (*hring*, *béag*) could be any circular adornment and as well as finger-rings included armbands, bracelets, neck-rings, and the like and was extended to treasure in general. Ring-giving becomes not simply the dispensing of treasure but the outward symbol of the lord's fulfillment of his role, and just as a thane's worth is judged through his ability to fulfill his oath, the king's worth becomes defined through his generosity. Ring-giving is so central to the concept of the king that in Old English poetry a "ring-giver" (*béaggyfa*, *béaga brytta*) signifies a king.

Aspects of this *comitatus* relationship and its expression through ring-giving are especially evident in the Old English poem *Beowulf*. Kings are called not only ring-givers (*béaggyfa*, *béaga brytta*) but gold-givers (*goldgyfa*), gold-friends (*goldwine*), and treasure-givers (*sincgifa, sinces brytta*); the site of the ring-giving becomes a ring-hall (*hringsele, béahsele*) or a gold-hall (*goldsele*). Good kings are extolled for their generosity while the prime sin of the bad king is hoarding—Heremod, the exemplum of the bad king in the poem, is condemned because "not at all did he give rings to the Danes for glory" (*nallas béagas geaf Denum æfter dóme* [1719–20]). He failed to honor his side of the lord-thane bond; the poem shows us an example of thanes failing to honor their side, and again the giving of rings becomes paramount in its symbolic value. After Beowulf's thanes desert him as he battles the dragon, Wiglaf upbraids them, reminding them of "when we promised to our lord in the beer-hall, he who gave us rings, that we would repay him" (*þonne wé gehéton ússum hláforde in bíorsele, ðé ús ðás béagas geaf, þæt wé him . . . gyldan woldon* [2634–6]). *Beowulf* is not unique in this regard, and heroic poetry like the *Battle of Maldon*, elegies like *The Wanderer*, and even religious poetry (with God/ Christ as lord) all feature this *comitatus* relationship expressed through ring-giving.

Tolkien explores this in a number of ways, perhaps most obviously through the Rohirrim who are based in many ways upon Anglo-Saxon society, and their king, Theoden (*ðeoden* means "king" in Old English). In addition Isildur's insistence on taking the Ring "as weregild for my father, and my brother" (*FR*, II, ii, 256) suggests an Anglo-Saxon attitude—as well as securing the lord-thane bond the giving of treasure could pay for a death and thus avoid feud (*weregild* literally means "man-price"). But of course the main ring-giving that takes place is Sauron's gift of rings. Sauron "dealt them out" (*S*, 288)—seven to Dwarves and nine to men, and the nine become ring-wraiths, Nazgûl, in a perversion of the lord-thane relationship. While the nine are loyal thanes indeed, the reciprocity, the key aspect of the *comitatus* relationship symbolized through ring-giving, has been lost, and the Ring becomes a symbol not of mutual obligation but of servitude.

YVETTE KISOR

Further Reading

Klaeber, Fr., ed. *Beowulf and the Fight at Finnsburg.* 3rd ed. Lexington, MA: D.C. Heath & Co., 1950.
Liuzza, R.M., trans. *Beowulf: A New Verse Translation.* Toronto: Broadview Press, 2000.
Stratyner, Leslie. "Ðe Us ðas Beagas Geaf (He Who Gave Us These Rings): Sauron and the Perversion of Anglo-Saxon Ethos." *Mythlore* 16 (1989): 5–8.

See also **Battle of Maldon; Kingship; Northern Courage;** *Wanderer*

RINGS

The ring image derives from a long tradition older than that of the Christian cross and is found in nearly all European historical and literary periods including Greek, Roman, Germanic, Norse, Celtic, and Arthurian. Tolkien's employment of rings in his mythology is similar to what one finds in early medieval epics and romances. Rings occupied a foundational space within those cultures Tolkien found so fascinating, specifically the Anglo-Saxon and Danish world of *Beowulf* and the Icelandic/Scandinavian culture of *The Prose Edda* and *The Volsunga Saga*. Some argue that Tolkien was also inspired by Wagner's adaptation of the *Niebelungenlied* though he claimed that outside of the fact that both were round there was no connection.

The symbolism of the ring appears often in Tolkien's works. The Maharaxar is the name of the circle around which the Valar sit to pronounce their judgments, hence it is called the Ring of Doom (from the Old English *dom*: judgment). There is also the stone wall encircling the tower of Orthanc, which is called the Ring of Isengard. Tolkien also refers to Middle-earth as Morgoth's Ring since Morgoth suffused his power throughout that created realm.

Most of the ring imagery in Middle-earth, however, refers to rings worn on the hand. The events surrounding their forging, exchange, disappearance, recovery, and use occupy much of Tolkien's imagination. The twenty Rings of Power appearing in the well-known rhyme ("Three Rings for the Elven-Kings under the Sky") are central to *The Lord of the Rings*. Sixteen of these were made by the smiths of Eregion or *mirdain* and Celebrimbor with the aid of Sauron in the guise of Annatar. Nine were given to men, great kings and sorcerers, three of whom were from Númenor; these become the Ring-wraiths or Nazgûl. The remaining seven were bestowed upon the Dwarves. One of these was given to Durin III by Celebrimbor and later inherited by Thror, who wandered Middle-earth with the ring before being captured. This is Thror's Ring. Three rings, however, were made by the Elves in Eregion without the assistance of Sauron. They are Nenya the Ring of Adamant, also called the Ring of Water worn by Galadriel; Narya the Ring of Ruby, also called the Ring of Fire, given to Gandalf the Grey by Círdan the Shipwright; and Vilya the Ring of Sapphire, also called the Ring of Air worn by Elrond. The final ring of power, the One Ring, was forged by Sauron himself and was made to rule over all the rest. Sauron's plan was understood by the Elves, who quickly removed and hid their rings, and so they remained uncorrupted. All the Rings of Power, however, are bound to the fate of the One Ring.

Lesser rings also appear in Middle-earth. One known to exist into the Fourth Age is the Ring of Barahir. Barahir was a mortal given a ring for his bravery in the Dagor Bragollach by Finrod Felagund, brother to Galadriel. Barahir was slain by Orcs and his ring-adorned hand was cut off. Beren, his son, retrieved the hand, and the ring passed down through Elros to the chieftains of the north-kingdom until it is eventually bestowed on Aragorn at Imladris. The corrupted wizard Saruman too wears a ring, though its powers are never spoken of. That he possesses one at the time of Gandalf's imprisonment underscores his preoccupation with the One Ring.

All rings in Tolkien's mythology are symbolic. Barahir's ring is a gift and thus symbolizes Finrod's friendship. Vilya, Nenya, and Narya are worn by those most opposed to Sauron's might in the Third Age: Elrond, Galadriel, and (eventually) Gandalf. Though each of these rings has its own unique magic, all three reinforce support of the Valar's vision for Middle-earth. Vilya and Nenya preserve the idyllic beauty of Middle-earth and protect Imladris and Lorien respectively from moderate dangers from the outside. Their circles reflect the temporal cycles to which the Elves and the land are together bound. Narya, the ring later won by Gandalf, inspires Elves and mortals to feats of greater bravery and courage, its ruby suggesting the warmth and courage of the heart. Sauron's Ring, on the other hand, mocks creation, seduces its wearers with the promise of absolute power very much like what we find in Plato's passage on the ring of Gyges the Lydian. Supernatural and unnatural, it promises greater power while offering, in reality, an undoing of one's being and one's accomplishments. On a psychological level, the One Ring exposes the presence in most of the characters of a humbling frailty, a potential to become a hateful overlord. Only Tom Bombadil seems truly exempt from this rule.

CHRISTOPHER VACCARO

Further Reading

Day, David. *Tolkien's Ring*. London: HarperCollins, 1994.

See also: **Elrond; Galadriel; Gandalf; One Ring, The; Ring-Giving; Rings of Power; Sauron**

RINGS OF POWER

Rings of Power usually designate the magic rings created by the Noldor Elven-smiths of Eregion and Sauron between 1500 and 1590 SA. Of prominence are the greater Rings of Power, that is, the nine rings of men, the seven of the Dwarves, and the three Elven rings (for alternative distributions see *Shadow*, 269).

Each is made from a band of (precious) metal and contains a precious stone. Tolkien's conception of the history and the powers of these rings is closely linked to the development of the idea of the One Ring. The Rings of Power were designed to give their bearers the gift of longevity and special power in accordance with their nature. About ten years after the forging of the last Ring of Power, that is, 1600 SA, Sauron secretly wrought the One Ring in order to dominate all the others. The Elves, however, perceived Sauron's treason and hid the three Elven rings from him and did not use them as long as he was in possession of the Ruling Ring. Yet Sauron obtained all the other rings and tried to use them to ensnare men and Dwarves. He gave nine rings to kings of men, who faded and came under his dominion as the Nazgûl (Ringwraiths). To the Dwarves he gave seven to increase their wealth. Yet the children of Aule proved resistant, could not be dominated and did not fade, although their hunger for gold may have increased under the influence of the rings. Four of the Dwarf-rings were devoured, together with their hapless owners, by dragons and thus destroyed. In time, Sauron won back the remaining three, although Tolkien briefly played with the idea that the Dwarves, at the time of the Council of Elrond, might still possess Durin's ring (see *Shadow*, 398). This ring had been given to Durin III by the Elves and was believed to be the most powerful of the seven. As learn from Gandalf, it was taken from Thráin circa 2845 TA while he was kept prisoner at Dol Guldur.

The fate of the three Elven rings, Narya, Nenya, and Vilya, is better chronicled. Tolkien, at first, believed the three had been wrought with the help of Sauron, too (see *Treason*, 155). Later, he considered the possibility of making Fëanor, under the influence of Melkor, the creator of the three Elven rings (see *Treason*, 255). In the end, Tolkien made them the work of Celebrimbor, son of Curufin, grandson of Fëanor. Celebrimbor forged them in secret and Sauron never touched them. However, they still fell under the dominance of the One Ring and the thoughts of their bearers would be laid bare to Sauron, so they could not be used while Sauron possessed the Ruling Ring. The power of the Three did not lie in domination or wealth, but in making, healing, and preserving.

Nenya, the Ring of Water or Adamant (also called the White Ring; originally the Ring of Earth, see *Treason*, 260), is made from mithril and inset with a diamond. Celebrimbor himself gave it to Galadriel, who used it to enhance the beauty and power of Lórien. It is, in *Unfinished Tales* (325) called "chief of the Three," which stands in contrast to *The Lord of the Rings* (*RK*, VI, ix, 308), where the ring of Elrond is called "Vilya, mightiest of the Three." Nenya is the only Elven ring that stayed with its original owner throughout the ages.

Narya, the Ring of Fire or the Red Ring (inset with a ruby), was given to Gil-galad, who had also Vilya in his keeping. He later entrusted it to Círdan who kept it till the arrival of the Istari (c. 1000 TA) and who then gave it to Mithrandir/Gandalf to assist him in the long labors that lay ahead.

Vilya, the Ring of Air or Sky, also called the Blue Ring (made of gold and inset with a sapphire), was also first given to Gil-galad by Celebrimbor. Gil-galad passed it on to Elrond who bore it throughout the Third Age.

The three Elven rings were of great importance in the conflict with Sauron and the three bearers proved instrumental in helping the Fellowship of the Ring with the destruction of the One Ring, although this brought about the fading of the power of their rings and of all that has been wrought through them. This is not obvious at the inception of the tale, and the reader is initiated—along with the hobbit-protagonists—only gradually into the significance of the three rings. At the end of the Third Age, all three Elven ring-bearers, and with them the three rings, depart over the Sea and thus out of human reach.

THOMAS HONEGGER

Further Reading

Tolkien, J.R.R. "Of the Rings of Power and the Third Age." In *S*, 285–304.

See also Beowulf; **Elves; Magic; Rings; Sauron**

RIVENDELL

Rivendell, a translation of the Sindarin name *Imladris* (meaning "cut valley"), was founded by Elrond in SA 1697 during an assault of Sauron against Eriador. While leading a host of Elves in defense of Eriador, Elrond was outnumbered and nearly overwhelmed until help from the Dwarves of Khazad-dûm enabled him to escape. Retreating north to a deep valley on the western slopes of the Misty Mountains, he founded Rivendell as a "refuge and stronghold." There Elrond was soon besieged again by Sauron's army, but held out until 1700 when, in response to Gil-galad's call for aid, Númenórean ships arrived on the shores of Middle-earth. The Númenóreans quickly crushed Sauron's forces and drove them from Eriador, and shortly thereafter the first Council was held. The Council decided that an Elvish stronghold in east of Eriador was needed and that it should be at Rivendell. Gil-galad then appointed Elrond as his vice-regent and gave to him the ring Vilya, one of the three Elvish rings of power, which thereafter remained in Rivendell on the hand or in the hands of Elrond (*UT*, 238–39).

By the end of the Third Age, Rivendell (along with Lothlórien) was one of the chief strongholds against Sauron. Unlike Gondor, however, its strength came not as much from military might as from the power of Elrond. Tolkien described it as a "kind of enchanted sanctuary" (*Letters*, 153). When Black Riders try to cross the Ford of Bruinen into Rivendell in pursuit of Frodo, the river rises at Elrond's command and sweeps the Riders away. It was in Rivendell, under the care and nurture of Elrond, that Aragorn (after the death of his father Arathorn) was fostered and raised from the age of two until he was twenty years of age. And it is to Rivendell that Bilbo retires at the end of his life.

Like many aspects of the legendarium, Tolkien's concept of Rivendell develops slowly. The portrayal changes considerably in tone and detail from *The Hobbit* (where it is the "Last Homely House") to *The Lord of the Rings*, where it is described as a place of power able "to withstand the might of Mordor, for a while" (*FR*, II, i, 235). One of the first mentions of Rivendell's folk in *The Hobbit* is Gandalf's reference to them "hurrying along for fear of the trolls" (*H*, II, 83). And though Elrond himself is described as noble, fair, strong, wise, venerable, and kind (*H*, III, 94), the Elves of Rivendell are portrayed in the Hobbit as being almost silly. In *The Lord of the Rings*, by contrast, we see that Rivendell includes mighty Elven warriors like Glorfindel (who stands alone against several Black Riders) as well as Elladan and Elrohir, the twin sons of Elrond. Elrond and his realm of Rivendell are known far and wide for their wisdom, healing, and power, and many important councils are held at Rivendell at the end of the Third Age.

Through the developing portrayal, one thing that remains consistent is that Rivendell is a sanctuary. Even in *The Lord of the Rings*, it remains a "Homely House." As Douglas Anderson points out in *The Annotated Hobbit*, with reference to the OED, "homely" far from being derogatory, means very literally "characteristic of home"—a place one receives "kind treatment" (*H*, III, 89–90) In short, it is "a perfect house, whether you like food or sleep or story-telling or singing, or just sitting and thinking best, or a pleasant mixture of them all." Just to be there, as Frodo learned, "was a cure for weariness, fear, and sadness" (*FR*, II, I, 237).

MATTHEW DICKERSON

Further Reading

Dickerson, Matthew. *Following Gandalf: Epic Battles and Moral Victory in* The Lord of the Rings. Grand Rapids, MI: Brazos Press, 2003.

Helms, Randel. *Tolkien's World*. Boston, MA: Houghton Mifflin, 1974.

See also **Aragorn; Elrond; Elves; Lothlórien; Rings of Power**

ROAD GOES EVER ON, THE

This book consists of a collection of poems from and related to *The Lord of the Rings* and set to music by Donald Swann (1923–94). The book comes both with scores and with a recording of the songs. It is notable not only for its music, but also for its translations, philological notes, and decorations by Tolkien himself, and for its publication, in later editions, of a poem that had not before seen print.

The first edition of *Road* (1967) featured only poems that had already been published. The poems from *The Lord of the Rings* are "The Road Goes Ever On," "Upon the Hearth the Fire is Red," "In the Willow-meads of Tasarinan," "In Western Lands," "Namárië (Farewell)," and "I Sit Beside the Fire." Another poem, "Errantry," had appeared in *The Adventures of Tom Bombadil* (1962). For the second edition of *Road* (1978), the previously unpublished "Bilbo's Last Song" appeared, and for the third edition, published in Germany in 1993, "Lúthien Tinúviel," from *The Silmarillion* chapter 19, was added. The music for the latter song was not published in Britain until 1998, however, when it appeared in *The Songs of Donald Swann* (arr. John Jansson, Thames/ William Elkin). In 2002, a new edition of *Road* was published by HarperCollins, including all of the songs and a compact disc of the performances.

Donald Swann was best known to the British public as one half of the songwriting and performing duo Flanders and Swann. They first became known in 1956–57 for their musical revue *At the Drop of a Hat*, featuring their best-known song, "Madeira, M'Dear?" a witty account of a failed seduction. Flanders was the lyricist of the team; Swann was the composer. Swann's musical style is in the classical tradition and has incorporated opera, children's songs, folk music, music hall, and sacred music, among many other forms. Tolkien and his wife Edith saw a performance of the revue when it came to Oxford and enjoyed both Swann's music and Flanders' clever lyrics.

Swann was born to an Anglo-Russian family and grew up speaking both languages; his musical travels and his studies at Oxford made him familiar with several other languages, and it was partly his multi-lingual facility that attracted him to Tolkien's writings. But Swann's introduction to fantasy came through C.S. Lewis's space trilogy. With librettist David Marsh, Swann composed a rarely performed and almost-forgotten operatic version of the trilogy called *Perelandra*.

Thus, Swann was already well known, both generally and to the Inklings, when he and Tolkien began collaborating on the first edition of *Road*, and had established himself both as a popular composer and as one of unusual range. During their collaboration, Swann became a trusted colleague to Tolkien; indeed, there was much commonality in the two men's minds. In addition to their mutual love of languages, both men were believing Christians; both were combat veterans albeit of different world wars; and both shared a concern with ecological perspectives and issues. Swann's notes on Tolkien's writings, both in the various introductions to *Road* and in his autobiography *Swann's Way*, show him to be an intelligent and sensitive reader. That Swann was a trusted member of Tolkien's circle is shown also by the fact that, at Tolkien's funeral, Joy Hill— Tolkien's secretary and a close friend and neighbor of Swann—presented Swann with a copy of the then-unknown "Bilbo's Last Song," which Swann set to music and published in the second edition of *Road*.

Swann's compositions for *Road* are unique in that, unlike most musical adaptations of Tolkien's poetry, they do not attempt to reproduce a "medieval" or folk atmosphere. Instead, they take the form of classical Leider, sometimes stretching and compressing the meter of Tolkien's verse. Swann's melodies show a wide range of influences. For example, "Namárië" is based upon a Gregorian chant that Tolkien himself sang to Swann in the initial stages of their collaboration; while "Bilbo's Last Song" is based on a tune from the Isle of Man, merged with a Greek melody. Swann has described most of the other compositions as resembling Schubert or Grainger. The arrangements in Swann's scores are for the most part for piano and single voice, but some include optional parts for other voices or for a guitar. The recordings feature Swann on piano, accompanied by various solo operatic singers; Swann himself sings "Bilbo's Last Song," Clive McCrombie sings "Lúthien Tinúviel," and the other songs are sung by William Elvin (whose surname Tolkien referred to as "a name of good omen" when the songs were first performed). Elvin was a Scot, and Tolkien, working with him on Quenya and Sindarin pronunciation, intriguingly encouraged him to use his own accent when singing those languages.

Tolkien's "Notes and Translations" at the end of the volume represented one of the earliest opportunities for readers to see the full range of his linguistic creativity. Here, the theory in Appendices E and F of *The Lord of the Rings* is shown in application. The sections on "Namárië" (*FR*, II, viii, 394) and "A Elbereth Gilthoniel" (*FR*, I, iii, 88–89; *FR*, II, i, 250) feature the poems written in Tengwar; transcriptions into English letters including metrical, stress, and vowel-length markers; guides to pronunciation; literal translations of all the word elements; and idiomatic translations (reproduced from *The Lord of the Rings*), followed by commentaries on Quenya and Sindarin vocabulary, grammar, and prosody, along with notes on the mythological history and the place of the Elves within it.

CHESTER N. SCOVILLE

Further Reading

Carpenter, Humphrey. *J.R.R. Tolkien: A Biography*. London: Allen & Unwin, 1977.
Swann, Donald. *Swann's Way: A Life in Song*. 2nd ed. London: Arthur James, 1993.
Tolkien, J.R.R., music by Donald Swann. *The Road Goes Ever On: A Song Cycle*. 4th ed. London: HarperCollins, 2004.

See also **Adventures of Tom Bombadil; Alphabets, Invented; Art and Illustrations by Tolkien; Christianity; Environmentalism and Eco-Criticism; Grammar; Languages Invented by Tolkien; Lewis, C.S.;** *Lord of the Rings*; **Lyric Poetry; Music in Middle-earth; Poems by Tolkien; Poems by Tolkien in Other Languages; Popular Music; Rhyme Schemes and Meter;** *Silmarillion, The*

ROHAN

The land of Rohan, originally a region of Gondor named "Calenardhon," was given to Eorl the Young and the people of the North by Cirion, Steward of Gondor, in reward for their assistance against an enemy invasion. The land was called "The Mark" by its inhabitants, and the people who settled there were known to be masters of horsemanship and well acquainted with the plains.

The natural borders of the land are as follows: the River Isen to the west, the Limlight River and Fangorn Forest to the north, the river Anduin (The Great River) to the east, and the mouths of the River Entwash to the south. The river Adorn and the White Mountains separate Rohan from Gondor, which lies

to the southwest. Rohan is divided by the Entwash into two regions: the West Emnet and the East Emnet. Helm's Deep, the valley that serves as a natural protection of the fortress of the Hornburg, lies to the west as well, in the northwestern White Mountains.

The king of Rohan resides in Meduseld (Old English "mead-hall"), the golden hall of the courts of Édoras (OE "the Courts"). It is described by Legolas, upon first sight, as a great hall of Men, set upon a green terrace, thatched with gold, the phrase "the light of it shines far over the land" (*TT*, I, vi, 111) is an adaptation of *Beowulf*, line 311, "lixte se leoma ofer landa fela." Édoras is located in the West Emnet, near the White Mountains and along the North-South road. The description of Theoden's hall in fact owes something to William Morris's *House of the Wulfings*, and that source explains the otherwise anomalous "louver" that is described in the scene.

The people of Rohan were descended from a race of men who came from the land of Éothéod, a land that "lay near the sources of the Anduin, between the furthest ranges of the Misty Mountains and the northernmost parts of Mirkwood" (*RK*, Appendix A, 344). In the year 2510 of the Third Age, Gondor was attacked by men from the northeast and Orcs from the mountains. The steward of Gondor, Cirion, sent for help from the people of Éothéod and those riders answered the call. The forces of Gondor were saved by the riders of Éothéod and their leader, Eorl the Young. In gratitude for their services, Cirion gave the area of Calenardhon to the people of the North and thus, the land of Rohan was founded during the Second Age, in the year of 3320, and named "the Mark of the Riders." The people of that land called themselves "Eorlingas," after their lord, Eorl the Young. The people of Gondor referred to them as the "Rohirrim," or the Horse-Lords. The name given to the land by the people of Gondor (Rohan) is formed from the Sindarin word "roch" (horse) and the ending "-and" (land). Tolkien decided quite early in the composition of *The Lord of the Rings* that there would be some adventures involving the "Horse Lords," but the Rohan/Anglo-Saxon England connection developed significantly later.

Rohan was also known for the "mearas" (OE "horse"): great horses that would only bear the King of the Mark or his sons (that is, until Shadowfax; OE: "shadow pelt"). This dates back to Eorl the Young's father, who was killed by a horse. Eorl vowed to avenge his father by taming the horse and he did so, giving the horse the name "Felaróf." Eorl was able to ride him without bit or bridle, and it is upon this horse that he rode to the aid of Cirion and the people of Gondor. From that horse were descended the Mearas.

Rohan was faced with troubles long before the War of the Ring: in 2758, the land was attacked from the East while Gondor was attacked from the coastline. The people of Rohan were defeated, enslaved and killed mercilessly. It was at this time that King Helm Hammerhand took refuge in the valley of the Hornburg, which later became known as "Helm's Deep" (*RK*, Appendix A, 346–48). After this, Rohan suffered under a particularly cold winter known as "the Long Winter": the people suffered from starvation and plague. Long after Helm's death, Saruman took up residence in Isenguard. His true intentions were seen later, when his agent Gríma Wormtongue infiltrated the courts of Edoras and the thoughts of King Theoden.

The language of Rohan ("Rohirric") is a form of Old English: for instance, the "Mark" is related to the Old English "mearc," meaning "border, boundary or limit." The first king of Rohan, Eorl the Young, has a name that means simply "earl" in Old English. The Rohirrim, in fact, speak Old Mercian, the particular dialect of Old English that would have been spoke by Tolkien's ancestors in the West Midlands. However, Tolkien in Appendix F and elsewhere took considerable pains to separate his invented Riders from the historical Anglo-Saxons, arguing that the Rohirrim were really only like the Anglo-Saxons in being "a simpler and more primitive people living in contact with a higher and more venerable culture, and occupying lands that had once been part of its domain" (*RK*, Appendix F, 414 n1).

HILARY WYNNE

Further Reading

Shippey, Tom. *The Road to Middle-earth: Revised and Expanded Edition*. Boston, MA: Houghton Mifflin, 2003.

See also **Éomer; Goths; Gríma (Wormtongue); Old English; Old Mercian; Théoden**

ROMAN HISTORY

J.R.R. Tolkien wrote in the foreword to *The Lord of the Rings* that he "much prefer[red] history, true or feigned" to "allegory or topical reference." Given that authorial predilection, it is perhaps not surprising that, in addition to Middle-earth's Kingdom of Gondor exhibiting some parallels to Byzantium and Egypt, its "feigned history" can also be seen to contain a number of striking parallels to the "true history" of the (Western) Roman Empire in our primary world.

For instance, Æneas (*pius Æneas*, as Vergil calls him) and Elendil "the Faithful" both escape the wreck of their homelands (Troy, Númenor) to become founding rulers overseas. Additionally, Romulus and Remus are, like Isildur and Anárion, dynasty-founding brothers; rivalry between the two houses breaks out early in the Roman case, later in the Númenórean one. Further, as Judy Ann Ford has pointed out, the southern capital of the new empire is in both cases built in stone, a construction material not used in either case by the Germanic and/or Germanic-named indigenous barbarians to the north. Finally, both Rome and Gondor experience decadence and decline. As Faramir remarks to Frodo at Henneth Annûn, in aging Gondor the "Númenóreans still, as they had in their own kingdom and so lost it, hungered after endless life unchanging." In contrast to Rome, though, Gondor is granted an unexpected respite from complete downfall, in the person of Aragorn Elessar, whose coming results in the founding of a new royal house.

Not only the history of Gondor, but the history of Middle-earth itself inscribes a general arc of descent from the beginning, or at least since the First Age; it is made clear that the free will of flawed creatures is responsible. Galadriel speaks of having "fought the long defeat" (*FR*, II, vii, 372). Between battles in Gondor, Legolas and Gimli debate how Men (human beings) "fail of their promise" and have the potential to "come to naught in the end but might-have-beens." This fall from grace is consistent not only with Tolkien's Christian concepts of fallen man; but also with a Germanic sense of fate and doom; as well as with the classical idea of humankind's descent from a primeval Golden Age to a current Iron Age, as found in Hesiod.

Given these parallels with Roman imperial history and this arc of descent, one might suspect Tolkien's dependence on, or at least consultation of, Edward Gibbon's *Decline and Fall of the Roman Empire* (1776–81). However, if one compares Tolkien's Gondorian decline, fall and redemption with Gibbon's narrated decline, it becomes clear that the two narratives are far from parallel. Gibbon argued, for instance, that Rome's downfall was brought about by the supplanting of the early Roman virtue of secular patriotism by the lesser virtues of honor and religion, specifically the Christian religion (*Decline and Fall*, chap. 1 and throughout). Gibbon called the Christian cults of saints and martyrs introduced to Rome late in its history "gaudy and superfluous," practiced by those who "felt the strong intoxication of fanaticism, and perhaps of wine" (chap. 28). The redemption of Tolkien's fallen Númenóreans, by contrast, is constructed in mirror image to Gibbon's model: they must relinquish their racial and national pride in favor of a return to humility and (what might be called) piety. (One can see this change in microcosm in the character of Faramir, or by negative example in that of Denethor.)

SANDRA BALLIF STRAUBHAAR

Further Reading

Ford, Judy Ann. "The White City: The Lord of the Rings as an Early Medieval Myth of the Restoration of the Roman Empire." *Tolkien Studies* 2 (2005): 53–73.

Goffart, Walter. *The Narrators of Barbarian History*. Princeton, NJ: Princeton University Press, 1988.

Straubhaar, Sandra Ballif. "Myth, Late Roman History and Multiculturalism in Tolkien's Middle-earth." In *Tolkien and the Invention of Myth: A Reader*, edited by Jane Chance, 101–18. Lexington, KY: University Press of Kentucky, 2004.

See also **Gibbon, Edward:** *Decline and Fall of the Roman Empire*; **Men, Middle-earth**

ROMANCES: MIDDLE ENGLISH AND FRENCH

After flourishing in France for well over half a century, the romance genre appeared in English literature in the middle of the thirteenth century and continued through the time of Chaucer. *King Horn* and *Floriz and Blauncheflur*, which date from around 1240, are the earliest extant English romance texts; at the close of the fourteenth century, Chaucer's *The Franklin's Tale* and his *Tale of Sir Thopas* parodied the genre and thus essentially brought it to an end. Of the surviving English romances, only two, *King Horn* and *Havelock* (also thirteenth century), are based on the "matter of Britain" and thus on English subjects. In fact, almost every English romance, including *King Horn* and *Havelock*, had a precursor in an Old French original. As a genre, therefore, the English romance represented largely a French inheritance, more specifically the inheritance of the Breton Lai, a popular, nontextual, form of poetry sung by itinerant minstrels on the Armorican peninsula to the accompaniment of a harp or a rote. The origins of this form, however, are Celtic; and, it is assumed that the word "lai" was derived from the Celtic word for song. During the last third of the twelfth century, the Breton Lais were given textual and literary form in Britain by Marie de France, a gifted author trained in Latin and versed in classical literature, who wrote them up in the Old French vernacular for King Henry II Plantagenet. Marie's works were likely the principal source of importation of the Lai into the stock of English minstrels and authors. As Thomas Rumble has noted, there "are in Middle English eight tales that purport to be, or to be based upon, Breton Lays" (vii). Thomas Chestre's *Sir Launfal* and the anonymous

Lay le Freine, for example, are likely descended from Marie's *Lanval* and *Fresne*.

J.R.R. Tolkien's scholarship and his creative works are redolent with the presence and influence of the Breton Lai. He translated *Sir Orfeo*, and its opening lines: "We often read and written find, / as learned men do us remind, / that lays that now the harpers sing / are wrought of many a marvellous thing": place that text, and Tolkien's philological focus, squarely within the history of the genre. Line ten of the *Orfeo* prologue, however, provides the strongest connection between Tolkien's scholarship and his fiction, noting, about the Lais, that "some are tales of Faërie." Indeed, unlike any other medieval genre, the Breton Lais are fairy-stories in the truest Tolkienien sense in that they almost invariably describe encounters in the "Perilous Realm" and, in so doing, rely on the "arresting strangeness" of fantasy ("On Fairy-Stories," 139). The Breton Lais are in fact fantastic, in the semantic sense that Tolkien ascribed to that term. They deal "with images of things that are not only 'not actually present', but which are indeed not to be found in our primary world at all, or are generally believed not to be found there" ("On Fairy-Stories," 139). Hence we find, among other fantastic elements, the following in the works of Marie de France and in later English romance: encounters with fairies, voyages to enchanted lands, shape-shifting between human and other forms, animals with human characteristics, and creatures that are neither human nor animal according to our classifications. Tolkien's notions of recovery, escape, and the happy ending are also characteristic of fairy stories and can be found consistently in the Breton Lai and Middle English romance.

Jane Chance has noted that some of Tolkien's creative works, for example, the "Lay of Aoutrou and Itroun" and *Farmer Giles of Ham*, are mimetic parodies of the Breton Lai and Middle English romance combined with fabliau. In superficial appearance, they match the medieval genres, but they are in substance unlike fairy stories. Rather than escape, they depict struggle and the "difficulty of living in this primary world" (Chance, *Tolkien's Art*, 114); and, they do not end happily. The parodies also point to flaws in past generations. Shippey discerns a "stern morality" in "Aotrou and Itroun." And he also perceives an "aggressive point" in *Farmer Giles of Ham*: that preoccupation with present reward, luxury and style, especially when combined with ignorance of the lessons and values of the past, is a means to ruin.

In *The Lord of the Rings*, especially in the first two books, Tolkien relies frequently on songs to provide historical texture, backdrop, and context. Some of these songs could be construed as lays, and we know that their conception and initial composition predate *The Lord of the Rings* by a number of years. Two important examples are the "Song of Eärendil," sung by Bilbo in Rivendell, and the "tale of Tinúviel," told by Aragorn on Weathertop just prior to the attack by the Black Riders. This latter tale is part of the larger "Lay of Leithian" in which the story of Beren and Lúthien is supposedly told in its original setting. As Shippey points out, Tolkien, in the 1920s, had already versified parts of these stories, which would later be published posthumously in the *Lays of Beleriand*. Extended prose versions of the voyage of Eärendil and the exploits of Beren and Lúthien appeared in the *Silmarillion*, and it was among this material that Tolkien first sought a sequel to *The Hobbit*.

Eärendil, and Beren and Lúthien, are central to Tolkien's mythology. The former, a mariner, becomes "a herald star, and a sign of hope to men" (*Letters*, 385). The latter couple beget a line of descendants that will eventually include Elrond, Arwen, and Aragorn. The story of Beren and Lúthien also held great personal significance for Tolkien and his wife, Edith; their gravestone in fact bears those names. It is by no means insignificant that Tolkien conceived of these stories precisely as lays and not as other poetic forms. As lays, they could occupy a place in the forgotten past of oral cultures, such as the Celts, and thus could be construed as stories that once were lost but now have been recovered, at least partially. As songs from a hitherto undocumented and properly English tradition, they were also free from French influence. They thus possessed a depth and potential that no other form did, and so provided the substance and basis for the full elaboration of *The Lord of the Rings* and Tolkien's tale of the third age of Middle-earth. They also expressed the culture of that distant past in an authentic and personalized way, inflecting the poem with the melody, tone, and rhythm of the inimitable English voice.

GERALD SEAMAN

Further Reading

Bruckner, Matilda Tomaryn. "Marie de France." In *Literature of the French and Occitan Middle Ages: Eleventh to Fifteenth Centuries*, edited by Deborah Sinnreich-Levi and Ian S. Laurie, 199–208. Dictionary of Literary Biography 208. Detroit, Washington, DC, and London: Bruccoli, Clark, Layman, 1999.
Carpenter, Humphrey. *Tolkien: A Biography*. Boston, MA: Houghton Mifflin, 1977.
Chance, Jane. *The Lord of the Rings: The Mythology of Power*. Rev. ed. Lexington, KY: University Press of Kentucky, 2001.
———. *Tolkien's Art: A Mythology for England*. Rev. ed. Lexington, KY: University Press of Kentucky, 2001.
Gibbs, A.C. *Middle English Romances*. London: Edward Arnold Ltd., 1966.
Noel, Ruth S. *The Mythology of Middle-earth*. Boston, MA: Houghton Mifflin, 1977.
Rumble, Thomas C. *The Breton Lays in Middle English*. Detroit, MI: Wayne State University Press, 1965.
Shippey, Tom. *J.R.R. Tolkien: Author of the Century*. Boston and New York: Houghton Mifflin, 2000.
———. *The Road to Middle-earth*. Boston, MA: Houghton Mifflin, 1983.
Tolkien, J.R.R. *Farmer Giles of Ham*. Boston, MA: Houghton Mifflin, 1950.
———. "On Fairy-Stories." In *MC*, 109–61.
———, trans. *Sir Gawain and the Green Knight, Pearl, and Sir Orfeo*. Boston, MA: Houghton Mifflin, 1975.
West, Richard C. "Real-World Myth in a Secondary World: Mythological Aspects in the Story of Beren and Lúthien." In *Tolkien the Medievalist*, edited by Jane Chance, 259–67. London and New York: Routledge, 2003.

See also **Beren;** *Father Giles of Ham***; Lays of Beleriand; Lúthien; Mythology, Celtic; Old French Literature; "On Fairy-Stories";** *Pearl*

ROVERANDOM

Roverandom is the earliest-written of Tolkien's fictions for children (mid-1920s), though it was not published until 1998 in an edition prepared by Christina Scull and Wayne Hammond, the editors of *Tolkien's Art* (1995). Unlike *Mr. Bliss* (which went to Marquette), Roverandom (in several versions in part or whole) was in with the Tolkien papers that went to the Bodleian. There are in fact four versions, of which the earliest (in manuscript) is missing chapter 1 and part of chapter 2. The other three versions are in typescript, (1) an interlineated writing copy, (2) a revised and more neatly typed copy of the first part, and then (3) the final copy for submission to Allen & Unwin in 1936, and probably the copy submitted. It is roughly contemporaneous with *The Hobbit* (though started earlier, in 1925–27) and *Mr. Bliss*. The editors find (important) echoes of Edith Nesbit Bland's Psammead books–*Five Children and "It"* (1902), *The Phoenix and the Carpet* (1904), and *The Story of the Amulet* (1906)—important because the great wave coming over and drowning Atlantis is a scene from *The Story of the Amulet* (which appeared earlier as a serial and which Tolkien may have read on its original issue).

Scull and Hammond note an interesting similarity between the illustration (watercolor) *The Garden of the Merking's Palace*, with the whale Uin in the upper left corner, and the illustration of the leviathan in Kipling's "How the Whale Got His Throat" in *Just-So Stories* (1902). Despite *Tolkien's Art* and this edition of *Roverandom*, there is still work to be done linking the influences on Tolkien as artist/illustrator with the influences on Tolkien as writer/ storyteller. Also, there is room for more discussion of Tolkien's sense of humor, and the comment on Artaxerxes in *Roverandom* (74) that "the only thing he did like a fish was to drink" is an interesting example of adult humor in his children's story—not unlike the comment in *Farmer Giles* that the dragon did more damage in a short time than the King's foxhounds could have done in a year.

The story of Roverandom (the name was given by the Man-in-the-Moon) began when Michael left his little toy dog (made of lead) on the beach at Filey, in September of 1925, and then could not find him, nor could his father or his brother John (Christopher was too young really to look). So Tolkien told him a story of the enchanted dog that had become Michael's toy dog, Rover, and his adventures after meeting a comical sand-sorcerer Psamathos (this is the link to E. Nesbit's Psammead stories). He goes up the moon-path (recalling the full moon shining on the sea at Filey), meets the Man-in-the-Moon (who already has a moon-dog Rover, so this Rover becomes Roverandom), has various adventures there and with moon-dog Rover (including an adventure with the Dragon in the moon), eventually returns to earth, is caught up in the rivalry of the sand-wizard Psamathos with Artaxerxes (who was the original enchanter), is guided by the seagull Mew, meets the mer-people through the right whale Uin, and meets Artaxerxes (who has married a mer-lady), and returns again to earth and eventually to his true owner (his owner as a real dog—little boy Two [Michael] who owns the enchanted toy dog not being his real owner—but there are complications within complications here, and it turns out in the end the real dog belongs to little boy Two's grandmother).

The story was told several times over the years, as the five surviving illustrations bear witness (one is inscribed to Christopher Tolkien): it was rather a family favorite. Toward the end of the book, Rover (now back as a real dog) speaks briefly with Tolkien's voice (or paterfamilias comes into the story). The cars are racketing by "making all speed (and all dust and all smell) to somewhere" (87). "'I don't believe half of them know where they are going to, or why they are going there, or would know it if they got there' grumbled Rover" (see entry on World War II on coming Americanization after the War). And at the very end, we suddenly have Father Tolkien sounding a little Victorian—perhaps a little like "Uncle" Lewis Carroll: "But the [adventures] I have told you were the most unusual and most exciting. Only Tinker says she does not believe a word of them. Jealous cat!"

JARED LOBDELL

Further Reading

Hammond, Wayne and Christina Scull, eds. *Roverandom*. Boston, MA: Houghton Mifflin, 1998.

See also **Art and Illustrations by Tolkien; Literary Influences, Nineteenth and Twentieth Century;** *Mr. Bliss*

RUNES

The word "rune" (from Germanic *rūnō*- 'mystery, secret') is applied to the letters of a variety of alphabets, angular in form and used primarily for inscriptions carved in wood or stone. The word is sometimes more generally used to refer to symbols of a cryptic, mystical, or magical nature, but most commonly refers to the letters of the alphabets used by the Germanic peoples before their conversion to Christianity.

The most widely accepted theory on the origin of the runes derives them from one of the North Italic alphabets of the first and second centuries CE. The original runic alphabet or Elder Futhark, named for the first six letters of the alphabet (*fuþark*), consisted of twenty-four letters and was common to the various Germanic tribes. As the sounds of the individual Germanic languages changed, the runic alphabet was altered accordingly. Among these derived runic alphabets are the Scandinavian Younger Futhark of sixteen runes (from c. 800 CE) and the Old English *fuþorc* from the same period, consisting of twenty-eight to thirty-three runes.

The Old English runes are the basis for a number of runic alphabets created by Tolkien in the 1920s and 1930s for the representation of modern English. Examples of several of these have been published in "Early Runic Documents" (102–4, 114–16, 120). The most familiar runic alphabet of this sort, however, is that used on Thror's Map and the original dust jacket for *The Hobbit*, also used (with minor variations) in a 1947 postcard to Katherine Farrer (*Letters*, 125). As described in *The Annotated Hobbit* (27, 378–79), this alphabet consists of thirty-one runes, representing *a, b, c, d, e, f, g, h, i* (or *j*), *k, l, m, n, o, p, r, s, t, u* (or *v*), *w, x, y, z, ea, ee, eo, ng, oo, sh, st,* and *th*. The runes of this alphabet are found with the same values in genuine Old English inscriptions, with a few exceptions: the *k*-rune is a modified *c*-rune, the *ee*-rune is an Old English *æ*-rune, the *oo*-rune is a modification of another version of the Old English *æ*-rune, and the *sh*-rune is a reversed *s*-rune. Tolkien describes the *z*-rune as a "dwarf-rune," and though this rune does represent *z* in the *Angerthas Moria* (see below), it is also one of the forms of the original Germanic *z*-rune, which did not survive into the Old English *fuþorc*.

Tolkien also invented a number of alphabets that made use of the shapes of the historical Germanic runes, but in which these runes represented different values. The most familiar of these invented runic alphabets are the Elvish *Angerthas Daeron* (long rune-rows of Daeron) and the Dwarvish *Angerthas Moria* (*RK*, Appendix E, 401–4). The runes of these alphabets are called *cirth* (singular *certh*) in Sindarin. Examples of the Dwarvish *cirth* can be seen on the title pages of *The Lord of the Rings*, in the inscription on Balin's tomb (*FR*, II, iv, 333), and in the facsimile pages of the Book of Mazarbul (*Pictures*, no. 24). Early versions of the *cirth*, along with rounded cursive variants, can be found in the "Appendix on Runes" (*Treason*, 452–65).

The arrangement of the *Angerthas* is linguistically sophisticated and systematic, unlike the seemingly random order of the Germanic *fuþark*. The sequence of the *cirth* in the *Angerthas Daeron* is based on phonological relationships between the sounds that they represent. The shapes of the individual *cirth* are likewise based on such relationships. The *cirth* representing fricative consonants, for example, are reversed versions of the *cirth* representing the corresponding stops, a voiced consonant is generally indicated by the addition of a stroke to the *certh* representing its voiceless counterpart, and long vowels are indicated by similarly modifying the *cirth* representing short vowels. The *Angerthas Moria* is somewhat less systematic, due to a number of changes in value introduced by the Dwarves.

A similar, though less elaborate, relationship between form and value can be seen in the Gondolinic Runes, the earliest of Tolkien's invented runic alphabets, dating probably from the mid-1920s ("Early Runic Documents," 111–13). Another runic alphabet mentioned by Tolkien is the Taliskan *skirditaila* (runic series). This was a Mannish alphabet, derived from runes used by the Danian Elves, which appears to have been intended as a link between the Beleriandic and Germanic runes (*Treason*, 454–55).

That the Germanic runes were used for magical purposes is clear from historical and literary sources, and this function of the runes has become firmly rooted in the popular imagination. Such an association between runes and magic also appears in Tolkien's fiction. A prime example is the secret inscription on Thror's Map in "moon-letters," which are runes that can only be read when the light of a moon of a certain shape and season shines through them (*H*, III, 95). Runic inscriptions also appear on the swords Orcrist and Glamdring (*H*, III, 95–96), and the runes inscribed on Andúril apparently provide some sort of protective or strengthening power (*FR*, II, iii, 290). Gimli's song tells of "runes of power" upon the door of Khazad-

dûm (*FR*, II, iv, 330); these were presumably engraved on the eastern entrance to Moria and are not to be confused with the *tengwar* on the West-gate, which also had magical properties (*FR*, II, iv, 317–22).

The individual Germanic runes also had names that were full words, although the meanings of some these later became obscure. The first rune of the *fuþark*, for example, was called *fehu* "cattle, movable property" (Old English *feoh*, Old Norse *fé*). Tolkien gave the runes in some of his modified Old English runic alphabets modern English names of a similar acrophonic type (e.g., ash, birch, city), generally using the modern reflexes of the Old English names wherever possible ("Early Runic Documents," 120–21). If Tolkien ever invented names of this sort for the *cirth*, they do not appear to have survived, but the Quenya "full names" of the *tengwar* have a similar quality: *tinco*, "metal," *parma*, "book," and so on (*RK*, Appendix E, 400–1).

ARDEN R. SMITH

Further Reading

Elliott, Ralph W.V. *Runes: An Introduction*. 2nd ed. New York: St. Martin's Press, 1989.

Hyde, Paul Nolan. "The *Angerthas* & *The Hobbit*." *Mythlore* 13, no. 4 (Summer 1987): 43–47, 62.

Smith, Arden R. "*Certhas, Skirditaila, Fuþark*: A Feigned History of Runic Origins." In *Tolkien's Legendarium: Essays on the History of Middle-earth*, edited by Verlyn Flieger and Carl F. Hostetter, 105–11. Westport, CT: Greenwood Press, 2000.

Tolkien, J.R.R. "Early Runic Documents." Edited by Arden R. Smith. *Parma Eldalamberon* 15 (2004): 89–121.

———. *Pictures by J.R.R. Tolkien*. 2nd ed. with foreword and notes by Christopher Tolkien. Boston, MA: Houghton Mifflin, 1992.

See also **Alphabets, Invented; Languages Invented by Tolkien; Weapons, Named**

RUSSIA: RECEPTION OF TOLKIEN

Interest in J.R.R. Tolkien grew quickly in Russia after the publication of *Lord of the Rings* in 1955. Given that Tolkien's world is "fundamentally linguistic in inspiration," arising from his invention of languages, a dictionary of the English language is vital to readers, because this work of a preeminent Oxford philologist invites reading in the original. Some readers want to offer their own, improved and more precise interpretation of Tolkien's book, which perhaps explains why ten official translations of the epic have appeared since 1990, the year of the first Russian officially published translation. Other supplementary sources also help to reveal the trilogy's depths: histories of the English language, historical grammars, textbooks of Old English and Old Welsh, folktales, legends, and epics (principally Scandinavian), no doubt appear on many readers' bookshelves. Studies in mythology, heraldry, the Middle Ages, the history of English literature, and, of course, the Bible, also prove useful, given the erudition that shapes the trilogy.

During the time of the Iron Curtain, Russian concepts of twentieth-century English literature were distorted, and details extremely scanty. Translated foreign authors were carefully selected. That the publication of Kenneth Grahame's *The Wind in the Willows* was hindered because the censor considered the chapter "Piper at the Gates of Dawn" dangerous suggests the sort of resistance that Tolkien's books were destined to encounter.

The first attempt to get *The Lord of the Rings* published was made in the earlier 1960s. To circumvent the barriers of censorship, its translator had to make the trilogy resemble the literature that was acceptable in the USSR, which meant that Tolkien's text had to be reduced either to a fairy tale or to science fiction. The translation combined *The Hobbit* and the trilogy under the common title of *The Lay of the Ring*. The book was subjected to a considerable abridgment, and the translator provided a short "interlude" at the beginning of each chapter. The origin of "Tolkien's" renowned all-powerful Ring was explained scientifically as the Ring having been found when a drill core of basalt was melted. The heroes of the interlude record the Ring's history in a series of flashbacks, drawing the conclusion that the Ring is a special device, "a repository of information, which it releases when subjected to sparks." This approach was the translator's unsuccessful strategy to get Tolkien into print. Having failed to publish *The Lord of the Rings* as science fantasy, there was a new attempt to turn it into fairy fantasy, producing yet another version of the book. Despite all these machinations, disguising *The Lord of the Rings* as a fairy tale, peppering it with elements from Russian folklore, this abridged retelling also failed. The danger of *The Lord of the Rings* detected by some commentators was the hidden allegory "of the conflict between the individualist West and the totalitarian, Communist East." Nowadays Russian Communists think differently about this: they view the anti-industrial ideas of Tolkien's work as a return to primordial Communism and discuss the possibility of creating a type of Communist fantasy, whose father could be considered Tolkien.

The appearance of a new, maximally Russified and more emotionally specific than the original, translation of *The Lord of the Rings* in 1992 was a defining moment in the history of Russian Tolkienism. The entire text was treated as the personal experience of someone doing battle with the Soviet power structure. The book was thus transmogrified into a three-volume banner for the fight for freedom.

The Tolkienist movement began to take shape at Moscow State University in the earlier 1990s at the time of Perestroika when the two mentioned translations of Tolkien's work came out. Later the Russian Tolkienist Movement underwent an internal split: there are now scholarly Tolkienists whose primary interests are the study and translation of Tolkien's literary legacy, as well as the creation of original songs, poems, and art based on his works; and there are the gamers, for whom Tolkien's world is more than a simple game, but rather a lifestyle, a special ritual, demanding serious self-discipline. Thus the unflagging popularity of Tolkien in Russia has allowed this English author to expand the boundaries of the real world in order to make every day routine brighter and more profound.

O. MARKOVA

See also **Communism; Marxist Readings of Tolkien; Politics; Russian Language**

RUSSIAN LANGUAGE

Russian attracted Tolkien's attention chiefly as the largest representative of a major branch of the Indo-European language family. He gave himself a course in it whilst in hospital in the summer of 1918. Soon he encountered it professionally as well: his job as a part-time lexicographer for the *New English Dictionary* (1919–20) involved developing etymologies of English words in the range *waggle–warlock*, and that included citing cognates from Russian and Old Slavic (among other Indo-European languages).

He never got beyond a cursory familiarity with Russian. He wrote in 1953: 'the efforts spent on trying to teach me the fiddle in youth, have left me only with a feeling of awe in the presence of fiddlers. Slavonic languages are for me almost in the same category. I have had a go at many tongues in my time, but . . . the time I once spent on trying to learn Serbian and Russian have left me with no practical results, only a strong impression of the structure and word-aesthetic" (*Letters*, 173). It made an impression in his creation also, especially at the earliest (more eclectic and less systematic) stage; but it is not always possible to single out a particular Slavic language as the source.

The most evident Slavic element in Tolkien's languages is the Qenya word *velikë*, "great," known from the toponym *Haloisi Velikë*, "Great (Stormy) Sea" on the "World-Ship" drawing (*Lost Tales I*, 84), the *Gnomish Lexicon* (*LnG*, 22) and the *Qenya Lexicon*: *velikĭ-*, "great," *velikse*, "greatly," *velitya-*, "magnify" (*QQ*, 100). It has a perfect match in both sound and meaning in Russian *velik(ij)*, "great," *veliča(t')*, "glorify; style, address (by a title)," whose stem is related to Old Slavic *vel(ii)*, "big" and together with Welsh *gwala*, "enough, plenty," Greek *hális*, "enough," Tocharian A *wäl*, "king, prince," goes back to the Proto-Indo-European root *wel*-[3], "press, push" (Pokorny, *Indogermanisches*, 1138; Vasmer, *Ètimologicheskij*, 1289). (By a remarkable coincidence this root is in the range Tolkien dealt with, although the word *velike* predates his work for the *New English Dictionary*.) The Qenya word was eliminated later, and while Goldogrin *beleg*, "mighty, great," progressed in the same form into Noldorin, the stem BEL-, "strong" was declared to be absent from Qenya of the Etymologies (*Lost Road*, 352).

Other early words (from Qenya of the Lexicons) with correspondences in Russian (but perhaps accidental ones) are *patinka*, "shoe, slipper" (*QQ*, 72; cf. Russian *botinok*, "shoe") and *ulku*, "wolf" (*QQ*, 97; cf. Russian *volk* ditto). To these might be added the Q(u)enya diminutive suffix *-inke/-inka*, found in *katinka*, "candle" (< *kate*, "gleam, ray"; *QQ*, 45), *kilinke*, "little bell" (< *kilin*, "bell"; *QQ*, 46), *Atarinkë*, "Little Father" (Curufin's mother-name; *Peoples*, 353), *hérinkë*, "Miss" (*UT*, 195), *kirinki* a species of small Númenorean birds (*UT*, 169); compare the Russian suffixes of singulative nouns *-ink(a)* (*izjum-ink-a*, "raisin" < *izjum*, "raisins") and of diminutive adjectives *-en'k(ij)* (*mal-en'k(ij)*, "small" < *mal(yj)* ditto). And the Noldorin kenning *megli* < *mad-lī*,

"eat-honey" for "bear" (*Lost Road*, 369) follows a Slavic model: *medŭ-ěd-*, "honey-eat(er)," whence Russian *medved'*, "bear," Serbian *medved* ditto (Vasmer, *Ètimologicheskij*, 2589), and from these the name Medwed, the werebear Beorn's name in an early version of *The Hobbit* (Anderson, *Annotated*, 7–8).

Lastly, the Variags of Khand (*RK*, V, vi, 121, 123) are named in Russian (*varjag*, "Varangian; Viking, Norseman," from Old Norse *væring-r*), perhaps because these were northern mercenaries who fought for the lord of the southeastern land of Khand in the same way as the Varangian Guard served the emperors of Byzantium (Allen, 175).

IVAN A. DERZHANSKI

Further Reading

Allen, Jim. *An Introduction to Elvish*. Somerset: Bran's Head, 1978.

Anderson, Douglas. *The Annotated Hobbit*. Boston, MA: Houghton Mifflin, 2002.

Gilson, Christopher, Carl F. Hostetter, Patrick Wynne, and Arden R. Smith, eds. *Qenyaqetsa: The Qenya Phonology and Lexicon* (*QQ*). Parma Eldalamberon 12.

Gilson, Christopher, Patrick Wynne, Arden R. Smith, and Carl F. Hostetter, eds. *I·Lam na·Ngoldathon: The Grammar and Lexicon of the Gnomish Tongue* (*LnG*). Parma Eldalamberon 11.

Pokorny, Julius. *Indogermanisches Etymologisches Wörterbuch* (An Indo-European Etymological Dictionary). Bern Francke, 1959–69.

Vasmer, Max. *Ètimologicheskij slovar' russkogo jazyka* (An Etymological Dictionary of the Russian Language). Moscow: Progress Publishers, 1964–73.

See also **Languages Invented by Tolkien**

S

SACRIFICE

Tolkien's treatment of sacrifice in his literature is essentially self-sacrifice or sacrifice chosen to preserve good and defeat evil. His works therefore demonstrate his indebtedness to Christian theology and neo-Platonic philosophy, locating his view of sacrifice within an understanding of good and evil. Tolkien's works represent evil as the corruption of good, manifested in the pursuit of absolute power that destroys, desolates, and enslaves. As corrupted good, evil in Tolkien's works possesses embodiment and agency, and it must be resisted through the sacrifices of those who love good. Tom Shippey has outlined Tolkien's position on good and evil as a combination of the "orthodox Christian" view, based on Augustine and Boethius, and the Manichaean view: in one, evil is "the absence of good," while in the other, "Good and Evil are equal and opposite and the universe is a battlefield" (*Road*, 108). In Shippey's analysis, Tolkien unites these views through the Ring.

The Lord of the Rings is replete with accounts of self-sacrifices born of the desire to do good rather than evil. At the Council of Elrond, the "Free Peoples of the World," Elves, Dwarves, and Men, unite in their determination to make any sacrifice to protect Middle-earth and defeat Sauron (*FR*, II, iii, 289). To do so, the Free Peoples, notably the Elves and the Dwarves, must first sacrifice their pride, forgetting ancient rivalries to pursue a greater and far more urgent purpose. Other peoples, such as Theoden's Rohirrim, offer their lives in battle, while the Ents relinquish their rest to defeat Saruman.

Notable figures of sacrifice in Tolkien's works include Elvish women who forfeit eternal life to die with their human husbands. In *The Silmarillion*, Lúthien surrenders immortality for the sake of Beren, enduring tremendous grief (*S*, 195). Arwen Evenstar shares a similar anguish as she follows Aragorn into death, painfully divided from Elrond, her father (*RK*, VI, vi, 256; *RK*, Appendix A, 343). These sacrifices are redemptive because they unite the two kindreds of Elves and Men, as *The Silmarillion* emphasizes (*S*, 222). Elwing, wife of Eärendil, descends from Beren and Lúthien; Eärendil is born to Idril Celebrinbal and Tuor, a Man. Elwing and Eärendil, in their turn, are the parents of Elrond and Elros, ancestor of Aragorn.

The Silmarillion features many other characters who sacrifice themselves to save others: for example, Finrod Felagund dies defending Beren a sacrifice immortalized in the Lay of Leithian (201–2). Huan, the noble hound, gives his life to protect Beren from the wolf Carcharoth (219–0). Beren also sacrifices himself recovering the Silmaril, returning from the "dark borders of death" through Lúthien's care (385, 216). The greatness and goodness of Beren's descendants testify to the redemptive power of his and Lúthien's sacrifices.

In *The Lord of the Rings*, the Elves perform a notable sacrifice in their willingness to depart from Middle-earth to defeat Sauron. Galadriel tells Frodo and Sam that, despite the grief at their loss, "[the Elves'] will cast all away rather than submit to Sauron; for they know him now" (*FR*, II, vii, 380). Galadriel herself surrenders a chance for unlimited power when Frodo offers her the Ring. In her sacrifice, and in that of all the Elves, lies the salvation of Middle-earth: when the One Ring is destroyed, the Three Rings of the Elves lose their power.

Of many figures in *The Lord of the Rings* associated with sacrifice, one of the most eminent is Gandalf the Grey. In the mines of Moria, Gandalf sacrifices himself to save his companions from the Balrog, whom he confronts unaided: "he seemed small, and altogether alone" (*FR*, II, v, 345). His fall is later lamented in song by the Elves of Lothlórien and by Frodo (*FR*, II, vii, 374–75). After his return, Gandalf narrates his battle with the Balrog, his journey back from the depths and up to the mountains. "'I threw down my enemy,'" he says, "'. . . then darkness took me, and I strayed out of thought and time, and I wandered far on roads that I will not tell'" (*TT*, III, v, 105–06). He is healed by Galadriel in Lothlórien, rising again for the salvation of Middle-earth. In his confrontation with Saruman, he speaks of his resurrection: "'I am Gandalf the White, who has returned from death'" (*TT*, III, x, 189).

Aragorn likewise is a figure of sacrifice in *The Lord of the Rings*, suffering for the safety of others without their knowledge or recognition. He mentions these trials infrequently, but the hobbits perceive his pain (*FR*, I, x, 177), and Aragorn speaks of his struggles at the Council of Elrond (*FR*, II, ii, 261–62). At his first meeting with the hobbits, he declares his willingness to sacrifice himself for their sake: "I am Aragorn son of Arathorn, and if by life or death I can save you, I will" (*FR*, I, x, 183).

Frodo likewise sacrifices himself when he accepts the burden of the Ring at the Council of Elrond (*FR*, II, ii, 284). Initially, he gives up the life he knows to protect the Shire: "I should like to save the Shire, if I could" (*FR*, I, ii, 71). His friends likewise relinquish their lives at home to accompany him, despite their fear. In Mordor, as Frodo grows weaker, Sam takes up his burden, even in the face of seemingly certain death: "when the task was done, there they would come to an end. . . . There could be no return" (*RK*, VI, iii, 211). Ultimately, Frodo, still troubled by his wound, cannot even enjoy the deliverance of the Shire: "I tried to save the Shire, and it has been saved, but not for me" (*RK*, VI, ix, 309). Arwen's sacrifice of her own immortality eventually provides Frodo with healing; he takes her place and sails into the West with Gandalf, Elrond, and Galadriel (*RK*, VI, vii, 252–253; *RK*, VI, ix, 308–309).

Despite Frodo's enduring pain, his sacrifice is most significant. It demonstrates the greatness of the forgotten peoples, those not initially included among the Free Peoples. The hobbits' contribution is noted in *The Silmarillion*: "help came from the hands of the weak when the Wise faltered. For . . . it was the

Periannath, the Little People . . . that brought them deliverance".

CHRISTINA M. HECKMAN

Further Reading

Shippey, Tom. *The Road to Middle-earth*. Boston, MA: Houghton Mifflin, 1983.

See also **Aragorn; Arwen; Augustine of Hippo; Beren; Christian Readings of Tolkien; Dwarves; Elves; Ents; Fëanor; Finrod; Frodo; Free Will; Galadriel; Good and Evil; Hobbits; Lothlórien;** *Lord of the Rings***; Lúthien; Maiar; Men, Middle-earth; Morgoth and Melkor; Moria; One Ring, The; Plato; Redemption; Resurrection; Rings of Power; Sam; Saruman; Sauron; Shire;** *Silmarillion***; Theoden; Theological and Moral Approaches in Tolkien's Works; Tolkien Scholarship: Since 1980; Valar; Wizards**

SAINT BRENDAN

St. Brendan or Brennainn (484–577 or 583), Abbot and probably founder of the Abbey of Clonfert in Galway, was the hero of the *Navigatio Sancti Brendani* (ca. 1050), describing his voyages to the northern and western islands, *Hy Bréasail*, the Islands of the Blest, or possibly the Shetlands, Orkneys, Iceland, and even according to some commentators, North America. His importance for Tolkien lies in part in his exemplification of the "there-and-back-again" or "Well, I'm home" motif in the "Imram" Tolkien published (from his Middle-earth MSS) in *Time & Tide* in 1955 ("When Shannon down to Lough Derg ran / under a rain-clad sky / Saint Brendan came to his journey's end / to find the grace to die"). It also lies in a linking of the islands encountered in his voyages to Tolkien's Elvenhome ("of islands by deep spells beguiled / where dwell the elvenkind"), also to the Old Straight Road ("beyond the Door of Days, / where the round world plunges steeply down / but on the old road goes"), and by implication to the Celtic (and Egyptian) Ship of the Sun freighted with souls. In his search for the "fair elusive beauty that some call Celtic" Tolkien looked to the Celtic West, where days and souls are carried by the Ship of the Sun to the perpetual Summer Country. Some have linked the voyages of Brendan to the voyages of the Sons of Don. The *Time & Tide* "Imram" was published as the volumes of *The Lord of the Rings* were being published—and perhaps not coincidentally, as Tolkien's friend Lewis was writing his *Voyage of the 'Dawn Treader.'* The poem was apparently written earlier, but is reprinted in its 1955 form in *Sauron Defeated* in the *History of Middle-earth*.

JARED LOBDELL

Further Reading

Lobdell, Jared. "In the Far Northwest of the Old World." In *The World of the Rings*. Chicago, IL: Open Court 2004.
Oxford Dictionary of the Christian Church, 2nd ed. Oxford, 1961.
Shippey, Tom. *J.R.R. Tolkien: Author of the Century*. Boston, MA: Houghton Mifflin, 2001.

See also **Ireland**

SAINT JOHN

As revealed in the few glimpses available of "The Ulsterior Motive," an unpublished exploration of Tolkien and C.S. Lewis's friendship, Tolkien took St. John the Apostle as his patron saint. The exchange recorded, unfortunately, reveals much about certain weaknesses in their friendship: "Lewis stiffened," Tolkien wrote. "His head went back, and he said in the brusque harsh tones which I was later to hear him use again when dismissing something he disapproved of: 'I can't imagine any two persons more dissimilar.' We stumped along the cloisters, and I followed feeling like a shabby little Catholic caught by the eye of an 'Evangelical clergyman of good family' taking holy water at the door of a church" (Carpenter, *Inklings,* 51). In Roman Catholic theology, a person takes a saint as a companion and advocate in the court of heaven. According to Catholic practice, a person alive in this world prays to the deceased saint, asking for his prayers and influence with God.

That Tolkien chose St. John should not be surprising. St. John wrote the fourth Gospel of the Christian New Testament, and he labeled himself "the one whom Jesus loved." In his life of Christ, St. John focused on the Stoic nature of the Word as that which created the World and sustains the World and will ultimately redeem the World. The Word also "lighteth up every man," thus offering, as Tolkien would have interpreted it, the gift of imagination, the ability to perceive things greater than oneself. Tolkien was quite taken with St. John's poem at the beginning of his gospel—"In the beginning was the Word"—and often used its Anglo-Saxon translation as a text for his students to translate.

Most importantly for Tolkien, perhaps, St. John was also the only one of Jesus's twelve apostles to stand with Him under the cross and to stay with him to the bitter end of His death. In these actions, St. John fulfilled (or perhaps served as the inspiration for and definer of) Tolkien's understanding of true heroism. For the subordinate, Tolkien explained, "personal pride was therefore in him at its lowest, and love and loyalty at their highest." The subordinate's loyalty and sacrifice, in essence, is a purer, unadulterated love. The most profound heroism, then, stems from "obedience and love not of pride or wilfulness" (Tolkien, "Homecoming," 14). In this role, St. John appears as the model for Wiglaf in the *Beowulf* story, Sir Gawain in the Arthurian legend, and Samwise Gamgee in Tolkien's legendarium.

BRADLEY J. BIRZER

Further Reading

Carpenter, Humphrey. *The Inklings: C.S. Lewis, J.R.R. Tolkien, Charles Williams, and Their Friends*. London: Allen 8 Unwin, 1978.
Tolkien, J.R.R. "The Homecoming of Beorhtnoth Beorthelm's Son." In *Essays and Studies 1953*. London: John Murray.

See also **Beowulf; Catholicism, Roman; Christianity; Lewis, C.S.; Life; Saints; Sam; *Sir Gawain and the Green Knight***

SAINT OSWALD

The "Tolkienian" importance of St. Oswald lies in the reference in "*Beowulf*: The Monsters and the Critics" (32–33): "I will conclude by drawing an imaginary contrast [to *Beowulf*]. Let us suppose that our poet had chosen a theme more consonant with 'our modern judgement,' the life and death of St. Oswald. He might then have made a poem, and told first of Heavenfield, when Oswald as a young prince against all hope won a great victory with a remnant of brave men; and then have passed at once to the lamentable defeat of Oswestry, which seemed to destroy the hope of Christian Northumbria; while all the rest of Oswald's life and the traditions of the royal house and its feud with that of Deira might be introduced allusively or omitted" (*MC*, 32). This would be a greater thing that the straightforward recounting of Oswald's life and reign, but it would not reach the greatness of *Beowulf*. "Poetically it would be greatly enhanced if the poet had . . . much enlarged the reign of Oswald, making him old and full of years of care and glory when he went forth heavy with foreboding to face the heathen Penda"—but it still would not reach the greatness of *Beowulf*. "To match his theme with the rise and fall of poor 'folk-tale' Beowulf the poet would have been obliged to turn Cadwallon and Penda into giants and demons" (*MC*, 33).

In fact, Oswald, king of Northumbria (Bernicia and Deira), son of King Æthelfrith (of Bernicia and Deira), reigned only from his accession in 634 at the age of twenty-nine, to his death in battle in 642. Oswald had fled Northumbria when (St.) Edwin of

Deira seized the kingdom at Æthelfrith's death in 616, and in his exile was converted to Christianity by St. Columba and the monks at Iona. Edwin died in 633, succeeded by Oswald's brother Eanfrith in Bernicia and by Ælfric in Deira. Oswald reunited the kingdoms in 634; his brother Oswy succeeded in 642 but lost Deira in 644 to Oswine (Osric's son), who was succeeded by Æthelward Oswald's son in 651 and Alcfrith Oswy's son in 656, before Oswy succeeded in reuniting Bernicia and Deira again in 664.

Edwin, Oswald, and Oswy are counted among the Bretwaldas (overlords) of all Saxon England, in succession to Ælle of the South Saxons, Ceawlin of Wessex, Æthelbert of Kent, and Rædwald of East Anglia. Some count as Bretwalda, also, the last great pagan king, Penda of Mercia, son of Pybba. Penda made war on *Edwin* of Northumbria, and defeated and slew him, with his son Osfrith, at the battle of Heathfield, in 633; defeated and slew *Oswald* of Northumbria at Maserfeld in 642; about 645 drove Cenwealh of Wessex from his kingdom; and then made war on Anna, king of East Anglia, who had given shelter to Cenwealh. Anna was killed, and Penda compelled his brother and successor, Æthelhere, to join him in a campaign against Oswiu. The decisive battle was fought (655) at Winwidfield, where Penda and Æthelhere, with most of their allied chiefs, were slain.

JARED LOBDELL

Further Reading

Stenton, F.M. *Anglo-Saxon England.* 3rd ed. Oxford, 1968.
Tolkien, J.R.R. "*Beowulf*: The Monsters and the Critics." In *MC*.

See also **"*Beowulf*: The Monsters and the Critics"**

SAINTS

As a practicing Catholic, Tolkien believed in the Communion of Saints, a doctrine affirmed in the Apostles' Creed since the earliest days of the Church. The doctrine of the Communion of Saints asserts that the saints in heaven are in mystical and practical communion with the struggling souls on earth. The saints are able to help the souls on earth through their powerful prayers of intercession to God, in whose presence they are.

In a letter written in January 1969 Tolkien informed his correspondent that he had adopted St. John the Evangelist as his personal patron, entrusting him as his intercessor. Explaining that his own first name, John, was "a name much used and loved by Christians," he continued that "since I was born on the Octave of St. John the Evangelist, I take him as my patron—though neither my father, nor my mother at that time, would have thought of anything so Romish as giving me a name because it was a saint's" (*Letters*, 397).

In common with all Catholics, Tolkien revered the Mother of Christ (*Mater Christi*) as the Queen of All Saints (*Regina sanctorum omnium*), writing in 1941 that the "beautiful devotion to Our Lady . . . has been God's way of refining so much our gross manly natures and emotions, and also of warming and colouring our hard, bitter, religion."

In a letter written in 1953, in which Tolkien referred to *The Lord of the Rings* as "a fundamentally religious and Catholic work," Tolkien wrote reverently about "Our Lady, upon whom all my own small perception of beauty both in majesty and simplicity is founded" (*Letters*, 172). In another letter, written five years later, he agreed with a critic who had "asserted that the invocations of Elbereth, and the character of Galadriel as directly described (or through the words of Gimli and Sam) were clearly related to Catholic devotion to Mary." Much later, in 1971, he reiterated the Marian influence on the characterization of Galadriel, stating that "it is true that I owe much of this character to Christian and Catholic teaching and imagination about Mary." He stressed, however, that she should not be seen as simply a personification of Mary but as a fully developed character in her own right (*Letters*, 407).

Tolkien wrote at length about the many modern miracles attributed to the intercession of the Blessed Virgin at the shrine of Lourdes in France. Alluding specifically to the miraculous healing of a small boy in 1927, Tolkien connected it with the sudden joyous turn of events that he was trying to achieve at certain moments in his work: "At the story of the little boy (which is a fully attested *fact* of course) with its apparent sad ending and then its sudden unhoped-for happy ending, I was deeply moved and had that peculiar emotion we all have—though not often. It is quite unlike any other sensation. And all of a sudden I realized what it was: the very thing I have been trying to write about and explain. . . . For it I coined the word 'eucatastrophe': the sudden turn in a story which pierces you with a joy that brings tears. . . . And I was there led to the view that it produces its peculiar effect because it is a sudden glimpse of Truth."

JOSEPH PEARCE

Further Reading

Pearce, Joseph, ed. *Tolkien: A Celebration.* London: HarperCollins, 1999.
———. *Tolkien: Man and Myth.* London: HarperCollins, 1998.

See also **Angels; Catholicism, Roman; Christ; Christianity; Paradise**

SAM

Samwise Gamgee is the hobbit companion of Frodo Baggins in *The Lord of the Rings*. He alone accompanies Frodo entirely from Hobbiton to Mount Doom, pledging his faithfulness soon after they depart: "If you don't come back, sir, then I shan't, that's certain" (*FR*, I, i, 96). Unwavering loyalty, bravery, and innocence distinguish Sam in the novel; they also mark him, in Tolkien's own words, as "the chief hero" (*Letters*, 161).

At the beginning of *The Lord of the Rings* Sam is employed as gardener of Bag End, a job he has taken over from his father, Hamfast "Gaffer" Gamgee. At the urging of Merry and Pippin he uses the position to gather information about Bilbo's ring, but stops after Gandalf catches him eavesdropping. Gandalf punishes Sam by sending him to Rivendell with Frodo, and he accepts the responsibility happily. Having been trained by Bilbo in reading, poetry, and Elvish lore, Sam longs for the chance to meet Elves. It is largely through Sam's eyes that readers experience Elvish culture: "I feel as if I was *inside* a song, if you take my meaning" (*FR*, II, vi, 365).

Sam's trip to Mordor changes him significantly. He sets out with little understanding of evil, but is soon confronted by it. When Orcs attack the Fellowship at Parth Galen, Sam wisely anticipates Frodo's plan to continue alone and intercepts him. He attacks Shelob, rescues Frodo from Cirith Ungol, and crosses Gorgoroth. The trip also brings growth through moral struggle. Galadriel's mirror shows Sam a war-ravaged Shire, and he is forced to reevaluate his love of home and family before continuing the quest. Outside Cirith Ungol, he takes on the Ring-bearer's task when he believes Frodo is dead. Though largely unaffected by the ring, Sam still must wrestle with the temptation of becoming the world's greatest gardener, "Samwise the Strong, Hero of the Age" (*RK*, VI, i, 177). Sam gets hungry and impatient as they travel, and with Gollum he shows distrust and a lack of pity. For Tolkien this proves crucial: "For me perhaps the most tragic moment in the Tale comes . . . when Sam fails to note the complete change in Gollum's tone and aspect. . . . [Gollum's] repentance is blighted and all Frodo's pity is (in a sense) wasted" (*Letters*, 330).

Even as Sam learns of evil, he remains a voice of hope. From inside the darkness of Mordor, for example, Sam sees a single star and realizes "in the end the Shadow was only a small and passing thing: there was light and high beauty for ever beyond its reach" (*RK*, VI, ii, 199). The local hobbits cannot understand Sam's victories when he returns, but they make him a hero, allowing him to live out the happy ending Frodo cannot. Sam heals the landscape with Galadriel's gift of

Elvish soil; he marries Rosie Cotton, fathers thirteen children, and inherits Bag End; he is elected mayor of the Shire seven times; and at Rosie's death he travels to the Grey Havens and sails to the West.

Tolkien calls Sam "the most closely drawn character" (*Letters*, 330–31). His name means "half-wise" in Old English (*sām*, half; *wīs*, learned), which suggests not merely a half-wit, but someone with multiple kinds of wisdom. Sam displays a range of overlapping, conflicting, characteristics; his provincial conservatism, displayed through a love of home and immediate concerns, is balanced by his longing for Elves, history, and Oliphaunts, something fostered by Bilbo. Sam sees the practical sides of situations, perhaps more clearly than any other character, but also gleans their relation to the past. Sam's musings on life and story on the Stairs in Mordor were considered by Tolkien one of the highlights of *The Lord of the Rings*: "I expect they had lots of chances, like us, of turning back, only they didn't. . . . We've got—you've got some of the light of [Eärendil's Silmaril] in that star-glass that the Lady gave you! Why, to think of it, we're in the same tale still!" (*TT*, IV, ix, 321). At this moment Sam both grounds the scene in immediate, individual choice and simultaneously contextualizes it in Tolkien's larger mythology.

Sam also serves as mediator. After Gollum joins Sam and Frodo, for example, he provides balance to the trio, standing between two ring-bearers who battle with varying degrees of control by the ring. Sam articulates the personality divide that exists within Gollum: Slinker and Stinker. As Frodo becomes increasingly overwhelmed by the effects of the ring, Sam also becomes mediator for the reader, detailing events of the Frodo-Sam storyline. It is through Sam's eyes that readers discover Ithilien, enter Cirith Ungol, and ultimately witness the destruction of the ring. Finally, Sam becomes mediator of the physical text by completing the manuscript's final lines and passing down the Red Book of Westmarch through his ancestors.

One of the most problematic sets of roles Sam negotiates is that of servant and friend. His use of "master" continually reminds readers that a class distinction exists. The working-class Gamgees live in the same hill as the Bagginses, but Number Three Bagshot Row exists *below* Bag End, both geographically and socially. Sam's sacrifices blur the line between servant and friend; he often carries more weight than Frodo, eats less food, and stays awake longer. The most useful explorations of this bond have detailed the relationship between the World War I officers and their batmen (Carpenter, Hooker). Because Sam and Frodo's friendship is also one of the most developed, intimate relationships in the book, depicted more fully than the heroic love of Aragorn and Arwen or the chivalric love of Gimli for Galadriel, for example, scholars have considered various ways in which it reveals Tolkien's attitudes about friendship, sex, and homosocial bonds. Some praise Tolkien's skillful portrayal of male friendship, which he understood well, and others criticize his inability to depict adult heterosexual intimacy (Partridge).

Sam remained a vexed part of Tolkien's personal life. The author clearly loved the young gardener, calling him a "jewel among hobbits," but Sam's antics and colloquial speech came to represent for Tolkien the kind of writing that kept his "Silmarillion" from being published. After the 1937 publication of *The Hobbit*, readers wanted only a *Hobbit* sequel, not the stylized Elvish narratives that were closest to his heart. In his *Letters* Tolkien laments the problem, admitting that editors asked for less "hobbit talk," while at the same time refused his more serious manuscripts: "Sam is meant to be lovable and laughable. Some readers he irritates and even infuriates. I can well understand it" (*Letters*, 329). The comment ultimately reflects a conflict within Tolkien himself—a love of hobbit life which stood alongside, and seemingly in conflict to, a love of high narrative forms, poetry, and Elves. Tolkien had to negotiate similar conflicts in his Oxford life: as novelist writing for popular audiences, and medieval scholar whose colleagues ridiculed nonacademic pursuits. Heroism and naïveté thus come together in Sam the "half-wit," but they also reflect some of the enigmatic passions that Tolkien himself embodied.

STEPHEN YANDELL

Further Reading

Carpenter, Humphrey. *Tolkien: A Biography*. Boston, MA: Houghton Mifflin, 1977.

Clark, George. "J.R.R. Tolkien and the True Hero." In *J.R.R. Tolkien and His Literary Resonances*, edited by George Clark and Daniel Timmons, 39–51. Westport, CT: Greenwood, 2000.

Hooker, Mark T. "Frodo's Batman." *Tolkien Studies* 1 (2004): 125–36.

Partridge, Brenda. "No Sex Please—We're Hobbits: The Construction of Female Sexuality in *The Lord of the Rings*." In *J.R.R. Tolkien: This Far Land*, edited by Robert Giddings, 179–97. Totowa, NJ: Vision, 1984.

Robinson, Derek. "The Hasty Stroke Goes Oft Astray: Tolkien and Humour." In *J.R.R. Tolkien: This Far Land*, edited by Robert Giddings, 108–24. Totowa, NJ: Vision, 1984.

See also **Class in Tolkien's Works; Frodo; Gollum; Heroes and Heroism; Hobbits; Homosexuality; Sexuality in Tolkien's Works**

SARACENS AND MOORS

Saracens and Moors are two catch-all terms used by Europeans since the Middle Ages to apply to a number of Muslim peoples of the Near East and North Africa respectively, and both carrying connotations of extreme racial and cultural alterity.

J.R.R. Tolkien's constructions of the idea of "Saracens" would have been drawn partially from texts he would have studied as an academic medievalist. Among these would have been narratives of the Crusades as well as other celebrated battles of European Christians against Muslims, some of them quite fictional: texts such as the *Chanson de Roland*, the *Gesta Francorum*, the Middle English metrical romance of *Richard Coeur de Lyon*, and possibly the French *Roman de Saladin et Godefroi de Bouillon*. Many widely read late-medieval texts incorporated, like this last romance, types of the "virtuous Saracen," often in the person of the historical Egyptian-born sultan of Damascus, Saladin (Salah al-Din Yusuf bin Ayub, 1138–93), who defeated the Crusaders at Hattin in 1187. Dante Alighieri, for instance, put him in the first circle of Hell with other worthy heathens; and Giovanni Boccaccio characterized him in the *Decameron* as a man of great hospitality and courtesy. Tolkien was probably also familiar with such standard texts on the Crusades as Charles Mills' *History of the Crusades* (1820) and G.P.R. James' *History of Chivalry* (1830), both of which were widely read by popular audiences.

It is likely, though, that the most significant sources of Tolkien's notions of Saracens (like those of many educated people of his generation) would have been the various popular historical novels of the Crusades (themselves dependent on Mills and James), such as Sir Walter Scott's *The Talisman* (1825) and H. Rider Haggard's *The Brethren* (1904), which last certainly provided inspiration for C.S. Lewis's Calormenes.

The term "Moor" as such has generally been used for Muslims of African and Iberian origin specifically, even if their domicile was in Venice, as was the case in Shakespeare's *Othello*—a text that Tolkien certainly knew and that incorporates a celebrated ambivalence on issues of race and alterity. Tolkien also had firsthand experiences with real life Africans from his earliest years in South Africa.

All of these influences almost certainly played a part in Tolkien's creation of the Haradrim (Swertings or "Swarthy Men"; also called Southrons [Harad being Sindarin for "south"]), vassals of Sauron and hereditary foes of Gondor, black-haired "swarthy men in red" with a taste for gold adornments, who wore armor made of "overlapping brazen plates," launched "deadly darts" from their bows, and rode giant elephants (*mûmakil*). Those of "Far Harad" were darker yet, seeming (to the eyes of Gondorians) "black men like half-trolls with white eyes and red tongues." The general impression Tolkien leaves is of a noble and proud, very foreign, dark-skinned warrior people who have been misled—quite similar to the medieval and novelistic constructions of Saladin and his men mentioned above.

Easterlings and Variags were similarly alien tribal peoples in Middle-earth who fought for Sauron, but their real world roots are better sought with the Huns and Varangians, respectively.

SANDRA BALLIF STRAUBHAAR

Further Reading

Said, Edward. *Orientalism*. New York: Vintage, 1979.

See also **Easterlings; Huns; Men, Middle-earth; Race; Racism**

SARUMAN

A Wizard, one of the five Istari who appear in the Third Age to assist the people of Middle-earth in their struggle against Sauron, Saruman like the others of his order, was originally one of the Maiar—a lesser rank of the Valar empowered to complete and sustain the creation of Arda. In Valinor, Saruman's name was Curunír, a compound in Quenya meaning "man of skill." Consistent with the linguistic geography of Men in Middle-earth, which Tolkien modeled on real world relations between dialects in the Germanic language group, Saruman's name among the Men of Rohan is a compound of elements cognate with Old English (West-Saxon) *searu*, "clever, skillful, ingenious," and *mann*, "man." The resulting compound, *searumann*—an unattested but not impossible OE coinage—is thus a calque or loan translation of Curunír. Surviving forms in *Beowulf* and other OE manuscripts, including *searuginnn*, *searunett*, and *searecræft*—"wondrous gem," "armor, mail-coat," and "machine, engine, ingenious device"-suggest associations with smith-craft that are consistent with Saruman's interest in technology and his earlier connection with Aulë the smith. S*earu* (Mercian OE *saru*, Gothic *sarwa*, Old High German *saro*, Old Icelandic *sörvi*) appears in additional compounds including *searu-þancum* and *searu-niþ* ("wily thoughts," "cunning malice"), and *searu* itself has negative connotations associated with treachery and wily artifice that Tolkien also drew upon in his characterization of the fallen wizard.

Initially the head of the Istari, Saruman is portrayed as a character who succumbs to the unrestrained desire for power. Humiliated, stripped of power, and cast out of his order, he remains unrepentant to the end, treacherously murdered by his servant Gríma Wormtongue. Saruman is one of the few tragically unredeemed characters in the whole Middle-earth corpus, and unlike others—for example, Túrin Turambar, Boromir son of Denethor II—Tolkien does not mitigate his moral corruption, nor does he ameliorate his tragic demise by giving him—even after his downfall—any significant virtues or traces of fallen nobility.

As a traitor to the cause of freedom and goodness in Middle-earth, Saruman provides a strategic link between Sauron's opponents—including Gandalf, Elrond, and Théoden—and Sauron himself, with whom Saruman has communicated by means of the *palantír*. Gandalf recognizes the source of Saruman's policies and uses Saruman as an unwitting double agent to discern Sauron's secret plans. His tower fortress at Orthanc in Isengard is strategic in its proximity to Rohan, and—by capturing Merry and Pippin—the Orcs under his command are important in the narrative's bifurcation and forward movement in the second volume of the trilogy. Said by Treebeard to have "a mind of metal and wheels," (*TT*, III, iv, 76) Saruman is representative of a fascination with technology and industry at the expense of vegetative life and growth.

Significant as he is in the mechanics of the plot, the two scenes in which Saruman directly enters the narrative are brief. Just as the malevolent effect of Sauron's character is heightened by Tolkien's refraining from direct description, Saruman casts a longer shadow than can be attributed to his short appearances. Tolkien builds the portrait of this character largely by implication through other characters' references to him, his words, and his actions. In his account in "The Council of Elrond," Gandalf says Saruman "has long studied the arts of the Enemy himself," (*FR*, II, ii, 270) suggesting in his native curiosity he has yielded to the appeal of Sauron's deceit and lust for power. His report to the Council conveys a sense of Saruman's malevolence indirectly by presenting Saruman's side of the conversation without narratorial commentary and through the use of discourse verbs selected to reveal his spiteful, belittling tone of voice: for example, "he scoffed," "he sneered," and "he laughed" (*FR*, II, ii, 270).

Saruman's ability to influence others is attributed largely to his powers of speech. In the appropriately titled chapter "The Voice of Saruman"—the only extensive scene featuring him in the whole book and a tour de force among all Tolkien's characterizations — Éomer calls him "an old liar with honey on his forked tongue" (*TT*, III, x, 185). In his parley with Gandalf and Théoden, Saruman's voice modulates between carefully controlled flashes of anger and suave, melodious tones said to be in "very sound an enchantment" whereby he holds the others spellbound and enthralled (*TT*, III, x, 183). His rhetorical devices are varied; they include manipulation of his auditors' desire for approval and fear of reprisal, arrogant assertions of his superiority and belittling dismissal of others, flattery, appeals for pity, and the subtle use of understatement, false premises, logical non sequiturs, and false conclusions to win his hearers' allegiance. His mission is ultimately one of "compromise and calculation" (Shippey, *Author*, 75). Saruman's rhetorical ploys are comparable to those of Satan in Milton's *Paradise Lost*. Gandalf offers him a chance to repent, leave Orthanc, and forsake his ruinous path; like Milton's Satan, Saruman is shown in a brief moment of doubt, "loathing to stay and dreading to leave its refuge" (*TT*, III, x, 187–188). Saruman rejects the offer and, like Satan, is conquered by pride and hatred. His removal from Orthanc and his banishment from the order of Istari, pronounced by Gandalf, are presented as the result of his own free choice. Gandalf's final assessment is that Saruman is "a fool . . . yet pitiable" (*TT*, III, x, 188). Under the Orkish name "Sharkey," "old man," he appears considerably reduced in stature finally as an exiled vagabond in the Shire, a self-pitying character filled with malice, retaining only traces of his earlier verbal powers. He is shown pity by Frodo, who does not allow his execution but banishes him forever from the Shire. He is murdered moments later by the servile character Wormtongue—his last follower—recalling the murder of the exiled usurper Sigeberht in annal 755 of *The Anglo-Saxon Chronicle*. In a scene suggestive of the departure of his soul and its utter annihilation, upon his death a grey mist rises above his body, faces the undying West, but then is dissipated by a cold western wind and dissolves to nothing.

JONATHAN EVANS

Further Reading

Robinson, James. "The Wizard and History: Saruman's Vision of a New Order." *Orcrist: Bulletin of the University of Wisconsin J.R.R. Tolkien Society* 1 (1966–67): 13–17.

Ryan, J.S. "Saruman, 'Sharkey' and Suruman: Analogous Figures of Eastern Ingenuity and Cunning." *Mythlore* 12, no. 1 (1985): 43–44, 57.

Shippey, Tom. *J.R.R. Tolkien: Author of the Century*. Boston, MA: Houghton Mifflin, 2002.

———. *The Road to Middle-earth: Revised and Expanded Edition*. Boston, MA: Houghton Mifflin, 2001.

See also **Exile; Free Will; Maiar; Milton, John; Pride; Redemption; Theological and Moral Approaches; Valar; Wizards**

SATAN AND LUCIFER

The biblical picture of the devil, also known as Satan and in our modern imagination as Lucifer, is developed slowly over the entire course of scripture. The Hebrew word "sâtân" means "accuser"; as can be seen in the first two chapters of Job, Satan's primary role is to accuse men before God. In English, the words "devil" and "diabolical" come from the Greek "diabolé," which also means "accuser" or "slanderer." In English, the word "devil" has come to take many related meanings including the enemy of God, the ruler of Hell, a tempter, or a demonic being. The English word "diabolical" means having to do with the devil, but sometimes is used more generally to mean "exceedingly cruel."

The biblical character Satan is introduced first in Genesis 3 only as a wily serpent who seeks to deceive and tempt Eve. He later appears as an angel who rebels against God and is cast out of heaven (Isa. 14:12; Luke 10:18; Rev. 12:7–9) and as a dragon (Rev. 12:3ff.). As a mighty but fallen angel, Satan is associated with the Latin name Lucifer, whose root means "light," suggesting that Satan began as an angel of light. In addition to being an accuser, Satan is also a deceiver ("the father of lies" in John 8:44), a tempter (Mark 1:13), and devourer (1 Pet. 5:8). However it is not until the final book of the bible that all of these images are tied together in the person of Satan (see Rev. 12:9).

In Tolkien's writing, the diabolical nature is portrayed most completely in Morgoth, also known as Melkor (of whom Sauron is but a lieutenant.) Despite the influence of Norse gods on Tolkien's development of the Valar, Morgoth has far more in common with the biblical Satan and with Milton's Lucifer (from *Paradise Lost*, another work of Christian imagination) than with the devious and deceiving Norse god Loki, whose nature is more mischievous than entirely diabolical. Like Satan, Morgoth is portrayed as a fallen angel, a deceiver, a tempter, a devourer, and an accuser.

Morgoth is initially numbered among the angelic Valar, but he rebels against his creator Eru Ilúvatar. His fall is described as one "from splendour. . . through arrogance to contempt for all things save himself" (*S*, 31). This fall, like the fall described in Isaiah 14:12ff., stems from a desire to usurp the Creator's authority and to rule in his stead. Like Satan, Morgoth is also presented as being unable to create anything of his own; he can only corrupt that which Ilúvatar has created, as he does with the race of Orcs. Like the army of Satan in Revelation 12:7–9, Morgoth's chief servants, the Balrogs (or Valaraukar) are described as spirit-beings (Maiar) whom Morgoth leads in rebellion and who become "demons of terror" (*S*, 31). Though Morgoth does not appear as a dragon, he breeds dragons and is therefore called the Father of Dragons (*S*, 332), and is associated with consummate devourer Ungoliant. He uses deceit—the sowing of lies—in order to tempt the Elves to rebellion against the Valar (*S*, 68).

However, Morgoth's chief role in bringing about the fall of Elves might be seen as one of accusing and slandering. He first falsely accuses the Valar to the Noldor, suggesting that the Valar "had brought the Eldar to Aman because of their jealousy" (*S*, 68). He then helps turn the sons of Finwë against one another, again through accusations: to Fëanor, he accuses Fingolfin and the Valar of "plotting to usurp the leadership of Finwë and the elder line of Fëanor, and to supplant them"; to Fingolfin and Finarfin, he accuses Fëanor of plotting to drive them out of Túna (*S*, 68–69). Ultimately, therefore, and quite literally, Morgoth is a satan—an accuser and slanderer.

MATTHEW DICKERSON

Further Reading

Birzer, Bradley. *J.R.R. Tolkien's Sanctifying Myth: Understanding Middle-earth*. Wilmington, DE: ISI Books, 2002.

Flieger, Verlyn. *Splintered Light: Logos and Languages in Tolkien's World*. 2nd ed., rev. and exp. Kent, OH: Kent State University Press. 2002.

Dickerson, Matthew, and David O'Hara. *From Homer to Harry Potter: A Handbook on Myth and Fantasy*. Grand Rapids, MI: Brazos Press, 2006.

Purtill. *J.R.R. Tolkien: Myth, Morality, and Religion*. San Franciso: Harper 8 Row, 1984.

See also **Good and Evil; Morgoth and Melkor; Moral and Theological Approaches in Tolkien's Works; Valar**

SAURON

He begins as the Necromancer, in *The Hobbit*, and Tolkien found the Necromancer in Samuel Rutherford Crockett, *The Black Douglas* (1899), in the person of Gilles de Retz, though, as he remarked in 1967 (in an unfinished letter to his son Michael; *Letters*, 391), he never reread the book after school days (see also the entry on Tolkien's Childhood). Sauron, "in the Silmarillion and Tales of the First Age" (Tolkien remarks in his famous 1951 letter to Milton Waldman of Collins), "was a being of Valinor perverted to the service of the Enemy [Morgoth] and becoming his chief captain and servant. He repents in fear when the First Enemy is utterly defeated, but in the end does not do as he was commanded, return to the judgement of the gods. He lingers in Middle-earth. Very slowly, beginning with fair motives: the reorganising and rehabilitation of Middle-earth, 'neglected by the gods,' he becomes a reincarnation of Evil, and a thing lusting for Complete Power, and so consumed ever more fiercely with hate (especially of Gods and Elves)" (*Letters*, 151).

His temptation of Elves and Men was to make Western Middle-earth as beautiful as Valinor, a veiled attack on the gods, an incitement to try to make a separate independent paradise. "The Elves of Eregion made Three supremely beautiful and powerful rings, almost solely of their own imagination, and directed to the preservation of beauty" (*Letters*, 152). But "secretly, in the subterranean Fire, in his own Black Land, Sauron made One Ring, the Ruling Ring that contained all the powers of the others"—the Three, the Seven (of the Dwarves), and the Nine (of Mortal Men)—but also his own powers. From all this, of course, came the War of the Rings.

In his beginnings, in Tolkien's mind, it may have been that Sauron was a man (the Necromancer), as Bluebeard (Gilles de Retz) was a man. But as the story grows, we see that Sauron is not a man. In a letter to Major R. Bowen, June 25, 1957, Tolkien remarks that Sauron

> was always de-bodied when vanquished. The theory, if one can dignify the modes of the story which such a term, is that he was a spirit, a minor one but still an "angelic" spirit. According to the mythology of these things, that means that, though of course a creature, he belonged to the race of intelligent beings that were made before the physical world, and were permitted to assist in their measure in the making of it. Those who became most involved in this work of Art, as it was in the first instance, became so engrossed with it, that when the Creator made it real . . . they desired to enter into it, from the beginning of its "realization." They were allowed to do so, and the great among them became the equivalent of the "gods" of traditional mythologies; but a condition was that they would remain "in it" until the Story was finished. They were thus in the world, but not of a kind whose essential nature is to be physically incarnate. They were self-incarnated, if they wished; but their incarnate forms were more analogous to our clothes than to our bodies, except that they were more than are clothes, the expression of their desires, moods, wills, and functions.
> Sauron had been attached to the greatest of these, Melkor (Morgoth) (*Letters*, 259–60).

In a draft letter to Gunnar Urang (August 1967), Tolkien attempted (or began an attempt) once and for all to dispose of the Sauron/saurian connection, with its suggestion of Sauron as Serpent. It is "idle to compare chance similarities between names made from 'Elvish tongues' and words in exterior 'real' languages, especially if this is supposed to have any bearing on the meaning or ideas in my story. To take a frequent case; there is no linguistic connexion, and therefore no connexion in significance, between *Sauron*, a contemporary form of an older *èaurond* -derivative of an adjectival **èaura* from a base √THAW 'detestable,' and the Greek óáýñÜ 'a lizard'" (*Letters*, 380).

In the Fell Year (455 in the First Age), according to the *Grey Annals*, Sauron, who was known as *Gorsodh* in Beleriand, "took Minnas-tirith and made it into a watch-tower for Morgoth, and filled it with evil; for he was a sorcerer and a master of phantoms and terror. And the fair isle of Tolsirion became accursed and was called *Tol-in-Gaurhoth*, Isle of Werewolves; for Sauron fed many of these evil things" (*Jewels*, 54). In the year 460, when rumor of the deeds of Barahir enheartened those under Morgoth's domination, Morgoth sent Sauron to find and destroy the rebels, as is told in the *Quenta* and the *Lay of Leithian* (59). In 465, when Beren took on himself the quest for the Silmaril from the Crown of Morgoth, Sauron cast Beren and his companions into a pit in Tol-in-Gaurhoth, where Felagund, losing his own life, slew the (were)wolf that would have slain Beren (62).

In the later *Quenta Silmarillion*, Tolkien wrote first that "Sauron was the chief servant of the evil Vala [Melkor=Morgoth], whom he had suborned to his service in Valinor from among the people of the gods. He was become a wizard of dreadful power, master of necromancy, foul in wisdom" (*Jewels*, 239). This passage became "Now Sauron, whom the Noldor call Gorthú, was the chief servant of Morgoth. In Valinor he had dwelt among the people of the gods, but there Morgoth had drawn him to evil and to his service. He was now become a sorcerer of dreadful power, master of shadows and of ghosts, foul in wisdom."

As we learned from "The Tale of Years" in Appendix B to *The Lord of the Rings* (*RK*, Appendix B, 363–78), the First Age ended with the Great Battle, in which Morgoth was overthrown (and with him Sauron); then about the year 500 in the Second Age, Sauron began to stir; about the year 1000 he chose Mordor as a stronghold and began the building of Barad-dur; then the war of the Elves and Sauron began in SA 1695 and lasted to the first (or second) overthrow of Sauron in SA 3441; then again around the year 1000 in the Third Age, the Wise perceived the power of Sauron was growing again, and of course what happened thereafter is told in *The Lord of the Rings*, and (unlike the story of the First Age) need not be retold here.

JARED LOBDELL

See also **Childhood of Tolkien; Good and Evil; Morgoth and Melkor;** *Morgoth's Ring*

SAURON DEFEATED

With *Sauron Defeated*, Christopher Tolkien concludes his penetrating analysis of the evolution of *The Lord of the Rings*. Part 1 of *Sauron Defeated* treats the history of book 6, detailing Frodo's journey into Mordor, arrival at Orodruin, and the destruction of the Ring; Aragorn's ascendance to the crown; the hobbits' return to the Shire; and Frodo's departure from Middle-earth. In addition, Christopher Tolkien

presents for the first time an abandoned epilogue along with a letter from King Elessar to Samwise.

Overall, the drafts of book 6 are not vastly dissimilar to the published chapters; however, there are a few differences worth noting. The details of the Ring's destruction, for instance, offer some alternative glimpses. Though Tolkien devised the essential plan for the scene at the Sammath Naur as early as 1939, he contemplated having Sam sacrifice himself, *pushing* Gollum into the Cracks of Doom. He also pondered having Gollum repent; however, he discarded this as counter to the Ring's wholly corruptive power. Tolkien also considered staging a final face-to-face confrontation between Frodo and the Lord of the Nazgûl to bookend their previous encounter at Weathertop (obviously drafted before Tolkien conceived of his end at the hand of Éowyn).

Apart from numerous variations in names and dates, there are other, more salient divergences in the drafts of the closing chapters. For one, Gandalf accompanies the hobbits all the way to the Brandywine Bridge. For another, in *The Scouring of the Shire*, Frodo plays a more active, aggressive role in combating the ruffians and Saruman. And indeed, while sketching out the chapter, Tolkien vacillated over just who Sharkey was—whether the leader of the ruffians or the "Boss," Lotho Sackville-Baggins or, finally, Saruman himself. During the chapter's development, these questions found their ultimate answers. Sharkey became the last embodiment of the petty and wasted Saruman, and Frodo receded to a more secondary role, making good his claim in "The Land of Shadow" that "I do not think it will be my part to strike any blow again" (*RK*, VI, ii, 204).

The history of Tolkien's magnum opus reaches its final denouement with the hitherto unknown epilogue. Christopher Tolkien presents two versions, along with three drafts of Aragorn's letter to Sam. But apart from a sentimental peek at the Gamgees' home life, the epilogue failed to retain the mood of *The Grey Havens*, and Tolkien finally abandoned it. As he wrote to Naomi Mitchison in April 1954, "An epilogue giving a further glimpse . . . has been so universally condemned that I shall not insert it" (*Letters*, 179).

The remaining two parts of *Sauron Defeated* are concerned with an earlier overthrow of Sauron. Reaching far back into the Second Age, they deal with Sauron's corruption of Ar-Pharazôn and with the ensuing cataclysm that swallowed Númenor forever.

Part 2 presents a new work, *The Notion Club Papers*, with which Tolkien distracted himself while writing *The Lord of the Rings*. Tolkien evidently began it in 1945–46 while struggling with the transition from *The Two Towers* to *The Return of the King*; however, instead of the remote past, Tolkien set this new work many years in his own future. Yet at the same time, it taps into the Númenórean legend in quite a novel way.

The Notion Club Papers began as an avenue for Tolkien's ruminations on the works of his fellow Inklings, particularly Lewis, and caricatures of the Inklings and their meetings and mannerisms. Christopher Tolkien offers loose correlations between actual Inklings and the fictitious Notion Club members, but one should remember that these were very loose indeed, with traits often redistributed among the characters, or changed from draft to draft.

The work, insofar as it was developed, consists of two parts, following the form of secretarial reportage on successive meetings of the Club. In the first part, members of the Club argue about whether time and space travel is more or less believable in fiction than fairies and fantasy. In the second, discussion turns to the topic of *true dreams*—the notion that one can tap into the distant past (or future) through a kind of extraordinarily deep dreaming. As Tolkien expounded these ideas, the legend of Númenor continued to resurface until it essentially took over the narrative, dragging it away from simple caricature into more serious territory.

In the second part, two characters emerge as linked to this remote legend. Arundel Lowdham and Wilfrid Jeremy are revealed to be distant relatives and contemporary parallels of the pseudo-historical characters of Ælfwine and his companion, Tréowine, who themselves are descendents of the Númenóreans Elendil and Voronwë. And both pairs of companions experience a sort of echo of the events surrounding the Fall of Númenor—just as the narrative of *The Notion Club Papers* itself becomes an echo of another, earlier work, *The Lost Road*.

Part Three of *Sauron Defeated* presents additional variations on the Númenórean legend. First, Christopher Tolkien offers another version of "The Fall of Númenor," previously discussed in *The Lost Road and Other Writings*. Next, he introduces a parallel story, "The Drowning of Anadûnê," written contemporaneously with *The Notion Club Papers*. This story represents the Númenórean perspective, where "The Fall of Númenor" captured the Elvish tradition of the same tale. It also contains striking departures from the legend's original conception, including confusion between Aman and Tol Eressëa and ambiguity between the Eldar and Valar. But rather than a lapse, such disparities between the mannish and Elvish legends, and indeed between drafts of the same legend, are best construed as a deliberate statement about how such traditions evolve over time, wearing down to their essentials—the details eroding—in much the same way that words of ancient languages wear down and erode into present-day forms.

Which brings us to "Lowdham's Report on the Adunaic Language," which concerns the Númenórean language. Sadly incomplete, the essay goes little further than a description of phonology and morphology. Apart from noun declensions, the grammar and syntax are, unfortunately, omitted. Even so, the essay reveals many Adunaic words and touches on the relationship between Adunaic, Avallonian (that is to say, Quenya), and Khazadian (Dwarvish).

JASON FISHER

Further Reading

See also Ælfwine; Dreams; Eärendil; Fall of Man; History, Anglo-Saxon; *History of Middle-earth*; Inklings; Lewis, C.S.; *The Letters of J.R.R. Tolkien*; *Lord of the Rings*; *Lost Road*; Middle-earth: Men; Mordor; Mythology for England; Publications, Posthumous; *Return of the King*; Saruman; *The Return of the Shadow*; Sacrifice; Saint Brendan; Sauron; *Silmarillion, The*; Time Travel; Tol Eressëa; *The Treason of Isengard*; Valar; *The War of the Ring*

SAXO GRAMMATICUS

Saxo Grammaticus (c. 1150–1220) was the author of the Latin *Gesta Danorum*, or *History of the Danes*. The first nine books of the *Gesta* are composed largely of legendary material, often found elsewhere in Old Norse and Old English literature, but reworked to fit Saxo's own purposes and learned education.

Saxo's influence on Tolkien was probably mostly indirect. The *Gesta* was an important source for the critics whom Tolkien attacked for treating *Beowulf* as a mine for the reconstruction of early Germanic history in "*Beowulf*: The Monsters and the Critics." Book 5 is mostly concerned with the legendary king Frode (Old English *Froda*, Old Norse *Fróði*), whose story Shippey argues influenced Tolkien's naming and characterization of Frodo in *The Lord of the Rings*. Saxo appears to have turned to this figure repeatedly; there are six kings named Frode in the *Gesta*, many of which bear further traces of the legend.

Tolkien probably drew directly on Old Norse sources for such material and used the *Gesta* for comparison. Likewise, the Old Norse Aurvandil is more likely to have been an influence than Saxo's Orvendil in book 3. However, Tolkien may have drawn small details from Saxo's narrative, such as where an earlier King Frode receives a coat impenetrable to weapons in book 2. The *Gesta* may have also had a more general influence on Tolkien's work since, as a literary undertaking, it resembles his early ambitions to rework early legend into a national mythology and his personal taste for "feigned" history.

SCOTT KLEINMAN

Further Reading

Elton, Oliver, trans. *The First Nine Books of the Danish History of Saxo Grammaticus.* London: D. Nutt, 1894. Available online from The Online Medieval and Classic Library (OMACL) at http://sunsite3.berkeley.edu/OMACL/DanishHistory/.

Fisher, Peter, trans., and Hilda Ellis Davidson, ed. *The History of the Danes.* 2 vols. Cambridge: D.S. Brewer; Totowa, NJ: Rowman and Littlefield, 1979–80.

Flieger, Verlyn, and Carl F. Hostetter, eds. *Tolkien's Legendarium: Essays on the History of Middle-earth.* Westport, CT: Greenwood Press, 2000.

Olrik, Jørgen, and H. Ræder, eds. *Saxonis Gesta Danorum.* 2 vols. Hauniæ: Levin & Munksgaard, 1931–57. Available online from the Danish Royal Library at http://www.kb.dk/elib/lit/dan/saxo/lat/or.dsr/index.htm.

Shippey, Tom. *The Road to Middle-earth: Revised and Expanded Edition.* Boston, MA: Houghton Mifflin, 2001.

See also **Eärendil; Frodo; Mythology, Germanic; Old Norse Literature**

SAYERS, DOROTHY LEIGH (1893–1957)

Dorothy Sayers is a major figure in English letters. In mystery fiction she was important as a critic and anthologist and even more as an author, notably for her series of eleven novels and twenty-one short stories featuring Lord Peter Wimsey (a fragmentary twelfth novel was finished posthumously by Jill Paton Walsh). She was also a playwright for the stage and radio, perhaps best known for her dramatization of the life of Christ in *The Man Born to Be King* (1941–42), and a translator of medieval French and Italian, including an excellent version of Dante's *Divine Comedy* (her friend Barbara Reynolds completed the final volume after Sayers's death). She was an accomplished essayist, often writing on literary and Christian subjects, as in *The Mind of the Maker* (1941) and *The Other Six Deadly Sins* (1943). She was closely associated with Oxford (she was born there, educated at Somerville College, and in 1936 used the University as the setting for *Gaudy Night,* generally considered one of her finest novels), but she never attended a meeting of the Inklings. She was on very friendly terms with C.S. Lewis and Charles Williams, and much of the correspondence between them survives (Lewis thought her an outstanding writer of letters, and her collected letters now fill five volumes). She and Tolkien never met, but they read each other's works (Tolkien said he enjoyed the Wimsey novels initially but came to loathe them, yet he read all of them).

RICHARD C. WEST

Further Reading

Brabazon, James. *Dorothy L. Sayers: The Life of a Courageous Woman.* London: Victor Gollancz, 1981.

Reynolds, Barbara. *Dorothy L. Sayers: Her Life and Soul.* London: Hodder & Stoughton, 1993.

See also **Inklings; Lewis, C.S.; Williams, Charles**

SCHOLARS OF MEDIEVAL LITERATURE, INFLUENCE OF

Tolkien's thinking was dominated by the discipline in which he had been trained—comparative philology, the major achievement in the soft sciences of the nineteenth century. To understand this, one should remember that by the late eighteenth century the learned world of Europe had very largely forgotten its early past. No one could read Old English with any accuracy. Despite the efforts of a number of early collectors and antiquarians, Old Norse mythology was little known. The single manuscript of *Beowulf* lay almost undisturbed in the British Museum. Although the major manuscript of the Old Norse *Poetic Edda* had been discovered in an Icelandic farmhouse and sent to the Danish royal library, most of it had never been edited. Those who tried to read such texts could only guess at their meaning by comparison with surviving languages, such as Dutch and Icelandic.

This situation changed dramatically as a result of the work of several scholars. The Dane Rasmus Rask (1787–1832) brought out the first satisfactory grammar of Old Norse in 1811, and of Old English in 1817; the Icelander Grímur Thorkelin (1752–1829) had transcripts of *Beowulf* made in 1787–89, and finally brought out his edition of the poem in 1815; the brothers Grimm edited poems from the *Edda* and the Old High German *Hildebrandslied,* among many other works, in the early 1810s. Most significantly, Jacob Grimm (1785–1863) brought new order to the study of ancient Northern languages with his *Deutsche Grammatik,* which began to appear in 1819. Not only did this build on the work of Rask by providing adequate grammars of early languages, it also offered a system for explaining the way that languages changed. Armed by Grimm, scholars could (and did) correct error in early manuscripts and early editions, sometimes without seeing the manuscripts, and could "reconstruct" whole extinct languages, such as "Proto-Germanic" or "Early Indo-European."

They also became able to read surviving texts very much better, and during the early nineteenth century a whole string of poems suddenly became readable, including *Beowulf,* the *Poetic Edda,* the Middle High German *Nibelungenlied* and *Kudrun,* the Old French *Chanson de Roland,* as well as many prose sagas in Old

Norse. The rediscovery of some of these poems, however, created a problem for scholarship. They clearly dealt with events in preliterate periods. It seemed impossible that people without writing could develop long and complex poems, especially as the poems surviving were usually clearly the product of Christian writers. It was concluded that surviving epics, long, complex and Christian, must have been based on earlier, short, pagan poems, which the Germans called *Lieder* and English speakers "lays" or "ballads." Many German scholars decided that the thing to do was to dissect out the original (and in their opinion far superior) *Lieder* from the mass of later epic additions.

Pioneers in this field included Karl Lachmann (1793–1851), who edited the *Nibelungenlied* in 1840 as a compilation of twenty lays. In England, the historian Thomas (later Lord) Macaulay (1800–59) decided that what was thought about Germanic poetry was probably true of Latin history, and wrote a sequence of *Lays of Imperial Rome* (1842), presented as the original ballads on something like which the ancient historian Livy (d. CE 17) must have based his accounts of early Rome. Tolkien's first published poem, "The Battle of the Eastern Field," is a mock-heroic parody of Macaulay. In his *Lays of Beleriand* (1987), one can see him presenting the original poems on which (in his imagined history) later synopses like *The Silmarillion* would be based. It should be said that *Liedertheorie*, or "ballad-theory," while wildly speculative, was not without some grounds: the well-known *Saga of the Volsungs*, for instance, is clearly a synopsis based on earlier poems, though in this case many of the earlier poems survive—and Tolkien is known to have written a long poem, as yet unpublished, called "Volsungakviða En Nyja" or "The New Lay of the Volsungs," reorganizing and perhaps completing the poetic cycle on this subject (see *Letters*, 379 and n).

Besides Jacob Grimm, major figures in this era of scholarship include Jacob's brother Wilhelm (1786–1859), who also of course collaborated on the immensely influential *Grimms' Fairy-Tales*, first published in German in 1812. The Grimms were rivaled by the Dane N.F.S. Grundtvig (1783–1872), and succeeded in Germany by Karl Viktor Müllenhoff (1818–84): these two are probably the "old voices . . . now generally shouted down" who proclaim that *Beowulf* is a "mythical allegory" in Tolkien's allegory of Babel in "*Beowulf*: The Monsters and the Critics." Grundtvig published on *Beowulf* for fifty years between 1815 and 1865, and also wrote two very different versions of his work on *Nordens Mytologi*, or "The Mythology of the North," in 1808 and 1832, the latter rivaled by Jacob Grimm's *Deutsche Mythologie* of 1835 (later much expanded, and translated into English as *Teutonic Mythology* by J.S. Stallybrass,

4 vols., 1882–88). Stallybrass's careful retitling of Grimm's work should remind us that scholarship in this era was intensely nationalistic, a situation not eased by the fact that parts of Germany were ruled by Denmark till the Prusso-Danish war of 1864, while after that large areas of Denmark were ruled by Prussia. Grundtvig's work did a great deal to establish and preserve Danish identity at a time when it was under threat.

One other early philologist gave even more to his country. In the early nineteenth century a country doctor, Elias Lönnroth (1802–84) found himself in an ideal situation for a *Lieder*-theorist. Traveling in remote Finnish-speaking areas of Karelia, he began to collect *runor*, short poems on mythological themes sung by traditional nonliterate singers—just what *Liedertheorie* predicted. Lönnroth concluded, though, that rather than being the raw material for some future epic, these were the remains of an epic that must once have existed in complete form. He accordingly reassembled many of the *runor* into the epic now known as the *Kalevala*, first published in 1835, much expanded in 1849. His work was immensely successful both as literature and politically: some say that without the sense of ancient identity crafted by Lönnroth, Finland would not now exist as a nation. In 1910 or 1911, Tolkien discovered the *Kalevala* in W.F. Kirby's translation of 1907 and was deeply affected by it. The works of Grimm, Grundtvig, and Lönnroth give added point to Tolkien's stated aim of creating, or recreating, a mythology for his country, England. It should be remembered that in Tolkien's time as now "England" was not a political entity, its autonomy having been merged (some would say, lost) within the United Kingdom: Tolkien was not irrational in his belief that native tradition was as threatened in England as in Denmark or Finland.

Philology, however, did not catch on in England to anything like the same extent that it did elsewhere in northern Europe. British scholars in this field in the nineteenth century were mostly dismissed by the Germans and Scandinavians as mere amateurs. J.M. Kemble (1807–57) indeed brought out an edition, a second edition, and a translation of *Beowulf* between 1833 and 1837, and this had some effect on Jacob Grimm, to whom Kemble was devoted: Kemble was another who thought the poem contained strong elements of myth. But Kemble was cranky and unstable, and managed to alienate even Grimm in the end. Sharon Turner (1768–1847), a lawyer, had made a praiseworthy effort to popularize the poem even earlier, with successive editions of his *History of the Anglo-Saxons* from 1799, but he could not read or understand it even on the most elementary level—on his first reading he had got the pages in the wrong order.

Later on "old John Earle" (1824–1903), as Tolkien calls him, not entirely respectfully, had excitedly announced his solution to the origin of the poem in three articles in the *Times* in 1884–85, and repeated it in his 1892 translation: his view was based on odd scraps of information and never at any point taken seriously. One might almost say that the only serious philologists in Britain during the later nineteenth century were the Icelanders Guthbrandur Vígfusson (1827–89) and Eiríkur Magnússon (1833–1913): the former, for instance, had brought out the still-valuable *Corpus Poeticum Boreale*, or "Complete Set of the Poetry of the North," in 1883, with the assistance of F. York Powell.

By the time Tolkien reached Oxford, things were looking up. Hector Munro Chadwick (1870–1947) published his *The Origins of the English Nation* in 1907 and *The Heroic Age* in 1912. He and his wife, Nora Kershaw Chadwick (1891–1972), had a great influence on the field till her death, but were based in Cambridge, always competitive with Tolkien's Oxford. *Liedertheorie* had meanwhile, received a mortal wound from W.P. Ker's (1855–1923) work *Epic and Romance* (1897), which pointed out how unlikely it was that one could simply assemble short poems into a long one. Ker repeated his points in less academic form in his *English Literature: Medieval* (1912), dubbed Ker's "shilling shocker" by Tolkien in "The Monsters and the Critics," and they were rubbed home in much more academic form, for German scholars, by Andreas Heusler (1865–1949) in his *Lied und Epos* (1905). Tolkien paid tribute to Ker when he gave the Ker Memorial Lecture on "Sir Gawain and the Green Knight" in Glasgow on April 15, 1953, since printed in *The Monsters and the Critics and Other Essays* (1983). After Ker and Heusler *Liedertheorie* was effectively dead, but found no immediate replacement, especially in *Beowulf* studies.

Here there had been two major trends. The long and politically driven argument between German and Scandinavian scholars as to the origins of the poem seemed to have been settled decisively in favor of the latter. *Beowulf*, after all, was entirely set in Scandinavia; the claims of German scholars that it was nevertheless written in English, and English was not a Scandinavian but a West Germanic language, carried less weight, especially as a number of Scandinavian analogs had been found for the poem in the ever-increasing number of newly published sagas. Significant figures in this field included the Dane Axel Olrik (1864–1917), whose work on early Danish tradition was translated, not entirely faithfully, by Lee Hollander (1880–1972) as *The Heroic Legends of Denmark* in 1919. Olrik also very remarkably, like Tolkien, decided to rewrite another major lost poem, the *Bjarkamál*, in Old Norse, basing his work on surviving fragments and a Latin epitome.

Another prominent Scandinavian scholar was Sophus Bugge (1833–1907), whose argument that Eddic poems including the "Lay of Wayland" might have been the work of Norse settlers in England would have appealed to Tolkien.

Furthermore, something of a consensus was emerging among English-speaking scholars. The German Friedrich Klaeber (1863–1954) emigrated to Minnesota and there brought out his edition of *Beowulf* in 1922: in successive editions it has remained standard to this day. His 1911 article on "The Christian elements in *Beowulf*"—written in German, but now available in English—left no doubt that Christianity was too ingrained in the poem for this to be the work of a pagan author or authors, no matter how much it had been rehandled. The American W.W. Lawrence (1876–1958) published his *Beowulf and Epic Tradition* in 1928, in essence agreeing with Klaeber and Ker and Olrik and discarding *Liedertheorie*. In England, the major figure was R.W. Chambers (1874–1942).

If Tolkien had an academic role model in his early years, it is likely to have been Chambers. His first major work was the 1912 edition of the Old English poem *Widsith*, subtitled *A Study in Heroic Legend*. *Widsith* (the word is a nickname meaning "far-traveled") is a relatively short poem consisting largely of lists of kings and peoples. Despite its lack of narrative content, it had been read eagerly by early scholars (especially Müllenhoff) as seeming to offer a guide to a lost world of heroic story. Chambers's edition fleshed this out with detailed commentary and quotation from across the whole range of rediscovered poems and chronicles. In 1921 he did something like the same service for *Beowulf*, bringing out a work modestly titled *Beowulf: An Introduction*. Like Klaeber's edition, this was revised twice, the second time by one of Tolkien's Oxford successors and fellow Inklings, C.L. Wrenn (1895–1969), and is still one of the most useful aids a reader of the poem can have. What Chambers did in it was bring together long excerpts, in translation and also sometimes in the original language, from all other ancient works that seemed to cast any light on *Beowulf*. He added extensive commentary on problems that had seemed to defeat scholars; and he endorsed the Klaeber—Lawrence view of the poem, in essence descended from Olrik, which saw it as alluding to (without describing) the self-destruction of the Danish royal house, the Scyldings, and so being in a sense almost an antiheroic poem.

Among Chambers's other distinguished works was his long essay *On the Continuity of English Prose* (1932), which among other things praises the prose treatise *Ancrene Riwle*, on which Tolkien spent so much time. But the most important connection with

Tolkien lies in Chambers's style. Like Tolkien, Chambers wrote fluently, often colloquially, with more than a touch of the humor normally absent from philology. He was deeply affected by the romantic elements in what he edited, and especially by the romance of the lost works, which "gave glimpses of a large history in the background," forever "unattainable vistas"—qualities which Tolkien was to recognize and deliberately build into his own fiction (see *Letters*, 333). Commenting on one passage of *Widsith* that seems to mention the Burgundian and historically verified originals of the characters who became the heroes of the *Nibelungenlied*, Chambers cites lines from a late Roman poet, Sidonius Apollinaris, complaining about having to listen to barbarian, indeed Burgundian poetry, and breaks out indignantly: "how gladly now would we give all his [Sidonius's] verses for ten lines of the songs in which these 'long-haired, seven foot high, onion-eating barbarians' celebrated, it may be, the open-handedness of Gibica, or perhaps told how, in that last terrible battle, their fathers had fallen fighting around Gundahari." Tolkien surely sympathized with this attitude and may have been encouraged by the boldness with which Chambers matched literary and linguistic studies together.

Chambers, who held a chair at University College London, refused the chair of Anglo-Saxon at Oxford when this became vacant on the resignation of W.A. Craigie (1867–1957) in 1925. Tolkien applied for the chair, as did Kenneth Sisam (1887–1971). Sisam was older than Tolkien, had been his tutor, and already had a post at Oxford: he must have been very much the favorite candidate, though his only major work at this time was a student textbook, the *Fourteenth Century English Reader* (1921), to which Tolkien had contributed the *Glossary*. Just possibly the electors may have thought that philology had had quite enough student grammars and readers—another of Tolkien's teachers, Joseph Wright (1855–1930), produced little else, and while these might answer the question "what to teach," they strikingly did not say *why*. The edition of *Sir Gawain and the Green Knight* which Tolkien brought out with E.V. Gordon that year was not only unusually rigorous in a scholarly way, it was also lively and interesting in Chambers's manner. One would like to think that this consideration gave the casting vote to Tolkien.

When Tolkien gave his 1936 lecture to the British Academy on *Beowulf*, therefore, he could look back on 120 years of scholarly debate, much of which had proved completely fruitless, and on a relatively recent period in which there had been more general agreement. Both the early period and the later one, however, had shared one characteristic from which even Ker and Chambers were not immune. They wanted to read *through* the poem to reach something else, such as information about the origins of England (Chadwick), or the lost tale of the Fall of the House of the Scyldings (Chambers, Lawrence, and even Klaeber). Ker seemed not to like the poem much. All of them wanted more heroes and fewer monsters. The suggestion that the poem was primarily mythical, held in entirely different, and since discredited, ways by Kemble, Grimm, Grundtvig, and Müllenhoff, had been forgotten. It was Tolkien's achievement at this point to insist on the poem's autonomy, to force scholarly attention on to what it *did* do as opposed to what it *might* have done. Scholarship has followed his lead ever since; though it has failed to pay much attention to Tolkien's rather different views expressed in the Oxford lectures which were edited by A.J. Bliss (1921–85) and published in 1982 as *Finn and Hengest*.

Even more irritating than misguided scholarship, though, was what one might call subscholarship. A familiar image of the Anglo-Saxons was one of strong, dull, stupid barbarians, probably half-stupefied by beer, quite incapable of any literary subtlety. This was the kind of thing one found (and finds) in journalism, in elementary histories, in student textbooks, and far too often among critics of later literature. Tolkien found it all deeply offensive—especially when voiced by the French, so long hostile to *les anglo-saxons*, whether British or American—and though he cut much of his fulmination out of the published version of his 1936 lecture, one can see that he had a major target in J.J. Jusserand (1855–1932), whose now-forgotten *Literary History of the English People* came out in 1895. Tolkien's irritation appears much more prominently in the early drafts of the lecture since edited by Michael D.C. Drout as *Beowulf and the Critics* (2002).

Mention should also be made of the connection between medieval scholarship and fairy-tale studies, first made by the Grimms. A characteristic figure is Sir George Webbe Dasent (1817–96) who translated Snorri Sturluson's mythical handbook *The Prose Edda* in 1842, and Rasmus Rask's Old Norse grammar a year later, but also *Popular Tales from the Norse* in 1859, with an introduction (which Tolkien quotes) linking fairy tales and philology. Tolkien mentions Dasent in "On Fairy-Stories," and also repeatedly refers there to the fairy stories and fairy-story collections of Andrew Lang (1844–1912). Tolkien is known to have read Lang's 1873 essay on "Mythology and Fairy-Tales" in the *Fortnightly Review*. Lang returned to the topic at greater length in his "Introduction" to Margaret Hunt's 1884 translation of *Grimm's Household Tales*, offering among other things a critique of the views of Max Müller (1823–1900), whom Tolkien cited only to contradict.

Another important area of philological activity was the compilation of dictionaries, especially the *New English Dictionary on Historical Principles*, which was eventually retitled as the Oxford English Dictionary. The distinctive feature of this massive work is that it aims to give not only definitions of meaning, but also to show how meanings changed over the years: the dictionary gives citations from the earliest recorded uses to the present day. In 1919 Tolkien was hired to work on this project, which by that time had been continuing ever since 1878, by Henry Bradley (1845–1923), the dictionary's second editor. Tolkien learned a great deal while engaged in this work; his colleagues included the third and fourth editors, respectively, W.A. Craigie (see above), and C.T. Onions (1873–1965), another Birmingham man eventually responsible for the *Oxford Dictionary of English Etymology* (1966). Tolkien was to mock the OED's definition of "blunderbuss" in *Farmer Giles*, where his joking reference to "the Four Wise Clerks of Oxenford" is clearly to the OED's four first editors, James Murray (1837–1915), Bradley, Craigie, and Onions. In "On Fairy-Stories" he corrects one of the medieval citations given under "fairy"; and his images of creatures such as "elf," "dwarf" and "wraith" are often markedly different from what the OED tells us. Tolkien, however, had every respect for the aims and intentions of the OED, while reserving the right, as a lexicographer himself, to disagree with some of its conclusions.

Tolkien also worked closely for a while with E.V. Gordon (1896–1938), who succeeded him in the Leeds Chair of English Language, and whose publications—besides the coedited *Sir Gawain*—include an *Introduction to Old Norse* (1927), which has remained valuable to the present day, and an edition of *The Battle of Maldon* (1937), clearly in Tolkien's mind while working on "The Homecoming of Beorhtnoth." Gordon's widow Ida Gordon completed his edition of *Pearl* (1953), thanking Tolkien for his contributions to it. Another Leeds professor was Bruce Dickins (1889–1979), who succeeded Gordon and Tolkien in the Leeds Chair, and whose publications include an edition of *Runic and Heroic Poems* from 1915.

One may say in conclusion that Tolkien was deeply affected by the notion, strongly present to all philologists, of loss: lost languages, lost poems, lost manuscripts. His first extended attempt at fiction was *The Book of Lost Tales*. *The Silmarillion* itself is presented as a synopsis of much older stories in vanished works, while *The Lays of Beleriand* are seen as intermediate stages in the "Silmarillion" tradition. Tolkien was keenly aware of the glamour of "unattainable vistas" of story, and deliberately introduced a sense of it into *The Lord of the Rings*. Two works on "the lost literature of medieval England" that Tolkien

is accordingly likely to have read with interest and sympathy are, first, an essay by Chambers with that title published in 1925, and a longer book by R.M. Wilson (born 1908) with the same title, published in 1952 but based on articles that had appeared earlier.

TOM SHIPPEY

Further Reading

Aarsleff, Hans. *The Study of Language in England, 1780–1860*. London: Athlone Press, 1983.

Anderson, Douglas A. "'An Industrious Little Devil': E.V. Gordon as Friend and Collaborator with Tolkien." In *Tolkien the Medievalist*, edited by Jane Chance, 15–25. London and New York: Routledge, 2003.

Damico, Helen, ed. *Medieval Scholarship: Biographical Studies on the Formation of Discipline*. Vol. 2, *Literature and Philology*. New York and London: Garland, 1998.

Drout, Michael D.C. *Beowulf and the Critics*. Tempe, AZ: Arizona State University Press, 2002.

Flieger, Verlyn. "A Mythology for Finland: Tolkien and Lönnrot as Mythmakers." In *Tolkien and the Invention of Myth*, edited by Jane Chance, 277–83. Lexington, KY: University Press of Kentucky, 2004.

Gilliver, Peter M. "'At the Wordface': J.R.R. Tolkien's Work on the *Oxford English Dictionary*." In *Proceedings of the J.R.R. Tolkien Centenary Conference*, edited by Patricia Reynolds and Glen H. GoodKnight, 173–86. Milton Keynes: Tolkien Society; Altadena, CA: Mythopoeic Press, 1995.

Palmer, D.J. *The Rise of English Studies*. London: Oxford University Press, 1965.

Payne, Richard C. "The Rediscovery of Old English Poetry in the English Literary Tradition." In *Anglo-Saxon Scholarship: The First Three Centuries*, edited by Carl T. Berkhout and Milton McC. Gatch, 149–66. Boston, MA: G.K. Hall, 1982.

Shippey, Tom. "Introduction." In *Beowulf: The Critical Heritage*, edited by T.A. Shippey and Andreas Haarder, 1–74. London and New York: Routledge, 1998.

Yates, Jessica. "'The Battle of the Eastern Field': A Commentary." *Mallorn* 13 (1979): 3–5.

See also ***Beowulf* and the Critics; "*Beowulf*: The Monsters and the Critics"; Finland: Literary Sources; German Folktale: *Deutsche Mythologie*; Mythology, Germanic; Gordon, E.V.; Obituary for Henry Bradley; Old Norse Literature; Oral Tradition; *Sir Gawain and the Green Knight*, Edition by Tolkien and E.V. Gordon**

SEAFARER, THE

Preserved in the late tenth-century manuscript commonly called *The Exeter Book*, *The Seafarer* is an anonymous Old English poem written in 124 lines of alliterative verse. Along with *The Wanderer*, a poem generally considered to be its companion piece, *The Seafarer* may belong to the category of Old English "wisdom" literature and is typically classified as an elegy, although it differs from classical definitions of the genre. Like other Old English elegies, *The Seafarer* is a dramatic, self-reflective lyric poem that uses a first-person speaker to address issues characteristic of lament poetry and focuses its attention on the speaker's state of mind. It recounts the thoughts of a solitary sailor whose life of hardship on the sea leads him to mourn his separation from companionship and worldly comfort. Icy waves, storms battering stone cliffs, and the cries of seabirds emphasize the physical hardship and loneliness of the seafarer's life in contrast to the life of physical ease and companionship available to land dwellers. Yet, as attractive as life on land might seem in his imagination, a restless desire for the sea compels him to continue his self-imposed exile for he realizes that the material pleasures of youth and glory pass, while personal wealth is useless after death. In its closing, the poem advocates that the individual soul, exiled on earth by mortal life, should chart its course humbly, with good deeds and right behavior, toward its eternal home in God, which offers the only authentic existence.

Not only was Tolkien intimately familiar with *The Seafarer* through his work as a teacher and scholar of Old English language and literature, but he worked initially on a critical edition of this poem with his friend and colleague E.V. Gordon. Although Tolkien never completed the project, in the preface to her 1960 edition of *The Seafarer*, Ida Gordon remarks that she incorporated much of the original material written by her husband and Tolkien into her text, especially in the notes. In addition, Tolkien's fictional works are marked by themes evocative of those found in *The Seafarer*. In two of his unfinished works *The Lost Road* and *The Notion Club Papers*, Tolkien paraphrases portions of *The Seafarer* and even alludes directly to the Old English text. *The Seafarer*'s frequent use of gnomic phrases, statements conveying generally shared philosophical wisdom, similarly finds its way into many of Tolkien's works, especially *The Hobbit* and *The Lord of the Rings*. Most important, Tolkien incorporates the Old English poem's themes of exile, sea-longing, and the world's ephemerality into *The Lord of the Rings* and *The Silmarillion*. In both works, Tolkien presents the Noldor Elves particularly as exiles from their otherworldly home in the Undying Lands. Separated from their cultural roots by past inadequacies of leadership and current attachments to Middle-earth, Tolkien presents them as longing for their eternal and ancestral homeland. For them, like the Old English seafarer, the ordinary world of Middle-earth is a place of exile that in the end is unfulfilling. Reminding them of their beloved, the sea calls to the Elves' souls, especially in the cries of seabirds. Although he is not a Noldor and has never

been to the Undying Lands, Legolas expresses a similar sentiment in *The Return of the King* (*RK*, VI, iv, 234–35) in a poem that employs seabird imagery evocative of *The Seafarer*. Less direct parallels that incorporate seafaring motifs for character development and thematic expressions of cultural or eternal loss are found also in the presentation of the Númenóreans in general as well as the specific characters of Eärendil and Aldarion in *The Silmarillion* as well as *The Unfinished Tales*.

LESLIE A. DONOVAN

Further Reading

Crossley-Holland, Kevin, trans. *The Seafarer*. In *The Anglo-Saxon World: An Anthology*, 53–55. Oxford: Oxford University Press, 1999.
Gordon, Ida L., ed. *The Seafarer*. London: Methuen, 1960.
Krapp, George Phillip, and Elliot Van Kirk Dobbie, eds. *The Seafarer*. In *The Exeter Book*, 143–47. Anglo-Saxon Poetic Records 3. New York: Cambridge University Press, 1936.
O'Brien O'Keeffe, Katherine, ed. *Old English Shorter Poems: Basic Readings*. New York: Garland, 1994.
Orton, Peter. "Form and Structure of *The Seafarer*." In *Old English Literature: Critical Essays*, edited by R.M. Luizza, 353–80. New Haven, CT: Yale University Press, 2002.
Wilcox, Miranda. "Exilic Imagining in *The Seafarer* and *The Lord of the Rings*." In *Tolkien the Medievalist*, edited by Jane Chance, 133–54. New York: Routledge, 2002.

See also **Christian Readings of Tolkien; Elves; Exile; Gordon, E.V.; Gordon, Ida; Legolas; *Lost Road*; *Wanderer, The***

SEAFARER: IDA GORDON EDITION

The Seafarer is an Old English elegiac poem. It survives in a single manuscript: the Exeter Book, a late tenth-century collection of Old English poetry. *The Seafarer*'s speaker describes the physical hardships and the loneliness he has suffered at sea, but also his eager longing for another journey. Then he meditates on the contrast between the earthly and the heavenly life, lamenting his own state of exile and the transience of human splendor and happiness, and inviting his audience to seek out an eternal home with God.

Scholarly interpretations of the poem have varied widely over the last century, as summarized by Miranda Wilcox and the *Blackwell Encyclopaedia of Anglo-Saxon England* (*BEASE*). Early scholars believed the poem to be a dialogue between two speakers: one old and mindful of the trials of the seafaring life, the other young and eager to be off to sea. Others read the whole poem allegorically, interpreting the sea journey with its hardships as an extended metaphor of earthly life and the seafarer himself as mortal man in exile from heaven. Yet others insisted on a literal interpretation: C.W. Kennedy saw the poem as an account of real seafaring experience (1936); Dorothy Whitelock explained it more specifically, viewing the seafarer as a self-exiled "hermit-pilgrim," who goes to sea for the love of God, practicing a form of asceticism familiar to an Anglo-Saxon audience (1950). According to *BEASE*, current scholarship sees *The Seafarer* as a relatively unified monologue, in which the sea voyage symbolizes the life of the Christian ascetic, journeying through hardships towards his heavenly home (*BEASE*, s.v. "Seafarer"). This is the view of the poem most like Ida Gordon's in her 1960 edition, where she argues that the sea journey suggested earthly life symbolically rather than signifying it allegorically.

In theme and tone, *The Seafarer* resembles another Old English poem, *The Wanderer*. The speaker of the latter laments his exiled state, the loss of his lord, and the transience of earthly joys in general, but eventually achieves a stoic wisdom and places his trust in God.

In 1932, the London publisher Methuen launched Methuen's Old English Library, a series of small student editions of Old English works. Tolkien signed up to edit two Old English poems for this series, in collaboration with his friend and colleague, E.V. Gordon. One was *The Wanderer*; the other was *The Seafarer*. As Douglas Anderson relates in his history of this scholarly project, the plan for the two joint editions was that Tolkien would be the principal editor of the former, Gordon of the latter. As early as 1933, the two editions were announced as pending publication. Eventually, Tolkien and Gordon decided to combine both poems in a single volume, perhaps for the sake of a larger glossary (Anderson, "Industrious," 19).

In 1938, when E.V. Gordon died, the project was put on hold for several years. In 1960 Ida Gordon, E.V. Gordon's wife, published her own edition of *The Seafarer*; though she had initially intended to complete her husband's and Tolkien's work, developments in scholarship about the poem prompted her to produce an edition very different from Gordon and Tolkien's original project (*Seafarer*, vii).

Ida Gordon thanks Tolkien for "some notes given to [her] with his usual generosity" and acknowledges that her edition "incorporates much of the original material" (*Seafarer*, vii), especially in the explanatory notes, mostly concerned with grammar or vocabulary. However, she does not specifically pinpoint how Tolkien contributed to either the 1960 edition or the 1938 manuscript. She indicates that her own edition, which reads the poem symbolically, is "a view of the poem basically different from that of the original draft" (*Seafarer*, vii), but this does not reveal whether Tolkien and Gordon would have seen

The Seafarer as a dialogue or a monologue, his journey as an allegory or a symbol. As Wilcox points out, Tolkien's attitude to allegory is ambivalent: he repeatedly states his dislike of it, but admits its usefulness and begins his famous lecture "*Beowulf*: The Monsters and the Critics" with an extended, carefully wrought allegory of the poem and its scholarship. There is, in short, no clear evidence as to where Tolkien and E.V. Gordon's interpretation would have fallen in the critical spectrum described above.

ALEXANDRA BOLINTINEANU

Further Reading

Anderson, Douglas A. "'An industrious little devil': E.V. Gordon as Friend and Collaborator with Tolkien." In *Tolkien the Medievalist*, edited by Jane Chance, 15–25. London and New York: Routledge, 2003.

Dobbie, Elliott Van Kirk, and George Philip Krapp, eds. *The Wanderer*. In *The Anglo-Saxon Poetic Records: A Collective Edition*, 3:134–37. New York: Columbia University Press, 1931–53.

Gordon, I.L., ed. *The Seafarer*. London: Methuen & Co. Ltd, 1960.

Gordon, R.K., trans. *Anglo-Saxon Poetry*. Translated by R.K. Gordon. London: J.M. Dent & Sons Ltd. New York: E. P. Dutton & Co. Inc., 1962.

———, trans. "The Seafarer." In *Anglo-Saxon Poetry*, 76–78. London: J.M. Dent & Sons Ltd. New York: E.P. Dutton & Co. Inc., 1962.

———, trans. "The Wanderer." In *Anglo-Saxon Poetry*, 73–75. London: J.M. Dent & Sons Ltd. New York: E.P. Dutton & Co. Inc., 1962.

Lapidge, Michael, et al., eds. *The Blackwell Encyclopedia of Anglo-Saxon England*. Oxford; Malden, MA: Blackwell, 1999

Shippey, Tom. *The Road to Middle-earth: Revised and Expanded Edition*. Boston, MA: Houghton Mifflin, 2001.

Wilcox, Miranda. "Exilic Imagining in *The Seafarer* and *The Lord of the Rings*." In *Tolkien the Medievalist*, edited by Jane Chance, 133–54. London and New York: Routledge, 2003.

See also **Allegory; Gordon, E.V.; Old English;** *Seafarer*; *Wanderer*

"SECRET VICE, A"

The lecture published as "A Secret Vice" in *The Monsters and the Critics and Other Essays* in 1983 (*MC*, 198–223) was originally written in 1931. It was probably presented at a meeting of some philological society, and the manuscript was hastily revised for a second presentation some twenty years later. The title given in the manuscript is "A Hobby for the Home," but Tolkien later referred to the essay by the title "A Secret Vice," which Christopher Tolkien adopted for the published version (*MC*, 3–4).

The essay deals with the "secret vice" of language invention, which was a hobby of Tolkien's throughout his life. The lecture begins with a mention of Esperanto, in which Tolkien briefly discusses the need for an international language and his liking for Esperanto in particular. He then takes the essay in a very different direction, turning away from artificial languages that were created for a utilitarian purpose, and instead begins to discuss languages that were invented merely for the sake of their creators' own enjoyment. Since such creators tend to be shy about revealing their private languages to the world at large, as Tolkien notes, the essay relies primarily on Tolkien's own private languages for examples.

As a specimen of the "lower stages" of linguistic invention, Tolkien presents a sentence in Animalic: *dog nightingale woodpecker forty* (you are an ass). He notes that the inventors were young children, but does not reveal that they were his cousins, Mary and Marjorie Incledon (Carpenter, 35–36). He then goes on to discuss a more advanced stage of invention, exemplified by Nevbosh (the New Nonsense), which was created by Mary Incledon and Tolkien himself, and provides a limerick written in the language. Whereas the vocabulary of Animalic consisted entirely of English words, the Nevbosh vocabulary was derived (in various ways) from words in English, French, and Latin, though Nevbosh syntax is strictly English, the language being essentially a word-substitution code.

At this point Tolkien begins to discuss the role of pleasure: the "incipient pleasure found in *linguistic invention*," pleasure found in "the *contemplation* of the relation between sound and notion," and pleasure in the "very word-form itself." He cites Greek, Finnish, and Welsh as examples of "languages which have a very characteristic and in their different ways beautiful word-form" (*MC*, 206–7). Tolkien then goes on to show how characteristics of this sort can be applied to linguistic invention, giving a specimen of Naffarin, which was influenced by Latin and Spanish in its sound patterns and word-forms.

Tolkien states that his greatest interest in language construction is "in word-form in itself, and in word-form in relation to meaning" (*MC*, 211). He also mentions how language invention can satisfy philological, grammatical, and logical interests. Most significantly, he expresses his view that an "art-language" requires a concomitant mythology, or at least a sketch thereof, and that such a language will in fact *breed* a mythology. He also states that if one abides by the principles used in creating the language, one may even write "poetry of a sort."

Both the mythological and the poetic aspects of language creation are reflected in the examples that Tolkien gives of Qenya and Noldorin, the predecessors of the Quenya and Sindarin of *The Lord of the Rings*. Three Qenya poems appear in the essay:

Oilima Markirya (The Last Ark), *Nieninque*, and *Earendel*; an eight-line passage in Noldorin is also given. Translations of the texts are provided, and two other versions of *Oilima Markirya* (one earlier, one much later) are appended to the essay. Further material relating to these poems appears in "Early Qenya Poetry."

ARDEN R. SMITH

Further Reading

Carpenter, Humphrey. *Tolkien: A Biography*. Boston, MA: Houghton Mifflin, 1977.

Tolkien, J.R.R. "Early Qenya Poetry." Edited by Christopher Gilson, Patrick H. Wynne, Carl F. Hostetter, and Bill Welden. *Parma Eldalamberon* 16 (2006), forthcoming.

Wynne, Patrick, and Carl F. Hostetter. "Three Elvish Verse Modes: *Ann-thennath, Minlamad thent / estent*, and *Linnod*." In *Tolkien's Legendarium: Essays on the History of Middle-earth*, edited by Verlyn Flieger and Carl F. Hostetter, 113–39. Westport, CT: Greenwood Press, 2000.

See also **"English and Welsh"; Esperanto; Languages Invented by Tolkien; Poems by Tolkien in Other Languages; Language, Theories of**

SEXUALITY IN TOLKIEN'S WORKS

Tolkien's stories are "juvenile trash" (Wilson, 332) filled with characters who are essentially prepubescent boys (Muir, 11). So some critics of *The Lord of the Rings* have declared, even suggesting that Tolkien's fiction reflected his own sexual immaturity (Stimpson, 20). Fortunately for Tolkien's reputation, the publication of a broader range of his writings and a more careful examination of his fiction have provided us with a better understanding of sexuality in Tolkien's work and life.

Tolkien states some of his views on sexuality in a letter to his son Michael. Commenting on sexual temptation in the context of the fallen world of Christian belief, Tolkien explains that women are monogamous by nature, while men, who "could healthily beget. . . a few hundred children, and enjoy the process" (*Letters*, 51), are not. He also expresses reservations about the unrealistic idealization of women in the romantic chivalric tradition, though he admits that it can be "the highest ideal of love between man and woman" (*Letters*, 49). In contrast to this human world, where there is "no consonance between our bodies, minds, and souls" (*Letters*, 51), Tolkien presents a vision of harmony between flesh and spirit in "Laws and Customs among the Eldar" (*Morgoth*, 207–54). This essay describes Elvish sexuality, which is characterized by natural monogamy and procreative sex that is "both exalted and contained" in the early part of marriage (Rosenthal, 35–42).

Among his fictional characters, Tolkien represents several romantic heterosexual lovers. Aragorn and Arwen, Beren and Lúthien, and Thingol and Melian follow a chivalric paradigm in which a male is struck by the sight of a beautiful female of higher status and falls in love. A relationship that moves along somewhat faster is Éowyn and Faramir's, whose kiss is for many readers a memorable image of romantic passion. A subtler instance of erotic attraction is Éowyn and Aragorn's first meeting in which, according to Lewis and Currie, "Calm waters have been ruffled" (214), or in Smith of Wootton Major's dancing with the kilted maiden, a scene in which "the nostalgic erotic suggestion is delicate, but it is unmistakeable" (Rosebury, 132). Daniel Timmons makes a case for the sensuality of the hobbits in *The Lord of the Rings* when he points out their reactions on meeting Goldberry, Arwen, and Galadriel, all beautiful females (75–77).

The erotic attraction underlying some of these heterosexual relationships may result in the begetting of children, but characters who do not procreate have a less secure footing in Middle-earth than those who do. The Dwarves and Ents are fading races due to a lack—or complete loss—of females. Frodo's and, to some extent, Bilbo's involvement with the Ring cuts them off from their communities and prevents them from establishing prolific families like other hobbits (Timmons, 75). However, Sam's marriage to Rosie Cotton celebrates his successful return to the Shire and the promise of his future life there. While Frodo and his companions sail out of history, the last image in *The Lord of the Rings* is of Sam and his new family (Lewis and Currie, 227–28).

In contrast to these productive relationships, Tolkien also includes a range of sexual problems in his legendarium, although these are not attributed to an Eve figure, the traditional sexual temptress and cause of the Fall in biblical mythology (Crowe, 273). Instead, Rosenthal (35–42) attributes Finwë's inability to restrain his libido after the departure of Míriel as a cause leading to Fëanor's disastrous actions in *The Silmarillion*. Although Edith Crowe finds that Tolkien does not describe violence that targets only women, she does note that the Númenórean decline is marked by Ar-Gimilzôr forcing Inzilbêth into marriage or by Ar-Pharazôn constraining Tar-Míriel into an incestuous union that is "nothing less than rape" (Crowe, 276). Unwitting incest, on the other hand, occurs in the tragic story of Túrin Turambar. Elsewhere, Tolkien represents complex marriages with disastrous personal and political consequences, as in the stories of Aldarion and Erendis in *Unfinished Tales* or of Aredhel, Eöl, and their son Maeglin who, according to Lewis and Currie (201), contribute to a theme of

sexual degeneracy leading to the fall of Gondolin. More positive is one husband's love for and fidelity to his wife in "The Lay of Aotrou and Itroun"; however, if Tolkien's poem "The Fall of Arthur" were to be published beyond the few lines appearing in his biography (Carpenter, 171), we would have another story not only of sexual lust but probably also of adultery.

In discussions of Tolkien's representations of sexuality, one of the most controversial figures is Shelob. Some interpretations see Sam's fight with Shelob as an image of violent sexual intercourse with an "enormous, stenching bitch-castrator" (Stimpson, 19) who is a creation of Tolkien's misogynist imagination (Partridge, 187–91). While other critics agree that the description of the Shelob episode has sexualized elements, interpretations vary, as do the conclusions drawn about Tolkien's views on female and male sexuality.

However, the subject of male sexuality in the Shelob episode and elsewhere does raise questions about homoeroticism and homosexuality, especially in Frodo and Sam's relationship in *The Lord of the Rings*. Marion Zimmer Bradley states that "Frodo and Sam reach classical 'idealized friendship' equivalent in emotional strength to the ardor of Achilles and Patrocles or David and Jonathan: 'passing the love of women'" (83). Critics have suggested other historical contexts for understanding the homosocial and sexual elements of Frodo and Sam's relationship, such as Victorian romantic friendships between men (Rosenthal) or the male bonding of soldiers serving in World War One (Craig, Smol). Although Brenda Partridge interprets Sam's discovery of Frodo in the Tower of Cirith Ungol as the (presumably symbolic) consummation of a sexual affair, Valerie Rohy takes the Lacanian belief that "We never truly have or know the ones we love" (933) and reads homosexuality in *The Lord of the Rings* as "*amor interruptus*" (940), a love that is recognized but never completed.

Clearly, Tolkien's treatment of sexuality is more varied than some critics have thought. The evidence certainly suggests that opinions to the effect that there is no understanding of adult sexuality in Tolkien's fiction should finally be put to rest.

ANNA SMOL

Further Reading

Bradley, Marion Zimmer. "Men, Halflings, and Hero Worship." In *Understanding "The Lord of the Rings": The Best of Tolkien Criticism*, edited by Rose A. Zimbardo and Neil D. Isaacs, 76–92. Boston and New York: Houghton Mifflin, 2004.

Carpenter, Humphrey. *J.R.R. Tolkien: A Biography*. Boston and New York: Houghton Mifflin, 2000.

Craig, David M. "'Queer Lodgings': Gender and Sexuality in *The Lord of the Rings*." *Mallorn: The Journal of the Tolkien Society* 38 (2001): 11–18.

Crowe, Edith L. "Power in Arda: Sources, Uses and Misuses." In *Proceedings of the J.R.R. Tolkien Centenary Conference 1992*, edited by Patricia Reynolds and Glen GoodKnight, 272–77. Milton Keynes and Altadena: Tolkien Society and Mythopoeic Press, 1995.

Lewis, Alex, and Elizabeth Currie. *The Uncharted Realms of Tolkien: A Critical Study of Text, Context and Subtext in the Works of J.R.R. Tolkien*. Oswestry: Medea Publishing, 2002.

Muir, Edwin. "A Boy's World." *Sunday Observer*, November 27, 1955, 11.

Partridge, Brenda. "No Sex Please—We're Hobbits: The Construction of Female Sexuality in *The Lord of the Rings*." In *J.R.R. Tolkien: This Far Land*, edited by Robert Giddings, 179–97. London, Totowa, NJ: Vision; Barnes & Noble, 1983.

Rohy, Valerie. "On Fairy Stories." In *Modern Fiction Studies* 50, no. 4 (2004): 927–48.

Rosebury, Brian. *Tolkien: A Cultural Phenomenon*. Basingstoke: Palgrave Macmillan, 2003.

Rosenthal, Ty. "Warm Beds Are Good: Sex and Libido in Tolkien's Writing." *Mallorn: The Journal of the Tolkien Society*. 42 (2004): 35–42.

Smol, Anna. "'Oh . . . oh . . . Frodo!': Readings of Male Intimacy in *The Lord of the Rings*." *Modern Fiction Studies* 50, no. 4 (2004): 949–79.

Stimpson, Catharine R. *J.R.R. Tolkien*. New York: Columbia University Press, 1969.

Timmons, Daniel. "Hobbit Sex and Sexuality in *The Lord of the Rings*." *Mythlore* 23 (2001): 70–79.

Tolkien, J.R.R. "Aldarion and Erendis: The Mariner's Wife." In *UT*, 223–80.

———. "Laws and Customs among the Eldar." In *Morgoth*, 207–54.

———. "The Lay of Aotrou and Itroun." *Welsh Review* 4 (December 1945): 254–66.

———. "Smith of Wootton Major." In *Tales from the Perilous Realm*, 147–78. London: HarperCollins, 1998.

Wilson, Edmund. "Oo, Those Awful Orcs." In *The Bit Between My Teeth: A Literary Chronicle of 1950–1965*, 326–32. New York: Farrar, Straus & Giroux, 1965.

See also **Aragorn; Arthurian Romance; Arwen; Beren; Dwarves; Elves; Ents; Éowyn; Faramir; Feminist Readings of Tolkien; Finwë and Míriel; Frodo; Gender in Tolkien's Works; Goldberry; Hobbits; Homosexuality; *Letters of J.R.R. Tolkien*; *Lord of the Rings*; Lúthien; Marriage; Melian; Middle-earth: Men, Middle-earth; Monsters, Middle-earth; *Morgoth's Ring*; Poems by Tolkien; Sam; Shelob; *Silmarillion*; *Smith of Wootton Major*; Thingol; *Unfinished Tales*; Women in Tolkien's Works; World War I**

SHAKESPEARE

It would be easy to take Tolkien at his word and dismiss any possible influence by William Shakespeare on his work. After all, Tolkien held a well-known grudge against the playwright for his "unforgiveable part" in the "debasement" of the Elves of English folklore (*Letters*, 185) and cursed the "damned cobwebs" he wrapped them in (143n). He "cordially" disliked studying Shakespeare (213), and in a school debate took a strong anti-Shakespeare stance, disparaging the bard and "his filthy birthplace, his squalid surroundings, and his sordid character" (Carpenter, *Tolkien*, 40). Some of this invective could, of course, be put down to youthful bluster and "an impish delight in challenging established values" (Carpenter, *Inklings*, 25). In spite of this supposed hostility, Tolkien was comfortable enough with Shakespeare to lecture on *Hamlet* as part of a series of talks with Neville Coghill, Hugo Dyson, C.S. Lewis, C.L. Wrenn, and others during his early career at Oxford (Ryan, 50). He referred to *King Lear* and other plays numerous times in the longer versions of his Beowulf essay (for example, comparing *Lear* to its analogue in Layamon's *Brut*) (*B&C*, 7, 97, 140, 159, passim). However, Tolkien's later curricular reforms, besides reconciling "Lang." and "Lit." to some extent, did deemphasize what he felt was an unwarranted focus on Milton and Shakespeare to the exclusion of older materials (Carpenter, *Tolkien*, 137).

Tolkien's thoughts on fantasy on stage, particularly concerning *Macbeth*, form a vital part of his arguments on "secondary belief" in the seminal essay "On Fairy-Stories." Tolkien calls Drama "naturally hostile to Fantasy" (49), considering any representation of faerie on stage, no matter how good the stage-trickery, to require a tertiary level of belief impossible in an art form where the audience is by definition set apart from the performance. In reading, there are fewer barriers to complete immersion and one may more freely enter this other realm. Drama is also essentially "anthropocentric," and while it can deal competently and even harrowingly with the effects of the faerie world on humans, it fails if it also tries to present the faerie world itself (81). (Tolkien does, however, give stage drama its due in a letter reviewing a production of *Hamlet* which he attended. He does not say if the Ghost passed the test of tertiary belief, but does praise the production for making Ophelia's mad scene, which clearly did not produce "secondary belief" for him in reading, "moving, almost intolerably so" [*Letters*, 88].)

Antipathy, whether feigned or not, does not rule out influence. In many places in his fiction Tolkien engages in a dialogue with Shakespeare, sometimes overtly, often more subtly, using his plays as "argumentative foils" (Drout, in *B&C* 7). The best-documented example of this is the creative process that led to the Ents. In a 1955 letter to W.H. Auden, Tolkien very specifically details his disappointment with the way the prophecy concerning Birnam Wood marching on Dunsinane Castle was fulfilled in *Macbeth* (*Letters*, 212n). Shakespeare of course hewed fairly close to the historical events as described in Holinshed, so the prophecy could only be fulfilled by the trick of soldiers carrying "leavy screens" to hide their numbers. Tolkien wanted to see the trees actually "unfix their earthbound roots" and march on the traitorous Macbeth; and so he had his Ents march on Saruman's stronghold, tear down the walls, and drown his evil works. Similarly, Tolkien also responds to the prophecy that "none of woman born" can harm Macbeth. In Shakespeare's play, the answer is again a bit of a disappointing trick, dictated by history; Macduff is born by Caesarian section, not a fact obvious to the observer. Tolkien, however, plays fair with the reader; his Witch-king, subject of a similar prophecy ("not by the hand of man shall he fall"), is killed by the joint efforts of the hobbit Merry and the woman Éowyn (Croft, "'Bid the Tree'").

In his article on Tolkien's prose style, Michael D.C. Drout makes a comprehensive case for this scene and Denethor's self-immolation scene as parts of an extended dialogue with *King Lear*, principally in its linguistic features (especially the key phrase "come not between the dragon/Nazgûl and his wrath/prey" and the word "recreant"), but also in selected plot elements such as Éomer's rage at finding Éowyn apparently dead and Éowyn's breath on Imrahil's mirrored vambrace, as well as larger thematic issues of kingship, succession, and madness (Drout). Tom Shippey also draws attention to Tolkien's "rebuke" of *Macbeth*, his different philosophical and theological approach to prophecy, his stylistic and linguistic echoes (particularly in a comparison of a stanza from *Love's Labour's Lost* with a piece of Bilbo's poetry), and his "guardedly respectful" attitude toward Shakespeare in general (Shippey, *Century*, 192–96, *Road*, 177–85). *A Midsummer Night's Dream* is also an obvious influence, if only as an example of the diminution of faerie Tolkien was rebelling against with his fair and perilous Elves. However, Lisa Hopkins makes it clear that there are thematic and structural parallels between this play and *The Hobbit* as well, in the functions of the forests of Athens and Mirkwood as places of transformative adventure, in similar tricks played by Gandalf and Puck, and in the enchanting glamour of faerie (Hopkins). A collection of essays published in 2006 examines additional influences, parallels, and responses to *The Tempest*, *Richard II*, *Henry V*, *Hamlet*, *Twelfth Night*, *Othello*, and other plays, and explores the authors' shared interests in themes such as kingship and power, dramatic catharsis, the divided self, the place of women, race and otherness, and magic and wizardry (Croft, *Tolkien and Shakespeare*).

Both Tolkien and Shakespeare grew up in the Warwickshire countryside, absorbing its rich country folklore and traditions, and they dipped freely into the cauldron of story for their inspirations. Both have been dismissed as hacks with a shaky spot in the canon and lauded as geniuses for the ages and the authors of the defining works of their times. Both fascinate general audiences and scholars alike, and exploring their use of similar themes, motifs, and linguistic influences enriches our appreciation of both.

JANET BRENNAN CROFT

Further Reading

Carpenter, Humphrey. *The Inklings: C.S. Lewis, J.R.R. Tolkien, Charles Williams, and Their Friends*. Boston, MA: Houghton Mifflin, 1979.

———. *Tolkien : A Biography*. Boston, MA: Houghton Mifflin, 1977.

Croft, Janet Brennan. "'Bid the Tree Unfix His Earth-Bound Root': Themes from *Macbeth* in *The Lord of the Rings*." *Seven: An Anglo-American Literary Review* 21 (2004): 47–60.

———, ed. *Tolkien and Shakespeare: Influences, Echoes, Revisions*. Jefferson: Macfarland, 2006.

Drout, Michael D.C. "Tolkien's Prose Style and Its Literary and Rhetorical Effects." *Tolkien Studies* 1 (2004): 137–62.

Hopkins, Lisa. "*The Hobbit* and *A Midsummer Night's Dream*." *Mallorn* 28 (1991): 19–21.

Norman, Philip. *The Prevalence of Hobbits*. Interview. *New York Times*, 2001 (1967), http://www.nytimes.com/1967/01/15/books/tolkien-interview.html (July 1, 2002).

Ryan, John S. "J.R.R. Tolkien's Formal Lecturing and Teaching at the University of Oxford, 1929–1959." *Seven: An Anglo-American Literary Review* 19 (2002): 45–62.

Shippey, Thomas A. *J.R.R. Tolkien: Author of the Century*. Boston, MA: Houghton Mifflin, 2001.

———. *The Road to Middle-earth*. 2nd ed. Boston, MA: Houghton Mifflin, 2003.

Tolkien, J.R.R. "On Fairy-Stories." In *The Tolkien Reader*, 3–84. New York: Ballantine, 1966.

See also **Brut** **by Layamon; Coghill, Neville; Dyson, Hugo; Education; Ents; Éowyn; Lewis, C.S.; Oxford; Warwick**

SHAPING OF MIDDLE-EARTH

The Shaping of Middle-earth is the fourth book in the twelve-volume *History of Middle-earth* series compiled and edited by J.R.R. Tolkien's son, Christopher Tolkien, from the various unpublished manuscripts, drafts, notes, and archival materials left by his late father. It follows *The Book of Lost Tales I* and *II* and *The Lays of Beleriand*. First published in 1985 by Allen & Unwin, *The Shaping of Middle-earth* follows the development of J.R.R. Tolkien's vision of

Middle-earth through sometime in the 1930s, to the point at which he wrote *The Hobbit*.

The volume is divided into several sections. The first, "Prose Fragments Following The Lost Tales," include three brief works written around 1920. The first two excerpts are from the early piece *Turlin and the Exiles of Gondolin*, in which Turlin represents the character who later became the Noldorin Elf Turgon. The text adds to the tale *The Fall of Gondolin*, which is now found in *The Book of Lost Tales II*. The second text as well as the third fragment reflect the development of the story of the Noldor's departure from Aman, the Blessed Realm, and their arrival in Middle-earth.

The second section is "The Earliest 'Silmarillion' (The 'Sketch of the Mythology')," a piece first written in 1926 and revised through 1930. Literally, *The Silmarillion* means "the history of the Silmarils," or the jewels made by the Noldorin Elf prince Fëanor with the light of the Two Trees of Valinor. Although this text gives only a brief explanation of the early days of Tolkien's world of Arda, all further development of *The Silmarillion*'s mythology can be traced directly back to its chronology, making this text a vital artifact in the history of Tolkien's cosmology, creation myth, and the Elder Days of his universe.

The third section, "The Quenta," builds on the "Sketch of Mythology" and represents Tolkien's only completed account of the First Age. Tolkien apparently wrote "The Quenta" in 1930, and conceived of it as a condensed summary of a much longer work. The general organization and even specific sentences of "The Quenta" reveal the building blocks of what would become *The Silmarillion*, Tolkien's posthumously published account of the creation and early history of Middle-earth, also edited by his son Christopher. This section includes two appendices. The first is the "Fragment of a translation of the Quenta Noldorinwa into Old English, made by Ælfwine or Eriol; together with Old English equivalents of Elvish names." The second, the poem "The Horns of Yhnir," represents a song the Adan hero Tuor wrote for Eärendel (later Eärendil), his son, as described in "The Quenta."

Also included in *The Shaping of Middle-earth* is "The First 'Silmarillion' Map," which is essentially several maps of the lands of Arda as described in the history of the Silmarils: a central map and two extensions, one northern and one southern, all of which date to approximately 1926 and were heavily altered during subsequent years.

The fifth section, "The Ambarkanta," details Tolkien's universe and explains how the nature and very shape of the world changed due to great cataclysms, namely, the two Battles of the Gods and the Fall of Númenor. In this text, written in the mid-1930s,

Tolkien explains that the creator's First Design possessed a careful symmetry that was marred by subsequent events. First, after those in Valinor broke the underground fortress Utumno and chained its lord, the rebellious Ainu Melko (later Melkor), the waters of the world moved, so that the northern sea became a lake and the southern sea became a great ocean and joined the eastern and western waters. The greatest shift, however, occurred when the Númenóreans assaulted the Lands of the Gods in the forbidden quest for immortality: in response to Númenóreans' disobedience, the Earth became round, and the race of Man was severed from Valinor and the Gods who dwelled there.

"The Earliest Annals of Valinor" is the sixth section of the volume and represents Tolkien's drafts from the early 1930s. As Christopher Tolkien points out, this text is the first of several, and was followed by another "Annals of Valinor" later in the 1930s and a related version, "The Annals of Aman," probably in 1951 or 1952. Styled as the writing of Pengolod the Wise of Gondolin as translated by Eriol of Leithien (or Ælfwine of the Angelcynn), this earliest incarnation of the annals is an extended chronology tracing the history of Valinor and the rest of Arda from creation until the arrival of the Noldor in Middle-earth. It ends with an appendix, "Old English versions of the Annals of Valinor, made by Ælfwine or Eriol."

The last section, "The Earliest Annals of Beleriand," is, like its immediate predecessor, the first of several incarnations of similar chronologies, and its writing and subsequent rewriting parallels that of "The Earliest Annals of Valinor." This text, included in two versions ("AB I" and "AB II"), follows events in Beleriand, or the Land of the Elves, from the creation of the Sun and Moon through the great war against Morgoth, or Melkor, and the end of the Elder Days. The second, revised version of the annals presented in this section, AB II, depicts the coming of Men into Beleriand. The text also ends with an appendix of the Old English version, once again attributed to Ælfwine, or Eriol.

The Shaping of Middle-earth as a whole is a valuable addition to the *History of Middle-earth* series, analysis of *The Silmarillion*, and scholarship about Tolkien's writing for several reasons. It offers the only description Tolkien ever made of the physical nature of his created universe and its subsequent changes in form. It likewise offers Tolkien's only complete account of the Elder Days. Moreover, the details provided in the maps and various prose and poetry drafts provide a more complicated and thorough understanding of the early lore of Middle-earth, Tolkien's cosmographical vision, and the ways in which Arda's chronology and details, especially the stories later included in *The Silmarillion*, developed and changed from their inception until Tolkien's death in 1973.

AMY H. STURGIS

Further Reading

Carpenter, Humphrey. *J.R.R. Tolkien: A Biography*. Boston, MA: Houghton Mifflin, 1977.
Foster, Robert. *The Complete Guide to Middle-earth: Tolkien's World from A to Z*. Rev. ed. New York: Ballantine Books, 2001.
Shippey, Tom. *J.R.R. Tolkien: Author of the Century*. Boston, MA: Houghton Mifflin, 2000.
———. *The Road to Middle-earth: How J.R.R. Tolkien Created a New Mythology*. Boston, MA: Houghton Mifflin, 2003.
Tolkien, Christopher. *The History of Middle-earth Index*. New York: HarperCollins, 2002.

See also Ælfwine; Arda; Astronomy and Cosmology, Middle-earth; *Book of Lost Tales I*; *Book of Lost Tales II*; Eärendil; Elves; *History of Middle-earth*; *Hobbit, The*; Immortality; *Lays of Beleriand*; Maps; Middle-earth; Men, Middle-earth; Morgoth and Melkor; Poems by Tolkien; *Silmarillion, The*; Tolkien, Christopher

SHELOB

There is no way to be certain whether or not Tolkien's infantile encounter with a Bloemfontein tarantula is the source of his fictional spiders. In a 1955 letter to W.H. Auden, Tolkien makes light of the idea and claims not to "dislike spiders particularly" (*Letters*, 217); nonetheless villainous, oversized spiders play repeated roles in his literature, from Ungoliant in *The Silmarillion* to the Dungortheb spiders in "Of Beren and Lúthien," to *The Hobbit*'s Mirkwood spiders, to Shelob the Great in *The Lord of the Rings*. All are violent and vicious; all trap and feed; all live within a deeper than natural darkness.

Shelob, Ungoliant's "last child," closely resembles her mother. Ungoliant is the female counterpart to Melkor, as Shelob is to the Dark Lord; but neither accepts a master. Ungoliant turns on Melkor (Morgoth), whom she initially serves, and Shelob, living in close proximity to Sauron, serves "none but herself" (*TT*, IV, ix, 332). Ungoliant both hungers for light and hates it; Shelob finds light "intolerable." Neither is precisely a spider. Ungoliant chose to take "shape as a spider" (*S*, 73), and Shelob is "most like a spider," an "evil thing in spider-form" (*TT*, IV, ix, 334 and 332).

Females are clearly Tolkien's preference for the species, and Shelob's name, which combines *she* with *lob* (an Old English word for *spider*), emphasizes

her gender. (See *Letters*, 81 and 180.) Tolkien's other spiders are essentially genderless—though early *Hobbit* drafts suggest the Mirkwood spiders (descendants of Shelob) were originally female too, and the existence of males is suggested through passing references to Ungoliant and Shelob breeding with and then devouring their mates. Given this female emphasis, it seems likely that Tolkien saw entrapment and poisoning as forms of female evil. To this he adds an implied and aggressive sexuality. Like Ungoliant, Shelob has her "appetite," "lust," and "desire"; and more than one critic has pointed to the phallic thrust of Sam's sword, pricking "deep, deep" into Shelob's soft "shuddering belly" (*TT*, IV, ix, 338). Other critics place less emphasis on the Freudian. Tolkien was, after all, borrowing from a long tradition of monsters (male or female) who wait beneath water or earth and are vanquished by heroes carrying swords. Still, within this tradition, violent and lustful female monsters are strongly evident: the Morrígan and other cave-dwelling witches or female monsters in early Celtic tales; Grendel's mother in *Beowulf*; the troll-woman, Night, in the *Ala Flekks Saga*; Edmund Spenser's Errour from *The Faerie Queene*, and the figure of Sin in Milton's *Paradise Lost*.

Shelob is also carefully matched against Galadriel. Where Shelob takes life, Galadriel preserves life. Where Shelob (bloating and swelling from her feasts) lives for herself alone, Galadriel serves others and accepts diminishing. Where Shelob is called "Her Ladyship" (ironically), Galadriel is the "Lady." Where Shelob has her entrapping webs, Galadriel is falsely spoken of as weaving "webs of deceit" (*TT*, III, vi, 118). Where Shelob creates darkness, Galadriel's phial brings light into Shelob's tunnels, light that causes Shelob "unbearable" pain. Moreover, the light in Galadriel's phial came first from the Two Trees of Valinor, trees destroyed through Ungoliant's poison and her drinking of their light. The association with Valinor, inherited through her mother; their shared hatred and destruction of light, and Shelob's great age (nearly the same as Galadriel's) justifies Tolkien's claim that Shelob is "a survivor from the *Silmarillion* and the legends of the First Age" (*Letters*, 180).

MARJORIE BURNS

Further Reading

Abbott, Joe. "Tolkien's Monsters: Concept and Function in *The Lord of the Rings*. II. Shelob the Great." *Mythlore* 60 (Winter 1989): 40–47.
Burns, Marjorie. *Perilous Realms: Celtic and Norse in Tolkien's Middle-earth*. Toronto: University of Toronto Press, 2005.
Chance, Jane. *Tolkien's Art: A Mythology for England*. Rev. ed. Lexington, KY: University Press of Kentucky, 2001.

Goselin, Peter Damien. "Two Faces of Eve: Galadriel and Shelob as Anima Figures." *Mythlore* 6, no. 3 (Summer 1979): 3–4.

Partridge, Brenda. "No Sex Please—We're Hobbits: The Construction of Female Sexuality in *The Lord of the Rings*." In *J.R.R. Tolkien: This FAR Land*, edited by Robert Giddings, 179–97. London: Vision Press Ltd., 1983; Totowa, NJ: Barnes & Noble, 1984.

Petty, Anne Cotton. *One Ring to Bind Them All: Tolkien's Mythology*. University of Alabama Press, 1979.

See also **Caves and Mines; Darkness; Galadriel; Nature; Phial; Ungoliant**

SHIRE, THE

Always called *the* Shire, as Gandalf informs Radagast, this small district in Eriador, in west-central Middle-earth, is home to the beings known as hobbits. It is probably the best-defined geopolitical unit in all of Middle-earth, J.R.R. Tolkien having carefully fashioned its history, geography, and culture.

Hobbits inhabited the region later called the Shire from the eleventh or twelfth century of the Third Age onward. Its first formal grant of territory came in 1601 TA from King Argeleb II to Marcho and Blanco Fallohide; he granted them forty leagues in an east-west direction from the Brandywine River to the Far Downs and fifty leagues in a north-south direction, an original total of eighteen thousand square miles. In 2340 TA, hobbits settled in an enclave beyond the Brandywine River, which came to be known as Buckland. Much later, in FA 32, King Elessar granted lands from the Far Downs westward to the Tower Hills, a region designated the Westmarch; at the same time Buckland became officially the Eastmarch. The total area of the Shire is thus about twenty-one thousand square miles.

The Shire calendar, or Shire Reckoning, begins from the original grant and so is always 1,600 years behind the so-called King's reckoning. Even in the new count of the Fourth Age, the Shire kept its own reckoning. The population of the Shire is not recorded; a few hundred thousand would be a cautious estimate. The hobbits speak only Westron, or the Common Speech; before they arrived in the Shire, they tended to use the languages of their Mannish neighbors: the Rohirrim, for instance.

Some of the chief events in Shire history, expressed in Shire-reckoning, include:

SR 37 The Great Plague and following years of dearth
SR 1147 The Battle of the Greenfields, in the Northfarthing
SR 1311 The Fell Winter; White Wolves invade
SR 1419 The Battle of Bywater
SR 1420 The year of plenty and renewal

The first hobbit kindred to appear in Eriador was the Harfoots, followed by the Fallohides, and last by the Stoors. The Harfoots were the most numerous and most "typical" in appearance, being short and brown of skin. The fairer and taller Fallohides were less numerous but included some distinguished families: the Brandybucks and the Tooks, among others. Bilbo and Frodo are of Fallohide kin. The Stoors were stouter than other hobbits; they alone grew beards, and unlike most hobbits liked boating and fishing (Gollum was originally of Stoor stock).

Relatively isolated and content to be so, even though the Great East Road traverses the Shire, the hobbits divided their original grant of land into four districts called farthings, within which are various folklands (Tookland, for instance). Each farthing has its own characteristics:

Northfarthing: a hilly and dry country, perhaps the Shire's least fertile soil, although good barley for beer is grown there. The region is noted for hunting, and for frequent winter snow, although the general climate of the Shire is mild.

Southfarthing: even though the whole Shire is basically agricultural, the most notable products of the soil come from here: the famous red wine of Old Vinyards is a Southfarthing specialty, and fields of pipeweed grow Southfarthing Leaf.

Eastfarthing: probably has the most various land forms and land uses, since it includes wetlands like the Marish and abuts the lands beyond the Brandywine River, right up against the eaves of the Old Forest. Here Farmer Maggot grows his mushrooms, and across the River are Buckland, and Crickhollow, Frodo's home-to-be. Many Stoors live in the Eastfarthing.

Westfarthing: probably the most populous and politically important area, it contains many of the sizable towns and villages, such as Bywater, Hobbiton, and Michel Delving, the latter being the chief township of the whole Shire and the home of the mayor, of the Lockholes, usually storage tunnels but made into prisons by the ruffians during the War of the Ring, and of the museum or Mathom-house.

In these four areas, the topography of the Shire is pleasingly varied but tame: hills, brooks and rivers, woodlands and meadows.

The Shire has little government: there is a thain or honorary lord with mostly ceremonial duties, a mayor who actually administers civic matters, three shirriffs or constables in each farthing, boundary watchers or bounders, and a somewhat casual postal service. One of the real horrors the hobbits found on their return to the Shire after the War was the growth in government: in rules and prohibitions, in officials and enforcers, in taxes and penalties. For daily life, ridding the Shire of such pestilence was one of the happiest result of the Scouring. In later years, Sam Gamgee became mayor, Merry became master of Buckland, and Pippin became thain of the Shire.

No social extremes exist in the Shire. There are richer and poorer, but there are no plutocrats and no needy. There can be gentry and yeomanry, but little above or below these ranges. The economy of the Shire is farm based whether the crop is mushrooms or pipeweed; much of the nonfarm work of the Shire still meets rural needs: smithery, milling, brewing, and so on. Centers of social life (for male hobbits anyway) are inns and taverns like the famous Green Dragon at Bywater.

In some ways, the Shire is based on Tolkien's memory of his youth in the village of Sarehole, and more generally on rural and village life in the English West Midlands around the turn of the twentieth century. It is rich in what Tolkien loved: "gardens, trees, and unmechanized farmland" (*Letters*, 288). With its umbrellas and teatime, the Shire is certainly more English than the rest of Middle-earth. *The Hobbit* shows us the Shire as distinctly anachronistic, as T.A. Shippey has pointed out. Its anomalies are much less evident in *The Lord of the Rings*.

MICHAEL N. STANTON

Further Reading

Anderson, Douglas A. *The Annotated Hobbit*. 2nd ed., rev. Boston, MA: Houghton Mifflin, 2002.

Burger, Douglas A. "The Shire: A Tolkien Version of Pastoral." In *Aspects of Fantasy: Selected Essays from the Second International Conference on the Fantastic in Literature and Film*, edited by William Coyle. Westport, CT: Greenwood, 1986.

Carpenter, Humphrey. *Tolkien: A Biography*. Boston, MA: Houghton Mifflin, 1977.

Curry, Patrick. *Defending Middle-earth: Tolkien: Myth and Modernity*. Rev. ed. Boston, MA: Houghton Mifflin, 2004.

Fonstad, Karen Wynn. *An Atlas of Middle-earth*. Rev. ed. Boston, MA: Houghton Mifflin, 1998.

Hawkins, Emma. "Chalk Figures and Scouring in Tolkienland." *Extrapolation* 41 (2000): 385–96.

Shippey, T.A. *J.R.R. Tolkien: Author of the Century*. Boston, MA: Houghton Mifflin, 2000.

Stoddard, William H. "Law and Institutions in the Shire." *Mythlore* 70, 18, no. 4 (1992), 4–8.

Strachey, Barbara. *Journeys of Frodo*. London: HarperCollins, 1998.

See also **Bilbo; Calendars; Childhood of Tolkien; Class in Tolkien's Works; Frodo; Hobbiton; Hobbits; Languages**

SILMARILLION, THE

The term "Silmarillion" is used to refer to two distinct textual complexes in Tolkien. As *The Silmarillion*, it refers to the volume edited and published by Christopher Tolkien in 1977 (with the assistance of Guy Kay), as the first of the posthumous publications after his father's death. As the "Silmarillion (tradition)," the term refers to the whole of the corpus of variant texts, treating the matter of the Elder Days that Tolkien produced from the late 1910s to the end of his life in 1973. Even though the former was editorially put together using texts from the latter, the two are entirely different texts (textual complexes), and need to be considered separately.

History (Writing and Publication)

Tolkien started to write stories about an imagined past involving the Elves or fairies in what he called the *Book of Lost Tales* in the late 1910s. In this, he elaborated on the conceptions and mythological elements that emerged unexpectedly in his earlier poetry; the result was a more or less coherent storyline that became the foundation of the later "Silmarillion." Even though he eventually abandoned the *Lost Tales*, the stories remained in their essential form when in the 1920s he began casting two of the most important of them into long narrative poems (the alliterative "Children of Húrin" and the "Lay of Leithian"); it was to contextualize these for his old schoolmaster R.W. Reynolds that he wrote the first account of the full span of the mythology ("Sketch of the Mythology," 1925). Over the next fifteen years, Tolkien produced many versions of the mythological cycle in many different forms and conceptions, and it was in the course of this work that the "Silmarillion" as a collection of the mythological stories emerged. In 1930, Tolkien enlarged the "Sketch" into the "Qenta Noldorinwa," and also in the 1930s he started two annalistic accounts of the history, the (earlier) "Annals of Valinor" and the (earlier) "Annals of Beleriand." In the late 1930s, the compendious summary of the whole story was again revised (perhaps through a lost intermediary text) as the "Quenta Silmarillion" (perhaps 1937, interrupted before the end, but concluded by a similar account of the end of days that was present in the previous version), and both sets of Annals were also rewritten. The Lost Tale about the creation of the world was another text that was rehandled at this time, becoming the "Ainulindalë," strictly speaking independent of the "Silmarillion" proper (as the Quenta tradition). The story of the Second Age and the fall of Númenor was also first written in the second half of the 1930s, and attached to the main mythology.

The writing of *The Lord of the Rings* affected the "Silmarillion" complex in many ways: the latter book's connections with the earlier legendarium were of course not negligible, but the effect *The Lord of the Rings* had on the "Silmarillion" is perhaps more important, since the themes and motifs that emerged in the "new Hobbit" made necessary the revision of earlier stories (such as the character of Galadriel, or the One Ring itself). In the long period of writing, Tolkien occasionally took time to work on some of the "Silmarillion" texts; versions of the "Fall of Númenor" (together with its proposed presentation frame, the *Notion Club Papers*) were written at this time, and though the history of "On the Rings of Power" is little known, it seems to have been in existence by 1948 (which is not surprising, since Tolkien needed to work out the conception of the rings of power).

After the completion of *The Lord of the Rings*, Tolkien for a period wanted to publish it together with the "Silmarillion," and since after the success of *The Hobbit* the manuscripts belonging to the "Silmarillion" complex that he sent as possible sequels were rejected (although without in-depth reading or consideration) by Allan & Unwin (see Unwin, "Early"), having made contact with Milton Waldman of Collins, for a time Tolkien considered Collins a more promising prospective publisher. In about 1951, Tolkien wrote Waldman a long letter detailing the story and importance of the "Silmarillion." It was in this letter that he made the famous statement that he had intended to create a "body of connected legend" to "dedicate" to England. Tolkien's intention to bring the "Silmarillion" into publishable form can be seen in his efforts on the texts in this period: he returned to the "Quenta Silmarillion" in 1951–52, having already produced a new version of the "Ainulindalë" in the late 1940s, and evolving the first section of the "Quenta" into the independent "Valaquenta" sometime in the early 1950s. However, when Collins too turned down the publication of the two long books together, Tolkien finally reestablished contact with Allan & Unwin, and published *The Lord of the Rings* with them in 1954–55.

In the late 1950s, after the unexpected success of *The Lord of the Rings*, Tolkien enthusiastically turned again to the mythology intending to finish and publish it (partly to his own satisfaction, and partly to provide information for readers similarly minded, who wrote him long letters inquiring about details of history, mythology, and language), but realized that the legends have to be made consistent with *The Lord of the Rings*. He apparently intended to make a final version of the "Silmarillion," but what he actually wrote was another version of the "Quenta Silmarillion" (in about 1958), a new version of both sets of Annals ("Annals of Aman" and the "Grey Annals,"

both late 1950s), and a version of the "Fall of Númenor" (by 1958) that finally became the "Akallabêth." American scholar Clyde S. Kilby visited Tolkien in this period to help with the work of arrangement and organization, but Tolkien ultimately failed to concentrate effort and finish the comprehensive treatment of his mythology. This was doubtless partly due to his doubts as to the setting and the presentation frame of the stories: the later revisions of the "Silmarillion" narratives show him meditating on the very foundations of the cosmology, of which the "flat world" (earlier conception) vs. "round world" (later conception) problem is a representative example. Tolkien in fact was considering the recasting of the entire mythology and gave much thought to its integration into what finally became its presentation frame: the fiction of Bilbo's "translations from the Elvish" in Rivendell. In the last period of his life, he wrote shorter essays on problems he should have solved to continue work and never managed to establish any finished variant or even an authorized "canon" of what exactly belongs to the "Silmarillion."

At Tolkien's death in 1973, the mythology was therefore left unfinished, consisting of a great number of manuscript or typescript versions of the individual stories, the relationship of which it was nearly impossible to disentangle, and no clear indication as to the final version of stories, the "canon" of the "Silmarillion," or the presentation frame. As the literary executor of Tolkien's will, Christopher Tolkien then undertook to go through the manuscripts and (with the assistance of writer Guy Kay) produce a continuous narrative from them for publication. *The Silmarillion* (published in 1977) thus became, as its preface claimed, a compendious work not only in fiction but also in fact. The editorial work on this volume resulted in the *Silmarillion* canon: the "Ainulindalë," the "Valaquenta," the "Quenta Silmarillion," the "Akallabêth," and "Of the Rings of Power and the Third Age" are its textual units. In the preface, Christopher Tolkien described his work as "selecting and arranging," but as not all the relevant manuscripts were available or known to him at the time, the 1977 text might not in all details represent Tolkien's "last intentions."

At the time of the publication of *The Silmarillion*, Christopher Tolkien only spoke of setting out the development of this "continuing and evolving creation" in the preface; from 1984 to 1996, in twelve volumes, he undertook to present in a more scholarly and detailed fashion the creative work of more than half a century that Tolkien put into his mythology. With the exception of volumes 6, 7, and 8, and the first half of volume 9, which deal with the history of *The Lord of the Rings*, the series presents texts and their versions that Tolkien wrote for the "Silmarillion" stories from the late 1910s to his death. Although this is naturally still not a full edition of all the versions, the texts available in the *History* volumes make an enormous contribution toward the study of how Tolkien created and envisaged this extraordinarily complex structure of stories and fictionalized texts, and make an evaluation of the "Silmarillion" tradition possible.

On the tangled provenance of the "Silmarillion," more detailed accounts are available in Noad, Shippey (223–27), and in the volumes of *The History of Middle-earth.*

Summary and Themes

The narrative of the published *Silmarillion* had been largely fixed from its first emergence in *The Book of Lost Tales*; it tells the story of Tolkien's invented universe from its creation by the One divine being (Eru or Ilúvatar) with the assistance of his first spiritual creatures through three ages of more and more "earthbound" history, ending with the end of the Third Age as seen in *The Lord of the Rings*. The First Age shows the conflicts in the created world between the Valar (those spirits who descend into the created world to govern it) and their antagonist, a fallen Vala (Melkor, later called Morgoth), and the consequent playing out of conflicts in a world that now includes Eru's other creatures, Elves and humans, along with other beings like Dwarves and (in the end) hobbits. This age centers on Morgoth's theft of the Silmarils, artificial gems made by the Noldorin prince Fëanor, incorporating the light of the Two Trees of Valinor (destroyed by Morgoth), and the Elves' age-long struggle to recapture them. When the war to this ends in catastrophe, at the appeal of Eärendil (a joint representative of Elves and humans) the Valar take action, and finally defeat Morgoth. The Silmarils, however, are finally lost, and only one remains as a star on the firmament. The Second Age is human dominated, and its focus it the kingdom on Númenor, which the humans, faithful to the Elves and Valar, had received as reward. The narrative of Númenor deals with the eventual corruption of this realm by the incomprehension of death as the "gift of Eru" and by Sauron, Morgoth's escaped servant. The disobedience of the Númenoreans finally leads to the destruction of the island kingdom, which leaves only a handful of faithful humans to organize the assault on Sauron in Middle-earth, together with the remnant of the Elves. The Second Age ends with the defeat of Sauron by the Last Alliance, when the One Ring is taken from him. This Ring structures the history of the Third Age as the kingdoms in Middle-earth

strive with various servants of the again returning Sauron, finally to destroy the Ring and open the way to the Age of Men.

Even the main themes of *The Silmarillion* are several, and their complexity, especially if considered in the context of the underlying manuscript corpus, is considerable. The motif of light (as a metaphor for Eru's creative power) runs through the whole work, in close connection to the themes of (artistic) creation, shaping, and corruption. Tied to these is the origin of evil, located in pride and possessiveness (illustrated both on a theological and "earthly" plane as well, with the examples of Melkor and Fëanor). The relations between different cultures are also a prominent theme, foregrounding the several contexts in which stories are told, preserved, and used, relying on different concepts of heroism or service. The idea of history, or myth, shifting into history is also figured.

The Silmarillion is primarily a context for *The Lord of the Rings*, explaining a number of allusions and references in the latter work. It epitomizes the unheard and often unknown "past" that lies behind the narrative of *The Lord of the Rings* and casts light on the characters in the privileged position of possessing knowledge about it. Indeed, *The Silmarillion* enhances the other work's concern with the uses of the past, and provides us with useful clues as to the representation of culture as *The Lord of the Rings* conceives of it. If we know the stories referred to by Elrond, Gandalf, Galadriel, or Frodo, we see more clearly how those stories, although not themselves necessarily fully told in *The Lord of the Rings*, nevertheless work to determine it, and determine how the characters (especially Frodo and Bilbo) are shown to conceive of their world and their story; eventually, to write that story in terms of the older stories.

The number of names even in the published *Silmarillion* is very great. The "Silmarillion" tradition complicates this even more, since in the several layers of revision names and the person, group, geographical unit names refer to are frequently changed and can be clarified only by reference to Christopher Tolkien's erudite commentaries.

Reception and Criticism

The published *Silmarillion* was intensely awaited but naturally met with a much colder and in some cases explicitly disappointed reception. Tolkien fans naturally relished the information that it offered, but even they were sometimes baffled by the *Silmarillion*'s totally different attitude to character, story, and narrative. Tolkien was expecting this when he wrote about the "elvishness" and "heigh stile" of the prospected publication, and remarked that there were "no hobbits" to serve as mediators (*Letters*). Shippey attributes this to the fact that *The Silmarillion* relates to novelistic convention (the most easily accessible and most clearly operational reading strategy readers know) in a different way than *The Lord of the Rings* does and is in fact much closer to the conceptions of literature and literary representation that Tolkien's medieval sources manifest. *The Silmarillion* indeed negotiates between the modern and postmodern novel, and the genres of literary history that inspired Tolkien, and comes up in result with an extremely refined texture of literary and cultural history, coupled with surprisingly modern (as opposed to the usually supposed "obsolete" character of Tolkien's work) attitude to theoretical questions prominent at the end of the twentieth century.

Few critical works have dealt exclusively with *The Silmarillion*. The medieval models and parallels have been efficiently mapped (source study/comparative approach), and thus the work was situated in one of its many contexts. The sense in which Tolkien meant to dedicate the work "to England" has been the theme of a number of treatments, and consequently (also connected to the sources) the conception of mythology and myth that Tolkien's whole work comments on is also an issue of ongoing critical examination. The role of light and language in *The Silmarillion*, as Verlyn Flieger argued, owes something to Owen Barfield's theory about language and mythology. Especially if considered in the context of the manuscript corpus in its background, *The Silmarillion* can be seen as Tolkien's ultimate emphasis on the importance of texts, textual variants, and textual activities in the course of processes of cultural history that result in the complexes of mythologies and mythological texts. The creation of networks of stories and texts which tell the stories (translated, adapted, reduced, selected, versified, or summarized in prose) point out positions of reception and production, putting heavy stress on authors and readers; the final presentation frame of *The Silmarillion* (as Bilbo's selection and translation) opens up these positions and activities through the figure of Bilbo, and with the fiction of the text creates further author figures, sources, authorities, and traditions behind the text, thereby authentically capturing its compendious nature. While interpretation is of course a crucially important concept in this textual network, its role is not negligible in the story itself either. Light metaphors and the theology of creation enable a theorized reading where the main motif is meaning and its control; Eru, as in an authentic medieval world picture, functions as the totality of meaning and control over it who, in the levels of creation,

guarantees meaning and knowledge. Acts of good or evil are thus seen as interpretation or the forceful manufacturing of independent meanings (impossible since Eru's totality cannot be challenged). The creatures of the world, in all their (textual) actions of shaping, representation and preservation really interpret Eru's intentions, and make the story of Middle-earth into a model of how cultures deal with traditionally meaningful stories. The discourses that cultures use for this are also under scrutiny in *The Silmarillion*: theology, history, poetic or prose storytelling, and their selection, translation, and so on, are seen as so many different strategies to relate to stories, finally yielding a complex where Tolkien really investigates (models of) cultural representation and the uses of stories. Culture is the real central concept of *The Silmarillion*, circumscribed by such other terms as interpretation, textuality, and representation.

The 1977 *Silmarillion* is, in conclusion, a perfect device to highlight Tolkien's main themes: it is an editorial text in fiction as well as in fact, providing a context and a background for *The Lord of the Rings* in several ways, while also representing and foregrounding concerns that the manuscript "Silmarillion tradition" shows to be central: variance, the always unfixed and unfinished nature of meaning, interpretation, and text. By its nature, it ties the "Silmarillion" to the unfixedness of medieval manuscript culture and is able to suggest textual and even nontextual layers of tradition (like an underlying orality or lost poetic traditions) in the course of modeling cultural processes. The edited *Silmarillion* can therefore be seen as in an important sense the most significant of Tolkien's works, since it brings together the concepts, problems, and models Tolkien's whole work is apparently centered on.

GERGELY NAGY

Further Reading

Flieger, Verlyn. *Interrupted Music: The Making of Tolkien's Mythology*. Kent, OH, and London: Kent State University Press, 2005.

———. *Splintered Light: Logos and Language in Tolkien's World*. Rev. ed., Kent, OH, and London: Kent State University Press, 2002.

Kilby, Clyde S. *Tolkien and "The Silmarillion."* Berkhamstead: Lion, 1976.

Nagy, Gergely. "The Adapted Text: The Lost Poetry of Beleriand." *Tolkien Studies* 1 (2004): 21–41.

———. "The Great Chain of Reading: (Inter-)Textual Relations and the Technique of Mythopoesis in the Túrin story." In *Tolkien the Medievalist*, edited by Jane Chance, 239–58. New York and London: Routledge, 2002.

Noad, Charles. "On the Construction of 'The Silmarillion'." In *Tolkien's Legenadrium. Essays on "The History* of Middle-earth," edited by Verlyn Flieger and Carl F. Hostetter, 31–68. Westport, CT, London: Greenwood Press, 2000.

Shippey, Tom. *The Road to Middle-earth*. 3rd ed. Boston, MA: Houghton Mifflin, 2004.

Unwin, Rayner. "Early Days of Elder Days." In *Tolkien's Legenadrium. Essays on "The History of Middle-earth"* edited by Verlyn Flieger and Carl F. Hostetter, 3–6. Westport, Connecticut, London: Greenwood Press, 2000.

See also **Alliterative verse by Tolkien; Barfield,** *Owen***; Book of Lost Tales; Dwarves; Elves; Eru; Frame Narratives; Good and Evil; Heroes and Heroism; Light; Middle-earth: Men; Morgoth and Melkor; Mythology for England; Poems by Tolkien; Possessiveness; Pride; R.W. Reynolds; Rhyming Poetry; Sauron; Silmarils; The One Ring; Tolkien, Christopher; Two Trees; Valar**

SILMARILS

Anyone intent upon developing a fuller understanding of Tolkien's rich mythological framework must sooner or later confront the Silmarils. Among the most important artifacts of Tolkien's subcreation, the Silmarils of Fëanor significantly undergird the majority of the early legends and even find later echoes in the events of the War of the Ring. It is perhaps surprising, then, to realize that the Silmarils played only a very small and rather unexceptional role in the earliest drafts of Tolkien's mythology. It was only after much reworking of these early stories that, as Christina Scull explains, "Tolkien gradually made the Silmarils more powerful, more significant, more fateful, even holy, and eventually he referred to the whole *legendarium* as 'The Silmarillion'."

By the time of the published *Silmarillion*, the role of the Silmarils themselves as one of the chief underpinnings of the entire mythology had settled into its more or less final form. Fëanor created the three Silmarils and poured into them the light of the Two Trees of Valinor. As is said in the *Quenta Silmarillion*, "it may be that some shadow of foreknowledge came to him of the doom that drew near; and he pondered how the light of the Trees, the glory of the Blessed Realm, might be preserved imperishable" (*S*, 67). Fëanor first devised a new crystalline substance to house the Trees' radiance. He called this substance *silima*, a name that seems to mean "silver, shining white." Of the etymology of the Silmarils themselves, the appendix to *The Silmarillion* explains: "The Quenya word *Silmarilli* is said to derive from the name *silima* that Fëanor gave to the substance from which they were made" (*S*, 364). Delving a little deeper, one discovers the two fundamental elements of the word in Tolkien's "Etymologies": the root *Sil-*, meaning "shine silver,"

from which the words *silima* and Silpion (a name for Telperion, the elder of the Two Trees) derive; and the root *ril-*, "glitter," as seen in Idril and *mithril*. Putting the two together, one arrives at something like Tolkien's own loose translation of the word "Silmaril," as given in a letter to Milton Waldman: "radiance of pure light" (*Letters*, 148).

Within the context of the legends of the Elder Days, the Silmarils take center stage after Ungoliant, goaded and aided by Melkor, destroys the Two Trees. Their light lives on in Fëanor's jewels; however, the over-possessive Fëanor will not suffer the Silmarils to be broken open, even though the Two Trees could be saved thereby. His stubbornness, in the end, is moot—Melkor has already taken the Silmarils by force—but it puts Fëanor and his sons in the wrong for the rest of their days. The Valar cannot mollify Fëanor, and he swears with his seven sons a blasphemous oath to recover the Silmarils at any cost. Then he departs Aman in exile, leading the greater part of the Noldor with him to Middle-earth.

Fëanor meets his death soon after reaching its shores, but his sons continue in the relentless pursuit of their oath, ensnaring Elves and Men within its hopeless net. After much war and ruin, it is finally Beren and Lúthien—no Noldo or heir of Fëanor—who reclaim a Silmaril from Morgoth's iron crown. This, they deliver to Thingol as the bride-price for his daughter's hand, and Fëanor's Oath swiftly bears wicked fruit in that hidden realm also.

But the Silmaril was saved from the sack of Menegroth and passed down finally into the hands of Eärendil, who, perhaps guided by the Silmaril, and heralded by it certainly, ventures to sail into the Uttermost West. There he entreats the Valar on behalf of Men and Elves for succor in ridding Middle-earth of Morgoth's evil. The Valar will not permit Eärendil to return to Middle-earth; however, they place his ship in the heavens, with Eärendil at its helm and "the Silmaril . . . bound upon his brow" (*S*, 250). Thus the light of the Silmaril might be seen in Middle-earth, outshining the stars of Varda, forever after. And therein sounds an echo of the Silmaril eons later during the War of the Ring, for Galadriel captures its light, mingled with water from her Mirror, in the phial she gives to Frodo. And with this light, Frodo and Samwise defy Shelob, last descendent of Ungoliant—who herself thirsted insatiably for the light of the Silmarils.

Following the War of Wrath, the two remaining Silmarils are recovered from Morgoth's crown. Then, driven by their oath, Fëanor's last two living sons, Maedhros and Maglor, disgracefully seize the two jewels. But Varda had long ago hallowed the jewels, "so that thereafter no mortal flesh, nor hands unclean, nor anything of evil will might touch them, but it was scorched and withered" (*S*, 67) and therefore, neither Maedhros nor Maglor can bear to hold them, so evil had their oath made them. Maedhros "cast himself into a gaping chasm filled with fire," taking one Silmaril with him. The other, Maglor threw into the deep ocean. And so, as Mandos had foretold—that "the fates of Arda, earth, sea, and air, lay locked within them"—the three Silmarils took each its final place: in earth, sea, and air (*S*, 254).

The origins of the Silmarils in Tolkien's thought aren't quite so clear. But there is evidence to believe he may have modeled them, to some degree, on the mysterious *Sampo* of the Finnish national epic, *The Kalevala*, which Carpenter believes he first read around 1911. *The Kalevala* offered much early inspiration to Tolkien, yielding the underlying framework for the story of Túrin Turambar. But the *Sampo* may well be Tolkien's most remarkable borrowing. In *The Kalevala*, the *Sampo* is a strange and vaguely mythological object of power, over which the poles of good and evil struggle for control. But the inherent ambiguities of the *Sampo* permitted Tolkien to adapt it in whatever ways he wished—indeed, his choices may reveal something of his own personal ideas about the nature of the *Sampo*.

JASON FISHER

Further Reading

Carpenter, Humphrey. *J.R.R. Tolkien: A Biography*. London: Allen & Unwin, 1977.

Flieger, Verlyn. *Splintered Light: Logos and Language in Tolkien's World*. 2nd ed., revised and expanded. Kent, OH: Kent State University Press, 2002.

Helms, Randel. *Tolkien and the Silmarils*. Boston, MA: Houghton Mifflin, 1981.

Himes, Jonathan B. "What Tolkien Readlly Did with the Sampo." *Mythlore* 22, no. 4 (2000): 69–85.

Noad, Charles. "On the Constructions of 'The Silmarillion.'" In *Tolkien's Legendarium*. edited by Verlyn Flieger and Carl F. Hostetter, 31–68. Westport, CT: Greenwood, 2000.

Petty, Anne C. "Identifying England's Lönrott." *Tolkien Studies* 1 (2004): 69–84.

Scull, Christina. "The Development of Tolkien's *Legendarium*: Some Threads in the Tapestry of Middle-earth." In *Tolkien's Legendarium*, edited by Verlyn Flieger and Carl F. Hostetter, 7–18. Westport, CT: Greenwood, 2000.

Shippey, Tom. *J.R.R. Tolkien: Author of the Century*. Boston, MA: Houghton Mifflin, 2001.

———. *The Road to Middle-earth*. 2nd ed. London: Grafton, 1992.

Tolkien, J.R.R., and Donald Swann. *The Road Goes Ever On: A Song Cycle*. Boston, MA: Houghton Mifflin, 1967.

See also **Beren; *Christ*: "Advent Lyrics"; Cynewulf; Eärendil; Elements; Fëanor; Finland: Literary Sources; Galadriel; Jewels; Light; Lúthien; Morgoth and Melkor; Phial; Possessiveness; Shelob; Thingol; Two Trees**

SIN

Sin, in Christian theology, is defined as the purposeful disobedience of a creature to the known will of God—although more recently there has come into being the confusing designation "material sin" (not formal or mortal), which is a sin through mistaking the will of God. In the Apostolic Age, sin was considered as having roots in a man's character (Matthew), as a breach of the natural law written in man's conscience (Paul), and as a personal condition and responsibility residing in the human will (James). The condition of sin (or precondition for sin—either of these being designated by the term Original Sin) derives from the Fall. Alone of the Church Fathers, Origen suggested a premundane Fall or falls of created spirits who voluntarily separated themselves from the goodness in which they were created.

Probably the textus receptus for Tolkien on the Fall (of men and the celestial orders)—and thus of sin—is in "Myths Transformed" in part 5 of *Morgoth's Ring* (378–79). The influence of the Epistle of St. James is recognizable, and the lights of Melkor emphatically not without variableness and shadow of turning. The entire concept is in accordance with Origen, and (by a kind of Tolkienian pun) might be considered Original sin if not Original Sin. "Brother to him [Manwë the Blessed] was Melkor, the Potent, and he had, as has been told, fallen into pride and desire of his own dominion.... Measureless as were the regions of Eä, yet in the Beginning, where he could have been Master of all that was done—for there were many of the Ainur of the Song willing to follow him and serve him, if he called—still he was not content.... As a shadow Melkor did not then conceive himself. For in his beginning he loved and desired light, and the form that he took was exceedingly bright; and he said in his heart, 'On such brightness as I am the Children shall hardly endure to look'. . . . But the lesser brightness that stands before the greater becomes a darkness. And Melkor was jealous, therefore, of all other brightnesses, and wished to take all light unto himself" (*Morgoth*, 378–79).

The New Testament text here is this: "Do not err, my beloved brethren. Every good gift and every perfect gift is from above, and cometh down from the father of lights, in whom is no variableness neither shadow of turning. . . . For whosoever shall keep the law, and yet offend in one point, he is guilty of all" (James 1:16–17, 2:10). Now, sin is not the same thing as evil, not even as moral evil. It is fundamentally a theological concept. Post-Nicene theology has added little to the New Testament and Ante-Nicene discussion of sin (which includes the Seven Deadly Sins—Pride, Anger, Gluttony, Greed, Lust, Envy, and Sloth—given in that order to form the mnemonic "Paggles"). In present-day churches (as indeed in the second century CE) there is some variance (and even argument) over whether the important question is the forgiveness or remission of sin or of sins—the condition or the actions. St. Augustine (of Hippo 354–430) argued essentially for the Platonic view that sin is not a substance but a negative—privatio boni. The strength of Tolkien's description of sin (with Melkor = Morgoth) is that it gives substance to the negative, making it more understandable.

Arguably, Middle-earth at the end of the Third Age is neither fallen nor unfallen. Wrong use of power has necessarily affected the generations that came after, and there has come to be a vast accumulated power of sin in the world—but the presence of the Elves and the Men of the West has made things easier even in the Third Age. There is no Christ figure in *The Lord of the Rings*, but there is something of Christ in many of the figures. It has been argued (*Lobdell*, 66–67) that if Middle-earth is a prelapsarian world, "we should expect to find all seven virtues and only one of the sins would be deadly: the sin against the Holy Spirit." That is precisely what we find. "The intersection of the timeless moment with time in The Lord of the Rings is at the temptation of the Adam" (67). We have, indeed, Original (would it be Origenist?) sin (the sin of spirits as defined by Origen), but not Original Sin.

The Medieval view of sin as extrinsic (made up of sins committed) and of a kind of quantitative penance (or indulgences) is miles from Tolkien's view (and from that of the New Testament). Though Tolkien was Roman Catholic and a medievalist, his religious instruction was largely through the Oratorian Fathers (of St. Philip Neri, known for his humor and simple piety) and the founder of the Oratory in England was John Henry Newman, an expert on and profoundly influenced by the Ante-Nicene Fathers.

JARED LOBDELL

Further Reading

Cross, F.L., ed. *The Oxford Dictionary of the Christian Church*. 1961; 2nd ed. London: Oxford University Press 1974.
Lobdell, Jared. *The World of the Rings: Language, Religion, and Adventure in Tolkien*. Chicago and LaSalle, IL: Open Court, 2004.
Webster Rogers, Deborah. "Everyclod and Everyhero." In *A Tolkien Compass*. 1975, 1980, 2003.

See also **Good and Evil; Morgoth and Melkor; *Morgoth's Ring*; Theology in *The Lord of the Rings***

SIR GAWAIN AND THE GREEN KNIGHT, PEARL, SIR ORFEO, EDITED BY CHRISTOPHER TOLKIEN

After Tolkien's death his translations of three Middle English poems were edited by his son Christopher and published with a preface, introduction, glossary, appendix on the verse forms, and a translation of stanzas from another poem, to which Tolkien had given the title "Gawain's Leave-taking."

Tolkien first encountered the fourteenth-century poems *Pearl* and *Sir Gawain and the Green Knight* at school. *Pearl* describes a dream vision in which the narrator is consoled for the death of his young daughter by meeting her in heaven and being persuaded by her that she has been saved. Tolkien's translation was begun while he was working at Leeds in the 1920s, and stanzas from it were broadcast on August 7, 1936. The translation was set in type by Blackwells in 1940, but Tolkien failed to provide the introduction and notes, and publication was abandoned. *Sir Gawain* tells of the knight's testing by a mysterious Green Knight who survives decapitation. Tolkien and E.V. Gordon, his colleague at Leeds University, published an edition of *Sir Gawain* in 1925. A version of Tolkien's translation of the poem was complete by the early 1950s and was broadcast on the BBC Third Programme in December 1953, with a repeat in September 1954. Tolkien studied *Sir Orfeo* as an undergraduate. The poem is a romance from the late thirteenth or early fourteenth century that recounts a version of the myth of Orpheus in which Orfeo secures the release of his wife from the realm of faerie. Tolkien's translation of *Sir Orfeo* was probably made during the Second World War for a Cadets Training Course for which he also produced an edition of the Middle English text (published in Hostetter, 2004).

Publication of Tolkien's translations was much delayed both by his perfectionism, and by the difficulty of determining the scope of the introduction and notes: Tolkien hoped to reach, and satisfy, both general readers without access to the original Middle English texts and also students of the poems for whom his translations could function as a "commentary" on the originals. Many of his letters from 1944 onward contain references to Tolkien's attempts to ready the translations of *Pearl* and *Sir Gawain* for the press. In a letter written in 1965 to his grandson Michael, Tolkien claims that despite the difficulties of translating such demanding verse "anyone who reads my version, however learned a Middle English scholar, will get a more direct impression of the poem's impact (on one who knew the language)" (*Letters*, 352). In another letter Tolkien writes of his problems compressing and selecting notes and draws attention to the fact that he has had to do much "hidden" editorial and lexicographical work that is not immediately apparent to the reader of the translations (*Letters*, 364).

Christopher Tolkien assembled the introduction to the posthumous book from several sources: his father's notes, a radio talk on *Sir Gawain* given after the broadcast of his translation, and a passage on *Pearl* that Tolkien had contributed to the edition of that poem by his friend and collaborator E.V. Gordon. Christopher Tolkien supplied a brief note on *Sir Orfeo* himself and also compiled the glossary of archaic and technical vocabulary used in the translations. The appendix on verse forms was assembled from his father's unpublished notes. Verses printed at the end of the book as "Sir Gawain's Leave-taking" are the first three and the final stanzas of a fourteenth-century lyric that originally had nothing to do with Sir Gawain, but which was connected by Tolkien to the passage in *Sir Gawain* where the knight leaves Bertilak's castle for his meeting with the Green Knight at the Green Chapel.

The book's introduction begins with a discussion of what can be deduced about the anonymous poet believed by most scholars, including Tolkien, to have written *Sir Gawain*, *Pearl* and two other poems preserved in the same manuscript. Tolkien notes that the language, meter and scenery of his poetry indicate that "his home was in the West Midlands of England," an area with which Tolkien himself identified (later research has located the poem's dialect more precisely to an area on the boundary between Cheshire and Staffordshire). The language and alliterative meter employed by the poet are contrasted with the work of his contemporary, Chaucer.

The introduction to *Sir Gawain* focuses particularly on the poem's structure, its "moral" and its symbolism. The introduction to *Pearl* begins by considering whether the poem is, as it appears to be, a lament for the death of an infant girl or should rather be interpreted allegorically. Tolkien argues that the pearl is a symbol, but the poem as a whole is not allegory. In considering whether the narrative situation of a father mourning the death of his young daughter is fictionalized or autobiographical Tolkien argues that the "fictionalised I" had probably not yet appeared in literature in the fourteenth century. He then goes on to describe briefly the conventions of the dream vision genre to which *Pearl* belongs.

Tolkien's translations imitate closely the meters of the original poems, as described in the book's appendix on verse forms. In *Sir Gawain* the stanza consists of a variable number of unrhymed alliterative lines following by a short line known as a "bob" and then a four-line "wheel" rhyming *abab*, with the *b* lines rhyming with the end of the bob. The *Pearl* stanza consists of twelve lines rhyming *ababababbcbc*; there is also extensive alliteration that here performs a decorative rather than structural function. *Sir Orfeo* is composed in rhyming octosyllabic couplets.

The poet of *Pearl* and *Sir Gawain*, like other writers of alliterative verse, employs a specifically poetic vocabulary that includes words that were already archaic in the fourteenth century. Tolkien likewise employs archaic diction such as "carl" (man), "gramercy" (thank you), "liever" (rather): such words, and technical vocabulary referring to aspects of medieval life, are explained in Christopher Tolkien's glossary.

CARL PHELPSTEAD

Further Reading

Bliss, A.J., ed. *Sir Orfeo*. London: Oxford University Press, 1954.

Carpenter, Humphrey. *J.R.R. Tolkien: A Biography*. London: Allen & Unwin, 1977.

Gordon, E.V., ed. *Pearl*. Oxford: Clarendon Press, 1953.

Hostetter, Carl F. "*Sir Orfeo*: A Middle English Version by J.R.R. Tolkien." *Tolkien Studies* 1 (2004): 85–123.

Ryan, J.S. "The Wild Hunt, *Sir Orfeo* and J.R.R. Tolkien." *Mallorn: Journal of the Tolkien Society* 24 (1987): 16–17.

Shippey, Tom. "Tolkien and the *Gawain*-poet." In *Proceedings of the J.R.R. Tolkien Centenary Conference 1992*, edited by Patricia Reynolds and Glen GoodKnight, 213–19. Milton Keynes and Altadena: Tolkien Society and The Mythopoeic Press, 1995.

Tolkien, J.R.R. *Sir Gawain and the Green Knight, Pearl, Sir Orfeo*. Edited by Christopher Tolkien. London: Allen & Unwin, 1975. Paperback ed., London: HarperCollins, 1995.

Tolkien, J.R.R., and E.V. Gordon, eds. *Sir Gawain and the Green Knight*. Oxford: Clarendon Press, 1925.

See also **Alliterative Verse by Tolkien; Arthurian Literature;** *Orfeo, Sir*; *Pearl* **Poet;** *Sir Gawain and the Green Knight*: **Edition with E.V. Gordon;** *Pearl*: **Edition by E.V. Gordon**

SIR GAWAIN AND THE GREEN KNIGHT: EDITION WITH E.V. GORDON

J.R.R. Tolkien first read *Sir Gawain and the Green Knight* at King Edward's School in Birmingham; the text was one of his favorites and the source of some of his recitations to the Tea Club and Barrovian Society (T.C.B.S). Most significantly, *Sir Gawain* bookended Tolkien's scholarly career and, along with his writings and lectures on *Beowulf*, makes up the core of a comparatively small, but distinguished, body of scholarship. His 1925 edition with E.V. Gordon was a signal professional achievement. Tolkien's election to the Rawlinson and Bosworth Professorship of Anglo-Saxon at Oxford followed publication of *Sir Gawain* almost immediately. Later revised by Norman Davis, one of Tolkien's students, the edition became definitive and, in the graduate curriculum, remained the preferred text until very recently. In 1953, one of Tolkien's personal translations of *Sir Gawain* was produced and broadcast by the BBC. During his lifetime, no such translation was ever printed. As his published letters show, Tolkien was vexed toward the end of his life by distractions that kept him from finalizing the translation of what Shippey has called the author's first "academic hit." Along with translations of *Pearl* and *Sir Orfeo*, the translation of *Sir Gawain* was finally published posthumously by Christopher Tolkien. As an anthology, these three translations are used together in some undergraduate courses.

The Tolkien-Gordon edition of *Sir Gawain* is characterized by conservative editing, a feature that, at the time, set it apart from contemporary editions of Middle English texts. As the preface indicates: "The first endeavour of this edition has been to provide the student with a text which, treating the unique manuscript with all due respect, is yet pleasant for the modern reader to look at, and is free (as are few Middle English texts) from a litter of italics, asterisks, and brackets, the trail of the passing editor" (v). Leaving the text more or less untouched, the editors nonetheless contributed an introduction (treating the manuscript, the story, the history of the legend, the treatment of the source, the author and his work, the date, and the dialect); a select bibliography; notes; discussions of meter (focusing on the long alliterative lines, rhymed lines, and alliteration), and language (with sections on spelling, phonology, the Scandinavian element, the French element, and grammar); a glossary; and an index of names. Responsibility for the text and glossary was primarily Tolkien's; Gordon did most of the work on the notes. In its current form, the Tolkien-Gordon-Davis edition provides an "excellent conservative text and glossary" (Miller and Chance, 3) and a critical apparatus (e.g., the appendix on phonology, morphology, lexicon, and meter) that is "essential in coping with the difficult dialect of the *Gawain* poet" (Miller and Chance, 3).

Tolkien's coeditor, E.V. Gordon, was a friend and colleague at Leeds University, where Tolkien served on the faculty from the fall of 1920 until the beginning of the calendar year 1926, when he departed for Oxford. Gordon's term at Leeds began in 1922. For the following four years, Gordon and Tolkien were key members of the English department. "They formed a Viking Club for undergraduates, which met to drink beer, read the sagas, and sing drinking songs in Anglo-Saxon and Old Norse" (Anderson, 17). In 1926, Gordon replaced Tolkien as professor of English language, and in 1931 he also left Leeds in turn to become Smith Professor of English Language and Germanic Philology at the University of Manchester. In his lifetime, Gordon was a more prolific scholar than Tolkien. In 1927, he published *An Introduction to Old Norse*, which was revised by A.R. Taylor in 1957 with assistance from Ida Gordon. E.V. Gordon also published a translation of *Scandinavian Archaeology* and an edition of *The Battle of Maldon*, both in 1937, by which time he had also nearly completed an edition of *Pearl*. Had history unfolded differently, this latter edition might have borne Tolkien's name as coeditor. As it turned out, *Pearl* was left in Tolkien's hands to finish when Gordon, at the age of forty-two, died unexpectedly on July 29, 1938, from an attack of gallstones that was followed by surgery to remove his gallbladder. Tolkien never fully rose to the task, and the Gordon edition of *Pearl* was ultimately brought to print in 1953 without Tolkien as coeditor and thanks to a revision by E.V. Gordon's widow Ida.

In recent decades, scholars have begun to explore the connections between *Sir Gawain and the Green Knight* and *The Lord of the Rings*. Miriam Youngerman Miller detects thematic and technical links between the two texts and also observes generic similarities in plot. Most important to her argument, however, is the shared presence in each text of "carefully constructed Secondary Worlds" (347) and "two-tiered Other Worlds" (348). Based on these factors, Miller claims "an absorption on Tolkien's part of the *Gawain*-poet's work which borders perhaps on identification" (362). Roger Schlobin, also considering the *Lord of the Rings*, sees origins and parallels in *Sir Gawain*, with respect to their "absentee villains" (Sauron and Morgan le Faye), the failures of Gawain and Frodo at their "ultimate tests," and in their depictions of "responsible virtue." Verlyn Flieger, finally, contends that Tolkien has derived the character Treebeard from ancient literary sources and from vegetation myths—the Green World—of which the Green Knight is a clear embodiment.

GERALD SEAMAN

Further Reading

Anderson, Douglas A. "'An industrious little devil': E.V. Gordon as Friend and Collaborator with Tolkien." In *Tolkien the Medievalist*, edited by Jane Chance, 13–25. New York: Routledge, 2003.

Brewer, Elizabeth. *Sir Gawain and the Green Knight: Sources and Analogues*. Woodbridge, Suffolk: D.S. Brewer, 1973; 1992.

Carpenter, Humphrey. *Tolkien: A Biography*. Boston, MA: Houghton Mifflin, 1977.

Flieger, Verlyn. "The Green Man, the Green Knight, and Treebeard: Scholarship and Invention in Tolkien's Fiction." In *Scholarship and Fantasy: Proceedings of the Tolkien Phenomenon*, edited by K.J. Battarbee. *Anglicana Tukuensia* 12 (1993): 85–98.

Miller, Miriam Youngerman. "Of sum mayn meruayle, þat he my3t trawe": *The Lord of the Rings* and *Sir Gawain and the Green Knight*." *Studies in Medievalism* 3, no. 3 (Winter 1991): 345–65.

Miller, Miriam Youngerman, and Jane Chance, eds. *Approaches to Teaching Sir Gawain and the Green Knight*. New York: Modern Language Association of America, 1986.

Schlobin, Roger C. "The Monsters Are Talismans and Transgressions: Tolkien and *Sir Gawain and the Green Knight*." In *J.R.R. Tolkien and His Literary Resonances: Views of Middle-earth*, edited by George Clark and Daniel Timmons, 71–81. Westport, CT, and London: Greenwood Press, 2000.

Shippey, Tom. *J.R.R. Tolkien: Author of the Century*. Boston and New York: Houghton Mifflin, 2000.

———. *The Road to Middle-earth*. Boston, MA: Houghton Mifflin, 1983.

Tolkien, J.R.R., and E.V. Gordon, eds. *Sir Gawain and the Green Knight*. Oxford: Clarendon Press, 1925. Reedited by Norman Davis. Oxford: Oxford University Press, 1967.

Tolkien, J.R.R., trans. *Sir Gawain and the Green Knight, Pearl, and Sir Orfeo*. Boston, MA: Houghton Mifflin, 1975.

———. "Sir Gawain and the Green Knight." In *MC*, 72–108.

See also **Beowulf; Gordon, E.V.; Orfeo, Sir; Pearl: Edition by E.V. Gordon; Pearl, Sir Orfeo: Edited by Christopher Tolkien; Publications, Posthumous; Sir Gawain and the Green Knight; T.C.B.S**

SMITH, GEOFFREY BACHE (1894–1916)

Geoffrey Bache Smith was born in West Bromwich on October 18, 1894, the second of two children of Thomas and Ruth Annie Smith. Smith entered King Edward's School, Birmingham, in December 1904, shortly before his father's death early in 1905. Smith was two classes behind Tolkien at King Edward's School. After Tolkien left for Oxford in October 1911, he kept in close touch with his school friends, who called themselves the T.C.B.S. (for Tea Club and Barrovian Society). His friendship was Smith was cemented at a December 1911 performance of Sheridan's "The Rivals," in which both Smith and Tolkien had acted. Smith followed Tolkien to Oxford, entering Corpus Christi College in October 1913. After the outbreak of the First World War, Smith joined the Oxford and Buckinghamshire Light Infantry, and was posted to the Nineteenth Lancashire Fusiliers, training at Penmaenmawr in North Wales. At a Christmas 1914 meeting of the T.C.B.S., Tolkien had decided that he was to be a poet, and Smith's similar literary interests and ambitions brought them closer via an extensive correspondence. Smith published some poems in *The King Edward's School Chronicle* and in a college magazine, *The Pelican Record*. A few of his longer poems were intended as entries in the annual Newdigate poetry competition, for which a new topic was set each year. Smith contributed one poem ("Song on the Downs") to *Oxford Poetry 1915*, where it appeared with work by Tolkien ("Goblin Feet") and Smith's friend (who was also an officer in his battalion), H.T. Wade-Gery (1888–1972), with whom Smith shared Tolkien's poetry.

Smith was sent to the front by December 1915, and found it very dreary, but managed to finish his long poem "The Burial of Sophocles" in the trenches and sent it to Tolkien. Smith and Tolkien managed to meet a few times in France in 1916. Like other soldiers who survived the Battle of the Somme, Smith hoped to see the end of the war. But on November 29, 1916, as he walked along a road, he was hit in the right arm and buttocks by fragments of a bursting shell. The wounds did not seem life threatening, but after two days he developed gas-gangrene, and died at half past three in the morning of December 3, 1916. He was buried at Warlincourt Halte British Cemetery in France. Smith's older brother Roger was also killed in the war, eight weeks later, leaving his widowed mother alone.

Smith's expressed wish had been to have his poetry published, and Tolkien and R.W. Reynolds were soon at work on it. Tolkien had the primary responsibility for editing the book, but he was assisted by Christopher Wiseman. Reynolds helped in the search for a publisher. *A Spring Harvest* appeared in July 1918.

In February 1916, Smith had written to Tolkien: "My chief consolation is, that if I am scuppered to-night . . . there will still be left a member of the great TCBS to voice what I dreamed and what we all agreed upon. . . . May you say the things I have tried to say long after I am not there to say them, if such be my lot."

A number of Smith's books, particularly on Celtic themes, were bequeathed to Tolkien, becoming part of his personal library.

DOUGLAS A. ANDERSON

Further Reading

Garth, John. *Tolkien and the Great War: The Threshhold of Middle-earth*. London: HarperCollins, 2003.

Smith, Geoffrey Bache. *A Spring Harvest*. London: Erskine Macdonald, 1918.

See also **Childhood; Gilson, Robert Quilter; Reynolds, R.W.;** *Spring Harvest, A***; T.C.B.S.; Wiseman, Christopher; World War I**

SMITH OF WOOTTON MAJOR

The last short story Tolkien wrote, *Smith of Wootton Major* was also the last of his work to be published in his lifetime. It thus stands as his final, most definitive representation of human interaction with Faery, the Otherworld of the imagination that is the uncharted territory of the artist. This tale of a boy who swallows a magical star hidden in his slice of cake at a children's party and through its agency finds his way into Faery is markedly different in tone from Tolkien's other short works. Lacking the picaresque whimsy of *Roverandom*, the humor of *Farmer Giles of Ham*, or *Leaf by Niggle*'s pronounced allegorical overtones, *Smith of Wootton Major* is essentially a meditation on imagination and the creative process. Of all Tolkien's shorter works, *Smith* is at once the most deceptively simple yet thematically complex, interweaving concepts of creativity and imagination with the beauty and danger of the Otherworld and the inevitability of its eventual loss. The major character, Smith, is a simple artisan, a blacksmith whose craft is lifted to art by his possession of the star. He is an extraordinary ordinary man, a human whose travels in the perilous realm of Faery expose him to wonders, dangers, and mysteries that he can sometimes apprehend and often explore, but for which no explanations are given.

In this respect, *Smith of Wootton Major* might well be taken as the practical enactment of the first paragraph of Tolkien's 1936 lecture/essay "On Fairy-stories." In that essay he describes Faërie (his spelling of this word varied from work to work) as a "perilous land" containing "pitfalls for the unwary and dungeons for the overbold." It is a place where it is dangerous for the traveler to ask too many questions, "lest the gates should be shut and the keys be lost" (*MC*, 109). This is precisely what happens to Smith. After his many ventures into Faery and his unwary encounters with its pitfalls, he is forced to realize that the gates are shutting to him and that the star that is his key, though not lost, must be given back in order to be passed on to the next recipient.

As background to the story, Tolkien wrote a companion essay in which he developed and refined some of the ideas first expressed in "On Fairy-Stories" nearly thirty years earlier. More explicitly concentrated on Faery itself than on its place in fairy stories, the later essay examined the temporal, geographical, and psychological relationship of the Faery Otherworld to the real world (specifically Wootton Major). Most important, it developed and explored the possibility and significance of interaction between them.

Begun in 1964 and published in 1967, the story had a curious beginning in Tolkien's negative reaction to another short story, George MacDonald's *The Golden Key*. He had been invited by a publisher to write a preface for a new edition of that story. However, upon rereading the story in preparation for his preface, Tolkien not only reacted strongly against MacDonald's didacticism, but also disagreed with his concept of fairyland. The preface then grew into Tolkien's attempt to explain just where and how MacDonald had missed the mark, and the explanation gave way to his own story illustrating what Faery was really like.

The last paragraph of the never-finished preface began a parable about a cook who in making a cake for a children's party had the idea that it should be very sweet. The excessive sweetness of the cake illustrated what Tolkien considered to be the popular misconception of Fairyland and fairy stories, that they were saccharine confections meant primarily for children with undeveloped tastes. The preface broke off at this point, but the cook, the cake, and the children's party became the opening focus of the story, which went on to develop a life of its own. Keeping these three initial components, Tolkien enriched the mix by putting inside the cake the star that is the emblem of Faery, by having the star swallowed by the boy Smith who becomes the tale's protagonist, and by introducing the character of Alf the Apprentice, who is in reality the King of Faery. These added elements—opposing and refuting both the cake and its baker, the Master Cook unable of understanding the true nature of Faery-provide the plot.

The deceptively slight action of the story is simply the account of Smith's enchanting, often bewildering travels into Faery, and his final reluctant surrender of the star at Alf's behest so that it may pass to someone else. Despite Tolkien's initial reaction against MacDonald's didacticism, the ghost of allegory haunts his own story, for the cake and the star, which obviously have meaning beyond their ordinary natures, and the type-characters of the Cook and the Smith (both makers or creators but at different levels of art) invite symbolic interpretation. Thus, the story has been variously read as its author's farewell to his art, as a representation of the conflict between philology and literary studies (Faery, represented by Alf, opposed by literary criticism, represented by the Cook), or as an expression of grief and renunciation of powers at the approach of old age. Certainly, the two worlds of the story, the village where Smith works and lives and the Otherworld he is privileged to enter, suggest comparison with the two worlds of their creator, the everyday world of Oxford where Tolkien lived and worked and the Otherworld where his imagination and his fiction took him. Tolkien himself admitted that there was "some trace" of allegory, not in the Faërien elements but in the human ones. He suggested the Master Cook and the Great Hall as an allegory of the village church and its parson, their true function and role in the community steadily declining, and expressed some surprise that no reader had referred to this.

The book got a mixed critical reception when it was published in 1967. Some reviewers found it to be a haunting tale of delicacy and charm, while others found it a disappointing, too-slight follow-up to *The Lord of the Rings*, and missed the earthiness, robust humor, and individuality of that book's hobbit characters. Nevertheless, *Smith of Wootton Major* has been translated into over fifteen languages, and has appeared in a number of stand-alone editions, as well as being included in several collections of Tolkien's shorter works. The most enduring versions seem to be those retaining the original format and illustrations by Pauline Baynes.

VERLYN FLIEGER

Further Reading

Flieger, Verlyn and T.A. Shippey. "Allegory versus Bounce: Tolkien's *Smith of Wootton Major*." *Journal of the Fantastic in the Arts,* 12 (2(46)). 2001: 186–200.

See also **Enchantment; Magic; "On Fairy-Stories"**

SMITH OF WOOTTON MAJOR (CHARACTER)

Smith of Wootton Major is the title character of Tolkien's short story of 1967. As a boy of nine years attending the rare Twenty-four Feast (of Good Children), Smith eats the piece of Great Cake that has hidden within it a "fay-star." On his tenth birthday the star falls out of his mouth, and he instinctively places it on his forehead where it remains for almost forty-eight years, giving to Smith both the privilege of entering the realm of Faery and the longing to do so. As an adult, he grows in fame in Wootton Major and the nearby villages for his smith-work, which is marked with unusual beauty, grace, and strength. He also sings as he works, with a voice so beautiful that any who hear him stop to listen. Yet his main "business" is in Faery, where he becomes a wandering explorer, guarded from the Greater Evils and avoided by the Lesser Evils.

The story is not, however, an adventure tale. Of Smith's many adventures in Faery, only a few are recounted and only in brief. The emphasis is rather on how Faery changes Smith. He grows in wonder at the beauty of the land and its strangeness, grandeur, and power. He learns wisdom and humility, and in his own world he does not forge any weapons, though he could have made them with "power enough to become the matter of great tales." He also learns appropriate fear, shown most clearly when he meets the Elven Mariners.

Perhaps the most poignant emotions, and those most central to the tale, are regret and grief. Among the few adventures recounted by the narrator are Smith's encounter with the young birch and his two meetings with the Queen of Faery. When the young birch gives its leaves to save Smith from the "wild Wind," Smith is so saddened that he is unable to return to Faery for some time. Later, when he first meets the Queen, though he does not know who she is, he is abashed to discovered his own presumption. Toward the end of the tale, he responds to the Queen's summons and meets her a second time, and is given to understand even more; he is again deeply grieved at the poverty of his own people's image of the Queen. On his return to Wootton Major after this visit, Smith meets the King of Faery, who tells him it is now time to return the fay-star. Smith is overcome and at first angrily resists, knowing that once the star is gone he will never be allowed in Faery again. Yet with tears and a stab of pain, and feeling great bereavement, he submits and returns the star. As a reward, he is allowed to choose which child will receive it next. Though Smith was chosen by his grandfather, he does not choose any of his own descendants.

The character Smith has at least two important sources. The first is a similar character named Anados in George MacDonald's novel *Phantastes*. Anados is granted permission to enter "Fairy Land" when he opens a hidden chamber an old heirloom desk. Many of Smith's adventures, including encounter with watchful trees and great knights, are strikingly familiar to those of Anados. The second source is

J.R.R. Tolkien himself, who in his essay "On Fairy-stories" describes himself in terms startlingly similar to his description of Smith: as "a wandering explorer in the realm, full of knowledge but not of information" (*TL*, 9). This later connection between the Smith and Tolkien suggests that the story, like "Leaf by Niggle," also has autobiographical allegorical implications—a point argued by some scholars and disputed by others.

MATTHEW DICKERSON

Further Reading

Dickerson, Matthew, and Jonathan Evans. *Ents, Elves, and Eriador*. Lexington, KY: University Press of Kentucky, 2006.

Dickerson, Matthew, and David O'Hara. *From Homer to Harry Potter*. Grand Rapids, MI: Brazos Press, 2006.

Flieger, Verlyn. *A Question of Time: J.R.R. Tolkien's Road to Faerie*. Kent, OH: Kent State University Press, 1997.

Shippey, Tom. *J.R.R. Tolkien: Author of the Century*. London: HarperCollins, 2000.

See also **Allegory; Enchantment; Faerie; "Leaf by Niggle"; *Smith of Wootton Major*; *Tree and Leaf***

SOLOMON AND SATURN

Solomon and Saturn is the title given to a number of Old English dialogues written in poetry and prose, though it is the second poetic dialogue (commonly referred to as *Solomon and Saturn II*) that seems to have had a particular influence on Tolkien's own literary work. The dialogue takes the form of a riddling contest between the biblical figure of Solomon, who is reimagined as a Christian and demonstrates a peculiarly English brand of wisdom, and the classical figure of Saturn, who is reimagined as a Babylonian prince. The tone is agonistic, and the poem continually contrasts Saturn's pagan learning, which is clearly great, with Solomon's Christian wisdom, which is clearly greater. The two interlocutors exchange riddles on some of the traditional subjects of Old English wisdom poetry such as the seasons of the year and the workings of fate, as well as on less traditional topics such as the nature and uses of books, the story of the Tower of Babel, and Eastern as well as Christian traditions concerning doomsday.

The form of the riddling contest itself had an obvious influence on Tolkien, and he draws on *Solomon and Saturn* as well as on two Old Norse examples—the *Vafðrúðnismál*, one of the poems of the *Poetic Edda*, and a riddle contest in the *Saga of King Heidrek the Wise*—as sources for specific riddles in his riddling contest between Bilbo and Gollum in *The Hobbit*. Gollum's "hard and horrible" riddle, for which Bilbo's answer is "time" (*H*, V, 72–73), draws on one

of Saturn's riddles, wherein he asks what "beats at foundations" (*Solomon and Saturn* (*S&S*), line 274b; translations are my own) and describes how "to [this wonder] as food must go each of the years of earth-dwellers, sky-fliers, lake-swimmers" (*S&S*, 279b–81). Solomon's reply is not "time," but "old age," and he describes how "She overpowers the wolf, the wild bird; she outlives stones, she overmatches steel, she bites through iron with rust, so she does to us" (*S&S*, 290–92). Gollum's riddle is a simpler, more direct version of the same. Similarly, Gollum's "dark" riddle (*H*, V, 70) finds an analogue in *Solomon and Saturn II*, when Solomon asks, "Tell me what was not that was," and Saturn's reply, although riddling in itself, is clearly meant to be "darkness" or "shadow" (*S&S*, 330b–34). Furthermore, Tom Shippey has suggested that this understanding of shadow as both having a positive existence and being a form of absence or oblivion informs Tolkien's frequent use of the term "shadow" in *The Lord of the Rings*.

KATHRYN POWELL

Further Reading

Menner, Robert J., ed. *The Poetic Dialogues of Solomon and Saturn*. MLA Monograph Series 13. New York: Modern Language Association, 1941.

Shippey, Tom. *J.R.R. Tolkien: Author of the Century*. Boston, MA: Houghton Mifflin, 2000.

———. "Tolkien's Sources: The True Tradition." In *Readings on J.R.R. Tolkien*, edited by Katie deKoster, 153–61. San Diego, CA: Greenhaven Press, 2000.

See also **Darkness; *Hobbit, The*; *Lord of the Rings*; Old English; Old Norse Literature; Riddles; Riddles: Sources; Time**

"SOME CONTRIBUTIONS TO MIDDLE-ENGLISH LEXICOGRAPHY"

Tolkien's brief essay, "Some Contributions to Middle-English Lexicography," first appeared in *The Review of English Studies*, vol. 1, no. 2 in April of 1925 (pp. 210–15). The essay consists of a series of notes on twelve early Middle English words and seeks to give each word its proper etymology, definition, and modern English equivalent. In general, the method in each note is to identify the word in question; to discuss its earliest appearance in literature; to identify and reject the false, misleading, or incorrect gloss given by other scholars or editors; to set the word in its linguistic context by comparing it to Old English, Old Norse, Old French, Middle Low German, Middle High German, Middle Dutch, Dutch, Gothic, and other Middle English cognates (whichever happen to be most relevant); and then to give the most probable translation of the Middle English word based on a previously discussed (and more precise) etymology.

The essay begins with a declaration of the urgent need for Middle English dictionaries and suggests the value of publishing information related to such work, calling it "a service worth performing" (210). The essay that follows is divided into two major sections. The first section offers corrections to the N.E.D. (New English Dictionary) by considering two words, *long home* and *burde*, words clearly of special interest to Tolkien. He identifies the meaning of the first word group as "grave" (not "the future life" or "heaven"). The second, usually glossed as "lady" or "damsel," Tolkien proposes might be better identified as "embroideress." Tolkien's discussion of *burde* is his lengthiest and gives insight into his perception of gender roles, both female and male, in medieval literature.

The second section offers corrections to the glossary of the Early English Text Society (EETS) 1922 edition of *Hali Meidenhad* (which Tolkien proposes ought simply to be called *Meiðhad* since that is the form used in the Bodleian manuscript of the text, a manuscript Tolkien regarded as better than the Cotton Titus MS also used in the edition), reglossing ten words, the final two together: *wori* (Tolkien rejects "make war" in favor of "weary" or "wander, be confused, fall to pieces"), *mirð* (suggests misreading of the ms and substitutes *nurð*, "noise"), *nemman* (suggests misreading of the ms and substitutes *munnen*, "mention"), *heasci* (rejects "become exasperated" for "to show hostility, be wroth"), *suti* (rejects "sooty" or "filth" in favor of "grief"), *uleð* (rejects "uses" for "speak fair, flatter, cajole, wheedle"), *greni* (rejects "groan" for "gnash the teeth in anguish"), *medi* (rejects "meddle" for "reward them"), and *heme and hine* (rejects treating "heame" as an error for "heane" and proposes several possible readings, including "master and servant").

Though valuable for its philological, etymological, and lexicographical acuity, this essay also gives insight to readers interested in Tolkien's fascination with words generally, his intimate knowledge of the use of words in a wide range of Old English and Middle English texts (including *Handling Sin*, *The Fates of the Apostles*, *The Vision of Leofric*, Layamon's *Brut*, Alfred's *Orosius*, *Gawain and the Green Knight*, the *Exeter Book*, *Hali Meidenhad*, *Ancren Riwle*, Old English *Homilies*, the Katherine group, *Julianna*, *Beowulf*, and *The Owl and the Nightingale*), and his familiarity with medieval scholarship in his day (by such critics as Sisam, Bosworth-Toller, Napier, Cleasby-Vigfusson, Sveinbjörn Egilsson, Morris, Cockayne, Bradley-Stratmann, and Hall).

The essay also reveals Tolkien's knowledge of contemporary slang ("bird"), interest in ballads, and familiarity with the "modern poet" (210), William Morris. It is worth reading for all of these reasons.

JANE BEAL

See also **AB Language;** *Ancrene Wisse***; MS Bodley 34; Middle English; Philology; Scholarship**

SONG CONTESTS

The related motifs of a contest of knowledge through song and the magical power of song are known from several European folk and literary traditions and occur in at least two places in Tolkien's works. In the *Silmarillion*, Finrod Felagund and Beren magically take on the appearance of Orcs, but as they attempt to pass through the domain of Morgoth, Sauron becomes aware of them. After being made suspicious by Felagund and Beren's failure to report, as Orcs should, Sauron captures them. Felagund then fights Sauron using songs of magic, but Sauron proves more powerful and is able to remove their disguise, but not to find out who they are. The motif of the magical power of song is also alluded to in *The Lord of the Rings* when Frodo and Sam get Tom Bombadil's help in freeing Merry and Pippin from Old Man Willow: Tom threatens to sing the roots, leaves, and branches off of the willow if it does not release the two hobbits.

Tolkien draws from several Finnish and Scandinavian sources for his versions of the motifs. His primary source is the third poem of Elias Lönnrot's 1849 *Kalevala*, which is called *Kilpalaulanta* (The Singing Match) in Finnish. In this poem the young wizard Joukahainen challenges the ancient and powerful wizard Väinämöinen to a contest of knowledge. Joukahainen's knowledge is trivial in comparison to Väinämöinen's, and thus Joukahainen's challenge provokes Väinämöinen into a rage. Väinämöinen begins to sing, and because of his anger, "the earth shook/the copper mountains trembled/the firm stones cracked/the cliffs flew apart/the rocks on the shore shattered" (*Kilpalaulanta*, lines 295–300; my translation). Väinämöinen then begins to sing Joukahainen into the ground. Joukahainen is terrified and tries to bargain with Väinämöinen. Väinämöinen rejects all of Joukahainen's offers until Joukahainen promises to give his sister to Väinämöinen, at which point Väinämöinen relents and releases Joukahainen.

In addition to the song contest in the *Kalevala*, there are two poems from the *Poetic Edda* that are contests of knowledge, that were also sources for Lönnrot's *Kalevala*, and that were known to Tolkien. In *Vafðruðnismál*, Odin and the giant Vafðruðnir compete in a contest of knowledge that ends only when Odin asks the giant what Odin said into Baldur's ear after he died, a question that only Odin himself can answer. In the second Eddic poem, the *Alvíssmál*, Thor and the Dwarf Alvíss (a name meaning "all-wise") have a similar contest that ends at sunrise, when the Dwarf is turned to stone.

A final source for the motif of the power of song is the Danish ballad *Harpens Kraft* (The Power of the Harp). After a knight's beloved falls off a bridge and is captured by a kelpie, the knight calls for his harp, and through the power of the music he plays and the charm he sings, he forces the kelpie to return his beloved.

DAVID GAY

Further Reading

Larrington, Carolyne, trans. *The Poetic Edda*. Oxford: Oxford University Press, 1996.

Lönnrot, Elias. *Kalevala, the Land of Heroes*. Trans. W.F. Kirby, intro. By Michael Branch. London: Athlone Press, 1985; orig. 1907.

Olrik, Axel, ed. *A Book of Danish Ballads*. Trans. E.M. Smith-Dampier. Princeton, NJ: Princeton University Press, 1939.

See also **Charms; Epic Poetry; Finland, Literary Sources; Music in Middle-earth; Mythology, Germanic; Old Norse Literature**

SOUTH, THE

In Middle-earth, the South is little explored as a place and is the least symbolic of the four cardinal directions. Generally, it represents exotic peoples, then the unknown, with the added suggestion in *The Lord of the Rings* that a hot climate implies evil inhabitants.

In *Silmarillion*, the South is rarely mentioned. In Valinor, it is "lightless and unexplored" (*S*, 73), and in Beleriand, those who go south drop out of the story (*S*, 54; *Morgoth*, 324). The derivation of Quenya *hyarmen* (south) from *hyarya* (left) + *men* (place) shows that to the Elves, the South was a left turn taken during the journey West toward Elvenhome.

At the midpoint of the greater and more luminous east-west spectrum, the Elvish realms of Beleriand are south of Morgoth's evil kingdom in the North. A north-south axis defines the wars and the quest of the Silmarils in *Silmarillion*.

The Hobbit offsets but repeats this pattern. Although most of the adventure takes place in the eastern Wilderland, the South there tends to represent Men and civilization, while the North is the abode of evil Dragons and Goblins as well as the heroic Dwarves. Again, a north-south axis rules the climactic events of the quest, from Lake–town to the desolation of Smaug.

The Lord of the Rings displays a far more complex interaction of place, direction, and meaning. The North is no longer the location of any evil power, but is the story's geographic and moral home, as was established in *The Hobbit*. The story expands to the South, with a gentler climate and a long history of conflict. That is where Gondor, the declining Númenorean kingdom, is at continuous war with Mordor and its allies to the east and south.

Beyond Gondor, on the edge of the map and of the story, are the little-known nations of The Harad from Sindarin *harad* (south). These are hot lands whose fierce dark-skinned peoples, the Haradrim or "Southrons," are historically hostile to Númenor and Gondor (*S*, 293; *TT*, IV, iv, 267), and are allied with Sauron in the War of the Ring.

This is a fully expressed moral geography. The South flaunts imperial sophistication and decadence (*TT*, IV, v, 286), but regresses into hot savagery further south, and it is always secondary to the East, the primary locus of darkness and evil. Frodo's quest leads both South and East from his northwestern homeland, but Gondor in the southwest has virtues as well as failings. Mordor in the southeast is a virtual hell (Scheps, 45).

That the intemperate extremes of the South (and the North in earlier eras) tend toward evil in Middle-earth reflects similar prejudices and mythologies from a temperate medieval Europe, but this symbolism is not central to the story. For instance, the South is often referred to in *The Lord of the Rings* as sunny, but the sun as a symbol always belongs to the primary East-West opposition of light and darkness (Tolkien, "Guide," 192).

As a parallel to real historical lands in relation to northwestern Europe and England, Gondor is roughly equivalent to Italy and Mediterranean Europe and the Harad may be considered Africa. But Tolkien rejected easy allegories: Gondor also has echoes of Egypt and Byzantium (*Letters*, 211, 280), and the Haradrim have elements of the Near East, and even India (Kocher, 17).

Tolkien's use of Africanic images for the lands and peoples of the Harad have led to accusations of racism in his writing. Most scholars reject this, referring to his personal character, the interplay between good and evil in *The Lord of the Rings* that is irrespective of geography and race, and the consciously antiquated style of the story (Rearick, 861). Any racist imagery (*TT*, IV, iii, 254; *RK*, V, vi, 121) accurately reflects medieval European views of Africa, with which Tolkien was very familiar (Tolkien, "Sigelwara"; Sinex).

JOHN F.G. MAGOUN

See also **Astronomy and Cosmology, Middle-earth; Egypt: Relationship to Númenóreans; Hell; Jungian**

Theory; Maps: Middle-earth; Middle-earth: Peoples; Missions from Anglo-Saxon England; Mordor; *Morgoth's Ring*; Middle-earth: Men; Morgoth and Melkor; Race and Ethnicity in Tolkien's Works; Sauron; Symbolism in Tolkien's Works; *War of the Jewels*; Wilderland

Further Reading

Day, David. *The World of Tolkien*. New York: Gramercy Books, 2003.

Kocher, Paul. *Master of Middle-earth: The Fiction of J.R.R. Tolkien*. Boston, MA: Houghton Mifflin, 1972.

LeGuin, Ursula. "Rhythmic Pattern in *The Lord of the Rings*." In *Meditations on Middle-earth*, edited by Karen Haber. New York: St. Martins Press, 2001.

Rearick, Anderson. "Why Is the Only Good Orc a Dead Orc? The Dark Face of Racism Examined in Tolkien's World." *Modern Fiction Studies* 50, no. 4 (2004): 861.

Rosebury, Brian. *Tolkien: A Cultural Phenomenon*. Hampshire: Palgrave MacMillan, 2003.

Scheps, Walter. "The Fairy-Tale Morality of The Lord of the Rings." In *A Tolkien Compass*, edited by Jared Lobdell. La Salle, IL: Open Court, 1975.

Sinex, Margaret. "Tolkien's Haradrim and the Medieval Construction of the Other." Unpublished manuscript, 2005.

Tolkien, J.R.R. "The Etymologies." In *Lost Road*.

———. "Guide to the Names in *The Lord of the Rings*." In *A Tolkien Compass*, edited by Jared Lobdell. La Salle, IL: Open Court, 1975.

———. "Sigelwara Land." *Medium Ævum* 1 (1932): 182; and 3 (1934): 95.

SPAIN: RECEPTION OF TOLKIEN

The Lord of the Rings was first published by Allen & Unwin in 1954–55. More than two decades passed before readers of Spanish language could make the interior journey together with Frodo, Sam, and the Ring walking along the paths of Middle-earth. Francisco Porrúa, who eventually became the owner of Minotauro ediciones, had finally the chance to publish the works by J.R.R. Tolkien in 1971, barely two years before the author's death in September 1973.

But the story is a bit longer. By the early 1970s, some publishers in Spain were trying to buy the rights for a Spanish edition of *The Lord of the Rings*, and conversations with Allen & Unwin had almost led to the signature of a contract. Actually, Porrúa received the rights after being informed by the editors in England that he should contact one Mr. Costa, in Argentina, the man who was in charge of the rights for International Editors, the company that managed the edition of Tolkien's works overseas.

A phone call revealed that the rights for a translation of Tolkien's masterpiece had just been recovered almost for free. Then the work to translate *El Señor de los Anillos* started, a work that soon faced the difficulty of communicating to readers in a Romance tongue, the same flavor of ancient times and happiness under siege the book provides using the linguistic vest of modern English. Under the pseudonym of "Lluís Doménech," Francisco Porrúa was the translator of the first volume, *La Comunidad del Anillo*. The whole book was finally published in Spain in three volumes, from 1978 to 1980.

The translation of *Las dos Torres*, and *El retorno del Rey* demanded several months of hard work, together with a small crew whose expertise made possible to get those two volumes ready for publication. Francisco Porrúa also translated *El hobbit* in 1982, this time under the alias "Manuel Figueroa." *El Silmarillion* was the next piece to be edited, in 1984. Thereafter he became the supervisor for the translation and edition of Tolkien's corpus until his retirement from Minotauro, the official editor concerning J.R.R. Tolkien and *tolkieniana*, in 2001.

La Comunidad del Anillo was first published in Spain on May 15, 1978, and no promotion or campaign of any sort supported the release. Sales ranged from forty to fifty thousand copies a year from the early 1980s and through the 1990s, at times increasing up to sixty thousand. *El hobbit* was also a best-seller from the very beginning, and the figures ranged the same way. *El Silmarillion* sold about twenty thousand per year. Obviously, these figures belong to both Spain (55 percent) and South America (45 percent). *The Lord of the Rings* was recently translated into Catalán by Francesc Parcerisas (titled *El Senyor dels Anells*), while no translation into Galician or Basque, the other co-official languages in Spain, has been attempted.

On the other hand, Peter Jackson's version of Tolkien's classic for screen caused a deep impact on sales, increasing in the period 2000–5 up to an average of 900,000 copies a year, including the works by Tolkien and the books concerning the movies produced by New Line Cinema.

In 1992, enthusiastic readers all over Spain founded the Sociedad Tolkien Española. More than six hundred members have joined the association since. The society is still expanding after the successful release of the movies. Smials, as local groups are called, have spread all over the main cities and villages of Spain, dedicated to the study of Tolkien's life and works, as well as to the enjoyment of a common delight for literature.

Three doctoral dissertations have been presented from 1995 to 2001, and three more are currently in progress. Discussion panels, conferences, lectures, and scholar meetings have been held under the supervision of university scholars and professors from 1997 to date all over the country, showing a continuing interest for research and scholarship on philology and Middle-earth.

A final question arises concerning the success of "a mythology for England" in a Mediterranean context. The answer deals with the deep relation between myth and truth, a universal knowledge rooted in human desire and longing for Truth, History, and tales. It also points toward the bond between a land largely embedded in tradition and wisdom and the enchantment that legends, magic, and nostalgic beauty provide. In this sense, the Mediterranean seems quite an adequate context for Beleriand, Númenor, and Middle-earth.

EDUARDO SEGURA

Further Reading

Tolkien, Christopher, ed. *La Historia de la Tierra Media:El Libro de los Cuentos Perdidos 1*, Minotauro: Barcelona, 1990; *El Libro de los Cuentos Perdidos 2*, Minotauro: Barcelona, 1991; *Las Baladas de Beleriand*, Minotauro: Barcelona, 1997; *La formación de la Tierra Media*, Minotauro: Barcelona, 1998; *El Camino Perdido y otros escritos*, Minotauro: Barcelona, 1999; *La Caída de Númenor*, Minotauro: Barcelona, 2000. This volume also includes *Los papeles del Notion Club. El Anillo de Morgoth*, Minotauro: Barcelona, 2000, *La Guerra de las Joyas*, Minotauro: Barcelona, 2002, and *Los Pueblos de la Tierra Media*, Minotauro: Barcelona, 2002.
Tolkien, J. R. R. *Apéndices de El Señor de los Anillos*. Minotauro: Barcelona, 1987.
———. *Árbol y Hoja*. Minotauro: Barcelona, 1994.
———. *Los Cuentos Inconclusos*. 3 vols. Vol. 1, *La Primera Edad*, Barcelona, 1988; Vol. 2, *La Segunda Edad*, Barcelona, 1989; Vol. 3, including pts. 3 and 4, *La Tercera Edad* and *Los Drúedain, Los Istari, Las Palantíri*, Minotauro: Barcelona, 1989.
———. *Egidio, el granjero de Ham. Hoja, de Niggle. El herrero de Wooton Major*. Minotauro: Barcelona, 1981.
———. *El Hobbit*. Minotauro: Barcelona, 1982.
———. *Los Monstruos y los críticos y otros ensayos*. Minotauro: Barcelona, 1998.
———. *El Señor de los Anillos*:
I. *La Comunidad del Anillo*, Barcelona, 1978.
II. *Las dos Torres*, Barcelona, 1979.
III. *El retorno del Rey*, Barcelona, 1980.
———. *El Silmarillion*. Minotauro: Barcelona, 1984.

SPANISH LANGUAGE

Tolkien's fondness for Spanish is well known. Since the early years of his childhood in Birmingham, his mentor Father Francis Morgan's support, teachings, and encouragement, helped the young Ronald in his effort to learn and *taste* languages. But support was not the only help Father Francis provided. He also taught Tolkien the *sound* of Spanish, its texture. It eventually became his favorite among the Romance tongues: "Spanish came my way by chance and greatly attracted me. It gave me strong pleasure, and still does—far more than any other Romance language" (*MC*, 191).

Many years later, in a letter dated on February 8, 1967, to a Canadian reader who offered himself as a translator of *The Lord of the Rings*, and others, into Spanish, Tolkien wrote:

Dear Mr. Sands,

. . .

With regard to your project: a good translation of these for the Spanish market, I am interested. I have some acquaintance with the Spanish language on both sides of the Atlantic and I find it, *especially the European variety*, extremely attractive.

It can be argued that Tolkien's mind always remained focused on the sound of language—of any language—and not only on its richness of meaning. His opinions about the intimate relation between lit. and lang. are well known too. But in this letter, dealing with the chance of a possible translation into Spanish, his view illuminates the point: Tolkien wanted it to provide a pleasure from the point of view of sound, a translation into the *Spanish of Spain* since he found its euphony delightful *as a reader*, because "the basic pleasure in the phonetic elements of a language and in the style of their patterns, and then in a higher dimension, pleasure in the association of these word-forms with meanings, is of fundamental importance." (*MC*, 190).

Tolkien always thought there was an inherent relation between sound and meaning that was almost intuitive, and not only rational. He also made clear that his books had been written to be read aloud because his background as a reader was the literature of the ancient Europe, and also because the music of the words acted on the listeners as a spell: it was the right vehicle to a deeper understanding of the meaning of the plot, and also to a certain glimpse of the truth behind the immediate meaning of the invented languages—and beyond, of myth. Reading aloud was the right context for an epic, for a heroic elegy.

Tolkien's delight for Spanish has been explained by his biographers. They all agree, following Humphrey Carpenter's authorized study, that one of the invented languages the young Tolkien attempted was deeply influenced by Spanish. From rudimentary "Animalic" to "Nevbosh"a mixture of English, Latin, and French—Tolkien was able to develop a new language because to him Welsh was not available in sufficient quantity. So he turned to the collection of Spanish books at Father Francis's home. His guardian spoke Spanish fluently and Tolkien had often asked to be taught the language, but nothing came of it. He eventually became a good reader of Spanish, although he was never able to speak it fluently.

In those books he found the euphony he longed for and began work on an invented language he called "Naffarin," itself a Spanish-like phonetic combination according to the use of Spanish in the South of the country. "Naffarin" showed a great deal of Spanish influence, especially in sound, but it had its own phonetics and grammar, a development that Tolkien attempted from a very early stage of his training as an amateur philologist. "In 'Naffarin' the influences—outside English, and beyond a nascent purely individual element—are Latin and Spanish, in sound-choices and combinations, in general word-form" (*MC*, 209).

Finally, a few words must be said on the guidelines that Tolkien prepared to the translators of his masterpiece into other languages, the *Guide to the Names in The Lord of the Rings*, a book in itself that shows the author's deep familiarity with more than twenty languages. In this nomenclature, Tolkien provides a discerning linguistic knowledge in order to keep the flavor and atmosphere of the names for the Hobbits, and the geography of the Shire.

Finnish and Welsh are renowned as Tolkien's favorite languages. They are actually the basis for the Elven tongues, Quenya and Sindarin. No matter the importance of those real languages on the process of creation of Middle-earth, Tolkien always missed a deeper familiarity with Spanish. But his scholarship and formation led him to the languages of the German branch, and far from the Mediterranean. His mythology is also partly inspired by far-off materials deeply rooted in "the North." However, the flavor of Spanish-like sounds still remains in the translated names of the Shire: the texture of the same soil, the same remembrances of a happy folk and land.

EDUARDO SEGURA

SPENSER, EDMUND

Edmund Spenser is most well known for his epic work *The Faerie Queene*. Writing in the sixteenth century, a time where English poetry underwent refinement and experimentation, he strictly followed Sidney's conception of the poet's progression from pastoral to epic poetry (*Poesy*). As one of the earliest English epics, *The Faerie Queene* stands as an example for later epics. Similarly, Tolkien's *The Lord of the Rings* stands as one of the first works of modern fantasy, with numerous offshoots and derivative works by later authors. Spenser and Tolkien both drew from

similar sources although their goals and methods were different.

Spenser's work is primarily allegorical; he included a preface letter stating its purpose "is to fashion a gentleman or noble person in vertuous [*sic*] and gentle discipline" (*Edmund Spenser's*, 1). He used as his vehicle for this purpose the epic style of the classical poets and the legends of King Arthur. Tolkien's purpose in his creation of Middle-earth was to create a mythology for England and a vehicle for his invented languages. He looked to the work of the classical poets, the legends of England, including Arthur, and to Norse mythology. He expressly states his dislike of allegory in the foreword later added to *The Lord of the Rings*, citing the difference between applicability and allegory (*FR*, Foreword, 7).

Due to the similar source material with common themes, one can find similarity between *Rings* and *The Faerie Queene*. Tolkien's and Spenser's heroes follow the role of chivalric knight and epic hero generally, as do most mythological heroes (Campbell). Gandalf mirrors Merlin, in the archetype of the wise counselor aiding the heroes in their quest. Merlin's globe, Galadriel's mirror, and the *palantiri* all come from the same tradition of crystal balls and magic mirrors in myth and fairy tale.

Writing under the reign and eventual patronage of Elizabeth I, Spenser developed a female heroine, Britomart, as a way of representing the noble virtues of his queen (Roche). Britomart is one of the earliest strong female characters in English literature, and Tolkien's Éowyn and Lúthien bear strong resemblance to her. Britomart possesses the same skills as any other knight, defeating enemies in battle, including slaying the Amazon queen Radigund by whom the knight Artegall was captured and forced into servitude (*Queene*, Book III, Cantos v and vii). Éowyn slays the Witch-King in battle, an enemy who overcame Faramir and Theoden, and of whom it was prophesied that no living man would defeat (*RK*, V, vi, 116). Lúthien aids her beloved, Beren, in the quest for the *Silmaril*, and her power enables him to succeed where he would otherwise have failed (*S*, 208–22). She frees her love from imprisonment, as Britomart frees Artegall. Lacking Britomart's allegorical representation of Chastity, these women are not bound by allegorical strictures; thus, Éowyn rides with the Rohirrim against the express command of her uncle and king and Lúthien leaves against Thingol's wishes in aiding Beren.

In Spenser's work, however, each hero or heroine represents a specific noble virtue, overcoming allegorical wrongs in the process. Tolkien's heroes follow the heroic model but carry no allegorical one-to-one relationship in meaning; the symbolism is more generic, allowing the reader to make one's own determinations as to meaning and applicability.

JULAIRE ANDELIN

Further Reading

Campbell, Joseph. *The Hero with a Thousand Faces*. 2nd ed. Princeton, NJ: Princeton University Press, 1980.

Roche, Thomas P. *The Kindly Flame*. Princeton, NJ: Princeton University Press, 1964.

Sidney, Sir Phillip, "The Defense of Poesy." In *The Renaissance in England, Non-dramatic Prose and Verse of the Sixteenth Century*, edited by Hyder E. Rollins, Herschel Baker, 605–24. Prospect Heights, IL: Waveland Press, 1992.

Shippey, Tom, *The Road to Middle-earth: How J.R.R. Tolkien Created a New Mythology*, Rev. and expanded ed. New York: Houghton Mifflin, 2003.

Spenser, Edmund. *Edmund Spenser's Poetry*. 3rd ed. Edited by Hugh MacLean and Anne Lake Prescott. New York: W.W. Norton & Company, 1993.

———. *The Faerie Queene*. Edited by Thomas P. Roche and C. Patrick O'Donnell. London: Penguin Classics, 1979.

Woolf, Virginia. "*The Faery Queen*." In *The Moment and Other Essays*, 24–30. Orlando, FL: Harcourt Brace Jovanovich, 1976.

See also **Allegory; Aragorn; Arthurian Literature; Chaucer; Dante; Epic Poetry; Éowyn; Faramir; Feminist Readings of Tolkien; Gandalf; Gender in Tolkien's Works; Heroes and Heroism; Homer; Jungian Theory; Literature; Lúthien; Mythology for England; Milton; Old Norse Literature; "On Fairy-Stories"; Palantíri; Quest Narrative; Shakespeare; Symbolism in Tolkien's Works; Theoden; Theological and Moral Approaches in Tolkien's Works; 20th Century: Influence of Tolkien; Virgil; Women in Tolkien's Works**

SPRING HARVEST, A: G. BACHE SMITH, ED. J.R.R. TOLKIEN

A posthumous selection of the poetry of G.B. Smith (London: Erskine Macdonald, 1918), this was the first publication by a member of the T.C.B.S., the cultural clique Tolkien had formed at school. The first book to be edited by Tolkien, it is his sole contribution to mainstream modern literature. He worked on it with Christopher Wiseman at the request of Ruth Annie Smith, the dedicatee, after her son's death in 1916.

Long bracketing narratives, begun as entries for Oxford's Newdigate Prize, are the most ambitious and satisfying items. "Glastonbury" recounts in Tennysonian manner the fates of Bedivere and Lancelot according to Sir Thomas Malory. "The Burial of Sophocles," lost en route to the Western Front in 1915 and then presumably reconstructed by Smith, refutes the idea that those favored by the gods die young; his death long before "the splendid

harvest-tide" of old age lends a poignancy underlined by the title of the volume. An epigraph highlights the poet's pessimism for his "spoiléd sheaf / Of rime that scarcely came to harvesting."

The remainder consists of shorter pieces, mostly lyrical: "First Poems" dating from as early as 1910, and "Last Poems" from after the outbreak of war. Among the early influences are W.B. Yeats, A.E. Housman and Edward Marsh's *Georgian Poetry*, a 1913 anthology favored by Smith. Wiseman thought Smith was behind the times and "Victorian" but, in an era of literary innovation, A.D. Burnett-Brown (a college friend of Smith's) was pleased to find "no new experiments, and commendably few tricks of style." The cast is largely medieval (riders, hermits, warriors), the language antiquarian ("sere," "betwixt," "cramasy"). Trees, seas, and towers are buffeted by winds that bear rumors of ancient wars and mystic lands. Inaction is an abiding horror; death and glory are objects of yearning. Smith glimpses eternity on a medieval page or in sublime Romantic solitudes.

His war poems may seem pallid beside the slightly later, more confrontational verse of Robert Graves and his heirs, now regarded as the epitome of war poetry. Burnett-Brown, however, provides a contemporary soldier's view of *A Spring Harvest*: "War is seen throughout in its true perspective, as a stern, harsh, evil, and ugly thing, provocative only of a stern resolve." The collection records a shift from a peacetime fixation with nature and self-realization, through early wartime patriotism, to the demoralization of a serviceman on the Somme. Smith inveighs against the chattering classes at home and, misanthropically, welcomes war as a purgative. But particularly moving are "Ave Atque Vale," a farewell to Oxford; and "Let us tell stories of quiet eyes," written (like "R.Q.G") in memory of Rob Gilson, the other T.C.B.S. fatality.

Tom Shippey has noted that Smith shared Tolkien's interest in ancient roads and their decay in time; Verlyn Flieger identifies a spirit-kinship between "The Sea-bell" and Smith's "The House of Eld." The latter, describing "a far isle set in the western sea," stands alongside an invocation to "the old gods who wrought the world / And shaped the moon and sun" to suggest Smith shared some of Tolkien's earliest mythological conceptions. If so, this would elucidate his statement that the T.C.B.S. saw their "own finger" in Tolkien's writing; and that Tolkien might "voice what I dreamed and what we all agreed upon." Tolkien perhaps deliberately echoed Smith's *envoi*, "So we lay down the pen," in Eriol's epilogue to "The Book of Lost Tales": "so I lay down the pen, and so of the fairies cease to tell."

Several poems had appeared in the *King Edward's School Chronicle*, the *Pelican Record*, *The Oxford*

Magazine and *Oxford Poetry 1915*. Some have reappeared in war poetry anthologies such as Anne Powell's *A Deep Cry*.

JOHN GARTH

Further Reading

Burnett-Brown, A.D. Review. *Pelican Record* (Oxford, Corpus Christi College), June 1919, 105–7.
Flieger, Verlyn. *A Question of Time*. Kent, OH: Kent State University Press, 1997.
Garth, John. *Tolkien and the Great War*. London: HarperCollins, 2003.
Powell, Anne. *A Deep Cry*. Aberporth: Palladour, 1993.
Shippey, Tom. *The Road to Middle-earth*. Boston, MA: Houghton Mifflin, 2003.

See also **Gilson, Robert Quilter; Smith, Geoffrey Bache; T.C.B.S.; Wiseman, Christopher; World War I**

SUBJECT THEORY AND SEMIOTICS

Semiotics is conventionally the discipline of studying signs and sign systems. Its poststructuralist variety, postsemiotics, or the theory of the speaking subject, builds less on structuralist assumptions and more on a psychoanalytical model of the subject, inspired by the work of Jacques Lacan (1901–81), and theories of the discourses of culture influenced by Michel Foucault (1926–84). The theory of the speaking subject examines sign systems, linguistic utterances, and representations as products of subjects with their own internal processes (the microdynamics of the speaking subject) contextualized and partly determined by the discourses of culture and power (the macrodynamics of the speaking subject).

Tolkien's work offers fertile ground for interpretations concerned with such foci: on the one hand, through the constantly reflected textuality of his fiction, he is very sensitively foregrounding exactly the discourses of culture that the macrodynamics of the subject is interested in, and on the other hand in his stress on central characters as primarily users of the past (of past stories, texts, or traditions) he highlights the subject's embeddedness in these discourses. The microdynamics of the subject are also involved, since Tolkien's use of the concepts of language, body, identity/self, power, and desire are all aspects of such investigations and comment on the internal processes of the subject's production of meaning.

The individual subject's internal processes are perhaps best seen in the character of Gollum, where Tolkien consistently uses language, body, and power to problematize the effect of evil domination on the subject: as a result of Sauron's crude discourse of power, Gollum is stripped of his interpretive choices, and thus of the ability to produce meaning. Identity is seen as an aspect of the subject's ability to produce his/her own meanings. Sauron's power is figured (with the help of mythological parallels) in terms very similar to Foucault's model of the Panopticon (Chance, 20–25), a "technology of power" that is built on the constant visibility of the subjects, and the One Ring appears as Tolkien's ingenious device to bring to the center the concepts of desire and lack as constitutive aspects of the subject.

The discourses of culture and the ways these affect subjects in that culture are treated with considerable sophistication by Tolkien's emphasis on the textuality of his creation, the fact that whatever is written about the fictitious world and its history is usually supposed to be a text in that very fictitious world. This way, instead of producing simple unreflected fiction, Tolkien assigns representation its proper place, since every story that is told is determined by a number of elements such as its author, provenance, function, and use. For example, the theological explanation of the world in the "Ainulindalë" does not show an uncritical stance of mythological or religious discourse; on the contrary, Tolkien problematizes with it the status of such a mode of writing, pointing attention to its culturally determined nature (as with other modes of writing: history, poetry; and textual activities: translation, selection, adaptation).

These discourses and the individual subject's meaning producing activities are further connected in Tolkien's sensitive depiction of how individuals relate to these discourses and stories: the ways the subject sees itself in relation to the past is always presented as specific of culture and individual, and the question of identity is thus effectively tied also to the uses of cultural traditions. These attitudes can manifest in textual activities (like Bilbo's work on *The Silmarillion*) or be integrated into the story, and determine actual actions of the subject (like Frodo's and Sam's relating to the story of Beren and Lúthien).

GERGELY NAGY

Further Reading

Chance, Jane. *The Lord of the Rings: The Mythology of Power*. Rev. ed., Lexington, KY: University Press of Kentucky, 2001.
Curry, Patrick. *Defending Middle-earth: Tolkien, Myth, and Modernity*. London: HarperCollins, 1998.
Silverman, Kaja. *The Subject of Semiotics*. Oxford: Oxford University Press, 1984.

See also **Authorship; Gollum; The One Ring; Power in Tolkien's works; Sauron; *Silmarillion, The*; Textuality**

SUFFIELD FAMILY

Tolkien's mother, Mabel, was the second daughter of Emily Sparrow and John Suffield (Burns, personal correspondence with author). Tolkien lived with the Suffields for a time as a child after his father died (Carpenter, 18). He attributed his "tastes, talents and upbringing" to the Suffields, whose roots in the West Midlands contributed to his deep attachment to this region (*Letters*, 54).

The Suffields' trade was platemaking and engraving and Tolkien's calligraphy talents are considered an inherited trait (Garth, 13). Originally from Evesham in Worcestershire, they moved to Birmingham in the early 1800s and later to Edgbaston and Moseley. From 1812, Tolkien's great, great, great uncle William owned a Birmingham book and stationery shop. Converted to a drapery business by his brother, John Sr., in 1826, it operated until an 1886 redevelopment plan demolished the shop (Burns, personal correspondence).

Tolkien was named after Mabel's father, John Suffield (1833–1930.) He attended the Methodist College, worked in sales, and was a member of Birmingham's Central Literary Association. (Burns, personal correspondence). A strong, anti-Catholic Unitarian, he disowned Mabel when she converted to Catholicism; Tolkien felt this made her a "martyr," deepening both his own faith and the sense of loss in his life (Carpenter, 34).

Other significant Suffields include his mother's sisters, Jane (Neave), the owner of the "Bag End" farm (Carpenter, 197), and Edith May (Incledon), another Catholic convert (Pearce, 16).

Tolkien's dual Suffield and Tolkien heritage is seen to contribute to his inner conflict between academic and fictional pursuits and to "double-sided" characters like Bilbo and Gollum (Moseley, 58); John Suffield, Mabel, and her sisters have also been compared to "the old Took and his three remarkable daughters" (Carpenter, 196).

PATRICIA TUBBS

Further Reading

Burns, Margaret E. E-mail correspondence with author. Birmingham Central Library, September 15, 2000. Sources for her research include:
1851 census, Warwickshire, England
1881 census, Worcestershire, England
Birmingham Post-Office Directory, commercial and court sections, various dates
Kelly's Directory of Birmingham, commercial and court sections, various dates
Central Literary Magazine 1887–88
Birmingham Weekly Post, September 1928
Carpenter, Humphrey. *Tolkien, A Biography*. New York: Ballantine Books, 1977.
Garth, John. *Tolkien and the Great War*. Boston, MA: Houghton Mifflin, 2003.
Moseley, Charles. *J.R.R. Tolkien*. Plymouth: Northcote House, 1997.
Pearce, Joseph. *Tolkien: Man and Myth*. San Francisco: Ignatius Press, 1998.
Tolkien, J.R.R., and Priscilla Tolkien. *The Tolkien Family Album*. Boston, MA: Houghton Mifflin, 1992.

See also **Bilbo; Catholicism, Roman; Childhood of Tolkien; Death; Doubles; Family Background; Gollum; Neave, Jane; Sacrifice; Tolkien, Mabel**

SUICIDE

Some cultures (such as classical Roman or Japanese) have seen the taking of one's own life as honorable in certain circumstances, but in the Christian West it has traditionally been viewed as an act of despair that bars one from salvation. When Gandalf seeks to dissuade Denethor from killing himself and his own son, his argument is the thoroughly Christian one that the steward does not have authority to order the hour of his own death, and he speaks disparagingly of "heathen kings" in the past, under the domination of the Dark Power, slaying themselves in pride and despair (*RK*, V, vii, 853). Any good Catholic of Tolkien's generation might have argued the same.

Suicides are rare in Tolkien's fiction. There are instances where characters sacrifice themselves to save others, and Aragorn eventually orders the hour of his own death (but, unlike Denethor, he does have the authority to do so), but such actions are not suicidal by most standards, including Christian. Túrin tries to take his own life while deranged after finding he has accidentally killed his best friend Beleg but is forestalled by his companion (called varioiusly Flinding or Gwindor) and restored to some semblance of mental health by the waters of Eithel Ivrin (hallowed by the godlike power of Ulmo). Such an averted suicide would seem a proper deed in a Christian context. When Túrin's sister Nienor drowns herself in the horror of discovering that she has married her own brother and is pregnant with a child of incest, the action is all the worse by Christian standards because she has also killed her unborn child. Túrin, overwhelmed by all the innocent blood he has unwittingly shed and the evil fate that has dogged his family, finally does take his own life, falling on the cursed sword he has used to kill others. These suicides were in Tolkien's source in *The Kalevala*, and he depicts their horror very movingly. But, for a Christian, death is not the end, and Tolkien has Túrin and Nienor redeemed at the end of the world (*Lost Tales II*, 115–16).

In this he is in tune with recent Christian thought. The 1994 *Catechism of the Catholic Church* notes that grave psychological disturbances diminish the responsibility of one committing suicide and that God can provide opportunities for salutary repentance even after death. In Denethor's case, he had wrestled with Sauron's mind in the palantír and so had indeed been under the domination of the Dark Power, in addition to having grave psychological disturbances to endure (with one son dead, another near death, and his city facing destruction; *RK*, V, vii, 856–57). So a Christian like Tolkien need not entirely despair even of a character like Denethor.

RICHARD C. WEST

Further Reading

Catechism of the Catholic Church. Mahwah, NJ: Paulist Press, 1994.

See also **Aragorn; Denethor; Despair (Wanhope); Finnish Literature;** *Kalevala*; **Kullervo;** *Lays of Beleriand*; **Palantíri; Sauron; Túrin**

SWEDEN: RECEPTION OF TOLKIEN

Hompen, the first Swedish translation of *The Hobbit*, by Tore Zetterholm in 1947, was the first Swedish publication of a work by Tolkien. It seems not to have been reprinted, and it was another publishing house that engaged Åke Ohlmarks to translate *The Lord of the Rings*. His translation (excluding most of the appendices) appeared in 1959–61, only the Dutch one being earlier. It was called *Härskarringen*, but the first volume's title, *Sagan om Ringen*, came to be very often used for the entire work.

Tolkien had been annoyed by Zetterholm's turning of *hobbit* into *hompe*. With Ohlmarks, he was annoyed, not only by the sometimes unsatisfactory translation, but also by the translator's attitude in correspondence, and most by the description of himself in the introduction to the first volume. "*Who's Who* is not a safe source. . . . From it Ohlmarks has woven a ridiculous fantasy," Tolkien saw (*Letters*, 305). Swedish critics, however, mainly praised the work.

The success was enough to encourage a translation, also by Ohlmarks, of *Farmer Giles of Ham* in 1961 (*Gillis Bonde från Ham*), and a new translation of *The Hobbit* by Britt G. Hallqvist in 1962 (*Bilbo: En hobbits äventyr*). In the late 1960s a paperback edition brought *Härskarringen* to a wide readership; over the years the work has sold approximately two million copies. In the following decades many more of Tolkien's works were translated into Swedish:

Ringens värld (the appendices to *The Lord of the Rings*), 1971, Åke Ohlmarks
Tom Bombadills äventyr (*The Adventures of Tom Bombadil*), 1972, Åke Ohlmarks
Träd och Blad (*Tree and Leaf*), 1972, Åke Ohlmarks
Sagan om Smeden och stjärnan (*Smith of Wootton Major*), 1972, Britt G. Hallqvist
Om Beowulfsagan (*Beowulf, the Monsters and the Critics*; "Prefatory Remarks to a Prose Translation of Beowulf"; "English and Welsh"), 1975, Åke Ohlmarks
Tengwar och Cirth (App. E II to *The Lord of the Rings*, which was not included in *Ringens värld*), circa 1975 (rev. ed. 1991), the Mellonath Daeron [mostly Björn Fromén]
Breven från Jultomten (*Father Christmas Letters*), 1976, Åke Ohlmarks
Silmarillion (*The Silmarillion*), 1979, Roland Adlerberth
"Beorhtnoths hemkomst" ("The Homecoming of Beorhtnoth, Beorhthelm's Son"), 1980, Åke Ohlmarks (appended, along with *Tom Bombadills äventyr* and *Träd och Blad*, to an edition of *Ringens värld*)
Sagor från Midgård (*Unfinished Tales*), 1982, Roland Adlerberth
Herr Salig (*Mr. Bliss*), 1983, Roland Adlerberth
De förlorade sagornas bok (*The Book of Lost Tales*), vol. 1, 1986, and vol., 2 1988, Roland Adlerberth

The Tolkien Society of Sweden that was founded in 1968 was the earliest in Europe. It is now defunct, but the Forodrim Tolkien Society (from 1972) and Midgårds Fylking (from 1973) have been continuously active, and there are also a couple of younger societies. Generally, Swedish Tolkien societies are observant of "Middle-earthly" manners as to dress, naming, and so on. The Forodrim has its own ancient-style legal system, with a Grand Council ruling 'in the absence of the King' and awarding distinctions to the merited. Midgårds Fylking is a secret society.

At the same time, the large majority of Swedish Tolkien fans are not organized; some join dedicated fora and discussion groups on the Web. There have been a few academic papers on Tolkien. The present writer has edited several volumes of *Arda*, an annual for Tolkien studies and reviews (in Scandinavian languages and English).

Organized or not, many fans would read the original texts, and over the years awareness of the deficiencies of Ohlmarks' versions grew. In 2004–5 a new translation of *The Lord of the Rings* was published, named *Ringarnas herre*, by Erik Andersson (prose) and Lotta Olsson (verse) [also Gustav Dahlander (index)].

BEREGOND, ANDERS STENSTRÖM

Further Reading

Beregond, Anders Stenström. "Tolkien in Swedish Translation: From *Hompen* to *Ringarnas herre*." In *Translating Tolkien: Text and Film*, edited Thomas Honegger, 115–24. Zürich and Berne: Walking Tree Publishers, 2004.

See also **Fandom; Swedish Language**

SWEDISH LANGUAGE

Swedish is a Scandinavian language, which Tolkien must have encountered when he studied Old Norse as a special subject. Working for *The New* (or *Oxford*) *English Dictionary* (OED), in which Scandinavian cognates are routinely cited in etymologies of Germanic English words, Tolkien cited Swedish forms in well over a dozen entries. For such purposes words pass from one dictionary or philologist to another; s.v. Waggle nonstandard *vakla*, instead of *vackla*, betrays such secondhand usage.

For Scandinavian relations in *A Middle English Vocabulary* Tolkien mainly cited ON forms, but saw occasion to adduce three "OSwed.," two "Swed.," and one "OEastScand." (entries Gif(fe), Gyf(fe); Harwen; Hauer-cake; Scere; Trow(e); Waille). Again, there is evidence of unfamiliarity. The ME verb *harwen* is compared to "OSwed. *harva*, a harrow," rather than to the more apposite homonym *harva* 'to harrow'. Under Waille a supposed ON *veila* is mistakenly repeated as Swedish, presumably in place of the "Sw.dial. *väla*" cited under Wail in the OED (not one of Tolkien's entries).

In the following few years, Tolkien's grip of Swedish appears to have grown surer. E.V. Gordon, his colleague in Leeds, was especially interested in Scandinavian matters. Among the songs they shared with their students (eventually *Songs for the Philologists*) is the common Swedish "Gubben Noach" (two stanzas of Carl Michael Bellman's text, and three from an Icelandic rendering by Eirikur Björnsson). Their edition of *Sir Gawain and the Green Knight* contains a glossary by Tolkien, twice citing "Swed. dial." and once "Swed."; a "Scand.dials." is also pertinent (entries donkande; knaged; lurk(k)e; norne, nurne). The forms are aptly chosen and glossed. In *A Middle English Vocabulary* the etymology of *donkeþ* "moistens" said "Unknown"; here *donkande* "moistening" is compared to "Swed.dial. *dänka*."

In 1957 Tolkien received a letter in Swedish from Åke Ohlmarks, who was translating *The Lord of the Rings*. Commenting to Rayner Unwin, Tolkien notes his own "inadequate knowledge of Swedish," and his poor dictionary; but his reading seems accurate. Later, in an otherwise just criticism of the translation's introduction, he wrongly concluded that Ohlmarks

had misread "leathery soles" as "feathery soles." His dictionary doubtlessly lacked *trampdyna*: not a stuffed cushion but a "pad (part of a (usually animal) foot)." A month afterwards Tolkien had translated that text into English; published excerpts show an adequate understanding of vocabulary, grammar, and usage (*Letters*, 263, 304–7).

There is little evidence of Tolkien reading books in Swedish, but he did refer to *Det svenska rikets uppkomst* by Birger Nerman when lecturing on *Beowulf*. He submitted the first Swedish version of *The Hobbit* (1947) to an expert, but also himself examined the text (*Letters*, 188). "Guide to the Names in *The Lord of the Rings*" gives some attention to the Swedish and Dutch translations. In its opening Tolkien disclaims "any competence" in Scandinavian languages "beyond an interest in their early history." In general he deals sure-handedly enough with the Swedish material, knowing rare words like *vång* (though an obscurer *mård* defeats him). But he erred in thinking etymological translation does not work with *Greyhame (Gråhamn), and would work with Snowbourn (Snöbrunn)*.

The entry *Shire* reveals that Westron *Sûza* was inspired by ON *sýsla*. "The Shire" is *Sûzat*, with a definite ending rather than an article (see *The Peoples of Middle-earth*): a Scandinavian feature.

BEREGOND, ANDERS STENSTRÖM

Further Reading

Gilliver, Peter M. "At the Wordface: J.R.R. Tolkien's Work on the *Oxford English Dictionary*." In *Proceedings of the J.R.R. Tolkien Centenary Conference 1992*, edited by Patricia Reynolds and Glen GoodKnight, 173–86. Milton Keynes and Altadena: Tolkien Society and Mythopoeic Press, 1995.

See also **Danish Language; *A Middle English Vocabulary*; Norwegian Language; Old Norse Language**

SYMBOLISM IN TOLKIEN'S WORKS

A symbol is an image that has a meaning, or expressive force, beyond its literal sense. Two examples from Tolkien's fiction would be the symbol of a lidless Eye, used by Sauron to represent himself on the livery of his Orcs, and the symbol of an anvil and hammer surmounted by a crown with seven stars, used by Celebrimbor on the West-door of Moria to represent the sovereignty of the Dwarf-Lord Durin. A rather different example would be the ceremony of facing West before a meal, undertaken by Faramir's company: this symbolizes their reverence for the lost Númenor and for the Valar.

These examples show that the inhabitants of Middle-earth use symbolism in much the same ways as human beings in the real world. They do not, however, show that Tolkien as a writer used symbolism, in the sense that his images and narratives need to be construed in some nonliteral way if we are to understand them properly. If we are tempted to think, for example, that the facing West ceremony symbolizes (Christian) prayer, we need to remember that in the imagined world, the immortal realms of the far West actually materially exist. The fiction contains internally a sufficient explanation of its own elements.

Tolkien expressed in the foreword to *The Lord of the Ring*s a special dislike of allegory, the most systematic exploitation of symbolism, in which the main elements of a narrative collectively encode a "hidden" meaning. His objection was that allegory seeks the "domination" of the author, curtailing the reader's freedom (*FR*, Foreword, 7). Nevertheless, commentators have detected coded meanings in certain works. Tom Shippey and Verlyn Flieger have found allegory (of different kinds) in *Smith of Wootton Major*. "Leaf by Niggle" is unquestionably allegorical: it makes little sense unless Niggle's unwelcome journey is understood to symbolize death, the "Workhouse Infirmary" Purgatory, and so on. And in the cosmogonic images of *The Silmarillion*, such as the Music of the Ainur or the Light of the Two Trees, the literal and the symbolic can hardly be distinguished.

Medieval conceptions of symbolism with which Tolkien was closely familiar allowed for the superimposition of multiple significances upon a literal meaning. So, in *Pearl*, for example, which Tolkien studied and translated, the lost pearl of the poet's dream signifies his dead daughter, whom he imagines in heaven, and, more abstractly, the lost purity of his (or the human) soul, which requires redemption. It is up to each reader to recapture these significances and to judge their importance in the poem. The modernist idea of the poetic symbol as the unique formula for an otherwise indescribable emotion, rather than as the bearer of a definite encoded meaning, assigns still more autonomy to the reader's response. Tolkien was not sympathetic to modernism, but in his reluctance to constrain the reader through symbolizing codes he is, for once, in harmony with it.

We should be cautious, therefore, about symbolic interpretation of Tolkien's works. While, for example, Frodo's bearing the Ring into Mordor may be thought somewhat to resemble Christ carrying the Cross, the correspondences cannot be pressed very far without straining the sense of the text. Nor can the reductive claims—usually made with hostile intent—that details of Tolkien's invention simply "are" coded versions of real world phenomena (the Orcs "are" the working class, the Nazgûl "are" Nazis, etc.).

When, at the end of *The Lord of the Rings*, Frodo leaves his friends and sails into the West, many readers will feel that this departure symbolizes death. Numerous details of the surrounding narrative encourage such a reading. The sea is a natural symbol of eternity. The journey to the Havens, and the actual parting, take place in the evening. The walking song of Bilbo and Frodo, sung by the latter for the final time, now alludes mysteriously to "the hidden paths that run / West of the moon, East of the Sun" and prepares for Frodo's glimpse of paradisal "white shores' as his journey draws to a close" (*RK*, VI, ix, 308, 310). Yet it is left to the reader to intuit these significances and, in contrast to "Leaf by Niggle," the narrative makes complete sense without them: the supreme intensity and poignancy of this episode is grounded in a literal and comprehensive evocation of time and place.

BRIAN ROSEBURY

Further Reading

Flieger, Verlyn. *Splintered Light: Logos and Language in Tolkien's World*. Rev. ed. Kent, OH: Kent State University Press, 2002.

Pearce, Joseph. *Tolkien: Man and Myth*. London: HarperCollins, 1999.

Shippey. Tom. *J.R.R. Tolkien: Author of the Century*. London: HarperCollins, 2000.

Tolkien, J.R.R. *Smith of Wootton Major*. Edited by Verlyn Flieger. London: HarperCollins 2005.

———. "Leaf by Niggle." In *TL*, 75–95.

See also **Allegory; Arthurian Literature; Bible; Christian Readings of Tolkien; Dante; Darkness; Dreams; Heaven; Hell; Jungian Theory;** *Lembas*; **Light; Romances, Middle English and French; One Ring, The; Paradise; Silmarils; Spenser, Edmund**

T

TANIQUETIL

The highest peak of the Pelóri—the defensive mountain range the Valar raised on the eastern margins of Aman—Taniquetil is therefore the preternaturally highest mountain in all of Arda. Manwë and Varda dwell there in the Halls of Ilmarin, where it is said: "When Manwë there ascends his throne and looks forth, if Varda is beside him, he sees further than all other eyes, through mist, and through darkness, and over the leagues of the sea. And if Manwë is with her, Varda hears more clearly than all other ears the sound of voices that cry from east to west, from the hills and the valleys, and from the dark places that Melkor has made upon Earth" (*S*, 26).

But Taniquetil is more than a mere geographical curiosity of Valinor. Called "the Holy Mountain," Taniquetil embodies the reverence of the Valar and echoes the quasi-omniscience of Manwë and Varda, providing a preeminent vantage point for observing the travails of Middle-earth. And in a sense, Taniquetil pillars Arda up toward the ultimate reverence of Ilúvatar. The Holy Mountain is, in fact, a common mythological topos. In Norse legend, for example, Odin dwelt in his halls atop Hliðskjálf, while the Greek Pantheon held court at Olympos. Further examples abound—Apollo's Parnassos; Christianity and Judaism's Zion, Ararat, and especially Sinai; Meru, sacred to Buddhists, Hindus, and Jains.

In the context of Tolkien's own myth-making, Taniquetil makes a very early appearance in the 1915 poem, "The Shores of Faery," where "West of the Moon, East of the Sun / There stands a lonely Hill / Its feet are in the pale green Sea; / Its towers are white and still: / Beyond Taníquetil [*sic*] / In Valinor." Other nascent elements, such as the Two Trees, that would come to be fleshed out in *The Silmarillion*, also feature in the poem. Some years later, Taniquetil appears again in the 1926 "Sketch of the Mythology," where it is also given the Old English form, Timbrenting. Then in 1928, Tolkien captured the Holy Mountain in the breathtaking watercolor "Halls of Manwë on the Mountains of the World Above Faery." The painting depicts Taniquetil rising from the shores of Aman, the Sun and Moon on opposite shoulders (visually echoing the 1915 verse "West of the Moon, East of the Sun"), the rarified airs described in the *Ambarkanta* plainly delineated, and a Telerin sailing vessel in the foreground. At its summit, the hallowed halls of Manwë and Varda glimmer in the darkness among the stars.

The name Taniquetil derives from the Quenya roots *TĀ*- "lofty" + *NIK-W*- "whiteness as of snow" + *TIL*- "point, horn," thus giving us "*Taniqetil(de)* = High White Horn." Among its many other names, we have the Quenya Oiolossë, "Everwhite;" the Sindarin Amon Uiolos, with the same meaning; the Hill of Ilmarin (Quenya, "Mansion of the High Airs"); and Elerrína, also Quenya, signifying "Star-crowned."

It's also worth a passing mention that, although Taniquetil features most notably in the *Valaquenta* and early *Quenta Silmarillion*—even being named in the terrible Oath of Fëanor—it echoes on in later tales and in lesser forms. Indeed, as one travels east, one encounters a series of diminishing afterimages of

Taniquetil: Númenor's Meneltarma, Mount Taras (where Ulmo appeared to Tuor), Elostirion in the Tower Hills, Mount Mindolluin (where Aragorn would discover the scion of the White Tree)—even in direct reference in Galadriel's lament in Lothlórien. And finally, one might even suggest that the Tower of Barad-dûr stands in the furthest east as an obscene mockery of Taniquetil in the Uttermost West.

JASON FISHER

Further Reading

Burns, Marjorie. "Gandalf and Odin." In *Tolkien's Legendarium*, edited by Verlyn Flieger and Carl F. Hostetter, 219–32. Westport, CT: Greenwood, 2000.

Carpenter, Humphrey. *J.R.R. Tolkien: A Biography.* London: Allen & Unwin, 1977.

Flieger, Verlyn. *Splintered Light: Logos and Language in Tolkien's World.* 2nd ed., rev. and expanded. Kent, OH: Kent State University Press, 2002.

Hammond, Wayne G., and Christina Scull. *J.R.R. Tolkien: Artist & Illustrator.* London: HarperCollins, 1995.

Helms, Randel. *Tolkien and the Silmarils.* Boston, MA: Houghton Mifflin, 1981.

Scull, Christina. "The Development of Tolkien's *Legendarium*: Some Threads in the Tapestry of Middle-earth." In *Tolkien's Legendarium*, edited by Verlyn Flieger and Carl F. Hostetter, 7–18. Westport, CT: Greenwood, 2000.

Tolkien, J.R.R. *Pictures by J.R.R. Tolkien.* Foreword and Notes by Christopher Tolkien. London: Allen & Unwin, 1979.

See also **Art and Illustrations by Tolkien; Bible; Eru; Greek Gods; Heaven; Mountains; Mythology, Germanic; Old Norse Literature; Paradise; Symbolism in Tolkien's Works; Towers; Valar; Valinor**

TAVROBEL (OR TATHROBEL)

In *Interrupted Music*, Verlyn Flieger discusses Tolkien's efforts to find a "frame-narrative" in which to place his mythology of Middle-earth. That story-within-a-story was to provide a way for events in his invented history to become oral tales that were written down and preserved. Tolkien invoked a similar device in first paragraph of his "Prologue" to *The Lord of the Rings,* where he claims that that book and *The Hobbit* were derived from the Red Book of Westmarch.

Tavrobel plays a similar role to Westmarch in Tolkien's earliest attempt to create a frame-narrative for tales that he was working on in 1916–17. Although never completed, they influenced *The Silmarillion* and would later be edited and published by his son Christopher in *The Book of Lost Tales.* On page 292

of the second volume, Christopher Tolkien attempts a "coherent narrative:"

Coming to Tol Eressëa, an island located where England now lies, Eriol (also known as Ælfwine) lives in the Cottage of the Lost Play in Kortirion and listens to tales of Middle-earth history. He then travels to Tavrobel (sometimes spelled Tathrobel), a village on that same island, to stay with Gilfanon. In "The Tale of the Sun and Moon" (*Lost Tales I*, ch. VIII), Gilfanon describes his village as the "fairest of all the isle." There is also praise for the "guestkindliness" of Gilfanon at his House of a Hundred Chimneys, so it is an ideal place for a writer such as Eriol to stay. There he writes down tales that become the Golden Book.

There's an intriguing link between Tavrobel and Great Haywood, a Staffordshire village near which Tolkien received his military training between August 1915 and June 1916, when he went to France. His wife would live in Great Haywood after their marriage in March 1916. In the winter of 1916–17, Tolkien would stay with her at a cottage on the Teddesley Park Estate, recovering from trench fever and writing. Both villages have names connected with woods, and both have a bridge at the junction of two rivers. In *The Lost Road,* Christopher wrote that the bridge is the Essex Bridge, once used by packhorses, and the House of the Hundred Chimneys is possibly Shugborough Hall. A BBC article entitled "Tolkien's Staffordshire Past" (January 2003) reported that the Hall has eighty chimneys.

Although neither Tolkien nor his son Christopher seemed to have noticed the parallel, there are similarities between Gilfanon's home in Tavrobel and the post-Roman monasteries in Ireland and on islands between Ireland and Britain (such as Iona). Ancient books often survive in isolated communities where learning is kept alive far from wars and battles.

At the end of the "Appendix" to *The Lost Road,* Christopher mentions another Tavrobel, a "village of the Woodmen in Brethil." He speculates that this second use may be because his "father did not wish to finally abandon this old and deep association of his youth."

MICHAEL W. PERRY

Further Reading

Flieger, Verlyn. *Interrupted Music: The Making of Tolkien's Mythology.* Kent, OH: Kent State University Press, 2005.

See also **Frame Narratives; Mythology for England; Oral Tradition; Time Travel**

T.C.B.S. (TEA CLUB AND BARROVIAN SOCIETY)

A school clique that formed around Tolkien and encouraged his first mythological writings during the First World War, in which two members were killed, the T.C.B.S. had its origins in the friendship of Christopher Luke Wiseman and Tolkien when they played rugby for their house at King Edward's School, Birmingham; another friend, Vincent Trought (1892–1912), was also a de facto member. Witty and devoted to farce, the coterie also had an intellectual and cultural dimension: Wiseman was fascinated by science and music, Tolkien by philology, and Trought by the Romantics. With other friends, the clique wrested control of school cultural life from boys whom it saw as boorish.

In his final term, summer 1911, when Tolkien was school librarian, the group used the librarians' office to brew clandestine teas and eat smuggled treats, calling itself the Tea Club. Now perhaps eight-strong, it also met in the tea room of Barrow's department store, Birmingham, grandiosely naming itself the Barrovian Society. The designation "T.C., B.S., etc." was applied to members including Wilfrid Hugh Payton (1892–1965), his younger brother Ralph Stuart Payton (1894–1916), and Sidney Barrowclough (b. 1894) in an issue of the school *Chronicle* edited by Wiseman and Gilson. The T.C.B.S. lost a member when Vincent Trought died in January 1912, but by then Geoffrey Bache Smith had been enrolled.

At Oxford Tolkien formed new clubs, the Apolausticks and the Chequers, though neither proved a lasting substitute for the T.C.B.S., which meanwhile shifted its axis to Cambridge with Wiseman and Gilson as well as Thomas Kenneth Barnsley (1891–1917), Barrowclough, and the Paytons. The latter four "hangers-on" were blamed by Tolkien and Wiseman for reducing meetings to arenas of vapid wit and were ejected from the group shortly after the outbreak of international hostilities in late 1914.

For the remaining four, comprising also Smith and Gilson (who had both just enlisted in the army), the purpose of the T.C.B.S. became clear at a "Council of London," held at the Wiseman family home in Wandsworth on December 12, 1914. The society existed to nurture and amplify each member's creative powers, which should be used to restore various neglected values to a decadent and mechanized world——among them (as outlined by Tolkien) religious faith, human love, patriotic duty and the right to national self-rule. He felt the T.C.B.S. "had been granted some spark of fire—certainly as a body if not singly—that was destined to kindle a new light, or, what is the same thing, rekindle an old light in the world," and he likened the group to the Pre-Raphaelite Brotherhood. It would work through inspiration, rather than didacticism and confrontation. Each member hoped to make his own mark on the world (Smith through poetry, Gilson through the visual arts), but Tolkien seems to have been tacitly viewed as the guiding spirit of the group.

Tolkien credited the Council of London with an immediate opening-up of his creativity: he decided to become a poet, and soon produced his first poetry set in what later became Middle-earth, as well as an Elvish language, Qenya, to be spoken there. Along with Edith Bratt and Tolkien's former schoolteacher R.W. Reynolds, the T.C.B.S. became the first audience for his poetry, providing valuable criticism. They recognized their own influence in his work and believed that he was voicing a shared "TCBSian" vision.

After his own enlistment in the army, the four met one last time at a "Council of Lichfield" in October 1915, near his training camp. Around the turn of the year Smith and Gilson embarked for France, and Wiseman joined his battleship in Scotland. The TCBSian spirit was increasingly invoked to steel each to his duty—in defense of higher peacetime values—and to boost morale; it became an "oasis" during their travails, as Gilson put it. Facing a dangerous night patrol in No Man's Land in February 1916, Smith urged Tolkien to publish his work and declared, "I am a wild and whole-hearted admirer, and my chief consolation is, that if I am scuppered to-night . . . there will still be left a member of the great T.C.B.S. to voice what I dreamed and what we all agreed upon." Wiseman believed the group's divinely ordained purpose would ensure the survival of all its members.

The illusion was shattered on July 1, 1916 with the death of Gilson in the first assault of the Battle of the Somme. After Tolkien heard the news from Smith two weeks later, he was plunged into a crisis of faith in the greatness that had been expected of Gilson, and in the purpose of the T.C.B.S.: he declared the group finished. Angered, Smith defended Gilson and insisted that no individual death could dissolve the group; Wiseman agreed. Tolkien appears to have acquiesced, perhaps with relief, to the continuance of the fellowship.

Smith's death in December dealt a further blow. Wiseman visited for a "Council of Harrowgate" when Tolkien was convalescing in the Yorkshire town in April 1917, and the two corresponded in their habitual forthright manner. The two edited Smith's poetry for publication as *A Spring Harvest* (1918) and

Wiseman imagined them sharing a home in Oxford after the war. However, the deaths of Smith and Gilson perhaps overshadowed the T.C.B.S., and Wiseman lacked the innate sympathy for Tolkien's mythological project that might have made him a useful critic. Ultimately, C.S. Lewis took Wiseman's place, and the Inklings took the place of the T.C.B.S.

Although Wiseman had suggested that Edith Tolkien should be considered a member, the T.C.B.S. remained all-male: a fellowship of schoolboys, undergraduates, and then servicemen. Tolkien invoked its memory, tacitly, in his foreword to the second edition of *The Lord of the Rings* (1965), warning against assuming the Second World War was an influence on the book: "As the years go by it seems now often forgotten that to be caught in youth by 1914 was no less hideous an experience than to be involved in 1939 and the following years. By 1918 all but one of my close friends were dead."

Even at the end of his life, Tolkien signed his letters to Wiseman with the letters T.C.B.S.: a mark, perhaps, not of nostalgia, but of the enduring influence and impetus he had drawn from this youthful association.

JOHN GARTH

Further Reading

Carpenter, Humphrey. *J.R.R. Tolkien: A Biography*, Boston, MA: Houghton Mifflin, 1977.
Garth, John. *Tolkien and the Great War: The Threshold of Middle-earth*. London: Harper Collins, 2003.

See also **Gilson, Robert Quilter; Smith, Geoffrey Bache;** *A Spring Harvest***; Wiseman, Christopher; World War I**

TECHNOLOGICAL SUBCULTURES: RECEPTION OF TOLKIEN

The availability of *The Lord of the Rings* in paperback in 1965 increased the books' popularity on college and university campuses. Many of those discovering Tolkien were also discovering the mainframe computer and Tolkien's books proved particularly popular with scientists, engineers, and computer programmers. *The Lord of the Rings* proved so popular at the Stanford Artificial Intelligence Lab (SAIL) that the first printable fonts at SAIL were based on the Tengwar and Cirth characters Tolkien created for his Elvish languages. When Stanford required that rooms in the SAIL facility be numbered and named, the staff named each room after a place in Middle-earth and used the new fonts to create signs for each door.

These early "hackers," the term used for the extraordinarily proficient programmers, problem solvers, and engineers thriving in the mainframe environments of MIT in Cambridge, Massachusetts and SAIL at Stanford University in California, were often drawn to Tolkien's works because of the level of detail, particularly in terms of the languages, that Tolkien provided; indeed, these aspects of subcreation were often seen as qualities of the artificial worlds made possible by binary code and silicon memory systems, so much so that *The Lord of the Rings* entered hacker culture at the early stages, and flourishes there still. That Middle-earth was one of the inspirations for the nascent video game industry is well known. But Tolkien inspired terms of art have entered the hacker lexicon, or *The Jargon File*, as it is officially known. *Elder days* refers not only to Tolkien's First Age, before Morgoth was cast out (*RK*, "Appendix B") but to the early era of hackers at MIT and SAIL, and the ARPANET, the ancestor of the Internet. *Elvish* refers not only to Tolkien's invented languages, but to the Tolkien-derived fonts that most plotters, printers and mainframe operating systems supported as a sign of the early fascination of programmers, working on artificial binary languages, with Tolkien's artificial human languages, and the elegance they perceived in his character sets. While Tolkien used *Great Worm* to refer to Glaurung, the First of the dragons of Morgoth (*S*, 192, 332), to hackers the *Great Worm* is the destructive Internet worm Robert Tappan Morris released in 1988.

In 1985 Hugo Cornwall's *The Hacker's Handbook* advised would-be computer intruders, more properly known as "crackers" than hackers, to try passwords and IDs derived from Tolkien's works, as they were predictably common. To this day, password dictionaries routinely include names of people, places and things in Middle-earth, and password systems at universities routinely advise against using Tolkien's creations as password fodder because they are too popular to be secure. The mainframe hackers of MIT and SAIL passed on their admiration for Tolkien to the following generations, who have continued to draw inspiration and pay homage to Tolkien's creation in their own subcreations. Larry Wall, the creator of the Perl computer scripting language is not only given to frequently quoting Tolkien's works verbally, in the early versions of Perl, Wall embedded an appropriate quotation from *The Lord of the Rings* in the header of each Perl module. One Perl, module, designed to convert Middle-earth calendar dates, has made its way, in one form or another to most modern

Unix systems. On a Macintosh OS X system typing cat /usr/share/calendar/calendar.history | grep "LOTR" in any Terminal window will produce a list events from *The Hobbit* and *The Lord of the Ring* for a given date in the year. Similar commands work in various other flavors of Unix.

But Tolkien's popularity is not limited to hackers and engineers; it runs deeply and widely in academia. Between 1974 and 1990 twenty dorms were built at the University of California at Irvine and named after places in Middle-earth. A small asteroid discovered by M. Watt in 1982 is named "2675 Tolkien." Students, in a traditional MIT "hack" inspired by the December 2001 release of Peter Jackson's film *The Fellowship of the Ring* painted MIT's Great Dome with gold paint and the One Ring's inscription in red Tengwar characters.

LISA L. SPANGENBERG

Further Reading

Cornwall, Hugo [pseud. Peter Sommer]. *The Hacker's Handbook*. London: Century Communications, 1985.

Levy, Steven. *Hackers: Heroes of the Computer Revolution*. Garden City, N.Y.: Anchor Press/ Doubleday, 1984.

Peterson, T.F. *Nightwork: A History of Hacks and Pranks at MIT*. Cambridge, MA: MIT Press, 2003.

Raymond, Eric S. *The Art of Unix Programming*. Boston, MA: Addison-Wesley, 2004.

———. "The Jargon File, version 4.4.7." http://www.catb.org/~esr/jargon/ (May, 2005)

SAIL. "SAIL Farewell" http://www.db.stanford.edu/pub/voy/museum/pictures/AIlab/SailFarewell.html (May 2005)

University of California at Irvine Student Housing. "Middle-earth Residence Halls Description." http://www.housing.uci.edu/ug/ME/mehalldsp.htm#Me%20Res.%20Halls (May 2005)

See also **Gaming; Undersea Landscape: Features Named after Tolkien Characters**

TECHNOLOGY IN MIDDLE-EARTH

Technologies, comprising tools and techniques, are mentioned throughout Tolkien's work on Middle-earth. All manufactured objects, or natural ones put to artificial use, can be classed as technologies. Technologies used together may form complex, interdependent systems, such as ore-processing equipment at Isengard, urban architecture, such as Minas Tirith, or siege weaponry. Techniques include specific skills, such as picking mushrooms, or systematic sets of skills, such as farming.

Tolkien's descriptions of technology help to define the nature of each race in Middle-earth. Even as his choice of languages and lifestyles indicate Earthly prototypes for the races of Middle-earth, so do tools, architecture, and styles of warfare. Technologies became widespread in particular historical periods; referring to such objects invokes lifestyles and skills for the group that possesses them. All of Tolkien's races employ technology in some form, including those that are most in tune with their environments, the Elves and the Ents. Good and evil are distinguished by the way each uses technology, differing in ends, not means. Evil entities do not care about the impact their use of technology has upon their surroundings.

Hobbits use nineteenth-century technologies, including wastepaper baskets and wooden pipes, which were developed in the late eighteenth century. Bilbo's umbrella stand reflects the early eighteenth-century spread of umbrellas for rain protection in Western Europe. Bilbo possesses a mantel clock, the one instance of a mechanical timekeeping device explicitly described by Tolkien in Middle-earth. Bells are used elsewhere, including Rivendell and Gondor, to tell the time. The bells may or may not be mechanically regulated; the author does not say. The degree to which the hobbit community is a systematically-organized civic body is emphasized by the presence of a working postal service and the Michel Delving Museum. While hobbits possess some of the most recent technologies in Middle-earth, they are portrayed in a pastoral setting, cultivating fields, maintaining vegetable gardens, and milling grain. The mill is the source of the hobbits' flour, an important ingredient for their frequent meal schedule. When Saruman replaces the mill with a factory, the resulting structure fails to fulfill the same crucial purpose in the community.

Men employ a variety of crafts, but are neither magic-users nor industrialized. They live in fortified cities and rely on agricultural trades for their subsistence and income. Gondor cultivates extensive terraced fields, hops, orchards, and herds in the earthenwork-fortified Pelennor fields, while Rohan depends on grain and hay as its primary crops. Distinctly Medieval elements used by Men include the large wood-burning hearth in the center of the Golden Hall at Edoras. Central open hearths were generally replaced by chimneys and fireplaces during the fourteenth and fifteenth centuries.

The Elves are highly skilled in crafts, so much so that the goods they produce seem supernatural to other races, and are feared as magic. Their rope is seemingly obedient, their garden soil intensely fertile and their *lembas* nutrient-rich and long-lasting. They can build boats from metal and glass (*mithril* and Elven-glass) and capture the light of a star in a bottle.

It is unclear whether these results are achieved through craftsmanship or magic; to the Elves, there is no difference. Elvish crafts are unobtrusive and work harmoniously with their environments.

Dwarves have used up their best resources by the Third Age, but are still competent miners. Their forebears knew more about metalwork, including the working of the precious and versatile metal *mithril*. The Mines of Moria were overworked as the unique source of *mithril*, leading to the metal's substantially increased rarity and value. The subsequent Dwarvish decline reflects the perennial mining problem of overworking an inherited vein. In mining and building, the Dwarves continued to prosper, constructing paved roads and artificial waterways in Dale, and finishing the wall protecting the Pelennor fields.

Ents, named after legendary prehistoric stoneworking giants, craft bowls, jars, tables, and bed frames out of rock. Their skill in stone-working extends to stone-breaking in the destruction of Isengard. As tree-herds, herders of Huorns, they practice a craft described as more akin to sheep-herding than forestry.

While wizards often employ magic instead of tools, they seem to be the sole source of gunpowder production. Gandalf designs, builds, and sets off magically enhanced fireworks in elaborate displays. Bilbo's birthday party display is one of two possible instances of gunpowder use in Middle-earth; the Orcs use an unspecified flame-powered explosive device to blast a hole in the Deeping Wall in the Battle of Helm's Deep. The explosive is referred to as the "fire of Orthanc," implying that its source may be Saruman, another wizard. Gunpowder developed in China around the ninth century, and was imported into Western Europe as fireworks beginning in the late twelfth century. By the fifteenth century, when knowledge of saltpeter production became known to the West, gunpowder was increasingly employed for use in cannons and explosives.

The technological nature of Orcs is defined through their frequent associations with iron-working, although they are never clearly described as metal-workers. The Isengard furnaces produce cast iron, or possibly steel, which is used to make stronger and more flexible weaponry. Large-scale smelting of iron developed between the twelfth and fourteenth centuries. Ore processing scars the landscape through smoke, and the use of trees from Fangorn (possibly Huorns) as wood for fuel. Orkish involvement in the industrialization of Middle-earth helps labels the race as the enemy. Orkish architecture is built in stone, from small Orc-holds to large castles.

From the prehistoric Ents' hewn stone to the sophisticated Early Modern fireworks of the wizards, each race uses technologies that reflect their language and culture. The Hobbit gentleman-adventurers possess those quintessential nineteenth-century technologies, umbrellas and mantel-clocks, while the Anglo-Saxon culture of Rohan is embodied by the open hearth at Edoras. Through these tools, Tolkien helps his readers understand who the peoples of Middle-earth are.

SHANA WORTHEN

Further Reading

Crawford, Edward. *Some Light on Middle-earth. The Use of Scientific Techniques of Social Analysis to Reveal the Nature of the World of the Free Peoples.* Pinner, Middlesex, Tolkien Society, 1985.

Hood, Gwyneth. "Nature and Technology: Angelic and Sacrificial Strategies in Tolkien's The Lord of the Rings." *Mythlore* 19 (1993): 6–12.

Kranzberg, Melvin, and Carroll W. Pursell, Jr. *Technology in Western Civilization.* Oxford: Oxford University Press, 1967.

Pacey, Arnold. *Technology in World Civilization: A Thousand-Year History.* Boston, MA: MIT Press. 1991.

See also **Arms and Armor; Industrialization**

TELEVISION: U.S. COVERAGE

Tolkien often expressed his distaste for American culture. He particularly disliked the habits of so many Americans wantonly polluting and impoverishing their lands (*Letters*, 412). His feelings did not improve with the rise of *The Lord of the Rings's* fandom in the United States during the 1960s; Tolkien's name or slogans adopted from Tolkien permeated many aspects of American life, from graffiti to pins, folk songs to bumper stickers, poetry to fan fiction, fanzines to parody, criticism to books (Carpenter, 232–33). Tolkien's name on television in the United States, however, was not commonplace. Tolkien was not a man that sought fame or had much personal desire to appear in the public eye, nor did he take pleasure in giving interviews. In 1967 he refused to admit photographers into his study, stating in a letter to the reporters in question that he had better things to do with his valuable time then to sit and pose for pictures (*Letters*, 373). In his *Biography* of Tolkien, Carpenter discusses Tolkien's tendency to make some agreement as to an interview—mainly due to his Hobbitish good nature and inability to refuse a person immediately—only to abruptly retire, feigning prior engagement or other such business (*Biography*, 234). In a turnaround, Tolkien appeared in a BBC film in 1968: *Tolkien in Oxford*. Tolkien's distaste for being a cult icon in his own lifetime certainly lent to his virtual absence from American television.

In a letter written to his son in 1957, Tolkien amiably—albeit sarcastically—mentioned interest from the American audience for a film version of *The Lord of the Rings*. He also quoted what can be seen as a fated motto devised between himself and his British publisher Stanley Unwin: "Art or Cash" (*Letters*, 261). Tolkien viewed this notion as profitable either monetarily or by having the sole power to reject offensive or obnoxious suggestions. Unfortunately, none of Tolkien's letters concerning the sale of film rights to *The Lord of the Rings* or *The Hobbit* to United Artists in 1969 have hitherto been published. Tolkien's worst fears regarding the Zimmerman script proposed in 1958 were realized with the United States production of *The Hobbit* by Rankin-Bass studios in 1977. The Rankin-Bass *Hobbit* originally aired on US television. Ralph Bakshi followed suit in 1978 with *The Lord of the Rings*. When funding became unavailable for Bakshi to continue his version of *The Lord of the Rings*, Rankin-Bass picked up where Bakshi left off with their own interpretation of *The Return of the King* in 1980, which aired on American television.

Tolkien fans waited for two decades to have his name mentioned again on American airwaves. Once New Line Cinema released plans for a live-action interpretation of *The Lord of the Rings*, the media rush to get the scoop on film production was frenzied. Most of the media wars, however, took place not on American television, but via the Internet, and it was Jackson's name that was discussed, not Tolkien's. Prior to the release of the first installment of the Jackson films, American-based *TV Guide* produced a series of collectors' magazines featuring different *The Lord of the Rings* covers. *TV Guide* continued its marketing strategy for the next two film installments. The first of a series of hastily produced documentaries aired December 2001 on the Sci-Fi Channel: "A Passage to Middle-earth: The Making of *LotR*." The program aired repeatedly in prime time. Many of these documentaries lacked one important factor: a discussion of Tolkien, providing instead an insider's look into the making of the Jackson films. After the release of *The Lord of the Rings*, *The Lord of the Rings* became a staple in American entertainment television programs such as *Entertainment Tonight* with such television stories such as "The Hobbits Take Hollywood" (December 2002), "Hobbits Rule Hollywood" (December 2003), and "One 'Ring' To Rule Them All" (February 2004). In 2002 and 2003, National Geographic produced two documentaries, *Beyond the Movie—LotR: The Fellowship of the Ring* and *Beyond The Movie: LotR: The Return Of The King*. Both programs sought to link the blockbuster films to the man behind the creation: Tolkien. Rather than provide just another way for the public to see how the films were made, the National Geographic pieces explored what may have inspired Tolkien to write his tales of Middle-earth.

The popularity of the Jackson films, particularly airing on cable television in the United States, has contributed to the expansion of *The Lord of the Rings's* fan-base and continues to bring new generations of fans to Tolkien.

ANTHONY BURDGE and JESSICA BURKE

Further Reading

Carpenter, Humphrey. *J.R.R. Tolkien: A Biography*. Boston, MA: Houghton Mifflin, 2000.

See also **America in the 1960's: Reception of Tolkien; Bakshi, Ralph; Fandom; Film Scripts, Unused; Jackson, Peter; Rankin/Bass; Technological Subcultures: Reception of Tolkien**

TERTULLIAN

Tertullian, a church leader from the second century, asked "What has Athens to do with Jerusalem? What has the Academy to do with the Church?" This sentiment was later echoed by Alcuin in the seventh century when he asked Higbald, Bishop of Lindisfarne, "What has Ingeld to do with Christ?" Tolkien, in "The Monsters and the Critics," comments that Ingeld "the thrice faithless and easily persuaded is chiefly interesting as an episode in a larger theme, as part of a tradition that had acquired legendary, and so dramatically personalized, form concerning moving events in history" (16). Ingeld, Christ, Beowulf, Frodo are each the corner-stones in their stories and episodes, and each story builds upon other characters and a prior history leading up to the current tale they feature in. This statement echoes in the *Lord of the Rings*. While in the end it is Frodo and the destruction of the Ring that saves Middle-earth, each character, be it farmer or king, plays a small part in a much larger tale.

This dichotomy persists in the question "What does *Lord of the Rings* have to do with Christianity?" While *Lord of the Rings* contains many elements from Northern mythology such as Dwarves, Elves, and dragons, it has at its a heart several Christian themes and examples. One theme expressed through the trilogy is Christian mercy and pity, which is most clearly shown in the treatment of Gollum. Sam Gamgee clearly states that he and Frodo would be better off if they were to just kill Gollum. However, because of Frodo's pity he shows mercy to Gollum. Had he not, then Gollum could not have bitten off Frodo's finger, an act that resulted in the destruction of the One Ring and the salvation of Middle-earth.

Another example of the Christian themes in *The Lord of the Rings* is Gandalf's conversion into Gandalf the White. Gandalf the Grey descends into the depths of the Earth, defeats the Balrog and then returns as Gandalf the White. This descent and resurrection cycle is the same as Christ's Harrowing of Hell and resurrection. While the source of the Harrowing of Hell is apocryphal, it was well known in the Middle Ages.

Thus the themes of mercy and pity, as well as Gandalf's descent and return, answer the Tertullian question of "What has *The Lord of the Rings* to do with Christianity?"

JOHN WALSH

References and Further Reading

Hare, Kent G. "Christian Heroism and the West Saxon Achievement: The Old English Poetic Evidence." *Medieval Forum* 4 (2004).

TEXTUAL HISTORY: ERRORS AND EMENDATIONS

The publishing history of *The Lord of the Rings* is replete with examples of errors created during the printing process and emendations made by Tolkien as he revised his magnum opus since its publication in 1954, and indeed the revision process has continued long after the author's death. In 1993, Wayne G. Hammond and Douglas A. Anderson compiled an extensive list of typographical errors, printing or proofreading mistakes, and textual revisions in their book *J.R.R. Tolkien: A Descriptive Bibliography* (Hammond and Anderson), and other sources have uncovered additional errors and changes (see also Bratman; and Scull). The problems with the text arise in part from the conditions of the publishing and printing industries in the 1950s and subsequent decades, but the unfamiliarity of Tolkien's invented languages, landscapes, and peoples coupled with his habit of tinkering endlessly with details in his writing have added to the difficulties. A complete errata for *The Lord of the Rings* is beyond the scope of this article, but I will provide a timeline for the publication of the novel in its various forms along with an analysis of some of the most notable textual issues that have arisen both intentionally and accidentally

in different printings and editions. Hammond and Christina Scull cite the not entirely facetious remark of Tolkien's publisher Rayner Unwin that it will probably take three hundred years of emendation and correction to the text to achieve perfection (Hammond and Scull, xliv). Yet the many editorial efforts undertaken from the first Unwin & Allen edition in 1954 to the fiftieth anniversary edition have sought to bring the text as close to Tolkien's intentions as possible.

Tolkien struggled with the manuscript of *The Lord of the Rings* from 1937 through the 1940s and 1950s. George Unwin & Allen finally published his work after Tolkien briefly considered rival publisher Collins (a move that led to the writing of the often-reproduced letter no. 131 to the editor Milton Waldman), and Jarrold and Sons of Norwich did the printing. *The Fellowship of the Ring* appeared on July 29, 1954, *The Two Towers* on November 11, 1954, and *The Return of the King* on October 20, 1955. Tolkien fought with the proofreaders over his peculiar nomenclature as he wrote in an August 1954 letter: "Jarrold's appear to have a highly educated person as a chief proof-reader, and they started correcting my English without reference to me: *elfin* for *elven*; *farther* for *further*; *try to say* for *try and say* and so on" (*Letters,* 183). One dispute Tolkien won was over the use of the name "nastertians" instead of "nasturtiums" for the flowers in the garden of Bag End on page 33 of *FR*; sadly, however, the first printing of the Ballantine paperback nine years later quietly reinstated the offending "nasturtium." Mistakes in the Cirth inscriptions on the title page were changed for the first impression of *Return of the King* and subsequent impressions of *Fellowship of the Ring* and *Two Towers*. One printing error that collectors have long noted is the signature mark "4" and the sagging type in the first state of the first impression of *RK* (Hammond and Anderson, 86).

More problems and emendations followed in the subsequent impressions of the first Unwin edition. Jarrold and Sons did not keep the type of the first impression of *Fellowship of the Ring* standing and consequently had to reset the type for the second impression (December 1954), introducing approximately twenty new errors. The most notorious of these errors was the substitution of "bride-piece" for term "bride-price" in the discussion of the Silmaril that Thingol demanded of Beren for Lúthien's hand in marriage (*FR*, I, ix, 206). This error was not corrected for nearly two decades, leading Christopher Tolkien to speculate that this "most ancient and ineradicable" error "seems likely to become part of the English language in America to judge from the number of times it is quoted" (Hammond and Scull, 176). Tolkien himself introduced other changes in subsequent printings to clarify certain points in the story. In "The King of the Golden Hall" chapter of *Two Towers*, for example, he altered Gandalf's words to Wormtongue from "I have not passed through fire and flood to bandy crooked words with a serving-man" to "fire and death" with the third impression (*Two Towers*, III, iv, 118). As Tolkien commented in a letter, "Gandalf really 'died' and was changed," so his resurrection needed to be better emphasized (*Letters*, 201). Although "an index of names and strange words" was promised for the last volume, the 1958 index prepared by Nancy Smith was not included in the first edition in part to prevent cuts in the appendices (Hammond and Scull, 680–81).

The most substantial set of emendations to the text made by Tolkien appeared in 1965 as a result of the copyright controversy in the United States over the pirated Ace Books paperback edition. The first Houghton Mifflin editions of *The Lord of the Rings* were printed in Great Britain, and Ace Books, claiming that US copyright restrictions on imported books had been violated, published its own unauthorized paperback edition in the spring of 1965, leading what the press dubbed the "War over Middle-earth." Nancy Martsch has catalogued some of the typographical and copying errors in book 1 of this poorly edited version, including a number of "Americanisms" such as "around" for "round" or "drowned" for "drownded" (Martsch, 3). To secure American copyright protection and royalties, Tolkien undertook a number of revisions. This new version was first issued in late 1965 as the authorized Ballantine paperback edition; this edition then served as the basis for the hardcover revised edition that Unwin & Allen published in 1966 and the subsequent second edition Houghton Mifflin hardcover volumes.

Among the many changes and additions to the text were a new foreword, an expanded Prologue on hobbit customs, and Nancy Smith's index (although the 2005 impression of the Fiftieth Anniversary Edition substitutes a new, expanded index prepared by Hammond and Scull). Various revisions in the body of the text appeared in the various second edition paperback and hardcover volumes. Among these are changes to the geography between Weathertop and Rivendell that Christopher Tolkien has discussed in some detail (*Shadow*, 199–200), an altered account of what Gandalf knew about the *Palantír* that was first published in the second impression of the revised Allen & Unwin (see Hammond and Scull, 434–35), and expansions such as more on Merry's state of mind in "The Ride of the Rohirrim" and Gandalf's

dressing of Frodo in "The Field of Cormallen" (for an analysis of these and some other second edition additions, see J.S. Ryan). Tolkien continued to revise and correct various copies of the text, but not all of the changes were transferred into the various editions available in different countries. In the third printing of the Ballantine edition, for instance, Tolkien added Estella Bolger to the Brandybuck family tree as Meriadoc's wife, but that change never made it into the UK or US hardcover editions until 1987 (Hammond and Scull, 724).

Douglas Anderson's 2004 "Note on the Text" gives a concise summary of the printing history following Tolkien's death in 1973 up to the age of word processing that has simplified the task of hunting down errors. In 2004 the Fiftieth Anniversary Edition edited by Hammond and Scull was published by HarperCollins in the United Kingdom and Houghton Mifflin in the United States. They consulted with Christopher Tolkien and used an electronic version of the 2002 edition to produce as accurate a text as possible. The editors succeeded in correcting many long-standing errors such as the distance between Bucklebury Ferry and Brandywine Bridge, but for historical reasons they chose not to correct other inconsistencies such as the superseded version of Bilbo's Eärendil poem in "Many Meetings" or Gimli's declaration at Helm's Deep that he has not hewn anything but wood since Moria (Hammond and Scull, xliv; Hammond and Scull, xxi). Even that setting of the text has not been completely free of errors, though, for Hammond and Scull have had to fix several new mistakes produced by the editing software in a new 2005 printing of the Fiftieth Anniversary Edition.

Tolkien wrote to Joy Hill in October 1967 that he had by that time ceased to worry about small "discrepancies" he had introduced into the text; nevertheless, he qualified that statement in boldface: "*But errors in the text are another matter*" (quoted in Hammond and Scull, xix). The war Tolkien and his editors have waged to achieve a pristine text for *The Lord of the Rings* has truly been an arduous one, but the goal of perfection may ultimately be an impossible one given the vagaries of Tolkien's writing practices and the sheer length of the work.

DAVID D. OBERHELMAN

Further Reading

Anderson, Douglas A. "A Note on the Text." In *The Lord of the Rings* by J.R.R. Tolkien, xi–xvii. 50th Anniversary Edition. Boston, MA: Houghton Mifflin, 2004 [2005].

Bratman, David. "A Corrigenda to *The Lord of the Rings*." *Tolkien Collector* 6 (March 1994): 17–25.

Hammond, Wayne G., and Douglas A. Anderson. *J.R.R. Tolkien: A Descriptive Bibliography*. New Castle, DE: Oak Knoll Press, 1993.

Hammond, Wayne G., and Christina Scull. "Note on the 50th Anniversary Edition." In *The Lord of the Rings* by J.R.R. Tolkien. xviii–xxi. 50th Anniversary Edition. Boston, MA: Houghton Mifflin, 2004 [2005].

———. *The Lord of the Rings: A Reader's Companion*. London: HarperCollins, 2005.

Martsch, Nancy. "Differences between Houghton Mifflin/ Allen & Unwin and Ace Books Editions of *The Fellowship of the Ring*, Book I." *Beyond Bree* (August 2005): 1–7.

Scull, Christina. "A Preliminary Study of Variations in Editions of *The Lord of the Rings*." *Beyond Bree* (April 1985/August 1985).

See also **America in the 1960s: Reception of Tolkien; Family Trees;** *Lord of the Rings*: **Success of; Publishing History; Tolkien, Christopher**

TEXTUALITY

Notoriously difficult to define, textuality is a concept that has gained enormous importance in theories of literature and culture in the late twentieth century. The examination of the characteristics of representation in language and in conventional literary forms yields textuality as a specific form of cultural discourse, where representation is structured by the opportunities offered by the written text and its conventions (or the subversion of these) and characteristic features. In Tolkien, textuality means that the representation and creation of the fictitious world happens not only in writing (this is common in all literature), but the status of these texts is explicitly and doubly textual, and thus a layer of reflection is added to representation that characterizes Tolkien's relation to culture and its contents. Tolkien's texts are nearly always claimed to be texts inside his fictitious world as well, fictionalized *as texts* and largely about how texts and stories told in them are used by cultures and individuals (created by those very texts), Tolkien therefore represents and creates cultural processes and contents in terms of textual activities, by the device of various sorts of texts and their interrelations.

Tolkien's preoccupation with texts and what happens to (and in) them is clearly an influence of his profession, philology; as the philologist can only deal with older forms of language through texts that remain from those historical periods, Tolkien imagines his fictitious world and its events as parts and details of texts, and the whole as a necessarily textual complex, not merely a system of interrelated stories, but of texts standing in several relations to each other. Shippey brings the medieval manuscript culture's inevitable variance and diversity to bear on Tolkien's practices of creation (308–17), explaining that the depth that is sensed behind Tolkien's works (most notably *The Lord of the Rings*) is partly the result of the connection points any story or element of story brings into play, and the whole complex of variant stories has a meaning for the effect it has on the reader. Gergely Nagy and Verlyn Flieger argue further (based on relationships between Tolkien's variants and their claims, and Tolkien's argument in "On Fairy-Stories") that it is always the individual variant, 'the story as it is served up by its author or teller' (*MC,* 120, 47) of the story that criticism examines, that Tolkien's many variants and rewritings of his tales suggest a "philological space" where stories are connected to texts, and Tolkien's creation is in essence is the modeling of a fictitious complex of texts.

Tolkien's conception of a body of legend to be dedicated to England from the start involved the reference to storytelling in both its oral and its written form. Part of the Eriol/Ælfwine frame was the mediator figure's composing of a book or transcribing a book by a more authentic author (complete with colophon and defining of source); this finally (by default, in the lack of the final frame narrative) became the fiction of Bilbo Baggins collecting, selecting, and translating from Elvish the texts that make up (fictionally) the compendious *Silmarillion*. This frame is most convenient for the emphasis on textuality that Tolkien apparently wanted, since Bilbo's work, by its (real) philological background (the variants that actually lie behind the 1977 *Silmarillion* text) produces diversities and traces of the different textual activities that produce these texts: translation between languages or cultures, adaptation of poetry to prose, a mythological mode of writing to historical, or selection, exclusion or inclusion of other versions, variants or interpretations. The compendious text that gives the reader information about Tolkien's fictitious Middle-earth is seen as the result of not only the actual historical processes in that world, but also of emphatically writerly activities, and this (heavily metafictional) text functions as a context for *The Lord of the Rings* and *The Hobbit*, which also have their textual origin in the fiction (as Frodo's or Bilbo's texts). Tolkien's focus on the written text as the only appropriate medium in which the creation of a world can be performed leads to important theoretical considerations about the different discourses of culture (such as history, theology, economies, politics, etc.), observable in these texts, that shape a representation of any world. The insistence on texts as artifacts with Tolkien goes on even to his painstakingly constructing a few pages from the Book of Mazarbul, to be included in *The Lord of the Rings* (finally they were not).

GERGELY NAGY

Further Reading

Flieger, Verlyn. *Interrupted Music: The Making of Tolkien's Mythology.* Kent, OH, and London: Kent State University Press, 2005.

Nagy, Gergely. "The Great Chain of Reading: (Inter-)Textual Relations and the Technique of Mythopoesis in the Túrin story." In *Tolkien the Medievalist*, edited by Jane Chance, 239–58. New York and London: Routledge, 2002.

Noad, Charles. "On the Construction of 'The Silmarillion'." In *Tolkien's Legendarium: Essays on the History of Middle-earth*, edited by Verlyn Flieger and Carl F. Hostetter, 31–68. Westport, CT: Greenwood Press, 2000.

Shippey, Tom. *The Road to Middle-earth.* 3rd ed. Boston, MA: Houghton Mifflin, 2004.

Tolkien, J.R.R. "On Fairy-Stories." In *The Tolkien Reader*, 31–99. New York: Ballantine, 1966.

See also **Ælfwine; Authorship; Frame Narratives; *Silmarillion***

THEODEN

Lord of the Mark, First Marshal of the Mark and Seventeenth King of Rohan from 2984–3019. He was son of Thengel and Morwen of Lossarnach, and brother of Theodwyn, who was the mother of Éowyn and Éomer. Born in Gondor, the king returned to his place of birth to die, falling at the Battle of Pelennor Fields. He lay in state in Gondor before being borne back to Rohan to be laid to rest.

Theodon ascended the throne at the age of thirty-two after the death of his father, who ruled Rohan from 2953–80. Theoden thus ruled from 2980–3019, when he was succeeded by his nephew, Éomer. King Theoden's wife Elfhild died in childbirth, and he did not wed again. His only son, Theodred, was killed in the war against Saruman.

In the year 3014, Theoden began to take on the appearance of a man much older than his years. His health began to decline sharply (which was later understood to be due to the influence of his advisor, Gríma Wormtongue, an agent of Saruman). When Gandalf the White, Aragorn, Legolas, and Gimli arrived at the hall Meduseld, they were met with the sight of a man "so bent with age that he seemed almost a dwarf" (*TT*, III, vi, 116). After revealing Gríma's sorcery, Gandalf lifted the darkness from Theoden's eyes. He was henceforth referred to as "Theoden Ednew." He gathered his riders and traveled to meet his enemies at the battle of Helm's Deep, where the men of Rohan defeated Saruman's armies. Theoden then traveled to Isengard to confront Saruman before leading the men of Rohan to battle in Gondor in fulfillment of their ancient alliance.

Theoden fell at the Battle of the Pelennor Fields, crushed under his horse Snowmane. His niece Éowyn, with the help of Meriadoc the Halfling, slew the Lord of the Nazgûl, who had intended to finish Theoden off and, apparently, desecrate his body. Theoden passed the kingship to his nephew Éomer before dying.

The name "Theoden" relates to the Old English masculine noun, "Þeoden, es," which is defined by Bosworth as "the chief of a Þeod (a nation, people), a prince, a king." Cognates include Old Saxon "thiodan" and Icelandic "Þjoðann." His name as King, Theoden "Ednew," comes from the Old English ed-niowe, "To recover, renew."

Theoden may be contrasted with Denethor in his reaction to the overwhelming odds of Sauron's likely victory. Although he had despaired, he was renewed by Gandalf, and though he rode into battle without great hope of victory, he was victorious, and his attack saved the city of Minas Tirith from sack and destruction. The scene in which Theoden is healed by Gandalf ("The King of the Golden Hall") has often been taken as representative of an archetype of the winter king renewed. Certainly it is one of the great moments in *The Lord of the Rings* when Theoden brandishes his sword outside of Edoras and when he rallies the Rohirrim before their great charge into battle.

HILARY WYNNE

See also **Alliterative Verse by Tolkien; Éomer; Éowyn; Old English; Rohan; War**

THEOLOGICAL AND MORAL APPROACHES IN TOLKIEN'S WORKS

A discussion of theological and moral approaches in Tolkien's work should begin with the author's avowed distaste for intentional allegory, stated most famously in the foreword to the second edition of *The Lord of the Rings*. Though Tolkien wrote a conscious allegory in "The Monsters and the Critics," and there are allegorical implications in "Leaf by Niggle" and "Smith of Wooten Major", the effort to force an allegorical interpretation on most of Tolkien's work is likely to end in failure. Nonetheless there are important moral and theological implications stemming from Tolkien's Catholic Christianity in nearly all of his popular writings. In one personal letter, Tolkien wrote, "*The Lord of the Rings* is of course a fundamentally religious and Catholic work; unconsciously so at first, but consciously in the revision" (*Letters*, 172). In another he said, "I am a Christian (*which can be deduced from my stories*), and in fact a Roman Catholic" (*Letters*, 288, emphasis mine). And he also wrote that fantasy literature "*must* contain elements of moral and religious truth (or error)" (*Letters*, 144, emphasis mine). Thus, while Tolkien did not see his work as allegorical or religious, he did see it as morally applicable, theologically insightful, and deeply rooted in a Christian worldview.

Despite its various polytheistic influences, especially Norse, the legendarium is essentially a monotheistic mythology, where the Valar function as angelic beings under the authority of the creator Eru Ilúvatar. In *Morgoth's Ring*, there is a messianic prophecy of the incarnation of Ilúvatar within his creation as a final means of defeating the enemy Melkor. Many scholars have seen echoes of this in *The Lord of the Rings*, particularly in the ways that Gandalf, Aragorn, and Frodo collectively function as an image of Christ. This would make the theology of Middle-earth not only monotheistic, but specifically Christian.

That Tolkien's works have moral implications is widely accepted. It is his heroes' moral choices as well as their courage (rather than superhuman abilities) that define them as heroes—an idea seen most keenly in the choice of hobbits as primary heroes in *The Lord of the Rings*. Various statements from Gandalf, Galadriel, Aragorn, Faramir, and others suggest that it is more important to strive for moral virtue than for military victory—better to lose a battle than to win it by doing evil. Mark Eddy Smith identifies more than twenty moral virtues in *The Lord of the Rings,* including simplicity, generosity, hospitality, faith, sacrifice, wonder, trust, hope, submission, and courage. "Leaf by Niggle" and *Smith of Wootton Major* express the moral virtues of community, hard work, wonder, and self-sacrifice.

A less popular aspect of Tolkien's work is that these moral virtues are asserted to be not mere subjective preferences, or convenient social norms, but objective moral values that transcend any era, culture, or geographic location. This is made most clear in the words of Aragorn to Éomer when the two first meet: "Good and ill have not changed since yesteryear; nor are they one thing among Elves and Dwarves and another among Men" (*TT*, III, ii, 41). This objective morality has its basis in the author's theology. Moral law comes from God, and not from Man. Gandalf also points out numerous times that although no individuals can choose the time or place of his or her births, each must choose what to do with that time; everyone is responsible for the choices he or she makes. At the same time, Tolkien's works also communicate the Christian concept of grace: nobody is able fully to live up to God's moral law, so we must depend on God's grace for salvation. All of the efforts of the hero Frodo are insufficient; when he comes to the Crack of Doom he cannot destroy the Ring, and victory over evil is only accomplished by an act of grace. As explained in "On Fairy-Stories," one of the most important ways that fairy-tales reflect an underlying truth is in giving glimpses of the eucatastrophe of the Christian gospel.

Other important theological aspects of the legendarium include: that the universe was purposefully created and is not a byproduct of random chance, that the Creator remains actively at work within his creation, and that the Creator answers prayer. We see many of these ideas tied together in the presentation of the evil of the One Ring. Tolkien suggests in the legendarium that the greatest gift given by the creator Eru Ilúvatar to his children is the gift of moral freedom, represented as a kindling of the Imperishable Flame, and demonstrated through the possibility of heroism. The greatest moral evil is therefore to take away another's free will, which is central power of the Ring. T.A. Shippey points out that the ambiguous nature of the One Ring also provides a theological commentary on the nature of evil and on the Lord's Prayer (128ff.).

Specifics of Tolkien's Roman Catholicism can be seen in imagery of the Virgin Mary (especially Elbereth) and the Eucharist or Blessed Sacrament (Elven waybread). (See Birzer, 61–63.) Tolkien's Aristotelian and Thomist outlook can be seen in his emphasis on the orderliness of creation and the view of all creation having its source and purpose in the mind of God; the Ainur were the offspring of Ilúvatar's thought, and Eä, the creation, arose from the music or Theme of Ilúvatar (*S,* 15).

Tolkien's consistent moral and theological approach can be seen in many of his other works of fiction and nonfiction as well. The short story "Leaf by Niggle" conveys a message of moral responsibilities for one's actions in life, as well as a promise of an afterlife and a message of divine grace at work through a Christ-like Shepherd figure. "Smith of Wootton Major" also presents an eternal being from Faërie (the King of Faërie) who comes to live among humans as a figure of both grace and judgment. In "On Fairy-Stories," Tolkien puts forth a theological view of subcreation, and states that the truth of the Christian gospel of the incarnation as the source of all fairy stories. He believed that Christianity was the truth, or underlying reality of the universe, but that many non-Christian myths could acts as pointers back to reflections that truth.

MATTHEW DICKERSON

Further Reading

Birzer, Bradley. *J.R.R. Tolkien's, Sanctifying Myth: Understanding Middle-earth*. Wilmington, DE: ISI Books, 2002.

Dickerson, Matthew. *Following Gandalf: Epic Battles and Moral Victory in The Lord of the Rings*. Grand Rapids, MI: Brazos Press, 2003.

Flieger, Verlyn. *Splintered Light*. Logos and Languages in Tolkien's World. 2nd ed., Rev. and exp. Kent, OH: Kent State University Press, 2002.

Purtill, R. *J.R.R. Tolkien: Myth, Morality, and Religion*. San Francisco, CA: Harper & Row, 1984.

Smith, Mark Eddy. *Tolkien's Ordinary Virtues*. Downers Grove, IL: Inter Varsity Press, 2002.

Shippey, Tom. *J.R.R. Tolkien: Author of the Century*. London: Harper Collins, 2004.

Wood, Ralph. *The Gospel According to Tolkien. Visions of the Kingdom in Middle-earth*. Louisville, KY: John, Knox.

See also **Good and Evil; Heathenism and Paganism; Paradise; Satan and Lucifer;** *Tree and Leaf;* **Valar**

THEOLOGY IN *THE LORD OF THE RINGS*

According to biographer Humphrey Carpenter, Tolkien asserted that, "I dislike allegory wherever I smell it" (193). Nevertheless there is a decided element of allegory about *The Lord of the Rings*, not in the sense of portraying political events, but certainly in the sense of Christian parable.

The novel depicts the human condition and outlines the pilgrimage of the human soul in a fallen world. Christian theology, especially that as promulgated by the Roman Catholic Church, expresses the notion of the Edenic Fall of humankind in terms of 'original sin', a tendency to self-worship and to evil that humans inherit at conception. At baptism, this tendency is replaced by grace that in effect restores the soul to its essential integrity. To the Roman Catholic, the Christian life then depends upon the constant replenishing of sanctifying grace through the sacraments and offices of the church. Grace supplies the soul's refreshment and strength on its journey toward eternity through such symbolic forms as the sacrament of Communion, in which bread and wine are transformed into the Body and Blood of Christ, supplying spiritual food for the journey. *The Lord of the Rings* suggests this Catholic pilgrimage in its imagery and in its plot structure.

The title, the epigraph of the trilogy and the very first chapters are all concentrated on the notion of evil, although at first in the Shire it is confined to acts of pettiness and braggadocio, as in Lobelia Sackville-Baggins's theft of spoons and Bilbo's disappearing trick. As the plot progresses and sundry other evil characters materialize—from Ringwraiths and Orcs to Saruman and Shelob, and finally to the malevolent entity of Sauron himself—the sense of oppression is magnified.

What sets *The Lord of the Rings* apart from other fantasy works is that, whereas in conventional fantasy the hero's quest is usually to *gain* something, Frodo and his companions are on a quest to *lose* something. That the Ring can be seen as a representation of original sin is evident from the way it controls those who use it, tempting them to self-aggrandizement and to the misuse of power.

There are, additionally, images of the function of the church and the provision of sacramental grace. The spiritual food of bread and wine can be seen in the provision of the *miruvor*, the healing cordial of Imladris, and the *lembas*, the Elven way-bread, which strengthen and sustain the members of the fellowship—the pilgrims—in times of difficulty.

At Rivendell and Lothlorien, care and counsel are offered and moral and spiritual strength renewed. At Rivendell Frodo accepts the call on his life to be the Ring Bearer, though he admits, "I do not know the way" (*FR*, II, iii, 284) (The Way being the biblical name for Christianity). In Lothlórien, the person of Galadriel can be seen to symbolize the figure of the church in its feminine aspect of "the bride of Christ." Catholics refer to "our mother the church." Galadriel represents the church, not the Virgin Mary, because Galadriel is not a virgin. All the same, Galdriel is holy, and though she is not beyond the temptation to power offered by the ring, she rejects it.

The Elves seem to fulfill an ecclesiastical role in function if not in social structure and ceremony. Just as the Elves leave Middle-earth for the West once their roles have been fulfilled, so will the church cease to function on earth when its purpose has been accomplished. And of course, at the conclusion of the novel, the ring is destroyed thanks to the intervention of the Gollum.

Associated with the Gollum is the otherwise unnamed Deity of *The Lord of the Rings*. Bilbo had the opportunity to kill the Gollum during the events related in *The Hobbit*, but, as Gandalf tells Frodo, "It was Pity that stayed his hand. Pity and Mercy not to strike without need" (*FR*, I, ii, 68). And Frodo remembers Gandalf's words, "Even Gollum may have something yet to do. . . . But for him . . . I could not have destroyed the Ring" (*RK*, VI, iii, 225).

This passage suggests the subtle operation of a Divine presence. The capitalized words "Pity" and "Mercy" and the transitive verb "stayed" allow for personification, while the link between Gandalf's words and Frodo's at the demise of the Gollum indicates very strongly the existence of "a Providence that shapes their ends."

God, the church, sacraments and grace engaged in the battle with the forces of evil, all point to a very real allegorical and theological emphasis in *The Lord* of the Rings. Tolkien has clothed in myth and fantasy the image of the wayfaring Christian overcoming his fallen self on his journey to redemption.

Cath Filmer-Davies

Further Reading

Carson, H.M. "Roman Catholicism." In *The New International Dictionary of the Christian Church*, edited by J.D. Douglas et al., 853–56. Grand Rapids, MI: Zondervan 1978.
Humphrey Carpenter, *J.R.R. Tolkien: A Biography*. London: Allen & Unwin, 1977.

THINGOL

"In after days he became a king renowned, and his people were all the Elves of the Twilight, and King Greymantle was he, Elu Thingol in the tongue of that land. And Melian was his Queen, wiser than any child of Middle-earth; and their hidden halls were in Menegroth, the Thousand Caves in Doriath" (*S*, 46).

Thingol, King of Doriath plays an immensely important role in the tales of the First Age. He was one of the three Elves invited by the Vala Oromë to come to Aman and afterward convince the Elvish kindreds to journey into the west. *The Silmarillion* tells in short how he fell in love with the Maia Melian, founded the Sindar realm of Doriath, and fathered Lúthien the fair.

With the return of Melkor, peace in Middle-earth ends and Doriath is guarded by the Girdle of Melian. After Thingol learns of the Kinslaying at Alqualondë, he decides to take withdraw behind Melian's magical barrier and no longer be bound up with the War of the Jewels brought by Fëanor's sons to Beleriand. In the end, however, he enmeshes himself and the kingdom of Doriath in the fate of the Silmarils: "Bring to me in your hand a Silmaril from Morgoth's crown, "he commands Beren, "and then, if she will, Lúthien may set her hand in yours" (*S*, 165).

In *The Lays of Beleriand* the alliterative poems *The Lay of the Children of Húrin* and *The Lay of Leithian* are strongly bound up with the fate of Thingol and Doriath. He appeared first in the *Book of Lost Tales* as Linwë Tinto.

It is only with the publication of *The Silmarillion* that the scope of Thingol's deeds becomes evident. In both *The Hobbit* and *The Lord of the Rings* he is only mentioned in passing when the Dwarves are brought before Thranduil and in Aragorn's song of Beren and Lúthien. In the *Letters* he is only mentioned in answers to linguistic questions.

Thingol's growing lust for the Silmaril is the starting point for the hate between Dwarves and Elves repeatedly mentioned in both *The Hobbit* and

The Lord of the Rings. The possession of the Nauglamir, the Necklace of the Dwarves with the Silmaril set in it, leads to the Dwarves' murder of Thingol.

Helms relates Thingol to Untamo in the *Kalevala* who is a noble relative fostering Kullervo just as Thingol is fostering Turin (*S*, 7). The flight of Túrin after the death of Saeros resembles Kullervo's flight from Ilmarinen. Shippey identifies Thingol's oath to give Beren his daughter's hand in marriage as a story element of *Sir Orfeo* (Shippey 193).

The love between Thingol and Melian belongs to an archetypical representation of a relationship and is mirrored both in Beren and Lúthien as well as with Aragorn and Arwen. The men fall in love with a woman dancing or walking in a glade and are caught in a spell: "And suddenly even as he sang he saw a maiden walking on a greensward among the white stems of the birches; and he halted amazed (. . .)" (*RK*, Appendix A, 338).

Marcel R. Bülles

Further Reading

Flieger, Verlyn. *Splintered Light: Logos and Language in Tolkien's World*. Kent, OH: Kent State University Press, 2002.
Helms, Randel. *Tolkien and the Silmarils*, Boston, MA: Houghton Mifflin, 1981.
Shippey, Tom. *The Road to Middle-earth*. Boston, MA: Houghton Mifflin, 1983.

See also **Beren; Dwarves; Elves: Kindreds and Migrations; Jewels; Lúthien; Melian; Silmarils**

THORIN OAKENSHIELD

Thorin II was born in Erebor in 2746 of the Third Age, son of Thrain II, son of Thrór, the King of Durin's Folk. Thorin had a brother, Frerin and a sister, Dis, who bore Fili and Kili. Thorin never married. From a great distance he saw the devastation of Smaug when the Dragon overthrew Dale and Erebor in 2770. Thorin escaped the tumult with his family.

During the Battle of Azanulbizar (Dimrill Dale) in 2799 against the Orcs—a battle to avenge the savage death of his grandfather Thrór—Thorin's shield was broken. He found a stout oak branch nearby, which he wielded as both a shield and a club, never lagging during the battle. Thorin bravely killed many Orcs that day, and was thereafter named Oakenshield. His brother, Frerin, was killed in action at this time.

Following the battle, Thorin, his father Thrain, and some remaining Dwarves wandered aimlessly first to Dunland, then to Eriador. As an exiled Dwarf-folk, they finally settled just east of the Ered Luin mountain range in 2802.

After the disappearance of his father in 2845 Thorin Oakenshield became the King of Durin's folk. Over the next ninety-six years Thorin pondered more and more about the wealth stolen from his kin and the Dragon who wronged his house. It was a chance meeting with Gandalf in Bree in March of 2941 that changed the future of Thorin and his descendants, leading the Dwarves on the Quest of Erebor, the Lonely Mountain, with Bilbo the Hobbit.

At his best, Thorin was courageous, valiant, and loyal to close friends and family. He had strong leadership abilities and willingly took charge. These admirable qualities are evident throughout *The Hobbit*. However, he also possessed a thirst for vengeance, most strongly displayed in his determined desire to regain his family treasure—lying in Erebor—from Smaug the Dragon. Stubbornness, pride, and greed were also part of his makeup. These three character traits were most prominently shown at the Front Gate of the Lonely Mountain where Thorin steadfastly refused to consider a parley with the Men of the Lake and the Elves. He was also adamant about not giving to the Men of Esgaroth their rightful share of the wealth.

Thorin valued his family's lost gold and treasure, and assumed others coveted it. Bilbo the Hobbit, who was instrumental in aiding the Dwarves in their quest to regain Erebor, was even contracted (in writing), with Thorin promising the Hobbit a specific percentage of the treasure. Thorin believed that financial gain might have been the only reason the Hobbit agreed to join the Dwarves' quest, but as we find, this was not the case.

Despite Thorin's angry words and actions toward Bilbo for secretly taking the highly valued Arkenstone to Bard and the Elvenking as a bargaining tool to keep peace, Thorin redeemed himself, but only on his deathbed. In his last few minutes on Middle-earth, broken with fatal wounds, Thorin called for Bilbo, and apologized for his words and deeds at the Front Gate, recognizing that he was now going to a place where treasure is of no value. In his final farewell to Bilbo—akin to a blessing—Thorin graciously told him that there was more good in him than he realized—an unusually positive comment for this proud Dwarf, who, in the final episode of his time upon Middle-earth, surely atoned himself for his previous actions.

At the end of his very full and temperamental life, Thorin Oakenshield, King under the Mountain, parted from Bilbo the Hobbit in restored friendship in 2941—a poignant end to a somewhat tumultuous relationship.

In the epic poem *Völuspá* found in Iceland's *Eldar Edda* which Tolkien admired, Dwarves were bred in the earth and were like maggots in the flesh. The gods then held a council and decided to give them the appearance and intelligence of Men, although they still lived in the earth and in the rocks. The *Nibelungenlied*, an epic poem in Middle High German, similarly describes its Dwarves as subterranean creatures living in darkness—hostile and greedy in nature, having been born of maggots.

Tolkien claimed that although he did not strictly follow the Germanic or Scandinavian models of Dwarves, they did share some of the basic characteristics, especially those of the Germanic legends. Tolkien's Dwarves were not inherently evil or hostile to other races, but they did exhibit the very human traits of greed and jealousy.

Tolkien took the names of Thorin Oakenshield and the other Dwarves of Middle-earth verbatim from the *Völuspá*. The name Oakenshield is a direct translation of Eikinskjaldi, who is also one of the Dwarves listed in the *Edda*.

Jo-Anna Dueck, Paulina J. Gibson, Gerda Marz, and Sharon Tanhueco Schmitt

Further Reading

Day, David. *Tolkien's Ring: Illustrated by Allen Lee*. Barnes and Noble Books by arrangement with Pavilion Books Limited, 1999.

Foster, Robert. *The Complete Guide to Middle-earth*. New York: Ballantine Books, 2001.

Magee, Elizabeth, ed. *Legends of the Ring*. London: Folio Society, 2004.

Rutledge, Fleming. *The Battle for Middle-earth*. Grand Rapids, MI: Wm. B. Eerdmans, 2004.

Stanton, Michael N. *Hobbits, Elves and Wizards: Exploring the Wonders and Worlds of J.R.R. Tolkien's Lord of the Rings*. New York: Palgrave Macmillan, 2002.

See also **Arkenstone; Bilbo; Dwarves; *Hobbit, The*; Lonely Mountain (Erebor); Mythology, Germanic; Rankin/Bass; Redemption**

TIME

Tolkien's interest in and concern with time are manifest in the very early drafts of his "Silmarillion" mythology. The Tale of the Sun and Moon, most probably written some time in 1917–18, includes a segment called "The Weaving of the Days and Months and Years." This tells of Ranuin and Danuin, the children of Aluin (Time), who tether the sun and moon with invisible ropes, thus setting their paths across the sky and anchoring creation in the bonds of Time. Although the concept was later abandoned, it stands as an early indication of its inventor's continuing interest in the importance, the mechanics and the connotations of measured time. This marking of days, weeks, and years extends to centuries in the many Annals Tolkien went on to construct for his mythology. The various and often-reworked Annals of Valinor (later changed to "Aman") and Beleriand, (later changed to "Grey") are testament to his concern with the interdependence of time and history, and were clearly considered necessary accompaniment to the tales themselves. While most of the annals are attached to "The Silmarillion," "The Tale of Years," Appendix B of *The Lord of the Rings*, is a valuable chronology of and context for the events in that story.

The scrupulous attention to the passage of time, changes in weather, and the turning year apparent in *The Hobbit* and *The Lord of the Rings* is not simply the author's attempt to give both narratives the air of reality they so clearly possess. *The Hobbit* in particular also uses time as the natural marker of supernatural events. The clearest instance occurs when the celestial mechanics of Durin's Day, the simultaneous (and rare) appearance of sun and moon in the same sky, together with the (apparently) yearly action of the thrush, give Bilbo the key to entering the mountain. Time in *The Lord of the Rings,* although more subtly treated, is again both natural and supernatural. While more is said about this below, in the present context, the recurrent illnesses of Frodo on the anniversaries of each of his woundings serve as examples of cyclical time contained within linear time.

As his mythology developed, Tolkien's treatment of time moved from celestial mechanics and the calendar round into more exploratory dimensions, particularly during the thirties and forties of his century. In this period it became linked with time-travel effected through para-psychological regression into dream and ancestral memory.

The possible dimensions of time and space were areas of interest for both theoretical physicists and writers of speculative fiction in the early twentieth century, so that in writing time-travel Tolkien was following a trend at once philosophical and popular. The trend, indeed, was the genesis of Tolkien's 1936 agreement with C.S. Lewis that in order to get more of what both men liked to read (that is, fantasy and science fiction) they would have to write it themselves—Lewis taking space-travel and Tolkien time-travel. This apparently spur-of-the-moment bargain occurred at the start of a particularly fertile and productive period in Tolkien's creative life. His first attempt at science fiction, an unfinished time-travel story called *The Lost Road*, has been tentatively dated

by Christopher Tolkien to some time in 1936. In November of that same year, Tolkien delivered his ground-breaking lecture, "*Beowulf*: The Monsters and the Critics" (later published as an essay) to the British Academy. In December of 1937 he began *The Lord of the Rings*. A scant year and a half after that he delivered his equally important theoretical discourse on myth and fairy tale, "On Fairy-Stories" (also later published as an essay) as the annual Andrew Lang lecture at St. Andrews University, Scotland.

In all these works, time is a recurrent motif. The bargain with Lewis was thus a useful spur to direct his attention to the possible uses of time for conveying some of his most complex and important ideas. As these took shape, they became manifest not just in the two time-travel stories that were the direct outcome of the bargain, but in the essays and the greater fiction as well. Phrases such as "the fields of Time" and "within Time" from "*Beowulf*: the Monsters and the Critics," and reference to standing "outside Time," or "opening a door on Other Time" in "On Fairy-Stories" indicate, not least by their capitalization of the key word, the importance of these concepts to his imagination. Treated as theory in the essays, these ideas become explicit and experiential in the fiction.

Tolkien's treatment of time touches on all the concepts introduced in the essays—fields of Time, Other Time, standing outside Time—employing them as interdependent and interlocking motifs. Again and again, either directly or obliquely, one or another of his characters will enter into an extraordinary relationship with Time, opening a door on Other Time, experiencing both past and future in the field of Time, or standing somehow outside the passage of Time altogether. Tolkien includes not just other time-dimensions as a concept, or time-travel as a narrative device, but incorporates into both ideas of collective or ancestral memory, as well as the function of dream as a window or gateway into that memory and thus into Other Time. One source was traditional, the conventional fairy-tale time-warp dictating that entry into the Otherworld puts the traveler outside his own time, making years of mortal time pass in a single fairy day; or compressing apparent years of fairy time into one mortal moment.

As well as fairy stories, however, there were other important, more contemporary, extraliterary influences on his treatment of time. One was his own era's growing theoretical and scientific speculation, fueled by advances in theoretical physics, about the multiple dimensions of time and space. The other was the work and thought of his fellow-countryman, an aeronautical engineer named J.W. Dunne. Dunne's 1927 book *An Experiment with Time* exerted a formative influence on writers of speculative fiction in the middle decades of the twentieth century from the twenties to the forties. Tolkien's copy of the 1934 edition contains his notes on relevant passages. The concepts of "fields of Time," Other Time," and "standing outside Time" in Tolkien's essays, the various time-experiences of his characters, had Dunne's theory as their immediate catalyst. Dunne's major point was that Time is not, as generally supposed, divided into discrete categories of past, present, and future. Rather, it is, like space, a continuous field that can be perceived and moved into, most often through dreams, by anyone at any time and in any direction.

Tolkien's most direct use of Dunne's idea of dream as the entry portal into "Other time," comes in *The Lost Road* (1936) and its successor, *The Notion Club Papers* (1945–46), his second attempt at a time-travel narrative. In both stories, the protagonists dream themselves through time. Traveling by way of successively regressing inherited memories, they move back through periods of actual historic and prehistoric time to arrive finally at the entirely fictive time of the Downfall of Númenor. Such explicit Other Time travel is replaced in *The Lord of the Rings* by more subtle variations. There is, for example the moment (given without explanation) in Book I where Merry, rescued from the barrow, undergoes a brief flashback to the experience and death of a warrior in an ancient battle of which his present self knows nothing (*FR,* I, viii, 154). More immediately relevant is Frodo's sensation on first entering Lórien that he has stepped over a bridge of Time into a corner of the Elder days, a time that is no more. Another example is the experience of Frodo at the Mound of Cerin Amroth, where, observing another's experience rather than feeling it as his own, Frodo suddenly perceives Aragorn not as the travel-stained Ranger he presently is, but as the young man clothed in white that he was in time past (*FR,* I, vi, 366–67).

It is no accident that these last two episodes occur in Lórien, for Tolkien's most mystical and philosophical deployment of time comes in his treatment of Elves and Elven strongholds. Abandoning the earlier notion of their "fading" over time, he instead depicted the Elves as desiring to arrest time, to halt the natural processes of decay and death and thereby "stand outside" the normal progress of Time. Caught in timelessness, the Elves stand in marked and deliberate contrast to Men, forever subject to change and decay. Tolkien's purpose in making his Elves free from the constraints of time and death is, paradoxically, to validate both of these factors, and to support the natural processes of decay and death. Implicit in *The Lord of the Rings*, this is explicit in his

collected letters, where the Elves are characterized as "embalmers" of time, criticized for "wanting to have their cake and eat it." Disparity between time in the outside world and Time in Faërie is conveyed in his depiction of the Elvish strongholds of Rivendell and Lórien, where travelers experience these havens as outside their ordinary time. Frodo cannot tell how many days he has spent in Rivendell, while Bilbo remarks that time in Rivendell does not seem to pass, but just is. Sam Gamgee is unable to reckon up the days he has spent in Lórien, and speculates that time doesn't "count in there."

Tolkien's most immediate presentation of this Faërian time-warp comes in his last short story, *Smith of Wootton Major*, while his clearest explication appears in the long essay he wrote in conjunction with in that story. The essay devotes considerable space to plotting the particular contiguities of geography and time between the real word and Faërie (or Faery—the spelling varied), exploring how the two can be conjunct and communicable, yet separate. The story itself shows the two worlds in action. The hero of the story, Smith, can and does spend what seems to be many days wandering in Faery outside his ordinary time, yet the point is made repeatedly within the tale that he can go and return to his home in Wootton Major in the compass of a single day. Faërien timelessness and its corollary Deathlessness have one critical referent in the "*Beowulf*" essay, where Tolkien notes that in contrast to the northern mythology he defends, the "southern gods" are "timeless and do not fear death," whereas the northern gods are very much within time, and doomed to die. A similar reference occurs in his deliberate and only seemingly playful contrast in "On Fairy-Stories" between human fairy-stories with their offer of Escape from Death, and the "human-stories" of Elves that doubtless, or so he speculates, offer a parallel Escape from Deathlessness.

Tolkien addressed the contrast between human and faërian time most explicitly in a long unpublished essay on "Elvish time." Unfortunately the essay is unfinished as well as unpublished, and what we have of it says more about human concepts of time than Elven ones. Tolkien explores our concept of time as expressed in language (specifically English language) with a view to contrasting this with the disparate Elven concept. His discussion offers an enlightening look at how human (again English) language articulates time (often confusingly) in terms of space. The past is *behind* us, Tolkien points out, the future lies *ahead*, yet our ancestors come *before* us and our descendent*s follow* us. The argument is that the directional metaphors for past and future employed by analogy with space are confused and contradictory.

Despite the title, however, the essay does not go on to the expected discussion of Elven language in terms of time, though something can be inferred from the words for time, for aspects of time, or for describing concepts associated with time that make up a notable part of the early lexicons of his invented languages. The implied image of time as a road or path along which (or so the words suggest) humanity can look both backward and forward, gave Tolkien the metaphor for his time-travel story, "The Lost Road," in which two English philologists, using dream as their vehicle, travel the road of time through successive incarnations back into their own ancestral past.

VERLYN FLIEGER

Further Reading

Flieger, Verlyn. *A Question of Time*. Kent, OH: Kent State University Press, 1997.
———. *Interrupted Music*. Kent, OH: Kent State University Press, 2005.
Tolkien, J.R.R. *Smith of Wootton Major*. Edited by Verlyn Flieger. London: HarperCollins, 2005.
Zap, Jonathan. Time and Tolkien's Elves. www.alignment2012.com/timeandtolkienseleves.html - 30k.

See also **Lost Road, The**; **Memory**; *Sauron Defeated*; *Smith of Wootton Major*; **Time Travel**

TIME TRAVEL

"I'd give a bit for a time-machine," Tolkien wrote to his son Christopher in January 1945 (*Letters,* 108). The occasion was his reading of F.M. Stenton's *Anglo-Saxon England*, and the impetus was his desire to experience first-hand the history he read about. Yet for all his expressed interest in time-travel, which given his interest in England's past we can take as genuine, Tolkien's only explicit attempts at writing journeys into the past were his two science fiction stories, *The Lost Road* and *The Notion Club Papers*, both tangentially connected to his better-known mythology of Middle-earth. The first of the two, *The Lost Road*, was written as nearly as can be determined in late 1936. The occasion was Tolkien's self-described toss-up with C.S. Lewis over which of them was to write a space-travel tale and which a time-travel one. Tolkien got time-travel and the result was *The Lost Road*. The story was never finished, as Tolkien abandoned it after a few chapters to start work on *The Lord of the Rings*.

However, he made a second attempt with the same theme and treatment some ten years later in *The Notion Club Papers*. Though longer and better developed, this, too, gave way unfinished to Tolkien's ever-extending work on *The Lord of the Rings*. In both stories the leading characters, contemporary Englishmen of Tolkien's own century, were to regress through time and memory, inhabiting ever-earlier ancestral identities in episodes from English history and prehistory. Outline sketches for *The Lost Road* include incidents from Anglo-Saxon history, Irish mythology, the period of European cave paintings, and the Ice Age. In both stories the protagonists were to arrive finally at Tolkien's own prehistory of Middle-earth, inhabiting Númenórean identities and witnessing the downfall of Númenor. Though neither story was ever finished, both showed promise in a style unusual for Tolkien, that of the modern novel with contemporary characters and dialogue. The later and better developed of the two, *The Notion Club Papers*, featured characters based on members of his own literary discussion circle, the Inklings, and it gives some idea of what Tolkien felt Inklings' gatherings to be like.

Both *The Lost Road* and *The Notion Club Papers* use the dreaming mind as the vehicle for journeys into history and myth, and both rely on inherited memory to take their dreaming protagonists back into episodes from their ancestral past. *The Notion Club Papers* carries the idea further by having time-travel erupt into the present as the characters experience flashbacks to past lives that are witnessed by their contemporaries in the present. Rather than a Wellsian time machine or similar apparatus, Tolkien's time-travel is notable for being explicitly para-psychological. Other twentieth-century writers were working with the idea of travel into the past by means of shared or exchanged identities—Henry James's unfinished novel *The Sense of the Past* and John Balderstone's play *Berkeley Square* are two examples. While Tolkien's stories seem related in concept and execution to Carl Jung's theory of the collective unconscious, a theory Jung developed out of his work with his patients' dreams, there is this important difference—that Tolkien's unconscious memories were specifically ancestral, part of a lineage rather than a communal or collective experience.

Other, both more and less overt encounters with past time occur in scenes of *The Lord of the Rings*. In one brief episode in *The Fellowship of the Ring* Merry Brandybuck, awakening from the barrow, experiences a time-travel flashback to a long-ago battle with the men of Carn Dûm and relives an ancient warrior's death from a spear wound. The incident passes quickly and the memory is over in a moment, after which Merry (restored to his own identity and memory) is left with the sensation that he has been dreaming. Since there is no evidence to suggest that the dream is part of the personal past of Merry

Brandybuck, the episode seems based on some kind of collective memory, but whether this is inherited or simply inspired by Merry's experience in the barrow is unclear.

In a less explicit treatment of the concept, Frodo, entering Lórien, feels that he has stepped out of his own time into the Elder Days, that the land of Lórien is a memory from the First Age still preserved in the modern world. In early drafts of the Lórien chapter Tolkien considered presenting Lórien as outside Time altogether, and though he later rejected this idea, some elements of Lórien's ambiguous relationship to Time remain in the published book. Frodo's poignant vision of Galadriel on the shore of Lórien slipping backward to "forgotten shores" as the Anduin current catches the Elven boats in "mortal time" suggests Tolkien's own vision.

VERLYN FLIEGER

See also **Lost Road, The**; **Memory**; **Time**

TOL ERESSËA

The haunting beauty of the Lonely Isle, the gleam of its white city shining over the shadowy sea, is one of the most persistent and powerful images in Tolkien's works. Tolkien used the name Tol Eressëa for the island as early as the very first page of "The Cottage of Lost Play," and in the very earliest stages of Tolkien's mythology Tol Eressëa was in fact England and it was the place of Elvish exile from Valinor. The idea of a beautiful island far, far to the West of England is consistently found in English and Irish literature, its most famous appearance in medieval literature being in the story of the Irish Saint Brendan, and in nineteenth-century literature in Charles Kingsley's *The Water Babies*.

In *The Silmarillion*, Tol Eressëa is originally an island used by the Valar to transport the Elves from the shores of Beleriand to Valinor. When the host of Teleri led by Olwë comes into the bay of Eldamar, they ask the Vala Ulmo to stop their voyage there, and Ulmo has the island fastened in the midst of the bay. The Elves there are thus able to dwell beneath the light of the stars but within sight of the land of Aman. Through the Calacirya, the Pass of Light in the mountains of the Pelóri, the light of the Two Trees shines forth across the bay of Eldamar and onto the western shore of Tol Eressëa; the flowers that bloomed there were the first east of the mountains of the Pelóri.

After the War of Wrath and the destruction of Beleriand, most of the Noldor return from their exile but live in Tol Eressëa rather than in Valinor, their original home (although they are permitted to come to Valinor). The most far-sighted of the Dúnedain of Númenor were able to catch a glimpse of Tol Eressëa's great harbor and tower either from the summit of the Meneltarma or from a tall ship as far off the Western coast as was lawful. After the downfall of Númenor, a few lucky mariners might still find the Straight Road into the West and see the "lamplit quays of Avallónë" before they died.

This combination of beauty—the lamps shining on the sea, the white city on the green land—with deep loneliness is entirely characteristic of Tolkien's most aesthetically effective creations. Tol Eressëa and the sea Elves with their white ships and their songs is a poignant image that ties together Tolkien's works from the beginning of "The Cottage of Lost Play" to the end of *The Lord of the Rings*.

MICHAEL D.C. DROUT

Further Reading

Garth, John. *Tolkien and the Great War: The Threshold of Middle-earth*. Boston: Houghton Mifflin, 2003.

See also **Eldamar**; **Elves: Kindreds and Migrations**; **Saint Brendan**; **Valinor**

TOLKIEN READER, THE

The Tolkien Reader, first published in America in September of 1966 by Houghton Mifflin and illustrated by Pauline Baynes, is a reprint of material from various sources. Composed of five parts: "Tolkien's Magic Ring" by Peter Beagle, which first appeared in *Holiday,* "The Homecoming of Beorhtnoth Beorhthelm's Son," which first appeared in *Essays and Studies for 1953,* "Tree and Leaf" composed of "On Fairy-Stories" and "Leaf by Niggle" which was first published in the *Dublin Review* in January 1945, "Farmer Giles of Ham" (originally published by Allen and Unwin in 1949), and "The Adventures of Tom Bombadil."

"Tolkien's Magic Ring" is a brief essay by author Peter S. Beagle. In it Beagle reviews the plot, themes and major characters in the *Lord of the Rings* trilogy. This introduction serves as an effective primer for anyone unfamiliar with Tolkien's work.

The second part of *The Tolkien Reader* is "The Homecoming of Beorhtnoth Beorhthelm's Son." This short play is based on "The Battle of Maldon." In the play two servants come to the battlefield at Maldon to recover their master's corpse. Following the play is Tolkien's commentary, "Ofermod."

The next part of *The Tolkien Reader* is "Tree and Leaf," which is composed of "On Fairy-Stories" and "Leaf by Niggle." "On Fairy-Stories" is an essay that examines the themes of fantasy, recovery, escape and consolation as they appear in the genre. "Leaf by Niggle" is the story of an artist, Niggle, of limited ability who attempts to paint trees and leaves. In the end only a single leaf painted by Niggle survives in a museum. It is lost when the museum burns down, demonstrating that all things are impermanent.

"Farmer Giles of Ham" is the tale of an English farmer who, by the story's end, has become king of the region. During the course of the story Giles defends his farm from a giant, fights the dragon Chrysophylax and gets the dragon's horde.

"The Adventures of Tom Bombadil" is a collection of sixteen poems. The poems are set in Middle-earth and Tolkien, in the foreword to the section, attributes them variously to Bilbo, Frodo, and Sam Gamgee.

JOHN WALSH

See also **Tree & Leaf**; **"On Fairy-Stories"**; **Leaf by Niggle**; **Farmer Giles of Ham**; **The Homecoming of Beorhtnoth**; **The Adventures of Tom Bombadil**; **Poems by Tolkien**

TOLKIEN REMEMBERED: HUMPHREY CARPENTER

Tolkien Remembered is a made-for-television documentary short film (thirty-eight minutes) that was produced in 1992 by Jim Berrow and Alan Wallis for Central Productions (U.K.), and filmed in Oxford. It presents a thoughtful overview of Tolkien, as discussed by some of those closest to him and his work. The principal speakers are two of his children, Fr John and Priscilla; his publisher, Rayner Unwin; Tolkien scholar Tom Shippey; and his biographer Humphrey Carpenter, a lifelong resident of Oxford.

Carpenter, the primary speaker, offers a concise reaffirmation of his biography, at times negotiating a careful path between praise and criticism of Tolkien. He begins the film by declaring *The Lord of the Rings* to be the longest book in the English language that people reread regularly. He then relates the principal events of Tolkien's life, accompanied by archival family photographs, lending his unique perspective on the Oxford scene. He explains that Tolkien remained withdrawn from the world following World War I; was not a particularly remarkable lecturer; and describes his writing as a hobby, similar to model railways. However, Carpenter sums up by claiming Tolkien to be unique in terms of authors with which he has come into contact, and notes a genuine sadness about him.

Tolkien's children present a more intimate view, reminiscing about their father's story-telling at home. They note a special fondness for *The Father Christmas Letters*, with Priscilla appreciating the fact that her brothers did not spoil the magic, even after she suspected the letters' true origin. She describes *The Lord of the Rings* as, above all, a wonderful story, creating a convincing world in which readers are able to delightfully lose themselves for a time. Fr John provides some of the lighter moments in the film, relating several humorous anecdotes about his father, whom he describes at one point as a typical absent-minded professor.

Unwin shares his unique memories, recalling his review of *The Hobbit* as a child as the "best shilling" his firm ever spent, but describes Tolkien's attempts to have him read later manuscripts to be a terrible chore. He also acknowledges that more has been published posthumously by Tolkien than while he was alive. While explaining how Tolkien is both popular and unpopular in literary circles, Unwin claims that Tolkien's place in the field of literature is secure, but exactly what that place is remains unknown.

Shippey provides insight into the lasting meaning of Tolkien's works, vis-à-vis the century in which they were written. He begins by explaining that hobbits act as reader figures, symbolizing those forced to survive and manage in a larger, more complex, world. He informatively comments on Tolkien's perceived lack of activity within the academic community, and the resulting jealousy of his peers after the success of *The Lord of the Rings*. Shippey speculates that Tolkien, and *The Lord of the Rings*, may go down in literary history as being significantly representative of loss in the twentieth century.

The film's appeal is enhanced by selections from Tolkien's taped readings of *The Hobbit* and *The Lord of the Rings*, and also by the inclusion of many images of Tolkien's own artwork, shown with musical accompaniment. A camera pan-up of the mountain slope in Tolkien's water-color, *Halls of Manwë (Taniquetil)* is intended as a grand crescendo. However, the film also dwells on early movie proposals, animated adaptations of Tolkien's work, and the "cult phenomenon" of the late twentieth century, occasionally displaying an anti-American bias. As such, it may appear to be somewhat insular and dated.

As Douglas Anderson observes in his obituary of Carpenter, his "disillusionment with Tolkien reached its nadir" in the year of this production, as he had distanced himself from the subject of his earlier biography (Anderson, 222). Although he avoided television for most of his life, preferring to remain a radio broadcaster, then biographical writer, this film is imbued with Carpenter's engaging style and polished skills.

DON N. ANGER

Further Reading

Anderson, Douglas A. "Obituary: Humphrey Carpenter (1946–2005)." *Tolkien Studies.* 2, no. 1 (2005); 217–24.

Carpenter, Humphrey. *J.R.R. Tolkien: A Biography.* London: Allen & Unwin, 1977.

Hammond, Wayne G., and Christina Scull. *J.R.R. Tolkien: Artist and Illustrator.* London: HarperCollins, 1995.

Shippey, T.A. *J.R.R. Tolkien: Author of the Century.* Boston: Houghton Mifflin, 2001.

Tolkien, John, and Priscilla Tolkien. *The Tolkien Family Album.* London: HarperCollins, 1992.

Unwin, Rayner. "Publishing Tolkien." In *George Allen & Unwin: A Remembrance,* 71–135. Ludlow: Merlin Unwin, 1999.

See also **Art and Illustrations by Tolkien; Bakshi, Ralph; Fandom;** *Father Christmas Letters;* **Film Scripts, Unused; Oxford; Rankin/Bass; Tolkien, John; Tolkien, Priscilla; Tolkien Scholarship: Since 1980**

TOLKIEN SCHOLARSHIP: AN OVERVIEW

The scholarly and critical literature on Tolkien can be anatomized in a variety of ways. A chronological survey, for example, would identify four, partly overlapping, phases. First, long before the "Tolkien expert" was invented, came the book reviews, above all those of *The Lord of the Rings* (1954–55). Whether enraptured or dismissive, these, and the explanations and rebuttals they immediately prompted (in some cases from Tolkien himself), set the agenda for much subsequent controversy.

The second phase, coinciding with the Tolkien cult of the sixties and the subsequent reaction against it, showed twentieth century literary criticism slowly bringing its apparatus to bear upon Tolkien, striving—sometimes against the grain of its own assumptions—to evaluate his claims as a literary artist: landmark texts here would be the essays collected by Isaacs and Zimbardo in 1968 and Paul Kocher's *The Master of Middle-earth* (1972).

A key event of the third phase would be the publication in 1982 of Tom Shippey's *The Road to Middle-earth.* Shippey's book decisively changed the direction of much Tolkien criticism, by insisting—in the teeth of the "death of the author" ideology then dominant in literary studies—on approaching Tolkien's writings from Tolkien's point of view, through an understanding of his philological scholarship, and

the reflections on language and literature to which it had led him. Meanwhile, the writings of Humphrey Carpenter were providing at least a rudimentary framework of biographical information, and Tolkien's letters and main critical essays were collected and published. By the centenary year, 1992, the foundations for an adequately informed understanding of Tolkien had been laid.

The fourth and most recent phase is hard to characterize, other than by its very diversity—and by its massive scale, with more new or updated volumes now appearing in a year than appeared in a decade previously. The incentive provided by the popularity of Peter Jackson's films of *The Lord of the Rings* has clearly been at work since the millennium, but longer-term factors include the energetic exploitation of their Tolkien property by the publishers HarperCollins, and the dedicated work of the Tolkien Society and the Mythopoeic Society as focal points for conferences and specialist journals. Moreover, there are signs that the silent exclusion of Tolkien from serious consideration by mainstream academics is drawing to an end, perhaps because his cultural significance can now hardly be denied, even if his literary value is still doubted.

An alternative way of categorizing the Tolkien literature would be in terms of methodology. Some scholars, as already noted in the case of Shippey, have pursued approaches Tolkien would have understood from his own academic training in the first quarter of the twentieth century: they have examined his literary works as complex sites of language use or located him within the narratives and groupings of literary history (as a Romantic, an Inkling, a Catholic, or a First World War writer) or treated his work as a source of moral, religious or political wisdom. Other critics have followed the modernist doctrine that a literary work must be discussed independently of its author or context, in terms of a highly wrought poetics of narrative, imagery, and rhetoric. There is support for this essentially aesthetic approach in Tolkien's brusque dismissal of biographical criticism, and his insistence that the purpose of his work was not to convey a topical message but to "amuse. . . delight. . . and at times maybe excite or deeply move" readers (*FR,* Foreword, 6). But the exhaustive detail and ever-receding horizons of Tolkien's vision are far from conforming to the crystalline ideal of modernism, and the modernist expectation of pervasive irony also has to be set aside if he is to be appreciated. Even more inhospitable to Tolkien, for obvious reasons, were the social realist conceptions of fiction, whether Marxist or Leavisite in orientation, which influenced literary criticism in the years following the publication of *The Lord of the Rings.*

The post-1960, postmodernist, post-Marxist repertoire of "critical theory" has been relatively unproductive so far as Tolkien is concerned, the main exceptions being in psychoanalytical theory, which has quarried his work for symbols and archetypes, and feminist criticism, which has explored the presentation of female characters and gender stereotypes. The potential of "cultural studies" to produce an orderly analysis of the cultural phenomena derived from Tolkien's work is yet to be demonstrated. However, there is promising recent work in a number of fields. Analysis of Tolkien's style, or styles, is still underdeveloped and is likely to be enhanced by sensitive application of the techniques of contemporary linguistics. There is also increasing recognition that Tolkien has a place in intellectual history, more subtle than any assignment to a "school" of writers can suggest, and not limited to his debt to medieval sources. The annual refereed journal *Tolkien Studies*, launched in 2004, looks likely to host work in these fields, as well as consolidating other areas of Tolkien scholarship.

Finally, the range of attitudes to Tolkien's work deserves comment. It is a truism that his work divides readers, and his reputation may have benefited as little from the wholly absorbed enthusiasm of some (especially where this absorption seems to alienate the rest of literature), as from the studied indifference, or inflammatory denunciations, of others. One possible reason for controversy is the uncertainty over the genres to which his writings belong and so over the expectations that ought to be applied to them. In the extreme case, his work may be thought by its very nature to lie outside serious literature altogether. And where Tolkien is admitted into the purview of some accredited genre, such as fantasy, science fiction, or children's literature, discussion of his standing within that genre is often characterized by a kind of embarrassment, Tolkien featuring as a conservative icon, whose popularity blocks the path to the recognition of more radical and contemporary writing. In this combative atmosphere, attempts to be judicious about the varying merits of Tolkien's writings, to discriminate the best work from the less successful, in a way that is fairly normal with other writers, are still quite rare.

Given Tolkien's popularity, it is no surprise that attempts have also been made by sympathizers to appropriate him to various ideological positions. His traditional Catholicism and his Ruskinian hostility to "the machine" can hardly be disputed, but their expression in his writing has been translated by some commentators into a didactic discourse that he would have rejected. Tolkien's own hope that different readers would find for themselves "applicability" in his

work seems to be borne out by its diverse reception in countries across the world, as translations have multiplied. This internationalization of Tolkien will itself be a phenomenon worthy of future study.

BRIAN ROSEBURY

Further Reading

Carpenter, Humphrey. *The Inklings*. London: Allen & Unwin, 1978.
———. *J.R.R. Tolkien: A Biography*. London: Allen & Unwin, 1977.
Drout, Michael D.C., and Hilary Wynne. "Tom Shippey's *J.R.R. Tolkien: Author of the Century* and a Look Back at Tolkien Criticism since 1982." *Envoi* 9, no. 2 (2000): 101–67.
Johnson, Judith A. *J.R.R. Tolkien: Six Decades of Criticism*. Westport, CT: Greenwood Press, 1986.
Shippey, Tom. *The Road to Middle-earth*. 1st ed. London: Allen & Unwin, 1982.
West, Richard C. *Tolkien Criticism: An Annotated Checklist*. Kent, OH: Kent State University Press, 1970.
———. "A Tolkien Checklist: Selected Criticism 1981–2004," *Modern Fiction Studies* 50, no. 4 (2004): 1015–28.

See also **Children's Literature; Criticism of Tolkien, Twentieth Century; Fandom; Tolkien Scholarship: First Decades; Tolkien Scholarship: Institutions; Tolkien Scholarship: Since 1980**

TOLKIEN SCHOLARSHIP: FIRST DECADES: 1954–1980

The Lord of the Rings attracted the attention of scholars and lovers of literature immediately upon publication in 1954–55, and ever since then both academic and popular interest in Tolkien's body of work has not only been maintained but has grown enormously. Even many of the early book reviews went beyond succinct commentary to become thoughtful essays, whether mostly positive, as in those of W.H. Auden on the quest theme or C.S. Lewis on myth, or mostly negative, as in Edmund Wilson's review (which spurred many to refute its accusation of puerility).

Within a few years there were already several theses or dissertations devoted wholly or in part to Tolkien, pioneering lines of analysis that were developed more fully in the scholarship of the latter part of the century. Everett as early as 1957 provides a succinct biography, discusses not only *The Lord of the Rings* but also *The Hobbit* and *Farmer Giles of Ham*, and quotes background information from their author (later published in *Letters*, 257–59). Hart (1959) devotes a substantial section to *The Hobbit* and *The Lord of the Rings*, considering them better illustrations of C.S. Lewis's literary theory than Lewis was able to achieve in his own fiction. Reilly (1960) continues the association of Tolkien with the other Inklings, notably with Owen Barfield whose influence was long neglected by many other scholars. Levitan (1964) surveyed many aspects of *The Lord of the Rings* that were later much written about, such as the theme of power and the nature of the hero (he himself published several articles based on chapters in his thesis).

Nor were academic conferences on Tolkien's fiction long in coming. Probably the first was held in 1966 at Mankato State College in Minnesota. The keynote address by Bruce A. Beatie looked at Tolkien within the traditions of epic, long a staple of Tolkien scholarship. Other particularly notable contributions were George Burke Johnston's survey of Tolkien's poetry, Levitan on the epic hero and the quite different hero of fairy tale, and David M. Miller's early essay on what was to become the well-worn theme of Good and Evil in *The Lord of the Rings*.

J. S. Ryan (whose doctoral dissertation in 1967 was on Tolkien and other myth-makers) and Hugh Crago were the speakers at a seminar on Tolkien at the University of New England in Australia in 1969. The book that resulted covers the whole landscape of Tolkien scholarship at that time: biography (of which not much was then known), the influence of his medieval studies on his fiction, a look at all of his fiction then published, the Inklings as a group, the phenomenon of being a best seller, philology, writing style, mythology (especially Germanic), the history of fantasy literature, the use of archetypes, the quest story, the themes of power and of Good versus Evil, an annotated bibliography, and some ancillary material such as reprinting the early poem "Goblin Feet."

Much of the best scholarly work being done during this period was not in single books but in essays scattered in numerous journals. The 1968 collection edited by Isaacs and Zimbardo was a milestone that gathered some of the most significant such essays (those by Auden, Bradley, and Lewis, for example) and commissioned several new ones (notably by Mary Quella Kelly on Tolkien's poetry and John Tinkler on the use of Old English in *The Lord of the Rings*).

The honor of the first worthwhile book on Tolkien must go to Carter, who was widely read in literature from ancient times to the twentieth century, and his 1969 book surveys a long list of works behind *The Lord of the Rings* from all periods. Unfortunately, he did not have the scholarly training to do this with sufficient rigor and the book has many factual errors throughout, but his enthusiasm is infectious.

More and more books poured out, showing by example that Tolkien's oeuvre was of a complexity

to repay examination under any critical template: Freudian (Helms), Jungian (O'Neil), philosophical (Petty), and others. By consensus the finest book from this period is Kocher's *Master of Middle-earth* (1972), which looks closely and deeply at the whole body of Tolkien's work to that time. Its insights have held up well for decades. Kocher's later book on *The Silmarillion* is the earliest full study of that posthumous work and remains worthwhile.

Kilby's book on *The Silmarillion* in 1976 actually appeared well before *The Silmarillion* itself in 1977. It deals not with the work as published but with the background stories in manuscript, which Kilby knew well from having assisted the author in trying to put Tolkien's papers in order. Much of Kilby's scholarship focuses on C.S. Lewis, but he also published several articles on Tolkien in addition to his book on *The Silmarillion*.

Essays continued to be generated at gatherings of Tolkienists like the Conferences on Middle-earth organized by Jan Howard Finder. Jared Lobdell edited what he considered to be the best of these in a 1975 collection that has held up as well as the Isaacs and Zimbardo anthology. Among the most notable essays are those by Bonniejean Christensen on Tolkien's development of the character of Gollum in *The Hobbit*, David M. Miller on narrative pattern in *The Fellowship of the Ring*, Deborah Webster Rogers on the image of humanity in Tolkien's characters, and Richard C. West on the interlace structure of *Lord of the Rings*. But the gem of this collection is undoubtedly "Guide to the Names in The Lord of the Rings," notes on nomenclature prepared by Tolkien as a guide for translators of his work and edited by Christopher Tolkien. Alas, the 2003 reprint of *A Tolkien Compass* does not include this guide, but does have an introduction by T.A. Shippey commenting trenchantly on each of the essays.

Foster provided an important aid to scholars with his own guide to names and places in Tolkien's work, beginning in magazine articles and growing through a number of editions. Tyler has performed a similar service with the various editions of his *Companion*.

Carpenter's biographies of Tolkien and of the Inklings as a group were carefully researched and became the basis for all later work, though later scholars have corrected him on some points. Yet perhaps the greatest aid to scholars has been Tolkien's own *Letters*, edited by Carpenter with Christopher Tolkien, and a treasure trove of the author's considered thoughts on life and his art.

Citations to the major scholarship of this period may be found in the bibliographies by Johnson and West, both of which are annotated.

RICHARD C. WEST

Further Reading

Bradley, Marion Zimmer. *Men, Halflings and Hero Worship.* FAPA (Fantasy Amateur Press Association) booklet, 1961. Reprinted with corrections in *Niekas*, 16 (June, 1966), 25–44. Reprinted (slightly abridged) as a booklet, Baltimore: T-K Graphics, n.d. [c. 1973]. Reprinted (substantially abridged) in Isaacs and Zimbardo (q.v.), 109–27.

Carpenter, Humphrey. *The Inklings: C.S. Lewis, J.R.R. Tolkien, Charles Williams, and their friends.* London: Allen & Unwin, 1978; Boston: Houghton Mifflin, 1979.

———. *Tolkien: A Biography.* London: Allen & Unwin, 1977. Boston: Houghton Mifflin, 1977.

Carter, Lin. *Tolkien: A Look behind The Lord of the Rings.* New York: Ballantine, 1969.

Evans, Robley. *J.R.R. Tolkien.* New York: Thomas Y. Crowell, 1971.

Everett, Caroline Whitman. "The Imaginative Fiction of J.R.R. Tolkien." M.A. thesis, Florida State University, 1957.

Foster Robert. *A Guide to Middle-earth.* Baltimore: Mirage Press, 1971; New York: Ballantine, 1974. Revised and update as *The Complete Guide to Middle-earth: From The Hobbit to The Silmarillion* (New York: Ballantine, 1978).

Hart, Dabney Adams. "C.S. Lewis's Defense of Poesie." Ph.D. diss., University of Wisconsin, 1959.

Helms, Randel. *Tolkien's World.* Boston, MA: Houghton Mifflin, 1974.

Hillegas, Mark R., ed. *Shadows of Imagination: The Fantasies of C.S. Lewis, J.R.R. Tolkien, and Charles Williams.* Carbondale, IL: Southern Illinois University Press, 1969; new ed. 1979.

Isaacs, Neil D., and Rose A. Zimbardo, eds. *Tolkien and the Critics.* Notre Dame, IN, and London: University of Notre Dame Press, 1968.

Johnson, Judith A. *J.R.R. Tolkien: Six Decades of Criticism.* Westport, Conn.: Greenwood Press, 1986.

Kilby, Clyde S. *Tolkien and The Silmarillion.* Wheaton, IL: Harold Shaw Publishers, 1976.

Kocher, Paul H. *Master of Middle-earth: The Fiction of J.R.R. Tolkien.* Boston, MA: Houghton Mifflin, 1972. British edition as *Master of Middle-earth: The Achievement of J.R.R. Tolkien* (London: Thames & Hudson, 1972).

———. *A Reader's Guide to The Silmarillion.* Boston, MA: Houghton Mifflin, 1980.

Levitan, Alexis. "The Lord of the Rings." M.A. thesis, Columbia University, 1964.

Lobdell, Jared, ed. *A Tolkien Compass.* La Salle, IL: Open Court Publishing, 1975. New York: Ballantine, 1980. Reissued by Open Court in 2003 without Tolkien's "Guide to the Names in The Lord of the Rings" but with a new introduction by T.A. Shippey.

Manlove, C.N. *Modern Fantasy: Five Studies.* Cambridge University Press, 1975.

Nitzsche, Jane Chane. *Tolkien's Art: A "Mythology for England."* New York: St. Martin's, 1979. Rev. ed., Lexington, KY: University Press of Kentucky, 2001.

O'Neill, Timothy R. *The Individuated Hobbit: Jung, Tolkien and the Archetypes of Middle-earth.* Boston, MA: Houghton Mifflin, 1979.

Petty, Anne Cotton. *One Ring to Rule Them All: Tolkien's Mythology* Tuscaloosa, AL. University of Alabama Press, 1979.

Purtill, Richard L. *Lord of the Elves and Eldils: Fantasy and Philosophy in C.S. Lewis and J.R.R. Tolkien.* Grand Rapids, MI: Zondervan Publishing, 1974.

Reilly, R[obert] J. "Romantic Religion in the Work of Owen Barfield, C.S. Lewis, Charles Williams, and J.R.R. Tolkien." Ph.D. diss., Michigan State University, 1960. Updated in book form as *Romantic Religion: A Study of Barfield, Lewis, Williams, and Tolkien.* Athens, GA: University of Georgia Press, 1971.

Rogers, Deborah Webster, and Ivor A. Rogers. *J.R.R. Tolkien.* Twayne's English Authors Series, TEAS 304. Boston: Twayne Publishers, 1980.

Rossi, Lee Donald. "The Politics of Fantasy: C.S. Lewis and J.R.R. Tolkien." Ph.D. diss., Cornell University, 1972. Revised and published in book form under the same title (Ann Arbor, MI: UMI Research Press, 1984).

Ryan, John Sprott. "Modern English Myth-Makers, An Examination of the Imaginative Writings of Charles Williams, C. S. Lewis, and J.R.R. Tolkien." Doctoral diss., Cambridge University, 1967.

———. *Tolkien: Cult or Culture?* Armidale, New South Wales, Australia: University of New England, 1969.

Salu, Mary, and Robert T. Farrell, eds. *J.R.R. Tolkien, Scholar and Storyteller: Essays in Memoriam.* Ithaca and London: Cornell University Press, 1979.

Stimpson, Catherine R. *J.R.R. Tolkien.* Columbia Essays on Modern Writers No. 41. New York: Columbia University Press, 1969.

"The Tolkien Papers." *Mankato Studies in English,* No. 2. *Mankato State College Studies,* Vol. 2 (February, 1967).

Tyler, J.E.A. *The Tolkien Companion.* London: Macmillan, 1976. New York: St. Martin's, 1976. Revised and updated as *The New Tolkien Companion* (1979). 3rd edition as *The Complete Tolkien Companion* (2004).

Urang, Gunnar. *Shadows of Heaven: Religion and Fantasy in the Writing of C. S. Lewis, Charles Williams, and J.R.R. Tolkien.* Philadelphia: United Church Press, 1971.

West, Richard C. *Tolkien Criticism: An Annotated Checklist.* Kent, OH: Kent State University Press, 1970. Rev. and updated ed., 1981.

Wilson, Edmund. "Oo, those Awful Orcs!" *Nation* 182 (April 14, 1956): 312–13. Reprinted in his *The Bit between My Teeth: A Literary Chronicle of 1950–65* (New York: Farrar, Straus and Giroux, 1965), 326–32.

See also **Tolkien Scholarship: An Overview; Tolkien Scholarship: Since 1980**

TOLKIEN SCHOLARSHIP: INSTITUTIONS

University

Although Tolkien was a notable professor at Oxford University, it took some years before his literary legacy was accepted in the academic world, and the work is still in progress.

Since the publication of *The Hobbit* in 1937, the writings of J.R.R. Tolkien have been admired throughout the world. With the publication in the 1950s of *The Lord of the Rings*, Tolkien's writing began to attract academic attention in both the classroom and the world of scholarship. "While his tales and fantasies have found a lasting place in the popular culture, their roots lie deep in academe," Scott McLemee remarks. "Academic working on Tolkien inevitably fall under suspicion of being fans. But even before the author's death, in 1973, some readers were beginning to wonder about a different set of questions: how to understand the relationship between Tolkien's storytelling and his scholarship. In Middle-earth, the line between philology and fantasy was quite thin"

According to Jane Chance, "Tolkien has come to be accepted by high academic culture in varying ways." She acknowledges three milestones: the journal *Seven*, dedicated to the writings of the Inklings; the 1992 conference on Tolkien held at Oxford; and the acceptance of three sessions on Tolkien at the International Congress on Medieval Studies at Western Michigan University in Kalamazoo.

It has also been decisive the role of some eminent professors such as Jane Chance (Rice University), Michael D.C. Drout (Wheaton College), Verlyn Flieger (University of Maryland), and Tom Shippey (St Louis University). Their works, published in books, journals, and on the Web have reached out thousands of fans, and their academic courses gave an impulse to Tolkien scholarship and educated hundreds of students.

Marquette University Library

The collection of John Ronald Reuel Tolkien contains the original manuscripts and multiple working drafts for *The Hobbit* (1937), *Farmer Giles of Ham* (1949), and *The Lord of the Rings* (1954-1955), as well as the original copy of the children's book *Mr. Bliss* (published in facsimile form in 1982). The collection includes books by and about Tolkien, periodicals produced by Tolkien enthusiasts, audio and video recordings, and a host of published and unpublished materials relating to Tolkien's life and fantasy writings.

Tolkien manuscripts reside at Marquette because of the vision of William B. Ready (1914–81), director of libraries from 1956 to 1963. He recognized *The Lord of the Rings* as a masterpiece soon after its publication. With administrative approval, Ready

approached Tolkien in 1956 and an agreement was reached whereby Marquette purchased the manuscripts for 1,500 pounds (or less than $5,000). The first shipment of material arrived in 1957; *The Lord of the Rings* manuscripts arrived the next year.

The manuscripts for *The Lord of the Rings*, 1938–55, consist of 7,125 leaves (9,250 pages). They represent an important document of the creativity of J.R.R. Tolkien; in many cases there are several drafts of a single chapter. The history of the composition of *The Lord of the Rings* is presented in *The History of Middle-earth* series (in particular volumes 6–9, 1988–92), edited by Christopher Tolkien. The manuscripts also show drawings and sketches in the margins of the text or linguistic notes on the versos of the sheets.

Other manuscripts and typescripts at Marquette include *The Hobbit*, *Farmer Giles of Ham*, and *Mr. Bliss*. Marquette Library has been developing a significant collection of Tolkien's published works, of critical literature on Tolkien's fantasy and academic writings, of periodicals produced by Tolkien enthusiasts (over thirty-five titles). There is also a representative collection of literature in foreign languages, book reviews, obituaries, journal and anthology articles, studies of Elvish languages, conference announcements and programs, exhibit catalogs, as well as unpublished scholarly papers. Also included are poems and songs, dramatizations, and teaching materials, in addition to audio recordings of readings and radio adaptations and video recordings of movie adaptations, commemorative documentaries.

Generous bequests and gifts of books, research papers, and other secondary material by Tolkien scholars and collectors have contributed immeasurably to the holdings at Marquette. In 1987 Dr. Blackwelder, who donated to Marquette his collection of Tolkieniana—the largest single body of secondary sources on Tolkien—established the Tolkien Archives Fund at the university to provide support for the acquisition and preservation of Tolkien research material in the Department of Special Collections.

The manuscripts were microfilmed in 1983 and, in order to protect the physical integrity of the originals, researchers are asked to use only the microfilm. The Estate of J.R.R. Tolkien retains literary rights and copyright to the manuscripts, thus the documents may be photocopied or published only with the written permission of the Estate.

The Wade Center

The Marion E. Wade Center of Wheaton College, Illinois, publishes *Seven*, a literary review dedicated to seven Christian writers from Great Britain, including J.R.R. Tolkien. Published since 1980, *Seven* is a forum for both the general and the specialized reader.

An international study and research center, the Wade Center was established in 1965 and houses a major research collection of the books and papers of seven British authors: Owen Barfield, G.K. Chesterton, C.S. Lewis, George MacDonald, Dorothy L. Sayers, J.R.R. Tolkien, and Charles Williams. Overall, the Wade Center has more than 11,000 volumes including first editions and critical works. Other holdings on the seven authors include letters, manuscripts, audio and video tapes, artwork, dissertations, periodicals, photographs, and related materials. The Wade Center is open to the public; there is no charge to browse or do research. In September 2001, the Wade Center dedicated a new facility on the campus of Wheaton College.

Bodleian Library

The Bodleian Library opened in Oxford in 1602. It is the main research library of the University of Oxford and since 1610 it is also a copyright deposit library, where a copy of each book copyrighted in Great Britain must be deposited.

The Bodleian Library contains Tolkien's personal and academic papers, as well as his other literary manuscripts (e.g., *The Silmarillion* and "Leaf by Niggle").

The Tolkien Society

The Tolkien Society was founded in 1969 to spread further interest and study the works and life of J.R.R. Tolkien. Based in the United Kingdom and registered as an independent, nonprofit charity, the Society has an international membership that benefits from regular publications and events.

The largest gathering of the Tolkien Society is the annual Oxonmoot, held over a weekend in late September, often in a college of Oxford University. Events are many and varied and may include talks, slide shows, a guided walk around historic Oxford, and an opportunity to present music or drama.

The Society produces two regular publications: the bulletin *Amon Hen* and the journal *Mallorn*, more serious in nature with longer critical articles and essays. *Mallorn* has often been the place where Tolkien experts and scholars have shared their insights with curious fans.

The Tolkien Society has an Education team that develops educational projects for teachers and lectures not just about teaching Tolkien but using Tolkien in the classroom, public libraries, lecture halls, and other educational settings.

The Mythopoeic Society

The Mythopoeic Society was founded in 1967 as a nonprofit international literary and educational organization for the study, discussion, and enjoyment of fantastic and mythic literature, especially the works of J.R.R. Tolkien, C.S. Lewis, and Charles Williams. All scholars, writers, and readers of these literatures can be members of the Society.

Of the three periodicals the Society publishes, *Mythlore* is a peer-reviewed journal that focuses on the works of J.R.R. Tolkien, C.S. Lewis, Charles Williams, and contains scholarly articles on mythic and fantastic literature. Like *Mallorn* (the journal of the Tolkien Society) the older issues of *Mythlore* contain articles that are closer to fan appreciation than to scholarship, but underwent a remarkable evolution and now it is a referred journal.

Each summer the Society holds the Annual Mythopoeic Conference, whose themes have included images of women in mythopoeic fiction, Shakespeare and fantasy, and modern supernatural fiction. The Society also sponsors the Mythopoeic Scholarship Award in Inklings Studies, which is given to books on Tolkien, Lewis, and Williams that make significant contributions to Inklings, scholarship and the Mythopoeic Scholarship Award in Myth and Fantasy Studies, which is given to scholarly books on other specific authors in the Inklings tradition, or to more general works on the genres of myth and fantasy.

The Arda Format Project

The Stockholm Tolkien Society, Forodrim gave birth to the *Arda Format for Structural References to the Works of J.R.R. Tolkien*. As the various editions of the same book differ in layout, a structural reference identifies an element of the text by the help of its place in the text structure (e.g. the numbering of the Bible). In particular, the Arda format specifies in which work to look and, down to hierarchical levels, in what part of the work, then in what text paragraph.

The aim of the project is to ease the work of the scholars whatever language they read by using a universal method. Other countries (e.g., Spain) are adopting it. Forodrim also publishes such remarkable work as the *Tolkien Bibliography* by Ake Bertenstam.

The Lord of the Rings Research Project

The Lord of the Rings Research Project was launched by the University of Canterbury in New Zealand and the University of Wales, Aberystwyth, joined by researchers working in universities in twenty countries across the world. The project, based on Cultural Studies approaches, aims to find out what *The Lord of the Rings* (both J.R.R. Tolkien's novel and Peter Jackson's films) meant to different kinds of people in different countries, the reasons for the popularity of "a story which began in England, but seems to be loved and admired in most countries around the world." The research was conducted in thirteen different languages and is designed to target academic audiences as well as popular readers throughout the Web, where gathered materials and results will be published. The research has received almost 25,000 responses that can be the base of further study.

Tolkien Studies

Tolkien Studies is an annual journal of scholarship on J.R.R. Tolkien and his works. It is the first scholarly journal published by an academic press for the purpose of presenting and reviewing the growing body of critical commentary and scholarship about Tolkien's writings.

It is published by the West Virginia University Press. The founding editors are Douglas A. Anderson, Michael D.C. Drout, and Verlyn Flieger. The members of the editorial board are distinguished Tolkien scholars, including Tom Shippey.

Kalamazoo Medieval Congresses

The International Congress on Medieval Studies is held each year at Western Michigan University in Kalamazoo. The main goal of Tolkien Studies at Western Michigan University is presenting scholarship based on Tolkien's work at the Medieval Congress, in the special section Tolkien at Kalamazoo, which was first accepted for the conference in 2001. Several papers that have been presented through Tolkien at Kalamazoo later went on to be published in journals, theses and books.

Vinyar Tengwar

Vinyar Tengwar is the journal of the Elvish Linguistic Fellowship, devoted to the scholarly study of languages invented by Tolkien. It is indexed by the Modern Languages Association (MLA) and edited by Carl F. Hostetter. The first issue of *Vinyar Tengwar* appeared in 1988. This coincided with the greater frequency of publication of texts written by Tolkien himself; the journal is now dedicated primarily to such texts. Several of these texts were mentioned in volumes of the *History of Middle-earth*, edited by Christopher Tolkien, but not published in that series owing to their specialist or recondite nature.

CECILIA BARELLA

Further Reading

Drout, Michael D.C., and Scott McLemee. "Frodo Lives! And So Does Tolkien Scholarship."http://chronicle. com/colloquylive/2004/06/tolkien/ (June 3, 2004).

Drout, Michael D.C., and Hilary Wynne."Tom Shippey's 'J.R.R. Tolkien: Author of the Century' and a Look Back at Tolkien Criticism since 1982." http://members. aol.com/JamesIMcNelis/9_2/Drout_9_2.pdf.

McLemee, Scott. "Reaching for the Ring, Tolkien Scholars Embark on a Quest for Legitimacy in Academe." http:// contemporarylit.about.com/gi/dynamic/offsite.htm?site= http://chronicle.com/free/v50/i39/39a01101.htm (June 4, 2004).

Tolkien, A Webliography. http://tolkienwebliography.blog. tiscali.it/.

See also **Bodleian Library; Fandom; Manuscripts by Tolkien**

TOLKIEN SCHOLARSHIP: SINCE 1980

Books

The past two decades have seen a flood of significant and well-written contributions to Tolkien scholarship. Christopher Tolkien's *The History of Middle-earth* (which is both primary material and secondary scholarship), Hammond and Anderson's bibliography and Anderson's editions are the essential starting points for scholarship.

Additional recent posthumously published works of Tolkien's scholarship and literature include Michael D.C. Drout's edition of *Beowulf and the Critics*, which provides the draft lectures from which Tolkien drew his celebrated 1936 British Academy Lecture, "Beowulf: The Monsters and the Critics."

Wayne Hammond and Christina Scull's new edition of *Farmer Giles of Ham* provides significant additional material on this work, as does Verlyn Flieger's edition of *Smith of Wootton Major,* which prints for the first time an essay by Tolkien about this short story.

John Garth's *Tolkien and the Great War* is the most significant work of life-scholarship since Carpenter's 1977 *Tolkien: A Biography,* and has the benefit of being far more scholarly. Garth focuses on Tolkien's youth and his service in WWI, unearthing significant new information. He also publishes previously unknown material, and works through the development and origins of Tolkien's mythology more fully than any previous scholar.

Among the essential works of criticism, Tom Shippey's *The Road to Middle-earth* remains the benchmark against which all other works of criticism must be judged.

Shippey first demonstrated the deep interconnections between Tolkien's profession as a philologist and his imaginative creations, and he showed how cruces in medieval literature, tortured passages whose interpretation is disputed or unclear, were often the catalyst for Tolkien's imaginative creation. Despite having published *Road* before Christopher Tolkien's twelve-volume *History of Middle-earth,* Shippey's conjectures and conclusion have been for the most part borne out. Subsequent revised editions of *Road* have served more to augment the text rather than correct it.

Nearly as important and just as well written is Verlyn Flieger's *Splintered Light: Logos and Language in Tolkien's World.* Shippey explicates the way Tolkien worked; Flieger explains the goal Tolkien was working toward. Flieger shows the complexities of Tolkien's justification for the creation of new words and worlds. And Flieger has not only written the second-best book of Tolkien criticism: she has also written the third-best book: *A Question of Time: J.R.R. Tolkien's Road to Faerie* must be considered the definitive study of *The Lost Road* and "The Notion Club Papers," and it is also a major contribution to the study of *The Lord of the Rings* and *Smith of Wootton Major. A Question of Time* is similar to *Splintered Light* in that both books engage the complex and difficult intellectual project Tolkien set himself: to justify and explain his own desires—for subcreation and for deathlessness—that he feared contradicted the teachings of his faith. In response to this internal conflict, Tolkien developed a kind of double vision that allowed him to create a bridge between time present and time past. Tolkien was an exile speaking to exiles, Flieger writes, and he gave voice to his and their longing.

Joseph Pearce's *Tolkien: Man and Myth* focuses wholly upon a Catholic reading of the literature, using Tolkien's *Letters* in copious examples. Through this interpretation, Pearce is successful in pointing out that Tolkien was concerned to find a way to make his work fit within the rubric of orthodox Catholic theology.

Three other book-length studies of importance include Brian Rosebury's *Tolkien: A Critical Asseessment,* Jane Chance's *The Lord of the Rings: The Mythology of Power* and William Green's *The Hobbit: A Journey into Maturity.* Rosebury does an admirable job in beginning a discussion of Tolkien's style and he also makes the point that Tolkien should be analyzed as a twentieth-century writer. Chance argues that Tolkien's work is linked with the truth-producing institution of the university and the truth-producing discipline of philosophy. Green uses contemporary theory to argue that *The Hobbit* can be seen as representing personal, psychosocial development from childhood into maturity. The 1995 (U.K.) and 2000 (U.S.) paperback editions of *The Letters of J.R.R. Tolkien* also contain an exceptionally detailed and useful Index compiled by Christina Scull and Wayne G. Hammond.

Verlyn Flieger's *Interrupted Music: The Making of Tolkien's Mythology* examines in detail the ways by which Tolkien created his mythology. Focusing in particular on *The Silmarillion,* Flieger emphasizes that it is the unfinished nature of Tolkien's mythology that produces its most powerful aesthetic, effects: being unfinished is both its greatest strength and greatest weakness.

Marjorie Burns' *Perilous Realms: Celtic and Norse in Tolkien's Middle-earth* brings into one book these two sets of influences that has previously been treated both separately and in essays and book chapters scattered throughout the scholarly corpus. Burns' examination of the "two Norths" usefully augments other medieval-focused criticism that has tended to focus primarily on Anglo-Saxon, secondarily on Old Norse, and only slightly on Celtic influences.

Articles

Both of the journals *Mallorn* and *Mythlore* contain excellent scholarship: the trouble is that until the recent conversion of *Mythlore* to a more serious format, works of excellent scholarship were often mixed among works of lesser quality. The journal *Seven,* published out of Wheaton College in Illinois, also publishes quality works of Tolkien scholarship, though the journal's focus seems to be more on C.S. Lewis. Also worth mentioning is *Inklings:*

Jahrbuch für Literatur und Asthetik. Arda, the journal of the Swedish Tolkien Society, often publishes quality works of Tolkien scholarship.

Most useful is the *Proceedings* volume of the 1992 Tolkien Centenary Conference, sponsored jointly by *Mallorn* and *Mythlore*, and edited by Patricia Reynolds and Glen H. GoodKnight. There are at least fifteen first-rate articles in the volume, and many others of great interest. The best essays include those by Shippey (both of his, though they have been incorporated into *Author*), Flieger (incorporated into *A Question of Time*), Jessica Yates ("Tolkien the Anti-Totalitarian"), Wayne Hammond ("The Critical Response to Tolkien's Fiction"), Bruce Mitchell ("J.R.R. Tolkien and Old English Studies: An Appreciation") and Peter Gilliver ("At the Wordface: J.R.R. Tolkien's Work on *The Oxford English Dictionary*"). Reading the volume from cover to cover would give a prospective Tolkien scholar an excellent overview of the state of the criticism in 1992.

Two more recent essay collections also gather together examples of the work of most of the best current critics of Tolkien. *J.R.R. Tolkien and His Literary Resonances*, edited by George Clark and Daniel Timmons, includes essential essays by Flieger, Shippey, and Jonathan Evans. Geoffrey Russom's "Tolkien's Versecraft in *The Hobbit* and *The Lord of the Rings*" is the single best study of Tolkien's poetry yet published. The rest of the collection is somewhat uneven, but it is definitely still worth reading. Daniel Timmons's introduction does a good job condensing the long history of Tolkien criticism and the selected bibliography is most extensive.

More specialized than the Clark and Timmons collection, but of excellent scholarly quality, is Tolkien's *Legendarium: Essays on the History of Middle-earth*, edited by Verlyn Flieger and Carl F. Hostetter. The *Legendarium* collection focuses primarily on the posthumously published twelve-volume *History of Middle-earth*, edited by Christopher Tolkien, but of course studies of these texts are of necessity linked to *The Hobbit* and *The Lord of the Rings*, since *The History of Middle-earth* and these books created and drew upon Tolkien's series of interconnected legends. Among the essays, Charles E. Noad's painstaking work tracing the composition of *The Silmarillion* will not be easily surpassed. David Bratman's essay on "The Literary Value of The History of Middle-earth" is a fair-minded approach to analyzing the problem of whether or not *The History of Middle-earth* should be seen as literature or merely scholarly source material. Verlyn Flieger's "In the Footsteps of Ælfwine" is essential for understanding the links between English history, legend, and Tolkien's work, and Paul Edmund Thomas does an

admirable job of looking at Tolkien's style in his investigation of some of Tolkien's narrators. In terms of linguistic approaches, the essay "Three Elvish Verse Modes" Ann-thennath, Minlamad thent¶ estent, and Linnod" by Patrick Wynne and Carl F. Hostetter, is one of the clearest and most approachable efforts on this subject available.

Additional scholarly essay collections include three edited by Jane Chance: *Tolkien the Medievalist, Tolkien and the Invention of Myth* and *Tolkien's Modern Middle Ages*. These collections are somewhat uneven, with the inclusion of a relatively significant amount of somewhat shallow or trivial scholarship (and a surprising number of factual or interpretive difficulties), but they also include some of the most significant scholarship of the past decade. In particular, Gergely Nagy's essay "The Great Chain of Reading: (Inter-)textual Relations and the Technique of Mythopoesis in the Túrin Story," is the single most important article published in Tolkien scholarship in the past fifteen year. Nagy explains more effectively than any previous critic *how* Tolkien's impression of depth and the feeling of mythology in his works is created by a complex web of textual traditions.

Other significant essay collections include *The Lord of the Rings: 1954–2004: Scholarship in Honor of Richard E. Blackwelder*, edited by Wayne Hammond and Christina Scull. This collection gathers together work by leading Tolkien scholars who presented papers at the 2004 conference in honor of Blackwelder at Marquette University. Highlights include papers by Tolkien's former student Arne Zettersten (on the AB Language), Tom Shippey and John Garth. Robert Eaglestone's *Reading The Lord of the Rings* goes mostly outside the usual ranks of Tolkien scholars, attempting to analyze *The Lord of the Rings* through contemporary critical approaches. Some of the essays are less successful than others, but the volume does avoid the errors of the Giddings collection. Rose A. Zimbardo and Neil D. Isaacs *Understanding The Lord of the Rings: The Best of Tolkien Criticism* does not live up to its name, reprinting most of the old chestnuts from their original collection (including the dreadful "Power and Meaning in *The Lord of the Rings* by Patricia Meyer Spacks") and adding very little to current criticism.

Important articles published in journals include William Green's " 'Where's Mama?' The Construction of the Feminine in *The Hobbit*," one of the few effective applications of feminist approaches to Tolkien's texts, and David M. Craig's "Queer Lodgings: Gender and Sexuality in *The Lord of the Rings*," which is perhaps the first sensible discussion of sexuality in Tolkien's work. Craig compares ideals of male friendship in medieval texts, in World War I contexts and in Tolkien's fiction, arguing that Tolkien is able to avoid associations of his characters with homosexuality by making it "unimaginable" in his secondary world. Kathleen Jones's "The Use and Misuse of Fantasy" is a comprehensive examination of religious aspects of fantasy in *The Lord of the Rings* and perhaps the best article-length treatment of this topic. Helen Armstrong's "There Are Two People in This Marriage" discusses the balance between Christian hope and pagan honor as evidenced by a close analysis of the story of Aragorn and Arwen. Armstrong shows that a critic (feminist or otherwise) need not despair of finding women and their stories in *The Lord of the Rings*, but must be creative in extracting female stories from other tales. For example, the points of view of the women (Gilraen and Arwen) in the tale of Aragorn and Arwen are "nested within" the story of Aragorn's life, but they are indeed there. Finally Gene Hargrove's "Who is Tom Bombadil?" is the best scholarly treatment of this enigmatic figure.

Vinyar Tengwar is the journal of the Elvish Linguistics Fellowship, a group of scholars devoted to the study of Tolkien's invented languages, and *Parma Eldalamberon* is another journal of Tolkien linguistic studies. While much of the work published in these journals is exceptionally technical in nature, it is also of a very high quality. Not everyone goes in for Elvish linguistics, but scholars should take care to consult *Vinyar Tengwar* and *Parma Eldalamberon* before making judgments on Elvish words and phrases in Tolkien's work. Finally, there is the Tolkien scholarship that exists only in electronic form. It is important to remember that not all electronically published materials are refereed or otherwise quality controlled, but nevertheless, there are many insightful and intelligent Tolkien critics (amateur and professional) online.

HILARY WYNNE

Further Reading

Burns, Marjorie. *Perilous Realms: Celtic and Norse in Tolkien's Middle-earth*. Toronto: University of Toronto Press, 2005.

Chance, Jane, ed. *Tolkien The Medievalist*. New York: Routledge, 2003.

Chance, Jane, ed. *Tolkien and the Invention of Myth: A Reader*. Lexington, KY: University Press of Kentucky, 2004.

Chance, Jane and Alfred Siewers, ed. *Tolkien's Modern Middle Ages*. London: Palgrave Macmillan, 2005.

Drout, Michael D.C., and Hilary Wynne. "Tom Shippey's *J.R.R. Tolkien: Author of the Century* and a look back at Tolkien criticism since 1982." *Envoi* 9, no. 2 (2000) 101–34.

Drout, Michael D.C., Hilary Wynne, and Melissa Higgins. "Scholarly Studies of J.R.R. Tolkien and His Work (In English): 1984–2000." *Envoi* 9, no. 2 (Fall 2000), 135–65.

Eaglestone, Robert. *Reading The Lord of the Rings: New Writings on Tolkien's Classic*. London: Continuum, 2005.

Flieger, Verlyn. *Interrupted Music: The Making of Tolkien's Mythology*. Kent, OH: Kent State University Press, 2005.

Garth, John. *Tolkien and the Great War: The Threshold of Middle-earth*. London: Harper Collins, 2003. Boston, MA: Houghton Mifflin, 2003.

Hammond, Wayne and Christina Scull. *The Lord of the Rings 1954–2004: Scholarship in Honor of Richard E. Blackwelder*. Milwaukee, MN: Marquette University Press, 2006.

Hammon, Wayne and Christina Scull. *The Lord of the Rings: A Reader's Companion*. Boston, MA: Houghton Mifflin, 2005.

Rosebury, Brian. *Tolkien: A Cultural Phenomenon*. New York: Palgrave Macmillan, 2003.

Shippey, Tom. *The Road to Middle-earth: Revised and Expanded Edition*. Boston, MA: Houghton Mifflin, 2003. [Third edition.]

See also **Tolkien Scholarship: Early Years; Tolkien Scholarship: 1960–1980**

TOLKIEN, ARTHUR REUEL (1857–96)

The father of J.R.R. Tolkien, and a manager for some years with Lloyds Bank in Birmingham, England. Arthur Tolkien was born in Handsworth, Birmingham, around February 1857 to John Benjamin Tolkien and Mary Jane Stow (his father's second wife). Arthur was the oldest in this second family, and had at least five full siblings as well as stepbrothers and -sisters. He moved to South Africa in 1889 to improve his prospects so that he could marry and have a family, and the following year was appointed to an important branch in Bloemfontein, seven hundred miles from Cape Town, and capital of the Orange Free State. Discoveries of gold and diamonds had expanded the banking business there. Mabel Suffield, who had met and became engaged to Arthur Tolkien in Birmingham, left England in March 1891 to marry him. The ceremony took place the following month in Cape Town Anglican Cathedral. Their first son, John Ronald, was born in January the following year, and Hilary in 1894. In Bloemfontein the family lived "over the bank in Maitland Street: beyond were the dusty, treeless plains of the veldt." In April 1895 Mabel Tolkien and her sons sailed for England, in consideration of Ronald's health. The young child was coping badly with the heat of Bloemfontein. Arthur Tolkien remained, absorbed in his work responsibilities. He died soon after from rheumatic fever and severe haemorrhaging on February 15, 1896. Though so young, Ronald carried a vivid memory of his father painting "A.R. Tolkien" on their cabin trunk—a trunk he kept and treasured in later years—as Mabel and the boys prepared to leave for England. In one unfinished story, "The Notion Club Papers," he gave himself the fictional name of "John Arthurson."

COLIN DURIEZ

Further Reading

Carpenter, Humphrey. *J.R.R. Tolkien: A Biography*. London: Allen & Unwin, 1977.

Tolkien, John, and Priscilla Tolkien. *The Tolkien Family Album*. London: HarperCollins, 1992.

See also **Africa; Tolkien, Hilary; Tolkien, Mabel**

TOLKIEN, BAILLIE (1941–)

Baillie Klass was born in Winnipeg on December 10, 1941, the daughter of Alan and Helen Klass. Alan Klass (1907–2000) was a surgeon and a distinguished member of the Faculty of Medicine at the University of Manitoba. Baillie attended McGill University and the University of Manitoba, from which she received a BA in 1962. She also has an MA in English Language and Literature from Oxford (St. Hilda's College, 1964). She was briefly married to Brian Knapheis, a Rhodes Scholar from Winnipeg, and, as Baillie Knapheis, worked as secretary/personal assistant first to J.R.R. Tolkien and then Sir Isaiah Berlin, before her marriage to Christopher Tolkien on September 18, 1967. She and Christopher have two children, Adam Reuel Tolkien (b. 1969) and Rachel Clare Reuel Tolkien (b. 1971).

After J.R.R. Tolkien's death in 1973, the letters that he had written for his children in the guise of Father Christmas were found preserved in his papers. As Christopher Tolkien was busy with *The Silmarillion*, Baillie was chosen to edit the letters for publication and her involvement has continued since then. The first version, *The Father Christmas Letters*, was published in September 1976. The letters themselves began in 1920 and continued until 1943. Most of the letters were included in transcribed form, while (according to the introduction) "almost all of the pictures" were reproduced, all but a few of them in color.

In the wake of the publishing success of Nick Bantock's *Griffin & Sabine: An Extraordinary Correspondence* (1991), in which a fictional correspondence between two people is presented in book form with facsimile letters that could be pulled out of secured envelopes, this format was applied in 1995 to *The Father Christmas Letters*, hereafter more aptly renamed *Letters from Father Christmas*. This version includes a small amount of material not in the 1976 volume.

In 1999, *Letters from Father Christmas* was reworked in the style of an art book, with a larger format, and the opportunity was taken to expand the coverage by including previously unpublished letters and pictures. Unfortunately, as designed by the publisher, the placement of text and pictures is busy and overly crowded, with the text often distractingly printed on top of illustrations, and with a large number of designs repeated so as to fill up any leftover space on a page.

In 2004, the book was yet again redesigned and reformatted. This edition, containing all of the letters and illustrations, is vastly more reader-friendly, achieving a desirable balance of text and illustration.

For the 1976–77 exhibition of drawings by J.R.R. Tolkien, held at the Ashmolean Museum in Oxford, and afterward at the National Book League in London, Baillie Tolkien contributed a short introduction to the catalog, noting that "the difficulty in introducing the visitor to an exhibition of J.R.R. Tolkien's pictures is that his artistic work, like his writing, defies classification," and that "a deceptive combination of naturalism and formality characterizes his artistic work." She concluded perceptively that "though he disliked allegory, he was fascinated by symbols. . . . In seeing his pictures together one may come closer to such an understanding [of his imagination], for the variety and the unity are to be found in them."

DOUGLAS A. ANDERSON

Further Reading

Tolkien, Baillie. "Introduction" to *Catalogue of an Exhibition of Drawings by J.R.R. Tolkien*. Oxford: Ashmolean Museum, 1976.

See also **Art and Illustrations by Tolkien;** *Father Christmas Letters*; **Tolkien, Christopher**

TOLKIEN, CHRISTOPHER REUEL

Christopher Reuel Tolkien is probably best known as the dedicated and meticulous editor of his father's posthumous publications. Chr. Tolkien was born on November 21, 1924, while his father, J.R.R. Tolkien, was still working at the University of Leeds. He is the third and youngest son of Edith Tolkien (née Bratt) and John Ronald Reuel Tolkien. After J.R.R. Tolkien's appointment to the Rawlinson and Bosworth Professorship of Anglo-Saxon at Oxford in 1925, the entire family moved from Leeds to Oxford, where Christopher Tolkien grew up and where he attended the Dragon School and the Oratory School (Reading).

His interest in his father's work dates back to an early date and he and his elder brothers made up the original audience of *The Hobbit*. Yet Christopher also took an interest in the legends of the time before the Third Age of Middle-earth and when his father started working on a sequel to *The Hobbit* after 1937—which would grow into *The Lord of the*

Rings—he became deeply involved in the whole process. He not only made fair copies of some chapters, but also drew the maps that proved invaluable for Tolkien in his labor to synchronize events and that still provide today's reader with guidance in Middle-earth. Furthermore, most of book four of *The Lord of the Rings* (Frodo and Sam's journey into Mordor) was sent serially to Christopher who, from 1943 to 1945, trained as a pilot in South Africa with the Royal Air Force. It is also from this time that more than seventy letters written by J.R.R. Tolkien to his son survive, many of which were published in *The Letters of J.R.R. Tolkien* (1981).

Before joining the R.A.F., Christopher Tolkien had started studying at Oxford and after the war he returned to read English at Trinity College. He shared his father's enthusiasm for Old English, Middle English, Old Norse, and the related literatures and specialized in these subjects. He also continued attending the meetings of the Inklings, a group of literary-minded men who gathered around C.S. Lewis—who was for a while Chr. Tolkien's tutor—and that included, among others, J.R.R. Tolkien, Lewis brother W.H. Lewis, Nevill Coghill, Hugo Dyson, Charles Williams, and Owen Barfield. The Inklings would typically gather once a week, discuss questions of literature, theology, philosophy, and read out to each other from their work in progress (see Carpenter, *The Inklings*).

After graduating from university, Christopher Tolkien worked as a tutor and lecturer in the English Faculty while completing a B. Litt. thesis, a commented edition and translation of the Old Norse *Hervarar Saga*. The study was published in 1960 as *The Saga of King Heidrek the Wise*. It is also during the 1950s that Chr. Tolkien began to make a name for himself as a philologist and medievalist. He discussed the possible historical elements in the Old Norse poem "The Battle of the Goths and the Huns" and published the paper in 1955–56 in the *Saga-Book* (University College, London, for the Viking Society for Northern Research). In 1956 he wrote the introduction to E.O.G. Turville-Petre's edition of *Hervarar Saga ok Heithreks*, and two years later he coedited, together with Nevill Coghill, Chaucer's *Pardoner's Tale*, which was followed in 1959 by *The Nun's Priest's Tale* (also with Nevill Coghill). In the same year, Faith Faulconbridge, whom Christopher Tolkien had married in 1951, gave birth to their son Simon. Faith and Christopher separated in 1963 and Christopher married Baillie Klass in 1967 with whom he has a son, Adam (born 1969), and a daughter, Rachel (born 1971).

Elected to a Fellowship at New College, Oxford, in Autumn 1963, Christopher Tolkien continued to lecture on Old English, Middle English and Old Norse languages and literatures. In 1969, he coedited

(together with Nevill Coghill) another of Chaucer's tales, *The Man of Law's Tale*.

After the death of his father in 1973, Christopher Tolkien became his literary executor. The first two posthumous publications of his father's writings appeared in 1975. One, the "Guide to the Names in *The Lord of the Rings*," was published in Jared Lobdell's *A Tolkien Compass* (no longer included in the second edition, though) and is based on J.R.R. Tolkien's notes that he put together for translators of *The Lord of the Rings*. The other publication contains J.R.R. Tolkien's translations of the Middle English poems *Sir Gawain and the Green Knight*, *Pearl*, and *Sir Orfeo*.

Realizing that the task of identifying, deciphering, classifying and finally editing the numerous notes and manuscript pages would claim all his attention and energy, Christopher Tolkien resigned his Fellowship in 1975 and soon afterward moved with his family to southern France. There he dedicated the following decades to the daunting project of making available the material that illustrates and documents the growth of J.R.R. Tolkien's legendarium to a wider public. The first fruit of this labor was *The Silmarillion*, which appeared 1977 and which for the first time made accessible to the general reader much of the mythological and historical background of *The Lord of the Rings*. Christopher Tolkien also provided notes on some of his father's pictures that appeared in calendars in the years 1976–78, and he published in 1979 an annotated collection, *Pictures by J.R.R. Tolkien*, which presented another side of Tolkien's creative and artistic mind (and which has been superseded by Hammond and Scull's 1995 *J.R.R. Tolkien: Artist and Illustrator*). The next year saw the publication of *Unfinished Tales of Númenor and Middle-earth*, which features material written after the completion of *The Lord of the Rings*, that is, from the 1950s to the 1970s. In 1983, Christopher Tolkien edited *The Monster and the Critics and Other Essays*, a collection of scholarly papers by J.R.R. Tolkien, containing, among others, Tolkien's ground-breaking lecture on *Beowulf* from the year 1936 (see Drout's 2002 *Beowulf and the Critics by J.R.R. Tolkien* for an in-depth study of the development of this paper) and the important essay for the interpretation of *The Lord of the Rings* "On Fairy-Stories." *The Book of Lost Tales, Part One* was published in the same year and is the first volume of the twelve-volume *The History of Middle-earth*. From 1983 till 1996, Christopher Tolkien edited and published each year, with the exception of 1995, one volume of this series. The first two volumes, *The Book of Lost Tales I & II* (1983 & 1984), present the earliest forms of the legends and tales, dating back to the years 1916–20, that were later edited in *The Silmarillion*.

The third volume, *The Lays of Beleriand* (1985), comprises of J.R.R. Tolkien's epic poems that center on Túrin (*The Lay of the Children of Húrin*, 1920–25) and on Beren and Lúthien (*The Lay of Leithian*, 1925–31; *The Lay of Leithian Recommenced*, 1949–55). *The Shaping of Middle-earth* (1986) unites a collection of texts, maps and illustrations that pertain to the years 1926–30 and illustrate the development of the cosmogony of the Elder Days. Volume 5, *The Lost Road and Other Writings* (1987) gives the unfinished time-travel story that Tolkien wrote in 1936–37 and, with the presentation of other writings, brings up the coverage of the development of Middle-earth to the inception of the writing of *The Lord of the Rings* in 1937. Volumes 6–9 constitute a subseries (*The History of the Lord of the Rings*) within the *History of Middle-earth* in so far as they provide a detailed account of the writing of *The Lord of the Rings*. *The Return of the Shadow* (1988) gathers the drafts, sketches and versions from the years 1937–39 and ends with the Fellowship in the Mines of Moria. *The Treason of Isengard* (1989) covers the revisions and new writings made during the years 1939–42 and brings the protagonists to Lórien, describes the breaking of the Fellowship and the encounters with the Riders of Rohan and Treebeard. *The War of the Ring* (1990), containing the writings from the period between 1942–46, takes the story almost to its end ("The Last Debate"). *Sauron Defeated* (1992) brings *The History of The Lord of the Rings* to a close and relates the events that mark the end of the Third Age (written 1946–48). The volume also features *The Notion Club Papers*, taking up the time-travel theme already encountered in *The Lost Road*. It was composed 1945–46 and shows how the world of Middle-earth comes into contact with the modern world of the 1980s. Volumes 10 and 11 of the *History of Middle-earth* cover "The Later Silmarillion." Thus, *Morgoth's Ring* (1993) and *The War of the Jewels* (1994) contain material on the Elder Days that was composed after the conclusion of *The Lord of the Rings* (1948–60). The final volume, 12, *The Peoples of Middle-earth* (1996), collects a variety of texts related to the legendarium.

Christopher Tolkien's studies of medieval languages and literatures, his training as a philologist and editor of manuscripts as well as his intimate and first-hand knowledge of his father's writings made him an ideal candidate for the task of identifying, deciphering, ordering, transcribing, commenting on, and finally editing the vast bulk of papers related to Tolkien's literary production. It is due to a unique combination of talents, scholarship, energy and filial duty that the Tolkien community has now, after thirteen years of labor, a rare tool at their disposal for research into the literary genius of J.R.R. Tolkien.

The manuscripts and notes predominantly concerned with the linguistic aspects of Middle-earth—some three thousand pages—have been entrusted by Christopher Tolkien to a group of American linguists in the early 1990s. They have, since then, edited and published some of those equally complex materials.

Next to his work as editor of his father's writings, Christopher Tolkien also made several recordings of passages from *The Silmarillion* (*Of Beren and Lúthien*, 1977; *Of the Darkening of Valinor*, and *Of the Flight of the Noldor*, 1978). He thus continued a task he had already begun in the 1940s, when he had been appointed to read out aloud each new chapter of *The Lord of the Rings* at the meetings of the Inklings, who generally agreed that he did a much better job at this than his father. He also read the chapter The New Shadow (published 1996 in *The Peoples of Middle-earth*) at the Sheldonian Theatre in Oxford during the 1992 Tolkien Centenary Conference.

Furthermore, he appeared in at least one documentary (*J.R.R.T.: A Portrait of John Ronald Reuel Tolkien, 1892–1973* [Landseer Productions, 1992, longer version released on video 1996 as *J.R.R.T.: A Film Portrait of J.R.R. Tolkien*]).

Within the Tolkien Estate, which holds the copyright to most of the published works of J.R.R. Tolkien, Christopher Tolkien remains, as literary executor and general manager of the Company, the central figure.

THOMAS HONEGGER

Further Reading

Anderson, Douglas A. "Christopher Tolkien: A Bibliography." In *Tolkien's Legendarium*, edited by Verlyn Flieger and Carl F. Hostetter, 247–52. Westport, CT: Greenwood Press, 2000.
———. "Profile: Christopher Tolkien." *Canadian C.S. Lewis Journal* 92 (1997): 53–56.

I would like to thank Douglas A. Anderson for his help and willingness to share his expertise with me, and Christopher Tolkien for his kindness in factually correcting this article.

See also **Inklings; Lewis, C.S.; Life; Estate;** *History of Middle-earth*; **Oxford; Posthumous Publications;** *Silmarillion*; **Tolkien, Baille; Tolkien, Simon**

TOLKIEN, EDITH
See Marriage

TOLKIEN, FAITH
Faith Lucy Tilly Faulconbridge was born in 1928, the daughter of F.T. Faulconbridge, whom Tolkien had known in his youth as a fellow student at King

Edward's School, Birmingham. She read English at St. Anne's College, Oxford (BA 1950), and later studied sculpture at the Oxford City Art School. She married Christopher Tolkien on April 2, 1951. They had one son, Simon, born in 1959. Faith and Christopher Tolkien separated in 1964, and their marriage was dissolved in 1967.

Faith Tolkien was initially known for her portrait heads in bronze, some of which she exhibited at the Royal Academy as early as 1958. She made a bust of her father-in-law that the English Faculty at Oxford presented to Tolkien on his retirement in 1959. Around 1966, Tolkien had it cast in bronze, and it was placed in the English Faculty Library. Her other subjects have included Iris Murdoch and, posthumously, C.S. Lewis.

In 1958, she produced a seated Madonna and Child in bronze for the Catholic Chaplaincy at Birmingham University, and in the early 1980s she returned to religious themes, including ambitious work for the Corpus Christi Church, Headington, Oxford, and for the Church of the Sacred Heart, in Sutton Coldfield, near Birmingham. For the former she completed fourteen roundels, cast in resin bronze, forming a new sequence of Stations, while for the latter, she made a complex composition in relief to be fixed to the wall behind the altar. This later work was inspired by the apse mosaic in San Clemente, Rome.

DOUGLAS A. ANDERSON

Further Reading

Murray, Robert. "Faith Tolkien: A Theologian among Sculptors." *The Month* 255, no. 1520 (August 1994): 320–24.

See also **Tolkien, Christopher; Tolkien, Simon**

TOLKIEN, HILARY (1894–1976)

On February 17, 1894, Hilary Arthur Reuel, the younger brother of J.R.R. Tolkien, was born in Bloemfontein, South Africa. After his mother returned to England with them because of his older brother's health, they had an idyllic period residing in rural Warwickshire before moving into urban Birmingham. At that time local children, suspicious of their long hair (the custom for middle-class little boys) derisively called Tolkien and Hilary "wenches." Ronald nicknamed the flour-coated miller's son in the nearby Sarehole Mill "The White Ogre." Hilary remembered a farmer, nicknamed "The Black Ogre," who terrorized the local children. (He once chased Ronald for picking mushrooms.) When Mabel was confined by what proved to be terminal illness in the Oratory cottage at Rednall, Ronald would catch a train to school, walking more than a mile to the station. He started off early, and returned late, with Hilary sometimes meeting him with a lamp. With Mabel's death Father Francis Morgan became the boys' guardian and benefactor. After leaving school, Hilary helped run a farm in Nottinghamshire with his widowed aunt Jane Neave, before enlisting, at the outbreak of war in 1914, in the bugles and drums section of Third Birmingham Battalion (Sixteenth Royal Warwickshire Regiment). Being in that section meant that he became a stretcher-bearer. He was wounded in April 1916. Surviving the war, he bought a small orchard and market garden near Evesham, west of Oxford, the ancestral home of his mother's family, the Suffields. The brothers were able to keep in contact without too much difficulty. Hilary's great love for nature was shared by his brother Ronald.

COLIN DURIEZ

Further Reading

Carpenter, Humphrey. *J.R.R. Tolkien: A Biography*. Boston, MA: Houghton Mifflin, 1977.

See also **Morgan, Father Francis; Tolkien, Arthur; Tolkien, Mabel; Warwickshire**

TOLKIEN, JOHN (1917–2003)

John Francis Reuel Tolkien was born in Cheltenham on November 16, 1917, the first child of Edith and J.R.R. Tolkien. He was educated at the Dragon School, and at the Oratory School in Caversham, where in his final year he decided to prepare for the priesthood. On the advice of the Archbishop, he first read English at Exeter College, Oxford (BA 1939), before heading to the English College at Rome in November 1939. Although Italy had not yet entered the war, it was an ally of Germany, and soon it was not deemed safe to remain in Italy, so the College was removed to England, settling for six years at Stonyhurst in Lancashire. John was ordained as a priest at the Church of St. Gregory and Augustine in North Oxford in February 1946.

His first position was as a curate at the St. Mary and St. Benedict Church in Coventry, where from 1946–50, he taught weekly classes to sixty children and organized the rebuilding of church schools. From 1950–57, he ministered to some seven thousand parishioners as curate at the English Martyrs Church in Sparkhill, Birmingham. Thereafter he moved to North Staffordshire, where he was chaplain at the University College of North Staffordshire (which later became Keele University), and at two grammar schools, St. Joseph's College, Trent Vale, and

St. Dominic's High School, Hartshill. From 1966 to 1987 he was parish priest at the Church of Our Lady of the Angels and St. Peter in Chains, Stoke-on-Trent, where again he oversaw the building of a new school. Fr. John moved back to the Oxford area in 1987, settling in Eynsham, where he was the parish priest at St. Peter's Catholic Church until his retirement in 1994. Fr. John Tolkien died on January 22, 2003, after some years of failing health.

After Fr. John returned to Oxford, he and his sister Priscilla began identifying and cataloging the large collection of family photographs, and as the centenary of their father's birth approached, they collaborated on a book. *The Tolkien Family Album* contains many photographs and memories of their family, and gives an affectionate and anecdotal account of their father's life.

Fr. Tolkien had a passion for ecumenism, which he attributed to his father.

DOUGLAS A. ANDERSON

Further Reading

Tolkien, John, and Priscilla Tolkien. *The Tolkien Family Album.* Boston: Houghton Mifflin, 1992.
Weedon, Joan. "Father John Tolkien." *Round About Eynsham: Monthly News from Eynsham Churches*, no. 135 (February 1994): 3, 8.

See also **Oxford; Tolkien, Priscilla**

TOLKIEN (NÉE SUFFIELD), MABEL (1870–1904)

Described by J.R.R. Tolkien as "a gifted lady of great beauty and wit, greatly stricken by God with grief and suffering," Mabel Suffield was born into a family associated with Evesham, Worcestershire. Tolkien identified himself with these West Midland roots of his mother. He wrote: "Though a Tolkien by name, I am a Suffield by tastes, talents, and upbringing, and any corner of that county (however fair or squalid) is in an indefinable way 'home' to me, as no other part of the world is." That sense of home, emotionally linked to his mother, is realized in his creation of The Shire. The emotional links with his mother, heightened by her loss in boyhood, were further charged by her devotion to the Roman Catholic faith. Though he lost her at the age of twelve, Mabel Tolkien shaped his entire life. "It is to my mother, who taught me (until I obtained a scholarship)," wrote Tolkien, "that I owe my tastes for philology, especially of Germanic languages, and for romance."

Mabel was born in Birmingham early in 1870. Arthur Tolkien, who worked for Lloyd's Bank in Birmingham, proposed to her soon after her eighteenth birthday, before leaving in less than a year for South Africa to better his prospects with the Bank of Africa. It was not until 1891, with her coming of age, that Mabel's father allowed her to marry him. In March that year Mabel set out from Southampton on the steamer *Roslin Castle*. She and Arthur married in Cape Town Anglican Cathedral on April 16, 1891, and then Mabel had to adjust to life in Bloemfontein, deep in the dusty, hot interior. Here John Ronald Reuel Tolkien was born on January 3, 1892. Two years later, brother Hilary Arthur Reuel was born.

In April 1895 Mabel and her sons sailed for England, in consideration of Ronald's health. The toddler was coping badly with the heat of Bloemfontein. Arthur Tolkien remained, absorbed in his work responsibilities. The three stayed with Mabel's parents and sister, Jane, in their tiny family villa in Ashfield Road, King's Heath, Birmingham.

During this visit, Arthur Tolkien unexpectedly died—the family were about to return to South Africa. Mabel was now a single parent, with very limited means. Soon the three moved to Sarehole, in the more healthy countryside. Their new home, 5 Gracewell, was a smart and good-sized semi-detached cottage almost opposite the pond side of Sarehole Mill, then about a mile south of the city of Birmingham. Though so near, they were, in fact, in the very heart of rural Warwickshire. With only horses and carts, it was "long ago in the quiet of the world, when there was less noise and more green." Mabel, a highly talented and resourceful woman, educated her boys until they entered formal education. Amongst other things, Mabel taught Ronald to read, and later instructed him in calligraphy, drawing, Latin, French, piano, and botany.

Ronald's education was always a priority for Mabel. In 1900, he entered King Edward's School, a grammar school then located near New Street Station, Birmingham, his fees paid by an uncle. It was at this time that Mabel and her sister May Suffield were received into the Roman Catholic Church, alienating her relatives, heightening an anxious poverty to which Mabel was unused. In Tolkien's perception, her conversion to Catholicism intensified her suffering and hastened her death because of the coolness and rejection it created with her relatives on both the Tolkien and the Suffield side, who were Protestant. In his view, expressed over thirty-five years after her death, she experienced nothing less than "persecution of her faith." The family moved from their rural setting to just inside the city, to Moseley, somewhat nearer to The Birmingham Oratory. Founded by Cardinal Newman in 1859, this had become Mabel's spiritual home.

Moseley was on the tram route to the city centre, chosen by Mabel as it made it easier for Ronald to commute to school. The next year they had to move again. Later they moved to a mean house in Oliver Road in the Edgbaston district, a short walk from The Oratory and even closer to King Edward's School, for which, in 1903, Ronald gained a scholarship. Tolkien took his first Communion that year, marking his devotion to his mother's Roman Catholic faith.

Mabel and her sons had met Father Francis Xavier Morgan, who provided friendship, counsel and money for the fatherless family. With the boys often ill and the mother developing diabetes, he enabled them to move to the pretty cottage belonging to the Oratory, close by its rural retreat near Rednal village, deep in the Worcestershire countryside, for the summer of 1904. The rural atmosphere there was like that of Sarehole. Earlier that year, in April, Mabel had been in hospital, with her sons temporarily being sent to relatives, Ronald to his Aunt Jane in Hove. Mabel died in the cottage on November 14, 1904, aged only thirty-four. Father Morgan, who was now their guardian, promptly took on the responsibility of the orphaned boys. Mabel Tolkien was buried in the churchyard at St. Peter's Roman Catholic Church at Bromsgrove, not far from Rednal.

COLIN DURIEZ

Further Reading

Carpenter, Humphrey. *J.R.R. Tolkien: A Biography*. Boston, MA: Houghton Mifflin, 1977.
———, ed. *The Letters of J.R.R. Tolkien*. Boston, MA: Houghton Mifflin, 1981.
Tolkien, John, and Priscilla Tolkien. *The Tolkien Family Album*. Boston, MA: Houghton Mifflin, 1992.

See also **Catholicism, Roman; Childhood of Tolkien; Education; Morgan, Father Francis; Tolkien, Arthur; Tolkien, Hilary**

TOLKIEN, MICHAEL (1920–84)

Michael Hilary Reuel Tolkien was born in Oxford on October 22, 1920, the second son of Edith and J.R.R. Tolkien. He was educated at the Dragon School, and at the Oratory School then in Caversham. His study at Trinity College, Oxford, was interrupted by service in the Army in World War II. He defended aerodromes in the Battle of Britain, and later in France and Germany, but was invalided out of the Army. He returned to Oxford in 1944, and received a BA in Modern History from Trinity College in 1945.

In 1947 he began work as a school teacher at various Catholic boys schools, first at the Oratory School (relocated to Woodcote), and later at Ampleforth College in North Yorkshire, and, beginning in 1965, at Stonyhurst College in rural Lancashire. On November 11, 1941, he married Joan Audrey Griffiths (1916–82). Their three children are Michael George Reuel Tolkien (b. 1943), Joan Anne, later called Joanna Tolkien (b. 1945), and Judith Tolkien (b. 1951). Michael Tolkien died of leukemia on February 27, 1984.

Michael's involvement with his father as a storyteller began early. On a family holiday at Filey on the Yorkshire coast in the summer of 1925, Michael lost a toy dog on the beach, inspiring his father to tell the story, later written out and illustrated, of a real dog that was turned into a toy and had many adventures. The resulting short book, *Roverandom*, was published in 1998. When Michael was around eight years old, Tolkien wrote and illustrated a story based on his three sons' teddy bears and a toy car that was Christopher's. According to Michael's wife Joan, references to this tale appear in a diary Michael kept as a Dragon School summer holiday task in 1928. The story, *Mr. Bliss*, appeared in 1982.

Michael and his brothers also had a fondness for a children's book by E.A. Wyke-Smith called *The Marvellous Land of Snergs* (1927), in which one of the main characters is a half-high creature called a snerg who is named Gorbo. The boys' desire for more stories about snergs was fulfilled by their father's story about the half-high Hobbit named Bilbo. And Michael's abhorrence of spiders was the inspiration of Bilbo's encounter with the spiders in Mirkwood. Michael reminisced: "This is a chapter that I'm very proud to say was created almost entirely for my benefit to show however big a spider was, he could, in fact be overcome. And I *loved* the part where Bilbo plays hell with those spiders and this was heaven."

Some of Michael's concerns also found expression in *The Lord of the Rings*. Having witnessed a mass tree-felling, Michael told his father, who "listened seriously to my angry comments and when I asked him to make up a tale in which the trees took a terrible revenge on the machine-lovers he said: 'I will write one.' I had to wait many years, though not in vain, to read of the revenge of the Ents on the squalid industrialism of Saruman, the traitorous wizard, at Orthanc."

Michael shared with his father a recurrent dream of a great wave overwhelming trees and green fields, which Tolkien referred to as his Atlantis complex and which inspired the story of the downfall of Númenor. In his short obituary of his father, Michael mourned "a friend of half a century's standing, for he possessed the ability, rare in fathers of exceptional talent . . . of combining fatherhood and friendship."

DOUGLAS A. ANDERSON

Further Reading

Mills, Derek. "An Interview with Michael Hilary Reuel Tolkien." Transcribed by Gary Hunnewell and Sylvia Hunnewell from a tape-recording of a Radio Blackburn broadcast. *Minas Tirith Evening-Star*, 18, no. 1, and *Ravenhill*, 7 no. 4 (Spring 1989): 5–9.

Tolkien, Joan. "Origin of a Tolkien Tale." *The Sunday Times*, October 10, 1982.

Tolkien, Michael. "J.R.R. Tolkien—the Wizard Father." *Sunday Telegraph*, September 9, 1973.

See also **Ents; Oxford;** *Roverandom;* **Trees; Wyke-Smith, E.A.**

TOLKIEN, PRISCILLA (1929–)

Priscilla Mary Reuel Tolkien was born in Oxford on June 18, 1929, the fourth child and only daughter of J.R.R. Tolkien. Priscilla was too young to have been a member of the original audience for whom *The Hobbit* was written, but she did take an active part in the production of *The Lord of the Rings* by typing out some of the early chapters for her father when she was around the age of fourteen. She read English at Lady Margaret Hall, Oxford (BA 1951), and had a professional career as a social worker. She has lived and worked in the Oxford area for most of her life.

As Tolkien's only daughter, Priscilla has noted her father's "complete belief in higher education for girls; never in my early life or since did I feel that any difference was made between me and my brothers, so far as our educational needs and opportunities were concerned."

From late July through mid August 1955, Priscilla and her father took a two week holiday in Italy. There Tolkien found that "Venice seemed incredibly, elvishly lovely—to me like a dream of Old Gondor," and he and Priscilla delighted in attending an outdoor performance of Verdi's *Rigoletto*.

A few years after her father's death in 1973, Priscilla began to represent her family in occasional public appearances. She has done so with genuine charm and has frequently spoken with great insight on her father.

In a talk given at the time of the publication of *The Silmarillion*, Priscilla recalled her father's natural gift for story-telling: "From my earliest years I recall my father telling me stories at bed-time, and in the darkened room as I was falling asleep I have a vivid memory of him re-telling the story of Rapunzel and of how her prince sang to her at the foot of the tower where she was imprisoned, telling her to let down her golden hair. This was brought back to my mind when reading the 'Tale of Beren and Lúthien.'" Priscilla continued with an evaluation of the nature of her father's imagination: "In *The Silmarillion* we have many shorter tales woven into one large tale of Creation and History. . . . It was possible for my father to conceive stories on both the grand and on the small scale, and to have his imagination nourished by both the simplest fairy-tale and by great stories of the World."

Competing with her father's creative side, there were always practical matters. As an adult Priscilla came to understand "the very great strain suffered by the creative artist who has to meet the demands of a responsible professional life and work to support a family of four children, while at the same time trying to find spare time and energy to write the stories that were the most powerful expression of his being."

Beginning in 1987, after her brother John returned to the Oxford area, Priscilla and John worked together to identify and catalog the large collection of family photographs. This work developed into a book, *The Tolkien Family Album*, published in 1992 for the centenary of their father's birth. Illustrated with many photographs, it gives an affectionate and anecdotal account of their father's life. Priscilla also noted that the book "has enabled us to reflect on the vast changes in Britain that have taken place in the hundred years since my parents were born."

Also as part of the centenary celebrations, Priscilla traveled to her father's birthplace in Bloemfontein, South Africa, for the unveiling of a plaque honoring his memory at the Anglican Cathedral of St. Andrew and St. Michael, finding it particularly moving "to feel more in touch with his origins than I had ever felt before and with the grandparents I had sadly never known."

DOUGLAS A. ANDERSON

Further Reading

Gray, Rosemary, ed. *A Tribute to J.R.R. Tolkien.* Foreword by Priscilla Tolkien. Pretoria: University of South Africa, 1992.

Tolkien, John, and Priscilla Tolkien. *The Tolkien Family Album.* Boston, MA: Houghton Mifflin, 1992.

Tolkien, Priscilla. "Memories of J.R.R. Tolkien in His Centenary Year." *The Brown Book* [of Lady Margaret Hall, Oxford], December 1992, 12–14.

———. "Talk Given at the Church House [Bookshop] Westminster on 16 September 1977." *Amon Hen*, no. 29 (c. October 1977): 4–6.

See also **Oxford**

TOLKIEN, SIMON (1959–)

Simon Mario Reuel Tolkien was born in Oxford on January 12, 1959, the only child of Christopher Tolkien and his first wife, Faith Faulconbridge. His parents separated when he was five, and he grew up with his mother. He was educated at the Dragon School in Oxford, the Downside School (a Roman Catholic public school near Bath), and at Oxford University, where he read Modern History at Trinity College. In 1984 he married Tracy Steinberg (b. 1962), an American whom he met at Oxford in a university creative writing course. They have two children. Tracy Tolkien owns and operates a vintage clothing store in Chelsea and has published several books on vintage clothing and jewelry.

Simon Tolkien was called to the bar in 1994, and works as a barrister, specializing in criminal defense and prosecution. In January 2000, he began writing fiction, though feeling somewhat under the shadow of his grandfather's fame. His first novel, which he has called "a black comedy," was not accepted for publication, but his second, a courtroom drama, was published in the United States as *Final Witness* (2002) and in England as *The Stepmother* (2003). Some reviewers described it as a well-paced thriller with believable characters, while others found it uneven, with a disappointing ending. Simon's literary interests clearly run more toward John Grisham than to the works of his grandfather. He has said he would never write a fantasy book.

In the interviews given around the release of his novel, Simon Tolkien frequently complained of an estrangement with his father over the family's stance toward the Peter Jackson films of *The Lord of the Rings*. Simon favored participation with the filmmakers, while his father did not.

With this publicity surrounding both the films and his own novel, Simon published a short essay of recollections of his grandfather. As the only grandchild of his age in the Tolkien family, he felt special to both of his grandparents, and after his parents separated, he felt that his grandfather in particular took him under his wing: "My grandfather had the knack of being able to talk to a child without seeming like a voice coming from on high. He spent a great deal of time with me and his love and kindness helped me through difficult times." After his grandparents moved to Bournemouth in 1968, he frequently visited them: "I don't remember my grandfather writing when I went to stay with him. He played endless word games with me and did the Telegraph cross. While he worked out the clues, he'd embellish the newspaper with exquisite designs." Simon vividly recalled attending church with his grandfather in Bournemouth, where his father protested the change of the liturgy from Latin to English by responding loudly in Latin. Simon was fourteen when his grandfather died in 1973.

DOUGLAS A. ANDERSON

Further Reading

Tolkien, Simon. *Final Witness.* New York: Random House, 2002. London: Michael Joseph, 2003 [as *The Stepmother*] .
———. [Recollections of J.R.R. Tolkien]. *The Mail*, February 23, 2003. Reprinted at: http://www. simontolkien.com.

TOM BOMBADIL

Tom Bombadil is one of the most controversial beings in *The Lord of the Rings*. Though greatly loved by many readers, critics charge that he is an anomalous creation, out of place in the story, who could have been omitted without any effect on the narrative (and indeed was in the Peter Jackson film). The inspiration for Tom was a Dutch doll belonging to one of Tolkien's children. His appearance in literary form predates the publication of the trilogy by two decades. He was the main character in a long poem, "The Adventures of Tom Bombadil," first published in 1934 in *Oxford Magazine*. In its pre-Hobbit form, Tolkien referred to Tom as "the spirit of the (vanishing) Oxford and Berkshire countryside." The conversion of the poem into Middle-earth mythology or Hobbit folklore required only minor changes—for example, the feather in his hat was changed from peacock to swan-wing. He was known to the Hobbits of Buckland as "Tom Bombadil" (with Bombadil perhaps related to the Middle English words for "humming" and "hidden"), to the Dwarves as "Forn" (according to Grimm, associated with "old" and "sorcery"), to the Elves as "Iarwain Ben-adar" (probably meaning old and fatherless), and to Men as "Orald" (Old English for "very old, ancient, original). Yet, his true identity remains a mystery. This mystery is highlighted by three occasions in which the question "Who is Tom Bombadil?" is asked and discussed. In a letter to his proofreader in April 1954, Tolkien states that Tom was intentionally introduced into the trilogy as an enigma, that is, a mystery, a puzzle, something that seems to be discordant but isn't. Later in the same letter he explains that Tom, though not an important person in the narrative, serves an important function by showing that there are people and things in Middle-earth for whom the war with Sauron is largely irrelevant and unimportant. Tom has renounced power in a kind of "vow of poverty" and his life reflects "a natural pacifist view." Because he delights in nature for its own sake, Tom relates to the world through pure science and poetry rather than applied science and technology (representing a sharp contrast with the agricultural instrumentalism of the Entwives). Tom's status in Middle-earth is somewhat confused by the fact that Tom is called "the oldest" while Treebeard the Ent is referred to by Gandalf as "the oldest living thing." T.A. Shippey tries to resolve this conflict by suggesting that Tom is not living in the sense that the Nazgûl and the Barrow-wights are not dead. This solution, however, is problematic in that the Nazgûl and the Barrow-wights are beings who were formerly living beings in the ordinary sense. Another alternative is that while Treebeard is biotic, a product of the living ecosystems of Middle-earth, Tom is a visitor from another plane of existence (beyond the Void) like the Valar and the Maiar, and therefore not biotic. This interpretation is consistent with Tom's claim that he was in Middle-earth before the river and the trees, the first raindrop, and the first acorn, essentially, before the physical creation of Middle-earth by the Valar. Treebeard, in contrast, was at most an idea in the Song of Yavanna, part of the Music of the Ainur at the beginning of *The Silmarillion,* and only achieved physical existence along with the trees during the making of the world. Another controversy involves the first answer to Frodo's question "Who is Tom Bombadil?" when Goldberry simply states, "He is." In terms of medieval theology and philosophy, such a statement could be taken to suggest that existence is a predicate of Tom Bombadil and that he is therefore God. However, Tolkien seems to deny this possibility in a letter from September 1954, saying that the question asked is about names, about who Tom is, not about what he is. The answers to this question on the other two occasions are certainly focused on naming. On the second occasion, Tom insists that his name is the only answer and on the third occasion, the answer is merely a discussion of the various names Tom is called among various peoples. Goldberry's attempt to clarify Frodo's question does suggest a possible answer, when she explains that Tom, though a master who can control and dominate the beings in the Old Forest, does not own any of them, individually or collectively (they all belong to themselves). This lack of possessiveness may be an indication that Tom is Aulë the Smith, the third most powerful of the Valar, the master of all crafts, and the builder of the mountains, land, and the basins of the seas. Aulë's chief moral characteristic, in contrast to Melkor, was that he delighted in works of skill and was not envious of the works of others. This identification of Tom with Aulë would explain why Tom is the only powerful being in Middle-earth not worried that touching the Ring will corrupt him. The appearance of Goldberry, Tom's wife, at the end of the visit to the Old Forest also suggests that Tom is Aulë. Just as Yavanna appears to Elves as a tree crowned in light and with her feet as roots in the waters of Ulmo, she appears to the hobbits as "a sunlit flower" with "the glint of water on the dewy grass" under her dancing feet. The characterization of Goldberry as the River-woman's daughter does not necessarily refute this identification, for if Tom is not really Tom, it is not unlikely that Goldberry is misidentified in the folklore of Buckland as well. The early view that Tom is a nature spirit is consistent with Tolkien's pre-hobbit conception but is more an answer to "what is?" than "who is?" since there are no named nature spirits in Middle-earth. When Tolkien first introduced Tom into the early drafts of the trilogy, *The Return of the Shadow,* he was himself still unsettled on who and what Tom was. In answer to the question "Who are you, Master?" Tom originally answers that he is an "Aborigine," rather than "Eldest." Notes on the manuscript also indicate that Tolkien considered making Farmer Maggot a relative of Tom's and therefore not a hobbit. Because the term "aborigine" means a first inhabitant or native of a region, it is not inconsistent with Tom's claim that he was the first person to be in the Old Forest ("before the river and the trees" and "the first raindrop and the first acorn"). Tolkien may have dropped the term to avoid an association with the Woses or Drùedain, the carvers of the Púkel-men statues near Dunharrow and the primitives living in Druadan Forest. Tolkien also considered having Tom engage in a confrontation with Nazgûl or Barrow-wights riding horses, in which Tom brought them to a halt by raising his hand. Frodo's attempt to stop the Ringwraiths at the Ford of Bruinen was originally intended to be an attempt to imitate this power of Bombadil.

GENE HARGROVE

Further Reading

Hargrove, Gene. "Who Is Tom Bombadil?" *Mythlore* 13, no. 1(1986): 20–24.
———. "Who Is Tom Bombadil?" (expanded version) http://www.cep.unt.edu/~hargrove/bombadil.html (July 2004).
Isaacs, Neil D., and Rose A. Zimbardo, eds. *Tolkien and the Critics: Essays on J.R.R. Tolkien's The Lord of the Rings.* Notre Dame, IN: University of Notre Dame Press, 1968.
Jensen, Stuart. "What Is Tom Bombadil?" http://tolkien.slimy.com/essays/Bombadil.html (October 2002).
Noel, Ruth S. *The Mythology of Middle-earth.* Boston, MA: Houghton Mifflin, 1978.
Shippey, T.A. *The Road to Middle-earth.* Boston, MA: Houghton Mifflin, 1983.

TOUR IN THE ALPS, 1911

Before starting his first term at Oxford, Tolkien traveled through Switzerland with a "mixed party of about the same size as the company in *The Hobbit*." The tour, "on foot with a heavy pack," started in Interlaken and from there went south to Lauterbrunnen and Mürren, northeast to Grindelwald and Meiringen, southeast through the Grimsel Pass, and then southwest by the Aletsch glacier in the direction of the Matterhorn, arriving finally at Sion (*Letters*, 308–9). Scenes and episodes from this summer journey of 1911 remained with Tolkien throughout his life and left a noticeable mark on Tolkien's mountains and mountain settings, especially in *The Hobbit*, where (as Tolkien explains) certain adventures he himself experienced—a rock fall and a "thunder-battle," for example— reappear in Bilbo's crossing of the Misty Mountains. In a 1968 letter to his son, Michael, Tolkien shares further details about the journey and its influence on his writing. The hobbit's "journey from Rivendell to the other side of the Misty Mountains, including the glissade down the slithering stones into the pine woods, is based on my adventures in 1911." In this same letter Tolkien also cites the Alpine *Silberhorn*, "sharp against dark blue," as the source for what became his *Silvertine* (*Celebdril*) and once again describes how sun-loosened boulders rushed down upon them "at gathering speed." Two other incidents mentioned in this letter may also have left their mark on Tolkien's literature: the party's method of dealing with "harvestmen spiders" by dropping hot wax "onto their fat bodies" and a flood of "foaming water" created by releasing a dammed mountain rill (*Letters*, 391–93). Tolkien does not relate the Swiss spiders to his own villainous spiders; nor does he suggest that the rushing waters he and his companions released on an Alpine slope influenced Elrond's foaming flood at the Ford of Rivendell, but it is easy to speculate.

Elsewhere Tolkien writes how his "heart still lingers among the high stony wastes" and how he longs "to see the snows and the great heights again!" (*Letters*, 90–1 and 123).

MARJORIE BURNS

Further Reading

Anderson, Douglas A. *The Annotated Hobbit*. Rev. ed. Boston and New York: Houghton Mifflin, 2002.

Barnfield, Marie. "The Roots of Rivendell: or, Elrond's House Now Open As a Museum," Þe Lyfe ant Þe Auncestrye, no. 2 (Spring 1996): 4–18.

Carpenter, Humphrey. *J.R.R. Tolkien: A Biography*. London: Allen & Unwin; Boston, MA: Houghton Mifflin, 1977.

Green, William H. *The Hobbit: A Journey into Maturity*. New York: Twayne, 1995.

Hammond, Wayne, and Christina Scull. *J.R.R. Tolkien: Artist and Illustrator*. Boston and New York: Houghton Mifflin, 1995.

See also **Childhood of Tolkien; *Hobbit, The*; Mountains**

TOWERS

The motif of the tower has great significance in Tolkien's mythology and writing. Towers can signify creative impulses, the desire to transcend, or the yearning for the immortal of the divine. On the negative side, towers can also embody hubris, overreaching, and the opposition to creation or the power of good. Towers thus occupy an important symbolic place in Tolkien's invented landscapes, often serving as metonymic replacements for the major forces in his fiction (the White Tower for Gondor, Orthanc for Saruman, or the Dark Tower for Sauron) and as symbolic touchstones for the reader.

In "*Beowulf*: The Monsters and the Critics" Tolkien uses a tower as an allegorical representation of the poetic creativity versus the destructive tendencies of scholarship. The tower made with ancient stone stands for the poem *Beowulf* patched together from much older, now lost sources. The friends of the builder—or *Beowulf* scholars—find it interesting, but topple it to see where he and his forefathers had found the stones, thereby destroying the tower in a misguided effort to understand its building blocks. Tolkien laments, "But from the top of that tower the man had been able to look out on the sea" (*MC*, 8). Tom Shippey notes that this tower is "a strong and private image of Tolkien's own for what he desired in literature" (Shippey, 47) and points out similarities to other towers looking out over the sea in works such as his early poem "The Happy Mariners." In these instances, the seas connote artistic and even divine inspiration, and towers allow the mortal to rise up from the mundane level and be touched by the divine. In the legendarium this motif appears in the Elven towers on the Tower Hills—especially the tallest tower Elositirion that Gil-galad made for Elendil's *palantír* to gaze out toward Eressëa and the Undying Lands. The unpoetic, earth-bound Hobbits have never climbed those towers just as they don't perceive the greater life of the immortals on the borders of their land.

The "Silmarillion" accounts contain many towers that function as beacons or embodiments of celestial power, often removed from the mortal world. Taniquetil, the highest peak of Arda upon which Manwe and Varda have built their halls, is the prototypical "tower" like Odin's high throne from which he can survey creation; that seat is also echoed in the

Seat of Seeing on Amon Hen and in its dark counterpart, Barad-dûr from which the Eye of Sauron seeks the Ring (Wainwright, 33). Mindon Eldaliéva, Ingwë's tower in Tirion, the "Great Watch-tower," "whose silver lamp shone far out into the mists of the sea" (*S*, 59), is a feature that dates back to *The Book of Lost Tales* account. It is linguistically and emblematically related to the tower in the Land of the Dead from the Celtic myth of the god Íth. Íth spies Ireland from the summit of his tower and journeys there to his death just as the Noldor journey from the immortal realm of Eldamar to suffering in the mortal lands of Beleriand (Hostetter and Wynne). The tower of Avallonë in the Second Age also serves as a distant beacon of the now forbidden Undying Lands to the mariners of Númenor, a new tower that recalls but is lesser than the original.

The towers in *The Lord of the Rings* represent the ambition and cultural supremacy of Men in particular, but also the negative attributes of pride and the will to dominate. Arnor and Gondor, the "stone land" that is etymologically related to giants or the Old English *Ent* (Hostetter and Wynne, 49), are characterized by great citadels epitomizing the power of the Men of Westernesse. Yet many of the great towers built by the Dúnedain are in ruins or have been seized by the Enemy; Minas Morgul, the Tower of Cirith Ungol, and the Towers of the Teeth have all been transformed from structures of beauty and nobility into strongholds of sorcery and evil. These demonstrate how the great ideals and aspirations of the Men can become twisted into their opposites. Minas Tirith with its Tower of Ecthelion is the last outpost of Numenorean heritage. Its seven levels recall the seven-storied tower in David Lindsay's *A Voyage to Arcturus,* which represents a spiritual journey (Hoffman) or the famous seven hills of Rome (Wainwright, 62). Barad-dûr, the Dark Tower, stands against it as the physical incarnation of Sauron's lust for power, a distortion of the Gondorians' pride.

Tolkien's ambiguous title for the second published part of his novel, *The Two Towers,* underscores the symbolic functions of towers in his tale. In letter 140 Tolkien proposes that the title "might refer to Isengard and Barad-dûr, or to Minas Tirith and B[arad-dûr]; or Isengard and Cirith Ungol" (*Letters*, 170), and then in letter 143 he suggests Orthanc and Cirith Ungol, though he adds, "so much is made of the basic opposition of the Dark Tower and Minas Tirith, that seems very misleading" (*Letters*, 173). His proposed dust jacket sketches show Minas Tirith and Minas Morgul, though his final one features the two mentioned at the end of part 2, Orthanc and Minas Morgul (Hammond and Scull, 180).

The various pairings of towers figuratively suggest either the union of the forces of evil or the opposition of good and evil—order and chaos. Jane Chance, discussing Orthanc and Cirith Ungol, invokes the Tower of Babel when she proposes that the two towers figure expresses the "separation or perversion" of the mind and body (Chance, 163). Indeed, Orthanc's two meanings, "Mount Fang" in Sindarin and "Cunning Mind" in the language of the Mark, show how the tower embodies Saruman's fall from wisdom into evil. Towers thus serve as a symbolic shorthand for the thematic conflicts within Tolkien's universe.

DAVID D. OBERHELMAN

Further Reading

Chance, Jane. *Tolkien's Art: A Mythology for England*. Rev. ed. Lexington, KY: University Press of Kentucky, 2001.

Hammond, Wayne G., and Christina Scull. *J.R.R. Tolkien: Artist & Illustrator*. New York: Houghton Mifflin, 1995.

Hoffman, Curtiss. *The Seven Story Tower: A Mythic Journey Through Space and Time*. New York: Insight Books, 1999.

Hostetter, Carl F., and Patrick Wynne. "Stone Towers." *Mythlore* 19, no. 4 (1993): 47–55, 65.

Shippey, Tom. *The Road to Middle-earth: How J.R.R. Tolkien Created a New Mythology*. Rev. and Expanded ed. Boston, MA: Houghton Mifflin, 2003.

Wainwright, Edmund. *Tolkien's Mythology for England: A Middle-earth Companion*. Frithgarth: Anglo-Saxon Books, 2004.

See also **Gondor; Kôr; Power in Tolkien's Work; Pride; Symbolism in Tolkien's Works; Taniquetil; Tol Eressëa**

TREASON

To be true to one's word, to fulfill one's social and societal obligations and to get the priorities of one's loyalties right—this is what seems to distinguish virtuous protagonists in Tolkien's work (on the moral and ethical framework, see Weinreich). Treason, taken in the widest possible sense as a violation of any of these obligations, is thus a complex phenomenon that works on many levels. Although Tolkien did not discuss the nature of treason explicitly, we find numerous and variegated instances of treason in his work. The list comprises morally despicable acts for which no excuses are given, like the treason of Uldor the Accursed in the Battle of Unnumbered Tears (*The Silmarillion*), next to acts of betrayal that are likely to meet the reader's approval, such as Huan's desertion of his former master Celegorm (*The Silmarillion*). Most of Tolkien's traitors, however, occupy a middle ground. They may start out with honorable intentions and become corrupted with time (Saruman and

Denethor in *The Lord of the Rings*), or their treason is mainly due to a combination of outside pressure and inner desires (Gorlim, Maeglin, Mîm in *The Silmarillion*; Gríma Wormtongue in *The Lord of the Rings*). The tone of the passages relating the treason is mostly sober and matter-of-fact. Only once, in an early draft of "The Fall of Gondolin" (*Lost Tales* 2), does the style of the passage describing the treason of Meglin (>Maeglin) take on a rather melodramatic tone reminiscent of the Victorian adventure novels. Meglin betrayed Gondolin to Sauron, who then attacks the city. In the ensuing chaos, Meglin seizes Idril and her son Eärendel (>Eärendil) and wants to throw the latter into the flames of the burning town. Tuor arrives in the nick of time, rescues his wife and son, and kills the traitor. The difference in style may be seen best by comparing the two passages describing the same incident, one brief and matter-of-fact in *The Silmarillion* (293), the other with heightened dramatic effect in *The Book of Lost Tales* 2 (177f).

Tolkien—unlike Shakespeare—generally refrains from exploring and highlighting the struggles and the inner drama that must have taken place in the minds of his traitors. Yet even so it becomes clear that the act of treason is an act of the free will (see Dickerson and Weinreich) and that whatever the outside pressure applied, it is in the end the protagonist's inherent (moral) weakness of will that turns him traitor (see Húrin as an example of someone who successfully resists Morgoth). The reasons for committing an act of treason are manifold and so are the degrees of moral reprehensibleness of these acts. We have already mentioned Huan's desertion of Celegorm. This seems, at first sight, to constitute an act of treason, at least technically speaking (betrayal of trust, desertion of one's master). Yet upon closer consideration it becomes clear that Huan may indeed betray his former master, but the motivation to do so is the preceding treason committed by Celegorm. By serving Lúthien and Beren and helping them with their quest, Huan has chosen a higher good, which justifies his desertion of Celegorm.

A similar "choice between two goods" is laid before Gorlim (*S*, 195). He resists torture and does not betray the whereabouts of his comrades, yet when offered to be reunited with his wife, he gives in and betrays Barahir's hiding place to Sauron. Gorlim has thus put the good of his (and his wife's) private happiness over the general good of fighting evil in the form of Sauron and his Orcs. Needless to say, Gorlim himself has been betrayed and the wages of this tragic misapprehension are death.

Yet another form of betrayal is illustrated in the fate of Denethor, the steward of Minas Tirith. Although Sauron is not able to persuade him into an active betrayal, his resistance is undermined by what he sees in the Palantír so that he despairs at the crucial moment and does not lead his people into battle. It is an offence of default and as such a subtler form of treason, yet a betrayal of the trust received from the people and of the steward's responsibility toward the king nevertheless.

The betrayals committed by people in positions of power and responsibility (Denethor, Saruman) are all the more grievous since their knowledge and wisdom makes them largely invulnerable to direct threats and pressure. They have no excuse for their betrayals.

Although treason must be seen as a morally reprehensible act with dire consequences for most of the parties involved, it is not allowed to disrupt permanently the divine harmony of creation and may even become an instrument toward good, or, as Théoden remarks, "Oft evil will shall evil mar."

THOMAS HONEGGER

Further Reading

Dickerson, Matthew. *Following Gandalf. Epic Battles and Moral Victory in The Lord of the Rings*, Grand Rapids, MI: Brazos Press, 2003.
Weinreich, Frank. "Ethos in Arda. Charakteristika der Ethik in Mittelerde." In *Eine Grammatik der Ethik*, Thomas Honegger, Andrew Johnston, Friedhelm Schneidewind, Frank Weinreich, 111–34. Saarbrücken: Edition Stein und Baum, 2005.
———. "'It Was Always Open to One To Reject': Zur Möglichkeit philosophischer Interpretationen Tolkiens fiktionaler Werke am Beispiel der Willensfreiheit." *Hither Shore* 1 (2004): 71–83.
West, Richard C. "'And She Named Her Own Name': Being True To One's Word in Tolkien's Middle-earth." *Tolkien Studies* 2 (2005): 1–10.

See also **Fall of Gondolin (Book of Lost Tales I and II); Good and Evil; Silmarillion**

TREASON OF ISENGARD, THE

The Treason of Isengard is an account of the writing of *The Lord of the Rings* from late 1939 to early 1942, by Christopher Tolkien (CT), with detailed commentary, connective essays, and extensive excerpts from J.R.R. Tolkien's drafts and notes. It is volume 7 of *The History of Middle-earth* (*HoM-e*) series, and is the second of the four part subseries *The History of the Lord of the Rings* (*HoLR*).

"The Treason of Isengard" was Tolkien's title for book 3 of *The Lord of the Rings* before the three-volume format was imposed by the publishers in 1952 (1). CT revived it for this volume of *HoLR* because it introduces Tolkien's addition, in late 1940, of the complex subplot of Saruman, Rohan, and the Ents to the original linear plot of the quest of Mt. Doom. At least one edition of *The Lord of the Rings* has since been published as six individual books, with book 3 bearing the original title.

Treason is chronologically ordered and divides into three parts. Chapters 1–9 continue directly from volume 6, *The Return of the Shadow*. They complete the story of the achievement of the final form of most of *The Fellowship of the Ring* in 1940, from Bilbo's party to the Council of Elrond and on as far as Moria, the point at which Tolkien had paused, stymied. The major innovations are Gandalf's revelation that he was taken captive by a fellow wizard, Saruman, and Trotter's transformation into a Man who is the heir of Elendil.

Chapters 10–18 show Tolkien with renewed energy developing the story from Moria to the end of *The Fellowship of the Ring*. The most notable features are the death of Gandalf on the bridge, the invention of Lórien and the character of Galadriel, and the beginning of serious consideration of the geography of the southern part of Middle-earth as the quest began to approach Mordor and Gondor. In this section also are Tolkien's story-notes on the coming split in the Fellowship. These contain the first sketches and drafts for book 4 in *The Two Towers* and beyond, with Frodo's journey to Mordor, the war in Gondor, and the climax of the quest.

Only chapters 19–26 cover the textual development of *The Two Towers*, book 3, which recounts the struggle with the forces of Isengard. The history of the Riders of Rohan and the tale of the Ents of Fangorn grow even as Tolkien first writes them down. It is clear that the plot-diversion that led the Three Hunters, two hobbits, and Gandalf west to war with Saruman had not been anticipated by Tolkien in the story-notes presented just a few chapters earlier. Then, as CT explains in his introduction, for reasons of space he ends this volume abruptly at Edoras. He continues the story of the writing of book 3 and the rest of *The Lord of the Rings* in the next two volumes.

Several chapters contain remarkable information not directly related to the main history. There is an invaluable discussion with illustrations of the evolution of *The Lord of the Rings*' Map of Middle-earth. Critics have noticed that this material throws considerable doubt on Tolkien's claim that "I wisely started with a map and made the story fit"(Lewis and Currie, 138). There is an extensive investigation of Bilbo's *Eärendil* poem, documenting its development from the nonsense-poem *Errantry*, and proposing that the version intended for publication was accidentally mislaid and so not used. Also included here is a very

early fragment of *The Homecoming of Beorhtnoth Beorhthelm's Son*, discovered on the back of the first manuscript of *Errantry*. Discussion of the inscription on Balin's tomb in Moria leads to an appendix on Runes with an essay and illustrations by Tolkien on his various runic alphabets.

As a book to read, *Treason* is challenging. CT repeatedly refers to his difficulties in presenting Tolkien's reworked and illegible manuscripts in a coherent form. He succeeds brilliantly, but it is important to recognize that fully 50 percent of the book is commentary written by CT in his clear and logical but very closely argued style (Anderson, 131). *Treason* is thus best approached not as an edition of drafts by J.R.R. Tolkien, but rather as CT's scholarly history of the writing of *The Lord of the Rings* with very extensive quotations (Bratman, 83).

Scholars generally refer to material in *Treason* to examine Tolkien's process of creation by revision. Flieger establishes that Tolkien repeatedly changed his presentation of the different time-flow in Lórien, in order to make it less literal and specific; and she shows how Tolkien changed Frodo's dreams in Book I to become journeys in time as well as space (Flieger, 89, 175). Shippey finds in *Treason* examples of what he had previously argued was absent from *The Lord of the Rings*, concluding that Tolkien successfully struggled to overcome his own early inclinations toward excessive novelistic realism, and "soft-heartedness" about the fates of his characters (Shippey, 318). St. Clair demonstrates how Tolkien's revisions tend overall to darken the story from its first drafts (St. Clair, 146).

Treason provides material for other critical approaches also. Lewis and Currie draw on it extensively to argue that Tolkien connected *The Lord of the Rings* to the "Silmarillion" legends much later than is suggested by CT (Lewis and Currie, 96). Less successful is an essay that draws parallels between Tolkien's transformation of Trotter into Aragorn in *Treason,* and the screenwriters' changes to Aragorn's character in the New Line film adaptations (Paxson, 92).

Unlike the rest of *The History of Middle-earth, Treason,* and its *History of the Lord of the Rings* companions present drafts of work that Tolkien published in his own lifetime. Some critics feel that the series dedicates excessive energy and detail to presenting texts that Tolkien himself rejected as inferior (Rosebury, 3; Bratman, 71). Most feel that *The Treason of Isengard* and its companion volumes are an important resource for exploring the sources of Tolkien's ideas and the nature of his creativity, and provide a firm basis for all future textual scholarship on *The Lord of the Rings* (Drout and Wynne; Anderson, 134).

JOHN F.G. MAGOUN

Further Reading

Anderson, Douglas. "Reviews: The History of The Lord of the Rings." In *Arda 1988–91: Annual of Arda-Research*, edited by Anders Stenström, 128–35. Stockholm: Arda Society, 1994.

Bratman, David. "The Literary Value of The History of Middle-earth." In *Tolkien's Legendarium: Essays on the History of Middle-earth*, edited by Verlyn Flieger and Carl F. Hostetter, 69–91. Westport, CT: Greenwood Press: 2000.

Drout, Michael D.C. and moderator Scott McLemee. "Colloquy Live: Frodo Lives! And So Does Tolkien Scholarship." *The Chronicle of Higher Education*. http://chronicle.com/colloquylive/2004/06/tolkien/index.shtml (June 2004).

Drout, Michael D.C., and Hilary Wynne. "Tom Shippey's J.R.R. Tolkien: Author of the Century and a Look Back at Tolkien Criticism since 1982." *Envoi* 128 9, no. 2 (Fall 2000).

Flieger, Verlyn. *A Question of Time: J.R.R. Tolkien's Road to Faerie*. Kent, OH: Kent State University Press, 1997.

Lewis, Alex, and Elizabeth Currie. *The Uncharted Realms of Tolkien*. Oswestry: Medea, 2002.

Paxson, Diana. "Re-Vision: The Lord of the Rings in Print and On Screen." In *Tolkien on Film: Essays on Peter Jackson's The Lord of the Rings*, edited by Janet Croft, 81–99. Altadena, CA: Mythopoeic Press, 2004.

Rosebury, Brian. *Tolkien: A Cultural Phenomenon*. Hampshire: Palgrave MacMillan, 2003.

Shippey, Tom. *The Road to Middle-earth*. Rev. and expanded ed. New York: Houghton Mifflin, 2003.

St. Clair, Gloriana. "Tolkien as Reviser: A Case Study." In *Proceedings of the J.R.R. Tolkien Centenary Conference 1992*, edited by Patricia Reynolds and Glen Good-Knight, 145–50. Milton Keynes: Tolkien Society, 1996.

See also **Alphabet of Rúmil; Alphabets invented by Tolkien; Aragorn; Authorship; Doors and Gates; Elendilmir; Elessar; Elves; Ents; Éomer; Éowyn; Galadriel; Gandalf; Gollum; Gondor; Gríma (Wormtongue);** *History of Middle-earth*: Overview; *Homecoming of Beorhtnoth*; *Lord of the Rings*; **Lothlórien; Manuscripts by Tolkien; Maps; Mithril; Mordor; Moria; "Nomenclature of The Lord of the Rings"; Old English; Phial; Poems by Tolkien; Prose Style; Publications, Posthumous;** *Return of the Shadow*; **Rhyme Schemes and Meter; Rhyming Poetry; Rings of Power; Rohan; Runes; Saruman;** *Sauron Defeated*; **The One Ring; Theoden; Time; Tolkien Scholarship: Since 1980; Tolkien, Christopher; Treebeard;** *War of the Ring*; **Weapons, Named; Wizards**

TREE AND LEAF

Tree and Leaf is a collection of Tolkien's writings first published in 1964 by Allen & Unwin. The volume is unusual in that it contains works of two different genres: an essay titled "On Fairy-Stories" and a short story titled "Leaf by Niggle." A later 1988 edition, edited by Christopher Tolkien and published again under the title *Tree and Leaf*, adds a work of yet a third different genre: a previously unpublished poem called "Mythopoeia."

The combination of essay, story, and poem in the same volume is not a mere accident—a byproduct of their all having the same author. All three pieces deal with the importance of subcreative art and with the meaning and value of myth and fantasy, and this brings a cohesive unity to the collection despite the difference in genres. Three of the main points that run through *Tree and Leaf* are (1) that Man is a subcreator (as distinct from the Creator); (2) that the work of myth-making and subcreation is a part of what humans were created (by their Creator) to do; and (3) that myths, far from being lies, may be profound vehicles for communicating truth. To see this unity, a quick summary of the three pieces is necessary. (For further analysis on the individual pieces, readers are referred to their separate entries.)

"On Fairy-Stories" is a longer version of an essay delivered on March 8, 1939, as an Andrew Lang Lecture. It first appeared in print in 1947 in *Essays Presented to Charles Williams*, before being included in *Tree and Leaf* in 1964 with a new introduction by the author. The essay guides the reader toward an understanding, first, of what a fairy tale is (and is not) and, second, of why it is so valuable. "Leaf by Niggle," was written at least twenty years before publication in *Tree and Leaf*. It was sent to the editor of the *Dublin Review* in October of 1944, and in his introduction to the first edition of *Tree and Leaf* Tolkien claims it was written even earlier, in the same period as "On Fairy-Stories" (1938–39). Despite Tolkien's well-documented distaste for forced allegory, "Leaf by Niggle" can best be described as an autobiographical allegory—an argument made by Shippey (266–77). The poem "Mythopoeia" exists in seven different versions, with earlier titles including "*Nisomythos*: a long answer to short nonsense," "Misomythos," and "Philomyth to Misomyth." It is based on a conversation between Tolkien and C.S. Lewis that took place on 19 September, 1931, on the even of Lewis' conversion to Christianity. (One of the versions of the poem is marked "J.R.R.T. for C.S.L.") The poem contains Tolkien's refutation of a comment made by Lewis, prior to his conversion, that myths and fairy-tales were lies, albeit "lies breathed through silver."

"Mythopoeia" was the last of the three works to reach publication, but its composition predates both the essay and the story, and it is even quoted in the essay. Its final title refers to the making of myths, and in it Tolkien raises the idea of subcreation, referring to man as a "sub-creator" who is long estranged from his Creator, the "only Wise," but still refracts the

Light of that Creator in the things he makes. Tolkien explores this further in the essay. Though only God, the Creator, can go directly from thought to being, man can subcreate, drawing upon the material and reality of the creation in the making of new things, and thereby acting as God's vehicle for the enrichment of creation. This subcreative act is one of image-making, or imagination, and reaches its highest form in fantasy. In the poem, Tolkien specifically speaks of myth-making and legend-making—filling subcreated worlds with Elves, goblins, gods, dragons, and "things not found within recorded time"—as a human "right" that has not decayed. In the essay he similarly refers to it as a "natural human activity." The reason is simple, and is stated in both works, though in different ways: man creates because he is created in the image of a Creator.

These arguments are not stated in propositional form in "Leaf by Niggle," but they certainly inform the most important elements of the story. The auto-biographical allegorical interpretation sees Niggle as a Tolkien-figure, the Journey as death and afterlife, the workhouse as purgatory, and the Mountains as Heaven. The First Voice (a voice of justice) and the Second Voice (a voice of mercy) are described as a Board, relating them to the workhouse Doctor, thereby forming a Trinity. In Niggle's painting we see Tolkien's fantasy writings, and particularly his Middle-earth Legendarium. While the story makes painfully evident Niggle's shortcomings, it ultimately defends (especially through the Second Voice) Niggle for taking "a great deal of pains" with the subcreative process, and it shows the value of his subcreative art: the creation through paint and canvas of a fantasy world with strange birds, a mysterious forest, an unknown country, and distant wild mountains. The story also makes it clear that subcreation was a fundamental part of who Niggle was.

The poem, essay, and story all also point to the idea that our subcreative fantasy and myth-making can both reflect the truth and point back to it. The poem speaks of myth renewing "from mirrored truth the likeness of the True." The essay speaks of subcreative fantasy providing "a sudden glimpse of the underlying reality or truth." Specifically, Tolkien believed and suggested in all three works that even heathen mythologies may convey truth that leads people to Christ and Heaven. In his explanation of the consolation of the fairy tale—the joy of the happy ending—Tolkien created his "eucatastrophe," best described as a suddenly miraculous turn of events never to be counted on to recur. He argues that the eucatastrophe in fairy-tale is a reflection of and can lead one back to that which Tolkien considers the greatest eucatastrophe in history: the Gospel story

of the birth, death, and resurrection of Christ. A similar point is made in a more personal way in "Leaf by Niggle." The ultimate defense of Niggle's work—especially against the critique of the character Councilor Tompkins who sees art as valuable only insofar as it is economically useful—is that Niggle's painting becomes for many the best introduction to the Mountains. Taken as a whole, this collection not only provide key insights into the entire genre of fantasy literature, but probably the clearest insight into Tolkien's own writing and what he hoped to accomplish.

MATTHEW DICKERSON

Further Reading

Carpenter, Humphrey. *J.R.R. Tolkien: A Biography*. Boston, MA: Houghton Mifflin, 1977.

Kilby, Clyde S. *Tolkien and The Silmarillion*. Wheaton: Shaw, 1976.

Shippey, Tom. *Author of the Century*. London: HarperCollins, 2001.

See also **Alliterative Verse by Tolkien;** *Battle of Maldon*; **Mythopoeia; "On Fairy-Stories"; Literature, Twentieth Century: Influence of Tolkien**

TREEBEARD

Treebeard, also called Fangorn, appears in *The Lord of the Rings* as the chief Ent and the oldest living being on Middle-earth. Along with Leaflock and Skinbark, he is one of only three who remain of the first Ents. Although there are many other Ents still alive, Treebeard refers to himself as The Ent (*TT*, III, iv, 67). It is after him that Fangorn Forest, or Entwood, gets its name. He is a friend of Gandalf, and in an earlier age was acquainted with Celeborn and Galadriel.

In *The Two Towers*, the hobbits Merry and Pippin encounter Treebeard in Fangorn after escaping from the Orcs. Treebeard nearly mistakes the hobbits for Orcs, and refrains from killing them only because he likes their "nice little voices." When the hobbits bring news of events in the world, Treebeard is roused and decides to stop Saruman. He succeeds in rousing the Ents, even though their participation in the war might mean their doom. Leading the last march of the Ents, Treebeard conquers Isengard, destroys many Orcs, and imprisons the treacherous wizard. He then carries out the cleansing of the Ring of Orthanc, turning it into the Treegarth of Orthanc, which Aragorn later gives into his keeping.

With respect to Tolkien's eco-criticism, Treebeard is arguably the most important character in *The Lord of the Rings*. For example, Treebeard condemns Saruman for felling good trees in order to feed his fires. In naming the wizard an "accursed tree-slayer" (*RK*, VI, vi, 257), Treebeard pronounces the worst judgment an Ent can give. Moreover, Saruman often fells trees for no reason, leaving them to rot—an even worse crime than felling them for his fires, which is at least an excuse, although a bad one. Tolkien brings to mind factory chimneys when he has Treebeard also condemn Saruman for fouling the air with smoke. When Treebeard describes the wizard as having "a mind of metal and wheels," the factory imagery is furthered, suggesting a strong critique of industrialization. In Treebeard's reference to the wizard's possible blending of Orc and Men, and what a "black evil" that would be, Tolkien may even be prophesying genetic engineering, and condemning it as strongly as he condemns the rest of Saruman's practices. The foundation of this eco-criticism, however, is that Saruman does not care about growing things for their own sake, but only for their utilitarian value. Indeed, Treebeard even criticizes the Elves for not caring enough about trees (*TT*, III, iv, 76–89).

Two curious issues make Treebeard's role particularly interesting. The first is that Tolkien's earliest concepts involved a "Giant Treebeard" as a hostile force responsible for Gandalf's imprisonment (*Shadow*, 363). Clearly this conception changed as the story unfolded. However the second curious aspect may be related. Though Treebeard fights against Saruman and certainly views Sauron as an enemy, he is not politically aligned with Rohan or Gondor or even with the Elves. He makes this clear when he first meets the two hobbits, saying "I don't know about sides. I go my own way" (*TT*, III, iv, 69). And a little later, "I am not altogether on anybody's side, because nobody is altogether on my side, if you understand me" (*TT*, III, iv, 75). In this way, Treebeard represents an important form of environmentalism that transcends political boundaries and affiliations.

MATTHEW DICKERSON

Further Reading

Carpenter, Humphrey. *J.R.R. Tolkien: A Biography.* Boston: Houghton Mifflin, 1977.
Dickerson, Matthew, and Jonathan Evans. *Ents, Elves and Eriador: The Environmental Vision of J.R.R. Tolkien.* Lexington, KY: University Press of Kentucky, 2006.

See also **Ents; Gandalf; Merry; Pippin; Saruman; Théoden; Trees; Yavanna**

TREES

It would be difficult to overestimate the importance of trees in the writings of J.R.R. Tolkien. When Treebeard the Ent praises the Gandalf as the only wizard "that really cares about trees" (*TT*, III, iv, 69), he is echoing sentiments Tolkien expressed about himself in numerous letters. In a 1955 letter intended for Houghton Mifflin to use in response to publicity queries, Tolkien writes, "I am (obviously) much in love with plants and above all trees, and always have been; and I find human maltreatment of them as hard to bear as some find ill-treatment of animals" (*Letters*, 220) In a 1972 response to a newspaper article on forestry, he writes, "In all my works I take the part of trees as against all their enemies." This letter goes on to describe "the destruction, torture and murder of trees perpetrated by private individuals and minor official bodies" as incomparably beyond mere stupidity, whiling crediting the beauty of Lothlórien to a love of trees (*Letters*, 419–20). In his various writings, trees provide for Tolkien among other things: the most important mythic symbols in his Legendarium, a potent vehicle for his eco-criticism, centrally important images in his short stories "Leaf by Niggle" and "Smith of Wootton Major," and personal symbols to represent the competing A and B schemes of English language and literature education. Woods and forests also provide symbolic narrative regions of both rest and danger drawn from mythic and fairy-tale tradition.

Trees as Mythic Symbols

The most important mythic symbols in all of the legendarium are the Two Trees of Valinor: Telperion and Laurelin. It is said that "about their fate all the tales of the Elder Days are woven" (*S*, 38). The famed Silmarils of Fëanor contain the light of the Two Trees, as does, via the light of a Silmaril, the Phial of Galadriel (the "star-glass" given to Frodo). The Sun and Moon, known in Middle-earth as Isil and Anar, were made respectively from a hallowed flower of Telperion and a hallowed fruit of Laurelin (*S*, 99). The symbol of Aragorn's kingship is also a tree, the White Tree of Gondor, descended from Nimloth, the White Tree of Númenor, which itself was the symbol of the royal line of Númenor and was a descendant of Telperion. The destruction of Nimloth was symbolic of the downfall of Númenor, just as the discovery and transplantation by Aragorn of a sapling descended from the White Tree is a symbol of the return of the true King of Gondor.

It should furthermore be noted that the Two Trees of Valinor were sung into life by the Vala Yavanna, and she put into them the "thought of things that grow in the earth" (*S*, 38). To some extent, then, trees are symbolic of all plant life, or *olvar*, in

Middle-earth. This can be seen later when Yavanna foresees the hurt and marring that Morgoth and fallen Elves, Men, and Dwarves will cause to the growing things she has created. She sees trees not only as representative and "most dear" of all the *olvar*, but as the vehicles by which the rest shall be defended. "Would that the trees might speak on behalf of all things that have roots, and punish those that wrong them!" (*S*, 45). In light of this, it is not surprising that trees and Ents are the most important symbols and voices for the expression of eco-critical and environmental aspects of the Legendarium. For example the "evil ways" of Saruman are illustrated most clearly through his wanton destruction of the trees of Fangorn: his felling of "trees—good trees," sometimes just cutting them down and leaving them to rot, or carrying them off to feed his fires. Likewise, the most scathing criticism of Saruman comes from Treebeard the Ent who labels the White Wizard "a black traitor" and a tree-slayer, who "does not care for growing things" (*TT*, III, iv, 76–77).

Trees, Forests, Peace, and Hostility

Significant forests and trees also play an important role in *The Hobbit* and *The Lord of the Rings* narratives. It is in the forest of Mirkwood that Bilbo begins to develop as a hero and the real leader of his company in *The Hobbit*. (His earlier winning of the Riddle Game is accomplished by sheer luck.) When the four hobbits leave the Shire, their first adventure is with a tree, Old Man Willow, in the Old Forest, where they also meet Tom Bombadil. Though Tolkien, as noted earlier, claimed always to take the side of trees, Old Man Willow (along with the Huorns of Fangorn) serves to suggest both that nature itself has been corrupted by the fall, and also that because of the evil of Man there is now a state of hostility between Man and Nature. This hostility can be seen in the antagonistic relationship between the hobbits of the Shire and the Old Forest, as well as in the role of the fallen Númenóreans in the deforestation of Middle-earth (see *UT*, 262). Nonetheless, despite the dangers of the Old Forest and Fangorn, the forests of Lothlórien and Fangorn, the woods of Ithilien, and even Tom Bombadil's home in the Old Forest also serve as places of respite from evil.

Symbolic Significance

In his short story "Leaf by Niggle," Tolkien also uses a tree as a symbol of subcreative art in general and of his own fantasy literature in particular. The tree is described as having "innumerable branches," "fantastic roots," "strange birds" settled on its twigs, and glimpses through its branches "of a forest marching over the land, and of mountains tipped with snow." Initially the tree exists only in Niggle's painting, but at the end of the story it is given primary reality, showing the aspiration of subcreative art. The tree is also a fitting allegory of Tolkien's development of his own legendarium, in that it began with a single leaf "caught in the wind" (like the earliest philologically-inspired stories of *The Silmarillion*), that grew into a tree onto which his other leaf pictures (like *The Hobbit* and *The Adventures of Tom Bombadil*) were tacked (*TL*, 76). At least one other time, Tolkien also used a tree as a symbol of his life; after the death of his close friend C.S. Lewis, he wrote: "I have felt the normal feelings of a man of my age—like an old tree that is losing all its leaves one by one: this feels like an axe-blow near the roots" (*Letters*, 341).

Finally, there are two important trees in "Smith of Wootton Major," each appearing once. The second is the birch that rescues Smith from the wild Wind. To understand the significance of the latter of these, it must be noted that Tolkien used birch and oak particularly in a personally symbolic way to represent the so-called A-scheme and B-scheme of education. The A-scheme was a modern-literature-only approach. The B-scheme, which Tolkien introduced to Leeds, included philology and Old English literature as a foundation. Shippey has a succinct summary in *Author of the Century* of this symbolism. In the OE runic alphabet, A is for *ác* (OE for "oak"), and B for *beórc* (OE for birch). The birch tree thus becomes a symbol for Tolkien's preferred B-scheme, and the oak for the A-scheme. More specifically, Shippey explains, in the "particular and personal symbolic meaning for Tolkien," the birch "stood for philology." This connection can be seen in a poem Tolkien published in *Songs for the Philologist* in which he praises both the birch and the B-scheme. It can be seen more poignantly in the birch that gives itself (is stripped bare) to save the Tolkien-like figure Smith, and in the naming of the story's only completely nonsympathetic character Nokes, whose name relates to Okes, or Oaks. "It is as if Tolkien still . . . felt guilty about stripping philology for his own purposes," Shippey concludes (302–3). (Though Ents are not associated only with birches, it is probably not entirely insignificant that Ents, and especially Treebeard, are the philologists of Middle-earth.)

The other tree in "Smith of Wootton Major" is the King's Tree. Tolkien made it clear in personal letters that the story has religious symbolism and that the "Hall and Cook were allegories of the church and parson" (299). At the end of the story, readers learn that the King of Faery is Alf, also called Prentice. The King had left Faery and come as a child to the world of men, where he lived for a time, was despised by the Cook (allegorically the religious leader of the day), and then revealed in his glory before returning to Faery. There is, then, in the character Alf, something of the Christian story of the incarnation of Christ, the King of Heaven. The King's Tree, then, can be interpreted as a cross, which was also on a hill. This final symbolic connection of trees to the important cross of Tolkien's faith may explain some of the significance of many other trees in the body of Tolkien's work.

MATTHEW DICKERSON

Further Reading

Shippey, Tom. *J.R.R. Tolkien: Author of the Century.* London: Harper Collins, 2000.

Verlyn Flieger, *Splintered Light: Logos and Languages in Tolkien's World.* Grand Rapids, MI: Eerdmans, 1983.

See also **Ent; Huorn; Old Man Willow;** *Smith of Wootton Major*; *Tree and Leaf*; **Treebeard**

TRENCH FEVER

Trench fever, a communicable disease caused by a type of ricketsial organism, *Bartonella quintana*, is transmitted by the body louse, *Pediculus humanus*. After the victim is bitten, the disease usually takes five days to incubate. Then the symptoms begin to appear: fever, headache, back and leg pains, weakness, skin rashes, and malaise. Antibiotics are now found to be effective, but when the disease was first identified during World War I, antibiotics had not been discovered, so doctors could only treat the symptoms and insure that patients rested. Recovery took weeks, sometimes months, with relapse being common.

When J.R.R. Tolkien was in France during the Battle of the Somme, he lived with his comrades in the trenches, which were open to the weather and in the fall of 1916 were cold, damp, muddy holes. The soldiers lived, slept, ate, and defecated in the trenches. Hygiene was nearly impossible, and to add to the jeopardy, dead bodies were often piled in the trenches. Infestations of lice were difficult to avoid.

On October 27, 1916, Tolkien reported to the medical officer with a high temperature. He was cared for in France for a few days and then shipped back to England on November 8. After a few weeks in a

Birmingham hospital, he continued his convalescence under Edith's care at Great Haywood. He returned to light duty in April 1917 but relapsed again in August. During his recovery, he worked on his invented language, Quenya, and some of the stories in *Lost Tales*.

ELIZABETH A. WHITTINGHAM

TÚRIN

Túrin Turambar, son of Húrin the Steadfast, is a flawed hero, a study by Tolkien of the virtues and defects of the heroic ethos.

The saga of Túrin has its origin in Tolkien's desire (expressed in a letter of October 1914 [*Letters*, 7] to his future wife, Edith Bratt) to retell the tale of the Finnish hero Kullervo in a short story modeled on the romances of William Morris, in prose with some parts in verse. The character of Kullervo was virtually created by Dr. Elias Lönnrot by combining a number of traditional Finnish songs about unlucky heroes into one sequence in *runos* (poems) 31 through 36 of the national epic of Finland, *The Kalevala* (first published in 1835 and expanded in 1849). Kullervo possesses the enormous strength and courage proper to a hero and his intentions are good, but by ill fate he is responsible for many deaths among his kindred and friends. He and a sister he does not recognize unwittingly commit incest, and she drowns herself in remorse once she learns of their kinship. Finally Kullervo, devastated by the tragedies throughout his life, addresses his sword, which has drunk the blood of innocent and guilty alike, asking if it is willing to take his life, too; the the cursed sword speaks, agreeing to do so.

These elements survived in the saga of Túrin as it developed from a retelling of the Finnish source into an original and very long story within Tolkien's own legendarium, though it was greatly changed in its events and characters and was influenced by many other sources. The literary tradition of unwitting incest goes back at least to Oedipus, and analogues to incest between brother and sister are found in legends of Sigmund, King Arthur, and Charlemagne. The most notable addition, already present in the earliest extant version from 1919, is the dragon lore taken largely from the *Völsunga Saga*, the *Nibelungenlied*, and *Beowulf* to produce the dragon Glaurung (to use the final form of his name), who became one of the chief instruments of the curse on Túrin's family.

A common theme throughout Tolkien's oeuvre is the delicate balance between fate and free will. Túrin's father Húrin, captured after the Battle of

Unnumbered Tears but steadfastly refusing to collaborate with the Great Enemy, is enchanted to watch helplessly while his wife and children suffer under Morgoth's curse. Whatever the operations of fate, and however the people in the tale doom themselves by the very actions they take to avoid their doom, Tolkien is careful to show that they always have reasonable motivations. Túrin's tragic flaw is the very pride in his high lineage and vast prowess that makes him such a great hero, always justly admired by everyone he meets from Elf kings to human yeomen, ever laboring for the good of the people among whom he lives. He is always in the forefront of battle, but this is as rash as it is courageous, and the folk he leads to war are thereby opened to their eventual destruction: whether it is the outlaws of Dor-Cúarthol whom he makes fighters against marauding Orcs, the Elves of Nargothrond whose protecting river he causes to be bridged so that armies may go out but thus also allowing enemies to come in, or the villagers of Brethil whom he forges into an army (but this brings the Dragon against them). He is overly sensitive to any perceived slight to his honor. His pride sends him into self-imposed exile from Doriath after he slays an envious Elf, and keeps him from returning even after he is told of King Thingol's pardon. When he returns to his homeland of Dor-lómin, seeking news of his family, it is his pride that impels him to confront the lord of the invaders and slay him, bringing down vengeance on his countrymen. It is his rashness that leads him to strike out blindly in the dark to kill the Elf who was trying to rescue him from the Orcs, his best friend Beleg Strongbow, and to kill the man who tried to reveal that Túrin had inadvertently married his sister. The character of Túrin is Tolkien's examination of how the boldness that makes a great warrior can also be overboldness, which can be and highly dangerous, and also needs to be tempered by such humane values as patience and moderation.

No finished version of the tale exists, and in all likelihood none was ever written, though Tolkien worked on numerous recensions in both prose and verse. Each is incomplete, but in each there are unique details, or sections of narrative, or fuller development of some part of the story. Every volume in the *History of Middle-earth* series contains some mention of Túrin, but the main versions are these: "Turambar and the Foalókë" (1919) in *Lost Tales II*; *The Lay of the Children of Húrin* (1920–25), of which two different versions in alliterative verse exist, in *Lays; Narn i Hîn Húrin* "The Tale of the Children of Húrin" (1920s–1930s?) in *UT* (paradoxically the most finished version of the parts of the story that are covered); and

"Of Túrin Turambar," chapter 21 in *Silmarillion* (1977), which would be the most complete version except for its largely summary nature.

The story of Túrin is one of almost unrelieved gloom, but Tolkien's mythology provided for an ultimate happy ending after the apocalyptic ending of the world, when it is prophesied that Túrin and his sister will be cleansed of their sin, and Túrin will assist the forces of Good in overthrowing Morgoth and the forces of Evil.

RICHARD C. WEST

TURVILLE-PETRE, JOAN

Joan Elizabeth Blomfield Turville-Petre, noted teacher and scholar of Middle English, Old English, Old Norse, and Old Icelandic, published five volumes in the Viking Society for Northern Research Saga-Books between 1941 and 1981, including *Runes and the Gothic Alphabet* (vol. 12), *Hengest and Horsa* (vol. 14), *The Metre of Icelandic Court Poetry* (vol. 17), *Beowulf and Grettis Saga: A Excusion* (vol. 19), and *The Genealogist and History: Ari to Snorri* (vol. 20). While a university tutor at Oxford, she met and married Edward Oswald Gabriel Turville-Petre, who was a reader in ancient Icelandic literature from 1941 to 1953 and a professor from 1953, and with whom she had three children: Thorlac Francis Samuel (b. 1944), Merlin Oswald (b. 1946), and Brendon Arthur Auberon (b. 1948). In the early sixties, she wrote "Sources of the Vernacular Homily in England, Norway, and Iceland' for *Arkiv för Nordik Filologi* 75 (1960), 168–82, and "Translations of a Lost Penitential Homily" for *Traditio* 19 (1963), 51–57. Her essays "*The Metre of Sir Gawain and the Green Knight*" appeared in *English Studies* 57 (1976), 310–28, and "On Ynglingatal" in *Medieval Scandinavia* 11 (1978–79). After the death of her husband in 1978, she compiled his complete bibliography, published in 1981. She was then an Honorary Research Fellow at Somersville College, Oxford. In 1980, her work *Hetjukvaeði á Íslandi og Í Wales* was published in Icelandic. Her 1983 translation of Preben M. Sorenson's *The Unmanly Man: Concepts of Sexual Defamation in Early Northern Society* is now widely cited in medieval gender and sexuality studies, courses, and bibliographies. In 1998, her translation (with Terry Gunnell) of Jón Hnefill Aðalsteinsson's *A Piece of Horse Liver: Myth, Ritual, and Folklore in Old Icelandic Sources* into English appeared in print. Her most significant contribution to Tolkien scholarship is her 1981 edition of *The Old English Exodus:*

Text, Translation, and Commentary by J.R.R. Tolkien, published by Oxford University Press.

JANE BEAL

See also **Exodus, Edition of; Oxford; Tolkien, Christopher**

TWO TREES

The Two Trees stood on a green mound outside Valmar, the city of the Valar, in Valinor. Sung into being at the beginning of the Elder Days by Yavanna, the Valië (Queen of the Valar) who was the Giver of Fruits, they were Telperion the White, Eldest of Trees, and Laurelin the Golden, younger of the two. The radiance of their flowers, silver and gold, respectively, waxed and waned again every seven hours, beginning an hour apart; so the light of the one began to gather again an hour before the other ceased, and twice a day there were times of soft light when both were faint. Their lights mingled and flowed like water through the Calacirya or "Light Cleft", spilling into Eldamar and as far as Tol Eressëa. Not long after their creation, Varda, another Valië, used the silver dew of Telperion to create bright new stars for the coming of the Eldar. For this reason she was named by them the Queen (or Lady) of the Stars.

When the Eldar arrived in Eressëa, a cutting of Telperion was given to them by the Valar to plant there. This became Galalithion, renowned for its beauty although it emitted no light. This tree and its heirs were to outlive their luminous forebear. Later in the First Age, a seed of Galalithion was taken to Númenor and became Nimloth the Fair. The White Trees of Gondor, first brought to Middle-earth by Elenedil and his sons at the end of the Second Age, were its scions.

Long beforehand, however, Fëanor of the Noldor, the unequalled craftsman of all time, found a way to capture the light of the Two Trees in a substance that he then fashioned into the three jewels of the Silmarils. These were coveted and stolen by Morgoth, the fallen Vala—an act that, together with his pursuit to Middle-earth by the vengeful Noldor, led to the tragic War of the Jewels, which resulted in the cataclysmic end of the First Age. And before fleeing Valinor, Morgoth, aided by Ungoliant the giant spider, fatally poisoned the Two Trees.

Just before they died, however, Telperion bore a last flower and Laurelin a final fruit. Of these (in Tolkien's original mythology) the grieving Valar made the Moon and Sun. But the light of the Two Trees also survived in what we now know as Venus; after Earendil's voyage to the West with the aid of a Silmaril—the only one to be recovered by the Eldar—it was eventually placed in the heavens as a beacon of hope by Elbereth or Varda. (This star was what we know as Venus, which is both the Morning and the Evening Star.)

Tolkien's account of the Two Trees and their place at the heart of events both in the Undying Lands and Middle-earth reveals the iconic status of trees in both his work and his life. In addition to his autobiographical remarks, this is also perceptible in his portrayal of the trees of Lothlórien and Fangorn, and indeed the Party Tree in Hobbiton, with which the story of *The Lord of the Rings* starts.

PATRICK CURRY

See also **Earth; Eldamar; Environmentalism and Ecocriticism; Plants, Tol Eressëa; Valinor**

TYRANNY

Tyranny is the action or government of an absolute ruler who exercises power in an unjust, or unnecessarily severe manner. For Tolkien, the term additionally connotes a regime that is pro-industrial and anti-environmental. Most political systems can develop tyrannical aspects whether they are socialist, fascist, capitalist, or monarchal. Denethor displays at times a tyrannical nature, and his son, Boromir, possesses its potential too before he is slain. At a cosmogonic level, Morgoth is the quintessential tyrant, marring the world in his ancient struggle for obedience and control. However, Sauron is the most obvious example of a tyrannical ruler, seeking supreme power and commanding his realm of Mordor through fear and severe punishment. Moreover, Sauron's Lieutenant of the Tower of Barad-dûr most directly exemplifies the tyranny inherent in the Ring and its Dark Lord. Also called The Mouth of Sauron, this ancient Black Numenorean gloats with overconfidence before the troop of heroes outside the Black Gate where we learn of his impending rise to power: "He was to be that lieutenant, and gather all that remained of the West under his sway; he would be their tyrant and they his slaves" (*RK*, V, x, 166). The Black Númenúrean, we must assume, falls alongside his Dark Lord, and the threat of his tyranny is removed though a pathetic imitation of it is eventually realized in the Shire. The numerous sheriffs give too many orders, shut taverns, hoard provisions, curtail freedoms, and cut down trees for no other purpose than to exercise control. Pointing out the ease with which some people (even Hobbits) take to despotism, Tolkien exposes the danger of power: the inevitable desire for more.

CHRISTOPHER VACCARO

Further Reading

Chance, Jane. *The Lord of the Rings: The Mythology of Power*. Rev. ed. Lexington, KY: University Press of Kentucky, 2001.

Curry, Patrick. *Defending Middle-earth*. Boston, MA: Houghton Mifflin, 2004.

Petty, Anne C. *Tolkien in the Land of the Heroes*. Cold Spring Harbor, NY: Cold Spring Press, 2003.

Plank, Robert. "'The Scouring of the Shire': Tolkien's View of Fascism." In *A Tolkien Compass*. La Salle, IL: Open Court, 1975.

See also **Power in Tolkien's Works; Violence; War; World War II**

U

UNDERSEA LANDSCAPE: FEATURES NAMED AFTER TOLKIEN CHARACTERS

Undersea features of the Rockall Plateau, off the coast of Ireland, are named after significant elements from J.R.R. Tolkien's *Lord of the Rings* trilogy including: Rohan Seamount, Gondor Seamount, Eriador Seamount, Fangorn Bank, Edoras Bank, Lorien Knoll, Gandalf's Spur, and Isengard Ridge. All of the features are located between 52°25′ N and 56°00′ N, and 20°10′ W and 25° 20′ W. In accordance with international standards, multiple oceanographic features of similar types may be named after groups of mythical features and names should reflect the type of feature being named. The international organization responsible for compiling undersea nomenclature accepted Eriador Seamount and Lorien Knoll in 1985; dates the other features were named are not included in the scientific literature, nor does it list who named any of the features.

Eriador, the entire region of Tolkien's Middle-earth extending from the Misty Mountains to the Blue Mountains, contains all of the areas the oceanographic features were named for and has a similar topography. The undersea ridge is named after Isengard, the peak upon which Saruman's tower, Orthanc, was built. Isengard lay inside Gondor, next to Rohan. Edoras, Lorien, and Fangorn were areas abutting, but not in the mountains. The undersea counterparts are banks adjacent to the Eriador, Gondor, and Rohan seamounts. Gandalf's Spur is the only feature named for a character.

JENIFFER G. HARGROVES

Further Reading

Fonstad, Karen Wynn. *The Atlas of Middle-earth*. Boston: Houghton Mifflin Company, 1981.

General Bathymetric Chart of the Ocean Sub-Committee on Undersea Feature Names. "International Hydrographic Organization-Intergovernmental Oceanographic Commission General Bathymetric Chart of the Ocean (IHO-IOC GEBCO) Gazetteer of Undersea Feature Names" http://www.ngdc.noaa.gov/mgg/gebco/underseafeatures.html (August 2005).

Tolkien, J.R.R.. "On Fairy Stories." In *The Tolkien Reader*. New York: Ballantine Books, 1966. pp. 33–99.

See also **Maps; Merchandising; Middle-earth; Mountains; "Nomenclature of the Lord of the Rings"; Technological Subcultures: Reception of Tolkien**

UNFINISHED TALES

The *Unfinished Tales of Númenor and Middle-earth*, consists of a collection of stories concerning the History of Middle-earth from the Elder Days until the end of the War of the Ring. Going through the tales, the readers will hear the brilliant speech of Gandalf explaining his decision to send the Dwarves to the notorious meeting at Bag-End; they will vividly see the emergence of the sea-god Ulmo before the eyes of Tuor; or learn about ancient excerpts of the history of Númenor before the drowning and fall of the island. The book also contains a great deal of information on varied matters, such as the Five Wizards, the palantíri, the military organization of the Riders of the Mark of Rohan, and the only map of the island of Númenor sketched by Tolkien himself. A larger scale map of Middle-earth at the time of the War of the Ring is also included, as well as a revision of the map of Númenor, both made by Tolkien's third son, Christopher.

The volume was first published in 1980, three years after the publication of *The Silmarillion*. It is possible that as the compilation of the history of the *silmarilli* progressed, Christopher Tolkien projected the idea of another book to accomplish his father's desire of writing a 'mythology for England' in its widest sense. From this point of view, the *Unfinished Tales* have now become a crucial piece in the enormous literary tapestry that Christopher Tolkien has completed with the twelve-volume collection of *The History of Middle-earth*, a task that came to an end in 1997.

The tales have been presented according to a chronological pattern, in four parts:

    I. The First Age
   II. The Second Age
  III. The Third Age, and
   IV. The *Dúnedain*, the *Istari*, the *Palantíri*.

The information provided in each section deals with early versions of important tales (Tuor, the Lay of the Children of Húrin); with the description and history of the island of Númenor, and the tale of Aldarion and Erendis; with the history of such important characters in *The Lord of the Rings* as Galadriel and Celeborn, with the deeds of Isildur and the defeat at the Gladden Fields; with the friendship between Rohan and Gondor, sealed by an oath whose echoes still resonate over the mountains and plains in *The Lord of the Rings*, and also with the key role of Gandalf in the War of the Ring, from the early steps of Bilbo towards the Lonely Mountain until the closing of the Third Age and the parting of the Ring-bearers.

These can tales be understood without the rest of the books written by Tolkien. They are enjoyable, readable, as 'books', as the 'tales' they are intended to be, because sound and legend are powerful enough to provoke the reader's both delight and curiosity — say, fascination and enchantment. All along the book images reverberate in the imagination. The stories concerning the First Age date from an early stage of Tolkien's composition, and the tone of the epic remains archaic and sombre, reaching the solemnity of the published *Silmarillion*. It can be assumed that the *Unfinished Tales* are true to his mind also from the point of view of the adequate tone and consistency of both the text and the style of language as 'backcloth' for the main legends, those concerning Gondolin,

Turambar, Númenor, and especially the War of the Ring.

It was partly the intention of Tolkien to give the readers a glimpse of the landscape beyond the boundaries of Middle-earth, a remote vision of the blurry past behind the main stories connected with Bilbo, Frodo, and the Ring answers. That desire was deeply rooted in Tolkien's conviction of the striking effect far-off mountains, forests, and distant clouds have on both the intelligence and the imagination of any reader: places never to be visited, seas that will never be sailed. That was always his own experience as man and reader, something that can be checked out in many of his published letters. Longing for glittering silver peaks was truer to human hearts than stories of the deeds of brave climbers, despite their heroism and courage —they turned out to be nothing but the immediate elucidation of nostalgia. Glimpses of distant places provide recovery and consolation and the satisfaction of human desires, and these were some of Tolkien's writing most important aims. However, glimpses point always beyond the horizon, and human hearts need answers regarding the unknown.

At the same time, Tolkien felt extremely attractive the charge of granting the information many readers asked for, and especially the enquiry —almost the scholarship— on the history of the invented languages, as well as on the roots of the plot in the History of Beleriand and Middle-earth. In 1955, a few months after the publication of *The Two Towers*, he planned a volume of appendices for 'specialists' with detailed information, though he felt a bit upset because 'I am not all sure that the tendency to treat this whole thing as a kind of vast game is really good —certainly not for me, who finds that kind of thing only too fatally attractive.'

Now, the corpus edited under the title *Unfinished Tales* is exactly that: a part of the 'vast backcloth', branches of the big tree of his inspiration, heterogeneous as it is. In the introductory preface to the edition of the volume, Christopher Tolkien provides an explanation for the different treatment he gave to such a diverse corpus of texts. Being the result of more than fifty-five years of Tolkien's visions of a general *lógos*, re-visions of multiple texts, and invention of languages that became to him the adequate tool to sub-create a feasible, secondary world, the *Tales* truly look like a chronicle recovered from a distant but real world.

Unfinished Tales is not an exotic experiment to squeeze the success of an editorial phenomenon. The tales offer a wider perspective of Tolkien's mind and talent as a writer. At the same time, they have become essential for an upright understanding of the author's notion of Sub-creation in its radical sense, because to

Tolkien to sub-create really meant to *create a credible and feasible world where things could really happen.* This is something Aristotle had explained many centuries before Tolkien wrote the history of Middle-earth; but the very notion is the same: credibility in order to provide *free* applicability, for any reader at any time.

The atmosphere of *Unfinished Tales* remains true to its creator. The style, the resonance of language, and particularly the appearance of a chronicle written and compiled by different hands and minds working for centuries in order to preserve the echoes of a deeper past, equally filled with bliss and sadness, can be felt in every page. It points straight to the heart of Tolkien's desire as an artist: the desire of turning the stone into a living creature. Middle-earth was made of Tolkien's flesh and bone, it had been 'written with my blood, thin or thick', he even wrote to a friend. He always intended the whole corpus to be that 'mythology' he could dedicate 'simply: to England, to my country.'

EDUARDO SEGURA

UNGOLIANT (Q., UNGOL, SPIDER + LIANTE, TENDRIL)

(1) Araneiform spirit allied with Melkor, opposed by Eärendil. The name has varying forms, alternative etymology, and several aliases, including *Móru,* "Primeval Night" (*Lost Tales,* 288).

In *Lost Tales I*, Melko, having stolen the gems of the Noldoli, wanders south to Eruman, where Móru discovers him. A mystery even to the Valar, she is primal darkness, whose webs enmesh the stars. Melko seals an alliance with her by giving up all the gems but the Silmarils. They destroy the Trees, and Ungoliant escapes to the south while the Valar pursue Melko northward (151–154). Later, Manwe chooses the Sun's route in order to avoid them (182, 200). Christopher Tolkien compares this story with The *Silmarillion* version (*Lost Tales I* 157–158.) In *Lost Tales II*, a draft "Tale of Eärendel" refers to Ungewelianté (254, 256)—in later versions, he kills her. Changing conceptions can be traced in indices of *Lays* (392), *Shaping* (378) and *Morgoth* (466).

The Silmarillion suggests that Ungoliant entered Arda when "Melkor first looked down with envy" on it (73). Melkor deliberately seeks her out; the theft follows the attack on the Trees, and they quarrel over the Silmarils. Balrogs, coming to Melkor's aid, drive her off. She flees to Beleriand, mating with other spider creatures in Nan Dungortheb before returning to the south. Her end is a mystery (*S,* 73–77, 80–81).

The story of Morgoth and Ungoliant echoes Milton's *Paradise Lost*, where Satan must persuade Sin to unlock the gates of hell: sprung from his head, she conceived by him a child, Death. He promises food for their insatiable hunger, and they follow him as he flies to the new-made world.

(2) Original name for the spider on the border of Mordor in drafts of *LotR* (*War* 196).

JOHN WM. HOUGHTON

Further Reading

Chance, Jane. *Tolkien's Art: A Mythology for England.* Revised Edition: Lexington, KY: University Press of Kentucky, 2001.

See also **Book of Lost Tales I; Book of Lost Tales II; Eärendil;** *History of Middle-earth*: **Overview;** *Lays of Beleriand*; **Lord of the Rings; Melkor and Morgoth;** *Morgoth's Ring*; **Monsters, Middle-earth; Shelob;** *Silmarillion, The*; **South, The; Two Trees**

V

VALAR

The Valar are the Powers of Middle-earth. Among the Ainur ("rational spirits or minds without incarnation" [*Letters*, 284]) who were the offspring of Eru's thought and his vehicles in shaping Arda, were some who descended into Eä to assist in further creation. Their power was thereafter bounded in the World "so that they are its life and it is theirs" (*S*, 20). The lesser of these spirits were called the Maiar, while the greatest among them were known as the Valar. Verlyn Flieger describes as the original role of the Valar "to shape and light the world" (58). They created first the great lamps Illuin and Ormal whose light "flowed out over the Earth, so that all was lit as it were in a changeless day" (*S*, 35). They later create the Two Trees that were the light of Valinor, and the stars that lit Middle-earth, and eventually the Sun and Moon. Later their role become more one of governance.

Though not physical beings, the Valar could put on visible form as one wears a raiment, appearing fair and noble, alike to Elves in form but much greater in majesty and splendor. Some of the Valar take forms "as of a male and some as of female; for that difference of temper they had even from their beginning" (*S*, 21). They are fourteen in number. Those taking male forms are: Manwë, Ulmo, Aulë, Oromë, Námo, Irmo, and Tulkas. Those taking female form, called the Valier, are: Varda, Yavanna, Nienna, Estë, Vairë, Vána, and Nessa, Manwë is king over them all, under only Eru Ilúvatar himself, and Varda his queen.

As described in the Valaquenta, each of the Valar have a particular domain. The three mightiest of the lords were Manwë, lord of the winds and airs, Ulmo, lord of the waters, and Aulë whose lordship is over the substances of the earth. Among the Valier, Varda, also known as Elbereth, is the Lady of the Stars, and most beloved by the Elves. Yavanna, spouse of Aulë, is the giver of fruits; she seeded the plants and animals of Middle-earth, and sang into being the Two Trees. Flieger also summarizes what numerous scholars have alluded to: that these descriptions strongly "suggest the gods of pagan mythologies, since they have separate functions and each has a particular role in, or association with, an element of the earth—air, water, minerals, growing things," (55). More specifically, despite the numerous influences of Old Norse literature on the legendarium, Richard Purtill points out that the Valar "have a greater resemblance to the Olympian gods than to the Scandinavian gods such as Odin and Thor" (38).

Though imaginatively portrayed like gods of pagan myths, theologically Tolkien envisioned the Valar more as angelic beings; they "take the imaginative but not the theological place of 'gods'" (*Letters* 284). Some scholars have pointed out that the Elves' devotion to Varda bears close resemblance to Catholic devotion to Mary. In various other letters, Tolkien describes the Valar as "created spirits—of high angelic order" (*Letters*, 193), and as "regents under God," "angelic immortals (incarnate only at their own will)" (*Letters*, 411). The most important aspect of this is that the Valar are not to be worshipped.

Manwë is king of Arda, but he obeys Eru. For this reason, there are limits on power and knowledge of the Valar. When the Númenóreans rebel and attack Valinor, rather than exercising power and fighting against the Children of Ilúvatar, the Valar for a time lay down their authority.

Like angels (Greek for "messengers"), the Valar (especially Ulmo) and Maiar (especially Olórin) also act as messengers, bringing the word of Ilúvatar to Elves and Men often in dreams and visions. The fall of Morgoth, when he leads into rebellion many of the Maiar, is akin to the biblical fall of angels (Revelation 12:1–9). The Valar are also susceptible to both moral errors and errors of judgment. Aulë's creation of Dwarves is as a moral error, of which he repents. It is also suggested that the Valar's summons of the Elves to Valinor—opposed by Ulmo and others—was an error. Whether of judgment or a moral kind is uncertain, but when the summons is issued, Mandos says "so it is doomed" and the narrator comments that "from this summons came many woes that afterward befell" (S, 52). This moral error is seen not in the desire to protect the Elves, but the desire to have the Elves gathered at their knee; a suggestion that hints too much of worship, thus transplanting the proper worship of Ilúvatar.

MATTHEW DICKERSON

Further Reading

Birzer, Bradley. *J.R.R. Tolkien's Sanctifying Myth.* Wilmington, DE: IST Books, 2002.
Dickerson, Matthew. *Following Gandalf: Epic Battles and Moral Victory in The Lord of the Rings.*
Flieger, Verlyn. *Splintered Light. Logos and Language in Tolkien's World.* Kent, OH: Kent State University Press, 2002.
Purtill, R. *J.R.R. Tolkien: Myth, Morality, and Religion.* Ignatius Press, 2003.
Wood, Ralph. *The Gospel According to Tolkien.* Westminster: John Knox Press, 2003.

See also **Gandalf; Maiar; Melian; Morgoth and Melkor; Paradise; Satan and Lucifer; Two Trees**

VALE OF THE WHITE HORSE

At the highest point on the Berkshire Downs the visitor finds the hill-fort of Uffington Castle, the flat-topped Dragon Hill and White Horse Hill; a short distance away lies the long-barrow known, since at the least the mid-tenth century, as Wayland's Smithy. All four phenomena were well known to J.R.R. Tolkien who, as Carpenter tells us, visited the Berkshire Downs in the summer of 1912, and was a frequent visitor in the 1930s with his family. Christopher Tolkien, in *A Film Portrait of J.R.R. Tolkien,* recalls sitting on White Horse Hill with his father, and noting the intensity of Tolkien's awareness of the Hill; he believes that the area inspired Weathertop. It may clearly be seen that Dragon Hill is a low, flat-topped mound which could have been the inspiration for Weathertop as described by Tolkien in Chapter 11 of *The Fellowship of the Ring.* Similarly, Wayland's Smithy appears to have inspired the barrow in which Frodo and the others find themselves trapped after they part company from Tom Bombadil in Chapter 8. The description of the Barrow-Downs could easily be a description of the Berkshire Downs, with its short turf, its silence except for the cries of birds or the air moving across the grass, and the sky so close overhead.

The exact age of the chalk horse carved into the Berkshire hillside is unknown, but it is believed to be around three thousands years old; measuring some 365 feet from nose to tail, the White Horse is a stylised representation of a horse rather than an anatomically correct depiction. Seen from afar, as it was designed to be, the horse appears to be racing across the hillside. The horse clearly inspired Tolkien; the device of the Horse-lords of Rohan found on the shield given to Gimli in Chapter 6 of *The Two Towers* and on the banner carried by the Rohirrim in Chapter 5 of *The Return of the King* is a white horse on a green background. It appears that the old name for the area in which the White Horse is found also inspired Tolkien; the name given by the Rohirrim to their country is 'the Mark' and, as Shippey observes, the West Saxon name for the central area of England in which the Vale of the White Horse is located, was the *Mierce* (now Mercia); the name *Mierce* is derived from *Mearce*, which, says Shippey, was most likely to have been pronounced 'Mark.' In letter number 297, Tolkien records that he used Anglo-Saxon as the basis for the language of the Rohirrim, and Shippey explains in detail that the Rohirrim are like the Anglo-Saxons of legend and poetry (which Tolkien knew so well), rather than the actual historical Anglo-Saxons (who were not horsemen as are the Rohirrim). Throughout the eighteenth and nineteenth centuries, a "pastime" was held every seven years during which the White Horse was scoured, i.e. cleaned of the grass that grew over the chalk. It is probable that Tolkien was familiar with the practice of Scouring the White Horse, although it is not clear if *Sauron Defeated* that the phrase influenced his choice of the word for the chapter "The Scouring of the Shire"; Christopher Tolkien notes in the chapter was originally titled "The Mending of the Shire" (*Sauron,* 94). However, for those who know the area well, the influence of the Vale of White Horse on Tolkien's work is as clear as the White Horse itself.

MICHÈLE FRY

Further Reading

J.R.R.T.: A Film Portrait of J.R.R. Tolkien Dir. Derek Bailey. Written and Prod. by Helen Dickinson. Videocassette. Visual Corporation Limited, 1992.

The Letters of J.R.R. Tolkien. Carpenter, Humphrey Editor, with Christopher Tolkien. London: HarperCollins, 1995.

Carpenter, Humphrey. *J.R.R. Tolkien A Biography.* London: HarperCollins, 1992.

Higham, Roger. *Berkshire and the Vale of White Horse.* London: B T Batsford Ltd., 1977.

Shippey, T.A. *The Road to Middle-earth: How J.R.R. Tolkien created a new mythology.* London: HarperCollins, 1992.

Tolkien, Christopher. *The History of Middle-earth* Volume 9. London: HarperCollins, 1992.

Tolkien, J.R.R. *The Lord of the Rings.* London: HarperCollins, 1993.

See also **Old English; Old Mercian; Rohan**

"VALEDICTORY ADDRESS"

Tolkien's "Valedictory Address to the University of Oxford" is as the word "valedictory" suggests etymologically, a farewell, a "well-wishing." It is also, however, despite its humbly self-deprecating language, a parting shot in Tolkien's life-long battle against the marginalization of philology within the English Studies curriculum at Oxford.

The ice-breaking humor traditional in the opening phrases of such an address was in this case Tolkien's observation that, as he never delivered the expected inaugural address upon assuming the Rawlinson and Bosworth Chair 34 years earlier, he was in the awkward position of delivering an inaugural address upon retirement—still having found nothing to say. In an apology reminiscent of the themes of "Leaf by Niggle," Tolkien suggests that the genius required for a valedictory address is that of the larger view, the all-encompassing schematic mind, while his forte is the minute detail, "the implications of one word," the leaf rather than the forest. This passage sets the tone for the whole address: while seeming to disparage his penchant for niggling detail and for the philological approach, he actually decries the abandonment of philology for its opposite, which he dubs "misology."

Surveying the current state of the B. Litt. degree program at Oxford, Tolkien likens it to a sausage factory. On the graduate level, the preference for a "research" degree has led to "the loss of the M.A. as a genuine degree," a "premature attempt to add to knowledge" with research rather than reading more deeply among the fruits of earlier scholarship. Particularly inexcusable is the elimination of any Old English requirement in the English curriculum. Old English literature is too often dismissed as merely the "root" of a glorious plant that would later "flower" in the renaissance: Old English is itself a flower.

The remainder of the Valedictory Address is largely taken up by a lament for the artificial dichotomy of "language" and "literature" (*Lang* and *Lit*) subdivisions of the *Honour School of English*. In recalling his undergraduate days (1912–1915), Tolkien concedes that the battle lines were then already forming. The distinction is false both as to content and etymology, for surely literary criticism involves language, and both "literature" and its earlier cognate "letters" mean "language" (Greek *grammatike* and *philologia*). Furthermore, philology serves criticism: *Lang* rescued Chaucer from oblivion, though now he seems the exclusive province of *Lit*. Why is medieval spelling a matter of *Lang*, but Milton's spelling *Lit*? Students of all periods should study both disciplines.

After a final expression of pique that, as a native of South Africa, he should live to find his discipline subjected to an academic *apartheid*, the emotional tone of the address modulates to a warm appreciation of the fellowship of Oxford scholars of the past, whom he cites by name, and younger colleagues and students, to whom he addresses some dozen lines of Old English and Elvish verse, elegizing the passing of the great.

In his "Afterword" to *The Road to Middle-earth*, Tom Shippey sees Tolkien's assessment of the state of English studies in the Valedictory Address as an index of what is needed in Tolkien criticism. The "culture gap" between *Lang* and *Lit* exists even among Tolkien scholars, where it should be least at home. As a glimpse into Tolkien's professional life at Oxford, both its joys and its frustrations, the Valedictory Address is a valuable document. As a "final word" on the gulf between philology and criticism in English studies, it is anything but final. The breach may always be there, but the address might serve, if only for Tolkien's readers, as a call to do what can be done to close it.

JOHN R. HOLMES

Further Reading

Shippey, Tom. *The Road to Middle-earth: Revised and Expanded Edition.* Boston: Houghton Mifflin, 2003.

Tolkien, J.R.R. "The Oxford English School." *The Oxford Magazine* 48 (1930), 278–80, 782.

———. "Valedictory Address to the University of Oxford." In *The Monsters & the Critics and Other Essays.* London: HarperCollins, 1997, 224–240.

See also **Philology; Oxford; Tolkien Scholarship**

VALINOR

Valinor is the domain of the Valar, their followers the Maiar, and the faithful Elves (the Vanyar) on the continent of Aman, "the westernmost of all lands upon the borders of the world" (*S*, 37). It was also the location of the Two Trees, Laurelin and Telperion, before their destruction by Melkor and Ungoliant, and is site of the Halls of Mandos to which the spirits of Elves and Men go to their separate fates after death. The name comes from the Quenya *Valinórë*, the "people of the Valar," combined with the related word *Valandor*, "the land of the Valar" (*S*, 357); it also goes by epithets such as the "Guarded Realm," the "Blessed Realm," the "Uttermost West," and, along with Eldamar and Tol Eressëa, the "Undying Lands." It is bounded to the east, north, and south by the crescent-shaped fence of the Pelóri mountain range and to the west by the Encircling Sea, Ekkaia or Vaiya. Once a part of the physical world of Arda, Valinor became a hidden and forbidden realm, and following the Second Age has been completely removed from the Circles of the World, unreachable to all but the Elves.

Tolkien's depictions of Valinor draw upon Christian iconography of heaven and pagan images of the dwelling-place of the gods from Norse and other mythologies (2004). As a prototypical Otherworld like the "Perilous Realm" of *Faërie* Tolkien describes in "On Fairy-stories" (*MC* 114), Valinor represents an "earthly paradise" that now lies on "another plane of existence" (Flieger 2005, 123). In Norse mythology, the Vanir gods (the "Fair ones") reside in Vanaheim, which is often situated in the west Valinor. It also belongs to traditions such as the Celtic lore of a "deathless land to the West" from the Saint Brendan legends and Classical representations of Elysium (Roche 16). Thus Tolkien makes this land an embodiment of paradise lost in his legendarium, an Edenic place barred to mortals but still serving as a reminder of an unfallen world.

The Valar founded Valinor after Melkor destroyed the Two Lamps and ruined their former island home on Almaren. They raised the defensive barrier of the Pelóri, built their chief city, "Valmar of many bells" (*S*, 38), and made Valinor a land of light once Yavanna sang the Two Trees into being. Tolkien frequently changed the timeline for the history of Valinor: in the two *Annals of Valinor*, the realm was established in Valian Year (VY) 500, but the later *Annals of Aman* change the date to VY 3500. The blossoming of the Trees marked the first Year of the Trees (YT). The earliest reference to Valinor from the "The Cottage of Lost Play," the frame narrative for *The Book of Lost Tales*, includes the Olórë Mallë,

the Path of Dreams down which the "children of the fathers of the fathers of Men" would journey in their sleep (*Lost Tales I*, 19). The "Cottage of Lost Play" then housed those children left once Valinor was closed to the Gnomes (Noldor) who left for the Great Lands (Middle-earth), but Tolkien abandoned this concept in his later portrayals of the land.

The other accounts of Valinor published in the 1977 *Silmarillion* and in the volumes of *The History of Middle-earth* paint a rather consistent, if intentionally vague picture of the geography and nature of the Blessed Realm. As Karen Wynn Fonstad notes, "Tolkien left impressions of Valinor with a few strokes" rather than detailed descriptions of features with "meticulously calculated leagues" (6). Tolkien's cosmological work, the *Ambarkanta*, situates Valinor on the edges of the flat Arda before the sinking of Númenor. The air in Valinor is Ilmen, the celestial atmosphere in which the stars and later the Sun and Moon exist, rather than the earthly Vista, or breathable air. There is a chasm filled with Ilmen separating the western boundary of Valinor from the Enfolding Ocean Vaiya (Ekkaia), and Ulmo uses this gap to travel to the Earthroots to mix the waters of Middle-earth. Vista can flow into Eldamar, and if Valinor is darkened and the air is not cleansed by the light of the Blessed Realm, it takes the form of shadows and grey mists" (*Shaping*, 236); Tolkien even painted the lofty heights of Taniquetil during the time of the Sun and Moon when the mists are lowering upon the Blessed Realm (Hammond and Scull 1995, 54).

The land of Valinor itself contains the Valar's "houses, their gardens, and their towers" and is "more beautiful even than Middle-earth in the Spring of Arda" (*S, 37*). Time and decay do not affect it, for "naught faded nor withered, neither was there any stain upon flower or leaf in that land, nor any corruption or sickness in anything that lived; for the very stones and waters were hallowed" (*S*, 38). Before the diurnal rhythm of the Sun, the six-hour waxing and waning cycles of the Two Trees defined the twelve-hour day in Valinor. Though the land has no seasons, Yavanna has ordained periods of ripening and flowering for growing things, and harvest times are marked by feasts in praise of Eru. The Pelóri, reared to protect Valinor from Melkor's stratagems, are the highest mountains in Arda, and Manwë and Varda built their mansion Ilmarin with its star-spangled, webbed roof on the summit of Taniquetil, the greatest peak, from which they can survey the entire earth. On the plain beyond the mountains lies the city of Valmar, and before its western gate is the mound of the Ezellohar where the Two Trees stood and

Máhanaxar, the "Ring of Doom" where the Valar sit in council; this ring recalls the myths of the Norse gods holding their council under shade of Yggdrasil, the World Ash (Kocher, 39).

The abodes of the other Valar are scattered throughout Valinor, although few indications as to their locations appear in the various texts. Aulë's house borders a great vale and is full of webs woven with the stories of the music of the Ainur (*Lost Tales I*, 74). Tulkas has a many storied house in Valmar with a tower of bronze and pillars of copper in an arcade; he hold athletic contests in his court, but his wife Nessa retires to a lawn Oromë prepared for her (*Lost Tales I*, 75). Oromë has raised woods full of deer, bison, and horses, but he never hunts in Valinor, and his halls are lined with skins as well as spears, knives, and bows (*Lost Tales I*, 75). Lórien, the gardens of the Vala Irmo, are "the fairest of all places in the world, filled with many spirits" (*S*, 28), and Estë sleeps there during the day on an island in the lake Lórellin. To the west, near the borders of Valinor, lie the Halls of Mandos, the Houses of the Dead where Námo, Summoner of the Dead, maintains his vigil. Nienna resides near Mandos, her halls overlooking the Walls of the World (*S*, 28). Formenos, the fortress to which Fëanor and Finwe retreat, is situated in the northern reaches of Valinor. Eldamar lies beyond Valinor in the pass of the Calacirya (where Tirion upon Túna is located) to the Bay of Eldamar and Alqualondë, the city of the Teleri, with Tol Eressëa anchored nearby. West of the Pélori are the wastes of Araman and the ices of the Helcaraxê to the far north, and Avathar with its great mountain Hyarmentir, the hiding place of Ungoliant.

The Darkening of Valinor occurred in YV 2990 (*Annals of Valinor*) or YT 1495 (*Annals of Aman*), but Valinor itself remained a part of the world even after the subsequent exodus of the Noldor. The Nurtalë Valinóreva, the "Hiding of Valinor," however, occurred when the Valar created the Enchanted Isles as barriers to mariners coming from Beleriand. Only Eärendil, who sought the Valar's pardon for both Elves and Men, successfully navigated back to the shores of Aman and entered Valinor; for setting foot in the immortal land, he was exalted and his ship made to sail the skies. In SA 3319 Ar-Pharazôn broke the Ban of the Valar and invaded the Blessed Realm, getting as far as Túna. The Valar laid down their guardianship of Arda asked Eru to intercede, and thus "the world was indeed made round" with Aman being removed from the new globe (*S*, 281). Thereafter "only elven ships could sail into the 'true West' following the 'straight road,' and so rising above the Circles of the World to come again to Eldamar (Elvenhome)

on the shores of Valinor" (Hammond and Scull 2005, 11). Mortal flesh must be aided if it is to make the crossing through Ilmen to Valinor (*S*, 282).

In *The Lord of the Rings*, Valinor is mention by name only a handful of times, and Valmar once in Galadriel's Lament, but the image of the Elves leaving Middle-earth for the Undying Lands figures prominently in the novel. The Ringbearers—Bilbo, Frodo, and presumably Sam—and Gimli are the only mortals allowed to depart from the Grey Havens on the Straight Road to Aman, or more properly, Eressëa. Tolkien observes in his letters that those mortals do not gain immortality in the Undying Lands, but rather find relief from their suffering and a "purgatorial" purification (*Letters*, 198, 386). Frodo's vision of "white shores" and "a far green country under a swift sunrise" (*RK*, VI, ix, 310) is the only glimpse of the environs of Valinor found in the novel.

As the elusive paradisiacal Arda Umarred, that part Arda free from the taint of Morgoth (*Morgoth's*, 254), Valinor comes to embody a heaven that forbidden to human, but yet accessible to those worthy enough to enter it. It is a potent symbol in Tolkien's invented universe that orients his cosmology and stands in opposition to the realms of evil—Utumno, Angband, and Mordor—that figure so prominently in the struggle between good and evil.

DAVID D. OBERHELMAN

Further Reading

Burns, Marjorie. "Norse and Christian Gods: The Integrative Theology of J.R.R. Tolkien." In *Tolkien and the Invention of Myth: A Reader*. Jane Chance, Ed. Lexington: University of Kentucky Press, 2004, pp. 163–178.

Flieger, Verlyn. *Interrupted Music: The Making of Tolkien's Mythology*. Kent, OH: Kent State University Press, 2005.

Fonstad, Karen Wynn. *The Atlas of Middle-earth*. Revised Edition. Boston: Houghton Mifflin, 1991.

Hammond, Wayne G. and Christina Scull. *J.R.R. Tolkien: Artist & Illustrator*. Boston: Houghton Mifflin, 1995.

———. The *Lord of the Rings: A Reader's Companion*. London: HarperCollins, 2005.

Kocher, Paul H. *A Reader's Guide to The Silmarillion*. Boston: Houghton Mifflin, 1980.

Roche, Norma. "Sailing West: Tolkien, the Saint Brendan Story, and the Idea of Paradise in the West." *Mythlore* 17.4 (1991): 16–20, 62.

See also **Eärendil; Eldamar; Elves: Kindreds and Migrations; Frodo; Greek Gods; Kôr; Heaven; Maiar; Morgoth and Melkor; Mythology, Celtic; Mythology, Germanic; Saint Brendan; Taniquetil; Tol Eressëa; Two Trees; Valar**

VIKING RAIDS

The first Viking raid upon the British Isles occurred in 793 C.E. Alcuin of York, whose monastery, Lindisfarne, was attacked in that year, said this about the Vikings: "Never before has such a dreadful deed come to pass in Britannia as the one we now have been exposed to in the hands of a pagan people". This began several centuries of Viking attacks. Many entries of *The Anglo Saxon Chronicle* reported Norse devastations in early medieval England.

As professor of Anglo-Saxon at Oxford University, Tolkien lectured regularly on *Beowulf*, the episode of *Finn and Hengest* and the *Fight at Finnesburg*. The extensive fragment called *The Battle of Maldon* (fought in August 991 CE) was crucial to Tolkien's thinking about war. It romanticized the chivalry that the Ealdorman of Essex, Byrhtnoth (Beorhtnoth in the poem), showed in allowing his Viking foes to fight on the mainland. Tolkien wrote a one-act play, *The Homecoming of Beorhtnoth*, critiquing the warrior's false heroism, talking about his *ofermod*, "overconfidence".

Vikings raids in Anglo Saxon England appeared also in the early version of Tolkien's mythos of Ælfwine, the narrator who provides the framework for *The Book of Lost Tales*, although it wasn't published in *The Silmarillion*. Ælfwine was born in 869 CE, during the reign of King Alfred the reign, who had to fight the Viking for all his life. Tolkien's idea about Evil—that it is to some degree real not merely an absence—was probably influenced by King Alfred's personal translation of Boethius's *De Consolatione Philosophiae* into Old English, that he knew well.

ROBERTO ARDUINI

Primary Sources

Scagg, D.G. The Battle of Maldon. *Oxford: Oxford University Press, 1991.*

———. "The Homecoming of Beorhtnoth Beorhthelm's Son." In *The Tolkien Reader*. New York: Ballantine Books, 1966, pp. 1–27.

———. "*Finn and Hengest, the Fragment and the Episode*". Edited by Alan Bliss. London: George Allen & Unwin, 1983.

Further Reading

Houghton, John Wm. and Neal K. Keesee, "Tolkien, King Alfred, and Boethius: Platonist views of Evil in *The Lord of the Rings*" *Tolkien Studies*, 2 (2005): 131–59.

Shippey, Tom. *The Road to Middle-earth: Revised and Expanded Edition*. Boston: Houghton Mifflin, 2001.

See also **Alcuin; Ælfwine; *Battle of Maldon*; *Beowulf*: Tolkien Scholarship; *Finn and Hengest*; Good and Evil; History, Anglo-Saxon; *Homecoming of Beorhtnoth*; King Alfred**

VIOLENCE

J.R.R. Tolkien himself defined Faerie as "the Perilous Realm", that world in which Gawain lops off the Green Knight's head, Signy has her children slain, and King Arthur's knights die one by one in their quest for the Holy Grail. Fairy-stories, Tolkien reminds us, are not really for children, though it takes a child-like receptivity to appreciate them. One need only read the story of "Hansel and Gretel" or "The Juniper Tree" to discover their macabre and haunting qualities. *The Lord of the Rings* is such a story, and while it encourages readers to escape from the modern threat of atomic bombs and machine guns, it does little to protect them from the reality of violence.

Neither gods, nor elves, nor men escape its purview. Morgoth roused strife among the Noldor, leading to their crafting of weapons and armor and to their kin slaying at Alqualondë [Haven of the Swans] for which Fëanor was ultimately responsible. The first to spill blood in Valinor, Morgoth killed Fëanor's father, King Finwë. The Valar too brought about violence, marring the world in their battles with Morgoth.

Often the reader's attention is drawn back to a safe distance where violent events are not described in detail. Elves die in Gondolin, and Rohirrim are killed at Helm's Deep; however, the descriptions are left vague. At other times, Tolkien elaborates on the details: Túrin Turambar falls onto his sword, the Witch-king stabs Frodo at Weathertop, Boromir is feathered with arrows by Uruk-hai, and Gríma cuts Saruman's throat, "at the very door of Bag End" (*RK*, VI, viii, 300). Though he does not shy away from the violent scenes appropriate to a heroic narrative, Tolkien's *legendarium* hardly condones violence. Though the killing of orcs, Nazgûl, and trolls is always sanctioned, violently defending oneself against men, dwarves, or elves becomes an unfortunate necessity at best and a condemned moral failing at its worst.

The violence most hateful to Tolkien would have been the "ruining" of a tree, a natural beauty dear to his heart. Tolkien's love for trees is well acknowledged, as is his anger over their destruction. Often in his *legendarium*, violence against trees signifies one's opposition to the benevolent forces of the world: Morgoth and Ungoliant drain and poison Telperion and Laurelin; Sauron causes the destruction of Nimloth, the White Tree of Numenor and again fells a sapling of the White Tree at Minas Ithil; Saruman uproots hundreds of trees around Isengard; and ruffians pull down the Party Tree in Hobbiton. Even Hobbits sometimes act aggressively towards trees, as they did once against the Old Forest.

Tolkien has been accused of glorifying war, particularly in the battles at Helm's Deep and the Pelennor

Fields, and admittedly, the body count contest between Legolas and Gimli does make the experience out to be a good deal of fun (*TT*, III, vii 140–143). However, in both battle scenes, humankind was defending itself from occupation, slavery or worse, annihilation. This situation would have been familiar to anyone living during either one of the World Wars of the twentieth century. Concerning the reciprocity of violence during and after World War II, Tolkien reminds his son, Christopher, that, "you can't fight the Enemy with his own Ring without turning into an Enemy," (*Letters*, 94) and he not only remarks on the virtues of the German soldiers, but points to the orc-like behavior of some of the British.

Frodo Baggins and Samwise Gamgee provide a more compassionate perspective. Sam's sensitive reflection on the death of a Southron killed by the troops of Gondor humanizes the enemy (*TT*, IV, iv, 269). And Gandalf offers Frodo a moral lesson, which impacts the hobbit from that point on:

"Many that live deserve death. And some that die deserve life. Can you give it to them? Then do not be too eager to deal out death in judgment" (*FR*, I, ii, 69).

By the time Frodo returns to the Shire, his behavior approaches pacifism. His only objective is to keep the hobbits from killing the ruffians. Even when Saruman attempts to stab him with his dagger, Frodo exhibits extreme compassion, a trait we must assume he acquires through his suffering as Ring-bearer. Frodo is ultimately unsuccessful in preventing bloodshed in the Shire and reluctantly resigns himself to its necessity.

Tom Shippey argues that Frodo's pacifist behavior is a manifestation of the early medieval 'virtuous pagan' (Froda) whose failed attempts at peace are now lost amongst the more memorable heroic battles.

CHRISTOPHER VACCARO

Primary Sources

Tolkien, J.R.R. The Lord of the Rings. [1954–55] Boston: Houghton Mifflin, 1987.
———. *The Letters of J.R.R. Tolkien.* Ed. Humphrey Carpenter. 1981; Boston: Houghton Mifflin, 2000.

Further Reading

Garth, John. *Tolkien and the Great War.* Boston: Houghton Mifflin, 2003.
Shippey, Tom. *J.R.R. Tolkien: Author of the Century.* Boston: Houghton Mifflin, 2002.

See also **War**

VIRGIL

The Latin poet Virgil, Publius Vergilius Maro, lived in Italy during the I century BCE. He is the author of the *Aeneid*, the well-known epic poem of twelve books that became the Roman Empire's national epic. Modeled on Homer's both *Odyss* and *Iliad*, it tells the story of Aeneas who travels from the sacked Troy to the shores of Italy, where he settles to become the ancestor of the Romans.

Virgil was the Latin author whose success was continuous through the ages. He was integrated in the Christian culture and most appreciated by scholars during the Middle Age and Renaissance. Dante chose Virgil as his guide through the *Inferno* and the *Purgatorio*. Tolkien was introduced to the works of Virgil as a student (he learned Latin since his childhood) and as a scholar of medieval studies. Moreover, in a letter dated 22 September 1943 Tolkien wrote to his son Christopher about Lewis "new translation in rhymed alexandrines of the Aeneid" (but it wasn't published). Tolkien quotes Virgil several times in his essay *"Beowulf"*: The Monsters and the Critics where he claims that the Anglo-saxon poem Beowulf "was inpired by emulation of Virgil".

Similarities between Virgil and Tolkien are on the ideological side and the artistic side as well. The first point is that Tolkien wanted to write a mythology for England the same way Virgil had written a mythic history for Rome. In the *Aeneid* Tolkien appreciated the "impression of depth ... effect of antiquity... illusion of truth and perspective", as Shippey points out. Both Virgil and Tolkien conceived history as the whole of the human experience, myth being a true part of it.

In Tolkien own words: "Alas for the lost lore, the annals and the old poets that Virgil knew, and only used in the making of a new thing!". This statement represents the idea and the method Virgil and Tolkien adopted to build their masterpieces. During the years between the World Wars, writers such as T.S. Eliot and James Joyce developed the so-called "mythic method", though their style was very different one from the other.

As far as the narrative is concerned, the reader of *The Lord of the Rings* may similarities between Aeneas, Frodo and Aragorn, who are a find on a missions and have strong senses of duty. Aeneas and Frodo show a *pietas* that is lacking in the Nordic sagas such as *Edda* or *Kalevala*. Aeneas and Aragorn have to build a post-war society and, most impressive to the reader, they have to go through the underworld. This passage of the hero through the underworld is a typical step in the pattern of most mythical tales.

Gandalf is the guide of the fellowship as Virgil is the guide of Dante in the *Commedia*. Tolkien was a member of the "Oxford Dante Society" for a while and he and C.S. Lewis used to read Dante's works together.

A very important aspect both in Virgil and in Tolkien's work is a deep sense of nature, a love for country life that Tolkien portrayed in the Shire and Virgil dealt with in the *Georgics* and the *Bucolics* (or *Eclogues*). Virgil lived in Naples and Rome, that was the capital city of the Roman empire. To him countryside stood for the place where true human values were alive and where the Roman empire got its nourishment, both in a literally and in a symbolic sense.

Virgil and Tolkien gave a new start to literary genres that were non more much popular among their comtemporaries; actually, Virgil wrote an epic poem and Tolkien wrote stories with strong elements of fairy-tales.

CECILIA BARELLA

Further Reading

Greenman, David "Aeneidic and Odyssean Pattern of Escape and Return in Tolkien's *The Fall of Gondolin* and *The Lord of the Rings*" in *Mythlore* 18, no.2 (1992): 4–9

Houghton, John. "Commedia as Fairy-Story: Eucatasrophe in the Loss of Virgil" in *Mythlore* 17 no.2 (1990): 29–32

Morse, Robert E. *Evocation of Virgil in Tolkien's Art*. Oak Park, IL: Balchazy-Carducci Publishers, 1986

Obertino, James "Moria and Hades: Underworld Journeys in Tolkien and Virgil" in *Comparative Literature Studies* 30, no 2 (1993): 153–69.

See also **Homer; Joyce, James; Latin Language; Roman History**

WAIN, JOHN (1925–1994)

John Wain was an English author and critic and, for a time, a member of the Inklings. He came to Oxford as an undergraduate in 1943 and was tutored in English by C.S. Lewis. After his 1946 graduation, Wain spent another year at Oxford as a post-graduate fellow and then taught English at Reading University (1947–55) before becoming a full-time writer. Later, he served a term as Professor of Poetry at Oxford (1973–78).

Upon graduation, Wain was invited by Lewis to attend the Inklings and "became for two or three years a member of [this] informal circle" (179), to which he read poetry and criticism. Wain appreciated the opportunity for literary conversations with his seniors and shared their aversion to artistic modernism, but otherwise found himself out of sympathy with the Inklings' literary values and principles. He had no taste for fantasy, described Tolkien's theory of sub-creation as "manifestly absurd" (182), and found that *The Lord of the Rings* had "nothing to say" to him (*Contemporary Authors Autobiography Series* 4 (1986) 329). His description of the Inklings as a partisan cell was disputed by Lewis (*Encounter*, Jan. 1963, 81–2).

Wain's own literary sympathies were with the conservative realism that became prominent in the 1950s. He saw himself as a general man of letters, writing fiction, poetry, drama, criticism, and literary journalism alike. He was also active as editor, broadcaster, and teacher. Despite his differences of opinion with the Inklings, Wain remained devoted to Lewis's memory, writing several articles and reviews about him.

Some autobiographical writings cited above include his memories of and reactions to Tolkien.

DAVID BRATMAN

Further Reading

Wain, John. *Sprightly Running: Part of an Autobiography*. London: Macmillan, 1962.

See also **Inklings; Lewis, C.S.**

WANDERER, THE

The Wanderer, an anonymous Old English poem of 115 lines, presents the meditations of a lordless thane, who laments his former life of heroic companionship and worldly comfort. Along with its companion piece, *The Seafarer*, this lyric poem is included in a late tenth-century manuscript collection, *The Exeter Book*. The poem emphasizes a first-person speaker's state of mind as he passes from grief over the loss of his retainer status to resigned acceptance of the transitory nature of earthly life. Written in alliterative verse, *The Wanderer* has been classified as both an elegy and a work belonging to the larger category of wisdom literature. Through imagery characteristic of the Old English elegiac mode, such as ruined halls and lost hall-joys, as well as passages of gnomic wisdom, aphoristic sayings that present a general truth, *The Wanderer* establishes a picture of a solitary man unwillingly exiled from his homeland, bereft of personal attachments and future opportunities for glory, who wanders the earth seeking stability and consolation. Opening with a description of the speaker as a solitary dweller or exile (*anhaga*, line 1) and an earth-stepper or wanderer (*eardstapa*, line 6), the poem uses the bleak imagery of an icy, forbidding seascape on an early winter morning to portray the wanderer's feelings of isolation and hopelessness. He dreams of past material comforts and companionship, but wakes to his present suffering and the cries of seabirds who offer little fellowship. As he contemplates the mutability of human fate, the wanderer laments the loss of treasured tokens of the hall such as the horse, the byrnied warrior, and the bright cup. By the end of the poem, the wanderer has become wise in mind (*snottor on mode*, line 111) by accepting that the pleasures of mortal life are insufficient and transitory and that only the eternal life offers authenticity and permanence for the Christian soul.

As a teacher and scholar of Anglo-Saxon, Tolkien knew *The Wanderer* well and even began a collaboration on the poem with his friend and colleague E.V. Gordon, though this work was never completed. In Tolkien's fiction, themes recalling those of *The Wanderer* may be found in *The Lord of the Rings* and *The Silmarillion*, especially in connection with the Noldor Elves who have resided in Middle-earth after being exiled from their home in the Undying Lands beyond the sea. The seabird motif from *The Wanderer* appears in *The Lord of the Rings* in relation to Legolas's longing for the sea to highlight the separation of all Elves in Middle-earth from a homeland that some like the Noldor have lost, while others like Legolas have never known but still desire. Another of Tolkien's exiled groups, the Ents, also have their origins in a statement from *The Wanderer* about old giant's work (*eald enta geweorc*, line 87), as Tolkien explains in a letter to W.H. Auden (*Letters*, 212). Further resemblances to *The Wanderer's* themes in *The Lord of the Rings* appear in Tolkien's portrayal of the Dúnedain in general, but especially of Aragorn, who wanders the wilds with few attachments to others, always yearning for a noble past while seeking a more permanent future. One of Aragorn's many names, "Strider," may also be meant by Tolkien to echo the Old English wanderer's description as *eardstapa*. Early in Chapter 6 of *The Two Towers*, Aragorn recites a poem of the Rohirrim beginning "Where now the horse and the rider?" based directly on imagery from *The Wanderer*. Legolas describes this poem as reflecting "the sadness of Mortal Men," a theme evocative of the Old English elegy's insistence on the inadequacies of mortal life and earthly impermanence.

LESLIE A. DONOVAN

Primary Sources

Crossley-Holland, Kevin, trans. *The Wanderer*. In *The Anglo-Saxon World: An Anthology*. Oxford: Oxford University Press, 1999. pp. 50–52.

Krapp, George Phillip and Elliot Van Kirk Dobbie, eds. *The Wanderer*. In *The Exeter Book*. Anglo-Saxon Poetic Records 3. New York: Cambridge University Press, 1936. pp. 134–37.

Further Reading

Bjork, Robert E. "*Sundor æt rune*: The Voluntary Exile of *The Wanderer*." In *Old English Literature: Critical Essays*. Ed. R.M. Luizza. New Haven: Yale University Press, 2002. pp. 315–27.

Green, Martin, ed. *Old English Elegies: New Essays in Criticism and Research*. Cranbury, NJ: Associated University Presses, 1983.

Shippey, T.A. "*The Wanderer* and *The Seafarer* as Wisdom Poetry." In *Companion to Old English Poetry*. Ed. Henrik Aertsen and Rolf H. Bremmer, Jr. Amsterdam: VU University Press, 1994.

See also **Aragorn; Auden, W.H.: Influence of Tolkien; Christian Readings of Tolkien; Elves; Ents; Exile; Gordon, E.V.; Legolas; Men, Middle-earth; Seafarer, The**

WAR

The timing of *LotR's* publication in the decade following the Second World War led critics to assume that the work reflected directly on that war and the nuclear threat that dominated the post-war period. Tolkien, however, famously rejected a direct allegorical relationship to any contemporary historical events. This position needs to be understood not as a rejection of the connection between *LotR* and war but as resistance to an overly simplistic model of interpretation. *LotR* is not an allegory for any particular war; instead it reveals a characteristically twentieth-century understanding of war. Tolkien did acknowledge the effects on *LotR* of "the darkness of the present days" (*FR* Foreword, 7). In his letters he also makes a number of explicit links between the First World War and *LotR*, seeing, for example, Sam Gamgee as a typical batman, and comparing the landscape of the Dead Marshes to Northern France after the Somme (*Letters*, 111). Today, Thomas A. Shippey, Janet Brennan Croft, and Hugh Brogan, among many critics, consider a rich array of themes, including the influence of the First World War, the mythologizing of war, the role of heroism, fantasy as a genre for war writing, homoerotic attachments in the Ring-bearer's Company, and the othering of the enemy in the form of the Orcs.

Tolkien himself had intimate experiences of both the 1914–18 and the 1939–45 World Wars. At the start of the First World War he enlisted in the Oxford University Officer Training Corps whilst completing his B.A. In 1916 he joined the Lancashire Fusiliers and arrived in France in time for the Battle of the Somme where he acted as battalion signaling officer. By November he was invalided back to England suffering from trench fever, which kept him convalescent until just before the end of the war in November 1918. Two of Tolkien's closest school friends, G.B. Smith and Rob Gilson, with whom he had formed the "Tea Club and Barrovian Society" (T.C.B.S) died in 1916, a loss Tolkien referred to in the Introduction to the 1965 edition of *LotR*. During the Second World War, two of Tolkien's sons were in the armed forces: Michael served as an antiaircraft gunner and was invalided out in 1944 with "severe shock to the nervous system due to prolonged exposure to enemy action," whilst Christopher was an RAF pilot stationed in South Africa. Tolkien himself was active in Civil Defense throughout the war, and trained as a cryptographer for the Foreign Office in 1939.

Since the early nineties Shippey has done much to establish Tolkien's place as part of a generation of writers, including William Golding, C.S. Lewis, George Orwell, and T.H. White, for whom the Second World War intensified a concern with the role of evil. All of these writers, and the Americans Kurt Vonnegut and Ursula LeGuin, whom Shippey adds to the list in *J.R.R. Tolkien: Author of the Century* (2001), use fantasy or other non-realist fictional forms for the exploration of themes such as the dynamics of power, the individual's response to evil, and the nature of total warfare. Shippey terms these writers, including Tolkien, "traumatized authors."

Tolkien's choice of the fantasy genre made it difficult, at one time, to see his writing as part of the huge outpouring of First World War literature between 1914 and 1939. Until feminist criticism, in the 1980s, challenged the identification of war writing with the representation of frontline, combatant experience, war writing was defined very narrowly as realist and largely first-person, whether in the form of the soldier–poet's protest against the suffering of the frontline fighter, or the memoirs and autobiographical fiction that dwelt in minute detail on the miseries of trench warfare, shell shock, and the problem of returning to civilian life. Wilfred Owen, Siegfried Sassoon, Isaac Rosenberg, Ivor Gurney, and Edmund Blunden are still iconic of First World War poetry, while Robert Graves, Erich Maria Remarque, Richard Aldington, and Vera Brittain are famous for creating the image of a lost generation of youth survived by a cohort of scarred and disillusioned contemporaries to whom fell the task of recording the true horror of the War. As a result, the First

World War has been seen as the origin of a peculiarly twentieth-century commitment to irony as the dominant literary mode, with approaches such as David Jones's long mythological poem, *In Parenthesis* (1937), with which Tolkien has some commonalities, being minor offshoots (Fussell, 1975: 5).

It is no wonder that Tolkien's fairy stories and poems written during the War, such as "The Fall of Gondolin," "Kortirion among the Trees," and "The Cottage of Lost Play," and poems such as "The Lonely Isle," "An Evening in Tavrobel," and "Princess Ni," are still seen as predominately escapist (Croft, 17–18). In 1939, Tolkien linked his choice of genre to the war, stating that his "taste for fairy-stories was ... quickened to full life by war" ("On Fairy Stories" 42). Critics such as Croft and Verlyn Flieger point to the emergence in the thirties of Tolkien's understanding of the potential of fantasy to be more than welcome escape from the war. Flieger, for example, establishes a parallel between the incommunicable experience of Fairie and the veteran's inability to describe war experiences in later works such as "Looney" (*H*, XVIII, 346), revised and published as "The Sea-Bell" in 1962. The Battle of the Five Armies near the end of *The Hobbit* (1937) is described mainly from the point of view of Bilbo, whose role is anything but heroic and who sums up victory as "a very gloomy business" (263). A discussion of Northern courage and heroism is central to his 1936 essay, "*Beowulf*: The Monsters and the Critics," and Croft notes that the section on Escape in "On Fairy-stories" uses a contemporary political vocabulary such as "prisons and deserters, party lines and treachery, quislings and false patriotism" that belongs to the thirties (Croft, 19).

Although it is widely accepted that the First World War ushered in a new paradigm of post-industrial, mechanized warfare, it is too easy to see Tolkien's fantasy setting as mythologizing war by returning to a pre-war paradigm of romantic and chivalric heroism. This view is inaccurate in several ways. The post-war period saw a surge in religious forms of consolation. Protest and patriotism continued to coexist through the inter-war years as they had as early as 1914. Pro- and anti-war literature shared themes, such as the value of male comradeship and a stress on individual courage and honor in the soldiers, however horrific or pointless their deaths. In this context, Tolkien's interest in wartime heroism is not inevitably nostalgic. As an Anglo-Saxonist, Tolkien was committed to a historically accurate understanding of different codes of honor and the heroic; this can hardly be reduced to Fussell's picture of Victorian and Edwardian pseudo-medievalism. Tolkien compares different versions of heroism in *LotR*, as well as in *The Hobbit* or "Farmer

Giles of Ham,'' ranging from Boromir's redemption through a sacrificial death, through Aragorn's endurance and lofty purity, to Frodo's lonely endurance as Ring-bearer. The question of what constitutes moral courage in wartime is central.

Much remains to be explored about the place of war in Tolkien's writing, with the important contributions of critics including Croft and Garth having initiated many new lines of inquiry, such as Tolkien's debt to just war theory (Croft, 138), new attention to Tolien's early work in the context of war (Garth), the relationship of Eowyn's martial femininity to suffrage iconography in the early twentieth century (Malone), or the link between the abject and deadly maternal figure of Shelob and the powerful anti-maternal rhetoric that emerged out of the First World War and reached full force in the thirties (Malone). At the start of the twenty-first century, the most intriguing insight awaiting development must be the potential connection between wartime culture and Tolkien's soaring popularity after the release of Peter Jackson's film adaptation.

CLAIRE BUCK

Further Reading

Croft, Jane Brennan *War and the Works of JRR Tolkien*, Westport, CT: Praeger Publishers, 2004.
Flieger, Verlyn *A Question of Time: JRR Tolkien's Road to Faerie*, Kent, OH: Kent State University Press 1997.
Fussell, Paul *The Great War and Modern Memory*, Oxford: Oxford University Press, 1975.
Garth, John *Tolkien and the Great War: The Threshold of Middle-earth*, Boston: Houghton Mifflin, 2003.
Malone, Katherine *Lord of the Rings* gender structure in its World War One Context.'' Unpublished thesis, Norton, MA: Wheaton College, 2001.
Shippey, Thomas R. *JRR Tolkien: Author of the Century*. Boston: Houghton Mifflin, 2001.

See also **World War I; World War II**

WAR OF THE JEWELS, THE

The name given by Christopher Tolkien to Part XI of the History of Middle-earth. It forms, with *Morgoth's Ring* (*Morgoth*), a sub-set entitled ''The Later Silmarillion.'' Both volumes contain drafts and essays dating from the period after the completion of the *LotR* in 1949, and therefore represent Tolkien's last, albeit unfinished, version of the ''Silmarillion'' legendarium. The two books do not cover different periods of Tolkien's life; instead they are separated chronologically in relation to the fictional narrative. Therefore, while *Morgoth* describes some of the drastic revisions Tolkien made to his creation myths and

Valinorean histories, *Jewels* concerns itself with events in Beleriand during ''the last epoch of the Elder Days.'' The title itself was, in the editor's words, ''a term my father often used of the last six centuries of the First Age . . . after the return of Morgoth and the coming of the Noldor'' (*Jewels*, vii–viii). The dividing point between the two volumes is therefore the Hiding of Valinor.

Jewels is divided into four parts. The first part, an unfinished work entitled ''The Grey Annals,'' is actually two texts closely related, both written in the early 1950s, which together constitute Tolkien's third attempt at an ''Annals of Beleriand.'' They give an account of the early First Age as recorded by the ''Grey-Elves'' of Doriath and the Havens; events in Valinor are accordingly glossed over or reduced to quick references. Christopher Tolkien calls the Grey Annals ''the primary text'' for ''the structure and history of Beleriand'' (*Jewels*, 4), and used it extensively in the creation of the published Silmarillion.

The second part of the book is a heavily editorialized summary of the post-1949 revisions made by Tolkien to the ''Quenta Silmarillion,'' his last pre-war account of the First Age. *Jewels* contains the second half of the revised text, from Chapter Nine onwards; Chapters One to Eight can be found in *Morgoth*. The key difference between the pre-war Quenta and the 1950s text is a movement away from what David Bratman calls the curt ''Annalistic'' style of the former, and an attempt to return to the mythology ''some of the power and vividness of the earliest stories'' (Bratman, 72). This ''Later Quenta Silmarillion'' forms the central part of *S*, though it is an incomplete account and was necessarily expanded by the editor.

Part three is divided into five sections, of which three can be quickly dealt with: ''Maeglin'' was used extensively in the creation of Chapter 16 of *S*; ''Of the Ents and the Eagles,'' one of Tolkien's last pieces, was largely threaded into Chapter 2 of the same; ''Aelfwine and Dírhaval'' contains two versions of an introductory note to the poetic ''Tale of the Children of Húrin,'' written from the perspective of its supposed Elvish composer. Although these notes are summarized in *UT*, they are here given in full.

The third part also contains a major narrative entitled ''The Wanderings of Húrin.'' Apparently lost by Tolkien in his own lifetime, it describes the events that befell the father of the hero Túrin shortly after his release, aged sixty, from imprisonment in Morgoth's stronghold. Although intended as a continuation of the ''Grey Annals,'' the narrative evidently outgrew the annalistic format and evolved into a vivid and engaging tale; it was not included in the *S* because of its irreducible length and incompatible style. In seeking to place the text within the context of the legendarium, Charles E. Noad speculates that we ought to consider it "a part of the saga of the Children of Hurin 'retold', in the same way that the *LotR* can be interpreted as a retelling of Frodo's original writings in the Red Book" (Noad, 2000, 61). This text represents the latest part of the First Age chronology that was fully revised by Tolkien before his death; everything that comes after in the *S* narrative was drawn from pre-*LotR* sources.

The importance of the final text in part three, "The Tale of Years," is belied by its appearance. In form it is nothing more than a terse reduction of the two Annal traditions (those of Aman and Beleriand) into a summary of dates and events. However, due to a lack of any other late texts concerning the Ruin of Doriath, Christopher Tolkien and Guy Gavriel Kay were forced to rely heavily on it (in conjunction with earlier sources from "as far back as the Quenta Noldorinwa" of 1930) when constructing Chapter 22 of *S*. As Christopher Tolkien regretfully concedes, this has resulted in a published account of the Fall of Doriath that "in certain essential features has no authority whatever" in his father's own writings (*Jewels*, 354–6). The argument over how, and indeed if, the less coherent elements of the legendarium ought to have been published is an unresolved one (Bratman 2000, 71, 89–90).

Part Four contains just one text, "Quendi and Eldar," a very detailed essay on the Elvish names for themselves and their clans, and the derivation and meanings of those names. It also contains commentary on the language of the Valar (along with a small lexicon), and a description of the secret "gesture-language" of the Dwarves. Tolkien's belief that "a language requires a suitable habitation, and a history in which it can develop" (*Letters* 375) is amply demonstrated by the wealth of historical and cultural information tied up in these linguistic notes. An interesting appendix, "the legend of the Awakening of the Quendi," offers an entertaining and informative fairy-tale of the origins of the "Elf-fathers", naming them as Imin, Tata and Enel (One, Two and Three), and describing the earliest years of their respective kindreds.

The War of the Jewels has much to offer, from previously unpublished narrative work, to the latest drafts of key *S* texts, to some of the most detailed information about the Elvish languages available. But more than this, it offers a valuable insight into the editorial difficulties and discussions that surrounded the creation of the published *Silmarillion* itself.

MATT FENSOME

Further Reading

Bratman, David. "The Literary Value of The History of Middle-earth," in *Tolkien's Legendarium: Essays on the History of Middle-earth*. Eds. Verlyn Flieger and Carl F. Hostetter. Westport, CT: Greenwood Press, 2000.

Charles E. Noad. "On the Construction of the Silmarillion," in *Tolkien's Legendarium: Essay on the History of Middle-earth*. Eds. Verlyn Flieger and Carl F. Hostetter. Westport, CT: Greenwood Press, 2000.

See also **Aelfwine; Elves: Kindreds and Migrations; Frame Narrative;** *History of Middle-earth*: **Overview; Maps;** *Morgoth's Ring*; **Tolkien, Christopher;** *Unfinished Tales*

WAR OF THE RING, THE

War—the eighth volume in *The History of Middle-earth*, first published in 1990—documents each moment in the creative process Tolkien underwent when completing *LotR*. *War* is the third part of a sub-series within the twelve volume *HoM-e*. This sub-series, volumes VI–IX, entails how Tolkien brought *LotR* to completion. The title of this volume stems from the original title for Book V of *LotR*: "The War of the Ring," proposed by Tolkien to Raynor Unwin in 1953. The title was adopted by Christopher Tolkien when compiling and editing his father's manuscripts for this volume of *HoM-e*. *War* contains a profusion of narrative drafts, that expand upon the *LotR* proper.

There are three parts within *War*: "The Fall of Saruman," "The Ring Goes East," and "Minas Tirith." Written in 1942, "The Fall of Saruman" includes the last chapters of Book III, from a chronological introduction of "The Destruction of Isengard," to "The Palantír. Written in 1944, "The Ring Goes East," includes all of Book IV from "The Taming of Sméagol," to "Kirith Ungol." Part three was composed primarily from 1944–46 and includes Book V, which opens with an "Addendum to 'The Treason of Isengard'" and "Minas Tirith," to "The Black Gate Opens."

The opening chapter of *War* details "The Destruction of Isengard," which brings to light the chronological dilemmas Tolkien faced as his sub-creation unfolded. The entire 'Isengard story' was conceived and set down as one whole story, and interwoven with other chapters of *LotR*. In the early writing of *LotR* through to its completed form Tolkien created charts, lists and tables in order to keep track of the many threads and events of *LotR*—all of which has been referenced to as the *Scheme*. As new bits of story developed, Tolkien as sub-creator and perfectionist returned to the start, re-writing the story to incorporate new drafts with the proper moon cycles and calendar dates. A series of events in the tale would converge, causing chronological dislocation as pieces of the narrative were written. These issues of chronology were not limited to Tolkien's narrative scheme. Christopher Tolkien highlights the confusion in his father's papers as the earlier drafts versus the later versions of the narrative were sorted out. Tolkien had fixed narrative points and relations: Merry and Pippin in Wellinghall, the "story foreseen from Fangorn," (*War*, 4) Aragorn, Gimli and Legolas' encounter with Eomer (Day 1); the Entmoot, the return of Gandalf and smoke rising in Rohan (Day 2); the Golden Hall and the host of the Rohirrim setting out, including the Ents attack on Isengard. These three days of narrative would later dislodge the original opening of what would become "Helm's Deep."

One of the major tasks for Christopher Tolkien in arranging his father's manuscripts for the history of *LotR* was dating each of the versions to show the course of its creation and providing the reader with the earlier narrative. *War* contains the evolution of place names and character names as well. In Part One, we see the development of the naming of Helm's Deep from Heorulf's Clough to *Nothelm* and *Helmshaugh*, and finally *Helm's Deep*, as well as earlier renderings of Erkenbrand, which was a name Tolkien had contemplated utilizing for Trotter instead of Aragorn (*War*, 11).

"The Road to Isengard" also shows essential narrative differences in the overall tale. The diverse forms of this chapter, including its varied plot and narrative changes are included, was originally a continuing narrative with "The Battle of Helm's Deep." These alternatives include the events of Gandalf and Théoden after the end of the Helm's Deep battle, their not seeing the Ents after leaving the wood, not going down the Fords of Isen and meeting with Bregalad the Ent. The first part of *War* continues through "Flotsam and Jetsam" to "The Palantír" which continues to highlight chronological issues and expansive narrative from earlier drafts of *LotR*.

The introduction of Faramir, originally Falborn son of Anborn, and the "Window on the West" chapter, as it was later entitled, was achieved in little more than a week. According to Christopher Tolkien, it appears to have been a "time of intense and concentrated work" (*War*, 144). Faramir develops swiftly into one of Tolkien's more full developed characters—a character who Tolkien thought bore the most resemblance to Tolkien himself. Faramir often reflects Tolkien's personal views, inherent beliefs, and is generally "like him" (Hammond, 468) as Tolkien states in a 1956 letter. This new chapter, "Faramir," was initially the fourth

since "The Black Gate is Closed," and "Of Herbs and Stewed Rabbit," had not been created as separate chapters. The initial drafting of "The Forbidden Pool" originally ran as a singular narrative with the later chapter "Journey to the Cross-Roads."

The typescript for "Many Roads Lead Eastward," which later became "The Passing of the Grey Company," included large extensions to a later chapter entitled, "The Muster of Rohan." "The Muster of Rohan" narrative was almost achieved word for word in *RK*. Early story outlines of Book V show how the evolution of the characters and narrative differ greatly from the final version. This most notably includes the falls of Théoden and Éowyn. Tolkien had these two characters slain during the fight with the Witch King on the field of Pellenor. The funeral of Théoden and Éowyn is compared by Christopher Tolkien to the "...grief of Baldr," (*War*, 369). The death of Éowyn occurs in several outlines, yet is rejected for the popular scene we know in the final draft. This scene changes over several drafts, which include the death of the Witch King as Éowyn beheads his Nazgûl steed, and no role for Merry in the battle. The prophecy of Glorfindel, "...not by the hand of man will he fall," cited in "The Siege of Gondor" has been compared by scholars to those made of *Macbeth* in Shakespeare (Hammond, 362). This scene, as it appeared to Christopher Tolkien, was first composed in isolation from the rest of the story. The subsequent events of *War* "The Story Foreseen From Fronts (the north gate of the Pellenor Wall)," as Christopher Tolkien entitled this point in the story, deals with the Rohirrim pouring through the walls of Minas Tirith. This includes early conceptions of Denethor's role that are was not consonant with his final story of madness and suicide. "The Pyre of Denethor" through "The Last Debate," are the last chapters covering Book V of *LotR*, and "The Second Map" (notes and commentary on Tolkien's working map of Book V, conclude the volume.

ANTHONY BURDGE and JESSICA BURKE

Further Reading

Tolkien, Christopher, ed. Tolkien, J.R.R. *The War of the Ring*. Houghton Mifflin: Boston. 1990.

Hammond, Wayne G., Scull Christina. *The Lord of the Rings: A Readers Companion*. Houghton Mifflin: Boston. 2005.

Bratman, David. "The Literary Value of the History of Middle-earth" *Tolkien's Legendarium: Essays on the History of Middle-earth*. Verlyn Flieger, Carl E. Hostetter, ed. Greenwood Press: Connecticut and London. 2000.

See also **Éowyn; Faramir; Glorfindel;** *History of Middle-earth:* **Overview;** *Hobbit, The;* *Lord of the Rings, The;* **Théoden**

WARWICK

In June of 1913 Edith Bratt, then Tolkien's fiancée, and her cousin Jennie Grove, moved to Warwick, in England's Midlands. After her conversion to Catholicism, Edith was no longer welcome in Cheltenham. She lived in Warwick until shortly after her marriage to Tolkien in March of 1916.

On weekends when he had leave from the Lancashire Fusiliers, Tolkien would motorbike to Warwick. Edith Bratt married Tolkien at the Catholic church of St. Mary Immaculate in Warwick, March 22, 1916. When they returned from their honeymoon, Tolkien was posted to Rugeley Camp in Staffordshire, and Edith Tolkien moved to Great Haywood to be close to him until he left for Europe.

Tolkien would have known Warwick's Anglo-Saxon history as a town fortified against invading Danes in the tenth century, and as one of the royal towns in the kingdom of Mercia, the home of the Old Mercian dialect of Old English dear to Tolkien's heart. According to Carpenter's *Biography*, Tolkien found Warwick strikingly beautiful. The town, built around the Earl of Warwick's castle, is bordered by the river Avon and is not far from the forest of Arden. There are numerous groves and small forests, particularly around the castle. In a letter Tolkien wrote Edith Bratt on November 26, 1915 he mentions a poem he had been working on, "Kortirion Among the Trees," inspired by Warwick (*Letters* 8). Christopher Tolkien, who published three versions of "Kortirion Among the Trees," dates the earliest version to November, 1915. The latest version is one J. R. R. Tolkien sent to Raynor Unwin in February of 1962 for possible publication in *The Adventures of Tom Bombadil* (*Lost Tales I*, 32). In Tolkien's prehistory, Kortirion is an Elvish city at the center of the island of Tol Eressëa, the island which would eventually become England (*Lost Tales I* 24–5). In a prose preface preceding the 1915 version of the poem Tolkien makes it clear that the Elves named their city Kortirion after their former city of Kôr in Valinor (*Lost Tales I*, 25). The earliest version of the poem has a notation in Tolkien's handwriting dedicating the poem to Warwick. Kortirion is an allusion to an idealized Warwick, another city in the midst of trees, and featuring a castle standing on a hill. The great tower Ingil built in Kortirion parallels the great tower of Warwick castle, as the etymology of Kortirion parallels Warwick (*Lost Tales* II, 392).

The Warwick described in "Kortirion Among the Trees" is filled with the beauty of trees, passing seasons, and the music and dancing of the elves (or fairies). In later versions of the poem, Tolkien gradually moves away from the archaic diction of the 1915 text and increasingly emphasizes the fading of the elves, and of the beauty of the trees.

LISA L. SPANGENBERG

Further Reading

Carpenter, Humphrey. *J.R.R. Tolkien: A Biography*. London: George Allen & Unwin, 1978.

See also **Book of Lost Tales I; Great Haywood; Marriage; Mythology for England; Nature; Poems by Tolkien; Trees; Towers**

WEAPONS, NAMED

Naming weapons has long been part of our mythological past. In tales of heroic epic, the named weapon was of singular importance, and served as part of the hero, journey and a rite of passage. The weapons in Middle-earth are unique creations, imbued with their own story, connecting readers to ritualistic warfare.

A few examples which inspired the weaponry of Middle-earth can be seen in Gram, the sword of Sigurd the Volsung, the swords Naegling and Hrunting used by Beowulf, and Tyrfing from "The Waking of Agantyr" found in the Elder Edda. These swords are heirlooms passed from King to heir, father to son, or found in treasure hoards. Some fit within motif of the sword that was broken and re-forged.

The sword, for Tolkien, symbolized a code of physical warrior prowess. Tolkien preferred such a code for the heroes of his stories. The great weapons of legend are not always simple instruments of war; at times they break in battle and are re-forged with new names and inscriptions signifying the transfer of office and authority to a new bearer. The runes of power inscribe enchantment and history upon blade, enhancing the abilities of the warrior who bears it. These rites date back to the ancient world of Northern Europe. Such can be seen with Brynhilde's instructions to Sigurd to cut runes on his blade to insure victory and wisdom (Byock, 67–8). Tolkien's work incorporates various forms of these ceremonial instructions. From the First Age through the Third Ages of Middle-earth, Tolkien's characters bear such memorable arms as, Aiglos—The Spear of Gil-Galad, Sting, Orcrist, Glamdring, and Narsil. Telchar, most renown of the Dwarf-smiths, forged Narsil in the First Age (*S*, 294–5). Narsil was the sword of Elendil broken in combat with Sauron, used to cut the one ring from The Dark Lord's hand by Isildur, later re-forged, and renamed Anduril for Aragorn (*LotR*, 276–7). The Sword that was Broken has numerous links to the swords of Northern literature. The sword

Tyrfing, belonging to Oðin's grandson Svafrlami, was the work of two Dwarves: Dvalin and Durin. The Dwarves had been trapped and forced to Forge a sword to shine like gleaming fire (Terry, 250–3). Narsil, being forged by a Dwarf smith, parallels Tyrfing. Tolkien furthers the link by describing Andúril as shining with light of Sun and Moon. Andúril became known as the Flame of the West. In *Saga of the Volsungs*, King Sigmund fell under the spear of an enemy one–eyed and cloaked in black (Byock, 53). Sigmund gave his wife Hjordis his sword and, with his dying breath, requested it be re-reforged and re-named Gram (Byock, 53–4). Gram, later born by Sigmund's son, Sigurd, was described as having flames leaping from its edges as it passed from the forge (Byock, 59–60).

The connection to ancestral past through weapons runs throughout the text of *Beowulf*. Beowulf's named weapons, however, tend not to fulfill their purpose, failing when tested. The monster Grendel, who each night attacks Heorot, hall of Hrothgar, is impenetrable to weapons of war and bears no arms (*Beowulf*, 115–163). Beowulf decides to fight Grendel with use of his sword (*Beowulf*, 343–347; 381–386). The monster is soon defeated and is avenged by his mother (*Beowulf*, 710–836; 1537–1569). The sword, Hrunting, which Unferth gives to Beowulf, is said never to have failed any man, yet it proves useless against Grendel's mother (*Beowulf*, 1519–1528). *Beowulf* finds a sword hanging upon the wall within Grendel's lair and uses it against his foe, which succeeds in defeating the monster, but its blade melts from the enemy's blood (*Beowulf*, 1567–1569; 1605–1611). The sword used to defeat Grendel's mother serves as a connection to a past mythology even for Beowulf. Forged by the race of giants, the sword's origins written in runes upon the hilt. The blade explains a pre-history that may link tales from emerging Christianity and the ancient Nordic culture (*Beowulf*, 1659–1699). During the encounter with the dragon, Beowulf's sword Naegling breaks (*Beowulf*, 2575–2586). The dragon is defeated with a sword thrust from Wiglaf and a dagger strike Beowulf gives to the beast's belly (*Beowulf*, 2680–2705). The weapons utilized by Beowulf to defeat Grendel's mother and the dragon did not bear any names, and such nameless weapons succeeded in their task.

The transfer of a sword or weapon, through re-forging or re-finding, transfers historical significance to the current generation, giving new purpose for the bearer and lifting any hardship from its previous owner. Tyrfing passed to Agantyr and finally to his daughter the Valkyrie Hervor; Gram passed from Sigmund to Sigurd; Hrunting and Naegling both passed unto Beowulf. Further examples of such passage of time and transference of power via the sword can be seen in Narsil, and the blades of Orcrist, Glamdring, and Sting. These three swords, found in a troll-hoard by Thorin, Gandalf and Bilbo are forged in the First Age (*H*, II, 82–83; 94–95). Thorin bears the blade Orcrist, Goblin Cleaver. It is recognized by the Great Goblin, and it gleams in the darkness on Thorin's breast when he is laid to rest after the Battle of the Five Armies (*H*, IV, 110–111; XVIII, 350–351). Turgon made Glamdring—Foe-Hammer—and it is wielded by Gandalf throughout *H* and *LotR*. Bilbo takes a knife with no proper lineage. He names the weapon Sting after facing the spiders of Mirkwood (*H*, 208).

A catalogue of named weapons in Middle-earth are as follows:

- Aeglos, Aiglos: Spear of Gil-galad (*FR*, II, ii, 256, 243; *S*, 294; *UT*, 148)
- Andúril: 'Flame of the West' Narsil reforged for Aragorn (*FR*, II, iii, 290)
- Anglachel: sword made by Eöl, given by Thingol to Beleg, reforged for Túrin as Gurthang (*S*, 201–2, 206–10; *UT*, 148)
- Angrist: 'Iron-cleaver,' knife made by Telchar, used by Beren (*S*, 177, 181)
- Anguirel: sister-sword to Anglachel, made by Eöl (*S*, 202)
- Aranrúth: 'King's Ire,' Thingol's blade, passed unto kings of Númenor (*S*, 201; *UT*, 171)
- Belthronding: Beleg Cúthalion's bow (*S*, 208)
- Dragon-helm of Dor-lómin—Helm of Hador—passed unto Túrin (*S*, 199, 204–205, 211, 230; *UT*, 75–6, 77–9, 90, 94, 146, 152–5)
- Dramborleg (*UT*, 172)
- Glamdring, Beater, Foe-hammer: Gandalf's weapon (*H*, III, 82–83; IV, 94–95; *UT*, 54)
- Grond: battering-ram, mace of Morgoth, 'Hammer of the Underworld' (*S*, 154; *RK*, V, iv, 102)
- Gúthwinë: Éomer's sword (II, III, vii, 139)
- Gurthang: the 'Black Thorn of Brethil,' 'Iron of Death,' Anglachel reforged for Túrin (*S*, 210, 213, 216, 222, 224–6; *UT*, 110, 126, 128. 135, 137, 140–3)
- Herugrim: Théoden's sword (*TT*, III, vi, 123)
- Narsil: Sword of Elendil, made by Telchar, broken in combat with Sauron (*FR*, II, 256, 259; *TT*, III, vi, 115, *S*, 294–5)
- Orcrist, Biter, Goblin-cleaver (*H*, 82–83; 94–95, 110–111; 350–351)
- Ringil: Fingolfin's blade (*S*, 153–4)
- Sting: Bilbo's Elven blade, passed from Frodo to Sam (*H*, III, 82–83, VIII, 208)

ANTHONY BURDGE and JESSICA BURKE

Further Reading

Anderson, Douglas. *The Annotated Hobbit: Revised and Expanded Edition* Boston: Houghton Mifflin 2002.

Chickering, Howard D. (ed.) *Beowulf.* New York: Anchor Books, 1989.

Byock, Jesse (trans.) *The Saga of the Volsungs.* Los Angeles: University of California Press, 1990.

Petty, Anne C. *Tolkien in the Land of Heroes.* New York: Cold Spring Press, 2003.

Terry, Patricia (trans.) *Poems of the Vikings: The Elder Edda.* New York: The Bobbs-Merrill Company Inc, 1969.

See also **Aragorn; Arms and Armor; Bilbo; Charms; Gandalf; Runes; Old Norse Literature; Power in Tolkien's Works; Túrin**

WELSH LANGUAGE

Welsh is an Indo-European language, immediately descended from a Brythonic language of Roman Britain. One speaks of Early Welsh as developing from its Brythonic precursor around the time when Britain fell to the Saxons (and Angles and Jutes), and Old Welsh as being the language of Wales between the ninth and eleventh centuries CE Manuscripts of the laws of Hywel Dda and of early poetry date from this period, while some of the earliest Welsh documents are from the *Hen Ogledd*, the 'Old North' (of what is now England and southern Scotland). *Cymraeg Canol*, Mediaeval Welsh, covers the period from the twelfth to the fourteenth centuries. Most extant manuscripts of the *Mabinogi* are from this period, though the stories are older.

The principal present identifiable dialects of Welsh are *y Wyndodeg* (Venedotian, of the North-West), *y Bowyseg* (Powysian, of North-East and mid-Wales), *y Ddyfydeg* (Demetian, of the South-West), and *Gwenhwyseg* (of Gwent and Morgannwg in the South-East). The closest relatives of Welsh are the other p-Celtic languages, of which the other modern representatives are Cornish and Breton, which are also descendants of Brythonic.

Cumbrian, if it was indeed a distinct language, would also have been p-Celtic, and there was also a p-Celtic language, Gaulish, indigenous to the continent but long extinct. The p-Celtic languages use, for example, Map as the patronymic ("son of") rather than Mac- (Maq-) as in the q-Celtic languages like Gaelic. On Tolkien and the Welsh language, the basic text is Tolkien's O'Donnell Lecture on "English and Welsh" (1955), the form of the text used here being that in *The Monsters and the Critics and other Essays*, though the original publication was in *Angles and Britons* (University of Wales Press 1963). Tolkien is not past the first few minutes of the lecture when he remarks that he "would say to the English philologists that those who have no first-hand acquaintance with Welsh and its philology lack an experience necessary to their business" (163). But this is far from his most important reason for studying (and reading) Welsh.

A few minutes (or pages) later (166) comes the highly important quotation from Sjéra Tómas Sæmundsson: "Languages are the chief distinguishing marks of peoples. No people in fact comes into being until it speaks a language of its own; let the languages perish and the peoples perish too, or become different peoples. But that never happens except as the result of oppression and distress." This passage, which Sjéra Tomas applied to the Icelanders, Tolkien applies to the Welsh: "the words might apply as well to the Welsh of Wales, who have also loved and cultivated their language for its own sake ... and who by it and with it maintain their identity" (p. 166). Tolkien considered himself an amateur at Welsh: "I speak only as an amateur, and address the *Saxon* and not the *Cymry*; my view is that of a *Sayce* and not a *Waugh*. I use these surnames—both well known (the first especially in the annals of philology) since *Sayce* is probably a name of Welsh origin (*Sais*) but means an Englishman, while *Waugh* is certainly of English origin (*Walh*) but means a Welshman; it is in fact the singular of *Wales*" (167). The "Sayce" reference is presumably to the great Archibald Henry Sayce (1845–1933), Deputy Professor of Comparative Philology at Oxford, but might include also Olive Lenore Sayce, now Emeritus Fellow of Somerville, who edited the 1954 (2nd) edition of Joe Wright's *Grammar*.

Of *Waughs* in Tolkien's world we need only look to Evelyn, who found a very different kind of sustenance in the Roman Catholic Church, and his son Auberon, one of the more antagonistic reviewers of *The Lord of the Rings*. No wonder Tolkien would rather, in 1955, be a *Sayce* than a *Waugh*. For all his disclaimer, Tolkien, the *Sais*, has some highly important things to say about the Welsh language. "Old Welsh is used for the scanty records of a time roughly equivalent to that of the documents of Anglo-Saxon; and this we call Old English. But Old English and Old Welsh were not on a European basis old at all" (176) – both are "middle" speeches, well advanced toward the second stage of a language, though the "movement of Welsh was naturally not the same as that of English. It resembled far more closely the movement of the Romance languages." He remarks that the AS (OE) word for "interpreter" is "wealhstod"—an intermediary between those who spoke English and those who spoke a *waelisc* ("British") tongue—even if, in the case of King Oswald acting for St. Aidan, the *waelisc* tongue was *scyttisc* (181). In *Kulhwch and Olwen* the interpreter is Gwrhyr Gwalstawt Ieithoed, and the Bishop of those beyond the Severn in Bede was Uualchstod. "Walh" referred originally to any speaker of a Celtic or Latin tongue (as *vlachu* for the speaker of Rumanian), but it came in time to mean the speaker of Welsh, the last strong Celtic tongue (and the last spoken) in the Island of Prydain.

"For myself," Tolkien writes, "I would say that more than the interest and uses of the study of welsh as an adminicle of English philology, more than the practical linguist's desire to acquire a knowledge of Welsh for the enlargement of his experience, more even than the interest and worth of the literature, older and newer, that is preserved in it, these two things seem important: Welsh is of this soil, this island, the senior language of the men of Britain; and Welsh is beautiful" (189) "Most English-speaking people, for example, will admit that *cellar door* is 'beautiful', especially if dissociated from its sense (and from its spelling).... Well, then, in Welsh, for me, *cellar doors* are extraordinarily frequent, and moving to the higher dimension, the words in which there is pleasure in the contemplation of the association of form and sense are abundant" (190–191). "Modern Welsh is not, of course, identical with the predilections of such people [those who live in *Lloegr* and speak *Saesneg*]. It is not identical with mine. But it remains probably closer to them than any other living language ... It is the native language to which in unexplored desire we would still go home" (194), having just before this quoted the lines in no need of translation, "*Gogoniant i'r Tad ac i'r Mab ac i'r Ysbryd Glân, megis yr oedd yn y dechrau, y mae'r awr hon, ac y bydd yn wastad, yn oes oesoedd. Amen.*"

JARED LOBDELL

Further Reading

Lobdell, Jared. *The Rise of Tolkienian Fantasy* La Salle, IL: Open Court, 2005.
Tolkien, J.R.R. "English and Welsh." In C. Tolkien, ed., *Tolkien: The Monsters and the Critics.* Boston, MA: Houghton Mifflin, 1984.

See also **"English and Welsh"; Languages: Introduction and Early Interest; Language, Theories of**

WHITBY

A seaside town on the east coast of Yorkshire. Whitby is a site of historical importance both to the history of Catholicism in England and to the history of the Old English language. In 664, the Synod of Whitby established that Christianity in England would be unified on the Roman, not the Celtic

model, with regard both to the dating of Easter and to other ecclesiastical practices. Additionally, around the year 680, Caedmon is said to have written the first recorded English poem, "Caedmon's Hymn," near Whitby. Both of these events are accorded significance by the Venerable Bede in his *Ecclesiastical History of the English People*, and undoubtedly were of great interest to Tolkien.

Tolkien's only recorded visit to Whitby took place on a holiday in the summer of 1910. While there he made a number of pencil and ink drawings of Whitby's Old Town and of the ruins of Whitby Abbey. The drawings display the visual style that was characteristic of Tolkien throughout his life: a strong attention to detail and composition, a good eye for architecture, animals, and landscape, and a weakness in drawing the human figure. They also display Tolkien's characteristic calligraphy, both in his signatures and in his captions. His full signature on a drawing of the Abbey, "Ronald Tolkien," is unusual; Tolkien signed most of his artwork throughout his life with the initials "JRRT."

The drawings are now held in the Bodleian Library at Oxford University.

CHESTER N. SCOVILLE

Further Reading

Hammond, Wayne G. and Christina Scull. *J.R.R. Tolkien: Artist and Illustrator*. London: Harper Collins, 1995.

See also **Art and Illustrations by Tolkien; Artists' and Illustrators' Influence on Tolkien; Bede; Caedmon; Childhood of Tolkien**

WILDERLAND

In the Legendarium, *Wilderland*—sometimes called *Rhovanion*—is a wild and uninhabited region of Middle-earth, north of the realm of Gondor, east of Arnor, and historically a part of neither kingdom. In the "Nomenclature of *The Lord of the Rings*", Tolkien describes the word "Wilderland" as "an invention (not actually found in English), based on *wilderness* (originally meaning country of wild creatures, not inhabited by Men), but with side-reference to the verbs *wilder* 'wander astray' and *bewilder*". Not surprisingly, though people from all over Middle-earth—including hobbits, dwarves, ents, elves and wizards—refer to "Wilderland", its definition is vague and shifting, and depends somewhat on the background of the one speaking.

In *The Hobbit*, for example, the dwarf Balin comments that the company must "get through, or over, or under" the Misty Mountains before coming to

Wilderland, implying that Wilderland starts east of the mountains (*H*, 87). From a hobbit's point of view, however, Wilderland seems to refer to everything past the Edge of the Wild, a north-south line running through eastern Eriador past the Ford of Bruinen across the Loudwater near of Rivendell. Thus Tolkien's map of Wilderland—which appears in *The Hobbit* and presumably corresponds with Bilbo's viewpoint—includes Mirkwood, the Desolation of Smaug, and the Grey Mountains, as well as the Misty Mountains and even Rivendell.

In *The Lord of the Rings*, Wilderland again refers clearly to a land east of Misty Mountains: Thorin's company is described as still being on their way "towards Wilderland" when they are assailed by orcs in the Misty Mountains (*FR*, prologue, 20); and the "Great River" (Anduin) is said to be "on the edge of Wilderland" (*FR*, I, ii, 62). With reference to Pippin and Merry, Treebeard comments that "Orcs pursue[d] them down all the leagues of Wilderland" (*TT*, III, iv, 75); that pursuit ran from the Misty Mountains to the edge of Lothlórien.

There are outposts of order and civilization in Wilderland, These include Thranduil's kingdom in Mirkwood, Beorn's chiefdom west of Mirkwood, the settlements at Laketown and later Dale (in *The Hobbit*), and the kingdom of Dain (in *LotR*). When Legolas refers to "every Elf in Wilderland" (*TT*, III, v, 102), he is certainly including the elves in his father's kingdom, and his very use of the phrase implies that Wilderland is not uninhabited. Ultimately, however, these examples are little more than that: mere outposts of civilization in the midst of wilderness. The significance of the term *Wilderland* does not change: it is a primarily unsettled land, and wild, whose roads (if they exist) are dangerous at best. It is a place easy to wander astray.

MATTHEW DICKERSON

Further Reading

Dickerson Matthew, and Jonathan Evans. *Ents, Elves and Eriador: The Environmental Vision of J.R.R. Tolkien.* Lexington: University of Kentucky, 2006.

See also **Beorn; Lonely Mountain (Erebor); Mirkwood; Misty Mountains; Middle-earth; Maps**

WILLIAMS, CHARLES WALTER STANSBY (1886–1945)

Enigmatic in his writings and in his person, Charles Williams was introduced to the literary circle of Tolkien, C.S. Lewis, and friends the Inklings, in 1936. Nevill Coghill's copy of his novel, *The Place of the Lion*, had been passed around the group, then quite small. Williams exerted a deep and lasting influence on Lewis's thought and writings but not on Tolkien's. Though towards the end of Tolkien's life he distanced himself from Williams in some of his correspondence, this coolness is not borne out by earlier indications of a warm friendship. The two met frequently throughout the war years, usually in company with C.S. Lewis, and quite often outside of gatherings of the Inklings. It is clear that Tolkien respected Williams and appreciated his comments on chapters of the unfinished *The Lord of the Rings* as they were read. He contributed his essay, "On Fairy Stories," to a posthumous tribute, *Essays Presented to Charles Williams*. At one stage, Tolkien wrote an affectionate poem to Williams, complaining about difficulty in understanding his writings, but valuing his person nonetheless. It includes such lines as these:

> When your fag is wagging and spectacles are twinkling,
> when tea is brewing or the glasses tinkling,
> then of your meaning often I've an inkling,
> your virtues and your wisdom glimpse. . . .

In a wartime letter to his son Christopher, Tolkien noted Williams' perceptive understanding of the emerging draft of *The Lord of the Rings*: "C. Williams who is reading it all says the great thing is that its *centre* is not in strife and war and heroism (though they are understood and depicted) but in freedom, peace, ordinary life and good living."

Sometimes in the long, weary war years progress halted on the writing of the *The Lord of the Rings*. During one such hiatus Tolkien uncharacteristically wrote an allegory. *Leaf by Niggle* (1945) was a purgatorial story, perhaps written under the influence of Williams' growing fascination with Dante's *Purgatory*. Williams' novel *All Hallows Eve* had a purgatorial theme, as had Lewis's *The Great Divorce*, both read to the Inklings in the war years. It might be however that Tolkien's story was read first, and set the tone for the purgatorial explorations of Lewis and Williams.

Charles Williams' writings encompassed fiction, poetry, drama, theology, church history, biography and literary criticism. Anne Ridler perhaps captured the essence of Charles Williams when she wrote: "In Williams' universe there is a clear logic, a sense of terrible justice which is not our justice and yet is not divorced from love." For Ridler, "the whole man . . . was greater even than the sum of his works." Similarly, T.S. Eliot—who greatly admired Charles Williams—said, in a broadcast talk for the BBC: "It is the whole work, not any one or several masterpieces, that we have to take into account in estimating the importance of the man. I think he was a man of unusual genius, and I regard his work as important. But it has an importance of a kind not easy to explain."

Charles Williams was in his early forties when his first novel, *War in Heaven*, was published in 1930. Prior to this he had brought out several minor books, most of which were verse. His important work begins with the novels; it is after 1930 that his noteworthy works appear, packed into the last fifteen years of his life. During these final years over thirty books were published (an average of two a year) as well as numerous articles and reviews. The last third of these years of maturity as a thinker and writer were spent in Oxford as an evacuee from war-torn London. They involved Williams's normal editorial duties with Oxford University Press, lecturing and tutorials for the university (instigated by Tolkien and Lewis), constant meetings with the Inklings, and frequent weekends in his London home. Williams augmented the teaching of the Oxford English School with his wide knowledge of poetry, and his lectures were very popular with students. His wife stayed behind to look after the flat when Williams was evacuated to Oxford with the other staff of the OUP.

When Williams came to Oxford he made a vivid impact there, captured in John Wain's autobiography, *Sprightly Running*. Wain comments: "He gave himself as unreservedly to Oxford as Oxford gave itself to him." Williams's arrival in Oxford, and Lewis' friendship with him, was not entirely welcome to Tolkien, as it meant he had less of Lewis's attention. Indeed, in a late letter, Tolkien dates the end of the period when Lewis was his closest friend as 1940. In his wartime letters he often mentions seeing Lewis "and Williams" rather than Lewis alone. When Williams died suddenly in 1945 however Tolkien felt deep sorrow over the loss of his friend, writing a letter to his widow, Michal.

With Williams being a constant presence in Oxford during the war years Lewis soon came to see him as well as Tolkien as integral to his group of friends (most of whom attended the Inklings). This perception was brought out years later in his book, *The Four Loves* (1960), in his chapter on friendship, explaining the process by which friendship expands. In this extract "Ronald" is Tolkien, and "Charles" is Williams: "In each of my friends there is something that only some other friend can fully bring out. By myself I am not large enough to call the whole man into activity; I want other lights than my own to show all his facets. Now that Charles is dead, I shall never again see Ronald's reaction to a specifically Caroline joke. Far from having more of Ronald, having him 'to myself' now that Charles is away, I have less of Ronald. … We

possess each friend not less but more as the number of those with whom we share him increases."

While the Inklings was a small and intimate group in the thirties everything was very much to Tolkien's liking. But as the group expanded, particularly by embracing Charles Williams, he began to feel somewhat left out from Lewis's attentions. This may account for the coolness in his depiction in Williams in letters after the death of C.S. Lewis in 1963, which he felt very deeply. Tolkien in these late years was to describe Lewis as being under Williams's "spell," and clearly, with hindsight, did not approve of this, feeling that Lewis was too impressionable a man. Later also, he would refer to the Inklings as Lewis's "seance," alluding to Williams's fascination with the occult, a taste that had disturbed Tolkien.

COLIN DURIEZ

Primary Sources

Carpenter, Humphrey. *The Inklings: C.S. Lewis, J.R.R. Tolkien, Charles Williams and Their Friends.* George Allen and Unwin: London, 1978; Houghton Mifflin: Boston, 1979.

Duriez, Colin and David Porter, *The Inklings Handbook.* London: Azure, 2001.

Hadfield, Alice. *Charles Williams: An Exploration of His Life and Work.* Oxford: Oxford University Press, 1983.

King, JR., Roma A. (Ed.) *To Michal From Serge: Letters from Charles Williams to His Wife, Florence, 1939–1945.* Kent and London: The Kent State University Press, 2002.

Wain, John, *Sprightly Running: Part of an Autobiography.* Macmillan: London, 1962, 1965.

Further Reading

Dodds, David Llewellyn. *Arthurian Poets: Charles Williams.* Woodbridge, UK: The Boydell Press, 1991.

Williams, Charles. *The Descent of the Dove.* London: Collins, 1963.

Williams, Charles. *All Hallows' Eve.* New York: The Noonday Press (Farrar, Straus and Giroux), 1977.

Williams, Charles. *The Place of the Lion.* Grand Rapids, Michigan: William B. Eerdmans, 1978.

Williams, Charles. *A Charles Williams Reader.* Grand Rapids, Michigan: William B. Eerdmans, 2000.

Williams, Charles. Edited by Alice Mary Hadfield. *Outlines of Romantic Theology.* Grand Rapids, Michigan: William B. Eerdmans, 1990.

See also **Inklings; Lewis, C.S.; Wain, John; Oxford**

WISEMAN, CHRISTOPHER (1893–1987)

T.C.B.S. member and an influential early critic of Tolkien's work. They became friends playing rugby at King Edward's School, and named themselves "the Great Twin Brethren", despite contrasts in religion and outlook: Wiseman was a progressive, scientific liberal and son of Birmingham's leading Methodist minister. Musically adept, he thought Tolkien tone-deaf, but they shared an interest in British archaeology, Arthuriana, ancient scripts, and philology; Tolkien tried to involve him in one of his invented languages. Their debates, though bruising, reflected a shared sense of the inseparability of aesthetics, morals, and religious faith. Like the T.C.B.S., the clique they formed in 1911, Wiseman tended to combine the serious with the comic, and with R.Q. Gilson he edited witty issues of the school *Chronicle*.

In 1912 he entered Peterhouse, Cambridge, as a mathematics scholar. He spent much time with Gilson, but in 1914, dissatisfied with the increasingly supercilious T.C.B.S., he and Tolkien purged the group. The remaining four members held the 'Council of London,' pivotal in Tolkien's decision to become a writer, in December at Wiseman's new family home in Wandsworth. With a second-class degree, Wiseman joined the Royal Navy in 1915 and studied at Greenwich. From 1916 he was instructor-lieutenant on HMS Superb, which patrolled the North Sea and took part in the Battle of Jutland; then on HMS Monarch. He had a largely happy war but mourned Gilson and G.B. Smith deeply; he urged Tolkien, invalided home, not to return to the front, and hoped they might share a home after the war.

Wiseman greeted Tolkien's poetry in 1915 with amazement; he set one piece to music. Inspired by the rational universe, however, he questioned key aspects of Tolkien's fantasy project and urged him in 1917 to finish the "Lost Tales" and write something more realistic. Yet the Music of the Ainur seems to echo a view of art as process propounded by Wiseman in a 1916 letter ("the fugue is nothing on the page; it is only vital as it works its way out"). Self-deprecatingly, Wiseman said he had not found his T.C.B.S. cultural "weapon"; yet by challenging Tolkien's art (and by recruiting him to edit Smith's poems for *A Spring Harvest*) he helped "TCBSian" ambitions towards fruition.

The bond weakened after the war, and after *The Lord of the Rings* Wiseman imagined that Tolkien no longer had time for him. He taught at Cambridge and on HMS King George V; as senior maths master at Kingswood School, Bath; and from 1926 until 1953 as headmaster of Queen's College, Taunton, a Methodist public school, where his unconventional methods inspired Peter Mitchell, later a Nobel scientist. In 1946 Wiseman married Christine Irene Savage, who died in 1969 or 1971[?]; in 1972 he married Patricia Wragge. He had no children. A hardy, energetic

figure, he was active in village politics in Milford-on-Sea until the age of 90. There was a restrained rapprochement when Tolkien moved to nearby Bournemouth.

Wiseman probably appears in Tolkien's "The Battle of the Eastern Field" as Sekhet, reflecting his taste for Egyptology, and perhaps in *The Book of Lost Tales* as Tulkas. Tolkien named his third son after him.

JOHN GARTH

Further Reading

Carpenter, *J.R.R. Tolkien: A Biography*. Boston: Houghton Mifflin, 1977.
Garth, *Tolkien and the Great War: The Threshold of Middle-earth; King Edward's School Chronicle*. Boston: Houghton Mifflin, 2003.

See also **Gilson, Robert Quilter; Smith, Geoffrey Bache; *Spring Harvest, A*; T.C.B.S.; World War I**

WIZARDS

After twice intervening directly in the affairs of Middle-earth, the Valar in the Third Age decided to act more subtly to save it from resurgent evil. They therefore called upon various of their helpers, the Maiar, to go into Middle-earth as agents and stewards acting on their behalf. The function of these beings would be to guide and advise and train the natives of Middle-earth as the evil approached.

Called Istari, these agents came to Middle-earth in the guise of old men, revered figures endowed with the powers of mages, and called "wizards," according to our best understanding of their form and function. Tolkien said they could be thought of as "angelos," in the original Greek meaning of that term, "messengers" (*Letters*, 202).

The wizards began to arrive in the year 1000 of the Third Age, and paramount among them were five: Saruman, known as the White, was acknowledged the wisest and most authoritative, while Radagast the Brown was noted for his knowledge of and deep interest in the flora and fauna of his adopted Middle-earth. Two others were known as the Blue Wizards and apparently traveled eastward beyond the known lands of the West of Middle-earth. Fifth, and seemingly least in stature, was Gandalf the Grey. Unlike Saruman, who soon fixed his abode at Isengard, and Radagast, who lived at Rhosgobel, near the western edge of Mirkwood, Gandalf had no permanent dwelling-place, but traveled widely about Middle-earth, hence was known by several names. He was gently ridiculed by Saruman for his interest in the inconsequential race of Hobbits who lived in a small district called the Shire. Saruman soon immersed himself in the lore of the One Ring, just as Radagast became deeply and almost exclusively involved in the natural world.

As their preoccupations became obsessions, these two neglected their original roles as counselors and caretakers. In Saruman's case, indeed, his absorption in the Ring led to his actual falling away from good and becoming an ally (as he thought) and then a rival (as he later thought) but all the while (in fact) a servant of the Dark Lord Sauron. Only Gandalf kept faith with his original duties, keeping an eye on the Hobbits while learning as much as he could of the history, languages, and customs of Middle-earth's peoples the better to advise them when evil came.

Each of the three wizards thus had particular powers, and (as might be expected in Tolkien) each wizard's power was somehow connected with language. Saruman as presumed leader was a skilled rhetorician and an eloquent speaker. Radagast could talk to birds and animals and often used them for errands and messages. Gandalf seemed familiar with every tongue known in Middle-earth, and his gift for languages is repeatedly shown in *The Lord of the Rings*.

By the end of the Third Age, each wizard's part had been played. Radagast apparently disappeared into the forest, the corrupt Saruman was annihilated, and Gandalf, having faithfully completed his stewardship, returned to the West.

MICHAEL N. STANTON

Further Reading

Kocher, Paul. *Master of Middle-earth*. Boston: Houghton Mifflin, 1972.
Noel, Ruth. *The Mythology of Middle-earth*. Boston: Houghton Mifflin, 1978.

See also **Angels; Druids; Gandalf; Maiar; Saruman**

WOLVERCOTE CEMETERY

Wolvercote Cemetery is the final resting place of J.R.R. Tolkien, who passed away on September 2, 1973 at the age of eighty-one. The cemetery was formally opened and dedicated on March 12, 1894 and is located between Woodstock and Banbury Roads five miles north from the centre of Oxford.

Tolkien was laid to rest beside his wife, Edith, in the Roman Catholic section, which was established in 1956 and is the only burial ground for Catholics in Oxford. The burial took place on the afternoon of September 6 following a simple service held at the Church of St. Anthony of Padua in Headington. The requiem mass was celebrated by his son, Fr John Tolkien, his friend Fr Robert Murray, and by his parish priest, Mgr Wilfred Doran.

The headstone is made of grey, Cornish granite, and inscribed with the following:

Edith Mary Tolkien
Lúthien
1889–1971

John Ronald
Reuel Tolkien
Beren
1892–1973

It was Tolkien's own wish that the name Lúthien be part of the inscription. In a letter to his son Christopher, he noted, this "says for me more than a multitude of words....I never called Edith *Lúthien* - but she was the source of the story that in time became the chief part of the *Silmarillion*" (*Letters* 420).

Unlike the Silmarillion, however, in which "none saw Beren or Lúthien leave the world, or marked where at last their bodies lay" (*S* 188), Edith and Ronald are buried in plot L2–211. Small, simple way-markers point the way along the cemetery path to their grave.

ROBERT G. ANGER

Further Reading

Carpenter, Humphrey. *J.R.R. Tolkien: A Biography*. London: George Allen & Unwin, 1977.
Jackson's Oxford Journal, 13.10.1894, p. 6c.
Oxford Mail, 7 Sept. 1973, pg. 8.

See also **Beren; Lúthien; Marriage; Tolkien, John; Oxford; Roman Catholicism**

WOMEN IN TOLKIEN'S WORKS

Tolkien's depiction of women was influenced by several factors, most significantly his personal views on the roles and affinities of males and females, as influenced by his middle-class, Victorian, Roman Catholic upbringing, and the roles of women in the texts upon which his works were modeled. In a letter to his son Michael, Tolkien articulated a rather conventional view of professionally active men versus domestically inclined women (*Letters*, 50). Tolkien's female characters appear to resemble chaste medieval ladies of courtly romance, uninvolved in the stories beyond encouraging their heroes to great deeds (Myers, 14).

Female villains (Ungoliant and Shelob) are depicted as vile monsters, whom psychoanalytic critics characterize as oversexed Lilith figures (Goselin, 3). While Tolkien has fewer female than male characters, and most of the females seem to be relegated to the home, these women are extremely powerful figures that play prominent roles in his novels. They are either equal, or superior, to the men in their lives and not dependent upon them (Hopkins, 365). Additionally, Tolkien's critical attitude toward masculine power and destructiveness is compatible with that of contemporary feminists (Donovan, 106; Sanford, 19).

For Tolkien, gender was associated *a priori* with "modes of activity or influence" (Rawls, 6). As the Valar took material bodies, their genders reflected their interests, roles, and responsibilities in Middle-earth (S, 21; Sly, 114–115). At every level of being except that of the one God Eru, one finds at least one strong female character.

Two female Valar played crucial roles in Middle-earth. Varda, revered by the Elves as Elbereth, Lady of Stars, resembled the Virgin Mary in her role as Queen of Heaven (Crowe, 273). Yavanna, (surnamed Kementári, Queen of the Earth) whose sphere was the world of plants, created both the Two Trees of Valinor and the ents to guard plants against the axes of dwarves, her spouse Aulë's creations (S, 46). Typical of Tolkien's female characters, these deities were protectors and nurturers. The evil Ungoliant can be understood as Varda's opposite (if Varda is a Jungian anima, then Ungoliant is a shadow [Goselin, 3]); Ungoliant's hatred of light and her destruction of the Two Trees place her in opposition to both Varda and Yavanna.

The Maia Melian was the first immortal to enter into a "mixed" relationship (in this relationship and the others—Lúthien and Beren and Arwen and Aragorn—it is always the female member who is the higher being). As Thingol's spouse, she wove the protective Girdle of Melian around the kingdom of Doriath. Her daughter Lúthien, the most actively engaged female in all of Tolkien's works, defied her father to aid Beren in his quest for a Silmaril with which to win her hand; she both freed him from captivity and ransomed him from death, thereby losing her immortality. Arwen, despite her description as "the likeness of Lúthien...come on earth again " (FR, II, 239), is a "shadowy figure, a re-run of Lúthien who takes no part in [Aragorn's] adventures, and seems only to exist to provide a suitable bride for [him]" (Hopkins, 366). The under-development of Arwen was due to her being an afterthought; having originally planned to have Aragorn marry Éowyn, Tolkien revised his plan, married Éowyn off to Faramir, and inserted Arwen into the narrative as

Aragorn's love interest (Craig, 13). Another possible reason for Arwen's failure to participate fully in Aragorn's adventure is related to the High Elves' general withdrawal from active involvement in the Third Age. This follows a pattern already established for the Valar and the Maia Melian; the Eldar, while emotionally and spiritually engaged in the fight against Morgoth and later Sauron, were no longer actively, physically engaged in the happenings of Middle-earth, retreating instead to elvish havens like Rivendell and Lothórien preparatory to their leaving Middle-earth. Arwen, Halfelven until she married Aragorn, did not herself engage in his quest, but she was certainly emotionally and spiritually involved.

Galadriel is the most powerful female in Middle-earth and one of the few characters who spans all four Ages (Johnson, 11). Having left Valinor with the Noldor rebels (S, 90), she befriended Melian in Doriath and then created Lothlórien in its image (Johnson, 12). Like the other powerful females, Galadriel's role was not to fight, but to nurture, protect, and give counsel. Galadriel tested the members of the Fellowship (FR, II, vii, 372–73), and, as Craig points out, "... it is hard to imagine Tolkien using a male character in this way. It is therefore a gendered moment"(12). To Jungian critics, Galadriel represents the anima (Goselin, 3, 4); in the analysis of Campbell, she is a goddess (109); to Catholic readers, the Virgin Mary (Kotowski, 148), reinforced by Tolkien's description of her as "unstained" (Letters, 423) and her affinity with Elbereth as an elvish giver of light (cf. the gift of the phial containing light from Eärendil's Silmaril to Frodo [FR, II, viii, 393], a gift that later saves him from Shelob). Paralleling Ungoliant as the shadow to Varda's anima, Galadriel's opposite is Shelob, the antithesis of light (Sly, 117).

Criticism of Tolkien's treatment of women has echoed that of Stimpson, who characterizes him as "irritatingly, blandly, traditionally masculine" and his female characters as "hackneyed...stereotypes...either beautiful and distant, simply distant, or simply simple" (18). This criticism is certainly disproved by Éowyn, the most highly developed female character in *The Lord of the Rings*, and by most of the female characters in *The Silmarillion*, especially Lúthien. These women resemble the active heroines of Norse epics who "armed themselves and fought like men," (Bryce, 115). Éowyn, the only significant human female in *The Lord of the Rings*, defies attempts to domesticate her and goes into battle, partly out of unrequited love for Aragorn, but also out of despair at her being relegated to the home and out of love for her uncle Théoden. Her rejection of female domesticity ultimately fulfills the prophecy that the Witch

King of Angmar would not die by the hand of a man (RK, V, vi, 332).

CAROL A. LEIBIGER

Further Reading

Bryce, Lynn. "The Influence of Scandinavian Mythology on the Works of J.R.R. Tolkien." *Edda: Nordisk Tidsskrift for Litteraturforsknung* 83 (1983): 113–19.

Craig, David M. "'Queer Lodgings': Gender and Sexuality in *the Lord of the Rings*." *Mallorn* 38 (2001): 11–18.

Crowe, Edith L. "Power in Arda: Sources, Uses and Misuses." In *Proceedings of the J.R.R. Tolkien Centenary Conference*, Ed. Patricia Reynolds and Glen GoodKnight. Milton Keynes and Altadena, CA: The Tolkein Society and the Mythopoeic Society, 1995. pp. 272–77.

Donovan, Leslie A. "The Valkyrie Reflex in J.R.R. Tolkien's *the Lord of the Rings*." In *Tolkien the Medievalist*, Ed. Jane Chance. New York: Routledge, 2003. pp. 106–32.

Fenwick, Mac. "Breastplates of Silk: Homeric Women in *the Lord of the Rings*." *Mythlore* 21 (1996): 17–23, 50.

Flieger, Verlyn. "Who's Got the Goddess?" *Journal of the Fantastic in the Arts* 9. 1 (33) (1998): 3–14.

Goselin, Peter Damien. "Two Faces of Eve: Galadriel and Shelob as Anima Figures." *Mythlore* 6. 3 (21) (1979): 3–28.

Green, William H. "'Where's Mama?': The Construction of the Feminine in *the Hobbit*." *The Lion and the Unicorn* 22. 2 (1998): 188–95.

Hopkins, Lisa. "Female Authority Figures in the Works of Tolkien, C.S. Lewis, and Charles Williams." In *Proceedings of the Tolkien Centenary Conference*, Ed. Patricia Reynolds and Glen GoodKnight. Milton Keynes and Altadena: The Tolkien Society and the Mythopoeic Society, 1996. pp. 364–66.

Johnson, Janice. "The Celeblain of Celeborn and Galadriel." *Mythlore* 32 (1982): 11–19.

Maher, Michael W. "'A Land without Stain': Medieval Images of Mary and Their Use in the Characterization of Galadriel." In *Tolkien the Medievalist*, Ed. Jane Chance. New York: Routledge, 2003. pp. 225–36.

Myers, Doris T. "Brave New World: The Status of Women According to Tolkien, Lewis, and Williams." *Cimarron Review* 17 (1971): 13–19.

Partridge, Brenda. "No Sex Please–We're Hobbits: The Construction of Female Sexuality in *the Lord of the Rings*." In *J.R.R. Tolkien: This Far Land*, Ed. Robert Giddings. Totowa, NJ: Barnes & Noble, 1983. pp. 179–97.

Rawls, Melanie. "The Feminine Principle in Tolkien." *Mythlore* 10. 4 (38) (1984): 5–12.

Sanford, Len. "The Fall from Grace–Decline and Fall in Middle-earth." *Mallorn* 332 (1995): 15–20.

Sly, Debbie. "Weaving Nets of Gloom: 'Darkness Profound' in Tolkien and Milton." In *J.R.R. Tolkien and His Literary Resonances: Views of Middle-earth*, Ed. George Clark and Daniel Timmons. Westport, CT: Greenwood, 2000. pp. 108–19.

Stimpson, Catharine R. *J.R.R. Tolkien*. New York: Columbia University Press, 1969.

See also **Arwen; Elves; Ents; Éowyn; Galadriel; Gender in Tolkien's Works; Lúthien; Maiar; Melian; Old Norse Literature; Plants; Romances: Middle English; Sexuality in Tolkien's Works; Shelob: Valar**

WORLD WAR I

The First World War saw Tolkien lay the foundations of Middle-earth. Here, an outline of his creative output between 1914 and 1918, and a discussion of the war's influence on his life's work, must follow a summary of his wartime experiences—as a student, as an army officer in Britain and on the Western Front, and as a war invalid.

The Student

Hostilities broke out when Tolkien, 22, had completed the second year of his English degree course at Oxford University. When Britain declared war on Germany, on 4 August, he was on holiday in Cornwall. By October, despite pressure from his aunts and uncles, he had decided to defer enlistment in the armed forces until after his degree. He said later that this was because he did not relish military action; but at the time he told friends that as a young man with a fiancée and little money, he had to prioritize his future academic career.

In October, beginning his final undergraduate year, Tolkien joined the Officer Training Corps. Oxford was now full of soldiers, makeshift military hospitals and war refugees. Friends enlisted in the army, including G.B. Smith and R.Q. Gilson, whom he met up with in December 1914 in a "Council of London" that saw their clique, the TCBS, acquire a new moral and cultural sense of purpose.

The Soldier

Having achieved a first-class degree in June 1915, Tolkien quickly followed Smith into the Lancashire Fusiliers—celebrated for the gruelling Gallipoli landings that April—as a temporary second lieutenant, the lowest rank of commissioned officer. He trained from July 1915 with other officers at Bedford but was disappointed to not be assigned a place in the regiment's 19th Battalion, with which Smith would be going to war. Instead, in August Tolkien was placed with the 13th Battalion, purely a training unit, near Lichfield, Staffordshire, and as winter drew in he moved with it to bleak camps on Cannock Chase. Tolkien was bored by training, oppressed by military discipline and depressed by the war. At the start of 1916, Tolkien began to receive letters from Smith and Gilson describing the horrors of the Western Front. In March, Tolkien returned to Oxford for his official graduation and, in Warwick, married Edith Bratt, who then took lodgings at Great Haywood, near Cannock Chase. He had chosen to specialize in signals, which was a safer occupation than leading a platoon, and which appealed to his interest in codes; but his marks after a specialist course in Yorkshire that spring were average.

Into Battle

Embarkation orders arrived on June 2, 1916. Tolkien was sent via Folkestone and Le Havre to Le Touquet, where he received final training and awaited further orders for three weeks. He was despatched to meet his service unit, the 11th Lancashire Fusiliers, at the village of Rubempré on June 28 and was at Warloy-Baillon, five miles behind the front line, on July 1 when Britain and its allies launched the vast Somme offensive with immediate and tragic losses (20,000 British soldiers dead and 37,000 wounded on the first day). A few days later at Bouzincourt, a village just above the front line and reeking of death, he briefly met up with Smith. Tolkien stayed there at divisional signals H.Q. while the 11th Lancashire Fusiliers went into action and suffered their worst setback of the battle: the loss of an entire company which had advanced too far. Tolkien himself witnessed what he later described simply as "the animal horror of active service" when he went into action on July 14–16. He found the signals system in chaos and the battlefield choked with corpses, but his battalion took the surrender of hundreds of German soldiers and the entrenched hilltop of Ovillers-la-Boisselle.

On his return to Bouzincourt, Tolkien learned that Gilson had been killed on the first day of the offensive. The news undermined (perhaps only temporarily) his faith in the purpose of the TCBS and brought him into dispute with Smith and Wiseman, the other two surviving members. New duties as battalion signals officer from July 19 kept him busy amid what he called "the universal weariness" of war as the unit, uprooting itself every few days, rotated through rest, training and a series of trench duties: July 24–30 opposite Beaumont-Hamel, August 7–10 east of Colincamps, August 24 to September 5 in Thiepval Wood and north of Ovillers, September 27–29 in Thiepval Wood again (where the unit had made a minor attack on a German position), and finally from October 6 south of Regina Trench. The Somme turned to a mire, treacherous to navigate, littered with decaying corpses. With little or no ground gained in the campaign of attrition, demoralisation and shell shock

affected many soldiers. During a cold snap and a respite from rain on October 21, Tolkien ran the signals operation from a front-line dugout as his battalion joined others in capturing Regina Trench and many German prisoners.

Almost as soon as the battalion had marched out of the line for a series of congratulatory inspections, Tolkien succumbed to trench fever, a chronically debilitating, potentially fatal condition transmitted by lice in the unhygienic trenches. He reported sick on October 27 at Beauval, and the next day, as his battalion took the train to Ypres, Tolkien was taken to an officers' hospital instead. From October 29 to November 7 he was in another hospital at Le Touquet, on November 8–9 he crossed the English Channel in the hospital ship *Asturias*, and on November 10 he arrived at Birmingham University's wartime hospital.

The Invalid

Tolkien spent the remainder of the war either in hospital, convalescing at home or carrying out safer duties in England. Chronic ill-health almost certainly saved his life, as he was reminded by Edith, by Christopher Wiseman, and by the death of G.B. Smith on the Somme on December 3, 1916.

On December 9, Tolkien went to convalesce at Great Haywood. At the end of February 1917, he was sent to hospital in Harrogate, Yorkshire, for a month. On April 19, he joined the Lancashire Fusiliers' 3rd Battalion, which trained new recruits and guarded the coast of Yorkshire's Holderness peninsula. He was put in charge of a battalion outpost at the village of Roos, and then judged fit for general service in June. A relapse hospitalised him in Hull from August to October. Edith, who had moved several times to be near him, returned to Cheltenham to give birth to their son, John, on November 16. At the end of the dark "starvation year" of 1917, Tolkien was promoted to lieutenant but posted to the 9th Royal Defence Corps, a coastal unit of men too old or unfit to fight, based at Easington, near the tip of the peninsula.

The 11th Lancashire Fusiliers were wiped out near the River Aisne in May 1918. But Tolkien was far away, back at the Cannock Chase camps, in rural lodgings with Edith and John. At the end of June 1918 he was sent once more to the Hull hospital, with gastritis, and in October he was discharged from a convalescent hospital in Blackpool, Lancashire, unfit for military service and with permission to seek civilian employment. Around the armistice,

November 11, 1918, the lexicographer W.A. Craigie gave him a job as a sub-editor on the *Oxford English Dictionary*. Tolkien was officially demobilised on July 16, 1919, at Fovant, on Salisbury Plain, with a temporary disability pension.

Creative Output, 1914–18

The first poem of Tolkien's mythology, "The Voyage of Éarendel the Evening Star," arising from a reading of Cynewulf, was written at his aunt's farm in Nottinghamshire in September 1914 while he was under pressure to enlist. Back at Oxford, invigorated by infantry drill, he made progress on an adaptation of the story of Kullervo from the *Kalevala*. Fired with his own idiosyncratic patriotism, he gave a talk on this "Finnish national epic" in which he expressed the desire for "something of the same sort that belonged to the English": an anticipation of his entire creative *oeuvre*. Inspired by the "Council of London" with his TCBS friends, Tolkien produced a series of poems in April 1915 ranging from fairy-tale ("Goblin Feet") to epic ("The Shores of Faëry"). He also began constructing a "fairy" language, Qenya, alongside a complex of mythological conceptions centred on immortal Eldamar beyond the western ocean.

After enlistment, Tolkien continued to write poetry and work on Qenya. Training out in the open and among men from all walks of life in 1915–16, he composed landscape poetry set on his side of the western ocean, such as the ambitious "Kortirion among the Trees", as well as musings on mortality such as "Habbanan beneath the Stars". G.B. Smith carried "Kortirion" in the trenches "like a treasure", declared himself "a wild and whole-hearted admirer" and urged Tolkien to publish before going to war; but a collection, "The Trumpets of Faërie", was rejected by Sidgwick & Jackson.

Tolkien wrote or revised poetry a little in France, even in the trenches. However, return from the Somme unleashed a flood of creativity. In the Birmingham hospital, Tolkien began the story of "The Fall of Gondolin" and probably "The Cottage of Lost Play", the start of a framing narrative for such "Lost Tales". He started on a second language, to be spoken by the "Gnomes" in the ancient Europe of his imagination; Welsh-flavoured, it was the early prototype of Sindarin. The story of the elf-princess Tinúviel and her war-weary lover Beren was inspired by a walk at Roos in spring 1917 when Edith danced among the "hemlocks" (cow-parsley). Tolkien also began the "Tale of Turambar", drawing on the story of Kullervo. Meanwhile, at the request of

Smith's mother in 1917, he edited his friend's poetry with Wiseman for publication as *A Spring Harvest* in 1918.

Influence on Writing

Tolkien said that his a taste for fairy-stories was "quickened to full life by war" and that the idea of perpetual conflict between good and evil was a "conscious reaction" to the popular delusion that the Great War would end all wars. He also wrote that the approaches to Mordor had been coloured by the Somme battlefield landscape and Sam Gamgee was "a reflexion of the English soldier, of the privates and batmen I knew in the 1914 war, and recognised as so far superior to myself". However, his general reticence, combined with the tendency of early critics to see *The Lord of the Rings* as an allegory of the Second World War, delayed serious discussion of the First World War's impact until Hugh Brogan tackled it in 1989. John Garth's biographical *Tolkien and the Great War: The Threshold of Middle-earth* lays the ground for more informed discussion.

Tolkien might have written nothing of consequence if he had not been impelled by mortal peril (underlined by his TCBS friends). The First World War also furnished key themes, such as mortality and immortality. War probably contributed to his desire to create "a national epic", and (as an era rich in rumour and new coinages) may have also helped to reveal to him the interdependency of language and mythology. As C.S. Lewis first pointed out, war equipped him with the experience to write *The Lord of the Rings*. It showed him a world in fear and undergoing cataclysmic change; large-scale military actions; fellowships built and broken; individual heroism and despair; men, trees and villages destroyed with the aid of the machine. In addition, Garth has argued that many "fantasy" elements in Tolkien's work may be symbolist treatments of wartime experience, with Verlyn Flieger focusing on Tolkien's explorations of dream and exile. Tom Shippey has emphasized Tolkien's place among other witnesses of war in the 20th century who abandoned conventional realism to express their concerns. In a wider literary context, the pattern of Tolkien's "fairy-stories", in which ordinary people become heroes and experience "eucatastrophic" resurgences of inspiration against a backdrop of deepening despair, provides a striking contrast to the ironic, disenchanted work of soldiers such as Wilfred Owen whose work is now seen as the epitome of First World War writing.

JOHN GARTH

Further Reading

Brogan Hugh. 'Tolkien's Great War', in Gillian Avery and Julia Briggs (eds.), *Children and their Books: A celebration of the work of Iona and Peter Opie*, Oxford: Oxford University Press, 1989.

Carpenter Humphrey. *J.R.R. Tolkien: A biography*, London: George Allen & Unwin, 1977.

Flieger Verlyn. *A Question of Time*, Kent, OH: Kent State University Press, 1997.

Garth John. "Frodo and the Great War". Forthcoming in Wayne G. Hammond and Christina Scull (eds.), proceedings of the 2004 Marquette Tolkien conference.

Garth John. *Tolkien and the Great War: The Threshold of Middle-earth*. London: HarperCollins, 2003.

Lewis C.S. "The Dethronement of Power", *Time and Tide* 36 (22 October 1955); reprinted in Isaacs and Zimbardo, *Tolkien and the Critics*. South Bend, IN: University of Notre Dame Press, 1968.

Shippey Tom. *J.R.R. Tolkien: Author of the Century*. London: HarperCollins, 2000.

See also **Death; Despair (Wanhope); Eucatastrophe; Exile; Gilson, Robert Quilter; Good and Evil; Immortality; Quest Narrative; Sacrifice; Smith, Geoffrey Bache; T.C.B.S.; Tyranny; Violence; War; Wiseman, Christopher; World War II**

WORLD WAR II

For the United Kingdom, the Second World War began in 1939: it ended, as it did for the United States, in 1945. At the beginning was the "Phony War" followed by the German *blitzkrieg* into the West, the strung-out process of loss of British possessions in the East to Japan, the Fall of France, the replacement of Neville Chamberlain as Prime Minister by Tory-turned-Liberal-turned-Tory Winston Churchill, the Battle of Britain, the Blitz, expected invasion, the Narvik and North African campaigns, the coming of the Americans, the turn of the tide, and finally war on all fronts against that generation's Axis of Evil, and at the end, a kind of victory.

A brief chronology of the War from 1939 to 1943 more or less from the British point of view may be useful here. September 1, 1939 – Poland invaded by "Blitzkrieg." September 3, 1939 – England and France declared war on Germany. September 17, 1939 – Russia invaded Poland, Baltics, Finland November 30. September 27, 1939 – fall of Warsaw after twenty days bombardment. September 29, 1939 – German-Russian treaty partitioned Poland. December 13, 1939 – British sank German pocket battleship *Graf Spee* and recovered prisoners from Altmark February 16, 1940. May 10, 1940 – Western front attack began: Holland, Belgium, Luxembourg, France. Luftwaffe bombed Rotterdam Fort Eben Emael on Albert Canal. Churchill replaced Chamberlain as British PM - "I have nothing to offer but blood, toil. tears, and sweat" in speech to Parliament on May 13, 1940. May 13, 1940 – Ardennnes breakthrough into France. June 4, 1940 – Dunkirk fell after 338,000 were evacuated. July 10, 1940 – start of three-month air war; Goering vs. RAF, ends Oct 30 after 57-day Blitz on London. The British lose 832 fighters; Germany loses 668 plus 600 bombers. June 22, 1940 – Petain closed Indochina route to Chiang. Churchill closes Burma Road to avoid war with Japan. September 22, 1940 – Japanese troops crossed into Indochina; Vichy forced to agree. September 27, 1940 – Tripartite Pact with Japan, Germany, Italy. October 2, 1940 – Churchill decided to re-open Burma Road effective October 17. November 10, 1940 – torpedo planes from HMS *Illustrious* sink three Italian battleships in the shallow harbor of Taranto. December 9, 1940 – Wavell in Egypt defeats Italians and enters Libya.

Wavell takes Bardia Jan. 3, 1941, Tobruk Jan. 21, 1941, Derna Jan. 30, 1941. On Apil. 6, 1941 – Yugoslavia, Greece invaded. May 20, 1941 – airborne attack on Crete May 26, 1941 – German battleship *Bismarck* located off Brazil by U.S.-built PBY seaplane with U.S. pilot. June 22, 1941 – Operation Barbarossa began – 146 German divisions invaded Russia. Russian troops diverted west. June 24, 1941 – FDR extended Lend-Lease aid to Stalin. November 24, 1941 – U.S. Army to occupy bauxite-rich Dutch Guiana. December 7, 1941 – Combined Japanese air and sea attack on U.S. Naval installations at Pearl Harbor.

January 11, 1942 – Japan invaded Dutch Borneo, Timor, Celebes, seized Kendari airbase – finest in all East Indies. February 15 - Singapore fell - 130,000 under Percival who became "nonperson" Feb. 19, 1942 - Eisenhower appointed head of War Plans Division, urged BOLERO (buildup) and SLEDGEHAMMER (cross-channel invasion); Combined Chiefs of Staff agreed by June 18 on the ACROBAT plan for a joint landing in North Africa February 22, 1942 - Bomber Harris led British Bomber Command. Lancasters & B-17s began residential bombing of Lubeck, Essen, Cologne, Kiel. February 27, 1942 - Battle of Java Sea Mar. 10, 1942 - fall of Rangoon. Burma Road closed - fear of losing India. April 5, 1942 - Indian Ocean raid by Nagumo's First Air Fleet, but British kept Indian Ocean. April 28, 1942 - fall of Lashio. Gen. William Slim and Chinese 6th Army outnumbered. May 10, 1942 - Churchill announced invasion of Vichy Madagascar. Nov. 8, 1942 - TORCH landings began at 3 points: (1) Casablanca = 35000 US troops from US under Geoge Patton; (2) Oran = 39000 US troops from England under Lloyd Fredendall ; (3) Algiers = 33000 US and British under

Ryder. Nov. 11, 1942 – Gen. Mark Clark signed armistice with Vichy Admiral Darlan.

Jan 24, 1943 Casablanca Conference communiqué: (1) secure the Atlantic lifeline (2) "a paying investment" to aid Russia (FDR memo Jan. 23) (3) invade Sicily - operation HUSKY (4) BOLERO buildup, bomber offensive (5) Pacific operations, aid China. Then from July 10 to Aug. 17, 1943 – Operation HUSKY, the invasion of Sicily - only 90 miles from Africa - "greatest amphibious operation in history" - 38 day campaign. July 26 - fall of Mussolini due to success of Sicily - also, July 19 attack by 12th AF bombers on Rome. King Victor Emmanuel replaced Mussolini with Marshal Pietro Badoglio who favored Allies. (Hereafter events are well-known on both sides of the Atlantic.)

Tolkien and his family were, of course, significantly affected by World War II: his sons Michael and Christopher both served. Michael (who enlisted out of Trinity College at 18) was an anti-aircraft gunner in the Battle of Britain, and then after service in France and Germany was invalided out of the service in 1944. Christopher (who also enlisted out of Trinity College, age 18) was in the Royal Air Force in South Africa, his father's country of birth. Ronald Tolkien, as a nearly fifty-year-old veteran of the First War, was not called up for the Second, but served as Air Raid Warden and a member of the Firewatching Service. Oxford was not bombed, but Coventry, forty miles away, certainly was, and Tolkien returned home that night to tell Priscilla and Edith of the ever-increasing fiery glow over the horizon.

Priscilla was too young for the service (it will be remembered that the young Princess Elizabeth, three years her senior, did serve: that was certainly a possibility for Priscilla had the War lasted longer). John, the eldest son, had left Oxford for Rome in November 1939 to pursue his vocation. As the number of German troops in Rome increased, it became evident this was no place for a young English seminarian: after a five-day trip through Paris, John caught the last boat out of Le Havre and returned safely to England, much to the family's relief. During the rest of the War he was at the College at Stonyhurst and was ordained Priest at the Church of SS Gregory and Augustine [of Canterbury] in North Oxford in February 1946. In Oxford, Pembroke College (of which Tolkien was then a Fellow) was partly taken over by the Ministry of Agriculture ("FIRST FLOOR: PESTS"), and the dons had to make do – but on the other hand, the War brought the Oxford University Press and Charles Williams, and the University Naval Divison and Jim Dundas-Grant, to Oxford, swelling the ranks of the Inklings (and in Dundas-Grant's case the ranks of the Roman Catholics within the Inklings). It also changed the nature of the Oxford undergraduate, who in the years after 1945 was often a veteran himself (or, more rarely, herself).

The Tolkiens listened to the war news on Edith's huge old Pye radio. Tolkien writes (in a letter to Christopher in September 1944, *Letters*, p. 93): "The western war news of course occupies a great deal of our minds... Anxious times in spite of the rather premature shouting. The armored fellows are right in the thick of it and (I gather) think there is going to be a good deal more of the thick yet. I cannot understand the line taken by BBC (and papers, and so I suppose emanating from MOI) that the German troops are a motley collection of sutlers and broken men, while yet recording the bitterest defence against the finest and best equipped armies (as indeed they are) that have ever taken the field ... it is distressing to see the press groveling as low as Goebbels in his prime, shrieking that any German commander who holds out in a desperate situation ... is a drunkard and a besotted fanatic.... There was a solemn article in the local paper seriously advocating systematic extermination of the entire German nation as the only proper course after military victory; because, if you please, they are rattlesnakes and don't know the difference between good and evil! (What of the writer?)" (*Letters*, 93).

Of Tolkien's expectations of the War and what would follow, his letter to Christopher on 9 December 1943 (*Letters*, pp. 65–66) provides a good idea. "I must also admit that in the photograph [of Stalin, Roosevelt, Churchill], our little cherub W.S.C. actually *looked* the biggest ruffian present ... I love England (not Great Britain and certainly not the British Commonwealth (grrr!)), and if I was of military age I should, I fancy, be grousing away in a fighting service, and willing to go on to the bitter end – always hoping that things may turn out better for England than they look like doing. Somehow I really cannot imagine the fantastic luck (or blessing, oe would call it, if one could dimly see why we should be blessed – implying God) that has attended England is running out yet.... Our cherub above referred to can play a wily hand – one guesses, one hopes, one does not know..." (*Letters*, 65–66).

What did he actually expect from the War? This is from the same letter (65), and it seems to echo his delight (in a slightly later letter) at finding a pub not yet discovered by "Stars or Stripes" (*Letters*, 87). "The bigger things get, the smaller and duller and flatter the globe gets. It is getting to be all one blasted little provincial suburb. When they have introduced American sanitation, morale-pep, feminism, and mass production throughout the Near East, Middle East,

Far East, U.S.S.R., the Pampas, el Gran Chaco, the Danubian basin, Equatorial Africa, Hither Further and Inner Mumbo-land, Gondhwanaland, Lhasa, and the villages of darkest Berkshire, how happy we shall be. At any rate it ought to cut down travel. People will have no place to go. Some people will (I opine) go all the faster" (*Letters*, 65–66). He seems to have foreseen the Americanization that would follow the American victory in World War II, for victor and vanquished (and non-participant) alike. The comicality (and humor) of the "Old Uncle Tom Cobbleigh and all" list is characteristically British (it occurs in Surtees and in Thackeray's Christmas stories), though this may be its longest expression in Tolkien. Fundamentally, Tolkien supported the War, and would have served had he been younger, but he was not confident of any good outcome. It should not be necessary here to point out that The *Lord of the Rings* is not an allegory from World War II nor does the Ring have anything to do with the Atomic Bomb.

JARED LOBDELL

Further Reading

Carpenter, Humphrey. *J.R.R. Tolkien: A Biography*. Boston: Houghton Mifflin, 1977.

John and Priscilla Tolkien, *The Tolkien Family Album*. Boston: 1992.

Tolkien, J.R.R. *Letters*. ed. C. Tolkein. Boston: 1982.

See also **England, Twentieth Century; Oxford; Inklings**

WYKE-SMITH, E.A. AND *THE MARVELLOUS LAND OF SNERGS*

Edward Augustine Wyke-Smith (1871–1935) in some ways a typical Victorian gentleman, traveled around the world, worked in the American West, studied mine engineering, worked on the Suez Canal, and wrote stories for his children. He published eight novels, four of which were for children. His first, *Bill of Bustingforths* (1921), was printed concurrently with another of his stories, *The Last of the Barons*. The *Marvellous Land of Snergs*, Wyke-Smith's last book, was published in 1927.

Snergs, which has elements of *Alice in Wonderland* and *Peter Pan* in it, came to the attention of Tolkien after its publication, and he read it to his children, who enjoyed it immensely. Douglas A. Anderson, in his biography and introduction to the reprinted facsimile edition by Old Earth Books in 1996, provides a great deal of information regarding the influence of this book on Tolkien's inspiration for the hobbits. The Snergs are very similar to Hobbits in their general culture and physical features, and the writing style of *Snergs* and *The Hobbit* are similar as well. The names of the main characters of these two stories, Gorbo and Bilbo, also indicate an influence. Tolkien did not leave much evidence for his affection for the *Snergs* book, except for some notes in his Andrew Lang lecture "On Fairy Stories." There, he referred to it as an unconscious source for the hobbits; however, *Snergs* does fit very well into Tolkien's concept of subcreation, in that the Snergs are a people that have an entire history and culture that assists in their believability in the mind of the reader. The physical properties of the Land of Snergs is very similar to Middle-earth, in that it is somewhere in our current world but set apart and difficult to get to without a knowledgeable navigational guide. Given that there were very few books that Tolkien was impressed with in terms of believability among the Victorian fantasists, and that *Snergs* was one of them, requires its inclusion here.

Early drafts of *The Lord of the Rings* also show the influence of Gorbo's character on the hobbit Trotter, an early representation of Aragorn. Trotter was a well-traveled hobbit who Tolkien wrote into the "new *Hobbit*" to be Frodo's guide and companion during the trek from the Shire to Rivendell. The character of Aragorn eventually took over this role, but the fact that he guides Frodo and his companions from Bree to Rivendell in a manner similar to that of Gorbo in *Snergs* is very interesting.

Mention must be made of the original illustrations by George Morrow. This book not only captivated Tolkien and his children with its storytelling, but the illustrations themselves are unique, and contribute to the story in a way that complements and even assists in the subcreational realism of the story. Since Tolkien was himself an illustrator of his own works, the combination of both story and visual effects in this book probably had an influence on him as well.

BRADFORD LEE EDEN

Further Reading

Bratman, David. Review of *The Marvellous Land of Snergs*. Available at http://www.mythsoc.org/snergs.html

Williams, J. Michael. "Snergs as Hobbits." Available at http://www.tolkiencollector.com/snergs.htm

Wyke-Smith, E.A. *The Marvellous Land of Snergs*. Illustrated by George Morrow. A new facsimile edition, with an introduction by Douglas Anderson. Baltimore: Old Earth Books, 1996.

Y

YLFE, ÁLFAR, ELVES

References to elves are widespread in early Northern literature, as also in contemporary and current folk-tradition. They are, however, on the face of it curiously inconsistent, many negative, some positive, others neutral or uncertain. The *Beowulf*-poet, for instance, classes the *ylfe* or elves with *eotenas* (giants) and *orc-neas* (demon-corpses?). All three groups, like the man-eating monster Grendel, are the descendants of Cain, irrevocable enemies of the true human race. Old English charms tend to agree with him, seeing the *ylfe* as bringers of disease, possibly diabolical. On the other hand, the singular form is found in many presumably honorific names, such as Ælf-red, "Elf-counsel," and Ælf-wine, "Elf-friend," while there is also a continuing English tradition of the often fatal beauty and allure of the elves, male or female.

Norse tradition sometimes corroborates this, but is generally more respectful. In early poems the *álfar* are often linked with the *Æsir*, the Norse gods, while folk tradition seems unable to decide whether they are diabolical, hostile, or just alternative. The *Prose Edda* of Snorri Sturluson (1178?–1241), a handbook of pagan mythology compiled by a Christian scholar, meanwhile divides the elves into three groups, *ljósálfar*, *dökkálfar*, *svartálfar*, light-elves, dark-elves, swart-elves. Snorri seems to equate the last group with the dwarves.

Confronted with these and other contradictions, Tolkien's principles were twofold: in the first place he was not prepared to rule out any of the evidence he had as merely groundless; however, he was also determined to offer a consistent image of the elven race. One vital move was to separate Light-elves and Dark-elves, not by color, but by whether they had or had not seen the Light of the Two Trees in Valinor. The latter group might further equate in part with the Wood-elves, of whom we hear in Old English, and the former, again in part, with the Sea-elves, also mentioned in ancient times. As for the positive/negative reactions, these were to be explained by varying human responses to the same phenomenon: the allure, the beauty, the general physical and mental superiority of the elves, as also their longevity. In some humans this would generate love and respect, in others, envy and fear. Some would wish to be like them, others claim that for all the elves' long life, they had no souls and could never see Heaven. There was general agreement that to enter Elf-hill or go with the elves to Elf-home would play tricks with a human sense of time. In the reactions to the elves of Aragorn and Sam, of Boromir, Gimli, Éomer, and other more suspicious Riders, we can see the start of the traditions which have survived in our world.

Tolkien uses the information derived from his ancient and modern sources with great thrift and subtlety, to create an image the more convincing for its complexity. His long account of the First Age of the elves in *The Silmarillion* explains many outstanding problems in ancient texts, such as the often hostile but sometimes co-operative relations of elves and dwarves. In particular Eöl, the "Dark Elf" of chapter 16, unquestionably an elf but associated with the dwarves and always dressed in armor "black and shining like jet," seems designed to explain Snorri Sturluson's hesitant identification of dwarves and "swart-elves"; Tolkien shows how Snorri's view, while mistaken, could have arisen as a natural mistake. This is yet another example of a textual crux or apparent contradiction leading to the invention of story.

TOM SHIPPEY

Further Reading

Crossley, Robert. "A Long Day's Dying: the Elves of J.R.R. Tolkien and Sylvia Townsend Warner." In *Death and the Serpent: Immortality in Science Fiction and Fantasy*. Eds. Carl B. Yoke and Donald M. Hassler. Westport, CT: Greenwood Press, 1985. pp. 57–70.

Hickman, Michael R. "The Religious Ritual and Practice of the Elves of Middle-earth at the Time of the War of the Ring," *Mallorn* 26 (Sept. 1989): 39–43.

Loback, Tom. "The Kindreds, Houses and Population of the Elves during the First Age," *Mythlore* 14:1 [51] (Autumn 1987): 34–38, 56.

Shippey, Tom. "Light-elves, Dark-elves, and others: Tolkien's Elvish Problem," *Tolkien Studies* 1 (2004): 1–15.

———. "'Alias Oves Habeo': Elves as a Category Problem." In *The Shadow-walkers: Jacob Grimm's Mythology of the Monstrous*. Ed. Tom Shippey. Tempe, AZ: Arizona State University Press, 2005. pp. 157–87.

Talbot, Norman, "Where do Elves Go To: Tolkien and a Fantasy Tradition." In *Proceedings of the J.R.R. Tolkien Centenary Conference*. Eds. Patricia Reynolds and Glen H. GoodKnight. Milton Keynes: Tolkien Society, and Altadena, CA: Mythopoeic Press, 1995. pp. 94–106.

See also **Cruces in Medieval Literature; Elf-Shot; Mythology for England; Mythology, Germanic; *Silmarillion*, The**

INDEX